Middle East

Anthony Ham

James Bainbridge, César Soriano,

Amelia Thomas, Jenny Walker, Rafael Wlodarski

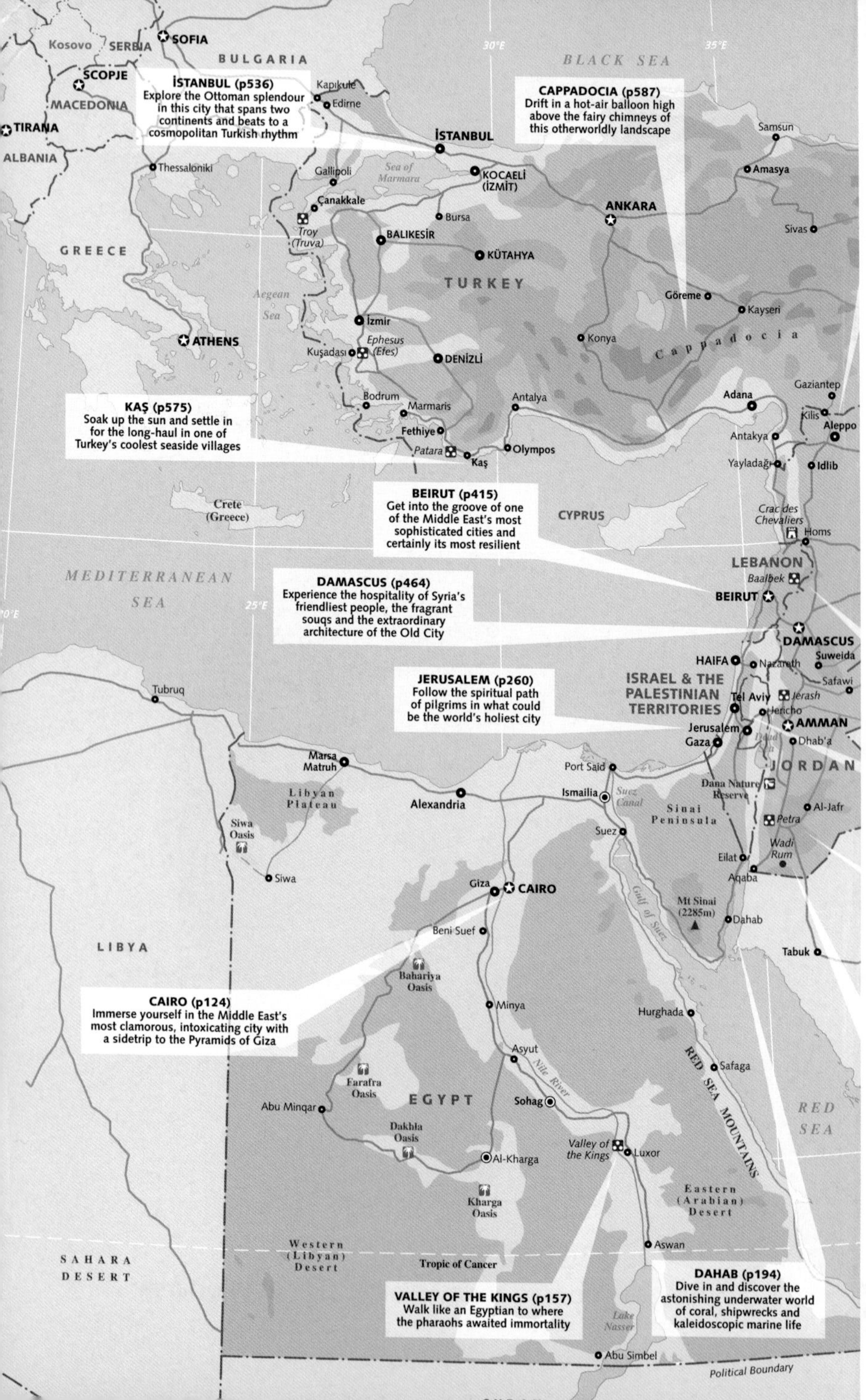

İSTANBUL (p536)
Explore the Ottoman splendour in this city that spans two continents and beats to a cosmopolitan Turkish rhythm
CAPPADOCIA (p587)
Drift in a hot-air balloon high above the fairy chimneys of this otherworldly landscape
KAŞ (p575)
Soak up the sun and settle in for the long-haul in one of Turkey's coolest seaside villages
BEIRUT (p415)
Get into the groove of one of the Middle East's most sophisticated cities and certainly its most resilient
DAMASCUS (p464)
Experience the hospitality of Syria's friendliest people, the fragrant souqs and the extraordinary architecture of the Old City
JERUSALEM (p260)
Follow the spiritual path of pilgrims in what could be the world's holiest city
CAIRO (p124)
Immerse yourself in the Middle East's most clamorous, intoxicating city with a sidetrip to the Pyramids of Giza
VALLEY OF THE KINGS (p157)
Walk like an Egyptian to where the pharaohs awaited immortality
DAHAB (p194)
Dive in and discover the astonishing underwater world of coral, shipwrecks and kaleidoscopic marine life
Kosovo
SERBIA
SOFIA
BULGARIA
SCOPJE
MACEDONIA
TIRANA
ALBANIA
GREECE
ATHENS
Thessaloniki
BLACK SEA
30°E
35°E
25°E
Kapıkule
Edirne
İSTANBUL
Gallipoli
Sea of Marmara
KOCAELİ (İZMİT)
Çanakkale
Troy (Truva)
Bursa
BALIKESİR
KÜTAHYA
ANKARA
Samsun
Amasya
Sivas
TURKEY
Aegean Sea
İzmir
Ephesus (Efes)
Kuşadası
DENİZLİ
Göreme
Kayseri
Konya
Cappadocia
Bodrum
Marmaris
Fethiye
Patara
Kaş
Olympos
Antalya
Adana
Gaziantep
Kilis
Aleppo
Antakya
Yayladağı
Idlib
Crete (Greece)
CYPRUS
Crac des Chevaliers
Homs
LEBANON
Baalbek
BEIRUT
DAMASCUS
Suweida
MEDITERRANEAN SEA
HAIFA
Nazareth
Safawi
ISRAEL & THE PALESTINIAN TERRITORIES
Tel Aviv
Jerash
Jericho
AMMAN
Jerusalem
Gaza
Dhab'a
JORDAN
Tubruq
Marsa Matruh
Port Said
Dana Nature Reserve
Libyan Plateau
Alexandria
Ismailia
Suez Canal
Sinai Peninsula
Al-Jafr
Petra
Siwa Oasis
Suez
Wadi Rum
Eilat
Aqaba
Siwa
Giza
CAIRO
Gulf of Suez
Mt Sinai (2285m)
Dahab
Beni Suef
Tabuk
LIBYA
Bahariya Oasis
Minya
Hurghada
Asyut
Nile River
Safaga
RED SEA MOUNTAINS
Farafra Oasis
EGYPT
Sohag
RED SEA
Abu Minqar
Dakhla Oasis
Valley of the Kings
Luxor
Al-Kharga
Kharga Oasis
Eastern (Arabian) Desert
SAHARA DESERT
Western (Libyan) Desert
Aswan
Tropic of Cancer
Lake Nasser
Abu Simbel
Political Boundary

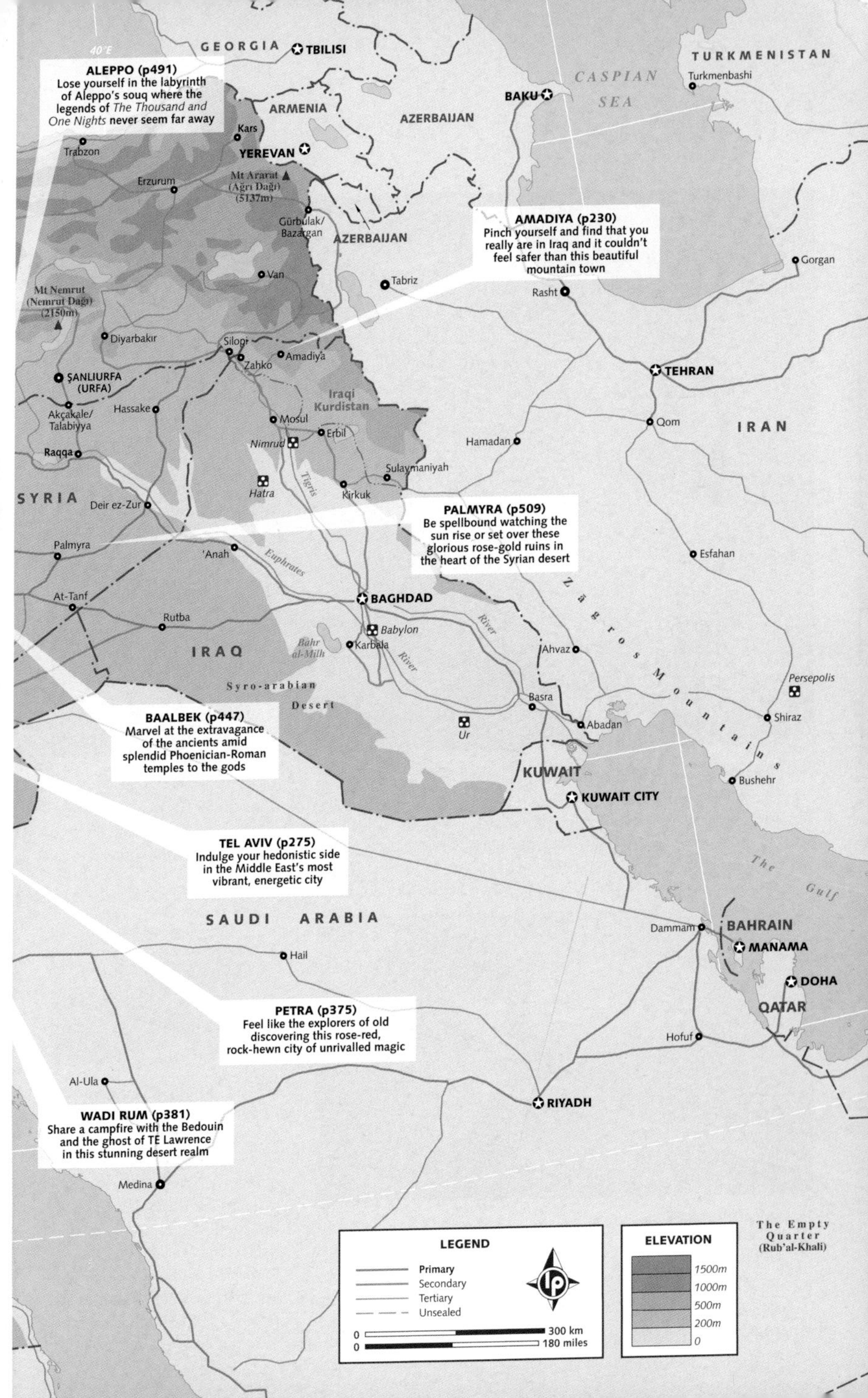
ALEPPO (p491)
Lose yourself in the labyrinth of Aleppo's souq where the legends of The Thousand and One Nights never seem far away
AMADIYA (p230)
Pinch yourself and find that you really are in Iraq and it couldn't feel safer than this beautiful mountain town
PALMYRA (p509)
Be spellbound watching the sun rise or set over these glorious rose-gold ruins in the heart of the Syrian desert
BAALBEK (p447)
Marvel at the extravagance of the ancients amid splendid Phoenician-Roman temples to the gods
TEL AVIV (p275)
Indulge your hedonistic side in the Middle East's most vibrant, energetic city
PETRA (p375)
Feel like the explorers of old discovering this rose-red, rock-hewn city of unrivalled magic
WADI RUM (p381)
Share a campfire with the Bedouin and the ghost of TE Lawrence in this stunning desert realm
GEORGIA
TBILISI
ARMENIA
AZERBAIJAN
YEREVAN
BAKU
CASPIAN SEA
TURKMENISTAN
Turkmenbashi
Kars
Trabzon
Erzurum
Mt Ararat (Ağrı Dağı) (5137m)
Gürbulak/Bazargan
Van
Tabriz
Rasht
Gorgan
Mt Nemrut (Nemrut Dağı) (2150m)
Diyarbakır
Silopi
Zahko
Amadiya
ŞANLIURFA (URFA)
Akçakale/Talabiyya
Hassake
Mosul
Iraqi Kurdistan
Erbil
Nimrud
TEHRAN
Qom
IRAN
Hamadan
Raqqa
Hatra
Tigris
Kirkuk
Sulaymaniyah
SYRIA
Deir ez-Zur
Palmyra
'Anah
Euphrates
Esfahan
Zagros Mountains
At-Tanf
BAGHDAD
Rutba
Babylon
IRAQ
Bahr al-Milh
Karbala
River
Ahvaz
Persepolis
Syro-arabian Desert
Basra
Shiraz
Abadan
Ur
KUWAIT
KUWAIT CITY
Bushehr
The Gulf
SAUDI ARABIA
Dammam
BAHRAIN
MANAMA
DOHA
QATAR
Hail
Hofuf
Al-Ula
RIYADH
Medina
The Empty Quarter (Rub'al-Khali)
40°E
LEGEND
Primary
Secondary
Tertiary
Unsealed
0
300 km
0
180 miles
ELEVATION
1500m
1000m
500m
200m
0

On the Road

ANTHONY HAM **Coordinating Author**

This photo finds me at one of my favourite places in all the world – Al-Nawfara Coffee Shop in the Old City of Damascus. Not long after the photo was taken, the sunset call to prayer rang out and Abu Shady spun tall tales from his storyteller's throne. I'd heard the same stories dozens of times before but his performance on this night was something special.

JAMES BAINBRIDGE Cappadocia's fairy chimneys and tuff valleys are extraordinary enough when seen from terra firma. Clapping eyes on them from a hot-air balloon 1000m above the ground, with snowy mountains glistening in the distance, added to the thrill. Equally amazing was gliding through the valleys, then rising to discover another balloon or a strange structure such as Uçhisar citadel.

CÉSAR SORIANO Walking into Amadiya, we soon attracted a crowd of giggling Kurdish children who led us on a tour of their ancient village. We followed them through a crack in the crumbling ruins of a stone gate, clambering over debris to reach a cliff with an endless view of green valleys and snow-capped mountains. I had to remind myself: 'This is IRAQ!'

RAFAEL WLODARKSI Wandering in a mesmerised daze, I spent over four hours at the Temples of Karnak in Luxor. It is impossible not to be awe-struck by this gargantuan feat of engineering, particularly the towering carved-pillar forest of the Great Hypostyle Hall.

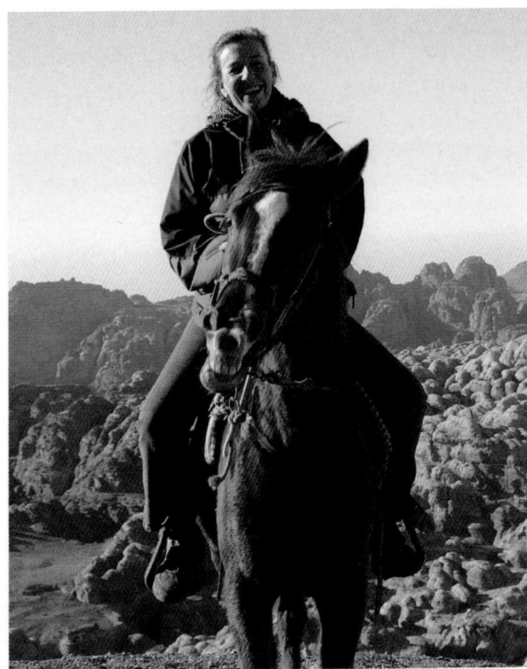

JENNY WALKER If a picture tells a thousand words, this shot ought to be censored. That's because Horse and I are poised on the edge of a precipice and instructions to step 'this way a bit' were nothing to grin about. This was meant to be the short cut to Petra's Treasury: needless to say, we opted for the long route home.

AMELIA THOMAS It's early morning in Old Jaffa, where a wooden Napoleon keeps watch over the slowly awakening cobbled streets, and my little tribe of researchers is, as usual, hungry. 'All right, everyone – say hummus!' I command, and manage one quick snap before we all head straight to breakfast at Ali Caravan, where a cauldron of Israel's finest – piping hot and thick with chickpeas – awaits.

For full author biographies see p672.

Middle East Highlights

The cradle of civilisation, the crossroad of continents and the coming together of the great empires of the past – ah, the history the Middle East has seen! This is where epic cities of antiquity rub shoulders with modern metropolises teeming with life, each overlaid with centuries of spiritual and architectural aspiration and inhabited by some of the friendliest people you'll ever meet. Venture beyond the cities and find landscapes of singular beauty and adventurous activities to match. The Middle East is like nowhere else on earth.

NOBORU KOMINE

1 THE DOME OF THE ROCK, JERUSALEM, ISRAEL

It's incredible to think that three of the world's religions can converge on a single spot, but here in Jerusalem's heady Old City, Christianity, Islam and Judaism do just that at the gilded, soaring Dome of the Rock mosque (p266). In Islamic tradition, it's the place from which Mohammed ascended to heaven; for observant Jews, it's the location of the holiest spot on earth; in Christianity, it's the former site of the Church of Holy Wisdom. And for me, each time I wander its beautiful, Byzantine perimeter, it's a reminder that despite the religious tensions simmering throughout the wider Middle East, there's still a little piece of serenity, sanctuary and silence in the midst of the mayhem.

Amelia Thomas, Lonely Planet author

MARK WEBSTER

3 PALMYRA, SYRIA

One morning I rose early. The sky, bizarrely for the desert, was grey and threatening. Then, as great forks of lightning struck, I ran through the majestic ruins of Palmyra (p509), weaving between the fluted columns of the avenues. Never had I seen such an exhilarating sight, and I doubt I will again. Don't be put off by the coachloads of tourists wandering through the ruins. Find yourself a quiet spot and imagine the life and bustle of this once-great city. Marvel at the remains of the great temples and theatre, but also at the reminders of a society as rich and sophisticated as ancient Rome.

Martin Wade & Suzanne West, Wales/UK

JULIET COOMBE

2 RED SEA, EGYPT

You'll never forget your first foray beneath the surface of the Red Sea (p184) – it's another world down there with vivid colours and an astonishing variety of marine life. You'll never forget the beauty, the sense of having stepped beyond the looking glass or the astonishing richness and variety of the natural world. By the water's edge, life is all about kicking back and getting into a groove that you'll find hard to give up.

Anthony Ham, Lonely Planet author

HOLGER LEUE

4 İSTANBUL, TURKEY

İstanbul (p536) is the sort of place where the glories of the past rub along nicely with the sophistication of the present. Whether it's in the Topkapı Palace, Aya Sofya (pictured) or beneath the cascading domes of the Blue Mosque, İstanbul is where East meets West and the result is more alluring than you could ever imagine.

Anthony Ham, Lonely Planet author

CÉSAR SORIANO

5 AMADIYA, IRAQ

Like a scene out of a fairytale, the village of Amadiya (p230) is perched on a high plateau that rises steeply above the valley floor. I thought it would be cool to walk the perimeter of the village. Walking and hiking are not popular pastimes in Iraq, so when a friend and I set out to explore the village on foot, we got a few stares, some questions, and pretty soon people were calling out to us from their homes and balconies. We attracted a parade of every child in the village, some as young as four. They motioned for us to follow them, crawling, through the crevice of the ancient, crumbling city wall. There, on the other side, was one of the most amazing scenic views I'd ever seen.

César Soriano, Lonely Planet author

JEAN ROBERT

6 PETRA, JORDAN

Visit Petra (p375) during the cooler months! This allows an amazing experience free from the throngs of peak-season visitors. We were able to walk down the Siq with only the sound of an echoing horse carriage and had parts of Petra all to ourselves. You can take fantastic, tourist-free photos of beautiful Petra and its Bedouin environment, camels and donkeys. More practical advantages include not having to carry so much water and enjoying a comfortable temperature for walks to the Monastery and Place of High Sacrifice.

Sharon Stark, New Zealand

JANE SWEENEY

7 OLD CITY, DAMASCUS, SYRIA

We fell in love with the narrow, cobbled streets of Damascus' Old City (p468) with its Roman gate arches leading to the bazaar and its offerings of olive-oil soap, musky fragrances, painted ceramic bowls, tablecloths, damascene and silver jewellery. It was like we'd gone back in time to an age where laid-back, gentle haggling over a cup of coffee and a chat about the world were the norm. Sitting at dusk in the city, drinking tea and snacking on *zaatar*-filled pita bread in a coffeehouse was pure magic.

Robin & Saima Nichols, Australia

8 BEIRUT, LEBANON

In Beirut (p415) we especially enjoyed walking along the waterfront and its opportunities for wonderful Lebanese food. We also spent a lot of time in Hamra. What caught our attention in the city was the diversity of its inhabitants, leaving us with the impression that this is a very cosmopolitan city.

Beatriz Castaño & Juan Olazabal, Spain

DJ PACO / PHOTOLIBRARY

RUSSELL MOUNTFORD

9 CAIRO, EGYPT

The hustle and bustle of modern Cairo (p124) is not for the faint-hearted. Once you get beneath the surface, though, it is a city whose wonders are infectious and people are endearing. Most travellers will understandably head towards the famous landmarks such as the pyramids (pictured) and the sphinx. While these are amazing, the true wonders of Cairo can be found in the most unexpected corners of this enchanting city.

Damien Bown, Australia

HOLGER LEUE

10 LUXOR, EGYPT

You can't help but feel you are in the very cradle of civilization when you visit Luxor (p153). The whole area abounds with opportunities to venture into and appreciate the wonders of ancient Egypt. The incredible size and scale of the monuments are only matched by the amazing detail and precision in the craftsmanship, which all amounts to an exhilarating experience.

Damien Bown, Australia

11 MADABA, JORDAN

For centuries the city of Madaba (p366) was a crossroad for trading caravans moving goods for sale, legions of armies pushing the borders of their empires and pilgrims driven by their own faith in search of the promised land. It was also a place where local cultures flourished. Madaba maintains marks of greatness among the old buildings, churches, museums, and of course, in the proud townspeople. Perhaps the best representation of their rich past is in the magnificent collection of mosaics.

Fernando Perego, Peru/USA

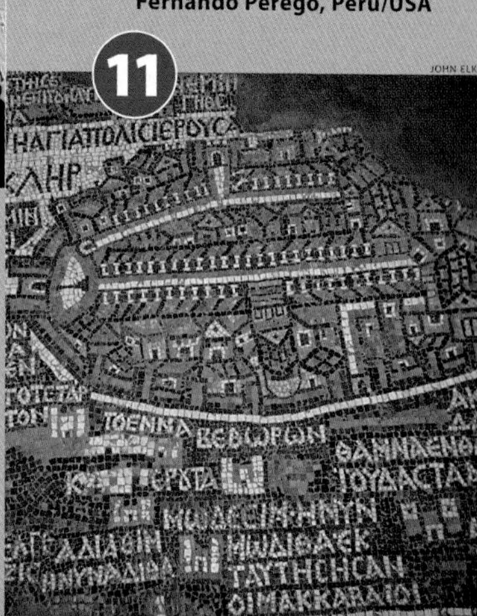

JOHN ELK III

HANAN ISACHAR

12 AMMAN & JERASH, JORDAN

If you thought Roman ruins were boring, think again. Jordan has some of the best I've ever seen. The Roman Theatre and Citadel in Amman (p343) were highlights of my trip, and wandering along the colonnaded street of Jerash (pictured; p355) was awesome. With its baths, temples, theatres and hippodrome, I could begin to imagine this Roman city in full swing. It must have been bustling with market traders, guards and gladiators – you can still see the grooves worn into the limestone floor by chariot wheels. This is history at its best!

Debbie Martin, UK

CAPPADOCIA, TURKEY

The moonscapes of Cappadocia (p587) leave a lasting impression in the minds of all who travel to see the region's stark beauty. The underground cities provide unique insights into the way different generations adapted their lifestyle to their surrounds in extreme circumstances. So unusual is its beauty, Cappadocia has been the backdrop for blockbuster films, such as the Star Wars series.

Damien Bown, Australia

13

DALLAS STRIBLEY

BOSRA, SYRIA

Bosra (p481) is an ideal place to stop on your way south to Jordan. The Roman ruins in black basalt are completely different from those of Baalbek and Palmyra. But the most interesting site to visit is the citadel, with its perfectly preserved ancient Roman theatre (pictured) inside. It's incredible to walk along the dark passageways and, without warning, emerge suddenly into the theatre in all its glory and immensity.

Beatriz Castaño & Juan Olazabal, Spain

14

MARK DAFFEY

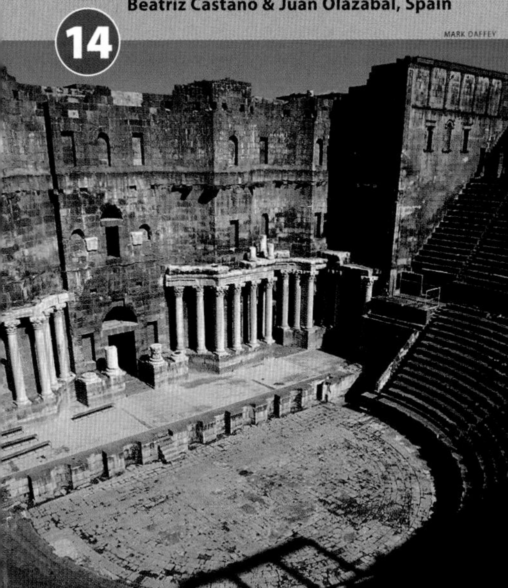

PATRICK BEN LUKE SYDER

15

DEAD SEA, JORDAN

The Dead Sea (p361) was definitely my highlight. It's amazing to think, standing on the shore, that all the mackerel and all the sticklebacks in the world are swimming around 1000ft above your head (because you are 1000ft below sea level) – and you don't even have to get your feet wet!

Sam Owen, UK

SYRIAN PEOPLE

It's quite disconcerting to have strangers shout at you in the street, but when they're saying, 'You are welcome in Syria,' it melts your heart. This kept happening wherever we went. On the train from Aleppo to Damascus, a man with a family struck up a conversation with us and invited us to stay at his house. At other times, taxi drivers would refuse to take fares or strangers would offer to be our guides. Sometimes the destination would be their brother's carpet shop, but more often there wasn't any ulterior motive. They were proud to show off their city and maybe to practise their English.

Martin Wade & Suzanne West, Wales/UK

JOHN ELK III

16 BAALBEK & BEKAA VALLEY, LEBANON

The ruins of Baalbek (pictured; p447) are better preserved than those of Palmyra and are equally spectacular – spend at least one full day here to appreciate their grandeur. Start early in the morning to avoid the crowds. It's also worth exploring the Bekaa Valley (p446) with so many fascinating landmarks and beautiful landscapes, some scarred by war, but they give a glimpse of the extraordinary natural riches of Lebanon.

Beatriz Castaño & Juan Olazabal, Spain

17

CLINT LUCAS

PAUL LINDSAY / PHOTOLIBRARY

18 MEDITERRANEAN COAST, TURKEY

It's little wonder that the rich and famous spend weeks on end floating along Turkey's Mediterranean coast (p569), a little slice of paradise, in their million-dollar yachts. You can easily let a week or two drift through you fingers as you lie back and enjoy the sights and sounds of Turkey's far south. A good spot to come ashore is Olympos, where tree houses sit among ancient ruins, before running back into the blue waters and pebble-covered beaches of the Mediterranean.

Damien Bown, Australia

Contents

Turkey 529

Regional Map Contents

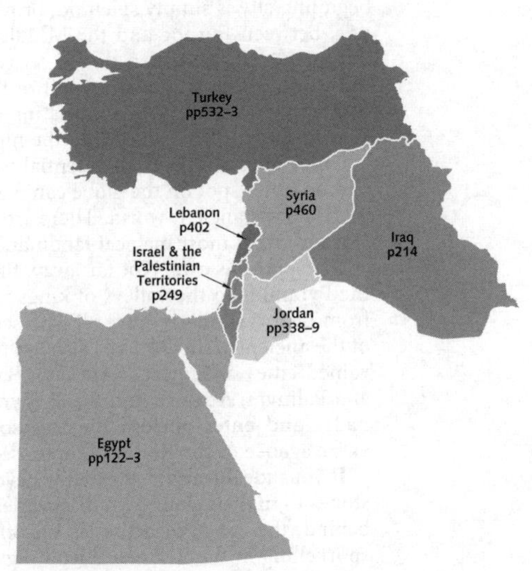

Destination Middle East

The Middle East is one of history's grand epics in the making. Once the cradle of civilisation, now a region where modern human history is daily being written upon the stones of the past, the Middle East is where the lines between history's story and the magic of the travel experience are forever being blurred.

Few places in the world can match the Middle East's roll-call of ancient ruins, landscapes of rare beauty and extraordinary cities whose personalities seem to spring from the tales of *The Thousand and One Nights*. More than that, the unforgettable travel moments that the Middle East has to offer are almost as diverse as the stunning backdrops in which to enjoy them. You'll never forget the wide-eyed wonder of that first time you dip below the surface of the Red Sea and discover an underwater world of dazzling colour and otherworldly coral. Or the feeling of well-being as you sit by the feet of the Middle East's last storyteller in Damascus and he weaves an intricate web of fact and fable worthy of Sheherezade. Or the spiritual stirrings in your soul the first time you hear the haunting call to prayer carried by the wind through the lanes of old Jerusalem.

Israel has the highest GDP per capita in the region (US$25,500), while the lowest is in the West Bank and Gaza Strip (US$1100). Otherwise, on average Turks earn US$12,900, Lebanese US$11,300, Egyptians US$5500, Jordanians US$4900, Syrians US$4500 and oil-rich Iraqis US$3600.

Many travellers fall irretrievably in love with the region in its cities. Cairo is known as 'the mother of the world'; it is a clamorous cultural hub for the Middle East, not to mention the home of the Pyramids of Giza. There's also something special about Damascus with its compelling claim to be the world's oldest continuously inhabited city (at least four other cities, all in the Middle East, make a similar claim); it is a place where the layers of history infuse every aspect of daily life. Call it what you like – Byzantium, Constantinople or İstanbul – but Turkey's most beguiling city is simply splendid, providing a bridge, in more ways than one, between Europe and the Middle East amid so many jewels of its Ottoman past. And then there's Jerusalem, a city sacred to almost half the world's population. If a whiff of the exotic is your thing, the souqs of Aleppo have no rivals. If pulsating nightlife gets you on your feet, Tel Aviv and Beirut rock deep into the night.

Cities have always been essential to the fabric of Middle Eastern life and no other spot on the globe can match the Middle East for the extant glories of its ancient world. There are no more stirring ruins than Petra (Jordan), that most magical landmark of antiquity where the only suitable response is awe. Not far away, the wonders of ancient Egypt, from the Pyramids to the valleys of kings and queens that sit across the Nile from Luxor, similarly leave all who see them spellbound by the wisdom of the ancients. The Romans also left their mark across the region; in the ruined cities of Ephesus (Turkey), Baalbek (Lebanon), Jerash (Jordan) and Palmyra, Apamea and Bosra (Syria) you'll stroll down great colonnades and enter ancient theatres so wonderfully preserved that the extravagance of the Roman Empire seems within your grasp.

If your ideal travel day extends beyond a diet of coffeehouses and old stones to making your own discoveries and leaving the madding crowds behind, the range of activities on offer can seem endless. Diving and snorkelling in the Red Sea – from Egypt, Jordan and, to a lesser extent, Eilat in Israel – is the ultimate aim for diving connoisseurs and beginners alike; combining this with lazy days along the Dahab shoreline could conceivably occupy weeks of your time. Sharing the desert with the soulful Bedouin in the extraordinary red sands of Wadi Rum with their echoes of *Lawrence of Arabia,* or leaving behind the last outpost of civilisation and losing yourself in the White and Black Deserts of the Egyptian Sahara, are also experiences with an almost spiritual dimension of solitude and silence. Hikers who take to the hills of Jordan invariably make a similar claim.

Such are the headline attractions of the Middle East. And yet it's the people of the region who will leave the most lasting impression. We've lost count of the number of times that we've received invitations to take tea, to pass the time in conversation or to eat in people's homes. The art of hospitality, with its strong roots in the desert cultures of Arabia and in Islam, is one of the most enduring constants in Middle Eastern life. '*Ahlan wa sahlan*' ('You are welcome') is a phrase you'll hear again and again because many Middle Easterners treat every encounter with guests in their country as a gift from their god.

This warmth that you'll experience often on your travels through the region is all the more remarkable given that life is a daily struggle for many people in the Middle East. Poverty and a lack of freedom are quotidian concerns for millions of people here. With the flawed exceptions of Turkey, Israel and Lebanon, political freedoms are heavily circumscribed and people chafe under the old guard of leaders who have, by some standards, singularly failed to better the lives of their citizens. Armed conflict and terrorism are rarer and more isolated in the Middle East than the mainstream Western media would have you believe, but they still darken the horizon of many, especially in Iraq and Gaza.

Far more paralysing are the conflicts over land that seem frozen in time and no nearer to a solution than they were six decades ago. Like a separation wall between historical conflict and a peaceful future, the enduring inability of Israel, the Palestinians, Syria and Lebanon to make peace with each other continues to cast a shadow over the region, hindering its economic growth and maintaining almost perpetual uncertainty for many.

All of these issues may be why nine out of 10 people polled will probably tell you the Middle East is too dangerous to visit (one of these nine will, most likely, be your mum). The Middle East does indeed have its problems and dangers. They are, however, far fewer than the prevailing stereotypes suggest. They're also far more likely to affect the people of the Middle East rather than travellers, for whom the risks are extremely small. You will come across relatively minor inconveniences, such as not being able to cross between Lebanon and Israel, or finding that an Israeli entry stamp in your passport means you cannot visit Syria or Lebanon. But we cannot emphasise it more strongly than this: many parts of the Middle East are safe to travel to.

To put it another way, the Middle East is a destination for discerning travellers, for those looking for the story behind the headline. It's the story of a region with its feet firmly planted on three continents, of a warm and hospitable people standing at the crossroads of history. And it's a story that, having visited the Middle East once, you'll find yourself returning to over and over again.

Getting Started

There's one question that every traveller to the Middle East wants answered: is it safe? The short answer is yes, as long as you stay informed. For the longer answer, turn to the boxed text, p627. Show it to your mum. Show it to all those friends who told you that you were crazy for travelling to the Middle East. Once you've realised that the region's reputation as a place that cannot be travelled to comes almost solely from people who've never been there, you can get down to the fun part of pretrip planning – tracking down a good read, surfing the net to learn other travellers' tales and renting a few classic Middle Eastern movies. And if the idea of scuba diving in the Red Sea, sleeping under the desert stars or skiing (yes, skiing in the Middle East) sounds like your kind of holiday, we recommend that you see Activities, p619) so that you can start dreaming. For the ultimate at-a-glance guide to planning your trip, see the Travel Planner, p32.

There are, of course, a few logistical matters that you should consider before setting out; primary among these is the question of visas. Although you can get visas on arrival in most countries, Syria could provide a road block if you don't plan ahead. For more information, see p523. You should also consult the Visa sections of the Directory in each individual country chapter, or for a general overview, see the table on p635.

DON'T LEAVE HOME WITHOUT...

- Checking the latest travel advisory warnings (see the boxed text, p626)
- Travel insurance (see p628) – accidents do happen
- Driving licence, car documents and appropriate car insurance if bringing your own car (see p650)
- Checking the status of border crossings in the region (see the boxed text, p635)
- A big appetite (see p97)
- Warm clothes for winter – the Middle East can be cold; desert nights can be freezing
- A universal bathplug – you'll thank us when you emerge from the desert
- An MP3 player – the desert can be beautiful but there are days when epic distances and empty horizons can do your head in
- Mosquito repellent – that unmistakeable high-pitched whine in the ear is death to sleep
- A small size-three football – a great way to meet locals
- A Swiss Army knife with a bottle and/or can opener – you never know when you might need it
- Photocopies of your important documents – leave a copy at home or email them to yourself before leaving
- Ear plugs – wake-up calls from nearby mosques can be *very* early
- Contraceptives – some local condoms have a distressingly high failure rate
- A phrasebook – an '*al salaam 'alaykum*', or 'peace be upon you', works wonders in turning suspicion to a smile
- Checking the status of visa rules for travel between Lebanon and Syria (see the boxed text, p524)
- A chic outfit if you're planning a night out in Beirut, İstanbul or Tel Aviv
- Hiking boots if you intend to get too far off the beaten track
- Patience – most things do run on time, but the timetable may be elusive to the uninitiated

If you're planning to visit Israel and the Palestinian Territories, remember that any evidence in your passport of a visit to Israel will see you denied entry to Syria, Lebanon and possibly Iraq. For advice on how to avoid this problem, see the boxed text, p332.

WHEN TO GO

Although the timing of your trip may owe less to personal choice and more to the caprices of your employer back home, there's nothing worse than arriving in the Middle East to discover that it's Ramadan and stinking hot.

Climate

The best time to visit the Middle East is autumn (September to November) or spring (March to May). December and January *can* be fairly bleak and overcast in the region. Any time from October through to March can see overnight temperatures plummet in desert areas. Unless you're like the ancient Egyptians and worship the sun, or you're a watersports freak, the summer months of June through to September may be too hot for comfort. In July and August visitors to the Pharaonic sites at Aswan and Luxor in Egypt, or to Palmyra in Syria, are obliged to get up at 5am to beat the heat. Don't even think of an expedition into the desert in summer.

For more details on weather conditions, see the Climate section in each individual country chapter and p625.

The most obvious exceptions to these rules are the mountain areas. The northeast of Turkey before May or after mid-October can be beset by snow, perhaps even enough to close roads and mountain passes.

Religious Holidays & Festivals

Although non-Muslims are not bound by the rules of fasting during the month of Ramadan, many restaurants and cafés throughout the region will be closed, those who are fasting can be understandably taciturn, transport is on a go-slow and office hours are erratic to say the least. If you're visiting Turkey, Kurban Bayramı, which lasts a full week, can be an uplifting experience, but careful planning is required as hotels are jam-packed, banks closed and transport booked up weeks ahead. In Israel and the Palestinian Territories quite a few religious holidays, such as Passover and Easter, cause the country to fill with pilgrims, prices to double and public transport to grind to a halt.

On the positive side, it's worth trying to time your visit to tie in with something like Eid al-Adha (the Feast of Sacrifice, which marks the Prophet's pilgrimage to Mecca) or the Prophet's Birthday, as these can be colourful occasions. Both of these religious holidays can be wonderful opportunities to get under the skin of the region and enjoy the festive mood. Remember, however, to make your plans early, especially when it comes to public transport and finding a hotel. See p628 for the dates of these and more Islamic festivals.

For a snapshot of the Middle East's best festivals, see the Travel Planner p32.

COSTS & MONEY

The Middle East is in the midst of an inflationary spiral driven by rising oil prices and it's difficult to predict how far it will go. Previously cheap countries such as Jordan, Egypt and Syria (where prices have almost doubled since we were last there) remain cheap by Western standards and travel staples – accommodation, meals and transport – are generally affordable for most travellers. The gap is, however, narrowing. The gap between prices in the West and Lebanon, Turkey and Israel and the Palestinian Territories long ago narrowed, and don't be surprised to pay the same for your latte in

Beirut, Tel Aviv or İstanbul as you would at home. Indeed, in many places, midrange and especially top-end travellers may find themselves paying prices on a par with southern Europe. Budget travellers should still, however, be able to travel economically in most countries of the Middle East.

'some of the best travel experiences cost nothing'

Although it's dangerous to generalise, if you're on a *really* tight budget, stay at cheap hotels with shared bathrooms, eat street food and carry a student card with you to reduce entry fees at museums, you could get by on around US$20 to US$25 a day. Staying in comfortable midrange hotels, eating at quality restaurants to ensure a varied diet, the occasional private taxi ride and some shopping will push your daily expenses up to between US$40 and US$60. In Lebanon, US$25 a day is the barest minimum, while US$45 is more realistic. In Israel and the Palestinian Territories, budget travellers could keep things down to $US40 per day if they really tried hard, while a more comfortable journey would require up to US$65.

When estimating your own costs, take into account extra items such as visa fees (which can top US$50 depending on where you get them and what your nationality is), long-distance travel and the cost of organised tours or activities, such as desert safaris and diving. And remember, some of the best travel experiences cost nothing: whiling away the hours taking on the locals at backgammon in Damascus, sleeping under the desert stars in the Sahara or watching the sun set over the Mediterranean.

For advice on the pros and cons of carrying cash, credit cards and/or travellers cheques, check out the Money section in the Directory of each individual country chapter. In general, we recommend a mix of credit or ATM cards and cash (see p629), but the situation varies from country to country.

READING UP

Books

Lonely Planet has numerous guides to the countries of the Middle East, including *Egypt, Turkey, Jordan, Cairo & the Nile* and *Syria & Lebanon.* There's also a city guide to *İstanbul,* a World Food guide to Turkey, as well as phrasebooks for Arabic, Farsi, Hebrew and Turkish.

TRAVEL LITERATURE

In *From the Holy Mountain,* William Dalrymple skips lightly but engagingly across the region's landscape of sacred and profane, travelling through Turkey, Syria and Israel and the Palestinian Territories in what could be an emblem for your own journey.

The 8:55 to Baghdad: From London to Iraq on the Trail of Agatha Christie and the Orient Express, by Andrew Eames, is a well-told tale retracing Agatha Christie's journey from Britain to archaeological digs in Iraq.

Travels with a Tangerine, by Tim Mackintosh-Smith, captures a modern journey in the footsteps of Ibn Battuta, a 13th-century Arab Marco Polo. The book begins in Morocco and takes in several countries of the Middle East.

Syria Through Writers' Eyes is one in a series of anthologies that brings together the best travel writing about the region down through the centuries. There are similar titles for Egypt, Persia and the Turkish coast.

The famous march to Persia by the Greek army, immortalised in Xenophon's *Anabasis,* has been retraced some 2400 years later by Shane Brennan in his fabulous tale, *In the Tracks of the Ten Thousand: A Journey on Foot Through Turkey, Syria and Iraq.*

Johann Ludwig (also known as Jean Louis) Burckhardt spent many years in the early 19th century travelling extensively through Jordan,

ONWARD TRAVEL: IRAN, SAUDI ARABIA & THE GULF STATES

If you can't bear your Middle Eastern journey to end and you've got Iran in your sights, pick up a copy of Lonely Planet's *Iran* guide. For Saudi Arabia, Oman, the UAE, Yemen, Bahrain, Kuwait and Qatar, see *Oman, UAE & Arabian Peninsula*, which features a special chapter for expats headed to the Gulf states. If Africa awaits, Lonely Planet's *Africa* covers the entire continent, while *Libya* and *Ethiopia & Eritrea* may also appeal.

Syria and the Holy Land. His scholarly travelogue *Travels in Syria and the Holy Land* is a great read.

Mark Twain's *The Innocents Abroad* is still many people's favourite travel book about the region. Twain's sharp humour and keen eye make the story still relevant 140 years after the fact.

OTHER GREAT READS

Nine Parts of Desire, by Geraldine Brooks, takes our fascination with the life and role of women in the Middle East and gives it the depth and complexity the subject deserves, but all too rarely receives. It includes interviews with everyone from village women to Queen Noor of Jordan.

In the Land of Israel, by one of Israel's most acclaimed writers, Amos Oz, introduces you to the people of Israel in all their glorious diversity. Letting ordinary people speak for themselves, Oz paints a rich, nuance-laden portrait of Israelis and the land they inhabit.

Once Upon a Country: A Palestinian Life, by Sari Nusseibeh, was described by the *New York Times* as 'a deeply admirable book by a deeply admirable man'. It's a personal journey through 60 years of history by one of the Palestinians' most eloquent voices.

You won't want to carry Robert Fisk's *The Great War for Civilisation* in your backpack (it's a weighty tome), but there has been no finer book written about the region in recent years.

You've seen the movie, now read the book – *Seven Pillars of Wisdom* by TE Lawrence. Not only was Lawrence one of the Middle East's most picaresque figures, he was also a damn fine writer.

The Thousand and One Nights resonates with all the allure and magic of the Middle East and its appeal remains undiminished centuries after its tales were first told with Cairo, Damascus and Baghdad playing a starring role.

Websites

For specific country overviews, the lowdown on travel in the region and useful links head to Lonely Planet's website (www.lonelyplanet.com), which includes the Thorn Tree, Lonely Planet's online bulletin board.

The following websites are an excellent way to get information about the Middle East.

Al-Ahram Weekly (http://weekly.ahram.org.eg) Electronic version of Egypt's weekly English-language newspaper.

Al-Bab (www.al-bab.com) Portal that covers the entire Arab world with links to dozens of news services, country profiles, travel sites, maps, profiles and more. A fantastic resource.

Al-Bawaba (www.albawaba.com) A good mix of news, entertainment and phone directories, with everything from online forums to kids' pages.

Al-Jazeera (http://english.aljazeera.net/news/middleeast/) The CNN of the Arab world provides an antidote to Western-driven news angles about the Middle East.

Al-Mashriq (www.almashriq.hiof.no) A terrific repository for cultural information from the Levant (Israel, Jordan, Lebanon, Palestinian Territories, Syria, Turkey). Some of the information is a bit stale but its range of articles, from ethnology to politics, is hard to beat.

Arabnet (www.arab.net) Excellent Saudi-run online encyclopaedia of the Arab world, collecting news and articles plus links to further resources that are organised by country.
Bible Places (www.bibleplaces.com) Interesting rundown on biblical sights in Jordan, Egypt, Turkey and Israel and the Palestinian Territories.
BBC News (www.news.bbc.co.uk) Follow the links to the Middle East section for comprehensive and excellent regional news that's constantly updated.
Great Buildings Online (www.greatbuildings.com) Download then explore digital 3D models of the Pyramids of Giza and İstanbul's Aya Sofya, plus lots of other info and images of monuments throughout the Middle East.
Jerusalem Post (www.jpost.com) Up-to-the-minute news from an Israeli perspective. Sections include a blog page, tourism news and a link to the 24-hour Western Wall webcam.

MUST-SEE MOVIES

The Middle East is so much more than a backdrop for Western-produced blockbusters such as *Lawrence of Arabia,* the Indiana Jones series and a host of biblical epics. For more on Middle Eastern film see p83. The following movies are likely to be available in your home country or online.

Lawrence of Arabia (1962) may be clichéd and may give TE Lawrence more prominence than his Arab peers, but David Lean's masterpiece captures all the hopes and subsequent frustrations for Arabs in the aftermath of WWI.

Yilmaz Güney's *Yol* (*The Way;* 1982) is epic in scale but at the same time allows the humanity of finely rendered characters to shine through as five Turkish prisoners on parole travel around their country. It won the coveted Palme d'Or in Cannes.

West Beirut (1998) begins on 13 April 1975, the first day of the Lebanese Civil War, and is Ziad Doueiri's powerful meditation on the scars and hopes of Christian and Muslim Lebanese. This is *the* film about the Lebanese Civil War.

Savi Gabizon's *Nina's Tragedies* (2005) begins with a Tel Aviv army unit telling a family that their son has been killed in a suicide bombing and ends with a disturbing but nuanced look at the alienation of modern Israel as it struggles for peace.

The average age of people living in the Gaza Strip is 16.2 years, while for the West Bank it's 18.7. Iraq (20.2) and Syria (21.4) also have young populations. Turkey (29), Israel (28.9) and Lebanon (28.8) have the highest average ages. The average age in the UK is 39.9 years.

Palestinian director Hany Abu-Assad's *Paradise Now* (2005) caused a stir when it was nominated for the Best Foreign-Language Film Oscar in 2005. It's a disturbing but finely rendered study of the last hours of two suicide bombers as they prepare for their mission.

The Yacoubian Building (2006), an onscreen adaptation of the best-selling Egyptian novel by Alaa al-Aswany, is a scathing commentary on the modern decay of Egypt's political system. Its release marked the rebirth of Egyptian cinema.

Caramel (2007) is a stunning cinema debut for Lebanese director Nadine Labaki. It follows the lives of five Lebanese women struggling against social taboos in war-ravaged Beirut.

The biggest budget Egyptian film in decades, *Baby Doll Night* (2008) is at once a thriller with the threat of terrorism at its core and a thoughtful evocation of the complexities in relations between the Muslim world and the West.

TRAVELLING RESPONSIBLY

Tourism has the potential to change for the better the relationship between the Middle East and the West, but the gradual erosion of traditional life is mass tourism's flipside. Sexual promiscuity, public drunkenness among tourists and the wearing of unsuitable clothing are all of concern. For more coverage on the impact of tourism in the Middle East, see p116. For a list of Middle Eastern businesses and sights that engage in sustainable environmental practices, see the GreenDex, p698.

Try to have minimal impact on your surroundings. Create a positive precedent for those who follow you by keeping in mind the following:

- Don't hand out sweets or pens to children on the streets, since it encourages begging. Similarly, doling out medicines can encourage people not to seek proper medical advice and you have no control over whether the medicines are taken appropriately. A donation to a project, health centre or school is a far more constructive way to help.
- Buy your snacks, cigarettes, bubble gum etc from the enterprising grannies trying to make ends meet, rather than state-run stores. Also, use locally owned hotels and restaurants and buy locally made products.
- Try to give people a balanced perspective of life in the West. Try also to point out the strong points of the local culture, such as strong family ties and comparatively low crime.
- Make yourself aware of the human-rights situation, history and current affairs in the countries you travel through.
- If you're in a frustrating situation, be patient, friendly and considerate. Never lose your temper as a confrontational attitude won't go down well and for many Arabs a loss of face is a serious and sensitive issue. If you have a problem with someone, just be polite, calm and persistent.
- Try to learn some of the standard greetings (see p662) – it will make a very good first impression.
- Ask before taking photos of people. Don't worry if you don't speak the language – a smile and gesture will be appreciated. Never photograph someone if they don't want you to. If you agree to send someone a photo, make sure you follow through on it.
- Be respectful of Islamic traditions and don't wear revealing clothing; loose lightweight clothing is preferable.
- Respect local etiquette. Men should shake hands when formally meeting other men, but not women, unless the woman extends her hand first. If you are a woman and uncomfortable with men extending their hand to you (they don't do this with local women), just put your hand over your heart and say hello.
- Public displays of physical affection are almost always likely to be misunderstood. Be discreet.
- Choose environmentally sustainable transport options (eg train, renting a bike, or sailing up the Nile) where they exist and support ecotourism initiatives and local environmental organisations (see the boxed text, p114).
- Consider offsetting the carbon emissions of your flights (see the boxed text, p639).
- Try not to waste water. Switch off lights and air-con when you go out.
- When visiting historic sites, consider the irreparable damage you inflict upon them when you climb to the top of a pyramid, or take home an unattached artefact as a souvenir.
- Do not litter.

For more specific advice in relation to diving responsibly, see the boxed text, p620, while hikers should check out the boxed text, p621.

A British organisation called **Tourism Concern** (☎ in the UK 020-7133 3330; www.tourismconcern.org.uk; Stapleton House, 277-281 Holloway Rd, London N7 8HN) is primarily concerned with tourism and its impact upon local cultures and the environment. It has a range of publications and contacts for community organisations, as well as advice on minimising the impact of your travels.

All countries of the Middle East have literacy levels above 80%, except for Iraq (74.1%) and Syria (79.6%). The highest literacy rates are for men in Israel (98.5%) and the Palestinian Territories (96.7%), while lowest are women in Egypt (59.4%).

Middle East Stories

Telling stories is an age-old tradition in the Middle East. Although public storytelling is a dying art form in the region, every traveller to the Middle East will return home with a bag full of unforgettable experiences. As Lonely Planet authors, we have been criss-crossing the region for years, listening to the ordinary people of the Middle East (the region's real storytellers), setting out on adventures, then returning home to write our own stories. What follows are some of our favourites.

EGYPT

Diving the Mighty Thistlegorm

Though other bubble-blowing pundits may be chafing at the bit to disagree, I stand by my conviction that Egypt's SS *Thistlegorm* is the premiere wreck dive in the world. This steam-powered, 126.5m-long British armed freighter was on her way to restock army supplies in Tobruk (Libya) when she was sunk in the northern Red Sea by German bombers in 1941. The ship was packed to the brim with cargo – munitions, trucks, armoured cars, motorcycles, uniforms, aircrafts and even locomotives. Now resting just 30m below sea level, the famed freighter is surrounded by the clear waters of the Red Sea with her full payload intact.

The site is 3½ hours by boat from Sharm el-Sheikh, so when diving the *Thistlegorm* I normally arrange a trip on an overnight live-aboard from Dahab or Sharm. Due to the sheer size of the wreck and the amount of well-preserved paraphernalia on board, the site is usually explored over two dives, though having said that, I have done half-a-dozen dives on this wreck and have yet to see all it has to offer. On our first dive, we circumnavigated the outside of the ship. Everything down here lies preserved exactly as it was when it sank, encrusted in a thick film of algae and barnacles. Fish teem all over the wreck, darting in and out of the deck's cabins, around the long barrels of heavy-calibre machine guns and deep in the bowels of the cargo hold. Lying a few hundred metres away from the ship on the sandy floor is a locomotive that was thrown off the deck during the original bombing raid. It is one thing to see a sunken ship lying underneath the sea, but the odd sight of a train wreck brings a whole new surreal edge to the dive. Along the top deck we swim through the captain's cabin and over the dismembered cargo hold where the fateful bombs hit. The highlight of the dive is rounding the stern to see the massive 2m brass propeller, which completely dwarfs the divers as they fin their way around it.

The SS *Thistlegorm* is just one of hundreds of dive sites scattered the length and breadth of the Red Sea. Pick up a copy of Lonely Planet's *Diving & Snorkeling the Red Sea* for detailed descriptions of more than 80 of the best dive sites in the area.

The second dive is where the adrenaline kicks in, as we penetrate the twisted bowels of the cargo hold. Using torches to find our way, we grapple along from one section of the ship's hold to another. Most of the original supplies are still found here: boots, lorries, munitions and more. The most impressive sight is the Bedford trucks, all lined up in a row and each with three perfectly preserved BSA motorcycles mounted on the back. Up close, you can make out the individual details of these 65-year-old relics – from the motorcycle handbrakes to the tachometers on truck dashboards. There are so many details to discover in this living museum of WWII artefacts that one tank of air is barely enough to skim the surface. Before too long we must make our ascent, most of us vowing before we even break the surface that we will return to one the world's greatest underwater war memorials.

Rafael Wlodarski

A Little Sheesha on the Sidelines

Ahh sheesha, my one weakness. My Achilles heel if you will. In every nook and cranny of the country, in any town of any size, you will always find a café of some description serving *shai* (tea) and catering to the archaic tradition of smoking tobacco from a sheesha, or water pipe. In Cairo, I love nothing more than plonking myself down on a makeshift table outside one of the thousands of cafés that line that city's maze of streets and alleys. Partaking in the daily sheesha ritual feels like I am part of the club – an initiated member of the puffing *galabeya*-clad contingent that sit here pondering the events of the world. As our tobacco smoke is languidly inhaled the soothing soundtrack of bubbles wafts through the air. Upon exhalation, each plume of the sweet-smelling haze is charged with the quiet whispers of political debate and friendly gossip. A small cup of sweetly brewed tea is always within arm's reach; the diligent staff rarely allow it to stay empty for long. For me this is the best way to experience Cairo – by taking time out of the city's hectic schedule to sit, rest, converse with friends and watch the world through a lethargic mist of blue tobacco clouds.

Rafael Wlodarski

For a unique insight into Cairo – its politics, personalities and gossip – pick up a copy of Khalid Al Khamissy's *Tales of Rides*, which is a fascinating collection of personal stories from Cairene taxi drivers.

IRAQ

Backpacking Iraq

It's not everyday that Iraqi Kurds see American backpackers traipsing through their countryside. In some places, I was simply a curious anomaly. But in rural areas where America is considered to be the Kurdish peoples' liberator, we Yanks were practically treated to a hero's welcome.

Late one afternoon, my mate Chase and I – both Americans – arrived in the hillside town of Akre. We had just begun hiking up the steep town to look for a hotel when a Kurdish Peshmerga soldier armed with an AK-47 rifle ran over to us, glanced at our rucksacks and cameras, and demanded to know who we were. 'We are tourists,' I said. 'Em geshtiyar in,' Chase repeated in Kurdish. The dumbstruck soldier took us to his boss, Peshmerga Commander Ayoub, a round, jovial man with a friendly face, who was even more incredulous. We were the first Western visitors they had ever seen, American or otherwise. With a big grin and outstretched arms, Commander Ayoub welcomed us with steaming cups of hot tea and promptly assigned two of his soldiers to escort us on a sightseeing trip through town. 'Americans good,' Ayoub exclaimed with a thumbs-up sign, 'President Bush VERY good!'

The pro-American hospitality would be repeated several times during my journey. In Haji Omaran, a local English teacher insisted I stay overnight with his family as a guest of the village. In Choman, a college student and his grandmother dragged me to their home and fed me a lunch fit for a king. In Gali Ali Beg, a family of Iraqi Kurds whipped out their cell phones and insisted on having their photographs taken with me. And in Shaqlawa, hotel manager Karim kept us up until the wee hours to chat politics over mugs of cold Heineken beer. 'We may not necessarily agree with American policies,' he said, 'but we love American people!'

César Soriano

In 1928, New Zealand engineer Sir AM Hamilton was commissioned to build a road from Erbil to Haji Omaran through some of the most inhospitable terrain in the world. He recounted his successful mission in his 1937 travelogue, *Road Through Kurdistan*. It remains a timeless, travel-writing classic and a wonderful insight into the psyche of Iraqi Kurdish people.

War Correspondents Invade Iraq

By February 2003 the US-Iraq war seemed like a foregone conclusion. At the time, I was working as an entertainment and celebrity reporter for *USA Today*. Because I was a US Army veteran I was tasked to be one of 800 civilian journalists who would be 'embedded' with military forces for a front seat to war. In early March, I flew to Bahrain and hopped a

IT SEEMS RIDICULOUS, BUT I'M REALLY ENJOYING IRAQ *Tony Wheeler*

In this condensed extract from his book *Tony Wheeler's Bad Lands: A Tourist on the Axis of Evil*, Lonely Planet founder Tony Wheeler crosses the border from Turkey into Iraq. The year is 2006...

The border is a chaotic, muddy mess and it's raining solidly again. Husni seems to know exactly which door to head for, which window to bang on, which queue to barge to the front of and exactly whom to bribe. I spot him slipping a note into my passport before he hands it over to one official. Nevertheless it takes over an hour of zigzagging from one ramshackle building to another before we make the short drive across the bridge that conveys us into Iraq.

Arriving in Iraq is like a doorway to heaven. Suddenly I'm sitting in a clean, dry, mud-free waiting room being served glasses of tea while we wait for the passports to be processed – Husni's too. The officials decide to put me through hoops, however, and I have to spend 20 minutes explaining why I want to visit Iraq and what I do for a living. Finally they relent, hand my passport over, and welcome me to Iraq. I've already been welcomed by half a dozen Peshmerga soldiers, photographed with two of them and had a chat, in French, with one.

Husni drops me in a car park, and I take a taxi to Zakho to look at the town's ancient bridge before continuing on to Dohuk for the night. As we drive in to the centre there are a surprising number of hotels. I take an instant liking to Dohuk. It's bright, energetic and crowded and has lots of fruit-juice stands. I wander around the town, try out an internet café – it had such a tangle of wires leading in to the building, I concluded it had to be the centre of the World Wide Web – search inconclusively for Dohuk's bit of decaying castle wall, look in various shops in the bazaar, check out the money-changing quarter (there are no ATMs that work and credit cards don't function either) and take quite a few photographs. Everybody is very enthusiastic about being photographed, a sure sign that there aren't many tourists around.

puddle jumper to *USS Constellation*, an aircraft carrier with a crew of 5000 that would be my home for the next month. As embedded journalists, we lived, slept, ate and worked alongside young sailors and marines and followed them anywhere they went, even into combat. We floated around the Gulf for several weeks of sheer boredom and anxiety, waiting for war. On 19 March the war began with a volley of air strikes and missile attacks that were dubbed 'shock and awe'.

Imperial Life in the Emerald City: Inside Iraq's Green Zone by *Washington Post* reporter Rajiv Chandrasekaran is a blunt, often hilarious account at America's attempt at nation building after the 2003 US-led invasion. It leaves many a reader laughing, crying and furious. A film adaptation by director Paul Greengrass will be released in 2009.

Itching to get to the front lines, I made my way to the Kuwait Hilton, where many journalists were assembling to cover the biggest story on the planet. On 9 April, Baghdad fell to US forces. Still, I hitched a ride with several journalists to Basra. With no guards or customs officials at the border, we strolled into Iraq easily, occasionally passing British and American troops. In Basra, Richard Leiby (*Washington Post* journalist) and I hired a taxi to the capital. No armed guards, no weapons, just two guys and a taxi on the road to Baghdad. We arrived late at night to find hundreds of other journalists encamped at the famous Palestine Hotel. By then, the invasion was over, but little did we know that the war was just beginning.

Over the next several years, I returned to Iraq many times, occasionally embedding with other US forces including the US Marine Corps and US Army. Because of the ongoing violence, being embedded is often the only safe way for reporters to work and travel around Iraq, but it's also the most restrictive. Contrary to popular belief, most journalists working in Iraq are not embedded or hunkered down in the Green Zone. These 'unilaterals', to use military parlance, live and work alongside Iraqi civilians, sharing their lives and the danger.

Since 2003, more than 130 journalists have been killed covering the war in Iraq.

César Soriano

Erbil is a delight as well. A sign announces the Kurdish Textile Museum. Recently opened and very well presented, the museum displays an eclectic collection of carpets, kilims, saddle bags, baby carriers and other local crafts along with well-presented displays and information about the Kurdish people and nomadic tribes. Lolan Mustefa, who established the museum, is a mine of information on Erbil and the surrounding region. I'm enormously impressed that he has put so much effort into creating an excellent tourist attraction when Iraq today has so very few tourists.

From the museum I continue to the citadel's mosque, visit the hammam (or bathhouse) and enjoy the view over the city from the citadel walls on the other side. Back down below the citadel walls I explore the bazaars, inspect the kilim shops, joke with the shoeshine guys, check the selection of papers on sale at the newsstands, photograph the photographers waiting for customers outside the citadel, snack on a kebab and drop in to a fruit-juice stand for an orange juice. It seems ridiculous, but I'm really enjoying Iraq.

WHAT'S CHANGED? *César Soriano*

I retraced Tony's steps in 2008 while researching this guidebook. Thankfully, the Ibrahim Khalil border crossing isn't as chaotic anymore – it took less than 45 minutes to get from Silopi (Turkey) to Zakho, including customs and immigration processes (for information on the crossing, see p246). Like Tony, I took an instant liking to Dohuk; it's a wonderfully addictive town with a youthful feel and growing tourism industry. Iraq is still a cash country, but some places, including Erbil's Kurdish Textile Museum, now accept credit cards. ATMs are also popping up, but at the time of writing they only worked for Iraq-held accounts. In late 2006, the citizens of Erbil's citadel were controversially paid off and evicted from the ancient mound to make way for redevelopment; most of the citadel is now a ghost town. Thankfully, the tasty fruit-juice stands are still common throughout Iraqi Kurdistan.

JORDAN

Vertigo on Horseback

She didn't look capable of much when I slipped into the saddle but I should have known better than to underestimate a glossy chestnut Arab with a star on her nose. 'You can ride, no?' asked Mahmoud as we edged the horses uphill in the opposite direction to the Siq. Odd time to be asking the question, I thought as we broke into a trot on the makeshift bridlepath out of town.

I hadn't intended to go riding but when offered a different way to reach Petra's Treasury I hopped into the saddle without a second thought. 'You first person ever to say yes,' said Mahmoud, pointing his horse in the direction of a distant plateau, 'you must be crazy woman!' It was breathtakingly beautiful, high above the stone turrets of Petra, the crisp winter sun drawing the colours from the rocky outcrops like a magnet.

Suddenly we reached the edge of the plateau and the horses lurched immediately from a canter into a gallop, snorting breath into the cut-glass air. I just about remembered to lift out of the saddle, leaning forward as one whole, magnificent horsepower urged at full speed across the slight rise. Caught somewhere between fear and exhilaration, I noticed the plateau was large…but not that large, and that it was surrounded on three sides by the end of the world. It was towards this aerial vacancy that we were now charging at full speed.

The path narrowed, the vague outline of Petra's tortured rock formations passed below on either side of us and the edge loomed terrifyingly into view. 'Stop. Stop! Sto…!' The last 'p' disappeared over the rim of the plateau, together with heart, lungs and stomach. The rest of me came to a perfectly poised four-legged tiptoe on the vertical edge. We dismounted.

'Come,' said Mahmoud, 'let me show you *my* Petra.' Flattened out against the rock and gingerly looking down, I spotted two climbers below us on the opposite ledge. They too were looking down. Somewhere in the dark end-of-day gloom, a trail of tiny figures marched in single file up through the gap in the rock. 'I said I'd bring you to the Treasury,' said Mahmoud, triumphantly dangling over the ledge, high above the monument. 'Coming down?'

Jenny Walker

For an intimate picture of the ways that the Bedouin, like Mahmoud, make Petra their own, read *Married to a Bedouin* by Marguerite van Geldermalsen. The author met her husband in 1978 while backpacking around Jordan and spent the next two decades living near his extended family within the ancient city, raising three children and running the local clinic.

Careful Handling in Wadi Rum

We gripped the frosty rails of Vehicle Number 1 and headed for a sandy rise, safe in the hands of our Bedouin driver. Having written our own off-road guide, we knew exactly what he would be thinking – is it the right speed for the incline? Will the engine cope? Can we reverse downhill if necessary? But today it wasn't our responsibility, so when Vehicle Number 1 ground to a halt, spraying sand from all four wheels independently, we just laughed.

Time for Vehicle Number 2: a stranger bundled us into his cosy pickup and sailed competently over the dune, finding time with one hand to wrap me in a goat-hair blanket while answering his mobile with the other. He was 'on business' at a nearby camp but detoured to unload us into Vehicle Number 3.

Number 3 was a work of art – dashboard padded with sheepskin, dangling talismans against the evil eye, a door attached with masking tape and an absent handbrake. Unfortunately, there was an absence of petrol too and so we unwrapped our picnic, resigned to a long wait. One bite into a cow-cheese triangle and Vehicle Number 4 arrived, backfiring like a mule on chilli. Five minutes aboard this bucking bronco and it sneezed out the drive shaft.

The sun sank behind great auburn pillars of sandstone and it was mind-numbingly cold so we were pleased when a whistle produced Vehicle Number 5 – with its 14-year-old driver. With superb skill he delivered us to base and drove off without waiting for thanks.

Our memorable journey was a seamless display of care. None of the drivers asked us for money; they simply delivered us hand-over-hand into safety. The Bedouin don't pay lip service to 'hospitality' – they live it.

Jenny Walker

TE Lawrence didn't have the luxury of mechanised transport in the desert but he did document the extraordinary hospitality (not to mention irascibility and stubbornness) of the Howeitat of Wadi Rum in *Seven Pillars of Wisdom*. This epic account of the Arab Revolt, in which he took part, remains the most intimate account of this region ever written in English.

ISRAEL

A Hard Day at the Beach

There's no better a day in Israel than one spent on the beach in September. The weather's perfect – hot but not blistering; breezy but not sand-blinding – and the Mediterranean's warm and glassy as a soothing bath. The crowds of international tourists have gone home, the Israeli kids are back at school, and the local, vocal lifeguards have closed their megaphones for the season, leaving vast swathes of sparkling sand for the rest of us to relish.

Our usual lazy location is a beach just north of Tel Aviv, since there's safe paddling for the children and a strong line in passionfruit margaritas for the grown-ups. We pick a shady spot, strip our tribe of toddlers down to the bare essentials, and settle in for sandcastles, sun and snacks. It's the most mellow day out you could hope for in the midst of the Middle East.

Today, I've brought along a British friend's two little children to play with our gang of four. Armed with buckets and spades, I head down the steps to the beach in sole charge of my group of six blonde-haired, blue-eyed under-4s, constantly counting the numbers to ensure no one's gone AWOL.

'French fries, everyone,' I call, as the legion of little children trots eagerly along behind me all the way to the waterfront. At this time of year, the beach's usual crowds have been replaced by a regular clientele of squawking old ladies, gossiping, smoking and playing cards beneath their parasols. I walk. The children follow. A hush descends among the ranks of pensioners. Mouths gape as the children parade past them like a gaggle of ducklings. 'They *can't* all be hers...can they?' I hear the crowd whispering. 'What *hard* work it must be!' It's very rare you see blonde toddlers in Israel. It's even rarer to see so many old ladies so quiet.

We reach the shoreline and I sink my toes into the sand. The ladies resume their squawking, I stretch out in my sarong and the children head for the open sea. A bronzed waiter appears. 'Chips for six, please,' I smile. He raises an eyebrow. 'And a margarita for their hard-working mother.'

Amelia Thomas

For a great beach read, pick up Israeli author David Grossman's novel, *The Zigzag Kid*, which tells the story of a 12-year-old boy's trials and adventures on the eve of his Bar Mitzvah. Grossman is one of Israel's most successful authors in translation and has also published several children's books.

PALESTINIAN TERRITORIES

A Light in the Darkness

On the road as a Lonely Planet author and journalist in the West Bank and Gaza, it often seems that the scales are balanced precariously between the good and the bad. There was the Christmas tree–lighting ceremony in Bethlehem's Manger Sq, beneath a magical snow flurry. The time, during Israel's Gaza disengagement of 2005, when I found myself holed up with a group of armed Jewish militant settlers inside an abandoned old hotel. An afternoon spent with the head of the militant Al Aqsa Martyrs Brigade in restive Jenin refugee camp. The cold beers sipped at Taybeh Brewery's happy hilltop Oktoberfest. The hours I queued pregnant at the Erez checkpoint after researching the Gaza Strip, hoping I wouldn't go into labour before complacent soldiers allowed me back into Israel.

Sometimes, when the scales seem to be tilting in favour of the bad, I remember a trip I took into the scruffy Aida Refugee Camp, on the outskirts of Bethlehem, where one determined man has made a difference to a generation of children's lives.

'Welcome!' Abdelfattah Abu Srour greeted me with a grin. 'Come on in!'

In Aida camp it's hard to imagine that anyone spends much time smiling. Immured behind Israel's 'security wall' and subjected to frequent military incursions, it's a place of concrete, curfews and barbed wire. But Abdelfattah has pledged to make life better for the kids of the camp, creating the Al Rowwad theatre centre as a stage on which to set free their everyday frustrations.

That afternoon I wandered its small rooms watching children rehearsing a new play, with Abdelfattah their diligent director. Other kids were taking music lessons, working on computers and surfing the internet. The centre is a blazing light in an otherwise dark world, providing hope and happiness for dozens of Palestinian children. We drank a cup of coffee. I listened to Abdelfattah's dreams for the centre's future and I knew that while people like him are hard at work ensuring children can continue to dream, the scales haven't tipped too far in the wrong direction.

Amelia Thomas

Get hold of a copy of *Growing Up Palestinian: Israeli Occupation and the Intifada Generation* by Laetitia Bucaille, for a glimpse into the lives of young Palestinians who have never experienced the world outside their refugee-camp homes.

TRAVEL PLANNER

	Egypt	Iraq	Israel & the Palestinian Territories
City Life	clamorous Cairo (p124), sophisticated Alexandria (p145)	beautiful Sulaymaniyah (p237)	soulful Jerusalem (p260), vibrant Tel Aviv (p275)
Mighty Ruins	the Pyramids (p128), Egyptian Museum (p132), Temples of Karnak (p155), Valley of the Kings (p157), Abu Simbel (p174)	Babylon (p223) & Nineveh (p226) - but not just yet	Caesarea (p292)
Outdoor Adventure	sailing a felucca up the Nile (p169), diving the Red Sea at Dahab (p195) or Sharm el-Sheikh (p191), 4WD safari into the White & Black Deserts (p178), climbing Mt Sinai (p199), kite-surfing at Hurghada (p185)	just being in Iraq is an adventure	watersports off Eilat (p311), hiking the Upper Galilee & Golan Heights (p303), night hiking in the Negev (p308)
Top Festivals	Ascension of Ramses II, Abu Simbel (22 Feb & 22 Oct; p204)	Nowruz Festival, Akre (21 Mar; p231)	Jerusalem Jazz Festival (Jun; p327), Karmi'el Dance Festival (Jul; p328), Beresheet Festival (Sep; p328)
Memorable Meals	Abou El Sid, Cairo (p140), Hood Gondol Seafood, Alexandria (p150), Sofra, Luxor (p163), on the banks of the Nile during your felucca trip (p169)	Park Restaurant, Erbil (p236), Restaurant Dunya, Sulav (p231), wherever you can find *masgouf* (p223)	pack a picnic at Mahane Yehuda Market, Jerusalem (p268), Douzan, Haifa (p291), Hummus Said, Akko (p294), Diana, Nazareth (p296)
Super Souqs	Khan al-Khalili Bazaar (p134)	Dohuk Bazaar (p228), Qaysari Bazaar, Erbil (p236)	Al-Balda al-Qadima souq, Nazareth (p295)
Off the Beaten Track	Western Oases (p175), Al-Quseir (p187), Ras Mohammed National Park (p189)	just about anywhere	Negev Desert (p307), West Bank (p315)

LEBANON

Breakfast on Mt Lebanon

It's early morning in the Mt Lebanon Ranges and I'm standing in a forgotten field that's full of ancient Greek ruins, en route to the ancient Lebanese port town of Byblos. Gunshots ring out in the clear morning air, echoing through ancient temple archways as I pick my way across the desolate, rock-studded site. Not another soul is in sight. Bang. Bang, bang. The volley is getting louder. Lebanon is a relatively peaceful place just now; I've picked a

Jordan	Lebanon	Syria	Turkey
multifaceted Amman (p343)	glamorous Beirut (p415), Mamluk Tripoli (p432)	timeless Damascus (p464), medieval Aleppo (p491), laid-back Lattakia (p503)	cosmopolitan İstanbul (p536), surprising Ankara (p583)
Petra (p373), Jerash (p355)	Baalbek (p447), Byblos (p429)	Palmyra (p509), Bosra (p481), Apamea (p490), Dura Europos (p517)	Ephesus (p563) Troy (p556), Mt Nemrut (p606)
diving & snorkelling the Red Sea (p386), hiking in the Dana Nature Reserve (p371), canyoning in Wadi Mujib Nature Reserve (p362), desert safari in Wadi Rum (p381)	caving in the Jeita Grotto (p428), skiing amid the Cedars (p438), hiking in the Qadisha Valley (p438)	camel safaris from Palmyra (p513)	hot-air ballooning over Cappadocia (p588), sea-kayaking over a sunken city near Kaş (p576), climbing Mt Ararat (p599), tandem paragliding in Ölüdeniz (p574)
Jerash Festival (Jul & Aug; p390), Distant Heat Festival, Wadi Rum & Aqaba (Jul; p390)	Baalbek Festival (Jul-Aug; p453), Beiteddine Festival (Jul-Aug; p453), Byblos International Festival (Jul-Aug; p453), Beirut International Film Festival (Oct; p453)	Bosra Festival (Sep or Oct; p522), Damascus International Film Festival (Nov; p522)	Kırkpınar Oil Wrestling Championship, Edirne (Jun or Jul; p611), International İstanbul Music p611), Mevlâna Festival, Konya (Dec; p611)
Umm Qais Resthouse, Umm Qais (p360), Kir Heres Restaurant, Karak (p370), Petra Kitchen, Petra (p379), under the stars with the Bedouin, Wadi Rum (p381)	Le Chef, Beirut (p424), Shahrazad, Baalbek (p450)	courtyard restaurants of Damascus (p476) & Aleppo (p500), Zekrayat Restaurant, Lattakia (p506)	Sofyalı 9, İstanbul (p549), Sultan Garden Restaurant, Kaş (p576), Dibek, Göreme (p590), Ziggy's, Ürgüp (p592)
catch a bus from Jordan to Damascus (Syria)	Tripoli (p433)	Damascus (p468), Aleppo (p494)	Grand Bazaar, İstanbul (p541), Şanlıurfa (p605)
Umm Qais (p359), desert castles (p363)	Tyre (p442), Deir al-Qamar (p445)	Rasafa (p518)	Diyarbakır (p602)

lull between political assassinations, Palestinian gun battles and Hezbollah upheavals. But still, I'm five months pregnant and in Lebanon you never know what's lurking around the corner. Bang. Bang. I hurry across grass crisp with frost towards the gatekeeper's hut, which was unmanned when I entered. The gatekeeper appears, grinning, with a rifle over his shoulder. 'Rabbits,' he declares, 'for breakfast.' He gazes at my tummy. 'Coffee?' He produces a battered kettle. 'Strong and sweet. Good for the baby.'

Amelia Thomas

Waxing Lyrical in Deir al-Qamar

Waxworks have never really been my cup of tea, so it seemed unfortunate that one of Lebanon's favourite national pastimes appeared to be traipsing around musty halls filled with the slightly skewed features of long-dead politicians, national heroes, and the odd tragic British princess or George Bush Sr. Everywhere I went in Lebanon, there was yet another waxworks – big, small, or downright bizarre – just waiting for me to step intrepidly inside, and Deir al-Qamar was no different.

Lebanon's contradictory nature – a place overshadowed by the threat of extreme violence, but offering relentlessly warm hospitality – is captured in all its tragic humanity in Robert Fisk's *Pity the Nation: Lebanon at War,* though unlike my morning in the mountains, he was often dodging real bullets.

We arrived back in the small, picturesque town – Lebanon's prettiest – after a long day trekking the trails of the vast Chouf Cedar Reserve. The late afternoon light was fading from pink to russet and bats were emerging from the eaves of ancient buildings surrounding the town square. The small grocery stores were closing their doors for the night, the café on the square was full of locals and tourists winding down over ice-cold beers, and yet, to my chagrin, the waxworks was still open, with reception lights blazing.

'Come in, come in!' the ticket clerk cried, as I peered reluctantly into the lobby.

'I wouldn't want to bother you if you're about to…'

'Nonsense! Our guide is honoured to show you our collection.' On cue, an ancient, near-deaf man in a dirty baseball cap stepped grinning eagerly from the shadows, 'Come in!'

I took a deep breath, assumed my most fascinated expression and put my best foot forward.

'Jumblatt…Jumblatt Junior…Senior…Senior's Father…Headless Jumblatt!' the old guide barked, in English and then in French, as he frog-marched us into our third long gallery, this one filled with weird wax renditions of the powerful Druze chieftain clan.

'Why is he headless?' I ventured.

'Quoi?' he yelled, cupping a hand to his ears and continued on regardless.

A full and excruciating 30 minutes later, the tour concluded with a final quick-fire bilingual round of 20 obscure historical figures and one hoarse old tour guide. We applauded with relief as he came to the end of his spiel. He bowed proudly.

'Mademoiselle,' he confided, leaning forward, 'it has been a pleasure to meet someone who appreciates beauty.'

'Well, I…' I began.

'So much so,' he seemed not to hear me, 'that there's a little something extra you might be interested to see.'

My heart sank. Visions of a hidden Albert Hall of wax dummies filled my mind.

'Allons-y,' he shuffled off, 'follow, please.'

Outside, night had closed in and bright strings of fairy lights illuminated the town square. I looked over with envy at the terrace café, where crowds sat listening to a local musician. The old man beckoned, producing a fistful of keys and fumbling with the lock in a heavy wooden door. I sighed and followed.

Up on the roof of the once-grand, abandoned summer palace, the view of the town was something from a dream. Low clouds rolled gently across the rooftops, mingling with woodsmoke from crooked chimneys. The lights on the square below twinkled. An owl hooted and swept by in a feathery hush. I surveyed the fairytale rooftop scene, reflected a thousand times in the broken window panes of the once-grand hall of the summer palace. This was well worth 30 minutes of morose, melting mannequins.

'It's beautiful,' I whispered to myself.

'Oui, mademoiselle,' the old man's hearing was suddenly sharp as a shard of broken window, '*almost* as beautiful as the waxworks.'

Amelia Thomas

Deir al-Qamar seems to have changed little in the last century or so. For a strong evocation of 19th-century Lebanon, delve into *The Rock of Tanios* by journalist Amin Maalouf, which tells a compelling tale of murder and mystery in a Lebanese village.

SYRIA

Damascus Nights

It was almost 10 years to the night since I had first walked down the steps behind the Umayyad Mosque in Damascus and through the doors of Al-Nawfara Coffee Shop. It was like coming home. For three months back in 1998, I had spent almost every evening here, arriving a couple of hours before the sunset call to prayer to find a quiet corner to write and chat with the locals before Abu Shady, the resident *hakawati* (storyteller), took his throne. Occasionally, in the manner of all live acts, his performance fell flat. But when it worked there was magic in the air as he wove fabulous tales, berated his audience and slammed down his sword for dramatic effect. In the time that I had been away from the Al-Nawfara Coffee Shop I had been drawn to the art of storytelling around the world. One time in particular, in the southern Spanish city of Granada, I had entered a tea room in the old Albaicín quarter and been assailed with apple-scented tobacco and the memories of stories told in Damascus.

But this time was different. The popularity of storytelling, that most noble of Middle Eastern art forms, is waning, displaced by gyrating pop divas beamed live from Beirut. Abu Shady had been one of my heroes. He was not a young man when I saw him last. That he was now the last heir to the Sheherezade throne had me worried – would I find him still telling tall tales?

I pulled up a chair in the corner of the shop, inhaled deeply and looked around. There in the corner, in the same seat that he has occupied for the past 10 years and probably longer, Mohammed was drawing long and hard on his nargileh. When I introduced myself and asked if he remembered me (he clearly didn't), he exhaled and said without hesitation, 'Yes, and you still owe me money.' I looked around at the other faces, most of which were lined with the passing years but unmistakeably the same. And there in the corner sat Abu Shady, chain-smoking and reminiscing about old times with his friends. When he donned his waistcoat and planted his tarboosh atop his head and climbed his throne, I felt a frisson of excitement. And then, with the manner of a kindly grandfather, with all the passion of an angry imam, he began to tell the story of the star-crossed lovers of Anta and Abla. The years melted away. When he was finished Abu Shady shuffled off into the night, leaving me to draw long draughts of reassurance from my nargileh.

In *Damascus Nights,* Rafik Schami, the exiled Damascene writer, tells the marvellous story of Salim the coachman, a storyteller in Damascus who loses his voice and only the seven stories of seven friends can bring it back. In its sense of magic, rambling digressions and larger-than-life characters, it's just like a night spent at Al-Nawfara Coffee Shop.

By interviewing Abu Shady for this book, I came to know a man with a passion for stories, a greengrocer by day who devours the classic works of world literature in his spare time, a man who believes that although he is one of the world's last storytellers, the tradition will never die. The world will, he assured me, always need stories, then he introduced me to his son, Shady, who promised that he stands ready to continue the tradition when his father retires.

Anthony Ham

Hospitality's Generation Next

As I picked my way through the ruins of Palmyra, I became accustomed to men with camels, men with portable eskies and men with 'old Roman coins, very cheap'. But Hamid, a local Bedouin boy, was different – he asked for nothing more than a coin to add to his collection. Finally, he settled on a 50¢ coin, forsaking the more-valuable €1 and €2 coins on offer because he already had them. He handed me a set of dusty postcards. Keep the postcards and the coin, I told him. Suddenly serious-faced, he gave back the coin, assuring me that he had never accepted money for nothing and didn't intend to start now.

A few weeks later, outside the citadel in Aleppo, I found Abdul lingering in my shadow. This quiet, gentle boy became my silent companion as I wandered through the souqs, translating for me when my Arabic wasn't up to it, always polite, never asking for anything in return. Later again, this time in the courtyard of the Umayyad Mosque in Damascus, a young girl named Fatima began by playing with my daughter and ended by inviting us to her family's home for a meal. I had long ago grown used to friendliness at every turn and gracious hospitality in Syria. I just wasn't expecting it to start so young.

Anthony Ham

To understand the Syrian love of hospitality at a deeper level, read *Damascus: Taste of a City* by Marie Fadel and Rafik Schami, while the lives of children across the region take centre stage in the enlightening *Children in the Muslim Middle East*, by Elizabeth Warnock Fernea.

TURKEY

Divriği's Divine Doors

It was a typical start to a Turkish journey. I took a taxi to the Sivas otogar, where the men shook their *şapkas* (hats) and said the next dolmuş to the southeast left in a few hours. As I had more than 350km to cover that day, I decided to tear up the thrifty traveller's rulebook and commandeer the taxi. The driver's eyes bulged behind his glasses, but he rapidly recovered and calculated the charge. We negotiated and haggled and bartered and frowned and, eventually, smiled and shook hands. Woohoo!

Bircan (the driver and I were now on first-name terms) steered us out of town. The rolling hills had one-mosque villages in their folds and stickmen shepherds on their ridges. Our first stop was Kangal, announced by a statue of a black-faced, pale-bodied, spiky-collared canine. Kangal dogs, originally bred to protect sheep from wolves and bears, are now man's best friend across Turkey.

Another type of creature had drawn me to this remote service town and I soon came face to scaly face with it at the Balıklı Kaplıca health spa. The warm water is inhabited by 'doctor fish', underwater ticklers that nibble fingers, toes and any other body part you offer them. The fish supposedly favour psoriasis-inflicted skin and the spa attracts patients from all over the world, but the school happily gets stuck into any patch of flesh. It's wonderfully therapeutic to dangle your feet in the water and feel nature giving you a thorough pedicure.

Shirking the recommended three-week treatment, we returned to the taxi. As the dry brown hills turned into snow-capped mountains, the road began to resemble a rollercoaster and Bircan's driving became increasingly inventive. Luckily, he was paying a rare visit to the right side of the white lines when we arrived at the military checkpoint.

Bircan's English was as lousy as my Turkish, but we always managed to communicate the important things. When the soldiers had examined our IDs and waved us on, he explained, 'PKK…terror!' The years of widespread insurgency in Kurdish southeastern Anatolia are over, but the area's fearsome reputation endures, as do military operations against the PKK (Kurdistan Workers Party).

Our last stop before taking the Big Dipper home was Divriği, a town dominated by Alevi Muslims in a valley between 2000m-plus mountains. It had a tense feel, but there was a good reason to come here. Three reasons, in fact. The Ulu Cami mosque and *medrese* (Islamic seminary), built in 1228 and named on the Unesco World Heritage list, has a trio of doorways carved in mind-boggling detail. Each door is decorated with a stone starburst of flowers, medallions, interlinking geometric forms and Arabic inscriptions.

When Bircan had finished praying, I asked him if he was glad I'd dragged him all this way. He smiled. The doors were so intricately carved, he said, that their craftsmanship proved the existence of God.

James Bainbridge

Above the Fairy Chimneys

Morning! For the first time in my life, I was happy to get up at 5am. I was taking a balloon flight over Cappadocia's unique landscape of fairy chimneys (rock formations). With 10 other passengers, I clambered into the basket and took a deep breath of crisp country air as we left the ground crew far below.

The valleys housing the chimneys looked as remarkable, if not as snigger-inducing, as the often-phallic formations; the wavy tuff (compressed volcanic ash) resembled a mound of wobbly blancmange. With the balloon's bulbous shadow falling on the curvy cliff faces, it was a symphony of surreal shapes.

Some 28 balloons fly most mornings and the multicoloured craft dotted the blue sky. The pilot was able to control the balloon's height to within a few centimetres, allowing us to descend into a valley to pinch some breakfast from an apricot tree in a secret garden. Around us, the rock was riddled with pigeon houses, traditionally used to collect the birds' droppings for fertilising the fields. As we used the katabatic currents of cool air to surf down the valleys, or rose on a warm anabatic wind, the only sound was the flame shooting into the balloon.

Leaving the fairy chimneys, we climbed almost 1000m and admired Erciyes Dağı (Mt Erciyes), which formed Cappadocia when it erupted. I had to pinch myself to check I hadn't overslept: moving effortlessly through the air above those flowing valleys was just like dreaming.

James Bainbridge

Andrew Eames recounts his journey to ancient sites in *The 8.55 to Baghdad*. On the eve of the Iraq War, he retraced the British crime writer Agatha Christie's life-changing train journey through the Balkans and the Middle East to Ur, Iraq. A chapter covers his Turkish adventures.

Former Lonely Planet author Tom Brosnahan's memoir, *Turkey: Bright Sun, Strong Tea,* begins high above the Atlantic Ocean, as the US writer-to-be flies to Turkey at the end of the 'Summer of Love', to work for the Peace Corps in İzmir.

History, Politics & Foreign Affairs

Five out of the Seven Wonders of the Ancient World were within the boundaries of the modern Middle East: the Temple of Artemis (Turkey), the Mausoleum of Halicarnassus (Turkey), the Hanging Gardens of Babylon (Iraq), Pharos of Alexandria (Egypt) and the Pyramids of Giza (Egypt).

The Middle East *is* history, home to a roll-call of some of the most important landmarks in human history. Mesopotamia (now Iraq) was the undisputed cradle of civilisation. Damascus (Syria), Aleppo (Syria), Byblos (Lebanon), Jericho (Israel and the Palestinian Territories) and Erbil (Iraq) all stake compelling claims to be the oldest continuously inhabited cities on earth. And it was here in the Middle East that the three great monotheistic religions – Judaism, Christianity and Islam – were born. Fast forward to the present and the great issues of the day – oil, religious coexistence, terrorism and conflicts over land – find their most compelling expression in the Middle East. It remains as true as it has for thousands of years that what happens here ripples out across the world and will shape what happens next in world history.

This section sketches out the broadest sweeps of Middle Eastern history – for further details see the more-specific history sections in the individual country chapters throughout this book.

CRADLE OF CIVILISATION

The Great Pyramid of Khufu (built in 2570 BC) remained the tallest artificial structure in the world until the building of the Eiffel Tower in 1889.

The first human beings to walk the earth did just that: they walked. In their endless search for sustenance and shelter, they roamed the earth, hunting, foraging plants for food and erecting makeshift shelters as they went. The world's first nomads, they carried what they needed; most likely they lived in perfect harmony with nature and left next to nothing behind for future generations to write their story. It was a difficult life, always on the move and vulnerable to predators and the elements. Increasingly, when they found a spot they liked, they stayed a little longer, either in caves or in shelters that would last long beyond the next morning. By observing the plants that bore food, they planted their first rudimentary crops and began to develop stone tools. Thus it was that they began to put down roots.

The first signs of agriculture, arguably the first major signpost along the march of human history, grew from the soils surrounding Jericho in what is now the West Bank, around 8500 BC. Forced by a drying climate and the need to cluster around known water sources, these early Middle Easterners added wild cereals to their diet and learned to farm them. In the centuries that followed, these and other farming communities spread east into Mesopotamia (a name later given by the Greeks, meaning 'Be-

TIMELINE

250,000 BC

The earliest traces of human presence appear in the Nile Valley. Little is known about them, but they are thought to be nomadic hunter-gatherers.

5000 BC

Al-Ubaid culture, the forerunner to the great civilisations that would earn Mesopotamia (now Iraq) the sobriquet of the cradle of civilisation, arises in the land between the Tigris and Euphrates rivers.

4000 BC

The Sumerian civilisation, immortalised in the *Epic of Gilgamesh,* takes hold in Mesopotamia. They would rule the region until the 24th century BC and invent cuneiform, the world's first writing.

THE MIDDLE EAST'S INDIGENOUS EMPIRES AT A GLANCE

Few regions can match the Middle East for its wealth of ancient civilisations, all of which have left their mark upon history.

Sumerians (4000–2350 BC) Mesopotamia's first great civilisation developed advanced irrigation systems, produced surplus food and invented the earliest form of writing.

Egyptians (3100–400 BC) This most enduring of ancient empires was a world of Pharaonic dynasties, exquisite art forms, the Pyramids and royal tombs. The monumental architecture of the empire reached new heights of aesthetic beauty.

Babylonians (1750–1180 BC) This empire further developed the cuneiform script and was one of the first civilisations to codify laws to govern the Tigris-Euphrates region from the capital at Babylon, one of the great centres of the ancient world.

Assyrians (1600–609 BC) Conquerors of territories far and wide and shrewd administrators of their domains from their exquisite capital at Nineveh, the Assyrians also developed the forerunners of modern banking and accounting systems. Their heyday was the 9th century BC.

Persians (6th–4th centuries BC) The relatively short-lived dynasties begun by Cyrus the Great ruled from India to the Aegean Sea and produced the stunning ancient city of Persepolis.

Ottomans (1300s–1918) The last of the great indigenous empires to encompass most of the Middle East. From the opulent capital in Constantinople, they governed from Iraq to North Africa before the decadence of Ottoman rule (and the ungovernable size of their realm) got the better of them.

tween Two Rivers'), where the fertile soils of the Tigris and Euphrates floodplains were ideally suited to the new endeavour. For some historians, this was a homecoming of sorts for humankind: these two rivers are among the four that, according to the Bible, flowed into the Garden of Eden. At around the same time, the enduring shift from nomadism to more sedentary, organised societies was gathering pace in the Nile River valley of ancient Egypt.

In the 6th century BC, a culture known as Al-Ubaid first appeared in Mesopotamia. We know little about it, largely because it was soon supplanted by the Sumerians who were the first to build cities and to support them with year-round agriculture and river-borne trade. In the blink of a historical eye, although almost 2000 years later in reality, the Sumerians invented the first known form of writing: cuneiform, which consisted primarily of pictographs and would later evolve into alphabets on which modern writing is based. With agriculture and writing mastered, the world's first civilisation had been born.

The Penguin Guide to Ancient Egypt, by William J Murnane, is one of the best overall books on the lifestyle and monuments of the Pharaonic period, with illustrations and descriptions of the major temples and tombs.

Elsewhere across the region, in around 3100 BC, the kingdoms of Upper and Lower Egypt were unified under Menes, ushering in 3000 years of Pharaonic rule in the Nile Valley. The Levant (present-day Lebanon, Syria, Jordan and Israel and the Palestinian Territories) was well settled by this time, and local powers included the Amorites and the Canaanites.

3100 BC

Along the banks of the Nile, Menes unites the kingdoms of Upper and Lower Egypt. Thus begins one of the great civilisations of antiquity, ancient Egypt of the pharaohs who would rule for almost 3000 years.

1800 BC

According to the Book of Genesis, Abraham, the great patriarch of the Jewish faith and prophet in both Christianity and Islam, is born in Ur of the Chaldees in Mesopotamia.

1750 BC

The Babylonian kingdoms are first united under Hammurabi, who brings much of Mesopotamia within Babylonian power, creating the capital, the Hanging Gardens of Babylon. They would rule the Tigris-Euphrates region for over 500 years.

BIRTH OF EMPIRE

With small settlements having grown into city-states, and with these city-states drawing outlying settlements into their orbit, civilisations were no longer content to mind their own business. The moment in history when civilisations evolved into empires is unclear, but by the 3rd century BC, the kings of what we now know as the Middle East had listened to the fragmented news brought by traders of fabulous riches just beyond the horizon.

The Cyrus Cylinder, which is housed at the British Museum with a replica at the UN, is a clay tablet with cuneiform inscriptions, and is widely considered to be the world's first charter of human rights.

The Sumerians, who were no doubt rather pleased with having tamed agriculture and inventing writing, never saw the Akkadians coming. One of many city-states that fell within the Sumerian realm, Akkad, on the banks of the Euphrates southwest of modern Baghdad, had grown in power, and, in the late 24th and early 23rd centuries BC, Sargon of Akkad conquered Mesopotamia and then extended his rule over much of the Levant. The era of empire, which would convulse the region almost until the present day, had begun.

Although the Akkadian Empire would last no more than a century, his idea caught on. The at-once sophisticated and war-like Assyrians, whose empire would, from their capital at Nineveh (Iraq), later encompass the entire Middle East, were the most enduring power. Along with their perennial Mesopotamian rivals, the Babylonians, the Assyrians would dominate the human history of the region for almost 1000 years.

In 333 BC, Persian Emperor Darius, facing defeat by Alexander, abandoned his wife, children and mother on the battlefield. His mother was so disgusted she disowned him and adopted Alexander as her son.

The 7th century BC saw both the conquest of Egypt by Assyria and, far to the east, the rise of the Medes, the first of many great Persian empires. In 550 BC, the Medes were conquered by Cyrus the Great, usually regarded as the first Persian shah (king).

Over the next 60 years, Cyrus and his successors Cambyses (r 525–522 BC) and Darius I (r 521–486 BC) swept west and north to conquer first Babylon and then Egypt, Asia Minor and parts of Greece. After the Greeks stemmed the Persian tide at the Battle of Marathon in 490 BC, Darius and Xerxes (r 486–466 BC) turned their attention to consolidating their empire.

Egypt won independence from the Persians in 401 BC, only to be reconquered 60 years later. The second Persian occupation of Egypt was brief: little more than a decade after they arrived, the Persians were again driven out of Egypt, this time by the Greeks. Europe had arrived on the scene and would hold sway in some form for almost 1000 years until the birth of Islam.

The Epic of Gilgamesh, written in 2700 BC and one of the first works of world literature, tells the story of a Sumerian king from the ancient city of Uruk (which gave Iraq its name).

HERE COME THE GREEKS

The definition of which territories constitute 'the Middle East' has always been a fluid concept. No-one, least of all the Turks, can decide whether theirs is a European or Middle Eastern country. And some cultural geographers claim that the Middle East includes all countries of the Arab world as

1600–609 BC

The Assyrian Empire, with its renowned administrative prowess and war-like conquests, rules from its capital at Nineveh (present-day Iraq) over a territory that reaches as far as Egypt. Its heyday is around 900 BC.

1500 BC

The Phoenicians set out to conquer the waters of the Mediterranean from their base in Tyre and Sidon (modern-day Lebanon). Primarily a trading empire, they establish ports around the Mediterranean rim and rule the seas for 1200 years.

15th Century BC

Hieroglyphic tablets make reference to a city called 'Dimashqa', which was conquered by the Egyptians. It's the first written record of a city (perhaps the world's oldest) that may date back to 3000 BC.

THE PHOENICIANS

The ancient Phoenician Empire (1500–300 BC), which thrived along the Lebanese coast, may have been the world's first rulers of the sea, for their empire was the Mediterranean Sea and its ports, and their lasting legacy was to spread the early gains of Middle Eastern civilisation to the rest of the world.

An offshoot of the Canaanites in the Levant, the Phoenicians first established themselves in the (now Lebanese) ports of Tyre and Sidon. Quick to realise that there was money to be made across the waters, they cast off in their galleys, launching in the process the first era of true globalisation. From the unlikely success of selling purple dye and sea snails to the Greeks, they expanded their repertoire to include copper from Cyprus, silver from Iberia and even tin from Great Britain.

As their reach expanded, so too did the Phoenicians' need for safe ports around the Mediterranean rim. Thus it was that Carthage, one of the greatest cities of the ancient world, was founded in what is now Tunisia in 814 BC. Long politically dependent on the mother culture in Tyre, Carthage eventually emerged as an independent, commercial empire. By 517 BC, the powerful city-state was the leading city of North Africa, and by the 4th century BC, Carthage controlled the North African coast from Libya to the Atlantic.

But the nascent Roman Empire didn't take kindly to these Lebanese upstarts effectively controlling the waters of the Mediterranean Sea, and challenged them both militarily and with economic blockades. With Tyre and Sidon themselves severely weakened and unable to send help, Carthage took on Rome and lost, badly. The Punic Wars (Phoenician civilisation in North Africa was called 'Punic') between Carthage and Rome (264–241 BC, 218–201 BC and 149–146 BC) reduced Carthage, the last outpost of Phoenician power, to a small, vulnerable African state. It was razed by the Romans in 146 BC, the site symbolically sprinkled with salt and damned forever.

far west as Morocco. But most historians agree that the Middle East's eastern boundaries were determined by the Greeks in the 4th century BC.

In 336 BC, Philip II of Macedonia, a warlord who had conquered much of mainland Greece, was murdered. His son Alexander assumed the throne and began a series of conquests that would eventually encompass most of Asia Minor, the Middle East, Persia and northern India.

Under Alexander, the Greeks were the first to impose any kind of order on the Middle East as a whole. Traces of their rule ring the eastern Mediterranean from Ephesus in Turkey to the oasis of Siwa in Egypt's Western Desert. Perhaps the greatest remnants of Greek rule, however, lie on the outer boundaries of the former Greek empire, in the Cyrenaica region of Libya where the glorious cities of the Pentapolis (Five Cities) bore all the hallmarks of Greek sophistication and scholarship.

In 331 BC, just five years after taking control, Alexander the Great's armies swept into what is now Libya, although the great man himself stopped at the border after the Cyrenaicans greeted him with promises of loyalty. Greek rule extended as far east as what is now the Libyan city of Benghazi, beyond which the Romans would hold sway. Ever since, the

Mesopotamia: The Invention of the City, by Gwendolyn Leick, takes a walk through the history of the great cities of Mesopotamia, including Babylon and Nineveh, and the civilisations that built them.

The southern Spanish city of Cádiz is the oldest continuously inhabited city on the Iberian Peninsula. It was founded as Gades by the Phoenicians in 1110 BC.

663 BC

After a series of military and diplomatic confrontations, Ashurbanipal, King of the Assyrians, attacks Egypt, sacks Thebes and loots the Temple of Amun.

550–610 BC

Cyrus the Great forms one of the ancient world's most enlightened empires in Persia, known for its tolerance and the freedoms granted to subject peoples. He and his successor Cambyses conquer Greece and Egypt.

586 BC

Babylonia's King Nebuchadnezzar marches on Jerusalem, destroys the Jewish temple and carries the Jewish elite and many of their subjects into Mesopotamian exile.

ALEXANDER THE GREAT

One of the greatest figures to ever stride the Middle Eastern stage, Alexander (356–323 BC) was born into greatness. His father was King Philip II of Macedonia, who many people believed was a descendant of the god Hercules, and his mother was Princess Olympias of Epirus, who counted the legendary Achilles among her ancestors. For his part, the precocious young Alexander sometimes claimed that Zeus was his real father.

Alexander was the ultimate alpha male, as well versed in poetry as in the ways of war. At the age of 12, the young Alexander tamed Bucephalus, a horse that the most accomplished horsemen of Macedonia dared not ride. By 13, he had Aristotle as his personal tutor. His interests were diverse – he could play the lyre, but he also learned Homer's *Iliad* by heart and admired the Persian ruler Cyrus the Great for the respect he granted to the cultures he conquered.

He rode out of Macedonia in 334 BC to embark on a decade-long campaign of conquest and exploration. His first great victory was against the Persians at Issus in what is now southeast Turkey. He swept south, conquering Phoenician seaports and thence into Egypt where he founded the Mediterranean city that still bears his name. In 331 BC, the armies of Alexander the Great made a triumphant entrance into Cyrenaica. After the Oracle of Ammon in Siwa promised Alexander that he would indeed conquer the world, he returned north, heading for Babylon. Crossing the Tigris and the Euphrates, he defeated another Persian army before driving his troops up into Central Asia and northern India. Eventually fatigue and disease brought the drive to a halt and the Greeks turned around and headed back home. En route, Alexander succumbed to illness (some say he was poisoned) and died at the tender age of 33 in Babylon. The whereabouts of his body and tomb remain unknown.

unofficial but widely agreed place where the Middle East begins and ends has been held to be Cyrenaica in Libya.

Upon Alexander's death in 323 BC, his empire was promptly carved up among his generals. This resulted in the founding of three new ruling dynasties: the Antigonids in Greece and Asia Minor; the Ptolemaic dynasty in Egypt; and the Seleucids. The Seleucids controlled the swath of land running from modern Israel and Lebanon through Mesopotamia to Persia.

But, this being the Middle East, peace was always elusive. Having finished off a host of lesser competitors, the heirs to Alexander's empire then proceeded to fight each other. The area of the eastern Mediterranean splintered into an array of different local dynasties with fluctuating borders. It took an army arriving from the west to again reunite the lands of the east – this time in the shape of the legions of Rome.

According to legend, Alexander's mother dreamed lightning struck her womb, while his father dreamed his wife's womb was sealed by a lion. A seer told them their child would have the character of a lion.

In 586 BC, the Babylonian king Nebuchadnezzar sacked Jerusalem and carried many Jews into exile. They were freed, given money to rebuild their temple and sent home by Cyrus the Great in 539 BC.

ROMAN MIDDLE EAST

Even for a region accustomed to living under occupation, the sight of massed, disciplined ranks of Roman legions marching down across the plains of central Anatolia must have struck fear into the hearts of people across the region. But this was a region in disarray and the Romans chose their historical moment perfectly.

536 BC

Cyrus the Great overruns Babylon, frees the Jewish exiles and helps them to return home to Jerusalem, complete with funds to rebuild the temple.

525 BC

The Persian king Cambyses conquers Egypt, rules as pharaoh then disappears with his army in the Saharan sands as he marches on Siwa.

334 BC

A youthful Alexander the Great of Macedonia marches out of Greece and doesn't stop until a vast empire stretching from Libya to India is within his grasp.

Rome's legionaries conquered most of Asia Minor (most of Turkey) in 188 BC, and as they moved south they easily swept aside the divided fiefdoms and city-kingdoms that the Middle East had become. Syria and Palestine fell, if not without a fight then without too much difficulty. In a classic pincer movement, Rome conquered the Phoenician/Punic port of Carthage (see the boxed text, p41) and much of Libya, leaving Egypt surrounded and, soon, suing for peace. When Cleopatra of Egypt, the last of the Ptolemaic dynasty, was defeated in 31 BC, the Romans controlled the entire Mediterranean world. This left the Middle East almost wholly within the Roman realm. Only the Sassanids in Persia held Rome at bay.

Foreign occupiers they may have been, but the Romans brought much-needed stability and even a degree of prosperity to the region. Roman goods flooded into Middle Eastern markets, improving living standards in a region that had long ago lost its title as the centre of the world's sophistication. New methods of agriculture increased productivity across the region and the largely peaceful Roman territories allowed the export of local products to the great markets of Rome. Olive trees, with their origins in Turkey and the Levant, were like the oilfields of today, a lucrative product and insatiable demand in Rome driving previously unimaginable growth for local Middle Eastern economies.

What the Mesopotamians began with their city-states, the Romans perfected in the extravagant cities that they built to glorify the empire but which also provided new levels of comfort for local inhabitants. Their construction, or development of earlier Phoenician and Greek settlements at Ephesus (p563), Palmyra (p509), Baalbek (p447) and Jerash (p355) announced that the Romans intended to stay.

So was the Roman Middle East a utopia? Well, not exactly. As just about any foreign power has failed to learn right up to the 21st century, Middle Easterners don't take kindly to promises of wealth in exchange for sovereignty. The fiercely independent nomads that occupied the empty spaces on the Roman map did as they pleased and the Romans largely left them to their own devices.

The same could not be said for the Jews who, living in Palestine at the heart of Roman rule, found themselves stripped of political power and operating in an ever-diminishing space of religious and economic freedom. By the middle of the 1st century AD, Jews across the Roman Empire had had enough. Primary among their grievances were punitive taxes, the Roman decision to appoint Jewish high priests and the not-inconsiderable blasphemy of Emperor Caligula's decision in AD 39 to declare himself a deity. The anti-Roman sentiment had been bubbling away for three decades, in part due to one rebellious orator – Jesus of Nazareth (see p78) – and to a Jewish sect called the Zealots, whose creed stated that all means were justified to liberate the Jews.

The Persian Empire, by Lindsay Allen, a landmark study of the empires that gave us Cyrus the Great, is littered with epic battles and enlightened rulers.

Alexander the Great, directed by Oliver Stone, made much of Alexander's supposed sexual ambiguity, but it's a spectacular Hollywood adaptation of the life of the great man.

Alexander the Great on the Web (www.isidore-of-seville.com/Alexanderama.html) contains good links to books and other references on the Middle East's youngest and most successful empire builder.

323 BC

Alexander the Great dies aged just 33. His empire is carved up among his generals, forming three dynasties: the Antigonids (Greece and Asia Minor); the Ptolemaic dynasty (Egypt); and the Seleucids (everywhere else).

3rd Century BC

The Nabataeans build their rock-hewn fortress of Petra and manage to hold out against the Romans until AD 106, partly through entrepreneurial guile, but also through military might and carefully negotiated treaties when the need arisen.

188 BC

The massed ranks of the Roman legionnaires conquer Asia Minor (Turkey), then continue south sweeping all before them. The Romans would rule the Middle East in some form for over six centuries.

The Middle East under Rome, by Maurice Sartre et al, is one of the few region-wide studies of Rome's rule over the Middle East. It combines academic research with an accessible writing style.

Petra is the most famous Nabataean city, but the sister city of Madain Saleh, in Saudi Arabia, has similarly spectacular, rock-hewn tombs. In 2008, it became Saudi Arabia's first Unesco World Heritage site.

Led by the Zealots, the Jews of Jerusalem destroyed a small Roman garrison in the Holy City in AD 66. Infighting within the revolt and the burning of food stockpiles in order to force wavering Jews to participate had disastrous consequences. Jerusalem was razed to the ground and up to 100,000 Jews were killed in retaliation; some Jewish historians claim that the number of dead over the four years of the revolt reached a million.

The failed uprising and the brutal Roman response (which came to be known as the First Jewish-Roman War) would have consequences that have rippled down through the centuries. Jerusalem was rebuilt as a Roman city and the Jews were sent into exile (which, for many Jews, ended only with the creation of the State of Israel in 1948). Few people in the Middle East dared to challenge the Romans after that.

In AD 331, the newly converted Emperor Constantine declared Christianity the official religion of the 'Holy Roman Empire', with its capital not jaded, cynical Rome but the newly renamed city of Constantinople (formerly Byzantium, later to become İstanbul). Constantinople reached its apogee during the reign of Justinian (AD 527–65), when the Byzantine Empire consolidated its hold on the eastern Mediterranean, while also recapturing the lost domain of Italy.

WHO WERE THE NABATAEANS?

The Romans may have left some spectacular cities all across the Middle East, but there's one city that captures travellers' imaginations above all others: Petra (p373). But who, if not the grandiose Greeks and Romans, was it who built this splendid rock-hewn city?

Petra was built by the Nabataeans in the 3rd century BC and was held by them almost for the entirety of the Roman era. The Romans did try to conquer the Nabataeans, but when they failed, they largely left them to their own devices as long as they posed no military threat. For their part, the Nabataeans never really possessed an 'empire' in the common military and administrative sense of the word, but rather, from about 200 BC, they had established a 'zone of influence' that stretched north to Rome and south into the Hadramaut (Yemen).

There are many theories about where the Nabataeans came from, although most scholars agree they were early Bedouins who lived a nomadic life before settling in the area as farmers in the 6th century BC. They developed a specialised knowledge of desert water resources (using water channels known as *qanats*) as well as the intricacies of the lucrative trade-caravan routes. These two skills would form the foundations of the Nabataean 'empire'.

Nabataean wealth, which had derived initially from plundering trade caravans, shifted to exacting tolls (up to 25% of the commodities' value) upon these same caravans as a means of securing protection and guiding the caravans to water. Through a mixture of shrewd diplomacy and military force, the Nabataeans kept at bay not just the Romans but also the Seleucids, Egyptians and Persians from their rock-hewn fortress.

Little is also known of what happened to them after the fall of Petra in AD 555, whereafter they disappeared from history to an unknown fate.

146 BC

The destruction of Carthage (in present-day Tunisia) by the Romans signals that more than a millennium of Phoenician/Punic dominance of the Mediterranean has finally come to an end.

64 BC

Pompey the Great abolishes the Seleucid kingdom, annexes Syria and transforms it into a province of the Roman Empire. Rome sets its sights on Egypt.

31 BC

The Romans defeat Cleopatra, bringing to an end the era of the pharaohs and drawing Egypt under their control. Unable to bear the ignominy of this historical landmark, Cleopatra commits suicide.

But the Byzantine (or Eastern Roman) Empire, as it became known, would soon learn a harsh lesson that the Ottomans (ruling from the same city; see p50) would later fail to heed. Spread too thinly by controlling vast reaches of the earth and riven with divisions at home, they were vulnerable to the single most enduring historic power in Middle Eastern history, stirring in the deserts of Arabia: Islam.

Under Ptolemaic patronage and with access to a library of 700,000 written works, scholars in Alexandria calculated the earth's circumference, discovered it circles the sun and wrote the definitive edition of Homer's work.

THE COMING OF ISLAM

No-one in sophisticated Constantinople, an opulent city accustomed to the trappings of world power, could have imagined that the greatest threat to their rule would come from a small oasis community in the desert wastes of Arabia. The Byzantines, it is true, were besieged in their coastal forts of the southern Mediterranean, their power extending scarcely at all into the hinterland. And the Sassanid empire to the east was constantly chipping away at poorly defended Byzantine holdings, creating a fault line between the two empires running down through what we know as the Middle East. But there was little to suggest to these heirs to the Roman domain that these were anything more than minor skirmishes on the outer reaches of their empire.

In the 7th century AD, southern Arabia lay beyond the reach of both the Byzantines and the Sassanids. The cost and difficulty of occupying the Arabian Peninsula simply wasn't worth the effort, home as it was only to troublesome nomads and isolated oases. Thus it was that when, far from the great centres of power, in the nondescript town of Mecca (now in Saudi Arabia), a merchant named Mohammed (b AD 570) began preaching against the pagan religion of his fellow Meccans, no-one in Constantinople paid the slightest attention. For full details on the birth of Islam and Mohammed's emergence as its most revered prophet, see p72.

The Golden Age of Persia, by Richard N Frye, is a fine historical work that traces myriad Persian contributions to civilisation from the rise of Islam to the 11th century.

Mohammed died in 632, but within a few short decades the entire Middle East would be under the control of his followers. Under Mohammed's successors, known as caliphs (from the Arabic word for 'follower'), the new religion spread rapidly, reaching all of Arabia by 634. The Byzantines still didn't get it: when Islam's armies first engaged the Byzantines in the Levant, the latter believed that Islam was merely a newly arisen Christian sect and would be swiftly put down. How wrong they were. The wafer-thin Byzantine defences were swept away and their army proved no match for the fearless zeal of the Muslim armies. By 646, Syria, Palestine and Egypt were all in Muslim hands, while most of Iraq, Iran and Afghanistan were wrested from the Sassanids by 656. By 682, Islam had reached the shores of the Atlantic in Morocco.

The unprecedented spread of Islam – as first conceived, it was a religious and social movement with no experience of political governance – was all the more remarkable because its custodians were deeply divided over the question of who should lead the Muslim community in

AD 0

Jesus of Nazareth, founder of the Christian faith, is born in Bethlehem (in the present-day Palestinian Territories), which was, at the time, fully incorporated into the Roman Empire.

AD 33

Jesus is crucified as a troublemaker by the Romans in Jerusalem. According to Christian tradition, he rises from the dead three days later, then ascends to heaven as his followers spread out across the world.

AD 39

The Roman emperor Caligula, not content with ruling much of the world, declares himself a deity, adding to the resentment already felt by Jews and Christians living across the Roman Empire.

AL-ANDALUS – THE HIGH POINT OF ISLAMIC CIVILISATION

In the distinguished annals of Islamic history, there has never been anything quite like Al-Andalus, the Islamic civilisation that flourished in southern Spain for over seven centuries.

The first successful Muslim expedition into Europe was launched from North Africa into Spain in 711. By 732, Muslim armies had taken the Iberian Peninsula and advanced as far north as Poitiers in France, before being pushed back across the Pyrenees. Although thereafter in a perpetual state of war with the Christian soldiers of the Spanish Reconquista (Reconquest), the Muslims retreated to their strongholds in Andalusia, built the unrivalled splendour of Córdoba and Granada – which were home to happily coexisting Jews, Muslims and Christians – and set about writing one of the most enlightened chapters in world history.

At the end of the first millennium, the intellectuals of Muslim Spain translated the classical works of medicine, astronomy, chemistry, philosophy and architecture, thus eventually bringing them to the attention of Christian Europe, and in turn laying the groundwork for the Renaissance. Words such as zenith, nadir, azimuth, algebra, algorithm – all of which have Arabic roots – are evidence of the legacy of Arabic scientists.

Undoubtedly the greatest contribution that the Arabs made to Europe was in mathematics. Until the 11th century, Europe laboured under the strictures of Latin numerals. Europe was well aware of the wellspring of learning that existed in the Muslim realm, and what amounted to intellectuals' study tours from Europe to Muslim Spain were common. It was after one such foray that the 'Arabic' numeral system – the system still in use today – was introduced to Europe. Most crucial among this system was 'zero', a concept that had thus far eluded Europe's imagination. Without 'zero' the binary system – central to much modern technology – could never have been devised.

Some also contend that it was first in the Muslim world that monarchs encouraged the learned to gather together and study a range of disciplines in one space, and it is from here that the concept of the university was conceived and spread to the West.

It all came to an end in 1492 when the Spanish Catholic monarchs, Ferdinand and Isabel, seized the last Muslim bastion of Granada and sent the Muslims into exile. In the same year, Columbus (who had been sponsored by Ferdinand and Isabel) reached the Americas, setting in course a pendulum swing that would see the Christian West in the ascendant for centuries to come.

The History of the Middle East Database (www.nmhschool.org/tthornton/mehistorydatabase/mideastindex.htm) has longish, informative essays on the great moments of Middle Eastern history and is especially good on the early Islamic period.

Mohammed's aftermath. With Mohammed having designated no successor, numerous candidates were openly at war with each other within just 12 years of the Prophet's death, even as their armies conquered the world. These battles for the caliphate opened a rift in Islam that grew into today's divide between Sunni and Shiite Muslims (see p72). The resulting civil war ended with the rise to power of Mu'awiyah, the Muslim military governor of Syria and a distant relative of Mohammed.

EARLY ISLAM

Having won the battle for supremacy over the Muslim world, Mu'awiyah moved the capital from Medina to Damascus and established the first great Muslim dynasty – the Umayyads. Thanks to the unrelenting success

AD 66–70

The Jews in Jerusalem and surrounding areas revolt against oppressive Roman rule. The uprising is brutally put down, the Jewish temple destroyed and, within four years, over 100,000 Jews are killed. Many more go into exile.

267–71

Queen Zenobia seizes power in Palmyra, defeats the Roman legion sent to dethrone her, briefly occupies Syria, Palestine and Egypt, and declares herself independent of Rome. Rome is not amused.

331

Emperor Constantine declares Christianity the official religion of the Roman Empire and moves his capital to Constantinople (previously known as Byzantium). This event marks the birth of the Byzantine Empire.

of his armies, Mu'awiyah and his successors found themselves ruling an empire that held sway over almost a third of the world's population.

The decision to make Damascus the capital meant that, for the first time in the Middle East's turbulent history, the region was ruled from its Levantine heartland. Already a well-established and relatively sophisticated centre of regional power, Damascus would prove to be a perfect choice for the Umayyads – by moving the capital here, the Umayyads were symbolically declaring that they had aspirations far beyond the rather ascetic teachings of the Quran. The Umayyads gave the Islamic world some of its greatest architectural treasures, including the Dome of the Rock (p266) in Jerusalem and the Umayyad Mosque (p469) in Damascus – lavish monuments to the new faith, if a far cry from Islam's simple desert origins.

History, however, has not been kind to the Umayyads. Perhaps seduced by Damascus's charms, they are remembered as a decadent lot, known for the high living, corruption, nepotism and tyranny that eventually proved to be their undoing. News of Umayyad excesses never sat well with the foot-soldiers of Islam and even confirmed their long-held suspicions about their adherence to Islamic tenets.

In 750, the Umayyads were toppled in a revolt fuelled, predictably, by accusations of impiety. Their successors, and the strong arm behind the revolt, were the Abbasids. The Abbasid caliphate created a new capital in Baghdad, and the early centuries of its rule constituted what's often regarded as the golden age of Islamic culture in the Middle East. The most famous of the Abbasid caliphs was Haroun ar-Rashid (r 786–809) of *The*

John Julius Norwich's concise *A Short History of Byzantium* – a distillation of three volumes on the Byzantines – does a fantastic job of cramming 1123 eventful years of history into less than 500 pages.

There is no finer work in English on the history of the Arabs, from the Prophet Mohammed to modern times, than *A History of the Arab Peoples*, by Albert Hourani – it's definitive, encyclopaedic and highly readable.

WHO ARE THE ARABS?

The question of who the Arabs are exactly is still widely debated. Fourteen centuries ago, only the nomadic tribes wandering between the Euphrates River and the central Arabian Peninsula were considered Arabs, distinguished by their language. However, with the rapid expansion of Islam, the language of the Quran spread to vast areas. Although the Arabs were relatively few in number in most of the countries they conquered, their culture quickly became established through language, religion and intermarriage. In addition to the original nomads, the settled inhabitants of these newly conquered provinces also became known as Arabs. In the 20th century, rising Arab nationalism legitimised the current blanket usage of the term to apply to all the peoples of the Middle East – except the Persians, Kurds, Israelis and Turks.

The most romanticised group of Arabs is no doubt the Bedouin (Bedu in Arabic). While not an ethnic group, they are the archetypal Arabs – the camel-herding nomads who roam all over the deserts and semideserts in search of food for their cattle. From among their ranks came the warriors who spread Islam to North Africa and Persia 14 centuries ago. Today, the Bedouin are found mainly in Jordan, Iraq, Egypt's Sinai Peninsula and the Gulf States. For a modern take on Bedouin life, see the boxed text, p382.

527–65

Emperor Justinian reigns over the Byzantine Empire during what is widely considered to be its golden age. Its realm extends through the Mediterranean including coastal North Africa and most of the Middle East.

570

The Prophet Mohammed is born in Mecca (present-day Saudi Arabia). In his humble origins, there is little to suggest that he will become the 25th and most revered prophet of the world's second-largest religion.

622

When his message from Allah, imparted to Mohammed by the Archangel Gabriel, is rejected by powerful Meccans, the Prophet flees to Medina. In the Islamic calendar, this flight is known as the Hejira and marks Year Zero.

The Court of the Caliphs, by Hugh Kennedy, is the definitive account of Abbasid Baghdad in its prime, blending careful scholarship and Arab sources with a lively and compelling style.

The Umayyads were descended from a branch of the Quraysh, the Prophet's tribe, known more for expediency than piety. Mu'awiyah's father was one of the last people in Mecca to embrace Islam and had long been Mohammed's chief opponent in the city.

Thousand and One Nights fame (see the boxed text, p90). Warrior-king Haroun ar-Rashid led one of the most successful early Muslim invasions of Byzantium, almost reaching Constantinople. But his name will forever be associated with Baghdad, which he transformed into a world centre of learning and sophistication.

After Haroun ar-Rashid's death, the cycle that had already scarred Islam's early years – a strong, enlightened ruler giving way upon his death to anarchy and squandering many of the hard-won territorial and cultural gains of his reign – was repeated. The empire was effectively divided between two of his sons and, predictably, civil war ensued. In 813, one son, Al-Maamun, emerged triumphant and reigned as caliph for the next 20 years. But Al-Maamun's hold on power remained insecure and he felt compelled to surround himself with Turkish mercenaries.

By the middle of the 10th century, the Abbasid caliphs were the prisoners of their Turkish guards, who spawned a dynasty of their own, known as the Seljuks (1038–1194). The Seljuks extended their reach throughout Persia, Central Asia, Afghanistan and Anatolia, where the Seljuk Sultanate of Rum made its capital at Konya. The resulting pressure on the Byzantine Empire was intense enough to cause the emperor and the Greek Orthodox Church to swallow their pride and appeal to the rival Roman Catholic Church for help.

What happened next would plant the seeds for a clash of civilisations, whose bitterness would reverberate throughout the region long after the swords of Islam and Christianity had been sheathed.

BAGHDAD THE BEAUTIFUL

When Haroun ar-Rashid came to power, Baghdad, on the western bank of the Tigris, had only been in existence for 24 years. By the time he died, it had become one of the world's preeminent cities.

Haroun ar-Rashid tried to rename the city Medinat as-Salaam (City of Peace). Although the name never caught on, everything else that Haroun ar-Rashid and his immediate successors did was an unqualified success. Baghdad was remade into a city of expansive pleasure gardens, vast libraries and distinguished seats of learning, where the arts, medicine, literature and sciences all flourished. It was soon the richest city in the world. The crossroads of important trade routes to the east and west, it rapidly supplanted Damascus as the seat of power in the Islamic world, which stretched from Spain to India. Al-Maamun, Haroun's son and successor, founded the Beit al-Hikmah (House of Wisdom), a Baghdad-based academy dedicated to translating Greek and Roman works of science and philosophy into Arabic. It was only through these translations that most of the classical literature we know today was saved for posterity.

Although the city would later be much reduced by wars, civil and otherwise, and be sacked by the Mongols, the name of Baghdad has never lost its allure. It's a reminder of the time when this was the most beautiful and intellectually creative city on earth.

632

After returning to Mecca in triumph at the head of Islam's first army in 630, the Prophet Mohammed dies in Mecca, his work done. The squabble over succession proves no impediment to his followers who carry the new religion across the world.

642

Islam's battle for succession reaches its critical moment with the death of Hussein, the son of Ali. Ever since this date, the Muslim world has been divided into strains – Sunni and Shiite.

646

Barely a decade after the death of Mohammed, Syria, Palestine and Egypt have all been conquered by the followers of Islam. Modern Israel aside, they have been predominantly Muslim ever since.

THE CRUSADES & THEIR AFTERMATH

With the Muslim armies gathering at the gates of Europe, and already occupying large swathes of Iberia, Pope Urban II in 1095 called for a Western Christian military expedition – a 'Crusade' – to liberate the holy places of Jerusalem in response to the eastern empire's alarm. Rome's motives were not entirely benevolent: Urban was eager to assert Rome's primacy in the east over Constantinople. The monarchs and clerics of Europe attempted to portray the Crusades as a 'just war', uncannily providing the language used by advocates of the Iraq war in 2003. In the late 11th century, such a battle cry attracted zealous support.

Bitterly fought on the battlefield, the Crusades have provoked similarly bitter debates among Muslim and Christian historians ever since, and this era remains one of the region's most divisive historical moments. For the Muslims, the Christian call to arms was a vicious attack on Islam itself, and the tactics used by the Crusaders confirmed the Muslim suspicion that Christianity had strayed far from its roots of tolerance and was more concerned with imperial conquest. So deep does the sense of grievance run in the region that President Bush's invasion of Iraq in 2003 was widely portrayed as the next Christian crusade. In the Christian worldview, the Crusades were a necessary defensive strategy, lest Islam sweep across Europe and place Christianity's very existence under threat.

After the Crusaders took Jerusalem and adopted many of the local customs, the nun's habit, the quintessentially Roman Catholic garment, was adopted and adapted from the veils that Muslim women wore in Palestine.

Whatever the rights and wrongs, the crusading rabble enjoyed considerable success. After linking up with the Byzantine army in 1097, the Crusaders successfully besieged Antioch (modern Antakya, in Turkey), then marched south along the coast before turning inland, towards Jerusalem, leaving devastation in their wake. A thousand Muslim troops held Jerusalem for six weeks against 15,000 Crusaders before the city fell on 15 July 1099. The victorious Crusaders then massacred the local population – Muslims, Jews and Christians alike – sacked the non-Christian religious sites and turned the Dome of the Rock into a church.

Curiously, even after the gratuitous violence of the Crusades, Christians and Muslims assimilated in the Holy Land. European visitors to Palestine recorded with dismay that the original Crusaders who remained in the Holy Land had abandoned their European ways. They had become Arabised, taking on eastern habits and dress – perhaps it was not an unwise move to abandon chain mail and jerkins for flowing robes in the Levantine heat.

The Crusades Through Arab Eyes, by Amin Maalouf, is brilliantly written and captures perfectly why the mere mention of the Crusades still arouses the anger of many Arabs today.

Even with their semi-transformation into locals, the Crusaders were never equipped to govern the massive, newly resentful Middle East. A series of Crusader 'statelets' arose through the region during this period. Contemporary Arab observers noted these regimes were relatively stable in contrast to Muslim political entities, where matters of succession were always occasions of bloodshed and armed conflict. Stable political institutions were very rarely created, a problem that continues in much of the Arab world to the modern day.

656

In the east, Islam takes hold in Iraq, Persia and Afghanistan, defeating the ruling Sassanids and building on the astonishing expansion of Islam, which had been born just a few decades before.

660

Mu'awiyah moves the capital of the Muslim world from Arabia to Damascus, shifting Islam's balance of power from the desert to the city. The Umayyad caliphate rules over an empire that encompasses almost the entire Middle East.

711

The armies of Islam cross from North Africa into Europe and the Iberian Peninsula is soon under their control. Al-Andalus, as the Muslim civilisation in southern Iberia was known, becomes a beacon for tolerance and the arts.

In 1118, the fanatical religious Order of the Knights Templar was founded in Palestine. The Templars later became a powerful force in Europe, until King Phillip IV of France executed thousands of them to capture their wealth.

These statelets aside, the Middle East remained predominantly Muslim, and within 50 years, the tide had begun to turn against the Crusaders. The Muslim leader responsible for removing the Crusaders from Jerusalem (in 1187) was Salah ad-Din al-Ayyoub, better known in the West as Saladin (see the boxed text, below).

Saladin and his successors (a fleeting dynasty known as the Ayyubids) battled the Crusaders for 60 years until they were unceremoniously removed by their own army, a strange soldier-slave caste, the Mamluks, who ran what would today be called a military dictatorship. The only way to join their army was to be press-ganged into it – non-Muslim boys were captured or bought outside the empire, converted to Islam and raised in the service of a single military commander. They were expected to give this commander total loyalty, in exchange for which their fortunes would rise (or fall) with his. Sultans were chosen from among the most senior Mamluk commanders, but it was a system that engendered vicious, bloody rivalries, and rare was the sultan who died of natural causes.

The Mamluks were to rule Egypt, Syria, Palestine and western Arabia for nearly 300 years (1250–1517), and it was they who finally succeeded in ejecting the Crusaders from the Near East, prising them out of their last stronghold of Acre (modern-day Akko in Israel) in 1291.

Saladin in his Time, by PH Newby, reads like a novel with surprising plot twists, epic events and picaresque characters brought to life.

THE RISE OF THE OTTOMAN TURKS

Turkey, saved for now from an Islamic fate by the Crusaders, had remained largely above the fray. But the Byzantine rulers in Constantinople felt anything but secure. The armies of Islam may have been occupied fighting the Crusaders (and each other) in the so-called Holy Lands, but the Byzantines looked towards the south nervously, keeping their armies of a state of high readiness. Little did they know that their undoing would come from within.

SALADIN – THE KURDISH HERO OF ARAB HISTORY

Saladin – or Salah ad-Din (Restorer of the Faith) al-Ayyoub – was born to Kurdish parents in 1138 in what is modern-day Tikrit in Iraq. He joined other members of his family in the service of Nureddin (Nur ad-Din) of the ruling Zangi dynasty. By the time Nureddin died in 1174, Saladin had risen to the rank of general and had already taken possession of Egypt. He quickly took control of Syria and, over the next 10 years, extended his authority into parts of Mesopotamia, but was careful not to infringe too closely on the territory of the now largely powerless Abbasid caliphate in Baghdad. In 1187, Saladin crushed the Crusaders at the Battle of Hittin and captured Jerusalem, precipitating the Third Crusade and pitting himself against Richard I (the Lion-Heart) of England. After countless clashes, the two rival warriors signed a peace treaty in 1192, giving the coastal territories to the Crusaders and the interior to the Muslims. Saladin died three months later in Damascus, where he is buried.

750

The first Arab dynasty, the Umayyad caliphate in Damascus, falls amid accusations of impiety and power shifts to Baghdad, the base for the Abbasids.

786–809

Haroun ar-Rashid rules the Abbasid world from his political and pleasure capital of Baghdad. This was the Abbasid heyday and provides the setting for many a tale told by Sheherezade in *The Thousand and One Nights*.

969

The Shiite general Jawhar lays the foundations for a new palace city, Al-Qahira (Cairo). Two years later, a new university and mosque complex, al-Azhar, is founded.

THE OTTOMAN CONQUEST OF EUROPE

Just as the forces of Christian Europe were on the verge of expelling Al-Andalus, the Islamic civilisation that ruled southern Spain from Christian soil (see the boxed text, p46), the Ottoman Turks, gathering in the east, opened a new front.

Horse-borne, and firing arrows from the saddle, the Ottoman Turks emerged from the Anatolian steppe in the 14th century, eager to gain a foothold on European soil. It was the boldest of moves, considering that the Abbasid advance on Constantinople had prompted the fierce European backlash of the Crusades. But the Ottomans were better equipped to take on war-weary Europe and advanced so swiftly – so seemingly miraculously – into Eastern Europe that Martin Luther openly wondered whether they should be opposed at all. The Ottoman Empire, at its greatest extent, reached from western Libya to the steppes of Hungary and the shores of the Red Sea.

The end of Ottoman expansion is variously pinpointed as the failed Vienna campaign in 1683 or the treaty of Karlowitz (in which the Ottomans lost the Peloponnese, Transylvania and Hungary) in 1699 when the Ottomans sued for peace for the first time.

In 1258, just eight years after the Mamluks seized power in Cairo and began their bloody dynasty, a boy named Osman (Othman) was born to the chief of a Turkish tribe in western Anatolia. He converted to Islam in his youth and later began a military career by hiring out his tribe's army as mercenaries in the civil wars, then besetting what was left of the Byzantine Empire. Payment came in the form of land.

Many of the tales recounted each night by Sheherazade in *The Thousand and One Nights* are set in Mamluk-era Egypt, particularly in Cairo, referred to as 'mother of the world'.

Rather than taking on the Byzantines directly, Osman's successors (the Ottomans) deliberately picked off the bits and pieces of the empire that Constantinople could no longer control. By the end of the 14th century, the Ottomans had conquered Bulgaria, Serbia, Bosnia, Hungary and most of present-day Turkey. They had also moved their capital across the Dardanelles to Adrianople, today the Turkish city of Edirne. In 1453 came their greatest victory, when Sultan Mehmet II took Constantinople, the hitherto unachievable object of innumerable Muslim wars almost since the 7th century.

Mehmet's siege of Constantinople coincided with a lunar eclipse (22 May 1453). The defending Byzantines saw this ill omen as presaging the fall of the city and the impending defeat of all Christendom. The city fell within a week.

Sixty-four years later, on a battlefield near Aleppo, an army under the gloriously named sultan, Selim the Grim, routed the Mamluks and assumed sovereignty over the Hejaz. At a stroke, the whole of the eastern Mediterranean, including Egypt and much of Arabia, was absorbed into the Ottoman Empire. By capturing Mecca and Medina, Selim the Grim claimed for the Ottomans the coveted title of the guardians of Islam's holiest places. For the first time in centuries, the Middle East was ruled in its entirety by a single Islamic entity.

LIFE UNDER THE OTTOMANS

The Ottoman Empire reached its peak, both politically and culturally, under Süleyman the Magnificent (r 1520–66), who led the Ottoman

1038–1194

The Seljuks, the former Turkish guards of the Abbasids, seize power, effectively ruling the Abbasid Empire. In addition to Turkey, they take Afghanistan, Persia and much of Central Asia.

1097

In response to a cry for help from the besieged Byzantines in Constantinople, the Christian Crusaders sweep down across the Middle East. Their mission? To liberate the Holy Land from Muslim rule.

1099

After a frightening campaign and a withering siege, the Crusaders enter Jerusalem, massacre everyone in sight regardless of their religion and claim the city for Christianity. The Dome of the Rock is turned into a church.

armies west to the gates of Vienna, east into Persia, and south through the holy cities of Mecca and Medina and into Yemen. His control also extended throughout North Africa. A remarkable figure, Süleyman was noted as much for codifying Ottoman law (he is known in Turkish as Süleyman Kanunı – law bringer) as for his military prowess. Süleyman's legal code was a visionary amalgam of secular and Islamic law, and his patronage of the arts saw the Ottomans reach their cultural zenith.

Zayni Barakat, by Gamal al-Ghitani, is full of intrigue, back stabbing and general Machiavellian goings-on in the twilight of Mamluk-era Cairo.

Another hallmark of Ottoman rule, especially in its early centuries, was its tolerance. In general, Christian and Jewish communities were accorded the respect the Quran outlines for them as 'People of the Book' (see the boxed text, p74) and were given special status. The Ottoman state was a truly multicultural and multilingual one, and Christians and Muslims rose to positions of great power within the Ottoman hierarchy. In a move unthinkable for a Muslim ruler today, Sultan Beyazit II even invited the Jews expelled from Iberia by the Spanish Inquisition to İstanbul in 1492.

But as so often happened in Middle Eastern history upon the death of a charismatic leader, things began to unravel soon after Süleyman died fighting on the Danube. The Ottomans may have held nominal power throughout their empire for centuries to come, but the growing decadence of the Ottoman court and unrest elsewhere in the countries that fell within the Ottoman sphere of influence ensured that, after Süleyman, the empire went into a long, slow period of decline.

Süleyman the Magnificent was responsible for achievements as diverse as building the gates of Jerusalem and introducing to Europe, via Constantinople, the joys of coffee.

Only five years after his death, Spain and Venice destroyed virtually the entire Ottoman navy at the Battle of Lepanto (in the Aegean Sea), thereby costing the Ottomans control over the western Mediterranean. North Africa soon fell under the sway of local dynasties. Conflict with the Safavids – Persia's rulers from the early 16th century to the early 18th century – was almost constant.

Although the campaigns waged against the Ottomans were driven, for the most part, by greedy local rulers desperate for a slice of the world's territory, there was also a sense in which the Turks were foreign rulers. The Turks may have been Muslim, but they were not and have never been Arabs (or Persians). During the period of Ottoman hegemony, they became known as *Shimaliyya* (Northerners) throughout the Arab world. This cultural, rather than religious, gulf between the rulers and the ruled would lead to simmering discontent almost for the duration of Ottoman rule.

The Ottoman sultan Murat (r 1421–51) was the most contemplative of the early Ottoman sultans – he abdicated twice to retire to his palace, but both times had to reclaim the throne in order to see off insurgencies in the Balkans.

To make matters worse, within a century of Süleyman's death, the concept of enlightened Ottoman sultans had all but evaporated. Assassinations, mutinies and fratricide were increasingly the norm among Constantinople's royals, and the opulent lifestyle was taking its toll. Süleyman was the last sultan to lead his army into the field, and those who came after him were generally coddled and sequestered in the fineries of the palace, having minimal experience of everyday life and little inclination to administer or expand the empire. The Ottomans remained

1171

The Kurdish-born general Salah ad-Din al-Ayyub (aka Saladin) seizes power from the Fatimid Shiite caliph in Egypt, restores Sunni rule and establishes the Ayyubid dynasty.

1187

Saladin retakes Jerusalem from the Crusaders and forever after becomes a hero to Muslims around the world. Fighting elsewhere between Saladin's forces and the Crusaders in their well-defended castles continues.

1192

Saladin signs a peace treaty with his long-time enemy, Richard the Lionheart. The Crusaders get the coast, the Muslims get the interior and Saladin dies three months later.

moribund, inward looking and generally unaware of the advances that were happening in Europe – the Ottoman clergy did not allow the use of the printing press until the 18th century, a century and a half after it had been introduced into Europe. As in Constantinople, so too for the rest of the empire, where the Ottomans were widely viewed as decadent despots known only for their corruption and their inability to adapt to the needs of their diverse subjects.

Miguel Cervantes was wounded fighting against the Ottomans at the battle of Lepanto. It is said that his experiences served as inspiration for some scenes in *Don Quixote*.

Just as it had under the similarly out-of-touch Umayyads in the 8th century, the perceived impiety of the sultans and their representatives gave power to local uprisings. And just as the Byzantines failed to understand the threat posed by the tribesmen of Arabia's Islamic heartland, thus it was that, in the 1760s, Abd al-Wahhab gained widespread support when he preached revolt against the Ottomans and a return to the core values of Islam.

The Ottoman Empire lumbered along until the 20th century, but the empire was in a sorry state and its control over its territories grew more tenuous with each passing year.

EUROPE & THE OTTOMAN DECLINE

If the power of the Ottomans was weakened by fratricidal battles among the sultans and growing unrest throughout the empire, two even more powerful forces would spell the end for the empire: European expansion and the rise of nationalism.

Ottoman Centuries, by Lord Kinross, is perhaps the definitive history of the Ottoman Empire, covering everything from the key events of Ottoman rule to the extravagances of its royal court.

Europe had begun to wake from its medieval slumber and the monarchs of France and Great Britain, in particular, were eager to bolster their growing prosperity by expanding their zones of economic influence. More than that, the prestige that would accompany colonial possessions in lands that had held an important place in the European imagination was undeniable. The reflected glory of 'owning' the Holy Lands or becoming the rulers over what was once the cradle of civilisation was too much for these emerging world powers to resist, and fitted perfectly within their blueprint for world domination. They may have talked of a 'civilising mission'. They may even have believed it. But it was prestige and greed that ultimately drove them as they cast their eye towards the Middle East.

In 1798, Napoleon invaded Egypt. It was not by accident that he chose the Middle East's most populous country as his first conquest in the region. By conquering the one-time land of the pharaohs, this ruler with visions of grandeur and an eye on his place in history announced to the world that France was the world power of the day. But it was merely the start: Napoleon saw Egypt as the first step towards building a French empire in the Middle East and India. The French occupation of Egypt lasted only three years, but left a lasting mark – even today, Egypt's legal system is based on a French model.

Lords of the Horizons: A History of the Ottoman Empire, by Jason Goodwin, is anecdotal and picaresque but still manages to illuminate the grand themes of Ottoman history.

The British, of course, had other ideas. Under the cover of protecting their own Indian interests, they forced the French out of Egypt in 1801.

1250

The Mamluks, a military empire forged from the ranks of the Muslim armies who fought the Crusaders, seize power for themselves and begin a 300-year rule over Egypt, Syria and Palestine.

1258

Baghdad is sacked by the Mongol hordes sweeping down out of Central Asia, destroying the city and officially ending the Abbasid Cailphate. In Anatolia, Osman (founder of the Ottomans) is born.

1291

With energy drained from the Crusader cause, the Mamluks drive the last Crusaders from their coastal fortress of Acre (now Akko in Israel) and from the Middle East, formally ending one of the region's bloodiest chapters.

Four years later, Mohammed Ali, an Albanian soldier in the Ottoman army, emerged as the country's strongman and he set about modernising the country. As time passed, it became increasingly obvious that Constantinople was becoming ever more dependent on Egypt for military backing rather than the reverse. Mohammed Ali's ambitions grew. In the 1830s, he invaded and conquered Syria, and by 1839 he had effective control of most of the Ottoman Empire.

At the Battle of the Pyramids, Napoleon's forces took just 45 minutes to rout the Mamluk army, killing 1000 for the loss of just 29 of their own men.

While it might have appeared to have been in Europe's interests to consign the Ottoman Empire to history, they were already stretched by their other colonial conquests and holdings (the British in India, the French in Africa) and had no interest, at least not yet, in administering the entire region. As a consequence, the Europeans prevailed upon Mohammed Ali to withdraw to Egypt. In return, the Ottoman sultan gave long-overdue acknowledgment of Mohammed Ali's status as ruler of a virtually independent Egypt, and bestowed the right of heredity rule on his heirs (who continued to rule Egypt until 1952). In some quarters, the Ottoman move was viewed as a wise strategy in keeping with their loose administration of their empire. In truth, they had little choice.

That the weakened Ottomans were struggling to hold their empire together and had become rulers in name only in many parts of the Middle East was not confined to their reliance upon the Europeans in dealing with Egypt. Not surprisingly, the Europeans were always at the ready to expand their influence in the region. In 1860, the French sent troops to Lebanon after a massacre of Christians by the local Druze. Before withdrawing, the French forced the Ottomans to set up a new administrative system for the area guaranteeing the appointment of Christian governors, over whom the French came to have great influence.

The Druze, by Robert Betts, only covers up to 1990, but this is otherwise the most comprehensive work on the Druze, a little-known people, and essential to understanding their reputation for fierce independence.

While all of this was happening, another import from the West – nationalism – was making its presence felt. For centuries, a multiplicity of ethnic groups had coexisted harmoniously in the Ottoman Empire, but the creation of nation states in Western Europe sparked a desire in the empire's subject peoples to throw off the Ottoman 'yoke' and determine their own destinies. The people of the Middle East watched with growing optimism as Greece and the Ottomans' Balkan possessions wriggled free, marking the final death knell of Ottoman omniscience and prompting Middle Easterners to dream of their own independence. In this, they were encouraged by the European powers, who may have paid lip service to the goals of independence, but were actually laying detailed plans for occupation. Mistaking (or, more likely, deliberately misinterpreting or ignoring) the nationalist movement as a cry for help, the European powers quickly set about filling the vacuum of power left by the Ottomans.

The Ottoman regime, once feared and respected, was now universally known as the 'sick man of Europe'. European diplomats and politicians condescendingly pondered the 'eastern question', which in practice

1453

After encircling the city during his Eastern European conquests, Sultan Mehmet II of the Ottoman Empire captures Constantinople, which had never before been in Muslim hands.

1492

Muslim Al-Andalus falls to the Christian armies of the Spanish Reconquista, ending seven centuries of enlightened but increasingly divided rule. The Jews will soon also be expelled and refugees begin arriving across the Middle East.

1520–66

Süleyman the Magnificent rules over the golden age of the Ottoman Empire, expanding the boundaries of the empire down into Arabia (including the holy cities of Mecca and Medina), Persia and North Africa.

WHAT HAPPENED TO THE ARMENIANS?

The final years of the Ottoman Empire saw human misery on an epic scale, but nothing has proved as enduringly controversial as the fate of the Armenians. For millennia, this large but disparate community had lived in eastern Anatolia, almost always as subjects of some greater state such as the Byzantines, Persians, Seljuks or Ottomans. In the early 20th century, the Orthodox Christian Armenians made the error of siding with the Russians against the Muslim Turk majority. It was an error for which they paid dearly.

The tale begins with eyewitness accounts, in autumn 1915, of Ottoman army units rounding up Armenian populations and marching them towards the Syrian desert. It ends with an Anatolian hinterland virtually devoid of Armenians. What happened in between remains one of the most controversial episodes in the 20th-century Middle East.

The Armenians maintain, somewhat compellingly it must be said, that they were subject to the 20th century's first orchestrated 'genocide'. They claim that over a million Armenians were summarily executed or killed on death marches and that Ottoman authorities issued a deportation order with the intention of removing the Armenian presence from Anatolia. To this day, Armenians demand an acknowledgement of this 'genocide'. Very few Armenians remain in Turkey, although there are significant Armenian communities in Syria, Iran and Israel and the Palestinian Territories.

Less compellingly, although with equal conviction, Turkey refutes any claims that such 'genocide' occurred. It does admit that thousands of Armenians died, but claims the Ottoman order had been to 'relocate' Armenians with no intention to eradicate them. The deaths, according to Turkish officials, were the result of disease and starvation, direct consequences of the tumultuous state of affairs during a time of war. A few even go so far as to say that it was the Turks who were subjected to 'genocide' by the Armenians.

Almost a century after the events, the issue remains contentious. In 2005, President Erdoğan encouraged the creation of a joint Turkish-Armenian commission to investigate the events; Orhan Pamuk, Turkey's most famous novelist and 2006 Nobel Prize Laureate, speaking in Germany, claimed that a million Armenians had been killed and that Turkey should be prepared to discuss it; and academics convened in İstanbul to discuss the issue. All three initiatives failed. Armenia flatly refused Erdoğan's offer, Pamuk was pursued by the courts for 'insulting Turkishness' (the charges were later dropped), and the conference attracted vehement protests from Turkish nationalists.

meant deciding how to dismember the empire and cherry-pick its choicest parts. In 1869, Mohammed Ali's grandson Ismail opened the Suez Canal. But within a few years, his government was so deeply in debt that in 1882, the British, who already played a large role in Egyptian affairs, occupied the country. It was a sign of things to come.

COLONIAL MIDDLE EAST

With the exception of Napoleon's stunning march into Egypt, Britain and France had slowly come to occupy the Middle East less by conquest than by stealth. European advisers, backed by armed reinforcements when

1571

Five years after the death of Süleyman the Magnificent, Spain and Venice defeat the Ottomans at the Battle of Lepanto in the Aegean. Ottoman power has peaked and will never be the same again.

1683

The Ottoman armies march on Vienna, but their defeat marks the end of Ottoman expansion and furthers the centuries-long period of Ottoman decline.

1760s

The Wahhabi movement in central Arabia calls for a return to Islam's roots and denounces the Ottoman rulers. Wahhabi Islam still prevails in Saudi Arabia and an extremist interpretation of the Wahhabi doctrine forms the basis for al-Qaeda thought.

A Peace to End All Peace: Creating the Modern Middle East, 1914–1922, by David Fromkin, is an intriguing account of how the map of the modern Middle East was drawn arbitrarily by European colonial governments.

When Zionist and British policy makers were looking for a homeland for the Jewish people, sites they considered included Uganda, northeastern Australia and the Jebel Akhdar in the Cyrenaica region of Libya.

'History is but a series of accepted lies' – TE Lawrence (of Arabia), referring to the broken promises of independence that the Allies made to the Arabs in return for their support during WWI. To see what he meant, you could read dry history books, but the film *Lawrence of Arabia* will bring the spirit of the age alive.

necessary, were increasingly charting the region's future and it would not be long before their efforts were rewarded.

With the outbreak of WWI in 1914, the Ottoman Empire made its last serious (and ultimately fatal) error by throwing its lot in with Germany. Sultan Mohammed V declared a jihad (holy war), calling on Muslims everywhere to rise up against Britain, France and Russia (who were encroaching on Eastern Anatolia). When the British heard the Ottoman call to jihad, they performed a masterstroke – they negotiated an alliance with Hussein bin Ali, the grand sherif (Islamic custodian and descendant of the Prophet Mohammed) of Mecca, who agreed to lead an Arab revolt against the Turks in return for a British promise to make him 'King of the Arabs' once the conflict was over. This alliance worked well in defeating the Ottomans.

There was just one problem. With the Ottomans out of the way, the British never had any serious intention of keeping their promise. Even as they were negotiating with Sherif Hussein, the British were talking with the French on how to carve up the Ottoman Empire. These talks yielded the 1916 Sykes-Picot Agreement – the secret Anglo-French accord that divided the Ottoman Empire into British and French spheres of influence. With a few adjustments, the Sykes-Picot Agreement determined the post-WWI map of the Middle East. Not surprisingly, this remains one of the most reviled 'peace agreements' in 20th-century Middle Eastern history.

In the closing year of the war, the British occupied Palestine, Transjordan, Damascus and Iraq. After the war, France took control of Syria and Lebanon, while Britain retained Egypt in addition to its holdings elsewhere. The Arabs, who'd done so much to free themselves from Ottoman rule, suddenly found themselves under British or French colonial administration, with the prospect of a Jewish state in their midst not far over the horizon thanks to the 1917 Balfour Declaration (see the boxed text, opposite).

When the newly minted League of Nations initiated its system of mandates in 1922, thereby legitimising the French and British occupations, the sense of betrayal across the region was palpable. As was the colonial way, no-one had thought to ask the people of the region what they wanted. As the Europeans set about programs of legal and administrative reform, their occupying forces faced almost continual unrest. The Syrians and Lebanese harried the French, while the predominantly Arab population of Palestine battled the British.

The problems in Palestine were particularly acute and would echo through the region for at least a century. Since taking control of Palestine in 1918, the British had been under pressure to allow unrestricted Jewish immigration to the territory. With tension rising between Palestine's Arab and Jewish residents, they refused to do this and, in the late 1930s, placed strict limits on the number of new Jewish immigrants. It was, of course, a crisis of Britain's own making, having promised to 'view with

1798

Napoleon invades Egypt, ushering in the period of colonial rivalry between France and Britain (who force the French out in 1801) that would ultimately redraw the map of the Middle East.

1839

Mohammed Ali of Egypt, an Albanian Ottoman soldier, establishes de facto control over declining Ottoman Empire from his base in Egypt. The dynasty he founded would rule Egypt until 1952.

1860

The massacre of Christians by the Druze in Lebanon's mountains prompts the French to send troops to restore order. The Ottomans remain nominal sovereigns, but the French never really leave.

ZIONISM: A PRIMER

Contrary to popular belief, Zionism, the largely secular movement to create a Jewish homeland in Palestine, began decades before the Holocaust. In the late 19th century, pogroms against Jews in the Russian Empire and the 1894 Dreyfus Affair (in which a French Jewish officer was wrongly accused of treason) shone uncomfortable light on racism against the Jews in Europe. Two years later, Theodor Herzl, a Hungarian Jew, published *Der Judenstaat* (*The Jewish State*), which called for the setting up of a Jewish state in Palestine. In 1897, Herzl founded the World Zionist Organization (WZO) at the First Zionist Congress in Basel. At the conclusion of the Congress, Herzl is said to have written in his diary: 'At Basel I founded the Jewish State. If I said this out loud today I would be greeted by universal laughter. In five years perhaps, and certainly in 50 years, everyone will perceive it.' Another leading Zionist, Chaim Weizmann, who would later become the first president of Israel, was instrumental in lobbying the British government for what became the 1917 Balfour Declaration, whose text assured Jews that the British government would 'view with favour' the creation of 'a national home for the Jewish people' in Palestine, provided that 'nothing shall be done which may prejudice the civil and religious rights of existing non-Jewish communities in Palestine'. Over the years that followed, the WZO funded and otherwise supported the emigration of Jews to Palestine under the catchcry 'A land without people for a people without land'. The Jews were indeed a people without land, but the rallying cry ignored the presence in Palestine of hundreds of thousands of Arabs who had lived on the land for generations. The WZO also set up numerous quasi-state institutions that were transplanted to the new Israeli state upon independence.

favour' the establishment of a Jewish state in Palestine in the Balfour Declaration of 1917.

As Iraq, Syria, Lebanon and Palestine simmered, Turkey was going its own way, mercifully free of both the Ottoman sultans and their European successors. Stripped of its Arab provinces, the Ottoman monarchy was overthrown and a Turkish republic was declared under the leadership of Mustafa Kemal 'Atatürk' (p531), a soldier who became Turkey's first president in 1923.

Orientalism, by Edward Said, is dense and academic but is *the* seminal work on the history of Western misconceptions and stereotypes about the Middle East from colonial times to the present.

His drive toward secularism (which he saw as synonymous with the modernisation necessary to drag Turkey into the 20th century) found an echo in Persia, where, in 1923, Reza Khan, the commander of a Cossack brigade who had risen to become war minister, overthrew the decrepit Ghajar dynasty. After changing his name from Khan to the more Persian-sounding Pahlavi (the language spoken in pre-Islamic Persia), he moved to set up a secular republic on the Turkish model. Protests from the country's religious establishment caused a change of heart and he had himself crowned shah instead. In 1934, he changed the country's name from Persia to Iran.

Looking back now at the turbulent years between the two world wars, it's easy to discern the seeds of the major conflicts that would come to define the Middle East in the late 20th and early 21st centuries: the Arab-Israeli conflict, the broken promises of the West, Iran's Islamic

1869

Ismail, the grandson of Mohammed Ali and ruler of Egypt, formally opens the landmark engineering feat that is the Suez Canal. Although Egypt is supposedly independent, Britain is heavily involved in Egyptian affairs.

1882

Weary of the Egyptian government's alleged financial ineptitude, the British formalise their control over the country, making it their first full-blown colonial possession in the Middle East.

1896

Theodor Herzl publishes *Der Judenstaat* (*The Jewish State*), in which he makes a call for a Jewish state in Palestine. This event is often described as the moment when Zionism was born.

Revolution and Turkey's struggle to forge an identity as a modernising Muslim country. If only we could turn back the clock…

The word 'Zionist' comes from Mount Zion, which lay in Jerusalem. 'Zion' later became a synonym for Jerusalem, and in the Bible, Jews are often referred to as the sons or daughters of Zion.

ISRAEL'S INDEPENDENCE

For the past 60 years, no issue has divided the Middle East quite like Israeli independence. Four major conflicts, numerous skirmishes and an unrelenting war of words and attrition have cast a long shadow over everything that happens in the region. If a way could be found to forge peace between Israel and the Palestinians, the Middle East would be a very different place.

There is very little on which the two sides agree, although the following historical chronology is *probably* among them: in early 1947 the British announced that they were turning the entire problem over to the newly created UN. The UN voted to partition Palestine, but this was rejected by the Arabs. Britain pulled out and the very next day the Jews declared the founding of the State of Israel. War broke out immediately, with Egypt, Jordan and Syria weighing in on the side of the Palestinian Arabs. Israel won.

One of Israel's best contemporary novels, Meir Shalev's *The Blue Mountain*, is about the early Zionists. It's a magic-realist novel set in an early kibbutz and is loosely based on the experience of Shalev's own family.

Beyond that, the issue has become a forum for claim and counter-claim to the extent that for the casual observer, truth has become as elusive as the peace that all sides claim to want. On both sides, there are now many shades of opinion, from extremists to moderate advocates of peace. At the time of writing, extreme opinions seem to hold the positions of greatest strength, whether held by Hamas in the Palestinian Territories or Israeli settlers and their allies in the right-wing Likud or Kadima parties. Equally, however, there are many Palestinians and Israelis who together occupy the middle ground and recognise the need for painful concessions in the cause of peace.

It wasn't always thus. What follows is our summary of the main bodies of opinion about Israeli independence among Israelis and Palestinians as they stood in 1948.

Israel was the last country in the region to achieve independence, following in the wake of Egypt (1922), Iraq (1932), Lebanon (1941), Jordan and Syria (both 1946).

The Israeli View

For many Israelis in 1948, the founding of the state of Israel represented a homecoming for a persecuted people who had spent almost 2000 years in exile. Coming so soon as it did after the horrors of the Holocaust, in which more than six million Jews were killed, Israel, a state of their own, was the least the world could do after perpetrating the Holocaust or letting it happen. The Holocaust was the culmination of decades, perhaps even centuries of racism in European countries. In short, the Jewish people had ample reason to believe that their fate should never again be placed in the hands of others.

Although the Jews were offered a range of alternative sites for their state, it could never be anywhere but on the southeastern shores of the Mediterranean. By founding a Jewish state in Palestine, the Jews were returning to a land rich in biblical reference points and promises – one

1897

Herzl helps found the World Zionist Organization. He writes after the World Zionist Congress in Basel: 'At Basel I founded the Jewish State. In five years perhaps, and certainly in fifty years, everyone will perceive it.'

1914

WWI breaks out. The Ottomans side with Germany, while the Allies persuade the Grand Sherif of Mecca to support them in return for promises of post-war independence for the Arabs.

1915

In the last years of the Ottoman Empire, Turkey's Armenian population is driven from the country. More than a million Armenians are killed in what Armenians claim was a genocide. Turkey denies the charge.

ISRAELI INDEPENDENCE: A PRIMER

In addition to the books listed below, *The War for Palestine: Rewriting the History of 1948,* edited by Eugene L Rogan and Avi Shlaim, brings together (on paper, if not in agreement) both Israeli and Palestinian scholars.

History by Israelis

- *1948: A History of the First Arab-Israeli War,* by Benny Morris – Israel's most prominent historian has drawn criticism from both sides.
- *The Birth of the Palestinian Refugee Problem Revisited,* by Benny Morris – an attempt to explain why 700,000 Palestinians ended up in exile.
- *The Arab-Israeli Wars: War and Peace in the Middle East,* by Chaim Herzog and Shlomo Gazit – although it covers more recent events, Herzog takes a long look at 1948.
- *The Ethnic Cleansing of Palestine,* by Ilan Pappe – a controversial text that challenges many of Israel's founding myths.

History by Palestinians

- *The Question of Palestine,* by Edward W Said – an eloquent, passionate, but fair-minded study of the issue by the late, leading Palestinian intellectual.
- *Expulsion of the Palestinians: The Concept of 'Transfer' in Zionist Political Thought, 1882–1948,* by Nur Masalha – revealing insights from Zionist archives.
- *The Iron Cage: The Story of the Palestinian Struggle for Statehood,* by Rashid Khalidi – looks at 1948 and the decades that preceded it.

of the most enduring foundations of Judaism is that God promised this land to the Jews. Indeed, it is difficult to overestimate the significance of this land for a people whose traditions and sacred places all lay in Palestine, especially Jerusalem. This may have been the driving force for many observant religious Jews. But the dream of a return had deeper cultural roots, maintained down through the generations during an often difficult exile and shared by many secular Jews. This latter branch of Jewish society hoped to create an enlightened utopia, an egalitarian society in which a strong and just Israel finally took its rightful place among the modern company of nations. It was, according to the popular Zionist song that would become Israel's national anthem, 'the hope of 2000 years'.

The freshest look at the early waves of Zionist immigration is in *The Founding Myths of Israel*, by political scientist Zeev Sternhell.

In 1997, Israeli agents poisoned Hamas activist Khaled Meshaal in Amman. Jordan's King Hussein insisted Israel hand over the antidote. Meshaal, who lives in Syria, later became leader of Hamas.

The Palestinian View

For many Palestinians in 1948, the founding of the state of Israel was 'Al-Naqba' – the Catastrophe. Through no fault of their own, and thanks to decisions made in Europe and elsewhere on which they were never

1916

Despite the promises Britain had made to the Arabs, the French and British conclude the secret Sykes-Picot Agreement, which divides the region between the two European powers in the event of an Allied victory.

1917

The British government's Balfour Declaration promises 'a national home for the Jewish people' in Palestine. Although promising not to prejudice the rights of the previous inhabitants, it gives unstoppable momentum to the Zionist movement.

1922

The League of Nations legitimises colonial rule in the Middle East, granting Syria and Lebanon to the French and Palestine, Iraq and Transjordan to the British. Egypt becomes independent but Britain remains in control.

consulted, the Palestinians were driven from their land. While the British were promising Palestine to the Jews in 1917, the Palestinians were fighting alongside the British to oust the Ottomans. Later, subject to British occupation, Palestinians suffered at the hands of Jewish extremist groups and found themselves confronted by an influx of Jews who had never before set foot in Palestine but who claimed equal rights over the land. Many Palestinians who had lived on the land for generations could do nothing without international assistance. No-one came to their aid. In short, when they were offered half of their ancestral homelands by the UN, they had ample reason to reject the plan out of hand.

As with the Israelis, it is difficult to overestimate the significance of this land for Palestinians, many of whose traditions and sacred places lay in Palestine. Jerusalem (Al-Quds) is the third-holiest city for Palestinian Muslims after Mecca and Medina (the Prophet Mohammed is believed to have ascended to heaven from the Al-Aqsa Mosque), and the holiest city on earth for Palestinian Christians. But this was never really about religion. Had they not lived alongside the Jews for centuries, many Palestinians asked, considered them equals and given them the respect that their religion deserved? For the Palestinians forced to flee, it was about the right to the homes in which people had lived and to the fields that they had farmed. As they fled into their own exile, they longed for a Palestinian homeland taking its rightful place among the modern company of nations.

In 1922, there were around 486,000 Palestinian Arabs and 84,000 Jews. By 1946, the Palestinian population had doubled to 1.1 million, whereas Jews had increased 550% to around 610,000.

ARAB (DIS)UNITY

The Arab countries that waged war against Israel were in disarray, even before they went to war. Newly independent themselves, they were governed for the most part by hereditary rulers whose legitimacy was tenuous at best. They ruled over countries whose boundaries had only recently been established and they did so thanks to centuries of foreign rule, ill prepared to tackle the most pressing problems of poverty, illiteracy and the lack of a clear national vision for the future. Although united in the common cause of opposing Israel, they were divided over just about everything else.

The disastrous performance of the combined Arab armies in the 1948 Arab-Israeli War had far-reaching consequences for the region. People across the region blamed their leaders for the defeat, a mood fuelled by the mass arrival of Palestinian refugees in Lebanon, Syria, Egypt and, most of all, Jordan, whose population doubled almost overnight. Recriminations over the humiliating defeat and the refugee problem it created laid the groundwork for the 1951 assassination of King Abdullah of Jordan. Syria, which had gained its independence from France in 1946, became the field for a seemingly endless series of military coups in which disputes over how to handle the Palestine problem often played a large part.

The history of Palestine during the British occupation is told through the stories of contemporary residents in the excellent *One Palestine, Complete* by Israel's best popular historian, Tom Segev.

1923

Kemal Atatürk, the towering figure in 20th-century Turkish history, becomes the first president of Turkey on a mission to modernise the country and create a secular state. Rezā Khān seizes power in Iran.

1920s & 1930s

Jewish immigration to Palestine gathers pace. The arrival of the immigrants prompts anger among Palestinian Arabs and the British impose restrictions on the number of arrivals.

1939–45

After decades of anti-Jewish racism in Europe, more than six million Jews are killed by the Nazis and their allies during WWII, giving fresh urgency to the call for a Jewish state.

But it was in Egypt, where the army blamed the loss of the war on the country's corrupt and ineffective politicians, that the most interesting developments were taking shape. In July 1952, a group of young officers toppled the monarchy, with the real power residing with one of the coup plotters: Gamal Abdel Nasser. King Farouk, descendant of the Albanian Mohammed Ali, departed from Alexandria harbour on the royal yacht, and Colonel Nasser – the first Egyptian to rule Egypt since the pharaohs – became president in elections held in 1956. His aim of returning some of Egypt's wealth to its much-exploited peasantry struck a chord with Egypt's masses. Egypt had its first ruler in centuries – Egyptian or otherwise – who placed the lot of ordinary Egyptians at the top of the priority list. He became an instant hero across the Arab world.

Nasser's iconic status reached new heights in the year of his inauguration, when he successfully faced down Britain and France in a confrontation over the Suez Canal, which was mostly owned by British and French investors. On 26 July, the fourth anniversary of King Farouk's departure, Nasser announced that he had nationalised the Suez Canal to finance the building of a great dam that would control the flooding of the Nile and boost Egyptian agriculture. A combined British, French and Israeli invasion force, which intended to take possession of the canal, was, to great diplomatic embarrassment, forced to make an undignified retreat after the UN and US applied pressure. Nasser emerged from the conflict the most popular Arab leader in history.

Such was Nasser's popularity that the Syrians joined Egypt in what would prove to be an ultimately unworkable union, the United Arab Republic. At the time, it seemed as if Nasser's dream of pan-Arab unity was one step closer to reality. But behind the staged photo opportunities in which the region's presidents and monarchs lined up to bask in Nasser's reflected glory, the region was as divided as ever. With the United Arab Republic at Jordan's borders to the north and south, King Hussein feared for his own position and tried a federation of his own with his Hashemite cousins in Iraq; it lasted less than a year before the Iraqi Hashemite monarchy was overthrown, and British troops were sent in to Jordan to protect Hussein. Egypt and Syria went their separate ways in 1961.

Meanwhile, Lebanon was taking an entirely different course, exposing the fault lines that would later tear the country apart. The Western-oriented Maronite Christian government that held sway in Beirut had been, in 1956, the only Arab government to support the US and UK during the Suez Canal crisis.

And yet, for all the division and gathering storm clouds, there was a palpable sense of hope across the Arab world. Driven by Nasser's 'victory' over the European powers in the 1956 Suez crisis, there was a growing belief that the Arab world's time was now. While this manifested itself in

Many Jews believe that when the Messiah comes, the Temple will simply reappear on the Temple Mount. Muslims, of course, prefer to keep the mosques on the Mount. Muslims call the area atop the Temple Mount the Haram ash-Sharif (Noble Sanctuary). Al-Haram (the Sanctuary) is the same name they also give to the Grand Mosque in their holiest city, Mecca, in Saudi Arabia.

Of the almost 11 million Palestinians, only five million live in Israel (1.3 million) or the Palestinian Territories (3.7 million). Palestinians comprise around 60% of Jordan's population, with around 400,000 in each of Lebanon and Syria.

No God but God: Egypt and the Triumph of Islam, by Genevieve Abdo, focusing on the Nasser and post-Nasser period, is one of the best books on the Egyptian Islamist movement.

1947

Britain hands the issue over to the newly formed UN, which decides to partition Palestine into two states, one Jewish, the other Palestinian. Arabs reject the plan.

1948

The British withdraw from Palestine, Israel declares independence and the Arab armies of neighbouring countries invade. The new State of Israel wins the war, increases its territory and hundreds of thousands of Palestinian refugees flee.

1951

King Abdullah I, the founder of modern Jordan, is assassinated as recriminations ripple out across the Arab world in the wake of their devastating defeat by Israel.

The officially secular Phalange army in Lebanon was established in 1936 by Pierre Gemayel as a youth movement, inspired by his observations of Nazi party organisation at the 1936 Berlin Olympic Games.

Pity the Nation: Lebanon at War, by Robert Fisk, ranges far beyond Lebanon's borders and is a classic account of the issues that resonate throughout the region. His *The Great War for Civilisation* is similarly outstanding, although not everyone agrees – Fisk's polemical style has made him a controversial figure, especially among right-wing Israelis.

Arafat, by the Palestinian writer Said K Aburish, is a highly critical look at one of the Middle East's most intriguing yet flawed personalities. *Arafat: The Biography*, by Tony Walker and Andrew Gowers, is also good.

the hope that the region had acquired the means and self-belief to finally defeat Israel when the time came, it was also to be found on the streets of cities across the region. Nowhere was this more true than in Beirut, which had become a regional economic powerhouse and was intent on celebrating the new Arab dawn. Starting in the early 1960s, Beirut became the Middle East's home of glamour, as it welcomed the private yachts of international superstars who skied the mountains by day and partied the night away in the city's seafront hotels. All hopes of a glorious Beiruti 'Paris of the East' would later die with the coming of the civil war in 1975, but it sure was fun while it lasted.

NEW FORCES OF ARAB RESISTANCE

All too often, the Arab-Israeli conflict, as with so many other events in the Middle East, has been explained away as a religious war between Jews and Muslims. There has at times indeed been a religious dimension, especially in recent years with the rise of Hamas in the Palestinian Territories and the religious right in Israel. But this has always been fundamentally a conflict over land, as was shown in the years following Israel's independence. Governments – from the Baath parties of Syria and Iraq to Nasser's Egypt – invariably framed their demands in purely secular terms.

It again became clear after the formation in 1964 of the Palestine Liberation Organisation (PLO). Although opposed by Jordan, which was itself keen to carry the banner of Palestinian leadership, the PLO enjoyed the support of the newly formed Arab League. The Palestine National Council (PNC) was established within the PLO as its executive body – the closest thing to a Palestinian government in exile. The PLO served as an umbrella organisation for an extraordinary roll-call of groups that ranged from purely military wings to communist ideologues. Militant Islamic factions were, at the time, small and drew only limited support.

Just as the PLO was at risk of dissolving into an acrimony born from its singular lack of a united policy, an organisation called the Palestine National Liberation Movement (also known as Al-Fatah) was established. One of the stated aims of both the PLO and Al-Fatah was to train guerrillas for raids on Israel. Al-Fatah emerged from a power struggle as the dominant force within the PLO, and its leader, Yasser Arafat, would become chair of the executive committee of the PLO in 1969 and, later, the PLO's most recognisable face. Despite paying lip-service to Muslim tenets and invoking the help of Allah, the PLO was more concerned with fighting to recover Palestinian land than waging holy war. Moderates the PLO's members were not, preaching fire and brimstone retribution upon the Israelis and their allies. But nor were they religious fanatics.

But Islam as a political force *was* starting to stir. Nasser may have been all-powerful, but there was a small group of clerics who saw him, Egyptian or not, as the latest in a long line of godless leaders ruling the

1952

Gamal Abdel Nasser leads a coup against the monarchy in Egypt and becomes the first Egyptian ruler over Egypt since the days of the pharaohs.

1956

Shortly after becoming Egyptian president, Nasser nationalises the Suez Canal, then successfully stares down Israel, Britain and France who attempt to seize it but are forced to retreat. Nasser's popularity soars across the Arab world.

1958–61

Egypt and Syria unite to form the United Arab Republic, a short-lived union that Nasser hopes will spark a pan-Arab mega-state that brings together all the Arab countries of the region.

country. Sayyid Qutb, an Egyptian radical and intellectual, was the most influential, espousing a return to the purity of grassroots Islam. He also prompted the creation of the Muslim Brotherhood, who would withdraw from society and prepare for violence and martyrdom in pursuit of a universal Muslim society. Qutb was executed by Nasser in 1966, but the genie could not be put back in the bottle, returning to haunt the region, and the rest of the world, decades later.

The Sayyid Qutb Reader, by Albert Bergesen, compresses the prolific writings of one of militant Islam's earliest scholars into an accessible form – an important text for understanding the later 'War on Terror'.

ARAB-ISRAELI WARS

With the Arab world growing in confidence, war seemed inevitable. In May 1967, the Egyptian army moved into key points in Sinai and announced a blockade of the Straits of Tiran, effectively closing the southern Israeli port of Eilat. The Egyptian army was mobilised and the country put on a war footing. On 5 June, Israel responded with a devastating pre-emptive strike that wiped out virtually the entire Egyptian air force in a single day. The war lasted only six days (hence the 'Six Day War'), and when it was over, Israel controlled all of the Sinai Peninsula and the Gaza Strip. The West Bank, including Jerusalem's Old City, had been seized from Jordan and the Golan Heights from Syria.

Although the 1973 war is painted as a victory and reassertion of Arab pride by many historians, by the time it ended, the Israelis actually occupied more land than when it began.

After more than a decade of swaggering between Cairo and Damascus, and empty promises to the Palestinians that they would soon be returning home, the unmitigated disaster that was the Six Day War sent shockwaves across the region. Not only were leaders like Nasser no match for the Israelis, despite the posturing, but also tens of thousands more Palestinian refugees were now in exile. The mood across the region was grim. A humiliated Nasser offered to resign, but in a spontaneous outpouring of support, the Egyptian people wouldn't accept the move and he remained in office. However, it was to be for only another three years; abruptly in November 1970, the president died of a heart attack, reportedly a broken man.

With Palestinian militancy on the rise, the year 1970 saw the ascension of new leaders in both Egypt (Anwar Sadat) and Syria (Hafez al-Assad). Preparations were also well under way for the next Middle Eastern war, with these radical new leaders under constant pressure from their citizens to reclaim the land lost in 1967. On 6 October 1973, Egyptian troops crossed the Suez Canal, taking Israel (at a standstill, observing the holy day of Yom Kippur) almost entirely by surprise. After advancing a short distance into Sinai, however, the Egyptian army stopped, giving Israel the opportunity to concentrate its forces against the Syrians on the Golan Heights and then turn back towards Egypt. Although the war preserved the military status quo, it was widely portrayed throughout the region as an Arab victory. True or not, the absence of overwhelming defeat restored to the region a large measure of the confidence it had lost in 1967.

Mezzaterra, by the Egyptian writer Ahdaf Soueif, is an eloquent series of essays on the modern Middle East, challenging Western stereotypes about the region while being rooted in the lives of ordinary people.

When the war ended in late 1973, months of shuttle diplomacy by the US secretary of state, Henry Kissinger, followed. Pressure on the USA to

1961

Kurds in northern Iraq launch a short-lived military campaign for an independent Kurdistan. The move fails and will become an important justification used by Saddam Hussein for later campaigns against the Kurds.

1964

Against the objections of Jordan and, of course, Israel, the Palestine Liberation Organisation (PLO), an umbrella group of Palestinian resistance groups, is formed. In the years that follow, Al-Fatah becomes the dominant group.

1967

After Egyptian manoeuvres in Sinai, Israel launches a pre-emptive strike and destroys Egypt's air force. Israel emerges from the resulting Six-Day War with much of the West Bank, Sinai, the Golan Heights and the Gaza Strip.

NATIONS WITHOUT A STATE: PALESTINIANS & KURDS

Everyone seems to agree there will one day be a Palestinian state, even if no-one dares to predict when it might come to pass. The same cannot be said for the Kurds, despite being more numerically significant. Why?

Well, for a start, the major Kurdish cities of Erbil and Sulaymaniyah just don't resonate in geopolitical circles in quite the same way as Jerusalem and the Holy Land, with their significance for the world's three largest monotheistic religions. Nor have the Kurds produced anyone with the charisma to capture the world's attention quite like Yasser Arafat – love him or loath him, the world could never ignore him. Although the Kurds have, from time to time, found favour with one world power or another, their shifting alliances and the short attention spans of world leaders have meant that the Kurds have never had a powerful backer consistently willing to champion their cause; not for nothing did John Bulloch and Harvey Morris call their 1993 history of the Kurds *No Friends but the Mountains*. Perhaps most importantly of all, given the chronic levels of instability already at large in the Middle East, no world leader would ever dare to suggest slicing off large sections of Turkey, Iraq, Iran and Syria to create a Kurdish state.

broker a deal was fuelled when the Gulf States embargoed oil supplies to the West 10 days after the war began. The embargo was relatively short-lived, but if the goal was to get the West's attention, it succeeded. The embargo's implications were massive, achieving nothing less than a shift in the balance of power in the Middle East. The oil states, rich but underpopulated and militarily weak, gained at the expense of poorer, more populous countries. Huge shifts of population followed the two oil booms of the 1970s, as millions of Egyptians, Syrians, Jordanians, Palestinians and Yemenis went off to seek their fortunes in the oil states.

PEACE & REVOLUTION

The Middle East had reached a temporary stalemate. On one side, Israel knew that it had the wherewithal to hold off the armed forces of its neighbours. But Israel also lived in a state of siege and on maximum alert, all the time facing escalating attacks at home and abroad on its citizens from Palestinian terrorist groups aligned to the PLO. On the other side, Arab governments continued with their rhetoric but knew, although none admitted it, that Israel was here to stay. To the north, Lebanon was sliding into a civil war that was threatening to engulf the region. Something had to give.

On 7 November 1977, Egyptian president Anwar Sadat made a dramatic visit to Israel to address the Israeli Knesset with a call for peace. The Arab world was in shock. That the leader of the Arab world's most populous nation, a nation that had produced Gamal Abdel Nasser, could visit Israeli-occupied Jerusalem had hitherto been inconceivable. The shock turned to anger the following year when Sadat and the hardline Israeli prime minister, Menachem Begin, shepherded by US president

1968–69

Saddam Hussein emerges as the key powerbroker in Iraq after a coup brings the Baath Party to power. A year later, Yasser Arafat becomes leader of the PLO, a position he will hold until his death in 2005.

1970

Hafez al-Assad assumes power in Syria after what he called 'The Corrective Revolution'. At the head of the Syrian Baath Party, he ruled Syria until his death in 2000.

1973

Egypt launches a surprise attack on Israel on the holy day of Yom Kippur. After initial gains, Israel recovers to seize yet more territory. Despite the defeat, the war is hailed as a victory in the Arab world.

Jimmy Carter, signed the Camp David Agreement. In return for Egypt's long-coveted recognition of Israel's right to exist, Egypt received back the Sinai Peninsula. Egypt did rather well out of the deal, but was widely accused of breaking ranks and betrayal for one simple reason: the Palestinians received nothing. Arab leaders meeting in Baghdad voted to expel Egypt from the Arab League and moved the group's headquarters out of Cairo in protest. The peace treaty won Sadat (and Begin) a Nobel Peace Prize, but it would ultimately cost the Egyptian leader his life: he was assassinated in Cairo on 6 October 1981.

Before his death, and with Sadat basking in the acclaim of the international community, one of the few friends he had left in the region was facing troubles of his own. Discontent with the shah of Iran's autocratic rule and his personal disregard for the country's Shiite Muslim religious traditions had been simmering for years. Political violence slowly increased throughout 1978. The turning point came in September of that year, when Iranian police fired on anti-shah demonstrators in Tehran, killing at least 300. The momentum of the protests quickly became unstoppable.

On 16 January 1979, the shah left Iran, never to return (he died in Egypt a year later). The interim government set up after his departure was swept aside the following month when the revolution's leader, the hitherto obscure Āyatollāh Ruhollāh Khomeini, returned to Tehran from his exile in France and was greeted by adoring millions. His fiery brew of nationalism and Muslim fundamentalism had been at the forefront of the revolt, and Khomeini achieved his goal of establishing a clergy-dominated Islamic Republic (the first true Islamic state in modern times) with brutal efficiency. Opposition disappeared, executions took place after meaningless trials and minor officials took the law into their own hands.

These two events – the Egypt–Israel peace treaty (and Sadat's subsequent assassination by Islamists) and Iran's Islamic Revolution – changed everything in the Middle East. Soon, the entire region would be in uproar and the effects are still being felt.

As a young Egyptian officer during WWII, Anwar Sadat was imprisoned by the British for conspiring with German spies.

The Hidden Face of Eve: Women in the Arab World, by Egyptian psychiatrist Nawal el-Sadaawi, is packed with insight and controlled anger in equal measure as she explores the role of women in Arab history and literature.

Covering Islam, by Edward Said, is a classic, exploring how the Iranian Revolution and Palestinian terrorism changed forever the way we view the Middle East.

BLOODY AFTERMATH

The Middle East's reputation for brutal conflict and Islamic extremism owes much to the late 1970s and early 1980s. It was the worst of times in the Middle East, a seemingly relentless succession of bloodletting by all sides. The religious fervour that surrounded Khomeini's Iran and the images of the masses chanting '*Marg bar amrika!*' ('Death to America!') also marked the moment when militant Islam became a political force and announced to the world that the West was in its sights. While this development applied to only a small proportion of the region's Muslims, the reputation has stuck.

The events that flowed from, or otherwise followed, the Iranian Revolution read like a snapshot of a region sliding out of control. In 1979, militants seized the Grand Mosque in Mecca. They were ejected several weeks later

1975

After years of tension, war breaks out in Lebanon between Palestinians and Christian militias. Other militia groups drawn from Lebanon's multiconfessional population join the fray. The fighting will last until 1990.

1977

Egyptian president Anwar Sadat's landmark visit to Jerusalem, during which he speaks before the Israeli Knesset, reverberates around the region. Egypt is expelled from the Arab League and Sadat is hailed around the world.

1979

Anwar Sadat and Israel's Menachem Begin sign the Camp David peace treaty. Egypt gets Sinai and recognises Israel's right to exist. Egypt's isolation from the rest of the Arab world is confirmed.

Voices from the Front: Turkish Soldiers on the War with the Kurds, by Nadire Mater, offers sometimes harrowing first-hand accounts of the Kurdish insurgency during the 1990s.

only after bloody gun battles inside the mosque itself, leaving more than 250 people dead inside Islam's holiest shrine. In November of that year, student militants in Tehran overran the US embassy, taking the staff hostage. They would be released only after 444 days in captivity. Away to the north, in 1980, Turkey's government was overthrown in a military coup, capping weeks of violence between left- and right-wing extremists. The same year, Saddam Hussein, supported by the US, invaded Khuzestan in southwestern Iran, on the pretext that the oil-rich province was historically part of Iraq. The resulting war lasted until 1988 and claimed millions of lives as trench warfare and poison gas were used for the first time since WWI.

In June 1982, Israel marched into Lebanon, joining Syria, the PLO and a host of Lebanese militias in a vicious regional conflict from which no side emerged with clean hands. The PLO had long been using the anarchy at large in Lebanon to set up a state within a state, from where they launched hundreds of rocket attacks across the Israeli-Lebanese frontier. Led by Defence Minister Ariel Sharon, Israel entered the war

WHO ARE THE KURDS?

The Kurds, the descendants of the Medes who ruled an empire over much of the Middle East in 600 BC from what is now northwestern Iran, are the Middle East's largest minority group. Kurds (who are predominantly Sunni Muslims) constitute significant minorities in Turkey (20% of the population), Iraq (15%), Iran (10%) and Syria (7 to 8%). The Kurdish homeland is a largely contiguous area split between southeastern Turkey, northeastern Syria, northern Iraq and northwestern Iran. Although they've been around longer than any other people in the region (since at least the 2nd century BC), the Kurds have never had a nation of their own.

Kurds in Turkey

Turkey's sparsely populated eastern and southeastern regions are home to perhaps seven million Kurds, while seven million more live elsewhere in the country, more or less integrated into mainstream Turkish society. Relations between Turks and Kurds soured after the formation of the republic, in which Atatürk's reforms left little room for anything other than Turkishness. Unlike the Christians, Jews and Armenians, the Kurds were not guaranteed rights as a minority group under the terms of the Treaty of Lausanne, which effectively created modern Turkey. Indeed, until relatively recently the Turkish government refused to even recognise the existence of the Kurds, insisting they be called 'Mountain Turks'.

Since 1984, when Abdullah Öcalan formed the Kurdistan Workers' Party (PKK), a separatist conflict raged in Turkey's Kurdish areas, prompting Turkey's government to declare a permanent state of emergency. After 15 years and the deaths of some 30,000 people, Abdullah Öcalan was captured in 1999. The insurgency died out.

In 2002, the Turkish government finally gave some ground on the issue of Kurdish rights, approving broadcasts in Kurdish and giving the go-ahead for Kurdish to be taught in language

1979

After brutal repression of opposition protests, the Shah of Iran, Reza Pahlavi, leaves Iran. The Islamic Revolution brings Āyatollāh Ruhollāh Khomeini to power as other groups that participated in the revolution are swept away.

1980–88

Counting on a weakened Iran in the wake of the Islamic Revolution, Saddam Hussein launches a surprise attack on Iran. Brutal fighting in one of history's most pointless wars would last until 1988.

1981

Anwar Sadat is assassinated in Cairo during a military parade, when a member of his armed forces (and also a secret member of an Islamist group) breaks away as the parade passes the presidential box.

claiming self-defence. But these claims lost considerable credibility when, weeks after the PLO leadership had already left Beirut for Tunis, Israeli soldiers surrounded the Palestinian refugee camps of Sabra and Shatila in Beirut and stood by as their Phalangist allies went on a killing rampage. Hundreds, possibly thousands, of civilians were killed. Israel withdrew from most of Lebanon in 1983, but continued to occupy what it called a self-declared security zone in southern Lebanon.

The Lebanese Civil War rumbled on until 1990, but even when peace came, Israel controlled the south and Syria's 30,000 troops in Lebanon had become the kingmakers in the fractured Lebanese polity. In the fifteen years of war, more than a million Lebanese are believed to have died.

Down in the Palestinian Territories, violence flared in 1987 in what became known as the 'first intifada' (the grass roots Palestinian uprising). Weary of ineffectual Palestinian politicians having achieved nothing of value for their people in the four decades since Israeli independence, ordinary Palestinians took matters into their own hands. Campaigns of

A Modern History of the Kurds, by David McDowall, has been updated to 2004 (although the body of the work finishes in 1996), and it remains an excellent primer on the social and political history of the Kurds, focusing on Turkey and Iraq.

schools. Emergency rule was lifted in the southeast. The government started compensating villagers displaced in the troubles and a conference entitled 'The Kurdish Question in Turkey: Ways for a Democratic Settlement' was held in İstanbul in 2006. Life for Kurds in the southeast has since become considerably easier: the press of harsh military rule and censorship has largely been lifted, and optimism has been fuelled by the outlook of accession with the EU. Although low-level fighting has resumed after the ceasefire was broken in 2004, few expect a return to the dark days of the 1980s.

Kurds in Iraq

Iraq is home to over four million Kurds, who live in the northern provinces of the country. The 1961 Kurdish campaign to secure independence from Iraq laid the foundations for an uneasy relationship between the Kurds and the Iraqi state. Cycles of conflict and détente have consistently characterised the relationship ever since. After the 1991 Gulf War, when an estimated two million Kurds fled across the mountains to Turkey and Iran, the Kurdish Autonomous Region was set up in northern Iraq under UN protection. Although ongoing Iraqi incursions and the bitter rivalry between the region's two main parties – the Patriotic Union of Kurdistan (PUK) and the Kurdistan Democratic Party (KDP) – frequently threatened the north, Kurdish Iraq became a model for a future federal Iraqi system.

After the fall of Saddam, there were fears that the Kurds would take the opportunity and go their own way. However, after the Kurds won 17% of the vote in the 2005 elections, Kurdish leaders restated their commitment to a federal but unified Iraq and have, along with Shiite leaders, been at the forefront of moves to build a democratic and plural Iraq. Jalal Talabani, a Kurd, was Iraq's president at the time of writing.

1982

Israel invades Lebanon, joining Syria and a host of local militias battling on Lebanese soil. In September, Israeli forces surround the Palestinian refugee camps, Sabra and Shatila, while Phalangists massacre thousands. Israel withdraws in 1983.

1983

Turkey returns to democratic rule after a succession of coups. The new constitution that forbids prior political participation suggests that the Turkish military remains the real power in the country.

1984

Abdullah Öcalan forms the Kurdistan Workers Party (PKK) and launches a brutal insurgency that paralyses Turkey's southeast and a forceful response from Turkey. The 'war' lasts until Öcalan is captured in 1999.

civil disobedience, general strikes and stone-throwing youths were the hallmarks of the intifada, which ran until 1993.

In the meantime, elsewhere in the region there were a few bright spots. Turkey had returned to democratic rule in 1983, albeit with a new constitution barring from public office anyone who had been involved in politics prior to the 1980 coup. In 1988, Iran and Iraq grudgingly agreed to a cease-fire. A year later, Egypt was quietly readmitted to the Arab League and Jordan held its first elections in more than 20 years. But these important landmarks were overshadowed by events in Lebanon, which had led many people to wonder whether the region would ever be at peace.

THE FALL, RISE & FALL OF HOPE

Just as the region was breathing a collective sigh of relief at the end of the Lebanese Civil War and the cessation of hostilities between Iraq and Iran, Iraq invaded Kuwait in August 1990. The 1990s were, it seemed, destined to repeat the cycle of violence that had so scarred the previous decade.

Fearful that Saddam Hussein had Saudi Arabia in his sights, King Fahd requested help from the USA. The result was a US-led coalition whose air and ground offensive drove Iraq out of Kuwait. In the process, Iraqi president Saddam Hussein (previously supported by the West in his war against Iran) became world public enemy number one. When the US-led coalition stopped short of marching on Baghdad, the Iraqi leader used his reprieve to attack the country's Shiite population in the south and the Kurds in the north with levels of brutality remarkable even by his standards. Not willing to wait around for Saddam's response to the Kurds' perceived support for the US-led coalition, hundreds of thousands of Kurds streamed across the border into Turkey in one of the largest refugee exoduses in modern history.

People Like Us: How Arrogance is dividing Islam and the West, by Waleed Aly, is one of the most important books written in recent years about relations between the Muslim world and the West.

But there was another, less immediately obvious consequence of the war. The presence of US troops on Saudi soil enraged many in a country known for its strict (some would say puritanical adherence) to Wahhabi Islamic orthodoxy. To have the uniformed soldiers of what many considered to be Islam's enemy operating freely from the same soil as the holy cities of Mecca and Medina was considered an outrage. From this anger, many respected analysts argue, would come al-Qaeda.

And yet from the ashes of war came an unlikely movement towards peace. While attempting to solicit Arab support for the anti-Iraq coalition, then-US president George Bush promised to make Arab-Israeli peace a priority once the Iraqis were out of Kuwait. Endless shuttling between Middle Eastern capitals culminated in a US-sponsored peace conference in Madrid in October 1991. It achieved little, but by late summer 1993 it was revealed that Israel and the Palestinians had been holding secret talks in Norway for 18 months. The 'Oslo Accord' was

1987

A grassroots uprising known as the intifada breaks out in the Palestinian Territories. Although the PLO later tries to claim credit, the intifada, which runs until 1993, is a spontaneous national rebellion.

1990

Saddam Hussein's Iraq invades Kuwait and remains there until the US-led coalition (operating from its bases in Saudi Arabia) drives him out in early 1991. Saddam turns on Iraqi Shiites and Kurds.

1991

Israel and its Arab neighbours sit down for the first time to discuss a comprehensive peace plan in Madrid. Talks dissolve in recrimination, but the fact that they do so face to face is seen as progress.

cemented with one of the most famous handshakes in history, between Yasser Arafat and Israeli prime minister Yitzhak Rabin on the White House lawn in September 1993.

An unprecedented era of hope for peace in the Middle East seemed on the horizon. Lebanon had just held its first democratic elections for 20 years and the mutually destructive fighting seemed well-and-truly at an end. In 1994, Jordan became the second Arab country to sign a formal peace treaty with Israel. But, sadly, it was not to last. The peace process was derailed by the November 1995 assassination of Rabin and the subsequent election to power of hardline candidate Binyamin Netanyahu. A blip of hope re-emerged when Netanyahu lost office to Ehud Barak, a prime minister who pulled his troops out of occupied south Lebanon and promised to open negotiations with the Syrians and the Palestinians. But critical momentum had been lost. When these talks came to nothing at two high-stakes summits at Camp David and in the Egyptian resort of Sharm el-Sheikh during the last months of the Clinton presidency, everyone knew that an opportunity had been lost.

Middle East History & Resources (www.mideastweb.org/history.htm) is a balanced examination of many of the region's thorniest political issues, with a rare commitment to fairness and accuracy.

In September 2000, after Ariel Sharon, by then the leader of the right-wing Likud Party, visited the Al-Aqsa Mosque in Jerusalem, riots broke out among Palestinians. This was the trigger, if not the ultimate cause, for the second Palestinian intifada that has continued in the years since. The election of that same Ariel Sharon – a politician as reviled by Palestinians as Yasser Arafat was by Israelis – as Israeli prime minister in 2001 was another nail in the coffin of the already much-buried peace process. Although the death of Yasser Arafat in November 2004 offered some signs for hope, the violent occupation of Palestinian land and bloody suicide bombings targeting Israeli citizens continued.

But by then, the hope that had spread like a wave across the Middle East in the early 1990s had come to seem like a distant memory.

THE MORE THINGS CHANGE

The Middle East may have a reputation for instability, but some things remain unchanged in the last 60 years. Israel and the Palestinians still trade accusations of bad faith and no solution has been found to the Arab-Israeli conflict. Hundreds of thousands of Palestinian refugees (including second- and third-generation exiles) languish in refugee camps, many still holding on to the keys of homes they left in 1948 or 1967. And wars great and small continue to flare around the region.

In 2003, US and UK forces, with support from a small band of allies, invaded Iraq. Their military victory was swift, driving Saddam Hussein from power, but the aftermath has proved to be infinitely more complicated. With large communities of Shiites, Kurds and the hitherto all-powerful Sunnis vying for power, the country has descended into a sectarian conflict with strong echoes of Lebanon's civil war. Hundreds of

1993

After a year and a half of secret negotiations between Israel and the Palestinians, Yasser Arafat and Yitzhak Rabin sign the Oslo Accords setting out a framework for future peace.

1994

Building on the goodwill generated by the Oslo Accords, Jordan under King Hussein becomes the second Arab country (after Egypt in 1979) to sign a peace treaty and normalise relations with Israel.

1995

Israeli prime minister Yitzhak Rabin is assassinated by a Jewish extremist who hoped to end the process Rabin had begun with the Oslo Accords. A year later, the right-wing Binyamin Netanyahu is voted into power.

thousands, perhaps millions of Iraqis have fled the fighting, placing huge pressure on the resources of neighbouring countries.

The 33-Day War: Israel's War on Hezbollah in Lebanon and its Consequences, by Gilbert Achcar and Michel Warschawski, makes an interesting read on the 2006 Israeli offensive in Lebanon.

In 2006, Israel and Hezbollah fought a bitter month-long war that shattered the Lebanese peace, while fighting broke out between Hezbollah and the Lebanese government in 2008. The power of Hezbollah, and the shifting of Palestinian power from Al-Fatah to Hamas in the Palestinian Territories, has confirmed a process that had begun with the PLO in the 1960s: the rise of nonstate actors as powerful players in the Middle East. Governments of Arab countries have singularly failed to meet the aspirations of their people, from bringing about a lasting peace between Israel and the Palestinians to providing the basic services necessary to lift them out of poverty. Little wonder, then, that many Middle Easterners have turned to organisations such as Hezbollah and Hamas who, in the eyes of many Arabs, have matched their words with actions. Both groups have built up extensive networks of social safety nets and, with some success, taken on Israel on the battlefield. That these groups are avowedly Islamic in focus, enjoy the support of arch-enemy Iran and have gained militarily in part through attacks on Israeli civilians has only served to widen the gulf between Israel (and the US) and its neighbours.

Hamas was founded in the living room of Sheikh Ahmed Yassin, in Gaza's Zeitoun neighbourhood. Yassin, a quadriplegic since the age of seven, was killed by an Israeli helicopter missile in 2004.

Peace talks, like war, come and go in the region without much ever changing on the ground. In 2008, Syria announced that it was holding indirect talks with Israel through Turkish mediators, Syria was talking increasingly with Lebanon and the seemingly endless talks between Israel and the Palestinians continued. But with Israel having shifted to the right, a resolution of the key issues – the Golan Heights, Israeli settlements and the separation wall built unilaterally by Israel through the West Bank, the boundaries of any future Palestinian state, the status of Jerusalem and the right of return for Palestinian refugees – seems as distant as at any time during the recent history of the Middle East.

Zoom in a little closer and you'll see that it remains, for the most part, business as usual. The generational change that sparked such hope in Syria with the death of Hafez al-Assad in 2000 has seen Syrians granted more freedoms; until his son and successor, Bashar al-Assad, can break free of the influence of his father's old-school advisers, however, the process of change promises to be slow. Father-to-son dynasties are also a feature in Jordan, although King Hussein (who died in 1999) is proving a hard act to follow for his son, King Abdullah II. In Egypt, Hosni Mubarak seems intent on outlasting the pharaohs, while Israel keeps recycling yesterday's politicians to lead the country (Tzipi Livni's ascension to lead the Kadima Party notwithstanding), and corruption allegations continue to swirl around the polity. For its part, Turkey is doing everything it can to join the EU, even as it struggles with its decades-old issues of the religious-secular divide and a Kurdish insurgency in the southeast.

2000

The second Palestinian intifada breaks out in the Palestinian Territories. In Damascus, Hafez al-Assad dies after 30 years in power and his son, Bashar, becomes president.

2003

The US and the UK, with a much smaller coalition and less international support than in 1990-91, invade Iraq, winning the war, but Iraq descends into looting and open insurgency. Saddam Hussein is captured in December.

2004

Evidence of the torture of Iraqi prisoners emerges from the US-controlled Abu Ghraib prison in Baghdad. The United States' reputation in the region sinks to an all-time low.

THE 2008 GAZA STRIP CONFLICT *Amelia Thomas*

On December 27 2008 Israel began an air, and subsequently ground, offensive in the Gaza Strip, stating its aim as the permanent prevention of missile strikes on southern Israel by Hamas fighters. Three weeks later, the BBC reported that the offensive had resulted in more than 1300 Palestinian fatalities, around 65% of them civilians, and at least 13 Israeli fatalities.

In mid-January, as this book went to press, Israel had declared a unilateral ceasefire and its troops had began withdrawing from the Gaza Strip. Israel claimed its operation's aims had been accomplished; senior Palestinian leader Ismail Haniyeh said on Hamas TV that Israel had failed to achieve its goals and that, despite 'all the wounds, our people didn't surrender, but demonstrated a legendary perseverance.'

Meanwhile, shell-shocked civilians began the painful process of salvaging what they could of their devastated homes and lives.

Iraq aside, most of the Middle East is nominally at peace. But it's a pretty weary peace, not to mention a fragile one. The region has reached something of an impasse with the issues of the past 60 years frozen into seemingly perpetual division that sometimes spills over into open warfare, but more often festers like an open wound. The Palestinian still dreams of returning home. The Israeli still dreams of a world free from fear. In the meantime, the two sides come no closer to a resolution. These are real issues that make life a daily struggle for ordinary people and the sad fact remains that, for many Middle Easterners, life is no easier than it was 60 years ago. But such a time frame is the mere blink of an historical eye for this part of the world, where moments of hope have all too often yielded to cycles of conflict.

2005

Yasser Arafat, the chairman of the PLO and leader of the Palestinian Authority, dies in Paris and is later buried in Ramallah, ending an eventful four decades at the frontline of Middle Eastern politics.

2006

After Hezbollah captures two Israeli soldiers, Israel launches a sustained air attack on Lebanon. The resulting war produces a stalemate and is widely portrayed throughout the region as a victory for Hezbollah.

2008

Civil war threatens again in Lebanon after Hezbollah besieges the government, although the crisis is later resolved. Syria admits to indirect talks with Israel through Turkish mediators, while relations improve between Syria and Lebanon.

Religion

The Middle East is where it all began for the three big monotheistic world religions: Judaism, Christianity and Islam. Infusing almost every aspect of daily life in the region, from the five-times-daily call to prayer and cultural norms to architecture and disputes over historical claims to land, these three religions provide an important back-story to your travels in the Middle East.

Muhammad: A Biography of the Prophet, by Karen Armstrong, is a sensitive, well-researched and highly readable biography of the Prophet Mohammed, set against the backdrop of modern misconceptions and stereotypes about Islam.

ISLAM

The Birth of Islam

Abdul Qasim Mohammed ibn Abdullah ibn Abd al-Muttalib ibn Hashim (the Prophet Mohammed) was born in 570. Mohammed's family belonged to the Quraysh tribe, a trading family with links to Syria and Yemen. By the age of six, Mohammed's parents had both died and he came into the care of his grandfather, the custodian of the Kaaba in Mecca. When he was around 25 years old, Mohammed married Khadija, a widow and merchant, and he worked in running her business.

At the age of 40, in 610, Mohammed retreated into the desert and began to receive divine revelations from Allah via the voice of the archangel Gabriel; the revelations would continue throughout Mohammed's life. Three years later, Mohammed began imparting Allah's message to the Meccans, gathering a significant following in his campaign against Meccan idolaters. His movement appealed especially to the poorer, disenfranchised sections of society.

The flight of Mohammed and his followers from Mecca to Medina (the Hejira) marks the birth of Islam and the first year of the Islamic calendar - 1 AH (AD 622).

Islam provided a simpler alternative to the established faiths, which had become complicated by hierarchical orders, sects and complex rituals, offering instead a direct relationship with God based only on the believer's submission to God (Islam means 'submission').

By 622, Mecca's powerful ruling families had forced Mohammed and his followers to flee north to Medina where Mohammed's supporters rapidly grew in number. In 630 Mohammed returned triumphantly to Mecca at the head of a 10,000-strong army to seize control of the city. Many of the surrounding tribes quickly swore allegiance to him and the new faith.

When Mohammed died in 632, the Arab tribes spread quickly across the Middle East with missionary zeal, in very little time conquering what now constitutes Jordan, Syria, Iraq, Lebanon and Israel and the Palestinian Territories. To the east, Persia and India soon found themselves confronted by the new army of believers. To the west, the unrelenting conquest swept across North Africa. By the end of the 7th century, the Muslims had reached the Atlantic and marched on Spain in 710, an astonishing achievement given the religion's humble desert roots.

Islam: A Short History, by Karen Armstrong, is almost like Islam 101, a readable journey through Islam's birth and subsequent growth with easy-to-follow coverage of the schism between Sunnis and Shiites.

Shiite & Sunni

Despite the Prophet Mohammed's original intentions, Islam did not remain simple. The Prophet died leaving no sons and no instructions as to who should succeed him. Competing for power were Abu Bakr, the father of Mohammed's second wife Aisha, and Ali, Mohammed's cousin and the husband of his daughter Fatima. Initially, the power was transferred to Abu Bakr, who became the first caliph, or ruler, with Ali reluctantly agreeing.

Abu Bakr's lineage came to an abrupt halt when his successor was murdered. Ali reasserted his right to power and emerged victorious in

RELIGIONS IN THE MIDDLE EAST

The following graph shows the approximate distribution of Christians, Sunni and Shiite Muslims across the Middle East. For updates on this information, see www.populstat.info.

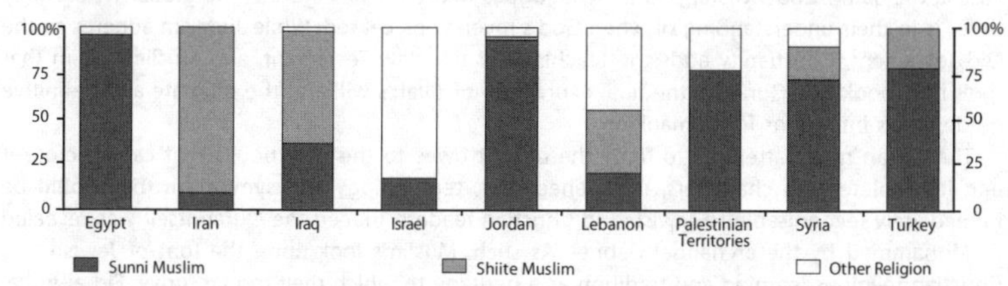

Jews make up around 80% of Israel's and around 15% of the Palestinian Territories' populations. Christians make up less than 10% of most Middle Eastern populations, except in Lebanon, where 39% of the population is Christian.

the ensuing power struggle, moving his capital to Kufa (later renamed Najaf, in Iraq), only to be assassinated himself in 661. After defeating Ali's successor, Hussein, in 680 at Karbala, the Umayyad dynasty rose to rule the majority of the Muslim world, marking the start of the Sunni sect. Those who continued to support the claims of the descendants of Ali became known as Shiites.

The Story of the Qur'an: Its History and Place in Muslim Life, by Ingrid Mattson, is a landmark 2007 text that's filled with insights into what it means to be a Muslim in the 21st century.

Beyond this early dynastic rivalry, there's little doctrinal difference between Shiite Islam and Sunni Islam, but the division remains to this day. Sunnis comprise some 90% of the world's Muslims, but Shiites are believed to form a majority of the population in Iraq, Lebanon and Iran. There are also Shiite minorities in almost all Arab countries.

The Quran

For Muslims the Quran is the word of God, directly communicated to Mohammed. It comprises 114 suras, or chapters, which govern all aspects of a Muslim's life from a Muslim's relationship to God to minute details about daily life.

It's not known whether the revelations were written down during Mohammed's lifetime, although Muslims believe that the Quran is the direct word of Allah as told to Mohammed. The third caliph, Uthman (644–56), gathered together everything written by the scribes (parchments, stone tablets, the memories of Mohammed's followers) and gave them to a panel of editors under the caliph's aegis. A Quran printed today is identical to that agreed upon by Uthman's compilers 14 centuries ago.

Some people are excused from the rigours of Ramadan, including young children and those whose health will not permit fasting. Travellers on a journey are also excused, although they are expected to fast on alternative days instead.

Another important aspect of the Quran is the language in which it is written. Some Muslims believe that the Quran must be studied in its original classical Arabic form ('an Arabic Quran, wherein there is no crookedness'; sura 39:25) and that translations dilute the holiness of its sacred texts. For Muslims, the language of the Quran is known as *sihr halal* (lawful magic). Apart from its religious significance, the Quran, lyrical and poetic, is also considered one of the finest literary masterpieces in history.

Five Pillars of Islam

In order to live a devout life, Muslims are expected to observe, as a minimum, the five pillars of Islam.

THE THINGS WE SHARE

Despite what you read in the papers, the differences between the three religions are fewer than you might think. As any Muslim will attest, the God invoked in Friday prayers across the Middle East is the same God worshipped in synagogues and churches around the globe. Where they differ is in their understanding of when God's revelations ceased. While Judaism adheres to the Old Testament, Christianity adds the teachings of the New Testament, and Muslims claim that their holy book, the Quran, is the final expression of Allah's will and the ultimate and definitive guide to his intentions for humankind.

The Quran never attempts to deny the debt it owes to the holy books that came before it and it's replete with characters, tales, anecdotes, terminology and symbolism that would be immediately recognisable to Jewish and Christian readers. Indeed the Quran itself was revealed to Mohammed by the archangel Gabriel. As such, Muslims look upon the font of Jewish and Christian religious learning and tradition as a heritage to which they too are privy. Eid al-Adha, for example, the Muslim festival that marks the end of the hajj, is based on the biblical tale of Abraham offering up his son for sacrifice. Some of the Quran's laws also closely resemble those of the other monotheistic faiths, particularly the doctrinal elements of Judaism and the piety of early Eastern Christianity. It's clear that the Muslim prohibition on the consumption of pork, for example, is based on the Jewish ruling. The Muslim month-long fast of Ramadan also bears similarities to Lent.

The suras contain many references to the earlier prophets – Adam, Abraham (Ibrahim), Noah, Moses (Moussa) and Jesus (although Muslims strictly deny his divinity) are all recognised as prophets in a line that ends definitively with the greatest of them all, Mohammed. Not surprisingly, given the shared heritage, Muslims traditionally attribute a place of great respect to Christians and Jews as *ahl al-kitab* (the people of the book; sura 2:100–15).

Originally the responsibility of the individual, zakat now often exists as a state-imposed welfare tax administered by a ministry of religious affairs with zakat committees overseeing the distribution of charitable donations.

Shahada This is the profession of faith, Islam's basic tenet: 'There is no god but Allah, and Mohammed is the Prophet of Allah.' This phrase forms an integral part of the call to prayer and is used at all important events in a Muslim's life.
Sala (sura 11:115) This is the obligation of prayer, ideally five times a day: at sunrise, noon, midafternoon, sunset and night. It's acceptable to pray at home or elsewhere, except for Friday noon prayers, which are performed at a mosque.
Zakat (sura 107) Muslims must give alms to the poor to the value of one-fortieth of a believer's annual income.
Sawm (sura 2:180–5) Ramadan, the ninth month of the Muslim calendar, commemorates the revelation of the Quran to Mohammed. As Ramadan represents a Muslim's renewal of faith, nothing may pass their lips (food, cigarettes, drinks) and they must refrain from sex from dawn until dusk. For more details on Ramadan see p628.
Hajj (sura 2:190–200) Every physically and financially able Muslim should perform the hajj to the holiest of cities, Mecca, at least once in his or her lifetime. The reward is considerable: the forgiving of all past sins.

Jihad is sometimes referred to as the sixth pillar of Islam. Widely interpreted in the West as 'holy war', the word actually means 'struggle' or 'striving in the way of the faith' – the interpretation preferred by most Muslims.

The Call to Prayer

Allahu akbar, Allahu akbar	God is great, God is great
Ashhadu an la Ilah ila Allah	I testify that there is no God but Allah
Ashhadu an Mohammed rasul Allah	I testify that Mohammed is His Prophet
Haya ala as-sala	Hurry towards prayer
Haya ala af-fala	Hurry towards success
Allahu akbar, Allahu akbar	God is great, God is great
La Ilah ila Allah	There is no God but Allah

This haunting invocation will soon become the soundtrack to your visit to the Middle East, a ritual whose essential meaning and power remain largely unchanged in 14 centuries.

Five times a day, Muslims are called, if not actually to enter a mosque to pray, at least to take the time to do so where they are. The call to prayer is made by the muezzin, who is a cantor who calls the faithful to prayer. The midday prayers on Friday, when the imam of the mosque delivers his weekly khutba, or sermon, are considered the most important. For Muslims, prayer is less a petition to Allah (in the Christian sense) than a ritual reaffirmation of Allah's power and a reassertion of the brotherhood and equality of all believers.

The act of praying consists of a series of predefined movements of the body and recitals of prayers and passages of the Quran, all designed to express the believer's absolute humility and Allah's sovereignty.

Historically, the muezzin climbed the minaret to make the call to prayer, but the growth of cities means that the call is now broadcast from minaret loudspeakers in all but the smallest villages.

Islamic Customs

In everyday life, Muslims are prohibited from drinking alcohol (sura 5:90–5) and eating carrion, blood products or pork, which are considered unclean (sura 2:165), the meat of animals not killed in the prescribed manner (sura 5:1–5) and food over which the name of Allah has not been said (sura 6:115). Adultery (sura 18:30–5), theft (sura 5:40–5) and gambling (sura 5:90–5) are also prohibited.

Islam is not just about prohibitions but also marks the important events of a Muslim's life. When a baby is born, the first words uttered to it are the call to prayer. A week later follows a ceremony in which the baby's head is shaved and an animal sacrificed in remembrance of Abraham's willingness to sacrifice his son to Allah. The major event of a boy's childhood is circumcision, which normally takes place between the ages of seven and 12. When a person dies, a burial service is held at the mosque and the body is buried with the feet facing Mecca.

If Muslims wish to pray but are not in a mosque and there's no water available, clean sand ('wholesome dust' according to the Quran) suffices; where there's no sand, they must go through the motions of washing (sura 5:5).

WHAT'S YOUR RELIGION?

Travelling in the Middle East involves some near-constants: you *will* be woken by the call to prayer, you *will* find yourself unable to sleep from all the tea and coffee you drink and you *will* be asked for your opinion on American foreign policy in the Middle East and the war in Iraq. Just as likely, at some point the conversation will turn to religion. More specifically, you'll probably be asked, 'What's your religion?' Given that most foreign travellers come from secular Western traditions where religion is a private matter, the level of frankness involved in some of these discussions can come as a surprise. On one level, there's no better way of getting under the skin of a nation than talking about the things that matter most in life. So how do you go about answering this question?

It's usually easy to explain that you are Christian or, in some circumstances, Jewish, although in the company of Hamas militants or on the unfamiliar streets of Baghdad is probably not the wisest moment to announce your Jewish faith to the world. However, the overwhelming majority of Muslims won't bat an eyelid and may even welcome the opportunity to talk about the common origins and doctrines that Judaism and Islam share. Christians and Jews are respected as 'people of the book' who share the same God (see the boxed text, opposite). In fact, many a Bedouin encounter begins with a celebration of that fact, with greetings such as 'Your God, my God same – *Salam* (Peace)!'

The question of religion gets complicated when it comes to atheists. 'I don't believe in God' can be a difficult answer because it calls into question the very foundation of a Muslim's existence. If you are concerned that your atheism will cause offence, perhaps say, 'I'm a seeker,' suggesting that you haven't quite made up your mind but may well do so in the future. Be aware that Muslims may respond by explaining the merits of Islam to you. If that's not how you planned to spend your afternoon, try saying, 'I'm not religious.' This will likely lead to understanding nods and then, perhaps on subsequent meetings, an earnest attempt at conversion. Words like 'You'll find God soon, God-willing' are a measure of someone's affection for you and a reasonable response would be *shukran* (thank you).

Jerusalem: One City, Three Faiths, by Karen Armstrong, is a comprehensive, unbiased history of a city believed to be holy by the three monotheistic religions.

Keeping the Faith Today

It's close to sunset in a coffeehouse in the shadow of the Umayyad Mosque in Damascus. The smell of scented tobacco from a dozen nargilehs hangs in the early evening air. Young men in designer jeans pause from their serious-minded conversations to watch respectfully as old men in traditional dress shuffle past. Women speak in conspiratorial whispers as children tumble down the steps. In the background, the latest Lebanese pop diva croons from the TV. Suddenly, the call to prayer rings out across the old city from the Minaret of Jesus. Nobody moves. Nobody breaks conversation. The coffeehouse owner may turn down the TV, but not necessarily. Someone calls for more coals to be brought for his or her nargileh. A bearded man orders a second round of tea.

Are most of the coffeehouse's temporary residents practising Muslims? Almost certainly. Does the failure to heed the muezzin's call suggest that the Muslims present aren't serious practitioners of the faith? Not in the least.

There are as many ways of practising Islam as there are Muslims, even as the fundamental beliefs remain constant. For some, Islam governs their every waking moment. For others, the formal rites of their religion form just one part of a life in which other underlying principles of Islam – the importance of community, hospitality and family to name just three – are treated with the utmost seriousness. In a city like Damascus, it's also highly likely that a sizeable portion of the people present is Christian, often sharing tables or lifelong friendships with fellow Syrians who happen to be Muslim. More than that, young Muslims are as savvy when it comes to the latest fashions and as eager to keep abreast of the latest musical icons of popular culture as their peers around the world.

Worldwide there are around 14 million (some say 18 million) people who either practise Judaism or are Jewish by birth, although this figure is disputed as there are ongoing debates about what defines a Jew.

Modern life requires daily compromises with any chosen religion. In this, and in many other aspects, there's not much that separates a person's life in the Muslim world from elsewhere in the world.

JUDAISM

Judaism is the first recorded monotheistic faith and thus one of the oldest religions still practised. Its major tenet is that there is one God who created the universe and remains omnipresent. Judaism's power is held not in a central authority or person, but rather in its teachings and the Holy Scriptures.

Until the foundation of the State of Israel in 1948, Jewish communities lived peacefully alongside their Muslim neighbours in all countries of the Middle East covered by this book; Iraq was home to a particularly large Jewish community. Tiny Jewish communities may remain in some Muslim countries, but most fled or were expelled in the years following 1948.

Essential Judaism: A Complete Guide to Beliefs, Customs and Rituals, by George Robinson, is aimed at Jews seeking to rediscover their traditions, but it covers everything from festivals and rituals to Jewish philosophy – the religion stripped of its political connotations.

Foundations of Judaism

The patriarch of the faith was Abraham who, according to the calculations of the Hebrew Torah, was born 1948 years after Creation and lived to the ripe old age of 175. According to Jewish belief he preached the existence of one God and in return God promised him the land of Canaan (the Promised Land in Jewish tradition), but only after his descendants would be exiled and redeemed. Accordingly, his grandson Jacob set off for Egypt, where later generations found themselves bound in slavery. Moses led them out of Egypt and received the Ten Commandments on Mt Sinai. Once they had returned to Israel, God assigned the descendants of Aaron (Moses' brother) to be a priestly caste. They became the Kohen (Kohanim), who performed specific duties during festivals and sacrificial offerings.

God's relationship with the Jews has not always been one of blessing: when he saw his chosen people straying from their faith he laid down punishment. In one biblical incident God allowed the Philistines to capture the *mishkan* (portable house of worship) used by the Kohen.

For a good grounding in Judaism, check www.jewfaq.org, which holds answers to a number of basic questions on the faith.

It was Rambam, the 12th-century Jewish rabbi, who laid out the 13 core principles of Jewish belief. These principles include the belief in one unique God to whom prayer must be directed; the belief that God rewards the good and punishes the wicked; and the belief in the coming of the Messiah and the resurrection of the dead. Having said this, Judaism doesn't focus on abstract cosmological beliefs. While Jews certainly contemplate the nature of God, the universe and the afterlife among other topics, there are no set definitions of these concepts, which leaves plenty of room for debate and personal opinion. Rather than a strict adherence to dogmatic ideas, actions such as prayer, study and performing mitzvah, which means adherence to the commandments, are of greater importance.

The Torah & Talmud

The basis for the Jewish religion is the Torah, the first five books of the Old Testament. The Torah contains the revelation from God via Moses more than 3000 years ago, including, most importantly, God's commandments (613 commandments in total). The Torah is supplemented by the rest of the books of the Old Testament, of which the most important are the prophetic books.

These books are, in turn, complemented by the Talmud, a collection of another 63 books. The Talmud was written largely in exile after the Romans crushed the Jewish state and destroyed the Temple in Jerusalem in AD 70, and within its pages is most of what separates Judaism from other religions. Included are plenty of rabbinical interpretations of the earlier scriptures, with a wealth of instructions and rulings for Jewish daily life.

Jewish Customs

The most obvious Jewish custom you'll experience in Israel is Shabbat, the day of rest. It begins on Friday night with sundown and ends at nightfall on Saturday. No work of any kind is allowed on Shabbat, unless someone's health is at stake. Tasks such as writing or handling money are forbidden. Starting a fire is also prohibited and in modern terms this means no use of electricity is allowed (lights can be turned on before Shabbat starts but must stay on until it ends). Permitted activities include visiting with friends and family, reading and discussing the Torah, and prayer at a synagogue. Sex is also allowed; in fact, it's a double mitzvah on Shabbat.

God's laws, as recorded in the Torah, govern every facet of an observant Jew's life, including issues like the prohibition of theft, murder and idolatry. There are other commandments to which Jews must adhere, such as eating kosher foods and reciting the *shema* (affirmation of Judaism) twice daily.

Some Jewish sects are easily recognised by their clothing, although most Jews wear Western street clothes. The most religious Jews, the Hasidim (or *haredim*) are identified by their black hats, long black coats, collared white shirts, beards and *peyot* (side curls). *Haredi* women, like Muslim women, act and dress modestly, covering up exposed hair and skin (except the hands and face).

Many Jews, both secular and orthodox, wear a kippa (skullcap). It's sometimes possible to infer a person's background, religious or even political beliefs by the type of kippa they wear. A large crocheted kippa, often in white, is a sign that the wearer is either a Braslav Hassid or a Messianist, perhaps an extreme right-wing settler. Muted brown or blue kippot (skullcaps) that are crocheted generally indicate strong Zionist beliefs; the IDF provides standard-issue olive kippot.

Christianity is the world's largest religion, with an estimated 1.9 billion followers. Islam comes next with around 1.1 billion adherents.

CHRISTIANITY

Jesus preached in what is present-day Israel and the Palestinian Territories, but Christians form only minority groups in all Middle Eastern countries. Lebanon's one million Maronites have followers all over the world, but by far the biggest Christian sect in the region is formed by the Copts of Egypt, who make up most of that country's Christian population. Originally it was the apostle Mark who established Christianity in Egypt, and by the 4th century it had become the state religion. The Coptic Church split from the Byzantine Orthodox Church in the 5th century after a dispute about the human nature of Jesus, with Dioscurus, the patriarch of Alexandria, declaring Jesus to be totally divine.

William Dalrymple observed Syrian Orthodox Christians at prayer in the 1990s, whereupon he wondered aloud if the Muslim prayer ritual could be based on the Christian, so uncannily similar were the series of genuflections and prostrations.

Otherwise, the Arab Christians of the Middle East belong to many churches in all main branches of the religion – Orthodox, Catholic and Protestant. The number of Christians in the Middle East is, however, in decline. The reasons are predominantly demographic. Over the centuries Christians, in Egypt and Syria in particular, have moved from the country to the city and this urbanisation has led to a fall in birth rates. Also, traditionally Christian church schools have provided a better education than Muslim state schools, which again has had the effect of lowering the birth rate. The professional qualifications resulting from the better education and subsequent wealth have also meant that Middle Eastern Christians emigrate far more easily. Syrian and Egyptian churches in particular have found it impossible to stem the flow of parishioners to Australia and the USA.

Foundations of Christianity

Jesus of Nazareth was born in Bethlehem in what is now the Palestinian Territories in the year zero (or AD 1, depending on who you believe) of the Christian calendar. After baptism by John the Baptist, Jesus was said to have been led by God into the desert, where he remained for 40 days and nights, during which time he refuted the temptations of the Devil. His ministry was marked by numerous miracles, such as healings, walking on water and the resuscitation of the dead (Lazarus). At the age of 33, Jesus was accused of sedition and condemned to death by Jerusalem's

THE BIBLE AS HISTORY

In Egypt, the wealth of tomb and temple texts and papyri has enabled historians to work out a detailed history of the country. For archaeologists in the 'Holy Lands', where the events related in the Bible's Old Testament are said to have taken place, the situation is far more complex. Little in the way of written archives has been found and historians cannot say for sure whether characters such as Abraham, Moses or even Solomon existed. The Old Testament was compiled from a variety of sources and probably set down in script no earlier than the 6th century BC. The stories it contains could be wholly or merely partly true, but believing in their veracity has become an article of faith for Jews, Christians and Muslims, rather than a proven fact.

When it comes to the New Testament and episodes related in the Gospels by Matthew, Mark, Luke and John, we do have some means of corroboration. This was the Roman era and there are plenty of other sources in the form of written accounts, inscriptions and works of art so we can say with certainty that figures such as Herod, Pontius Pilot and a man called Jesus did exist. Even so, many sites commonly held to be of biblical significance were only fixed in the 4th century, some 300 years after the death of Christ. They owe their status more to tradition than verifiable sources.

Roman governor Pontius Pilate. After being crucified, Christians believe that Jesus was resurrected and ascended to heaven. Although doctrinal differences have tied Christian scholars and adherents in knots for centuries – hence the proliferation of different sects – Christians believe that God's divine nature is expressed in the Trinity: God, Jesus Christ and the Holy Spirit.

The followers of Jesus came to be known as Christians (Christ is a Greek-derived title meaning 'Anointed One'), believing him to be the son of God and the Messiah. Within a few decades of Jesus' death, having interpreted and spread his teachings, his followers had formed a faith distinct from Judaism. A Greek-speaking Christian community emerged in Jerusalem in the mid-2nd century and the Greek Orthodox Church is now the largest denomination in Israel and the Palestinian Territories, having jurisdiction over more than half of Jerusalem's Church of the Holy Sepulchre and a bigger portion of Bethlehem's Church of the Nativity than anybody else. Numerous other denominations claim bits and pieces of other holy sites and ownership is fiercely defended, such as in November 2008 when a brawl between Greek Orthodox and Armenian monks broke out in the Church of the Holy Sepulchre (Jerusalem) in front of stunned pilgrims.

From the Holy Mountain: A Journey in the Shadow of Byzantium, by William Dalrymple, takes the reader through the heart of the Middle East and pays homage to the survival of Eastern Christianity.

Arts

ARCHITECTURE

Middle Eastern architecture ranges from the sublime to the downright ugly. On one hand, the graceful lines of Islamic architecture draw on the rich historical legacy left by the great empires that once ruled the region. On the other, the perennially unfinished cinder-block architecture of grim functionality that blights many city outskirts and smaller towns.

Dictionary of Islamic Architecture, by Andrew Petersen, is for those who can't quite distinguish a *sahn* (courtyard of a mosque) from a *riwaq* (arcade) and is useful primarily if your journey has whet your appetite to learn more.

Mosques

Embodying the Islamic faith and representing its most predominant architectural feature throughout the region is the *masjid* (mosque, also called a *jamaa).* The building, developed in the very early days of the religion, takes its form from the simple private houses where the first believers gathered to worship.

The house belonging to the Prophet Mohammed is said to have provided the prototype of the mosque. It had an enclosed oblong courtyard with huts (housing Mohammed's wives) along one wall and a rough portico providing shade. This plan developed with the courtyard becoming the *sahn,* the portico the arcaded *riwaq* and the house the *haram* (prayer hall).

The prayer hall is typically divided into a series of aisles. The central aisle is wider than the rest and leads to a vaulted niche in the wall called the mihrab; this indicates the direction of Mecca, towards which Muslims must face when they pray.

Islam: Art & Architecture, edited by Markus Hattstein and Peter Delius, is comprehensive, lavishly illustrated and one of those coffee-table books that you'll treasure and dip into time and again.

Before entering the prayer hall and participating in communal worship, Muslims must perform a ritual washing of the hands, forearms, neck and face (by washing themselves before prayer, the believer indicates a willingness to be purified). For this purpose mosques have traditionally had a large ablutions fountain at the centre of the courtyard, often fashioned from marble and worn by centuries of use. These days, modern mosques just have rows of taps.

Within these overarching architectural themes, each region developed its own local flourishes. The Umayyads of Damascus favoured square minarets, the Abbasid dynasty built spiral minarets echoing the ziggurats of the Babylonians and the Fatimids of Egypt made much use of

MIDDLE EASTERN ARCHITECTURE – OUR TOP TEN

- **Topkapı Palace**, İstanbul (p540)
- **Aya Sofya**, İstanbul (p540)
- **Süleymaniye Camii**, İstanbul (p541)
- The traditional architecture of **Cappadocia**, Turkey (p587)
- **Umayyad Mosque**, Damascus (p469)
- **Azem Palace**, Damascus (p472)
- **Citadel**, Aleppo (p497)
- **Dome of the Rock**, Jerusalem (p266)
- **Mosque of Qaitbey**, Cairo (p135)
- Oasis architecture of **Siwa**, Egypt (p179)

decorative stucco work. But it was the Ottoman Turks who left the most recognisable (and, given the reach of the Ottoman Empire, widespread) landmarks. Ottoman mosques were designed on the basic principle of a dome on a square, and are instantly recognisable by their slim pencil-shaped minarets. The Süleymaniye Camii (p541) in İstanbul and the Selimiye Mosque (p551) in Edirne, both the work of the Turkish master architect Sinan, represent the apogee of the style.

Islamic Art in Context: Art, Architecture and the Literary World, by Robert Irwin, one of the premier scholars on the Arab world, traces the development of Islamic arts from the 5th to the 17th centuries against the backdrop of prevailing social and political upheaval.

Urban Buildings

It's in the cities of the Middle East that you'll find the region's major architectural landmarks. Beyond the soaring mosques that adorn city skylines at almost every turn, it's the private world of palaces and homes that truly distinguishes urban Middle Eastern architecture. Often hidden behind high walls, these palaces were built on the premise of keeping the outside world at bay, allowing families to retreat into a generous-size refuge.

Usually built around a courtyard, these private homes and palaces were perfectly adapted to the dictates of climate and communal living. The homes often housed up to a dozen families, each with their own space opening onto the shared patio. The palaces worked on the same principle, containing the royal living quarters with separate rooms for women and domestic staff. Most such residences included a cooling central fountain and an *iwan* (arched alcove that served as a summer retreat), and were adorned with tilework, wood-carved lintels and elegant arches. Comfortable and stylish, private and largely self-contained, these homes were ideally suited to a region with long, hot summers and where complicated rules of engagement existed between the public and private spheres. You'll find such architecture in most Middle Eastern cities, but the most splendid examples are in Damascus.

Per capita, Cairo has one of the lowest ratios of green space to urban population on earth with just one footprint-sized plot of earth per inhabitant.

The Middle East's cities are also where the failure of architecture and urban planning to keep pace with burgeoning populations is most distressingly on show. Take Cairo, for example. In 1950, Cairo had a population of around 2.3 million. Now as many as 17 million people live cheek-by-jowl within greater Cairo's ever-expanding boundaries. The result is an undistinguished sprawl of grime-coated, Soviet-style apartment blocks and unplanned shanty towns, often without even the most basic amenities.

Another major issue is the decay of the beautiful homes of the old cities that once formed the core of Damascus, Aleppo and other cities. Throughout the 20th century, the trend was for old-city residents to leave homes that had been in their families for generations and move into modern homes in newer parts of town. Emptying old cities with ageing infrastructure were left behind and vulnerable to developers.

Belatedly, but perhaps just in time, something is being done to halt the decline. Since 1994, Unesco, the local Aleppo government and the German Agency for Technical Cooperation have been involved in an ambitious program of rehabilitation to make the remaining areas of Aleppo's old town more liveable. For more information, see the boxed text, p496. A similar plan is also in its early stages in Damascus. Tourism is playing an important role in bringing Syria's old cities back to life – many courtyard homes in Damascus and Aleppo have been saved from the wrecker's ball, painstakingly restored and converted into boutique hotels.

Architecture and Polyphony: Building in the Islamic World Today is an exciting work stemming from the Aga Khan Award for Architecture. It's filled with the innovations of modern Middle Eastern architecture – an antidote to the dominance of mosques in the aesthetics of Middle Eastern cities.

Even more ambitious has been the attempt to impose some order onto Cairo's unsightly sprawl. Funded by the Aga Khan Development Network (see the boxed text, p82), the first stage of the US$30 million project involved creating the 30-hectare Al-Azhar Park on land reclaimed from what had been a rubbish dump for 500 years. The project also involved

AGA KHAN: ISLAMIC ARCHITECTURE'S SAVIOUR

If there is one figure who has been responsible above all others for reviving Islamic architecture worldwide, it's the Aga Khan. The Aga Khan IV, the current imam (religious teacher) of the largest branch of the Ismaili Shia Muslims, inherited a vast family fortune upon succeeding to this hereditary position in 1957. Ever since, he has set about putting the money to good use.

Through the Aga Khan Development Network (www.akdn.org), one of the largest private development organisations in the world, the Aga Khan funds programs encompassing public health, education, microfinance, rural development and architecture. His interventions in the field of architecture in a region blighted by decades of ill-conceived development and urban decay have been particularly eye-catching.

The main focus of his efforts has been the Historic Cities Program, which aims to rescue, restore and bring back to life public buildings across the Islamic world. Egypt and Syria have been the main beneficiaries in the Middle East. Rather than focusing solely on bricks and mortar, the projects prioritise improvements in social infrastructure and living conditions in surrounding areas, thereby transforming architectural restoration into wider projects for social renewal.

A further pillar in the Aga Khan's masterplan has been the triennial Aga Khan Award for Architecture (www.akdn.org/akaa.asp), one of the world's most prestigious architecture awards. The award's primary aim is to promote excellence and creativity in Islamic architecture within a framework of heritage values and contemporary design, with special consideration given to social, historical and environmental issues. Winning projects since the award was announced in 1977 have included İstanbul's Topkapı Palace, Cairo's Citadel of Saladin and Aleppo citadel.

restoring 1.5km of the 12th-century Ayyubid Wall, rescuing a number of dilapidated mosques and an integrated plan for improving housing, infrastructure and living conditions in the adjacent Darb al-Ahmar, one of Cairo's poorest districts and home to more than 90,000 people; many of the rooftops were fitted with solar heating systems, water cisterns and vegetable gardens. It's one of the most exciting projects for urban renewal seen in the Middle East for decades. Let's hope it encourages other governments to do the same.

Gertrude Bell described the beehive houses of central Syria as 'like no other villages save those that appear in illustrations to Central African travel books'.

Rural Buildings

Architecture in rural areas of the Middle East has always been a highly localised tradition, determined primarily by the dictates of climate. In the oases, particularly the Saharan towns of Egypt's Western Oases, mud-brick was easy to manufacture and ensured cool interiors under the baking desert sun. Although perfectly adapted to ordinary climatic conditions, these homes also proved extremely vulnerable to erosion and rains, which explains why so few examples remain across the region.

Among other natural building forms in the Middle East, the extremely sturdy conical beehive houses of central Syria (see the boxed text, p487) are among the most distinctive. They owe their endurance to the whitewashing of the unusually thick mud walls, which reflects the sun and slows the ageing of the underlying structural materials. But the undoubted star when it comes to unique traditional architecture is Cappadocia (Kapadokya; p587), where homes and churches were hewn from the weird and wonderful landscape of caves, rock walls and soft volcanic tuff.

Unrelenting urbanisation in Middle Eastern cities has seen them grow at an alarming rate and this same urbanisation has stripped rural areas of much of their lifeblood. The result has been the widespread abandonment of traditional forms of architecture. Rural poverty has led to government-housing programs, which have chosen modern concrete constructions rather than the more expensive adaptations of the indigenous forms that coexisted in perfect harmony with the environment for centuries. The simple truth about the future of rural architecture in the Middle East is this: unless places become established as tourist attractions, their traditional architecture will disappear within a generation, if it hasn't done so already.

Your first order of business if you're buying a carpet should be to read *Oriental Rugs Today*, by Emmett Eiland, an excellent primer on buying new oriental rugs.

CARPETS

Carpets are among the most accessible art forms in the Middle East – you'll find them adorning storefronts across the region wherever there's a fair chance of a tourist passing by. That said, your relationship to these icons of Middle Eastern travel is more likely to be as a prospective purchaser rather than casual admirer: however averse you may be to the idea, you're likely at some stage to find yourself in a carpet shop. Resistance is futile.

As it's likely to be one of the major purchases of your trip, a little knowledge can go a long way. Carpets are made with Persian knots, which loop around one horizontal thread and under the next; or Turkish knots, looped around two horizontal threads, with the yarn lifted between them. For more on the art of buying a carpet, see the boxed text, below.

The Root of Wild Madder: Chasing the History, Mystery and Lore of the Persian Carpet, by Brian Murphy, is a travelogue through the countries of finest carpet production and a buyer's guide to quality, interwoven with stories told by individual designs.

CINEMA

Middle Eastern film stands at a crossroads. On one level, a small, elite company of directors is gaining unprecedented critical acclaim, picking up awards at international festivals and inching its way into the consciousness of audiences around the world. But the industry as a whole

CARPET-BUYING 101 *John Vlahides*

Due diligence is essential for perspective carpet-buyers. Though you may only want a piece to match your curtains, you'll save a lot of time and money if you do a little homework.

A rug's quality depends entirely on how the wool was processed. It doesn't matter whether the rug was hand-knotted if the wool is lousy. The best comes from sheep at high altitudes, which produce impenetrably thick, long-staple fleece, heavy with lanolin. No acids should ever be applied; otherwise the lanolin washes away. Lanolin yields naturally stain-resistant, lustrous fibre that doesn't shed. The dye should be a vegetable-based pigment. This guarantees saturated, rich colour tones with a depth and vibrancy unattainable with chemicals.

The dyed wool is hand-spun into thread, which by nature has occasional lumps and challenges the craftsmanship of the weavers, forcing them to compensate for the lumps by occasionally changing the shape, size or position of a knot. These subtle variations in a finished carpet's pattern – visible only upon close inspection – give the carpet its character, and actually make the rug more valuable.

Dealers will hype knot density, weave quality and country of origin, but their importance pales in significance compared to the crucial matter of finding out how the wool was treated. A rug made with acid-treated wool will never look as good as the day you bought it. Conversely, a properly made rug will grow more lustrous in colour over time and will last centuries.

Here's a quick test. Stand atop the rug with rubber-soled shoes and do the twist. Grind the fibres underfoot. If they shed, it's lousy wool. You can also spill water onto the rug. See how fast it absorbs. Ideally it should puddle for an instant, indicating a high presence of lanolin. Best of all, red wine will not stain lanolin-rich wool.

If you're looking for a gorgeous pattern that will look great in your living room, pack a few fabric swatches from your sofa and draperies. Patterns range from simple four-colour tribal designs of wool to wildly ornate, lustrous multicoloured silk carpets that shimmer under the light. Once in the stores, plan to linger long with dealers, slowly sipping tea while they unfurl dozens of carpets.

has spent much of the last two decades in crisis, plagued by a critical lack of government funding, straining under the taboos maintained by repressive governments or fundamentalist religious movements, and facing unprecedented competition from Middle Easterners' unfettered access to satellite TV channels from around the world. All of this comes at a time when these same satellite TV channels, which face no such constraints, have fostered politically aware audiences with a newly acquired taste for diverse opinions and subject matter.

For an introduction to Iranian cinema, and reading recommendations, see Lonely Planet's *Iran* guidebook.

The rise of other media is, of course, a problem faced by film industries around the world. It's just that the problem is particularly acute in the Middle East where many directors are expected to produce popular, high-quality films with one hand tied behind their backs.

A few brave directors are gently trying to expand the frontiers of acceptable political and social dialogue but, unless they go into exile, they're forced to do so on budgets that would make Hollywood directors weep. Syrian filmmaker Meyar al-Roumi, who lives in France and is best known for the 2006 *Rabia's Journey*, summed up the difficulties in a 2007 interview with the BBC: 'The establishment is the only source of funding films. Producers are much more interested in TV as its revenues are higher.' And then there's the issue of political boundaries: 'My work relies on self-criticism,' said al-Roumi, 'of my life, my friends and my country because I love it. But this made my films unwelcome here.'

The *Companion Encyclopedia of Middle Eastern and North African Film*, edited by Oliver Leaman, opens a window on the film industries in, among other countries, Egypt, Iran, Iraq, Lebanon, Libya, the Palestinian Territories, Syria and Turkey.

Some of the constraints have, of course, always been there. Producing films under the watchful eye of Saddam Hussein or Hafez al-Assad, from within the violence of Lebanon's Civil War, or under the threat of violence from Egypt's Islamist groups provided challenges that never cast a shadow over even the most stressed Western director. The way most Middle Eastern directors survived under such conditions was to produce films that either overtly supported the government line and strayed dangerously close to propaganda, or to focus on the microscopic details of daily life, using individual stories to make veiled commentaries on wider social and political issues. It is in this latter body of work, schooled in subtlety and nuanced references to the daily struggles faced by many in the region, that Middle Eastern film truly shines.

For all the difficulties, there are signs that a new breed of directors and production companies are emerging, particularly in Egypt, where adversity is being transformed into an opportunity. It's the most exciting development to happen in local film for decades and, if successful, promises a bold new future for Middle Eastern film.

For our pick of the best in Middle Eastern film, turn to p24.

The first Arab feature-length film, *The Call of God* (1927; which was also released entitled *Laila*) was produced by a woman, the Egyptian Aziza Amir.

Egypt: Coming of Age

In its halcyon years of the 1970s, Cairo's film studios turned out more than 100 movies a year, filling cinemas throughout the Arab world. These days the annual figure is closer to 20 and most are soap-opera–style genre movies that rely on slapstick humour, usually with a little belly-dancing thrown in for (rather mild) spice. Just how long these low-grade classics endure was revealed to us when one Lonely Planet author found himself assailed by such a movie on a Syrian bus journey in 2008, only to discover halfway through that it was the same film he appeared in as an extra during filming in Cairo 10 years before. The bus passengers were enthralled, although most had seen it many times before. The Lonely Planet author hung his head in shame and pretended to be asleep…

For all the gloom that has hung over the local film industry in recent years, Egypt's creative talents have set about reclaiming the country's once-undisputed title as the Middle East's cinematic powerhouse. The revival relies on a bold, ground-breaking willingness to confront social taboos in a way that few Egyptian filmmakers have dared for decades. For more details, see the boxed text, below.

Popular Egyptian Cinema, by Viola Shafik, demystifies all the melodrama of mainstream Egyptian films, placing them in their historical context and opening a window on the Egyptian soul in the process.

Despite signs that the Egyptian government censors are lightening up, directors in the country must still be wary of a conservative backlash. The portrayal of a lesbian kiss in *Until Things Get Better* saw the director Khaled Youssef threatened with arrest on moral grounds.

The new trend towards controversial subject matter must have come as music to the ears of Youssef Chahine, Egypt's premier director for more than half a century. This Alexandria-born stalwart of international film festivals, who died in Cairo aged 82 in June 2008, directed over 40 films in an illustrious career that saw him given the lifetime achievement award at the Cannes Film Festival in 1997. Known for championing free speech and for his willingness to take on authoritarian Egyptian governments, Western meddling in the Middle East and religious fundamentalism, Chahine, more than any other figure, laid the foundations for the brave new world of Egyptian cinema. His final film *Heya Fawda* (*Chaos;* 2007), which confronted police brutality and corruption, was a fitting epitaph to a stirring career.

Arab Film Distribution (www.arabfilm.com) is the Amazon.com of Arab cinema, with a large portfolio of DVDs that you just won't find on the shelves of your local rental store.

Israel & the Palestinian Territories: Worlds Apart

The conflict between the Israelis and the Palestinians not surprisingly weighs heavily upon films from this troubled land, but some outstanding movies have emerged from both sides of the divide. There is rarely conflict between the directors from these two cultures, as most tend to belong to the liberal, more-moderate strands of Israeli and Palestinian society.

NEW EGYPTIAN CINEMA – THREE FILMS

The first sign that Egyptian film was entering new territory came with *The Yacoubian Building,* a 2006 adaptation of Alaa al-Aswany's novel of the same name. Egyptian film audiences had rarely seen anything like it, with the issues of homosexuality, police torture, government corruption, sexual violence and terrorism all being highlighted through the prism of tenants' lives in an ageing Cairo apartment block. Directed by Marwan Hamed, the film provoked protests from conservative sectors of Egyptian society. The director's response was to argue that, 'We need to talk about the taboos, and we need to cancel the word "taboos" from our lives.' The film broke box-office records.

That a willingness to confront taboos was no passing fad became evident in 2008 when *Hassan and Morqos* was released. The film, which stars Egyptian-born Omar Sharif and comic legend Adel Imam – better known for slapstick movies of questionable quality – follows two moderates, a Muslim preacher and a Coptic priest, forced to go into hiding and swap roles to avoid the extremists in both communities. The movie tackled head-on tensions between Egypt's Muslim and Coptic Christian communities and Adel Imam showed particular courage in his portrayal – he has been accused of preaching Christianity in the role. His response? 'I hope Christians and Muslims will leave the cinema and embrace and kiss one another.'

But it was the 2008 release of *Baby Doll Night,* produced by the ground-breaking new-media company Goodnews4Film, headed by new-media mogul Adel Adeeb, that took the willingness to confront previously taboo subjects well and truly into the mainstream. The film, with an unprecedented US$8 million budget, took on the vexed issue of misunderstandings between the West and the Arab world post-9/11. Like *The Yacoubian Building, Baby Doll Night* was produced for both local and international release, a model that could raise the profile of Egyptian cinema and help ease the funding crisis in the industry as a whole.

ISRAEL

Film directors from elsewhere in the Middle East must look with envy at the level of government funding and freedom of speech enjoyed by Israeli filmmakers. It's a freedom that Israeli directors have used to produce high-quality films that have been praised for their even-handedness by juries and audiences alike at international film festivals.

A readiness to confront uncomfortable truths about Israel's recent history has long been a hallmark of Amos Gitai (b 1950) who has won plaudits for his sensitive and balanced portrayal of half a century of conflict. He became a superstar almost overnight with *Kadosh* (1998), which seriously questioned the role of religion in Israeli society and politics. He followed it up with *Kippur* (1999), a wholly unsentimental portrayal of the 1973 war, and *Kedma* (2001), which caused a stir by questioning many of the country's founding myths through the lens of the Israeli War of Independence. If Israeli cinema is entering a period of international acclaim, as many believe, Gitai is more responsible than anyone else for the renaissance.

Israeli films have received more Oscar nominations (six) for Best Foreign-Language Film than films from any other Middle Eastern country, although they've yet to win the prize.

But Gitai has not been the only director to produce the works of national self-criticism that set Israeli apart from other Middle Eastern film industries. Avi Mograbi goes a step further than Gitai with no-holds-barred depictions of the difficulties of life for the Palestinians under Israeli occupation.

Beyond the politically charged films that are causing a stir, there's also a feeling within Israel that the country's film industry is entering something of a golden age. Highlighting the sense of excitement, Shira Geffen and Etgar Keret won the Caméra d'Or for best film by debut directors at the 2007 Cannes Film Festival for *Meduzot (Jellyfish)*. At the same festival, Eran Kolirin's *The Band's Visit* won the Jury Prize of the International Federation of Film Critics. Kolirin's film, which follows an Egyptian police band that gets lost while touring Israel, marked what may ultimately be seen as a more important cinematic landmark: in 2008, it was shown to a select audience at a Cairo hotel, the first Israeli film to be shown in Egypt since the peace treaty between the two countries was signed almost 30 years ago.

PALESTINIAN TERRITORIES

The picture for Palestinian directors could not be more different. Starved of funding and living in occupation or exile, Palestinian filmmakers have done it tough, but have nonetheless turned out some extraordinary movies.

The *Encyclopedia of Arab Women Filmmakers*, by Rebecca Hillauer, is one of few works to challenge the male dominance in Middle Eastern film-making.

One Palestinian director who has made an international impact is the Hebron-born Michael Khalifa, whose excellent *Images from Rich Memories, The Anthem of the Stone* and *Wedding in Galilee* were all shot covertly inside the Palestinian Territories. Rasheed Masharawi has been rejected in some Palestinian circles for working with Israeli production companies, but the quality of his work is undeniable. Elie Suleiman's work – which includes *Cyber Palestine, Divine Intervention* and the notable *Chronicle of a Disappearance* – is a wonderful corpus of quietly angry and intensely powerful films.

Apart from the daily difficulties of maintaining a Palestinian film industry, some directors have fallen foul of Israeli censors. In 2004 the Israeli High Court finally overturned a ban on *Jenin, Jenin*, a documentary film by Israeli-Arab filmmaker Mohammad Bakri, even as the court called the film a 'propagandistic lie'. The film had been the first to be banned in Israel for 15 years. Palestinian director Hany Abu-Assad's *Paradise Now,* about the last 24 hours of two Palestinian suicide bombers, was nominated for a Best Foreign-Language Film Oscar in 2005, but had to withstand a massive campaign in Israel against the film. These are rare cases, but a reminder that some directors are freer than others in Israel and the Palestinian Territories.

Other Middle Eastern Countries

The career of the French-based exile, Randa Chahal-Sabbagh, arguably Lebanon's premier director, is a study in the bravery and endurance of Middle Eastern directors in the face of censorship. Her 90-minute, 1998 film *Civilised,* which encouraged the Lebanese people to stop blaming others for the war, was cut to just 43 minutes by Lebanese government censors. As a result, Chahal-Sabbagh refused permission for it to be screened in her native country. But she outlasted the government in question, won the Venice Festival's Silver Lion award for her 2002 film *The Kite* (which portrays a young girl in a village on the Lebanese–Israeli border) and, for good measure, was even awarded the Order of the Cedar, Lebanon's highest civilian honour, in 2003.

Young Lebanese director Ziad Doueiri, whose slick debut *West Beyrouth* (1998) is considered one of the best films about the Lebanese Civil War, was Quentin Tarantino's lead cameraman for *Pulp Fiction* and *Reservoir Dogs*.

Turkey's film industry, like Egypt's, is reemerging strongly from the long decline that followed its 1970s heyday. In 2007, 40 Turkish films were produced, compared with over 300 in 1972. Perhaps more importantly for the health of the industry, the four most popular films in Turkish cinemas in 2007 were all home-grown.

Syria's small film industry has produced some fine directors, despite the fact that the Syrian government's Public Establishment for Cinema has only produced two films a year since 1969. Leading lights include Meyar al-Roumi, documentary filmmaker Omar Amiralay, whose *Daily Life in a Syrian Village* (1976) won an award at the Berlin International Film Festival, but his much-awaited follow-up, *A Flood in Baath Country* (2005), has been banned in Syria. Abdellatif Abdelhamid's 2007 film *Out of Coverage,* which follows the life of a disappeared man (the implication is that he is a political prisoner), somehow slipped through the censors' net. Whether this suggests a new liberalisation by the Syrian government remains to be seen, although Abdelhamid is optimistic, telling the BBC that his film represents 'a new page in a new chapter'.

Filming the Middle East: Politics in the Cinemas of Hollywood and the Arab world, by Lina Khatib, takes a look at both sides of the cinematic fence and includes coverage of films from Egypt, Lebanon, Syria and Palestine.

At the 2005 Cannes Film Festival, Hiner Saleem marked the tentative resurgence of Iraqi cinema with the stirring *Kilometre Zero.*

YILMAZ GÜNEY: MIRROR TO TURKISH HISTORY

The life of Yilmaz Güney (1937–84) provides a fascinating window onto late 20th-century Turkey. In particular, the life story and films of this Turkish-Kurdish director speak volumes for the often fraught relationship between Turkey's governments and the country's creative talents.

Güney began his professional life as a writer, before becoming a hugely popular young actor who appeared in dozens of films (up to 20 a year according to some reports), before again changing tack to become the country's most successful film director. But behind that seemingly steady rise lies a life that reads like a scarcely believable film plot. Güney was first arrested in 1961 for writing what was condemned as a communist novel, then again in 1972 for sheltering anarchist students. In 1974, he was convicted of killing a public prosecutor. He wrote many of his screenplays behind bars – including the internationally acclaimed *The Herd* (1978). In 1981, he escaped from prison and fled to France.

It was from exile that Güney produced his masterpiece, the Palme d'Or–winning *Yol* (*The Way;* 1982), which was not initially shown in Turkish cinemas; its portrait of what happens to five prisoners on a week's release was too grim for the authorities to take. His following within Turkey was also never as widespread as his talents deserved, not least because his portrayal of the difficulties faced by Turkey's Kurds alienated many in mainstream Turkish society.

Calligraphy is an expression of the belief that Arabic is a holy language revealed by Allah to the Prophet Mohammed in the Quran. Derived from the Greek words *kala* (beautiful) and *graphos* (writing), calligraphy was a way of glorifying the word of God.

DECORATIVE ARTS

The serpentine swirl of a calligrapher's pen. The exquisite intricacy of exotic arabesques, geometric patterning and illuminated manuscripts. The microscopic detail of thousands of mosaic pieces combined to create large-scale masterpieces. These are the images that rank among the greatest signifiers of the Middle East's artistic and aesthetic richness.

Islam's restriction on the portrayal of living figures could have sounded the death knell for Middle Eastern artists. Instead, the exploration of the artistic possibilities of the Arabic script and the application of geometric principles to the world of decorative arts produced a distinctive and highly original artistic tradition very much rooted in the region's cultural and religious history. Wedded to these post-Islamic forms were adaptations from the long-standing figurative art traditions of Asia Minor, Persia and areas further east. Granted special dispensation to glorify the sacred, the illuminated manuscripts from Turkey and Iraq, and miniature paintings from Iran, provided a bridge to earlier art forms and depth to a decorative arts tradition of extraordinary diversity.

In the areas of calligraphy, metalwork, ceramics, glass, carpets and textiles, Islamic art has had great influence on the West. Middle Eastern artisans and craftspeople (Armenians, Christians, Jews and Muslims) have for more than 1200 years applied complex and sumptuous decorations to often very practical objects to create items of extraordinary beauty. Plenty such items are on view in the region's museums, including the Topkapı Palace (p540) in İstanbul. However, to appreciate the achievements of Islamic art, visit one of the older mosques in which tiling, wood carving, inlaid panelling and calligraphy are often combined in exaltation of Allah.

Contemporary Art in the Middle East, Nadine Monem (ed), which came out in early 2009, is the first overview of the region's modern art; it includes essays about the state of the art and leading contemporary artists.

Decorative Islamic art is, for a Muslim, foremost an expression of faith, and nowhere is this more important than in the most sophisticated of these arts – calligraphy. Early calligraphers used an angular script called Kufic that was perfect for stone carving. Modern calligraphy uses a flowing cursive style, more suited to working with pen and ink.

Another of the region's signature art forms is the mosaic, traditionally made from tiny squares called tesserae, chipped from larger rocks. The tesserae are naturally coloured, and carefully laid on a thick coating of wet lime. Mosaics depicting hunting, deities and scenes from daily life once adorned the floors and palaces of the Byzantine Middle East and, before them, the extravagant public and private buildings of the Romans. The art of mosaic making continues in such places as Madaba (p366) in Jordan, but is absent from most other Islamic countries.

VISUAL ARTS

Some countries in the region have long and distinguished traditions in fine arts – the Belzalel Academy of Arts and Crafts in Jerusalem opened in 1906, official painting and sculpture academies operated in Turkey as part of Atatürk's secularising overhaul of the country and Lebanon's first art school, the Académie Libanaise des Beaux-Arts, was established in 1937. In other countries such as Jordan and Syria, secular governments and the partial liberalisation of Islamic norms has seen a flourishing of artistic expression. Wander around the old cities of Jerusalem, İstanbul, Damascus, Beirut and Amman and you'll come across an eclectic range of independent, contemporary art galleries.

To learn more about how the stories of *The Thousand and One Nights* came together, read the excellent introduction by Husain Haddawy in *The Arabian Nights*.

One distinct visual art form, particularly strong within Palestinian society, is the political cartoon. Female Palestinian cartoonist Omayya Joha (see www.omayya.com) and the late Naji al-Ali are two of the best-known creators in the genre. Their work is characterised by bitter criticism of

Israel, the USA and, in the case of Omayya, Palestinian society itself. Her husband, an alleged Hamas operative, was killed in an Israeli army raid in Gaza in 2003. Al-Ali was assassinated in London in 1987, but his work seems just as timely today.

An Introduction to Arabic Literature, by Roger Allen, is a worthy addition to the canon of literary criticism, with extensive translations of seminal texts and lively analysis; it's especially good on *The Thousand and One Nights.*

LITERATURE

The Middle East is the cradle of storytelling. The telling of tales that are both mischievous and reveal the social and political times from which they arise has always occupied centre stage in Middle Eastern life, from the epic tales from the 8th-century Baghdad court of Haroun ar-Rashid, so wonderfully brought to life in *The Thousand and One Nights* (see the boxed text, p90) to the wandering storytellers that once entertained crowds in the coffeehouses and theatres of the region. It's a heritage with two tightly interwoven strands: entertainment through suspense and comedy, and thinly veiled commentaries on the issues of the day. The region's literary talents are worthy heirs to this ancient tradition and it's these storytellers – the poets and novelists – far more than government-controlled newspapers and 'information' ministries, who serve as the great chroniclers of Middle Eastern life.

Like Middle Eastern filmmakers, the writers of the region face many challenges, from government repression and a lack of funding to the stellar rise of satellite TV. But perhaps of far greater importance is the lack of a book-buying culture in Arabic-speaking countries. Storytelling in the Middle East, including poetry, was always a predominantly oral tradition and it was not until the 20th century that the first Arabic-language novels appeared. The audiences never really made the transition from the public performance to the printed page. Incidentally, although printed stories have not taken off, public storytelling is dying out – only one professional storyteller remains in the entire Middle East; see p478.

According to one UN estimate, Spain translates more books each year than have been translated into Arabic in the past 1000 years.

But performing the last rites for Arabic literature (note that Israeli writers face few such challenges) would be premature. Unable to sell many books at home, many writers in the region have learned to survive from international sales. The Palestinian poet Mahmoud Darwish, for example, combined a devoted local audience, which he cultivated through hugely popular public readings, with an equally devoted international following, so much so that he is the bestselling poet in France.

The Egyptian novelist Alaa al-Aswany also enjoyed international success for his 2006 novel *The Yacoubian Building.* But by selling the film rights to what became a successful movie in his home country (see the boxed text, p85), al-Aswany drew a whole new local audience into his grasp.

Whether the successes of Darwish and al-Aswany are a prototype for the future or isolated cases remains to be seen.

Poetry

The Lebanese-born poet Khalil Gibran (1883–1931) is, by some estimates, the third biggest-selling poet in history behind Shakespeare and Lao Tse. Born in Bcharré in Lebanon, he spent most of his working life in the US, but it didn't stop him from becoming a flag-bearer for Arabic poetry. His masterpiece, *The Prophet* (1923), which consists of 26 poetic essays, became, after the Bible, America's second biggest-selling book of the 20th century.

Nights and Horses and the Desert: An Anthology of Classical Arabic Literature, edited by Robert Irwin, traces the roots of Arabic poetry from the Quran to the modern day.

Mahmoud Darwish (1941–2008) has become one of the most eloquent spokesmen for Palestinian rights, his more than thirty volumes of poetry reading like a beautifully composed love letter to the lost land of his childhood. At his funeral in August 2008, one mourner told the BBC that he 'symbolises the Palestinian memory'. Another leading Arab poet and one

THE THOUSAND & ONE NIGHTS

After the Bible, *The Thousand and One Nights* (in Arabic, *Alf Layla w'Layla*, also known as *The Arabian Nights*) must be one of the best-known, least-read books in the English language. It owes its existence in the popular consciousness almost entirely to the Disneyfied tales of *Aladdin, Sinbad* and *Ali Baba and the 40 Thieves,* but it's equally revered by literature scholars and historians for its use (some would say invention) of classic storytelling devices and illuminating historical descriptions. It's from this book, more than anywhere else, that the Middle East gets its whiff of the exotic in the popular imagination.

That few people have read the actual text is unsurprising considering that its most famous English-language edition (translated by the Victorian adventurer Sir Richard Burton) runs to 16 volumes. The appeal of reading the volumes is further reduced by the old Middle Eastern superstition that nobody can read the entire text of *The Thousand and One Nights* without dying.

With origins that range from pre-Islamic Persia, India and Arabia, the stories as we now know them were first gathered together in written form in the 14th century. *The Thousand and One Nights* is a portmanteau title for a mixed bag of colourful and fantastic tales (there are 271 core stories). The stories are mainly set in the semifabled Baghdad of Haroun ar-Rashid (r AD 786–809), and in Mamluk-era (1250–1517) Cairo and Damascus. For the latter two cities in particular, *The Thousand and One Nights* provides a wealth of period detail.

All versions of *The Thousand and One Nights* begin with the same premise: the misogynist King Shahriyar discovers that his wife has been unfaithful, whereafter he murders her and takes a new wife every night before killing each in turn before sunrise. The wily Sheherezade, the daughter of the king's vizier, insists that she will be next, only to nightly postpone her death with a string of stories that leaves the king in such suspense that he spares her life so as to hear the next instalment.

Devotees of the collection wondered for centuries what happened next – on the 1002nd night if you like – and one possible answer was provided by the Nobel Prize–winning Egyptian novelist Naguib Mahfouz. In 1979, his masterful sequal *Arabian Nights and Days* appeared in Arabic, then the English-language translation arrived in 1995. To write a sequel to the best-loved tales in history must be one of world literature's most daunting tasks, but Mahfouz carried it off with aplomb. *Damascus Nights,* by Rafik Schami, is another series of Sheherezade-esque tales.

Modern Arabic Poetry, by Salma Khadra Jayyusi, can be a bit dense for the uninitiated, but there's no more comprehensive work about the Middle East's most enduring and popular literary form.

of the great celebrities of the Arab literary scene is Syria's Nizar Qabbani (1923–98), who was unusual in that he was able to balance closeness to successive Syrian regimes with subject matter (love, eroticism and feminism) that challenged many prevailing opinions within conservative Syrian society. His funeral in Damascus – a city that he described in his will as 'the womb that taught me poetry, taught me creativity and granted me the alphabet of jasmine' – was broadcast live around the Arab world.

Novels

The novel as a literary form may have come late to the Middle East, but that didn't stop the region producing three winners of the Nobel Prize for Literature: Shmuel Yosef Agnon (1966), a Zionist Israeli writer whose works are published in English under the name SY Agnon; Naguib Mahfouz (1988); and Orhan Pamuk (2006).

Naguib Mahfouz: His Life and Times, by Rasheed El-Elnany, is the first (and, it must be said, long-overdue) English-language biography of the Arab world's most accomplished and prolific novelist.

Much of the credit for the maturing of Arabic literature can be given to Naguib Mahfouz (1911–2006), who was unquestionably the single most important writer of fiction in Arabic in the 20th century. A life-long native of Cairo, Mahfouz began writing in the 1930s. From Western-copyist origins he went on to develop a voice that is uniquely of the Arab world and draws its inspiration from storytelling in the coffeehouses and the dialect and slang of the streets. Although widely respected throughout the Arab world, he fell foul of Egypt's fundamentalist Islamists, first for his 1959 novel *Children of Gebelawi* (which was banned for blasphemy in

Egypt) and later for defending Salman Rushdie; Mahfouz was seriously injured in an assassination attempt in 1994. His best-known works are collectively known as *The Cairo Trilogy*, consisting of *Palace Walk*, *Palace of Desire* and *Sugar Street*.

Orhan Pamuk (b 1952) is Turkey's latest literary celebrity. His works include an impressive corpus of novels and an acclaimed memoir of İstanbul, *Istanbul – Memories of a City*. His work has been translated into more than 50 languages and, like Mahfouz, Pamuk has never shirked from the difficult issues; in *Snow* (2004), Pamuk unflinchingly explores the fraught relationship between two of the great themes of modern Turkish life: Islamic extremism and the pull of the West. Also like Mahfouz, Pamuk is known as a staunch defender of the freedom speech.

In 2006, Orhan Pamuk was charged with 'insulting Turkishness' for claiming that a million Armenians and 30,000 Kurds had been killed in Turkey in 1915. The charges were dropped after an international outcry.

Among the region's other best-known writers are Turkey's Yaşar Kemal (b 1923) and the Israeli writer, Amos Oz; Oz's name regularly appears as a candidate for the Nobel Prize for Literature and his work includes essays and award-winning novels with themes that speak to the pride and angst at the centre of modern Israeli life. Of the native Lebanese writers, the most famous is Hanan al-Shaykh (b 1945), who writes poignant but humorous novels that resonate beyond the bounds of the Middle East. Also worth tracking down are the works of Jordan's Abdelrahman Munif (1933–2004), Egypt's prolific Nawal el-Saadawi (b 1931) and Lebanese-born Amin Maalouf (b 1949).

THE BEST OF MIDDLE EASTERN LITERATURE

- *Arabic Short Stories,* translated by Denys Johnson-Davies, is an excellent primer with tales from all over the Middle East.
- *The Prophet,* by Khalil Gibran, somehow expounds in poetic form on the great philosophical questions while speaking to the dilemmas of everyday life.
- Choose anything by Orhan Pamuk and you won't be disappointed, but it was with *The Black Book* that he leapt onto the international stage.
- Naguib Mahfouz rarely sounds a wrong note. Choose anything from *The Cairo Trilogy,* but if you have to choose just one Mahfouz title, *The Harafish* would be our desert island choice.
- *The Map of Love,* by Ahdaf Soueif, is the Booker-nominated historical novel about love and clashing cultures by this London-based Anglo-Egyptian writer, but *In the Eye of the Sun* is simply marvellous.
- *Memed My Hawk,* by Yaşar Kemal, deals with near-feudal life in the villages of eastern Turkey and is considered perhaps the greatest Turkish novel of the 20th century.
- Amos Oz fans will no doubt have their favourites but *My Michael* masterfully captures the turmoil of Jerusalem during the Suez Crisis of 1956, as reflected in the private torment of a woman in an unhappy marriage.
- *Pillars of Salt,* by Fadia Faqir, is a skilfully conceived work exploring social divisions and the vulnerability of women set against the backdrop of the British Mandate in Jordan.
- *Beirut Blues,* by Hanan al-Shaykh, deals with the fallout of the Lebanese Civil War, as seen by a young woman trying to decide whether to stay or flee abroad.
- *The Stone of Laughter,* by Hoda Barakat, is a lyrical work by a young Lebanese writer that beautifully charts Lebanon's civil war through the eyes of a character torn apart by issues of identity and sexuality.
- *The Yacoubian Building,* by Alaa al-Aswany, has been anointed as heir to Naguib Mahfouz' larger-than-life chronicling of life on the Cairo street.

Of the new wave of Middle Eastern writers, the names to watch include Alaa al-Aswany (Egypt), Ahdaf Soueif (Egypt), Khalid al-Khamisi (Egypt), Laila Halaby (Lebanon) and Dorit Rabinyan (Israel).

Arab Gateway – Music (www.al-bab.com/arab/music/music.htm) has everything from clear explanations of the basics for the uninitiated to links and downloads of contemporary Arab music.

MUSIC

If you're a music-lover, you'll adore the Middle East, which has home-grown music as diverse as the region itself. Yes you'll hear Bob Marley and other Western icons in traveller hang-outs such as Dahab, but this is one part of the world where local artists dominate airtime and you're far more likely to hear Umm Kolthum, soulful Iraqi oud (Middle Eastern lute) or the latest Lebanese pop sensation.

Arab

CLASSICAL & TRADITIONAL

Tonality and instrumentation aside, classical Arabic music differs from that of the West in one important respect: in the Middle East the orchestra has traditionally been there primarily to back the singer. Such orchestras are a curious cross-fertilisation of East and West. Western-style instruments, such as violins and many of the wind and percussion instruments, predominate, next to local species including the oud and *tabla* (drum). It's

PEERLESS DIVAS

Umm Kolthum

It's difficult to overestimate the importance of Umm Kolthum (1904–75), one of the towering figures of 20th-century world music. A favourite of Egyptian president Gamal Abdel Nasser, Umm Kolthum had the ability to stop a nation whenever she performed; rumour has it that the coup that brought Libyan leader Colonel Muammar Qaddafi to power on 1 September 1969 was delayed so as not to clash with an Umm Kolthum concert.

From the 1940s through to the '70s, her voice was that of the Arab world, a region that has never fallen out of love with her music nor with the fervour and hope of those tumultuous times that she represented. The passion of her protracted love songs and *qasa'id* (long poems) was nothing less than the very expression of the Arab world's collective identity. Egypt's love affair with Umm Kolthum (where she's known as *kawkab ash-sharq,* meaning 'Nightingale of the East') was such that on the afternoon of the first Thursday of each month, streets would become deserted as the whole country sat beside radios to listen to her regular live-broadcast performance.

Fairouz

A Lebanese torch singer with a voice memorably described as 'silk and flame in one', Fairouz (b 1935) has enjoyed star status throughout the Arab world since recording her first performances in Damascus in the 1950s. Along with her writers, the Rahbani brothers, Fairouz embraced a wide range of musical forms, blending Lebanese folk tales with flamenco and jazz. For all her experimentation, her lyrics embodied the recurring themes of love, loss, Lebanon and religious praise. During the 1960s and '70s her music – and three starring roles in Lebanese films – made her the embodiment of freewheeling Beirut. During the Lebanese Civil War she became at once a symbol of hope and an icon for Lebanese identity, resolutely refusing to sing inside Lebanon while her countrymen continued to kill each other.

Fairouz returned to the Lebanese stage after the war and her 1995 comeback concert in downtown Beirut drew a crowd of 40,000; across the Arab world, 125 million tuned in. That her popularity extends far beyond the Middle East was confirmed in 1999 with a concert in Las Vegas that drew the biggest crowd since Frank Sinatra. Although in her seventies, Fairouz maintains a vice-like grip over the affections of the region – her 2008 arrival in Damascus after an absence of 20 years brought Syria to a stand-still. Her record sales have now topped 80 million.

a style that was popularised by such icons as Umm Kolthum and Fairouz (see the boxed text, opposite). More recently, Lebanon's Ghada Shbeir is a name to watch for her mix of traditional Arab-Andalusian sounds backed by the oud, *qanun* (plucked zither), *ney* (flute) and percussion.

If one instrument has come to represent the enduring appeal of classical Arabic music, it's the oud, an instrument that has made the transition from backing instrument to musical superstar in its own right. The oud is a pear-shaped, stringed instrument and is distinguished from its successor, the Western lute, by its lack of frets, 11 strings (five pairs and a single string) and a neck bent at a 45- to 90-degree angle. Oud-players are to be found throughout the region, but its undisputed masters are in Iraq, where the sound of the oud is revered as a reflection of the Iraqi soul.

The former Led Zeppelin vocalist Robert Plant once said that one of his lifetime ambitions was to reform the Middle Eastern Orchestra, Umm Kolthum's group of backing musicians.

But it's Syria that produced the Arab world's so-called 'King of the Oud', Farid al-Atrache (1915–74). Sometimes called the 'Arab Sinatra', he was a highly accomplished oud player and composer, who succeeded in updating Arabic music by blending it with Western scales and rhythms and the orchestration of the tango and waltz. His melodic improvisations on the oud and his *mawal* (a vocal improvisation) were the highlights of his live performances and recordings of these are treasured. By the time of his death, he was considered – and still is by many – to be the premier male Arabic music performer of the 20th century.

Another outstanding exponent of the art is the Jordanian oud-player Sakher Hattar.

The other defining feature of classical Arabic music is the highly complicated melodic system known as *maqam*. The foundation for most traditional music in the Arab world, *maqam* is based on a tonal system of scales and intervals and is wholly different from Western musical traditions. Master *maqam* and you've mastered the centuries-old sound of the region. Put it together with the oud and you're somewhere close to heaven.

Al-Mashriq – Music (www.almashriq.hiof.no/base/music.html) offers more links to Arabic music than you can poke a stick at, from Umm Kolthum to traditional folk music with plenty of detours into Arabic pop along the way.

Each of the minorities in Arab countries also has its own musical traditions. The most high profile is the Nubian music of southern Egypt. The Nubian sound is extremely accessible, mixing simple melodies, soulful vocals, a rhythmical quality that's almost sub-Saharan African and a brass sound that could be from New Orleans. Probably the biggest name is Ali Hassan Kuban, who has toured all over Europe as well as in Japan, Canada and the US. He and other artists have been recorded on the German Piranha label.

Although not as high profile as the Nubians, other notable Arab folk music comes from the Bedouin. Whether produced by the Bedouin of Egypt, Jordan or Syria, the music is raw and traditional with little or no use of electronic instruments. The sound is dominated by the *mismar*, a twin-pipe clarinet, and the *rabab*, a twin-stringed prototype cello.

POP

Seemingly a world away from classical Arabic music, and characterised by a clattering, hand-clapping rhythm overlaid with synthesised twirlings and a catchy, repetitive vocal, the first true Arabic pop came out of Cairo in the 1970s. As Arab nations experienced a population boom and the mean age decreased, a gap in popular culture had developed that the memory of the greats couldn't fill. Enter Arabic pop. The blueprint for the new youth sound (which became known as *al-jeel*, from the word for generation) was set by Egyptian Ahmed Adawiyya, the Arab world's first 'pop star'.

Your could buy your music from Amazon.com, but Maqam (www.maqam.com) claims to be the world's largest distributor and online retailer of Arab music, with a sideline in cinema and musical instruments.

During the 1990s there was a calculated attempt to create a more upmarket sound, with many musicians mimicking Western dance music. Tacky electronics were replaced with moody pianos, Spanish guitars and

MUSICIANS FOR PEACE

It's not every American musician who can claim to have learned to play the oud (Middle Eastern lute) like an Iraqi, mastered the complexity of the *maqam* scale system and played love songs on a Baghdad street in the dangerous aftermath of the US invasion of Iraq. But then Cameron Powers is not your ordinary musician.

Together with his wife, singer Kristina Sophia, Powers was seriously disillusioned with his country's response to the terrorist attack on 11 September 2001. When we caught up with them in Lattakia, Syria, in May 2008 on their fifth visit to the region, Powers and Sophia spoke of how they performed with a Palestinian musician in Boulder, Colorado two weeks after the attacks, a concert that only went ahead when the word 'Palestinian' was removed from the promotional material. Experiences such as these prompted the couple to make their first trip to the Middle East in November 2002, hoping to build bridges between Western and Arab cultures through what they call 'the warmth, beauty and sensuality of Arab music'.

The welcome they received from ordinary Arabs convinced them to return. In spring 2003, impromptu performances for the Iraqi visa-issuing authorities and border officials saw Powers and Sophia granted permission to enter Iraq – 'music is an instant passport' is his explanation. Unable to find any functioning concert venues in post-invasion Baghdad, they simply began performing on the streets. 'The fact that we were on the streets of Baghdad singing Iraqi love songs showed the Iraqi people that Americans could also invade with music,' Powers told us. He later wrote a book, *Singing in Baghdad* (available from www.gldesignpub.com), about the experience. A performance before 60,000 people in Cairo followed the same year.

Struck by the warmth of the welcome they received in the Middle East, the couple realised that American audiences needed to hear an alternative vision of the Middle East as much as ordinary Arabs needed to feel their solidarity. Since then, the couple has covered more than 60,000km and performed at over 200 presentations in universities, schools and churches across the US. Nonetheless, they still find themselves confronted with the suspicions of post-9/11 America: 'We encounter fear first and then openness to the music. It used to be the other way around.' To learn more about their work and travels, visit their website, www.musicalmissions.com.

Not content with the power of performance, Powers and Sophia have set up a secular NGO, Musical Missions of Peace (www.musicalmissionsofpeace.org), which is based on the premise that 'people who have learned and sung each others' popular love songs together are less likely to war with one another than those who have not'. The NGO provides support to Iraqi musicians and refugees in exile in Jordan and Syria and promotes education and performance of international music in the US.

thunderous drums. Check out the Egyptian singer Amr Diab, whose heavily produced songs have made him the best-selling artist ever in the Arab world (achieved with his 1996 album *Nour al-Ain)*.

Amr Diab World (www.amrdiabworld.com) is the glitzy homepage of the Arab world's most famous modern pop star; it covers all the vacuity and strangely compelling kitsch that is modern Arab celebrity.

Heading the current crop of megastar singers (the Arabic music scene is totally dominated by solo vocalists, there are no groups) are Majida al-Rumi of Lebanon, Iraqi-born Kazem (Kadim) al-Saher and the enduring legend of Iraq's Ilham al-Madfai who founded the Middle East's first rock band back in the 1960s.

In the largely shrink-wrapped world of pop, regional influences are minimised and most artists have a tendency to sound the same, no matter where they come from. Arab pop music is like its Western counterpart in that fashions change almost as regularly as the stars change hairstyles. Watch Arab MTV and you'll soon learn what's hot, although that doesn't necessarily mean that they'll be around tomorrow.

Turkish

Traditional Turkish music is enjoying something of a revival with Sufi music, dominated by traditional instrumentation, leading the way. Sufis

MIDDLE EASTERN MUSIC – OUR TOP TEN ALBUMS

- *The Lady and the Legend,* Fairouz (Lebanon)
- *Al-Atlaal,* Umm Kolthum (Egypt)
- *Awedony,* Amr Diab (Egypt)
- *Bare Footed,* Kazem al-Sahir (Iraq)
- *Le Luth de Baghdad,* Nasseer Shamma (Iraq)
- *Asmar,* Yeir Dalal (Israel)
- *The Idan Raichel Project,* The Idan Raichel Project (Israel)
- *Nar with Secret Tribe,* Mercan Dede (Turkey)
- *Deli Kızın Türküsü,* Sezen Aksu (Turkey)
- *Les Plus Grands Classiques de la Musique Arabe,* various artists

are religious mystics who use music and dance to attain a trancelike state of divine ecstasy. Sufi music's spiritual home is Konya and the sound is bewitchingly hypnotic – a simple repeated melody usually played on the *nai* (reed pipe), accompanied by recitations of Sufi poetry.

Sufi music's growing popularity beyond Turkey's borders owes much to the work of artists like Mercan Dede (www.mercandede.com) whose blend of Sufism with electronica has taken the genre beyond its traditional boundaries and into a mainstream audience. He even doubles as a DJ with the stage name Arkin Allen, spinning hardcore house and techno beats at rave festivals in the US and Canada. Not surprisingly, one Turkish newspaper described him as a 'dervish for the modern world'.

Songlines (www.songlines.co.uk) is the premier world music magazine. It features interviews with stars, extensive CD reviews and a host of other titbits that will broaden your horizons and prompt many additions to your CD collection.

Traditional Turkish folk music has also undergone a revival in recent years, as 'Türkü' – an updated, modern version often using electronic instruments coupled with traditional songs.

But Turkey's most pervasive soundtrack of choice is Turkish pop and its stars rank among the country's best-known celebrities. Sezen Aksu is not known as 'the Queen of Turkish music' for nothing; she launched the country's love affair with the genre with her first single in 1976. Combining Western influences and local folk music to create a thoroughly contemporary sound, she's also an independent spirit not afraid to speak out on environmental issues and Turkey's treatment of its minorities.

If Sezen Aksu laid the foundations for pop music's current popularity, Tarkan took it to a whole new level. His 'Simarik' (written by Aksu and a track better known to Western audiences as 'Kiss Kiss') was covered by chart popper Holly Valance and became the catchy, feel-good anthem of Turkey in the late 1990s. Other super-popular pop stars include 'arabesque' luminary İbrahim Tatlises (also a constant fixture on Turkish TV), Çelik, Serdat Ortaç and Mustafa Sandal.

Popular Culture in the Arab world, by Andrew Hammond, offers a timely look at thriving popular Arab culture from Al-Jazeera to pop superstars, with detours into the world of tele-imams (think Muslim televangelists) and the mass media.

Relatively new to Turkey and with its roots in the Turkish Diaspora of Germany, rap music has found a growing following within Turkey with a younger audience drawn to its counter-culture voice of protest. Many of the groups are based in Germany, among them Cartel (the first group to make it big), KMR and Aziza-A.

Israeli

Israeli music will sound familiar to many travellers, not least because many of its roots lie in European soil. But the country's thriving music scene has become more nuanced in recent years, both in recognising the

DANIEL BARENBOIM

No figure in the Middle Eastern arts has done as much to promote peace and understanding between Israelis and Palestinians as Daniel Barenboim (b 1942), the Israeli pianist and conductor. Barenboim is best known for having cofounded the West-Eastern Divan Orchestra, a collection of young, talented Israeli, Palestinian, Lebanese, Syrian, Jordanian and Egyptian classical musicians, with his friend, the late Palestinian intellectual Edward Said, in 1999. From its base in Seville in Spain, the symphony orchestra (conducted by Barenboim) tours the world, including Israel and the Palestinian Territories. Back in Seville, the Barenboim-Said Foundation, which was set up to promote coexistence and dialogue and is funded by the local Andalusian government, holds summer workshops for young musicians from the Middle East, while it also supports a range of projects, including musical education programs in the Palestinian Territories. In 2002, Barenboim and Said were jointly awarded Spain's prestigious Príncipe de Asturias Prize for 'improving understanding between nations'.

But Barenboim has never been content to let his music alone do the talking. An outspoken critic of Israel's policies and an advocate of Palestinian rights, Barenboim has performed in the West Bank, including a piano recital he performed after secretly entering the Palestinian Territories under the cover of darkness when the Israeli government refused permission for the concert to go ahead. After a concert in Ramallah in January 2008, he accepted honorary Palestinian citizenship, a month after he and an international orchestra were refused permission by Israeli border guards to enter Gaza, where they were scheduled to perform a baroque-music concert. In 2005, he also refused to be interviewed by uniformed reporters for Israeli Army Radio as a mark of respect for the Palestinians who were present.

Perhaps not surprisingly, Barenboim has become a hate figure for many on the Israeli right, and was described by the former Israeli Minister of Education, Limor Livnat, in 2005 as 'a real Jew hater' and 'a real antisemite'. Undeterred, Barenboim pointedly refused to participate in the celebrations surrounding Israel's 60th anniversary in March 2008 as a gesture of solidarity with the Palestinians.

To learn more about Barenboim and the West-Eastern Divan Orchestra, track down Paul Smaczny's documentary, *Knowledge is the Beginning,* which won an Emmy Award in 2006.

multinational origins of Israel's population and in excavating distinctive Jewish rhythms from broader European traditions.

Perhaps the most successful example of this latter phenomenon is *klezmer,* which has taken the world-music scene by storm in recent years. With its foundations laid by the Jewish communities of Eastern Europe, *klezmer's* fast-paced, instrumental form was ideally suited to Jewish celebrations and it has sometimes been branded as Jewish jazz, in recognition of its divergence from established musical styles. The modern version has added vocals – almost always in Yiddish.

Sterns World Music (www.sternsmusic.com) is a reputable and independent London-based seller of world music CDs that allows you to search by country, artist or even region.

If *klezmer* takes its inspiration from Jewish Diaspora roots in Europe, the Idan Raichel Project (www.idanraichelproject.com), arguably Israel's most popular group, casts its net more widely. Israeli love songs are their forte, but it's the Ethiopian instruments, Jamaican rhythms and Yemeni vocals that mark the group out as something special. Although originally rejected by leading local record labels for being 'too ethnic', the Idan Raichel Project's building of bridges between Israel's now-multicultural musical traditions struck a chord with audiences at home and abroad.

Another artist to have adapted ancient musical traditions for a modern audience is Yasmin Levy, who sings in Ladino, the language of Sephardic Jews, who lived in Andalusia for centuries until 1492. The flamenco inflections in her music speak strongly of what she calls 'the musical memories of the old Moorish and Jewish-Spanish world'. Crossing frontiers of a different kind, Yair Dalal is an outstanding Israeli oud player who has collaborated with Palestinian and other Arab musicians.

Food & Drink

Eating is one of the grand passions of Middle Eastern life. For all the religious, political and social issues that divide the region, an emphatic belief in the importance of good food is one thing on which all the people of the Middle East agree. And little wonder given what's on offer.

Middle Eastern cooking draws on a range of influences, from sophisticated Ottoman and Persian sensibilities or the spare improvisation of the desert cooking pot to a Mediterranean belief in letting fresh ingredients speak for themselves. That's why eating in the Middle East is akin to a journey through the flavours of history, telling stories of the civilisations who have called the Middle East home through the ages. But the cooks of the region long ago took the best the world had to offer and transformed Middle Eastern food into a genre all its own.

Iraqi Family Cookbook: From Mosul to America, by Kay Karim, fills a long-neglected branch of Middle Eastern cookery with home-style Mosul cooking adapted for Western kitchens. It won the 2007 Gourmand World Cookbook Award.

The Middle East's gastronomic traditions may be relatively simple when it comes to a meal's constituent elements, but excitement lies in the astonishing variety at large in its feasts of colour and complementary tastes. Innovation comes more in the form of combining dishes of almost endless variety than in tampering with the basic elements of regional cuisine. Thus it is that Middle Eastern food revels in its broad brush strokes and bold colours (think a banquet of mezze), even as it holds fast to its mainstays (think kebabs cooked to perfection with a lingering hint of charcoal). The result is magnificent.

Lebanon, Turkey and Syria are undoubtedly the Middle East's culinary stars. Then there are the lesser-known delights of the Bedouin cooking in Jordan and the surprises brought to bear upon Israeli tables by the arrival of Jewish immigrants (for more information see the boxed text, p259), which are also quintessentially Middle Eastern and just as likely to live in the memory of a visitor. In Iraq, subtle Persian and Kurdish flavours are wedded to an Arab love of lamb and rice, thereby adding more contours to the region's culinary map. The Palestinian Territories and Egypt (think good, honest peasant fare) may be considered the Middle East's poor cousins when it comes to food culture, but eat in a Palestinian or Egyptian home presided over the matriarch of the family and you're unlikely to agree. Apart from anything else, where would the traveller be without those Egyptian staples of fuul (fava-bean paste) and *kushari* (noodles, rice, black lentils, fried onions and tomato sauce)?

The Spice Routes, by Chris and Carolyn Caldicott, is a fascinating overview of the history of the international spice trade and includes a number of recipes from the Middle East region.

But for all its glories, food is only part of the Middle Eastern dining experience. Just like their Mediterranean counterparts in Spain, Italy and Greece, Middle Easterners see eating as a way of life, as an event to be shared with family and friends and to mark the most important moments in life, and as a pastime that's worth spending hours over. In short, life revolves around food, which is, in turn, the most enjoyable way to celebrate all the good things in life.

And yet the Middle East has something that the renowned food cultures of the Mediterranean rim simply can't offer: the hospitality that transforms eating into a celebration where everyone is welcome. Hospitality may manifest itself in a restaurant, on public transport or when you're invited to share a family's meal. In fact, if you're invited to eat in a family home, you'll have arrived in gastronomic heaven. There's nothing that pleases an Arabic, Jewish or Turkish host more than a satisfied guest. They'll spend hours preparing their full repertoire and then sit down with great pleasure to share it with you, all the time pressing

EATING ETIQUETTE

Sharing a meal with a local is a great way of cementing a newly formed friendship. Most people in the Middle East are too polite to say anything if you break one of the region's eating taboos, but to avoid making your hosts feel uncomfortable, there are a few simple guidelines to follow:

Eating in Someone's House

- Bring a small gift of flowers, chocolates or pastries, fruit or honey.
- It's polite to be seen to wash your hands before a meal.
- Remember to always remove your shoes before sitting down on a rug to eat or drink tea.
- Don't sit with your legs stretched out – it's considered rude during a meal.
- Always sit at the dinner table next to a person of the same sex unless your host(ess) suggests otherwise.
- Use only the right hand for eating or accepting food.
- When the meal begins, accept as much food as possible when it's offered to you. If you say 'no thanks' continually, it can offend the host.
- Conversely, it's good manners to leave a little food on your plate at the end of the meal: traditionally, a clean plate was thought to invite famine.
- Your host will often lay the tastiest morsels in front of you; it's polite to accept them.
- The best part – such as the meat – is usually saved until last, so don't take it until offered.

Eating in a Restaurant

- Picking teeth after a meal is quite acceptable and toothpicks are often provided.
- Be sure to leave the dining area and go outside or to the toilet before blowing your nose in a restaurant.
- Take food from your side of the table; stretching to the other side is considered impolite.
- It's polite to accept a cup of coffee after a meal and impolite to leave before it's served.

the tastiest morsels upon you and urging you to eat until you can eat no more. That's because the people of the Middle East consider their food to be the perfect symphonic accompaniment to life as it should be lived. We're inclined to agree.

STAPLES & SPECIALITIES

Mezze

The word 'mezze' is derived from the Arabic *t'mazza,* meaning 'to savour in little bites'.

Mezze (meze in Turkish) ranks alongside Spanish tapas and Italian antipasto as one of the world's greatest culinary inventions. A collection of appetisers or small plates of food, mezze allows you to sample a variety of often complementary tastes and takes the difficulty out of choosing what to order – choose everything! As it appears on restaurant menus, mezze mirrors the time-honoured practices of hosts throwing a party, offering up for their guests a banquet of choice. Largely vegetable-based and bursting with colour and flavour, it's the region's most compelling culinary flourish.

Although it's usually perfectly acceptable for diners to construct an entire meal from the mezze list and forgo the mains on offer, there are subtle differences from country to country in just how far you can take this mezze obsession. Mezze is the headline act when it comes to Levantine cuisine, but it's the understudy to kebabs in Turkey and the trusted warm-up to the region's other cuisines, guaranteed to get the audience enthusiastic for what's next on the culinary bill.

Among the seemingly endless candidates for inclusion in a list of the Middle East's most popular mezze specialties, we've narrowed it down to the following dishes (spellings on menus differ from country to country).

baba ghanooj – literally 'father's favourite', it's a purée of grilled aubergines (eggplants) with tahina and olive oil
basturma – a cold, sliced meat cured with fenugreek
borek – pastry stuffed with salty white cheese or spicy minced meat with pine nuts; also known as *sambousek*
fatayer – triangular deep-fried pastries stuffed with spinach, meat or cheese
hummus bi tahina – cooked chickpeas ground into a paste and mixed with tahini, lemon, olive oil and garlic; sometimes served with meat on top
kibbeh – minced lamb, burghul wheat and pine nuts made into a lemon-shaped patty and deep-fried
labneh – thick yogurt flavoured with garlic and sometimes with mint
loobieh – French bean salad with tomatoes, onions and garlic
mouhamarra – walnut and pomegranate syrup dip
muttabal – purée of aubergine mixed with tahini, yogurt and olive oil; similar to but creamier than baba ghanooj
shanklish – tangy, eye-wateringly strong goat's cheese served with onions, oil and tomatoes
tahina – paste made of sesame seeds and served as a dip
wara ainab – stuffed vine leaves, served both hot and cold; in Egypt also called mahshi

A New Book of Middle Eastern Food, by Claudia Roden, brought the cuisines of the region to the attention of Western cooks when it was released in 1968. It's still an essential reference, as fascinating for its cultural insights as for its great recipes.

Breads

As the Syrian writer Rafik Schami has said, 'only a Middle Easterner could have written the Lord's Prayer' with its invocation to 'give us this day our daily bread'. Bread *(khobz* or *a'aish,* which means 'life') is considered a gift from God and the essential accompaniment to any Middle Eastern meal. It is a regional obsession and for all the variety of the Middle Eastern table, bread is the guaranteed constant, considered such a necessity that few Middle Eastern restaurants dare to charge a cent for it. Governments also know this lesson well: with the price of bread subsidised in many countries, it's a brave government indeed that dares to increase the price of bread. If you're wandering through the streets of an Arab city in the morning and you see a large queue forming at an otherwise innocuous hole in the wall, you've almost certainly stumbled upon the local bakery. Fresh bread is the only way that Middle Easterners will have it.

Literary foodies will enjoy *The Language of Baklava,* by Diana Abu Jabr, which combines an autobiographical novel with a home-style Jordanian recipe book, offering authentic recipes for *mouhamarra, kunafa* and shish kebab, among others.

The staple Middle Eastern bread follows a 2000-year-old recipe. Unleavened and cooked over an open flame, it's used in lieu of cutlery to scoop dips and ripped into pieces to wrap around morsels of meat. Dinner is always served with baskets of bread to mop up mezze, while kebabs are often served with a tasty bread canopy coated in tomato, parsley and spices.

There are variations on the theme and a multiplicity of forms. Depending on where you are, your day may start with a French-style croissant filled with *zaatar* (a fragrant mix of sun-dried thyme and sesame seeds with olive oil) or a crusty white loaf to accompany white cheese, tomatoes, cucumbers and olives. In Turkey, Egypt and Jordan you'll encounter a chewy, sesame-encrusted bread ring known respectively as a *simit, semit* or *ka'ik.* Lunch could be a felafel or shwarma stuffed into a freshly baked bread pocket *(shammy),* or a *zaatar*-smeared type of pizza known as a *manaeesh.* Other lunch or snack dishes include the Turkish *gözleme* (a thin pancake baked on a concave griddle over an open fire

Damascus: Tastes of a City, by Rafik Schami, is one of the most engaging books written about Middle Eastern food, introducing you to the kitchens and characters of Old Damascus.

and filled with cheese, potato, spinach or mushrooms) or the Levantine equivalent, *saj*.

Salads

If you don't order salad in the Middle East most waiters will ask, 'Would you like a salad with that?' That's because it's inconceivable for people in the region to eat a meal without salad. In summer, it's almost sacrilegious, considering the zest and freshness that Middle Eastern salads bring to a meal, perfectly complementing a piping hot kebab. You may find a long list of 'international' salads on menus in restaurants frequented by tourists. But Middle Easterners are loyal to their basic salads and don't mind eating them meal after meal. Elaborations or creative flourishes are rare and simplicity is the key: crunchy fresh ingredients (including herbs), often caressed by a shake of oil and vinegar at the table. Salads are eaten with relish as a mezze or as an accompaniment to a meat or fish main course. Three salads, found throughout the region, form an integral part of the local diet:

In 2001 an Armenian chef saw Israeli and Palestinian chefs working together in Italy and he got an idea: Chefs for Peace. Many culinary stars have since joined to promote coexistence through special events and benefits. Contact chefsforpeace@shabaka.net.

fattoosh – toasted *khobz,* tomatoes, onions and mint leaves, sometimes served with a smattering of tangy pomegranate syrup
shepherd's salad – also known as oriental salad, a colourful mix of chopped tomatoes, cucumber, onion and pepper; extremely popular in Turkey, where it's known as *çoban salatası*
tabbouleh – the region's signature salad combines burghul wheat, parsley and tomato, with a tangy sprinkling of sesame seeds, lemon and garlic

Snack Foods

Forget the bland international snack food served up by the global chains; once you've sampled the joys of Middle Eastern street food you'll never be able to face a quick snack in a fast-food giant again.

The regional stars of the snack food line-up are shwarma and felafel, and they are both things of joy when served and eaten fresh. Shwarma is the Arabic equivalent of the Greek *gyros* sandwich or the Turkish döner kebap – strips are sliced from a vertical spit of compressed lamb or chicken, sizzled on a hot plate with chopped tomatoes and garnish, and then stuffed into a pocket of bread. Felafel is mashed chickpeas and spices rolled into balls and deep-fried; a variation known as ta'amiyya, made with dried fava beans, is served in Egypt. The felafel balls are stuffed into a pocket of bread that's been smeared with tahina (sesame paste) and then the whole thing is topped with some fresh salad, or sometimes with pickled vegetables. Delicious!

Arabesque: Modern Middle Eastern Food, by Greg and Lucy Malouf, lists the 42 essential ingredients from the region and offers insights into how they can be used to create authentic dishes.

Of course, each country has its particular snack food specialty. In Egypt look out for shops sporting large metal tureens in the window: these specialise in the vegetarian delight *kushari,* a delicate mix of noodles, rice, black lentils and dried onions, served with an accompanying tomato sauce that's sometimes fiery with chilli. An alternative more often seen at Israeli sandwich stands is *shakshuka,* a Moroccan dish of eggs poached in tangy stewed tomatoes, which makes a good breakfast but is eaten any time.

In Lebanon, nothing beats grabbing a freshly baked *fatayer bi sbanikh* (spinach pastry) from one of the hole-in-the-wall bakeries that dot city streets. In Turkey, visitors inevitably fall deeply in love with melt-in-the-mouth *su böreği,* a noodle-like pastry oozing cheese and butter. Fast-food vendors in Syria, ever the culinary polyglot, have never been shy of borrowing these snacks and claiming them as Syria's own.

Variations of the pizza abound, one of the most delicious being Egypt's *fiteer,* featuring a base of thin, filo-style pastry. Try it topped with salty haloumi cheese, or even with a mixture of sugar-dusted fruit. In Turkey, the best cheap snack is pide, the Turkish version of pizza, a canoe-shaped dough topped with *peynirli* (cheese), *yumurtalı* (egg) or *kıymalı* (mince). A *karaşık pide* will have a mixture of toppings.

The most unassuming of all Middle Eastern fast foods is also one of the most popular. Fuul is mopped up by bread for breakfast and ladled into a pocket of bread for a snack on the run. You'll find it in Egypt (where it's the national dish), Syria, Jordan, Lebanon and Iraq.

Kebabs & Other Meats

There are more variations on the kebab in this part of the world than you could poke a skewer at. Every country has its specialities – Syria has the delicious *kebab Halebi* (Aleppine kebab, served with a spicy tomato sauce), Turkey is understandably proud of its luscious *İskender kebap* (döner kebap on a bed of pide bread with a side serving of yogurt) and Lebanon has an unswerving devotion to shish tawooq (grilled chicken kebab, often served with a garlic sauce).

The kebab might be king, but when it comes to meat dishes there are courtiers waiting in the wings. Primary among these is *kibbeh,* which is a strong candidate for the right to be called Lebanon's national dish. Indeed, these croquettes of ground lamb, cracked wheat, onion and spices are considered the ultimate test of a Lebanese cook's skills. Before the arrival of food processors, the matron of the household or village pulverised lamb for the *kibbeh* in a mortar and pestle. To produce an even texture requires great skill and strength in the arms. Driving through the mountains of Lebanon on a Sunday morning you can still hear the chimes of these stone 'food processors' like church bells calling the faithful to eat.

British soldiers stationed in the Middle East during WWII used to call *kibbeh* 'Syrian torpedoes', which describes their shape rather well.

Kibbeh may be elevated to an art form in Lebanon, but you'll find them in different variations across the region. In Damascus they're shaped into mini footballs and stuffed with spiced lamb, pine nuts and walnuts, then shallow-fried until golden brown. In Beirut they're served raw like a steak tartare, accompanied with fresh mint leaves, olive oil and spring onions. Raw *kibbeh* (*kibbeh nayye*) has many variations. In northern Lebanon you often find mint and fresh chillies mixed through the meat. In Aleppo, a chilli paste is layered on top of the *kibbeh* with walnuts and onions. *Kibbeh saniye* is *kibbeh* flattened out on a tray with a layer of spiced lamb and pine nuts in between. This is served with natural yogurt on the side.

Another culinary star is *kofta* (spiced ground meat formed into balls; *köfte* in Turkey), which is served in innumerable ways and is the signature element of the Egyptian favourite *daood basha* (meatballs cooked in a *tagen* pot with pine nuts and tomato sauce).

In Syria and Egypt *fatta* (an oven-baked dish of bread soaked in tahini, chickpeas and minced meat or chicken) is a favourite breakfast dish – it will either set you up for the day or have you counting down the hours until your siesta, such is its density.

Even more common than these dishes is one simple but delicious meal that you'll find throughout the region: roast chicken accompanied by salad, bread and hummus or tahini.

Rice Dishes

Although not native to the Middle East, rice is the unsung hero of Middle Eastern cuisine. It's a region-wide staple that's ever-present in home cooking but far less common on restaurant menus. Usually cooked with lamb or chicken, a subtle blend of spices and sometimes saffron, its arrival as the centrepiece of an already groaning table is often a high point of the meal. Indeed, there's no more dramatic moment in a home-cooked meal than when a proud host, with considerable flourish for effect, removes the pyramidal lid to reveal an enormous mound of steaming rice. Now the real business of eating can begin, he or she seems to be saying, now none of my guests shall leave hungry. It's also the point at which you wish you hadn't eaten so much mezze.

Cooking courses are few and far between in the Middle East, but Petra Kitchen (p379; www.petrakitchen.com) in Wadi Musa, near Petra in Jordan, is worth the wait, with local Bedouin teachers and plenty to learn and sample.

If your average Middle Easterner loves rice, it's the Bedouins who revere it. When eating with Bedouins, you'll even wonder whether they'd be perfectly happy if they ate nothing else for the rest of their days. Easy to store, transport and cook, rice was perfectly suited to the once-nomadic lifestyle of many Bedouin. Although they now lead more sedentary lives, rice has been transformed from convenience food to one that no self-respecting Bedouin can live without. For this hardy desert people, *mensaf* (lamb served on a bed of rice and pine nuts and accompanied by a tangy yogurt sauce) is what it's all about. In its true Bedouin form, *mensaf* comes complete with a gaping sheep's head and is best enjoyed from a communal bowl around the campfire beneath a million stars as desert winds make the flames of the fire dance. Such is *mensaf's* popularity, however, that you'll find it on menus, including some far from the desert, in the Palestinian Territories, Jordan and Syria (especially around Palmyra).

Another regional rice specialty that won't disappoint is *makhlooba* (literally 'upside-down') rice, which Damascenes adore. It's cooked in stock and spices with chickpeas, onions and off-the-bone lamb shanks, then pressed in a deep bowl and turned upside down to reveal a delicious work of art. The vegetarian version incorporates eggplants with almonds and pine nuts.

In Syria, sole is known as *samak moossa,* or Moses fish. Because of its thinness, it is said to have been cut in half when Moses divided the Red Sea.

Seafood

When on the Mediterranean and Black Sea coasts (particularly in İstanbul, Alexandria, Tripoli and, to a lesser degree, Lattakia), you'll undoubtedly join the locals in falling hook, line and sinker for the marvellous array of fresh seafood on offer. Local favourites are calamari, red mullet, sea bass and sole. Oddly enough, it's difficult to find good seafood in other parts of the region and the further inland you go, the more you'll pay for your prawns (up to three times the price of other main dishes in Damascus).

Vegetables

Unlike their Western counterparts, locals do not prepare vegetables that are out of season; here tomatoes are eaten when they're almost bursting out of their skins with sweet juices, corn is picked when it's golden and plentiful, and cucumbers are munched when they're crispy and sweet.

There are a number of vegetables that are particular to Middle Eastern cuisine, including *molokhiyya* (aka *moolookhiye* or *melokhia*), a slimy but surprisingly sexy green leafy vegetable known in the West as mallow. In Egypt it's made into an earthy garlic-flavoured soup that has a glutinous texture and inspires an almost religious devotion among the locals. In Syria and Lebanon *molokhiyya* is used to make strongly spiced lamb and chicken stews.

The Turkish dish *imam bayıldı* ('the imam fainted') is aubergine stuffed with onion and garlic, slow-cooked in olive oil and served cold. Legend has it that an imam fainted with pleasure on first tasting it.

The region also has a particularly distinctive way of serving vegetables, known as *dolma* (stuffed with rice or meat and slow-cooked in olive oil; also called *dolmeh* or *mahshi*). The most famous example of this style of cooking is the Turkish dish *imam bayıldı*.

Desserts & Sweets

If you have a sweet tooth, be prepared to put it to good use on your travels in this part of the world. The prince of the regional puds is undoubtedly *muhalabiyya* (also known as *mahallabiye*), a blancmange-like concoction made of ground rice, milk, sugar, and rose or orange water, topped with chopped pistachios and almonds. Almost as popular is *ruz bi laban* (rice pudding, known as *fırın sütlaç* in Turkey). All Middle Easterners love their sweets but they come closest to worshipping them in Syria and Turkey. Some say Turks' adoration of sweets may be attributed to the Quranic verse, 'To enjoy sweets is a sign of faith.' Just in case you missed the point, a local proverb adds that 'sweets are equated with a kind heart and a sugary tongue'.

Seasonal fresh fruit is just as commonly served, and provides a refreshing, light finale to a mezze-and-kebab–laden feast.

But best of all are the pastries. Although these are sometimes served in restaurants for dessert, they're just as often enjoyed as an anytime-of-the-day snack. Old favourites include *kunafa*, a vermicelli-like pastry over a vanilla base soaked in syrup; and the famous baklava, made from delicate filo drenched in honey or syrup. Variations on baklava are flavoured with fresh nuts or stuffed with wickedly rich clotted cream (called *kaymak* in Turkey, *eishta* elsewhere).

The popular Egyptian dessert of *umm ali* (dessert of filo pastry, butter, raisins and nuts baked in milk) is said to have been introduced into the country by Miss O'Malley, an Irish mistress of Khedive Ismail, the viceroy of Egypt.

DRINKS

Tea & Coffee

Drinking tea *(shai, chai* or *çay)* is the signature pastime of the region and it is seen as strange and decidedly antisocial not to swig the tannin-laden beverage at regular intervals throughout the day. The tea will either come in the form of a tea bag plonked in a cup or glass of hot water (Lipton is the usual brand) or a strong brew of the local leaves. Sometimes it's served with *na'ana* (mint) and it always comes with sugar. Be warned that you'll risk severe embarrassment if you ask for milk, unless you're in a tourist hotel or restaurant.

Surprisingly, Turkish or Arabic coffee *(qahwa)* is not widely consumed in the region, with instant coffee (always called Nescafé) being far more common. If you do find the real stuff, it's likely to be a thick and powerful Turkish-style brew that's served in small cups and drunk in a couple of short sips. Always ready with a proverb, the Turks strongly believe that 'coffee should be black as hell, strong as death and sweet as love'. Given that love is clearly the most appealing of the three options, Turkish coffee is usually served very sweet; if you want less sugar ask for it to be served *wassat* (medium sweet) or *sada* (without sugar).

Although it's not as popular as tea in public cafés, coffee is invariably served in people's homes. An Arab host will always refill his guest's coffee cup. A good guest will accept a minimum of three cups but when you've had enough, gently tilt the cup from side to side (in Arabic, 'dancing' the cup).

Legend has it that in society Ottoman-era houses chefs made baklava with over 100 pastry-sheet layers per tray. The master of the house would test the softness of the pastry with a gold coin: if it fell to the bottom of the tray the chef kept the coin.

Alcoholic Drinks

Though the region is predominantly Muslim and hence abstemious, most countries have a local beer. The best are Turkey's Efes, Egypt's Stella and Sakkara, Lebanon's famous Almaza and Jordan's Amstel, a light brew made under licence from the popular Dutch brewer Amstel. Less impressive are Syria's Barada (Damascus) and Al-Charq (Aleppo), and Israel's Maccabee, the dark-draught Gold Star and light Nesher. The most interesting ale is the preservative-free Taybeh. The product of the Arab world's first microbrewery (in Ramallah), it comes in light and malt-heavy dark varieties. Rumour has it that they also make a green-label, alcohol-free halal version in honour of Hamas.

When drinking Turkish-style coffee, you should never drink the grounds in the bottom of your cup. You may want to read your fortune in them, though – check out the website of İstanbul's longest-established purveyor of coffee, Kurukahveci Mehmet Efendi (www.mehmetefendi.com) for a guide.

Wine is growing in popularity in the Middle East, thanks largely to the fine vintages being produced in Lebanon. Lebanon's winemaking, which is based on the 'old-world' style, began with the French winemaker Gaston Hochar who took over an 18th-century castle, Château Musar in Ghazir,

THE CAFÉ & COFFEEHOUSE EXPERIENCE

There's nothing more authentically Middle Eastern than spending an hour (or an afternoon) soaking up the ambience and fragrant nargileh smoke at a *qahwa* (coffeehouse; *ahwa* in Egypt); in Turkey they're called *çay bahçesis* (tea gardens). Most serve up more tea than coffee and all have loyal, predominantly male, clients who enjoy nothing more than a daily natter and a game of dominoes or *towla* (backgammon). Adding to the atmosphere in more ways than one is the smoke from countless water pipes, a fragrant cloud of lightly scented tobacco that's one of the Middle East's most distinctive sensory experiences.

Called a nargileh in Turkey, Lebanon, Jordan and Syria and a sheesha in Egypt, the water pipe is a tradition, an indulgence and a slightly naughty habit all wrapped into the one gloriously relaxing package. A feature of coffeehouses from Ankara to Aswan, it's as addictive as it is magical. Consider yourselves warned.

When you order a water pipe you'll need to specify the type of tobacco and molasses mix you'd like. Most people opt for tobacco soaked in apple juice (known as *elma* in Turkey and *tufah* in Egypt), but it's also possible to order strawberry, melon, cherry or mixed-fruit flavours. Some purists order their tobacco unadulterated, but in doing this they miss out on the wonderfully sweet aroma that makes the experience so memorable. Once you've specified your flavour, a decorated bulbous glass pipe filled with water will be brought to your table, hot coals will be placed in it to get it started and you'll be given a disposable plastic mouthpiece to slip over the pipe's stem. Just draw back and you're off. The only secret to a good smoke is to take a puff every now and again to keep the coals hot; when they start to lose their heat the waiter (or dedicated water-pipe minder) will replace them. Bliss!

This being the Middle East, however, not all cafés and coffeehouses are created equal, at least not for women. Wandering into a traditional café as a woman will always turn heads, but in Damascus, Beirut and parts of Amman, the clatter of domino chips will quickly resume and you're unlikely to feel uncomfortable. In Egypt, Turkey, the Palestinian Territories and the coffeehouses of smaller towns across the region, you'll be far more of an attraction for far longer than you'd like to be.

There are many classic Middle Eastern coffeehouses, but if we had to choose just two classics among classics, they would be **Al-Nawfara** (p478) in the Old City in Damascus and **Fishawi's** (p141) in Cairo.

24km north of Beirut, in 1930. Together with his sons, Hochar created a wine that, despite the civil war, was able to win important awards in France, including the prestigious Winemaker's Award for Excellence. Ninety per cent of their produce is exported. The main wine-growing areas are Kefraya and Ksara in the Bekaa Valley and we particularly recommend the products of Château Musar and Ksara's Reserve du Couvent. For more information on some of Lebanon's wines see the boxed text, p447.

You can drink arak neat, but most devotees first pour about two fingers of arak, then add water and finish off with one ice cube.

In Turkey, the two largest producers are Doluca and Kavaklıdere. Doluca's best wines are its Özel Kav (Special Reserve) red and white. Kavaklıdere's most popular wines are the quaffable Yakut red and Çankaya white. Elsewhere, Egypt has a growing viticulture industry, but the product is pretty unimpressive – Grand de Marquise is the best of a lacklustre bunch. Syrian wine is diabolically bad, and most of the local tipplers stick to the Lebanese drops, which are also available. Israeli wine is improving, and Carmel, Golan, Barchan, Tishbi and Tzora all have reasonable reputations. For more coverage of Israeli wines, see the boxed texts, p259 and p304.

If there is a regional drink, it would have to be the grape-and-aniseed firewater known as rakı in Turkey and as arak (lion's milk) in the rest of the region. The aniseed taste of these two powerful tipples perfectly complements mezze. You'll find many Middle Easterners for whom mezze without arak (combined with water and served in small glasses) is just not taking your mezze seriously.

WATER WARNING

Many locals don't drink the tap water and we recommend that you follow their lead. If you do decide to risk the local stuff, the safest places to do so are in Israel, Syria and Turkey. Don't even *think* of drinking from the tap in Egypt, Iraq, the Palestinian Territories or Lebanon. Some expats may try to convince you otherwise with various degrees of conviction – one foreigner living in Cairo told us, 'You *can* drink the water in Cairo, I swear. It just tastes less than delicious.' Cheap bottled water is readily available throughout the region.

Nonalcoholic Drinks

Juice stalls selling cheap and delicious freshly squeezed *asiir* (juices) are common throughout the region. Popular juices include lemon (which is often blended with sugar syrup and ice, and sometimes with mint), orange, pomegranate, mango, carrot and sugar cane, and you can order combinations of any or all of these. For health reasons, steer clear of stalls that add milk to their drinks.

The Turks love *boza,* a viscous mucus-coloured beverage made from fermented burghul with water and sugar that has a reputation for building strength and virility.

Other traditional drinks include *aryan,* a refreshing yogurt drink made by whipping yogurt with water and salt to the consistency of pouring cream. This is widely available throughout the region and is a ubiquitous accompaniment to kebabs. Another favourite is the delicious and unusual *sahlab* (*sahlep* in Turkey), a drink made from crushed tapioca-root extract and served with milk, coconut, sugar, raisins, chopped nuts and rosewater. Famed for its aphrodisiacal properties, it is served hot in winter and cold in summer.

In the baking heat of an Egyptian summer, coffee and tea drinkers forgo their regular fix for cooler drinks such as the crimson-hued, iced *karkadai,* a wonderfully refreshing drink boiled up from hibiscus leaves, or *zabaady* (yogurt beaten with cold water and salt).

CELEBRATIONS

Food plays an important part in the religious calendar of the region and holy days usually involve a flurry of baking and hours of preparation in the kitchen.

The Arab Table: Recipes and Culinary Traditions, by May Bsisu, takes a holistic approach that blends practical recipes with discursive sections on Arab culinary philosophy, with a special focus on celebratory meals.

Ramadan & Other Islamic Celebrations

The region's most important religious feasts occur during Ramadan (Ramazan in Turkish), the Muslim holy month. There are two substantial meals a day during this period. The first, *imsak* (or *sahur*), is a breakfast eaten before daylight. Tea, bread, dates, olives and pastries are scoffed to give energy for the day ahead. *Iftar,* the evening meal prepared to break the fast, is a special feast calling for substantial soups, rice dishes topped with almond-scattered grilled meats and other delicacies. *Iftar* is often enjoyed communally in the street or in large, specially erected tents. In Turkey, a special round flat pide is baked in the afternoon and collected in time for the evening feast.

The end of Ramadan (Eid al-Fitr) is also celebrated in great culinary style. In Turkey, locals mark this important time with Şeker Bayramı (Sugar Festival), a three-day feast in which sweet foods (especially baklava) occupy centre stage.

Jewish Celebrations

The Shabbat (Sabbath) meal is an article of faith for most Jews and central to that weekly celebration is the bread known as *challah* (Sabbath bread), which is baked each week by Jewish householders in Israel and the Palestinian Territories. A slowly cooked heavy stew called *cholent* is another Sabbath tradition widely enjoyed in Israel. Fatty meat, beans, grains, potatoes, herbs and spices stewed for hours in a big pot will heartily serve the family as well as their guests.

The Pesah (Jewish Passover) is celebrated even by the nondevout, which comprises the majority of Israelis. Unleavened bread is the best-known ingredient. During Hanukkah, potato pancakes and special jam doughnuts (*soofganiot*) are traditional dishes, while Rosh HaShanah means eating sweet foods like apples, carrots or braided *challah* bread dipped in honey.

The Complete Middle East Cookbook, by Tess Mallos, is full of easy-to-follow recipes and devotes individual chapters to national cuisines including those of Turkey, Iraq, Iran, Egypt and Israel.

Easter

Easter heralds another round of feasting, with Good Friday's abstinence from meat bringing out dishes such as *m'jaddara* (spiced lentils and rice) or *shoraba zingool* (sour soup with small balls of cracked wheat, flour and split peas) in Lebanon and Syria. *Selak,* rolls of silver beet (Swiss chard) stuffed with rice, tomato, chickpeas and spices, are also served. The fast is broken on Easter Sunday with round semolina cakes called *maamoul* (which also appear as desserts on some Damascus restaurant menus) stuffed with either walnuts or dates. The Armenian Christmas, the Epiphany (6 January), has the women busy making *owamaut* (small, deep-fried honey balls).

Aromas of Aleppo: The Legendary Cuisine of Syrian Jews, by Poopa Dweck, is a universally acclaimed tour of the Jewish roots that helped create one of the Arab Middle East's culinary capitals.

Rites of Passage

In the Middle East, food is always associated with different milestones in an individual's and a family's life. When a baby is born, Egyptians mark the birth of a son by serving an aromatic rice pudding with aniseed called *meghlie*; in Syria and Lebanon it's called *mighlay* and is made of rice flour and cinnamon. The same dish is called *mughly* in the Palestinian Territories, where it is believed to aid lactation.

In Syria and Lebanon, chickpeas and tooth-destroying sugar-coated almonds are the celebratory treats when the baby's first tooth pushes

FOOD ECHOES FROM THE HOLY BOOKS

- During the daily *iftar* feast of Ramadan, platters of dates on the table remind diners of the Prophet Mohammed's only source of food while fasting in the desert.
- Turks eat *aşure Bayramı* on the 10th day of Muharram (the first month of the Muslim calendar) to celebrate Noah, his ark and the great glory of God. The story goes that when the flood waters were subsiding, Noah asked his wife to cook up all the food left in the pantry. She formulated a bizarre 40-ingredient pudding that included beans, barley, chickpeas, cinnamon, sultanas and burghul, and called it *aşure.*
- In Jewish tradition, *challah* (Sabbath bread) is baked to commemorate the Israelites being given a double portion of manna on their sixth day in the wilderness to provide for the succeeding seventh day.
- While two pieces of *matzah* (unleavened cracker bread) on the table are customary for the Jewish Sabbath, three are required for Passover. This is so that one can be broken at the start of the meal, emblematic of the sustenance of downtrodden slaves who made their escape to freedom in too much haste for bread to rise.
- The sourness of the Easter dish *shoraba zingool* reminds Christians of the vinegar on the sponge offered by the Roman centurion to Christ on the cross.
- For Christians in the Palestinian Territories, traditional Easter dishes include stuffed lamb or ribs accompanied by stuffed *kibbeh,* a pointed meatball encased in cracked wheat and fried, symbolising the spear that pierced Jesus' side.

through. In Egypt, *ataïf* (pancakes dipped in syrup) are eaten on the day of a betrothal and biscuits known as *kahk bi loz* (almond bracelets) are favourites at wedding parties. Turkish guests at engagement parties and weddings are invariably served baklava, providing sugary stamina for the rollicking hours of party-making ahead, not to mention the couple's wedding night.

In the 17th century 1300 workers slaved away in the kitchens of İstanbul's Topkapı Palace, producing food for around 10,000 people every day.

Mourning carries with it a whole different set of eating rituals. A loved one is always remembered with a banquet. This takes place after the burial in Christian communities, and one week later in Muslim communities. The only beverages offered are water and bitter, unsweetened coffee. In Israel and the Palestinian Territories, Muslims may serve dates as well, while Christians bake *rahmeh,* a type of bun commemorating the soul of the departed. For some, a North African Arab dish, named *mughrabiyeh* (Arab pasta formed by rolling wheat grains in flour to make small, round beads) is made when someone dies. Muted varieties of much-loved sweets, such as *helva* and *lokum* (Turkish delight), are commonly part of the mourning period in Turkey; a bereaved family will make *irmik helvası* (semolina helva) for visiting friends and relatives.

When observant Jews mourn the dead, religious dictates urge them to sit around the deceased for seven days and then have a solemn meal of bread to signify sustenance, and boiled eggs and lentils, whose circular forms invoke the continuation of life.

Go to www.inmamaskitchen.com and select 'Jewish Cooking'. Contributors to this thoughtful site will take you from the history of the Diasporas to a recipe file that spans the globe.

WHERE & WHEN TO EAT & DRINK

Eating patterns and styles differ throughout the region, but one rule stands firm in each and every country: the best food is always served in private homes. That's not to say there aren't some outstanding meals to be had in restaurants. But if you're fortunate enough to be invited to share a home-cooked meal, don't think twice.

While restaurant food can be disappointing in Egypt, Israel and Jordan, it can soar to the culinary heavens in Lebanon, Syria and Turkey, particularly in the big cities. The widest selection of regional dishes is, of course, to be found in capital cities and larger towns such as İstanbul, Aleppo, Tripoli and Alexandria.

When you do eat out, you'll find that the locals usually dine at a later hour than in many Western countries (it's normal to see diners arrive at a restaurant at 10pm, particularly in summer). They also dine as large family groups, order up big, smoke like chimneys and linger over their meals. The main meal of the day is usually lunch, which is enjoyed at around 2pm. In most places restaurants open from late morning until late into the night, meaning that you can usually keep hunger at bay at most times of the day while your body clock becomes accustomed to the unfamiliar hours. If not, you're never far from some local form of fast-food outlet serving shwarma or falafel. See under Business Hours in each country's Directory section for the usual opening hours for restaurants.

To ask, 'Do you have any vegetarian dishes?' in Egypt say, '*Andak akla nabateeyya?*' In Turkey ask, '*Etsiz yemekler var mı?*' (Is there something to eat that has no meat?) In other countries ask for dishes that are '*bidoon lahem*' (without meat).

VEGETARIANS & VEGANS

Though it's quite normal for the people of the Middle East to eat a vegetarian meal, the concept of vegetarianism is quite foreign. Say you're a vegan and they will either look mystified or assume that you're 'fessing up to some strain of socially aberrant behaviour. There is a sprinkling of vegetarian restaurants in big cities such as Beirut and İstanbul, but the travelling vegetarian certainly can't rely on finding them elsewhere.

Fortunately, it's not difficult to find vegetable-based dishes. You'll find yourself eating loads of mezze and salads, fuul, tasty cheese and spinach

VEG-A-WHAT? TRAVAILS OF A VEGETARIAN TRAVELLER IN TURKEY *Miriam Raphael*

As someone whose favourite part of the day is deciding what to eat, I was salivating at the thought of several months in Turkey. All that glorious bread! All that wonderful cheese! But on arrival in İstanbul I began to think, 'All that meat…' I recalled my friends warning me that as a vegetarian I would die in Turkey. After a week I had to agree; if something didn't change I was going to die. Not of starvation but of a surfeit of Welsh rarebit!

But if you are up for a challenge, being a vegetarian in Turkey can be done. First, learn the phrases, *'Etli mi?'* (Does it have meat?) and *'Sebze yemekleri var mı?'* (Are there any vegetable dishes?) And get used to walking into the kitchen to check things out for yourself (because Turkish 'vegetarians' sometimes eat no animal but chicken). Then get acquainted with all the vegetarian salads and mezes on offer. A couple of these and some piping hot bread is often more than enough for lunch. Cheap lokantas (restaurants) are great for vegetarians. Not only can you see what you are ordering, but also they offer lots of hearty dishes – stuffed aubergines, plates of green beans, okra and peppers – with an obligatory pile of rice on the side. Better restaurants often have vegetable *güveç* (stew in a clay pot) on the menu. Covered in cheese and baked in the oven, it's nothing short of scrumptious. *Menemen,* a stir-fried omelette with tomatoes and hot peppers, is also popular. Unfortunately, most soups, even *ezo gelin* (lentil and rice), are made with meat stock. Every town has a *börekci* that serves flaky pastry stuffed with white cheese and parsley. And don't miss *gözleme,* a Turkish pancake filled with spinach, cheese or potato. If all else fails, there's always dessert!

pastries, the occasional omelette or oven-baked vegetable *tagens* (stews baked in a terracotta pot) featuring okra and aubergine.

The main source of inadvertent meat-eating is meat stock, which is often used to make otherwise vegetarian pilafs, soups and vegetable dishes. Your hosts may not even consider such stock to be meat, so may assure you that the dish is vegetarian. Chicken and mutton are the biggest hide-and-seekers in the region's food, often lurking in vegetable dishes and mezze. Be careful.

The best country for vegetarians is Israel, where kosher laws don't permit the mixing of meat and dairy products, resulting in a lot of 'dairy' restaurants where no meat in any form is served.

The earliest physical evidence of an international spice trade is found in the wall reliefs of the Funerary Temple of Hatshepsut in Luxor, Egypt.

EATING WITH KIDS

Setting yourself up as a babysitter in the Middle East would have to be one of the more ill-conceived career choices. That's because, with the possible exception of Turkey, it's usual to eat out as a family group – you'll often see young children dining with their parents and friends in restaurants until the early hours. Waiters are either welcoming or, at the very least, accepting of children and will often go out of their way to be helpful, whether happily heating baby food to offering the tried-and-true favourite – fried potato chips. Best of all, the cuisine of the region is very child-friendly, being simple and varied, although you should always make sure the meat is well cooked.

On the downside, Middle Eastern ice creams may be too much of a risk for tender young stomachs and, although some places have high chairs, they're in the minority. Kids' menus are rare except in Western-style hotel restaurants.

For more information on travelling with children, see p623.

Environment

'The true servants of the most gracious are those who tread gently on the earth.'

Quran, sura 25, verse 63

The Middle East is home to some of the most pressing environmental issues of our time. Indeed, there are few regions of the world where the human impact upon the environment has been quite so devastating. More than that, as one of the world's largest oil-producing regions, the Middle East's size far outweighs its contribution to the gathering global environmental crisis. There *are* pockets of good news, but the governments of the region have, in general, yet to realise the urgency of the situation. Given that environmental issues – especially water scarcity – are invariably transformed into security concerns in this part of the world, such delays in addressing environmental issues are luxuries that few governments will soon be able to afford.

For more information on travelling responsibly in the region, see p24.

Climate Change: Environment and Civilization in the Middle East, by Arie Issar and Zohar Mattanyah, is a sobering study of how the rise and fall of civilisations in the Middle East has always been intricately tied to environmental issues.

THE LAND

Wrapping itself around the eastern Mediterranean and with its feet on three continents, the Middle East acts like a pivot for some of the oldest inhabited regions on earth. Appropriately, for such an important crossroads, the Middle East is home to some epic landforms, from the deserts that engulf much of the region and high mountain ranges of the north to some of history's most famous and important rivers.

Egypt has four of the world's five officially identified types of sand dunes, including the *seif* (sword) dunes, so named because they resemble the blades of curved Arab swords.

Deserts

The world's largest desert, the Sahara, does more than occupy Egyptian territory – it covers 93% of the country. Although the Egyptian case is extreme, other countries of the region face a similar situation with all of the attendant issues for land-use and water scarcity: 77% of Jordanian and Iraqi territory is considered to be desert, while the figure for Israel and the Palestinian Territories is 60%. Although deserts dominate much of the region, they're rarely home to the sandy landscapes of childhood imaginings. Apart from the Saharan sand seas in parts of Egypt, sand dunes of any great significance are rare in a region where stony gravel plains are the defining feature.

Deserts, or at least the oases strung out across the wastes, have played an important role in the history of the region. Nowhere is this more evident than in the Syrian oasis of Palmyra (p509), which became a crucial watering point for caravans travelling the Silk Road and between Mesopotamia and the Mediterranean. The oases of Egypt's Western Desert (p175), especially Siwa, served a similar function for trans-Saharan caravans.

The most accessible desert for travellers is Jordan's Wadi Rum (p381) with its exceptional sandstone and granite jebels rising from the sands. Stirring expeditions are also possible in Egypt's Western Desert (which forms part of the Sahara) and the Negev (p307) in southern Israel and the Palestinian Territories. For more information on desert expeditions, see p619.

Mountains

Although deserts dominate most popular perceptions of Middle Eastern landscapes, mountains provide plenty of their own drama, especially in Turkey and Lebanon. Eastern Turkey is simply glorious with seriously high mountains rising above 5000m – the 5137m-high Mt Ararat (Ağrı

Dağı) is the highest mountain in the countries covered by this book, although Mt Damavand (5671m) in neighbouring Iran is the Middle East's highest peak. Southeastern Anatolia offers windswept rolling steppe, jagged outcrops of rock that spill over into far north Iraq.

Elsewhere in Turkey, both the Black Sea and Mediterranean coasts cower beneath towering peaks, before giving way to the vast, high plateau of rolling steppe and mountain ranges of Central Anatolia.

In Lebanon, the Mt Lebanon Range forms the backbone of the country and towers over the Mediterranean. The range rises steeply with a dramatic set of peaks and ridges; the highest peak, Qornet as-Sawda, southeast of Tripoli, reaches over 3000m. South of Beirut are the beautiful Chouf Mountains. To the east the Mt Lebanon Range gives way steeply to the Bekaa Valley, which in turn yields to the Anti-Lebanon Range, a sheer arid massif averaging 2000m in height, which forms a natural border with Syria. Lebanon's mountains peter out to the north, crossing the frontier with Syria, whose Mediterranean coast is separated from the rest of the country by the Jebel Ansariyya.

Rivers

It's difficult to overestimate the significance of the rivers that flow into and through the Middle East. The Nile, which runs for 6695km, 22% of it in Egypt, is the longest river on earth and along its banks flourished the glorious civilisation of ancient Egypt. Other Middle Eastern rivers resonate just as strongly with legends and empires past. According to the Bible, the Euphrates and Tigris are among the four rivers that flowed into the Garden of Eden and they would later provide the means for the cradle of civilisation in Mesopotamia. The Jordan River, the lowest river on earth, also features prominently in biblical texts.

But the significance of these rivers is anything but old news. Even today, they provide the lifeblood for the people of Egypt (90% of whose population lives along the Nile), Israel and Palestinian Territories, Iraq, Jordan and eastern Syria, many of whom cling to the riverbanks for life support. Were it not for the rivers that run through these lands – hence providing a water source and narrow fertile agricultural zones close to the riverbanks – it's difficult to see how these regions could support life at all.

For more information on the Euphrates River, turn to the boxed text, p515.

Natural Selections: A Year of Egypt's Wildlife, written and illustrated by Richard Hoath and published locally by the American University in Cairo Press, is a passionate account of the creatures that make Egypt their home.

WILDLIFE

Animals

Occupying the junction of three natural zones, the Middle East was once a sanctuary for an amazing variety of mammals. Hardly any are left. The list of species driven to extinction by hunting and other consequences of human encroachment – among them, cheetahs, lions and Nile crocodiles – tells in microcosm the story of the irreparable damage that humankind has wrought upon the Middle Eastern environment. If you see anything more exciting than domesticated camels, donkeys and water buffaloes, you'll belong to a very small group of lucky Middle Eastern travellers. To make matters worse, despite a growing awareness of what has been lost, official government policies to protect wildlife are as rare as many of the animals.

There are exceptions to this otherwise gloomy outlook. The most famous of these is the campaign to save the Arabian oryx (see the boxed text, opposite), while the Israeli initiative known as Hai Bar (literally 'wildlife') has also provided a small beacon of hope.

Begun more than 40 years ago, Israel's Hai Bar program set itself the most ambitious of aims: to reintroduce animals that roamed the Holy Land during biblical times by collecting a small pool of rare animals, breeding them, then reintroducing them to the wild. As a result, the wild ass, beloved by the Prophet Isaiah, has turned the corner and may soon be off the endangered list. But the story of the Persian fallow deer is the one that really captured the public imagination. A small group of the species was secretly flown in from Iran in 1981 on the last El Al flight to leave before the Islamic revolution. These shy animals have taken hold in the Galilee reserve of Akhziv and around the hills that lead to Jerusalem.

Although casual wildlife sightings are rare, a dedicated expedition away from well-travelled routes, or a visit to a wildlife reserve (see p113), will definitely increase your chances of success. Desert expeditions in Egypt's Sinai or Sahara offer the chance to see gazelle, rock hyraxes, fennec fox and even the graceful Nubian ibex. Trekking in the Chouf Mountains, south of Beirut, might also yield a rare sighting of wolves, wild cats, ibex and gazelle. Oryx, ostrich, gazelle and Persian onager, all of which are being reared for reintroduction to the wild, are on show at Jordan's Shaumari Wildlife Reserve (p364) in eastern Jordan, while Jordan's striking caracal (Persian lynx), a feline with outrageous tufts of black hair on the tips of its outsized, pointy ears, is occasionally seen in Wadi Mujib (p369) and Dana (p371) nature reserves. The rare loggerhead turtle nests on some of Turkey's Mediterranean beaches, including Dalyan (p571).

The Zoo on the Road to Nablus: A Story of Survival from the West Bank, by Lonely Planet's own Amelia Thomas, is a sometimes depressing, sometimes inspirational account of the last zoo in the Palestinian Territories.

In *The Natural History of the Bible* (2006), Daniel Hillel, a world-renowned soil physicist and expert in water management, sheds light on the local ecology's influence on the people and world of the Holy Scriptures.

BIRDS

In contrast to the region's dwindling number of high-profile wildlife, the variety of bird life in the Middle East is exceptionally rich. As well as being home to numerous indigenous species, the Middle East, despite the critical loss of wetlands in Jordan and Iraq, continues to serve as

SAVING THE ARABIAN ORYX

For many in the Middle East, the Arabian oryx is more than just an endangered species. Thought by some to be the unicorn of historical legend, the herbivorous oryx is a majestic creature that stands about a metre high at the shoulder and has enormous horns that project over half a metre into the air.

Adapted well to their desert environment, wild oryx once had an uncanny ability to sense rain on the wind. One herd is recorded as having travelled up to 155km, led by a dominant female, to rain. In times of drought, oryxes have been known to survive 22 months without water, obtaining moisture from plants and leaves.

Their white coats offered camouflage in the searing heat of the desert, providing a measure of protection from both heat and hunters, but the oryxes and their long, curved horns were highly prized and they were stalked relentlessly for them. In 1972, the last wild Arabian oryx was killed by hunters in Oman, which lead officials to declare the oryx extinct in the wild. Nine lonely oryxes left in captivity around the world were pooled and taken to the Arizona Zoo for a breeding program. They became known as the 'World Oryx Herd' and eventually grew to over 200 in number.

In 1978 four male and four female oryxes were transported to Jordan and three more were sent from Qatar the following year. In 1979 the first calf, Dusha, was born and the oryx began the precarious road to recovery. By 1983 there were 31 oryxes in Shaumari Wildlife Reserve in eastern Jordan, where large enclosures and their treatment as wild animals served to facilitate their eventual release into the wild. In a landmark for environmentalists the world over, a breeding group of oryxes was reintroduced into the wild in the Wadi Rum Protected Area in 2002, a measure that has sadly not been as successful as hoped. Further efforts to reintroduce the oryx into the wild are continuing in other parts of the country.

a way-station on migration routes between Asia, Europe and Africa. Twice a year, half a billion birds of every conceivable variety soar along the Syro-African rift, the largest avian fly way in the world, which is compressed into a narrow corridor along the eastern edge of Israel and the Palestinian Territories.

Birdlife International (www.birdlife.org) is a global alliance of conservation organisations with a fantastic database of birds and the best places in the Middle East to view them.

Israel claims to be the world's second-largest fly way (after South America) for migratory birds and the **Society for the Protection of the Nature of Israel** (SPNI; Map p276; ☎ in Israel 03-566 0960; www.teva-tlv.org/eng_home.html) has an excellent map and guide, the *Bird Trails of Israel,* detailing 14 bird-watching centres.

Other organisations worth contacting include the following:

International Birding & Research Centre (www.birdsofeilat.com)

International Birdwatching Center of the Jordan Valley (☎ in Israel 04-6068396; www.birdwatching.org.il)

International Center for the Study of Bird Migration (www.birds.org.il)

Egypt's Sinai Peninsula and Al-Fayoum Oasis, and Wadi Araba in Jordan also receive an enormous and varied amount of ornithological traffic. Egypt alone has recorded sightings of over 430 different species.

MARINE LIFE

The Red Sea teems with more than 1000 species of marine life, and is an amazing spectacle of colour and form. Fish, sharks, turtles, stingrays, dolphins, corals, sponges, sea cucumbers and molluscs all thrive in these waters.

Coral is what makes a reef a reef – though thought for centuries to be some form of flowering plant, it is in fact an animal. Both hard and soft corals exist, their common denominator being that they are made up of polyps, which are tiny cylinders ringed by waving tentacles that sting their prey and draw it into their stomach. During the day corals retract into their tube, displaying their real colours only at night. Most of the bewildering variety of fish species in the Red Sea – including many that are found nowhere else – are closely associated with the coral reef, and live and breed in the reefs or nearby sea-grass beds.

It's well known that the world's coral reefs and other marine life are under threat from the effects of global warming, but there are plenty of local causes that threaten a more imminent death. This is especially the case in the Red Sea waters off Hurghada where, conservationists estimate, more than 1000 pleasure boats and almost as many fishing boats ply the waters. Fifteen years ago, there was nothing to stop captains from anchoring to the coral, or snorkellers and divers breaking off a colourful chunk to take home. However, due largely to the efforts of the **Hurghada Environmental Protection & Conservation Association** (Hepca; www.hepca.com) and the Egyptian National Parks Office in Hurghada, the Red Sea's reefs are at last being protected. Set up in 1992 by 15 of the town's more reputable dive companies, Hepca's program to conserve the Red Sea's reefs includes public-awareness campaigns, direct community action and lobbying of the Egyptian government to introduce appropriate laws. Thanks to these efforts, the whole coast south of Suez Governorate is now known as the Red Sea Protectorate. Over 570 mooring buoys have been set up at popular dive sites around Hurghada and marine rangers from the Egyptian National Parks Office police the waters. A symbolic 'reef conservation tax' has also been introduced.

Three of a small group of the critically endangered northern bald ibis have been tagged in Syria. Satellites so far have tracked Sultan, Salam and Zenobia on a 3100km journey to Ethiopia.

Although less celebrated, the marine environment of the Mediterranean also faces considerable challenges. As late as the mid-1990s Lebanon still did not have a single functioning wastewater treatment plant, and raw sewage was pouring into the sea. A number of treatment plants have since been rehabilitated and new ones built, but offshore water quality remains a concern. In 2006, during the Israel-Hezbollah war, things again took a turn for the worse after Israeli aircraft bombed the coastal power plant at Jiyyeh, south of Beirut. An estimated 15,000 tonnes of fuel oil spilled into the sea, threatening wildlife, marine life and delicate ecosystems, as well as the livelihoods of local fishermen.

Plants

Middle Eastern flora tends to be at its lushest and most varied in the north, where the climate is less arid, although after millennia of woodcutting Turkey and Syria are now largely denuded. Only the Mediterranean coast west of Antalya and the Black Sea area and northeast Anatolia still have forests of considerable size.

In Lebanon, the Horsh Ehden Forest Nature Reserve is the last archetype of the ancient natural forests of Lebanon and is home to several species of rare orchids and other flowering plants. The cedars for which Lebanon is famous are now confined to a few mountain-top sites, most notably at the small grove at the Cedars ski resort (p438) and the Chouf Cedar Reserve (p446) in the Chouf Mountains. For more information about Lebanon's cedars see the boxed text, p446.

NATIONAL PARKS & WILDLIFE RESERVES

In a region where governments face a legion of serious social, political and security issues, it's perhaps remarkable that there are any national parks at all. As it is, most of the region's officially protected areas are national parks and wildlife reserves in name only. Optimists may call them admirable statements of intent. The cynics would probably prefer to describe them as attempts to create token projects as a means of showing goodwill without having to do much at all to protect the environment. The truth, which varies from country to country, lies somewhere in between. Yes, it's a good thing that these parks and reserves exist, even if only because their resemblance to recreation areas encourages locals to actively experience and thus think more about their environment. But most parks are poorly patrolled and poorly funded, calling into question their long-term effectiveness.

Forests cover 26% of Turkish territory, 8% of Lebanon, 6% of Israel and the Palestinian Territories and less than 1% in Syria, Jordan and Egypt.

Syria and, for understandable reasons, Iraq are bottom of the class when it comes to setting aside protected areas. Apart from a handful nature reserves that you may never realise you've passed through, Syria has one of the lowest ratios of protected areas to total land area of any country in the Mediterranean region.

Next comes Egypt, which has set aside 23 'protected areas', although their status varies wildly and government funding is negligible. The Nile Islands Protected Area, which runs all the way from Cairo to Aswan, suffers from the fact that no one really knows, least of all the government, which islands are included, and most are inhabited and cultivated without restriction. At the other end of the scale, Ras Mohammed National Park (p189) in the Red Sea is an impressive symbol of what can be done when the government puts its mind to it.

Nearly 25 years ago the Jordanian government established 12 protected areas, totalling about 1200 sq km, amounting, in total, to just 1% of Jordan's territory. Some were abandoned, but the rest survive thanks to the **Royal Society for the Conservation of Nature** (RSCN; www.rscn.org.jo), Jordan's major environmental agency. Its activities include saving animal, plant and bird species from extinction; conducting public-awareness programs among Jordanians, especially children; sponsoring environmental clubs throughout the country; training guides; promoting ecotourism; fighting

At the disappearing wetlands of Azraq Wetland Reserve (p364) in Jordan, 347,000 birds were present on 2 February 1967. On the same date 33 years later there just 1200.

See Sıfır Yok Oluş (www.sifiryokolus.org) for information on Turkey's 266 Key Biodiversity Areas, outlined by Turkey's wing of the international coalition, Alliance for Zero Extinction.

against poaching and hunting; and lobbying against mining. The limited resources of the RSCN are used to maintain and develop six of Jordan's reserves, including the impressive the Shaumari Wildlife Reserve (p364) and Dana Nature Reserve (p371).

Lebanon comes under the category of 'trying hard, but could do better'. Most national parks have a 'Friends Association', offering both environmental and practical information for visitors. The most impressive site is undoubtedly the Chouf Cedar Reserve (p446), which, at 50,000 hectares, covers an astonishing 5% of the country's entire area and is home to 30 mammal species and six cedar forests, including three that contain old-growth cedars.

In recent years, thanks to EU aspirations, Turkey has stepped up its environmental protection practices. The growing number of protected areas includes 33 national parks, 16 nature parks and 35 nature reserves. It also includes 58 curiously named 'nature monuments', which are mostly protected trees, some as old as 1500 years. Sometimes the parks' regulations are carefully enforced, but at other times a blind eye is turned to such problems as litter-dropping picnickers. Visitor facilities are rare.

The Middle East's star environmental performer is undoubtedly Israel due to its strong regulation of hunting and a system of nature reserves comprising some 25% of the land. However, the parks are not without their problems. Many are minuscule in size and isolated, providing only limited protection for local species. Moreover, many of the reserves in the

LOCAL ENVIRONMENTAL ORGANISATIONS

Middle Eastern governments may be lagging behind the rest of the world when it comes to environmental protection, but they're being shown the way by others. There are a number of impressive NGOs with an environmental focus in the region, such as **Friends of the Earth Middle East** (www.foeme.org) with Israeli, Jordanian and Palestinian offices, or one of the following organisations:

Israel & the Palestinian Territories

For more information on Israeli environmental groups, see the boxed text, p258.

Galilee Society (www.gal-soc.org) Israel's leading Arab-Israeli environmental activism group.
House of Water & Environment (www.hwe.org.ps) An up-and-coming Ramallah-based NGO with strong professional staff and expertise in water.
Life & Environment (www.sviva.net) An umbrella group that's a valuable portal for reaching dozens of Israel's grassroots environmental groups.
Palestine Hydrology Group (www.phg.org) A very professional, water-oriented NGO that conducts research and projects, primarily in the West Bank.
Society for the Protection of Nature in Israel (SPNI; www.aspni.org) The largest and oldest of Israel's environmental organisations.

Jordan

Royal Society for the Conservation of Nature (RSCN; www.rscn.org.jo) The Jordanian environment's best friend.

Lebanon

Association for Forests, Development and Conservation (www.afdc.org.lb) Runs reforestation, firefighting and ecotourism programs.
Greenline (www.greenline.org.lb) One of Lebanon's biggest volunteer-based environmental NGOs.
Society for the Protection of Nature in Lebanon (www.spnlb.org) A dynamic organisation that's committed to conserving Lebanon's wildlife.

south are also used as military firing zones. One of the best reserves to visit for wildlife in Israel is Ein Gedi (p306), on the shores of the Dead Sea.

The Marsh Arabs, by Wilfred Thesiger, is a classic account of the marshlands of southern Iraq before Saddam ordered them drained in one of the worst environmental crimes of the 20th century.

ENVIRONMENTAL ISSUES

Name an environmental issue and chances are that the Middle East is struggling with it.

Water scarcity is undoubtedly the primary long-term environmental concern for most people in the Middle East; see p118 for details. But as long as water keeps coming out of the taps, daily lives more often involve struggles of a more immediate kind. Levels of waste – whether industrial outflow, sewage discharge or everyday rubbish – have reached critical levels across the region; recycling is almost nonexistent. At one level, the impact is devastating for local fishing industries, agricultural output, freshwater supplies and marine environments – Lebanon did not have functioning wastewater treatment plants until the mid-1990s, while up to 75% of Turkey's industrial waste is discharged without any treatment whatsoever and only 12% of the population is connected to sewage treatment facilities. At another level, the great mounds of rubbish and airborne plastic bags provide an aesthetic assault on the senses for traveller and local alike.

The related issue of air pollution is also threatening to overwhelm in a region where the motor vehicle is king. Take Cairo, for example, which is close to claiming the dubious title of the world's most-polluted city. Airborne smoke, soot, dust and liquid droplets from fuel combustion constantly exceed World Health Organisation (WHO) standards (up to 259 micrograms per cubic metre of air, when the international standard is 50), leading to skyrocketing instances of emphysema, asthma and cancer among the city's population. A startling feature article by Ursula Lindsey published in a March 2005 edition of *Cairo* magazine asserted that as many as 20,000 Cairenes die each year of pollution-related disease and that close to half a million contract pollution-related respiratory diseases every year. Cairo may be an extreme case, but it's a problem facing urban areas everywhere in the Middle East.

Pollution in a Promised Land: An Environmental History of Israel (2002), by Alon Tal, is a comprehensive and inspirational ecological journey through Israel's past century.

Desertification, which is caused by overgrazing, deforestation, the overuse of off-road vehicles, wind erosion and drought, is another significant problem faced by all Middle Eastern countries, with the possible exception of Lebanon. The seemingly unstoppable encroachment of the desert onto previously fertile, inhabited and environmentally sensitive areas is resulting in millions of hectares of fertile land becoming infertile and, ultimately, uninhabitable. Jordan, Egypt and Iraq are on the frontline, but even largely desert-free Turkey is casting a worried eye on the future. While hotel owners in Cappadocia happily equip their rooms with Jacuzzis and mini-hamams, environmentalists fear that much of Turkey could be desert by 2025.

In the 149-country 2008 Environmental Performance Index, Israel ranked highest among Middle Eastern countries at 49th, followed by Jordan (70th), Egypt (71st), Turkey (72nd), Lebanon (90th), Syria (99th) and Iraq (135th).

And then there are the perennial issues of loss of biodiversity, soil erosion and unfettered building developments.

Those grasping for a glimmer of good news – and it's only a glimmer – can take some comfort in the fact that reforestation programs have maintained (albeit meagre) forest levels for the past decade. There's also a tiny but growing movement towards renewable energy sources as an alternative to fossil fuels. Israel has had commercial wind farms since 1992, while, for once, this is one area where Egypt has something to crow about. One of the largest wind farms in Africa and the Middle East is located at Zafarana, approximately halfway between Cairo and Hurghada. Due to the success of this project, numerous other wind farms are planned in towns along the coast.

According to the US Department of Energy, Israel has the largest carbon footprint (10.8 metric tonnes of CO_2 emissions per capita) and is the 29th worst offender in the world followed by Lebanon (4.1), Syria (3.72), Turkey (3.14), Jordan (3.07), Iraq (2.97) and Egypt (2.21). Qatar is the world's worst with 69.2.

Africa & the Middle East: A Continental Overview of Environmental Issues, by Kevin Hillstrom, contains an excellent exploration of the Middle East's environmental past and future, with a special focus on how human populations affect the environment.

Tourism

Has tourism placed serious strains on the environment in the Middle East? Yes. Is tourism itself part of the solution? Yes again.

The Middle East is not alone in having greedily eyed the benefits of mass tourism and thumbed its nose at environmental sustainability. In Egypt, for example, some of the coastal resorts of the Red Sea and Sinai Peninsula are textbook cases of ill-conceived development that threaten to destroy the pristine natural beauty that drew tourists in the first place. Stretches of the Mediterranean coasts of Lebanon and Turkey aren't far behind. Indeed, **Greenpeace Mediterranean** (www.greenpeace.org/Mediterranean) considers tourism to be one of the major causes of coastal destruction in Lebanon. It cites the dozens of yacht ports, 'land reclamation' projects and hotels that have been established illegally along the coast. Further afield, sites such as Petra are now considering limiting the number of visitors to lessen the human wear and tear on the monuments and surrounding landscape.

The environmental impact of mass tourism on such places extends beyond the visible scarring that destroys the views. Destroyed coral reefs and the overexploitation of finite resources such as water are just a few of the environmental consequences for a place that's being loved to death by tourists. Flow-on effects include rising prices for locals and local economies that are dependent upon tourism, leading to the abandonment of traditional industries (such as fishing) and ways of life.

But things are changing, albeit slowly. Private tourism operators and, to a lesser degree, the governments of the region are finally waking up to the fact that environmental sustainability is an important consideration for many travellers. Crucially, they're also discovering that self-funding efforts to reverse environmental destruction and protect the last vestiges of wilderness will be amply rewarded by this new breed of traveller.

Consequently, ecotourism initiatives, though still very much in the minority, are appearing across the region. Israel and the Palestinian

WATER WARS

It's often said that the next great Middle Eastern war will be fought not over land but over water. There are already signs of tension. Syria and Iraq have protested to Turkey because it is building dams at the headwaters of the Tigris and Euphrates, while Egypt has threatened military action against Sudan or any other upstream country endangering its access to the waters of the Nile. But the greatest potential for a conflict based on water centres on Israel and the outstanding water disputes it has with all of its neighbours.

A third of Israel and the Palestinian Territories' fresh water comes from rain, melting snow and natural spring water from the Israeli-occupied Golan Heights. The Sea of Galilee, known to Israelis as Lake Kinneret and a popular recreational area for Israelis, receives all of its water from the Golan's run-off and from the Jordan River, which passes through the disputed territory. The Golan is also home to an increasing number of Jewish settlers, not to mention profitable farms.

And yet this is land that will almost certainly have to be returned if there is ever to be peace between Israel and Syria. Not surprisingly, given the significance of the Golan Heights to Israeli agriculture, there has been strong opposition within Israel to any deal that cedes the Golan to Syria. As one Israeli farmer told the BBC in 2008, 'For us it's life and death. I wouldn't count upon anyone else to say it's going to be OK. I'd rather the water be in my hands, especially round here – you can't trust people's words.' For their part, local Palestinian farmers and the Syrians argue that Israel has already abused the finite resources of the region and can't be trusted to care for the Golan's natural resources. To support their argument, they point to dangerously low water levels, rising salinity and increasing levels of toxic algae in the Sea of Galilee; experts agree that excessive human activity is to blame.

Territories is leading the way with Jordan also putting in an extremely strong showing thanks to the tireless work of the RSCN, whose projects in the Dana Nature Reserve (p371) in particular are models for marrying tourism to environmental sustainability. Lebanon's ecotourism projects are few but increasingly impressive, while Turkey is (very) slowly getting its act together. Egypt and ecotourism are taking a long time to come together with only a handful of private programs, although the work being done by the Hurghada Environmental Protection & Conservation Association to overturn decades of tourist-related damage to coral reefs is an initiative worth supporting. Syria and Iraq still lag far behind. Given that the latter has next to no tourists, Syria is undoubtedly bottom of the class, although its efforts to preserve its old cities are worthy of praise.

The Middle East is home to 4.5% of the world's population and around half of the world's oil supplies, but only receives 2% of the world's rainfall and possesses just 0.4% of the world's recoverable water supplies.

This general scorecard of the countries in the region is reflected in our GreenDex (p698), which recognises sustainability at tourist sites and businesses, whether for their environmental practices or for preserving traditional ways of living. In particular, the Israel and Palestinian Territories and Jordan have a number of exciting initiatives on offer.

For information on how to reduce your environmental impact, see p24. And for a look at the broader impact of tourism on the Arab world,

THE DEAD SEA IS DYING *Dr Alon Tal*

The Dead Sea is the lowest place on earth and probably one of the hottest. The high resulting evaporation produces an astonishing salinity of 31%, about nine times higher than the oceans, making a dip in the Dead Sea a very salty experience. The high mineral concentrations mean incredible buoyancy and great photo opportunities – get a snapshot of your travel companions happily sitting upright on the water reading newspapers. The water's oily minerals also contain salubrious properties. German health insurance covers periodic visits to the Dead Sea for psoriasis patients to luxuriate in the healing waters.

Sadly, no natural resource in the Middle East shows more signs of impact from relentless population growth and economic development than the Dead Sea. Technically, the sea is a 'terminal lake' into which the Jordan River, along with other more arid watersheds, deposits its flow. Despite the folk song's characterisation of the River Jordan as 'deep and wide', in fact it has never been much of a gusher. When Israeli and Jordanian farmers began to divert its water to produce a new agricultural economy in the 1950s, the flow was reduced to a putrid trickle and the Dead Sea began to dry up.

In 1900, the river discharged 1.2 trillion litres a year into the Dead Sea, but water levels in the river today are barely 10% of the natural flow. The Jordanian and Israeli potash industries in the southern, largely industrial Dead Sea region exacerbate the water loss by accelerating evaporation in their production processes. The impact is manifested in sink holes, created when underground salt gets washed away by the infiltrating subsurface freshwater flow. Particularly ubiquitous on the western, Israeli side of the Dead Sea, the ground literally opens up – with people, farming equipment and even trucks falling in. Perhaps the most acute environmental consequence, though, is the 27m drop in the sea's water level and the long and discouraging walks now required to reach the edge of the retreating beach.

Several solutions have been considered to bring water back to the Dead Sea. A 'Med–Dead' canal utilising the height drop from the Mediterranean Sea was discarded because of the prohibitively expensive price tag. But a similar pipeline from the Red Sea is seriously being considered. Dubbed the 'Peace Conduit', the project would pipe water from the Gulf of Aqaba to the Dead Sea's southern shore, producing hydroelectricity as well as a desalination plant that would provide water to Amman. Environmentalists question the anticipated unnatural water chemistry reaction and the seismic instability of the area. The World Bank, however, recently decided that the US$5 billion project was sufficiently serious to justify a $15 million feasibility study.

Dr Alon Tal is a professor in the Desert Ecology Department at Israel's Ben-Gurion University.

pick up a copy of the excellent *Beaches, Ruins, Resorts: The Politics of Tourism in the Arab World* by Waleed Hazbun.

Water

Water in the Middle East (www.columbia.edu/cu/lweb/indiv/mideast/cuvlm/water.html) hosts numerous links to articles on the Middle East's most pressing environmental issue.

To understand the extent of the Middle East's water-scarcity problem, consider this: Jordan has just 140 cubic metres of renewable water per capita per year, compared to the UK's 1500. Jordan's figure is expected to fall to 90 cubic metres by 2025. Anything less than 500 cubic metres is considered to be a scarcity of water. Another study suggests that Jordan currently uses about 60% more water than is replenished from natural sources. By some estimates, Jordan will simply run out of water within 20 years. Although many of these problems are attributable to growing populations in an arid land, poor water management practices are to blame – half the water consumed in Amman and the neighbouring cities of the Palestinian Territories is lost in leakage.

Relatively rich Israel must also shoulder its share of the blame. Since the 1960s Israel and the Palestinian Territories has drawn around one-third of its water from the Jordan River (which is also used by Jordan and the Palestinian Territories). The river has now been reduced to a trickle, half of which is 50% raw sewage and effluent from fish farms. But Israel remains optimistic about its future water supplies, largely because of its use of reverse osmosis technology, which will soon manufacture 20% of Israel's water supply. A breakthrough in the efficiency of the membranes through which sea water is filtered has allowed for a substantial drop in prices: for 50¢, new drinking-water plants along the Mediterranean coast can produce 1000L of water. The energy demands of these facilities are prodigious, and their discharged brine, which contains concentrations of chemicals and metals, adds to marine pollution when returned to the sea.

Power and Water in the Middle East: The Hidden Politics of the Palestinian-Israeli Water Conflict, written by Mark Zeitoun in 2008, is a timely study of how water resources could be central to any future regional conflict.

For its part, Jordan has begun to allocate millions of dollars to water projects. The joint Syrian-Jordanian Wahdah Dam on the Yarmouk River was recently completed, giving power to Syria and water to Jordan (mainly for Amman and Irbid). Jordan is also building a 325km pipeline from Disheh to Amman at a cost of US$600 million to tap nonrenewable fossil water from Diseh near Wadi Rum, and has plans for a series of desalination plants.

Egypt

'It has more wonders in it than any other country in the world and provides more works that defy description than any other place.' (Herodotus, 5th century BC)

The land that gave birth to the first great civilisation needs little introduction. The pyramids, the minarets, the Nile – the scope of Egypt is magnificent.

Visitors are surprised to discover that those legendary pyramids are merely the tip of the archaeological iceberg. Pharaonic nations, ancient Greeks, Romans, Christians and Arab dynasties have all played their part in fashioning Egypt's embarrassment of architectural wealth.

Cairo's chaos whirrs around a medieval core that has remained unchanged since the founding days of Islam. Upriver, Luxor, the site of ancient Thebes, is lined with warrens of opulent burial chambers and boasts some of the most formidable monuments in all antiquity. Further south at Aswan, even more geometrically imposing temples write a testament to the power of archaic gods and omnipotent pharaohs. It is here that the Nile is best explored by ancient sail, on a felucca (Egyptian sailing boat) at the hands of the prevailing currents and winds.

Out west, Egypt's ocean of sand stretches infinitely to the Sahara, with a handful of oases feeding solitary islands of green. Hivelike, medieval fortresses cower out here, interspersed with bubbling springs and ghostly rock formations. Meanwhile, the deep, crystal waters of the Red Sea lie brilliantly awash in coral, surrounded by an aquatic frenzy of underwater life. In the deserts of Sinai's interior, visitors can climb the mount where God had word with Moses, and spend their remaining days in halcyon bliss at coastal Dahab's backpacker Shangri-La.

Though it is one of the more politically stable countries in the region, modern-day Egypt is not without strife. Thirty years of authoritarian rule, an erratic economy and rising living costs fan the flames of social unrest. Still, Egyptians are a resilient lot, and visitors making the journey here will find as much ancient history as they will modern hospitality.

FAST FACTS

- **Area** 997,739 sq km
- **Capital** Cairo
- **Country code** ☎ 20
- **Language** Arabic
- **Money** Egyptian pound (E£); US$1 = E£5.35; €1 = E£8.39
- **Official name** Arab Republic of Egypt
- **Population** 81.7 million

CLIMATE & WHEN TO GO

Egypt's climate is easy to summarise: hot and dry, except for the winter months of December, January and February. Temperatures increase as you travel south and while Alexandria receives the most rain, in Aswan, in the far south, rain is rare.

Summer temperatures range from 31°C on the Mediterranean coast to a scorching 50°C in Aswan. At night in winter, the temperatures sometimes plummet to as low as 8°C, even in the south of the country. In the mountains of Sinai, night-time temperatures in winter can fall well below zero.

June to August is unbearable in Upper Egypt (the area extending south of Cairo to the Sudan), with daytime temperatures soaring to 40°C or more. Summer in Cairo is almost as hot, and the combination of heat, dust, pollution, noise and crowds makes walking the city streets a real test of endurance.

For visiting Upper Egypt, winter is easily the most comfortable time – though hotel rates are at a premium. In Cairo, from December to February skies are often overcast and evenings can be colder than you'd think, while up on the Mediterranean coast, Alexandria is subject to frequent downpours.

The happiest compromise for an all-Egypt trip is to visit in spring (March to May) or autumn (October and November). For more weather details, see Climate Charts, p625.

HISTORY

About 5000 years ago an Egyptian pharaoh named Menes (Narmer) unified Upper and Lower Egypt for the first time. For centuries the fertility and regularity of the annual Nile floods had supported communities along long Nile valley. These small kingdoms eventually coalesced into two important states, one covering the valley, the other consisting of the Delta itself. The unification of these two states in about 3100 BC set the scene for the greatest civilisation of ancient times.

Little is known of the immediate successors of Menes except that, attributed with divine ancestry, they promoted the development of a highly stratified society, patronised the arts and built numerous temples and public works. In the 27th

EGYPT IN...

One Week

Upon arrival in **Cairo** (p124), spend your first day braving the crowds to view the magnificent exhibits at the **Egyptian Museum** (p132). Another whole day could easily be spent wandering Islamic Cairo and the medieval **Khan al-Khalili Bazaar** (p134), where you can hone your haggling skills with gregarious stall owners. Day three is reserved for the seventh wonder of the ancient world, the **Pyramids** (p128). You'll need at least four hours here, and should explore the interior of at least one of these monolithic stone structures. From Cairo, catch the overnight train up the Nile valley to **Aswan** (p167), from where a day visit to the awesome **Abu Simbel** (p174) and a **felucca trip** (p170) are an absolute must. For the remainder of your first week, train it up to **Luxor** (p153) and spend a few days marvelling at the dozens of **tombs and temples** (p155) that remain from the ancient capital Thebes.

Two Weeks

Complete the trip outlined above in your first week and then you will have to make a hard choice between desert adventure or beach-side frolics. Either head off to the **Western Oases** (p175) to see the ancient fortified forts of **Dakhla** (p176), the eerie rock formations of the **White Desert** (p178) and the crystal clear springs of **Siwa** (p179). Be warned that from Siwa it will be a long slog on several buses to get to Taba/Nuweiba for the border crossing to Israel/Jordan. Alternatively, spend your last week in **Sinai** (p189), partying in **Sharm el-Sheikh** (p191), climbing Moses' famed **Mt Sinai** (p198), and diving and chilling in the backpacker nirvana of **Dahab** (p194). From Dahab, it's a short bus ride to the Nuweiba ferry for Jordan, or the land border of Israel at Taba.

Join the Itineraries

Israel and the Palestinian Territories (p248)

century BC, Egypt's pyramids began to materialise. Ruling from nearby Memphis, the Pharaoh Zoser and his chief architect, Imhotep, built what may have been the first, the Step Pyramid at Saqqara.

For the next three dynasties and 500 years (a period called the Old Kingdom), the power of Egypt's pharaohs and the size and scale of their pyramids and temples increased dramatically. The immense dimensions of these buildings served as a reminder of the pharaoh's importance and power over his people. The last three pharaohs of the 4th dynasty, Khufu (Cheops), Khafre (Chephren) and Menkaure (Mycerinus), left their legendary mark by commissioning the three Great Pyramids of Giza.

By the beginning of the 5th dynasty (about 2494–2345 BC), the pharaohs had ceded some of their power to a rising class of nobles. In the following centuries Egypt broke down into several squabbling principalities. The rise of Thebes (Luxor) saw an end to the turmoil, and Egypt was reunited under Montuhotep II, marking the beginning of the Middle Kingdom. For 250 years all was well, but more internal fighting and 100 years of occupation by the Hyksos, invaders from the northeast, cast a shadow over the country.

The New Kingdom, its capital at Thebes and later Memphis, represented a renaissance of art and empire in Pharaonic Egypt. For almost 400 years, from the 18th to the 20th dynasties (1550–1069 BC), Egypt was a formidable power in northeast Africa and the eastern Mediterranean. But by the time Ramses III came to power (1184 BC) as the second pharaoh of the 20th dynasty, disunity had again become the norm. Taking advantage of this, the army of Alexander the Great took control of Egypt in the 4th century BC.

Alexander founded a new capital, Alexandria, on the Mediterranean coast, and for the next 300 years the land of the Nile was ruled by a dynasty established by one of the Macedonian's generals, Ptolemy. Romans followed the Ptolemaic dynasty, and then came Islam and the Arabs, conquering Egypt in AD 640. In due course, rule by the Ottoman Turks and the Europeans followed (the French under Napoleon, then the British) – shifts of power common to much of the Middle East (see p53).

HOW MUCH?

- **Cup of tea** E£2 to E£4
- **Newspaper** E£1
- **One-minute phone call to the UK** E£3.75
- **Internet connection per hour** E£5 to E£10
- **Museum admission** E£40

LONELY PLANET INDEX

- **Litre of petrol** E£1.75
- **Litre of bottled water** E£3
- **Bottle of Stella beer** E£8
- **Souvenir T-shirt** E£35
- **Fuul or ta'amiyya sandwich** E£1

Self-rule was finally restored to the Egyptians as a result of the Revolution of 1952. Colonel Gamal Abdel Nasser, leader of the revolutionary Free Officers, ascended to power and was confirmed as president in elections held in 1956. That same year, ruminants of the colonial yoke were dramatically shaken off in full world view when Nasser successfully faced down Britain, France and Israel over the Suez Canal. Nasser was unsuccessful, however, in the 1967 war with Israel, and died shortly after of heart failure. Anwar Sadat, his successor, also fought Israel, in 1973, a war that paved the way for a peace settlement, culminating in the Camp David Agreement in 1979. In certain quarters, Camp David was viewed as a traitorous abandonment of Nasser's pan-Arabist principles and it ultimately cost Sadat his life at the hands of an assassin in 1981.

Sadat's murderer was a member of Islamic Jihad, an uncompromising terrorist organisation that aimed to establish an Islamic state in Egypt. Mass roundups of Islamists were immediately carried out on the orders of Sadat's successor, Hosni Mubarak, the vice president and a former air force general, who declared a state of emergency when he assumed power that continues to this day.

Mubarak was able to rehabilitate Egypt in the eyes of the Arab world without abandoning the treaty with Israel. For almost a decade, he and his National Democratic

EGYPT

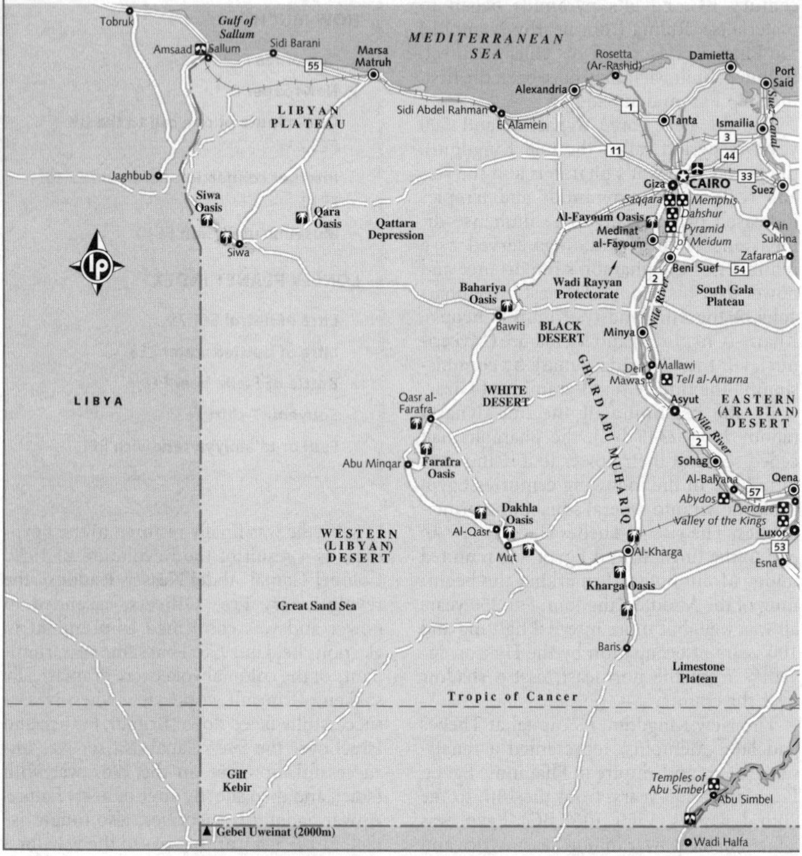

Party (NDP) managed to keep the domestic political situation calm – with the constant presence of the armed forces always in the background. In the 1980s, however, discontent brewed among the poorer sections of society as the country's economic situation worsened. With a repressive political system that allowed little or no chance to legitimately voice opposition, it was almost inevitable that the Islamist opposition would resort to extreme action.

Frequent attempts were made on the life of the president and his ministers, and regular clashes with the security forces occurred. The government responded with a heavy-handed crackdown, arresting thousands and continuing to outlaw the most popular Islamist opposition group, the Muslim Brotherhood. By the mid-1990s, the violence had receded from the capital, retreating to the religious heartland of middle Egypt where, in 1997, members of the Gama'a al-Islamiyya (Islamic Brotherhood) carried out a bloody massacre of 58 holidaymakers at the Funerary Temple of Hatshepsut in Luxor.

The massacre destroyed grassroots support for militant groups and the Muslim Brotherhood declared a ceasefire the following year. Things were relatively quiet until October 2004, when a bomb at Taba, on the border with Israel, killed 34 and signalled the start of increasing social unrest. In early 2005, President Mubarak bowed to growing international pressure and put forth a constitutional amendment aiming to introduce competitive presidential elections that

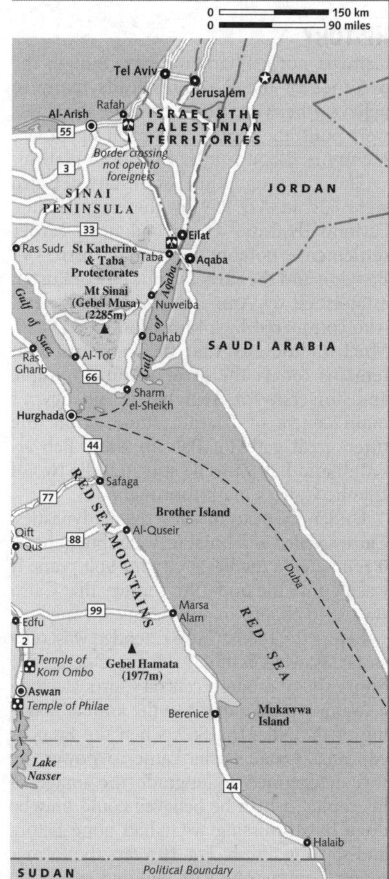

year. Though ostensibly a step in the right direction, many pundits saw it as a charade. Opposition groups such as the Muslim Brotherhood, by now seen by many as the most effective challengers to the incumbent government, were still banned and other independent candidates were required to have the backing of at least 65 members of the NDP-dominated lower house of parliament. When opposition groups loudly voiced their unhappiness, security forces cracked down and threw many leaders in jail on questionable charges. Soon after, the banned Muslim Brotherhood took responsibility for two isolated terrorist incidents aimed at foreign tourists in Cairo. The bombs continued at popular tourist hotspots in Sharm el-Sheikh in 2005 and Dahab in 2006, claiming a total of 122 lives, many of them Egyptian. Several groups claimed responsibility, the dissatisfaction with Egypt's recent entanglement in the Gaza strip adding momentum to extremist factions.

Things didn't change much in the 2008 council elections, when a further 800 members of the Muslim Brotherhood were jailed. Few voters even bothered to turn up – members of the NDP were running uncontested for about 90% of seats. More recently, rising global food inflation has further fanned the flames of social unrest, reaching flashpoint in 2008 during violent clashes over spiralling bread prices. The government raised its already high subsidies for wheat and sent in the army to guarantee supplies, hardly appeasing a populace tired of nearly three decades of life under a state of emergency.

Egypt Today

On the surface, it seems that Egypt's economy has heaved forward in recent years: growth hovers at 7%; record foreign investment floods in from moneyed Arab states; and tourism seems to have rebounded from Sinai's spate of bombings. Unfortunately, the vast majority of Egyptians still live in a grinding poverty that tarnishes any outward signs of success. While the threat of an Islamic uprising seems remote, the deep dissatisfaction with the status quo will continue as long as basic wages keep falling far behind the spiralling costs of staples such as food, fuel and building materials. Ballooning government subsidies for basic goods alleviate some of this shortfall (at the cost of a sizeable budget deficit), though many today feel that more profound changes are needed to take the country forward.

THE CULTURE

With the second-highest population in Africa, Egypt is also the most populous country in the Arab world.

As for the genealogy of present-day Egypt, one Italian traveller summed it up best: 'I look at the Pharaohs, I look at the Egyptians… I just don't see it.' While the blood of ancient Egypt no doubt flows in the veins of Egypt today, centuries of invading Libyans, Persians, Greeks, Romans and Arabs have helped dilute this to a trickle. Traces of independent indigenous groups do survive, most notably the nomadic

Bedouin tribes that settled in Sinai and Egypt's deserts, Berbers around the Oasis of Siwa, and dark-skinned Nubians, originating from the regions south of Aswan that were swallowed up by the High Dam.

With the largest population growth in the Arab world and limited arable land, the strain on Egypt's crumbling infrastructure is an ongoing problem. Signs of social unease have been bubbling to the surface in recent years, provoked by extreme inequality and a general dissatisfaction with the pace of political change.

RELIGION

> 'If you want to move people, you look for a point of sensitivity, and in Egypt nothing moves people as much as religion.'
>
> *Naguib Mahfouz*

About 90% of Egypt's population is Muslim; much of the remainder is Coptic Christian. Most of the time, the two communities happily coexist. While Islam permeates most aspects of Egypt's culture, from laws to mores to social norms, fundamentalist flavours of this religion are still quite rare.

CAIRO القاهرة

☎ 02 / pop 18 million

Upon arrival, the choreographed chaos here hits you like a ton of bricks. It doesn't take long, however, to acclimatise to Cairo's wall of noise, snarl of traffic, cry of hawkers and blanket of smog, and get drawn into the hypnotising charm of this pulsating metropolis. Known to its nearly 20 million residents as *Um ad-Dunya* (Mother of the World), modern Cairo is a hotchpotch of recent growth barely superimposed on a dense bed of history. Wander down to Islamic Cairo and you'll be sucked in through the looking glass to a bygone medieval era. Head out west to Giza's famed pyramids and the time warp sets you back a full 4000 years. Meanwhile, the city's main museum bursts at the seams with the priceless wealth of ancient Egypt's antiquities. But the real allure of Cairo lies somewhere in the quiet moments in between: sipping a sugary *shai* or puffing leisurely on a sheesha while watching the life of the city whirl past as it has for eons.

HISTORY

Cairo is not a Pharaonic city, though the presence of the Pyramids leads many to believe otherwise. At the time the Pyramids were built, the capital of ancient Egypt was Memphis, 22km south of the Giza plateau.

The core foundations of the city of Cairo were laid in AD 969 by the early Islamic Fatimid dynasty. There had been earlier settlements, notably the Roman fortress of Babylon and the early Islamic city of Fustat, established by Amr ibn al-As, the general who conquered Egypt for Islam in AD 640. Much of the city that the Fatimids built remains today: the great Fatimid mosque and university of Al-Azhar is still Egypt's main centre of Islamic study, while the three great gates of Bab an-Nasr, Bab al-Futuh and Bab Zuweila still straddle two of Islamic Cairo's main thoroughfares.

Under the rule of subsequent dynasties, Cairo swelled and burst its walls, but at heart it remained a medieval city for 900 years. It wasn't until the mid-19th century that Cairo started to change in any significant way.

Before the 1860s, Cairo extended west only as far as what is today Midan Opera. The future site of modern central Cairo was then a swampy plain subject to the annual flooding of the Nile. In 1863, when the French-educated Ismail Pasha came to power, he was determined to upgrade the image of his capital, which he believed could only be done by dismissing what had gone before and starting afresh. For 10 years the former marsh became one vast building site as Ismail invited architects from Belgium, France and Italy to design and build a brand-new

PLAYING CHICKEN IN CAIRO

It may sound silly, but the greatest challenge most travellers face when travelling through Egypt is crossing the street in Cairo. Roads are frantically busy and road rules are something that the average Cairene has heard of, but only in jokes. Our advice is to position yourself so that one or more locals form a buffer between you and oncoming traffic, and then cross when they cross – they usually don't mind being used as human shields. Basically, it's a game of chicken. Never, ever hesitate once you've stepped off the footpath; cross as if you own the road. But do it fast.

European-style Cairo beside the old Islamic city. This building boom has continued until the present day, with the city's boundaries constantly expanding into the surrounding desert to support an ever-growing populace.

ORIENTATION

Finding your way around the vast sprawl of Cairo is not as difficult as it may first seem. Midan Tahrir is the centre. Northeast of Tahrir is Downtown, a noisy, busy commercial district centred on Sharia Talaat Harb. This is where you'll find most of the cheap eateries and budget hotels. Midan Ramses, location of the city's main train station, marks the northernmost extent of Downtown.

Heading east, Downtown ends at Midan Ataba and Islamic Cairo takes over. This is the medieval heart of the city, and is still very much alive today. At its centre is the great bazaar of Khan al-Khalili.

Sitting in the middle of the Nile is the island neighbourhood of Zamalek, historically favoured by ruling colonials and still a relatively upmarket enclave with many foreign residents, a few midrange hotels and innumerable restaurants and bars.

The west bank of the Nile is less historical and much more residential than areas along the east bank. The primary districts, north to south, are Mohandiseen, Agouza, Doqqi and Giza, all of which are heavy on concrete and light on charm. Giza covers by far the largest area of the four, stretching some 20km west either side of one long, straight road (Pyramids Rd, also known as Sharia al-Haram) that ends at the foot of the Pyramids.

INFORMATION

Bookshops

American University in Cairo (AUC) bookshop Downtown (Map pp130-1; ☎ 2797 5370; Sharia Mohammed Mahmoud; 9am-6pm Sat-Thu); Zamalek (Map p137; ☎ 2739 7045; 16 Sharia Mohammed Thakeb; 9am-6pm Sat-Thu, 1-6pm Fri) The best English-language bookshop in Egypt, with stacks of material on the politics, sociology and history of Cairo, Egypt and the Middle East. It also has plenty of guidebooks and some fiction. The Zamalek branch is the smaller of the two.

Diwan (Map p137; ☎ 2736 2582; www.diwanegypt.com; 159 Sharia 26th of July, Zamalek; 9am-11pm) A cosy, modern bookshop with English- and French-language books, novels and guidebooks as well as a neat little café.

Lehnert & Landrock (Map pp130-1; ☎ 2392 7606; 44 Sharia Sherif; 9.30am-2pm & 4-7.30pm Mon-Fri, Sat morning) Good selection of books about Cairo and Egypt, as well as second-hand books and vintage postcards and photographs. There's a branch opposite the Egyptian Museum (Map pp130–1).

Emergency

Ambulance (☎ 123)
Fire department (☎ 180)
Police (☎ 122)
Tourist police (☎ 126)
Tourist police office (Map pp130-1; ☎ 2390 6028; Downtown) On the 1st floor of a building in the alley just left of the main tourist office.

Internet Access

Five St@rs Net (Map pp130-1; ☎ 2574 7881; Midan Talaat Haarb; per hr E£5; 8am-1am) Has air-con, does printing and burns CDs. There's another branch near Midan Tahrir (Map pp130-1; Sharia Talaat Harb).

Hany Internet Cafe (Map pp130-1; ☎ 2395 1985; 16 Sharia Abdel Khalek Sarwat, Downtown; per hr E£3; 10am-1am) Near the corner of Sharia Talaat Harb.

Internet Egypt (Map pp130-1; per hr E£10; 9am-midnight) In the basement of the Nile Hilton shopping mall. Students receive a 20% discount.

InterClub (Map pp130-1; ☎ 2579 1860; per hr E£5; 8am-2am) New computers with LCD screens. Near Estoril restaurant.

Zamalek Centre (Map p137; ☎ 2736 4004; Sharia Ismail Mohammed, Zamalek; per hr E£5; 8am-12am) Friendly surfing in Zamalek.

Medical Services

Many of Cairo's hospitals have antiquated equipment and a cavalier attitude to hygiene, but there are some exceptions, including the Ma'adi branch of **As-Salam International Hospital** (Map pp126-7; ☎ 2524 0250, emergency 2524 0077; Corniche el-Nil, Ma'adi).

Pharmacies abound in Cairo and almost anything can be obtained without a prescription. Pharmacies that operate 24 hours and deliver include **Al-Ezaby** (Bulaq ☎ 19600; Arcadia Mall, Corniche el-Nil; Heliopolis ☎ 19600; 1 Sharia Tayseer).

Money

The Banque Misr branches at the Nile Hilton (see Map pp130–1) and Mena House Oberoi (near the Pyramids of Giza; see Map p129) are open 24 hours. Otherwise, there are banks and forex bureaus all over town – forex offices give slightly better rates on cash. There are oodles of ATMs throughout the city.

CAIRO

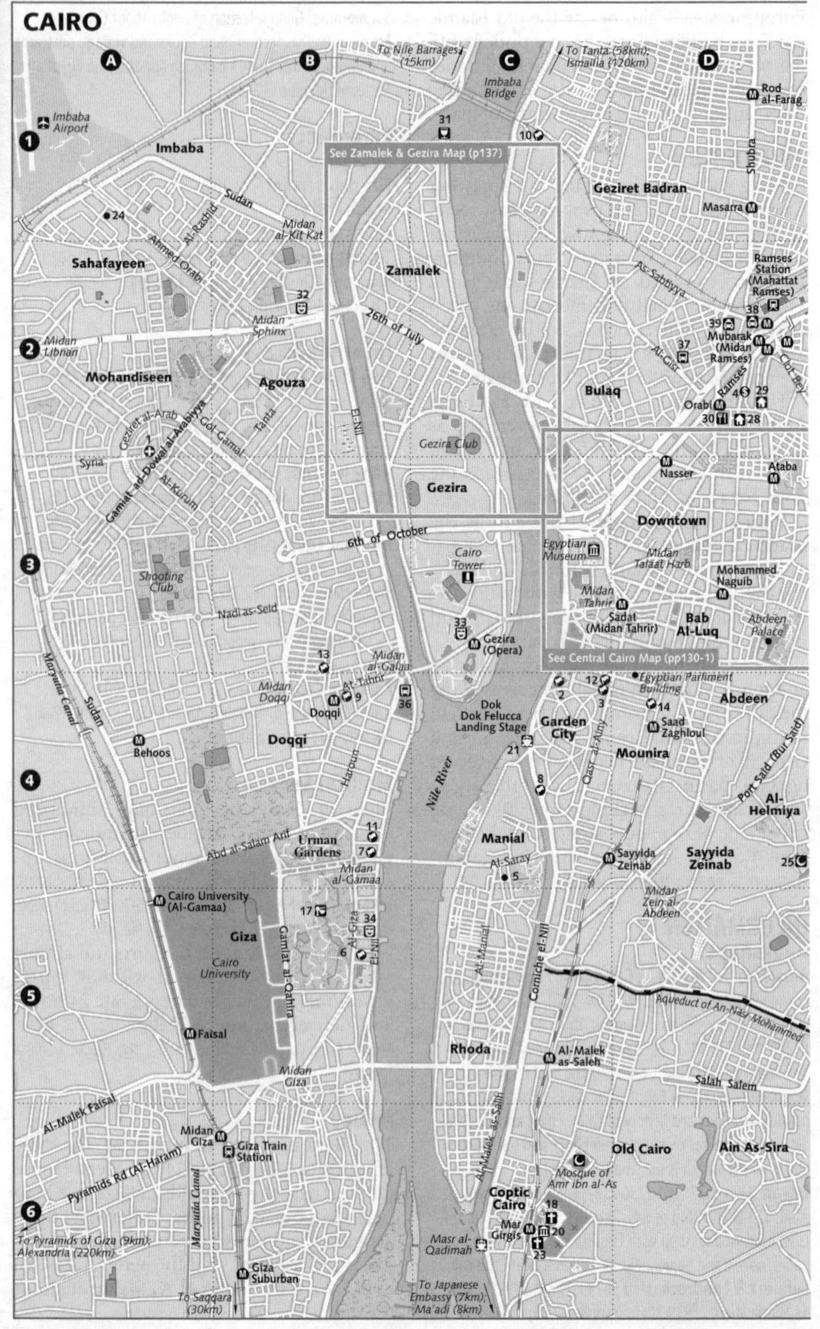

To Nile Barrages (15km)
To Tanta (58km); Ismailia (120km)
Imbaba Bridge
Imbaba Airport
Imbaba
See Zamalek & Gezira Map (p137)
Gezirat Badran
Rod al-Farag
Shubra
Masarra
Sudan
Al-Rashid
Ahmed Orabi
Midan al-Kit Kat
Sahafayeen
Zamalek
As-Sabtiyya
Ramses Station (Mahattat Ramses)
26th of July
Midan Sphinx
Midan Libnan
Mohandiseen
Agouza
Mubarak (Midan Ramses)
Al-Gisr
Ramses
Clot Bey
Bulaq
Orabi
Gezirat al-Arab
Gamiat ad-Dowal al-Arabiyya
Gol Gamal
Tanta
El-Nil
Syria
Al-Kurum
Gezira Club
Gezira
Nasser
Ataba
Downtown
6th of October
Egyptian Museum
Midan Talaat Harb
Cairo Tower
Shooting Club
Mohammed Naguib
Nadi as-Seid
Midan Tahrir
Sadat (Midan Tahrir)
Bab Al-Luq
Abdeen Palace
Gezira (Opera)
See Central Cairo Map (pp130-1)
Midan al-Galaa
Egyptian Parliment Building
At-Tahrir
Midan Doqqi
Doqqi
Dok Dok Felucca Landing Stage
Garden City
Abdeen
Saad Zaghloul
Maryutia Canal
Sudan
Behoos
Doqqi
Mounira
Qasr al-Ainy
Haroun
Nile River
Port Said (Bur Said)
Al-Helmiya
Urman Gardens
Abd al-Salam Arif
Manial
Sayyida Zeinab
Sayyida Zeinab
Al-Saray
Midan al-Gamaa
Cairo University (Al-Gamaa)
Midan Zein al-Abdeen
Giza
Gamiat al-Qahira
Al-Giza
El-Nil
Cairo University
Al-Manial
Corniche el-Nil
Aqueduct of An-Nasr Mohammed
Faisal
Rhoda
Al-Malek as-Saleh
Midan Giza
Salah Salem
Al-Malek Faisal
Midan Giza
Giza Train Station
Old Cairo
Ain As-Sira
Pyramids Rd (Al-Haram)
Mosque of Amr ibn al-As
Al-Malek as-Salih
Coptic Cairo
Maryutia Canal
Mar Girgis
Masr al-Qadimah
To Pyramids of Giza (9km); Alexandria (220km)
Giza Suburban
To Saqqara (30km)
To Japanese Embassy (7km); Ma'adi (8km)

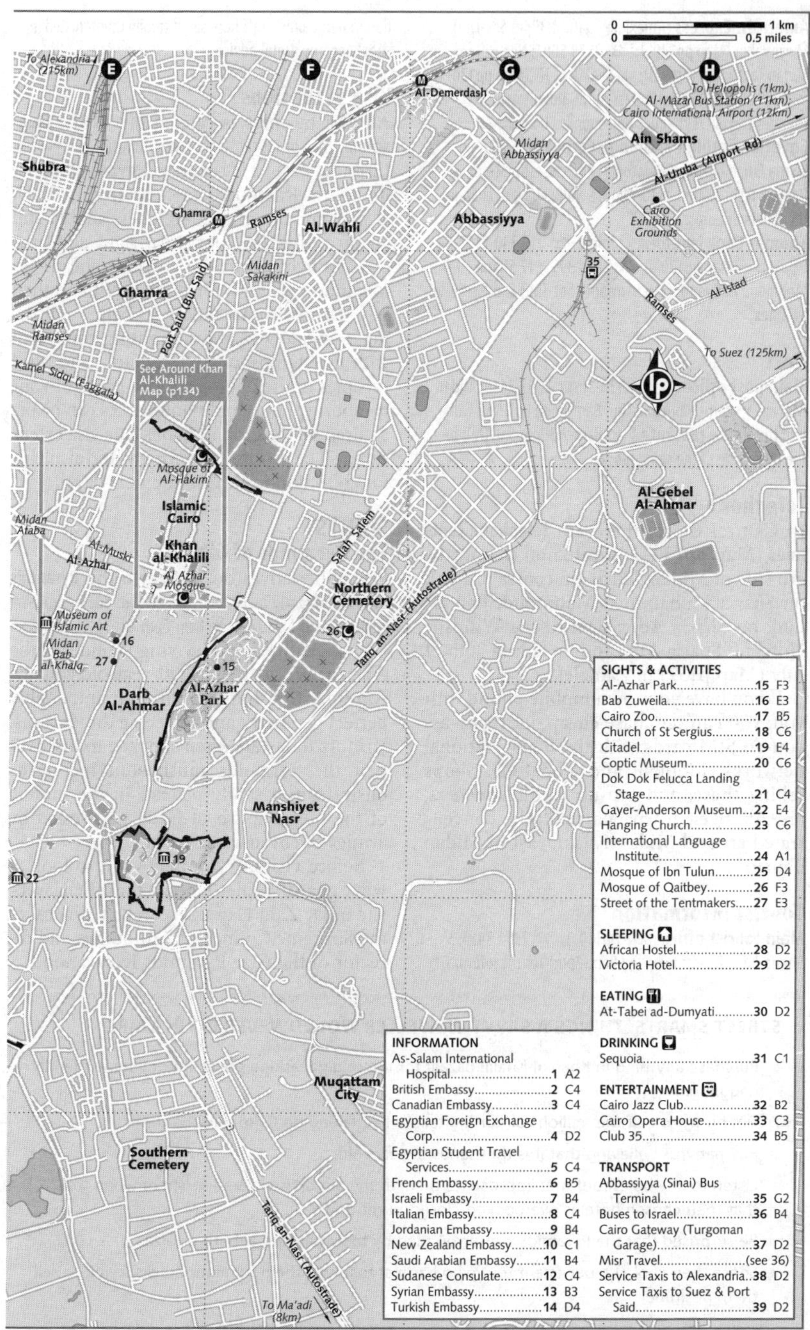
0 1 km
0 0.5 miles
E
F
G
H
To Alexandria (215km)
Al-Demerdash
To Heliopolis (1km); Al-Mazar Bus Station (11km); Cairo International Airport (12km)
Midan Abbassiyya
Ain Shams
Al-Uruba (Airport Rd)
Shubra
Cairo Exhibition Grounds
Ghamra
Ramses
Al-Wahli
Abbassiyya
35
Midan Sakakini
Ghamra
Port Said (Bur Said)
Al-Istad
Ramses
Midan Ramses
To Suez (125km)
Kamel Sidqi (Faggala)
See Around Khan Al-Khalili Map (p134)
Mosque of Al-Hakim
Islamic Cairo
Khan al-Khalili
Al-Gebel Al-Ahmar
Midan Ataba
Al-Muski
Al-Azhar
Salah Salem
Al Azhar Mosque
Northern Cemetery
Tariq an-Nasr (Autostrade)
Museum of Islamic Art
26
Midan Bab al-Khalq
16
27
15
Darb Al-Ahmar
Al-Azhar Park
Manshiyet Nasr
19
22
Muqattam City
Southern Cemetery
Tariq an-Nasr (Autostrade)
To Ma'adi (8km)
SIGHTS & ACTIVITIES
Al-Azhar Park........15 F3
Bab Zuweila........16 E3
Cairo Zoo........17 B5
Church of St Sergius........18 C6
Citadel........19 E4
Coptic Museum........20 C6
Dok Dok Felucca Landing Stage........21 C4
Gayer-Anderson Museum....22 E4
Hanging Church........23 C6
International Language Institute........24 A1
Mosque of Ibn Tulun........25 D4
Mosque of Qaitbey........26 F3
Street of the Tentmakers.....27 E3
SLEEPING
African Hostel........28 D2
Victoria Hotel........29 D2
EATING
At-Tabei ad-Dumyati........30 D2
DRINKING
Sequoia........31 C1
ENTERTAINMENT
Cairo Jazz Club........32 B2
Cairo Opera House........33 C3
Club 35........34 B5
TRANSPORT
Abbassiyya (Sinai) Bus Terminal........35 G2
Buses to Israel........36 B4
Cairo Gateway (Turgoman Garage)........37 D2
Misr Travel........(see 36)
Service Taxis to Alexandria..38 D2
Service Taxis to Suez & Port Said........39 D2
INFORMATION
As-Salam International Hospital........1 A2
British Embassy........2 C4
Canadian Embassy........3 C4
Egyptian Foreign Exchange Corp........4 D2
Egyptian Student Travel Services........5 C4
French Embassy........6 B5
Israeli Embassy........7 B4
Italian Embassy........8 C4
Jordanian Embassy........9 B4
New Zealand Embassy........10 C1
Saudi Arabian Embassy........11 B4
Sudanese Consulate........12 C4
Syrian Embassy........13 B3
Turkish Embassy........14 D4

American Express (Amex; 9am-4.30pm Sat-Thu) Midan Tahrir (Map pp130-1; 2578 5001; Nile Hilton, Midan Tahrir, Downtown); Sharia Qasr el-Nil (Map pp130-1; 2574 7991; 15 Sharia Qasr el-Nil, Downtown) Exchanges travellers cheques and supplies US dollars.
Egyptian Foreign Exchange Corp (Map pp126–7; Sharia Emad ad-Din, Downtown) The closest place to Ramses train station, a 10-minute walk away, to change US dollars or euros.
Thomas Cook (emergency hotline 010 140 1367) Downtown (Map pp130-1; 2574 3955; 17 Sharia Mahmoud Bassiouni; 8am-5pm Sat-Thu) Same services as Amex.

Post

Main post office (Map pp130-1; 2391 2615; Midan Ataba; 8am-10pm Sat-Thu, 8am-noon Fri). You will find the **Poste restante** (8am-2.30pm Sat-Thu) on the other side of the same block.

Telephone

In Central Cairo, there are **Telephone centrales** (Map pp130–1) located on the northern side of Midan Tahrir (in central Cairo); on Sharia Mohammed Mahmoud, Bab al-Luq; on Sharia Adly; next to the Windsor Hotel off Sharia Alfy; and on Sharia 26th of July (Map p137) in Zamalek.

If you have your own mobile phone with you, you can purchase cheap, local pay-as-you-go SIM cards with the major national networks, MobiNil and Vodafone. Shops selling these, and top-up credit vouchers, are all over town, particularly concentrated around Midan Falaki, east of Midan Tahrir.

Tourist Information

Main tourist office (Map pp130-1; 2391 3454; 5 Sharia Adly, Downtown; 9am-7pm) Tourist information in name only; staff here seem totally uninterested in supplying any useful advice.

Visa Extensions

All visa business is carried out at the **Mogamma** (Map pp130-1; Midan Tahrir, Downtown; 8am-1.30pm Sat-Wed), a 14-storey Egypto-Stalinist monolith. Rumoured to close around 2009, at the time of writing foreigners should still go up to the 1st floor, turn right and proceed straight down the corridor ahead. Go to window 12 for a form, fill it out and then buy stamps from window 43 before returning to window 12 and submitting your form with the stamps, one photograph, and photocopies of the photo and visa pages of your passport (photos and photocopies can be organised on the ground floor). The visa extension will be processed overnight and available for collection from 9am the next day.

SIGHTS

The Pyramids of Giza

Few superlatives do justice to the **Pyramids of Giza** (Map p129; tourist office 3383 8823; admission adult/student E£50/25; 8am-6pm Oct-May, 8am-6pm Jun-Sep). As the only surviving Wonder of the Ancient World, these 4000-year-old goliaths continue to astound with their impossibly perfect geometry and towering dimensions. Visitors today are often shocked to discover that the pyramids mushroom incongruously from a sandy plateau in the middle of the busy suburb of Giza, garrisoned by armies of enthusiastic touts.

Before visiting, you may want to look at www.guardians.net/hawass, the official website of Dr Zahi Hawass, secretary general of the Supreme Council of Antiquities and director of the Giza Pyramids Excavation.

STREET SMARTS: THINGS A SAVVY TRAVELLER WOULD NEVER DO IN CAIRO

- Purchase anything in Khan al-Khalili Bazaar for the original asking price without some friendly haggling.
- Get hit by one of the millions of darting taxis while taking on Cairo's insane traffic.
- Buy papyrus believing that it is thousands of years old.
- Listen to any hotel tout that approaches them in the airport/train station/street when told that their chosen hotel is overbooked/closed/burnt down.
- Be surprised that the Pyramids are surrounded by the sprawling suburb of Giza.
- Loose their cool at a persistent tout who has just followed them for eight blocks trying to sell them perfume.

If you're keen to ride around the site on a horse, camel or in a carriage, there are stables encircling the plateau. 'Official' rates are E£35 per hour, less for donkeys, though bargaining is still often required.

There are extra charges for entry to each of the three Pyramids and the solar barque.

GREAT PYRAMID OF KHUFU (CHEOPS)

The oldest pyramid at Giza and the largest in Egypt, the Great Pyramid of Khufu stood 146.5m high when it was completed in around 2600 BC. Although there isn't much to see inside the pyramid, the experience of the steep climb through such an ancient structure is unforgettable, though completely impossible if you suffer from even the tiniest degree of claustrophobia.

Entry to the Great Pyramid costs E£100/50 per adult/student, and tickets are limited to 300 per day – 150 in the morning and 150 in the afternoon. These go on sale at 7.30am and 1pm at the dedicated ticket box north of the pyramid. Queue ahead of time. Cameras are not allowed into the pyramid; you must surrender them to the guards at the entrance, who will ask for baksheesh before returning them.

PYRAMID OF KHAFRE (CHEPHREN)

Southwest of the Great Pyramid, and with almost the same dimensions, is the Pyramid of Khafre. At first it seems larger than that of Khufu, his father, because it stands on higher ground and its peak still has part of the original limestone casing that once covered the entire structure. This pyramid features the substantial remains of **Khafre's funerary temple**, located outside to the east. Entry costs E£25/15 per adult/student and tickets are obtained from the ticket box in front of the pyramid.

PYRAMID OF MENKAURE (MYCERINUS)

At a height of 62m (originally 66.5m), this is the smallest of the three Pyramids. Extensive damage was done to the exterior by a 16th-century caliph who wanted to demolish all the Pyramids, though he gave up after eight months, still far from his goal. Visitors are no longer allowed inside this pyramid as it is closed for restoration.

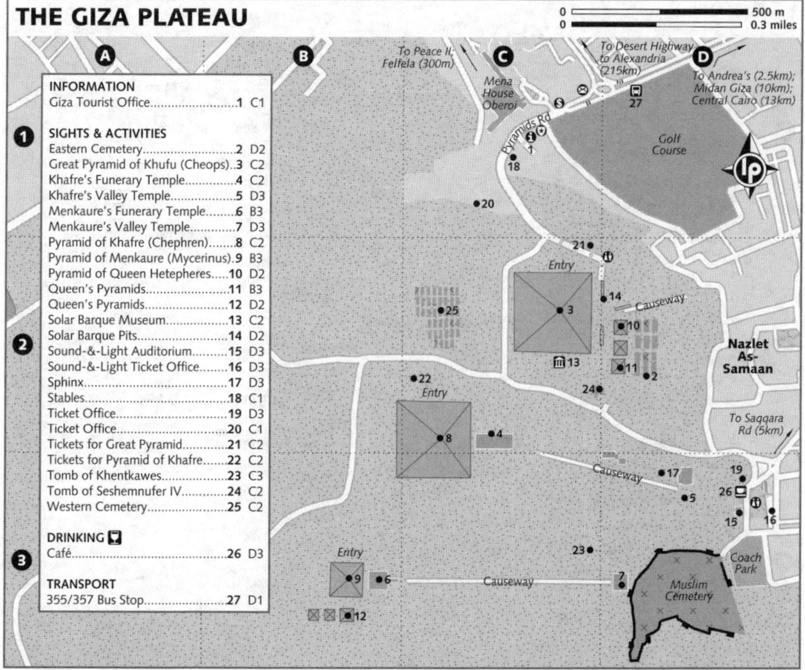

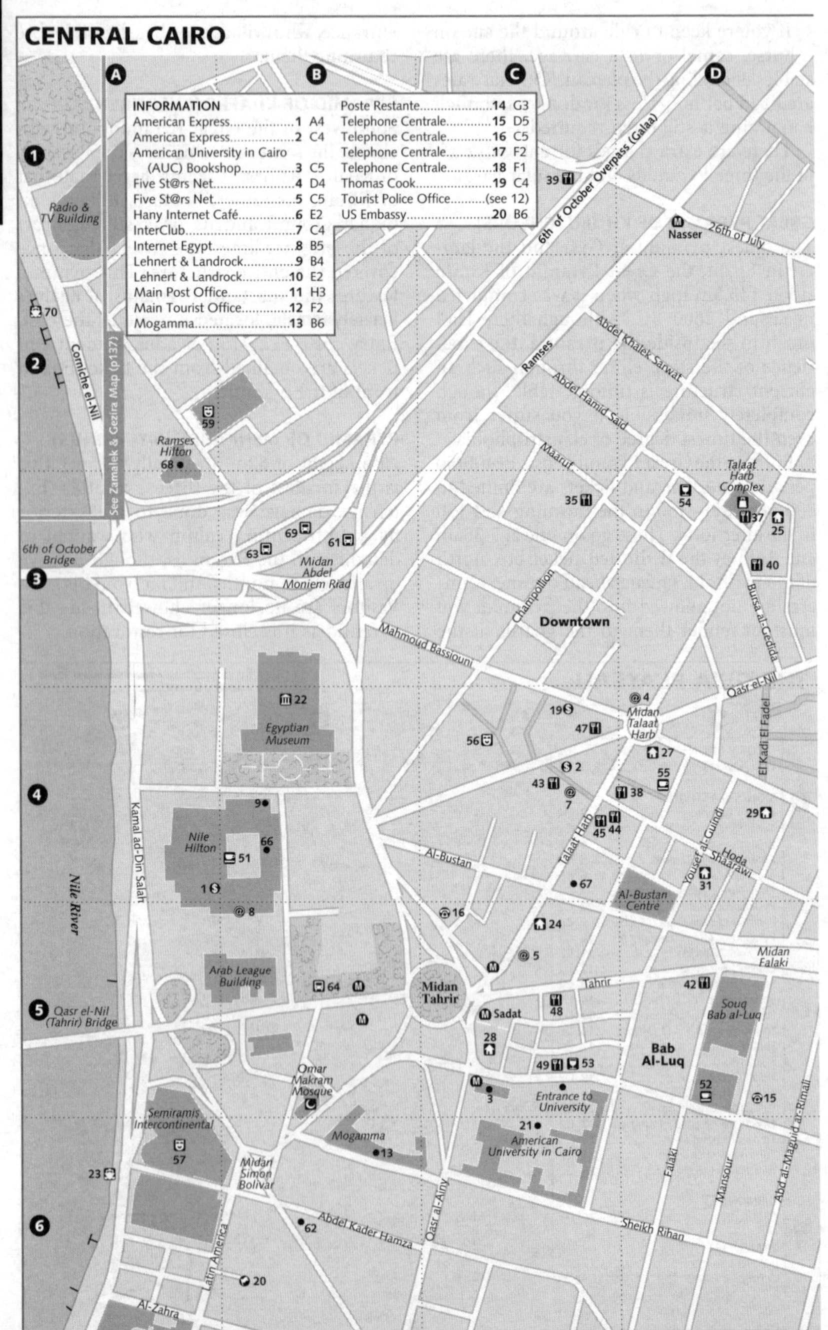

CENTRAL CAIRO
A
B
C
D
1
2
3
4
5
6
INFORMATION
American Express....................1 A4
American Express....................2 C4
American University in Cairo
(AUC) Bookshop....................3 C5
Five St@rs Net....................4 D4
Five St@rs Net....................5 C5
Hany Internet Café....................6 E2
InterClub....................7 C4
Internet Egypt....................8 B5
Lehnert & Landrock....................9 B4
Lehnert & Landrock....................10 E2
Main Post Office....................11 H3
Main Tourist Office....................12 F2
Mogamma....................13 B6
Poste Restante....................14 G3
Telephone Centrale....................15 D5
Telephone Centrale....................16 C5
Telephone Centrale....................17 F2
Telephone Centrale....................18 F1
Thomas Cook....................19 C4
Tourist Police Office....................(see 12)
US Embassy....................20 B6
Radio & TV Building
See Zamalek & Gezira Map (p137)
Corniche el-Nil
6th of October Overpass (Galaa)
Nasser
26th of July
Ramses
Abdel Khalek Sarwat
Abdel Hamid Said
Maaruf
Ramses Hilton
Talaat Harb Complex
6th of October Bridge
Midan Abdel Moniem Riad
Champollion
Downtown
Mahmoud Bassiouni
Bursa al-Gedida
Qasr el-Nil
Egyptian Museum
Midan Talaat Harb
El Kadi El Fadel
Kamal ad-Din Salah
Nile Hilton
Nile River
Talaat Harb
Yousef al-Guindi
Hoda Shaarawi
Al-Bustan
Al-Bustan Centre
Midan Falaki
Arab League Building
Tahrir
Midan Tahrir
Sadat
Souq Bab al-Luq
Qasr el-Nil (Tahrir) Bridge
Bab Al-Luq
Omar Makram Mosque
Entrance to University
Semiramis Intercontinental
Mogamma
American University in Cairo
Midan Simon Bolivar
Qasr al-Ainy
Falaki
Mansour
Abd al-Maguid ar-Rimali
Abdel Kader Hamza
Sheikh Rihan
Latin America
Al-Zahra

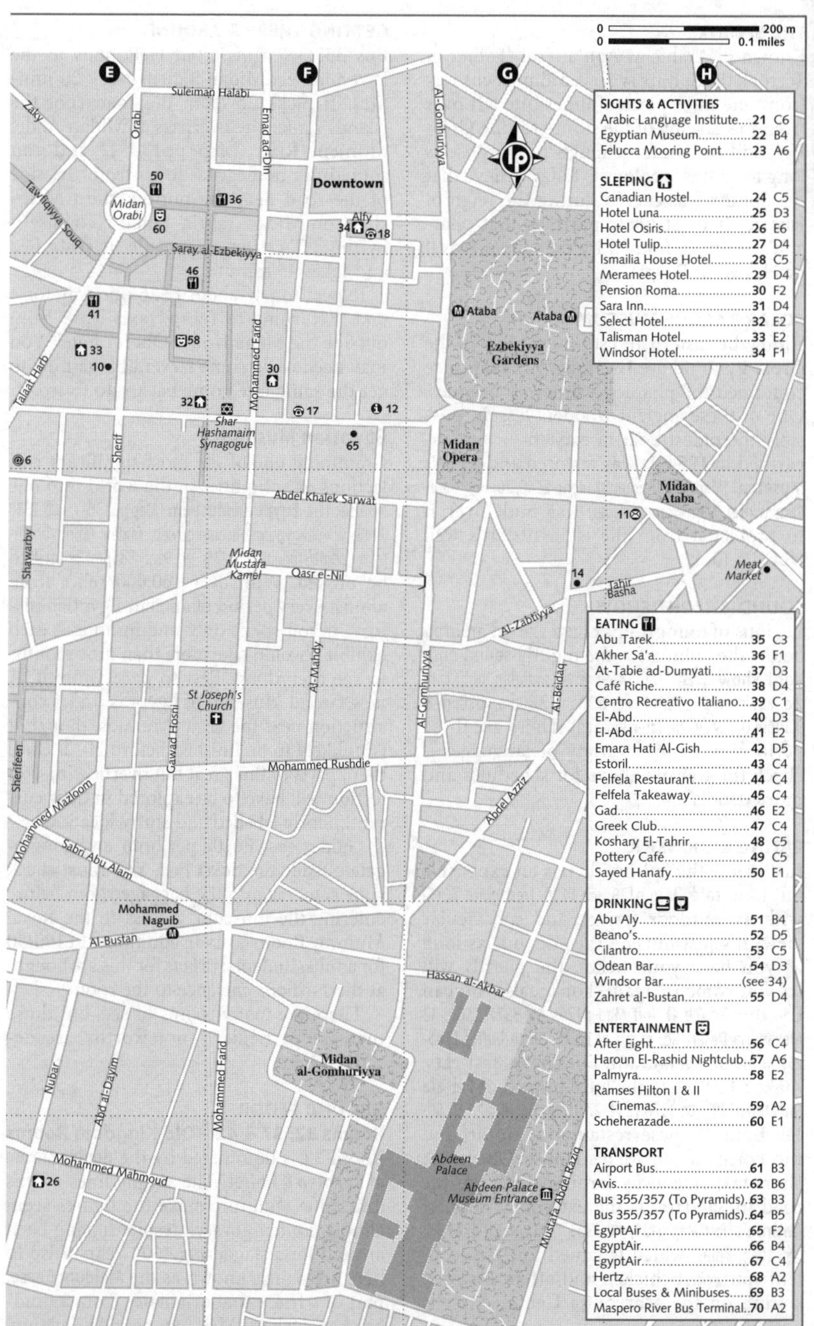
0 200 m
0 0.1 miles
E
F
G
H
SIGHTS & ACTIVITIES
Arabic Language Institute....21 C6
Egyptian Museum...............22 B4
Felucca Mooring Point.........23 A6
SLEEPING
Canadian Hostel..................24 C5
Hotel Luna.........................25 D3
Hotel Osiris........................26 E6
Hotel Tulip..........................27 D4
Ismailia House Hotel...........28 C5
Meramees Hotel..................29 D4
Pension Roma.....................30 F2
Sara Inn..............................31 D4
Select Hotel.........................32 E2
Talisman Hotel.....................33 E2
Windsor Hotel......................34 F1
EATING
Abu Tarek............................35 C3
Akher Sa'a...........................36 F1
At-Tabie ad-Dumyati............37 D3
Café Riche...........................38 D4
Centro Recreativo Italiano....39 C1
El-Abd.................................40 D3
El-Abd.................................41 E2
Emara Hati Al-Gish..............42 D5
Estoril.................................43 C4
Felfela Restaurant...............44 C4
Felfela Takeaway.................45 C4
Gad....................................46 E2
Greek Club..........................47 C4
Koshary El-Tahrir.................48 C5
Pottery Café........................49 C5
Sayed Hanafy......................50 E1
DRINKING
Abu Aly...............................51 B4
Beano's...............................52 D5
Cilantro...............................53 C5
Odean Bar...........................54 D3
Windsor Bar.....................(see 34)
Zahret al-Bustan..................55 D4
ENTERTAINMENT
After Eight...........................56 C4
Haroun El-Rashid Nightclub..57 A6
Palmyra...............................58 E2
Ramses Hilton I & II
Cinemas..............................59 A2
Scheherazade......................60 E1
TRANSPORT
Airport Bus..........................61 B3
Avis....................................62 B6
Bus 355/357 (To Pyramids)..63 B3
Bus 355/357 (To Pyramids)..64 B5
EgyptAir..............................65 F2
EgyptAir..............................66 B4
EgyptAir..............................67 C4
Hertz...................................68 A2
Local Buses & Minibuses......69 B3
Maspero River Bus Terminal..70 A2
Suleiman Halabi
Zaky
Orabi
Emad ad-Din
Al-Gomhuriyya
Downtown
Tawfiqiyya Souq
Midan Orabi
Alfy
Saray al-Ezbekiyya
Ataba
Ezbekiyya Gardens
Talaat Harb
Mohammed Farid
Shar Hashamaim Synagogue
Sherif
Midan Opera
Midan Ataba
Abdel Khalek Sarwat
Shawarby
Midan Mustafa Kamel
Qasr el-Nil
Meat Market
Tahir Basha
Al-Zabtiyya
Al-Mahdy
St Joseph's Church
Al-Beidaq
Gawad Hosni
Sherifeen
Mohammed Rushdie
Mohammed Mazloom
Abdel Azziz
Sabri Abu Alam
Mohammed Naguib
Al-Bustan
Hassan al-Akbar
Midan al-Gomhuriyya
Nubar
Abd at-Dayim
Mohammed Mahmoud
Abdeen Palace
Abdeen Palace Museum Entrance
Mustafa Abdel Raziq

THE SPHINX

Known in Arabic as Abu al-Hol (Father of Terror), the Sphinx is carved almost entirely from one huge piece of limestone left over from the carving of the stones for the Great Pyramid of Khufu. Though its purpose is long forgotten, geologists today believe that the Sphinx was carved during the reign of Kharfe. It most likely portrays that pharaoh's features, framed by the *nemes* (royal headdress of Egypt).

SOLAR BARQUE MUSEUM

Along the eastern and southern sides of the Great Pyramid are five long pits that once contained the pharaoh's funerary barques. One of these ancient wooden vessels, possibly the oldest boat in existence, was unearthed in 1954. It was restored and a glass **museum** (Map p129; adult/student E£40/20; 9am-4pm winter, 9am-5pm summer) was built over it to protect it from the elements. It's well worth a look.

SOUND-&-LIGHT SHOW

Legions of tour groups converge on an area below the Sphinx for the nightly **sound-and-light show** (3386 3469; www.soundandlight.com.eg; adult/child E£75/44; 6.30pm, 7.30pm, 8.30pm & 9.30pm Oct-May, 2hr later Jun-Sep). There are three performances in a variety of languages – check the website above for schedules and more details.

EATING & DRINKING

Just below the Sphinx there's an expensive outdoor **café** (Map p129; tea E£10, fresh juice E£15) with an outdoor terrace and spectacular view. It's just outside the site, but as long as you have your ticket, the guards will let you come in again. For meals, you can try the **Peace II** (off Map p129; 3377 7500; 13 Alexandria Desert Rd; meals E£12-75, lunch buffet E£35-75) seafood restaurant. For cheap, fast eats, make a beeline to the local branch of **Felfela** (off Map p129; 3376 1234; 27 Desert Rd; meals E£1.50-10). Both of these restaurants are around the corner from Mena House Oberoi. A short taxi ride away (around E£7), on the road to Saqqara, is the extremely popular **Andrea's** (off Map p129; 3383 1183; mains E£15-25; 10am-8pm), which is famed for its succulent spit-roast chicken and offers a garden setting on the Maryoutia Canal. A Stella costs E£20.

GETTING THERE & AROUND

Bus 355/357 runs from Heliopolis to the Pyramids via Midan Tahrir every 20 minutes. It picks up from the road (not the island) under the overpass at Midan Abdel Moniem Riad (Map pp130–1) and can sometimes be flagged down from the side of the road near the northwestern Metro stairs on Midan Tahrir. You'll recognise it by the 'CTA' sign on its side. It costs E£2 and takes 45 minutes.

Expect to pay about E£25 one way for a taxi. Returning to Cairo, taxis leave from outside the Mena House Oberoi hotel. You may need to do some fervent bargaining to get the same fare going back into Cairo.

Egyptian Museum

Cramming one of the most significant collections of antiquities in the world into one space, the **Egyptian Museum** (Map pp130-1; 2578 2448; www.egyptianmuseum.gov.eg; Midan Tahrir, Downtown; adult/student E£50/25; 9am-6.45pm) is not to be missed. With over 100,000 relics from almost every period of ancient Egyptian history, if you spent only one minute at each exhibit it would take more than nine months to see everything. Best to pace yourself. A new Grand Museum of Egypt is under construction near the Giza pyramids, though it is unlikely to be finished before 2012. Until then, parts of this great but overflowing collection will have to be explored in their current, poorly labelled and stuffy location.

Guides cost E£100 per hour and congregate outside the ticket box. You must check your cameras into the baggage room before entering the museum. Access to the Royal Mummy Room costs an additional E£100/50 for adults/students; tickets for this are bought at the 1st-floor entrance to the room.

There are many rooms to see, but those that are particularly noteworthy are described here.

GROUND FLOOR

Rooms 32, 37 & 42 – Old Kingdom Rooms

Room 32 is dominated by the **double statue of Rahotep & Nofret**. The simple lines of this limestone sculpture make the figures seem almost contemporary, despite having been around for a staggering 4600 years. Also in here are panels known as the **Meidum Geese**, part of a frieze that originates from a mud-brick mastaba at Meidum, near Al-Fayoum.

Room 37 contains the **tomb of Queen Hetepheres**, mother of Khufu, builder of the Great Pyramid at Giza. Room 42 holds what some consider to be the museum's masterpiece – a larger-than-life-size **statue of Khafre (Chephren)**, builder of the second Pyramid at Giza.

Room 3 – Amarna Room

This room is devoted to **Akhenaten** (1352–1336 BC), the 'heretic pharaoh' who set up ancient Egypt's first and last monotheistic faith. Compare the bulbous bellies, hips and thighs, and the elongated heads and thick, Mick Jagger–like lips of these statues with the sleek, hard-edged norm of typical Pharaonic sculpture. Also very striking is the delicate, but unfinished, **head of Nefertiti**, Akhenaten's wife.

1ST FLOOR

Room 2 – Royal Tombs of Tanis

This is a glittering collection of gold- and silver-encrusted amulets, gold funerary masks, daggers, bracelets, collars, gold sandals, and finger and toe coverings from five intact New Kingdom tombs found at the Delta site of Tanis.

Rooms 3, 7 & 8 – Tutankhamun Galleries

The exhibit that outshines everything else in the museum is without doubt the treasure of this young and comparatively insignificant pharaoh, who ruled for only nine years. About 1700 items are spread throughout a series of rooms. Room 3 contains an astonishing **death mask** made of solid gold, while rooms 7 and 8 house the four **gilded shrines** that fitted inside each other and held the gold sarcophagus of Tutankhamun at their centre.

Room 56 – Royal Mummy Room

This darkened and somewhat ghoulish gallery houses the bodies of 11 of Egypt's most illustrious pharaohs and queens, who ruled Egypt between 1552 and 1069 BC, including **Ramses II**. There's a separate mummy room you can enter on the same ticket, off room 46 across the building, where you can see the chickenpox-scarred remains of **Ramses V**.

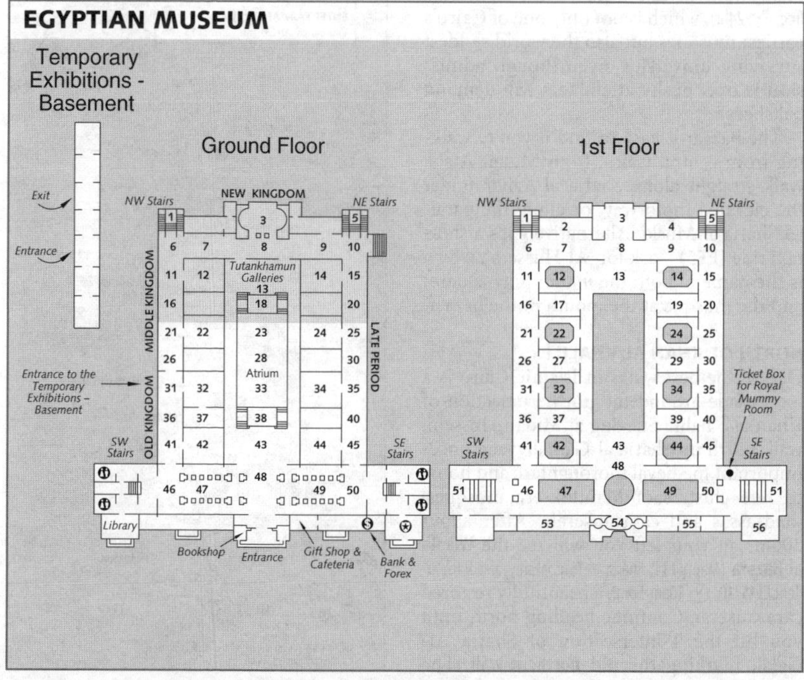

Islamic Cairo مصر الاسلامية

KHAN AL-KHALILI BAZAAR

The best place to start exploring this ancient part of the city is in the medieval cacophony of the great bazaar, **Khan al-Khalili** (Map p134). Here, a Byzantine maze of alleys meander their way past archaic gates, packed with shopkeepers selling everything from antiques to gaudy trinkets to pungent spices and everyday household wares. Note that bargaining is required, and expected, in most of the tourist-oriented shops.

After wandering around the bazaar and fending its eager touts, there's nothing better than sheltering for a while in **Khan el-Khalili Restaurant & Mahfouz Coffee Shop** (Map p134; ☎ 2590 3788; 5 Sharia Sikket el-Badistan; snacks E£13-23, mains E£35-60; ⏲ 10am-2am; ❄), a quiet space with a luxurious Moorish-style interior. Perfect for a tea (E£10) or Stella (E£8) and a sheesha (E£9), it's also good (but pricey) for snacks and meals. See p141 for details of the bazaar's most famous and atmospheric coffeehouse, Fishawi's.

While you're here, it's worth taking time out to visit one of Cairo's most historic institutions, **Al-Azhar Mosque** (Map p134; admission free; ⏲ 24hr), which is not only one of Cairo's earliest mosques but also the world's oldest surviving university. Even though admission is free, pushy attendants will demand baksheesh.

The bazaar is easy to find if you're walking from central Cairo: from Midan Ataba walk straight along Sharia al-Azhar under the elevated motorway, or along the parallel Sharia al-Muski. Alternatively it's a short taxi ride (E£5) – ask for 'Al-Hussein', which is the name of both the *midan* (city square) and the mosque at the mouth of the bazaar.

NORTH OF KHAN AL-KHALILI

One of the best walks in Islamic Cairo is a loop made around the northern section of Khan al-Khalili. Starting at Midan Hussein, walk north up Sharia al-Gamaliyya, a once-important medieval thoroughfare and home to fine clusters of Mamluk-era mosques, madrassas and caravanserais. After about 300m, on your left you will see the **Wikala al-Bazara** (Map p134; Sharia al-Tombakshiyya; adult/student E£15/10; ⏲ 10am-5pm), a beautifully restored caravanserai. Continue heading north until you hit the T-intersection of Sharia Al-Galal, marking the old **northern wall**. The recently restored ancient gates here include the square-towered **Bab an-Nasr** (Gate of Victory; Map p134) and the rounded **Bab al-Futuh** (Gate of Conquests; Map p134), built in 1087 as the two main northern entrances to the new walled Fatimid city of Al-Qahira. Passing through Bab al-Futuh and heading south again, you can return to the bazaar via

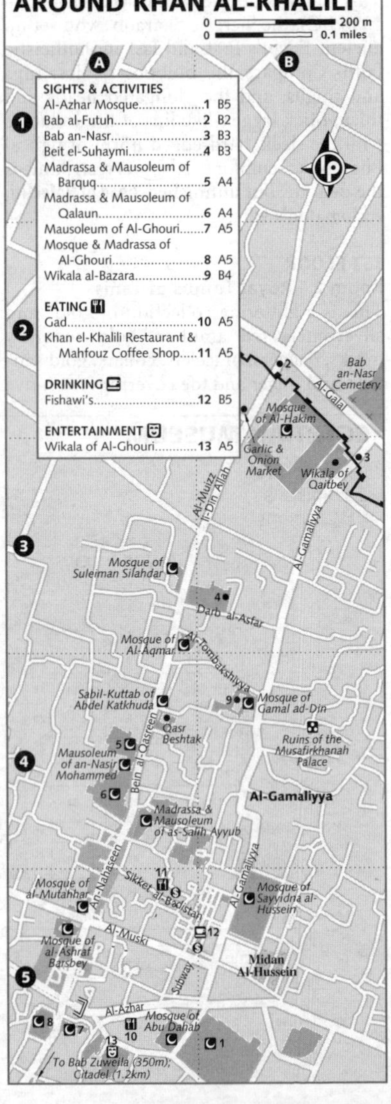

CITY OF A THOUSAND MINARETS

Anyone who has stood on a Cairo rooftop, or woken to a thousand calls to prayer, will tell you that Cairo has been justifiably nicknamed 'Madeenet el alf Midhana' – the city of a thousand minarets. The first minarets of Cairo were built at the corners of its first mosque, the mosque of 'Amr, commissioned by the caliph Mu'awiya in 673 AD. While these no longer exist, mosques and minarets were added by the successive Fatimid, Mamluk and Ottoman rulers until the skyline was filled to the brim with Cairo's landmark spires.

Sharia al-Muizz li-Din Allah. Don't miss the spectacular **Beit el-Suhaymi** (Map p134; Darb al-Asfar; adult/student E£25/15; 9am-5pm), an extensively restored complex of three houses. You'll find it tucked down a small alley on your left. This part of Islamic Cairo is also home to the city's most historic and architecturally significant madrassas, including the **Madrassa & Mausoleum of Barquq** (Map p134; baksheesh requested; 6am-9pm) and the **Madrassa & Mausoleum of Qalaun** (Map p134), which at the time of research remained closed for restoration.

EAST OF KHAN AL-KHALILI

If you walk east from Midan Al-Hussein along Sharia al-Azhar and bear right after breasting the top of the hill, walking under the overpass and straight on, you'll come to the fascinating **Northern Cemetery** (commonly known as the 'City of the Dead,' home to the splendid **Mosque of Qaitbey** (Map pp126–7).

SOUTH OF KHAN AL-KHALILI

On the other side of Sharia Al-Muski, a busy market street runs due south down past the **Mausoleum of Al-Ghouri** (Map p134; closed for renovation at the time of research) and the exquisite **Mosque & Madrassa of Al-Ghouri** (Map p134; admission free) to the twin minarets of **Bab Zuweila** (Map pp126-7; adult/student E£10/5; 9am-5pm), the sole surviving gate from the old city's southern wall. The view from the minarets is about the best in Cairo. Continuing south from Bab Zuweila, you pass through the **Street of the Tentmakers** (Map pp126–7), a covered bazaar filled by craftsmen specialising in appliqué work.

Commenced by Saladin (Salah ad-Din al-Ayyoub) back in the 12th century, the **Citadel** (Map pp126-7; 2512 1735; Midan al-Qala'a, Al-Helmiya; adult/student E£40/20; 8am-5pm Oct-May, 8am-6pm Jun-Sep) is one of the city's busiest tourist attractions – but we're not quite sure why. Its walls encircle an assortment of three very different and not terribly impressive mosques, and several palaces housing some fairly indifferent museums. The best part of any visit is marvelling at the view from the two terraces; on a clear day you can see all the way to the Pyramids of Giza.

Don't miss the **Mosque of ibn Tulun** (Beit al-Kritliyya, Al-Helmiya; Map pp126-7; Sharia ibn Tulun; admission free; 8am-6pm), 800m southwest of the Citadel. It's quite unlike any other mosque in Cairo, mainly because the inspiration is almost entirely Iraqi – the closest things to it are the ancient mosques of Samarra. Right next door to Ibn Tulun is the **Gayer-Anderson Museum** (Map pp126-7; 2364 7822; Sharia ibn Tulun, Al-Helmiya; adult/student E£30/15, video E£20; 8am-4pm), two 16th-century houses restored and furnished by a British major between 1935 and 1942. It's well worth a visit.

Old Cairo مصر القاديمة

Once known as Babylon, this part of Cairo predates the coming of Islam and remains the seat of the Coptic Christian community. You can visit the **Coptic Museum** (Map pp126-7; 2363 9742; www.copticmuseum.gov.eg; Sharia Mar Girgis, Coptic Cairo; adult/student E£40/20; 9am-4pm), with its mosaics, manuscripts, tapestries and Christian artwork, and **Hanging Church** (Kineeset al-Muallaqa; Map pp126-7; Sharia Mar Girgis, Coptic Cairo; admission free; mass 8-11am Fri, 7-10am Sun), which is the centre of Coptic worship. Among the other churches and monasteries here, the **Church of St Sergius** (Map pp126-7; Sharia Mar Girgis, Coptic Cairo; admission free; 8am-4pm) is supposed to mark one of the resting places of the Holy Family on its flight from King Herod.

The easiest way to get here from Midan Tahrir is by Metro (E£1) – get out at the Mar Girgis station.

ACTIVITIES

Cruising along the Nile on a traditional sail boat can be the perfect way to spend an afternoon. You can hire **feluccas** for about E£30 per hour from the mooring point by the Semiramis Intercontinental, on the Corniche. However, the best place to hire feluccas is about 800m to the south at the **Dok Dok felucca landing stage** (Map pp126–7), just short of the bridge over to Le Meridien hotel.

CAIRO FOR CHILDREN

There is plenty to keep children entertained in Cairo. If the **Pyramids** (p128) and **Egyptian Museum** (p132) aren't enough to keep them happy, they can feed the animals (25pt per feeding) at the **Cairo Zoo** (Guineenat al-Haywanet; Map pp126-7; ☎ 3570 8895; Midan al-Gamaa, Giza; admission 25pt; 9am-4pm); pretend to be a pirate on a **felucca ride** (p135); or investigate the manicured **Al-Azhar Park** (Map pp126-7; 10am-10pm), home to one of the few children's playgrounds in the city. For slightly older kids, **Fun Planet** (Map p137; Arkadia Mall, Corniche el-Nil, Bulaq; 3 games E£10; 3-11pm Sat-Thu & 1-11pm Fri) is an indoor amusement centre offering oodles of rides and loud games.

TOURS

Myriad companies and individuals offer tours of sights within and around Cairo. We often recommend Salah Muhammad's **Noga Tours** (☎ 2205 7908, 012 313 8446; www.first24hours.com), as he employs knowledgeable English-speaking guides, Egyptologists and drivers, and has properly maintained vehicles. To give you an idea of tour costs, Noga tours charges US$25 plus entry fees per person for a full-day trip to the Giza Pyramids, Memphis and Saqqara. Its half-day tour of Dahshur costs US$20. Places like the Canadian Hostel charge around E£150 per car for a Pyramids, Memphis and Saqqara trip.

If you're keen to explore at your own pace and wish to hire a car and driver for the day, reliable **Khaled Ibrahim** (☎ 0103 437 981) is an ex-taxi driver who runs a fleet of comfortable cars with drivers. Rates start at around E£25 per hour.

SLEEPING

Budget

Inexpensive hostels, hotels and pensions are concentrated in Downtown, mainly on the upper floors of buildings on and around Sharia Talaat Harb. All tend to be very hot in summer and have at least a few rooms facing the busy street – request a rear room if you're a light sleeper. All include a rudimentary breakfast.

Ismailia House Hotel (Map pp130-1; ☎ 2796 3122; www.ismailiahousehotel.com; 8th fl, 1 Midan Tahrir, Downtown; dm E£16-17, s/d E£140-160, s/d without bathroom E£55/90;) As any real-estate agent will tell you: location, location, location. Yes, the older rooms here verge on the dingy, and yes, the fancier rooms are hardly glamour incarnate, but one look at the strategic view over the *midan* and the Nile and you'll be sold. Be sure to ask for a front-facing room to get the most out of this place.

Meramees Hotel (Map pp130-1; ☎ 2396 2318; 32 Sharia Sabri Abu'Alam, Downtown; d E£120, dm/s/d without bathroom E£35/60/100) It's been around for a while, but the Meramees clings to its original standards of cleanliness and comfort. Most rooms share bathrooms and come with fans – the downstairs singles are particularly nice. There's free use of the kitchen, free tea and coffee, and free airport pick-ups for guests staying three or more nights. One LP reader raved about the service as 'always eager to solve every problem and respond to every question'.

Sara Inn (Map pp130-1; ☎ 2392 2940; www.sarainnhostel.com; 7th fl, 21 Sharia Yousef al-Guindi, Downtown; dm E£40, s/d with air-con E£120/140, s/d without bathroom E£60/80;) If your grandma had an Egyptian trinket fetish and decided to open a hotel – this would be it. With low ceilings brightly decked out in Bedouin tarps and cushions aplenty, the cosy Sara Inn lies cocooned in a blanket of hush. There are rooms for most budgets here, though the shared showers can be in high demand.

African Hostel (Map pp126-7; ☎ 2591 1744; africanhousehotel@hotmail.com; 15 Emad El-Din, Downtown; s/d US$15/19, without bathroom US$10/15;) While the approach to this 19th-century building borders on the post-apocalyptic, the cheerily painted walls of the African Hostel subscribe to the 'exploding crayon' school of interior design. The rooms are basic and make the necessary concessions to hygiene, but the big appeal here is the quiet location (away from the hubbub of downtown) and a laid-back, backpackery vibe.

Pension Roma (Map pp130-1; ☎ 2391 1088; http://pensionroma@pensionroma.com.eg; 4th fl, 169 Sharia Mohammed Farid, Downtown; d/tr E£110/140, s/d/tr without bathroom E£50/82/120) We doff our hats to the Roma: this French-Egyptian run veteran of the budget scene is a bastion of simple sophistication. The Cairo-of-yesteryear rooms are fastidiously maintained and the atmosphere is friendly and intimate – free wi-fi seems to be about the only concession to the 21st century. Particularly popular

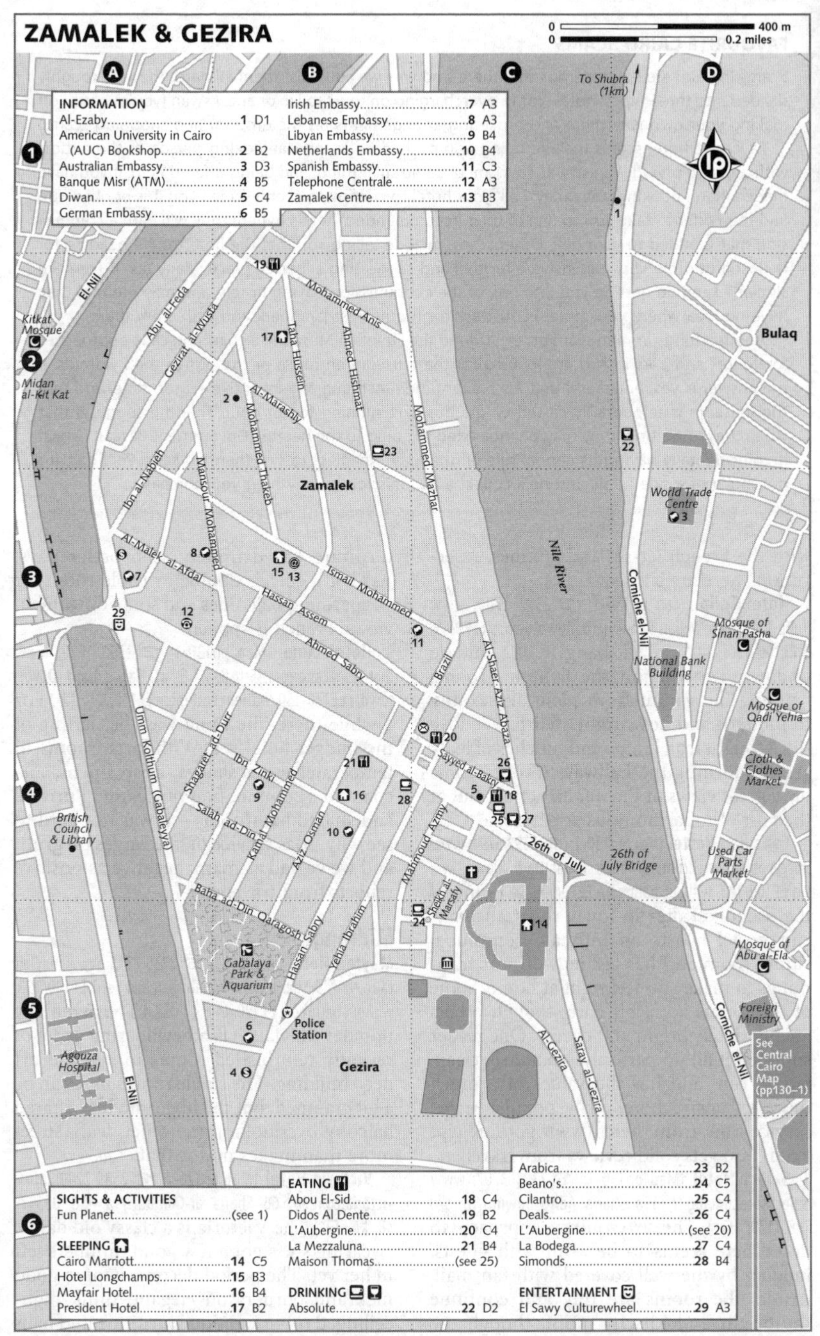
ZAMALEK & GEZIRA
0 400 m
0 0.2 miles
INFORMATION
Al-Ezaby....1 D1
American University in Cairo (AUC) Bookshop....2 B2
Australian Embassy....3 D3
Banque Misr (ATM)....4 B5
Diwan....5 C4
German Embassy....6 B5
Irish Embassy....7 A3
Lebanese Embassy....8 A3
Libyan Embassy....9 B4
Netherlands Embassy....10 B4
Spanish Embassy....11 C3
Telephone Centrale....12 A3
Zamalek Centre....13 B3
To Shubra (1km)
Kitkat Mosque
Midan al-Kit Kat
El-Nil
Abu al-Feda
Gezirat al-Wusta
Mohammed Anis
Taha Hussein
Ahmed Hishmat
Mohammed Mazhar
Al-Marashly
Mohammed Thakeb
Mansour Mohammed
Ibn al-Nabieh
Zamalek
Bulaq
World Trade Centre
Nile River
Corniche el-Nil
Al-Malek al-Afdal
Ismail Mohammed
Hassan Assem
Ahmed Sabry
Brazil
Al-Shaer Aziz Abaza
Mosque of Sinan Pasha
National Bank Building
Mosque of Qadi Yehia
Cloth & Clothes Market
Umm Kolthum (Gabaleyya)
Shagaret ad-Durr
Ibn Zinki
Kamal Mohammed
Salah ad-Din
Aziz Osman
Sayyed al-Bakry
Mahmoud Azmy
26th of July
26th of July Bridge
Used Car Parts Market
British Council & Library
Baha ad-Din Qaragosh
Hassan Sabry
Yehia Ibrahim
Sheikh al-Marsafy
Gabalaya Park & Aquarium
Mosque of Abu al-Ela
Police Station
Foreign Ministry
Agouza Hospital
Gezira
Al-Gezira
Saray al-Gezira
See Central Cairo Map (pp130–1)
SIGHTS & ACTIVITIES
Fun Planet....(see 1)
SLEEPING
Cairo Marriott....14 C5
Hotel Longchamps....15 B3
Mayfair Hotel....16 B4
President Hotel....17 B2
EATING
Abou El-Sid....18 C4
Didos Al Dente....19 B2
L'Aubergine....20 C4
La Mezzaluna....21 B4
Maison Thomas....(see 25)
DRINKING
Absolute....22 D2
Arabica....23 B2
Beano's....24 C5
Cilantro....25 C4
Deals....26 C4
L'Aubergine....(see 20)
La Bodega....27 C4
Simonds....28 B4
ENTERTAINMENT
El Sawy Culturewheel....29 A3

FAVOURITE CAIRO SCAMS

Scams in Cairo are so numerous that there's no way we could list them all here. They are roughly divided into three types: hotel scams, overcharging on tours to Luxor and Aswan (you're better off making your own way there and brokering arrangements on the ground) and shopping scams.

Favourite hotel scams include being approached by an official-looking person at the airport with a badge saying 'Ministry of Tourism' or some such thing, and being offered help. If you have made a hotel booking, they may 'call' your hotel to confirm this, only to tell you it is booked out, and then offer to take you to one of their 'recommended' hotels (where they will earn a commission that is added to your bill). Other scams include telling you that the hotel you're heading for is closed/horrible/very expensive/a brothel and suggesting a 'better' place. Many taxi drivers are similarly keen on getting you into one of their commission-paying hotels, and may pretend they have no idea where your hotel is. Just ask for the nearest landmark and walk from there.

Another long-running scam occurs around the Egyptian Museum: a charming chap approaches foreigners and asks if they are looking for the museum entrance or the bus to the Pyramids. If the answer is yes, he asserts that it's prayer time/lunchtime/any-inventive-reason time, and that the museum is temporarily closed or the bus isn't running for an hour. Then he suggests that while they're waiting, they may be interested in going to the nearby 'Government Bazaar', which is coincidentally having its annual sale on that day. Needless to say, there's a sale every day, it's not much of a sale at all, and he'll collect a commission on anything you purchase…

with the French jet-set and families, reservations here are a must.

Hotel Tulip (Map pp130-1; ☎ 2392 2704; www.tulip-hotel.com; Midan Talaat Harb, Downtown; s E£70-85, d E£100-130; 💻) Smack-bang in the middle of downtown's action, the Tulip has rooms running the gamut from plain and comfy to modern and downright stylish. We love the wrought iron lamps and touches of leafy green adorning the hallways. Front rooms have great views of the *midan* action, but at the cost of inharmonious street noise.

Canadian Hostel (Map pp130-1; ☎ 2392 5794; www.thecanadianhostel.com; 5 Sharia Talaat Harb, Downtown; s/d E£100/120, without bathroom E£70/90; 💻) One of the friendliest digs in town, this Canadian-run hostel boasts an intimate communal sitting room and has lashings of neat trimmings to make you feel right at home. Some of the rooms are a bit dark, though others are blindingly bright and cheery. One reader summed it all up perfectly: 'spotlessly clean, family run, and has the values of a much more expensive hotel'. The popular travel service run from here (www.gotouregypt.com) also gets solid reviews from travellers.

Select Hotel (Map pp130-1; ☎ 2393 3707; www.selecthotel.unblog.fr; 19a Sharia Adly, Downtown; s/d E£80/120; 💻) The arty/quirky approach to decor here seems to be a hit with guests, judging by the wall covered with fan mail. Inside, the rooms are tidy and continue the bright and kitschy motif, though the furniture has definitely seen better days. Ask for a corner double or triple room for wraparound balconies and some downtown views. French is spoken.

Hotel Luna (Map pp130-1; ☎ 2396 1020; www.hotellunacairo.com; 5th fl, 27 Sharia Talaat Harb, Downtown; r E£110-150, without bathroom E£100; ❄ 💻) For a while there, the Luna was the darling of the budget hotel set. With large rooms in temperate pastel shades, crisp linens, air-con and a combination of gleaming private and shared bathrooms – it was not hard to see why. Alas service of late verges on gruff, and we've had as many negative as positive reports from travellers.

Midrange

Mayfair Hotel (Map p137; ☎ 2735 7315; www.mayfaircairo.com; 9 Sharia Aziz Osman, Zamalek; s/d E£140/190, without bathroom E£120/140; ❄ 💻) The perenially popular Mayfair has a bewildering array of recently refurbished rooms in a grand art deco building. The single rooms here can be a bit cramped, but the huge and lush shared balcony overlooking the quiet, leafy street more than makes up for that.

Victoria Hotel (Map pp126-7; ☎ 2589 2290; info@victoria.com.eg; 66 Sharia al-Gomhuriyya; s/d US$37/48; ❄ 💻) The Victoria is a classy old dame, swearing she's got a few good numbers left in her yet. The period decor is kept in good nick and borders on elegant: think high-ceilinged rooms, antique furniture and halls lined with gilded mirrors. Their rooms all have good beds and satellite TV, though it's a shame it's not more centrally located.

Windsor Hotel (Map pp130-1; ☎ 2591 5277; www.windsorcairo.com; 19 Sharia Alfy, Downtown; s/d US$48/58, with shower & hand basin only US$38/48;) Riding on the coattails of it's former glory, the Windsor is more ambience than substance. The outside is dilapidated, the inside only slightly less so, and the rooms dim and crumbling. Still, nostalgia goes a long way: the worn marble stairs, creaking elevator, art deco travel posters and smoky, charming lounge/bar help make this an interesting stay.

our pick Hotel Osiris (Map pp130-1; ☎ 2794 5728; www.hotelosiris.over-blog.com; 48 Sharia Nubar, Downtown; r €30-35;) A knock-out winner in the midrange division, this chic French-run establishment is beautifully finished with Euro-Egyptian flair. Here, fetching Arabesque decor meets bright, airy modern minimalism, with many of the faultless rooms sporting balconies with sweeping Cairo vistas. There's a Bedouin-styled rooftop terrace and the breakfasts, which include fresh juice and crepes, are *magnifique*!

Hotel Longchamps (Map p137; ☎ 2735 2311; www.hotellongchamps.com; 21 Sharia Ismail Mohammed, Zamalek; s US$48-54, d US$68-75;) Run with ruthless efficiency and filled with eclectic decor (um, what's with the WWII telephone exchange?), this wonderful Zamalek stalwart nonetheless feels more like a second home. The standard rooms on offer are generous and immaculately scrubbed – pay a little extra and they'll throw in a mini bathtub and balcony to boot. Best of all, the small, leafy balcony and welcoming lounge invite lingering or surfing their free wi-fi. Book ahead.

President Hotel (Map p137; ☎ 2735 0718; preshotl@thewayout.net; 22 Sharia Taha Hussein, Zamalek; s/d US$65/70;) If breakfast is the most important meal of your day, then this the place for you: the in-house patisserie supplying the morning meal is one of the best in the city. Unfortunately the rooms are a tad downtrodden, newly renovated bathrooms not withstanding. Some abodes have views over the Nile, others onto a concrete wall – ask for the former.

Top End

our pick Talisman Hotel (Map pp130-1; ☎ 2393 9431; www.talisman-hotel.com; 5th fl, 39 Sharia Talaat Harb, Downtown; s/d €60/80;) This exquisite boutique hotel is straight out of the pages of *The Thousand and One Nights*. Rooms are individually decorated in coloured themes and sumptuously equipped; common areas are equally impressive, featuring antique furniture, *objets d'art* and rugs. The suites (€120) are quite simply works of art. Reservations are essential. To find it, turn off Sharia Talaat Harb into the alley opposite A l'Americaine Coffee Shop and enter the first building entrance on the right, where you'll see a sign for the Minerva Hotel.

Cairo Marriott (Map p137; ☎ 2728 3000; www.marriott.com/CAIEG; Sharia Saray al-Gezira, Zamalek; r from US$220;) Despite the addition of two very modern towers that house all the rooms, the former palace that serves as the lobby adds some historic cachet to this institution. Rooms flaunt plasma TVs and comfy beds, and the popular garden café downstairs and lovely pool are favourite places to hang out. Breakfast costs an extra US$22.

EATING

Restaurants

In central Cairo, most budget eateries are concentrated around Midan Talaat Harb, while the city's more interesting eats are over the river in Zamalek. In this section and other Eating sections throughout this chapter, restaurants reviewed are booze-free, except where noted.

At-Tabie ad-Dumyati (Map pp126-7; ☎ 2575 4211; 31 Sharia Orabi, Downtown; mains E£2-8; 6am-1am) About 200m north of Midan Orabi, this highly recommended enterprise whips up lip-smacking, dirt cheap meals. Grab a choice of four salads from their large array (E£3.25), add a small plate of shwarma (E£5.50) and an eggplant sandwich (75pt) and you're sorted. There's also a branch in the food court of the Talaat Harb Complex (Map pp130–1).

Felfela Restaurant (Map pp130-1; ☎ 2392 2833; 15 Sharia Hoda Shaarawi, Downtown; mezze E£2-5, mains E£20-35; 8am-midnight;) Perpetually packed with tourists, coach parties and locals, Felfela deserves its popularity. A bizarre jungle theme rules the decor, but the food is straight-down-the-line Egyptian and consistently good, especially the mezze. A Stella costs E£12.

Didos Al Dente (Map p137; ☎ 2735 9117; 26 Sharia Bahgat Ali, Zamalek; pasta E£7.50-25;) This cute eatery gets packed with students from the nearby AUC, all clambering for a taste of the best pasta in town. It's tiny, so be prepared to wait on the street for a table.

Estoril (Map pp130-1; ☎ 2574 3102; 12 Sharia Talaat Harb, Downtown; mezze E£7, mains E£29-56;) Often packed to the rafters with locals and in-the-know expats, this Egyptian-French restaurant has been serving up the goods since 1959. Chain-smoking and heated debate are de rigueur here, and you should come early if you want a table, or otherwise prop yourself up at the bar to sample their tasty mezze and ice-cold beer.

Greek Club (Map pp130-1; ☎ 2577 4999; 3 Sharia Qasr el-Nil, Downtown; mains E£8-30; 7am-2am Tue-Sun) With its great neoclassical interior, soaring ceilings and outdoor terrace, this Cairene institution drips faded charm. The menu is fairly typical, with a few token Greek touches like moussaka (E£12) and Greek salads (E£8), and the food is nothing to write home about. Still, a meal on the lovely summer balcony is hard to beat. A Stella costs E£7, wine E£50 by the bottle, and there's an entry fee of E£5 for those of us not of Hellenic origin. You'll find it above the Groppi Patisserie (entrance on the side).

Pottery Cafe (Map pp130-1; ☎ 2796 0260; 35 Mohammed Mahmoud, Downtown; mains E£10-50; 8am-10pm; V) For a menu that strays a little off the familiar 'chicken and kebab' path, try this popular student haunt. Here you'll find soups, salads and light vegetable dishes (billed as being 'for dieters!') as well as standard-issue pizzas and pastas.

Centro Recreativo Italiano (Map pp130-1; ☎ 2575 9590; 40 Sharia 26th of July, Downtown; pizza E£15-30; 7-11pm) Cairo's Italian social club has recently flung open its doors to non-Italian visitors – hoorah! Yummy pasta, thin crust pizza and sensibly priced red wine are served on their outdoor terrace in summer, or in a snug, wood-panelled room in winter. Unless you can convince them of your Roman roots, there's an E£10 entry fee.

Emara Hati Al-Gish (Map pp130-1; ☎ 2796 2964; 32 Sharia Falaki, Downtown; meals E£15-40; 11am-11pm;) You can almost hear the meatatarians salivating at this popular, upmarket charcoal-grill house. Just grab a seat, choose the hunk of meat you want grilled (E£15 to E£33), add some token vegie sides (E£5 to E£15) to your order, and tuck in!

Café Riche (Map pp130-1; ☎ 2392 9793; 17 Sharia Talaat Harb, Downtown; mains E£12-25; 8am-midnight;) Once the favoured drinking spot of Cairo's intelligentsia, in recent years it's been a reliable spot to enjoy a meal and a glass of wine in a dash of old-world ambience.

Abou El-Sid (Map p137; ☎ 2735 9640; 157 Sharia 26th of July, Zamalek; mezze E£12-28, mains E£18-62; noon-2am;) A sumptuous orientalist fantasy of a restaurant-bar, the über-hip Abou El Sid serves traditional Egyptian food to wannabe pashas amid moody and low-hanging lamps, oversized cushions and brass tables. A beer costs E£25 and reservations are a must, darling. Look for the massively tall wooden doors.

La Mezzaluna (Map p137; ☎ 2735 2655; 118 Sharia 26th of July, Zamalek; mains E£17-36; 7am-11pm; V) A funky little Italian-inspired hideaway, this favourite of the arts and letters set whips up sound breakfasts, panini, pastas and lots of vegetarian dishes. It's a cosy place, with polished wooden panelling and a tiny, relaxed outdoor patio that's perfect for a post-meal espresso.

L'Aubergine (Map p137; ☎ 2738 0080; 5 Sharia Sayyed al-Bakry, Zamalek; mains E£18-50; noon-2am; V) The noncarnivorous among you will love the massive vegie menu on offer at this dimly lit, Western-style bistro. Not as hot on the hipster calendar as it used to be, the minimalist, almost Japanese fusion decor, ever-changing menu, occasional live jazz and upstairs bar still draw in the punters.

Maison Thomas (Map p137; ☎ 2735 7057; 157 Sharia 26th of July, Zamalek; sandwiches E£23-43, pizzas E£25-35; 24hr;) Most people come here for arguably the best Italian pizza in Egypt, but secretly, we love it for the awesome *futurama*, space age–inspired art deco lampshades. They do take-away and delivery, plus there's a deli selling quality cheeses and meats on site.

Quick Eats

Akher Sa'a (Map pp130-1; 8 Sharia Alfy, Downtown; meals E£3-4; 24hr) A frantically busy fuul (fava bean paste) and ta'amiyya takeaway place with a no-frills cafeteria next door, Akher Sa'a has a limited menu but its food is fresh and good.

Gad (Map pp130-1; ☎ 2576 3583; 13 Sharia 26th of July, Downtown; meals E£3-8; 7am-1am;) This Western-style fast-food eatery is always packed to the rafters with a constant stream of young Cairenes sampling its fresh, sensibly priced food. The *fiteer* (Egyptian pancake/pizza) with Greek cheese (E£9.50) is scrumptious, and the quarter chicken with rice and salad (E£10) is both flavoursome and top value. There are branches all over town, including opposite Khan al-Khalili (Map p134; Sharia Al-Azhar).

Unbeknownst to first-time visitors new to *kushari* (a mix of noodles, rice and lentils among other things), a secret war is being waged in Cairo over the title for 'best *kushari* joint' in town. We'll take the role of the UN here, and declare **Koshary El-Tahrir** (Map pp130-1; Sharia Tahrir, Downtown; kushari E£3-5; 7am-12am), **Abu Tarek** (Map pp130-1; 40 Sharia Champollion, Downtown; kushari E£3-5; 24hr) and **Sayed Hanafy** (Map pp130-1; Midan Orabi, Downtown; small/medium/large kushari E£2/3/4; 24hr) all equally praiseworthy.

For mouth watering fuul and ta'amiyya sandwiches, try **Felfela takeaway** (Map pp130-1; Sharia Talaat Harb, Downtown), and for sweet oriental pastries be sure to pop by **El-Abd** (Map pp130-1; 8am-midnight; Sharia 26th of July Downtown; Sharia Talaat Harb cnr Sharia Talaat Harb & Bursa al-Gedida, Downtown) – everyone else does.

DRINKING

Cafés

Cairenes have only recently discovered the joys of espresso coffee, but there's no stopping them now. Slick, modern coffee shops have multiplied all over the city and serve up all manner of caffeinated beverages and snacks; some even offer free wi-fi. For more traditional coffeehouses, called *ahwas*, see right.

Cilantro (Downtown Map pp130-1; 2792 4571; 31 Sharia Mohammed Mahmoud; Heliopolis 2415 0167; 4 Sharia Ibrahim Korba; Ma'adi (2521 1190; 17 Rd 219; Ma'adi City Centre 2520 4410; Carrefour; Zamalek Map p137; 2736 1115; 157 Sharia 26th of July) One of the most prolific of the coffee shop chains, the Cilantro outlets are small and clean, with open fridges displaying packaged sandwiches, cakes and salads (E£8 to E£16) to eat in or take away. We heart the brownies (E£4).

Beano's (Downtown Map pp130-1; 2792 2328; 39 Mohammed Mahmoud; Heliopolis 2690 3484; 15 Sharia Baghdad; Zamalek Map p137; 2736 2388; 8 Midan al-Marsafy) This chain offers more of the same Starbucks-style drinks.

Simonds (Map p137; 2735 9436; 112 Sharia 26th of July, Zamalek) A Zamalek institution, the barista here has been preparing cappuccino (E£7) for over half a century – and judging by his grumpiness he hasn't taken a break in all that time. Be sure to grab a croissant (E£2.50) to go with your frothy coffee.

Arabica (Map p137; 2735 7982; 20 Sharia El Marashly; snacks E£10-35) This super-funky upstairs café is all 'Starbucks goes art-house', with painting-draped walls and a dedicated following of hip young things plopped upon the modern furniture. International tunes waft in the air, and you can munch on *fiteer*, soups, salads or wraps while watching the street scene below.

Ahwas

There are hundreds of traditional coffeehouses, or *ahwas*, in every nook and cranny of Cairo. Below are some of the most famous ones.

Fishawi's (Map p134; Khan al-Khalili; tea E£4, sheesha E£6; 24hr) Nearly as old as Cairo itself, this *shai*-sipping, sheesha-smoking institution is not to be missed. Filled with tourists and local shopkeepers in equal measure, this is a time-capsule of the Cairo of bygone days. It's a few steps off Midan Hussein.

Abu Aly (Map pp130-1; sheesha E£11, tea E£14; 10am-4am) Located in a tented courtyard at the Nile Hilton, this shi-shi café is a magnet for well-heeled Cairenes.

Zahret al-Bustan (Map pp130-1; tea E£3, sheesha E£5; 24hr) Sprawling across a laneway off Talaat Harb near Midan Talaat Harb, this *ahwa* is a Mecca for Cairo's young intelligentsia. Come evening time, the entire street is abuzz with the heady air of important conversation.

Bars & Nightclubs

Absolute (Map p137; 2579 6512; Corniche el-Nil; minimum charge E£75; 1pm-3am) Near the Conrad Hotel, this chic bar is the current place to see and be seen. While competent DJs thump out house tunes like there's no tomorrow, the cool crowd here groove on the spot while warming up for the popular dance floor. Reservations required.

Windsor Bar (Map pp130-1; 2591 5277; 19 Sharia Alfy, Downtown; 6pm-1am) The whiff of colonial history here will hit you in tandem with a thick wall of smoke upon entering the bar of the Windsor Hotel (p139). Its heyday may have been early last century, but the remaining shreds of atmosphere still make it a top spot for a nightcap.

La Bodega (Map p137; 2735 0543; 157 Sharia 26th of July, Zamalek; 7pm-1am) You can grab a drink either at the super-swanky lounge-bar (and restaurant) or by diving into their cubicle-sized bar, Barten, replete with psychedelic swirls and a thumping soundtrack. La Bodega has been known to attract the who's who of the Cairo jet-set.

L'Aubergine (Map p137; ☎ 2738 0800; 5 Sharia Sayyed al-Bakry, Zamalek; noon-2am;) Popular with the younger, black-is-back fashion brigade, this relaxed bar sits above L'Aubergine restaurant (p140).

Club 35 (Map pp126-7; ☎ 3573 8500; Four Season First Residence, 35 Sharia Giza, Giza; 7pm-3am) It's only in the wee hours that this nightclub comes alive, particularly at weekends as crowds pour in to get their after-hours wiggle-on.

Sequoia (Map pp126-7; ☎ 2576 8086; 3 Sharia Abu al-Feda, Zamalek; minimum charge Thu-Fri E£90, Sat-Wed E£65; 1pm-1am) This sprawling outdoor lounge-bar at the tip of Zamalek panders to Cairo's art crowd. While the minimum charge is not hard to meet (Stellas are E£25, sheesha E£15 to E£25), the moodily lit ambience in the evenings and Nile location are hard to beat. Can get chilly at night.

Other drinking spots include:

Odeon Bar (Map pp130-1; ☎ 2576 7971; 6 Sharia Abdel Hamid Said; 24hr) Musty old-timer on a downtown rooftop, good for an emergency drink any time of the day or night.

Deals (Map p137; ☎ 2736 0502; 2 Sharia Sayyed al-Bakry, Zamalek; 6pm-2am) Rowdy and smoky den, jam-packed at weekends, pleasant at other times.

ENTERTAINMENT

Sufi Dancing

There are regular, impressive displays of feverish Sufi dancing by the **Al-Tannoura Egyptian Heritage Dance Troupe** (☎ 2512 1735; admission free; 7pm Mon, Wed & Sat Oct-May, 8pm Jun-Sep) at Wikala of Al-Ghouri (Map p134) in Khan al-Khalili. Make sure you're there at least one hour before to score a seat.

Belly-Dancing

The best belly dancers often perform at Cairo's five-star hotels. The current favourite is **Haroun El-Rashid nightclub** (Map pp130-1; ☎ 2795 7171, ext 8011; Corniche el-Nil, Downtown; admission E£300-630; 11pm-3.30am, closed Fri & Mon) at the Semiramis Intercontinental, where the famous Dina undulates. Performances usually don't begin until around 1am.

For something a little more prosaic, bordering on the sleazy, try **Palmyra** (Map pp130-1; off Sharia 26th of July, Downtown; admission E£6; 10pm-4am). In a cavernous, dilapidated 1950s dance hall, it has a full Arab musical contingent, belly dancers who get better the more money is thrown at them, and an occasional singer or acrobat. A similar option around these parts is **Scheherazade** (Map pp130-1; 1 Sharia Alfy, Downtown; admission E£5; 10pm-4am), with an elegantly decorated interior, though a less than elegantly behaved clientele.

Cinemas

To catchup on the latest Hollywood fodder, try the **Ramses Hilton I & II cinemas** (Map pp130-1; ☎ 2574 7435; Sharia Galaa) at the Ramses Hilton shopping mall. Tickets to day sessions cost E£10, evening showings E£25.

Live Music

For live music try the **Cairo Jazz Club** (Map pp126-7; ☎ 2345 9939; 197 Sharia 26th of July, Agouza) or **After Eight** (Map pp130-1; ☎ 2574 0855; 6 Sharia Qasr el-Nil, Downtown; minimum charge Fri-Wed E£60, Thu E£90; 8pm-2am). Table reservations recommended at both.

Several nights a week, concerts of everything from electronic fusion to classical to Nubian music are held at the **El Sawy Culturewheel** (Map p137; ☎ 2736 6178; www.culturewheel.net; Sharia 26th of July, Zamalek). The **Cairo Opera House** (Map pp126-7; ☎ 2739 8144; www.operahouse.gov.eg; Gezira Exhibition Grounds) has two auditoriums hosting performances by the Cairo Opera and Symphony Orchestra, as well as concerts by local and international jazz and classical musicians.

GETTING THERE & AWAY

Air

EgyptAir (Corniche el-Nil Map pp130-1; ☎ 2577 2410; Nile Hilton, Corniche el-Nil, Downtown; Sharia Adly Map pp130-1; ☎ 2392 7680; 6 Sharia Adly, Downtown; Sharia Talaat Harb Map pp130-1; ☎ 2393 0381; 9 Sharia Talaat Harb, Downtown) has a number of offices. The main sales office is on Sharia Adly.

Bus

Cairo's main bus station is the **Cairo Gateway** (Turgoman Garage; Map pp126-7; Sharia al-Gisr, Bulaq), 1km northwest of the intersection of Sharias Galaa and 26th of July. It's too far to walk from central Cairo – the best way to get here is by taxi (E£5 from Downtown). While the majority of buses leave from here, there are two other bus stations: **Al-Mazar bus station** (off Map pp126–7), near the airport, where some international services depart and where most other services stop en route out of Cairo; and **Abbassiyya (Sinai) Bus Terminal** (Map pp126-7; Sharia Ramses, Abbassiyya), where all of the services from Sinai arrive (confusingly, these leave from Cairo Gateway).

For details of international bus services from Cairo, see p208.

ALEXANDRIA & THE MEDITERRANEAN COAST

All services leave from Cairo Gateway. **West Delta Bus Co** (☎ 2575 2157), commonly referred to as 'West Delta', travels to Alexandria (E£23 to E£25, 2½ hours) roughly every hour between 4.45am and 1.15am. **Superjet** (☎ 2575 1313) runs just as frequently (E£25). Six services a day go on to Marsa Matruh (E£40 to E£46, 5½ hours).

LUXOR & ASWAN

Upper Egypt Bus Co (☎ 2576 0261) buses depart from Cairo Gateway. There's one daily service going to Luxor (E£91, nine to 10 hours) at 5pm, going on to Aswan (E£91, 10 to 12 hours). Note that you're much better off getting the train. Superjet has a nightly service to Luxor departing from Cairo Gateway at 11.45pm (E£90).

RED SEA

Superjet leaves from Cairo Gateway to Hurghada (E£70, six hours) at 7.30am, 2.30pm and 11.45pm. Over a dozen Upper Egypt Bus Co services head to Hurghada (E£55 to E£60) between 8am and 1am.

There are three afternoon Upper Egypt Bus Co services to Marsa Alam (E£80 to E£90, 11 to 12 hours) via Al-Quesir (E£65 to E£75, nine hours).

SINAI

Confusingly all Sinai buses leave from Cairo Gateway, but return to Abbassiyya.

East Delta Bus Co (☎ 2574 2814) has a dozen services going to Sharm el-Sheikh (E£60 to E£70, seven hours) departing between 6.30am and 1.45pm. The 7.15am, 1pm, 5pm and 12.15am services go on to Dahab (E£70 to E£80, nine hours).

There are three daily buses to Nuweiba (E£70 to E£80, seven hours) and Taba (E£70 to E£80, nine hours) at 6.30am, 9.30am and 10.15pm. Two daily services to St Katherine's Monastery (E£40, seven hours) leave at 11.30am and 1.30pm.

Superjet also runs three, slightly more comfy, services to Sharm el-Sheikh (E£80).

SUEZ CANAL

All Suez buses leave from Cairo Gateway. East Delta Bus Co travels to Suez (E£8, 1½ hours) every 30 minutes between 6am and 8pm. Buses to Port Said (E£14 to E£16, three hours) leave every 30 minutes between 6am and 9.30am, and then every hour until 9.30pm. Superjet also runs equally frequent buses to Port Said (E£22).

WESTERN OASES

All Western Oases buses leave from Cairo Gateway. To get to Siwa, East Delta runs a once-weekly direct bus service departing Wednesdays at 7.45pm (E£50, 10 to 11 hours). Otherwise, you must take a bus to Alexandria or Marsa Matruh and change for a connecting service.

There are three Upper Egypt Bus Co services per day to Bahariya (E£27, five hours), Farafra (E£46, eight to 10 hours) and Dakhla (E£50 to E£55, 10 to 12 hours) departing at 7am, 8am and 6pm. Direct buses to Al-Kharga leave at 9.30pm and 10pm (E£35 to E£40, eight to 10 hours).

Service Taxi

Most service taxis depart from taxi stands around Ramses train station and Midan Ulali (see Map pp126–7). Service taxis depart for Alexandria (E£17, three hours), Port Said (E£15, two hours) and Suez (E£8, one hour).

Train

Ramses station (Mahattat Ramses; Map pp126-7; ☎ 2575 3555; Midan Ramses, Downtown) is Cairo's main train station. It has a left-luggage office charging E£2.50 per piece per day, a **post office** (🕑 8am-8pm), a pharmacy and a **tourist information office** (☎ 2579 0767; 🕑 8am-8pm).

LUXOR & ASWAN

The **Abela Egypt Sleeping Trains** (☎ 2574 9274; www.sleepingtrains.com) leave for Upper Egypt at 8pm and 9.10pm. They arrive in Luxor at 5.15am and 6.10am the next morning and in Aswan at 8.15am and 9.30am respectively. To either destination, it costs US$60/80 per person one way in a double/single cabin. Children four to nine years of age pay US$45. There are no student discounts and tickets must be paid for in US dollars, euros or with credit cards (for an extra US$2 fee). The price includes a basic dinner and breakfast. The ticket office is next to the tourist information office near the station's main entrance. In the October to April high season you are advised to book several days in advance.

Aside from the sleeping train, foreigners can only travel to Luxor and Aswan on train 980, departing Cairo daily at 7.40am; train 996, departing at 10pm; and train 1902, departing at 12.30am. To Luxor, 1st-/2nd-class fares are E£80/50, to Aswan they're E£90/60. It's around E£5 cheaper if you take the slower morning train. The trip takes 10 hours to Luxor, and around 13 hours to Aswan. Tickets can be bought from the ticket office beside platform 11, which is on the other side of the tracks from the main hall. You must buy your ticket at least a couple of days in advance. Student discounts are available for both classes.

ALEXANDRIA

The best trains running between Cairo and Alexandria are the *Turbini* (E£46/29 in 1st/2nd class, two hours). They depart from Cairo at 8am, 2pm and 7pm. The next best trains are the five *Espani* (Spanish) services, which cost the same as the *Turbini* and leave between 9am and 10.30pm. Six slower trains, known as *Francese* (French; E£35/19 in 1st/2nd class, three hours), leave between 6am and 8pm. Student discounts are available on all tickets.

PORT SAID

Trains to Port Said (E£18 to E£20, four hours) leave at 8.45am, 12.30pm, 2.30pm and 7.10pm. To Suez (E£18 to E£20, 2½ hours), trains depart from Ain Shams station, 15km northeast of Ramses station (accessible via metro), at 6.30am, 9.20am, 1.10pm, 4.15pm and 6.45pm.

GETTING AROUND

To/From the Airport

Cairo International Airport (Terminal 1 ☎ 2265 5000; Terminal 2 ☎ 2265 2222) is 20km northeast of Cairo. There are four terminals in all, but two terminals about 3km apart handle most passenger traffic. Terminal 1 services EgyptAir's international and domestic flights and Terminal 2 services all international airlines except Saudi Arabian Airlines. You'll find ATMs and exchange booths in the arrivals halls.

Bus 356 is air-conditioned, and runs at 20-minute intervals from 7am to midnight between both terminals of the airport and Midan Abdel Moniem Riad (Map pp130–1), behind the Egyptian Museum in central Cairo (E£2, plus E£1 per large luggage item, one hour). There is a far less comfortable 24-hour service on bus 400 (50pt), which leaves from the same places. Note that between the hours of midnight and 6am, this bus only stops at Terminal 1.

If you arrive at Terminal 1, you'll see the bus-parking area to the side of the arrivals hall. If you arrive at Terminal 2, walk out of the arrivals hall, cross the road, go down the stairs or escalator, cross through the car park and wait on the opposite side of the street at the end of the car park to flag the bus down.

If you decide to grab a black-and-white taxi, the going rate to central Cairo is around E£50 to E£60 (it's E£35 to E£40 back to the airport). You'll get the best rate if you walk down to the car park rather than relying on the taxis right outside the arrivals hall. Limousines cost anything from E£60 to E£100.

Bus & Minibus

Cairo's main local bus and minibus stations are at Midan Abdel Moniem Riad (Map pp130–1). From there, services leave for just about everywhere in the city.

Metro

The Metro system is startlingly efficient, and the stations are cleaner than any other public places in Cairo. It's also surprisingly inexpensive. You're most likely to use the Metro if you're going down to Old Cairo (served by a station called Mar Girgis) or Giza train station. A short-hop ticket (up to nine stations) costs E£1. The first and (sometimes) second carriages are reserved for women only.

Microbus

Destinations are not marked, so microbuses are hard to use unless you're familiar with their routes. Position yourself beside the road that leads where you want to go and when a microbus passes, yell out your destination – if it's going where you want to go and there are seats free, it'll stop. Fares range between 50pt to E£2 depending on distance.

River Bus

The **Maspero river bus terminal** (Map pp130–1) is on the Corniche in front of the big round Radio & TV Building. From here boats depart at 8am, 2pm and 9pm for Doqqi, Manial, Giza and Misr al-Qadima (Old Cairo). The trip takes 50 minutes and the fare is E£1.

Taxi

By far the easiest way of getting anywhere is by taxi. They're cheap enough to make buses, with their attendant hassles, redundant. Use the following table as a rough guide to what you should be paying for a taxi ride around Cairo. It's best to hail a trusty Peugeot 504 rather than one of the diabolically unroadworthy Fiats.

TAXI FARES FROM DOWNTOWN

Destination	Fare (E£)
Abbassiyya (Sinai) Bus Terminal	15
Airport	35-40*
Citadel	10
Heliopolis	15-20
Khan al-Khalili	5
Midan Ramses	3
Pyramids	25-30
Cairo Gateway	5
Zamalek	7

* Note: Airport to Downtown, E£50-60

AROUND CAIRO

MEMPHIS, SAQQARA & DAHSHUR

دهشور & سقارة ممفيس

There's little left of the former Pharaonic capital of **Memphis**, 24km south of Cairo. It's worth visiting, however, for its open-air **museum** (adult/student E£25/15; 8am-4pm Oct-Apr, 8am-5pm May-Sep), centred on a gigantically impressive limestone statue of Ramses II.

A few kilometres away is **Saqqara** (adult/student E£50/25; 8am-4pm Oct-Apr, 8am-5pm May-Sep), a massive necropolis covering 7 sq km of desert and strewn with pyramids, temples and tombs. Deceased pharaohs and their families, administrators, generals and sacred animals were interred here. The star attraction is the **Step Pyramid of Zoser**, the world's oldest stone monument and the first decent attempt at a pyramid. Surrounding it is Zoser's pyramid complex, which includes shrines and a huge **court**. Other attractions include the **Mastaba of Ti** and the **Pyramid of Teti**.

Ten kilometres south of Saqqara is **Dahshur** (adult/student E£25/15; 8am-4pm Oct-Apr, 8am-5pm May-Sep), an impressive 3.5km-long field of 4th- and 12th-dynasty pyramids, including the **Bent Pyramid** (unfortunately off limits to visitors) and the wonderful **Red Pyramid**. If your budget is limited, there's a lot to be said for visiting Dahshur and exploring the interior of this, the oldest true pyramid in Egypt, rather than spending a fortune at Giza.

It's possible to visit Memphis, Saqqara and Dahshur in five hours, but you will need your own transport to get here, travel around the sites (parking at each site costs E£2 to E£5) and bring you back to Cairo. A taxi will cost around E£150 to E£200 shared among a maximum of seven people. Stipulate the sights you want to see and how long you want to be out, and be ready for some fancy bargaining. Otherwise, organise a day tour (p136).

MEDITERRANEAN COAST

ALEXANDRIA الاسكندرية

03 / pop 4.1 million

Although Alexandria today has barely an ancient stone to show for its glorious past, it is in its cosmopolitan allure and Mediterranean pace of life that the magic lies. Sprawling necklace-like along a curving bay, this town vies with Cairo for the title of Egypt's culture capital. Our vote lies with Alexandria – be sure to scope out its splendid cluster of restaurants, its moody, antediluvian cafés and vibrantly active youth scene and cast your vote.

History

Established in 332 BC by Alexander the Great, the city became a major trade centre and focal point of learning for the entire Mediterranean world. Its ancient library held 500,000 volumes and the Pharos lighthouse was one of the Seven Wonders of the Ancient World. Alexandria continued as the capital of Egypt under the Roman Empire and its eastern offshoot, the Byzantine

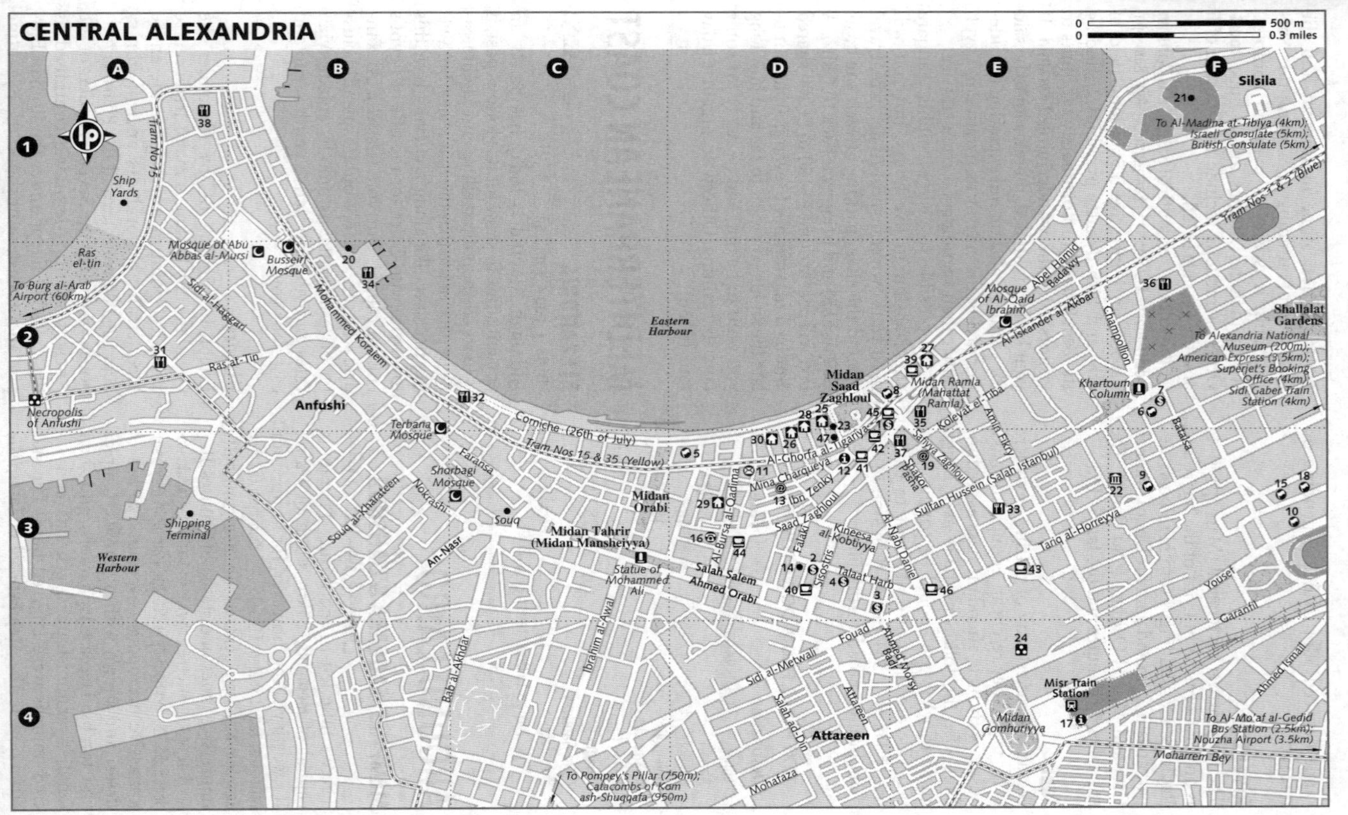
CENTRAL ALEXANDRIA
0 500 m
0 0.3 miles
Eastern Harbour
Western Harbour
Anfushi
Ras el-Tin
Ship Yards
Tram No 15
Necropolis of Anfushi
To Burg al-Arab Airport (60km)
Shipping Terminal
Mosque of Abu Abbas al-Mursi
Busseiri Mosque
Sidi al-Haggari
Ras al-Tin
Mohammed Koraiem
Terbana Mosque
Shorbagi Mosque
Faransa
Nokrashi
Souq al-Kharateen
An-Nasr
Souq
Bab al-Akhdar
Corniche (26th of July)
Tram Nos 15 & 35 (Yellow)
Midan Tahrir (Midan Mansheiyya)
Midan Orabi
Statue of Mohammed Ali
Ibrahim al-Awal
To Pompey's Pillar (750m); Catacombs of Kom ash-Shuqqafa (950m)
Salah Salem
Ahmed Orabi
Al-Bursa al-Qadima
Mina Charqueya
Al-Ghorfa al-Tigariya
Ibn Zenky
Saad Zaghloul
Falaki
Sisostris
Kineesa al-Kobtiyya
Talaat Harb
Al-Nabi Daniel
Midan Saad Zaghloul
Midan Ramla (Mahattat Ramla)
Safiyya Zaghloul
Shakor Pasha
Koleyat el-Tiba
Amin Fikry
Sultan Hussein (Salah Istanbul)
Tariq al-Horreyya
Ahmed Morsy Badr
Attareen
Fouad
Sidi al-Metwali
Salah ad-Din
Mohafaza
Mosque of Al-Qaid Ibrahim
Abdel Hamid Badawy
Al-Iskander al-Akbar
Champollion
Khartoum Column
Batalsa
Shallalat Gardens
To Alexandria National Museum (200m); American Express (3.5km); Superjet's Booking Office (4km); Sidi Gaber Train Station (4km)
Silsila
To Al-Madina at-Tibiya (4km); Israeli Consulate (5km); British Consulate (5km)
Tram Nos 1 & 2 (Blue)
Yousef
Garanfil
Ahmed Ismail
Misr Train Station
Midan Gomhuriyya
To Al-Mo'af al-Gedid Bus Station (2.5km); Nouzha Airport (3.5km)
Moharrem Bey

Empire. From the 4th century onwards, the city declined into insignificance. Napoleon's arrival and Alexandria's subsequent redevelopment as a major port attracted people from all over the world, but the Revolution of 1952 put an end to much of the city's pluralistic charm.

Orientation

Alexandria is a true waterfront city, nearly 20km long from east to west and only about 3km wide. The focal points of the city are Midan Ramla (Mahattat Ramla) and adjacent Midan Saad Zaghloul. Around these two *midan*s are the main tourist office, restaurants, cafés and most of the cheaper hotels. To the west of this central area are the older quarters of the city, such as Anfushi. To the east are newer, and swishier suburbs stretching 15km along the coastline to easternmost Montazah.

Information

INTERNET ACCESS

Internet cafés open and close in the blink of an eye in Alexandria. Two of the more reliable:

MG@Net (per hr E£2; ⌚ 10am-midnight) Conveniently near Midan Saad Zaghloul.

Zawia Computer Internet Café (☎ 484 8014; Sharia Dr Hassan Fadaly; per hr E£4; ⌚ 11am-11pm) Off Sharia Safiyya Zaghloul.

MEDICAL SERVICES

Al-Madina at-Tibiya (☎ 543 2150/7402; Sharia Ahmed Shawky, Rushdy) Well-equipped private hospital, accustomed to dealing with foreign patients.

MONEY

For changing cash, the simplest option is to use one of the many exchange bureaus on the side streets between Midan Ramla and the Corniche. For travellers cheques and forex services you can also go to:

American Express (☎ 420 1050; 14 Mai, Elsaladya Bldg, Smouha; ⌚ 9am-5pm Sun-Thu) Also a travel agency.

Thomas Cook (☎ 484 7830; www.thomascookegypt.com; 15 Midan Saad Zaghloul; ⌚ 8am-4pm)

POST & TELEPHONE

The **main post office** (Sharia al-Bursa al Qadima; ⌚ 8.30am-3pm Sat-Thu) is two blocks east of Midan Orabi. There is a 24-hour **Telephone centrale** (⌚ 24) on Midan Gomhurriya. Mobile phone SIM and top-up cards are available everywhere.

TOURIST INFORMATION

Main tourist office (☎ 485 1556; Midan Saad Zaghloul; ⌚ 8.30am-6pm) Only marginally informative; in the southwest corner of the *midan*.

Tourist office (☎ 392 5985; ⌚ 8.30am-6pm) At Misr train station.

VISA EXTENSIONS

Passport office (☎ 482 7873; 28 Sharia Talaat Harb; ⌚ 8am-1.30pm Sat-Thu) Off Sharia Salah Salem.

Sights

BIBLIOTHECA ALEXANDRINA

The boldly modern **Bibliotheca Alexandrina** (☎ 483 9999; www.bibalex.org; Corniche al-Bahr, Chatby; admission adult/student E£10/5, Antiquities Museum adult/student E£20/10, Manuscript Museum adult/student E£20/10; ⌚ 11am-7pm Sun-Thu, 3-7pm Fri & Sat) seems

INFORMATION

ATM....1 D2
Banque du Caire (ATM)....2 D3
Banque Misr (ATM)....3 D3
Banque Misr (ATM)....4 D3
French Consulate....5 D3
German Consulate....6 F2
HSBC Bank (ATM)....7 F2
Irish Consulate....(see 6)
Italian Consulate....8 E2
Lebanese Consulate....9 F3
Libyan Consulate....10 F3
Main Post Office....11 D3
Main Tourist Office....12 D3
MG@Net....13 D3
Passport Office....14 D3
Saudi Arabian Consulate....15 F3
Telephone Centrale....16 D3
Tourist Office....17 E4
Turkish Consulate....18 F3
Zawia Computer Internet Café..19 E3

SIGHTS & ACTIVITIES

Alexandria Dive....20 B2
Bibliotheca Alexandrina....21 F1
Graeco-Roman Museum....22 F3
Mena Tours....23 D2
Roman Amphitheatre (Kom al-Dikka)....24 E4

SLEEPING

Cecil Hotel....25 D2
Crillon Hotel....26 D3
Egypt Hotel....27 E2
Hotel Union....28 D2
Swiss Canal Hotel....29 D3
Windsor Palace Hotel....30 D3

EATING

Abu Ashraf....31 A2
El-Qobesi....32 C2
Elite....33 E3
Fish Market....34 B2
Gad....35 E2
Hood Gondol Seafood....36 F2
Mohammed Ahmed....37 E3
Qadoura....38 A1
Tikka Grill....(see 34)

DRINKING

Athineos....39 E2
Brazilian Coffee Store....40 D3
Brazilian Coffee Store....41 D3
Delices....42 D3
Pastroudis....43 E3
Sofianopoulo Coffee Store....44 D3
Trianon....45 D2
Vinous....46 E3

TRANSPORT

EgyptAir....(see 27)
West Delta Booking Office....47 D3

A MAGICAL HYSTORY (CAFFEINATED) TOUR

In case you hadn't noticed, Alexandria is a café town – and we're not talking Starbucks double-decaf-soy-lowfat-vanilla-grande lattes here. Ever since the first half of the 20th century, Alexandria's culture has centred on these venues, where the city's diverse population congregate to live out life's dramas over pastries and a cup of tea or coffee. Many of these old haunts remain and are definitely worth a visit for nostalgic purposes, historical associations and grand decor, but not always for the food.

As good a place to start as any is at **Athineos** (☎ 487 7173; 21 Midan Saad Zaghloul), an establishment that lives and breathes nostalgia. The café part on the Midan Ramla side still has its original '40s fittings, period character, and quite possibly some of its original customers – a loyal following of old men drinking tea who haven't moved for decades. Also facing Midan Ramla is **Trianon** (56 Midan Saad Zaghloul; from 7am;), a favourite haunt of the Greek poet Cavafy, who worked in offices above.

Next, stroll around the corner to check out **Delicies** (46 Sharia Saad Zaghloul; from 7am;). This enormous old tearoom drips with atmosphere and can actually whip up a decent breakfast. If you're starting to tire, pop in next door for a strong kick-start espresso at the counter (no seats) of old java haunt **Brazilian Coffee Store** (Sharia Saad Zaghloul;). Popular with local businessfolk and old Greek men, it also has a branch on Sharia Salah Salem (with seats).

Vinous (☎ 486 0956; cnr Sharias al-Nabi Daniel & Tariq al-Horreyya; 7am-1am) is an old-school patisserie with more grand deco styling than you can poke a puff pastry at, but really we love it for the period scales labelled with the 'Just' brand. From here you can make a historical detour to the place where the famous **Pastroudis** (Tariq al-Horeyya; 7am-1am) still stands. This was a frequent meeting point for the characters of Lawrence Durrell's *Alexandria Quartet*.

Finally, exhausted, you might just need one last pick-me-up coffee. Head over to Sharia Saad Zaghloul and **Sofianopoulo Coffee Store** (Sharia Saad Zaghloul), a gorgeous coffee retailer that would be in a museum anywhere else in the world.

a fitting 20th-century replacement for the near-mythical library of Alexandria. The original library was founded in the late 3rd century BC and was the pre-eminent centre of learning, considered one of the greatest of all classical institutions. The modern counterpart resembles a gigantic angled discus, with the ancient wealth of learning lyrically evoked on the curved exterior walls by giant letters, hieroglyphs and symbols from every known alphabet. Inside there's room for eight million books in the vast, completely windowed, main rotunda.

GRAECO-ROMAN MUSEUM

The **Graeco-Roman Museum** (☎ 486 5820; 5 Sharia al-Mathaf ar-Romani; adult/student E£30/15; 9am-4pm) is home to one of the most extensive collections of Graeco-Roman art in the world, with over 40,000 objects in its collection. Look for the collection of realistic **terracotta statuettes** (*tanagra*) from the Hellenistic period, **carved heads** representing the city's founder, Alexander, and an impressive wall-hung **mosaic** from the 3rd century BC. There also are lots of examples of the melding of Greek and Egyptian culture here, as well as just about the only historical depictions of the **Pharos** in Alexandria.

Unfortunately, this museum was closed for renovations at the time of research, scheduled to be reopened in 2009.

ALEXANDRIA NATIONAL MUSEUM

The excellent **Alexandria National Museum** (☎ 483 5519; 110 Sharia Tariq al-Horreyya, Challalate; adult/student E£30/15; 9am-4pm) sets new benchmarks for summing up Alexandria's impressive past. Its small, thoughtfully selected and well-labelled collection does a sterling job of relating the city's history from antiquity to the modern period. Look for it in a beautifully restored Italianate villa.

CATACOMBS OF KOM ASH-SHUQQAFA

Dating back to the 2nd century AD, these eerily fascinating **tombs** (☎ 484 5800; Carmous; adult/student E£25/15; 9am-5pm) would have held about 300 corpses. The centrepiece of the catacombs, the **principal tomb**, is the prototype for a horror-film set, with a miniature funerary temple decorated with a weird synthesis of ancient Egyptian, Greek and Roman death iconography. No cameras are allowed. You'll find the catacombs in the southwest of the city, a five-minute walk from the famed, misnamed and disappointing **Pompey's Pillar** (☎ 484 5800; Carmous; adult/student E£15/10; ⌚ 9am-4pm).

ROMAN AMPHITHEATRE (KOM AL-DIKKA)

The 13 white marble terraces of the only **Roman Amphitheatre** (☎ 486 5106; Sharia Yousef; adult/student E£15/10; ⌚ 9am-5pm) in Egypt were discovered in 1964. Worth seeing is the 'Villa of the Birds' **mosaic** (adult/student E£10/5) in the grounds.

Activities

As most of old Alexandria has slipped into the oceans, the underwater archaeology scene has recently managed to dredge up ancient pavements, platforms, statues and columns in the eastern harbour and around Fort Qaitbey. **Alexandra Dive** (☎ 483 2045; www.alexandra-dive.com; Corniche) runs diving tours of the submerged harbour sites, though visibility is often shockingly bad.

Sleeping

Alexandria is one of the few Egyptian cities where hotel rates stay the same year-round.

Swiss Canal Hotel (☎ 480 8373; 14 Sharia al-Bursa al-Qadima; s/d E£70/90, with air-con E£100/123; ❄) Fresh from a transformational makeover, the bright upstairs rooms here have whimsically pink walls and oodles of fresh pine trim, and range from small and cute to huge, bright and airy. Don't be tempted by the discount unrenovated rooms – they're icky.

Hotel Union (☎ 480 7312; 5th fl, 164 Corniche; s E£70-140, d E£90-160; ❄) This used to be the budget place of choice in Alexandria, but the Union let it go to its head a bit – with standards slipping and prices creeping. The smallish rooms are still quite charming, relatively well maintained and come in a bewildering mix of bathroom/view/air-con options and rates. Our rates quoted include their complicated mix of taxes and add-ons, but no breakfast.

Crillon Hotel (☎ 480 0330; 3rd fl, 5 Sharia Adib Ishaq; s/d from E£72/99) Two blocks west from the Cecil Hotel, the Crillon is a budget hotel poster child. The staff are friendly and attentive. Rooms are big and glistening, some sporting original '60s decor, while regular renovations deck out other rooms with more modern trimmings. Look at a few chambers – the best ones have polished wooden floors and French windows that open onto balconies with that great harbour view. Reservations recommended.

Egypt Hotel (☎ 481 4483; 1 Sharia Degla; s E£270-320, d E£320-350; ❄) The new kid on the block, the Egypt fills a desperate niche for decent midrange digs. The rooms are supercomfy, with plush beds and lots of frilly period touches thrown in for good measure. All have perfectly neat bathrooms, and either sea or street views, and there's a homey sitting room filled with antique-ish furniture.

Windsor Palace Hotel (☎ 480 8123; www.paradiseinnegypt.com; Sharia ash-Shohada; s US$125-135, d US$145-155; ❄ 💻) This bejewelled Edwardian gem is an institution unto itself, keeping a watchful eye on the Med since 1907. After a much-needed nip and tuck in the 1990s, the rooms sport the sort of old-world, green- and gold-flavoured pizzazz that wouldn't be out of place on the Orient Express. The pricier rooms have splendid sea views.

Cecil Hotel (☎ 487 7173; www.sofitel.com; 16 Midan Saad Zaghloul; s/d US$205/245, with sea view US$265/306; ❄ 💻) The historic Cecil Hotel, an Alexandria legend now managed by the international Sofitel chain, has been refitted several times over the last couple of decades, only sometimes for the better. The rooms are fully equipped, though a little sombre, while the grand lobby and famous bar (now relocated to the 1st floor) have retained only a fraction of the lustre they had when Durrell and Churchill came to visit. The big consolation is the sweeping view over Eastern Harbour.

Eating

The main place for cheap eats is around the area where Sharia Safiyya Zaghloul meets Midan Ramla. There are plenty of little fuul and ta'amiyya stands here, as well as sandwich shops and the odd *kushari* stand. Anfushi is where to head to sample some of Alexandria's best and freshest seafood.

Elite (☎ 486 3592; 43 Sharia Safiyya Zaghloul; mains E£4.50-30; ⌚ 9am-midnight) One of those Alexandrian time-warp affairs, Elite is cut from the same cloth as an old US diner – sealed in a 1950s bubble and almost slipping back in time. The menu traverses from the oriental to the occidental and tries to cover everything in between, though it's best to stick to the simple things. Beer is served.

our pick Hood Gondol Seafood (☎ 476 1779; cnr of Omar Lofty & Mohammed M Motwe; meals around E£25) For a quick fix of delicious, fresh and ridiculously cheap seafood – make a beeline for this local favourite. A massive plate of mixed seafood, including prawns, calamari, spicy clams and fried fish, as well as salads and bread, will barely make a dint in your wallet at E£25. It's located down an unmarked alley; ask for directions as everyone knows it by name.

Abu Ashraf (☎ 481 6597; 28 Sharia Safar Pasha, Bahari; mains E£35-60; 24hr) Make your selection from the day's catch, then take a seat under the green awning and watch it being cooked. Sea bass stuffed with garlic and herbs is a speciality as is the creamy shrimp *kishk* or casserole. Price is determined by weight and type of fish, ranging from grey mullet at E£40 per kilo to jumbo prawns at E£150 per kilo.

Qadoura (☎ 480 0405; 33 Sharia Bairam at-Tonsi, Bahari; meals E£35-80; 9am-3am) This is one of Alexandria's most authentic fish restaurants. Pick your fish from a huge ice-packed selection, which usually includes sea bass, red and grey mullet, bluefish, sole, squid, crab and shrimp, and often a lot more. A selection of mezze is served with all orders (don't hope for a menu). Most fish average E£40 to E£80 per kilo, prawns E£180 per kilo.

Fish Market (☎ 480 5119; Corniche, Bahari; mains E£50-80; noon-2am) Fish Market is the most upmarket fish restaurant in Alexandria. With prime views over the Eastern Harbour and flashy silver service, you can pick your own seafood and have it cooked to perfection any way you wish. It's on the Corniche beside the Kashafa Club.

Tikka Grill (☎ 480 5114; Corniche) With the same owners as Fish Market, and situated on the floor below it, Tikka Grill dishes up a similar, but more meat-centric, dining experience.

For quick eats, try the following:

Gad (Sharia Saad Zaghloul; snacks E£1-9; 24hr) Chain of absurdly popular take-away joints. Try the filled sandwiches, kebabs, ta'amiyya or mouth-watering shwarma.

Mohammed Ahmed (☎ 483 3576; 17 Sharia Shakor Pasha; mains E£2-5) The king of Alexandria's fuul and ta'amiyya scene.

El-Qobesi (☎ 486 7860; 51 Corniche; juices E£3-6; 24hr) The best darn mango and fruit shakes in Egypt.

Getting There & Away

AIR

Direct international flights fly into Alexandria's international airport, **Burg al-Arab** (☎ 459 1483), 60km west of the city, from Athens, Frankfurt and London as well as many Middle East capitals. There's a second, smaller airport at **Nouzha** (☎ 425 0527) where some flights land. **EgyptAir** (☎ 487 3357; 19 Midan Saad Zaghloul) has several daily flights to Cairo (from E£150 one way) and one daily flight to Sharm el-Sheikh (E£550 one way).

BUS

Long-distance buses all leave from the Moharrem Bey bus station **Al-Mo'af al-Gedid** (New Garage). It's several kilometres south of Midan Saad Zaghloul, reachable by microbus from Misr train station (50pt), or by taxi (E£10 to E£15 from the city centre).

West Delta (☎ 362 9685) and the slightly fancier **Superjet** (☎ 363 3552) both operate from here, as well as a few East Delta and Upper Egypt buses. West Delta has a convenient city centre **booking office** (☎ 480 9685; Midan Saad Zaghloul; 9am-10pm). Superjet's **booking office** (☎ 543 5222; Sidi Gaber train station; 8am-11pm) is opposite the Sidi Gaber train station.

Superjet has buses to Cairo (also stopping at Cairo airport) about every hour from 5am to 1am (2½ hours, E£25 to Cairo, E£35 to Cairo airport). West Delta has buses to Cairo every 30 minutes between 5am and 2am and charges E£23 to E£25, and E£35 to the airport.

For the North Coast and Siwa, West Delta has around 20 daily buses to Marsa Matruh (E£17 to E£30, four hours) between 6am and 1.30am. Many of these continue on to Sallum (E£28, nine hours) on the border with Libya. Four services go to Siwa (E£27 to E£30, eight hours) at 8.30am, 11am, 2pm and 10pm. Otherwise just take any Marsa Matruh bus and change there.

If you're heading to Sinai, Superjet has a daily 9pm service to Sharm el-Sheikh (E£100, nine hours) while West Delta has one at 9pm (E£80).

For the Red Sea and the Suez Canal, Superjet has a daily service to Hurghada (E£85, nine hours) at 8pm. West Delta has several services a day to Port Said (E£22 to E£25, four hours), four services to Suez (E£25 to E£30, 3½ hours) and buses to Hurghada at 9am and 6.30pm (E£80, nine hours). The Upper Egypt Bus Co runs three daily Hurghada buses (E£80).

SERVICE TAXI

Many service taxis in Alexandria are minivans, all departing from the main bus station in Moharrem Bey. From here taxis travel to Cairo (E£15 to E£18, three hours).

TRAIN

There are two train stations in Alexandria. The main terminal is **Misr Train Station** (☎ 426 3207), about one mile south of Midan Ramla. **Sidi Gaber Station** (☎ 426 3953) serves the eastern suburbs.

At Misr Train Station, 1st- and 2nd-class air-con tickets must be bought from the ticket office next to the tourist information booth; 2nd-class ordinary and 3rd-class tickets are purchased from the front hall. Cairo-bound trains leave from here at least hourly, from 4.30am to 10pm. The best trains, the *Turbini* and *Espani*, don't stop again until 2½ hours later when they arrive in Cairo. There are seven of these trains between 7am and 10.15pm (E£46/29 in 1st-/2nd-class air-con).

The next-best trains, the *Faransawi*, make a few extra stops and take three hours to get to Cairo. There are seven trains between 6am and 8pm (E£35/19 in 1st/2nd class).

Getting Around

TO/FROM THE AIRPORT

To get to the international airport, take bus 555 (E£6 plus E£1 per bag, one hour) from near the Cecil Hotel. A taxi should cost no more than E£100.

EgyptAir flights sometimes land at the smaller Nouzha airport, 10km from the city centre. To get there, catch minibus 711 or 703 (50pt) from Midan Orabi or Ramla. A taxi should cost around E£15.

BUS & MINIBUS

As a visitor to Alexandria, you won't use the buses much – the trams are a much better way of getting around. There are no real set departure points or stops for microbuses, but most whizz by Midan Saad Zaghloul or Midan Ramla and cost about 50pt for short trips. Just point yourself in the right direction, wave to flag one down, and yell out your destination.

TAXI

A short trip within town (eg Midan Ramla to Misr train station) will cost E£5. Midan Ramla to Sidi Gaber or Fort Quaitbey costs around E£10, to San Stefano E£15, and to the eastern beaches around E£25.

TRAM

Midan Ramla is the main tram station; from here, yellow-coloured trams go west and blue-coloured ones go east. Tickets cost 25pt. The most useful routes:

Tram No	Route
1 & 2	Ramla to Victoria, via the sporting club & Rushdy
6	Moharrem Bey to Ras el-Tin
15	Ramla to Ras el-Tin via El-Gomruk & Anfushi
16	Midan St Katerina to Pompey's Pillar
25	Ras el-Tin to Sidi Gaber, via Ramla
36	Ras el-Tin to San Stefano & Sidi Gaber

ROSETTA (AR-RASHID)

☎ 03 / pop 194,693

It is hard to believe that this dusty town that sits on the western branch of the Nile was once Egypt's most significant port. But its

THE ROSETTA STONE

The Rosetta Stone is the most significant find in the history of Egyptology. Unearthed in 1799 by a French soldier near Rosetta, this dark granitic stele records a decree issued by the priests of Memphis in 196 BC, on the anniversary of the coronation of Ptolemy V (205-180 BC). In order to be understood by Egyptians, Greeks and others living in Egypt, it was written in the three scripts current at the time – hieroglyphic, demotic (a cursive form of hieroglyphs) and Greek. At the time of its discovery scholars had still not managed to decipher hieroglyphs, and it was quickly realised that these three scripts would help crack the hieroglyph code and recover the lost world of the ancient Egyptians.

When the British defeated Napoleon's army in 1801, the original Rosetta Stone was taken as a spoil of war and shipped to London, where it can still be seen at the British Museum.

THE BATTLE OF EL ALAMEIN

In June 1942 the Afrika Korps, headed by German Field Marshal Erwin Rommel ('Desert Fox'), launched an all-out offensive from Tobruk, Libya, determined to take control of the strategically important Suez Canal. The Axis powers and their 500 tanks came within nearly 100km of their goal before the Allies, under the command of General Bernard Montgomery, stopped their advance with a line of defence at El Alamein. In October 1942 Montgomery's 8th Army swooped down from Alexandria with a thousand tanks, and within two weeks routed the combined German and Italian forces and drove them back to Tunisia. More than 80,000 soldiers were killed or wounded at El Alamein and in subsequent battles. Today a **war museum** (☎ 046-410 0031/0021; adult/student E£10/5; ⏲ 9am-4pm) and the Commonwealth, German and Italian **war cemeteries** mark the scene of one of the biggest tank battles in history.

The easiest way to visit is to organise a car and English-speaking driver through **Mena Tours** (Map p146; ☎ 03-480 9676; menatoursalx@yahoo.com; ⏲ 9am-5pm Sat-Thu) in Alexandria for approximately E£450 to E£500 per car. Otherwise, a private taxi will charge between E£200 to E£300 to take you to the museum and cemeteries and bring you back to Alexandria.

Alternatively, you can catch any of the Marsa Matruh buses from Al-Mo'af Al-Gedid station in Alexandria. You'll be dropped on the main road about 200m down the hill from the museum. Some have found the return trip to Alexandria more of a challenge – you'll need to try and flag down a minivan or passing bus by the side of the highway.

strategic position, between the Mediterranean and the Nile, made Rosetta an important military site. Today, the town's windy streets lie packed with market stalls selling produce while donkey carts still manage to outnumber cars. The major draw here are the attractive Ottoman-era merchant houses, several of them restored to former glistening-wood glory. Rosetta is also most famous as the discovery place of the stone stele that provided the key to deciphering hieroglyphics (see p151).

There is no tourist office, though the eager staff at the **tourist police** (Museum Garden) can point you in the right direction.

Sights

Rosetta's beautifully crafted **Ottoman-era merchants' houses** were built in the traditional Delta style in red and black flat-brick. Many of these three-storey structures are adorned with ornate *mashrabiyyas*, which are intricately assembled wooden screens. Among the 22 impressive buildings hiding along Rosetta's streets, several have been restored and are open to the public. These include the **House of Amasyali**, **House of Abu Shaheen**, and the wonderful **Hammam Azouz**, a 19th-century bathhouse. Sites are open from 9am to 4pm; tickets can be bought at the House of Amasyali and cost E£12/E£6 for adults/students and allow entry to all sites.

Sleeping & Eating

Rasheed International Hotel (☎ 045 293 4399; www.rosettahotel.jeeran.com; Museum Garden Sq; s/d E£90/123; ❄) Proudly Rosetta's newest, finest and first rodent-free hotel. This skinny, 11- storey hotel has austerely decorated but spotless new rooms, all with satellite TV, mini-bar and balconies with top views of town and the Nile.

The hotel's **restaurant** (☎ 045 293 4399; ❄) serves some of the better food in town. Alternatively, you can hunt down a few ta'amiyya stands and roast chicken places in the town's market streets.

Getting There & Away

The easiest way to make the 65km trip from Alexandria is by service taxi or microbus (both cost E£3 to E£5; one hour) from **Al-Mo'af Al-Gedid**, the long-distance bus station in Alexandria. Coming back it's easy to get a microbus from Rosetta's main roundabout, at the southwest entrance to town. A private taxi from Alexandria to Rosetta costs E£100 to E£160, including waiting time.

NILE VALLEY وادى النيل

In this part of the country, the life-giving Nile snakes its way through Egypt's desolate belly, as an over-abundance of ancient riches line its green shores.

LUXOR الأقصر

☎ 095 / pop 451,000

Built upon the once-brilliant 4000-year-old city of ancient Thebes, modern-day Luxor won the antiquity jackpot when it inherited the relics of one of history's most prosperous and powerful empires. Many of these relics seem to mushroom directly from the sprawl of this bustling modern Egyptian town. For most visitors, the opulent cache of tombs and funerary temples scattered across the West Bank make this Egypt's must-see destination.

History

Following the collapse of centralised control at the end of the Old Kingdom period, the small village of Thebes emerged as the main power in Upper Egypt under the 11th- and 12th-dynasty pharaohs. Rising against the northern capital of Heracleopolis, Thebes reunited the country under its political, religious and administrative control and ushered in the Middle Kingdom period. The strength of Thebes' government also enabled it to re-establish control after a second period of decline, liberate the country from foreign rule and bring in the New Kingdom dynasties.

At the height of their glory and opulence, from 1550 to 1069 BC, all the New Kingdom pharaohs (with the exception of Akhenaten, who moved to Tell al-Amarna) made Thebes their permanent residence. The city had a population of nearly a million, and the architectural activity was astounding.

Orientation

Luxor actually consists of three separate areas: the town of Luxor itself on the east bank of the Nile; the village of Karnak, 2km to the northeast; and the towns of Gurna, New Gurna and Al-Gezira near the monuments and necropolis of ancient Thebes on the west bank of the Nile.

Information

INTERNET ACCESS

Europa Internet (Map p154; ☎ 012 866 5558; Main Rd, Al-Gezira; per hr E£5; 8am-2am) Conveniently near the ferry stop on the West Bank.

Friends Internet Café (Map p154; ☎ 236 7260; Sharia Salah ad-Din; per hr E£10; 9am-11pm) Air-conditioned East Bank café serving up fast ADSL connections, ideal for Skyping or IMing.

Gamil Centre (Map p154; Lower Corniche; per hr E£10; 24hr) On the East Bank.

Rainbow Net (Map p154; ☎ 238 7938; Sharia Yousef Hassan; per hr E£6; 9am-midnight) East Bank café, up a laneway, posted from the street.

MEDICAL SERVICES

International Hospital (Map p154; ☎ 238 7192-4; Sharia Televizyon) The best medical care Luxor has to offer.

MONEY

Most banks have branches in Luxor offering ATMs and foreign exchange services. Money can be changed at a slew of forex offices around town. For travellers cheques, visit:

American Express (Map p154; ☎ 237 8333; 9am-4.30pm)

Thomas Cook New Winter Palace Hotel (Map p154; ☎ 237 2196; New Winter Palace Hotel; 8am-2pm & 3-8pm); Sharia Khalid ibn al-Walid (Map p154; ☎ 237 2620; 8am-2pm & 3-8pm)

POST

Main post office (Map p154; Sharia al-Mahatta; 8.30am-2.30pm Sat-Thu) There's also a branch in the Tourist Bazaar on the Corniche (Map p154).

TELEPHONE

Cardphones are scattered around town, and mobile phone shops selling local SIM cards and top-up vouchers are concentrated along Sharias al-Mahatta and Televizyon.

Telephone centrales can be found at the Old Winter Palace Hotel (Map p154; 8am-10pm); on Sharia al-Karnak (Map p154; 24hr); and at the train station (8am-8pm).

TOURIST INFORMATION

Main tourist office (Map p154; ☎ 920 0004; Corniche el-Nil; 8am-8pm) Opposite Luxor Museum, down along the waterfront. Branches at the train station (☎ 237 0258) and airport (☎ 237 2306) keep the same hours.

Tourist police (Map p154; ☎ 237 6620) In the bazaar south of Luxor Temple.

VISA EXTENSIONS

Passport office (Map p154; ☎ 238 0885; Sharia Khalid ibn al-Walid; 8am-2pm Sat-Thu) Almost opposite the Isis Pyramisa Hotel, south of the town centre. There's a branch in the West Bank, near the Antiquities Inspectorate Ticket Office.

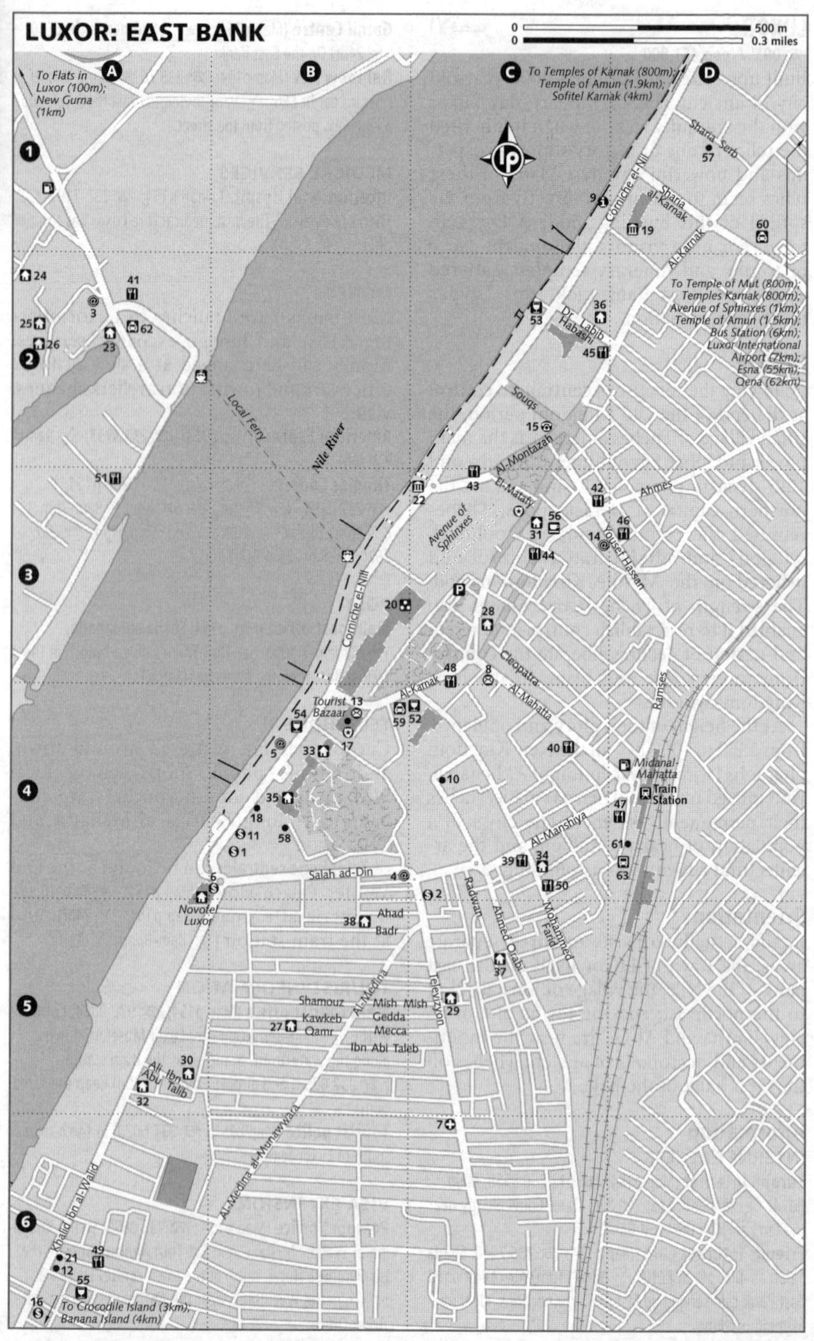
LUXOR: EAST BANK
0 500 m
0 0.3 miles
To Flats in Luxor (100m); New Gurna (1km)
To Temples of Karnak (800m); Temple of Amun (1.9km); Sofitel Karnak (4km)
To Temple of Mut (800m); Temples Karnak (800m); Avenue of Sphinxes (1km); Temple of Amun (1.5km); Bus Station (6km); Luxor International Airport (7km); Esna (55km); Qena (62km)
Nile River
Local Ferry
Corniche el-Nil
Sharia Serb
Sharia al-Karnak
Al-Karnak
Dr Labib Habashi
Souqs
Al-Montazah
El-Matafy
Avenue of Sphinxes
Ahmes
Youssef Hassan
Cleopatra
Al-Mahatta
Ramses
Tourist Bazaar
Midan al-Mahatta
Train Station
Al-Manshiya
Salah ad-Din
Novotel Luxor
Ahad
Badr
Radwan
Ahmed Orabi
Mohammed Farid
Shamouz
Kawkeb
Qamr
Mish Mish
Gedda
Mecca
Ibn Abi Taleb
Al-Medina
Televizyon
Ali Ibn Abu Talib
Al-Medina al-Munawwara
Khalid Ibn al-Walid
To Crocodile Island (3km); Banana Island (4km)

Sights

EAST BANK

Temples of Karnak

Simply referred to as **Karnak** (Map p154; ☎ 238 0270; adult/student E£50/25, tripod E£20; ⌚ 6am-5.30pm Oct-May, 6am-6.30pm Jun-Sep), the vast complex of extraordinary temples, pylons, obelisks and sanctuaries is quite possibly the most incredible sight in all of Egypt. A stunning representation of the power and prestige of the pharaohs and their Theban gods, one can only feel Lilliputian when confronted with this sprawling 2-sq-km site. Built, modified, enlarged and restored over a period of 1500 years, this was the most important place of worship in Egypt during the New Kingdom, and the main structure, the **Temple of Amun**, is considered to be the largest religious building ever built.

A **sphinx-lined path** that once went to the Nile takes you to the massive **1st Pylon**, from where you end up in the **Great Court**. To the left is the **Temple of Seti II**, dedicated to the triad of Theban gods – Amun, Mut and Khons. In the centre of the court is the one remaining column of the **Kiosk of Taharqa**, a 25th-dynasty Ethiopian pharaoh.

Beyond the **2nd Pylon** is the unforgettable 6000-sq-metre **Great Hypostyle Hall**. Built by Amenhotep III, Seti I and Ramses II, this hall is a pylon garden of 134 gargantuan, papyrus-shaped stone pillars that can only be described as humbling.

You can also visit an **Open Museum** (adult/student E£25/15) off to the left of the first court, where you can see a collection of statuary found throughout the complex, as well as three well-preserved chapels.

The prerequisite **sound-and-light show** (☎ 237 2241; www.soundandlight.com.eg; adult E£75, video camera E£40) is held here nightly. There are three or four performances in a variety of languages: check with the tourist office for the schedule or see the website.

A stampede of tour groups descends upon the site daily. It's best to come here in the early morning, late afternoon, or around tour-group lunchtime.

Microbuses make the short run to the temples from Luxor's centre for 50pt. A *calèche* (horse-drawn carriage) costs E£10 from Luxor Temple; a taxi costs E£10 to E£15.

Luxor Temple

Built on the site of an older sanctuary dedicated to the Theban triad, **Luxor Temple** (Map p154; ☎ 237 2408; adult/student E£40/20, tripod E£20; ⌚ 6am-9pm Oct-May, 6am-10pm Jun-Sep) is a strikingly graceful piece of Nile-side architecture. Largely built by the New Kingdom pharaoh Amenhotep III, Tutankhamun, Ramses II, Nectanebo, Alexander the Great and various Romans all

INFORMATION
American Express (see 35)
Banque du Caire & ATM 1 B4
Banque Misr & ATM 2 C4
Europa Internet 3 A2
Friends Internet Café 4 B4
Gamil Centre 5 B4
HSBC Bank & ATM 6 B4
International Hospital 7 C6
Main Post Office 8 C3
Main Tourist Office 9 C1
Nada Travel Service 10 C4
National Bank of Egypt & ATM 11 B4
Passport Office 12 A6
Post Office 13 B4
Rainbow Net 14 C3
Telephone Centrale (see 35)
Telephone Centrale 15 C2
Thomas Cook (see 33)
Thomas Cook 16 A6
Tourist Police 17 B4

SIGHTS & ACTIVITIES
Jolley's Travel & Tours 18 B4
Luxor Museum 19 D1
Luxor Temple 20 B3
Magic Horizons 21 A6
Mummification Museum 22 C3

SLEEPING
Al-Gezira Hotel 23 A2
Amon Hotel 24 A2
El-Fayrouz Hotel 25 A2
El-Nakhil Hotel 26 A2
Happy Land Hotel 27 B5
Horus Hotel 28 C3
Little Garden Hotel 29 C5
Morris Hotel 30 A5
Nefertiti Hotel 31 C3
New Pola Hotel 32 A5
New Winter Palace Hotel 33 B4
Oasis Hotel 34 C4
Old Winter Palace Hotel 35 B4
Philippe Hotel 36 C2
Princess Hotel 37 C5
Sherief Hotel 38 B5

EATING
Abou El-Hassan El-Shazly 39 C4
Abu Ashraf 40 C4
Africa Restaurant 41 A2
Chez Omar 42 C3
Jamboree Restaurant 43 C3
Lotus Restaurant 44 C3
Oasis Café 45 C2
Restaurant Elzaeem 46 D3
Salt & Bread Café 47 D4
Snack Time 48 C3
Snobs 49 A6
Sofra 50 C4
Tutankhamun Restaurant 51 A3

DRINKING
Ali Baba Café 52 C4
Cocktail Sunset 53 C2
King's Head Pub (see 21)
Metropolitan Café 54 B4
Murphy's Pub 55 A6
New Oum Koulsoum Coffee Shop 56 C3

TRANSPORT
Convoy Departure Point 57 D1
EgyptAir 58 B4
Local Taxis 59 B4
Service Taxi Station 60 D1
Superjet Ticket Office 61 D4
Taxi & Pick-up Parking Lot 62 A2
Upper Egypt Bus Co Ticket Office & Minibuses to Bus Station 63 D4

WEST BANK SITES

Tickets to the following sites must be purchased at the Antiquities Inspectorate Ticket Office (Map p158). Opening hours are from 6am to 4pm daily October to May, and 6am to 5pm June to September. Deir al-Bahri and the Valleys of the Kings and Queens have dedicated ticket offices and opening hours. All sites are shown on the map on p158.

Site	Adult/student (E£)
Assasif Tombs (Tombs of Kheruef & Ankhhor)	25/15
Assasif Tombs (Tomb of Pabasa)	25/15
Deir al-Medina Temple & Tombs (excl. Peshedu)	25/15
Deir al-Medina (Tomb of Peshedu)	10/5
Dra Abu'l Naga (Tombs of Roy & Shuroy)	12/6
Medinat Habu (Funerary Temple of Ramses III)	25/15
Ramesseum	25/15
Temple of Seti I	25/15
Tombs of the Nobles (Tombs of Khonsu, Userhet & Benia)	12/6
Tombs of the Nobles (Tombs of Menna & Nakht)	20/10
Tombs of the Nobles (Tombs of Neferronpet, Dhutmosi & Nefersekheru)	20/10
Tombs of the Nobles (Tombs of Ramose, Userhet & Khaemhet)	25/10
Tombs of the Nobles (Tombs of Sennofer & Rekhmire)	20/10

left their mark with additions to it over the centuries. Not to be outdone, the Arabs also built a mosque in an interior court in the 13th century.

Museums

The **Luxor Museum** (Map p154; Corniche el-Nil; adult/student E£75/35; 9am-3pm & 4-9pm Oct-May, 9am-3pm & 4-10pm Jun-Sep) is definitely worth a peek for its selective and excellently displayed collection, dating from the Old Kingdom to the Malmuk period. In the main downstairs hall, don't miss the finely crafted and well-preserved **relief of Tuthmosis III**, **statue of Thuthmosis III**, alabaster **figure of Amenhotep III**, and rare **Theban relief** dating from the Old Kingdom of Unas-ankh. The newest wing of the museum showcases the splendour of Thebes during the New Kingdom, with the highlight being two unwrapped royal mummies of **Amhose I** and possibly **Ramses I**, eerily presented in darkened rooms.

For mummy buffs (and who isn't one?), visit the small but interesting **Mummification Museum** (Map p154; Corniche el-Nil; adult/student E£40/20; 9am-2pm & 4-9pm Oct-May, 9am-2pm & 4-10pm Jun-Sep), down the steps opposite the Mina Palace Hotel. Its well-thought-out displays tell you everything you ever wanted to know about mummification and the journey to the afterlife.

WEST BANK

The lush Egyptian countryside of the bucolic West Bank conceals what has come to be known as the largest open air museum in the world. It was here, on the flood plains of the Nile and under the watchful gaze of the Theban hills, that the pharaohs built their memorial temples as a standing reminder of their immortality. Hundreds of tombs were excavated into the hills, built for kings, queens, royal children, nobles, priests, artisans and even workers. The most impressive burial chambers housed the bodies of mighty rulers, along with their wealth, their families, servants and anything else that might come be useful in the afterlife.

To see every site would cost nearly E£500 (without student card), take many days, and be utterly exhausting. It's best to select a handful of sites that you are most interested in and plan one or two days for your visit. Except for Deir al-Bahri (the Funerary Temple of Hatshepsut) and the tombs in the Valleys of the Kings and Queens, you can't pay for admission at the individual sites. Instead you must buy tickets in advance at the **Antiquities Inspectorate Ticket Office** (Map p158; 6am-4pm Oct-May, 6am-5pm Jun-Sep) on Main Rd, 500m west of the Colossi of Memnon. Tickets are valid only for the day of purchase, no refunds are given and students pay half price. Note that photography is strictly forbidden in all the West Bank tombs; if you're caught using a camera, guards will confiscate the film or memory card.

To give you an idea of the distances involved on the West Bank, from the local ferry landing it is 3km straight ahead to the Antiquities Inspectorate Ticket Office, past the Colossi of Memnon. From there it's 1km to the Valley of the Queens and 5km to the Valley of the Kings.

It should cost around E£100 to hire a taxi to bring you here from the East Bank and transport you from site to site. Alternatively, you can hire a bicycle on the East Bank and bring it over on the ferry. If you're footing it, you can catch the ferry, take a local pick-up truck (25pt; ask for 'Gurna') to the Antiquities Inspectorate Ticket Office, and then hire a rattletrap bike from the **bike hire place** (Map p158; per day E£10) next to the Nour el-Gourna hotel and pedal yourself around.

Colossi of Memnon

These 18m-high statues (Map p158; admission free) are all that remain of a temple built by Amenhotep III. The Greeks believed that they were statues of Memnon, who was slain by Achilles in the Trojan War.

Temple of Seti I

This pharaoh expanded the Egyptian empire to include Cyprus and parts of Mesopotamia. The temple (Map p158) is seldom visited, but is well worth a look.

Valley of the Kings

Once called the Gates of the Kings and the Place of Truth, this famous **royal necropolis** (Map p158; ☎ 231 1662; adult/student E£70/35; 🕑 6am-4pm Oct-May, 6am-5pm Jun-Sep) is dominated by the barren **Al-Qurn** (Horn) mountain. The tombs were designed to resemble the underworld; a long, inclined, rock-hewn corridor descends into either an antechamber or a series of halls, and ends in a burial chamber. Over 60 tombs have been excavated here, but not all belong to pharaohs. Only a few of the tombs are open to the public at any one time, though the most impressive tombs of **Tuthmosis III**, **Amenhotep II** and **Horemheb** were open at the time of research. Other tombs open to visitors include **Ramses VII**, **Ramses IV**, **Ramses IX**, **Ramses II**, **Merneptah**, **Ramses V/VI**, **Ramses III**, **Siptah**, **Queen Tawosret/Sethnakht**, **Seti II**, **Ramses I**, **Seti I**, **Montuhirkopshef** and **Tuthmosis IV**.

The **tomb of Tutankhamun** was found in 1922 by Howard Carter and is far from the most interesting. It requires an extra ticket (adult/student E£80/40) bought at the second ticket box when you enter the site, where the ludicrous toy train (E£1) stops. It's only worth paying the exorbitant entry fee if you've been to Cairo's Egyptian Museum and wish to see where this extraordinary cache was found.

Hiking across the **Theban Hills** from the Valley of the Kings to Deir al-Bahri is spectacular, and highly recommended if you have the energy, decent hiking shoes and an adequate supply of water. To start, ascend the steep cliff opposite the tomb of Seti I. Ask a guard to point you in the right direction as there's no signage. When you start climbing, souvenir vendors will offer to guide you to the ridge in return for a tip; be prepared for them to hawk their bits and pieces of tourist tat all the way. Once on the ridge, follow the path to the left and continue left when you come to a fork in the path. Follow the path around the ridge, passing a police post on your distant left, until you eventually see Deir al-Bahri down the sheer cliff to your right. Continue along the ridge, ignoring the steep trail that plunges down the cliff face, and almost complete a circle to descend in front of the ticket office to Hatshepsut's magnificent temple. The walk takes 50 minutes and is extremely steep in parts.

Deir al-Bahri (Funerary Temple of Hatshepsut)

Rising out of the desert plain in a series of terraces, the **Funerary Temple of Hatshepsut** (Map p158; adult/student E£25/15; 🕑 6am-4.30pm Oct-May, 6am-5pm Jun-Sep) merges with the sheer limestone cliffs of the eastern face of the Theban mountain. It was desecrated and vandalised by her bitter successor, Tuthmosis III, but retains much of its original magnificence, including some fascinating reliefs.

Assasif Tombs

Three of these 18th-dynasty tombs (Map p158) are open to the public – those of **Pabasa**, **Kheruef** and **Ankhhor**. Like the Tombs of the Nobles further south, the artwork concentrates on events from everyday life, such as fishing and hunting.

Tombs of the Nobles

There are at least 12 tombs (Map p158) in this group worth visiting; the most colourful are those of **Ramose & Userhet**, **Rekhmire** and **Nakht**. Tickets are sold for groups of two or three tombs.

Dra Abu'l Naga

Though 114 tombs of nobles and rulers were found here, most were plundered long ago. Two tombs that remain intact and are worth visiting include those of **Roy** and **Shuroy**.

Ramesseum

Ramses II was pretty busy during his lifetime building monuments to his greatness, and his **funerary temple** (Map p158) was to be the masterpiece. Sadly, it lies mostly in ruins.

Deir al-Medina

This small Ptolemaic temple (Map p158), dedicated to the goddesses Hathor and Maat, was later occupied by Christian monks – hence its name, literally 'the monastery of the city'.

Valley of the Queens

The 75-odd **tombs** (Map p158; adult/student E£25/15; 6am-4.30pm Oct-May, 6am-5pm Jun-Sep) in this valley belong to queens and other royal family members from the 19th and 20th dynasties. Only three – the tombs of **Titi**, **Amunherkhepshuf** and **Khaemwaset** – are currently open to the

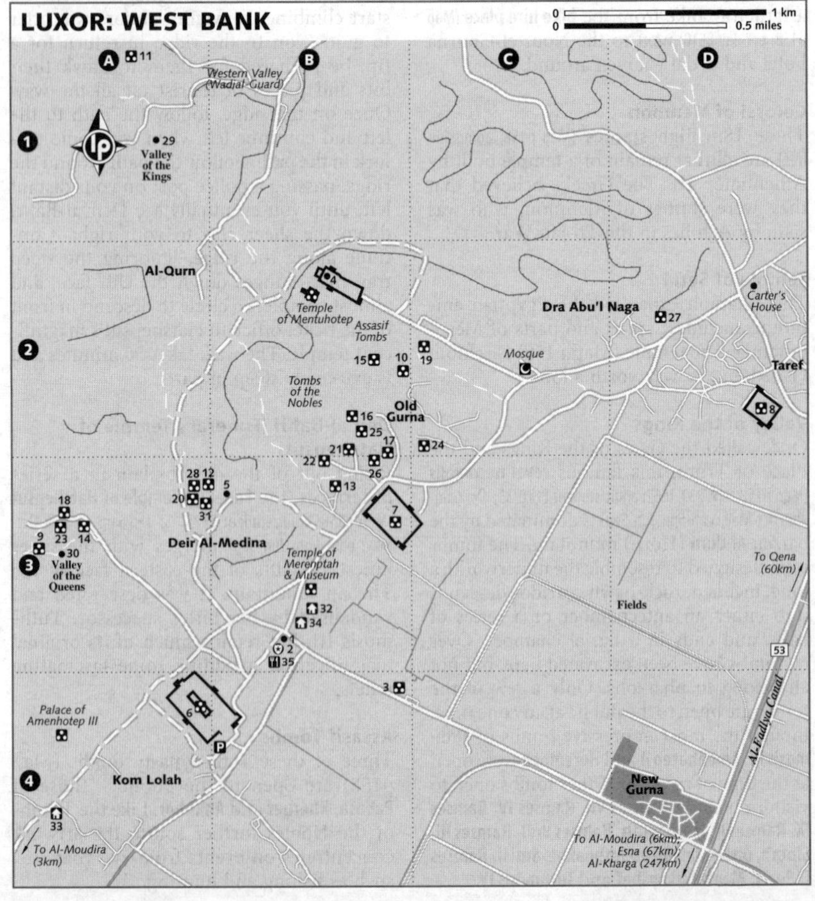

LIFE AFTER DEATH

Ancient Egyptians had developed an intricate belief system around death and the afterlife. Life in the beyond was believed to be a vast improvement on life on earth, a place where you literally could take everything with you. Burial chambers were packed with life's necessities – household goods, riches, and even family members and slaves – anything that might come in handy for a long and comfy life ever after. Corpses were ritually cleaned, hollowed out and mummified to create a body that would be useful for an eternity on the other side.

Belief had it that after death the deceased would travel along a treacherous river to the Hall of Final Judgement, where one's life would be reviewed by Anubis, god of mummification. A balance scale was used to measure the weight of one's heart against the 'feather of truth'. The heart was thought to hold a record of all the deeds of one's life, and if a heart was lighter than the feather (and thus chaste), eternal life with the gods was granted. If the heart was heavy with guilt and outweighed the feather, the deceased was consumed by Ammit, a hybrid crocodile, lion and hippopotamus creature, to disappear forever.

public. The crowning glory of the site, the **Tomb of Nefertari**, is still closed to the public until further notice due to restoration.

Medinat Habu

The temple complex of Medinat Habu is dominated by the enormous **Funerary Temple of Ramses III** (Map p158), inspired by the temple of his father, Ramses II. The largest temple after Karnak, it has an enthralling mountain backdrop and some fascinating reliefs. The best time to visit is in the late afternoon, when the setting sun interacts amazingly with the golden stone.

Activities

FELUCCA RIDES

Feluccas cruise the Nile throughout the day, and cost between E£30 and E£50 per hour per boat, depending on your bargaining skills. Captains will regularly ambush you along the Corniche, so it's easy to shop around for the best boat and price. The most popular trip is 5km upriver to Banana Island, a tiny, palm-dotted isle where locals grow fruit and vegetables. The trip takes between two and three hours, and is best timed so that you are on your way back in time to watch the sunset over Luxor from the boat.

BALLOONING

Sunrise balloon rides are offered by several companies, including **Magic Horizons** (Map p154; ☎ 236 5060; Sharia Khalid ibn al-Walid). Flights can be booked at most hotels – expect to pay between US$60 to US$100 (including transfers from your hotel and breakfast).

HORSE RIDING

A sunset ride around the West Bank temples is an unforgettable experience. Two West Bank stables offer guided horse rides, the best being **Arabian Horse Stables** (☎ 231 0024, 010 504 8558; 🕒 7am-sunset), which is known for its well-kept horses and tackle. If you phone

INFORMATION

Antiquities Inspectorate Ticket Office 1 B3
Tourist Police 2 B3

SIGHTS & ACTIVITIES

Bike Hire (see 34)
Colossi of Memnon 3 B4
Deir al-Bahri (Funerary Temple of Hatshepsut) 4 B2
Deir al-Medina 5 B3
Medinat Habu (Funerary Temple of Ramses III) 6 A4
Ramesseum 7 B3
Temple of Seti I 8 D2
Tomb of Amunherkhepshef 9 A3
Tomb of Ankhhor 10 B2
Tomb of Ay 11 A1
Tomb of Ipy 12 A3
Tomb of Khaemhet 13 B3
Tomb of Khaemwaset 14 A3
Tomb of Kheruef 15 B2
Tomb of Menna 16 B2
Tomb of Nakht 17 B2
Tomb of Nefertari 18 A3
Tomb of Pabasa 19 C2
Tomb of Peshedu 20 A3
Tomb of Rekhmire 21 B2
Tomb of Sennofer 22 B3
Tomb of Titi 23 A3
Tombs of Khonsu, Userhet & Benia 24 C2
Tombs of Neferronpet, Dhutmosi & Nefersekheru 25 B2
Tombs of Ramose & Userhet 26 B3
Tombs of Roy & Shuroy 27 D2
Tombs of Sennedjem & Inherka 28 A3
Valley of the Kings 29 A1
Valley of the Queens 30 A3
Workmen's Village 31 A3

SLEEPING

Marsam Hotel 32 B3
Nour al-Balad 33 A4
Nour el-Gurna 34 B3

EATING

Nour el-Gurna (see 34)
Restaurant Mohammed 35 B3

ahead to book, staff will collect you from the East Bank in a launch. Rides usually take three hours and cost E£25 per hour. They also offer camel (E£25 per hour) and donkey rides (E£20 per hour).

Tours

Travel restrictions for foreigners in the Nile Valley make independent travel a pain in the butt – it's considerably easier to visit sites north and south of Luxor on an arranged day tour. American Express and Thomas Cook (see p153) arrange tours for around US$35 to U$60 per person per half-day.

Jolley's Travel & Tours (Map p154; ☎ 237 2262; 🕐 9am-10pm) Has a fine reputation for its budget day trips.

QEA (☎ 231 1667; www.questfortheegyptianadventure.com) A British-and-Egyptian-run agency that tailors tours in and around Luxor and the Western Desert. A percentage of its profits go towards charitable projects in Egypt.

Sleeping

Though Luxor has some first-rate sleeping options, the cost of accommodation is a rollercoaster driven by demand. Many hotels drop their charges by 50% in the May to September low season. The second half of January is Luxor's busiest season as Egyptians travel over the school holidays – book ahead at this time.

It's best to decide whether to stay on the East or the West bank before you arrive, as getting between the two is not easy. The West Bank is quieter, has fewer touts and is closer to Luxor's main tombs and temples. There is a great selection of midrange accommodation choices, but it's pretty isolated and eating options are limited. The East Bank is where most of the shopping and entertainment action is, as well most of Luxor's budget hotels and cheap eateries. It's home to the Karnak and Luxor temples, Luxor Museum and a battery of *calèche* drivers, hotel touts and shop owners who seem to revel in hassling tourists.

Avoid the dodgy hotel touts who pounce on travellers as they get off the train – they get a 25% to 40% commission for taking you to certain hotels (which ends up being factored into your bill). They're also renowned for telling fibs about hotels that refuse to pay them commission.

EAST BANK

Budget

Princess Hotel (Map p154; ☎ 012 431 3699; Sharia Ahmed Orabi; s/d E£15/30, without bathroom E£10/20) Offering one of the cheapest places to kip in Luxor, this pad is a welcome addition to the ultra-budget scene. Don't expect fireworks; rooms are neat but uncomplicated, though the hallways have been gussied up with heartfelt murals. Staff are easygoing and chatty, and there's a scruffy, be-cushioned rooftop terrace. Bonus brownie points: you can order a cold Stella on the rooftop (E£10). Breakfast is E£5 extra.

Oasis Hotel (Map p154; ☎ 010 496 1848; Sharia Mohammed Farid; d E£40, s/d without bathroom E£20/30; 💻) This superb budget hotel is one of the best bang-for-buck deals in town. Scrupulously maintained by friendly staff, the generous, Smurf-blue rooms here are good enough to put your fussy grandma in. There's a lovely, rooftop terrace scattered with (blue) cushions, bike rental, free afternoon tea and free internet. Don't confused it with the subpar Nubian Oasis Hotel down the road.

Sherief Hotel (Map p154; ☎ 237 0757; sheriefhotel@yahoo.co.uk; Sharia Badr; s/d E£40/60, without bathroom E£25/50; ❄ 💻) Also called Bob Marley Home, this cosy establishment is down a hushed dead-end street and is plastered with posters of everyone's favourite Rastafarian. Attracting not only the dreadlock brigade, the small rooms at this hotel are very tidy, sporting ornate frilly touches. The extremely friendly owner Abdul promises a big breakfast of yoghurt and fruit, and the rooftop has views over the Nile. Student discounts available.

Happy Land Hotel (Map p154; ☎ 237 1828; www.luxorhappyland.com; Sharia Qamr; s/d E£65/74, without bathroom E£40/46; ❄ 💻) Perennially popular and often full, Happy Land has been attracting backpackers for eons. Managed by the animated Mr Ibrahim Abdul, this place has squeaky clean, freshly painted rooms, half of which have air-con and private bathrooms. The sometimes harried atmosphere can be a little much for some, but throw in generous breakfasts, soap and mosquito coils and most punters are happy. There's a rooftop lounge with satellite TV, bikes for hire and free laundry facilities.

Horus Hotel (Map p154; ☎ 237 2165; Sharia al-Karnak; s/d E£45/60) Frills are at a premium at this strategically situated old-timer. The rooms here have white tiles slapped on nearly every available surface and are kept just above minimum hygiene levels. While the management have a cavalier attitude to service, the view from the front-facing rooms is the Horus' saving grace – the balconies practically hang over the Luxor temple. Street noise can be an issue.

Nefertiti Hotel (Map p154; ☎ 237 2386; www.nefertitihotel.com; btwn Sharia al-Karnak & Sharia as-Souq; s/d E£50/80;) You can't beat this location: right in the thick of the market action and surrounded by *ahwas* on every side. This splendid budget option has unfussy but faultlessly maintained rooms with small private bathrooms and air-con. The roof terrace has views over to the West Bank, and the top-floor lounge has a pool table and satellite TV. A generous breakfast is included. Nice one.

Midrange

Little Garden Hotel (Map p154; ☎ 227 9090; www.littlegardenhotel.com; Sharia Radwan; s/d US$18/24;) Located down a side street in the bustling heart of the city, this slightly older hotel is a reliable midrange choice. The promised garden patio is small but cute and there's a rooftop restaurant with oriental offerings and 24-hour room service. Inside, the white/green rooms are kept in mint condition, and the service here is some of the most efficient in town. A 10% student discount is available.

Philippe Hotel (Map p154; ☎/fax 238 0050; Sharia Dr Labib Habashi; s US$20-35, d US$30-50;) While the Philippe's foyer is a ornate gallery of Egyptian artefacts and knick-knacks, the rooms are decidedly less elaborate. Still, they're comfortable enough and if you go for a deluxe room you'll get polished floorboards and some extra pine furniture thrown in. There's a rooftop pool here and discounts are often available.

New Pola Hotel (Map p154; ☎ 227 5081; www.newpolahotel.com; Sharia Khalid ibn al-Walid; s/d E£150/200;) Officially a three-star hotel, the amenities here flirt with four-star hotel standards and include a rooftop swimming pool, 24-hour room service and a pleasant downstairs restaurant and bar. Rooms from the 4th floor up have top Nile views, and while bordering on kitsch, all come with satellite TV, comfortable pink beds and other mod cons. Great value.

Morris Hotel (Map p154; www.hotelmorrisluxor.com; ☎ 227 9833; Sharia Ali Ibn Abu Talib; s/d E£170/250;) Don't let the overdone green marble and faux gold-leaf in the foyer put you off – the rooms at the four-star Morris take it easier on the glitz and are actually pretty smart. Abodes all come with satellite TV, a safe, full-sized baths and a mini-bar. There's an astroturf rooftop café here with a decent-sized pool next to it boasting great views and muzak on tap.

Top End

Sofitel Karnak (off Map p154; ☎ 237 8020; www.sofitel.com; Sharia Az-Zinai Gebly; r US$120-250;) This mammoth hotel lies sheltered among lush gardens several kilometres north of Karnak temple. A tranquil refuge from the bustle of town, the Moorish-inspired architecture and abundant greenery do wonders for its appeal. The garden bungalows here have all the expected mod cons, and extras include several restaurants, bars and cafés, a riverside pool, sauna, Jacuzzi, gym, tennis/squash courts and even a nearby golf course. Shuttle buses do pick-ups and drop-offs to and from town.

Old Winter Palace Hotel (Map p154; ☎ 238 0422; www.accorhotels.com; Corniche el-Nil; r Pavilion Bldg US$135-400, old wing US$250-1250;) This dainty Victorian relic on the Corniche, set amidst sprawling manicured gardens, is a significant monument in its own right. Built to house and impress visiting European nobility, the spectacularly adorned foyer and towering hallways alone are the stuff of legend. The new Pavilion Building in the garden is home to 118 comfortable rooms overlooking the large pool area, while the rooms in the old wing are much smaller, with half of them flaunting Nile views.

New Winter Palace Hotel (Corniche el-Nil; r US$95-135) Adjoining its older namesake, this hotel is package-tour territory, proffering 136 rooms that are sorely in need of a refit. Breakfast costs an extra E£81 to E£110.

WEST BANK

Budget

Marsam Hotel (Map p158; ☎ 237 2403; marsam@africamail.com; Gurna; s/d E£70/140, without bathroom E£45/90) Marsam easily scoops the 'best budget hotel on the west bank' plaudit. Built in the 1920s to house visiting archaeologists, the rooms at this tranquil hotel are simple, but kept faultlessly clean. The whole mud-brick building stays refreshingly cool in summer and there's a beautiful garden café overlooking a lush carpet of rice paddies. As a bonus, these guys support up-and-coming local artists, often displaying their works throughout the hotel. Reservations are a must. Situated near the Temple of Merneptah.

El-Gezira Hotel (Map p154; ☎ 231 0034; www.el-gezira.com; Al-Gezira; s/d with air-con E£70/100; ❄) Though showing its age, El-Gezera remains a popular west bank budget fave. Rooms all have air-con and are kept in good nick, with several boasting balconies overlooking the Nile. A fresh orange-on-orange paint job helps spruce the place up a little, and the relaxed lagoon-side café is ideal for an afternoon *shai* – though mosquitoes muster here in the evenings. Situated opposite the taxi stand.

Midrange

El-Fayrouz Hotel (Map p154; ☎ 231 2709; www.elfayrouz.com; Al-Gezira; s E£80/120, d E£120-150; ❄ 💻) This pink monolith brandishes arabesque arches and sleeping quarters, though views are at a premium. While the regular rooms are nothing to write home about, the two recently completed rooftop doubles – harbouring tall, brightly painted domed ceilings and lovingly adorned throughout – are where we'd put our money.

Nour el-Gourna (Map p158; ☎ 231 1430; www.nourelgournahotel.com; Gurna; s E£100-150, d E£150-300; ❄) Natural materials abound in this mud-brick, thatch-roofed little hotel opposite the Antiquities Inspectorate office. Rooms are stylishly decorated (some even have air-con) and there's a great shaded and cushioned indoor/outdoor restaurant serving food made from home-grown ingredients.

our pick **Nour al-Balad** (Map p158; ☎ 206 0111, 010 129 5812; Kom Lolah; s/d E£150/200) We absolutely love this bucolic, boutique hotel getaway. Hidden among greenery in the quaint village of Kom Lolah, this unique building flaunts its extensive and creative use of natural materials throughout. Here, trees sprout from mud-brick hallways open to the sky and light wells lead to tiny indoor courtyards. The generous rooms are super-cosy inside, using curved nooks in the mud walls to house lamps and crafty knick-knacks. There are both indoor and outdoor eating areas and the whole venture has an intimate and friendly vibe.

Amon Hotel (Map p154; ☎ 231 0912; www.amon-hotel-luxor.com; Al-Gezira; s/d €22/29, without bathroom €18/25; ❄) This family-run place is a favourite haunt of foreign archaeological missions. It dishes up great food, friendly service and speck-less rooms for reasonable prices. Comfortable rooms in the new wing have private bathrooms and balconies overlooking the attractive central courtyard garden. Five old-wing rooms have air-con, and some also have private bathrooms. The triple rooms on the roof terrace of the old wing boast breathtaking 360-degree views over to the Theban Hills and East Bank.

El-Nakhil Hotel (Map p154; ☎/fax 231 3922; www.el-nakhil.com; Al-Gezira; s/d €20/30; ❄) New on the hotel scene, this swish and attractive hotel presents an array of well-appointed rooms, including garden villas modelled on traditional Nubian abodes and a few dome-roofed numbers. You can get views either of the Nile or of rolling wheat fields, though their top-floor restaurant has vistas of both.

Top End

our pick **Al-Moudira** (off Map p158; ☎ 012 3251 307; www.moudira.com; Daba'iyya; r/ste €180/230; ❄ 🏊 💻) Built to resemble a Damascene courtyard house, this gorgeous hotel features luxurious rooms, whimsical interiors, a wonderful pool area and a stylish bar and restaurant. Some guests revel in its seclusion (it's a 15-minute taxi ride from the ferry landing), others end up feeling as if they're trapped in a gilded cage. We're of the former opinion: highly recommended.

Flats in Luxor (☎ 010 356 4540; www.flatsinluxor.co.uk; per week from US$330; ❄ 🏊 💻) If you're staying a week or more in Luxor, then renting one of these impressive flats could be for you. The main flats are located between Al-Gezira and New Gurna, are run by a British–Egyptian couple and feature three bedrooms (sleeping six), large sitting/dining areas, satellite TV and fully equipped kitchens. The two upper-floor flats have balconies with views over to the Theban Hills. There's a panoramic roof terrace with a pool table and sun lounges, and a downstairs area with a pool and Jacuzzi.

Eating

EAST BANK

Chez Omar (Map p154; ☎ 236 7678; Midan Yousef Hassan; salads E£3.50, mains E£15; 🕑 24hr) With both indoor seating and street-side tables near a small green *midan*, relaxed Chez Omar is a pleasant spot for a casual meal. The menu plays it pretty safe with modest Egyptian dishes, including kebabs and pigeon. With a nudge-nudge and a wink-wink, you can get Stella here for E£12.

Lotus Restaurant (Map p154; ☎ 238 0419; Sharia As-Souq;) For some great people observation with your dinner conversation, this spotless restaurant on the 1st-floor above the *souq* is a sure bet. The Egyptian dishes are dependable – try the lentil soup (E£6) or yummy chicken *tagen* (E£23) – or you can order European standbys like spaghetti napolitana (E£16).

Jamboree Restaurant (Map p154; ☎ 235 5827, 012 781 3149; Sharia al-Montazah; 10.30am-2.30pm for snacks & oriental mains, 6-10.30pm for full menu;) If you're hankering for a jacket potato (E£15 to E£23), spaghetti carbonara (E£31) or something else decidedly non-Egyptian, this British-run restaurant could be your cup of tea. Relax on the pleasant rooftop terrace or dine inside in the plain but speckless air-conditioned dining room. A selection from the salad bar costs E£15. As one traveller summed it up: 'good prices, great service, wonderful view – what more could one ask for?'

Oasis Café (Map p154; ☎ 237 2914; mains E£20-45; 10am-10pm;) Set in several rooms of a beautifully restored 1920s building, this elegant, modern café leaves little to be desired. There's art on the brightly coloured walls, soft jazz wafting through the air, smoking and nonsmoking rooms and free copies of *New Yorker* magazine. Lovely. Come for their enticing pastas (E£35 to E£42), succulent grilled meats (E£35 to E£50) or hearty sandwiches (E£22 to E£35), then linger a while over their selection of pastries and excellent coffee.

Snobs (Map p154; ☎ 227 6156; Sharia El Rwda; mains E£30-60;) In the heart of Luxor's self-styled British expat district, this smart-looking spot has etched itself a reputation for especially well-prepared fare. The menu runs the whole gamut from the oriental to the occidental, with a long list of chicken and meat dishes, pastas, pizzas, salads, soups and sandwiches on offer for both lunch and dinner.

our pick **Sofra** (Map p154; ☎ 235 9752; www.sofra.com.eg; 90 Sharia Mohammed Farid; mains E£14-50) For opulent, pasha-style dining that won't cost an arm and a leg, do not miss this place. Housed in several adorned private rooms and over a second-floor terrace, this beautiful restaurant is decked out with fanciful Arabesque flair: think wrought-iron lamps, hand-carved wooden furniture and enormous painted trays for tables, all illuminated by sensual lighting. The menu comprises interesting Egyptian dishes and is very sensibly priced, and service is very attentive. Best of all, you can relax and take in the surrounds over several varieties of herbal tea (E£6) or a sheesha (E£3) after your meal.

Snack Time (Map p154; ☎ 237 5405; Sharia al-Karnak; mains E£8-24;) This refreshingly modern and bright eatery is popular with students checking emails on the free wi-fi and gossiping about the day. The top-floor terrace looks right onto Luxor temple, and the food is an original mix of salads, wraps, baguettes, panini and pizzas. Try their frozen blended shakes – we dig the Oreo milkshake (E£9).

Also try the following:

Salt & Bread Café (Map p154; mains E£15-30) serves up the usual suspects of Egyptian cuisine. Go for the vegie moussaka (E£15), it's yummy. Opposite the train station.

Abou El-Hassan El-Shazly (Map p154; ☎ 238 0017; Sharia Mohammed Farid; mains E£15-25) The most genuinely friendly welcome in Luxor, with flavourful, no-frills Egyptian victuals.

Abu Ashraf (Map p154; Sharia al-Mahatta; mains E£4-15) Popular restaurant and takeaway serving decent *kushari*, pizza and kebabs.

Sharia al-Mahatta has a number of fine sandwich stands, juice stands and other cheap-eat possibilities. One of the most popular fast-food joints in town is **Restaurant Elzaeem** (Map p154; 24hr), where you can grab a table and enjoy tasty *kushari* (small/medium/large E£4/7/10) or spaghetti (E£7 to E£12). Situated halfway down Sharia Yousef Hassan.

WEST BANK

Nour el-Gourna (Map p158; ☎ 231 1430; Gurna; meals E£15-50) The restaurant of this little boutique hotel (see opposite) serves up delicious and hearty Egyptian food in either a pleasant courtyard or a cool dining room. The food is made using fresh home-grown ingredients and is definitely commendable.

Restaurant Mohammed (Map p158; ☎ 231 1014; Gurna; set meals E£25; 24hr) This laid-back family restaurant is set in and around the peaceful courtyard of Mohammed Abdel Lahi's mud-brick house, fronted by a 600-year-old tree. Mohammed's mum cooks up a yummy *kofta tagen* (meatballs cooked in a *tagen;* E£25), served with home-grown salad leaves; it goes down a treat with a cold Stella (E£10) or fresh lemon juice (E£3).

Africa Restaurant (Map p154; ☎ 012 266 1003; set menu E£25; ⏲ 10am-11pm) Not a bad place to get away from the West Bank hustle, the Africa is in a pleasant secluded and green courtyard. Popular with tour groups, they serve up large and flavourful set meals of chicken, fish, *kebab hala* (kebabs in a tomato sauce) or *kofta* with an avalanche of side dishes. If you ask nicely, the waiter can usually find a cold Stella (E£10) somewhere under the counter.

Tutankhamun Restaurant (Map p154; ☎ 231 0918; mains E£35-45) Just south of the ferry dock, this outdoor terrace restaurant is run by a cook who once worked on one of the French archaeological missions in Luxor. He serves up respectable set meals of roast chicken, duck *à l'òrange, kebab hala* or chicken curry, accompanied by a generous array of vegetable dishes, bread, soup, salad and tahina. The view here is top-notch.

Drinking

our pick Cocktail Sunset (Map p154; ☎ 237 2480; Corniche el-Nil; Stella E£11, cocktails E£48) This funky, retro lounge-bar is on a two-storey, fading yellow houseboat that looks like it's been dragged straight from the Mississippi (replete with flashing '50s neon 'Cocktail' sign). In the intimate, gently rocking upstairs lounge you can sip on some seriously dangerous (and pricey) cocktails, drink cheap beer and wine, snack on nibbles or sample some fancy-pants ice-creams (E£24). Belgian run, this bar oozes the sort of old-world elegance Luxor craves.

New Oum Koulsoum Coffee Shop (Map p154; coffee & sheesha E£4) A people-watching haven, this is deservedly the most popular *ahwa* in town. It's in the *souq*, next to the Nefertiti Hotel.

Metropolitan Café (Map p154; Corniche; Stella small/large E£10/15) This chain of terraced, Nile-side cafés (run by the same people as the identical Kebabgy cafés) is great for an evening tipple, though views are often obscured by moored cruise ships and the food is average.

Ali Baba Cafe (Map p154; Sharia al-Karnak, opp Luxor Temple) On a second floor terrace looking onto Luxor temple, this place has oodles of shade, awesome views and a cool Nile breeze – perfect for a quick *shai* or cold Stella (E£8).

The **Kings Head Pub** (Map p154; ☎ 228 0489; Sharia Khalid ibn al-Walid; ⏲ 10am-2am) is a British-style watering hole where you can watch English football on satellite TV over an Indian curry and wash it down with a cold beer (E£13). Not sure about you, but darts and pool feel just plain wrong to us in this heat. **Murphy's Pub** (Map p154; ☎ 238 8101; Sharia al-Gawazat; ⏲ 10am-2am), Kings Head's Irish counterpart, is nearby.

Getting There & Away

AIR

The **EgyptAir office** (Map p154; ☎ 238 0580; Corniche el-Nil; ⏲ 8am-8pm) is next to Amex. There are several daily connections with Cairo (E£356 one way) and Aswan (E£200 one way), and thrice-weekly flights to Sharm el-Sheikh (E£470 one way). Flights to Abu Simbel (E£550 one way) operate only in the high season, when there are one or two departures a day via Aswan. These entail ridiculously long transits, so you're much better off organising transport from Aswan.

BUS

The **bus station** (off Map p154; ☎ 232 3218; Sharia al-Karnak) is way out of town, located near the airport. There's an **Upper Egypt Bus Co ticket office** (Map p154; ☎ 237 2118; Midan al-Mahatta) just south of the train station. Taxis often wait to transfer passengers from the booking office to the bus station for around E£20 to E£30. There is one daily services to Cairo (E£91, 10 to 12 hours), departing at 7pm – it's best to book ahead for this service. There are six daily services to Aswan (E£20, four to five hours) via Esna (E£5, one hour), Edfu (E£10, two hours) and Kom Ombo (E£15, three hours). Nine buses run to Hurghada (E£30 to E£40, five hours) between 8.30am and 9pm, all travelling onto Suez (E£45 to E£60, eight to nine hours). There's one service at 5pm daily for Sharm el-Sheikh (E£110, 12 to 14 hours) and Dahab (E£120, 14 to 16 hours).

There is also a **Superjet ticket office** (Map p154; ☎ 236 7732; Midan al-Mahatta) near the train station. Superjet offers a slightly more comfortable service to Cairo at 8pm (E£90).

There are sometimes buses to Aswan (originating in Cairo) at 4am and 3pm (E£15), though the train is a much more reliable and comfortable option.

If you wish to head to Al-Kharga and the Western Oases, you'll need to catch the Cairo-bound train to Asyut and change for a bus to Al-Kharga there.

If you are travelling to the Red Sea coast, you'll need to catch a Hurghada-bound bus to Qift (minutes before Qena), from where you can hop on the 11am, 3.30pm or 6pm bus to Al-Quseir (E£15, three hours) and Marsa Alam (E£30, five hours).

CONVOY

It is usually compulsory for foreigners with private transport (including private taxis) to travel out of Luxor in a police convoy. At the time of research you were forced to travel by convoy to Aswan, Esna, Edfu, Kom Ombo, Hurghada, Dendara, Abydos, Qena, and part way to Marsa Alam and Al-Quseir. There are 10 checkpoints between Luxor and Hurghada and nine between Luxor and Aswan, so your chances of travelling outside the convoys are close to zilch.

The convoys to Hurghada leave at 8am, 2pm and 6pm daily, travelling via Qena and Safaga. The 8am convoy also stops at Dendara and Abydos, and the 2pm stops at Dendara but not Abydos. If you're travelling to Al-Quseir, you need to travel the first part of the trip with the Hurghada convoy.

Convoys to Aswan leave at 7am, 11am and 3pm. The 7am convoy makes stops at Esna, Edfu and Kom Ombo. If you're travelling to Marsa Alam, you need to travel the first part of the trip with the Aswan convoy.

All convoys leave Luxor from a road off the Corniche, north of the general hospital and Luxor Museum (Map p154).

CRUISES

The best times of the year for cruising are October/November and April/May. During the high season (October to May), an armada of cruise boats travels the Nile between Aswan and Esna (for Luxor), stopping at Edfu and Kom Ombo en route. You should be able to negotiate a decent discount on the usually high cruise price if you make your way to Esna and deal directly with the boat captains rather than booking through a travel agency. Feluccas can also be organised from Esna, but most travellers prefer to travel the other way (Aswan to Luxor), as this is how the current runs. See p173 for more information.

SERVICE TAXI

The service taxi station (Map p154) is on a street off Sharia al-Karnak, but because of police restrictions you will have to take an entire car and travel in convoy. This means paying about E£400 to Hurghada and E£250 to E£300 to Aswan. Be at the taxi stand 30 minutes before the convoy is due to leave.

With some gumption and perseverance, you may be able to persuade the police to let you travel the new direct road to Al-Kharga. If you can convince a taxi driver to take you, he will charge anywhere between E£400 to E£800 for the trip (three to four hours) due to the extra police hassle involved.

TRAIN

Luxor's **train station** (Map p154; Midan al-Mahatta) is conveniently located in the centre of town and contains a post office and left luggage facilities.

The **Abela Egypt Sleeping Train** (☎ 237 2015; www.sleepingtrains.com) services leave at 8pm and 9.30pm daily, arriving in Cairo at 5.45am and 6.45am the next morning. The trip costs US$60/80 per person one way in a double/single cabin and includes a basic dinner and breakfast. Children four to nine years old pay US$45. There are no student discounts and tickets must be paid for in US dollars or euros.

The only other Cairo trains that foreigners are allowed to take are train 981, departing at 9.30am; train 1903, departing at 9pm; and train 997, departing at 11.30pm. All trains stop in Qena (E£18/13 in 1st/2nd class) and Asyut (E£36/22 in 1st/2nd class). The trip to Cairo takes approximately 10 hours and costs E£91/40 in 1st/2nd class. Student discounts are available on all three services.

Foreigners are permitted to take three daily services to Aswan. These are train 996 (E£41/25 in 1st/2nd class), leaving at 7am; train 1902 (E£41/25), leaving at 9.20am; and train 980 (E£41/25), departing at 5pm. The trip takes three hours and student discounts are available. All three of the Aswan trains stop at Esna (E£14/12 in 1st/2nd class, 45 minutes), Edfu (E£19/15, 1½ hours) and Kom Ombo (E£25/18, 2½ hours).

In theory, there's a train from Luxor to Al-Kharga every Thursday at around 7am (E£11/10.25 in 2nd/3rd class, at least eight to 10 hours). In practice, full solar eclipses appear more frequently than this train.

Getting Around

TO/FROM THE AIRPORT

Luxor International Airport (☎ 237 4655) is 7km east of town. A taxi will cost around E£30 to E£40 to East Bank destinations and E£70 to E£90 to West Bank destinations. There are no buses between the airport and town.

BICYCLE

Easily the most pleasant way to get around both the East and West Banks, bicycles can be rented from most hotels for around E£10 to E£15. Be sure to check the roadworthiness of your two-wheeled steed, and take plenty of water if you plan on cycling in the heat of the day. It's no problem to take a bicycle on the ferry connecting the East and West Banks.

CALÈCHE

The most interesting way to get around town is by horse and carriage, called a *calèche* or *hantour*. Rates range from E£20 to E£50 per hour and are subject to haggling, bickering and – occasionally – yelling. You can usually bargain a short trip down to E£10. Be sure to agree on the price in Egyptian pounds, or you may subsequently be told to pay in British pounds or, more interestingly, the fictional 'Nubian' pounds (which are, naturally, worth more than their Egyptian equivalent).

FERRY & BOAT

Regular *baladi* (municipal) ferries carry passengers between the East and West Banks. You'll find the East Bank stop down a flight of stone stairs in front of the Luxor Temple, and the West Bank stop in front of the dusty car park where the pick-ups congregate. A ticket costs E£1 each way. Private launches charge E£5 each way for the same trip.

PICK-UP

On the West Bank, colourful pick-up trucks shuttle passengers from the ferry dock to various destinations for 25pt. To catch one, you flag it down from the side of the street; when you want to alight, push the bell on the inside of the partition between the driver and passengers. You can also hire one of these pick-ups as a private taxi for E£5.

NORTH OF LUXOR

Dendara دندرة

☎ 096

The wonderfully preserved **Temple of Hathor** (adult/student E£25/15; 🕑 7am-6pm) at Dendara is one of the most impressive temples in Egypt. Built at the very end of the Pharaonic period, its main building is still virtually intact, with a great stone roof and columns, dark chambers, underground crypts and twisting staircases, all carved with hieroglyphs. Hathor, the goddess of pleasure and love, is figured on the 24 columns of the Outer Hypostyle Hall, and on the walls are scenes of Roman emperors as pharaohs. The views from the roof are magnificent.

Dendara is 4km southwest of Qena on the west side of the Nile and an easy day trip from Luxor.

The tourist police actively discourage independent travel to Dendara, preferring travellers to take a day cruise from Luxor, or to travel by taxi or tour bus in the daily 8am and 2pm convoys. A taxi from Luxor to Dendara return will cost E£160 to E£220. If you decide to try your luck getting here under your own steam, your best bet is the bus to Qena, and a taxi from there to the site (E£20 to E£30 return). You may have to put up with a tourist police escort. See p164 for details.

Novotel's **MS Le Lotus** (☎ 238 0925; h1083@accor-hotels.com; adult/child E£355/177) cruises to Dendara on Sunday, Tuesday and Friday during the winter tourist season, leaving at 7am. Tickets include lunch and entry fees.

SOUTH OF LUXOR

Esna أسنا

The hypostyle hall, with its 24 columns still supporting a roof, is all that remains of the **Temple of Khnum** (adult/student E£15/10; 🕑 6am-4pm Oct-May, 6am-5pm Jun-Sep), constructed by Egypt's Ptolemaic rulers. Dedicated to the ram-headed creator god who fashioned humankind on his potter's wheel using Nile clay, its pillars are decorated with hieroglyphic accounts of temple ceremonies.

Trains running between Luxor and Aswan stop here (see p165 and p173), but the station is on the opposite side of the Nile, making this visit complicated. It's much easier to take a day tour or travel in a private taxi (from E£120 return) in the 7am daily convoy from Luxor.

UNLIKELY SOUVENIRS

The sights of Egypt have been attracting visitors for hundreds of years. In the 19th century, a perfectly common memento of a trip to Egypt was a mummy, either whole or in pieces. Hands and heads were particularly popular, as they packed well into one's luggage!

Edfu أدفو

The **Temple of Horus** (adult/student E£40/20; 6am-4pm Oct-May, 6am-5pm Jun-Sep) is the star attraction here, 53km south of Esna, as the most completely preserved Ptolemaic temple in Egypt. It was one of the last great Egyptian attempts at monument building on a grand scale (it took about 200 years to complete) and was dedicated to the falcon-headed son of Osiris. Walking through this awesome temple's halls, many filled with detailed inscriptions of temple rituals and priesthood rites, is both mesmerising and eerie.

Trains running between Luxor and Aswan stop here (p165 and p173); though the station is approximately 4km from the temple. Pick-ups travel between the station and town for E£8 (for the whole truck). Again, it's easier to take a day tour or travel in a private taxi (E£150 to E£200 return) in the 7am daily convoy from Luxor.

Kom Ombo كوم أمبو

The temple of **Temple of Sobek & Haroeris** (adult/student E£25/15; 6am-4pm Oct-May, 6am-5pm Jun-Sep), spectacularly crowning an outcrop at a bend in the Nile, is unique for its dual dedication to the crocodile and falcon gods Sobek and Haroeris. The symmetrical main temple dates from the Ptolemaic times, and among the halls and shrines inside you can view the remains of mummified crocodiles, which were once plentiful here as they basked on the Nile's shores.

The easiest way to visit Kom Ombo is to take a day tour or travel by private taxi in the morning convoys between Luxor and Aswan. A return taxi from Luxor to Edfu and Kom Ombo costs E£250 to E£300. If you're travelling from Luxor by train (p165), you can stop here and catch a pick-up from the station to the town (50pt), and then another (25pt to 40pt) from the town to the boat landing near the temple (4km). A taxi from town to the temple is around E£10. If you're coming from Aswan you can also catch the train (p173) or bus (p173).

ASWAN أسوان

☎ 097 / pop 1.2 million

With a pace of life as slow as the meandering Nile in this part of Egypt, picturesque Aswan will have you reaching for your point-and-shoot every few minutes. Just north of the first cataract and the southernmost boundary of ancient Egypt's empire, contemporary Aswan is a sleepy Nile-side town fringed by palms and sandy expanses and the river is dotted with flocks of graceful feluccas. Outside the summer months, when daily temperatures soar to 50°C, Aswan is an ideal place to sail the Nile the ancient way, or to base yourself as you explore the fantastic ruins of nearby Abu Simbel.

Orientation

The train station is at the northern end of town, with bus station a few kilometres further north. The lively souq (Sharia as-Souq) runs south from the square in front of the train station, parallel to the Corniche, which is home to banks, restaurants, shops and most of the public utilities. The southern end of the Corniche is where you'll find the Nubia Museum and a few of the city's better hotels.

Information

INTERNET ACCESS

Aswan Internet Café (Map p170; ☎ 231 4472; Corniche el-Nil; per hr E£10; 9am-midnight) In the oddly shaped El-Tagdiffe (Rowing) Club building on the Corniche.

Aswanet (Map p170; ☎ 231 7332; Keylany Hotel; per hr E£10; 9am-11pm)

Net Café (Map p170; per hr E£10) Air-conditioned, with fast, flat-screen PCs; located next to Nuba Nile Hotel.

MONEY

The main banks all have branches (with ATMs) on the Corniche. **Banque Misr** (Map p170) has a **foreign-exchange booth** (8am-3pm & 5-8pm) in its main building and there's an **Egypt Exchange office** (Map p170; 8am-6pm) on the Corniche. For travellers cheques and purchasing US dollars, try:

American Express (Map p168; ☎ 230 6983; Corniche el-Nil; 🕑 9am-5pm)
Thomas Cook (Map p170; ☎ 304 011; Corniche el-Nil; 🕑 8am-2pm & 5-9pm)

POST

Main post office (Map p170; Corniche el-Nil; 🕑 8am-2pm Sat-Thu)

TELEPHONE

Telephone centrale (Map p168; Corniche el-Nil; 🕑 24hr) At the southern end of town; international call can be made here.

TOURIST INFORMATION

Tourist office (Map p170; ☎ 231 2811; Midan al-Mahatta; 🕑 8am-3pm & 6-8pm) Next to the train station.

VISA EXTENSIONS

Passport office (Map p168; 🕑 8.30am-1pm Sat-Thu) On the 1st floor of the police building that's on the Corniche.

Sights

NUBIA MUSEUM

This little-visited but fascinating **museum** (Map p168; Sharia Abtal at-Tahrir; adult/student E£40/20; 🕑 9am-1pm & 5-9pm) showcases the history, art and culture of Nubia, and the collection ranges from prehistoric times to the present day. The extensive and clearly labelled collection is housed in a building that references traditional Nubian architecture. Make sure you have a good look at the 'Nubia Submerged' exhibition, which

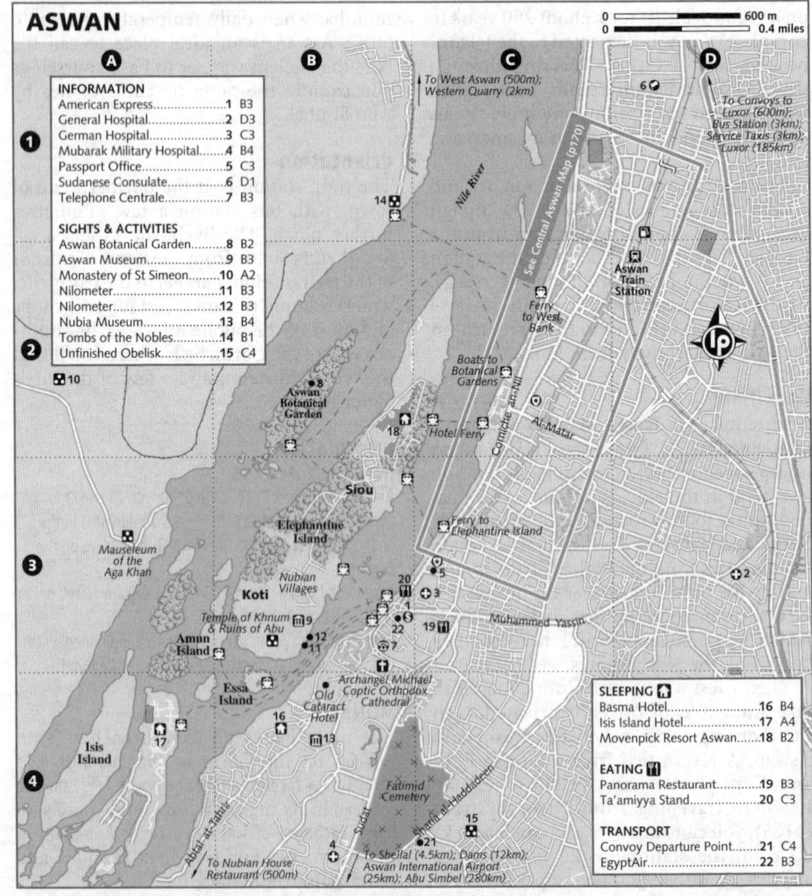

CRUISING THE NILE FELUCCA STYLE

It wasn't so long ago that the length of the Nile was swarming with the white-tipped sails of feluccas, the traditional wooden sail boats that have been cruising this river for eons. Motorised barges and colossal cruise boats may have taken some of the wind out of the felucca's sails, but this time-tested craft remains an idyllic way to travel the Nile.

Particularly popular around Aswan, it is here that a flock of 3400 swan-like vessels ply the river's gently sluicing waters. Trust us when we say the best way to experience this river is from the bow of a felucca as it lazily meanders its way from bank to bank. This is definitely not the fastest mode of transport around – one Egyptian proverb advises: 'the one who voyages the Nile must have sails made of patience' – but that's exactly the appeal. At the leisurely pace of the wind, you are immersed in the life of the river, passing within arm's reach of river-bank villages, fishermen plying their trade and palms swaying leisurely as the desert sunset burns bright. If you decide to take an overnight trip, you'll also be rewarded with the blinding vista of the night-time stars.

With so many boats and boat captains around, it's not hard to find an eager skipper willing to organise a multiday trip towards Luxor (that way currents will propel you if the wind fails). Feluccas are decked out in comfy cushions and usually hold six to eight passengers, making for a far more intimate experience than large cruise boats. Trips can be arranged from Aswan to the temples at Kom Ombo, Edfu or Esna and last between two and five days. Each evening, feluccas will moor and set up camp either on the shore or on the boat. Food will be prepared on the boat, and often captains and crew will burst into song and dance at the slightest provocation. Best of all, the fast-flowing bits of water south of Luxor are less likely to contain the nasty bug bilharzia (see p657), making a post-temple dip in the cool Nile a joy. For prices and practicalities, see p173.

includes photographs of Philae, Abu Simbel and Kalabsha before they were resited. The museum is a 15-minute walk from the town centre.

UNFINISHED OBELISK

This huge discarded **obelisk** (Map p168; adult/student E£25/15; 🕑 7am-5pm Oct-Apr, 8am-6pm May-Sep) lies on the edge of the northern granite quarries that supplied the ancient Egyptians with most of the hard stone used in pyramids and temples. Three sides of the 42m-long, 1168 tonne shaft were completed, *sans* inscriptions. It would have been the largest single piece of stone ever handled if a flaw had not appeared in the granite. Private taxis will charge around E£10 to bring you here from the centre of town.

ELEPHANTINE ISLAND

Aswan's earliest settlement, over 5000 years ago, was on this Nile **island** (Map p168). You can still see the ruins of the ancient community, called **Abu**, and two impressive **Nilometers** that lie at the southern end of the island, within the grounds of the small and humdrum **Aswan Museum** (Map p168; adult/student E£25/15; 🕑 8am-5pm Oct-Apr, 8.30am-6pm May-Sep). If you're keen to visit the museum or the two small colourful Nubian villages on the island, go down the stairs to the pontoon opposite the Thomas Cook office to catch a regular ferry (E£1). Note that women sit up front, men at the back.

ASWAN BOTANICAL GARDEN

Lord Kitchener turned this island into a verdant **botanical garden** (Map p168; admission E£10; 🕑 8am-5pm Oct-Apr, 8am-6pm May-Sep). You can still admire the remnants of his labours today, though you'll need to hire a boat or felucca to get here.

MONASTERY OF ST SIMEON

This well-preserved 6th-century mudbrick Coptic Christian **monastery** (Map p168; adult/student E£20/10; 🕑 8am-4pm Oct-Apr, 7am-5pm May-Sep) looks like a fortress and is a half-hour hike from the felucca dock near the Mausoleum of the Aga Khan. If you decide to take a camel or donkey instead of walking, you can usually get a return ride for E£30 after bargaining.

TOMBS OF THE NOBLES

A few of the Old and Middle Kingdom **tombs** (Map p168; adult/student E£20/10; 🕑 8am-4pm Oct-Apr, 8am-5pm May-Sep) of local dignitaries are worth exploring for their wall paintings and biographical hieroglyphics.

Activities

Top of the priority list for most visitors is a quick sluice between Aswan's many islands on a felucca. The afternoon is the ideal time to do this, as the fiery sun plonks itself down over Aswan's dunes. The 'official' price for hiring a felucca for one to eight people is E£25 to E£30 per hour; with a bit of bargaining you should be able get a boat for three hours for about E£60 to E£70, enough time to sail to Seheyl Island and back. For multiday trips, see p173.

Sleeping

Aswan's accommodation scene isn't nearly as good value as Luxor's. Be warned that hotels in the centre of town, particularly those on the Corniche, can be noisy at night.

BUDGET

Nubian Oasis Hotel (Map p170; ☎ 231 2123/6; nubian oasis_hotel_aswan@hotmail.com; Sharia as-Souq; s/d with air-con E£30/40, without bathroom E£25/30;) Worth considering only if you're on a super-shoestring budget, this tattered hotel barely makes concessions to minimum standards of cleanliness. To top it off, the staff here seem spectacularly uninterested in the whole endeavour.

Hathor Hotel (Map p170; ☎ 231 4223; fax 230 3462; Corniche el-Nil; s/d E£55/80;) What this hotel lacks in charisma it more than makes up for in cleanliness. The sometimes gloomy rooms are covered in bleach-cleaned tiles and proffer boxy bathrooms and air-con. A big bonus here is the great pool on the rooftop with breathtaking Nile vistas.

Keylany Hotel (Map p170; ☎/fax 231 7332; www.keylanyhotel.com; Sharia Keylany; s E£55-66, d E£70-93;) The pick of the town's budget bunch, the longstanding Keylany is run like clockwork. Their newer, freshly painted air-conditioned rooms are kept hospital-clean, though the cheaper fan rooms in the older section are showing their age. The big draw here is the quiet location and a lovely rooftop café that's kitted out in natural materials, with lots of shade and hearty breakfasts served every morning. There's a small kiddie pool on the roof to help you cool down and you can use wi-fi for E£25 per 24 hours.

Ramses Hotel (Map p170; ☎ 230 4000; Sharia Abdal al-Tahrir; s/d E£85/120;) The friendly management almost make you forgive the tattered '60s decor inside this high-rise hotel.

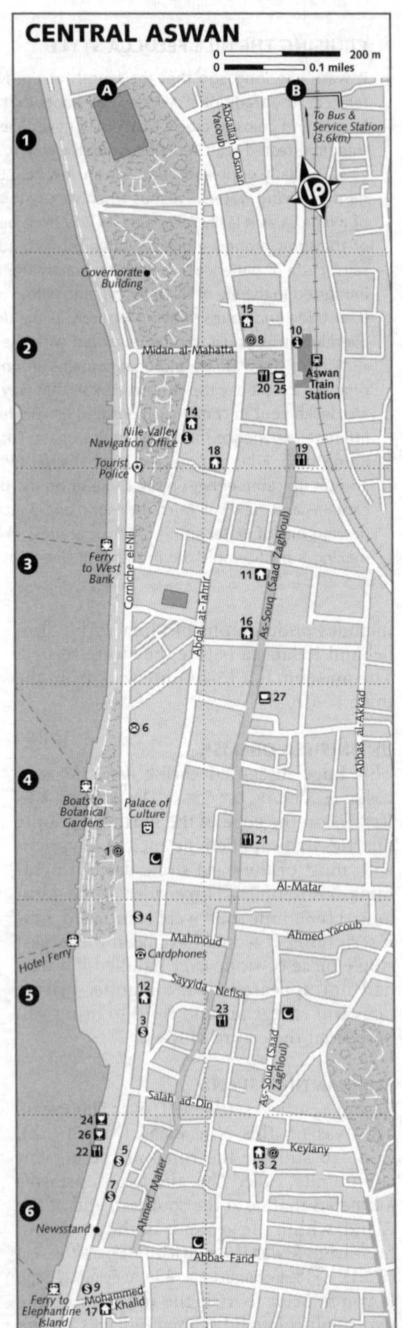

Don't expect fireworks: rooms here are just comfy enough, and some even manage to eke out a slim view of the Nile.

Nuba Nile Hotel (Map p170; ☎ 231 3267; www.nubanile.com; s/d E£100/130;) You will be pleased to discover that the rooms here surpass the low expectations set by the disappointing foyer. These freshly painted abodes all have bathrooms and air-con; some bright rooms sport balconies overlooking the street, though others wallow in windowless darkness – check out a few. It's next to a popular *ahwa* near the station, convenient for backpackers dragging big bags.

MIDRANGE & TOP END

At the time of research Aswan's grandest and most impressive establishment, the Old Cataract Hotel, was closed for renovations and scheduled to reopen sometime in 2010. Check the Sofitel website (www.sofitel.com) for the latest information.

Orchida St George (Map p170; ☎ 231 5997; www.orchida-sg-hotel.com; 9 Sharia Mohammed Khalid; s US$25-35, d US$35-45;) In a quiet spot well off the main drag, the tidy and slightly tacky rooms here aim for homely comfort rather than style. The pricier abodes have large balconies to appreciate the great views from here and the keen management seems amenable to giving discounts.

Cleopatra Hotel (Map p170; ☎ 231 4001/3/4; fax 231 4002; Sharia as-Souq; s/d US$47/59;) A dependable midrange option, this attractive hotel hovers right over the main *souq*. With a spacious and elegant foyer, inside the Cleopatra plays it safe with unpretentious, trim rooms offering satellite TV and private bathrooms. The small rooftop pool is a nice bonus.

Marhaba Palace Hotel (Map p170; ☎ 233 0102/4; www.marhaba-aswan.com; Corniche el-Nil; s US$56-83, d US$88-99;) The spiffy Marahaba leaves much of its midrange competition in the Aswan dust. The rooms here are top notch: bright, modern, fastidiously clean and attractively finished in light-coloured pine furniture (IKEA eat your heart out). Throw in a roof terrace with Nile views, a fitness centre and spa and – drum roll – we have a winner.

Basma Hotel (Map p168; ☎ 231 0901; www.basmahotel.com; Sharia Abtal at-Tahrir; s/d US$120/165;) Concrete reigns supreme at this shipshape four-star hotel, opposite the Nubia Museum. Basma has a neat garden, a huge pool as well as enticing Nile views, especially from the terrace rooms at the end of the building. Breakfast is extra.

our pick Movenpick Resort Aswan (Map p168; ☎ 230 3455; www.moevenpick-aswan.com; s/d from US$130/150;) Fresh from a whopping US$15 million facelift, and with its major competition the Old Cataract closed for renovations, this five-star resort is easily the best place to bed down in Aswan. Ignore the ugly '80s concrete tower: inside, the contemporary, minimalist decor is slick if not downright stylish. The hotel has all the usual amenities, including a massive pool, restaurants and a funky bar that wouldn't be out of place in New York's hippest hangouts. It's located on Elephantine Island with a free 24-hour ferry shuttling guests to and from the mainland.

Isis Island Hotel (Map p168; ☎ 231 7400; www.pyramisaegypt.com; Isis Island; s/d from US$147/190;) Set on its own private island (reachable by a free ferry), this pink monolith of a hotel looks like it escaped from Barbie's house-set collection. The rooms here are perfectly comfortable, though more chintzy than glamorous, and all dish up great vistas over the Nile. The hotel is a big hit with tour groups and is set among manicured lawns. It sports a massive pool with swim-up bar, mini-golf for the kiddies, a gym, spa and wi-fi.

INFORMATION

Aswan Internet Café	1	A4
Aswanet	2	B6
Banque du Caire (ATM)	3	A5
Banque Misr (ATM)	4	A5
Egypt Exchange Office	5	A6
Foreign-exchange booth	(see 4)	
Main Post Office	6	A4
National Bank of Egypt (ATM)	7	A6
Net Café	8	B2
Thomas Cook	9	A6
Tourist Office	10	B2

SLEEPING

Cleopatra Hotel	11	B3
Hathor Hotel	12	A5
Keylany Hotel	13	B6
Marhaba Palace Hotel	14	A2
Nuba Nile Hotel	15	B2
Nubian Oasis Hotel	16	B3
Orchida St George	17	A6
Ramses Hotel	18	B2

EATING

Chief Khalil	19	B2
El-Tahrir Pizza	(see 25)	
Fiteer Stand	20	B2
Kushari Store	21	B4
MonaLisa Caffee	22	A6
Shawish	23	B5

DRINKING

Aswan Moon Restaurant	24	A6
Cafés	25	B2
Emy	26	A6
Noba Coffee Shop	27	B4

Eating

Nubian House Restaurant (off Map p168; ☎ 232 6226; mezze E£4-5, mains E£7-20) The afternoon views of the First Cataract from the terrace of this chilled and friendly eatery are utterly breathtaking and shouldn't be missed. As well as serving authentic Nubian dishes, it's equally welcoming to guests who come to linger over a tea (E£4) and a sheesha (E£3). Be warned that gaggles of tour groups often book out the tables with the best views. To get here, follow the road from the Basma Hotel and veer right after 15 minutes, when it comes to a fork past a development of upmarket housing. Don't attempt the walk at night – catch a taxi.

Shawish (Map p170; Sharia as-Souq; set meal E£7) This hole-in-the-wall eatery swarms with famished locals come chow time. The set meals are finger-licking good and comprise meat or chicken and rice, salad, bread, vegies, soup and the best damned tahina sauce this side of Lake Nasser. Best of all, it will barely make a dent in your wallet at E£7. It's down a blind alley of the main *souq*.

Panorama Restaurant (Map p168; ☎ 230 6169; Corniche el-Nil; mains E£8-15) Creaking under the weight of its arabesque trinket collection, this is one of the most atmospheric eateries along Aswan's Nile. Serving up fish *tagen* (E£17) as well as a wide range of herbal and medicinal teas (E£3), the food here is good, though not as great as we remember it. Romantics will love the outside terrace, which is dripping with foliage and has premier river views.

MonaLisa Caffee (Map p170; Corniche el-Nil; meals E£10-18) This Aswan old-timer has recently had the full 'Bedouin' makeover, with cosy floor-cushioned sitting spaces, Bedouin tents and a separate intimate terrace looking onto the river. The staff seem ever eager to please, and the tagines are economically priced and darned tasty. You can get Stella here for E£7.50.

El-Tahrir Pizza (Map p170; Midan al-Mahatta; pizzas E£10-25; 🕑 24hr) This corner café, opposite the train station, does a roaring trade in scrumptious Egyptian pizza. Cheekily, prices are inflated on the English version of their menu – if you can convince them that you understand the Arabic menu you'll pay half as much for pizzas.

Chief Khalil (Map p170; ☎ 231 0142; Sharia as-Souq; meals E£25-50; ⛝) This tiny but busy seafood eatery grills delicious fresh fish from Lake Nasser and the Red Sea over coals and serves it up with salads, and rice or French fries.

For a quick bite, the most popular place in town is the **ta'amiyya stand** (Map p168) next to the Aswan Coffee Shop. It's opposite a public oven and uses freshly baked bread in its sandwiches. For good, cheap *fiteer*, hit the **fiteer stand** (Map p170) on the southern side of Midan al-Mahatta. To scratch a *kushari* itch, try the **kushari store** (Map p170; Sharia as-Souq; koshary E£3-5) with a couple of outdoor tables on Sharia as-Souq, just around the corner from Sharia al-Matar.

Drinking

Nubian House Restaurant (☎ 232 6226) Easily the most atmospheric tea-and-sheesha spot in town. It also serves meals (left).

Noba Coffee Shop (Map p170; Sharia Saad Zaghloul) Right in the middle of Aswan's hot stretch of *souq*, this is a nifty place to rest and sip a *souq*-side *shai* or sheesha (E£5 each).

The **cafés** (Map p170) on the busy corner of Midan al-Mahatta and Sharia as-Souq are great places to linger over a honey-drenched baklava and a glass of tea.

If you haven't yet been accosted along the Corniche and want to meet up with some felucca captains, two popular hangouts are **Aswan Moon Restaurant** (Map p170; ☎ 231 6108; Corniche el-Nil; mezze E£4-9, mains E£18-30) and **Emy** (Map p170; ☎ 230 4349; Corniche el-Nil; meals E£8-15). Located on a floating pontoon/houseboat respectively, the cheap food at these places sure ain't nothin' to rave about, but they remain popular with tourists and boat captains alike – particularly for the cheap beers (E£7 to E£8) and evening Nile breeze.

Getting There & Away

AIR

EgyptAir (Map p168; ☎ 231 5000; Corniche el-Nil; 🕑 8am-8pm) offers several daily flights between Aswan and the capital (around E£450 one way, 1¼ hours). The hop to Luxor starts at around E£200 one way (30 minutes) and leaves daily at 9am. Flights to Abu Simbel (E£785 return) depart at 6.30am and 9am.

BOAT TO SUDAN

See p645 for details of the weekly ferry to Wadi Halfa.

BUS

The bus station is 3.6km north of the town centre. A taxi to the town centre (including the hotels near the Nubia Museum) will cost around E£10; a seat in one of the regular service taxis is 50pt. Buses leave for Cairo (E£91, 13 hours) at 3.30pm, though the train is a far more comfortable option. There are six daily services to Luxor (E£20, four to five hours) via Kom Ombo (E£5, one hour), Edfu (E£10, two hours) and Esna (E£15, three hours). To Suez (E£60 to E£70, 12 hours), buses leave at 6am and 5pm, travelling via Hurghada (E£45 to E£55, seven hours). Extra services to Hurghada run at 8am and 3.30pm. There is also one 6.30am service to Marsa Alam (E£25, six hours). Note that there is a supposed to be a limit of four foreigners per bus, so it pays to book ahead of time or arrive early.

CONVOY

It is compulsory for foreigners with private transport to travel between Luxor and Aswan by convoy, and the nine checkpoints along the way mean that it is unlikely you can skirt the long arm of the law. Two daily convoys leave Aswan from the **departure point** (Map p168) in front of Fatimid Cemetery. The 8am convoy travels via Esna, Edfu and Kom Ombo, allowing stops at each of these sites, while the 2pm convoy travels direct to Luxor and barely allows one brief toilet stop en route. From Luxor, the convoy continues to Hurghada.

See p175 for details of the daily convoys to Abu Simbel.

FELUCCA

Aswan is the best place to arrange overnight felucca trips (see also boxed text p169). The most popular trips are to Kom Ombo (one night, two days) or Edfu (two to three nights, three to four days), but some people go on to Esna (four nights, five days).

Prices are usually based on six people travelling on the felucca; if there are fewer passengers the price per person will be higher. The standard cost is E£36 per person for one night, E£65 for two nights and E£80 for three nights. Be sure to pay at the end – trips have been known to be shortened for so-called 'breakdowns'. All passengers must pay an extra E£5 per person for a permit, plus the cost of food and drink supplies. Some tips before you head off: check the river-worthiness of your vessel; establish what the price includes and try to go along for the food shopping; and try to meet fellow passengers beforehand – you'll be sharing a very tight space with them for a few days.

SERVICE TAXI

At the time of writing, the police in Aswan were forbidding foreigners from taking service taxis between Aswan and Luxor, often turning them back at the checkpoint just north of town. In general it's better to take the bus or train, or else get a group of people together and hire a private taxi (which can travel with the convoys). A taxi to Luxor will cost E£200 to E£250; or E£250 to E£300 if you stop at Kom Ombo, Edfu and Esna en route.

TRAIN

Aswan Train Station (Map p170) is at the northern end of the As-Souq. The **Abela Egypt Sleeping Train** (☎ 230 2124; www.sleepingtrains.com) services leave at 5pm and 6.30pm, arriving in Cairo at 5.45am and 6.45am the next morning. Tickets cost US$60/80 per person one way in a double/single cabin. Children four to nine years old pay US$45. There are no student discounts and tickets must be paid for in US dollars or euros. The price includes a modest dinner and breakfast.

Other air-conditioned tourist trains to Cairo (E£110/56 in 1st/2nd class, 13 hours) via Luxor (E£42/26 in 1st/2nd class, three hours) leave at 6am, 6pm and 8pm, with tickets booked in advance. Extra Luxor-only trains also leave at 8am and 4pm; tickets for these are bought on board the train. A student discount is available on these tickets for both classes.

All of these trains stop at Kom Ombo (E£21/12 in 1st/2nd class, 45 minutes), Edfu (E£27/18, 1¾ hours) and Esna (E£35/21, 2½ hours).

Getting Around

TO/FROM THE AIRPORT

Aswan International Airport (☎ 248 0333) lies about 25km southwest of town; the taxi fare into town should be no more than E£30. A service taxi between the airport and the centre of town costs E£1.

THE HIGH PRICE FOR EGYPTIAN COTTON

World over, high-quality Egyptian cotton is revered among textile merchants and savvy cloth connoisseurs alike. Unbeknownst to most fabric-fondling cognoscenti, but knownst to us, the humble cotton plant was single-handedly responsible for bankrupting Egypt and ushering in nearly 70 years of colonial rule.

The story goes back to the thriving cotton plantations of the USA's deep south. During the American Civil War, the Confederate government froze lucrative cotton exports to Europe in an attempt to blackmail Britain into supporting the Confederate cause. Snubbing their collective noses at this, British and French merchants turned to Egypt for their supplies. This consortium invested heavily in the region's plantations, enticing Egypt's leader Ismail Pasha to borrow heavily from European banks. The end of the Civil War in 1865 resulted in a crash in cotton prices as cheap exports from the USA resumed. As a result, Egypt's spiralling economy soon found itself facing bankruptcy, and by 1875 Ismail was forced to sell his 44% stake in the Suez Canal to Britain. A year later, control of Egypt's finances was completely relinquished to its debtors and the country watched helplessly as it was eventually annexed by the British Empire in 1882.

Cotton is still grown in Egypt, and this region's particular variety boasts longer fibres than any other cotton in the world – allowing extremely fine, lustrous and durable yarns to be spun from it. But really, what a high political price to pay for some extra-snug bed sheets.

CALÈCHE

A *calèche* trip along the Corniche will cost around E£10.

FERRY

Public ferries shuttle regularly throughout the day from Aswan to Elephantine Island and the West Bank. Fares are E£1 each way.

TAXI

A 3½-hour taxi tour to the Temple of Philae, High Dam and Unfinished Obelisk costs around E£35. A taxi anywhere within town costs E£5.

AROUND ASWAN

Philae (Aglikia Island) معبد فيله

The dreamy **Temple of Philae** (adult/student E£40/20; 7am-4pm Oct-Apr, 7am-5pm May-Sep), just south of Aswan, was dedicated to god Isis who found the heart of her slain brother, Osiris, on Philae Island (now submerged). Relocated stone by stone in the 1970s to save it from being flooded by the High Dam (an ambitious construction project completed by the British in 1902), Philae today retains a regal grandeur that's bound to impress. Most of the temple was built by the Ptolemaic dynasty and the Romans. Early Christians later turned the hypostyle hall into a chapel.

Tickets are purchased from the small office before the boat landing at Shellal, south of the Old Dam. You'll pay around E£30 for a taxi to bring you here, wait for an hour or so and then bring you back to town. You'll need to negotiate a price for a boat to take you between the ticket box and the island – the captains have formed a cartel, so it's very hard indeed to organise a return trip for less than E£40 per boat, particularly at night. It's often best to hop on a boat with a larger tour group, where you can easily negotiate the price down to E£5 each return.

A nightly **sound-and-light show** (☎ 230 5376; www.soundandlight.com.eg; adult/child E£80/44), lasting 1½ hours, is held at the temple. Check the website or the tourist office (p168) in Aswan for performance times and languages.

Abu Simbel أبو سمبل

☎ 097

Ramses II, never one to do things by halves, surpassed even himself when he had the magnificent **Great Temple of Abu Simbel** (☎ 400 325; adult/student E£80/44; 6am-5pm Oct-Apr, 6am-6pm May-Sep) carved out of a mountainside. The temple was dedicated to the gods Ra-Harakhty, Amun and Ptah as much as to the deified pharaoh himself. Guarding the entrance, the four famous colossal statues of Ramses II sit majestically, each more than 20m tall, with smaller statues of the pharaoh's mother, Queen Tuya, his beloved wife, Nefertari, and some of their children.

The other temple at the Abu Simbel complex is the rock-cut **Temple of Hathor**, fronted by six 10m-high standing statues. Four represent Ramses and the other two Nefertari.

Both temples were moved out of the way of the rising waters of Lake Nasser in the 1960s and relocated here.

Sound-and-light shows (www.soundandlight.com.eg; adult/child E£80/44) are performed here each night. The website and the tourist office (p168) in Aswan will have the latest schedules.

There are banks in town, but no ATMs. You can eat at the **Seti Abu Simbel** or at a clutch of ramshackle **eateries** (including ta'amiyya and shwarma stands) on the main street.

SLEEPING

Abu Simbel Village (☎ 012 363 9794; s/d E£80/110; ❄) Catering to the budget set, the rooms wear the BBC (Basic But Clean) moniker with pride. Frills are at a premium; don't expect much more than a concrete courtyard and wheezing air-con.

Eskaleh (☎ 012 368 0521; fikrykachif@genevalink.com; s €30-35, d €40-60; 💻) A self-styled Nubian cultural centre, this sensational little hotel is housed in traditionally constructed mud-brick buildings and filled with local furniture and crafts. Rooms are simple but have more sparkle than most, and the modern tiled bathrooms are a welcome addition. There's a lovely restaurant-lounge, a roof terrace with views over the lake and serenity aplenty. The friendly owner Mr Fikri Hassan (described by one Thorn Tree poster as 'a true gentleman') serves three-course meals (E£50) featuring produce grown in their organic vegetable garden and hosts regular performances of Nubian music and dance.

GETTING THERE & AWAY

Most foreigners travel to Abu Simbel in one of the two official daily convoys from Aswan. These leave at 4am and 11am, take 3½ hours to get to the site and allow two hours before returning. No taxis are allowed to travel in the convoy, so your only options are luxury coach (if you're part of a tour group) or more cramped minibuses (if you've paid for a tour through one of Aswan's hotels or travel agencies). You'll need to shop around to get the best deal for a day tour – Thomas Cook charges E£280 for a seat on its bus while most of the budget hotels in town sell return seats for around E£55 to Abu Simbel, or E£65 with stops at the High Dam, Temple of Philae and the Unfinished Obelisk.

The only way to avoid the convoy is to travel on the services offered by the Upper Egypt and El Gouna Bus Cos. These leave from the Aswan bus station at 8am and 11.30am, take four hours and cost E£25 one way. Officially, a maximum of four foreign tourists are allowed on each bus; best to arrive at the bus station well ahead of time. Bring your passport, as there are two checkpoint stops. In Abu Simbel the buses depart from the front of the Wady El Nile Restaurant on the main street.

EgyptAir has two daily flights from Aswan to Abu Simbel (E£785 return), leaving at 6.30am and 9am.

WESTERN OASES
الواحات الغربية

The vast sandy expanses west of the Nile make up the Western Desert, a natural wonder as unfathomable as it is inhospitable. Stretching all the way to the Great Sea of Sand, five major oases lie in this formidable khaki ocean – islands of fresh water and verdant greenery. On the valley floor of the oases you can explore crumbling Roman forts, flourishing palm plantations and the ruins of medieval, labyrinth-like fortified towns. It's also here that you'll find the eerie rock formations of the White and Black Deserts, a dreamscape of white pinnacles eroded into an alien landscape of surreal shapes, as well as the almost forgotten oasis of Siwa.

Paved roads now connect the oases, and while travel in this region takes time, the Western Desert vaunts some of the most jaw-dropping scenery and photogenic journeys in all Egypt.

KHARGA OASIS الواحات الخرجة

☎ 092

Kharga is one of those places that hides its treasures under a veneer of provincial insignificance. Unfortunately this, the largest of the oases, is often blighted by over-exuberant tourist police who insist on shadowing all foreigners in the name of 'safety'.

Information

The helpful **Nile Valley Tourist Office** (☎ 792 1206; Midan Nasser; 🕐 8am-3pm Sat-Thu) is at the northern end of town. The **Banque du Caire** (off Sharia Gamal Abdel Nasser) has an ATM and will change cash and travellers cheques.

Sights & Activities

The town itself, **Al-Kharga**, is of little interest, though it houses the impressive **Antiquities Museum** (Sharia Gamal Abdel Nasser; adult/student E£25/15; ⌚ 8am-5pm). Just 2km north of town is the well-preserved **Temple of Hibis** (adult/student E£25/15; ⌚ 8am-5pm Oct-Apr, 8am-6pm May-Sep), built in honour of the god Amun by the Persian emperor Darius I. To the east are the remains of the **Temple of An-Nadura** (admission free), built by the Romans, and just north is the Coptic **Necropolis of Al-Bagawat** (adult/student E£25/15; ⌚ 8am-5pm Oct-Apr, 8am-6pm May-Sep), dating as far back as the 4th century. South of the town are the fortified Roman temples of **Qasr al-Ghueita** and **Qasr az-Zayyan** (per site adult/student E£25/15; ⌚ 8am-5pm Oct-Apr, 8am-6pm May-Sep).

Sleeping & Eating

Hamadalla Hotel (☎ 792 0638; fax 792 5017; off Sharia Abdel Moniem Riad; s/d E£40/55, with air-con E£65/85; ❄) A hotel popular with overland tour groups, Hamadalla has hygienic rooms that are unfortunately gloomy and garnished with ruffled furniture. There are a number of different room configurations, so ask to see a few.

Kharga Oasis Hotel (☎ 792 4940; Midan Nasser; s/d E£70/95; ❄) Another modern homage to concrete, the '60s Kharga Oasis nonetheless serves up the best-value nap in town. A favourite of desert adventurers, it sports generous and comfortable rooms and friendly, courteous staff, and has a lush, palm-filled garden and terrace. Construction of some great, traditional mud-brick bungalows in the palm groves out back may have been completed by the time you read this.

Pioneers Hotel (☎ 792 9751-3; www.solymar.com; Sharia Gamal Abdel Nasser; s/d half board from €99/132; ❄ 🏊 💻) While the salmon-pink, low-rise construction is reminiscent of a hollowed-out sponge cake, the hotel does offer a level of comfort that was until recently unimaginable in the oases: a swimming pool, fitness area, Bedouin café, ATM, billiards and a children's playground all connected by ridiculously lush grass. It is the only joint in Al-Kharga where you can count on getting alcohol.

Getting There & Away

The airport is 5km north of town, from where private flights run by **Petroleum Surface Company** are tentatively scheduled to Cairo. A 15-seater plane leaves Cairo on Sundays at 8am and returns from Al-Kharga at 4pm the same day (€50 each way, 1½ hours). Contact the Tourist Information Office for schedules and bookings.

Upper Egypt Bus Co (☎ 792 0838; Midan Sho'ala) operates buses from the station behind Midan Basateen to Cairo (E£35 to E£40, eight to 10 hours) at 7am, 9.30pm and 11pm. The 7am bus goes via Asyut. There are seven other buses to Asyut (E£9 to E£10, three to four hours) leaving between 6am and 9pm. At the time of writing, to get to Luxor by public transport you had to head to Asyut and change there for a bus or train to Luxor.

The **service-taxi station** (Midan Sho'ala) is next to the bus station, with destinations including Asyut (E£10, three to four hours) and Dakhla (E£10, three hours). Thanks to a new road, private taxis can get you to Luxor (via Jaja) in three hours, but it will set you back at least E£400. Cairo (six to seven hours) costs E£600 for the car (maximum seven people), but expect a long, hot, cramped ride.

Al-Kharga's **train station**, on the road south to Baris, has one weekly departure to Luxor, supposedly leaving on Fridays at 7.30am (E£11/10.25 in 2nd/3rd class). Be warned that this phantom train rarely *actually* runs.

DAKHLA OASIS الواحات الدخلة

☎ 092

Dakhla exemplifies the sort of lethargic pace, shaded by swaying oasis palms, that is life in the Western Desert. The oasis is centred around two small towns, Mut and Al-Qasr, though the former is the bigger of the two and has most of the hotels and facilities.

Information

The **tourist office** (☎ 782 1685/6; Sharia as-Sawra al-Khadra, Mut; ⌚ 8am-3pm & some evenings) is on Mut's main road. To get googling, albeit at carrier-pigeon speeds, try **MidoNet** (per hr E£1; ⌚ 8am-late) on the way to the Anwar Hotel. The **Bank Misr** (Sharia Al-Wadi, Mut) in Mut will change cash and give advances on Visa and MasterCard, but it doesn't have an ATM.

Sights & Activties

Eager explorers will find over 600 **hot springs** in the area – make sure you investigate a few. The biggest highlight remains the remarkable mud-brick citadel at Al-Qasr, also home to a small **Ethnographic Museum** (Al-Qasr; admission E£3; 9am-sunset). Local guides are happy to take you through the citadel's narrow winding lanes and into its half-hidden buildings (tip of around E£10 expected).

Sleeping

Gardens Hotel (782 1577; Sharia al-Genaye, Mut; s/d E£19/24, with shower E£18/23) Low prices and a prime location help keep the rooms occupied at this ramshackle but popular budget hotel. There's a bamboo café on the roof here, though the shared bathrooms can be pretty dire and single women may feel uncomfortable. Breakfast is extra and the hotel rents bicycles for E£10 per hour.

El-Negoom Hotel (782 0014; fax 782 3084; north of Sharia as-Sawra al-Khadra, Mut; s/d E£60/70, with air-con E£70/90;) On a quiet street behind the tourist office and near a selection of restaurants, this extra-friendly hotel has a span of trim little abodes with bathrooms, some even with air-con and TV. One of the most dependable options in town.

Bedouin Oasis Village (012 669 4893; s/d E£70/150, full board E£100/200) A relative newcomer on a rise above the town, this pad has well-designed, traditional-style buildings replete with a deluge of domes, arches and vaults. Nifty and arty touches in the humble-but-cosy rooms and in the communal areas really spruce the place up, and the restaurant (dinner around E£20) has splendid views. There's a 'Bedouin spa' (ie a natural spring pool) on the premises.

Al-Qasr Hotel (787 6013; Al-Qasr; s/d/tr E£10/20/30) The sprightly and ever-helpful Mohamed captains this great little guesthouse, which sits above a café near the old town of Al Qasr. The bucolically charming rooms have screens, balconies and even fortress views. There's a breezy upstairs communal sitting area, and for E£2 you can sleep on a mattress on the roof. The ground-floor coffeehouse and restaurant serve good, hearty fare (breakfast E£3 extra). Mohamed rents bikes for E£5 a day and arranges camel tours.

Desert Lodge (772 7061/2, in Cairo 02-690 5240; www.desertlodge.net; Al-Qasr; s/d half board €75/100;) The swishest accommodation in Dakhla also has the best views of Al-Qasr. This thoughtfully designed mudbrick fortress of a lodge crowns a hilltop overlooking the town and comprises 32 large rooms in traditionally styled clusters. The restaurant is adequate, and there is also a bar and many of the services you would expect for the hefty price.

Eating

Ahmed Hamdy's Restaurant (782 0767; Sharia as-Sawra al-Khadra, Mut; meals E£2-15) On the main road west of Mut, Ahmed Hamdy's popular restaurant serves delicious chicken, kebabs, vegetables and a few other small dishes. The freshly squeezed lime juice is excellent and you can request beer (E£12) and sheesha.

Said Shihad (Sharia as-Sawra al-Khadra, Mut; meals E£6-15) Owner Said is onto a great thing here: grilling up a meat-centric feast nightly to a dedicated following of hungry locals. The lamb *shish-kebab* is the thing to go for – yum!

Getting There & Away

All buses leave from near the new mosque on the main square in Mut. From here, **Upper Egypt Bus Co** (782 4366; Midan al-Gamaa, Mut) runs a 7pm and 8.30pm service to Cairo (E£50 to E£55, 10 to 12 hours) via Al-Kharga (E£10, two hours) and Asyut (E£20, four hours). Other Asyut buses leave at 6am, 8.30am and 10pm. Different buses leave at 6am and 7pm for Cairo via Farafra Oasis (E£20, three hours) and Bahariya Oasis (E£35, seven hours). There's a booking office in Mut at Midan al-Tahrir. The **Herz Bus Company** (782 4914; Microbus & Service taxi station) runs a daily bus to Cairo at 8pm (E£45).

Microbuses leave when full from the old part of Mut, near the mosque, and cost E£10 to Al-Kharga, E£20 to either Farafra or Asyut and around E£60 to Cairo.

Crowded pick-ups, Peugeots and microbuses head out from town to Al-Qasr, Balat and Bashendi from in front of the hospital for E£1.

FARAFRA OASIS الواحات فرافرا

092

Blink and you'll miss the smallest, and probably dustiest, of the oases. Farafra can be an alternative setting-off point for trips into the spectacular White Desert (see box p178), but is hardly worth visiting

THE WHITE & BLACK DESERTS

Upon first glimpse of the **White Desert** (Sahra al-Beida) dreamscape, you'll feel like a modern Alice fallen through the desert looking-glass. Beginning just 20km northeast of Farafra, the yellow desert sands here are pierced by chalky rock formations, sprouting almost supernaturally from the ground. Blindingly white spires of rock reach for the sky, each frost-coloured lollipop licked into an ever-odder shape by the dry desert winds. The surreal shapes soon start to take on familiar forms: chickens, camels, hawks and other uncanny shapes. They are best viewed at sunrise or sunset, when the sun turns them hues of pink and orange, Salvador Dali–like, or under a full moon, which gives the landscape a ghostly, arctic, whipped-cream appearance. A few kilometres north of here, the desert changes again and becomes littered with quartz crystals, best viewed at the famous Crystal Mountain.

Further north, the change in the desert floor from beige to black signals the beginning of the **Black Desert** (Sahara Suda). Here, layers of mountain-eroded black powder and rubble lie strewn all over the sandy earth. The landscape here stands in stark contrast to the nearby White Desert.

Only 4WD vehicles can enter deep into the deserts, so you'll need to arrange a tour to get the most out of your visit. Though closer to Farafra Oasis, **Bahariya Oasis** (see below) is the most popular jumping off-point into these areas and has hundreds of eager tour operators offering overnight adventures in the sand. For an overnight camping trip, expect to pay anywhere between E£150 to E£400 per day.

otherwise. The only tourist attraction in the town is **Badr's Museum** (☎ 751 0091; donation E£5; 🕑 8.30am-sunset). We salute the effort put into this place by enthusiastic local artist Badr Abdel Moghny.

Sleeping & Eating

Al-Waha Hotel (☎ 016 209 3224, 012 720 0387; wahafarafra@yahoo.com; d with/without bathroom E£45/35) A small, primitive hotel opposite Badr's Museum, Al-Waha has basal two- and three-bed rooms with barely acceptable shared bathrooms. Frills are definitely in short supply here.

Al-Badawiya Safari & Hotel (☎ 751 0060, 012 214 8343; www.badawiya.com; s/d US$22/32, s/d villa with air-con US$39/50;) The Ali brothers dominate Farafra tourism with their massive hotel and slick safari outfit. Al-Badawiya has a wide choice of stylishly designed and traditionally themed rooms and is dotted with cushioned sitting areas, has a refreshing pool, and parades more than its fair share of arches and domes. Breakfast costs E£20. Camel and jeep trips into the Western Desert are arranged from here.

Dining choices are limited. The restaurant in the **Al-Badawiya Hotel** (meals E£25-50) serves meals and has a solid reputation. You'll find a shack on the main road called **Al-Tamawy Restaurant** (mains E£2-10) that serves up tea and staples at a few tables. Alcohol isn't available in Farafra.

Getting There & Away

Buses travel to Cairo (E£46, eight to 10 hours) via Bahariya (E£20, 2½ hours) daily at 10am and 10pm. Buses coming from Cairo travel on to Dakhla (E£20, 4½ hours, two daily) and pass by at around 1pm and 2pm. Buses leave from outside the shops at the Dakhla end of the main street. Tickets are issued on board.

Occasional microbuses travel to Dakhla and Bahariya for the same prices.

BAHARIYA OASIS الواحات البحرية

☎ 02

Bahariya is the Western Desert's most bustling and visited oasis. Set among hills and dotted with innumerable palms and springs, Bahariya is also the most convenient jumping-off point for the White and Black Deserts (see boxed text, above). Be warned that there is ferocious competition among tour guides offering trips into the deserts. It might be helpful to speak to your hotel or contact the tourist office for a list of reputable guides.

Buses will drop you at **Bawiti**, the dusty main village. Attractions include the **Temple of Alexander**, 26th-dynasty tombs at **Qarat Qasr Salim** and the 10 famous Greco-Roman **Golden Mummies** on show near the **Antiquities Inspectorate Ticket Office** (admission to 6 sites adult/student E£35/25; 🕑 8.30am-4pm), just south of the main road in Bawiti.

Information

The **tourist office** (☎ 3847 3900; Main St, Bawiti; 8am-2pm & 7-9pm Sat-Thu) is on the town's main roundabout. Helpful office manager Mohamed Abd el-Kader can also be contacted on his mobile (☎ 012 373 6567). You can get online at **M&N Internet** (per hr E£10; 8.30am-9.30pm Sat-Thu), on the main road near Popular restaurant. The **National Bank of Development** (8am-2pm Sun-Thu), in the first street on the right after the tourist office, has no ATM but will change money (though not travellers cheques).

Sleeping & Eating

Desert Safari Home (☎ 3847 1321, 012 731 3908; www.desert-safari-home.com; dm E£15, s/d E£50/65, with air-con E£80/120, without bathroom E£35/50) The friendly family that runs this guesthouse looks ready to sign your adoption papers the minute you walk in the door. Whitewashed rooms encircle cute, garden gnome–inspired greenery, and a vine-shaded sitting area is refreshingly cool. Their restaurant serves a full dinner for E£20 and has beer. It's a long walk from town, but pick-you-ups are available, as are bicycles for hire.

New Oasis Hotel (☎ 3847 3030; max_rfs@hotmail.com; s/d E£50/80, with air-con E£100/120) A study in curvaceous construction, this small but homely hotel by El-Beshmo spring has several teardrop-shaped rooms, some with balconies overlooking the expansive palm groves nearby. Inside, the rooms are aged but kept in fine condition, though someone's been a little overzealous with the powder-blue paint.

Old Oasis Hotel (☎ 3847 3028, 012 232 4425; www.oldoasissafari.com; s/d E£80/140, with air-con E£120/180) This is one of the most charming places to stay in Bawiti. The Old Oasis Hotel sits above a pretty, shaded garden of palm and olive trees by El-Beshmo spring and has 13 homely and impeccably maintained fan rooms, as well as a few fancier, stone-walled air-conditioned rooms. A large pool receives steaming hot water from the nearby spring; the runoff waters the hotel garden. A fine restaurant serves full meals (dinner E£30), and you can rent motorbikes from here (E£150 per day) and access the internet (E£10 per hour).

Badr Sahara Camp (☎ 3847 2955, 012 792 2728; www.badrysaharacamp.com; Gebel al-Ingleez; huts per person E£25) A couple of kilometres from town, isolated Badr Sahara Camp has a handful of bucolic, African-influenced, two-bed huts, each with small patio sitting areas out front. Hot water and electricity can't always be counted on, but cool desert breezes and knockout views of the oasis valley can. Free pick-ups available.

Qasr el-Bawity Hotel & Restaurant (☎ 3847 1880, in Cairo 02-2754 7383; www.qasrelbawity.com; s/d half board €55/75, ste from €100) The relatively new Qasr el-Bawity boasts the swankiest accommodation in Bahariya. With a finely trained eye for environmentally friendly design, this hotel has sumptuous rooms finished in cool stonework, sporting ornate domed roofs, fine furniture and decorative arty touches. There are two pools (one natural and one that's chlorinated) and the restaurant here is suitably good.

Food options are limited to the hotels, a modest cafeteria near the petrol station or the town's most popular restaurant, aptly named **Popular Restaurant** (☎ 847 2239; meals E£15-20; 5.30am-10pm). The decent set meal here comprises soup, roast chicken, rice, pickles, salad, vegetable dishes and bread. Beer is available.

Getting There & Away

Six daily buses run by the **Upper Egypt Bus Co** (☎ 3847 3610) depart for Cairo (E£27, five hours) between 6.30am and midnight.

Heading to Farafra (E£20, two hours) or Dakhla (E£40, five hours) you can pick up one of the buses from Cairo. These pass by at around midday and midnight and stop in front of the Upper Egypt Bus Co ticket office on the main road.

Occasional microbuses travel to Farafra and Cairo for the same ticket costs.

There are no services to Siwa; you will have to hire a private four-wheel drive for the rough journey. A permit is required for this trip, and recent changes in legislation make it easy to arrange these permits in Bahariya (US$5 per person).

SIWA OASIS الواحات سيوه

☎ 046

Easily the prettiest, and most remote, of Egypt's oases, sleepy Siwa is the perfect antidote to the commotion of bustling Egyptian cities. Isolated for centuries from the rest of the country, Siwa today hasn't managed to stray from its traditional roots – donkeys still outnumber combustion engines and Siwi, the local Berber language, dominates. Worth the long detour from the Nile Valley, Siwa rewards those who trek out here with gorgeous freshwater springs, a dash of ancient history, and generous helpings of tranquillity among palm-shaded streets.

Information

To the north of the main square you'll find a branch of the **Banque du Caire** (8.30am-2pm & 5-8pm) with ATM, as well as a post office and a helpful **tourist office** (460 1330, 010 546 1992; 9am-2pm Sat-Thu, plus 5-8pm Oct-Apr). **El Negma Internet Centre** (460 0761; per hr E£10; 9am-midnight) is near the Fortress of Shali.

Sights & Activities

Apart from date-palm groves, Siwa's major attractions are its profusion of dazzling, fresh-water **springs**. The remains of the **Temple of Amun**, which once housed the famed oracle of Amun, and some Greco-Roman **tombs** can easily be visited on a day trip. The town centre is marked by the jagged remnants of the medieval mud-brick **Fortress of Shali**. At the edge of town are the towering dunes of the **Great Sand Sea**.

For a glimpse into traditional Siwan life, check out the **House of Siwa Museum** (adult/student E£10/5; 10am-3pm Sun-Thu), housed in a restored traditional mud-brick abode and showcasing Siwan crafts and traditions.

There are innumerable safari companies in Siwa, most of which charge around E£30 for a tour of Siwa town and environs, E£80 to visit the Great Sand Sea and E£300 to E£500 per vehicle for an overnight camping trip into the desert. Note that permits (US$5 per day plus E£11, arranged by your guide) are needed for desert trips. You can hire **sand boards** (E£10 to E£20) at several places around town.

Several shops around town sell local crafts, such as basketware and jewellery, but the quality is less than stellar. The local dates and olives on sale throughout town are delicious.

Women need to be very careful if wandering alone among the palm groves or bathing in the springs. There have been reports of assaults.

Sleeping

Make sure your hotel room has screened windows; the mosquitoes in Siwa are particularly insatiable.

Yousef Hotel (460 0678, 010 952 3957; central market sq; dm E£10, s/d E£15/30; without bathroom E£10/20) With the cheapest beds in town, Yousef is perennially full with backpacking budgeters. The rooms are a bit tattered and kept barely above minimum hygiene standards, but the rooftop has both great views of the oasis and a kitchen for guests to use.

Palm Trees Hotel (460 1703; salahali2@yahoo.com; Sharia Torrar; s/d E£35/45, without bathroom E£15/25, bungalows E£50) This deservedly popular budget hotel has sufficiently tidy (though ageing) rooms, all with screened windows, fans and balconies. The shady, tranquil garden with date-palm furniture is delightful (but mosquito filled), and a few ground-level bungalows have porches spilling onto the greenery. Breakfast costs E£5.

Siwa Dream Lodge (460 1745, 010 099 9255; www.siwadreamlodge.com; s/d E£120/160;) Just north-east of Siwa, this quiet and intimate midrange place is one of our faves. The eight neat and spacious chalets here are all unique, some sporting big domed roofs, others with bathrooms inlaid with pebbles, and all are finished with natural materials and traditional Siwan rock-salt and mud brick. Rooms even have TVs and fridges, and are decorated with local craft. There's a small dipping pool here as well as a fireplace for chilly nights. Lovely.

Shali Lodge (460 1299; info@eqi.com.eg; Sharia Subukha; s/d E£260/340;) This beautiful mud-brick hotel, owned by environmentalist Mounir Neamatallah, lies nestled in a lush palm grove about 300m from the main square. The palms are a feature of the building wherever possible and the seven large, decadently comfortable rooms have lots of curving mud brick goodness and massive exposed brick bathrooms and all lie arranged courtyard style. Tasteful and quiet, this is how small hotels should be. Breakfast not included.

Al-Babinshal (460 1499; s/d E£260/340) Literally attached to the Fortress of Shali, this intimate hotel continues the ecolodge footprint left by the owner of Shali Lodge. The cunning architects have seamlessly grafted a mud-brick hotel onto the front of Shali fort. A maze of tunnels and stairways connects the spacious and cool cave-like rooms, making it impossible to tell where the hotel ends and the fort begins. Entirely made from the same materials as the original fort, each intimate abode has wood floor panelling, traditional wooden-shuttered windows and exposed palm-log supports. Some locals, however, are not convinced that this augmentation of their town's landmark is necessarily for the better.

Eating

There are cheap chicken-and-salad joints on the central market square. No alcohol is served in Siwan restaurants.

Nour al-Waha (☎ 460 0293; Sharia Subukha; mains E£5-20) A popular hangout in a palm grove opposite Shali Lodge, Nour al-Waha has shady tables and plenty of games on hand for those who just want to while away the day in the shade. The food is a mixture of Egyptian and Western, and while it couldn't be called gourmet, it is generally fresh and good.

Abdu's Restaurant (☎ 460 1243; central market sq; mains E£5-25; 🕒 8.30am-midnight) Before internet and mobile phones, there were places like Abdu's – a village hub where people gathered nightly to meet, catch up and swap stories. This is the longest-running restaurant in town and remains the best eating option around, with a huge menu of breakfast, pasta, traditional dishes, vegetable stews, couscous, roasted chickens and fantastic pizza.

Tanta Waa Coffeeshop & Restaurant (☎ 010 472 9539; meals E£7-25; 🕒 8am-late) This super-chilled and creatively clad mud-brick café, located at Cleopatra spring, is the perfect spot for a cool drink or scrumptious meal between splashes in the spring. The food here is surprisingly delicious, with a small selection of salads, pastas, meat dishes and fruit juices/smoothies. Trust us when we say their lasagne alone is worth the trip out here (E£12). Slung with hammocks and with a background of funky tunes, it's easy to laze away an entire day at this haven.

Al Babinshal (☎ 460 1499; meals E£8-35) On the roof of the hotel by the same name, this might just be the most romantic dining spot in the oases. Moodily lit in the evenings, it's attached to the Fortress of Shali and has sweeping views over all of Siwa. Alas the food, while good, does not always live up to the promise of its ultra-chic ambience.

There are several places dotted around the square where you can have a sheesha or a cup of coffee and play some backgammon.

Getting There & Around

Buses depart from the **bus stop** opposite the Tourist Police station, where it is recommended to buy your tickets in advance. There are three daily buses to Alexandria (E£27 to E£30, eight hours), stopping at Marsa Matruh (E£12, four hours) leaving at 7am, 10am and 10pm. There's an extra Alexandria bus leaving at 3pm in the winter and 5pm in the summer, and a service to Marsa Matruh only departs at 1pm. Most recently, a once-weekly direct service to Cairo has started running, departing Thursdays at 8pm (E£50, 10 to 11 hours).

Service taxis and microbuses to Marsa Matruh (E£12) leave from the area in front of Abdu's Restaurant. These tend to leave in the early morning or after sunset.

A battered desert road links Siwa to Bahariya Oasis, passing through some awesome desert landscapes. Enterprising Siwan drivers are willing to make the 10-hour trip in a 4WD for round E£800 to E£1500 per car, though a permit is required (US$5 per person, organised through the tourist office).

Bicycles are by far the best way to get around town and can be rented from most hotels and a number of bike shops. The going rate is E£10 per day.

Donkey carts, or *caretas*, are a much-used mode of transport for Siwans and can be a more amusing, if slower, way to get around. After some haggling, expect to pay about E£25 for two to three hours, E£5 for a short trip.

SUEZ CANAL قناة السويس

An engineering marvel by any measure, the 1869-built canal that severs Africa from Asia is darned impressive. Though the region is hardly geared for tourists, intrepid travellers are rewarded not only with a few picturesque colonial-built cities but also the unforgettable sight of behemoth supertankers virtually gliding through the deserts that make up the Isthmus of Suez.

PORT SAID بور سعيد

☎ 066 / pop 550,000

At the mouth of the Suez Canal's Mediterranean entrance, wealthy Port Said tips its hat to a prosperous past. Abuzz with the energy of a lively port city, its grand but faded New Orleans–style wooden buildings still manage to cling to some colonial charm. The busy shop-lined Corniche attracts legions of hip, young locals, summering Egyptians and visitors alike. Alexandria eat your heart out.

The town is effectively built as an island, connected to the mainland by a bridge to the south and a causeway to the west.

Information

The main banks all have branches with ATMs in town, mostly along Sharia al-Gomhuriyya. **Thomas Cook** (☎ 322 7559; Sharia al-Gomhuriyya; 8am-4.30pm) sits where Sharia Orabi meets Sharia al-Gomhuriyya and will change travellers cheques and sell US dollars. If you urgently need to update your Facebook profile, try **Compu.Net** (per hr E£3; 9am-midnight), just opposite the main post office. The friendly **tourist office** (☎ 323 5289; 8 Sharia Palestine; 8am-6pm Sat-Thu, 9am-2pm Fri) is along the waterfront, near the ferry to Port Faud, and supplies maps of the town.

Sights & Activities

The **National Museum** (☎ 323 7419), at the top end of Sharia Palestine, was closed for renovation at the time of research. The small **Military Museum** (☎ 322 4657; Sharia 23rd of Jul; admission E£5; 9am-4pm Fri-Wed, 9am-10pm Thu) has some interesting relics from the 1956 Anglo-French War and the 1967 and 1973 wars with Israel.

The easiest way to explore the canal is to take the **free public ferry** from near the tourist office across to Port Fuad and back.

Sleeping

Hotel de la Poste (☎ /fax 322 4048; 42 Sharia al-Gomhuriyya; s E£37-52, d E£50-62;) Though starting to show its considerable age, the rooms at this elegantly faded hotel are nonetheless scrubbed clean and decent value. Facilities vary room to room: the better ones offer satellite TV, balconies and air-con. Best of all, there's a neat street-side café downstairs from where you can watch the hubbub of downtown.

Helnan Port Said (☎ 332 0890; www.helnan.com; Sharia Adef El Sadat; s/d US$120/150, ste from US$300;) Based in a massive modern monolith of a building, this five-star establishment manages to feel stylish while reining in the sort of over-the-top glitz so popular in this hotel class. Comfortably luxurious rooms are very well finished and most have swell views over the canal and the Mediterranean. Breakfast costs E£30 to E£45 and there are some first-rate restaurants on site.

> **SUEZ CANAL: FAST FACTS**
>
> - **Construction** Begun 1859, completed 1869
> - **Length** 190km
> - **Surface width** 280-345m
> - **Depth** 22.5m
> - **Speed limit** 11-14kph
> - **World trade passing through canal** 14%
> - **Vessels passing annually** Over 20,000

Eating & Drinking

There's a swathe of fast-food establishments on the New Corniche up from the Helnan Port Said hotel. This is also where most of the night-time action is.

Pizza Pino (☎ 323 9949; cnr Sharias 23rd of Jul & al-Gomhuriyya; pasta E£10-25, pizza E£15-25) Moodily lit and decked out in comfy seats, it's no wonder people linger here well after dinner is over. Friendly service, good Italian-influenced food, fresh juice and a wide range of ice-cream sundaes draws a packed crowd nightly – come early to get a seat.

Abou Essam (☎ 323 2776; Sharia Adef as-Sadat; meals E£20-30) Looking like a massive glass greenhouse, replete with draping foliage, this eatery does a great Egyptian salad buffet, as well as flavoursome meats, grilled fish and pastas to go with it.

There's a popular terrace *ahwa* at the front of the Grand Albatross Building on the New Corniche where locals linger over sheeshas.

Getting There & Away

BOAT

For details of boats from Port Said to Cyprus and Israel, see p644 and p209.

BUS

The bus station is 3km from the centre of town.

Two companies travel to Cairo. **East Delta Bus Co** (☎ 372 9883) has buses (E£14 to E£16, three hours) nearly hourly between 6am and

10pm. Superjet buses (E£22, three hours) also leave hourly, between 7am and 8pm.

To Alexandria, East Delta Bus Co has six services (E£22 to E£25, four hours) between 7am and 7pm.

There are buses to Suez (E£11 to E£13, three hours) at 6am, 10am, 1pm and 4pm.

A taxi from the bus station into town costs between E£3 and E£5. Taxis within town cost E£2.

SERVICE TAXI

These leave from an area in the bus station. Fares include Cairo (E£15 to E£18) and Suez (E£12).

TRAIN

Slow and uncomfortable trains to Cairo leave daily at 5.30am, 9.45am, 1pm, 5.30pm and 7.30pm (E£11/18 without/with air-con, 2nd class, five hours).

SUEZ السويس

☎ 062 / pop 555,000

Suez is a convenient spot to break up the long journey between Sinai and the capital. Though there is little to see in town but the famed canal, watching the cargo-laden maritime behemoths that ply the city's waterways can be truly mesmerising. From a slight distance, it almost seems that these giants are eerily slicing their way through the desert at the edge of the city.

The town is in two parts: Suez proper, the chaotic main settlement, and Port Tawfiq, at the mouth of the canal. The latter, a catatonic suburb boasting wide boulevards and some colonial buildings, is the best place for ship-spotting.

Information

There are ATMs at Banque Misr and BPN Bank, on or just off Sharia al-Geish, as well as several other banks in town.

Al Jezeera (off Sharia al-Geish; per hr E£3; 🕑 10am-4am) Fast internet access, just south of Al-Khalif restaurant in Suez.

Tourist office (☎ 333 1141; 🕑 8am-8pm Sat-Thu, 8am-3pm Fri) The extremely helpful tourist office in Port Tawfiq overlooks the canal.

Sleeping

Hotels choices are pretty limited and are fully booked during the month of the hajj.

Arafat Hotel (☎ 335 5992; 7 Sharia Arafat, Port Tawfiq; s/d E£45/55, without bathroom E£35/45) The only real budget pad in Port Tawfiq, this friendly place has very spartan abodes and shared bathrooms that haven't seen a mop since the '52 revolution. Do yourself a favour and go for the private bathroom option.

Red Sea Hotel (☎ 333 4302; www.redseahotel.com; 13 Sharia Riad, Port Tawfiq; s/d with city view E£282/354, with canal view E£324/398; ❄ 💻) Immaculate inside and out, this option has speckless rooms, some with balconies right over the canal. There's free wi-fi here, with air-con and satellite TV being standard. The 6th-floor restaurant has a panoramic view and serves decent fresh seafood meals (E£30 to E£40).

Eating & Drinking

Pizza Pronto (☎ 330 4443; Sharia as-Salaam; pizzas E£14-26) Expect fast service, a decent stab at making a pizza, and lines of hungry punters at this popular pizza joint on the main drag in Suez town.

Al-Khalifa Fish Centre (☎ 333 7303; Sharia as-Salaam; salads E£1.50-2, mains E£16-35; ❄) A no-nonsense restaurant that sells nothing but fresh fish cooked any way you like it. There's a picture menu helping you choose from tuna, calamari, shrimp or the catch of the day. Look for the big glass windows and fishy decor.

The main cheap-eats area is in the street between Al-Khalifa Fish Centre and the White House Hotel, off Sharia as-Salaam. The best of these is probably **Koshary Palace** (Sharia Saad Zaghloul, Suez; meals E£1.50-5), just around the corner from Al-Khalifa Fish Centre.

Getting There & Away

BOAT

For details of international boats from Suez, see p645.

BUS

The bus station (New Bus Station) is inconveniently located 5km from central Suez, on the road to Cairo. Arriving by bus, it's possible to get off before the bus station at the highway on the edge of the centre. Taxis (E£5 to E£10) and microbuses (50pt to E£1) congregate here to take passengers into the centre of town or Port Tawfiq. A taxi between the bus station and Suez costs E£10 to E£15.

Upper Egypt Bus Co (☎ 356 4258) buses to Cairo (E£8, 1½ hours) leave every 30 minutes from 6am to 9pm. Four services travel to Alexandria (E£25 to E£30, 3½ hours) at 7am, 9am, 2.30pm and 5pm. To Hurghada

(E£35 to E£40, four to five hours), buses depart about every two hours from 5am to 11pm. Services to Luxor (E£45 to E£60, seven to eight hours) depart at 5am, 5pm and 8pm. Buses to Aswan (E£60 to E£70, 12 hours) leave at 5am and 5pm. Buses leave at 11am and 3pm for Al-Quseir (E£45, seven hours).

East Delta Bus Co (☎ 356 4853) has six buses to Port Said (E£11 to E£13, 2¼ hours) between 7am and 3.30pm.

East Delta Bus Co buses also travel along the direct route down the Gulf of Suez to Sharm el-Sheikh (E£30 to E£35, 5½ hours) at 8.30am, 11am, 1.30pm, 3pm and 6pm. The 11am bus goes on to Dahab (E£40, 6½ hours) and Nuweiba (E£45, 7½ hours). Services travel to Nuweiba (E£45, four hours) via Taba (E£45, three hours) at 11am, 1.30pm and 3pm. A bus leaves for St Katherine's Monastery (E£26, five hours) at 2pm.

MICROBUS & TAXI

Small blue microbuses travel between Port Tawfiq and Suez (25pt). A taxi will cost E£3 to E£5.

SERVICE TAXI

Clapped-out taxis depart from beside the bus station to Cairo (E£8 to E£10), Ismailia (E£6), Port Said (E£12) and Nuweiba (E£35). There is an occasional service to Hurghada (E£35). To get to Sharm el-Sheikh you'll need to travel to Al-Tor (E£18) and catch an onward service.

TRAIN

Six trains daily depart for Cairo (E£4/1.50 in 2nd/3rd class, three hours) between 5.45am and 9.25pm, but they make it only as far as Ain Shams, 10km northeast of central Cairo. There is also one daily slow train (E£6, four hours) to Cairo's Ramses train station at 3.20pm.

RED SEA COAST
ساحل البحر الاحمر

The long stretch of Egyptian coastline that meets the Red Sea, extending from Suez to Sudan, is fringed by world-class coral reefs and clear aqua waters. It is here that Moses parted the Red Sea and early Christians established the first monasteries. These days, however, the legions of holiday-makers that descend here en masse are more keen on sun-bathing than biblical navel-gazing.

Hurghada is the sprawling concrete heart of the European package tourist scene. Ravenous development has steam-rolled its way through here to leave behind some of the most unsightly and environmentally disastrous expansion this coast has ever seen. To rub Red Sea salt into the wounds, a recent spate of bombings in Egypt has put a dint in tourist numbers, scarring the coastline with the concrete husks of unfinished future resorts. Further south, Al-Quseir and Marsa Alam have mostly been spared the 'developer's touch', though the government has grand plans for an expanding string of behemoth, high-end resorts.

HURGHADA الغردقة

☎ 065 / pop 115,000

If your ideal holiday involves rowdy package tours and jostling for beach-towel space on emaciated, crowded beaches in an overpriced, Las Vegas–inspired, faux ancient Egyptian metropolis, look no further! Hailed by Egyptian tourist authorities as a success story, Hurghada is a poster-child for everything that can go wrong with mass tourism. Uninhibited growth over the years has disfigured this part of the Red Sea coast with its relentless concrete spread, destroying much of the fringing reef ecosystems along the way. Nevertheless, there are a few low-key resorts that manage to retain shreds of calm, and for many touring the Nile Valley it remains the most accessible part of the Red Sea. Hurghada is the jumping-off point for boats to Sharm el-Sheikh and Sinai. For details of the somewhat belated efforts to rescue the region's green credentials, see p112.

Orientation

Most budget hotels are in the main town area, Ad-Dahar, at the northern end of a long stretch of resorts. A main road connects Ad-Dahar with Sigala, where the town's port is. South of Sigala, a road winds 15km down along the coast through the chintzy 'resort strip', which is the town's upmarket tourism enclave.

Information

Banks are scattered all over Hurghada: most have ATMs. Many upmarket hotels also have ATMs in their lobbies.

El Baroudy Internet (Sharia Sheikh Sabak, Ad-Dahar; per hr E£5; 24hr)

Main post office (Sharia an-Nasr) Towards the southern end of Ad-Dahar.

Passport Office (446 727; Sharia an-Nasr; 8am-2pm Sat-Thu) For visa extensions.

Speed.Net (Sharia al-Hababa, Sagala; per hr E£10; 10am-midnight)

Telephone centrale (Sharia an-Nasr; 24hr) Northwest of the main post office.

Thomas Cook Ad-Dahar (354 1870/1; Sharia an-Nasr; 9am-2pm & 6-10pm); Sigala (344 3338; Sharia Sheraton; 9am-3pm & 4-10pm) Changes travellers cheques.

Tourist office (344 4421; 8am-8pm) On the resort strip.

Activities

There's little to do in Hurghada itself other than sit on a beach and dream of more secluded places. The **public beach** in Sigala is less than appealing, though many resorts offer preferable sun-and-sand options (nonguest access charges range between E£20 and E£60).

Kite surfing is becoming hugely popular: the beach area just north of Jasmine Village on the resort strip is packed with surfers. Contact **Tommy Friedl** (010 667 2811; Jasmine Village) kite surfing school for two-day beginner courses (€210 including kit) or basic kit rental (from €90 per day).

If you decide to go diving or snorkelling, there are many operators that do day trips to local, over-dived and mostly destroyed reefs, as well as longer live-aboard safaris to some of the Red Sea's better sites. If you're angling for a scuba course, have a look at the boxed text, p194.

Sleeping

AD-DAHAR

Snafer Hotel (/fax 354 0260; s/d E£60/90;) Off the beach and just next to the National Hospital, the Snafer has refreshingly helpful staff and some of the best-value budget digs in town. Some abodes offer a slim view of the sea, and all rooms offer spotless midrange standards for budget prices.

Geisum Village (354 6692; Corniche; s/d €25/40;) This family-friendly resort has a lovely winding pool and its own thin slice of beach out front. Rooms are definitely tattered around the edges these days, but all have balconies looking onto a trim garden. All in all, pretty a favourable bang-for-buck ratio.

SIGALA

White Albatross Hotel (344 2519; walbatross53@hotmail.com; Sharia Sheraton, Sigala; s/d E£90/160;) This is a great place to base yourself if your mission is Sigala's thumping nightclubbing scene. Though slightly dated, the Albatross manages to keep up with the Joneses with a sterile level of cleanliness and sharp service. Top-floor doubles (E£200) have sea views and some respite from the street noise.

RESORT STRIP

Jasmine Village (346 0461; jasmine@tut2000.com; s/d full board US$32/54;) To get the full resort effect at bargain-basement prices, come to Jasmine Village. Though half of Russia seems to decamp here during much of the year, there should be plenty of room among the immense complex of 500 comfy, if basic, faux-brick rooms. Most people don't bother leaving the grounds, and with a private beach, restaurants, swimming pools and a list of facilities and activities as long as your arm, why would they need to?

Oberoi Sahl Hasheesh (344 0777; www.oberoihotels.com; Sahl Hasheesh; ste from US$350;) This utterly indulgent hotel features stunning suites decorated in minimalist Moorish style that come complete with sunken marble baths, walled private courtyards, and panoramic sea views. Some even have private pools.

Eating

AD-DAHAR

Portofino (354 6250; Sharia Sayyed al-Qorayem; mains E£22-65;) An old-fashioned trattoria serving up generous homemade pasta and meat dishes to a constant stream of tourists. The food is very good and made from fresh local ingredients. Stella is E£11, wine E£16 by the glass.

Gaucho (354 7007; Corniche; mains E£35-110;) If you like to see your dinnertime meat rations measured in kilograms, do not miss this succulent Argentinian steak house. A massive T-bone steak with all the trimmings will set you back E£110.

Cheap eateries include the toothsome **Pizza Tarboush** (☎ 354 8456; Sharia Abdel Aziz Mustafa; medium pizzas E£12-30), on the edge of the souq.

SIGALA

Hefny Restaurant (Shari Shedwan;, meals E£15-45) This isolated fish restaurant is located near the port – so you know the fish didn't have to travel far to get to your plate. It's little more than a collection of tables, but the fish served here (sold by weight) is expertly prepared.

RESORT STRIP

Felfela Restaurant (☎ 344 2410/1; Sharia Sheraton; mains E£10-60; 8.30am-midnight) Perched on the coastline and overlooking the turquoise sea, this branch of the Felfela chain wins a prize for its view, which you can enjoy while dining on serviceable Egyptian classics at reasonable prices.

Da Nanni… Non Solo Pizza (☎ 010 663 3162; Sharia Hadaba; mains E£25-80;) Just south of Sigala along the inland road (near La Perla Hotel), this very popular restaurant is run by bona-fide Italians and prides itself on its service and the quality ingredients used in its top-notch Italian fare.

Drinking & Entertainment

Papas Bar (www.papasbar.com; Sharia Sheraton) Probably the most popular hangout in Hurghada, this Dutch-run bar has loads of atmosphere and is packed nightly with diving instructors and other foreign residents. There's a Papas II located in Ad-Dahar – both feature a constantly changing entertainment program.

Several internationally renowned nightclubs have set up franchises in Hurghada, including the **Ministry of Sound** (www.ministryofsoundegypt.com) and **HedKandi** (www.hedkandibeachbar.com). Music ranges from house to techno to disco to R&B, with admission prices up to E£100 – check their respective websites for details. At the time of research, both these places had plans to move to the swish new marina complex at the northern end of Sakalla.

El-Arabi Coffee Shop, situated opposite Seagull Resort, is a popular local tea-and-sheesha spot.

Getting There & Away

AIR

Hurghada International Airport (☎ 344 2592) is located 6km southwest of town. **EgyptAir** (☎ 346 3034-7), with an office on the resort strip, has several daily flights to Cairo (from E£400 one way), though prices fluctuate wildly with demand. There are no buses between the airport and town; a taxi costs somewhere between E£15 and E£25.

BOAT

A luxury high-speed ferry operated by **International Fast Ferries Co** (☎ 344 7572, 012 190 1000; www.internationalfastferries.com; one way adult E£250 or US$40, child 3-12 half price) plies the waters of the Red Sea between Hurghada and Sharm el-Sheikh, departing at 4.30am each Wednesday, and 9.30am each Saturday, Monday, Tuesday and Thursday from the port in Sigala. The trip takes 1½ hours, but is often cancelled or can take longer when seas are rough (particularly in January and February). There is no student discount on tickets.

It's sensible to buy a ticket the day before the trip; you'll need to make your way to the ticket box at the harbour 30 minutes before departure time to grab a boarding pass. The ticket office is in the Fantasia building opposite the Hurghada Touristic Port entrance. The rate of the dollar against the Egyptian pound and the whim of the ferry officials determine which currency you'll need to use to purchase the ticket. Come prepared with dollars, but be prepared to convert them to pounds.

For details of boats to Duba in Saudi Arabia see p645.

BUS

Three bus companies operate services from Hurghada.

The **Upper Egypt Bus Co bus station** is at the southern end of Ad-Dahar. There are at least 10 daily buses to Cairo (E£55 to E£60, six hours) between 9am and 1am; the 7.30pm service goes on to Alexandria (E£80, nine hours). There are around eight buses per day to Luxor (E£30 to E£40, five hours), with the 10.30am, 10.30pm and midnight services travelling on to Aswan (E£45 to E£55, seven hours). There are three daily buses to Marsa Alam (E£30 to E£35, five hours) via Al-Quseir (E£20, three hours), leaving at 5am, 8pm and 1am. To Suez (E£35 to E£40, four to five hours), buses depart every two hours between 7am and midnight.

The **Superjet** (☎ 355 3499) bus station is 500m south of the Upper Egypt bus station in Ad-Dahar. It has services to Cairo (E£70, six hours) at noon, 2.30pm, 5pm, midnight and 2am. The 2.30pm and 2.30am service continues to Alexandria (E£85, nine hours). One daily bus to Luxor leaves at 7am (E£30, five hours)

The newly established **El Gouna Bus Co** (☎ 355 6188; Sharia al-Nasr) has a bus station a few hundred metres south of Superjet in Ad-Dahar. It has at least a dozen daily services to Cairo (E£60 to E£70) between 8am and 3am.

CONVOY

It is officially compulsory for foreigners with private transport to travel from Hurghada to Cairo and Luxor by police-escorted convoy. Although we have met many travellers who have had no problems driving themselves independently to Cairo, it's not possible to dodge the convoy to Luxor (there are 10 checkpoints). The convoys to Cairo leave from the first checkpoint on the road to Cairo in Al-Gouna, 20km outside Hurghada, at 2.30am, 11am and 5pm. Convoys to Luxor depart from Safaga, 53km south of Hurghada, at 7am, 9am and 4pm.

SERVICE TAXI

The service taxi station is near the telephone centrale in Ad-Dahar. Taxis go to Cairo (E£35), Al-Quseir (E£15 to E£20), Marsa Alam (E£20 to E£25) and Suez (E£25 to E£30). They cannot take you to Luxor or Aswan except on a private basis in a police convoy. With bargaining, it costs about E£400 per vehicle (up to seven passengers) to Luxor.

Getting Around

Local minibuses function as service taxis in Hurghada. These can be hailed from the side of the road. To travel from the resort strip to Sigala costs around E£1, and E£2 to Ad-Dahar. The trip between Sigala and Ad-Dahar costs 50pt. A taxi from Sigala to Ad-Dahar or the resort strip costs E£5 to E£10; it costs E£15 between Ad-Dahar and the resort strip. You'll need to bargain to get these prices.

El Gouna Bus Co operates a more comfortable service (E£5) between Al-Gouna, Ad-Dahar and the end of Sharia Sheraton in Sigala about every half hour, beginning at 9am. You can flag the bus down at any point along the way and pay on board.

AL-QUSEIR القصير

☎ 065 / pop 29,000

It's hard not to fall in love with this sleepy Red Sea town: it moves at the sort of sedate pace that's a perfect antidote to the Egypt hustle. While there's barely a handful of things to see in town, it's still worth a stopover to soak in some ocean-side serenity.

Until the 10th century, Al-Quseir was one of the most important exit points for pilgrims travelling to Mecca, later becoming an important entrepôt for Indian spices destined for Europe.

There's a 24-hour telephone centrale, a Misr Bank branch with a 24hr ATM, and a post office. For internet access try **Crazy Net** (per hr E£3; 🕓 10am-12am) behind the Fort.

Sights & Activities

The main sight in town is the 16th-century **Ottoman fortress** (admission adult/student E£10/5; 🕓 9am-5pm), still largely intact, though later modified by French and British colonials. Beautiful old coral-block buildings line the waterfront and a maze of dusty laneways snake inland. Look out for intricately carved wooden balconies and the domed tombs of various saints – mostly pious pilgrims who died en route to or from Mecca.

You can arrange diving trips or excursions into the Eastern Desert with **Mazenar Tours** (☎ 333 5247, 010 653 2964; www.rockyvalleydiverscamp.com; Sharia Port Said), located along the waterfront.

Sleeping & Eating

Sea Princess Hotel (☎ 333 1880; Sharia al-Gomhuriyya; s/d E£100/120, without bathroom E£25/40) The only shoestring choice in Al-Quseir provides prison-cell rooms filled with fumes from next door's petrol station. The newer upstairs rooms are more satisfactory, but overpriced.

Al-Quseir Hotel (☎ 333 2301; 112 Sharia Port Said; s/d E£100/150) This charming hotel is in a renovated 1920s merchant's house on the seafront. The six humble but spacious rooms are filled with glistening wood, and the shared bathrooms are flawlessly clean. Look for the 'diving world' sign.

Mövenpick Sirena Beach (☎ 333 2100; www.movenpick-quseir.com; r from €160; ✱ ■ □) This low set, domed ensemble, 7km north of the town centre, is top of the line in Al-Quseir, and one of the best resorts along the coast. There are restaurants, a Subex diving centre and a refreshing absence of the schmaltz so common in other resort hotels.

Dining options are limited. There are the usual ta'amiyya and fish stands around the seafront and the bus station. The most popular place in town is **Restaurant Marianne** (☎ 333 4386; Sharia Port Said; mains E£15-35), which serves yummy grilled fish on beach-side tables. They can also arrange jeep (€25) and quad-bike (€25 to €35) desert trips to visit nearby Bedouin camps. Another place to check out is **Sahraya Coffeehouse** (Sharia Port Said), also on the waterfront, which serves snacks.

Getting There & Around

The bus and service-taxi stations are next to each other, about 1.5km northwest of the Safaga road, and about 3km from the telephone centrale (E£3 to E£5 in a taxi).

BUS

There are seven daily buses to Cairo (E£65 to E£75, nine hours) via Hurghada (E£20, three hours), departing from 5am to 11.30pm. The 5am service continues to Suez (E£45, seven hours). Services to Marsa Alam (E£10, two hours) depart at 7am, 2pm, 7pm, 9pm and 10.30pm. For Luxor, catch a bus to Qift at either 5am or 3pm (E£15, three hours) and change there.

MICROBUS

You'll find that microbuses run along Sharia al-Gomhuriyya from the roundabout near Sea Princess Hotel north to the administrative buildings on the road to Safaga. Some also go to the bus and service-taxi stations. Fares range between 50pt and E£1.

SERVICE TAXI

Destinations include Cairo (E£60 to E£70), Suez (E£45 to E£50), Qena (E£20), and Hurghada (E£15). As in Hurghada, you have to hire the entire taxi for the trip to Luxor, Qena or Aswan (all routes via Safaga). Expect to pay from E£350 after negotiating.

MARSA ALAM مرسى علم

☎ 065

The Red Sea coast around Marsa Alam shelters some of the most impressive diving in the world. While just a decade ago these sites were accessible only by boat from Hurghada and Sharm, in recent years resorts and dive camps have sprung up to provide an easy jumping-off point to these pristine, world-class reefs.

Marsa Alam itself is not much more than a dusty T-junction where the road from Edfu meets the coastal road. Word on the street has it, however, that this area is about to get a major makeover, with an extravagant marina and several monstrously big luxury hotels moving in for the kill.

Just south of the main junction is a modest collection of shops, a pharmacy, a telephone centrale and a bustling market.

Activities

Apart from the marvellous diving opportunities offered by the dive camps along this coast, trips to the fascinating sites of the Eastern Desert can also be organised with **Red Sea Desert Adventures** (☎ 012 399 3860; www.redseadesertadventures.com; Marsa Shagra). This recommended safari outfit has tailored walking, camel and jeep safaris throughout the area. Prices start at approximately US$100 per person per day; they vary considerably depending on mode of transport, length of trip and number of people travelling. Try to book multiday safaris at least one month in advance so that the necessary permits can be arranged.

Sleeping & Eating

There's very little choice if you want to stay in Marsa Alam village itself, but along the coast is an ever-expanding array of resorts, plus a handful of simpler, diver-oriented 'ecolodges' (diving camps). These usually offer no-frills bungalows with generator-provided electricity and a common area for meals. They are run together with a dive centre, and offer a more down-to-earth alternative to the resort scene, though prices stubbornly hover around the mid-budget range. Most hotels and camps can also arrange desert excursions.

Riff-Villa Samak (☎ 372 0001, 012 462 4933; www.riff-villa.ch; Marsa Alam; r per person €20, full board €25) The only sleeping option in Marsa Alam, this cosy Swiss-German–run diving homestay is right on the beach, about 1km south of town. There's a hotch-potch of big and small rooms on offer, all spick and span and some with attached bath. Meals are taken together family style, and there are daily dives on the great house reef as well as further afield. Bookings recommended.

Shaqara Eco-Lodge (☎ in Cairo 02-337 1833; www.redsea-divingsafari.com; Marsa Shagra; full board per person in tents/huts/chalets €35/40/50) One of the first camps set up on this stretch of coastline, Shaqara is owned by lawyer, committed environmentalist and diving enthusiast Hossam Helmi. It has elementary, squeaky-clean and comfortable accommodation designed to be as kind to the environment as possible, plus first-rate diving. It has the only hyperbaric chamber in the region and arranges 4WD safaris into the desert. It's along the main road, 24km north of Marsa Alam.

Awalad Baraka (☎ 010 646 0408; www.aquarisuredsea.com; 14km south of Marsa Alam; hut per person €35, without bathroom per person €25) This is one of the prettier dive camps lining this bay 14km south of Marsa Alam. They offer accommodation in robust, and darned cute, African-styled huts all handsomely finished with hanging rugs and frilly touches. The en-suite huts are roomier and sit on a hill with sea views, and there are some neat chillout spaces in the compound that lie sunk into the ground. There's daily diving on the house reef, and this is one of the closest spots to popular offshore sites like Elphinstone reef.

In Marsa Alam, there are a couple of cafés at the junction in town where you can find ta'amiyya and similar fare, and there's a small supermarket with a modest selection of basics.

Getting There & Away

AIR

Marsa Alam International Airport (☎ 370 0005) is 67km north of Marsa Alam along the Al-Quseir road. There is no public transport, so you'll need to arrange a transfer in advance with your hotel. The airport is currently used only by charters.

BUS

There is no bus station in Marsa Alam. For transport to the Nile Valley, wait at the petrol station in Marsa Alam, or at the T-junction about 1km further along on the Edfu road. Buses from Shalatein pass Marsa Alam en route to Aswan (E£25, six hours), via Edfu (E£20, four hours), at around 7am, 9am and 12am daily.

There are four daily buses to Al-Quseir (E£10, two hours) and Hurghada (E£30, five hours), between 5am and 8pm. There's a direct bus to Cairo (E£80 to E£90, 11 to 12 hours) at 6pm and 8pm.

SINAI

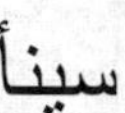

The breathtaking region of Sinai is one of the most unique in all Egypt. Famed as the place where Moses received the Ten Commandments from the big man in the sky, it's also here that ancient and modern armies fought and Bedouin tribes established their homes. This striking desertscape rolls straight into the turquoise waters of the Red Sea, offering countless opportunities for exploration of both the mountainous desert and pristine underwater ecology. Visitors can take their pick of places to stay while exploring the peninsula: the glitzy resorts of Sharm el-Sheikh, the chilled-out vibes of Dahab, or the remote and low-key Nuweiba and St Katherine's Monastery.

In recent years Sinai resorts have been the targets of terrorist bombs. In October 2004 a bomb in Taba, on the border with Israel, killed 34 people; in July 2005 three bombs in Sharm el-Sheikh and Na'ama Bay claimed 64 lives; and bombs in Dahab in 2006 took another 24 lives. Though tourism was relatively unaffected by the Taba and Dahab bombs (the notable exception being tourism from Israel), international arrivals immediately dropped as a result of the Sharm el-Sheikh and Na'ama Bay bombings, taking months to stabilise.

RAS MOHAMMED NATIONAL PARK محمية راس محمد

Declared a **national marine park** (admission per person/vehicle US$5/5; 8am-5pm) in 1988, the headland of Ras Mohammed lies about 20km west of Sharm el-Sheikh. The waters surrounding the peninsula are considered the jewel in the crown of the Red Sea, and the park is inundated with more than 50,000 visitors annually, enticed by the prospect of marvelling at some of the world's most spectacular coral-reef ecosystems. Camping permits cost US$5 per person per night and are available from the visitors centre inside the park, but camping is allowed only in designated areas. Take your passport with you, and remember that it is not possible to go to Ras Mohammed National Park if you only have a Sinai permit in your passport.

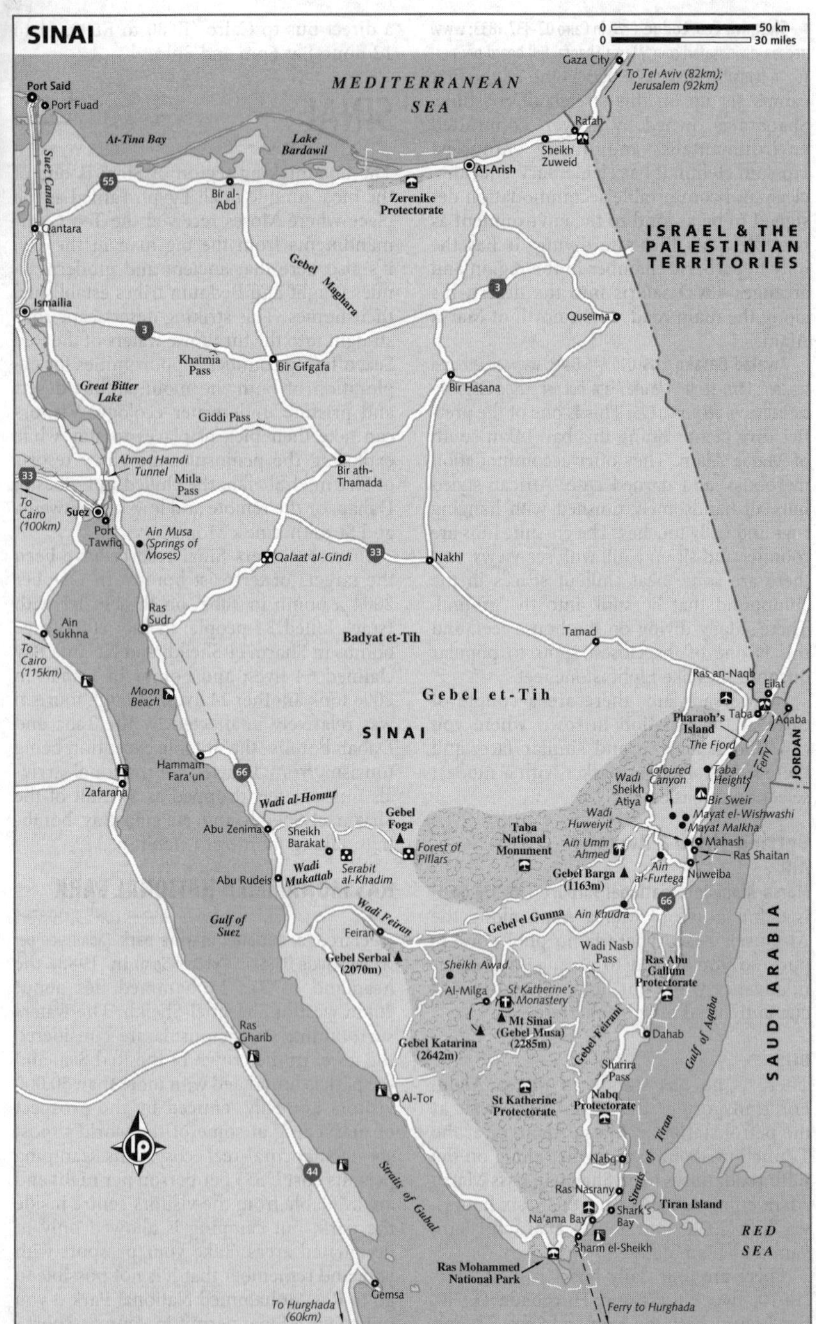
SINAI
0 50 km
0 30 miles
MEDITERRANEAN SEA
Gaza City
To Tel Aviv (82km); Jerusalem (92km)
Rafah
Port Said
Port Fuad
At-Tina Bay
Lake Bardawil
Suez Canal
Sheikh Zuweid
Al-Arish
Bir al-Abd
Zerenike Protectorate
Qantara
ISRAEL & THE PALESTINIAN TERRITORIES
Gebel Maghara
Ismailia
Quseima
Khatmia Pass
Bir Gifgafa
Bir Hasana
Great Bitter Lake
Giddi Pass
Ahmed Hamdi Tunnel
Mitla Pass
Bir ath-Thamada
To Cairo (100km)
Suez
Port Tawfiq
Ain Musa (Springs of Moses)
Qalaat al-Gindi
Nakhl
Ain Sukhna
Ras Sudr
To Cairo (115km)
Badyat et-Tih
Tamad
Ras an-Naqb
Eilat
Moon Beach
Gebel et-Tih
Taba
Aqaba
SINAI
Pharaoh's Island
The Fjord
JORDAN
Ferry
Hammam Fara'un
Zafarana
Wadi al-Homur
Coloured Canyon
Wadi Sheikh Atiya
Taba Heights
Bir Sweir
Gebel Foga
Wadi Huweiyit
Mayat el-Wishwashi
Mayat Malkha
Abu Zenima
Sheikh Barakat
Forest of Pillars
Taba National Monument
Ain Umm Ahmed
Mahash
Ras Shaitan
Wadi Mukattab
Serabit al-Khadim
Gebel Barga (1163m)
Ain al-Furtega
Nuweiba
Abu Rudeis
Wadi Feiran
Ain Khudra
Gulf of Suez
Feiran
Gebel el Gunna
Gebel Serbal (2070m)
Wadi Nasb Pass
Ras Abu Gallum Protectorate
SAUDI ARABIA
Sheikh Awad
Al-Milga
St Katherine's Monastery
Mt Sinai (Gebel Musa) (2285m)
Gebel Katarina (2642m)
Gebel Feirani
Gulf of Aqaba
Ras Gharib
Dahab
Sharira Pass
Nabq Protectorate
Al-Tor
St Katherine Protectorate
Straits of Tiran
Nabq
Straits of Gubal
Ras Nasrany
Tiran Island
Na'ama Bay
Shark's Bay
Sharm el-Sheikh
RED SEA
Ras Mohammed National Park
Gemsa
To Hurghada (60km)
Ferry to Hurghada

You can hire a taxi from Sharm el-Sheikh to bring you here for around E£150 for the day. If you don't mind company, the easiest option is to join one of the many day tours by jeep or bus from Sharm el-Sheikh and Na'ama Bay, most of which will drop you at the best beaches and snorkelling sites. Expect to pay from E£150.

To move around the park you'll need a vehicle. Access is restricted to certain parts of the park and, for conservation reasons, it's forbidden to leave the official tracks.

SHARM EL-SHEIKH & NA'AMA BAY

شرم الشيخ & خليج نعمة

☎ 069 / pop 35,000

Sharm is the main jumping-off point for spectacular, world-class diving found just off its turquoise shores. Alas, in recent years a development frenzy has turned this once-sleepy fishing village into a sterile enclave of resorts. With most traces of Egypt sanitised for Western consumption, Sharm today has all the charisma of a shopping mall. Still, it's not nearly as bad as Hurghada – yet – and can be worth a stopover for those eager for some thumping night-life or desperate to get at those famed underwater vistas. Package tourism is de rigueur here so budget and independent travellers may want to head straight for Dahab.

Na'ama Bay is a throbbing, purpose-built resort, while Sharm el-Sheikh, initially developed by the Israelis, is a long-standing settlement. They are 6km apart, but being joined by a fast-growing, suburban-like sprawl. Around 12km northeast of Na'ama Bay is Shark's Bay, home to the area's best budget accommodation.

Information

There are ATMs every few metres in Na'ama Bay. Most major banks have branches in Sharm (with ATMs) and can change cash.

Thomas Cook (☎ 360 1808/9; Gafy Mall, Sharm-Na'ama Bay Rd, Na'ama Bay; 🕑 9am-2pm & 6-10pm), just west of Sinai Star hotel, will cash travellers cheques.

The **post office** (Sharm el-Sheikh; 🕑 8am-3pm Sat-Thu) is on the hill. There's a **telephone centrale** (🕑 24hr) nearby.

To access the internet try **Maxim Internet** (Old Market; E£20 per hr; 🕑 10am-2am) opposite the Old Market in Sharm or **Speednet Internet Café** (Sharm-Na'ama Bay Rd, Sharm el-Sheikh; per hr E£10; 🕑 24hr) in the Delta Sharm complex in Na'ama Bay.

In Sinai, visa extensions are available only from the passport office in Al-Tor, approximately 90km northwest of here.

> **TOP RED SEA DIVE SITES**
>
> - **Thistlegorm** This WWII cargo ship is, arguably, the best wreck dive in the world; access it from Sharm el-Sheikh (left).
> - **Ras Mohammed** (p189) A national marine park teeming with more fish life than you can poke a regulator at.
> - **Blue Hole** The famed sinkhole near Dahab (p194) that is as dangerous as it is gorgeous.
> - **Elphinstone** A remote and virgin reef off the shore of Marsa Alam (p188), the perfect place for shark spotting.
> - **All of them** Best bet is to get greedy and arrange a multiday, live-aboard diving safari that will take you to all the major dive sites the Red Sea has to offer.

Activities

Some of the best windsurfing in Egypt is found at Moon Beach, 270km from Sharm – ask around to arrange transport and rentals.

Any of the many dive clubs and schools in Sharm can give you a full rundown on the superb underwater possibilities in the area (see also box above). If you're hankering to don fins for the first time and learn to scuba, you may want to check out our box, Choosing a Dive School, (p194).

Sleeping

Be warned that budget digs are very thin on the ground in Sharm.

SHARM EL-SHEIKH

Youth Hostel (☎/fax 366 0317; City Council St, Hadaba; per person E£55, member/nonmember without bathroom E£25/50; ❄) The only real budget option in town, this massive, institutionally white complex has bland but decent rooms. It's way off the beach and is popular with non-youths and Egyptians alike.

Amar Sina (☎ 366 2222/3; www.minasegypt.com; Hadaba; r from US$90; ❄ 🏊 💻) This huge, huge arabesque fort of a hotel is like a city in itself. Encircling a lovely oasis-like pool area, there are arches, wooden balconies and domes aplenty, all draped with an eclectic slew of arty decor. The rooms continue the Moorish theme and all face the pool area. Loads of facilities are also on site, including fitness and diving centres, a Jacuzzi, sporting facilities and more.

Creative Mexican Sharm (☎ in Cairo 02-257 7029; www.worldofcreative.com; Hadaba; r from US$95;) The bold colours and Mexican flair of this themed hotel seem strangely apt among the swaying palms and bright blue skies of Sinai. Whitewashed, two-storey chalets are very comfy and dripping with green vines along their exterior. The friendly atmosphere here is a big hit with vacationing families. You must book ahead as walk-ins are not accepted.

NA'AMA BAY

Camel Hotel (☎ 360 0700; www.cameldive.com; King of Bahrain St, Na'ama Bay; s/d with street view from €48/78, with pool view €54/91;) This popular and central spot is your one-stop shop for some solid accommodation options, diving activities and scrumptious food at one of their three restaurants. Efficiently run and relatively quiet, it even has five rooms specially equipped for guests in wheelchairs. Rates are discounted if you book in advance by email. Breakfast costs extra.

SHARK'S BAY

Shark's Bay Umbi Diving Village (☎ 360 0942; www.sharksbay.com; s/d huts without bathroom €12/15, cabins €20/30, cliffside chalets €30/40;) Once a quiet bay 6km north of Na'ama Bay, these days this small stretch of beach bustles with bronzed bodies packed like sardines. The diving camp here, run by a Bedouin family, has expanded to try to facilitate the rush and somehow still manages to feel more laid back than the rest of Sharm. You can stay in some of their top-value original beach huts, opt for swishier beach bungalows or go for the even more robust cliffside chalets. There's a relaxing bar/café and restaurant here serving decent grub, a small supermarket and a popular diving centre. They do pick-ups from the airport; otherwise the only way to get here from Na'ama Bay is by very overpriced taxi (E£40).

Eating

SHARM EL-SHEIKH

King (mains E£1.50-7; from 7am) With cheap and quick Egyptian eats like fuul and ta'amiyya being whipped up at lightning speed, it's no surprise there's always a line out the door of this popular take-away joint.

Felfela (☎ 012 915 4345; City Centre Mall, Old Market; meals E£8-45;) This branch of the popular Cairo eatery serves up a whopping menu of Egyptian favourites in sparkling, modern and bright surroundings. There's outdoor seating here to enjoy the sun, or an air-con indoor dining area to escape the heat. Try the roast pigeon (E£30 for two).

Red Sea Fish (☎ 366 4250; Old Market; meals E£15-40) One of the best-value seafood restaurants in Sharm, these guys do wonderful things to the catch of the day.

Ristorante & Beach Club El-Fanar (☎ 366 2218; Ras Um Sid; mains E£40-170) Perched on the side of a cliff next to the lighthouse, this glamorous Italian restaurant has the best location in Sharm. While the decor drips with Bedouin-influenced charm, the Italian menu is as authentic as the Colosseum. Expect to see the usual pastas, well-prepared mains and thin-crust pizzas, all promising fresh ingredients like mozzarella, anchovies and capers aplenty. You can buy imported wine by the glass here.

The reasonably priced **Sharm Express Supermarket** (8am-2am), in front of the Old Market, sells a limited range of toiletries, drinks and food.

NA'AMA BAY

There are lots of cushioned places around Na'ama Bay where you can chill and have a *shai* and sheesha, though it's best to steer clear of the food – it's nothing special.

Gado (24hr) This 'nouvelle Egyptian' fast-food eatery, at the start of the mall, has a pleasant outdoor terrace and a refreshingly cheap (for Sharm) price list. Felafel sandwiches cost E£2, shwarma sandwiches E£7 and fuul E£4 to E£5.

Abou El Sid (☎ 360 3910; Na'ama Bay; meals E£35-80;) Above the Hard Rock Café, this remarkable arabesque hideaway is as intimate as it gets. It has low ceilings and is filled with massive, painted tray tables, carved seats and low-slung wrought-iron lampshades. The food experiments with the more exotic end of Egyptian and Middle Eastern cuisine and is commendably prepared, their specialty being an ancient recipe for Circassian chicken with walnut sauce (E£50). There's an outdoor roof patio that opens after 5pm.

Little Buddha (☎ 360 1030; www.littlebuddha-sharm.com; Na'ama Bay; mains E£62-110; ❄) This restaurant and sushi bar is not only one of the plushest places to eat in town, it also serves up the best Pan-Asian food in Sinai. Owned by the same folk who brought you the Buddha in Paris, the menu covers everything from Thai to Japanese – local expats rave about the Red Fire curry shrimp (E£94).

Drinking & Entertainment

Popular watering holes include the ubiquitous **Hard Rock Café**, in the mall at Na'ama Bay, and the **Camel Roof Bar** (☎ 360 0700; Camel Hotel, Na'ama Bay).

On most nights, dive instructors and expats make a beeline for **Papastavern** (☎ 012 778 5509; Aqua Park, Hadaba), which holds BBQ nights and boasts an outdoor patio and billiards.

For something a little more glam, don't miss the über-hip lounge at **Little Buddha** (☎ 360 1030; Na'ama Bay; 🕑 1pm-3am), where DJs spin those proprietary Buddha Bar sounds well into the night.

If you're up for some serious clubbing, the most popular option is **Pacha** (☎ 360 0197, ext 300; www.pachasharm.com; Sanafir Hotel; admission Fri-Wed E£85, Thu E£155; 🕑 10pm-4am), which absolutely heaves on Thursday nights. International DJs tend to play Friday to Sunday, when a heftier entrance fee also applies.

Getting There & Away

AIR

Sharm el-Sheikh International Airport (☎ 360 1140) is about 10km north of Na'ama Bay at Ras Nasrany. **EgyptAir** (☎ 366 1057; Sharm el-Sheikh; 🕑 9am-9pm), at the beginning of the road to Na'ama Bay, has at least 10 daily flights to Cairo (from E£400 one way) and thrice-weekly flights to Luxor (from E£470 one way). There's also one daily flight to Alexandria (E£550 one way).

Microbuses charge E£2 to E£3 for the trip between the airport and Na'ama Bay or Sharm el-Sheikh; taxis charge E£20/40.

BOAT

A luxury high-speed ferry operated by **International Fast Ferries Co** (☎ 360 0936, 012 791 0120; www.internationalfastferries.com; one way adult/child E£250/150) runs between Sharm el-Sheikh and Hurghada, departing at 5pm each Saturday, Monday, Tuesday and Thursday and at 6pm on Wednesdays from the port west of Sharm el-Maya. The trip takes 1½ hours, but can be cancelled or take longer when seas are rough, particularly in January and February. There is no student discount on tickets and you need to be at the port one hour ahead of departure time to organise your boarding ticket.

Ferry tickets can be bought from various travel agencies in town. They are also sold at the ferry office at the port on the days that the ferry runs, beginning at 3pm (two hours before departure time).

If you're arriving by ferry, don't be pressured into getting one of the overpriced taxis close to the ferry building's exit. If you walk up the hill to the gates, you'll be able to pick up a taxi for half the price (E£15 to the bus station, E£25 to Na'ama Bay).

BUS & SERVICE TAXI

The bus station is behind the Mobil Station, halfway between Na'ama Bay and Sharm el-Sheikh. Superjet has services to Cairo (E£80, seven hours) at noon, 1pm, 3pm, 7pm, 11pm and 11.30pm. The 3pm service travels on to Alexandria (E£100, nine hours); there's also an East Delta Bus Co service to Alexandria (E£80) at 9pm. East Delta Bus Co has at least eight daily services to Cairo (E£60 to E£70, seven hours), starting at 7am and ending at 5.30pm. Buses to Suez (E£30 to E£35, five hours) leave at 7am, 9am and 10am daily.

East Delta Bus Co goes to Dahab (E£11 to E£15, 1½ hours) and Nuweiba (E£22 to E£25, 2½ hours) at 9am, 2.30pm and 5pm. The 9am bus then continues all the way to Taba (E£30, three to four hours). If enough travellers get off the ferry from Hurghada and want to transfer directly to Dahab, an extra service may be provided. For St Katherine's Monastery, you'll have to catch the 7.30am bus to Dahab and change there. To Luxor (E£110, 12 to 14 hours), there's one daily East Delta Bus Co service at 6pm.

Service taxis congregate around the bus station and charge slightly more per ticket than the bus. A private taxi to Dahab will cost around E£200.

Getting Around

The prices of local taxis and microbuses are regulated by the municipality. Microbuses travel regularly between Sharm el-Sheikh and Na'ama Bay for E£1. A taxi costs E£15, with larger Peugeots being slightly more expensive.

DAHAB دهب

☎ 069

Little Dahab has come a long way from its origins as a mandatory stopover on the overland hippie trail. Even though prices have crept up, the touts have multiplied, the promenade has been paved and a Hilton has opened further south, Dahab manages to cling to its 'chill or be chilled' roots. Based around a Bedouin village, backed by dramatic desert cliffs and fronted by unforgettable dive sites, Dahab's laid-back appeal has been known to suck in travellers for weeks or months at a time. You have been warned.

Orientation

There are two parts to Dahab: the purpose-built Dahab City is home to several five-star hotels and the bus station, while Assalah, once a Bedouin village, is about 2.5km north of here. Assalah now has more budget travellers and Egyptian entrepreneurs than Bedouin in residence and is divided into two sections, Masbat and Mashraba. Note that, confusingly, 'Assalah' is used to refer both to the tourist area and to the separate, original town to the north.

Information

INTERNET ACCESS

Download.Net (per hr E£8; 24hr) Next to the Nesima Resort in Mashraba.

Aladdin Internet (per hr E£8; 24hr) On the main strip, next to Nirvana.

Seven Heaven Internet Café (per hr E£8; 8am-midnight) In the camp of the same name.

MEDICAL SERVICES

Dr Sherif Salah (☎ 012 220 8484) A recommended local doctor. His office is at the Hilton Dahab Resort.

MONEY

Banque du Caire (9am-2pm & 6-9pm Sat-Thu, 9-11am & 6-9pm Fri) Near Inmo Diver's home.

National Bank of Egypt (9am-10pm) Has a branch in Dahab City and two on the promenade in Masbat, all with ATMs and forex services.

POST & TELEPHONE

The **post office** (8.30am-2.30pm) and **telephone centrale** (24hr) are both in Dahab City. There are a number of cardphones and a postbox near Ghazala Market in Masbat.

CHOOSING A DIVE SCHOOL

With hundreds of dive outfits around the Red Sea, choosing a diving school can be overwhelming. Here's some advice you might find useful when considering donning flippers for the first time.

- Even though you're on holiday, do your homework. You are probably about to spend a chunk of money and put your life in a stranger's hands, so it pays to take your time to walk around and visit several outfits.
- Have a look at the equipment. New equipment is great, but old equipment can be just as good if well maintained. Though you may have no idea what to look for, check to see how well the equipment is treated and stored. Stay away from shops with BCDs and regulators left out in the sun or strewn about their equipment room.
- While big schools have the reputation, lots of instructors and shiny equipment, they can be crowded and feel like impersonal diving factories. Some smaller outfits, without all the glitzy goodies, can offer a more personal touch.
- Choosing a good instructor is paramount: here's where asking other travellers for their experiences comes in handy. If possible, try to find someone who speaks your native language – it will definitely help when you're trying to understand dive tables for the 3rd time. Talk to several instructors and go with the one you feel most comfortable with. Since they will be your new best friend, you should at least get along with them.
- Check to see if your travel insurance covers diving accidents. If not, see what sort of insurance the school provides. Find the location of the nearest hyperbaric chamber – it's always a good idea know where to go for help should the need arise.

Activities

Without a doubt the most popular activity in Dahab is loafing, though developing a serious sheesha addiction is purely optional. Those who manage to drag themselves away from those comfy beachside couches, however, will also find some of the best and most accessible dive sites in the Red Sea. Nearly a hundred dive shops in Dahab offer all manner of diving possibilities: from boat/car/camel diving safaris to beginner scuba diving courses. Picking a shop to dive with is not always easy, particularly if you're a first-timer who's new to the game. Our box, Choosing a Dive School, (opposite) should help you get started.

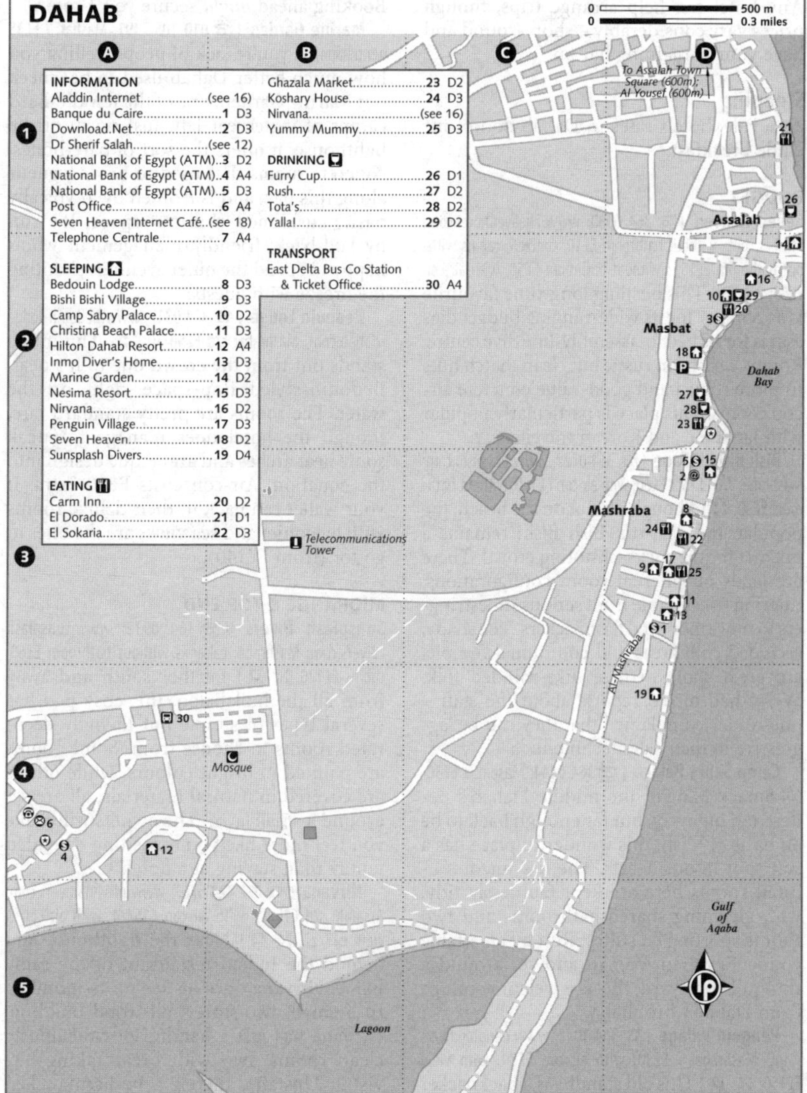

For above-the-water adventures, there are loads of options for camel and car safaris around Sinai, including day trips to the heavily touristed **Coloured Canyon** (from E£160), the fascinating **Abu Gallum** desert protectorate (around E£180), or to nearby St Katherine's Monastery (E£60 to E£120). All-inclusive three-day trips into the interior will set you back about E£600 to E£900. Any hotel can help arrange trips, though prices vary considerably – shop around and have your bargaining hat on.

Sleeping

As a rule, hotels rates in Dahab do not include breakfast.

BUDGET

Seven Heaven (☎ 364 0080; www.7heavenhotel.com; Masbat; huts without bathroom E£10, concrete cabins without bathroom E£15, r without bathroom E£50, with air-con E£60; ❄ 💻) This bustling long-time favourite is as popular for its wide-ranging budget digs as it is for its hectic, assembly-line dive centre. Rooms vary from rustic but clean thatch huts to more robust and good-value concrete air-con rooms. This place is particularly popular with Japanese and Korean travellers.

Bish Bishi Village (☎ 364 0727; www.bishbishi.com; Mashraba; dm E£15, r E£60, with air con E£180, without bathroom E£30; ❄) Though it's not on the beach, the popular and well-run Bish Bishi remains a magnet for the rucksack-toting crowd. There are loads of different room configurations, catering to everyone from serious shoestringers to more moneyed flashpackers. The shady, secluded chill areas and communal fire pits are great spots to meet like-minded folk. We've had mixed reports about the staff – one reader complained that they can be 'aggressive in their sales techniques'.

Camp Sabry Palace (☎ 364 0444; Masbat; r E£30-60) Smack-bang in the middle Dahab's pedestrian highway, but far enough back to be an oasis of hush, this wonderful place has a soft spot in our hearts. The few uncomplicated rooms here are kept faultlessly tidy, with gleaming shared bathrooms and two rooms sporting en suites. Run by an affable young Egyptian woman and set around a tranquil courtyard, this is a welcome refuge from Dahab's brouhaha.

Penguin Village (☎ 364 1047; www.penguindivers.com; Mashraba; r E£30, with air-con E£80, with view E£150; ❄ 💻) This old standby is a backpacker Venus fly-trap – somehow nearly everyone just ends up here. Not too surprising really; it has a sweet beach location, a dive centre, a wide selection of bargain-basement rooms as well as several upmarket rooms, and a lively beachside restaurant. Even though the service borders on brusque and cleanliness standards occasionally slip, it's still one of the better and more social options around. Booking ahead *might* secure you a room.

Marine Garden (☎ 010 105 2491; Masbat; r E£35 per person) If you're sick of people telling you how much better Dahab used to be, check out Marine Garden, one of the few die-hard camps of yesteryear left. Just north of the lighthouse, it offers the sort of bare-bones, concrete rooms that used to be de rigueur along this bay, and is fronted by a typically basic, cushioned chill-out space. It's run by laid-back, friendly management who's happy to spend the quiet evenings shooting the breeze with guests.

Bedouin Lodge (☎ 364 0317; www.bedouin-lodge-dahab.com; Mashraba; s/d E£50/70; ❄) This place stands out from the crowd due to it's neat, Bedouin-styled flop-space right on the water. The rooms are pretty standard fare, though the hotel does manage to sneak some neat arches and arabesque design into the equation. Air-con costs E£10 extra. If your wallet can hack it, their deluxe rooms with balconies and sea views are the ones to go for (from E£140).

MIDRANGE & TOP END

Sunsplash Divers (☎ 364 0932; www.sunsplash-divers.com; Mashraba; cabanas without bathroom E£60, cabins E£120; ❄ 💻) Further south and away from all the hullabaloo, this cosy pad has several types of simple but lovingly decorated rooms to choose from. Some rooms are painted in bright colours, while others are covered in natural materials; all are set around a small lawn. The owners will make you feel more like you're visiting extended family than staying at a hotel.

Nirvana (☎ 012 424 6762; www.nirvanadivers.com; Assalah; s/d €10/15, with air-con €15/24, with air-con & view €17/27; ❄ 💻) Near the lighthouse and behind the Indian restaurant of the same name, Nirvana does justice to its moniker. In a small, two-storey, all-wood building, Nirvana has just a handful of ridiculously clean rooms, two with breathtaking bay vistas. Upstairs, there's a be-hammocked

2nd-floor patio that's ideal for whiling away time, while the garden rooms out the back offer some air-conditioned respite.

Inmo Divers Home (☎ 364 0370; www.inmodivers.de; Mashraba; s/d US$37/46;) Though you don't have to be a diver to stay at this excellent, long-standing German-run resort, it will definitely help if you want to have something to chat about with fellow guests. Rooms are comfortable, attractively decorated and very orderly, with the architectural style delivering plenty of polished wood and white-domed goodness. The dive centre here has a solid reputation and the children's playground makes it a hit with families.

Christina Beach Palace (☎ 364 0390; www.christinahotels.com; Mashraba; s/d €32/40;) We are rather partial to the whitewashed rooms here, all finished with curving balconies, lots of glistening wood and neat spiral staircases. Inside, the rooms are very comfy and continue the polished wood theme. You can pay €4 extra for air-con.

Nesima Resort (☎ 364 0320; www.nesima-resort.com; Mashraba; s/d €44/57;) A solid midrange choice, popular Nesima has oodles of garden green and shady walkways. The place has a slightly more intimate feel than most and makes good use of its curved archways and high domed ceilings. Rooms are dark and cool, but kind of cosy and helped along by pretty decorations and arty touches. The beachside pool is very Club Med.

Hilton Dahab Resort (☎ 364 0310; www.hilton.com; Dahab City; r from US$100;) Far away from the Assalah action, this was the first big-spending resort to see the potential in Dahab's shiny shores. Designed around a garden-and-lagoon concept, it manages to retain a classy and tranquil atmosphere. Leisure facilities are impressive: a large pool area, a sand beach on the (real) lagoon where you can windsurf, a kids' club and the highly regarded Sinai Divers Dive Centre. Rooms are extremely comfortable and the suites are stocked with hammock-equipped terraces.

Eating

The long curve of Dahab Bay is a string of waterside restaurants eagerly vying for tourist custom. It's hard to recommend one over the other: they typically have the same slightly pricey menu of passable food – though they do make up for it in atmosphere with groovy cushioned seats, mood lighting and wafting, funky tunes. Best bet is to partake in the traditional Dahab evening stroll to find a place that tickles your fancy. The restaurants mentioned below stand out from the crowd.

El Sokaria (☎ 364 0459; Mashraba; mains E£8-25; 24hr) Along the main road in Mashraba, this friendly local establishment dishes up superb value by Dahab standards. Expect Egyptian usuals, where breakfasts are cheap and filling (E£7 to E£10), and the pizzas are top-notch (E£12 to E£20) – ask for them 'Italian style'.

Carm Inn (☎ 364 1300; Masbat; mains E£18-60; V) While not right on the water, this busy and snug place is tastefully bedecked in natural materials and abundant greenery. The inventive list of dishes strays well off the usual Dahab menu path, preparing Indonesian, Thai, Italian and Moroccan victuals as well as heaps of vegie options. Healthy eating is the call of the day; everything is made fresh to order from local ingredients (and hence may take a while to prepare). Bonus: the milkshakes here (E£9.50) are the best in town – trust us on this one.

Al Yousef (Assalah; mains E£20-40) One of several fish joints lining the main market square in the town of Assalah, a few kilometres north of the bay, this is the place to come for the best and cheapest seafood in Dahab. Period. Choose your fish from the fishmongers next door (where most restaurants also get their goods), grab a cold Stella (E£7) from the nearby Drinkies shop, and plop down on their streetside tables awaiting your marine-morsel delights.

Nirvana (☎ 012 424 6762; Mashraba; mains E£20-45) Don't go past Nirvana without sampling some of the most authentic Indian food in Egypt. You'll love the big range of curries and usuals like *paratha, samosas* and *naan,* but we'll bet our underpants that it's their phenomenal *masala chai* (spiced Indian tea; E£5) that will have you coming back for more.

El Dorado (☎ 364 1027; Masbat; mains E£35-65) As you'd expect from an Italian place run by genu-*ine* Italians, the dishes here are second to none. You can dine in their comfy, covered eating area or al fresco on the beach, sampling the winning thin-crust pizzas (E£35 to E£50), the pastas (E£50 to E£65) or, best of all, mouth-watering carpaccio with rocket and parmesan cheese (E£70). Real parmesan cheese! Be sure to leave room for tiramisu (E£30) and authentic espresso.

Yummy Mummy (☎ 010 580 0944; Mashraba; mains E£40-80) Though the word on the street is that this is the best of the ocean-side restaurants, we're not completely convinced. The grub is fine, though definitely on the spendy side, and the moody lamp-lit ambience is sublime indeed. Alas the surly staff don't do much to bolster the fine dining experience.

For a quick bite in Mashraba, pop into the **Koshary House** (koshary E£3-5), next to the taxi drop off point. The **Ghazala Market** (🕒 24hr) is in Masbat, with smaller satellite stores all over Dahab, and is well stocked with a range of food and sundries.

Drinking

Two main bars vie for punters' drinking attention on any given night: the grungy **Tota's** (in Masbat), an unmistakable two-storey bar shaped like a giant ship, and **Rush** (in Masbat), a slightly classier outdoor joint just a few doors down. Both try to outdo each other with nightly events that range from drink specials to trivia nights to foam parties. It's best to hop between the two to scope out which one has the more happening scene.

For a quieter tipple, try the **Furry Cup** (Blue Beach Club, Mashraba; 🕒 noon-2am), popular with dive instructors and other expat residents. Otherwise, the top-floor bar at the new **Yalla!** (in Masbat), on the main Dahab strip, is not a bad place for an afternoon beer or cocktail.

Getting There & Around

BUS

The **East Delta Bus Co station and ticket office** (🕒 7.30am-11pm) is located in Dahab City, close to the mosque. The most regular connection is to Sharm el-Sheikh (E£11 to E£15, 1½ hours), with 10 buses between 8am and 10pm. There are three daily buses to Nuweiba (E£11, 1¼ hour) at 10.30am, 4pm and 6.30pm, with the 10.30am service going on to Taba (E£22). There is a bus at 9.30am going to St Katherine's Monastery (E£20, 2½ hours). Buses to Cairo (E£70 to E£80, nine hours) leave at 8.30am, 12.30pm, 2.30pm, 4pm and 10pm. Buses for Suez (E£40 to E£45, seven hours) depart at 8am and 4pm, and there's one daily service to Hurghada (E£100, 12 to 14 hours) and Luxor (E£120, 14 to 16 hours) at 4pm. If you're going to Luxor, this is a cheaper and faster (but less comfortable) option than the bus-ferry-bus alternative.

Pickups meet all incoming buses and charge around E£5 to get to Assalah.

TAXI

A taxi (usually a pick-up) between Assalah and Dahab City costs E£5.

ST KATHERINE'S MONASTERY
دير القديسة كاترينا

☎ 069 / elevation 1570m

This unmissable ancient monastery traces its roots all the way back to AD 330, when Byzantine empress Helena built a small chapel and refuge here. Based at the foot of Mt Sinai, this was the supposed site of the biblical burning bush, where God first had word with Moses. In the 6th century, Emperor Justinian had a fortress built around the original chapel, also throwing in a basilica and monastery, to house and protect the small monastic community that had coalesced here. The monastery is dedicated to the legendry martyr of Alexandria, St Katherine, who had the misfortune to be tortured on a spiked wheel and beheaded.

Today there are just over 20 Greek Orthodox monks living in this ancient compound. There's no charge to visit the actual **monastery** (🕒 9am-noon Mon-Thu & Sat, except religious holidays), but you'll need to pay to see the wonderful collection of manuscripts and icons in the **Sacred Sacristy** (adult/student E£25/10), also known as the iconography museum. Be warned that the monastery is inevitably overrun by tour groups and can be packed to the rafters.

St Katherine Protectorate (adult/student US$3/US$2) is a 4350-sq-km national park that encompasses Mt Sinai and the monastery. To enter the area you'll need to purchase a ticket at the booth near the last police checkpoint, 10km before the monastery. At the ticket office, you can also arrange official guides for the climb up Mt Sinai (E£85) and camel transport (E£85 each way), though both are also easily organised at hotels in town and at the monastery itself. You can also set out on all-inclusive camel safaris for around E£150 per person per day.

CLIMBING MT SINAI *Mary Fitzpatrick*

Rising out of the desert and jutting above the other peaks surrounding the monastery is the towering 2285m Mt Sinai, known locally as Gebel Musa. Although some archaeologists and historians dispute Mt Sinai's biblical claim to fame, it is revered by Christians, Muslims and Jews, all of whom believe that God delivered his Ten Commandments to Moses at the summit. The mountain is beautiful and easy to climb, and – except at the summit, where you'll invariably be overwhelmed by crowds of visitors – it offers a taste of serenity and mountain magnificence.

There are two well-defined routes – the camel trail and the Steps of Repentance – that meet about 300m below the summit at a plateau known as Elijah's Basin. Here, everyone must take a steep series of 750 rocky and uneven steps to the top. Most people make the climb in the predawn hours to take in the magnificence of the sun rising over the surrounding peaks, and then arrive back at the base at 9am when the monastery opens for visitors.

The **camel trail** is the easier route, and takes about two hours to ascend at a steady pace. En route are several kiosks selling tea and soda, and vendors hiring out blankets (E£10) to ward off the chill at the summit. It's also possible to hire a camel at the base, just behind the monastery (E£85 each way), to Elijah's Basin. Note that it's easier on the anatomy to ride a camel up the mountain, rather than down.

The alternative path to the summit, the harsh 3750 **Steps of Repentance**, was laid by one monk as a form of penance. The steps are made of roughly hewn rock and are steep and uneven in many places, requiring strong knees and concentration in placing your feet.

During the summer, try to avoid the heat by beginning your hike by 3am. Although the trail is wide and clear, it can be a bit difficult in parts and a torch is essential. Bring sufficient food and water, warm clothes and ideally a sleeping bag. It gets cold and windy, even in summer, and light snows are common in winter. The start of the camel trail is reached by walking along the northern wall of the monastery, past the end of the compound. The Steps of Repentance begin outside the southeastern corner of the compound. Be prepared to share the summit with up to 500 other visitors, some carrying stereos, others Bibles and well-worn hymn books.

Information

In the village of Al-Milga, about 3.5km from the monastery, there's a **post office**, **telephone central**, and a handful of hotels as well as a few shops and cafés. The **Banque Misr** (10am-1pm & 5-8pm Sat-Thu) here will change cash and give Visa and MasterCard advances. The only ATM machine is found near the entrance to St Katherine Monastery.

Sleeping & Eating

Monastery Guesthouse (☎/fax 347 0353; s/d half board US$32/55) Definitely the most atmospheric place to bed down, this guesthouse lets you sample monastic life. Adjacent to the monastery, the hotel has spartan rooms, all with sanitary private bathrooms, comfortable beds and plenty of blankets for cold mountain nights. There's a reasonable restaurant that serves beer and wine as well as an outdoor café with primo mountain views.

Fox Desert Camp (☎ 347 0344; faragfoxsi@hotmail.com; r without bathroom per person E£20-25) In Al-Milga, this rudimentary camp can't be missed at night thanks to the brash neon signage. Rooms here offer little more than a bed, some heavy blankets and four walls. Several rooms share clean bathrooms between two, while the cheaper options share the more whiffy communal toilets. Still, there's a neat Bedouin-style setup, with friendly management and camp fires at night to ward off the chill. They cook up breakfast (E£10) and other meals (E£20 to E£30) on request, and sometimes have beer too boot.

In Al-Milga there's a bakery opposite the mosque and a couple of well-stocked supermarkets in the shopping arcade. A few small restaurants are just behind the bakery.

Shopping

Fansina Bedouin Crafts (☎ 470 155; 10am-3pm Sat-Thu) If you have the time, pop by this great, EU-funded workshop that supports local women by helping to re-establish traditional weaving crafts. The gift shop sells numerous wares, displaying some of the best-quality hand-woven fabrics, clothes and accessories we've seen in Egypt.

Getting There & Away

BUS

All buses leave from the East Delta Bus Co office behind the mosque in Al-Milga. A daily bus at 6am travels to Cairo (E£40, seven hours) via Suez (E£26, four hours) and another Cairo service leaves at 1pm. For Dahab (E£20, 2½ hours), where you can change for Nuweiba or Sharm el-Sheikh, there's a bus at 1pm.

SERVICE TAXI

Service taxis travel in and out of Al-Milga village irregularly and infrequently, although there are plenty available if you are willing to pay for the extra places to fill the vehicle (up to seven people). Per person fares are E£35/50 to Dahab/Sharm el-Sheikh.

NUWEIBA نويبع

☎ 069

Though endowed with the same natural resources as nearby Dahab, Nuweiba has somehow always found itself somewhere between obscurity and oblivion. The beaches here are golden, the water crystal clear, the desert mountains shimmering pink, and yet for most of the year Nuweiba has the catatonic feel of a post-apocalyptic beach resort. If you want to avoid the scenes at Sharm and Dahab and just relax solo on a tranquil beach, it could well be the place for you. For even more isolation and shush, check out some of the rudimentary beach camps north of Nuweiba, remote getaways where the hippy vibe soldiers on.

Orientation

The town is divided into three parts. To the south is the hectic and ugly port area, with the bus station and several banks. About 8km further north is Nuweiba City, a small but spread-out settlement with a few accommodation options, a small bazaar and several cheap places to eat. About a 10-minute walk further north along the beach is Tarabin, which is a throwback to Dahab's more rustic backpacker days of yesteryear.

Information

The post and telephone offices are next to the tiny bus station in the Nuweiba Port area. The Banque Misr, Banque du Caire and National Bank of Egypt branches near the bus station have ATMs but will not always supply US dollars, meaning that you should bring these with you if you intend to buy ferry tickets to Aqaba. Neither will they change Jordanian dinars. The Nuweiba branch of the **National Bank of Egypt** (🕑 9am-1pm & 7-9pm Sat-Thu, 9-11am Fri) is conveniently located in front of the Nuweiba Village hotel and has an ATM. The **Almostakbal Internet Café** (per hr E£6; 🕑 10am-midnight) is behind Dr Sheesh Kebab in Nuweiba City.

Activities

Apart from lazing on the beach and soaking in the plentiful peace, underwater delights are the feature attraction, with scuba diving and snorkelling keeping many visitors busy. **Diving Camp Nuweiba** (☎ 012 399 5828; www.scuba-college.com), in the Nuweiba Village hotel, and **Emperor Divers** (☎ 352 0695; www.emperordivers.com), which operates out of the Nuweiba Coral Hilton Resort, have solid reputations.

Nuweiba is the place to organise Jeeps or camel treks to sights such as **Coloured Canyon**, **Khudra Oasis**, **Ain Umm Ahmed** (the largest oasis in eastern Sinai) and **Ain al-Furtaga** (another palm-filled oasis). Most hotels and beach camps along the coast will be able to organise a trip for you, with all-inclusive camel treks costing around E£300 per day.

Sleeping

Big Duna (☎ 010 610 8731; huts per person E£15-20) About 2km south of Nuweiba town along an unmarked track between some trees, this secret hideaway hoards a perfectly curving bay all to itself. The accommodation here is little more than crumbling reed huts with mats on the floor, but that doesn't faze most of the long-haired backpackers who manage to find their way here.

Soft Beach Camp (☎ 364 7586, 012 634 4756; www.softbeachcamp.com; s without bathroom E£40-60, d without bathroom E£60-80; 💻) With one of the best beach settings in Nuweiba, Soft Beach manages to draw in the punters and avoid the graveyard emptiness of most other Nuweiba establishments. Their beach huts are pretty run-down and nothing special, but the friendly welcome and neat restaurant with hammocks, offering plenty of lazing space, go some way to making up for that. All rooms share bathrooms, and meals are available for E£25 to E£40.

Nakhi (☎ 350 0879; www.nakhil-inn.com; s/d US$30/44; ❄ ☒) Easily winning the Nuweiba 'best value' plaudit, Nakhi boasts several wonderfully designed rooms at the far northern end of the beach. The abodes here have room enough to swing several cats in and are lovingly finished and maintained. Some even have floor-to-ceiling windows for unbeatable panoramic vistas. There's a private beach here to relax on, satellite TV in the rooms, wi-fi all round and a modern restaurant serving meals. To top it off, the gregarious and welcoming owner has a small dive shop on site and organises desert safaris. Nice one.

Swisscare Nuweiba Village (☎ 350 0401; www.swisscare-hotels.com; s/d from US$60/70; ❄ ☒ ☐) This low-key, midrange resort offers a nod to chain-hotel design, with solid rooms decked out with the essential mod cons. On the beach out front there's a stocked bar, a pool, an area for beach volleyball and a kiddie playground. The abodes lie scattered around a pretty garden, and there's even a tiny organic vegie patch with vegetables for sale.

Dolphin Camp (☎ 345 0401-3; s/d E£40/50) Next door to Swisscare Nuweiba Village, this place provides simpler digs for the budget conscious in colourful and breezy hexagonal, huts – though be sure to ask for a mozzie net. A popular dive camp is based here.

NORTH OF NUWEIBA

Basata (☎ 350 0480; www.basata.com; 20km north of Nuweiba; campsites per person €10, huts per person €14, chalets €60) This German-run, commune-esque ecolodge is a self-styled beach oasis for ecominded folk and their families. Offering very basic huts as well as more robust, curvy walled chalets, the owners sell organic produce and provide the use of their well-stocked kitchen for guests to prepare their own meals. The beach chill-out space here is a great place to laze and meet fellow, like-minded wanderers. Basata lives up to their eco-promise by recycling waste, doing beach clean-ups, desalinating their own water and actively supporting the local community.

Ayyash Camp (☎ 010 444 2147; 10km north of Nuweiba; s/d E£30/40) This friendly and laid-back camp, near the breezy Ras Shaitan headland, sits on its own bay and maintains accommodation in austere huts. Ayyash has gained some notoriety among travelling Israeli and international musicians, who come here to jam and record music in the small onsite recording studio. Meals are E£30 to E£40, but be warned: if talk of chakras and the smell of petunia oil scares you, you may want to give this place a wide berth.

Eating

Eating options in Nuweiba are limited.

Dr Sheesh Kebab (☎ 350 0273; ⏰ 7am-11pm) The friendly Dr Sheesh has a remedy to cure all: yummy kebabs (E£25) and *kofta* (E£22), with a prescription of ta'amiyya, salad and bread (E£8) if pain persists. It's in Nuweiba City.

Cleopatra Restaurant (☎ 350 0503; ⏰ 8am-midnight) Opposite the Nuweiba Domina Resort, Cleopatra serves staples such as grilled chicken (E£22) and mezze (E£5 to E£20) in a small courtyard and serves Stella (E£10) to wash it all down.

There are a couple of supermarkets and a sprinkling of open-air eateries among the camps on Tarabin's promenade.

Getting There & Away

BOAT

For information on ferries to Aqaba in Jordan, see p209.

BUS

Buses going to or from Taba stop at both the port and its nearby bus station. You can also request that they stop outside the hospital in Nuweiba City, but this is on the whim of the driver. Buses don't stop at Tarabin. A seat in a service taxi from the bus station to Tarabin costs E£5; the whole taxi will cost E£15. The drivers will always try to charge more, so be ready to haggle.

East Delta Bus Co (☎ 352 0371) has three daily buses to Cairo (E£70 to E£80, nine hours) via Taba (E£15, one hour) at 9am and 3pm. Buses to Sharm el-Sheikh (E£22 to E£25, 2½ hours) via Dahab (E£11, one hour) leave at 6.30am, 10.30am and 4.30pm. One bus leaves for Suez (E£45, four hours) at 6am. There's no direct service to St Katherine's, but you can often catch the 6.30am Dahab-bound bus and make a connection there (see p198).

SERVICE TAXI

There is a service taxi station by the port, but unless you get there when the ferry has arrived from Aqaba, you'll have to wait a long time for the car to fill up. Per person fares (multiply by seven for the entire car) average about E£30 to Sharm el-Sheikh,

E£15 to Dahab and E£60 to Cairo (usually changing vehicles in Suez).

TABA طابا

☎ 069

This busy border crossing between Egypt and Israel is open 24 hours. There's a small **post & telephone office** opposite the New Taba Beach Resort in the 'town', along with a few shops. You can change money at the 24-hour Banque Misr booth in the arrivals hall, and there's an ATM just outside the border. The Taba Hilton can change travellers cheques.

Upon entering Egypt, when you exit the arrivals hall, the bus station is a 10-minute walk straight ahead on the left-hand side of the road. **East Delta Bus Co** (☎ 353 0250) has buses to Nuweiba (E£15, one hour) at 7am, 9am, 12pm and 3pm. A bus from Cairo to Nuweiba also passes by at around noon. Buses to Cairo (E£70 to E£80, nine hours) leave at 10.30am and 4.30pm. Services to Sharm el-Sheikh (E£30, 3½ hours) via Dahab (E£20, 2½ hours) depart at 9am, 3pm and 9pm. A bus heads out to Suez at 7am (E£45, three hours).

Peugeot taxis and minibuses function as service taxis. Per person rates are E£15 to Nuweiba, E£35 to Dahab, E£45 to Sharm el-Sheikh, E£60 to Cairo or St Katherine's. As you may be in for a long wait before each car is full, you're better off catching the bus; otherwise you can hire the whole car for about seven times these rates (less with vigorous haggling).

EGYPT DIRECTORY

ACCOMMODATION

Though youth hostels in Egypt are rare, there are loads of excellent budget hotels around. Decent midrange hotels, on the other hand, are harder to find. When it comes to the top end, travellers are spoilt for choice, with the major international chains represented in most of the larger cities.

Generally speaking, winter (December to February) is the tourist high season and summer (June to August) the low season in all parts of the country except on the coasts, and to a lesser degree in Cairo. Hotel prices reflect this distinction. Prices cited in this chapter are for rooms in the high season and include taxes. Breakfast and private bathrooms are included in the price unless indicated otherwise in the review. Some accommodation options offer 'half board', which includes bed, breakfast and one main meal. We have defined budget hotels as any that charge up to around E£100 (US$20) for a double room, midrange as any that charge between E£100 and E£540 (US$20 to US$100) and top end as any that charge more than E£540 (US$100) for a room. In the low season you should be able to negotiate significant discounts at all hotels, including those at the top end.

Hotels rated three-star and up generally require payment in US dollars. They are increasingly accepting credit-card payments but you shouldn't take this for granted.

ACTIVITIES

Visitors are spoilt for choice when it comes to activities, with plenty of nonarchaeological pursuits on offer. These include trekking, desert safaris, horse riding, sand-boarding, windsurfing, ballooning and world-class diving and snorkelling. Activities are mentioned throughout the chapter.

BUSINESS HOURS

The following information is a guide only. The official weekend is Friday and Saturday. Note that during Ramadan, all banks, offices, shops, museums and tourist sites keep shorter hours.

Banks Open 8.30am to 1.30pm Sunday to Thursday. Many banks in Cairo and other cities open again from 5pm or 6pm for two or three hours, largely for foreign-exchange transactions. Some also open on Friday and Saturday for the same purpose. Exchange booths are open as late as 8pm.

Government offices Open 8am to 2pm Sunday to Thursday. Tourist offices are generally open longer.

Post offices Generally open from 8.30am to 2pm Saturday to Thursday.

Private offices Open 10am to 2pm and 4pm to 9pm, except Friday and holidays.

Restaurants Open between noon and midnight daily. Cafés tend to open earlier and close a bit later, usually operating from 7am to midnight.

Shops Open 9am to 1pm and 5pm to 10pm Jun-Sep, 10am to 6pm Oct-May. Most large shops tend to close on Sunday and holidays.

CHILDREN

Though Egyptians are extraordinarily welcoming to children, Egypt's budget and midrange hotels rarely have child-friendly

PRACTICALITIES

- *Egyptian Gazette* (50pt) is Egypt's flimsy and embarrassingly bad English-language daily newspaper. *Al-Ahram Weekly* (www.ahram.org.eg/weekly; E£1) appears every Thursday and does a much better job of keeping English-speaking readers informed of what's going on. *Egypt Today* (E£15) is an ad-saturated general-interest glossy with good listings.
- You can pick up the BBC World Service (www.bbc.co.uk/worldservice) on various frequencies, including AM 1323 in Alexandria, the Europe short-wave schedule in Cairo and the Middle East short-wave schedule in Upper Egypt. In Cairo, FM95 broadcasts on 557kHz between 7am and midnight daily, including news in English at 7.30am, 2.30pm and 8pm. Nile FM (104.2kHz) is an English-language music station broadcasting out of Cairo.
- Satellite dishes are common in Egypt, and international English-language news services such as CNN and BBC World can be accessed in hotel rooms throughout the country.
- Electrical current is 220V AC, 50Hz in most parts of the country. Exceptions are Alexandria, and Heliopolis and Ma'adi in Cairo, which have currents of 110V AC, 50Hz. Wall sockets are the round, two-pin European type.
- Egypt uses the metric system for weights and measures.

facilities (the five-star chains do). Towns and cities don't have easily accessible public gardens with playground equipment, or shopping malls with amusement centres. Fortunately, there are other things kids find cool: felucca and camel rides, exploring the interiors of pyramids and snorkelling on Sinai reefs are only a few. Restaurants everywhere are very welcoming to families.

Formula is readily available in pharmacies, and supermarkets stock disposable nappies. High chairs are sometimes available in restaurants. Baby-sitting facilities are usually available in top-end hotels only.

COURSES

If you're serious about learning Arabic, the best option is to sign up at the **Arabic Language Institute** (Map pp130-1; ☎ 02-797 5055; www.aucegypt.edu; 113 Sharia Qasr al-Ainy, Downtown, Cairo), a department of the American University in Cairo. It offers intensive instruction in both modern standard Arabic and Egyptian colloquial Arabic at elementary, intermediate and advanced levels in semester courses (US$8532) running over five months. The institute also runs intensive summer programs (US$4128).

A less expensive option is studying at the **International Language Institute** (ILI; Map pp126-7; ☎ 02-346 3087; www.arabicegypt.com; 4 Sharia Mahmoud Azmy, Sahafayeen, Cairo). This place has courses in modern standard Arabic and Egyptian colloquial Arabic over eight levels. Prices start at US$250 for 32 to 48 hours' tuition over four weeks.

DANGERS & ANNOYANCES

With the exception of over-zealous touts and the odd scam (see p138) in the major tourist hotspots, Egypt is generally a safe place to travel around. Violent crime is rare, and most cities are safe to walk around at night, the exception being if you are an unaccompanied foreign woman (see also p207).

We receive increasing reports of items and money going missing from locked hotel rooms, and even hotel safes. Where possible, it's best to keep your documents, cash and valuables on you at all times.

Note that terrorist bombings targeting foreign tourists, such as those most recently carried out in 2004, 2005 and 2006 in Sinai, do occur. The government has prioritised security, particularly in heavily touristed areas, and the resulting police checks, convoys and police escorts have been known to slow down independent travel in parts of the country.

DISCOUNT CARDS

If you have an officially recognised student card you'll be eligible for major discounts at museums and sites throughout Egypt. The best is the International Student Identity Card (ISIC), and it's possible to organise this in Egypt if you didn't get a chance before you left home. You'll need one photo, proof of being a student, a photocopy of the front page of your passport and E£80. There are no age limits.

In Luxor you can get ISIC cards at the **Nada Travel Service** (NTS; Map p154; ☎ 095-238 4490; Petra Travel Agency Bldg, Sharia Ahmed Orabi; ⏰ 8am-11pm), near Luxor Temple. In Cairo, go to **Egyptian Student Travel Services** (ESTS; Map pp126-7; ☎ 02-2531 0330; www.estsegypt.com; 23 Sharia Manial, Midan el-Mammalek, Roda).

EMBASSIES & CONSULATES

If you are looking for the Egyptian embassy in a country other than Egypt, there is a comprehensive listing of Egyptian diplomatic and consular missions at www.mfa.gov.eg.

Embassies & Consulates in Egypt

Most foreign embassies and consulates are open from around 8am to 2pm Sunday to Thursday.

Australia (Map p137; ☎ 02-2575 0444; www.egypt.embassy.gov.au; 11th fl, World Trade Centre, 1191 Corniche el-Nil, Bulaq, Cairo)

Canada (Map pp126-7; ☎ 02-2791 8700; www.dfait-maeci.gc.ca/cairo; 26 Sharia Kamal el-Shenawy, Garden City, Cairo)

France Cairo (Map pp126-7; ☎ 02-3567 3200; www.ambafrance-eg.org; 29 Sharia Charles de Gaulle, Giza); Alexandria (Map p146; ☎ 03-487 5615; www.ambafrance-eg.org; 2 Midan Orabi, Mansheyya)

Germany Cairo (Map p137; ☎ 02-2728 2000; www.german-embassy.org.eg; 8 Hassan Sabry, Zamalek); Alexandria (Map p146; ☎ 03-486 7503; 9 Sharia El-Fawateem, Azarita)

Ireland Cairo (Map p137; ☎ 02-2735 8547; 3 Sharia Abu el-Feda, Zamalek); Alexandria (Map p146; ☎ 03-485 2672; 9 Sharia el-Fawateem, Azarita)

Israel Cairo (Map pp126-7; ☎ 02-3332 1500; info@cairo.mfa.gov.il; 6 Sharia ibn al-Malek, Giza); Alexandria (off Map p146; ☎ 03-544 9501; 15 Sharia Mena Kafer Abdou, Rushdy)

Italy Cairo (Map pp126-7; ☎ 02-2794 3194; www.ambilcairo.esteri.it; 15 Sharia Abdel Rahman Fahmy, Garden City); Alexandria (Map p146; ☎ 03-487 9470; www.consalessandria.esteri.it; 25 Sharia Saad Zaghloul)

Japan (off Map pp126-7; ☎ 02-2528 5910; www.eg.emb-japan.go.jp; 81 Corniche el-Nil, Maadi, Cairo)

Jordan (Map pp126-7; ☎ 02-2748 6169; fax 02-2760 1027; 6 Sharia Gohainy, Doqqi, Cairo)

Lebanon Cairo (Map p137; ☎ 02-2738 2823; fax 02-2738 2818; 22 Sharia Mansour Mohammed, Zamalek); Alexandria (Map p146; ☎ 03-484 6589; 64 Tariq al-Horreya)

Libya Cairo (Map p137; ☎ 02-2735 1269; fax 02-2735 0072; 7 Sharia el-Saleh Ayoub, Zamalek); Alexandria (Map p146; ☎ 03-494 0877; fax 03-494 0297; 4 Sharia Batris Lumomba, Bab Shark)

Netherlands (Map p137; ☎ 02-2739 5500; www.hollandemb.org.eg; 18 Sharia Hassan Sabry, Zamalek, Cairo)

New Zealand (Map pp126-7; ☎ 02-2461 6000; fax 02-2461 6099; North Tower, Nile City Bldg, Corniche El Nil, Ramlet Beaulac, Cairo)

Saudi Arabia Cairo (Map pp126-7; ☎ 02-2749 0775; fax 02-2795 5038; 2 Sharia Ahmed Neseem, Giza); Alexandria (Map p146; ☎ 097-482 9911; 9 Sharia Batalsa, Alexandria); Suez (☎ 062-497 7591; 12 Sharia El-Guabarty, Port Tawfiq)

Spain (Map p137; ☎ 02-2735 6462; embespeg@mail.mae.es; 41 Sharia Ismail Mohammed, Zamalek, Cairo)

Sudan Cairo (Map pp126-7; ☎ 02-2794 9661; fax 02-2354 2693; 3 Sharia al-Ibrahimy, Garden City); Aswan (Map p168; ☎ 097-230 7231, fax 097-234 2563; Bldg 20, Atlas)

Syria (Map pp126-7; ☎ 02-2749 4528; fax 02-2749 4560; 18 Abdel Rahim Sabry, Doqqi, Cairo)

Turkey Cairo (Map pp130-1; ☎ 02-2794 8364; turkemb@idsc.gov.eg; 25 Sharia al-Falaky, Downtown); Alexandria (off Map p146; ☎ 03-393 9086; 11 Sharia Kamel el-Kilany)

UK Cairo (Map pp126-7; ☎ 02-2794 0852-8; www.britishembassy.org.eg; 7 Sharia Ahmed Ragheb, Garden City); Alexandria (off Map p146; ☎ 03-546 7001-2; 3 Sharia Mena, Rushdy)

USA (Map pp130-1; ☎ 02-2797 3300; http://egypt.usembassy.gov; 8 Sharia Kamal el-Din Salah, Garden City, Cairo)

FESTIVALS & EVENTS

Surprisingly, there aren't very many headline events on the national cultural calendar. The most notable are the **Cairo International Book Fair** in January/February, the **Ascension of Ramses II** at Abu Simbel on 22 February and 22 October each year, and the **Egyptian Marathon** (egyptianmarathon@egypt.net) in February, when competitors race around the monuments on Luxor's West Bank.

GAY & LESBIAN TRAVELLERS

While homosexuality is not actually illegal according to Egypt's penal code, arrests on the charge of 'debauchery and contempt of religion' do occur. The website www.gayegypt.com is a good source of information.

HOLIDAYS

In addition to the main Islamic holidays (p628), Egypt celebrates the following public holidays:

New Year's Day 1 January

Coptic Christmas 7 January – only Coptic businesses are closed for the day

Coptic Easter March/April – only Coptic businesses are closed for the day

Sham an-Nessim (The Smell of the Breeze) First Monday after Coptic Easter
Sinai Liberation Day 25 April
May Day 1 May
Liberation Day 18 June
Revolution Day 23 July
Wafa'a el-Nil (The Flooding of the Nile) 15 August
Coptic New Year 11 September (12 September in leap years)
Armed Forces Day 6 October
Suez Victory Day 24 October
Victory Day 23 December

MONEY

The official currency is the Egyptian pound (E£) – in Arabic, a *guinay*. One pound consists of 100 piastres (pt). There are notes in denominations of 5pt, 10pt, 25pt and 50pt, and one, five, 10, 20, 50, 100 and 200 *guinay*. Coins in circulation have denominations of five, 10, 20 and 25 piastres. You should try to hoard as many E£1 and E£5 notes as you possibly can, as these come in very handy for baksheesh and taxi fares.

See the table for the rates for a range of currencies at the time of going to press.

Country	Unit	Egyptian pound (E£)
Australia	A$1	3.67
Canada	C$1	4.66
Euro zone	€1	7.21
Israel and the Palestinian Territories	1NIS	1.47
Japan	¥100	6.11
Libya	1LD	1.57
New Zealand	NZ$1	3.29
UK	UK£1	8.23
USA	US$1	5.56

ATMs

These have spread rapidly throughout the country; you'll find them everywhere in Cairo, Hurghada, Luxor, Alexandria and Sharm el-Sheikh, and less commonly in Aswan and Dahab. They are very rare in the Western Desert and in smaller towns throughout the country. ATMs are run by a number of different banks and not all are compatible with credit cards issued outside Egypt. In general, those belonging to Banque Misr, Egyptian American Bank, Banque du Caire, the National Bank of Egypt and HSBC will accept Visa and MasterCard and any Cirrus- or Maestro-compatible cards.

Credit Cards

These have become widely accepted in Egypt over recent years, but keep in mind that they usually aren't accepted in budget hotels and restaurants, nor in remote areas such as Siwa and the Western Oases. Visa and MasterCard can be used for cash advances at Banque Misr, the National Bank of Egypt and Thomas Cook offices. To report lost cards in Egypt:

Amex (☎ 02-2480 1530) In Cairo.
Diners Club (☎ 02-2578 3355) In Cairo.
MasterCard (☎ 02-2797 1179, 02-2796 2844) In Cairo.
Visa (☎ 02-2510-0200) In Cairo.

Moneychangers

Money can be officially changed at commercial banks, foreign exchange (forex) bureaus and some hotels. Rates don't tend to vary much but forex bureaus generally offer marginally better rates than the banks and they usually don't charge a commission fee.

Look at the money you're given when exchanging and don't accept any badly defaced, shabby or torn notes as you'll have great difficulty offloading them.

Taxes

Taxes of up to 25% will be added to your bill in most restaurants. There are also hefty taxes levied on upmarket accommodation; these have been factored into the prices we have quoted.

Tipping & Bargaining

Bargaining is a part of everyday life in Egypt and people haggle for everything from hotel rooms to clothes. There are rare instances where it's not worth wasting your breath (supermarkets, for example), but in any tourist-type shop, even marked prices can be fair game.

Tipping, called baksheesh, is another fact of life in Egypt. Salaries are extremely low and are supplemented by tips. In hotels and restaurants the 12% service charge goes into the till; an additional tip of between 10% and 15% is expected for the waiter. A guard who shows you something off the track at an archaeological site should be given a pound or two.

Travellers Cheques

There is no problem cashing well-known brands of travellers cheques at major banks and at Amex and Thomas Cook offices, but most forex bureaus don't take them. Most banks charge a small commission per cheque plus E£2 or E£3 for stamps. You must have your passport with you.

POST

Postcards cost E£1.50 to post and will take four or five days to get to Europe and around a week to 10 days to the USA and Australia. Letters of 20g cost between E£1.60 and E£2.20 (depending on the destination) and 1kg parcels cost between E£150 to E£200 to send by air mail. If you use postboxes, blue is for international airmail, red is for internal mail and green is for internal express mail.

SHOPPING

Even if you were not born to shop, you will be born again when you hit the *souqs* (markets) in Egypt. The country is awash with antediluvian bazaars selling all manner of pretty, shiny things for that perfect souvenir or memento. You can find nearly everything here including papyrus scrolls, fine metal work, antiques, sheeshas (a must-buy), and a whole slew of cheesy tourist tat. Often the quality on offer is pretty sub-par, but those with some patience and a keen eye are bound to find a deal.

The primo shopping spot in the country has to be Cairo's Khan al-Khalili bazaar (p134), where sleazy touts and rip-offs come part and parcel with awesome shopping opportunities. Hard bargaining here is nearly always required. Other towns with well-stocked souqs include Luxor and Aswan. Also look out for traditional Siwan, Bedouin and Nubian handcrafts in Siwa, Dahab and Aswan respectively.

TELEPHONE & FAX

Fax

Fax services are available at the main Telephone centrales in the big cities. A one-page fax costs around E£8 to send.

Mobile Phones

Egypt's mobile-phone network runs on the GSM system.

There are two main mobile-phone companies operating in Egypt: **MobiNil** (in Cairo ☎ 02-2760 9090; www.mobinil.com) and **Vodafone** (in Cairo ☎ 02-2529 2000; www.vodafone.com.eg). If your mobile phone from home is unlocked for use on other networks, local SIM cards for these companies can be bought for only E£10 to E£30, giving you a local number and access to cheap local calls. To top up your phone credit, both companies sell convenient prepaid cards from many retail outlets across the country in various denominations. The credit you purchase usually has a validity period of 30 days, though airtime credit is carried over if you recharge the card before the end of the validity period. Vodafone sells a Mobile Connect card that enables connection to the internet through your laptop.

ESSENTIAL EGYPTIAN VOCAB *Elbee*

Insha'Allah Literally: God willing, but takes on the meaning 'hopefully' or is just thrown into a sentence to spice things up.
Mafeesh Mushkila No problem, dude!
Malish Whatever, don't worry about it, okay. The official catch-all word in Egypt that goes along with the Egyptian lifestyle.
Khalas It's over, finished, okay, understand?
Alhamdulillah Literally 'Praise be to God', but also used to mean 'I'm fine'. Ie 'How are you?', 'Alhamdulillah.'
Mumkin Possibly or please or maybe.

What's your recommendation?
www.lonelyplanet.com/middle-east

Phone Codes

The country code for Egypt is ☎ 20, followed by the local area code (minus the zero), then the subscriber number. Local area codes are given at the start of each city or town section. The international access code (to call abroad from Egypt) is ☎ 00. For directory assistance call ☎ 140 or ☎ 141.

Phonecards

Two companies have card phones in Egypt. Menatel has booths that are yellow and green, while Nile Tel's are red and blue. Cards are sold at shops and kiosks and come in units of E£10, E£15, E£20 and E£30. Once you insert the card into the telephone, press the flag in the top left corner to get instructions in English.

There are different rates for peak (8am to 8pm Sunday to Thursday) and off-peak

(8pm to 8am Sunday to Thursday and all day Friday and Saturday) calls. Rates average E£3 per minute to the USA and Canada (E£2.25 off-peak); E£3.50 per minute to Europe (E£3 off-peak); and E£4.50 per minute to Australasia (E£3 off-peak).

Telephone Centrales

Alternatively, there are the old telephone offices, known as centrales, where you can book a call at the desk, which must be paid for in advance (there is a three-minute minimum). The operator directs you to a booth when a connection is made.

TRAVELLERS WITH DISABILITIES

Egypt for All (☎ 02-311 3988; www.egyptforall.com; 334 Sharia Sudan, Mohandiseen, Cairo) specialises in organising travel arrangements for travellers who are mobility-impaired.

VISAS

Most foreigners entering Egypt must obtain a visa. The only exceptions are citizens of Guinea, Hong Kong and Macau. There are three ways of getting a visa: in advance from the Egyptian embassy or consulate in your home country; at an Egyptian embassy abroad; or, for certain nationalities, on arrival at the airport. This last option is the cheapest and easiest of the three.

The processing times and the costs for visa applications vary according to your nationality and the country in which you apply. Visas at the airport are available for nationals of all Western European countries, the UK, the USA, Australia, all Arab countries, New Zealand, Japan and Korea. Nationals from other countries must obtain visas in their countries of residence. At Cairo airport the entire process takes only 20 minutes or so and costs US$15 or €15. If you are travelling overland you can get a visa at the port in Aqaba, Jordan, before getting the ferry to Nuweiba, but if you are coming from Israel, you *cannot* get a visa at the border unless you are guaranteed by an Egyptian travel agency. Instead, you have to get the visa beforehand at either the embassy in Tel Aviv or the consulate in Eilat.

A single-entry visa is valid for three months and entitles the holder to stay in Egypt for one month. Multiple-entry visas (for three visits) are also available, but although good for presentation for six months, they still o[...] a total of one mont[...]

Sinai Entry Stamps

It is not necessary to [...] visit is confined to the a[...] Sharm el-Sheikh and Taba (o[...] border), including St Katherine's Monastery. Instead you are issued with an entry stamp, free of charge, allowing you a 15-day stay. Note that this does not allow you to visit Ras Mohammed National Park. Points of entry where such visa-free stamps are issued are Taba, Nuweiba (port), St Katherine's (airport) and Sharm el-Sheikh (airport or port).

Travel Permits

Military permits issued by either the Ministry of the Interior or the border police are needed to travel in the Eastern Desert south of Shams Allam (50km south of Marsa Alam), on or around Lake Nasser, off-road in the Western Desert, or on the road between the oases of Bahariya and Siwa. These can be obtained through a safari company or travel agency, usually at least a fortnight in advance of the trip.

Visa Extensions & Re-entry Visas

Extensions of your tourist visa can easily be obtained. These cost E£11 for an extension of less than six months, E£16 for less than one year and E£46 for one year, and are obtained at passport offices. You'll need one photograph and photocopies of the photo and visa pages of your passport. You have a short period of grace (usually 14 days) to apply for an extension after your visa has expired. If you neglect to do this there's a fine of approximately E£100 and you'll require a letter of apology from your embassy.

If you don't have a multiple-entry visa, it's possible to get a re-entry visa that's valid to the expiry date of your visa and any extensions. Re-entry visas for one/two/several entries cost less than US$3.

WOMEN TRAVELLERS

Egypt is a conservative society and a woman's sexuality is, by and large, controlled by her family. Not only are most Western women outside these strictures but, thanks to a steady diet of Western films and soap operas, they are perceived as sexually voracious and available. The comparatively libe[...]

...r of some tourists reinforces these ...ces.

...s a result, while the country is gener-...y safe for women, hassling is more or less constant. Sometimes it is in the form of hissing or barely audible whispers; usually it is a lewd phrase. Very occasionally there is physical harassment. Rape is rare. Commonsense tips to avoid problems include wearing a wedding ring, dressing conservatively (ie no shorts, tank tops or above-the-knee skirts except in beach resorts), ignoring verbal comments, trying to sit beside women on public transport and avoiding eye-contact with men unless you know them. Take care not to get yourself into a situation of close proximity with men and stay alert in large crowds, particularly at *moulids* (religious festivals).

A couple of useful Arabic phrases for getting rid of unwanted attention are: *la tilmasni* (don't touch me); *ihtirim nafsak* (behave yourself); or *haasib eedak* (watch your hand). Swearing at would-be Romeos will only make matters worse.

TRANSPORT IN EGYPT

GETTING THERE & AWAY

Entering Egypt

If you enter the country via Cairo airport, there are a few formalities. After walking past the dusty-looking duty-free shops you'll come to a row of exchange booths, including a Thomas Cook booth. If you haven't already organised a visa, you'll need to pay US$15 or €15 here to receive a visa stamp. You then fill in one of the pink forms available on the benches in front of the immigration officials before queuing to be processed.

Air

Egypt has a few airports, but only seven are international ports of entry: Cairo, Alexandria, Luxor, Aswan, Hurghada, Sharm el-Sheikh and Marsa Alam. Most air travellers enter Egypt through Cairo, Alexandria or Sharm el-Sheikh. The other airports tend to be used by charter and package-deal flights only.

Egypt's international and national carrier is **EgyptAir** (☎ 0900 70000; www.egyptairm... 8am-8pm), though its service isn't ...arly good and its fleet is in need of an upgrade. You'll do better flying internationally with a different airline.

Air tickets bought in Egypt are subject to hefty government taxes, which make them extremely expensive. Always try to fly in on a return or onward ticket.

DEPARTURE TAX

If you're leaving Egypt by air your departure tax will usually have been prepaid with your ticket. If you're departing by land, you'll need to pay E£2 (travellers who entered Egypt on a Sinai-only visa are exempt).

Land

Egypt has land borders with Israel and the Palestinian Territories, Libya and Sudan, but for the latter there is no open crossing point. The only way to travel between Egypt and Sudan is to fly or take the Wadi Halfa ferry (p645).

Note that almost all international bus and ferry tickets must be paid for in US dollars.

ISRAEL & THE PALESTINIAN TERRITORIES

There are officially two border crossings with Israel: Rafah and Taba.

Rafah

At the time of research, the Rafah border crossing, which services a direct route from Cairo to Tel Aviv through the Gaza Strip, was closed to all independent travellers. While the border is now jointly policed by the Palestinian Authority and the Egyptian government, the political situation in the area is strained to say the least. Foreigners are unlikely to be able to use the border crossing in the near future.

Taba

This border crossing is used for the vast majority of travel between Egypt and Israel. Travellers making their way to Taba can simply walk across the border (open 24 hours) into Israel. An Israeli visa is not required for most nationalities. Once the border is crossed, taxis (40NIS) or hourly buses (6.40NIS) can be taken to Eilat (4km from the border), from where there are frequent buses onwards to Jerusalem and Tel Aviv.

Coming from Israel to Egypt, you must have a visa in advance unless your visit is limited to eastern Sinai (p207) or you have prearranged your entry with an Egyptian tour operator. Leaving Israel you'll need to pay an exit tax (69NIS) and, once in Egypt, an Egyptian entry tax (E£30) at a booth about 1km south of the border on the main road.

Vehicles can be brought into Egypt from Eilat (though not the other way); the amount of duty to pay depends on the type of vehicle, but averages about 32NIS/E£180 for exit/entry taxes.

At the time of research, **Misr Travel** (Map pp126-7; ☎ 02-3335 5470; Cairo Sheraton, Midan al-Galaa, Doqqi) and the Israeli travel company **Mazada Tours** (☎ 03-544 4454; www.mazada.co.il) were running an express service (US$60, 12 to 14 hours) that left the Cairo Sheraton on Sunday and Thursday at 7.30am (10 to 12 hours), travelling via Taba to Tel Aviv and then on to Jerusalem. Contact them for details.

JORDAN

From Cairo, there's a Superjet service to Amman (US$95), leaving Al-Mazar Garage on Saturday, Sunday, Tuesday and Friday at 11pm. There is also a daily East Delta Bus Co service to Aqaba (US$50) at 8pm.

From Alexandria, there's one daily Superjet service to Amman (US$85) on Saturdays, Tuesdays and Thursdays at 4pm, and one daily service to Aqaba (US$45) at 6pm.

These services use the ferry between Nuweiba and Aqaba, so you will be liable for the ferry ticket and port tax (see above).

LIBYA

The border crossing point of Amsaad, just north of the Halfaya Pass, is 12km west of Sallum. Hourly buses and frequent service taxis from Marsa Matruh to Sallum cost E£15. Service taxis run up the mountain between the town and the Egyptian side of the crossing for E£4. Once through passport control and customs on both sides (you walk through), you can get a Libyan service taxi on to Al-Burdi. From there you can get buses on to Tobruk and Benghazi. Note that Libyan visas are not issued at the border.

From Cairo, one Superjet service leaves Al-Mazar Garage for Benghazi (E£170) at 7am on Monday, Tuesday, Friday and Saturday. East Delta Bus Co services also travel to Tripoli (E£255) de[...] Wednesday, Thursday [...]

From Alexandria, t[...] ices to Benghazi on Mo[...] and Friday at 3pm (E£135), [...] on Tuesday, Thursday and Sunday [...] leaving at 10am.

Sea & Lake

For information on ferries between Egypt and Cyprus, Saudi Arabia or Sudan, see p644. All Egyptian international ferries charge US$10 port tax per person on top of the ticket price.

ISRAEL

There's been talk about resuming the boat service from Port Said to Haifa in Israel, though this has remained just talk for several years now. Contact **Canal Tours** (☎ 066-322 5742, 323 3376l; canaltour@bec.com.eg, 12 Sharia Palestine, Port Said) for the latest information.

JORDAN

There's an excellent **fast-ferry service** (☎ 069-352 0365; www.abmaritime.com.jo) between Nuweiba in Egypt and Aqaba in Jordan that leaves Nuweiba at 3.30pm daily (except Saturday) and takes one hour. One-way tickets cost US$70 for adults and US$55 for children aged three to 12 years old (including a port tax of US$10). Note that while long departure delays are becoming the norm, you must still be at the port entrance at least two hours before departure so as to go through the shambolic formalities in the main ferry terminal building.

Tickets must be paid for in US dollars (these are not always available at the banks in Nuweiba) and can be purchased on the day of departure only at the **ticket office** (🕑 9am-noon), which is in a small sand-coloured building near the port. To find the office turn right when you exit the bus station, walking towards the water, and turn right again after the National Bank of Egypt. Continue one long block, and you'll see the ticket-office building ahead to your left. The office stops selling tickets approximately one hour before the ferry leaves.

There's also a slow ferry (US$60/50 per adult/child including US$10 port tax, 2½ hours) leaving at 2pm daily, though th[...] more comfortable fast ferry is worth ev[...] cent of the extra US$10.

ST ACROSS THE BORDER: WADI RUM & PETRA, JORDAN

If you're in the Sinai region of Egypt, it would be criminal not to hop across the border to Jordan and check out the beautiful desert valley of Wadi Rum (p381) or the breathtaking spectacle that is the lost city of Petra (p373). For those with limited time, both of these can be visited easily over a few days from Sinai.

To get to Jordan, catch one of the early buses from your home base in either Sharm el-Sheikh (p193) or Dahab (p198) to Nuweiba to connect with the daily 3.30pm ferry (p209) to Aqaba, Jordan. Free Jordanian visas are organised on the boat for most nationalities.

From the ferry terminal, grab a taxi into Aqaba – if you're heading directly to Wadi Rum you'll have to charter a taxi for the one-hour trip (see p388). If you want to head out by public transport, you'll need to spend the night in Aqaba (for hotels see p386) and catch one of two public buses the next morning (p388).

If you plan on making a beeline for Petra instead, you can charter a taxi on your day of arrival in Aqaba to Wadi Mousa (for Petra, two hours, see p388), or overnight it in Aqaba and catch morning public transport (see p388). Rest up in Wadi Mousa for the night (see p378), because you have some serious sightseeing action ahead of you over the next few days.

No student discounts are available on these ferry services. Note that boats are always full during the hajj, and you'll need to purchase your ticket through a travel agency a long way in advance.

Free Jordanian visas can be obtained on the ferry if you have an EU, US, Canadian, Australian or New Zealand passport. Fill out a green form on board, give it and your passport to the immigration officers and – hey presto – your passport and visa are collected when you pass through Jordanian immigration at Aqaba. Other nationalities will need to organise a visa in advance.

GETTING AROUND

Air

EgyptAir (☎ 0900 70000; 🕑 8am-8pm) is the main domestic carrier. Iffy as their safety record might be, flights can be dirt cheap at certain times of the year, though fares will sky-rocket and planes get booked up during the October to April high season. Prices quoted in this book reflect average mid-season prices.

Bus

Buses service just about every city, town and village in Egypt. Deluxe buses travel between some of the main towns such as Cairo, Alexandria and Luxor, as well as und Sinai. These buses are reasonably rtable, with decent seats, air-con d Arabic videos. The best of the s companies is Superjet – try to travel with it whenever possible. The bulk of buses servicing other routes are horribly uncomfortable, dirty and noisy. Arabic pop or Quranic dirges are played at ear-splittingly loud levels – it's a good idea to take earplugs.

Often the prices of tickets for buses on the same route will vary slightly according to whether or not they have air-con and video, how old the bus is and how long it takes to make the journey – the more you pay, the greater comfort you travel in and the quicker you get there.

Tickets can be bought at the bus stations or often on the bus. Hang on to your ticket until you get off, as inspectors almost always board the bus to check fares. There are no student discounts on bus fares.

Car & Motorcycle

Driving in Cairo seems like sheer madness to the uninitiated, but in other parts of the country, at least in daylight, it isn't so bad. You should avoid intercity driving at night. Driving is on the right-hand side and you'll need an International Driving Permit. When travelling out of Cairo, remember that petrol stations are not always plentiful; when you see one, fill up.

The official speed limit outside Cairo is 90km/h and 100km/h on major motorways. If you are caught speeding, your driving licence will be confiscated and you will have to pick it up (and pay a fine) at the nearest traffic police station several days later. Roads throughout the country have checkpoints, so make sure you have all of your documents with you, including your passport.

Several car-hire agencies have offices around Egypt, particularly around touristy resorts like Sharm el-Sheikh or Hurghada. The following are all found in Cairo.

Avis (www.avisegypt.com) Airport (☎ 02-2265 4249); Nile Hilton (Map pp130-1; ☎ 02-2579 2400; Corniche el-Nil, Downtown)

Budget (www.budget.com) Airport Terminal 2 ☎ 02-2265 2395)

Europcar (www.europcar.co.eg) Airport Terminal 1 & 2 (☎ 02-2267 2439); Heliopolis Sheraton (☎ 02-2267 1815; 6M, 1226 Sq, behind Florida Mall)

Hertz (www.hertzegypt.com) Airport Terminal 2 (☎ 02-2265 2430); Ramses Hilton (Map pp130-1; ☎ 02-2575 8914; Corniche el-Nil, Downtown)

Their rates match international charges and finding a cheap deal with local dealers is virtually impossible. You are much better off organising cheap car hire via the web before you arrive in Egypt.

As a rough guide, rates are around US$50 a day for a small Toyota (100km included, US$0.25 per kilometre after this) to US$90 a day for a Cherokee 4WD (US$0.40 for the extra kilometres). Note that this doesn't include taxes.

Local Transport

Travelling by *servees* (… of the fastest ways to … Service taxis are eithe… Peugeot 504 cars that ru… Drivers congregate near bus … tions and tout for passengers by shouting their destination. When the car's full, it's off. A driver won't leave before his car is full unless you and/or the other passengers pay for all of the seats.

Train

Although trains travel along more than 5000km of track to almost every major city and town in Egypt, the system is badly in need of modernisation (it's a relic of the British occupation) and most services are grimy and battered and a poor second option to the deluxe buses. The exceptions are some of the trains to Alexandria and the comfy tourist and sleeping trains down to Luxor and Aswan – on these routes the train actually is the preferred option rather than the bus. For more info, you can try the government's irregularly working website www.egypttrail.gov.eg.

Students with an ISIC card can get discounts of about 33% on all fares except the sleeping-car services.

Iraq

Torn between its glorious past as the cradle of civilisation and the turmoil of its recent bloody history, Iraq is a country of contradictions. It is the birthplace of writing, thus beginning the recorded history of the human race. It is the legendary home of the Garden of Eden, the Tower of Babel, Hanging Gardens of Babylon and the Epic of Gilgamesh. But it is also a place of death and unimaginable violence.

Ancient Iraq was known as Mesopotamia, from the Greek meaning 'land between two rivers'. It was here that humans first began to cultivate their land in the fertile valleys between the mighty Tigris and Euphrates Rivers. The Sumerians, the world's first great civilisation, invented written communication and the wheel, and refined agriculture, science, mathematics and law. Later, the Akkadians, Babylonians and Assyrians all made Iraq the centre of the ancient world. The Abbasid caliphs built Baghdad, making it the centre for learning and development during the Islamic Golden Age.

Since its beginnings, Iraq has been a land of turmoil and conquest. Alexander the Great, the Persians, Mongols, Ottomans, British and Americans have all made their mark. Saddam Hussein's regime was marked by political repression and conflicts with Iran, Kuwait, Shiite Muslims, Kurds and Western armies, culminating in the 2003 US-led invasion of the country. The ongoing insurgency has made Iraq one of the most dangerous places on earth.

Today, Iraq is a country in transition. Violence has dropped dramatically since 2007, but with the exception of Iraqi Kurdistan, it remains a dangerous country. Getting the green light for 2009 provincial elections was a major government accomplishment – Iraq is, in the opinion of some, now one of the most democratic countries in the Middle East. Its future remains uncertain, but with its rich history, warm hospitality and natural beauty, Iraq could again become one of the great travel destinations of the Middle East, *insha' Allah*.

FAST FACTS

- **Area** 437,072 sq km
- **Capital** Baghdad
- **Country code** ☎ 964
- **Languages** Arabic, Kurdish (Kurmanji and Sorani)
- **Money** Iraqi dinar (ID); US$1 = ID1194; €1 = ID1547
- **Official name** Republic of Iraq
- **Population** 28.2 million

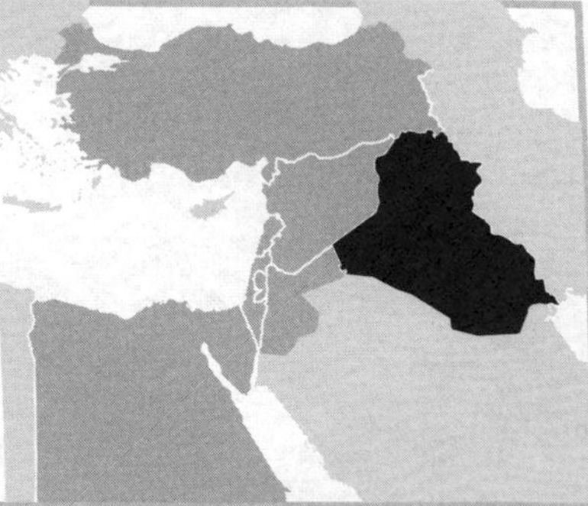

WARNING

Iraq is a war zone. The majority of the country has been in a state of war since the US-led invasion of Iraq in 2003. The situation is dangerous, volatile and unpredictable. The ongoing conflict is a complex and multifaceted war with no discernible battlegrounds, front lines or combatants.

After six years of war in Iraq, the death toll had reached 100,000 Iraqi civilians, 10,000 Iraqi soldiers and police, 4500 coalition soldiers (mostly from the US) and 135 journalists. Tens of thousands more have been injured or maimed. The UN High Commissioner on Refugees estimates at least 3.4 million Iraqis have either fled the country or are internally displaced.

The risks are omnipresent and varied: terrorist attacks, military combat operations, suicide bombings, improvised explosive devices (IEDs), land mines, sectarian violence, kidnappings, highway robberies and petty crime. Foreigners are the primary targets of militant groups such as Al-Qaeda in Iraq. Attacks can occur anywhere, at anytime.

The majority of violence in Iraq is concentrated in the southern two-thirds of the country that has a predominantly Arab population, particularly in the so-called 'Sunni Triangle'. Consequently, Arab Iraq should be considered completely off-limits to foreign travellers including – but not limited – to the cities of Baghdad, Basra, Babylon, Mosul, Kirkuk, Najaf and Karbala. Nationwide, the security situation across Iraq has improved dramatically since mid-2007 but still has a long way to go before the bulk of the country is open for business.

The sections on Baghdad, southern Iraq and northern Iraq in this chapter are intended solely for the use of readers who are in Iraq because they must be, for example, military, journalists, diplomats, contractors and members of non-governmental organisations (NGOs).

Iraqi Kurdistan – 'The Other Iraq' – is the only area of the country currently safe for travel. The pro-Western, Kurdish Regional Government–controlled provinces of Dohuk, Erbil and Sulaymaniyah are stable and peaceful with a growing tourism industry. Violence is rare, but not unheard of. Suicide bombers struck government offices in Erbil in 2004 and 2007, killing at least 54 people. In March 2008 a small bomb exploded outside Sulaymaniyah's Palace Hotel, killing one. Turkish and Iranian forces occasionally bomb the remote and mountainous border areas of northern Iraq in their fight against Kurdistan Workers' Party (PKK) militant separatists.

> **DISCLAIME**
>
> Due to the u we were unabl outside of Iraqi chapter. The sectio Iraq (including Baghdad) are based the author's extensive experiences in the as a war correspondent and journal 'embedded' with the US military. Arab Ira is currently completely off-limits to travelle

Staying Safe

No visit to Iraq is without risk. But there are steps you can take to minimise that risk.

You are the only one responsible for your security, and this should never be delegated to anyone else. Preparing for travelling or working in Iraq is critical. Even for the most seasoned, independent traveller, Iraq can be an assault on the norms. It is essential to take the time to learn about the country, culture, customs and current information on the security situation.

Military and security experts stress the need to maintain 'situational awareness'. In this case, information will be your greatest asset. The situation in Iraq can change in an instant. Keep abreast of the news from Iraq before and during your trip. For a list of good sources, see p244. Register your whereabouts with your country's embassy in Baghdad. Keep in regular contact with family and friends via the internet or phone.

Avoid any place that might present an attractive target to terrorists such as military bases, government buildings and large crowds. When travelling by road, it is extremely important that your vehicle not come too close to any US or coalition military convoy. They are the primary targets of suicide car bombs and IEDs. Coalition soldiers may shoot vehicles that approach too close without warning. Never attempt or allow your driver to overtake these convoys – regardless of how slow they are moving.

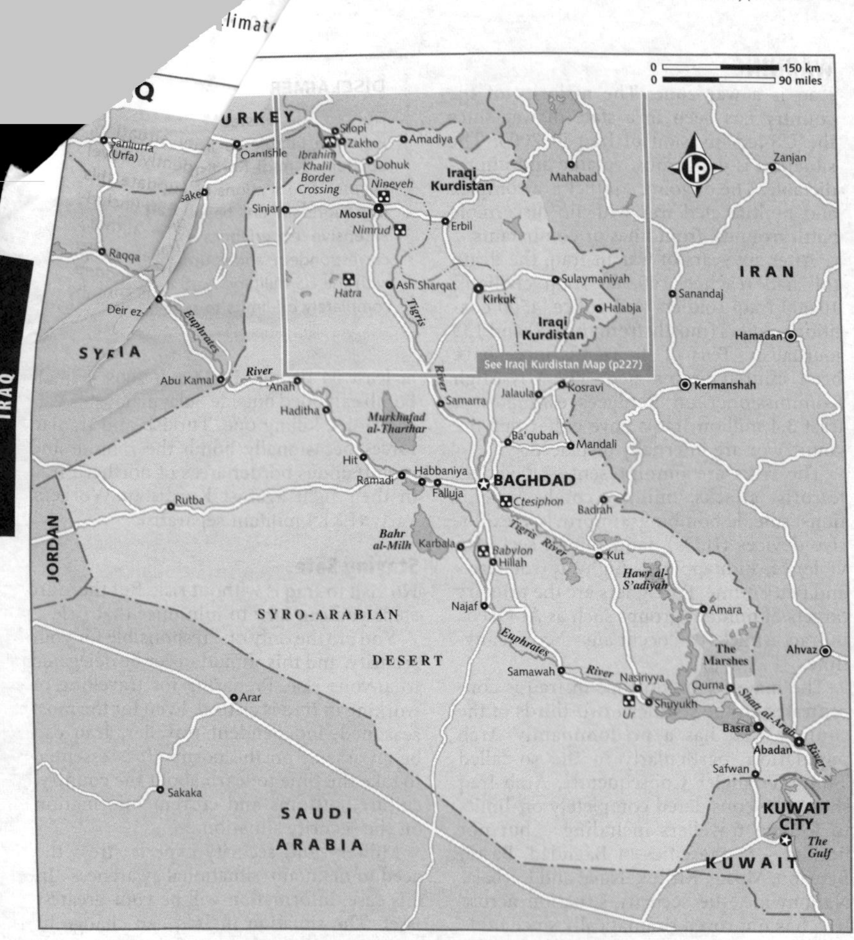

In Iraqi Kurdistan, land mines pose the biggest danger. Decades of war and internal conflicts have left Iraq littered with mines and unexploded ordnance (UXO), particularly along the northern Iraq–Iran border. Limit your risk by sticking to paved and hard surfaces. When travelling by road, stay on the road even when taking a toilet break. Stay away from unused roads, paths, irrigation canals and culverts. Some minefields are marked by red triangle signs bearing a skull and crossbones. Others are marked by simple piles of rocks painted red, but most are unidentified. When in doubt, go back – land mines are laid to be invisible.

Always follow the instructions issued by military, police, security and border control officials. In Iraqi Kurdistan, Peshmerga (Iraqi Kurdistan's army) forces maintain strict control over their tranquil piece of the country. Checkpoints and random stops by plain-clothed agents are common. Some security officials are more suspicious of outsiders than others (our author was briefly detained twice). If you are stopped or detained, remain calm and composed. It's a good idea to have the name and phone number of an Iraqi Kurd who can vouch for you.

CLIMATE

Iraq's climate is unforgiving. Summers in central and southern Iraq are brutally hot and dry. The average summer (May to September) temperature in Baghdad is 34°C and frequently hits 50°C. In southern Ir[aq] the stifling heat is made even worse by the unbearable humidity. The cool mountains of northern Iraq offer the only respite during summer months. Blinding sandstorms are common in central and southern Iraq. Winters can be cold and wet. The average winter temperature in Baghdad is 11°C. Heavy snowfalls and below-freezing temperatures are common in the Kurdish provinces. Nationwide, the most comfortable months are April and October.

HISTORY

Ancient Mesopotamia

Iraq's story begins with the Sumerians who flourished in the rich agricultural lands surrounding the Tigris and Euphrates Rivers from around 4000 BC. In 1750 BC, Hammurabi seized power and went on to dominate the annals of the Babylonian empire. He developed the Code of Hammurabi, the first written codes of law in recorded history. Despite constant attacks from the Hittites and other neighbouring powers, Babylon would dominate the region until the 12th century BC, after which it went into a slow decline.

By the 7th century BC, the rival Assyrian civilisation had reached its high point under Ashurbanipal, whose capital at Nineveh was one of the great cities of the world with cuneiform libraries, luxurious royal courts and magnificent bas-reliefs that survive to this day. But his expensive military campaigns against Babylonia and other neighbours drained the kingdom of its wealth and manpower. In 612 BC, Ninevah and the Assyrian Empire fell to Babylonian King Nabopolassar,

The Neo Babylonian Empire returned Babylon to its former glory. Nabopolassar's son, Nebuchadnezzar II, built the famous Hanging Gardens of Babylon and conquered Jerusalem. In 539 BC, Babylon finally fell to the Persian Empire of Cyrus the Great. The Persians were in turn defeated by Alexander the Great, who died in Babylon in 323 BC. For the next 1000 years, Mesopotamia was ruled by a string of empires, among them the Seleucid, Parthian and Sassanid.

Islamic Iraq

In AD 637 the Arab armies of Islam swept north from the Arabian Peninsula and occlaim. Their mo[illegible] Kufa, Bagh[illegible] go on t[illegible] first Abb[illegible] ing of Bagh[illegible] and [illegible] become, by so[illegible] the[illegible] Mansur saw the city [illegible] in the world (see [illegible]ts, the greatest city [illegible] 1258 Hulagu – grandson of the feared [illegible] ruler Chingiz (Genghis) Khan – laid wast[illegible] Baghdad and killed the last Abbasid caliph. [illegible] political power in the Muslim world shifted elsewh[illegible]

By 1638, Iraq had come under Ottoman rule. After a period of relative autonomy, the Ottomans centralised their rule in the 19th century, where after Iraqi resentment against foreign occupation crystallised even as the Ottomans undertook a massive program of modernisation. The Ottomans held on until 1920, when the arrival of the British saw Iraq submit to yet another occupying force, which was first welcomed then resented by the Iraqis.

Independent Iraq

Iraq gained its independence from the British in 1932. The period that followed was distinguished by a succession of coups, counter-coups and by the discovery of massive reserves of oil. During WWII, the British again occupied Iraq over fears that the pro-German government would cut oil supplies to Allied forces. On 14 July 1958, the pro-British monarchy was overthrown in a military coup and Iraq became a republic. In 1968 a bloodless coup brought the Ba'ath Party to power.

The 1970s marked a glory decade for Iraq. The oil boom of the 1970s brought wealth and prosperity. Oil profits were heavily invested in education, health care and infrastructure. Baghdad became a gleaming cosmopolitan city with new hotels, shopping centres, bridges and roads. Women achieved social and economic equality with men.

Iraq's heyday ended on 16 July 1979, when an ambitious Ba'ath official named Saddam Hussein Abd al-Majid al-Tikriti wangled his way into power. Saddam's first duty as president was to secure his power by executing political and religious opponents.

The Iran-Iraq War

Meanwhile, next door, the Islamic Revolution was busy toppling Iran's pro-Western

...ni
...erned
...ment. Saddam – ...on in his
...lim – became incre...ths of sabre
...bout the threat of a Sh 22 September
own country. After s of the USA, the
rattling, Iraq invad...ral Arab and Euro-
1980 with the fu...
Soviet Union a...
pean states. ...had the upper hand but
At first, ...self at an impasse. The eight
soon foun...ar were characterised by Iranian
years of ...
hum...-wave infantry attacks and Iraq's use
of chemical weapons against Iranian troops
and civilians. The Iran-Iraq war ended as a stalemate on 20 August 1988. Each side suffered at least 200,000 deaths and US$100 billion in war debts.

In the closing months of the war, Saddam launched a genocidal campaign against the ethnic Kurds of northern Iraq who had long opposed his regime. Saddam tapped his ruthless cousin Ali Hassan Al-Majid to spearhead Operation Al-Anfal, Arabic for 'the spoils of war'. Al-Majid's savage use of chemical weapons against civilians earned him the nickname 'Chemical Ali'. When it was all over, between 50,000 and 100,000 Kurds were dead and at least 4000 Kurdish villages destroyed.

Saddam Hussein's brutal legacy is epitomised by the horrific events that took place in the small Kurdish village of Halabja. On the morning of March 16, 1988, Iraqi forces bombed the village with poison gas as retribution for Kurdish support of Iranian forces. In less than an hour, more than 5000 men, women and children were killed.

The Gulf War

The wounds of the Iran-Iraq war had barely healed when Saddam turned his attention to Kuwait. In July 1990 Saddam accused the Kuwaitis, (with some justification) of waging 'economic warfare' against Iraq by attempting to artificially hold down the price of oil and of stealing oil by slant-drilling into the Iraq side of the border. On 2 August 1990, Iraq invaded Kuwait, whose small armed forces were quickly overrun. Six days later, Iraq annexed Kuwait as its 19th province. It was a costly miscalculation.

Led by the US President George W Bush Snr, an international coalition of nearly one million troops from 34 countries amassed on Iraq's borders. On 17 January 1991, Operation Desert Storm began with a massive five-week bombing campaign, followed by a ground offensive that drove Iraqi forces from Kuwait. Widely varied figures estimate that between 20,000 and 100,000 Iraqis were killed. As part of the ceasefire agreement, the UN ordered Iraq to destroy all chemical, nuclear and biological weapons and long-range missile programs. The 'Mother of All Battles' ended badly for Saddam, but even worse for Iraqi civilians.

Shortly before the war ended, Iraqi Shiites and Kurds took up arms against Saddam, encouraged by the impending victory and promises of coalition support. But help never arrived. Saddam's forces quickly crushed the rebellion, leaving thousands more dead. Other Saddam opponents were imprisoned, tortured or simply vanished. Coalition forces later established no-fly zones in southern and northern Iraq to protect the Shiites and Kurds, but it was too little, too late.

UN economic sanctions did little to undermine Saddam's regime, but they brought untold misery to the people of Iraq in the form of malnutrition, poverty, inadequate medical care and lack of clean water. The subsequent UN oil-for-food program suffered widespread corruption and abuse. In 1998 US and UK forces launched a four-day bombing campaign as punishment for Saddam's repeated interference with UN weapons inspections. Sporadic bombings and sanctions would continue for years, but Saddam remained defiantly in power.

The 2003 Iraq War

In a 12 September 2002 speech to the UN General Assembly, US President George W Bush Jnr set the stage for war by declaring that Iraq was manufacturing weapons of mass destruction (WMDs) and harbouring Al-Qaeda terrorists, among other claims. Saddam disputed the claims but reluctantly agreed to allow weapons inspectors back into the country. UN inspectors concluded that Iraq had failed to account for all its weapons, but insisted there was no evidence WMDs had existed. Meanwhile, a 'coalition of the willing' led by American and British troops was massing in Kuwait. On 20 March 2003 – without UN authority – the coalition launched its second war on Iraq. Allied forces easily overran Iraqi forces, with relatively few casualties. Baghdad fell on 9

April 2003, but Saddam escaped. On 1 May 2003, Bush declared victory under a banner that read 'Mission Accomplished'. But the war was just beginning.

Allied forces were at first welcomed by Iraqis as liberators. But initial optimism quickly vanished, and it soon became clear that planning for post-war Iraq had been woefully inadequate. Iraq descended into chaos and anarchy. Looting was widespread. The Iraqi Museum was robbed of priceless artefacts. The Iraqi Army was disbanded and former Ba'ath party members were excluded from the new Iraqi government, suddenly leaving millions of unemployed men on the streets. The country was spiralling into a guerrilla war with a growing insurgency.

In July 2003, Saddam's feared sons Uday and Qusay were killed in a fire fight with US forces. Five months later, a dishevelled and bearded Saddam was found cowering in a spider hole near his hometown of Tikrit. Saddam was executed in December 2006 for crimes against humanity.

In 2004 things went from bad to worse. The insurgency exploded, led by such groups as Al-Qaeda in Iraq, a feared Sunni militant group whose gruesome tactics included the videotaped beheadings of several Western contractors. That same year, photos emerged of American soldiers abusing Iraqi prisoners at Abu Ghraib prison, creating an international backlash against the occupation. Two major battles in the Sunni city of Fallujah did little to stem the bloodshed. On 22 February 2006, the holy Shiite shrine in Samarra was bombed, kicking off a wave of sectarian violence. The world watched in horror as Iraqi Sunnis and Shiites slaughtered each other by the thousands.

By its fifth anniversary in March 2008, the war had killed more than 4000 US and allied soldiers, tens of thousands of Iraqi civilians (figures range from 100,000 to over one million) and hundreds of contractors and journalists. Financially, the war was costing US citizens US$2 billion per week.

Iraq Today

Despite uncertainty about its future, Iraq is sowing some seeds of optimism. In 2005 Iraqis elected a transitional government and ratified a new constitution. In 2006 the country held elections to form Iraq's first permanent democratic government, led by Prime Minister Nouri al-Maliki. Iraq's infrastructure remains dilapidated; there is a severe shortage of basic services including electricity, clean drinking water, sewage treatment and, ironically, gasoline (petrol).

In 2007 the tide began to turn against the insurgency. The US deployed 20,000 more troops to quell the violence. Iraqis began to reject the insurgency. US-funded Sunni militias calling themselves The Awakening (or Sons of Iraq) rose up against Al-Qaeda. The Shiite Mahdi Army militia led by fiery anti-American cleric Muqtada al-Sadr declared a ceasefire. By mid-2008, violence had fallen dramatically. Newly elected US President Barack Obama vowed to withdraw US combat troops by early 2010; the Iraqi parliament ordered all US troops to leave the country by 31 December 2011. Only time will tell if Iraq can move towards peace and re-emerge as a major democratic power in the Middle East.

THE LONELY PLANET GUIDE TO INVASIONS

In a 2007 BBC documentary, former US ambassador Barbara Bodine admitted that the Iraq invasion and post-war reconstruction plans were partially based on an outdated, copy of Lonely Planet's *Middle East*. 'It's a great guidebook, but it shouldn't be the basis of an occupation', she told the BBC. Lonely Planet founder Tony Wheeler responded on his blog: 'We don't write our books with invasion, coups, revolutions and general mayhem in mind…but I have to admit our books sometimes get used in ways I don't approve of'.

THE CULTURE

The National Psyche

You would think that decades of war would have left Iraqis demoralised and bitter. On the contrary, Iraqis are resilient, warm and welcoming people. Nowhere is this truer than in Iraqi Kurdistan, where the Kurds are renowned for their hospitality. Strangers are offered food and lodging within minutes of meeting. Americans in particular are given a hero's welcome in Iraqi Kurdistan, where former US President George W Bush Jnr is considered a saviour of the Kurdish people.

Iraqis are well known for their sense of humour, even in the face of suffering and misery. Iraqis have an acute sense of pride and honour and are fiercely proud of their history and homeland. They are well read and surprisingly knowledgeable about the world. It is a country where formality and politeness are all important.

Democracy has brought capitalism – and materialism – to the country. Iraqis have embraced Western pop culture, fashion, cars and technologies banned under Saddam such as mobile phones, satellite TV and the internet. With the grip of violence now loosening and the economy improving, Iraqis are looking to the future with a guarded sense of optimism.

Daily Life

Iraqi life revolves around the family and extended family, a bond that took on added significance during years of war, sanctions and international isolation. Family dominates all aspects of Iraqi life, with great importance on honour and reputation. It's a paternalistic, patriarchal and conservative society, especially in rural areas. Iraq is primarily a tribal society. Allegiance to one's ethnic group often takes precedent over any party, provincial or national loyalties, and ethnic interests play an important role in the shaping of government and public policy.

The role of women is complex. Legally, men and women have the same rights. Women are commonplace in government, politics, media, private business and universities. Nevertheless, women are still expected to take on the traditional role as wife and mother. Arranged marriages are the norm, usually between first cousins. So-called honour killings are, sadly, not uncommon. Sectarian violence that swept through Iraq in 2006 forced many women back into the home and to adopt a more conservative style of dress. Men and women socialise separately and public displays of affection are taboo.

Population

Iraq's population is one of the most multicultural in the Middle East. About 75% of the population is Arab, 15% Kurdish and the rest made up of Turkomans, Assyrians, Persians, Chaldeans, Palestinians, Yazidis and nomadic Bedouins. Iraq is a predominantly urban society, with 74% living in cities. Iraq has a youthful population, with about 40% under the age of 15.

> **COMEDY OF ERRORS**
>
> Iraqis are well known across the Middle East for their satirical sense of humour, even in the face of adversity. Black comedy and political satire have been raised to an art form on TV, while Iraqi comedies poke fun at everything from the Iraqi government and the US occupation to suicide bombings, sectarian violence and electricity blackouts. Under Saddam Hussein, such criticism would have been unthinkable. Now, it's a national pastime. Popular shows include *Caricatures*, a variety sketch show that lampoons daily life in post-war Iraq, and *Hurry Up, He's Dead*, Iraq's answer to *The Daily Show with Jon Stewart*.
>
> Comedy isn't without its risks. In a 2004 interview, *Caricatures* star Walid Hassan told me Iraqis use comedy as a survival mechanism. 'We laugh because we are done crying,' he said. Two years later Hassan was shot dead while driving home, just another in Iraq's long line of tragedies.

RELIGION

Islam is the official religion of Iraq. Muslims make up 97% of the population – about 60% Shiite and 40% Sunni. There are also small but historically significant communities of Christians who belong to various sects including Chaldeans, Assyrians, Syrian and Roman Catholics, Orthodox Armenians and Jacobites. Other religious minorities are the Yazidis, Sabeans, the Mandeans (followers of John the Baptist) and a handful of Jews.

ENVIRONMENT

The Land

Iraq's terrain is mainly characterised by broad plains. The upper plain stretches northwest from Hit and Samarra to the Turkish border between the Euphrates and Tigris River, the most fertile region. The lower plain stretches southeast to the Gulf and contains the marshes, a wetland area flanked by high reeds. Iraq's deserts lie to the west of the Euphrates, stretching to the borders of Syria, Jordan and Saudi Arabia. The Tigris and

Euphrates converge near Baghdad, diverge and then meet again at Qurna (the legendary site of the Garden of Eden) to form the wide Shatt al-Arab River that flows through Basra and into the Gulf. Northeast Iraq along the Turkish and Iranian borders contains the country's most dramatic landscapes, with soaring mountains, deep canyons, natural springs, raging rivers and waterfalls.

Environmental Issues

The draining of the southern marshes by Saddam Hussein in the 1990s threatened many species of birds and led to displacement of the Marsh Arabs, an indigenous culture who inhabited the area for thousands of years. Since 2003, about 40% of the marshlands have been restored and wildlife and people are slowly returning. Iraq's primary environmental concerns stem from pollution or diversion of its rivers. Turkish dams on the Euphrates River have threatened Iraq's precarious water supplies. Excessive irrigation methods such as flooding have left the soil waterlogged with high levels of soil salinity, reducing the mount of arable land in the once-fertile Tigris and Euphrates valley. Desertification, littering, and air and oil-well pollution are other areas of concern. The use of depleted uranium weapons by all sides during Iraq's various wars is a major environmental and public health concern.

BAGHDAD بغداد

☎ 01 / pop 7 million

All roads lead to Baghdad, the capital of Iraq and once the centre of the Islamic world. Baghdad's very name invokes images of golden domes, towering minarets, sunlight filtering through exotic bazaars and tales of Ali Baba, Sinbad and *Arabian Nights*. The harsh reality is that Baghdad is now a city in ashes, ravaged by nearly three decades of war and neglect.

As the seat of Iraq's new government and headquarters of the US military, Baghdad has been the focal point of the 2003 war. Suicide bombings, mortar attacks, kidnappings, murder and crime are a daily fact of life. The vast majority of visitors to Baghdad these days are soldiers, diplomats, journalists, contractors and aid workers. Security is slowly improving, but for the time being Baghdad remains unsafe for foreign travellers.

HISTORY

Baghdad was founded in AD 762 by Abu Ja'far Al-Mansur, the second caliph of the Abbasid dynasty. The fortified city was built on the western bank of the Tigris River and surrounded by a circular wall, hence its nickname, the 'Round City'. During the 8th and 9th centuries, Baghdad was at the heart of the Islamic Golden Age. Scholars from around the known world travelled to Baghdad to study at the Bait al-Hikma, a leading learning centre known as The House of Wisdom, which contained the greatest collection of human knowledge.

From the 10th century onwards, Baghdad's power declined by a series of natural disasters, invasions and internal strife. In 1258 Baghdad was sacked and destroyed by Mongol conqueror Hulagu Khan – grandson of Chingiz (Genghis) Khan; the caliph was killed along with up to one million inhabitants. In 1534 the city was conquered again, this time by the Ottoman Turks. In 1921 it came under control of the British, who drew the lines of modern Iraq.

Baghdad's greatest modern development occurred in the 1970s, when oil revenues transformed the city into a cosmopolitan metropolis that attracted jet-set travellers. But the glory days were short-lived. The Iran-Iraq war, the 1991 Gulf War and the 2003 Iraq War all took their toll on Baghdad, once the crown jewel of the Middle East. These days, Baghdad is in the news every day for all the wrong reasons. It is a war-torn city of destroyed, looted and abandoned buildings, divided by concrete barricades and razor wire, military bases, police checkpoints and invisible sectarian lines.

ORIENTATION

Baghdad extends along both sides of the Tigris River. The eastern side is known as Rusafah and the western side as Karkh. The Tigris bisects the city from northwest to southeast, looping around the Karada Peninsula – an affluent modern area that is home to the University of Baghdad. The old city centre, Sheikh Omar, lies on the northeastern side of the river and contains traditional antiques and gold bazaars and many of Baghdad's oldest tourist attractions. The

IRAQ

BAGHDAD

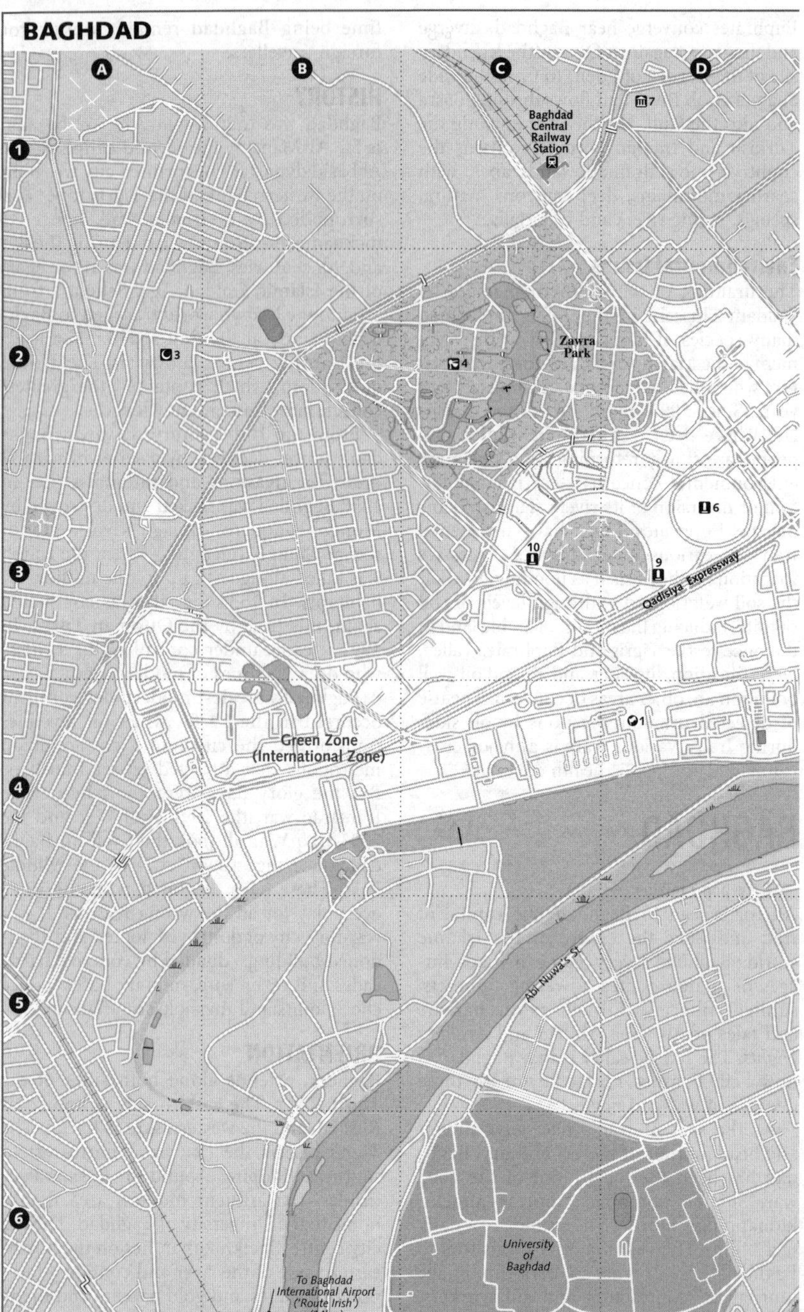

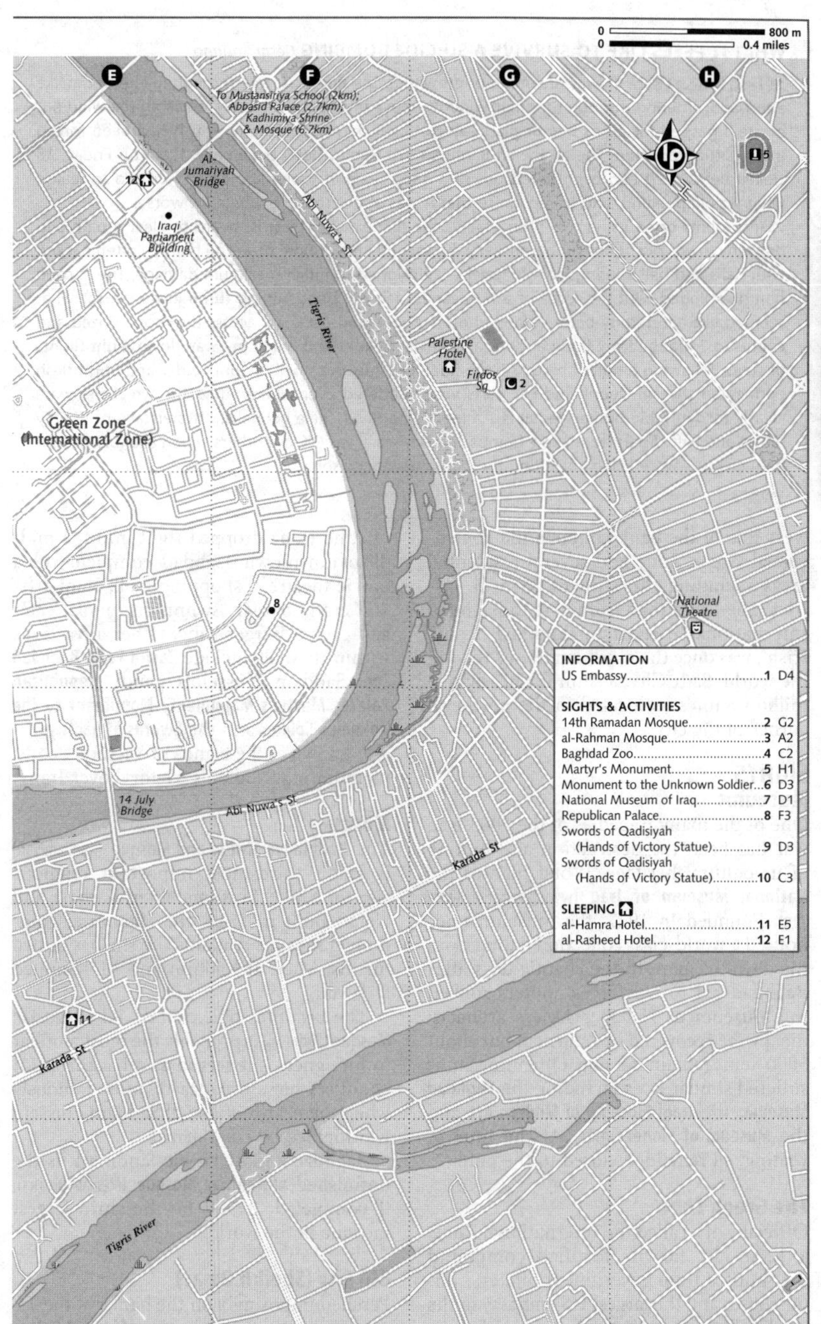
0 800 m
0 0.4 miles
E
F
G
H
To Mustansiriya School (2km); Abbasid Palace (2.7km); Kadhimiya Shrine & Mosque (6.7km)
Al-Jumariyah Bridge
12
Iraqi Parliament Building
Abi Nuwa's St
Tigris River
5
Palestine Hotel
Firdos Sq
2
Green Zone (International Zone)
8
National Theatre
14 July Bridge
Abi Nuwa's St
Karada St
11
Karada St
Tigris River
INFORMATION
US Embassy....1 D4
SIGHTS & ACTIVITIES
14th Ramadan Mosque....2 G2
al-Rahman Mosque....3 A2
Baghdad Zoo....4 C2
Martyr's Monument....5 H1
Monument to the Unknown Soldier...6 D3
National Museum of Iraq....7 D1
Republican Palace....8 F3
Swords of Qadisiyah (Hands of Victory Statue)....9 D3
Swords of Qadisiyah (Hands of Victory Statue)....10 C3
SLEEPING
al-Hamra Hotel....11 E5
al-Rasheed Hotel....12 E1

WHAT IT FEELS LIKE TO SURVIVE A SUICIDE BOMBING *César Soriano*

At first, I wasn't sure if I was dreaming or drowning. The first blast tore through my bedroom like a tornado, entering through the small window above my bed and literally knocking the wind out of me. I gasped for air as bits of glass rained down on my rigid body, which had been forced into a sitting position. The attack on Baghdad's Al Hamra Hotel began at 8.12am on Friday, 18 November 2005. I had been jolted out of a deep sleep. It took me a second or two to realise what was happening, and to recognise that it was about to get a whole lot worse.

Insurgents often use a two-prong tactic: the first, smaller blast is meant to clear a path and draw in crowds of curious rubberneckers; the second, much-more powerful bomb – often packed with nails and ball bearings for shrapnel – is designed to inflict maximum damage. The second bomb exploded with the force of a hurricane. I felt my body hurling through the air for what seemed like an eternity before I landed on my head and back, 3m across the room. Dazed and confused, I grabbed my body armour and Kevlar helmet and made my way down eight flights of stairs, following a trail of blood on the floor. Outside, the smell of gunpowder and burnt flesh permeated the air. Debris and car parts were scattered everywhere. Amid the wreckage were clearly recognisable human remains – a leg, half a head, male genitalia. I hysterically called my editor and wife. Apart from a few bumps and bruises, I was OK, but others weren't so lucky. Eight Iraqi civilians were killed, including the hotel manager's son.

west side of the bank contains the controversial Green Zone and several residential areas including the affluent Mansur district. The 12km road from here to Baghdad International Airport, nicknamed 'Route Irish', was once the most dangerous road in the world. Sadr City, a slum for nearly one million Shiites, is located in the northeast corner of the city.

SIGHTS

Museums

One of the many tragedies of the 2003 Iraq war has been the destruction and looting of its cultural heritage. Worst hit was the **National Museum of Iraq** (www.theiraqmuseum.org). Founded in 1923, the museum once housed a world-class collection dating from the dawn of man. In the chaotic days after Baghdad fell to US forces, looters robbed the museum of 15,000 priceless artefacts; most were recovered or returned, but about 5000 items remain missing. Other museums suffered similar fates including the **Baghdad Museum**, the **Iraqi Museum of Modern Art** and the **Museum of Pioneer Arts**. At the time of writing, all remained closed to the public.

The Green Zone

Officially, it's called the International Zone, a 12-sq-km, heavily fortified compound that houses Iraqi government offices, military bases and the largest US embassy in the world. The Green Zone is a surreal piece of Americana dropped right into the middle of downtown Baghdad, complete with a movie theatre, a shopping mall, Iraqi arts-and-crafts bazaar, swimming pools, cafés and even a Burger King. Other attractions within its walls include **Zawra Park, Baghdad Zoo**, Saddam Hussein's gaudy **Republican Palace**, **Martyr's Monument**, **Monument to the Unknown Soldier** and the **Swords of Qadisiyah** – also known as the Hands of Victory – commemorating Saddam's 'victory' over Iran.

Mosques

The **Kadhimiya Shrine and Mosque** (Kadhamiyah) is Iraq's third-most important religious site for Shiite Muslims, after Karbala and Najaf. Built in 1515, the elaborate, gold-domed mosque contains the shrines of two imams, Musa al-Kadhim and Mohammed al-Jawad.

The beautiful blue-domed **14th Ramadan Mosque** (Firdos Sq) is probably the most familiar to foreigners – it served as a backdrop for countless news broadcasts, most famously when the nearby statue of Saddam Hussein was toppled by US Marines.

Baghdad's most visible landmark is the unfinished **al-Rahman Mosque** (Mansur District); if completed, it will be the third-largest mosque in the world.

Old City (Sheikh Omar)

Perched imposingly on the banks of the Tigris River, the 13th-century **Abbasid Palace**

MASGOUF: THE TASTE OF IRAQ

For Iraqis, good food is a way of life. Eating is a ritual. Sharing food expresses hospitality and friendship, and being invited into an Iraqi home for dinner is considered a huge honour. As in other parts of the Middle East, Iraqis have an insatiable appetite for meat, particularly lamb dishes such as *quzi* – grilled whole lamb stuffed with rice, almonds, raisins and spices. But without a doubt, Iraq's national dish is *masgouf* – a whole-skewered fish barbequed on an outdoor grill.

Masgouf is popular across Iraq, but particularly in cities along the Tigris River; at ID20,000 per plate, it's considered a delicacy reserved for special occasions. Each restaurant has its own special recipe but the basics are the same. The fish is a bony, mild freshwater carp native to the Tigris. Fishermen still catch it as they have for centuries by casting large nets into the Tigris River, but most carp is now farmed. The fish is butterflied open, spiced with salt, pepper and tamarind, placed on wooden skewers and slow cooked next to a roaring fire. It's usually served with grilled vegies and fresh nan bread.

And the taste? Absolutely divine – sweet, buttery and flaky with a smoky wood flavouring. Just mind those bones.

is one of Baghdad's architectural wonders, with detailed brickwork and arches.

Just south along the river stands **Mustansiriyya School**, one of the oldest Islamic universities in the world.

SLEEPING & EATING

Most foreign visitors stay in military or government housing in the Green Zone. At the time of writing, there were only two hotels safe for foreign guests: the once-ritzy **al-Rasheed Hotel** (Green Zone; r from $75;) and **al-Hamra Hotel** (☎ 776 1805; www.alhamrasuitehotel.com; Jadriyah St; r from $60;).

Please note that it remains unsafe for foreigners to dine in public.

SOUTHERN IRAQ

Southern Iraq is the spiritual homeland of the Shiites. The sacred cities of Najaf and Karbala attract pilgrims from around the world. The region is also awash with legends of the past, from the port city of Basra – where Sinbad the Sailor set out on his epic journeys – to the ancient sites of Babylon, Ur and the Garden of Eden. The Marsh Arabs, whose culture has changed little in millennia, make their homes among the reeds of the marshlands.

BABYLON بابل

Babylon is Iraq's most famous archaeological site, and one of the most important in the world. Its very name has become synonymous with depravity and hubris. Babylon dates back to at least 2300 BC. It was the capital city of two of the most famous kings of antiquity: Hammurabi (1792–1750 BC), who introduced the world's first law code, and Nebuchadnezzar (604–562 BC), who built the Hanging Gardens of Babylon, one of the Seven Wonders of the Ancient World.

Today, little remains of ancient Babylon except for several mounds and the famous Lion of Babylon, a basalt statue carved more than 2500 years ago. The original Ishtar Gate and Processional Way are now located in Berlin's Pergamon Museum. In the 1980s, Saddam Hussein rebuilt the Ishtar Gate and several palaces, stamping his name into every brick. After the 2003 invasion, coalition forces built a military camp on Babylon that severely damaged the site. After international outcry, coalition forces turned over Babylon to the Iraqi Cultural Ministry. It remains off limits to visitors.

KARBALA كربلاء

☎ 032 / pop 572,300

Located 108km southwest of Baghdad, Karbala is one of Shiite Islam's holiest sites and of great significance to all Muslims. It's best known for the Battle of Karbala in AD 680, whereafter Islam would forever be divided between Sunni and Shiite sects (see p72). Hussein ibn Ali, grandson of the Prophet Mohammed, and his half-brother Abbas ibn Ali were killed in the battle. Both are buried in shrines under two golden-domed mosques that attract millions of pilgrims every year, particularly on the Day of Ashura. Banned under Saddam Hussein, the holy day commemorates the death of

Ali and is marked by mourning, praying, fasting and even self-inflicted injury – devout men practice self-flagellation, repeatedly striking their body with chains and knives until they are covered in blood.

In March 1991, Saddam cracked down on Karbala to punish Shiites for rebelling against his regime. Hundreds of people were killed and the shrines were heavily damaged. Since 2003, terrorists have repeatedly bombed Karbala. On the 2004 Day of Ashura, nearly 200 pilgrims were killed in a series of attacks. The danger has not stopped pilgrims from coming, but it remains unsafe for tourists.

NAJAF النجف

☎ 033 / pop 506,000

The holy Shiite city of Najaf, 160km south of Baghdad, was once a major centre of learning with many *madrassas* (religious schools) and libraries. In the middle of the city stands the **Shrine of Ali ibn Abi Talib** (AD 600–61), who was the cousin and son-in-law of the Prophet Mohammed. It's a breathtaking mosque covered in gold, with two 35m-high golden minarets. The other major attraction is the **Wadi al-Salam Cemetery**, the largest cemetery in the world. Both attract millions of pilgrims every year. In July 2008, Najaf opened a new US$250 million international airport with hopes of attracting more pious visitors.

Najaf is also the centre of Shiite political power in Iraq. It is the home of the Grand Ayatollah Ali Sistani, the most influential religious and political leader for Shiite Muslims. Radical cleric Muqtada al-Sadr and his Mahdi Army occupied Najaf in 2004, culminating in a three-week battle with US forces in the cemetery until Sistani brokered a cease-fire.

UR أور

The ancient Sumerian city of Ur, 15km south of Nasiriyya, is one of the most impressive archaeological sites in Iraq. Some believe it is the Ur of the Chaldees mentioned in the Bible as the birthplace of Abraham.

Ur dates back to at least 4000 BC but reached its heyday during the third and last Sumerian dynasty (2112–2004 BC). The dynasty's founder, Ur Namma, built the **Great Ziggurat of Ur** to honour the Sumerian moon god Nanna. It was restored in the 6th century BC by Nebuchadnezzar II and remains one of the finest and best-preserved ziggurats still standing. Ur is now located within the perimeters of a coalition military base and is off limits to visitors.

BASRA البصرة

Pop 1.76 million

Iraq's third-largest city, 550km southeast of Baghdad, was once known as the 'Venice of the Middle East' for its canal waterways and location on the Shatt al-Arab river. The fictional voyages of Sinbad the Sailor began here, but modern reality is less inspiring.

Basra was founded by caliph Omar bin Khattab in AD 637 as a military base. It rapidly became the hub of the Arab sea trade to points as far as China. Its strategic position made it a repeated target of Mongol, Persian and Turk conquerors. The British captured Basra during WWI and modernised its port. After a brief period of peace, the city was heavily damaged during the 1980s Iran-Iraq war.

In the 2003 invasion, the British returned to Basra, where they have repeatedly clashed with Shiite militias and insurgents. In December 2007, the British relinquished the city to Iraqi officials. Chaos followed as Islamic fundamentalists battled each other for control of the city. In March 2008, Iraqi forces stormed Basra to drive out the Shiite militias. At least 200 people were killed in the fighting. More worrisome, at least 1300 Iraqi soldiers and police deserted or refused to fight. Basra's security has improved, but remains a dangerous city.

NORTHERN IRAQ

Northern Iraq is caught between a rock and a hard place. To its south lies the volatile Sunni Triangle; to the north and east lies the Kurdish Regional Government (KRG), which is slowly annexing Arab lands into its territory. It is home to a complicated ethnic mix of Arabs, Christians, Kurds and smaller minorities who have lived together peacefully for centuries – until now. While security has improved in central and southern Iraq since 2007, northern Iraq has only gotten worse. The two major cities, Mosul and Kirkuk, are no-go areas. It's a shame, because northern Iraq boasts some of the country's most significant archaeological sights including Nimrud, Nineveh, Hatra and Khorsabad. For now, don't even think of visiting.

KIRKUK كركوك

☎ 050 / pop 755,700

The oil-rich city of Kirkuk is a kaleidoscope of ethnic groups, and a tinderbox waiting to explode. Kurds, Arabs and Turkmen all lay claim to Kirkuk. Kurds consider it part of their historical homeland and are seeking to make it the capital of the Kurdish Regional Government. Arabs and most Turkomans want the city and its oil wealth to remain under central government control. Lawmakers have proposed a power-sharing plan, but at the time of writing, the 'Kirkuk Question' remained unanswered. A referendum asking Kirkuk residents whether they want to be part of Arab Iraq or Iraqi Kurdistan has been repeatedly delayed.

Apart from oil, Kirkuk has little to offer. Bombings and shootings are common, giving this dismal city a feeling of the old 'Wild West.'

MOSUL الموصل

pop 3 million

Mosul is Iraq's second-largest city, and its most ethnically diverse. It has the country's

THE BIG DIG

'I think it's true to say that Iraq, more than anywhere else, is the cradle of civilisation and the country is one vast archaeological site,' says Dr John Curtis, keeper of the British Museum's Middle East department. Just how many sites there are is impossible to quantify, he says. 'With the exception of the desert, anywhere you dig in Iraq you will find an archaeological site. That reflects the fact that there have been continuous civilisations and settlements here for 8000 years and it was very prosperous in antiquity,' says Curtis.

The most important archaeological sites in Iraq are Ashur, Babylon, Hatra, Khorsabad, Nimrud, Nineveh, Samarra and Ur. The three that follow are located in and around Mosul.

Nineveh

The ancient ruins of Nineveh are located on the outskirts of modern-day Mosul. Some historians now believe the fabled Hanging Gardens of Babylon may have been confused with gardens that actually did exist in Ninevah.

Nimrud

Nimrud, the second capital of Assyria, is 37km southeast of Mosul and contains several buildings, the most impressive being King Ashurnasirpal II's palace and the Temple of Nabu, the God of Writing.

Hatra

Hatra, 110km southwest of Mosul, is one of the best preserved and youngest of Iraq's archaeological sites, dating to the 1st century AD. A Unesco World Heritage site, it's covered by dozens of temples, tombs and columns. If it looks familiar, it's because Hatra was used in the opening scene of the 1973 film *The Exorcist*.

Iraqi archaeologists are undertaking a few small-scale excavations around the country, but since the 2003 war began, it has been too dangerous for foreign archaeologists to visit. Archaeological work in Iraq has mainly switched from research to protecting and preserving sites from looting and damage. The British Museum's Iraq Project has been at the forefront of that mission. Dr Curtis and his colleagues have made several brief trips to Iraq to assess damage at several sites, including a 2004 visit to Babylon that led to a scathing report highly critical of coalition military activity around the ruins.

The international community including Unesco, the Global Heritage Fund and the State Board for Antiquities and Heritage in Iraq are working hard to save Iraq's cultural heritage. Ashur and Samarra were recently added to Unesco's list of World Heritage sites; Babylon is a candidate for future inclusion. Until then, archaeologists – and tourists – are waiting for the day when they can return to explore this rich history.

largest number of Christians and significant numbers of Kurds, Assyrians, Turkomans and Yazidis. Since 2003, thousands of minorities have fled the predominantly Arab city to escape violence and ethnic strife. As of late 2008, the area between Mosul and Tal Afar was one of the last strongholds for Al-Qaeda in Iraq and other terrorist groups, making it one of the most dangerous cities on earth.

History

Mosul dates back to at least 6000 BC. Around 700 BC, Assyrian kings Sennacherib and later his grandson Ashurbanipal built Nineveh – on the east bank of the Tigris River across from present-day Mosul – into one of the great cities of the ancient world. The epic Battle of Gaugamela, in which Alexander the Great defeated the Persian King Darius in 331 BC, is believed to have been fought somewhere east of Mosul. The city later became an important trade city because of its position on the caravan route from India and Persia to the Mediterranean. Mosul's chief export was cotton; the word 'muslin' is derived from its name.

Mosul was destroyed by the Mongols in the 13th century but began to revive under the Ottomans. The British occupied the city after WWI. Since the 2003 war, Mosul has been a hotbed of insurgency activity in northern Iraq. In July 2003, Saddam Hussein's sons Uday and Qusay were killed in a gun battle here with US forces. Despite several major coalition military operations, Mosul remains plagued by violence.

Sights

Mosul was once known as the 'Pearl of the North' for its great marble buildings like **Mosul House**. The **ruins of Nineveh** are located on the eastern bank of the Tigris. The **Mosul Museum** once housed a large collection of artefacts from Nineveh and Nimrud until looters ransacked it in 2003. The **Mosque of Nebi Yunus**, believed to be the burial place of Jonah, attracts Muslim and Christian pilgrims.

IRAQI KURDISTAN

Leave your misconceptions behind and discover one of the newest travel destinations in the Middle East – Iraqi Kurdistan. The region's slogan, 'The Other Iraq', could not be more fitting. This is the Iraq you don't see in the news. It's a safe and tranquil oasis with happening cities, soaring mountains and warm, welcoming people. It's a surreal kind of place, where Americans receive a liberators' welcome and former US president George W Bush Jnr is considered a national hero.

Iraqi Kurdistan is technically part of Iraq, but it might as well be a separate country. It has its own prime minister and parliament, its own passport stamps, its own languages and culture and its own army – the Peshmerga, meaning 'those who face death'. The red, white and green Kurdish flag, with its blazing yellow sun in the centre, seems to flutter from every building, car and hill top.

The semi-autonomous Kurdish Regional Government administers the Iraqi provinces of Dohuk, Erbil, Sulaymaniyah and a few northern bits of Ninawa and Tamim. The region has enjoyed de facto autonomy since 1991, when the US military established a no-flight zone to protect the long-oppressed Kurds from Saddam Hussein's brutal regime. The status was formalised in 2005 when the new Iraqi Constitution recognised Iraqi Kurdish sovereignty.

For early visitors to Iraqi Kurdistan, it's a chance to witness nation building first-hand. In the cosmopolitan cities of Erbil and Sulaymaniyah, cranes outnumber minarets as a construction boom gives rise to new luxury hotels, museums, shiny malls and tourist resorts. Iraqi Kurdistan's real attraction is its stunning natural beauty: snowcapped mountains, deep canyons, gorgeous waterfalls and raging rivers, all just waiting to be explored.

ZAKHO زاخو

☎ 062 / pop 90,000

Sooner or later, everyone ends up in Zakho. This hustling, bustling border town is just a hop, skip and a jump from the **Ibrahim Khalil Border**, the main crossing point between Turkey and Iraq. Zakho is just 20km from Silopi, Turkey, so overland travellers to Iraqi Kurdistan inevitable start or end their journey here. Like many border towns around the world, trade is the lifeblood of the local economy. At any given time, hundreds of trucks line up on either size of the border, waiting to ply their trade. Zakho is pleasant but there is little of interest for tourists.

Orientation & Information

The main road through town is Bederkhan St, also called Sehid Salih Yousifi St, where you'll find dozens of hotels, restaurants, pharmacies, supermarkets and internet cafés.

ZakhoNet (Bederkhan St; 10am-10pm; internet per hr ID1500), under the Zozek Hotel, has an internet café, international calling centre and MoneyGram money-wiring service.

Sights

Zakho's most famous attraction is the ancient **Delal Bridge**, a beautiful stone arch over the Khabur River. Unfortunately, the history of the old bridge has been forgotten over time. Near the bridge, you'll find a small **amusement park** and pleasant cafés overlooking the river. A major landmark is the huge Kurdish flag flying proudly above the roundabout in the town centre.

Sleeping & Eating

There are dozens of hotel and restaurant options along Bederkhan St. For cheap grub, check out the many kebab stands across the street from Jamal Restaurant.

Jamal Hotel (457 2832; Sehid Salih Yousifi St; s/d ID20,000/40,000) The Jamal has clean, pleasant rooms and friendly staff. It's located behind the best eatery in town, **Jamal Restaurant** (mains ID5000-10,000; 8am-midnight), where you can feast on a huge mixed grill plate, mezze and desert for about ID10,000.

Bazaz Hotel (418 7190; Bederkhan St; s/d/tr/ste ID30,000/47,000/59,000/77,000;) The nicest, largest hotel in town with huge beds, Western toilets and a decent but pricey restaurant.

DOHUK دهوك

☎ 062 / pop 130,000

Cradled by two mountain ranges about 40km southeast of Zakho, Dohuk is a busy, energetic and curiously appealing place. The name means 'small village', but in reality, the provincial capital of Dohuk (the province and capital go by the same name) is the third-largest city in Iraqi Kurdistan. A university town with a youthful vibe and growing arts scene, Dohuk is successfully marketing itself as a safe, regional tourist destination. It's so safe that even American troops come here to enjoy a bit of R&R.

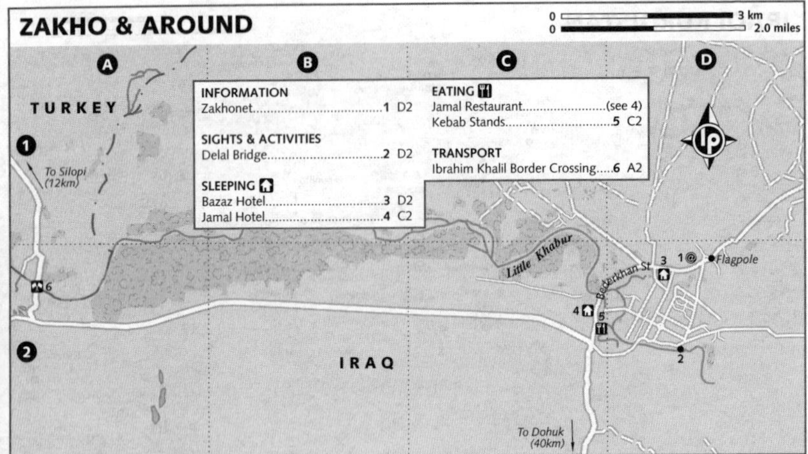

Located in a fertile valley, Dohuk is well known for its fruits and nuts such as pomegranates, apples, grapes, pears, almonds and walnuts. Don't leave town without sampling one of the many fresh-fruit-juice stands on Kawa Rd.

Dohuk makes a perfect base for visiting the nearby attractions of Lalish and Amadiya, but it's so appealing that you might end up spending more time here than you originally planned!

Orientation & Information

There are two main roads through town: Zakho Way runs through the modern, affluent west side of town, while Kawa Rd includes the old city and bazaar area. Both roads intersect near Mankal Restaurant.

There are numerous internet cafés around town, most charging ID1500 per hour. Try **Kani Net** (Kawa Rd, 10am-1am) across from the Hotel Bircin.

The main **money exchange centre** on Kawa Rd has better rates than banks.

Jeziri Bookshop (☎ 722 7017; cnr Zakho Way & Kawa Rd, 9am-7pm) sells English, Kurdish and Arabic books.

Sights

Dohuk's most popular attraction is **Dream City** (admission ID1500, rides ID1000-2000; 7pm-late) a large amusement park/resort with a towering Ferris wheel and other thrill rides, plus a video arcade, bowling, swimming, restaurants hotels and vacation homes. The place really gets cranking on Thursday and Friday nights, when local women turn out in their dazzling colourful traditional dresses.

Corniche promenade is a popular walking path and people-watching spot, especially in the late afternoon and early evening and weekends. It has inviting benches, water fountains, sculptures, cafés and an outdoor amphitheatre.

Dohuk Bazaar is a traditional old market with a maze of alleyways and colourful stalls selling everything from candy and spices to Kurdish clothing. The **Grand Mosque** and its colourful tiled minaret, located in the heart of the bazaar, is one of the oldest mosques in Dohuk.

Dohuk Art Gallery (☎ 722 5830; Kawa Rd; admission free; 9am-1pm & 3-6pm) displays and sells paintings and sculptures by Kurdish artists.

The domed **Church of St Ith Llaha** is located on a hill in west Dohuk and dates back to the 6th-century AD. The current building is clearly newer and includes a cute little blue-and-beige outdoor chapel dedicated to the Virgin Mary.

Just north of downtown, **Dohuk Dam** and its manmade lake and waterfall is a popular family picnic spot.

Sleeping & Eating

You'll find dozens of budget and midrange restaurants and hotels along Kawa Rd. Modern and pricier hotels and restaurants are located on Zakho Way near Dream City. Unless noted, most hotels have squat toilets.

our pick **Hotel Parleman** (☎ 722 1361; Kawa Rd; r ID10,000; ❄) The best of the cheapies, the bright-pink Hotel Parleman is quickly gaining a reputation as *the* backpacker hotel in Iraq. The basic but clean rooms include a fridge, TV and private bath. The centrepiece of the gaudy marble lobby is a framed photo of George W Bush Jnr standing side by side with Iraqi Kurdistan President Massoud Barzani. The hidden, coffin-shaped entrance is around the corner by the shoeshine guys.

Hotel Bircin (☎ 722 8182; cnr Kawa & Cinema Rds; s/d/tr ID49,000/65,000/95,000; ❄) Hotel Bircin, also spelled 'Birjin', is the tallest landmark in Dohuk city centre. All rooms are large and clean and include double beds, TV, Western toilets and bathtubs. The owner's son speaks English.

Dilshad Palace (☎ 722 7601; www.dilshad-palace.com; Dohuk Main St; s/d/ste ID150,000/180,000/450,000; ❄ 💻 V) Opened in 2007, Dilshad Palace is the first truly modern, five-star hotel in Iraq. All 106 rooms have king-sized beds; enormous marble bathrooms with Western toilets and tub; exquisite furnishings, flatscreen TVs, minibar and safe. There are four restaurants and bars, including one featuring nightly Lebanese music and belly dancing. If that's not enough, there's 24-hour room service.

Mankal Restaurant (☎ 762 4747; cnr Zakho Way & Kawa Rd; mains ID5000-10,000; ⏰ 10am-midnight) Come here hungry, because the portions

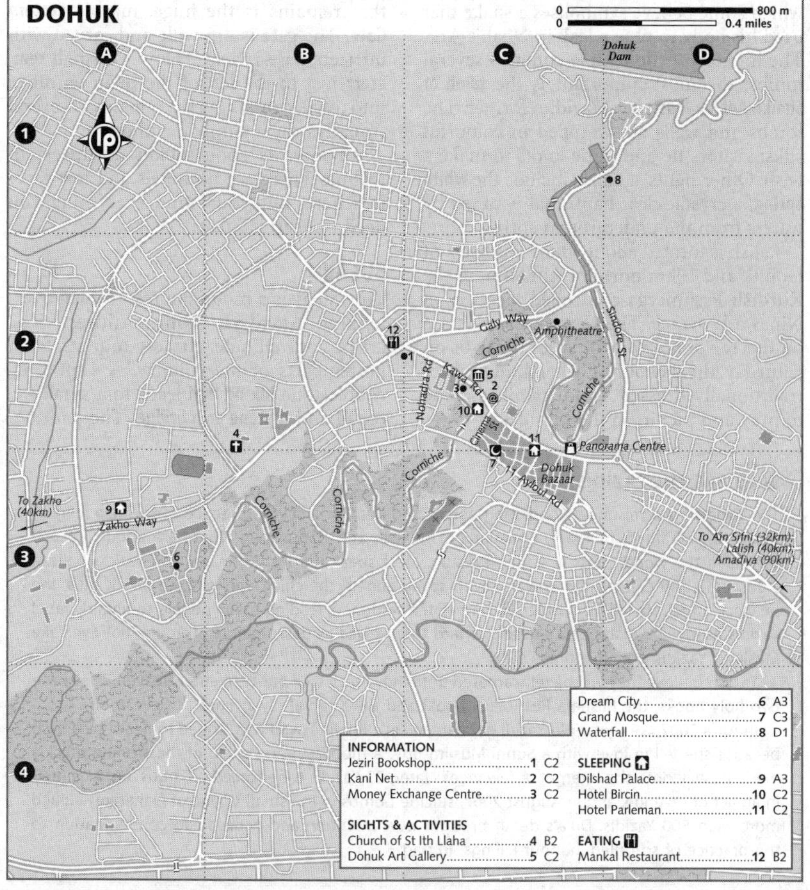

IRAQ

are absolutely HUGE. The lamb *quzi* is the house speciality, and big enough to feed an army.

LALISH لاليش

Hidden in a deep, green valley, Lalish is the most sacred place on earth for practitioners of the Yazidi faith (see boxed text, below). At least once in their lifetime, each Yazidi must make a pilgrimage to Lalish, where their chief deity Malak Taus – the peacock angel – first landed. Some also believe Noah's Ark came to rest here. Visitors must walk barefoot through the complex.

The focal point of Lalish is the **Sanctuary**, a temple topped by two large pyramids. The entrance is guarded by a stone relief of a black snake slithering into a hole in the wall, which some believe symbolises a snake that used his body to plug a leak in Noah's Ark. The interior of the temple contains several tombs; the most important is the **tomb of Sheikh Adi ibn Mustafa**, a Yazidi reformer. The tombs and walls are wrapped in colourful silks; visitors tie and untie knots to make a wish. Other sights at Lalish include the **White Spring**, a crystal-clear baptismal pool fed by waters from the underground spring.

Lalish is located about 30km southeast of Dohuk and 10km north of Ain Sifni, in the Kurdish Peshmerga-controlled territory of Ninawa Province. The best days to visit are on the Yazidi holy day of Wednesday or on Saturday, the day of rest, when hundreds of traditionally dressed Yazidi families come to pray and picnic on the hillsides.

AMADIYA العمادية

Like a village in the clouds, amazing Amadiya – or Amedi – is built on a high plateau 1200m above sea level. The village is breathtakingly picturesque, surrounded by magnificent mountains and endless green valleys. The city is a mix of Muslims and Christians, and there are several fine churches in town.

The most visible landmark is the 30m-high **minaret** of **Amadiya Mosque**, near the centre of town and built by Sultan Hussein Wali. It's about 400 years old and pock-marked with bullet holes from the Kurdish Civil War. It's possible to climb the spiral staircase to the top of the minaret, if you can find the imam who holds the key. The city was once a high-walled citadel, but all that remains is the huge, marble **Eastern Gate**. The gate is 4m wide and carved with intricate base reliefs. There is a small **cemetery** just to the left of the main entrance into town, containing the remains of several Amadiya royal family members.

Amadiya is about 60km northwest of Dohuk. There are no hotels and few services here, but you'll find everything you need in nearby Sulav.

SULAV سولاف

Tiny Sulav is a mountain resort town overlooking Amadiya, 5km northwest. The crisp, cool climate attracts tourists from hotter parts of the country. A 1km-long, cobblestone **hiking trail** leads to a small **waterfall** and a **stone arch bridge**. The path be-

WHO ARE THE YAZIDIS?

The Yazidis are a misunderstood, long-persecuted Kurdish sect who practice Yazidism, a religion that is an amalgam of Islam, Christianity, Judaism and Zoroastrian. There are about 500,000 Yazidis in the world, most in Iraqi Kurdistan. Most speak Kurdish Kurmanji. The Yazidis believe a supreme god created the universe with seven angels, the chief among them Malak Taus, the peacock angel. He fell from grace but was later pardoned, leading many people to unfairly label Yazidis as 'devil worshippers'. Yazidis regard themselves as descendents of Adam, not Eve. Like Muslims, Yazidis pray five times a day.

Yazidis believe they will be reincarnated until they reach soul purity to enter Heaven. They have two holy books, the Mishefa Res (black book) and the Kitab al-Jilwa (Book of Revelation).

In April 2007, a 17-year-old Yazidi girl named Du'a Khalil Aswad was stoned to death by a mob because she fell in love with a Sunni Muslim boy. A mobile-phone video of the stoning quickly made its way onto the internet. A few weeks later, 23 Yazidis were forced off a bus and executed in an act of revenge, and in August 2007, suicide bombs in the small village of Qahataniya killed more than 500 Yazidis. Du'a's death brought new attention and widespread condemnation to the practice of so-called 'honour killings' in Iraq.

gins near the Sulav Hotel, behind the cheesy man-made waterfall.

Sleeping & Eating

There are several hotels, restaurants, cafés, shops and even liquor stores along the one and only road through Sulav.

Sulav Hotel & Restaurant (r per person ID20,000) A small, family-run hotel with recently renovated rooms with balconies and shared bathroom. One room has a small, babbling brook running through it. The terraced restaurant offers magnificent views of Amadiya and the valley below.

Restaurant Dunya (6am-midnight; mains ID3000-10,000) Opened in April 2008, Dunya has good traditional food and panoramic views of Amadiya from its glassed walls.

BARZAN بارزان

The small village of Barzan, about 52km east of Amadiya, is the ancestral home of the Barzani family who dominate Kurdish politics. Chief among them was Mullah Mustafa Barzani, the father of the Kurdish independence movement and a national hero who fought Baghdad's government for decades. His son, Massoud Barzani, is the current president of the Kurdish Regional Government and leader of the Kurdish Democratic Party (KDP). His grandson, Nechirvan Barzani, Massoud's nephew, is the KRG Prime Minister.

The town of Barzan is itself rather boring and nondescript, yet many Kurds make pilgrimages here to visit the **grave of Mustafa Barzani**, who is buried in a simple plot on a hill overlooking the town and surrounded by KRG and KDP flags. Just a few metres away, a massive **Barzani Memorial Centre** is under construction.

AKRE عقره

Like a bit of Santorini plopped into the Middle East, the ancient city of Akre (also spelled Aqrah) is built into a steep hillside above a thriving old market. Located about 23km south of Barzan along a scenic mountain road, Akre once had a substantial Jewish population – former embattled Israeli defence minister Yitzhak Mordechai was born here. The mountain overlooking Akre has a flat plateau called **Zarvia Dji**, meaning Land of the Jews, and once used for Jewish celebrations. Today it is the site of the region's largest **Nowruz festival**, celebrating the Kurdish New Year on 21 March, when huge bonfires and fireworks light up the night skies around Akre.

The best way to explore the town is on foot – uphill. Narrow alleyways and hidden staircases climb past clusters of colourful houses. The opposite hill contains an old **cemetery** with great views of old Akre.

The valley floor at the base of the old city houses the town's two focal points, the **bazaar** and the white-and-green-trimmed **Akre mosque**. The crumbling **town hall** in the city centre has seen better days, but it's a fine example of British colonial architecture. Just north of the city centre, a hiking path leads to **Sipa Waterfall**.

As there is no real tourism industry here, sleeping and eating options are limited. **Sepal Hotel** (New Akre, r ID50,000;) is a new hotel with modern amenities, but when we stayed our room was filthy and the staff rude.

GALI ALI BEG & THE HAMILTON ROAD قلي علي بيك

Prepare yourself for one of the most amazing sights in the Middle East. The northeast corner of Iraqi Kurdistan is an unheralded area of beauty marked by cascading waterfalls, soaring snowcapped mountains, deep gorges cut by raging rivers, rolling green hills and lush valleys. It is, without a doubt, the most beautiful and awe-inspiring place in Iraq.

In 1928 New Zealand engineer Sir Archibald Milne Hamilton was commissioned to build a road from the Kurdish capital of Erbil to Haji Omaran on the Iranian border. This 'short cut' allowed the creation of a strategic and direct overland route from the Mediterranean cities of Beirut and Alexandretta (now Iskenderun) to the Caspian Sea, Tehran and on to India. Hamilton completed his road in 1932 and detailed its construction in his travelogue, *Road Through Kurdistan*.

Named for its builder, **The Hamilton Road** remains a remarkable feat of engineering through some of the world's most impassable and inhospitable terrain. Kurds also call it the Haji Omaran road, and it crosses at least five mountain ranges and rises from 409m in Erbil to about 1850m on the Iranian border. The most scenic portion of the drive is the 55km stretch from Gali Ali Beg to Haji Omaran.

In *Road Through Kurdistan,* Hamilton called **Gali Ali Beg Canyon** 'one of the grandest formations of nature to be found in the world'. This Grand Canyon of the Middle East extends 12km between the Korak and Bradost mountains and is cut by two rivers that form to create the **Great Zab River**. The Hamilton Road traverses the canyon from west to east. At the western entrance to the canyon at the Peshmerga checkpoint, the road splits into upper and lower halves.

The **Lower Hamilton Road** runs parallel to the river past high, red limestone walls that rise almost vertically from the canyon floor. Halfway along the canyon is **Gali Ali Beg Waterfall**. Located about 100km northeast of Erbil, the waterfall is Iraq's most famous, appearing on the back of the ID5000 note, and the falls tumble 80m into a frigid tidal pool that offers wading possibilities.

Upper Hamilton Road hugs the rim of the canyon along a series of hairpin turns. It's not for the faint hearted. Road signs depict cars driving off cliffs, a reminder for drivers to watch their speed. The road eventually arrives at **Bekhal Waterfall**, a raging whitewater falls that appears to pour straight out of the side of a mountain and down several steps. Both falls have pleasant cafés where you can sit and enjoy the scenery.

At the eastern end of the Upper Hamilton Road, on a high plateau overlooking the city of Rawanduz, sits **Pank Resort** (☎ 066-353 0105, 0750 412 8910; http://rawandoz.com; admission ID3000; 4-/8-person villa ID145,000/195,000; 🕑 8am-midnight). Built by an enterprising Kurdish-Swedish businessman, Pank features a rollercoaster, Ferris wheel, minigolf, restaurants and three helicopter landing pads.

The roads meet again in the dusty town of **Rawanduz**, a former British colonial outpost. From here, the road begins its most dramatic climb, running parallel to the Choman River. The regional market town of **Choman** is a city of about 10,000 people surrounded by unparalleled beauty and snowcapped mountains.

The Hamilton Road ends at the border town of **Haji Omaran**, the last city before the Iranian frontier. It's a major point of legal and not-so-legal trade. Iranian and Kurdish men in traditional clothing haggle over goods on the roadside. At 1828m above sea level, the air here is cold and crisp and surrounded by mountains that are covered in snow even in the summer. Some reach peaks of 3600m. In another time and place, this could be a ski resort. But for now, there is little of consequence in Haji Omaran apart from its natural beauty. Here, one can truly appreciate the Kurdish proverb, 'No friends but the mountains'.

Haji Omaran is one of the busiest border crossings between Iraq and Iran. Unfortunately, it is not possible to cross the border from here into Iran without a prearranged Iranian visa.

SHAQLAWA شقلاوة

About 50km northeast of Erbil at the base of Safeen Mountain is the resort town of Shaqlawa. At 966m above sea level, the cool temperatures and lush, green environment have long attracted wealthy Iraqi tourists from the hotter Arab regions of the country. Shaqlawa is a predominantly Assyrian Christian town with several new churches.

A strenuous one-hour hike leads up into a canyon on the side of Safeen Mountains. Hidden in a rock crevice near the top of the mountain are the ruins of the **Rabban Beya Monastery**. Dating to the 4th century AD, the ruins consist of a stone arch and three crumbling, small rooms. The real reward here is the stunning view of the Beya Valley and Shaqlawa below. The steep trail is mostly a dirt and gravel path barely half a metre wide, definitely not for those afraid of heights. Bring plenty of water and sturdy footwear.

Shaqlawa has at least four hotels, several restaurants, falafel shops, supermarkets and liquor stores.

our pick **Motel Saffin** (Shaqlawa; motel_saffin@yahoo.com; 066 256 5126, 0770 652 5516; 4-/8-person r ID72,000/90,000) has large bungalow-style rooms surrounding a large garden. All rooms have kitchenettes, TV, private entrance, four or eight beds and both Western and squat toilets. Kind manager Karim speaks English, Armenian, Arabic and Kurdish, and will happily let you use his internet connection.

ERBIL أربيل

☎ 066 / pop 1 million

Erbil (Kurdish: Hawler) is the capital of the Kurdish Regional Government and the largest city in Iraqi Kurdistan. It is one of the oldest continuously inhabited cities in the world. Today, Erbil is where it's all happening. It's the fastest-growing city in Iraq, with dozens of ambitious projects under construction including the tallest building in Iraq (the Korek Tower), an 8000-store shopping complex (Nishtiman Mall), a five-star luxury hotel (Park Kempinski Hotel) and a new airport with a runway long enough to land the double-decker Airbus 380, or even the Space Shuttle.

Billboards advertise luxury Western-style homes in posh subdivisions with names such as 'Dream City' or 'English Village'. Erbil's Master Plan even calls for championship golf courses, a wildlife safari, amusement parks and a Grand Prix racetrack. Erbil, dare we say, is the new Dubai. It's a tolerant, diverse city full of big dreams and optimism that serves as a model for all of Iraq.

History

There is archaeological evidence that Neolithic peoples roamed the area 10,000 years ago. The first written record of Erbil dates back to 2000 BC when it was called Arbilum. The city was consecutively invaded by Akkadians, Sumerians, Assyrians, Persians and Greeks. Around 100 AD, Erbil became a centre of Christianity until Muslims conquered it in 642 AD. Erbil prospered as a centre of learning and trade during the Islamic Golden Age. Over the next several hundred years, Erbil passed through many powerful hands including the Abbasids,

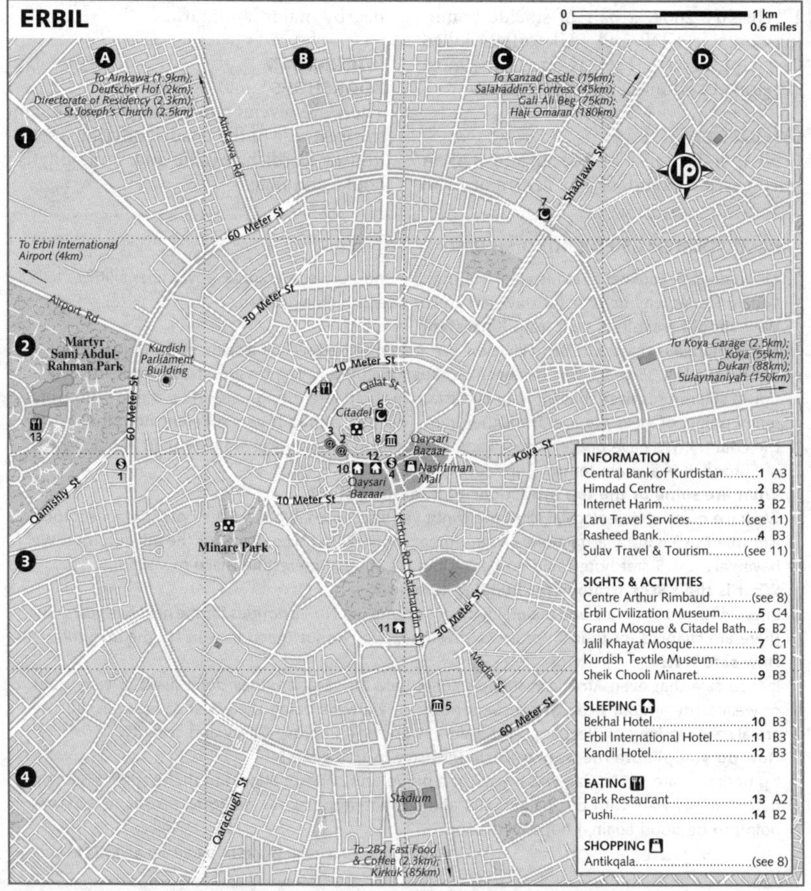

Moguls, Turkomans, Persians, Ottomans and British. For centuries, Erbil has revolved around its citadel, an enormous city on a manmade hill built up by a succession of civilisations.

During the mid-1990s, Erbil was caught in the middle of the Iraqi Kurdish Civil War between the armies of the two major political parties, the Kurdish Democratic Party (KDP) and the Patriotic Union of Kurdistan (PUK). Erbil was PUK territory until it was captured by the KDP in 1996. Thousands were killed during the fighting until the parties signed a peace treaty in 1998.

Since the 2003 US-led invasion, Erbil has enjoyed relative peace and stability, but there have been a handful of attacks. On 1 February 2004, a pair of suicide bombings outside KDP and PUK offices killed 98 people. Today, Erbil is one of the most developed and modern cities in Iraq.

Orientation

Erbil is 84km east of Mosul and 320km northeast of Baghdad. The centre of Erbil is the citadel, the city's primary landmark that dominates the skyline. Major roads radiate out from the citadel like spokes on a bicycle wheel. A series of ring roads encircle the citadel; the closest is Qalat St, followed by 30 Meter St, 60 Meter St and 100 Meter St. The Christian suburb of Ainkawa and Erbil International Airport are located in the outskirts of northwest Erbil. Most roads are known by several names, so the shiny new blue road signs written in English and Kurdish are practically useless. Roads are most commonly known by their ultimate destination, so people will refer to them as 'The Road to Kirkuk' (Salahaddin St) or 'The Road to Shaqlawa' (Pirman St). When using taxis, it's best to give the exact destination or a nearby major landmark.

Information

BOOKSHOPS

There are several bookstores on Qalat St on the west side of the citadel, offering a selection of Kurdish, Arabic and some English books and maps.

PACK YOUR BAGS FOR KURDISH IRAQ

Mr Nimrud B Youkhana, Minister of Tourism for the Kurdish Regional Government (KRG), tells Lonely Planet why its time for travellers to consider a holiday in Iraq.

Why should travellers visit Iraqi Kurdistan?

Mesopotamia is the cradle of civilisation. We are a multi-ethnic, multifaith, multicultural country. But for the last 35 years, Iraq has been famous for all the wrong reasons. Nationwide, the situation is still not resolved, but for Iraqi Kurdistan this is an interesting time and place to visit. From many points of view, we are 'The Other Iraq'. This part of Iraq is very different from the rest of the country. We have peace, security and low crime. It's more peaceful here than in many parts of Europe. It is a virgin territory ripe for discovery.

What are some of the top attractions of Iraqi Kurdistan?

We have many archaeological sites, many not yet discovered. We have the potential for ecotourism thanks to natural attractions like our great mountains. It is a place for the adventurous. We have very few 5-star hotels and no beach, but it's still an interesting place to visit.

What is the KRG's strategy for building tourism?

Improving infrastructure and maintaining security are our No 1 priorities for the next five years. But there are chances for tourism projects. It will happen. We just need to wait for the investors.

How safe is it?

It is so safe that even American soldiers come here for vacation; they don't need to carry guns or wear body armour here. Of course, terrorists are always doing their best to reach us. But we are always working on keeping our borders strong and improve safety and security.

How do you picture the Iraqi tourism industry in five years?

Up until the late 1970s, Iraq was known as a prime tourist destination. But then Saddam Hussein began all his wars with our neighbours and all that stopped. It's going to take time, but it is going to be good again, I hope, very soon.

Mr Nimrud B Youkhana works as a tourism minister in Iraq.

INTERNET ACCESS

There are several internet cafés located in and around the old bazaar.

Himdad Centre (Bazaar; ☎ 222 3248; per hr ID2500; 8am-midnight)

Internet Harim (Bazaar; per hr ID2000; 8am-10pm, closed Fri)

MONEY

The **Central Bank of Kurdistan** (cnr 60 Meter St & Qamishly St; 9am-noon & 2pm-5pm) and **Rasheed Bank** (Qalat St; 9am-noon & 2pm-5pm) can wire money anywhere in the world. Rasheed Bank offers MoneyGram services.

TRAVEL AGENCIES

Laru Travel Services (☎ 0750 455 4411; Erbil International Hotel; 9am-5pm) Can help book flights to and from Erbil International Airport.

Sulav Travel & Tourism (☎ 0750 769 0202, 0750 769 0303; 30 Meter St; 9am-5pm, closed Fri) Across from Erbil International Hotel.

VISA EXTENSIONS

Directorate of Residency (Shlama Rd, Ainkawa; 8am-3pm, closed Fri) In the Ministry of Interior satellite building.

Sights

THE CITADEL

The heart of Erbil is the **citadel** (Kurdish: Qalat Hawler), claimed to be the longest continuously inhabited urban area on earth. This imposing *tell*, or mound, covers an area of 102,000 sq metres and rises 32m above street level, built on layers of successive settlements. A ring of fortified honey-yellow walls tops the citadel. Inside this city within a city are hundreds of little stone and mud-brick homes, many built directly into the walls. In the centre of town is the **Grand Mosque** and **Citadel Bath**, built in 1775 on top of an older structure and featuring a colourfully tiled minaret.

The citadel has been continuously inhabited for at least 8000 years – sort of. Until recently, it was home to more than 3000 of Erbil's poorest people, many of them refugees who had fled war-torn regions of Iraq. Human action was wreaking havoc on the citadel. So in a controversial November 2006 move, the KRG paid off and resettled residents to make way for redevelopment. Most of the citadel is now an eerie, crumbling ghost town, but one family remains in order to not break the continuous habitation streak. Unesco and the KRG recently announced plans to renovate the citadel.

The main entrance into the citadel is the **South Gate**, guarded by a **colossal statue** of 12th-century historian Mubarek Ahmed Sharafaddin. Pass through the gate and make an immediate right to reach three fine, 19th century buildings that now house museums and shops.

The **Kurdish Textile Museum** (☎ 251 1660; www.kurdishtextilemuseum.com; admission free; 9am-6pm) contains a fascinating, colourful collection of Kurdish carpets, clothing and other goods. The museum's wonderfully addictive gift shop accepts MasterCard and Visa. Next door, **Antikqala** is an eclectic and pricey antiques shop that also accepts credit cards.

The last house on this street is home to **Centre Arthur Rimbaud** (☎ 0750 477 7636; www.ar-erbil.org; admission free), a French and Kurdish cultural exchange centre. It occasionally hosts exhibits by Iraqi artists. On most Saturday nights, French and European films with English subtitles are screened in the centre's open-air courtyard.

Take time to stroll through the abandoned alleyways and structures of the citadel, a city frozen in time.

MARTYR SAMI ABDUL-RAHMAN PARK

Also known as Erbil Park, **Martyr Sami Abdul-Rahman Park** (60 Meter St; admission free; 8am-midnight), across from the Kurdish Parliament Building, is one of the most beautiful urban spaces in Iraq. Opened in 2006, this oasis of fountains, lakes and gardens was built over what was previously a military base for Saddam Hussein's feared 5th Corps Army. On Fridays, the park is packed with families and young couples enjoying picnics. Take the time to stop and smell the many rose gardens. The large lake in the centre of the park rents swan-shaped paddleboats and speedboat rides. There are many cafés and restaurants around the park, including the popular Park Restaurant (p236).

The park is named for the KRG deputy prime minister who was killed in a 2004 suicide bombing. A large black obelisk memorial near the entrance to the park lists the names of the 98 people killed in that attack.

IRAQ

QAYSARI BAZAAR

Erbil's huge **bazaar** (8am-late, closed Fri) is one of the oldest in the world. It wraps around the entire southern half of the citadel, where you can literally find anything. It's a maze of narrow alleys and streets, much of it covered by a corrugated metal roof to protect shoppers from the blazing Iraqi sun. The bazaar is divided into various sections. The western side has many book stalls. The south side is filled with clothing stores and shops selling fresh yogurt and honey and cheese. The east side contains hardware, electronics and bootleg DVDs and video games. It's easy to get lost in here, but that's part of the fun.

ERBIL CIVILIZATION MUSEUM

This small museum (Ministry of Antiques, Salahaddin St; admission free; 9am-1.30pm, closed Fri) inside the Ministry of Antiques houses a collection of Iraqi archaeological finds, some dating back to 6000 BC. But compared to its sister museum in Sulaymaniyah, this place is rather ordinary. Many items on display are copies of artefacts located in the still-closed National Museum of Iraq in Baghdad.

MOSQUES & CHURCHES

Erbil has more mosques than any city in Iraqi Kurdistan. Just southwest of the citadel, the 36m-tall **Sheik Chooli Minaret** (Kurdish: Minare) is all that remains of a grand mosque that once stood here. The broken, leaning minaret was built between 1190 and 1232 during the reign of Sultan Mudhafaraddin Kokburi.

The minaret stands on a 14.5m octagonal base and is made of baked bricks and gypsum with highly detailed tiled ornamentation. The minaret is located in the new **Minare Park**. Driving into the city from Shaqlawa, you can't miss Erbil's largest and grandest mosque, the **Jalil Khayat Mosque**. Opened in 2007, it's inspired by İstanbul's famed Blue Mosque. The main dome is 45m high, flanked by two 65m tall minarets.

The Christian neighbourhood of Ainkawa has several churches. The largest is **St Joseph's Church**, a Chaldean Christian church built in 1978.

Sleeping

There are many budget hotels in and around the bazaar. Most have squat toilets unless otherwise noted.

Kandil Hotel (066 222 9230, 0750 453 2233; cnr Qalat St & Salahaddin St; s/d ID10,000/ID20,000) This clean and friendly cheapie offers the best deal for the dinar. It's located directly across from the main gate of the citadel. Most rooms have shared bathrooms.

Bekhal Hotel (222 509, 407 2810; Bazaar; r per person ID25,000;) Located in the bazaar about a block southwest of the citadel, this orange hotel is hard to miss. It's impeccably clean with Western toilets, fridge, TV and private bathroom. The owner speaks basic English.

Erbil International Hotel (223 4460; 30 Meter St & Salahaddin St; www.erbilinthotel.com; s/d ID240,000/300,000;) Better known by locals as 'The Sheraton,' the Erbil is a luxury hotel favoured by Western visitors. Amenities include two swimming pools, tennis courts, a Turkish bath, six bars and restaurants and 24-hour room service. Surrounded by high, bomb-blast walls and tight security, it has all the warmth of a military bunker.

Eating & Drinking

Many budget kebab shops and food vendors can be found in the bazaar.

our pick **Deutscher Hof** (0750 488 3981, 253 6274; Ainkawa; deutscher-hof-international@web.de; mains ID10,000-20,000; noon-midnight) The only German restaurant and beer garden in Kurdistan, this spot was founded in 2006 by former German soldier Gunter Voelker. The menu features typical German dishes such as bratwurst, schnitzel, steak and plenty of mugs of cold German beer. *Prost!*

Park Restaurant (0750 401 0339, 251 9812; Erbil Park; restaurantpark@yahoo.com; mains ID5000-12,000; noon-midnight) Perhaps the most scenic restaurant in Erbil, the Park Restaurant overlooks the lake at Martyr Sami Abdul-Rahman Park. The menu has a range of Middle Eastern and Western dishes including lamb *quzi*, kebabs, fried chicken and, yes, beer and wine.

Pushi (454 0431, 253 6717; Ainkawa Rd; mains ID8000-12,000; noon-midnight) Pushi Restaurant is an Erbil institution, serving up Turkish and Kurdish specialties such as *İskender kebaps* and fish dishes.

2B2 Fast Food & Coffee (255 5050; Salahaddin St under Swan Hotel; www.2b2.cc; mains ID3000-11,000; 11am-midnight) Tired of eating kebabs? This American-style fast-food joint serves greasy hot dogs, burgers and pizza. But the real draw is the top floor café, featuring real coffee drinks, milkshakes, fresh-squeezed juices and ice cream sundaes.

Getting There & Away

International flights arrive at **Erbil International Airport**, (www.erbilairport.net), 6km northwest of the city centre.

If you're coming overland from Shaqlawa and all points north, no problem. But travelling to/from Dohuk is another matter; the main highway between Erbil and Dohuk traverses the very dangerous city of Mosul. We strongly discourage travellers from using long-distance buses because they often stop in or near Mosul. The best and safest option is to hire a private taxi and travel via Ain Sifni and Bararash to bypass Mosul. Always settle on a price and route before getting into a taxi.

To get to Sulaymaniyah, avoid travelling into or near the hotspot of Kirkuk. This is easy enough done. Start by taking a local taxi to the Koya Garage. From there, hire a shared taxi to Koya (ID5000), where you can catch another shared taxi to Sulaymaniyah (ID10,000).

Getting Around

Taxis within Erbil are cheap and plentiful. A short ride in town should cost between ID3000 to ID5000 and a bit more to the suburbs of Ainkawa and the airport.

AROUND ERBIL

Khanzad Castle

Located 15km north of Erbil on the road to Shaqlawa, Khanzad Castle dates back to the Soran Period. The stone castle features a squat turret on each of its four corners. Saw-toothed battlements top the turret and main building of the castle. The castle was recently renovated and now looks a little too new.

Just up the road from the castle is **Khanzad Hotel & Resort** (☎ 066-224 5273; Erbil-Shaqlawa Hwy; www.khanzadresort.com; info@khanzadresort.com; s/d/ste ID208,000/260,000/338,000;) a five-star hotel with all the comforts of home.

Salahaddin's Fortress

Salahaddin's Fortress (Kurdish: Qalat Salahaddin) is a spectacular ruin perched on a high ridge overlooking two valleys. A small path leads up to several stone walls and five turrets that survive intact. The history of this fortress, also called Deween Castle, is open to debate. According to the KRG Tourism Ministry, it was established by princes of the Zarzariya Tribe, who were associates of Shadi bin Marwan, the grandfather of 12th-century Kurdish conqueror Saladin (Salah ad-Din) – see p50.

Getting here is the hard part; there are no signs and even locals have never heard of the fortress. It's located about 15km north of the city of Salahaddin, itself about 30km northeast of Erbil. From Salahaddin, a scenic drive traverses through a goat-herding region of tiny villages with mud-brick homes.

Warning: The last 5km to the fortress is a gravel road lined by minefields, identified by piles of rocks painted red. Never venture off hard surfaces.

DUKAN دوكان

Dukan, 65km northwest of Sulaymaniyah, is a resort town on the banks of the Dukan Lake, the largest man-made lake in Iraq. It was created in 1959 when a dam was built on the Little Zab River to control flooding and provide hydroelectric power to the region. The massive, triangle-shaped lake behind the dam covers an area more than 150 sq km. The lake is a popular place for swimming and boating. Several hotels and holiday cabins have been built around the southern shores of the lake. On Fridays, the banks of the river below are swarmed with families enjoying the Kurdish national pastime of picnicking.

SULAYMANIYAH السليمانية

☎ 053 / pop 700,000

Beautiful and cosmopolitan Sulaymaniyah (Kurdish: Slemani) is Iraqi Kurdistan's second-largest city, and easily the most liberal and Westernised city in Iraq. Born in 1784, Sulaymaniyah is a young city by Mesopotamian standards. That youthful vibrancy gives Sulaymaniyah something of a European vibe – trendy, fashion forward, chic, sophisticated, free spirited. It has a strong arts and cultural scene with great museums and several world-class universities including the new American University of Iraq. Sulaymaniyah is a place of natural beauty, located at 883m above sea level on a rolling plain at the foothills of the Zagros Mountains, a mere 40km from the Iranian border. Get here now before the masses discover this gem.

IRAQ

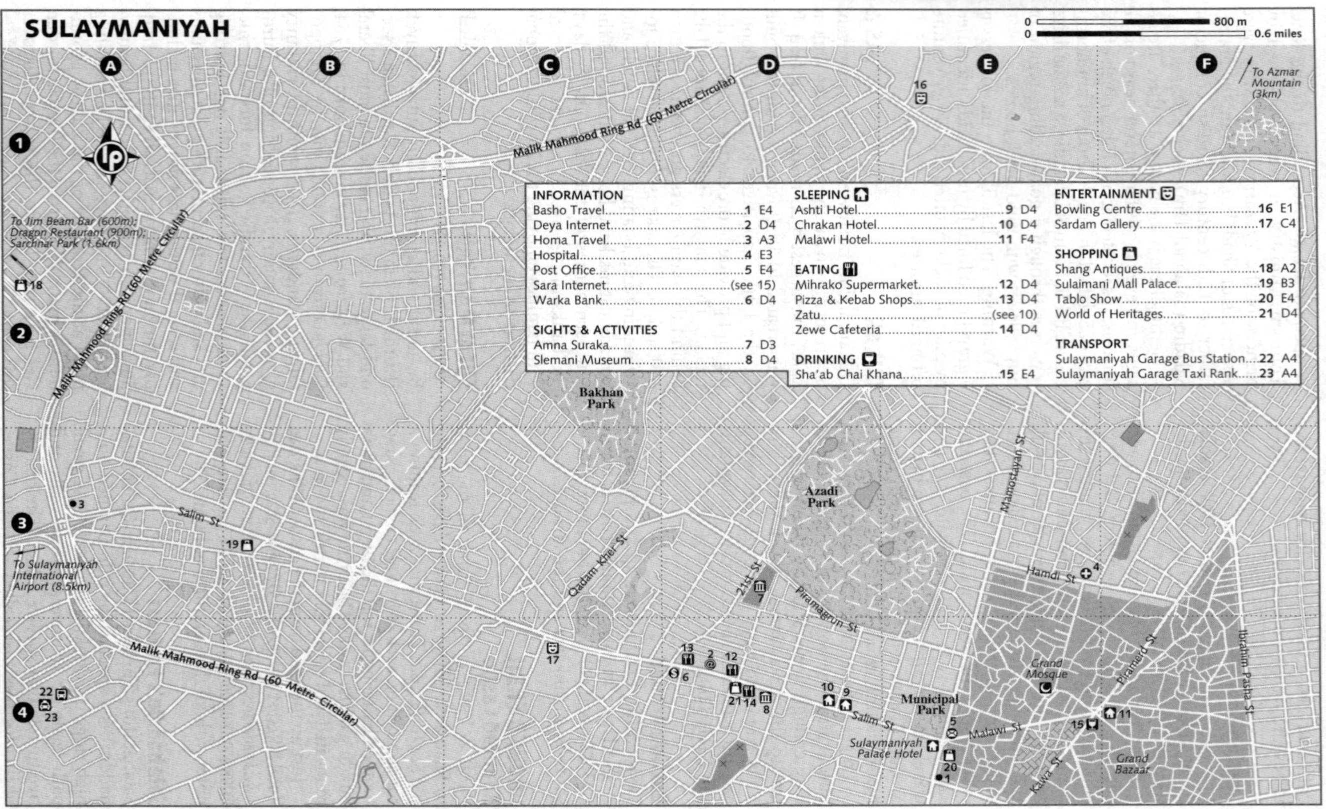
IRAQ
SULAYMANIYAH
0 800 m
0 0.6 miles
To Azmar Mountain (3km)
To Jim Beam Bar (600m); Dragon Restaurant (900m); Sarchnar Park (1.6km)
To Sulaymaniyah International Airport (8.5km)
Malik Mahmood Ring Rd (60 Metre Circular)
Salim St
Qadam Kher St
21st St
Piramagrun St
Mamostayan St
Hamdi St
Malawi St
Piramerd St
Kawa St
Ibrahim Pasha St
Bakhan Park
Azadi Park
Municipal Park
Grand Mosque
Grand Bazaar
Sulaymaniyah Palace Hotel
INFORMATION
Basho Travel 1 E4
Deya Internet 2 D4
Homa Travel 3 A3
Hospital 4 E3
Post Office 5 E4
Sara Internet (see 15)
Warka Bank 6 D4
SIGHTS & ACTIVITIES
Amna Suraka 7 D3
Slemani Museum 8 D4
SLEEPING
Ashti Hotel 9 D4
Chrakan Hotel 10 D4
Malawi Hotel 11 F4
EATING
Mihrako Supermarket 12 D4
Pizza & Kebab Shops 13 D4
Zatu (see 10)
Zewe Cafeteria 14 D4
DRINKING
Sha'ab Chai Khana 15 E4
ENTERTAINMENT
Bowling Centre 16 E1
Sardam Gallery 17 C4
SHOPPING
Shang Antiques 18 A2
Sulaimani Mall Palace 19 B3
Tablo Show 20 E4
World of Heritages 21 D4
TRANSPORT
Sulaymaniyah Garage Bus Station 22 A4
Sulaymaniyah Garage Taxi Rank 23 A4

History

If Iraq is the cradle of civilisation, Sulaymaniyah is a newborn baby. It was founded in 1784 by Kurdish prince Ibrahim Pasha Babanm, who named it for his father Sulaiman Pasha. During WWI, the city was the centre of Kurdish nationalism. In May 1919 Sheikh Mahmmud Barzanji led the first revolt against the British Mandate of Iraq. Barzanji was defeated and exiled to India. In 1922 he returned to Sulaymaniyah and declared himself the first king of Kurdistan. The short-lived kingdom ended when the British again defeated Barzanji in 1924.

The PUK, one of two major political parties in Iraqi Kurdistan, was founded in Sulaymaniyah in 1975. During and after the Iran-Iraq War, Saddam Hussein brutalised Sulaymaniyah's residents until the Kurdish uprising of 1991.

In 1994 civil war broke out between forces of the PUK and the KDP. The fighting between the two went nowhere until 1996, when the KDP made a deal with the devil: with the help of Saddam's Iraqi forces, the KDP captured the PUK-held cities of Erbil and Sulaymaniyah, driving the PUK into Iran. Much of Sulaymaniyah was destroyed in the fighting. Peace finally prevailed in 1998 when Washington mediated a power-sharing deal between KDP leader Massoud Barzani and PUK leader Jalal Talabani.

Today, 'Sulay' as its called by locals, has been rebuilt into a model city. It is the provincial capital of Sulaymaniyah (the capital and province go by the same name), the cultural centre of the Sorani-speaking Kurds, and an important economic centre of Iraqi Kurdistan. Since the 2003 war began, Sulaymaniyah has managed to avoid the violence that has plagued much of the country, making it one of the safest and most-prosperous cities in Iraq.

Orientation

Sulaymaniyah is shaped like a pair of puckered lips, outlined by the Malik Mahmood ring road (also known as the 60 Metre Circular). The eastern skyline is dominated by the striking Zagros Mountains. The main commercial thoroughfare is Salim St, which runs roughly west to east uphill to the city centre; numbered streets run north to south.

The city centre's main intersection is Sulaymaniyah Circle, where Salim, Mamostayan and Malawi Sts all meet. The Sulaymaniyah Palace Hotel, a major area landmark, is on the southwest corner of this intersection. East of Sulaymaniyah Circle, a giant arched gate leads to Malawai St, a mostly-pedestrian road that runs through the bazaar and old quarter.

The city's largest park, Azadi, is located smack in the middle of the city, about 1km northwest of the Sulaymaniyah Circle.

Sulay is a very hilly city; get ready to walk up lots of steep inclines.

Information

EMERGENCY

Hospital (☎ 327 0511; cnr Pashai Kora & Hamdi Sts)
Police and fire (☎ 104)
Police headquarters (☎ 210 4058, 312 2811; Salim St)

INTERNET ACCESS

Deya Internet (☎ 0770 192 9325; Salim St; per hr ID1500; 9am-midnight) One block west of Mihrako Supermarket.
Sara Internet (Kawa St; sarahinernet2008@hotmail.com; per hr ID2000; 8am-11pm)

MONEY

Most banks can wire money internationally. **Warka Bank** (Salim St; 9am-4pm, closed Fri) offers Western Union services.

POST

The **post office** (☎ 313 0873; Malawi St; 8am-1.30pm), located near the bazaar and run by the Kurdish postal service, is fast, cheap and reliable. It costs ID1000 to mail a postcard to Europe, and ID1500 to Australasia and North America. Postcards take four or five days to get to Europe, and about a week to 10 days to Australia and the USA.

TELEPHONE

KurdTel payphones are common throughout Sulaymaniyah. Most require prepaid cards, available from many shops and street vendors. Mobile-phone service is very reliable. The main service provider is AsiaCell. SIM cards are widely available in the bazaar and high street shops.

TRAVEL AGENCIES

Basho Travel (☎ 312 4730, 0770 214 3070; basho.travel@yahoo.com; Mamostayan St; 10am-6pm) One block south of Sulaymaniyah Circle.

Homa Travel (☎ 319 0111; Azmar Air Bldg, cnr Salim & Malik Mahmoud Sts; ⌚ 10am-6pm, closed Fri)

Sights

AMNA SURAKA (RED SECURITY)

The **Amna Suraka** (21st St; admission free; ⌚ 9am-noon & 2-4pm Sat-Thu), Kurdish for Red Security, was once a house of unspeakable horrors. Under Saddam Hussein's regime, this imposing red building served as the northern headquarters of the notorious Iraqi Intelligence Service, or the Mukhabarat. Thousands of people, mainly Kurds, were imprisoned and tortured here. Many more simply vanished. In 1991 the Kurdish Peshmerga attacked and liberated the prison. In 2003 Hero Ibrahim Ahmed, wife of Iraqi President Jalal Talabani, spearheaded a plan to turn the building into the country's first war-crimes museum. The Amna Suraka now stands out as the most impressive museum in Iraq.

Upon entering the complex gates, the first thing you notice is the **Amna Suraka** building itself. Its red facade has been kept exactly as it appeared after the 1991 uprising, pockmarked from bullet holes, shattered windows and blackened from fires. The courtyard contains a **weapons display** of Iraqi tanks, artillery, mortars and other instruments of death. The first stop indoors is the **Hall of Mirrors**, a 50m-long narrow hallway lined by 182,000 shards of mirrored glass, one for every victim of Saddam's Anfal campaign (see p215). The ceiling twinkles with 5000 lights, one for every Kurdish village destroyed under Saddam. The next room features a replica of a traditional **Kurdish village home**.

Passing through exterior corridors covered by barbed wire, you enter the main building that contains several **prison cells** and **torture chambers**. Many rooms contain lifelike sculptures of Kurdish prisoners, created by local artist Kamaran Omer. In one particularly gruesome exhibit, a Kurdish man is hanging by his wrists from a metal hook with electrical wires attached to his earlobes while a recording of an interrogation plays. The basement of the museum is a graphic **photo gallery** showing the aftermath of Saddam's chemical attack on Halabja.

Museum guides, many whom speak English, conduct free tours of the complex. Visitors should come prepared for an experience likely to be disturbing and difficult to forget.

SLEMANI MUSEUM

The **Slemani** (☎ 312 0609; Salim St; admission free; ⌚ 8.30am-2.30pm, closed Fri), or Sulaymaniyah Museum, is a timeline of Mesopotamian history dating back to the Palaeolithic Age from 15,000 BC. The museum is divided into several galleries featuring an array of archaeological artefacts. Some of the more interesting finds include a ceramic coffin containing the skeleton of a 6000-year-old woman found near Dohuk, and a Greek statue of Hercules dating to 334 BC. There is also a fine display of Islamic ceramic arts from the Islamic Golden Age. Most of the exhibits have Kurdish and English signs.

PARKS OF SULAYMANIYAH

Sulaymaniyah is a green city blessed with many beautiful public parks.

Azadi Park (Parki Azadi; ☎ 0770 149 6061, 329 0690; admission free; amusement park ID1000, rides ID500-1000; ⌚ 8am-midnight) is Sulaymaniyah's answer to Central Park and Coney Island all rolled into one. It's a huge place filled with gardens, playgrounds, restaurants, cafés and a small lake. It's a popular place for jogging, picnicking and people-watching. The best day to come is Friday night, when the park is packed with families and young people. The northwest corner of the park is a separate, fenced-in amusement park with a Ferris wheel, kiddie rides and plenty of junk-food vendors.

Municipal Park (Salim St at Sulaymaniyah Circle) is a small park popular with the lunchtime crowd from nearby Sulaymaniyah University.

Northwest of the city, just outside the ring road, is **Sarchnar Park** (admission ID1000; ⌚ 8am-midnight), a large family park with outdoor garden restaurants, a small amusement park with the obligatory Ferris wheel, and a sad little zoo containing such 'exotic' caged animals as dogs, pigeons, squirrels and goats.

Further afield, **Azmar Mountain**, about 6km northeast and above the city, is a stunning picnic spot with million-dinar views.

THE GRAND BAZAAR

Sulaymaniyah's **bazaar** (along Malawi St, ⌚ 8am-6pm) may be the largest traditional market in Iraqi Kurdistan. You can find anything here including and up to the proverbial kitchen sink. This place is HUGE, stretching nearly 1.5km along Malawi and Goran Sts from the Sulaymaniyah Palace Hotel to Ibrahim Pasha St. The bazaar is an intermingled mix of tiny shops, traditional market stalls and street vendors.

The real heart of the market is the **covered bazaar** between Malawi and Kawa Sts – a chaotic and colourful treat for all five senses. The smells of spices and kebabs waft through the dark narrow alleys, beckoning shoppers into the depths of the bazaar. Claustrophobics should be aware that the tight quarters can get very crowded. As most of the market is covered, it's very easy to get lost; follow the light at the end of the tunnels to get back to Malawi or Kawa Sts.

Sleeping

There are lots of budget choices in the bazaar, particularly near the roundabout that intersects Kawa, Malawi, Goran and Piramerd Sts. Many modern hotels are located along Salim St.

ourpick Chrakan Hotel (☎ 312 6991; Slemani St; s/d ID30,000/35,000; ❄) A fantastic budget choice in a convenient location. The large, clean rooms all have a fridge, TV and air-con. Street-front rooms have balconies but can get a bit noisy. There's also a small bar and restaurant on the premises. Super owner Omar speaks English, Kurdish, Arabic, Swedish, Turkish and Hebrew!

Malawi Hotel (☎ 312 0147; cnr Malawi & Kawa Sts; r ID30,000; ❄) This ageing but clean hotel is located in the heart of the bazaar. The surprisingly quiet rooms have TV, air-con and Western toilets.

Ashti Hotel (☎ in the UK 704 312 0435; ashtihotel@hotmail.com; cnr Salim & 15th Sts; r ID107,000; ❄) This ugly, dated and overpriced hotel is the most popular upscale hotel in town. It has a nice bar and restaurant.

Eating

Many new and modern restaurants are located on Salim St. The bazaar is the place to go for cheap grub. There is also a small strip mall of **pizza and kebab shops** near the corner of Salim and 21st Sts that is popular in the evenings.

Mihrako Supermarket (☎ 210 1414; www.mihrako.com; Salim St below Mihrako Hotel; 🕑 9am-9pm) Stock up on provisions at this giant grocery store that has hundreds of products from around the world. The real attraction is its French bakery, the first in Sulaymaniyah.

Zewe Cafeteria (☎ 0770 153 6949; Salim St next to Slemani Museum; mains ID3000-8000; 🕑 9am-10pm) Zewe is a popular lunch spot with traditional Iraqi and Kurdish dishes. The lamb *quzi* is fan-fracking-tastic! The upstairs is a desert and coffee shop.

ourpick Zatu (☎ 158 1363; cnr Salim & 15th Sts; mains ID3000-6000; 🕑 noon-midnight) This great food-find is located directly under Chrakan

IRAQ

THE AMERICANIZATION OF MC-KURDISTAN *César Soriano*

'Yo, man! You like 50 Cent?' I turned in my tracks and did a double take at the grinning little boy wearing blue Levi's jeans. I wasn't sure which was more shocking – the fact that this Iraqi Kurdish kid on a street corner in Dohuk could speak English, or that he knew the music of American rapper 50 Cent. Since the 2003 US invasion, Iraqi Kurds have become obsessed with Americana. It's so prevalent that some parts of Kurdistan look more like Kentucky. There's no KFC in Iraqi Kurdistan yet, but 'Kan Tacky Fried Chikin' (sic) is a popular item on many restaurant menus. And Sulaymaniyah doesn't have a McDonald's, but it does have a MaDonal.

Across Iraqi Kurdistan, billboards advertise such products as Microsoft, Motorola, Tide laundry detergent and a FedEx knock-off service called PelePost. In 2008 Erbil opened the first Coca Cola plant in Iraq. Need a car? The Kurdish capital has the country's first Chevrolet auto dealership; just look for the bright yellow, US$60,000 Hummer H2 parked out front. Competitor Ford has dealerships here and in Sulaymaniyah. Considering college in Kurdistan? Wealthy young Iraqis are flocking to enrol at the new American University of Iraq in Sulaymaniyah, where tuition to the private university costs US$10,000 per year. Ready to settle down? The American Village in Kanzad, 15km north of Erbil, is modelled after an upscale American suburb, complete with American-like prices – US$585,000 for the top-end 'palace' model.

During my travels, I constantly looked for places to get away from this American invasion of Iraq. So in Erbil, I trekked up a narrow stairwell to reach the citadel, home of one of the oldest civilisations in the world. As I'm walking up, something on the retaining wall catches my eye. There, spray-painted in English, a bit of graffiti slaps me back to the reality of the new Iraq: 'I LOVE 50 CENT'.

Hotel and famous for its tasty kebabs. Other menu options include *shwarmas*, grilled chicken and pizza.

Dragon Restaurant (☎ 319 4440; Sarchnar Rd; mains ID5000-20,000; ⏰ 11am-2.30pm & 6pm-10.30pm) Chinese food anybody? Dragon serves up traditional favourites such as stir-fried beef, spicy shrimp and fried noodles. The sweet-and-sour chicken is to die for. The great food makes up for lack of decor or customer service.

Drinking

Staying in tonight? There are dozens of liquor stores around town, particularly on Salim and Mamostayan Sts.

Jim Beam Bar (☎ 0770 533 9449; ⏰ 6pm-1am) Its real name is Nenkasy, named after the legendary Mosul woman who was the first to brew beer in Iraq. But locals know this place better as the Jim Beam Bar because every square inch of the interior is covered in Jim Beam whiskey memorabilia. It's situated less than 1km west of the city centre.

Sha'ab Chai Khana (Kawa St; tea ID500; ⏰ 6am-7pm) Just to the right of Sara Internet, through an unmarked door, is the most famous men's teahouse in town. It's a traditional smoky establishment where old guys slap dominos loudly on the table and young blokes watch football on the telly. Peruse through the many old books and photos of Sulaymaniyah while drinking tiny, tulip-shaped cups of sweet tea. Sorry ladies, men only.

Entertainment

Bowling Centre (0770 366 8705; Malik Mahmoud St; bowling ID5000; ⏰ noon-midnight) Opened in 2007, this mammoth ten-pin bowling alley has 16 lanes, a bar, snack shop and outdoor café. The huge upstairs hall contains a video arcade, pool tables, foosball (table football), air hockey, an internet café and bumper cars. On weekend nights, this is *the* place to see and be seen.

Sardam Gallery (Salim St; admission free). This new art gallery, inside the Sardam Publishing House, features rotating exhibits by local Kurdish artists. On Saturday afternoons, the gallery screens US and European movies in their original language, with Arabic subtitles.

Shopping

You can find most anything under the sun at the Grand Bazaar (p240).

For something different, **The World of Heritages** (☎ 313 1582; Salim St; ⏰ 9am-noon & 3-7pm, closed Fri) is an eccentric shop selling unique antiques, souvenirs and trinkets.

Shang Antiques (☎ 319 5444, 0770 152 3256; Sarchnar Rd; ⏰ 9am-9pm, closed Fri) has a wonderful collection of gold and silver jewellery, antiques and women's clothing.

For carpets, **Tablo Show** (☎ 0770 155 0460, 312 1788; Mamostayan St across from Sulaymaniyah Palace Hotel; ⏰ 8am-8pm) has a nice selection of handmade carpets at reasonable prices.

Sulaimani Mall Palace (Salim St; ⏰ 9am-6pm) is a gleaming new shopping mall selling all the latest Western fashions.

Getting There & Away

International flights arrive at **Sulaymaniyah International Airport** (www.sulairport.net), about 15km west of the city.

Long-distance shared taxis and buses arrive and depart from **Sulaymaniyah Garage**, located in the southwest corner of the city just outside the ring road. Drivers will be standing outside their vehicles, yelling the name of their destinations. To Erbil, avoid dangerous Kirkuk by taking a shared taxi to Koya (ID10,000), where you can hire another shared taxi to Erbil (ID5000).

Getting Around

Taxis around town are cheap and plentiful and should cost between ID2000 and ID5000 depending on time and destination. Always agree on a price and route before getting in.

AHMADAWA احمداواه

The resort village of Ahmadawa, 62km southeast of Sulaymaniyah near the Iranian border, is a wonderful place of natural beauty with plenty of opportunities for hiking, swimming and picnicking. Hidden in a deep and narrow green gorge, the resort is surrounded by walnut, pomegranate and fig trees, attracting visitors to their cool shade. A small cascading river runs along the base of the canyon. From the entrance of the gorge, hike up the 3km very rough dirt road to reach a spectacular 30m-high waterfall.

On Fridays, busloads of Kurds in colourful traditional dress descend on Ahmadawa to enjoy weekend picnics, filling the canyon with Kurdish music and the smells of barbecues. There are several kebab restaurants at the entrance to the gorge.

HALABJA حلبجة

Mention the name 'Halabja' to Iraqi Kurds and you'll be met with looks of sadness and sorrow. What happened in Halabja on the morning of 16 March 1988 was one of the darkest days in Kurdish history.

Halabja was once a bustling city. In the final days of the Iran-Iraq war, it found itself on the front lines, occupied by Iranian troops and Kurdish Peshmerga forces allied with Iran. On the morning of 16 March 1988, Saddam Hussein's Ba'athist forces launched a counter strike, bombarding the city with conventional air strikes and artillery. At about 3pm, Iraqi jets flying low overhead began dropping an unusual kind of bomb that left a smell of sweet apples – chemical weapons. In less than 30 minutes, 5000 men, women and children were dead and 7000 injured. Human Rights Watch has declared the massacre as an act of genocide.

More than 20 years on, Halabja has never fully recovered. It's a poor, run-down village with high rates of poverty and unemployment. As you enter the town, the first thing you'll notice is a small roadside **statue** modelled on the most famous photograph of the massacre, depicting a lifeless elderly man on the ground shielding his dead grandson. The road behind the statue leads to the controversial **Monument of Halabja Martyrs**, a 30m-tall cenotaph and museum. In 2006 villagers stormed the monument and set it on fire, angry that the government was spending money on the dead instead of helping the living. The monument is being rebuilt and scheduled to open in early 2009.

In **Halabja Cemetery**, thousands of victims of the chemical attack are buried in **mass graves** under giant, black-and-white marble blocks. Nearby, a grassy field contains hundreds of neatly arranged white **headstones** bearing the names of the dead. A sign at the entrance of the cemetery is unforgiving: 'It is not allowed for Ba'athists to enter.'

IRAQ DIRECTORY

ACCOMMODATION

For a developing country emerging from decades of war, Iraq is a surprisingly expensive place. Hotel rooms that went for US$5 before the war are now going for US$50. It all comes down to supply and demand.

For the purpose of this guide, we are assuming that readers are only travelling to Iraqi Kurdistan.

The Kurdish Regional Government is focusing all its energies on building four- and five-star luxury hotels. Hostels and campgrounds are nonexistent. Thankfully, family-run budget hotels are quite common. Older hotels usually have squat toilets, but Western toilets are increasingly common, especially in newer midrange and top-end establishments. With the exception of Kurdish mountain resorts, nearly all hotels in Iraq have air conditioning – a necessity in this desert climate. Unfortunately, electricity is still a luxury (see below) – the more you pay, the more likely your hotel will have a generator.

BUSINESS HOURS

Officially, government offices, banks and private businesses are usually open 8am to 6pm, Sunday to Wednesday and until 1.30pm on Thursday. Unofficially, business hours in Iraq are whenever the employees feel like showing up to work. Go with the flow. In the summer, bazaars and restaurants are open well past midnight, when Iraqis come out to enjoy the cooler weather.

DANGERS & ANNOYANCES

We've said it once (p213) and we'll say it again: Iraq is a war zone. In Iraqi Kurdistan, violence and crime are rare, but not unheard of. Take the same precautions you'd take in any big city. Open hostility towards Western visitors – including Americans – is rare in Iraqi Kurdistan. In fact, Americans are treated like heroes by Kurds. The biggest annoyance is the sheer amount of security officers including Kurdish Peshmerga soldiers, policemen and undercover intelligence officers. Expect to be stopped and questioned several times during your trip through Iraqi Kurdistan. Normally it's just a minor inconvenience. But on occasion you may run into a few overzealous officials. Remain calm and follow the officer's instructions. It's a good idea to have an Iraqi contact who can vouch for you.

ELECTRICITY

Electrical current is 230 AC, 50Hz. Wall sockets are the three-prong, British-type plug. Since 2003, war, looting and neglect have devastated Iraq's infrastructure. Twenty-four hour power is rare, especially in Baghdad. Most homes and businesses supplement the lack of power with generators.

EMBASSIES & CONSULATES

Most countries strongly advice their citizens not to travel to Iraq. Foreign embassies in Iraq can only provide limited consular services, if any. Travel at your own risk.

Australia (☎ in Australia 02-6261 3305; www.iraq.embassy.gov.au; Baghdad International Zone)
Czech Republic (☎ 01-541 7136, 01-542 4868; www.mzv.cz/baghdad; baghdad@embassy.mzv.cz; al-Mansour district, Baghdad)
Germany (☎ 01-543 1470; www.bagdad.diplo.de; al-Mansour district, Baghdad)
Netherlands (☎ 01-778 2571, in the US 914-360-3982; iraq.nlembassy.org; bad@minbuza.nl; Baghdad International Zone)
Romania (☎ 01-778 2860; ambrobagd@yahoo.com; Arassat Al-Hindia St, Baghdad)
Switzerland (☎ 01-719 3091; bag.vertretung@eda.admin.ch; Baghdad)
UK (☎ 0790 191 1684; www.britishembassy.gov.uk/iraq; britishconsulbaghdad@yahoo.co.uk; Baghdad International Zone)
USA (Map pp220-1; ☎ in the US 240-553-0581 ext 2413, 0770 443 0287; iraq.usembassy.gov; austemb.baghdad@dfat.gov.au; Baghdad International Zone) Note, the first phone number listed here requires you to dial the US, but it rings in Baghdad.

GAY & LESBIAN TRAVELLERS

Homosexuality is illegal in Iraq. A 2006 UN human-rights report found that armed Islamic groups and militias have been actively targeting gays and lesbians with violence and murder. Families have engaged in so-called honour killings of gay relatives. That said, there is no reason why gay and lesbian travellers should not visit Iraq as long as they refrain from overt displays of affection in public. For up-to-date information, visit iraqilgbtuk.blogspot.com.

HOLIDAYS

Shiite Muslims always seem to be mourning the death of some religious figure. In addition to the main Islamic holidays (p628), Iraq also observes the following:

Nowruz (21 March) Kurdish New Year, Iraqi Kurdistan only.
Baghdad Liberation Day (9 April) Anniversary of the fall of Saddam Hussein's regime in 2003.
Ceasefire Day (8 August) End of Iran-Iraq war.

INTERNET ACCESS

Most big-city internet cafés, which typically keep very long hours, are filled with cigarette smoke and charge about ID1000 to ID2000 per hour.

INTERNET RESOURCES

Backpacking Iraqi Kurdistan (backpackiraq.blogspot.com) The original and still the best blog on travelling in Kurdish Iraq.
British Museum Iraq Project (www.britishmuseum.org/iraq) The British Museum's project to protect and preserve Iraq's cultural heritage.
Institute for War & Peace Reporting (www.uniraq.org) Independent reports by Iraqi journalists.
Iraq Updates (iraqupdates.com) Latest news and incident reports.
Iraqi Kurdistan Tourism Ministry (tourismkurdistan.com)
Iraqi Ministry of Foreign Affairs (mofa.gov.iq) Includes news and listings of Iraqi embassies abroad.
Iraq Slogger (iraqslogger.com) News and scoops from Iraq.
Kurdish Regional Government (krg.org)
Operation Iraqi Freedom (www.mnf-iraq.com) Official website of coalition military forces in Iraq.
The Other Iraq (theotheriraq.com)
Soma Digest (soma-digest.com) English-language Kurdish newspaper.
UNAMI (www.uniraq.org) UN Assistance Mission for Iraq.

LANGUAGE

Arabic and Kurdish are the official languages of Iraq. Arabic is spoken by 80% of the population. The Kurds speak a language that is widely known as Kurdish, but in reality Kurds speak one of two Indo-European languages: Kurmanji and Sorani. Sorani is spoken in the cities of Erbil and Sulaymaniyah, while Kurmanji is spoken in Dohuk. Persian is widely spoken along the Iranian border. Other minor languages include Assyrian, Assyrian Neo Aramaic, Chaldean Neo-Aramaic and Turkmani. English is widely spoken in urban centres. In Iraqi Kurdistan, English education is now compulsory, so many young people understand at least a bit of English.

MONEY

With a few rare exceptions, Iraq is a cash country. You should plan to bring enough cash – preferably US dollars – to last your entire trip.

The official unit of currency is the Iraqi Dinar (ID). Current banknotes include 50,

250, 500, 1000, 5000, 10,000 and 25,000 dinars. Coins are no longer used. US dollars are also widely accepted. Businesses often list prices in both dinars and dollars. US notes should be undamaged and printed after 2003.

In Iraqi Kurdistan, dollars, euros, British pounds and Turkish lira can usually be changed quite easily. Anything else and you're pushing your luck. Money can be changed in banks, but for the best exchange rate, hit one of the street-corner exchange stands and look for the guys holding giant wads of cash. Current exchange rates are posted on finance.yahoo.com/currency.

The following were official bank rates at the time of writing:

Country	Unit	Iraqi dinar (ID)
Euro zone	€1	1547
UK	UK£1	1765
USA	US$1	1194

ATMs are starting to pop up, but at the time of writing, most only work for accounts held in Iraq. Credit cards and travellers cheques are even more useless. Many banks now offer international transfers. MoneyGram and Western Union money wire services can be found in Baghdad, Erbil and also in Sulaymaniyah.

Tipping & Bargaining

As in other parts of the Middle East, tipping, or baksheesh, is a fact of life in Iraq. Waiters and taxi drivers expect 10%. Bargaining is expected in bazaars, and tolerated by taxi drivers and family-run hotels and shops.

POST

In Iraqi Kurdistan, the postal service is fast, cheap and reliable. It costs ID1000 to mail a postcard to Europe and ID1500 to Australasia and North America. Postcards take four or five days to get to Europe, and about a week to 10 days to Australia and the USA.

In Arab Iraq, forget about it.

TELEPHONE

The country code for Iraq is ☎964, followed by the local area code (minus the zero), then the subscriber number. Due to the poor state of Iraq's landline telephones, most residents and businesses rely on mobile phones. Considering the mobile phone has only been around since 2003, Iraq has surprisingly reliable and widespread network. The main service providers are Iraqna, Asia-Cell and Korek. SIM cards and pay-as-you-go phones are widely available. Pay phones are only common in Sulaymaniyah.

TOILETS

Most toilets in public places and older hotels are the squat variety. Toilet paper is rarely provided, but readily available in grocery stores and bazaars. Most newer hotels and buildings have Western-style 'throne' toilets.

WOMEN TRAVELLERS

Iraqi Kurdistan is safe for female travellers, and women are generally treated with courtesy and respect. Some women who have recently travelled solo in Iraq have reported that they had no problems. Still, we recommend that it is best to always travel in pairs or groups. As in most parts of the Middle East, it's important to dress conservatively – no bare shoulders or legs, cleavage or other excessive skin should be on display. Iraqi Kurdistan is a secular society, so there is no need to cover your hair. Western clothing is common throughout Iraq and in liberal Sulaymaniyah, blue jeans and tight tops are de rigueur.

VISAS

Visas are required for everyone entering Iraq.

The Republic of Iraq issues visas for Arab regions of the country such as Baghdad and Basra, and they are only available to people with official business in the country such as journalists, diplomats, contractors and aid workers. Visas must be obtained prior to departing your home country and cost US$20 to US$50.

The Kurdish Regional Government issues its own tourist visa, good for travelling within Iraqi Kurdistan only. Citizens of most countries including Australia, the EU, New Zealand and USA are automatically issued free, 10-day tourist visas at the point of entry. Travellers of Arab descent need prior premission to enter Iraqi Kurdistan. Thirty-day visa extensions can be obtained at the Directorate of Residency in Erbil.

TRANSPORT IN IRAQ

Iraq has a good network of roads. A rail line connecting Mosul, Baghdad and Basra recently reopened. But at the time of writing, Arab Iraq was not safe for travel. Independent travellers should stick to Iraqi Kurdistan only.

GETTING THERE & AWAY

For information on visas and entry requirements, see p245.

Air

Iraqi Kurdistan has two international airports: Erbil and Sulaymaniyah. Tourist visas to Iraqi Kurdistan are issued upon arrival. Only those who absolutely *must* fly into Baghdad should do so. Flights into Baghdad often land in a hair-raising corkscrew manoeuvre to avoid the threat of missile attacks. Flying anywhere into Iraq is very expensive due to high insurance costs and limited competition.

Royal Jordanian (www.rj.com) and **Iraqi Airways** (www.iraqiairways.co.uk) fly to Erbil, Sulaymaniyah, Baghdad and Basra from both Amman and Dubai. **Turkish Airlines** (www.thy.com) flies between İstanbul and Baghdad once a day, five days a week. **Austrian Airlines** (www.aua.com) flies between Erbil and Vienna; **Azmar Air** (www.azmarairline.org) serves Sulaymaniyah from İstanbul and Dubai. There are also a handful of fly-by-night charter airlines.

Land

Iraq is bordered by six countries. At the time of writing, the only safe overland crossing is the Ibrahim Khalil border crossing between Silopi, Turkey and Zakho, Iraq. It may be possible to enter or exit Iraqi Kurdistan through the Haji Omaran Border with a prearranged Iranian visa, but this has not been tested by us. All other borders are dangerous no-go zones.

IBRAHIM KHALIL BORDER CROSSING

Arriving into Silopi by bus, you'll be met at the station by a crowd of taxi drivers yelling, 'Zakho! Zakho!' Pick any one; the price is set at US$50 per taxi. Bring 10 photocopies of your passport's photograph page. From Silopi, it's a five-minute drive to the border, where your driver will manoeuvre through a maze of checkpoints and handle the paperwork. You may be searched and interviewed by Turkish border guards. Warning: the Kurdish issue is a very sensitive topic in Turkey. Never refer to your destination as 'Kurdistan'. It's 'Iraq' and 'Iraq' only!

Finally, you'll reach the big 'Welcome to Iraqi Kurdistan Region' sign. You'll be led into a small office, offered tea and interviewed by one or more Kurdish Peshmerga officials. Be honest. It helps to have the name and phone number of an Iraqi Kurdish contact. After receiving your 10-day tourist-visa stamp, your driver will drop you off at a nearby taxi lot where you must change into an Iraqi taxi to continue to Zakho, Dohuk or beyond.

GETTING AROUND

Air

Iraqi Airways flies several domestic routes including between Erbil and Sulaymaniyah, but it is so unreliable it's not worth it.

Bus

Iraq's bus transport network is very poor. The few routes that exist are crowded and unsafe. Travellers in Iraqi Kurdistan are advised not to use intercity buses because they often travel through or stop in dangerous cities such as Mosul and Kirkuk.

Taxi

Taxis are the main mode of public transport in Iraq. In cities, they are cheap and plentiful, usually costing no more than ID5000. For intercity travel within Iraqi Kurdistan, you have two choices: private taxi or cheaper, shared taxis. Shared taxis depart and arrive from a city 'garage', or large parking lot; drivers will be standing outside their vehicle, yelling the name of their destination. Shared taxis leave when they are full. Expect to pay between ID5000 to ID20,000. When travelling between major cities in Iraqi Kurdistan, ensure you stay within Kurdish Peshmerga-controlled territory. Agree on price and route before getting in.

Israel & the Palestinian Territories

There's an old Israeli backpackers' joke that goes something like this:

An Israeli backpacker in Thailand gets talking about his homeland with a local café owner. 'How many Israelis are there, anyway?' the café owner asks.

'About seven million,' the backpacker replies.

The man thinks for a minute. 'And how many are there in Israel?'

It's hard to believe that a country as diminutive as Israel, along with the even smaller Palestinian Territories, has so often taken centre stage in world politics and religion. But with Jerusalem at the region's disputed heart, the Golan Heights at its disputed head, and Gaza dipping its disputed toe into the crystalline Mediterranean Sea, it's not hard to see why.

A trip to this area, whether you come for the spiritual, the political or the decidedly hedonistic is a high-paced ride that will challenge your preconceptions of this beautiful, friendly yet deeply troubled land. Ponder the foundation stones of Christianity, the promised land of the Jews, and some of the holiest places in all Islam. Bathe in three seas – the Med, the Dead and the Red – or do a spot of breaststroke where Jesus once walked on water. Hike mountains, shifting dunes and desert craters. Marvel at ancient fortresses and consider contentious modern 'security walls'. Go dancing in Tel Aviv, then seek out silence in a Palestinian monastery or mosque.

Most of all, talk to the Israeli Jews, Arabs, Ethiopians, Palestinian Muslims and Christians, Druze, Samaritans, Bedouins and others; the children of refugee camps and teen soldiers who people the troubled landscape. It's the best way to gain your own perspective, quite apart from the shocking news headlines and propaganda, on why Israel and the Palestinian Territories' complicated, volatile but intoxicating reputation far outstrips its geographical size.

FAST FACTS

- **Area** 20,770 sq km; Gaza Strip and the West Bank 6220 sq km
- **Capital** Jerusalem (disputed)
- **Country code** ☎ 972
- **Languages** Hebrew, Arabic
- **Money** new Israeli shekel (NIS); US$1 = 3.48NIS; €1 = 5.45NIS
- **Official name** Medinat Yisra'el (State of Israel)
- **Population** 7.1 million; Gaza Strip and the West Bank 4.1 million

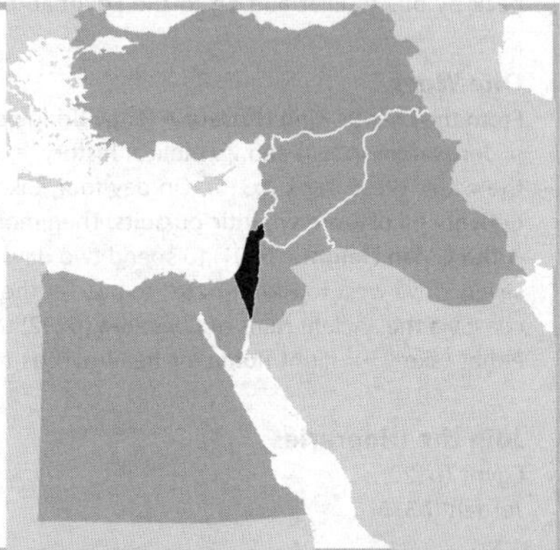

CLIMATE & WHEN TO GO

Israel and the Palestinian Territories enjoy a warm Mediterranean climate for much of the year, although winter (November to March) sees rain and cool temperatures in coastal areas, chilly nights in Jerusalem, and the occasional snowfall in the north, especially up in the Golan Heights. Summer (April to October) is hot and dry throughout the region and peaks in July and August, when daytime temperatures of 45°C aren't uncommon. In the evenings – especially in the highlands and deserts – temperatures may drop as much as 30°C to 40°C below the daytime highs. See Climate Charts, p625, for more.

The high tourist seasons in Israel are July and August and during the Jewish religious holidays; in the Palestinian Territories, the only peaks to speak of are in Bethlehem around Christmas and Easter. Bear in mind that if you visit during Israeli religious holidays, many businesses may be closed, public transport is limited and accommodation prices double or triple. During the fasting period of Ramadan (see p628 for when Ramadan occurs each year), it's impolite to eat, drink or smoke in public during daylight hours in the Palestinian Territories and East Jerusalem. See p328 for details on holidays.

HISTORY

Though the history of Israel and the Palestinian Territories is as fraught with disagreement as its troubled present, it's generally agreed that the first inhabitants of the land were the Canaanites, who migrated here as early as the 20th century BC. Around 2800 BC, Pharaonic Egypt claimed Canaan as part of its empire, and it was still under Egyptian control when, 1000 years later, Abraham led his nomadic tribe – the Israelites – here from Mesopotamia, to what is now known in Israel as the Judean Hills. Though his descendents were forced to move on to Egypt due to drought and famine, Moses (grandson of Abraham) led them back, via Sinai, in 1250 BC, to end their servitude under Egyptian rule.

At around the same time, however, the maritime civilisation known as the Philistines arrived and established a coastal government between present-day Ashdod and Gaza. The Israelites, threatened by the Philistines' political superiority, soon consolidated their 12 disparate tribes under one king, Saul. Upon Saul's death, the tribe of Judah supported

ISRAEL & THE PALESTINIAN TERRITORIES IN...

Three Days

From Israel/Jordan's southern Yitzhak Rabin Crossing (p396), head to **Eilat** (p310) for an underwater adventure, before taking the night bus (p313) to party city **Tel Aviv** (p275), for a day of shopping, eating, and relaxing on the sands. On your second evening, hop on a train to **Jerusalem** (p260), before taking tea, or something stronger, at East Jerusalem's historic **American Colony hotel** (p271). Head by train or taxi to Ben-Gurion airport (p331) to catch your flight home, or go back by bus to Eilat and on to the Egyptian border at Taba (p332).

One Week

From the chaotic King Hussein/Allenby Bridge crossing (p333) start your week with a full-day tour of **Jerusalem** (p260) and its biblical history, and two days' exploration of **Bethlehem** (p318) and the wider **West Bank** (p315). On day four, take a train ride from Jerusalem to **Tel Aviv** (p275) to get your fill of more sybaritic pursuits. Then rent a car, if you can, and head north to **Upper Galilee & the Golan Heights** (p301) to spend two days hiking stunning national park trails (p303). On day seven, drive west to **Haifa** (p287) to gaze at the famous **Baha'i Gardens** (p289), then on down the coast via the ancient ruins of **Caesarea** (p292) to deposit your car at Ben-Gurion airport (p331) and either take your flight home, or head by bus to Eilat and the Egyptian Taba crossing (p332).

Join the Itineraries

Egypt (p120)
Jordan (p336)

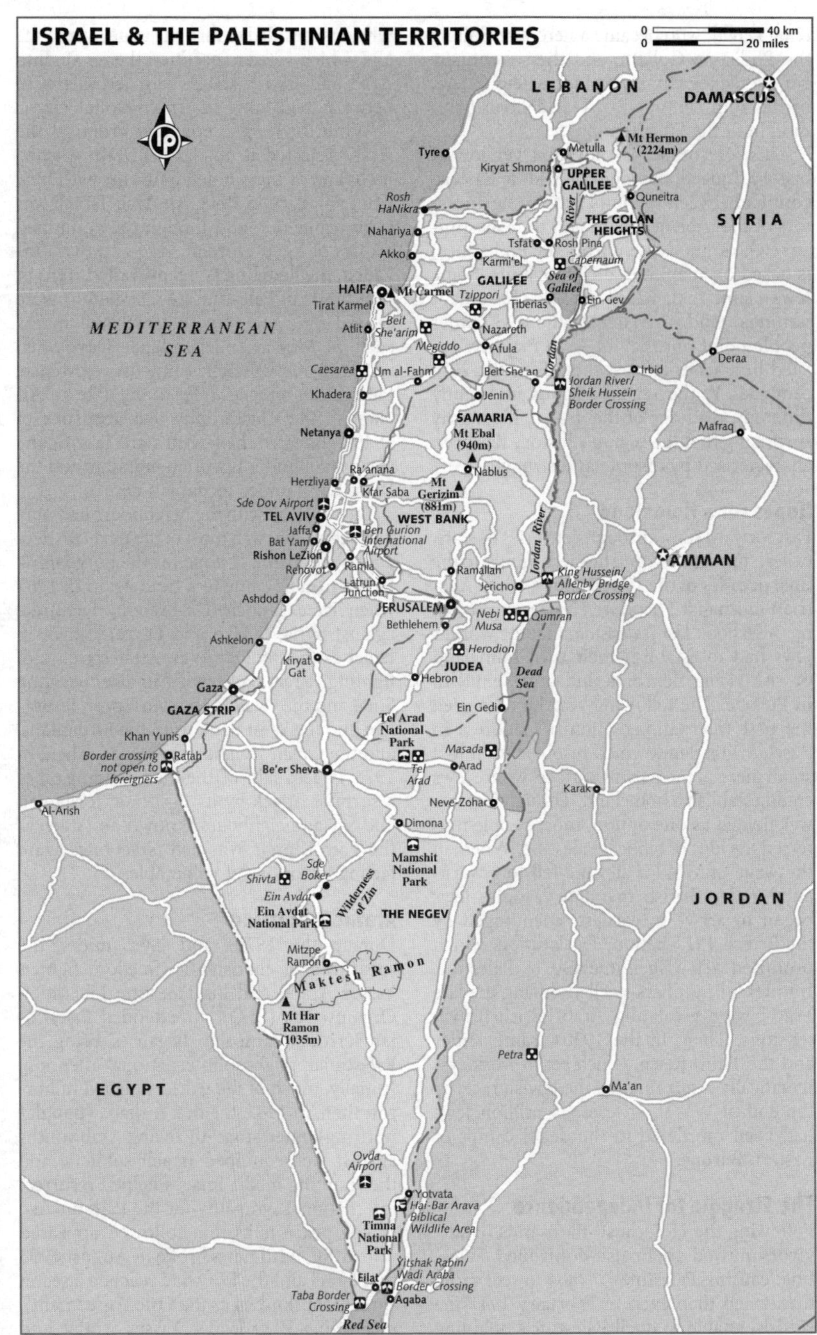
ISRAEL & THE PALESTINIAN TERRITORIES
0 40 km
0 20 miles
LEBANON
DAMASCUS
Mt Hermon (2224m)
Tyre
Metulla
Kiryat Shmona
UPPER GALILEE
Quneitra
Rosh HaNikra
River
THE GOLAN HEIGHTS
SYRIA
Nahariya
Tsfat
Rosh Pina
Akko
Karmi'el
Capernaum
GALILEE
Sea of Galilee
HAIFA
Mt Carmel
Tzippori
Ein Gev
Tirat Karmel
Tiberias
MEDITERRANEAN SEA
Atlit
Beit She'arim
Nazareth
Megiddo
Afula
Jordan
Deraa
Caesarea
Um al-Fahm
Beit She'an
Irbid
Jordan River/ Sheik Hussein Border Crossing
Khadera
Jenin
SAMARIA
Netanya
Mt Ebal (940m)
Mafraq
Nablus
Ra'anana
Herzliya
Kfar Saba
Mt Gerizim (881m)
Sde Dov Airport
TEL AVIV
WEST BANK
Jaffa
Ben Gurion International Airport
Bat Yam
Rishon LeZion
Jordan River
AMMAN
Rehovot
Ramla
Ramallah
King Hussein/ Allenby Bridge Border Crossing
Latrun Junction
Jericho
Ashdod
JERUSALEM
Nebi Musa
Qumran
Bethlehem
Ashkelon
Herodion
Kiryat Gat
JUDEA
Dead Sea
Gaza
Hebron
GAZA STRIP
Ein Gedi
Tel Arad National Park
Khan Yunis
Masada
Border crossing not open to foreigners
Rafah
Be'er Sheva
Tel Arad
Arad
Karak
Al-Arish
Neve-Zohar
Dimona
Mamshit National Park
Shivta
Sde Boker
Ein Avdat
Wilderness of Zin
JORDAN
Ein Avdat National Park
THE NEGEV
Mitzpe Ramon
Maktesh Ramon
Mt Har Ramon (1035m)
Petra
EGYPT
Ma'an
Ovda Airport
Yotvata
Hai-Bar Arava Biblical Wildlife Area
Timna National Park
Yitshak Rabin/ Wadi Araba Border Crossing
Eilat
Taba Border Crossing
Aqaba
Red Sea

King David, who became a hero after killing the Philistine Goliath, and they eventually conquered the city-state of Jerusalem. There, in the 10th century BC, David's son Solomon built the First Temple.

This, of course, is only one version of history. Indeed, the modern Middle Eastern conflict between the Jews (said to be ancestors of the tribe of Judah) and the Palestinians (who argue descent from the Philistines) is based on manifold ancient claims. Some Jews claim that, based on Old Testament writings, 'God gave Israel to the Jews'; other people point out that an Arab majority existed here from at least the 7th to the 20th centuries. With so many various, and subtly different, readings of the 'truth', it's hardly surprising that the region's history has been characterised by dispute and struggle.

Hopes for a Homeland

Fast forward now, through centuries of wars, exiles, suppressions and homecomings, to the final decades of the 19th century, when Austrian journalist Theodore Herzl surmised in his 1896 book *Der Judenstaat* that the world's Jews had to establish their own homeland or risk rising pogroms and anti-Semitism in Europe. The following year he organised the first International Zionist Congress in Basel, Switzerland, which resolved to 'find a small piece of the Earth's surface' where Jews could establish a homeland. Though Uganda was floated as one option, most people preferred the idea of biblical Palestine. When, in the wake of WWI, Palestine fell to governance under British mandate, Zionist Jews began to arrive in earnest, encouraged by the British 1917 Balfour Declaration, which promised a Jewish homeland in Palestine. Immigrant numbers swelled during the late 1920s, soon escalating Arab/Jewish/British tensions. Then, in the 1930s, came Hitler and the Third Reich, which set to work systematically exterminating the Jewish race; by the end of WWII, at least six million Jews had been murdered in the death camps of Eastern Europe.

The Struggle for Independence

Following the Holocaust, thousands of survivors moved to British-controlled Palestine, causing Palestine's Arabs to feel more threatened than ever. In February 1947 the British, unable to quell Palestine's bubbling tensions, decided to turn the issue over to the UN, which voted to partition the region into Arab and Jewish states, with Jerusalem, in between, becoming an 'international' city.

While the Jews accepted the proposal, the Arabs rejected it outright. Britain washed its hands of the whole affair and withdrew from Palestine in 1948. An Arab-Israeli war soon broke out, and though the combined armies of Egypt, Jordan, Iraq and Syria invaded, the fledgling Israel prevailed. Tens of thousands of Palestine's Arabs fled or were chased out, and though Israel still marks each 14 May as Independence Day, when in 1948 Israel officially came into existence, Palestinian refugees refer to the date as 'Al-Naqba', the Catastrophe. An armistice of 1949 delineated the Jewish state, leaving the Gaza Strip under Egyptian mandate and the West Bank under Jordanian control.

But tensions with the neighbours had only just begun. Though most of the next two decades were a time of hope for the burgeoning Israel, trouble came to a head again in 1967 when Israel launched a pre-emptive strike against Syria, Jordan and Egypt, known in Israel as the Six Day War. After six days of fighting, Israel had tripled in size, wresting Sinai and the Gaza Strip from Egypt, Jerusalem and the West Bank from the Jordanians, and the Golan Heights from Syria. Then, in 1973, Israel's skin-of-the-teeth fending off of a surprise attack by its Egyptian, Jordanian and Syrian neighbours (known, in Israel, as the Yom Kippur War) left Israel once again feeling victorious, if vulnerable.

Arafat & Uprising

During the 1970s and '80s, under the spearhead of charismatic 'freedom fighter' Yasser Arafat and his Palestine Liberation Organisation (PLO), an extended Palestinian terrorist campaign began to bring the Palestinian plight to international attention. Initially, much of the world watched in horror; then, in 1987, the first intifada (popular uprising) pitted stone-throwing Arab youths against well-equipped Israeli soldiers, and the resulting media images helped resurrect international sympathy for the Palestinians.

The peace talks that followed appeared unfruitful, until news broke in August 1993 that Israel and the PLO had reached a secret agreement (known as the Oslo Agreement), prompting PLO leader Yasser Arafat and the Israeli prime minister Yitzhak Rabin to make their famously premature, but Nobel Prize–winning, handshake on Washington's White House lawn. As a result, the Gaza Strip and most of the West Bank were handed over to Palestinian rule, with Yasser Arafat ostensibly at the helm.

Despite the Washington show, though, mutual trust between Rabin and Arafat was shaky, and there remained quite a few details to be hashed out, not least of which were the status of Jerusalem (Palestinian, Israeli or neutral?) and the future of the four million Palestinian refugees spread across the Arab world. Added to this was a fractious relationship with Syria, centred on the disputed Golan Heights, and a continued military confrontation with the terrorist Hezbollah (Party of God) organisation in southern Lebanon; see p406 for more on Hezbollah.

The Second Intifada Erupts

Progress was set back once again with the assassination of Yitzhak Rabin by a disgruntled Jewish extremist on 4 November 1995. Rabin's death marked the beginning of several years of stalled negotiations that came to an ultimate collapse when a deal for a two-state solution, brokered by Bill Clinton in 2000, was rejected by Arafat, despite support by Israel and pressure from the US government. Meanwhile, tit-for-tat violence escalated, and within months the fighting grew into a second fully fledged intifada. When Israeli voters had the opportunity, they chose the controversial, and reputedly ruthless, ex-army general Ariel Sharon to lead them through the storm.

Whilst most moderate Israelis and Palestinians continued to support the cause of peace and the creation of a Palestinian state, Sharon and Arafat soon got down to what they both seemed to do best. Blows were exchanged in the form of Palestinian suicide attacks, and Israel Defence Force (IDF) action that ranged from bulldozing Palestinian homes to full-scale aerial and ground assaults.

Israel: A Pariah State?

By late 2004 the death toll was grim, and the intifada was also taxing national morale as Sharon's hardball tactics were threatening to make Israel a pariah state among European governments. The economy suffered too: Israel's tourist industry collapsed and the Palestinian economy suffered US$14 billion in losses. But the war was to be Arafat's swan song; despite a lifetime of fighting for an independent state, he never realised this achievement, dying of an unknown disease in a Paris hospital on 11 November 2004.

Arafat's passing sparked a mood for change that fell on the shoulders of longtime PLO bureaucrat Mahmoud Abbas (aka Abu Mazen). Three months after Arafat's death, Sharon shook hands with his new Palestinian counterpart at a summit for peace in Sharm el-Sheikh.

Encouraged by the internationally supported 'Road Map for Peace', the Palestinian Authority and Israeli cabinet resumed talks and took several positive steps, including the withdrawal of Jewish settlers from Gaza and four West Bank towns in August 2005, and the release of hundreds of Palestinian prisoners from Israeli jails.

The Rise of Hamas

Yet paths to peace always move slowly, and with Sharon's hospitalisation in early 2006, and his subsequent slipping into a seemingly permanent coma, Israeli leadership soon fell to the less popular Ehud Olmert, whom many soon saw as ineffectual and corrupt. And while suicide attacks, by 2008, had thinned to a trickle, Israel's controversial 'Security Fence', ostensibly separating Israel and the West Bank (but in actual fact veering significantly into Palestinian land) continued to cause dissent and resentment among Palestinians. In 2006, moreover, encouraged largely by Mahmoud Abbas's Fatah party inefficacy at securing either peace or prosperity, the controversial Hamas party was democratically voted into power in both the West Bank and Gaza. While life in the West Bank has remained fairly calm ever since, warring Palestinian factions in Gaza (primarily Hamas versus Abbas's Fatah group) have created a mini civil war and effectively isolated Gaza (nicknamed 'Hamastan') from the outside world.

Onwards & Upwards

And Israel's troubles haven't stopped with the missiles incessantly being lobbed across the fence from Gaza. In summer 2006, the country embarked on a month-long war with Hezbollah, sending ammunition hurtling

WHO IS HAMAS?

Hamas had its beginnings in 1987 in Gaza, when a group of Islamic leaders founded the Harakat al-Muqaama al-Islamiya; its acronym, Hamas, means 'enthusiasm' and 'courage' in Arabic. A charter declared its doctrine: 'Allah is its goal, the Prophet is its model, the Quran is its institution, jihad ('strive' or 'struggle') is its path, and death for the sake of Allah is its most coveted desire.' Its militant 'military wing', named after a Syrian preacher who perished in a struggle against the British in the 1930s, soon proved itself willing and ready to uphold these ideals.

By the early 1990s, Hamas was gaining popularity among Palestinians, who were tiring of Yasser Arafat's administration and its apparent corruption and inefficacy. In contrast, Hamas (with around US$50 million raised from Gulf States and, later, Iran) was busy funding hospitals, youth groups, schools and clinics.

In 1993, as Arafat signed the Oslo Agreement and peace seemed a possibility, Hamas stepped up its terrorist activities; Arafat, caught between the West and the growing power of Hamas, attempted to juggle the two, ordering mass arrests of militants while simultaneously assuring Hamas sheikhs that this was simply a show to pacify the outside world. He consistently praised the terrorist 'martyrs', yet in doing so ensured that the West would never take him seriously as a figure for peace or the leader of an independent Palestinian state.

As the first, and then second, intifadas erupted, Hamas emerged as a prolific source of suicide bombings against Israel, with Israel hitting back in dozens of 'targeted attacks'. It wasn't until Arafat's death and the inauguration of the new president, Mahmoud Abbas, that Hamas began to diversify from military action to politics. In January 2006, the world watched as Hamas swept victorious through the national, democratic elections, winning 76 seats out of 132 in the Palestinian Legislative Council (the parliament), trouncing Fatah (who won only 45 seats) and signalling that the Palestinian people were ready to take a chance on change.

Since 2006, however, little seems to have changed for the better under Hamas' leadership. With Gaza plagued by both Israeli army action and inter-party armed conflict, and the West Bank still locked down by roadblocks and checkpoints, it's not yet apparent whether voters are satisfied with progress. Few Western countries are willing, as yet, to accept Hamas as a legitimate political force (at least until the group disbands its 'military wing') and it might seem to many onlookers that the majority of Hamas members are simply out to grab local power and prestige, just as Fatah was before it.

toward Lebanon, and leaving both countries tired and shell-shocked. In the aftermath, Hezbollah claimed victory and started about rearming more extensively than ever.

As Sharon still languishes in a hospital bed and the current prime minister's resignation, due to his investigation for fraud (only topped by former president Moshe Katsav's ongoing court case for alleged rape), has resulted in new elections scheduled for February 2009, the chances for peace look scant in the region. Street fighting in Gaza remains common; West Bank poverty is rife. Hezbollah claims to be gaining in both firepower and popularity near Israel's northern border, and Hamas' influence throughout the region continues to grow. As the Israeli business world and tourist industry goes from strength to strength, and Palestinians remain immured in camps across the Middle East, peace in this complicated, unpredictable region remains as far-off a dream as it has been for millennia.

THE CULTURE

The National Psyche

As the only Jewish state, Israel and its society are unique in the Middle East – and in the world. Yet Israeli society is surprisingly diverse, encompassing sizeable communities of Israeli Arab Christians and Muslims, Druze and Bedouins, as well as Jews ranging from entirely secular to non-Zionist ultra-Orthodox.

The majority of Israelis, though, (around 76%) are Jewish, a tie that binds in a collective memory of persecution at the hands of the Holocaust, and in the state's history of defending its existence against its mostly Muslim neighbours. The army, to which young Israeli men and women (excluding most Israeli Arab Muslims and Christians, and ultra-Orthodox Jews) are drafted at the age of 18 (men for three years, women for almost two), creates strong bonds of unity within its youthful population, though in recent years, growing numbers of 'refuseniks' are challenging the necessity of compulsory military service. There are increasingly options – mostly for women – to perform community service instead. Nevertheless, most Israeli men under the age of 40 carry out one month of military service per year, and there remains a strong sense of the necessity of constant defence against would-be attackers, fuelled by regular skirmishes with Lebanon's Hezbollah, the Palestinian Territories' Hamas and other militant groups.

Despite being planted very much at the heart of the Middle East, Israel leans toward Europe, and increasingly to America, in its lifestyle, culture and business proclivities. For Israel, inclusion in European events, especially the Eurovision Song Contest (a country-wide favourite) and the Euroleague basketball and football championships are a chance to commune with the neighbours on the opposite side of the Med. In the business world, too, Israel has forged strong and successful links to Europe and the USA. It had one of the world's highest GDPs in early 2008, created by a keen sense of entrepreneurism and huge advances in the fields of high-tech and medical research. Large numbers of young Israelis still depart each year to study and work in Europe and the US; ask most, though, and they'll tell you that they miss the sunshine, the family and the hummus, and that they're planning to return home one day.

The Palestinian Territories, just across the disputed border, has a national psyche based on a troubled recent history of hardship, violence and deprivation. While Islam plays a major role in its worldview, its key defining characteristic is the desire for an independent homeland. For many civilian Palestinians, years of deprivation, unemployment, poverty and food shortages have led to a collective sense of desperation and powerlessness. For others, these factors still lead to a need to stand up against their 'oppressors', joining militant organisations in order to fight for Palestinian freedom, using any tactic possible.

Recently, increasing numbers of Palestinians have left home to seek a better life abroad: for example, Bethlehem's Christian population has shrunk considerably, as those who have sought refugee status overseas. Like Israeli emigrants, though, their ties to the homeland remain strong, and many hope to return eventually.

HOW MUCH?

- **Newspaper** 10NIS
- **Dorm bed in guesthouse** 35NIS to 80NIS
- **Internet connection per hour** 15NIS
- **City bus ticket** 5.50NIS
- **Museum admission** 25NIS to 40NIS

LONELY PLANET INDEX

- **Litre of petrol** 6.50NIS
- **Litre of bottled water** 8NIS
- **Bottle of Maccabee beer** 18NIS
- **Souvenir T-shirt** 20NIS to 30NIS
- **Shwarma** 15NIS

Daily Life

Though Israel and the Palestinian Territories are, in many ways, like chalk and cheese, there are a number of elements of daily life that are remarkably similar on either side of the 'security wall'. For both populations, family life is of prime importance; many Israeli families eat dinner together each Friday night, before the younger generation head off to nightclubs and the older generation to bed. Similarly, extended families are highly valued in the Palestinian Territories, and grandparents frequently live with or close by their younger family members. For both Israelis and Palestinians, religious holidays – be it Christmas, Eid or Rosh Hashanah – are the perfect excuse for big family celebrations, with meals, parties and barbeques stretching for up to a week at a time.

The second uniting factor between the two populations is the importance of food to daily life. Food is everywhere, all the time; in Tel Aviv, Ramallah, Bethlehem or Haifa, it's very difficult to go hungry. This takes on different forms. In Tel Aviv sophisticated restaurants are packed with diners around the clock. In Palestinian villages, the local coffee haunt is filled with old-timers playing backgammon and snacking on sticky baklava. And come lunchtime, in any Israeli or Palestinian town, village or city, cafés dispensing hummus to the hungry masses are filled to bursting.

Much of Israel was founded on the principles of socialism and the shared community life on the kibbutz, though many contemporary Israelis have converted to a suburban, comfortable, consumer-driven existence. New-found wealth and a love of the outdoors have made them an active lot; sports, outdoor pursuits, travel and other leisure activities take the edge off an otherwise stressful position in the Middle East. But while Tel Avivans are out clubbing on Friday nights, the Jerusalem Orthodox are busy maintaining strict religious laws, which inhibit any sort of work (for the most religious, this even means turning on light bulbs) from sundown Friday to after sundown on Saturday. And while gays and lesbians live an open lifestyle in Tel Aviv and other cities, their lifestyle in Jerusalem is more cautious and conservative. Secular Israelis usually have two or three children; the religious may have a dozen or more.

Israeli women enjoy a freedom and prestige on par with their European counterparts and have historically played significant roles in the economy, the military and politics. (Israel was one of the first countries to elect a female prime minister, Golda Meir, in 1969). But a number of challenges remain: most troubling is the fact that matters of marriage and divorce (and subsequent child custody) remain in the hands of religious courts. This, equally, is a challenge for Palestinian women, whose family matters are also dominated by religious rulings.

Palestinians earn far less than the average Israeli (an annual per-capita income of just US$1100), a troublesome statistic that has done much to keep the Arab-Jewish conflict simmering. With an unemployment rate of around 30% (in some places over 60%), and a spectacular birth rate (around 7.5 children per woman), the Palestinian home is both overcrowded and poor. In recent years, though, Palestinians have encouraged women to go to school and work outside the home, leading to an educated middle class at odds with the image of the desperate, illiterate militant often portrayed in the media. While the election of Hamas to national government in 2006 has led to fears of growing Islamic extremism, the West Bank, unlike highly troubled Gaza, retains for now its quite moderate outlook, and Ramallah in particular contains its fair share of Western trappings, including fast cars, health clubs and late night bars.

Population

For more than 50 years Israel has served as a melting pot for the Jewish faithful. Economic opportunities, the hope for a better life, or spiritual convictions have ushered in Jews from Morocco, Russia, Yemen, Syria, Iraq, India and beyond. Israel's law of *Aliyah* confers full citizenship on any Jew, from anywhere in the world, who requests it.

Though in recent years, the Israeli middle class is tending towards the larger family (three or four children per couple is fast becoming the norm), the Israeli government continues to encourage immigration – offering cash incentives to young Russian and American Jews who move to Israel. Though never explicitly stated, the undertones are unavoidable: Israel's Arab populations are far more prolific in child production, and demographers report that in 20 years the Arab minority will increase from 20% to 30%.

In Gaza, 99.3% of the population is Muslim and just 0.7% Christian; in the West Bank, Christians comprise around 8%. Christian Palestinians – traditionally more moneyed and educated – have opted, where possible, for emigration in recent years (some estimate that at least 35% of the original Palestine Christians have emigrated since 1967) though Bethlehem, Ramallah and plenty of West Bank villages still hold thriving Christian populations.

SPORT

Football (soccer) is Israel's national obsession, with a number of clubs representing various cities across the country. Beitar Jerusalem FC, which won the Israeli championship in 2007, has the biggest following and the most raucous fans. Football crosses cultural boundaries, and several Arabs play on Israel's national side. After star strikers Abbas Suan and Walid Badir scored key goals for Israel during the 2005 World Cup qualifiers, an Arab member of the Knesset (Israeli parliament) suggested changing the popular slogan of the Jewish right from 'No Arabs, no terrorism' to 'No Arabs, no goals'.

The Palestinian Territories has its own national football squad, although in qualifying matches it's grouped in Asia, while Israel is grouped in Europe. In 2002 it made a surprising debut in the World Cup qualifiers, finishing second in its opening-round group ahead of Malaysia and Hong Kong. There's also a national women's football team; see p319 for more.

Basketball is another favourite Israeli sport and professional teams are a combination of local talent and American imports. The country's best club, Macabee Tel Aviv, has also enjoyed international success, winning several Euroleague titles including back-to-back championships in 2004 and 2005, though nothing much since.

RELIGION

Alongside the 76% of Israel that's Jewish, Muslims make up another 16%, Christians a further 2%, and other sects, including Druze, the remaining 6%.

Jewish doctrine states that Jews exist as a conduit between God and the rest of mankind. As God's 'chosen people', Jews have recorded his law in the Torah, the first five books of the Old Testament. The Torah contains 613 commandments that cover fundamental issues such as the prohibition of theft, murder and idolatry. The remainder of the Old Testament (the prophetic books), along with the Talmud (commentary on the laws of the Torah, written around AD 200), make up the teachings that form the cornerstone of Jewish study.

Judaism includes several sects of varying degrees of religiosity, the most religious being the Hasidim (Haredim) ultra-Orthodox Jews, easily identified by their black hats, long black coats, collared white shirts, beards, and *peyot* (side curls). Hasidic women, like observant Muslim women, act and dress modestly, covering exposed hair and skin (except hands and face). Many male Jews, of varying degrees of piousness, wear a kippa (skullcap), generally thought to be more of a tradition than a commandment.

Islam and Judaism – and Christianity too – share many ancient, holy sites, including, for example, the Temple Mount (p266) in Jerusalem and the Cave of Machpelah (p321) in Hebron, as well as prophets and ancestors, including Adam, Noah, Abraham, Isaac, Jacob, Joseph and Moses. Although historically Palestinians have been moderate Muslims, the strongest centre of Islam here is Gaza, where militant Islamic groups have found ready ears among those disenchanted with false promises of peace. For more on the Islamic, Christian and Jewish faiths, see p72.

Despite its origins in Israel and the Palestinian Territories, Christian populations in the region are small, and most of the holy sites are administered by overseas churches. The balance of power tilts toward the Greek Orthodox Church, which has jurisdiction over more than half of Jerusalem's Church of the Holy Sepulchre (p266) and a large proportion of Bethlehem's Church of the Nativity (p319). The Armenians, Copts, Assyrians, Roman Catholics and Protestants also lay claim to various holy sites, and disputes arise frequently over how to share their stewardship.

Smaller faiths include the Druze, an offshoot of Islam, whose small communities are based mainly in northern Israel, especially Haifa (p287) and Mt Carmel. Haifa is also the centre of the fast growing Baha'i faith (see boxed text, p289), a development of a Muslim mystical movement, founded in Persia in 1844.

ARTS

Israel and the Palestinian Territories might be small in size, but they're big in artistic output, be it literature, the visual arts, music, or, increasingly, film. For a bit of everything, check out the annual **Israel Festival** (p327). In recent years, Palestinian festivals have been few and far between, victims of limited funding, but keep an eye out for events at the **International Centre of Bethlehem**, also known as Dar Annadwa (p319), which regularly hosts art exhibitions, film screenings and other cultural events.

Literature

Israel's three most popular and widely-translated contemporary novelists are Amos Oz, David Grossman and AB Yehoshua. Oz is probably the best known worldwide, with his recent *How to Cure a Fanatic* (2006) offering two thought-provoking essays on the Israeli-Palestinian conflict. For more classic literature, look up the works of SY Agnon, Israel's first Nobel Literature Prize winner, whose 1931 *The Bridal Canopy* remains a cherished read.

Across the Green Line, poetry has historically been the literary medium of choice, and the late Mahmoud Darwish was the leading light. Two recent collections *Unfortunately, it was Paradise* and *Why Did You Leave the Horse Alone?* are good introductions to his lyrical, often political works. Meanwhile, it's worth getting hold of the works of Emile Habibi, a long-time Arab member of the Israeli Knesset. His novel *The Secret Life of Saaed the Pesoptimist* was translated into 16 languages, and tells the tragi-comic tales of Palestinians who took on Israeli identity after 1948. Another novelist – whose career was cut short by a Beirut car bomb in 1972 – worth dipping into is Ghassan Khanafani, whose debut *Men in the Sun*, a novella and short story collection, is simply stunning.

Cinema

Israeli and Palestinian filmmakers have been coming into their own in recent years. The acclaimed and controversial *Paradise Now* (2005), telling the story of two would-be suicide bombers, and the moving *Syrian Bride* (2004), in which a young Druze woman sets out to leave Israel forever for a marriage in Syria, are two greats. Likewise, the charming *The Band's Visit* (2007), which tells the tragi-comic tale of an Egyptian marching band's misadventures in a small Negev town, and the harrowing, animated *Waltz With Bashir* (2008) are international successes that you should definitely check out.

Though, as with all the arts, a lack of funding continues to plague the Palestinian film scene, change is definitely in the air. The AM Qattan Foundation (www.qattanfoundation.org) has embarked on an ambitious film education program for talented young Palestinian filmmakers, and grassroots projects have sprung up across the West Bank and Gaza. Look up the West Bank's Balata Refugee Camp Collective (www.balatacamp.net/website/balata.htm) and Gaza's Qisat Nas Community Film School (www.qisatnas.org.uk/home/) to learn more.

With such a spectrum of subjects on offer, the documentary scene, too, is thriving in the region. Poignant as ever are the now classic *Jenin, Jenin* (2002) by Mohammed Bakri, and *Death in Gaza* (2005), during which British director James Miller was killed by Israeli gunfire. Tel Aviv's annual DocAviv documentary festival (p327) is the best opportunity to catch the newest titles doing the rounds.

Music

Though Israelis are pretty Eurovision-mad, there's more to Israel's music scene than Dana International. Classic performers worth listening out for include Shlomo Artzi, Arik Einstein, Matti Caspi and Shalom Hanoch, all of whom produce anthemic-type songs that will have you humming along in no time. Idan Raichel, who introduces Ethiopian influences into his music, is a popular younger figure, as are Assaf Amdursky and Aviv Geffen, both of whom you're likely to spot frequenting the bars and cafés of Tel Aviv.

Israel also has a particularly strong classical music tradition, largely as a result of Jewish musicians who fled persecution in Europe during WWII. The Israeli Philharmonic Orchestra is world-class, while Klezmer music – a sort of Eastern European whirligig 'soul' music – has recently grown in popularity, and its annual festival in Tsfat (p327) is a giddy musical delight.

In the Palestinian Territories, music lessons have become increasingly important to children in recent years, as a therapeutic escape from the rigours of every day life. Teenagers and 20-somethings have expanded into hip-hop and rap, the two most popular outfits currently being Gaza-based PR (Palestinian Rappers) and Israeli Arabs Dam Rap (www.dam3rap.com) who rap in a heady mixture of Arabic, Hebrew and English.

If you're looking for something more traditional, the Palestinian Territories' love of classical Arab music is still very much alive; jump at the chance to attend local weddings or celebrations where there will often be a live band. With haunting melodies created with the oud (lute), *daf* (tambourine) and *ney* (flute), their melodies will remain in your mind long after the performance is over.

Theatre & Dance

Theatre is vibrant in Israel, with plenty of small repertory companies alongside the stalwarts, and lots of well-attended festi-

PARTY PURSUIT *zmagen*

Tel Aviv night life On par with other leaders in the nonstop nightlife field, Tel Aviv (p275) offers a parade of ever changing, innovative dance clubs, from megadomes housing thousands where international DJ stars play every weekend, to neighbourhood dance bars open till far after dawn, decadent gay friendly day clubs, and street parties in broad daylight.

Outdoor rave parties Israel is one of the world leaders in the psychedelic trance music genre, and has been for the past few decades. As such, it's surprising to note how underground and hush-hush the outdoor rave parties in Israel can be. Nevertheless, ask the right people, and you might be in for the experience of a lifetime.

Ethnic music festivals As spring emerges and valleys fill with flowers and wildlife, annual long-running ethnic music festivals are held in the lush north and scenic desert down south, as well as in the citrus-laden Sharon area. These feature music concerts and workshops for the entire family and provide an organic-spiritual environment for the so inclined.

What's your recommendation?
www.lonelyplanet.com/middle-east

vals countrywide. Perennially popular are the works of late, great playwrights such as Hanoch Levin and Nissim Aloni, and the contemporary Yehoshua Sobol. The oldest, most respected theatre company is Habima (p284), founded by Russian immigrants of the 1920s and '30s.

Social commentary theatre is also highly popular, tackling subjects from religion to terrorism to suicide and sexuality; *Phallus HaKadosh* (The Holy Phallus), a male response to the *Vagina Monologues,* and the international hit *Plonter,* with a mixed Jewish and Arab cast, have been two recent highlights.

Though not as far-reaching, theatre struggles on in the Palestinian Territories, despite a dearth of funding and the problems of movement for audiences, caused by roadblocks, curfews and checkpoints. The Palestinian National Theatre (www.pnt-pal.org) in East Jerusalem and the Al Kasaba Theatre in Ramallah (p317) keep up a ready schedule of performances. Palestinian youth groups, too, have seized on theatre as a way of venting everyday frustrations; visit Jenin's Freedom Theatre website (www.freedomtheatre.org) or Al Rowwad theatre (www.alrowwad.virtualactivism.net) in Aida refugee camp just outside Bethlehem, for two of the best.

Israelis and Palestinians alike love dance, albeit of different kinds. In Israel, contemporary dance troupes abound; Tel Aviv's Bat Sheva group, founded by Martha Graham, is probably the best known, with acclaimed choreographer Ohad Naharin. Israel's folk dance of choice is *hora,* with its origins in Romania; a great place to see it in action is at the Carmiel Dance Festival (p327). Palestinians, meanwhile, go in for *dabke* folk dancing. Check out El-Funoun Palestinian Popular Dance Troupe (www.el-funoun.org) based in Al-Bireh in the West Bank, to see some for yourself.

ENVIRONMENT

With an area of nearly 28,000 sq km, Israel and the Palestinian Territories are geographically dominated by the Great Rift Valley (also known as the Syrian–African Rift), which stretches from Southern Turkey to Lake Kariba on the Zambia–Zimbabwe border.

Between the mountain-fringed rift and the Mediterranean Sea stretches the fertile, but sandy, coastal plain where the bulk of the population and agriculture is concentrated. The lightly populated Negev, the country's southern wedge, is characterised by mountains, plains and wadis, and punctuated by military bases and irrigation schemes to transform the desert.

Due to its position at the junction of these three natural zones, Israel and the Palestinian Territories support an incredibly diverse wealth of plant and animal life. In the wet, mountainous Upper Galilee, otters dive in highland streams and golden eagles circle dense laurel forests; in the southern desert, ibex water at date palm–shaded wadis. Birdlife, too, is rich, since Israel is on countless species' migratory paths: go to www.birds.org.il, www.birds-eilat.com or www.birdingisrael.com to find out more.

National parks throughout the country, comprising around 25% of Israel's total area, have created sanctuaries safe from the

ALL THINGS ECO

To get yourself acquainted with the Israeli (and Palestinian) eco-scene, dip into some of the following internet resources.

- **Arava Institute for Environmental Studies** (www.arava.org) A research and teaching centre uniting Israelis, Palestinians and Jordanians.
- **Blaustein Institutes for Desert Research** (http://bidr.bgu.ac.il/bidr/) Your first stop for information on desertification and sustainable desert living.
- **Eco-Tourism Israel** (www.ecotourism-israel.com) A good guide to Israel's ecotourism options.
- **Friends of the Earth Middle East** (www.foeme.org) A regional branch of the global group with triparate Israeli/Jordanian/Palestinian partnership.
- **Galilee Society** (www.gal-soc.org) Israel's leading Arab-Israeli environmental activism group.
- **Israel Nature & National Parks Protection Authority** (www.parks.org.il) The central authority managing Israel's scores of national parks and archaeological sites.
- **Ministry of Environment** (www.sviva.gov.il) Offers good, basic English-language information on the state of the region's environment.
- **Society for the Protection of Nature in Israel** (SPNI; www.teva.org.il) An excellent source of information, the society also runs trips, treks and field schools countrywide.

unrelenting building work that has attacked so much of the region, and Israel is increasingly looking to 'green' concerns. Although the Palestinian Territories doesn't benefit from the same parks system or ecologically-minded organisations, the West Bank is sparsely populated outside major cities. Many communities here still rely on goat-herding or agriculture for their livelihood, meaning that the area's great open spaces, for now at least, remain so.

Environmental Issues

When Theodore Herzl suggested planting 10 million trees in Palestine, his colleagues thought he was crazy. But 100 years later the people of Israel proved that they could indeed 'make the desert bloom'. Unfortunately, the Zionists' zeal to populate the land has had a much greater environmental impact than the afforestation project. Demands on the land from increased urbanisation have resulted in the same problems found in many parts of the world – air and water pollution, overuse of natural resources and poor waste management. Recycling is in its infancy, gas-guzzling Hummers are de rigeur, and you only need to drive along Israel's 197km of coastline to see the sorry effects of building right up to the shoreline. Things are even worse on the coast of Gaza, where the problem of pollution is overshadowed by civil strife.

Israel and the West Bank's most publicised environmental threat, though, is the drying up of the Dead Sea, which has continued unabated for 30 years – the direct result of overuse of its main water source, the Jordan River. The dramatic decline in the Dead Sea water level threatens not only Israel, but also Jordan and the Palestinian Territories, and in recognition of this, the three sides have entered into talks on how to reverse the problem. A number of solutions have been proposed, including one long-floated plan to build a canal that would bring water from the Red Sea to the Dead Sea. To get up-to-date on the Dead Sea situation, see p117 and visit the Friends of the Earth Middle East's 'Save the Dead Sea' campaign at www.foeme.org.

FOOD & DRINK

Food is a national obsession on either side of the 'separation wall', and the one dish that probably unites the two nations more than any other is the humble hummus. Ask any Israeli or Palestinian who makes the best hummus and you're likely to instigate a long, animated debate. Ask how they like it best, and you'll be lectured on the pros and cons of hummus with fuul (fava bean paste), tahina (sesame seed paste), or the version containing soft whole chickpeas, known as *masabacha*.

Dining out is common for both Israelis and Palestinians. Tel Aviv, Jerusalem and Ramallah are filled with top-end restaurants covering every conceivable cuisine, while even the smallest village will usually have a place or two dispensing the ubiquitous felafel, shwarma, or local specialities.

Vegetarians won't find it hard to maintain a varied and tasty diet, particularly in Israel where kosher laws dictate that many restaurants eschew meat for a 'dairy' menu. Some dishes to watch out for are *shakshuka*, a rich egg-and-tomato breakfast dish served in a frying pan, the Yemenite weekend speciality *jachnun* (rolled pastry served with slow-boiled egg, strained tomatoes and fiery *zhug* (a Yemenite hot pepper and garlic relish), and *sabich*, a felafel alternative whereby roast aubergine, boiled egg and potato, salads and spicy *amba*, a mango sauce, are all stuffed into a pita.

A real treat is the variety of juices, which are freshly squeezed and sold at streetside stands almost everywhere. Try pomegranate juice for a vitamin-kick – but watch out for resultant blue-stained teeth. Coffee in all its permutations – instant, cappuccino (*afuch* in Hebrew) or Turkish (*qahwa bi-hel;* or in Hebrew, *kafé turki*) with cardamom – is popular throughout; Cup of Joe, Aroma and Arcaffe are the local chain equivalents of a certain white-and-green worldwide favourite. Tea is a Palestinian favourite, usually with fresh mint *(shai bi-naana;* or in Hebrew: *tey im naana*), especially refreshing on a blazing summer's day.

ISRAEL & THE PALESTINIAN TERRITORIES

THE WORLD ON A PLATE & HEAVEN IN A GLASS

Israel's culinary scene is blessed with a wide variety of dishes that Jewish immigrants brought with them from all over the world. Look out for these cuisines on your travels through the country; each dish generally costs less than 50NIS.

- **Persian** Try *gondi nochodi* (vegetarian or chicken balls with chickpeas, served in a soup or with rice) and *kroma sabzi* (herbed beef with vegetables).
- **Eastern European** Meaty *kreplach* (similar to dumplings); chopped liver with fried onions, and grilled goose with mashed potatoes and gravy.
- **Moroccan** Meatballs with gravy on rice; chicken with couscous and steamed vegetables, stuffed courgettes, and *mossaca* (ground meat on a bed of aubergine).
- **Upper Galilee Arabic** Homemade kebabs, stuffed lamb and *sinea* (ground beef with pine nuts and tahina).
- **Ethiopian** *Tibs Wat* (beef cooked in tomato and garlic sauce) and huge vegetarian combination plates, perfect for sharing.

Due to a combination of entrepreneurship, expertise and great conditions for growing grapes, Israel is experiencing a rise in independent boutique wineries, spread throughout the country. These guys produce an amazing variety of excellent wines; top wines will come in at well under 100NIS per bottle. Here's a list of our best wineries:

- **Zmora Winery** (www.zmorawinery.co.il) Produces full-bodied, powerful and fruity reds; the 2005 shiraz is a top drop.
- **Vitkin Winery** (www.vitkin-winery.co.il) Strong and fruity blends. Try the Cabernet Frank 2005 if you have the chance.
- **Clos De Gat Winery** (www.closdegat.com) Produces dark reds with flowery aromas. Look out for the 2004 Herel Syrah.
- **Chillag Winery** (www.preker.co.il/israelwines/chillag/eorna.html) This winery's rich and delicious Primo Merlot 2004 (90% merlot, 10% Cabernet Sauvignon) has won local awards.
- **Tulip Winery** (www.tulip-winery.co.il/) Another award winner; try the spicy 2006 vintage Tulip Syrah Reserve.

Compiled with the help of Yoran Bar, Tel Aviv.

Alcohol is available everywhere, but observant Muslims don't drink at all and observant Jews drink very little. In city centres, though, there's no end of bars serving up cocktails by the bucketful, local beers and an abundance of Israeli wines. The main brands of local beer are Maccabee, Gold Star and Nesher, all very nice indeed when served ice cold, while Taybeh Beer produces the only Palestinian brew, from the Middle East's sole microbrewery in the West Bank (see p317).

Note that in both Israel and the Palestinian Territories, tipping around 10% of the bill is as much of an established practice as it is in the West.

JERUSALEM

ירושלים القدس

☎ 02 / pop 729,100

Jerusalem, Israel's ancient, enigmatic and stunning capital, is without doubt one of the world's most fascinating cities, as well as one of its holiest, most beautiful – and most oft disputed. Here you'll find an enchanting blend of religions, lifestyles and monuments to three of the world's great monotheistic faiths, with a good bit of tension, turmoil and turbulence thrown into the mix.

HISTORY

Jerusalem, originally a small Jebusite settlement, occupies the slopes of the biblical Mt Moriah, where according to the Old Testament Abraham offered his son Isaac as a sacrifice. In 997 BC King David captured the city and made it his capital, and his son and successor, Solomon, built the great First Temple. The temple was destroyed by the Babylonian king Nebuchadnezzar in 586 BC and the Jews were exiled into the wilderness.

After 50 years, the Babylonians were pushed off the land by the Persians and it was under Cyrus the Great that the Jews were allowed to return and reconstruct a 'Second Temple', which was completed in 515 BC. Power shifted between subsequent invading armies until the Romans marched on Jerusalem in 63 BC, and installed Herod the Great as King of Judea. Herod launched a massive building campaign in Jerusalem, and the city was thereafter ruled by a series of procurators. It was the fifth of these, the renowned Pontius Pilate, who ordered the crucifixion of Jesus.

The swell of Jewish discontent with Roman rule escalated into the First Revolt in AD 66, resulting in the destruction of the Second Temple. A Second Revolt in AD 132 took the Romans four years to quell. The Jews were banished from Jerusalem and the Emperor Hadrian razed the city and rebuilt it as Aelia Capitolina, the basis of today's Old City.

Christianity soon became the official state religion, forcing the conversion of many local Jews and Samaritans, and building work started on Christian shrines; work on the Church of the Holy Sepulchre commenced in 326. Jerusalem's importance as a centre of Christian worship soon spread through the Eastern Roman Empire, until it was on a par with Antioch, Rome, Alexandria and Constantinople.

In 638, however, after weathering a short-lived Persian invasion and occupation, Byzantine Jerusalem fell to a new power: Islam, and the Dome of the Rock was completed in AD 691. But despite its significance to Islam, Jerusalem's political and economic fortunes fell into decline, the result of its distance from the imperial capitals of Damascus and Cairo.

By the 11th century, Palestine had fallen to the Seljuk Turks, who stopped Christian pilgrims from visiting Jerusalem. Thus, between 1095 and 1270, Western Christians led a series of Crusades to deliver the Holy Land from Arab occupation. The Crusaders took Jerusalem in 1099 but lost it in 1187 to Saladin (Salah ad-Din), a sultan, warlord and founder of the Ayyubid dynasty.

In 1250 the city came under the influence of the Mamluks, successors to Saladin's Ayyubid dynasty, who ruled from Egypt and turned the city into a centre of Islamic learning. In 1517 the Ottoman Turks defeated the Mamluks in battle near Aleppo, and thereby absorbed Jerusalem into their expanding empire. The city remained under loose Turkish rule from Constantinople for the next 400 years.

A lack of central authority from the 18th century on resulted in squabbles between landowners, and in the mid-19th century the power vacuum seemed to invite portions of the Jewish Diaspora to return to their ancestral homeland. Subsequently, Jerusalem became a hotbed of Arab and Jewish rivalry. The Ottomans rejected a British proposal to create an international enclave in the city, a decision that made the city a battleground again in 1948. When the fighting ended, a ceasefire, or 'Green Line', divided the city, with Israel on the west and Jordan to the east. After the Six Day War of 1967, Jerusalem was reunified under Israeli rule, but the control of the Holy City remains a sore point for Palestinians, who still claim the city as their capital today.

ORIENTATION

Jerusalem is divided into three distinct parts, each with an extremely individual character: the ancient walled Old City with its four quarters (Jewish, Muslim, Christian and Armenian); the predominantly Arab enclave of East Jerusalem; and the Israeli New City, also known as West Jerusalem. The main street in the New City is Jaffa Rd, which runs east to west between the Old City and the central bus station. The city's main shopping areas are concentrated on King George V, Ben Yehuda and Hillel Sts.

INFORMATION

Bookshops

Educational Bookshop (Map pp262-3, ☎ 628 3704; 22 Salah ad-Din St; 🕑 8am-8pm) This fantastic East Jerusalem bookshop has a range of books illuminating the Israeli-Palestinian conflict, along with a selection of Palestinian music CDs.

Sefer VeSefel (Map p269; ☎ 624 8237; 2 Ya'Avetz St; 🕑 8am-8pm Sun-Thu, 8am-2.30pm Fri, 8.30-11.30pm Sat) A Jerusalem institution housing floor-to-ceiling new and secondhand fiction and nonfiction titles.

T'mol (Map p269; ☎ 623 2758; www.tmol-shilshom.co.il; 5 Yoel Salomon St; 🕑 8.30am-midnight Sun-Thu, 8.30am-4pm Fri, 8pm-midnight Sat) Bohemian café and used bookshop, often hosting poetry readings or lectures by authors and journalists.

Emergency

Central police station (Map p269; emergency ☎ 100) Near the Russian Compound in the New City.

Fire department (☎ 102)

First aid (☎ 101)

Police (☎ 100)

Internet Access

There's no shortage of tiny internet cubbyholes in the Old City, where you can you check your email in a centuries-old cavern, surrounded by online game-playing Arab teenagers.

Freeline (Map p264; ☎ 627 1959; 8th station, 51 Aqabat al-Khanqah St; per hr 12NIS; 🕑 10am-midnight)

Internet Café (Map p269; ☎ 622 3377; 31 Jaffa Rd; per hr 15NIS; 🕑 9.30am-4am) In the New City; located beside the Main post office.

St Raphael@Internet (Map p264; Jaffa Gate; per hr 15NIS; 🕑 10am-midnight Mon-Sat)

Laundry

Laundry Place (Map p269; ☎ 625 7714; 12 Shamai St; 🕑 8.30am-8pm Sun-Thu, 8.30am-3pm Fri) Washes laundry at 10NIS per kilo.

Media

Jerusalem Post (www.jpost.com) A good source of local news and events listings, with an extensive 'What's On' weekend supplement published on Fridays.

Medical Services

Hadassah Hospital (Map pp262-3; ☎ 684 4111) On Mt Scopus, with another enormous branch above Ein Kerem (off Map pp262-3; ☎ 677 7111).

Magen David Medical Centre (Map pp262-3; ☎ 652 3133; 7 Himem Gimel St, Romema; 🕑 24hr) Five minutes' walk from the central bus station.

Orthodox Society (Map p264; ☎ 627 1958; Greek Orthodox Patriarchate Rd; 🕑 8am-3pm Mon-Fri, 8am-1pm Sat) In the Old City's Christian Quarter, the Orthodox Society operates a low-cost medical and dental clinic that welcomes travellers.

Money

There are banks with ATMs all over town; remember that Old City ATMs are not in service during Shabbat (Friday dusk to Saturday just after dusk). The best deals for changing money are at the private, commission-free change offices to be found in every district of Jerusalem. Many, especially around Ben Yehuda St, will also change travellers cheques.

American Express (Map p269; ☎ 624 0830; 18 Shlomzion HaMalka St) Cashes travellers cheques (note that the Tel Aviv office doesn't do this) and replaces lost ones.

Post

Main post office (Map p269; ☎ 624 4745; 23 Jaffa Rd 🕑 7am-7pm Sun-Thu, 7am-noon Fri)

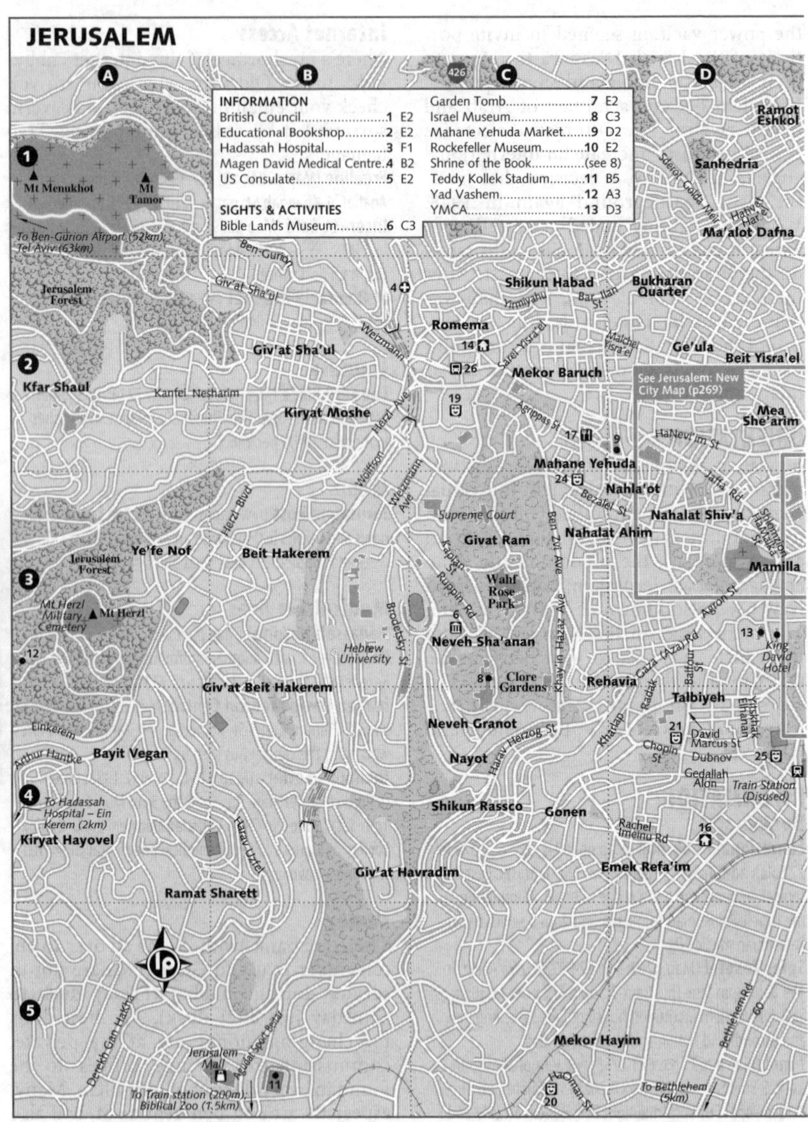

Tourist Information

Alternative Information Centre (Map p269; ☎ 624 1159; www.alternativenews.org; 2nd fl, 4 Shlomzion HaMalka St; 9.30am-8pm) A good point of contact for countrywide NGOs, this political group also produces information on the Israeli-Palestinian conflict.

Christian Information Centre (Map p264; ☎ 627 2692; Omar Ibn al-Khattab Sq; 8.30am-noon Mon-Sat) Opposite the entrance to the Citadel; provides information on the city's Catholic sites, maps for walking tours, and can arrange tickets to Jerusalem and Bethlehem Christmas church services.

Jaffa Gate Tourist Office (Map p264; ☎ 627 1422; www.tourism.gov.il; Jaffa Gate; 8.30am-5pm Sun-Thu) Offers free maps and can arrange informal meetings with Christian, Orthodox Jewish and Muslim families.

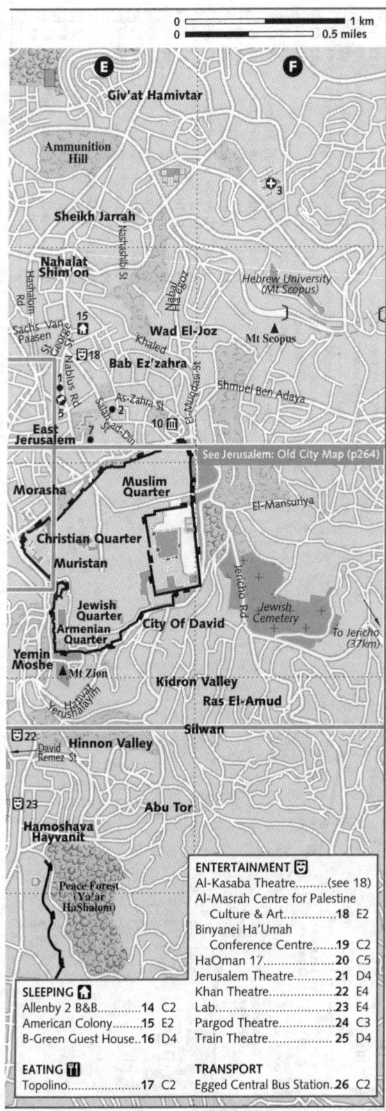

Travel Agencies

ISSTA New City (Map p269; ☎ 625 7257; 31 HaNevi'im St); Zion Sq (Map p269 ☎ 621 1888; 4 Herbert Samuel St, Zion Sq) Organises inexpensive flight tickets.

Mazada Tours (Map p269; ☎ 623 5777; www.mazada.co.il; Pearl Hotel Bldg, 15 Jaffa Rd) Operates tours and buses to Cairo and Jordan, and tours throughout Israel, Egypt and, on request, Syria. Also has a branch in Tel Aviv (see p279).

SIGHTS

Old City

Bounded by 16th-century stone ramparts, the magical, mysterious Old City is divided into Jewish, Muslim, Christian and Armenian Quarters, each with a distinct and intoxicating character. Home to some of the world's most important Christian, Jewish and Muslim sites, it's also home to hundreds of Jews and Arabs, to labyrinths of enticing bazaars, to good food, to Muftis, monks and moneylenders, and to a good bit of history, legend and controversy.

WALLS & GATES

The sturdy Old City walls are the legacy of Süleyman the Magnificent who built them between 1537 and 1542, though they've since been extensively renovated. The **Ramparts Walk** (Map p264; adult/child 16/8NIS; 9am-4.30pm Sat-Thu) is a 1km jaunt along the top – beginning at the top of the stairs just inside Jaffa Gate, and heading on to Lion's Gate (also called St Stephen's Gate), via New, Damascus and Herod's Gates, and from Jaffa Gate south to Dung Gate (also called Gate of the Moors), via Zion Gate.

The **Jaffa Gate** (Map p264), so named because it was the beginning of the old road to Jaffa, is now the main entrance to the Old City from the New City. Moving clockwise, the 1887 **New Gate** (Map p264) was built by Sultan Abdul Hamid and also gives access to/from the New City. Down the hill, **Damascus Gate** (Map p264), the most attractive and crowded of all the city gates, opens into bustling Arab East Jerusalem. Here, you'll see vendors selling their wares as they have for centuries, and armed Israeli soldiers peeping out from atop Süleyman's magnificent gateway. **Herod's Gate** (Map p264) also faces Arab East Jerusalem, and it was near here in 1099 that the Crusaders first breached Jerusalem's walls.

Lion's Gate (Map p264), facing the Mount of Olives, has also been called St Stephen's Gate after the first Christian martyr, who was stoned to death nearby. It was from here that Israeli fighters took the Old City in the 1967 Six Day War. **Zion Gate** (Map p264) became known as the Gate of the Jewish Quarter in late medieval times and is still pocked with reminders of the fierce fighting here in Israel's 1948 Arab-Israeli War.

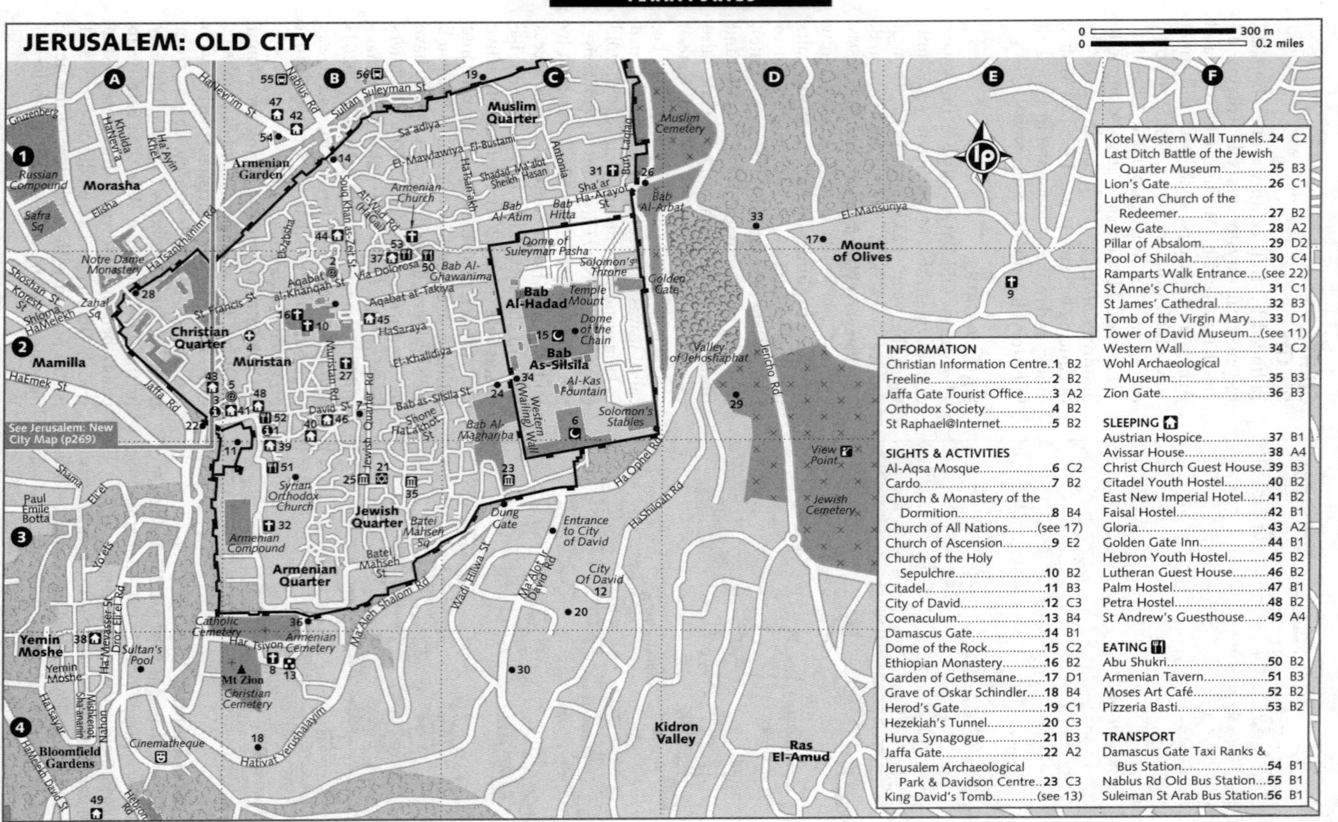
JERUSALEM: OLD CITY
0 300 m
0 0.2 miles
INFORMATION
Christian Information Centre..1 B2
Freeline..2 B2
Jaffa Gate Tourist Office..3 A2
Orthodox Society..4 B2
St Raphael@Internet..5 B2
SIGHTS & ACTIVITIES
Al-Aqsa Mosque..6 C2
Cardo..7 B2
Church & Monastery of the Dormition..8 B4
Church of All Nations..(see 17)
Church of Ascension..9 E2
Church of the Holy Sepulchre..10 B2
Citadel..11 B3
City of David..12 C3
Coenaculum..13 B4
Damascus Gate..14 B1
Dome of the Rock..15 C2
Ethiopian Monastery..16 B2
Garden of Gethsemane..17 D1
Grave of Oskar Schindler..18 B4
Herod's Gate..19 C1
Hezekiah's Tunnel..20 C3
Hurva Synagogue..21 B3
Jaffa Gate..22 A2
Jerusalem Archaeological Park & Davidson Centre..23 C3
King David's Tomb..(see 13)
Kotel Western Wall Tunnels..24 C2
Last Ditch Battle of the Jewish Quarter Museum..25 B3
Lion's Gate..26 C1
Lutheran Church of the Redeemer..27 B2
New Gate..28 A2
Pillar of Absalom..29 D2
Pool of Shiloah..30 C4
Ramparts Walk Entrance..(see 22)
St Anne's Church..31 C1
St James' Cathedral..32 B3
Tomb of the Virgin Mary..33 D1
Tower of David Museum..(see 11)
Western Wall..34 C2
Wohl Archaeological Museum..35 B3
Zion Gate..36 B3
SLEEPING
Austrian Hospice..37 B1
Avissar House..38 A4
Christ Church Guest House..39 B3
Citadel Youth Hostel..40 B2
East New Imperial Hotel..41 B2
Faisal Hostel..42 B1
Gloria..43 A2
Golden Gate Inn..44 B1
Hebron Youth Hostel..45 B2
Lutheran Guest House..46 B2
Palm Hostel..47 B1
Petra Hostel..48 B2
St Andrew's Guesthouse..49 A4
EATING
Abu Shukri..50 B2
Armenian Tavern..51 B3
Moses Art Café..52 B2
Pizzeria Basti..53 B2
TRANSPORT
Damascus Gate Taxi Ranks & Bus Station..54 B1
Nablus Rd Old Bus Station..55 B1
Suleiman St Arab Bus Station..56 B1
See Jerusalem: New City Map (p269)
Muslim Quarter
Christian Quarter
Jewish Quarter
Armenian Quarter
Muristan
Mamilla
Morasha
Russian Compound
Armenian Garden
Mount of Olives
Kidron Valley
Ras El-Amud
Valley of Jehoshaphat
Muslim Cemetery
Jewish Cemetery
View Point
Temple Mount
Bab Al-Hadad
Bab As-Silsila
Dome of Suleyman Pasha
Solomon's Throne
Dome of the Chain
Al-Kas Fountain
Solomon's Stables
Golden Gate
Western (Wailing) Wall
Dung Gate
Entrance to City of David
City Of David
Mt Zion
Christian Cemetery
Catholic Cemetery
Armenian Cemetery
Armenian Compound
Syrian Orthodox Church
Armenian Church
Notre Dame Monastery
Yemin Moshe
Bloomfield Gardens
Sultan's Pool
Cinematheque
Mishkenot Sha'ananim
Jaffa Rd
Nablus Rd
Sultan Suleyman St
HaNevi'im St
Via Dolorosa
Jericho Rd
El-Mansuriya
Ha Ophel Rd
HaShiloah Rd
Ma'Aleh Shalom Rd
Hativat Yerushalayim
Wadi Hilwa St

JEWISH QUARTER

Largely residential, the wheelchair-friendly Jewish Quarter was almost entirely flattened during 1948 fighting, and was reconstructed following its recapture by Israel in 1967. Consequently, there are few historic monuments above ground level, but excavations have unearthed a number of archaeological sites. One not to miss is the **Cardo** (Map p264; 8am-6pm Sun-Thu, 8am-4pm Fri), the main north–south street of Roman and Byzantine Jerusalem, part of which has been restored to approximate its original appearance, while another part has been reconstructed into a less authentic shopping arcade, replete with thoroughly modern gift shops. The Cardo also includes the **Last Ditch Battle of the Jewish Quarter Museum** (Map p264; admission free; 10am-3pm Sun-Thu, 9am-1pm Fri), which documents the 1948 campaign for control over the city.

At Hurva Sq, east of the Cardo, a graceful brick arch is the most prominent remnant of the **Hurva Synagogue** (Map p264), Jerusalem's main synagogue in the late 19th century. Down a narrow alleyway east of the square is the impressive **Wohl Archaeological Museum** (Map p264; 628 8141; admission 15NIS; 9am-5pm Sun-Thu, 9am-1pm Fri), which features a 1st century home and several Herodian archaeological sites, bringing to life the lavish lifestyle enjoyed by residents of this part of Herod's city.

The iconic **Western Wall** (Wailing Wall; Map p264), the only remnant of Judaism's holiest shrine, was built about 2000 years ago as a simple retaining wall, supporting the Temple Mount upon which stood the Second Temple (the 'wailing' moniker stems from the Ottoman period, during which Jews would arrive here to express sorrow over the destruction of the temple). The area immediately in front of the wall now serves as an open-air synagogue; the right side is open to women (who must dress modestly, covering their arms and legs), and the left side to men (who must wear a kippa; paper ones are provided). It's accessible 24 hours a day, and up-to-the-minute live pictures can be viewed online at www.aish.com/wallcam. Look out for the prayers on slips of paper stuffed into cracks in the wall, which are thought to have a better chance than others of being answered. These days, the faithful – or hopeful – with limited time can send prayers by email, also at www.ai sh.com.

If subterranean is your thing, be sure to head to the **Kotel Western Wall Tunnels** (Map p264; 627 1333; www.thekotel.org; adult/child 25/15NIS), an amazing 488m passage dug out by archaeologists that delves down to Jerusalem's original street level, in an area thought to have been the city's shopping district. Hour-long tours operate several times daily, but must be booked in advance, preferably about a week ahead.

On the southern side of the Western Wall, the **Jerusalem Archaeological Park & Davidson Centre** (Map p264; 627 7550; www.archpark.org.il; Dung Gate; adult/child 30/16NIS; 8am-5pm Sun-Thu) includes an interesting virtual tour of the Temple Mount as it looked 2000 years ago, bringing to life what's now a collection of ruins.

MUSLIM QUARTER

Running from the Damascus Gate east and southward towards the Temple Mount, this is the most exhilarating, sensory and densely populated area of the Old City, while simultaneously being the most claustrophobic, confusing and crowded. You'll inevitably get lost in the tangle of trade and teeming humanity, relieved by the tempting aromas emanating from spice shops, coffee corners, bakeries and tiny restaurants. Wander its Mamluk and medieval alleyways, and you'll be transported back to a different century – if, that is, you can just ignore the children with their flashing, whirring toy guns and the tinny whine of Arabic pop.

St Anne's Church (Map p264), near the Lion's Gate, is perhaps the finest example of Crusader architecture in Jerusalem, and is traditionally thought to have been the home of Joachim and Anne, parents of the Virgin Mary. With perfect acoustics, you're welcome to burst into song, as long as it's of the ecclesiastical variety.

The road leading from the Lion's Gate into the heart of the Old City is known as **Via Dolorosa** (The Way of Sorrows) or **The Stations of the Cross**, the route that tradition claims was taken by the condemned Jesus as he lugged his heavy cross to Calvary. At 3pm on Fridays, the Franciscan Fathers lead a solemn procession here, while you're also likely to encounter groups of Italian or Spanish tourists lugging their own huge (rented) cross up the hill. Explanations on plaques at each of the nine 'stations' along the way illuminate the biblical story (the final five stations are all in the Church of the Holy Sepulchre; see right.

The **Temple Mount** (Haram ash-Sharif; Map p264; www.noblesanctuary.com, www.templemount.org; admission free; 7.30-11am & 1.30-2.30pm Sun-Thu) is one of the most instantly recognisable icons of the Middle East. The massive, open stone plaza, dotted with cypress trees, was built over the biblical Mt Moriah, the location, according to Jewish tradition, of the foundation stone of the world itself. It was here, says the Talmud, that Adam, Cain, Abel and Noah performed ritual sacrifices, and where Abraham offered his own son, Isaac, to God in a supreme test of faith. And its significance doesn't stop there. It was also the location of Solomon's First Temple, where the Ark of the Covenant was housed, and the site of the Second Temple (home to the 'Holy of Holies', the sacred altar to which only high priests were permitted), destroyed by the Romans in AD 66. Later, the Romans erected a temple to Zeus on the site, which then became a Christian church.

But Temple Mount is not only holy to Jews. To Muslims, it's the 7th-century site of Mohammed's ascension to heaven *(miraj)* to join Allah, making it Islam's third-holiest site after Mecca and Medina. The site is still in the custody of Muslim leaders today, having been handed over to them by Israeli commander Moshe Dayan, following the 1967 Six Day War. This has never gone down well in extreme Jewish circles, whose plots to destroy the Muslim sites and build a Third Temple (www.thirdtemple.com) have increased tensions at the now heavily guarded site, but have so far failed.

The centrepiece of the Temple Mount today is the gold-plated, mosaic-adorned **Dome of the Rock** (Map p264), completed in AD 691, which covers the slab of stone on which Abraham prepared his sacrifice, and from which Mohammed ascended to heaven. The nearby **Al-Aqsa Mosque** (Map p264) is a functioning house of worship, believed to be a partial conversion of a 6th-century Byzantine church, with columns donated – oddly enough – by Benito Mussolini.

Entrance to the Temple Mount by non-Muslims is through the Bab al-Magharibа gate (Gate of the Moors), at the Western Wall. Non-Muslims can walk around the Temple Mount, but are barred from entering the Dome of the Rock or the Al-Aqsa Mosque. Remember that the area is closed to visitors on Islamic holidays, and that conservative dress, including a headscarf for women, is required. Always be prepared for random closures, and for long waits due to security checks.

CHRISTIAN QUARTER

The quiet, soothing Christian Quarter, with its mixture of souvenir shops (crowns of thorns, holy water, pieces of the true cross, anyone?), pilgrims' hostels and religious institutions, makes a calm antidote to the excitements of the Muslim Quarter. Its centrepiece is the sombre, stately **Church of the Holy Sepulchre** (Map p264; 5am-9pm Apr-Sep, 4am-7pm Oct-Mar), at the site also known as Calvary or Golgotha – the place where the Catholic, Greek Orthodox, Ethiopian and Coptic churches all believe that Jesus was crucified, buried and resurrected. The church itself represents a collision of architectural traditions. The original Byzantine structure was extensively rebuilt by the Crusaders and tweaked by numerous others over the years; today, its keys are in the hands of a Muslim family who open and shut-up-shop each day, to prevent rivalry between the notoriously uppity Christian factions in residence. It's open daily to anyone who's modestly dressed, and with its blend of candles, robed figures, icons and incense, might seem to some worthy of an Indiana Jones opening scene.

It's also worth visiting the tower of the neighbouring **Lutheran Church of the Redeemer** (Map p264) for excellent views over the Old City, and the **Ethiopian Monastery** (Map p264), on the northwest corner of the Holy Sepulchre complex, where a few Ethiopian monks reside in a highly atmospheric Medieval cloister.

The Jaffa Gate area is dominated by the Crusader **Citadel** (Map p264), which includes Herod's Tower and the Tower of David minaret. The tower is occupied by the highly worthwhile **Tower of David Museum** (Map p264; ☎ 626 5333; www.towerofdavid.org.il; Jaffa Gate; adult/student/child 30/20/15NIS; 10am-4pm Sun-Thu, 10am-2pm Fri & Sat), which tells the entire history of Jerusalem in a concise and easily digestible format. Guided tours in English are conducted at 11.30am daily.

A FEW OF MY FAVOURITE THINGS IN JERUSALEM

Local Jet van Wijk shared her favourite places to visit while in the ancient city of Jerusalem:

- Aimlessly meandering the narrow streets of the Old City until you find those steps leading up to the roof of the **Church of the Holy Sepulchre** (p266). Nothing beats entering the church via the Ethiopian village and chapel on top, then just hanging in the church and observing the various pilgrims and religious rituals.
- Refreshments at the **American Colony hotel** (p271). OK, so the service may not always be up to par and the menu might seem a tad overpriced. The ambiance, however, makes up for everything. Keep an eye out for well-known Palestinian negotiators, European diplomats, foreign correspondents and Mordechai Vanunu, the convicted atomic-secrets spy, who, now that he has done his time but is barred from leaving the country, frequents the place.
- A walk through the **Mahane Yehuda Market** (p268). Just wander around and make sure you bring your camera, and don't skip the Iraqi section, where old men often sit outside playing backgammon.
- The Jewish neighbourhood of **Mea She'arim** (p268). It's a world of its own. Dress for the occasion if you're a woman, though – or just drive through, though better not during Shabbat.
- Taking a drive out of Jerusalem towards the **Dead Sea** (p306). The landscape is absolutely spectacular, even though recent road works have destroyed some its charm. Keep an eye out for shepherds herding their flocks, Bedouin tents and camels. It's best in the early morning or late afternoon, when the mountain rifts shift to shades of red and pink.

Jet van Wijk works as a journalist in Jerusalem.

ARMENIAN QUARTER & MT ZION

Though it might strike you as strange that the Old City has a dedicated Armenian Quarter, Armenia was in fact the first nation to embrace Christianity, in AD 303. Quite hidden and less touristed than the rest of the Old City, the Armenian Quarter seems to exist as it has for centuries, its 1500-strong population insular and traditional, its gates locked daily at dusk.

A worthwhile visit is the Armenian **St James' Cathedral** (Map p264; Armenian Orthodox Patriarchate Rd; 6.30-7.15am & 2.45-3.25pm Mon-Fri, 2.30-3pm Sat to Sun), which has a sensuous aura of ritual and mystery, though you'll have to be nippy since it's only open for services (visit on a Sunday to see its nine hooded Armenian priests).

From the Armenian Quarter, Zion Gate leads out to Mt Zion, site of the **Coenaculum** (Cenacle, Dining Room; Map p264; Mt Zion; 8am-5pm Sun-Thu, 8am-1pm Fri), traditionally held to be the site of the Last Supper. At the back of the same building is the traditional site of **King David's Tomb** (Map p264; ☎ 671 9767; Mt Zion; 8am-6pm Sun-Thu, 8am-2pm Fri), and around the corner, the **Church & Monastery of the Dormition** (Map p264; 8am-noon, 2-6pm), where Jesus' mother Mary fell into 'eternal sleep'.

Brush up on your Spielberg before your visit, then take a wander to the small cemetery containing the unelaborate **grave of Oskar Schindler** (Map p264; Christian Cemetery, Mt Zion; 8am-1.30pm Mon- Fri) just south of King David's Tomb; it's a bit tricky to find, so ask the caretaker to point the way or keep your eyes peeled for a small sign.

Mount of Olives, Mount Scopus & the Kidron Valley

To the east of the Old City, outside Lion's Gate, the land drops away into the lovely **Kidron Valley**, then rises again up the slopes of the Mount of Olives. For Christians, this hillside holds special significance as the site where Jesus took on the sins of the world, was arrested and later ascended to heaven. Predictably, several churches have been built here, but visitors can still wander the old olive groves at Gethsemane (see p268) and the **Tomb of the Virgin Mary** (Map p264; 6am-noon & 2.30-5pm). Equally impressive is the panorama of the Old City from the summit – visit early in the morning for the best light.

The Kidron Valley, historically the oldest area of Jerusalem, has more than four millennia of archaeological remains. Because of the steep terrain, it's more isolated than other areas of Jerusalem, making it all the more worth exploring. At the top of the valley sits the 1st-century **Pillar of Absalom** (Map p264), the legendary tomb of David's son. Below Jerusalem's current city walls are the remains of the **City of David** (Map p264; ☎ 1-800-252423; www.cityofdavid.org.il; admission 23NIS; 9am-5pm Sun-Thu, 9am-1pm Fri), the Canaanite settlement captured by King David some 3000 years ago. The main attraction here is the extraordinary 500m-long **Hezekiah's Tunnel** (Map p264), an underground passage of knee-deep water that ends at the **Pool of Shiloah** (Map p264), where it's said a blind man was healed after Jesus instructed him to wash in it. You'll need good shoes, a strong torch, and a sense of adventure.

Nearby **Mount of Olives** (Map p264), with its spectacular views of Jerusalem, earns its biblical significance from being the place, according to Zechariah, where God will redeem the dead when the Messiah returns on the Day of Judgement. If that's not in progress on the day you're visiting, keep yourself busy exploring the more than half-dozen churches, most commemorating events in Jesus's life. All are open daily, closing for a couple of hours from around noon, and admission to all is free. Highlights include the **Church of the Ascension** (Map p264; 8am-5.30pm Mon-Sat), with stunning views from its 45m-high tower, and the gold-mosaiced **Church of All Nations** (Map p264; 8.30-11.30am & 2.30-4pm), situated amid the gardens of **Garden of Gethsemane** (Map p264; 8am-noon & 2-6pm), containing several ancient olive trees that were probably already standing there during Jesus's lifetime. To get to the Mount of Olives, walk from St Stephen's Gate in the Old City or from East Jerusalem, or take bus 75 (5.50NIS) from the bus station on Sultan Suleiman St .

East Jerusalem

Modern, workaday, predominantly Arab East Jerusalem is filled with hustle, bustle, some lovely crumbling architecture, and a number of worthwhile sights. On Sultan Suleiman St, just outside the Old City walls, the **Rockefeller Museum** (Map pp262-3; ☎ 628 2251; www.imj.org.il/rockerfeller/; cnr Jericho Rd & Sultan Suleiman St; adult/student 26/16NIS, entry free with a ticket from the Israel Museum; 10am-3pm Sun, Mon, Wed & Thu, 10am-2pm Sat) once boasted the most impressive archaeological collection in the region; today it's a bit musty but still worth a visit.

Behind a heavy stone wall on Nablus Rd is the beautiful **Garden Tomb** (Map pp262-3; ☎ 627 2745; www.gardentomb.com; 2-5.30pm Mon-Sat), an ancient stone tomb and garden that are believed to have once been the property of Joseph of Arimathaea. It's thought by some to be the site of Jesus's crucifixion and resurrection, an alternative location to the Church of the Holy Sepulchre. Most archaeologists, though, would beg to differ.

Appropriately located on the former Green Line that once divided East and West Jerusalem and now divides Orthodox Jewish neighbourhood Mea She'arim from secular West Jerusalem, is the **Museum on the Seam** (Map p269; ☎ 628 1278; www.coexistence.art.museum; 4 Chel Handasa St; adult/senior/student 25/10/20NIS; 9am-5pm Sun-Thu, 9am-3pm Fri), a powerful multimedia exposition that deals with conflict and coexistence through the use of art.

New City

The New City is roughly centred on the triangle formed by Jaffa Rd, King George V St and the pedestrianised Ben Yehuda St (the latter two are great bets for shopping). The most colourful and aromatic district, though, is **Mahane Yehuda Market** (Map pp262-3; 8am-sunset Sun-Thu, 9am-2pm Fri), the city's fabulous, fascinating food market: a perfect place to pick up provisions for a picnic or grab gifts to take back home.

Possibly one of the world's most reluctant tourist attractions, the ultra-Orthodox Jewish district of **Mea She'arim** (Map p269) is reminiscent of a *shtetl* (ghetto) in pre-Holocaust Eastern Europe, with the customs and dress-code to go with it. Dress conservatively (crucial if you're female), don't take photos without permission and avoid the area during Shabbat – though Thursday night and Friday daytime before Shabbat are particularly lively times to visit.

MUSEUMS

Holocaust museum **Yad Vashem** (Map pp262-3; ☎ 644 3769; www.yadvashem.org; admission free; 9am-5pm Sun-Thu, 9am-2pm Fri) is a moving memorial to the millions of victims of the Nazi Holocaust. A visit here is both enlightening and tear-jerking: the Children's Memorial, for example, is an underground chamber with a solitary flame commemorating the 1.5 million Jewish children exterminated in the Holocaust, whilst the Hall of Remembrance's

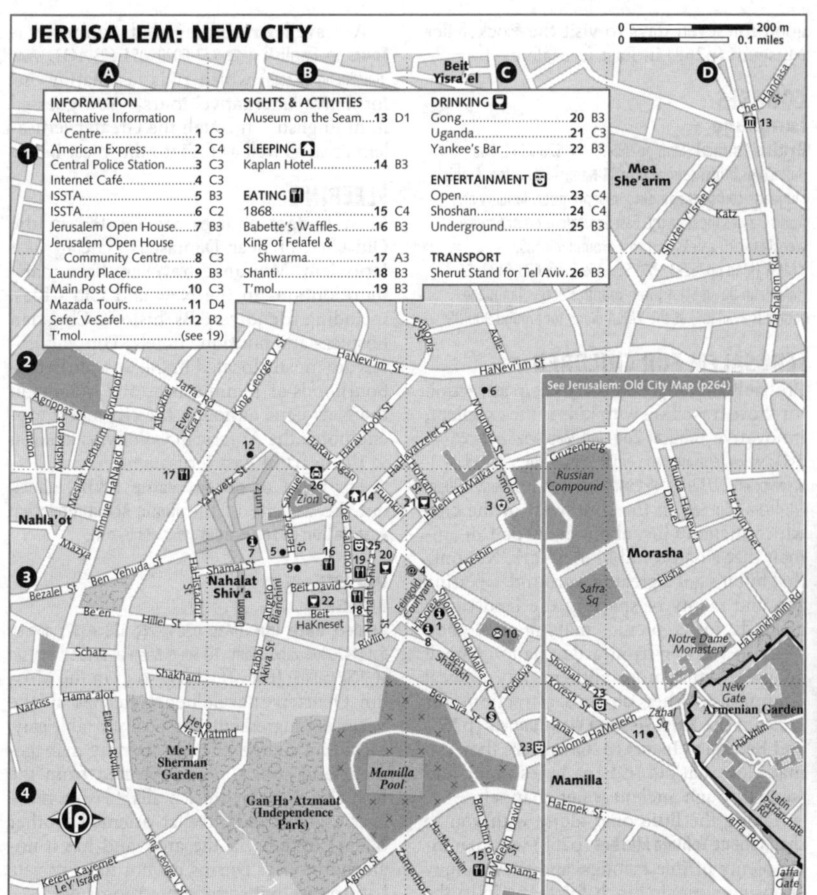

floor is inscribed with the names of victims. A tour of the whole complex takes around three sombre hours. To get here, take Egged bus 99, which stops in the car park, or bus 13, 18, 20, 23, or 27, which all drop you within a 10-minute walk of the museum.

The **Bible Lands Museum** (Map pp262-3; ☎ 561 1066; www.blmj.org; 25 Granot St, Neveh Sha'anan; adult/child/student 28/15/18NIS; ⏲ 9.30am-5.30pm Sun-Tue & Thu, 9.30am-9.30pm Wed, 9.30am-2pm Fri, 11am-3pm Sat, reduced hours in winter) illuminates the history of the Holy Land with a wealth of well-displayed artefacts and background information. Free guided tours in English run daily at 10.30am and on Wednesday at 5.30pm.

A good initial briefing on Israel and its 5000 most recent years of history can be found at the **Israel Museum** (Map pp262-3; ☎ 670 8811; www.imj.org.il; Rupin St, Neveh Sha'anan; adult/child/student 40/20/30NIS; ⏲ 10am-5pm Sun, Mon, Wed, Thu & Sat, 4-9pm Tue, 10am-4pm Fri), just west of the New City. An assemblage of several major collections of national historical and artistic significance, it also includes a peaceful sculpture garden and the jar-shaped and architecturally inspiring **Shrine of the Book**. Here you'll see background displays and examples of the famous Dead Sea Scrolls, which were uncovered at Qumran between 1947 and 1956. Note that a 'campus renewal program' is underway at the museum until summer 2010, resulting in the temporary closure of some parts of the museum. Check the website for up-to-date details. Your ticket is also good for seven days to visit the Rockefeller Museum (p268) in East Jerusalem.

COURSES

Language

British Council (Map pp262-3; ☎ 626 7111; issa.faltas@ps.britishcouncil.org; 31 Nablus Rd) Offers Arabic language courses beginning in September, January and April. Classes meet at the East Jerusalem branch twice weekly for 10 weeks and cost around 900NIS.

YMCA (Map pp262-3; ☎ 569 2692; fax 623 5192; 26 HaMelekh David St) A three-month Hebrew language course is available at the YMCA *ulpan* for around 900NIS.

JERUSALEM FOR CHILDREN

Probably the single best Jerusalem attraction for those travelling with kids is the excellent, innovative **Biblical Zoo** (off Map pp262-3; ☎ 675 0111; www.jerusalemzoo.org.il; Masua Rd; adult/child 3-8/senior 40/32/32NIS; 9am-6pm Sun-Thu, 9am-4.30pm Fri, 10am-5pm Sat) in the southwest of the city, which includes just about every pair of animals that Noah could fit in his ark. Not only that but it's got a great playground, a petting zoo and plenty of space in the landscaped grounds for a picnic, making it a good place to recover from a day hauling small people around more authentically biblical landmarks. Other obvious attractions for kids are the **Kotel Western Wall Tunnels** (p265) and **Hezekiah's Tunnel** (p268) where they can make like that old Indiana Jones again, and wade through ancient water channels.

Taking the little ones along with you to the **Mahane Yehuda Market** (p268) will guarantee plenty of free tastings, and they'll enjoy choosing a picnic lunch for that trip to the zoo. To beat the heat, check the schedule at the popular **Train Theater** (Map pp262-3 ; ☎ 561 8514; www.traintheater.co.il; Liberty Bell Park; admission 15-40NIS), a puppet theatre with regular performances for children aged four and upward.

TOURS

A good introduction to the city is Egged's **Route 99 Circular Line** (☎ 530 4704; per person 45NIS). This coach service cruises past 35 of Jerusalem's major sites, making a loop every two hours; meaning that you can hop on and off to visit sites thoroughly. The first bus departs at 9am from the central bus station, and stops at Jaffa Gate at 9.34am and the King David Hotel (Map pp262–3) at 9.38am. The last bus departs the central bus station at 4pm.

A traveller-recommended company is **Tours in English** (☎ 777 0020, 054 693 4433; www.toursinenglish.com) which runs fascinating, informative 'alternative' tours – you guessed it, in English – through the Greater Jerusalem area, as well as on into the West Bank.

SLEEPING

Most budget choices are located in the Old City, or near Damascus Gate in East Jerusalem. Midrange travellers have many more options in the New and Old Cities, including friendly B&Bs, historic Christian hospices and boutique hotels. Top-end hotels are mostly located in the upscale neighbourhoods of Yemin Moshe and Mamila in the New City, although the city's best top-end hotel, the American Colony, is a haven in the heart of East Jerusalem.

For a list of decent value B&Bs, check out the website of the **Home Accommodation Association of Jerusalem** (www.bnb.co.il).

Old City

BUDGET

Golden Gate Inn (Map p264; ☎ 628 4317; goldengate442000@yahoo.com; 10 Souq Khan al-Zeit St; dm/s/d 30/100/150NIS) Just off a busy souq in the Muslim Quarter, the Golden Gate has all the necessary ingredients for a comfortable stay, including a large kitchen, friendly management and cool rooms protected from the heat and noise by thick walls. It isn't, however, as jovial and traveller-oriented as other budget options in the area, and has a no-alcohol policy. Dorms do not have private bathrooms, but some other rooms do.

Petra Hostel (Map p264; ☎ 628 6618; www.inisrael.com/petra; Omar Ibn al-Khattab Sq; d with/without bathroom 150/120NIS, roof mattresses/dm without bathroom 5/35NIS;) Converted from a grand old hotel (which once hosted Mark Twain and Herman Melville), the Petra is a fairly grimy shadow of its former self, but still retains a cheerful atmosphere due to its backpacking guests. Its biggest draw is the convenient Jaffa Gate location and spectacular views over the Old City.

Hebron Youth Hostel (Map p264; ☎ 628 1101; ashraftabasco@hotmail.com; 8 Aqabat at-Takiya St; d with/without bathroom 160/100NIS, dm without bathroom 35NIS;) This venerable old hostel, with a magnificent stone interior, is buried inside the Muslim Quarter's Souq Khan al-Zeit. There are lockers to protect your valuables, but beware the hot water - or rather, the potential absence of it – in the winter months.

Citadel Youth Hostel (Map p264; ☎ 628 5253; www.citadelhostel.com; 20 Mark St; d 190-250NIS, without bathroom 110-150NIS, dm without bathroom 40NIS; 🖳) This centuries-old building has a mixed bag of rooms, all nicely decorated in an Arabic style, but those on higher floors get a bit hot in summer months. Travellers consistently praise the super-friendly management; bring your sleeping bag in summer to snooze on the roof, and your laptop to avail of the free wi-fi.

East New Imperial Hotel (Map p264; ☎ 628 2261; Jaffa Gate; s/d/tr US$35/50/75; 🖳) Quirky, antiquated and a little murky in the corners, this rambling, dishevelled old hotel was built in 1885 on the site of Bath Shebiye, where King David supposedly saw the wife of Uriah bathing in a pool. It's got loads of character, and consequently is one of those places you'll either love or loathe; don't count on hot water but do expect a friendly welcome.

MIDRANGE

our pick **Lutheran Guest House** (Map p264; ☎ 626 6888; www.luth-guesthouse-jerusalem.com; St Mark's St; s/d/tr from US$44/70/83; ❄) The historic Lutheran gets our vote for its great views, comfortable rooms, rose garden and medieval kitchen – the perfect place to rustle up a shared banquet and swap Middle Eastern travelling tips. Rates include breakfast.

Christ Church Guest House (Map p264; ☎ 627 7727; www.itac-israel.org; Omar Ibn al-Khattab Sq, Jaffa Gate; s/d US$50/80, extra person US$25) A prime location, relaxed atmosphere and simple, clean rooms with domed ceilings make this Christian hospice a solid-value choice. A mixed staff of Jews, Muslims and Christians makes for a model of cooperation and tolerance, sometimes sadly wanting outside the front door. A percentage of your bill will go toward local community projects.

Austrian Hospice (Map p264; ☎ 627 1466; www.austrianhospice.com; 37 Via Dolorosa; dm/s/d/tr €18/48/78/108) If you're looking for a location to imagine chain-rattling ghosts or Christian Crusaders, this sometimes eerie but otherwise terrific castle-like guesthouse is the cavernous place for you. The front porch and leafy garden are nice places to share a beer with your fellow guests, while the Viennese café whips up a awfully mean apple strudel.

Gloria (Map p264; ☎ 628 2431; www.gloria-hotel.com; 33 Latin Patriarchate Rd; s/d from US$80/100; ❄) With comfortable, airy rooms, a well-stocked bar and a friendly reception, this is a good, solid choice for midrange digs in the Old City.

East Jerusalem

BUDGET

Faisal Hostel (Map p264; ☎ 628 7502; faisalsam@hotmail.com; 4 HaNevi'im St; dm/d without bathroom 25/80NIS; 🖳) Political opinions run rife in this Palestinian-run guesthouse, making it a popular meeting point for freelance journalists, political activists and wannabe anarchists, who come here for the company and the chat, rather than for the comfort level. There's free internet access, so you can stay connected to your NGOs while sipping on your complimentary cuppa.

Palm Hostel (Map p264; ☎ 627 3189; 6 HaNevi'im St; dm/d without bathroom 25/80NIS; 🖳) The Palm, reached through a small vegetable stand, is cleaner than its neighbour Faisal, but dimly lit, with less sociopolitical talk and consequently less character. There's free internet, though, and the dorm beds are a bargain.

TOP END

American Colony (Map pp262-3; ☎ 627 9777; www.americancolony.com; 23 Nablus Rd, East Jerusalem; d from US$325; ❄ 🖳 🏊) Offering luxury and class like no other hotel in Israel, this place is in a league of its own. Despite its high-brow status, it remains unpretentious, a rendezvous point for journalists and scholars as well as a temporary home for visiting celebrities. Former guests include Winston Churchill, Mikhail Gorbechov, Jimmy Carter, Bob Dylan, Ingrid Bergman and John Steinbeck. If the sky-high room rates are too much, head here for a courtyard lunch, afternoon tea, or to prop up the Cellar Bar, like so many notables before you.

New City

BUDGET

Kaplan Hotel (Map p269; ☎ 625 4591; www.mznet.org/kaplanhotel; 1 HaHavatzelet St, Zion Sq; s US$35-45, d US$45-65; ❄ 🖳) One of the few budget hotels in the city centre, this small place has a great location next to Zion Sq, and gets good reviews from travellers for its worn but very clean rooms. With free internet and the use of a small, shared kitchen, it might not be exceptional in any way, but nevertheless makes for a comfy night's stay.

B-Green Guest House (Map pp262-3; ☎ 566 4220; www.bnb.co.il/green/index.htm; 4 Rachel Imeinu Rd, German Colony; s/d US$50/60) A simple but lovely choice in an attractive, lively area 15 minutes' walk or a short bus ride from the Old City. Each fan-cooled room has private facilities and a kitchenette, while futons are available for a third guest at no extra charge.

Allenby 2 B&B (Map pp262-3; ☎ 052 257 8493; www.bnb.co.il/allenby; 2 Allenby Sq, Romema; s US$25-55, d US$35-70;) A comfortable, friendly nine-room B&B, a convenient two minutes' walk from the central bus station. The irrepressible owner is a font of knowledge on the city and beyond, as well as a delightful host. Rates include breakfast and use of the communal kitchen.

MIDRANGE

St Andrew's Guest House (Map p264; ☎ 673 2401; www.scotsguesthouse.com; 1 David Remez St, Yemin Moshe; s/d/tr US$85/115/135;) With colonial charm aplenty, you'll be expecting to run into a bagpiper at this ecclesiastical hospice, which has a nice quaint feel, thanks to the fireplace, novel-stuffed reading room and old-world, wicker-heavy café. The guesthouse also has a well-equipped apartment sleeping four, from US$225 per night.

Avissar House (Map p264; ☎ 625 5447; www.jeru-avisar-house.co.il; 12 Ha'Mevasser St, Yemin Moshe; apt US$81-243;) Owner and documentary filmmaker Yossi offers four well-kept apartments, sleeping from two to six people. It's one of the closest midrange places to the Old City, located in a cobbled area with lots of flowers, staircases, and even a bona fide windmill. There's a minimum three-night stay.

EATING

You'll never have to look far in Jerusalem to find something to munch; fine and fancy, cheap and cheerful, quick and Kosher, Jerusalem has it all. Most of the finer dining options are spread throughout the New City; eating in the Old City is more about grabbing a bite on the hoof while you're hitting the sights. For a self-catering extravaganza, visit the Mahane Yehuda Market (see p268).

Old City

For quick eats in the Old City, head straight to the Muslim Quarter, where there are hole-in-the-wall stores aplenty vending felafel, freshly ground coffee, shwarma, cookies and pastries, while informal stalls and stands sell mountains of fresh fruit and vegetables, olives and pickles.

Moses Art Café (Map p264; ☎ 628 0975; Omar Ibn al-Khattab Sq; mains from 35NIS; ⏲ 7.30am-1am) A friendly and informal Lebanese choice just inside Jaffa Gate; offers good-value steaks, kebabs, hummus and the like.

Armenian Tavern (Map p264; ☎ 627 3854; 79 Armenian Patriarchate Rd; meat mains 35-55NIS; ⏲ 11am-10.30pm Tue-Sun) Walk down a flight of stairs near Jaffa Gate to find a beautiful stone-and-tile interior complete with a gently splashing fountain. Try the *khaghoghi derev,* a spiced minced-meat mixture bundled in vine leaves, or the excellent Armenian pizza.

Abu Shukri (Map p264; ☎ 627 1538; 63 Al-Wad Rd; mains from 20NIS; ⏲ 7am-6pm) If you're hungry for hummus, jostle for elbow-room at this popular Muslim Quarter joint, near the 5th Station of the Cross, which dishes up hearty portions of the beige stuff to Jews, Christians and Muslims alike.

Pizzeria Basti (Map p264; ☎ 628 4067; 70 Via Dolorosa; pizzas from 25NIS; ⏲ 7.30am-9pm) Though pizza may not always have been on the menu, a restaurant has graced this spot near the 3rd Station of the Cross for a century, to which photos on the walls attest. Twenty varieties of pizza all make for a good lunchtime carbs boost, before heading back out on the Old City sight-seeing trail.

One ever-popular felafel option is the unnamed stall at the bottom of the steps on the road into the Old City from Damascus Gate, in the narrow frontage between two forking lanes; the crowd outside will ensure you won't miss it.

New City

The New City offers diners a world of choice, and the places listed here are just a teeny taster of what's on offer. To find your own dining gems, go awandering: Jaffa Rd has a number of trendy, loungy places; the Mamilla and German Colony districts have lots of delis and informal café stops; Yoel Solomon St has a string of simple, tourist-orientated choices; and Aza Rd hosts some funky places popular with the student population.

1868 (Map p269; ☎ 622 2312; 10 HaMelekh David St; starters 35-70NIS, mains 80-120NIS; ⏰ noon-midnight) This sophisticated kosher gourmet restaurant is set in one of the oldest buildings in West Jerusalem, built (unsurprisingly) in 1868. Hearty wines complement a menu of succulent lamb chops and roast beef.

Babette's Waffles (Map p269; ☎ 625 7004; 16 Shamai St; waffles from 20NIS; ⏰ 8am-10pm Sun-Thu, 8am-2pm Fri) For when the mood for something sweet strikes, this teensy place specialises in heavenly hot chocolate and melt-in-the-mouth waffles.

our pick Topolino (Map pp262-3; ☎ 622 3466; 62 Agrippas St; pasta mains 35-47NIS; ⏰ 10am-11pm Sun-Thu) For delicious, well-priced and home-made Italian food, look no further than this tiny green-awninged eatery, a few steps away from the Mahane Yehuda Market. The menu changes regularly, but try the heavenly blue cheese ravioli if it's featuring, or, for something unusual, the cherry ravioli in chilled sheep's yogurt, with mint and lemon.

Shanti (Map p269; Nakhalat Shiv'a; ☎ 624 3434; mains from 30NIS; ⏰ lunch-late Sun-Fri) This cosy, wooden pub-type bar-restaurant, hidden away in a cute courtyard, is the place to escape to for a draught beer and a hearty dinner. The spicy pumpkin soup is gorgeous, the hot ham sandwiches are a local favourite, and meals come with little complimentary pots of tapas.

T'mol (Map pp262-3; ☎ 623 2758; 5 Yoel Salomon St; mains from 20NIS; ⏰ 8.30am-midnight Sun-Thu) This legendary boho-style place is more café than restaurant but serves great kosher light meals – and strong coffee – in the company of a distinctly literary set. It's also a gay and lesbian–friendly joint, with a 10% discount for members of the Jerusalem Open House (see Gay & Lesbian Jerusalem, p274), and sometimes hosts impromptu concerts.

For a fast bite, one of the most popular stands with locals is **King of Felafel & Shwarma** (Map p269; felafel from 10NIS; ⏰ 8am-midnight), on the corner of King George V and Agrippas Sts.

DRINKING

East Jerusalem and the Old City roll up their pavements at sundown and only a hike into the New City will provide an alternative to a beer in your bedroom or hotel bar. Yoel Salomon and Rivlin Sts in the New City are lined with late-night bars and cafés, particularly popular with tourists and American teenagers in town on semesters abroad. Most bars serve good food or bar snacks to satisfy cocktail-induced cravings.

Gong (Map p269; ☎ 625 0818; 33 Jaffa Rd; ⏰ 7pm-2am) It's a dimly lit Japanese-influenced place with black lacquer furniture, blood-red lighting and blaring hip-hop sounds, serving great sushi snacks on the side.

Yankee's Bar (Map p269; ☎ 625 6488; 12 Yoel Salomon St; ⏰ 4pm-9.30am) This beer bar in a narrow alley just off Yoel Salomon St is all about live music, all-you-can-drink beer nights, karaoke, and DJ nights, for lots of raucous fun.

Uganda (Map p269; ☎ 623 6087; 4 Aristobulos St; ⏰ noon-3am Sun-Thu, noon-5pm & 9pm-3am Fri, 8pm-3am Sat) Quirkily named after the country Israel might have been located in had Herzl agreed to the British suggestion, this shrine to everything alternative is a great local hang-out for a coffee, a glass of wine or something stronger. Peruse a comic book from its on-sale stocks and relax along to the good music.

ENTERTAINMENT

Nightclubs

HaOman 17 (Map pp262-3; ☎ 678 1658; 17 HaOman St, Talpiot; admission 50-80NIS; ⏰ 11pm-late Thu & Fri) With its warehouse location, booming sound system and great lighting, 17 is one of Jerusalem's ultimate clubbing venues. There are around eight other clubs on the street, so take your pick if HaOman's queue is too long: the new Hata'asia ('The Industry') club gets terrific reviews from locals, as does Campus Nightclub, with similar entrance prices and opening hours.

Open (Map p269; ☎ 622 2622; 17 Shlomzion HaMalka St, Mamilla; ⏰ 7pm-late Sun-Thu) As the name subtly suggests, this is a pick-up bar supreme, where you should head if you want to dance, nibble on tapas, and, well, be picked up.

Underground (Map p269; ☎ 054 677 2856; 1 Yoel Salomon St, Nahalat Shiv'a; ⏰ 9pm-6am) A cave-like bar and club that reels in teenage tearaways and first-time tourists.

Gay & Lesbian Venues

Shoshan (Map p269; ☎ 623 3366; 4 Shoshan St. Mamilla; ⏰ 9.30pm-2am) A small, slick bar at the end of a quiet alley south of Safra Sq. Dance parties are held Thursday and Friday, while Sunday is lesbian night.

> **GAY & LESBIAN JERUSALEM**
>
> Though the gay and lesbian scene is far more subdued in Jerusalem than in coastal Tel Aviv, there are still plenty of ways to get involved and connected.
>
> Your first point of contact should be the **Jerusalem Open House** (Map p269; ☎ 625 3191; www.worldpride.net; 7 Ben Yehuda St, Nahalat Shiv'a), which offers a mine of info on groups, events, and gay and lesbian–friendly venues. Its **community centre** (Map p269; 2 HaSoreg St, Mamilla; 🕓 10am-5pm Sun-Thu) hosts all kinds of regular events, social evenings and screenings.

Live Music

Lab (Map pp262-3; ☎ 673 4116; 28 Hebron St, Hamoshaya Havanit; adult/student 65/40NIS; 🕓 10pm-3am Mon-Sat) Crafted out of a disused railroad warehouse, this innovative bar and theatre hosts young artists, musicians and dancers mainly interested in alternative and 'experimental' arts, hence the name. Call ahead for upcoming events.

Pargod Theatre (Map pp262-3; ☎ 625 8819; 94 Bezalel St, Mahane Yehuda) Great for jazz; jam sessions take place every Friday from 2.30pm to 5.30pm.

Theatre & Classical Music

Jerusalem Theatre (Map pp262-3; ☎ 561 7167; www.jerusalem-theatre.co.il; 20 David Marcus St, Talbiyeh) The theatre offers simultaneous English-language translation headsets for certain performances. It's also home to the Jerusalem Symphony Orchestra.

Khan Theatre (Map pp262-3; ☎ 671 8281; www.khan.co.il; 2 David Remez Sq, Yemin Moshe; adult/student 150/120NIS) Occasional English-language performances.

Binyanei Ha'Umah Conference Centre (Map pp262-3; ☎ 622 2481; 1 Shezar Rd) The residence of the Israel Philharmonic Orchestra.

Off Salah ad-Din St in East Jerusalem, **Al-Masrah Centre for Palestine Culture & Art and Al-Kasaba Theatre** (Map pp262-3; ☎ 628 0957; Abu Obeida St, East Jerusalem) stages plays, musicals, operettas and folk dancing in Arabic, often with an English synopsis.

Sport

The **Teddy Kollek Stadium** (Map pp262–3), seating a respectable 20,000, is home to the two Jerusalem football teams, Beitar Jerusalem and Ha'poel Jerusalem, with their rowdy and relatively relaxed fans, respectively. If you're steeled for the experience, tickets can be bought at the stadium on the day of the match. To get here, take bus 31 from King George St or bus 6 from the central bus station.

GETTING THERE & AWAY

Air

Jerusalem has no civilian airport. For information on air travel into the country, see p331.

Bus

From the sparkling **Egged central bus station** (Map pp262-3; ☎ 694 4888; Jaffa Rd), buses connect to all major cities and towns around the country. Popular routes include bus 405 to Tel Aviv (17.70NIS, one hour, every 15 minutes); bus 940 or 947 to Haifa (39NIS, 2½ hours, every 15 mins); bus 962 to Tiberias (42NIS, 2½ hours, hourly); bus 446 or 470 to Be'er Sheva (32NIS, 1½ hours, every 30 mins); and bus 444 to Eilat (65NIS, 4½ hours, six daily). For day trips to the Dead Sea, bus 421, 444 or 486 depart for Ein Gedi (32NIS, two hours) or bus 444 or 486 to Masada (39NIS, 2½ hours); be sure to leave on the first service of the day (8.45am) or you will find yourself pressed to get back the same day. To get to the Palestinian West Bank, it's best to take a sherut (shared taxi).

For information on buses to Egypt, see p332.

Sherut

Sheruts (service or shared taxis) are much faster than buses, depart more frequently and cost only a few shekels more; they're also the only way to travel during Shabbat. Sheruts for Tel Aviv (20NIS per person on weekdays, 30NIS on Friday and Saturday) depart from the corner of Harav Kook St and Jaffa Rd (Map p269).

Sheruts for all West Bank destinations depart from the ranks opposite Damascus Gate in East Jerusalem.

Train

Jerusalem's **train station** (Map pp262-3; www.israil.org.il.english; ☎ 577 4000) is located in the southwest of the city. Trains depart hourly

ISRAEL & THE PALESTINIAN TERRITORIES

to Tel Aviv (adult/child 19/17NIS, 45 minutes) from 6.10am to 9.10pm, Monday to Thursday. The last train to Tel Aviv leaves at 3pm on Friday. To get to the station, take bus 6 from Jaffa Rd or the central bus station; check the website for up-to-date information on fares and times.

GETTING AROUND

To/From the Airport

Bus 947 runs the 51km from the central bus station to Ben-Gurion airport (20NIS, 40 minutes, hourly) between 6.30am to 8.30pm Sunday to Thursday, 6am to 4.30pm Friday, and 8.20pm to 10pm Saturday. Allow yourself plenty of time in case you get stuck in traffic, though, since there's no dedicated bus lane. Alternatively, **Nesher service taxis** (☎ 625 3233, 625 5332; 45NIS per person) takes prebooked passengers from their hotel, 24 hours a day.

Bus

Jerusalem is laced with a very good network of city bus routes (5.50NIS per ride). If you need to transfer, ask for a *Ma'avar* ticket, for 6.40NIS. Pick up a colour-coded route map (in Hebrew) from the Jaffa Gate tourist office (p262).

Taxi

Plan on spending 25NIS to 35NIS for trips anywhere within the central area of town. Always insist on using the meter, or agree to the price in advance.

MEDITERRANEAN COAST

The Israeli coast comprises a long band of white-sand beach along glistening blue-green Mediterranean sea, backed by a flat, fertile coastal plain and interrupted by low coastal hills. Most of Israel's burgeoning population is concentrated on the coast, and unfortunately, with the Israeli penchant for packing in as many apartment complexes as possible, open spaces beachside – aside from national parks – are fast becoming few and far between.

TEL AVIV תל-אביב تل أبيب

☎ 03 / pop 382,500

A universe away from historical – and sometimes hysterical – Jerusalem, secular party-city Tel Aviv, barely a century old, is many things that Jerusalem is not: easy, breezy, sometimes garishly ugly, and open for business 24/7. It's a city of diners, drinkers and dog owners; here, you'll find people out for a burger at 1am, doing their laundry at 3am, and taking an early morning dip in the sea at 5am. You'll also find hardcore left-wing activists, pockets of crumbling Bauhaus buildings unpainted since the 1950s, kite surfers, sunbathers, scores of young professionals with a couple of kids, a designer dog and cash to burn, and, increasingly, tourists from Europe arriving for a sunny weekend on budget airline flights.

WHITE CITY?

In 2003, Tel Aviv was pronounced a Unesco-rated city for its beautiful and abundant Bauhaus architecture, an art deco–like style built in the 1930s and '40s, with planning designed by Sir Patrick Geddes.

Though the moniker 'White City' is proudly applied, you'd sometimes be hard-pressed to find anything in town even approaching that colour. Every summer seems to herald garbage collector strikes, and in a city not known for its cleanliness in the first place, this wreaks havoc. Tel Avivans, moreover, just love their dogs, with a couple squeezed into every tiny apartment in town, making things often quite perilous underfoot. Add to this the fact that many of those beautiful Bauhaus buildings are slowly succumbing to the elements, and you're not exactly approaching pristine. Still, you've got to love Tel Aviv, especially now that those Bauhaus beauties are slowly being restored: just remember to hold your nose if there's a garbage strike.

For more on exploring Tel Aviv's Bauhaus masterpieces, go to www.white-city.co.il. A free English-language guided **Bauhaus tour** departs from 46 Rothschild Blvd every Saturday at 11am. The **Bauhaus Centre** (Map p278; ☎ 522 0249; www.bauhaus-center.com; 99 Dizengoff St; 10am-7.30pm Sun-Thu, 10am-2.30pm Fri) also has a variety of architecture-related maps and plans of the city, along with postcards of Tel Aviv back in its gleaming heyday.

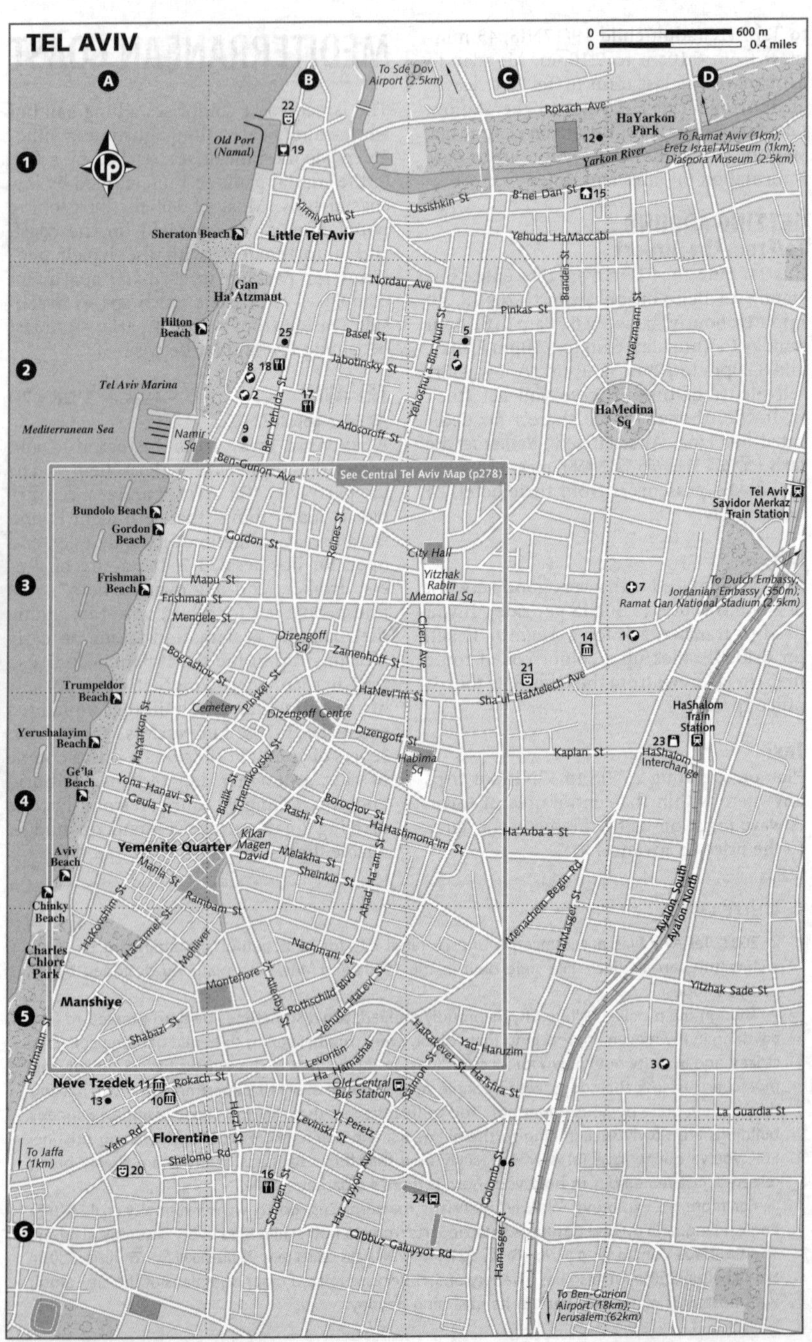
TEL AVIV
0 600 m
0 0.4 miles
To Sde Dov Airport (2.5km)
Old Port (Namal)
HaYarkon Park
Rokach Ave
Yarkon River
To Ramat Aviv (1km); Eretz Israel Museum (1km); Diaspora Museum (2.5km)
Ussishkin St
B'nei Dan St
Yirmiyahu St
Sheraton Beach
Little Tel Aviv
Yehuda HaMaccabi
Gan Ha'Atzmaut
Nordau Ave
Brandeis St
Weizmann St
Pinkas St
Hilton Beach
Basel St
Jabotinsky St
Yehoshu'a Bin Nun St
Tel Aviv Marina
Ben Yehuda St
HaMedina Sq
Mediterranean Sea
Namir Sq
Arlosoroff St
Ben-Gurion Ave
See Central Tel Aviv Map (p278)
Tel Aviv Savidor Merkaz Train Station
Bundolo Beach
Gordon Beach
Gordon St
Reines St
City Hall
Yitzhak Rabin Memorial Sq
Frishman Beach
Mapu St
Frishman St
Mendele St
To Dutch Embassy; Jordanian Embassy (350m); Ramat Gan National Stadium (2.5km)
Dizengoff Sq
Zamenhoff St
Chen Ave
Bograshov St
Pinsker St
HaNevi'im St
Sha'ul HaMelech Ave
Trumpeldor Beach
Cemetery
Dizengoff Centre
HaShalom Train Station
Yerushalayim Beach
HaYarkon St
Dizengoff St
Tchernikovsky St
Habima Sq
Kaplan St
HaShalom Interchange
Ge'la Beach
Yona Hanavi St
Geula St
Bialik St
Borochov St
Rashi St
HaHashmona'im St
Ha'Arba'a St
Aviv Beach
Yemenite Quarter
Kikar Magen David
Melakha St
Sheinkin St
Ahad Ha'am St
Menachem Begin Rd
Ayalon South
Ayalon North
Chinky Beach
Marla St
Rambam St
HaKovshim St
HaCarmel St
Mohliver
Nachmani St
HaMasger St
Charles Chlore Park
Montefiore St
Allenby St
Rothschild Blvd
Yehuda HaLevi St
Yitzhak Sade St
Manshiye
Shabazi St
HaRakevet St
Yad Haruzim
Kaufmann St
Levontin
Ha Hamashal
Salmon St
HaTsfira St
Neve Tzedek
Rokach St
Old Central Bus Station
Yl Peretz
Levinski St
La Guardia St
Herzl St
Yafo Rd
Florentine
To Jaffa (1km)
Shelomo Rd
Colomb St
Schoken St
Har Zion Ave
Qibbuz Galuyyot Rd
Hamasger St
To Ben-Gurion Airport (18km); Jerusalem (62km)

INFORMATION	Home of Shimon Rokach....10 A5	**DRINKING**
Australian Embassy....1 D3	Nahum Gutman Museum....11 A5	Whisky a Go Go....19 B1
British Embassy....2 B2	Sportek....12 C1	**ENTERTAINMENT**
Canadian Embassy....3 D5	Suzanne Dellal Centre....13 A5	HaOman Tel Aviv....20 A6
Egyptian Embassy....4 C2	Tel Aviv Museum of Art....14 C3	New Cameri Theatre....21 C3
Mazada Tours....5 C2	**SLEEPING**	TLV Club....22 B1
Physicians for Human Rights....6 C6	HI Tel Aviv Youth Hostel....15 C1	**SHOPPING**
Tel Aviv Medical Centre (Ichilov) Hospital....7 D3	**EATING**	Azrieli Centre....23 D4
Turkish Embassy....8 B2	24 Rupees....16 B6	**TRANSPORT**
SIGHTS & ACTIVITIES	Batya....17 B2	Central Bus Station....24 C6
Azrieli Observatory....(see 23)	Benedict....18 B2	O-Fun....25 B2
Gordon Ulpan....9 B2		

Orientation

Tel Aviv's bustling central area focuses on five roughly parallel north–south streets that follow 6km of seafront. Nearest the sand is Herbert Samuel Esplanade which runs along the main beach area, while the hotel-lined HaYarkon St lies a block inland. Next to the east is Ben Yehuda St, home to backpackers and an odd assortment of post-Eastern bloc immigrants, and the fourth parallel street is the trendy shopping street, Dizengoff St, which marks the geographic centre of the city. Further east again, Ibn Gvirol St forms the eastern boundary of the city centre. The smart Neve Tzedek and scruffy, but increasingly Boho, Florentine districts mark the southernmost reaches of the city centre; HaYarkon St and the Tel Aviv port (Namal) mark the northernmost.

MAPS

The English-language *Tel Aviv-Jaffa Tourist* map is an excellent resource and available from the Tourist Information Centre (see p279). Most hotels also have the free *Tourist Map of Tel Aviv*. The Bauhaus Centre (see the boxed text, p275) has plenty of Bauhaus-slanted maps on offer.

Information

BOOKSHOPS

These bookshops are open from 9am to 6pm Sunday to Thursday, and 9am to 4pm on Friday.

Halper's (Map p278; ☎ 629 9710; 87 Allenby St) Specialist in used English-language titles.

Lametayel (Map p278; ☎ 616 3411; www.lametayel.com; Dizengoff Centre) Specialist shop for travel books, Lonely Planet titles and maps, and has a useful travellers' notice board.

Steimatzky (Map p278; ☎ 522 1513; 109 Dizengoff St) Chain bookstore; this branch has a decent array of English-language titles.

EMERGENCY

Ambulance (☎ 101)

Fire department (☎ 102)

Police (☎ 100)

Tourist police (Map p278; ☎ 516 5832; cnr Herbert Samuel Esplanade & Geula St)

INTERNET ACCESS

All of the internet places listed below are open 24 hours per day, seven days a week.

Log-In (Map p278; 21 Ben Yehuda St; per hr 15NIS)

Private Link (Map p278; ☎ 529 9889; 78 Ben Yehuda St; per hr 13NIS)

Surf-Drink-Play (Map p278; per hr 10NIS) Dizengoff St (☎ 529 1618; 112 Dizengoff St); Ibn Gvirol St (☎ 695 8750; 65 Ibn Gvirol St); King George V St (☎ 629 1311; 77 King George V St)

INTERNET RESOURCES

www.tel-aviv.gov.il/english Official municipality website.

www.tel-aviv-insider.com Excellent tips on activities, dining and nightlife.

LAUNDRY

There are countless, nameless self-service laundromats (12NIS washing machine, 5NIS dryer; open 24 hours) to be found across the city, especially on Ben Yehuda St. If you're looking for something a bit better than a neon-lit wasteland, try **dizi** (Map p278; ☎ 629 4559; www.dizi.co.il; 13 Ben Ami St/Dizengoff Sq; 8am-midnight) where you can drink a gourmet coffee, make use of free wi-fi and wash your smalls in one convenient, trendy location.

LEFT LUGGAGE

Left-luggage facilities are available at Ben-Gurion airport for US$4 per day. Most guesthouses and hotels in Tel Aviv have a left-luggage room, charging between 2NIS and 10NIS per day. For security reasons, the

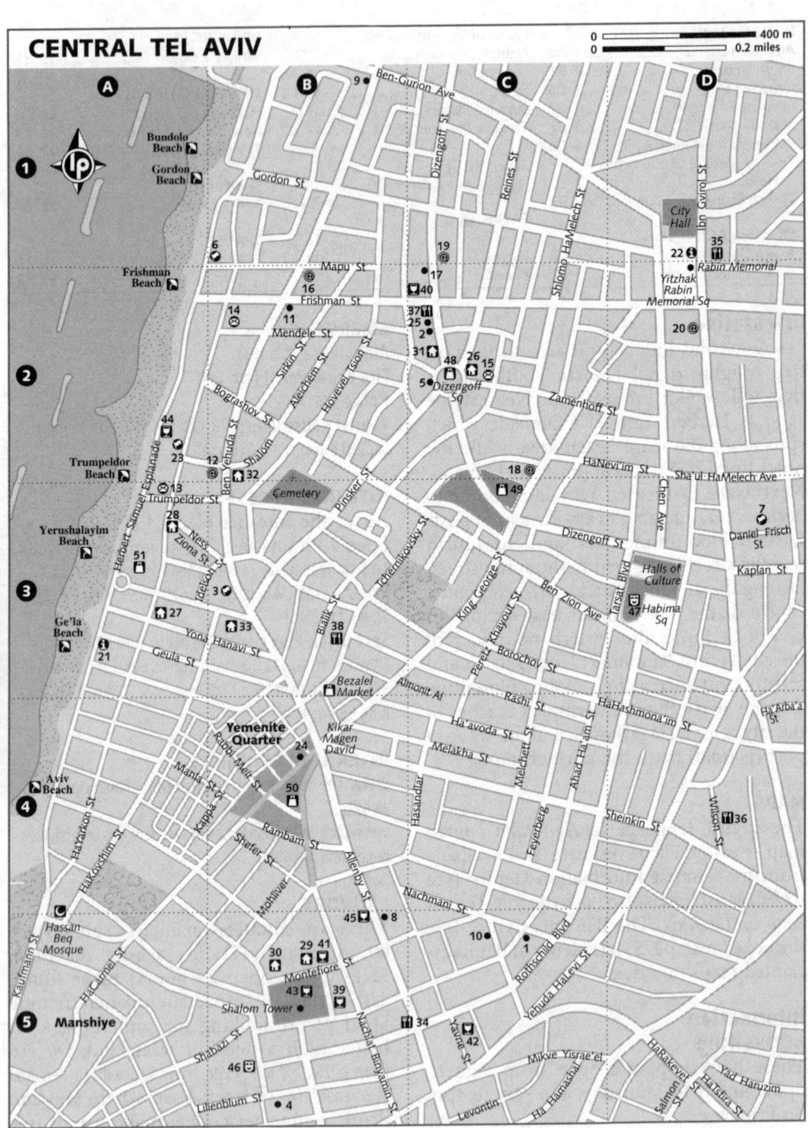

bus and train stations have no left-luggage options.

MEDIA

Time Out Tel Aviv, produced bi-monthly, is a great resource for what's on in the city. It is available at the Tel Aviv Tourist Information Centre and at most hotels. *Ha'aretz* newspaper – particularly the weekend edition – carries events listings and can be bought at newsstands citywide. If you are in town for a longer period, consider investing in the glossy *City Guide Tel Aviv* (US$24.95), with sumptuous pictorial listings of all the very coolest bars, shops and cafés.

INFORMATION		SIGHTS & ACTIVITIES		EATING	
Association of Gay Men, Lesbians, Bisexuals & Transgenders	1 C5	Carmel Market	24 B4	Benedict	34 C5
Bauhaus Centre	2 C2	Le-an Ticket Agency	25 C2	Brasserie M&R	35 D1
British Consulate	3 B3			Dizengoff Centre	(see 49)
CLAF	4 B5	**SLEEPING**		Pasta Mia	36 D4
Dizi	5 C2	Cinema Hotel	26 C2	Sabich Stall	37 C2
Dr Ayaldan	(see 49)	Hayarkon 48 Hostel	27 A3	Tchernikovsky 6	38 B3
French Embassy	6 B1	Hotel de la Mer	28 A3		
German Embassy	7 D3	Hotel Montefiore	29 B5	**DRINKING**	
Halper's	8 B5	Hotel Sun Aviv	30 B5	Betty Ford	39 B5
Irish Embassy	(see 7)	Kikar Dizengoff Apartments	31 C2	Bukowski	40 C2
ISSTA	9 B1	Momo's Hostel	32 B2	Carpe Diem	41 B5
Kibbutz Hotels Reservations Office	10 C5	Mugraby Hostel	33 B3	Evita	42 C5
Kibbutz Program Centre	11 B2			Lanski	43 B5
Lametayel	(see 49)			Mike's Place	44 A2
Log-In	12 B2			Minerva	45 B5
Opera Tower Shopping Centre	(see 51)				
Post Office	13 A3			**ENTERTAINMENT**	
Post Office	14 B2			Breakfast Club	46 B5
Post Office	15 C2			Habima Theatre	47 D3
Private Link	16 B2				
Steimatzky	17 C2			**SHOPPING**	
Surf-Drink-Play	18 C2			Antiques Market	48 C2
Surf-Drink-Play	19 C1			Dizengoff Centre	49 C3
Surf-Drink-Play	20 D2			Nahalat Binyamin Crafts Market	50 B4
Tourist Information Centre	21 A3			Opera Tower Shopping Centre	51 A3
Tourist Information Centre	22 D1				
Tourist Police	(see 21)				
US Embassy	23 A2				

MEDICAL SERVICES

Dr Ayaldan (Map p278; ☎ 525 4186; Dizengoff Centre; ⏲ 4-8pm Mon, 3-7pm Tue & Thu, 10am-2pm Fri) For dental services, try this reasonably priced dentist in the Dizengoff shopping centre.

Physicians for Human Rights (Map p276; ☎ 687 3718/3027; fax 687 3029; 52 Golomb St; ⏲ 5-7pm Sun, Tue & Wed) This clinic provides free medical assistance for visitors who aren't covered by health insurance in Israel.

Tel Aviv Medical Centre (Ichilov) Hospital (Map p276; ☎ 697 4000/4444; www.tasmc.org.il; 6 Weizmann St) Massive central hospital, with 24-hour emergency room, and a travellers' clinic (the Malram Clinic) for immunisations.

MONEY

The best currency exchange deals are at the private bureaus that don't charge commission, and there are plenty of them, especially on Dizengoff, Allenby and Ben Yehuda Sts, and there's another with good rates at the base of the **Opera Tower shopping centre** (Map p278) escalator. Most post offices also change travellers cheques, commission-free. ATMs are widespread throughout the city; but beware that many run dry by Friday night or mid-Saturday, so if you need lots of cash for the weekend, try to withdraw it in advance.

POST

There are three useful branches of the **post office** (www.postil.com; ⏲ 8am-6pm Sun-Thu, 8am-noon Fri); HaYarkon St (Map p278; ☎ 510 0218; 61 HaYarkon St); Herzl St (Map p278; ☎ 682 5856; 61 Herzl St); Ibn Gvirol St (170 Ibn Gvirol St; Map p278; ☎ 604 1109).

TOURIST INFORMATION

Tourist Information Centre (Map p278) City Hall (☎ 521 8214; 69 Ibn Gvirol St, Lobby, City Hall); Downtown (☎ 516 6188; 46 Herbert Samuel Esplanade)

TRAVEL AGENCIES

ISSTA (Map p278; ☎ 521 0555; www.issta.co.il; 109 Ben Yehuda St; ⏲ 9am-6pm Sun-Thu, 8.30am-1pm Fri) Student travel agency that can sometimes come up with well-priced airline tickets. It's on the corner with Ben-Gurion.

Mazada (Map p278; ☎ 544 4454; www.mazada.co.il; 141 Ibn Gvirol St; ⏲ 9am-5pm Sun-Thu) Operates buses to Egypt and Jordan, as well as tours throughout the region.

Sights

It would be perfectly understandable if you couldn't bear to tear yourself away from Tel Aviv's beaches, shops and cafés to do anything remotely more cultural; likewise, you might well be too partied out to do anything but lounge beside the sea. But if you do summon the energy for less sybaritic pursuits, there's a couple of interesting museums and some neighbourhoods well worth a wander.

BEACHES

All Tel Aviv's beaches are clean, safe and well-equipped with umbrellas, beach bars and irritatingly vocal lifeguards, but each has its own particular character. **Gordon** and **Frishman beaches** (Map p278) are the most all-encompasssing, and are packed with a real cross-section of locals and tourists.

Chinky Beach (Map p276) draws drummers and dancers on Friday afternoons and evenings; **Ge'la, Yerushalayim and Trumpeldor beaches** (Map p276), all attract a teenage crowd, and **Aviv Beach** (Map p278) is reserved for water-sporters. The **Hilton Beach** (Map p276), is the city's unofficial gay beach; don't confuse it with the next one along (Nordau Beach), which is for the Orthodox religious folks. Here Sundays, Tuesdays and Thursdays are reserved for women only (a good place, too, for non-Orthodox women to escape male beach hassle). Mondays, Wednesdays and Fridays are for men only, and Saturday is open to both sexes.

MUSEUMS

The diverting **Diaspora Museum** (off Map p276; ☎ 640 8000; www.bh.org.il; Beit Hatefutsoth, 2 Klausner St, Matiyahu Gate, Ramat Aviv; adult/student 34/24NIS; 🕑 10am-4pm Sun-Tue, 10am-6pm Wed) is a well-conceived and fascinating collection of dioramas, films and displays chronicling 2500 years of Jewish culture in exile. It's on the grounds of Tel Aviv University, 2.5km north of the Yarkon River. Take bus 25 from King George V St or bus 27 from the central bus station.

Eretz Israel Museum (off Map p276; ☎ 641 5244; 2 Chaim Levanon St, Ramat Aviv; adult/student 35/27NIS; 🕑 9am-4pm Sun-Wed, 10am-8pm Thu, 10am-2pm Fri & Sat), south of the Diaspora Museum, consists of 11 small themed collections (glass, ceramics, folklore etc) constructed around the Tel Qasile archaeological site, and is quite interesting to take a stroll around.

Home to a superb permanent collection of Impressionist and post-Impressionist works, the **Tel Aviv Museum of Art** (Map p276; ☎ 607 7000; www.tamuseum.com; 27 Sha'ul HaMelech Ave; adult/student 40/32NIS; 🕑 10am-4pm Mon, Wed & Sat, 10am-10pm Tue & Thu, 10am-2pm Fri) also has some fine 20th century avant-garde pieces. Works by Picasso, Matisse, Gauguin, Degas and Pollock feature prominently.

YEMENITE QUARTER

The Yemenite Quarter's maze of narrow, cobbled streets and crumbling buildings seems at odds with the clean-cut modernism of the rest of Tel Aviv. Imbued with an oriental flavour, the **Carmel Market** (Map p278; 🕑 8am-5pm Sun-Fri) is one of the few places in the city that reminds visitors of Tel Aviv's Middle Eastern location. Push past the first few metres of knock-off brand-name clothing and trainers to reach the more aromatic and enticing stalls of fresh fruits and vegetables, hot breads and spices.

NEVE TSEDEK

Cute and characterful Neve Tsedek, with its narrow streets and historic houses, has fast become one of Tel Aviv's most upmarket

SUCH A PERFECT DAY *Amelia Thomas*

Though Tel Aviv manages to be at once cool and hot on every day of the week, Fridays are my own personal favourite. Everyone's out on the streets, at the park, or at the beach all day. A magical hush descends as the light softens at about 5pm, as city dwellers head home to prepare for a family dinner followed by a late night out. Here's my recipe for a perfect Tel Aviv Friday.

First, pick up the weekend *Ha'aretz* newspaper from a newsstand, then head out for a long, lingering breakfast at one of the tiny cafés on Sheinkin, Shabazi or Bograchov Sts, and take a wander around the boutiques of the cute little Neve Tsedek district (above), or head over to Nachlat Binyamin to taste the happy atmosphere of the **craft market** (p284).

Grab lunch on the go at the city's favourite **sabich stall** (p283), then wander along Rothschild Blvd with the dog walkers and frolicking families to soak up some beautiful Bauhaus architecture. Head back towards the beach for an afternoon in the waves, and stroll the promenade as the sun goes down. Saunter towards Jaffa, where the air hangs heavy with smoke as Jews and Arab Israelis alike break out the barbeques.

After dinner at one of our recommendations (see p282), rev up for a night on the tiles; the hip bars and clubs in Tel Aviv's Old Port (Namal) make a good starting (and finishing) place (see p284). After that, it just depends how long you can keep up the pace: there are after-parties and after-after-parties. Otherwise, head off for a post-party breakfast, along with legions of exhausted Tel Avivans, before spending Saturday recovering on the city sands.

neighbourhoods. In the late 19th century it was the choice area for intellectual Jews looking for a prestigious address; nowadays it's for well-to-do young families and artsy professionals, who you'll find patronising its cafés, boutiques and bars at all hours of the day. Most of the action takes place on Shabazi St.

The **Suzanne Dellal Centre** (Map p276; ☎ 510 5656; www.suzannedellal.org.il; 5 Yechieli St), a former school and cultural centre, serves as a venue for festivals, exhibits and cultural events, as well as a relaxing place to look at artistic murals and spend a sunny afternoon. On weekends, you can visit the historic 1887 **Home of Shimon Rokakh** (Map p276; ☎ 516 8042; www.rokach-house.co.il; 36 Rokakh St; admission 10NIS; 10am-4pm Sun-Thu, 10am-2pm Fri & Sat), outlining life in 19th-century Tel Aviv, and a tribute to the man who conceived the building of Tel Aviv. On the same street is the **Nahum Gutman Museum** (Map p276; ☎ 516 1970; www.gutmanmuseum.co.il; 21 Rokakh St; adult/child 20/10NIS; 10am-4pm Sun, Mon, Wed & Thu, 10am-7pm Tue, 10am-2pm Fri, 10am-5pm Sat), which displays 200 lively and fanciful works by the 20th-century Israeli artist.

Courses

Tel Aviv's most popular Hebrew-language program, **Gordon Ulpan** (Map p276; ☎ 522 3095; hadas.goren@012.net.il; LaSalle 7), charges around 670NIS per month, plus a 70NIS registration fee.

Tel Aviv for Children

If you can drag your little ones away from the beach, there's lots to keep them occupied in this most child-friendly of cities. For active older kids, the **Sportek** (Map p276) has basketball courts, a skate park, mini-golf, a climbing wall (50NIS for three hours) and trampolines. Ultimate Frisbee matches are held here every Friday at 4.45pm and Saturday at 4.30pm. The neighbouring **HaYarkon park** (Map p276) has lots of space to play, boats for hire, playgrounds, pony rides and animal enclosures.

The **Azrieli Observatory** (Map p276; ☎ 608 1179; Azrieli Centre; 22NIS; 10am-8pm Tue-Thu & Sat, 10am-6pm Fri) on the top floor of the shopping centre of the same name, offers great views over Tel Aviv and beyond – on a clear day, you can see well into the West Bank.

More intellectual activities are often on offer at the **Tel Aviv Museum of Art** (opposite) – give them a call to check what's on while you're in town. A great place for lunch with children is the **Old Port** (Namal; Map p276), packed with child-friendly restaurants and a couple of playgrounds, as well as a wide and undulating wooden boardwalk on which to let off steam.

Sleeping

BUDGET

Tel Aviv's lively budget hostels are concentrated near the centre of town, meaning you can spend the day on the beach, pop back for a shower, then head out on foot for the night. Those who prefer a little more serenity may want to consider staying in nearby Jaffa (p285).

Mugraby Hostel (Map p278; ☎ 510 2443; www.mugraby-hostel.com; 30 Allenby St; dm €12, s/d from €41/46;) Cleanliness and colour make up for the slight shabbiness of this place, which has a nice roof for a cold drink. There's free wi-fi and breakfast is served from 5am, perfect for the early-morning swimmer. Double rooms have air-con and cable TV.

Hayarkon 48 Hostel (Map p278; ☎ 516 8989; www.hayarkon48.com; 48 HaYarkon St; dm €14; s with/without bathroom €52/46; d with/without bathroom €58/52;) The best, but pricy, budget option in town, this clean, friendly and colourful hostel sits just two blocks from the beach and has excellent facilities including a kitchen, hot showers and a free breakfast. Booking through its website will net you a dollar discount on double rooms, meaning that it just scrapes in at the very top of the budget category.

Momo's Hostel (Map p278; ☎ 528 7471; www.momoshostel.com; 28 Ben Yehuda St; dm without bathroom 62NIS, d 140-220NIS, tr 280NIS;) This slightly scruffy but cheerful place has an attached bar-café and a central location. Rates include a light breakfast and use of the kitchen. In summer you may be able to sleep on the roof for 40NIS.

HI Tel Aviv Youth Hostel (Map p276; ☎ 544 1748; telaviv@iyha.org.il; 36 B'nei Dan St; dm without bathroom US$28, d US$84) With less of an international party vibe than the other hostels, this is nevertheless a clean and well-kept place with all the necessary amenities, situated close to the buzzing Old Port. Dorms are definitely budget; the slightly overpriced doubles are well into the midrange price category.

MIDRANGE

Hotel Sun Aviv (Map p278; ☎ 517 4847; www.sun-aviv.co.il; 9a Montefiore St; d US$85-125;) With just four beautifully decorated rooms, including the 'Aphrodite' equipped with a Jacuzzi (which the hotel suggests is 'ideal for marriage proposals') this is a warm and intimate choice. Situated at the heart of the city, the hotel is well placed for nights out on Rothschild Blvd.

Kikar Dizengoff Apartments (Map p278; ☎ 524 1151; www.hotel-apt.com; 89 Dizengoff St; s US$110-130, d US$110-170, ste US$180-210;) Overlooking Dizengoff Sq, these are secure and comfortable self-contained units equipped with cable TV, safes and kitchenettes. Some even have a Jacuzzi and neat balconies for watching the world go by.

Hotel de la Mer (Map p278; 510 0011; www.delamer.co.il; 2 Ness Ziona St, cnr HaYarkon; s/d from US$135/155;) Fancifully branding itself a 'Feng Shui hotel', the de La Mer gets top marks from travellers for its airy pastel-shaded rooms, great spa, personal attention by staff and sea views. The extensive breakfast, too, comes highly recommended and is sure to set you up for the day.

TOP END

Of course, you could stay in one of the well-known chains hugging the seaside: comfortable, corporate-feel branches of the Renaissance, Hilton, and Dan hotel chains are all up for grabs. Or you could try something a little different, as Tel Aviv slowly begins to cotton on to the notion of the boutique abode.

Cinema Hotel (Map p278; ☎ 520 7100; www.atlashotels.co.il; 2 Zamenhoff St; US$225/331;) Part of an Israeli hotel chain, the Cinema is located in an old namesake, and manages to be charming and individual, complete with old bits of projectors, cinema posters and old stage lighting.

Hotel Montefiore (Map p278; ☎ 564 6100; 36 Montefiore St; d US$350-450;) Antique-filled, bright and decadent, this is the newest, hottest place in town for travellers to splash out on a night of luxury in one of the 12 deliciously decorated rooms.

Eating

RESTAURANTS

It's hard to recommend just a handful of Tel Aviv restaurants, since it's rare to have a bad meal here. Here are a selection of favourites, but don't neglect to branch out and discover your own.

Brasserie M&R (Map p278; ☎ 696 7111; 70 Ibn Gvirol St; mains 50-100NIS; noon-5am) Wannabe French 'matradies' (complete with surly attitude) serve up mouth-watering steak and chicken dishes, in a dimly lit brasserie that stays busy even until the wee hours. It's quietly known as a meeting place for local celebrities, but still maintains a bustling neighbourhood atmosphere.

Benedict (Map p278; ☎ 686 8657; 29 Rothschild Blvd; 24hr) Where do you go if you're craving blueberry pancakes or eggs Benedict at five in the afternoon, or, for that matter, in the morning? This constantly crowded 24-hour breakfast place, with two branches in Tel Aviv, makes light work of breakfast in all its manifold forms, with pastries baked on site and nutella pots on the tables. The second branch is located at 171 Ben Yehuda St (Map p276).

our pick **Tchernikovsky 6** (Map p278; ☎ 620 8729; 5 Tchernikovsky St; mains from 45NIS; noon-midnight Mon-Fri, noon-6pm Sat & Sun) If it's a cool, calm night out you're after, you can't go wrong with this lovely local bistro run by a friendly young husband-and-wife team. There are cocktails and a delicious menu that changes almost daily; carnivores will melt at the 'butcher's cuts', while vegetarians will delight in gorgonzola salad, homemade gnocchi or polenta with grilled asparagus.

Pasta Mia (Map p278; ☎ 561 0189; 10 Wilson St; mains 30-60NIS; noon-midnight) Yum. That's all we can say to this little neighbourhood trattoria that produces fresh pasta daily and lets you match the pasta of your choice to any of a variety of sauces. It's tiny, candlelit and just like a little slice of Tuscany in a grubby Tel Aviv backstreet. The antipasti is great and the homemade limoncello's suitably stirring.

Batya (Map p276; ☎ 527 3888; 197 Dizengoff St; mains 28-55NIS; 11am-10pm Sun-Thu, 11am-6pm Fri) For hearty Jewish food just like your Polish grandmother used to make, pile up your plate at this Tel Aviv institution, with all your *gefilte fish* (poached fish patties), corned beef and *kneidelach* (dumpling) requirements. Though the menu's meat-heavy, the vegetable plate is huge and satisfying; go for mashed potato with just the right ratio of lumps, and the *gevetch*, a tomatoey vegie stew.

GAY & LESBIAN TEL AVIV

With its gay and lesbian–friendly air, and an annual Gay Parade in June to attest to it, Tel Aviv is without doubt the Middle East's most gay-friendly city.

The **Association of Gay Men, Lesbians, Bisexuals & Transgenders** (AGUDAH; Map p278; ☎ 620 5591; www.glbt.org.il; 28 Nachmani St) is a good place to pick up information on current events, though their *Pink Times* is in Hebrew only. Alternatively, try **CLAF** (Map p278; ☎ 516 5606; www.gay.org.il/claf; 22 Lilienblum St).

The hottest gay-friendly and gay-orientated clubs and bars in town change fast. Pick up *Time Out Tel Aviv* (p278) for up to the minute listings. Three long-standing favourites are.

- **Evita** (Map p278; ☎ 566 9559; 31 Yavne St; noon-late) This preppy café mutates into a saucy gay lounge-bar by night. There's plenty of pelvic shaking and free-flowing alcohol. It's located on a quiet alley a half block south of Rothschild Blvd.
- **Carpé Diem** (Map p278; ☎ 560 2006; 17 Montefiore St; 8pm-late) A relaxed atmosphere pervades this great loungey place. Tuesdays are for women only.
- **Minerva** (Map p278; ☎ 560 3801; 98 Allenby St; 10pm-late) Dedicated lesbian bar, with DJ dance parties every Thursday.

Beachgoers might want to check out (and be checked out at) the Hilton Beach, Tel Aviv's unofficial gay beach.

24 Rupees (Map p276; ☎ 681 8066; 14-16 Schoken St; thalis from 30NIS; noon-midnight; V) Head straight to Varanasi at this delicious Indian thali hangout, unprepossessingly located above a motorbike showroom on a hot and dusty industrial street. Slip off your shoes, slide onto a floor cushion, and munch on vegetarian food served on tin thali platters. The momos are fat and juicy, and the *gulab jamun* (dough dumplings in syrup) will satisfy all those who've craved it since leaving Delhi.

QUICK EATS

Fast food joints are never more than a few steps away in Tel Aviv, and Ben Yehuda, Allenby and Ibn Gvirol Sts in particular have a cauldron-full of them, dishing up everything from pizza to pancakes, sushi to sandwiches.

On Thursday evenings the **Dizengoff Centre** (Map p278) is overrun with food stalls, which you can take out to eat on the street. At the intersection of Frishman and Dizengoff Sts, you'll find the deservedly popular **sabich stall** (Map p278), open daily, except Saturday, from morning to late. This Iraqi-derived snack food consists of roast aubergine, boiled egg and potato, salad, hummus, pickles and spicy *amba* (mango) sauce, all stuffed into a pitta. Beware: it's highly addictive.

SELF-CATERING

Some of the best fresh fruit and vegetables to be found anywhere in town are sold at the Carmel Market (p280).

Tel Aviv is now overrun by two small chains of convenience supermarket, both offering a good selection, reasonable prices, and late-night hours. These are the AM-PM and Tiv Taam in the City: there's no point listing branches, as you'll barely walk 50 yards without passing one.

Drinking

Drinking is a serious business in Tel Aviv, and though locals don't go out to get plastered, they do like to prop up uber-hip bars till the wee hours, sipping on good wines or sophisticated cocktails combinations. The bars strung along Lillenblum St, Rothschild Blvd, Sheinkin St and dotted about the cute Neve Tsedek district are the current coolest locations.

Lanski (Map p278; ☎ 517 0043; 1st fl, Shalom Tower; 6 Montefiore St; 9pm-late Sat-Thu, 10pm-late Fri) Built in the shape of an 'H' for maximum eye-contact opportunities, this bar makes claim to being the biggest in the Middle East, an assertion we won't try to dispute. Sunday is bartender's night, when Tel Aviv's barmen come in to swap war stories.

Betty Ford (Map p278; ☎ 510 0650; 48 Nachalat Binyamin St; noon-late) A cool-as-Chardonnay lounge bar on a strip teeming with great small bars and eateries. This is a hip choice for a late night tipple, or a good spot for a tasty lunch, with lots of bar snacks gracing a good-value menu.

Bukowski (Map p278; ☎ 523 2323; 39 Frishman St; ⌚ 10pm-late) A cool, brick-walled hangout hidden behind an unassuming, unmarked exterior. As you might expect, it has a slightly literary feel and attracts a cool crowd, from students to Tel Aviv professionals.

Whisky a Go Go (Map p276; ☎ 544 0633; Old Port; ⌚ 9pm-late) One of a bevvy of trendy drinking destinations at Tel Aviv's Old Port, this massive, highly designed place is a delight for fans of burnished steel, matte wood, glass and chandeliers. The music's great, the drink portions are generous, and the crowd is a 20s-to-40s mix.

Mike's Place (Map p278; ☎ 052 267 0753; 86 Herbert Samuel Esplanade; ⌚ 4pm-late) On the beach, this is the place to go for live music. Blues and rock bands play nightly from 10.30pm. There's also a sizable menu of grill-style meals, cocktails and, especially, beer. Happy hour lasts from 4pm to 9pm, and all day on Saturday.

ISRAEL & THE PALESTINIAN TERRITORIES

Entertainment

Tel Aviv is well known for its nightlife, and the mind-boggling variety of spots can keep you crawling all night long.

NIGHTCLUBS

Tel Aviv has a number of world-class, party-till-dawn clubs, most without any of the ridiculous dress codes imposed, for example, in London. Check out *Time Out Tel Aviv* (p278) for club night listings.

Breakfast Club (Map p278; 6 Rothschild Blvd; ⌚ midnight-late) Night owls rejoice. One of the hippest clubs in town doesn't get going till around 3am, and only lets out when the sun comes up. A line-up of Israel's top DJs completes the picture; admission varies depending on which high musical priest is guarding the decks.

HaOman Tel Aviv (Map p276; 88 Arbanael St; admission 100NIS; ⌚ 1am-late) If you missed it in Jerusalem, catch this megaclub in its equally vast Tel Aviv incarnation. Five floors of mayhem, picky bouncers (dress your best) and an in-house sushi bar to boot.

TLV Club (Map p276; ☎ 544 4194; Old Port; admission 50-100NIS ⌚ midnight-late Mon, Fri & Sat) This massive party place in the port often hosts well-known Israeli rock stars. Admission prices vary depending on who is performing on the night.

THEATRE

New Cameri Theatre (Map p276; ☎ 606 0900; www.cameri.co.il; Golda Meir Centre, cnr Leonardo da Vinci St & Sha'ul HaMelech Ave) Hosts theatre performances in Hebrew, with simultaneous English translation of its most popular shows three times per week.

Habima Theatre (Map p278; ☎ 629 5555; Habima Sq, Tarsat Blvd) Home to Israel's national theatre company, Habima stages performances with simultaneous English-language translation most Thursdays.

Shopping

In case you lose the battle with your worthier instincts, the best clothes shopping districts are Sheinkin St (with lots of small boutiques), Dizengoff St (with Israeli designer stores toward the northern end), and the tiny one-of-a-kind shops dotting the Florentine and Neve Tsedek neighbourhoods.

If it's markets you're after, a **Nahalat Binyamin Craft Market** (Map p278; ⌚ 9.30am-5.30pm Tue, 9am-4pm Fri) runs twice weekly on Nachlat Binyamin St, with a festival-like atmosphere enhanced by some pretty good buskers. On Dizengoff Sq, an **'antiques' market** (Map p278) is held on the same days; haggle hard for the gems amongst the junk. The Carmel Market (p280) is the place for more perishable goods.

For shopping centres, try the central, sprawling, and confusingly-designed **Dizengoff Centre** (Map p278) or the **Azrieli Centre** (Map p276), which is a slightly classier experience. The Dizengoff Centre hosts **Designers Boutique** every Friday from 10.30am to 4pm, where young clothes designers take over the lower floor of the centre to sell their wares.

Sports

Tel Avivans are passionate about their football team, the Maccabee Tel Aviv. Big matches are played October to June at Ramat Gan National Stadium (Map p276), reached from downtown bus 20, 42 or 67. Buy your ticket at the stadium on game day for 40NIS to 120NIS or in advance from **Le-an ticket agency** (Map p278; ☎ 524 7373; 101 Dizengoff St).

Getting There & Away

AIR

See p331 for details of local and international air travel into Ben-Gurion airport and the smaller Sde Dov airport.

BUS

From Tel Aviv's enormous **central bus station** (Map p276; ☎ 694 8888; Levinski St) outgoing intercity buses depart from the 6th floor, where there's also an efficient information desk. Suburban and city buses use the poorly signposted stalls on the 4th floor. Tickets can usually be bought from the driver as well as from the company desks. Note that during Shabbat you'll have to resort to sheruts.

Buses 405 leaves from here for Jerusalem (17.70NIS, one hour, every 15 minutes); bus 910 for Haifa (23NIS, 1½ hours, every 20 minutes); and buses 830, 835 and 841 for Tiberias (42NIS, 2½ hours, every hour from 6am to 9pm). There are also services to Be'er Sheva (14NIS, 1½ hours, two to three hourly) and Eilat (65NIS, five hours, roughly hourly from 6.30am to 5pm), with an overnight Eilat service departing at 12.30am.

For services to Egypt, see p279.

SHERUT

The sheruts (shared taxis) line up outside the central bus station and run to Jerusalem (20NIS) and Haifa (25NIS). On Saturday, they leave from HaHamashal St just east of Allenby St and charge about 50% more than the weekday fare.

TRAIN

Tel Aviv has two train stations: the main station, **Tel Aviv Savidor Merkaz Train Station** (Map p276; ☎ 577 4000; www.israrail.org.il/english), and the smaller **HaShalom Train Station** (Map p276; HaShalom Interchange) – convenient for the Azrieli Centre. From Tel Aviv Merkaz, you can travel to Haifa (26.50NIS, one hour, hourly from 5am to midnight Sunday to Thursday, 5am to 3pm Friday), and on to Akko (35NIS, 1½ hours). Trains to Jerusalem depart hourly (19NIS, 45 minutes). Heading south, you can travel as far as Be'er Sheva (26NIS, 1¼ hours, hourly 6am to 10pm Sunday to Thursday, 7am to noon Friday). To reach Tel Aviv Merkaz from the centre, take bus 61 or 62 north from Dizengoff St. Trains don't run until after dusk on Saturdays.

Getting Around

Getting around the compact centre is easiest on foot, avoiding traffic snarls, packed buses and unscrupulous taxi drivers.

TO/FROM THE AIRPORT

From the central bus station, take bus 475 (11.70NIS), departing every 20 to 30 minutes. At least two trains per hour also service the airport from Tel Aviv Merkaz station (13NIS) between 3.30am and 11pm daily, but with limited services on Saturdays. A metred taxi from the centre of town to the airport should cost around 100NIS.

BICYCLE

Tel Aviv is flat and easy to get around by bike, though you might have to negotiate traffic, dogs, pedestrians, roadworks and other hurdles. A good rental option is **O-Fun** (Map p276; ☎ 544 2292; www.rentabikeisrael.com; 197 Ben Yehuda St), which rents bikes for 60NIS per day, including lock and helmet.

BUS

Tel Aviv city buses follow an efficient network of routes. The single fare is 5.20NIS, but for 12NIS you can buy a daily pass *(hofshi yomi)*, which allows unlimited bus travel around Tel Aviv and its suburbs. The city centre is well covered by bus 4, which travels from the **central bus station** (Map p276; ☎ 694 8888) to the Reading Terminal via Allenby, Ben Yehuda and northern Dizengoff Sts. Bus 5 is another useful one, running from the central bus station to Dizengoff Sq. Buses don't run on Shabbat (Saturday), until the evening.

SHERUTS & TAXIS

Sherut 4 follows the same route as bus 4 and operates on Shabbat, when the bus doesn't (for double the price), from the northern end of Ben Yehuda St to the bottom of Allenby St. If you're taking a taxi, make sure the driver turns the meter on; minimum fare is around 20NIS.

JAFFA יפו يافا

☎ **03 / pop 46,400**

After Noah was catapulted to watery fame, one of his sons, Japheth, headed for the coast and founded a new city named Jaffa (Yafo in Hebrew) in his own honour. During Solomon's time, it came to prominence as a major port city, and it's allegedly from here Jonah set sail to have his encounter with that famous whale.

Today, Jaffa's Old City is cute and gentrified. It's home to Jewish artists and craftspeople, while much of the remainder of this sprawling town is impoverished, home to Arab Muslims and Christians, and, increasingly, Tel Avivans looking for a more 'authentic' alternative to the dull high-rise Tel Aviv suburbs. This has sent prices in Ajami, a seaside Jaffa neighbourhood just south of the Old City, sky-rocketing, sometimes creating a new pocket of inter-faith tolerance, sometimes causing tension between Arab fishing families who've been here for generations, and their new, company car–owning neighbours.

Sights & Activities

For thousands of years, **Old Jaffa** was a thriving commercial and fishing port. The once-active residential community of longshore-men and market traders of today, however, is a pretty – if staid – maze of art studios, galleries and outdoor cafés. It centres on Kikar Kedumim (Kedumim Sq), ringed with restaurants and galleries and dominated by the pastel-shaded **St Peter's Church** (⌚ 8-11.45am & 3-5pm).

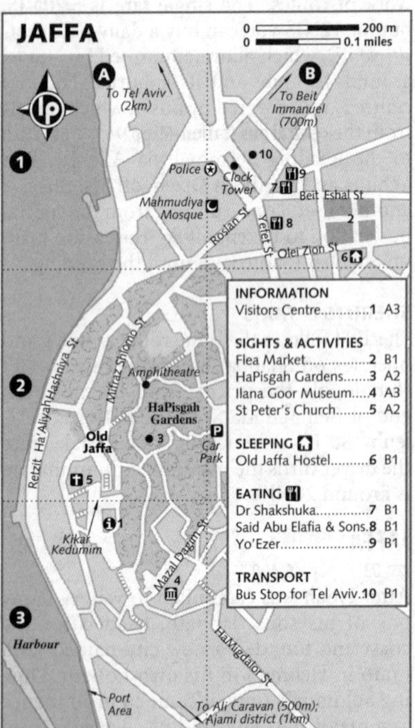

In an underground chamber at the centre of the square, a small **Visitors Centre** (⌚ 10am-6pm) describes the history of Jaffa from its beginnings as a Canaanite settlement nearly 4000 years ago, and offers a 15-minute film on its history. To the east of the square, the **HaPisgah Gardens** have a nice view north up the coast to Tel Aviv, and make a pretty stroll past some ancient Egyptian ruins.

Nearby, the **Ilana Goor Museum** (☎ 683 7676; www.ilanagoor.com; 4 Mazal Dagim St; adult/child/student/senior 24/14/20/20NIS; ⌚ 10am-4pm Sat-Thu, 10am-6pm Fri), housed in an 18th-century stone hostel on the aquatically named 'Lucky Fish' St, is a small museum featuring the sculptures and furniture of its artist-owner namesake.

If you're in the market for a lamp the shape of a Spanish guitar or a delightful formica table, head without delay to the teeming **flea market** (☎ 8am-6pm Sun-Thu, 8am-3pm Fri), which makes up the heart of 'new' Jaffa. Here, you can also satisfy all your nargileh, incense and Indian floaty clothing requirements, and munch on good-value meals in tiny local lunch joints.

After that filling lunch, walk down to the **Ajami** district, where gentrified Ottoman homes still exist side-by-side with tiny, ramshackle fishermen's shacks, for a taste of the real lives of Jaffa residents.

Sleeping

If the big city–style of Tel Aviv's not your thing, consider basing yourself in Jaffa, where the pace is a little less frenetic.

our pick Old Jaffa Hostel (☎ 682 2370; www.inisrael.com/old jaffahostel; 8 Olei Zion St; dm 68NIS, r 190-350NIS) In a beautiful old Turkish home, decorated with historic Arabic furniture and *objets d'art*, this place offers rather small but definitely cosy private rooms, and a lovely, breezy rooftop garden. Some travellers have recently complained about standards of cleanliness, but our visit found the hostel spick, span, and extremely welcoming.

Beit Immanuel (☎ 682 1459; www.beitimmanuel.org; 8 Auerbach St; dm 85-90NIS, s/d/tr 210/300/390NIS) Clean and tidy, this tucked-away guesthouse and hostel, attached to a Messianic community worship centre, is a great alternative to Tel Aviv's party-vibe hostels. It's perfect for those seeking a little

THE HUMMUS TO END ALL HUMMUS *Amelia Thomas*

Throughout your trip, you'll doubtless be subjected to many disagreements over where exactly sells the region's best hummus. But in this author's humble opinion (along with that of hundreds of in-the-known natives) there's no question that the world's hummus throne is housed within Jaffa's diminutive, unassuming **Ali Caravan** (Abu Hassan; Dolphin St; hummus portions from 20NIS; around 7am-2pm Sun-Thu).

This tiny restaurant, which you'll spot by its constant queue of locals waiting outside, is to the hummus-hungry as Jerusalem is to the God-fearing. It dishes up its hummus from huge cauldrons, serves it up alongside chunks of raw onion (for dipping) and vinegary chilli sauce (for pouring) and closes when the pots runneth dry. But beware: this will be one of your quickest lunch experiences ever. Your order appears almost before it's been placed, and you're expected to gobble it down at high speed, since other patrons are hovering just behind your shoulder waiting to take your seat. For a real bowl of manna from heaven, order the 'triple', a hummus-fuul-tahina combination, or the melt-in-the-mouth *masabacha* (a version of hummus containing whole chickpeas). Go. Queue. Enjoy. But don't tell the locals I told you.

tranquillity. The hostel welcomes families with children, and is housed in a lovely old building, built in 1884 by actor Peter Ustinov's father. Guesthouse rates include breakfast.

Eating

Said Abu Elafia & Sons (☎ 681 2340; 7 Yefet St; 24hr) This legendary bakery is where locals flock after a hard night on the tiles. Pastries, *sambusas* (a sort of Middle Eastern samosa), and Arabic takes on pizza, perfect for those late-night munchies.

Dr Shakshuka (☎ 682 2842; 3 Beit Eshal St; meals 35-50NIS; 8am-midnight Sun-Thu, 8am-3pm Fri) Don't miss this eccentric, family-run place, hurling out *shakshuka* from multiple gas burners at an incredible rate. There's also some mighty tasty couscous and a table-full of small salad plates.

Yo'Ezer (☎ 683 9115; 2 Ish Ha'bira St; mains from around 90NIS; 12.30pm-1am Sun-Thu, 11am-1am Fri & Sat) For a culinary treat – many say one of the best in Israel – you can't get better than Yo'Ezer. Hundreds of wonderful wines by the glass, a meat-heavy menu (though there's blue cheese and truffle-infused noodles for vegetarians) and a cozy, candle-lit atmosphere await.

Getting There & Away

From the centre of Tel Aviv, it's a pleasant 2.5km seafront stroll to Old Jaffa, though at the time of writing, parts of the seafront were being torn up in preparation for a new pedestrian boulevard. Alternatively, take bus 46 from the central bus station, bus 10 from Ben Yehuda St (or the train station), bus 26 from Ibn Gvirol St, bus 18 from Dizengoff St or bus 18 or 25 from Allenby St, and get off at the clock tower. To return to the centre, take bus 10 from immediately north of the clock tower.

HAIFA חיפה حيفا

☎ 04 / pop 267,000

The attractive multilevel city of Haifa spills down the wooded slopes of Mt Carmel and takes in a busy industrial port area, a trendy German Colony centred on Ben-Gurion Ave, and the landmark Baha'i Gardens. While Jerusalem is swathed in historical mystique and Tel Aviv buzzes with hedonism and *joie de vivre*, Haifa, Israel's third-largest city, might seem a bit provincial in comparison. Still, it's a nice place to wander for a couple of days, especially at the end of the year when the city's famously tolerant intercultural mix puts on its best face with the **Christmukkah** (joint Christmas/Eid-ul-Fitr/Hanukkah) festival.

Orientation

Haifa occupies three main tiers on the slopes of Mt Carmel. New arrivals by bus, train or boat are ushered into Haifa in the Port Area, also known as downtown. Uphill lie the busy Arab commercial district of Wadi Nisnas and the predominantly Russian Hadar district. The Carmel Centre district at the top of the mountain is home to the university, exclusive residences and trendy bars and eateries.

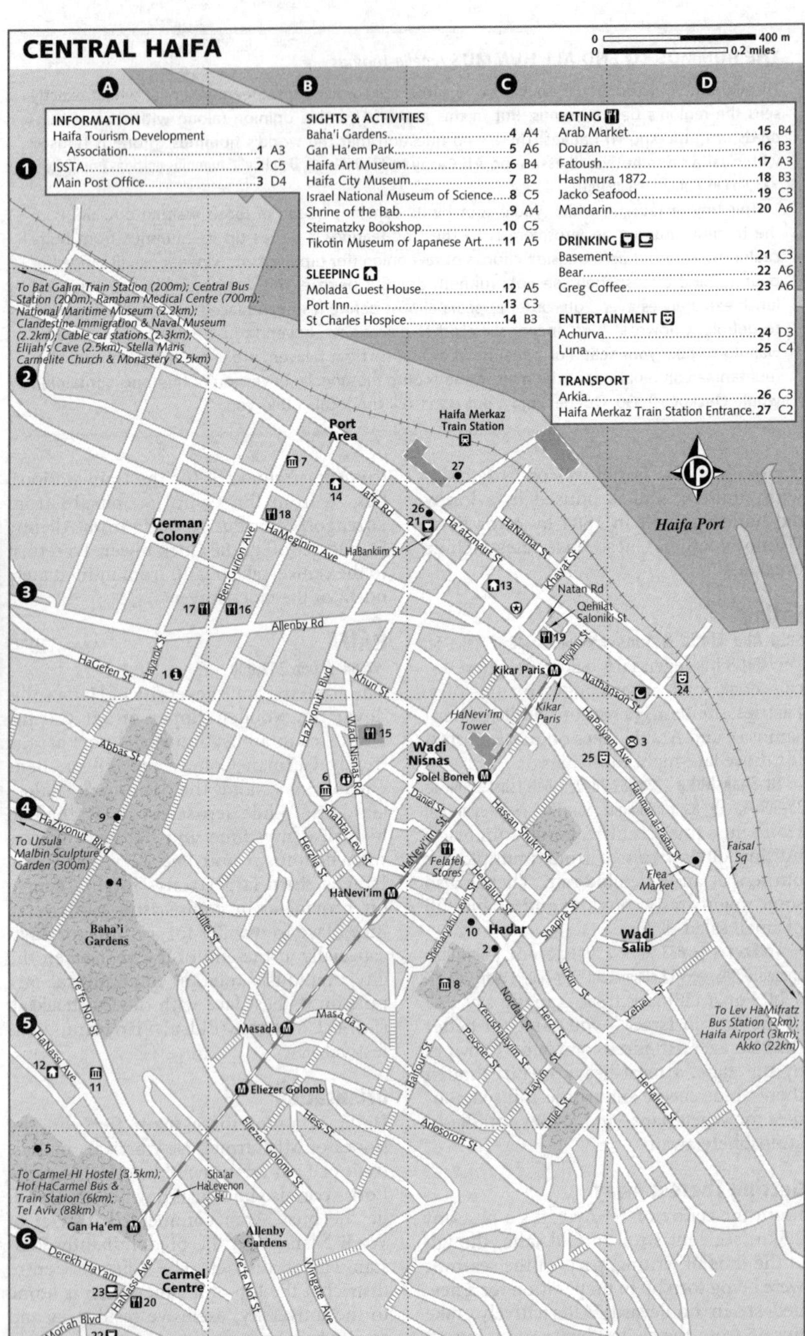
CENTRAL HAIFA
0 400 m
0 0.2 miles
A
B
C
D
1
2
3
4
5
6
INFORMATION
Haifa Tourism Development Association 1 A3
ISSTA 2 C5
Main Post Office 3 D4
SIGHTS & ACTIVITIES
Baha'i Gardens 4 A4
Gan Ha'em Park 5 A6
Haifa Art Museum 6 B4
Haifa City Museum 7 B2
Israel National Museum of Science 8 C5
Shrine of the Bab 9 A4
Steimatzky Bookshop 10 C5
Tikotin Museum of Japanese Art 11 A5
SLEEPING
Molada Guest House 12 A5
Port Inn 13 C3
St Charles Hospice 14 B3
EATING
Arab Market 15 B4
Douzan 16 B3
Fatoush 17 A3
Hashmura 1872 18 B3
Jacko Seafood 19 C3
Mandarin 20 A6
DRINKING
Basement 21 C3
Bear 22 A6
Greg Coffee 23 A6
ENTERTAINMENT
Achurva 24 D3
Luna 25 C4
TRANSPORT
Arkia 26 C3
Haifa Merkaz Train Station Entrance 27 C2
To Bat Galim Train Station (200m); Central Bus Station (200m); Rambam Medical Centre (700m); National Maritime Museum (2.2km); Clandestine Immigration & Naval Museum (2.2km); Cable car stations (2.3km); Elijah's Cave (2.5km); Stella Maris Carmelite Church & Monastery (2.5km)
Port Area
Haifa Merkaz Train Station
German Colony
Haifa Port
Jaffa Rd
HaMeginim Ave
Ha'atzmaut St
HaBankiim St
HaNamal St
Khayat St
Ben-Gurion Ave
Natan Rd
Qehilat Saloniki St
Allenby Rd
HaGefen St
Hayarok St
Kikar Paris
Eliyahu St
Nathanson St
Khuri St
HaZiyonut Blvd
Wadi Nisnas Rd
HaNevi'im Tower
Kikar Paris
HaPalyam Ave
Abbas St
Wadi Nisnas
Solel Boneh
Daniel St
Hassan Shukri St
Hammam al-Pasha St
HaZiyonut Blvd
To Ursula Malbin Sculpture Garden (300m)
Shabtai Levi St
HaNevi'im St
Felafel Stores
Faisal Sq
Flea Market
Herzlia St
HaNevi'im
HeHalutz St
Shemaryahu Levin St
Shapira St
Hadar
Wadi Salib
Baha'i Gardens
Hillel St
Sirkin St
Yehiel St
Ye'fe Nof St
Nordau St
Herzl St
Masada St
Masada
Yerushalayim St
Pevsner St
To Lev HaMifratz Bus Station (2km); Haifa Airport (3km); Akko (22km)
HaNassi Ave
Balfour St
Hayim St
Eliezer Golomb
HeHalutz St
Hillel St
Hess St
Arlosoroff St
Eliezer Golomb St
To Carmel HI Hostel (3.5km); Hof HaCarmel Bus & Train Station (6km); Tel Aviv (88km)
Sha'ar HaLevanon St
Gan Ha'em
Allenby Gardens
Derekh HaYam
Carmel Centre
HaNassi Ave
Ye'fe Nof St
Wingate Ave
Moriah Blvd

THE BAHA'I

After a trip to Haifa's Baha'i Gardens and Akko's Tomb of Mizra Hussein Ali (below), you might well wonder what the Baha'i are all about, except for having an eye for landscape gardening.

The Baha'i faith is one of the world's youngest religions, its origins lying in Shiraz, Iran with one Ali-Muhammed (1819–50), who declared that he was 'Al-Bab' (the gate) through which prophesies would be told. Though he quickly gathered followers, longevity wasn't one of his virtues: he was executed by firing squad for heresy in Tabris, at the age of 31.

His most notable successor was Mizra Hussein Ali, who proclaimed himself the messianic figure of whom Ali-Muhammed had spoken, and who was equally unpopular throughout the region. Exiled to Baghdad, Constantinople and Adrianople, he ended his days in Akko, but before his death laid out the principles of the Baha'i faith, whose name stems from the Arabic word *baha,* meaning glory.

Today, there are between 5 and 6 million Baha'i worldwide, who all adhere to the faith's central tenets of equality and unity, and who become Baha'i by choice after the age of 15. Haifa is of key importance to Baha'i across the world: each member must perform a pilgrimage here at least once in their life, walking the 1400 leg-acheing steps up the Baha'i Gardens. For more information, go to www.bahai.org.

Information

The Bank Leumi and Hapoalim Bank main branches are both on Jaffa Rd, and you'll find lots ATMs along most city streets; there are plenty of exchange places around Hadar. Post offices on HaPalyam and Ben-Gurion Ave will change travellers cheques.

Haifa Tourism Development Association (☎ 853 5605, toll free 1-800-305090; www.tour-haifa.co.il; 48 Ben-Gurion Ave) Immediately at the foot of the Baha'i Gardens, this tourist office distributes several useful maps and publications.

ISSTA (☎ 868 2227; www.issta.co.il; Bei Hakranot Bldg, 20 Herzl St) Books air tickets and sells student ID cards.

Main post office (19 HaPalyam Ave; 🕑 8am-12.30pm & 3.30-6pm Sun-Tue & Thu, 8am-1pm Wed, 8am-noon Fri)

Rambam Medical Centre (☎ 1-700-505-150; Bat Galim) A large, state-of-the-art hospital, 1km north of Haifa's port area.

Steimatzky Bookshop (☎ 866 4058; 16 Herzl St; 🕑 10am-7pm Sun-Thu, 10am-3pm Fri)

Sights

BAHA'I GARDENS

The stunning, immaculately kept multiple terraces of the dizzily sloped **Baha'i Gardens** (☎/fax 831 3131; www.terraces.bahai.org; admission free; 🕑 9am-5pm) are themselves alone a reason to visit Haifa. Apart from the top two tiers, the gardens are accessible to the general public only on hour-long guided tours (daily, except Wednesday), which must be prebooked well in advance by phone or fax. Baha'i pilgrims, however, can organise individual entry.

Amid the perfectly manicured gardens, fountains and walkways rises Haifa's most imposing landmark, the golden-domed **Shrine of the Bab** (🕑 9am-noon). Completed in 1953, this tomb of the Baha'i prophet, Al-Bab, integrates both European and oriental design, and is considered one of the two most sacred sites for the world's five million Baha'is (the other is the tomb of Mizra Hussein Ali; see p294). Visitors to the shrine must remove their shoes and dress modestly (no shorts or bare shoulders).

Near the upper entrance to the Baha'i Gardens you will find the **Ursula Malbin Sculpture Garden** (www.malbinsculpture.com; Gan HaPesalim; HaZiyonut Blvd), a small park filled with 'hands-on' sculptures, where families come to relax amid the greenery.

STELLA MARIS MONASTERY & ELIJAH'S CAVE

The neo-Gothic **Stella Maris Carmelite Church & Monastery** (☎ 833 7748; 🕑 6am-noon & 3-6pm), with its wonderful painted ceiling, was originally established as a 12th-century Crusader stronghold. The monastery was later used as a hospital for the troops of Napoleon in 1799, but was subsequently destroyed by the Turks. In 1836 it was replaced by the present structure. The easiest access to Stella Maris is via the **cable car** (☎ 833 5970; one way/return 16/22NIS; 🕑 10am-6pm) from the highway below.

Below Stella Maris, close to the highway, is the grotto called **Elijah's Cave** (admission free; 8am-5pm Sun-Thu, 8.30am-12.45pm Fri), considered holy by Christians, Jews and Muslims alike. Here the prophet Elijah hid from King Ahab and Queen Jezebel after slaying the 450 priests of Ba'al (Kings 1:17-19). The adjacent garden is a favoured picnic site for local Christian Arabs. Take bus 44 or 45 from downtown.

GAN HA'EM (MOTHER'S PARK)

Rest weary calf muscles after climbing Haifa's steep streets at this attractive green **park** (837 2390; adult/child 30/15NIS; 8am-5pm Sun-Thu, 9am-4pm Fri) on the crest of Carmel Centre, with its amphitheatre, cafés and attractive small zoo. Bus 21, 28 or 37 from downtown will drop you near the zoo.

MUSEUMS

The **Haifa Art Museum** (852 3255; www.haifamuseums.org.il; 26 Shabtai Levi St; adult/senior/child/student 29/14.50/22/22NIS; 10am-4pm Sun-Wed & Sat, 10am-9pm Thu, 10am-1pm Fri) is three museums in one – ancient art, modern art, and music and ethnology. The same ticket (good for three days) also admits you to the following museums, all with the same opening hours as the Art Museum: **Haifa City Museum** (851 2030; 11 Ben-Gurion Ave), with exhibitions by local artists; the wonderful **Tikotin Museum of Japanese Art** (838 3554; 89 HaNassi Ave) and its unique collection of Far Eastern works; and the **National Maritime Museum** (853 6622; 198 Allenby Rd), which presents the history of Mediterranean shipping.

The **Clandestine Immigration & Naval Museum** (853 6249; 204 Allenby Rd; adult/child 10/5NIS; 8.30am-4pm Sun-Thu) is a surprisingly interesting place to brush up on Israel's naval history and the Zionists' 1930s and '40s attempts to migrate into British-blockaded Palestine with its centrepiece boat, the *Af-Al-Pi-Chen*, which attempted to carry 434 Jewish refugees here in 1947.

If you're stuck with a very occasional rainy day, a great place to take kids is the hands-on **Israel National Museum of Science** (862 8111; www.madatech.org.il; Technion Bldg, Shmaryahu Levin St, Hadar; over 5s/students 60/30NIS; 9am-4pm Sun-Wed, 9am-8pm Thu, 10am-2pm Fri, 10am-6pm Sat). For a 'sensory cinema' experience (allegedly the world's first and only), pay an extra 20NIS to experience the Cinematrix, suitable for everyone aged over six.

Tours

The **Haifa Tourism Development Association** (toll free 1-800-305090, ext 101/102; www.tour-haifa.co.il; 48 Ben-Gurion Ave) offers a number of tours, including a four-hour walking or bus tour of the city, and a dramatised tour of the German Colony. Drop in, or check out the website for more details. Telephone tour bookings can be made.

Sleeping

our pick **Port Inn** (852 4401; www.portinn.co.il; 34 Jaffa Rd; dm without bathroom 70NIS, s with/without bathroom 180/210NIS, d with/without bathroom 250/300NIS;) The simply furnished, bright, clean dorms and rooms of the Port Inn make for the most comfortable central budget stay. There's a kitchen available for use and a nice quiet garden. Dorm beds cost an extra 25NIS if you want breakfast thrown in (not to the bunk, of course); with private rooms, it's included in the price.

Carmel HI Hostel (853 1944; www.iyha.org.il; dm/s/d US$20/37.50/56;) Comfortable and friendly, this place is close to the Hof HaCarmel train and bus station, but less convenient for Haifa's main tourist attractions. Take bus 3 or 114 from the Hof HaCarmel station or bus 43 or 45 from downtown.

St Charles Hospice (855 3705; stcharls@netvision.net.il; 105 Jaffa Rd; s/d/tr US$35/60/75) With a lovely garden, this place is owned by the Latin Patriarchate and run by the Catholic Rosary Sisters. Rooms all have fans and private showers and rates include a filling breakfast. The gate is often locked so you'll need to ring the bell to enter.

Molada Guest House (838 7958; www.rutenberg.org.il; 82 HaNassi Ave; s/d US$60/76;) Run by the Rutenberg Institute for Youth Education, this welcoming guesthouse has clean, comfortable rooms, some with balconies that offer sea views.

Eating

RESTAURANTS

Hashmura 1872 (855 1872; 15 Ben-Gurion Ave; mains 45-105NIS; noon-midnight Sun-Thu, noon-8pm Fri & Sat) Situated in the heart of the German Colony, this place comes with hearty recommendations from both locals and visitors. To start, try the aubergine terrine; for mains, there's lots of French-style meat and fish dishes, and veggie pasta options. A glass floor reveals the extensive wine cellar in the historic 1872 basement, where there's also an atmospheric pub.

Jacko Seafood (☎ 866 8813; 12 Qehilat Saloniki St; mains 65-85NIS; ⌚ noon-midnight Sun-Thu, noon-8pm Fri & Sat) A reliable seafood option, this place has been offering an excellent variety of fish (including salmon, bream, bass, shark, triggerfish and St Peter's fish) and seafood (calamari, crab or shrimp), for the last three decades.

Fatoush (☎ 852 4930; 38 Ben-Gurion Ave; mains 50-70NIS; ⌚ 8am-1am) All decked out in Bedouin style, Fatoush is an atmospheric German Colony place serving good salads, mezze and Mediterranean fare. In summer, its outdoor area is a good spot for watching the world go by.

our pick **Douzan** (☎ 852 5444; 35 Ben-Gurion Ave; mains from 30NIS; ⌚ 10am-1am) Look no further for delicious, authentic Middle Eastern food, dished up in a great, central location. The home-cooked feel of the food, with its French influences, is all down to the family recipes rustled up by owner Fadi Najar's mother Leila, who's out to ensure that diners don't leave hungry.

QUICK EATS

Around the HaNevi'im St end of HeHalutz St, you'll find a wide range of excellent felafel and shwarma cubbyholes, as well as bakeries selling sweet pastries, sticky buns and other delights. The other prime shwarma area is Allenby Rd, around HaZiyonut Blvd. For fruit and vegetables, shop at the great little Arab Market in Wadi Nisnas on Wadi Nisnas Rd.

Drinking & Entertainment

For an evening out, locals head for the slick bars and cafés along Moriah Blvd and the environs of Carmel Centre. A handful of bars and nightclubs are clustered around downtown.

Bear (☎ 838 1703; 135 HaNassi Ave; meals 35-75NIS; ⌚ 6pm-3am Sun-Wed, 11am-4am Thu-Fri, 5pm-3am Sat) The Bear, Haifa's only Irish-style pub, is regarded as the city's main expat hangout and sports bar. For meals, you can choose between salads, sandwiches, chicken, steak and seafood, washed down with your choice of 12 different draught beers.

Basement (☎ 853 2367; 2 HaBankiim St; ⌚ 9pm-3am) Dim, hedonistic and rowdy, this alternative rock bar is popular with young Haifans. Live music is featured on Saturdays while Sunday is open-mike night; aspiring rock stars will have a captive audience.

Greg Coffee (3 Derekh HaYam St; ⌚ 7am-1am) If it's a good cup of joe you're after, or some fantastic brownies to munch while availing of the free wi-fi, try this cute little café in Carmel Centre.

Downtown dance places, such as **Luna** (HaPalyam St; ⌚ midnight-late Thu-Fri) and **Achurva** (Captain Steve St; ⌚ midnight-sunrise Thu) all charge from around 70NIS, and open on weekends; don't even think of hitting the dancefloor before about 1am.

Getting There & Away

AIR

Arkia (☎ 861 1600; www.arkia.com; 80 Ha'Atzmaut St) connects Haifa with Eilat (one-way from around US$68, 1¼ hours). The airport is around 3km from the town centre.

BUS

Arriving from the south, passengers are dropped off at the new Hof HaCarmel bus station (adjacent to the train station of the same name) from where you can take bus 103 downtown. The old **central bus station** (HaHaganah Ave) handles city buses northwest of town. Buses to Akko, Nahariya and Galilee use the eastern bus terminal at Lev HaMifratz.

During the day, bus 910 departs every 20 minutes for Tel Aviv (23NIS, 1½ hours); bus 940 or 947 leaves every 15 minutes for Jerusalem (39NIS, 2½ hours). Heading north, bus 251 and 252 (express) stop at Akko (15NIS, 30 to 50 minutes). Eastbound, bus 430 goes to Tiberias (35NIS, 1½ hours) and bus 332 goes to Nazareth (22NIS, 45 minutes). The amount of departures per day for Akko, Tiberias and Nazareth varies greatly; check for details at the bus station.

TRAIN

Haifa has three train stations: **Haifa Merkaz**, near the port; **Bat Galim**, adjacent to the central bus station (accessible via the passage from platform 34); and **Hof HaCarmel**, at the new southern bus terminal of the same name. From Haifa Merkaz, trains depart around every 20 minutes for Tel Aviv (26NIS, 1½ hours), and north to Nahariya (16.50NIS, 45 minutes) via Akko (13NIS, 30 minutes).

Getting Around

The only underground in Israel, the **Carmelit** (☎ 837 6861; per person 5.50NIS; 6am-10pm Sun-Thu, 6am-3pm Fri, 7pm-midnight Sat), connects Kikar Paris with Carmel Centre, via the Hadar district. Visitors can ride to the top and see the city sights on a leisurely downhill stroll.

CAESAREA קיסריה قيصريا

☎ 04 / pop 3400

First developed by the Persians in the 6th century BC, Caesarea never amounted to much until about 30 BC when Herod the Great made it the headquarters of the Roman government in Palestine. The palaces, temples, churches and mosques built by Herod and subsequent conquerors have all but disappeared, but their ruins, stretching along the Mediterranean for over 1km, are a world-class archaeological site, making an easy day trip from Tel Aviv or Haifa.

Sights & Activities

The **Caesarea National Park** (☎ 636 1358; adult/child 23/12NIS; 8am-5pm), contains the remains of a Crusader city, with its citadel and harbour. Beyond the walls to the north stretch the beachfront remains of an impressive **Roman aqueduct**. A hippodrome lies to the south, and beyond this, a reconstructed **Roman amphitheatre**, which serves as a modern-day concert venue. It makes a great wander, especially for children who can clamber the ruins to their hearts' content; look out for the colonies of squabbling bats that roost in the ancient archways. There are several restaurants, cafés and shops on site, so you can take a break from your explorations for a leisurely waterfront lunch.

Getting There & Away

From Tel Aviv, take any bus headed north along the coastal road towards Khadera, where you can disembark and connect with bus 76 to Caesarea. Coming from Haifa, get off at the Caesarea intersection and hike the last 3.5km to the site. Alternatively, take the train to Binyamina from Tel Aviv (22NIS, 45 minutes) or Haifa (17.50NIS, 30 minutes) and pick up a taxi for the last 7km.

AKKO (ACRE) עכו عكا

☎ 04 / pop 45,900

Akko, a Unesco World Heritage–rated stone-walled fortress town on the Mediterranean, is small but perfectly formed. Here, you can wander narrow alleyways and explore vaults, ramparts and towers, with barely a trace of tourist-orientated tat. Unlike Old Jaffa further south, Old Akko's beautiful stone houses remain homes to local families rather than well-heeled artists, and its souq and quays are still home to fishermen, rather than boutiques and gentrified cafés.

History

Akko is the Crusader city of Acre, under whom it rose to prominence as a port, receiving ships from as far afield as Venice and Amalfi, and playing host to a young Marco Polo on his way to the court of Khublai Khan. Its modern history has ensured it retains many of the features Polo himself might have observed: during the Jewish immigration of the 1930s, Akko was a hotbed of Arab hostility, meaning that few Jews chose to settle in the Old City. Since then, things have remained pretty much the same, and Old Akko remains a predominantly Arab place.

Orientation

From the bus and train stations, it's roughly a 2km walk to Old Akko. From the bus station, exit to the left on Derekh HaArba'a St and continue one long block to the traffic lights. There, turn right (west) onto Ben Ami St. After two blocks turn left onto Weizmann St and you'll see the city walls ahead. The train station is about 300m further east from the bus station.

Information

Public Library (9am-7pm Sun-Thu, 9am-3pm Fri) Located 200m north of the old city walls, the library offers internet access for 7NIS per 30 minutes.

Tourist office (☎ 995 6707; www.akko.org.il; 1 Weizmann St; 8.30am-6pm Sat-Thu & 8.30am-5pm Fri in summer, 8.30am-5pm Sat-Thu & 8.30am-3pm Fri in winter) Located north of the Festival Garden, inside the Crusader Citadel, the tourist office can arrange guided tours, boat trips and offers lots of info on Akko and around.

Sights

OLD AKKO

A visit to Old Akko begins by stepping through city walls built by Ahmed Pasha al-Jazzar in 1799 following Napoleon's thwarted attempt to capture Akko. Immediately, you'll be thrust back, time-machine–like, into another century.

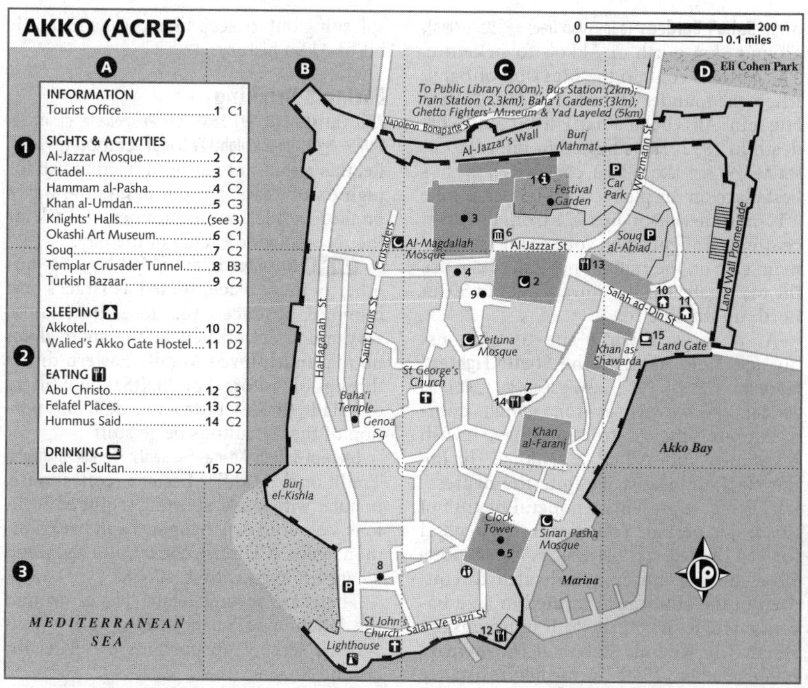

The 1781 **Al-Jazzar Mosque** (admission 6NIS; 8am-5pm Sat-Thu, 8-11am & 1-5pm Fri), with its green, Turkish dome and minaret, is the dominant element on the Akko skyline. North of the mosque is the rambling **Citadel**, built by the Turks in the 17th century on 13th-century Crusader foundations. Here you'll find the tourist office where you can buy a great value **combination ticket** (adult/child 46/39NIS), which allows admission to most of Old Akko's sights, including the Citadel, Knight's Halls, Hammam al-Pasha, Okashi Art Museum and the Templar Crusader Tunnel. After a short film about the city, grab a free audio headset to lead you around the **Knight's Halls** (adult/child 27/24NIS; 8.30am-5pm Sun-Thu, 8.30am-2pm Fri), an atmospheric series of vaulted halls that 8m below street level, once headquarters of the crusading Knights Hospitallers. Today, the annual October **Akko Fringe Theatre Festival** is staged here.

From here, a series of winding passages will take you to a **Turkish Baazar**. Turn right from here to reach the **Hammam al-Pasha** (Turkish Bath), housed in the 1780 bathhouse built by Al-Jazzar, which remained in use until the 1940s. The hammam now contains a 30-minute **multi-media show** (adult/child 25/21NIS; 8.30am-5pm Sun-Thu, 8.30am-2pm Fri) called 'Balan, The Bath Attendant'. From the hammam walk back towards the Citadel to the **Okashi Art Museum** (adult/child 10/7NIS; 8.30am-5pm Sun-Thu, 8.30am-2pm Fri), an art gallery that's dedicated to one of Old Akko's few Jewish residents, Avshalom Okashi (1916–80).

From the Citadel, follow the alley south into the **souq**, the Old City's main, workaday marketplace. Beyond the souq lies the **Khan al-Umdan (Inn of the Pillars)**, once a grand khan (caravanserai or inn) that served camel trains carrying grain from the hinterlands, and whose courtyard now often hosts impromptu football games. En route to the harbour, don't miss the amazing **Templar Crusader Tunnel** (adult/child 10/7NIS; 8.30am-5pm Sun-Thu, 8.30am-4pm Fri), an underground passageway that connected the port to a Templar palace.

NEW AKKO

The complementary attraction to Haifa's Baha'i Gardens (p289), are Akko's very own **Baha'i Gardens** (admission free; 9am-4pm), around 3km north of Akko's town centre. The gardens contain the Mansion of Bahji, where the founder of the Baha'i faith, Mizra Hussein Ali (Baha'u'llah) lived until his death in 1892. He is buried in the adjacent **shrine** (9am-noon Fri-Mon), considered the holiest place on the planet for the Baha'i. Take a 10-minute ride on bus 271 from the town centre, and alight when you see the gardens' main gate on the right. Only Baha'i can use the main gate: use the entrance about 500m north up the side road.

Another worthwhile site to visit just outside New Akko is the **Ghetto Fighters' Museum** (995 8052; www.gfh.org.il; adult/child 20/18NIS; 9am-4pm Sun-Thu), which commemorates the ghetto uprisings, Jewish resistance and Allied assistance during the Nazi Holocaust. Despite the depressing theme, it presents a hopeful picture of this tragic period. Your ticket is also good for **Yad Layeled** (9am-4pm Sun-Thu, 10am-5pm Sat) a moving museum dedicated to children of the Holocaust, located in an adjacent circular structure. Both museums are situated in Kibbutz Lohamei HaGheta'ot, established in 1949 by former resistance fighters from the ghettos of Germany, Lithuania and Poland. To get here, take bus 270 or 271 north to Nahariya and ask your driver to drop you at the kibbutz.

Sleeping

Walied's Akko Gate Hostel (991 0410; fax 981 5530; Salah ad-Din St; dm 30NIS, s/d 200/220NIS, s/d without bathroom 120/140NIS;) In this split personality guesthouse, you've a choice of decent street-side rooms with attached bathrooms, or stuffy nonattached rooms that overlook a grubby yard filled with discarded metal bunk beds. Owner Walied can arrange trips to the Golan Heights (200NIS) when there is enough demand. Call for a free pick up from the station.

our pick **Akkotel** (987 7100, 981 0626; Salah ad-Din St; d US$165-250) This gorgeous place, recently opened by an Arab Catholic local with the dream of rejuvenating Old Akko, offers 16 boutique hotel rooms – the suites are particularly opulent – each individually designed and decorated, with 18th-century stone walls built by Al-Jazzar himself. Once an Ottoman guard HQ, and later a boys' school and magistrates court, it's well worth splashing out to sleep like a pasha in a little bit of Akko history.

Eating & Drinking

Abu Christo (991 5653; Sea Promenade; mains 50-90NIS; 10am-midnight) A local seafood favourite, this restaurant has been dishing fish for nigh on 60 years. Eat out beside the waves on the lovely terrace in summer, and ask for the recommended catch of the day.

our pick **Hummus Said** (6am-2pm) Yet another of those places touted as Israel's best hummus producer, this local institution, very much entrenched in the souq, doles up that much-loved Middle Eastern dip to throngs of visitors. For 20NIS, you'll fill up on salads, pickles, pitta and a delicious portion of the ubiquitous beige stuff.

Leale al-Sultan (Khan as-Shawarda; 9am-midnight) Traditional Middle Eastern coffeehouse, popular with locals, sporting sequined cushions, colourful wall hangings and backgammon tables. A Turkish coffee costs 5NIS, and a nargileh to go with it, 10NIS.

There are several felafel places around the junction of Salah ad-Din and Al-Jazzar Sts, serving up portions of felafel for around 5NIS.

Getting There & Away

Akko's bus terminal and train station lie about a 1.7km or 20-minute walk from the main entrance to the Old City. For Haifa, buses 251 and 252 depart frequently (15NIS, 30 to 50 minutes). The most pleasant way to travel between Akko and Haifa (13NIS, 28 minutes), however, is by train along the beachfront railway. Trains pass in both directions around three times per hour. Tel Aviv trains run twice an hour between 1am and 10pm (35NIS, 1½ hours).

GALILEE الجليل הגליל

With its lush scenery and religious heritage, Galilee's green valleys, verdant forests, fertile farmland and, of course, the Sea of Galilee, all provide relief from the drier lands to the south. It's a popular weekend getaway for southerners, as well as a firm favourite for those on the Christian tour-group itinerary, who come to Galilee to follow in Jesus's footsteps, except, of course, on that one particularly watery walk.

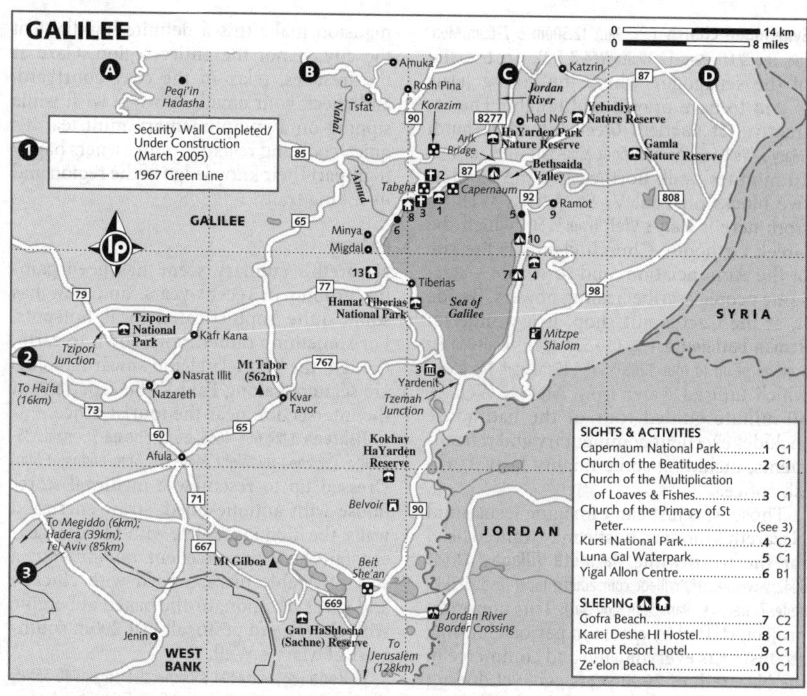

NAZARETH نצרת الناصرة

☎ 04 / pop 64,600

If you've already been to Bethlehem, don't expect something anywhere near as bucolic and serene when you pull up (probably not on a donkey) at the childhood home of Jesus. Modern Nazareth is chaotic, fume-filled and the largest Arab city in Israel. But still, peel away that traffic-clad exterior and you'll find charming vestiges of the past: the crumbling mansions of the Old City, the myriad churches scattered through town, and the colourful old souq. Armed with a portion or two of local *kunafa* (syrupy curd cheese pastry) to provide energy for all those sights, you might just find that you'd like to stick around after all.

Orientation & Information

Most sites of pilgrim interest are concentrated around the Old City, centring on Paul VI St and El-Bishara St (also called Annunciation or Casa Nova St). On El-Bishara St, just above the Paul VI intersection, is the helpful **tourist office** (☎ 657 0555; www.nazarethboard.org; 8.30am-5pm Mon-Fri, 8.30am-2pm Sat).

Sights

Nazareth's revered Roman Catholic **Basilica of the Annunciation** (El-Bishara St; 8.30-11.45am & 2-5.30pm Mon-Sat) is the largest church in the Middle East and stands on the site where Catholics believe the Angel Gabriel announced to the Virgin Mary that she would bear the Son of God. Its rather bland 1969 exterior is redeemed somewhat by remnants of earlier Crusader and Byzantine churches inside the dimly lit 'lower church' downstairs.

At the **Sisters of Nazareth Convent** (☎ 655 4303; admission by appointment), a school for deaf and blind children just up the street, you can see one of the best examples of a Herodian tomb, a type of tomb sealed by a rolling stone, which lies under the present courtyard. The nearby **Church of St Joseph** (El-Bishara St; 8.30-11.45am & 2-5.30pm Mon-Sat), built in 1914, occupies the traditional site of Joseph's carpentry shop, over the remains of a medieval church.

The **Al-Balda al-Qadima souq** (9am-5pm Mon, Tue, Thu & Fri, 9am-2pm Wed & Sat), west of upper El-Bishara St, occupies a maze of narrow streets. In its midst sits the **Greek Catholic**

Synagogue-Church (9am-12.30pm & 2-6pm Mon, Tue, Thu & Fri, 9am-12.30pm Wed & Sat), on the site of the synagogue where the young Jesus is said to have prayed and taught. The attractive **St Gabriel's Greek Orthodox Church** (Mary's Well Sq; 8am-6pm Mon-Sat) lies about 10 minutes' walk northeast of the basilica, two blocks off Paul VI St. Across Well Sq from here is **Mary's Well** (Paul VI St), which the Greek Orthodox Church claims is the site of the Annunciation, and to whose waters some people ascribe healing powers. Beside it, at the Cactus gift shop, is a wonderful **Roman bathhouse** (050 538 4343; admission for a group of up to four 120NIS; 10am-7pm Mon-Sat), which utilised water from Mary's Well. A 40-minute guided tour of the bathhouse includes excellent commentary and refreshments, including some mighty tasty Turkish coffee.

Those who just can't imagine Jesus amid Nazareth's modern bustle may want to head for the worthwhile **Nazareth Village** (645 6042; www.nazarethvillage.com; adults/under 18s 50/22NIS, under 7s free; 9am-5pm Mon-Sat). This nonprofit project, staffed by actors in period clothing, reconstructs everyday life and commerce in the Nazareth of 2000 years ago, yet doesn't trespass into distressingly tacky theme-park territory. It's a 15-minute walk due west from the basilica, just beyond Al-Wadi al-Jawani St.

Sleeping

Sisters of Nazareth Convent (655 4304; fax 646 0741; dm US$8, s/d US$28/46;) With dormitories and 30 private rooms, this is a nice, well-furnished and airy choice. Kitchen facilities are available, and private room rates include breakfast. Look for the door marked 'Religieuses de Nazareth', and ring the bell. Reception opens at 4pm and closes at 9.30pm.

Casa Nova Hospice (645 6660; fax 657 9630; El-Bishara St; s/d US$30/60;) Opposite the basilica, the Casa Nova caters mainly to Italian pilgrimage groups; its austerity offset by fantastic Italian food and a heavenly espresso (breakfast and dinner included in room rates). There's a 10pm curfew, and it's worth booking in advance to ensure there's room at the inn.

our pick **Fauzi Azar Inn** (602 0469; www.fauziazarinn.com; dm/d/tr from 67/400/480NIS;) Ten rooms in a beautifully restored Old City mansion make this a definite highlight of the city, if not the entire region. Gaze at the frescoes, relax in the cozy courtyard, and check your email with free wi-fi while sipping on a complimentary mint tea. It's quiet, cool, and relaxing, with owners happy to impart their knowledge of the region and its hiking trails.

Eating

Nazareth's culinary scene has been gaining ground in recent years, and now has some quite sophisticated local hotspots. For something rather more down to earth, though, the best felafel and shwarma joints are scattered along Paul VI St, especially at the intersection near the tourist office.

Tishreen (608 4666; 56 El-Bishara St; mains 35-75NIS; noon-midnight Mon-Sat, 5pm-midnight Sun) Dressed up to resemble a medieval storehouse with antique-lined, straw-encrusted walls, the menu is replete with Middle Eastern fare. Try the excellent *muhammar*, a sort of Arabic pizza topped with chicken and slices of onion, or the baked aubergine with cheese and pesto, all just 200m southwest of Mary's Well.

El-Reda (608 4404; Albesharah St; mains 40-55NIS; 1pm-2am Mon-Sat, 7pm-2am Sun) Dine on heavenly delights in a century-old restored mansion, with incredible views from the roof terrace and a family-run ambience. Try the roast chicken in yogurt sauce for a particularly lip-smacking luncheon.

our pick **Diana** (657 2919; Paul VI St; mains 55-75NIS; noon-midnight) Considered by locals and tourists alike as one of the best sources of Arabic cuisine in northern Israel, don't miss a dinner at Diana. Behind the unassuming exterior, you'll find dozens of delicious mezze to fill you to bursting.

Getting There & Away

From **Nazareth Bus Station** (656 9956; Paul VI St) bus 431 runs hourly to Tiberias (21.50NIS; 45 minutes). Other services include bus 332 to Haifa (22NIS, 45 minutes); bus 343 to Akko (25NIS, one hour); and bus 824 to Tel Aviv (15NIS, 2½ hours) via Afula. To get to Jerusalem, take bus 355 or 356 to Afula (7NIS, 20 minutes) and change there. Sheruts to Tiberias leave from in front of Hamishbir department store on Paul VI St. For Haifa and Tel Aviv, they leave from the Paz petrol station on Paul VI St.

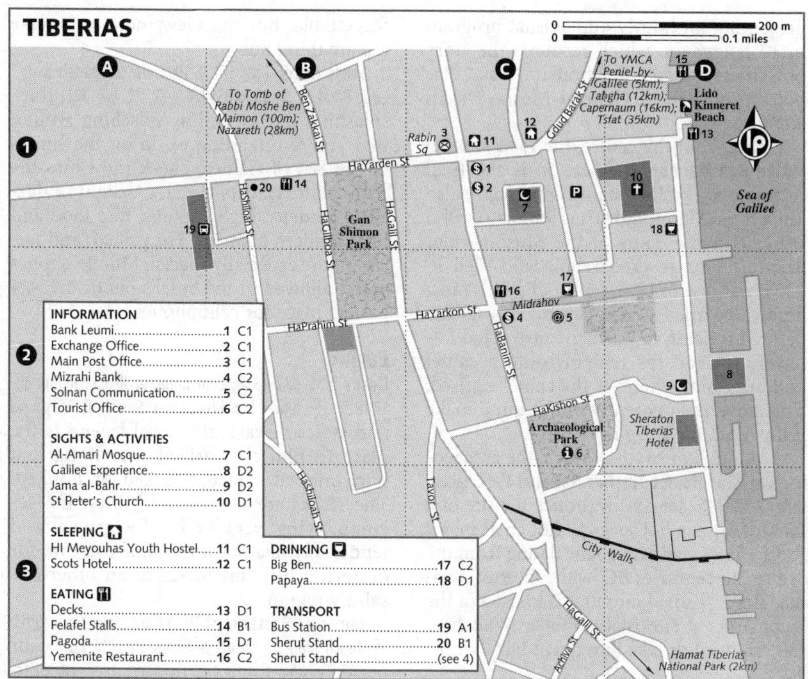

TIBERIAS טבריה طبريا

☎ 04 / pop 40,100

Though not exactly an attractive lakeside town in the fashion of European hotspots like Garda or Geneva, Tiberias makes a convenient jumping-off spot for exploring the Sea of Galilee. With its tombs of Jewish sages and ancient ritual baths, it's a popular holidaying spot for the ultra-Orthodox, who crowd its concrete high-rise hotels in high season. Come expecting the picturesque, though, and you'll be sorely disappointed. Most of the town itself is a '70s throwback decidedly lacking in glam or intrigue. You'll need to head out further around the shores of the Sea of Galilee to find that magical, mystical feeling associated with the evocative, biblical name.

Information

Bank Leumi (HaBanim St) and **Mizrahi Bank** (HaBanim St) both charge a 4% commission.

Exchange Office (HaBanim St; 10am-7pm) No commission money changer.

Main post office (cnr HaYarden & HaBanim Sts; 7am-6pm Sun-Thu, 7am-noon Fri) Also changes travellers cheques.

Solnan Communication (☎ 672 6470; 3 Midrahov; per hr 20NIS; 8am-11pm) Internet café and international phone office.

Tourist office (☎ 672 5666; 9 HaBanim St; 9am-4.30pm Sun-Thu, 9am-1pm Fri) Located in the Archaeological Park, this office has free maps of Tiberias, Nazareth and the Galilee area.

Sights

The dignified but utterly incongruous mid-18th-century **Al-Amari Mosque** is one of the few historic structures in Tiberias' Old Town; a second mosque, the waterfront **Jama al-Bahr** (1880), with a special entrance for those arriving by boat, now stands forlorn and abandoned. The pretty **St Peter's Church** (mass 6pm Mon-Sat, 8.30pm Sun), also on the waterfront, was originally built by 12th-century Crusaders, but the present structure dates from 1870. The boat-shaped nave is a nod to St Peter's piscatorial profession.

If experiencing Tiberias itself is not enough, you could always spend some time at the **Galilee Experience** (☎ 672 3620; adult/student US$6/5; 9am-10pm Sun-Thu, 9am-4pm Fri), presenting an hourly audiovisual program in 12 languages, which recounts the story of Galilee, bringing in Abraham, Jesus, Napoleon and Israeli General Moshe Dayan along the way.

Uphill from the centre, the **Tomb of Rabbi Moshe Ben Maimon** (Ben Zakkai St) is the final resting place of the Spanish physician, also known as Maimonides or Rambam, who worked in the court of the Muslim ruler Saladin. This revered rabbi, who died in 1204, was one of 12th-century Egypt's most highly regarded sages. Legend has it that before his death in Cairo, he instructed followers to load his remains onto a camel and bury him wherever the camel expired. The creature apparently didn't quite make it downhill for a dip in the lake.

Around 2km south of town, the archaeological site **Hamat Tiberias National Park** (adult/child 12/6NIS; 8am-5pm) was once the site of a famous Roman hot springs, though its major feature is a small synagogue dating from the 3rd to 5th centuries BC, with a beautiful zodiac floor. A small museum is housed in the reconstructed Turkish bathhouse. Walk here (30 minutes) or take infrequent bus 2 or 5.

Tours

If you're a keen archaeologist, get in touch with **Tiberias Excavations** (02-582 5548; www.tiberiasexcavation.com) which holds annual week-long digs just outside Tiberias, run by the Hebrew University of Jerusalem. Costs for participation and accommodation vary; contact the group for more details.

Sleeping

HI Meyouhas Youth Hostel (672 1775; 2 HaYarden St; dm/s/d 90/180/270NIS) Once upon a time the swish Hotel Tiberias, built in 1862, this is a reasonable hostel though unsurprisingly lacking in the atmosphere of its glory days. Bare rooms are brightened with a few personal touches, and the views from the balconies are lovely. Take a room at the back to avoid traffic noise.

our pick **YMCA Peniel-by-Galilee** (672 0685; www.ymca-galilee.co.il; s/d 200/290NIS;) Put all thoughts of dingy, metal bunk beds aside and head to this beautiful, serene and secluded location around 5km north of Tiberias. There's a quiet pebble beach for a spot of paddling, and a natural pool fed by warm springs. The 13 rooms might be forgettable, but the views across the lake are anything but.

Scots Hotel (671 0710; www.scotshotels.co.il; 1 Gdud Barak St; s/d from US$320/400;) If it's splashing out as well as splashing around that you're intending to do on the shores of the Sea of Galilee, check right into the 19th-century Scots Hotel, a delight of dazzling gardens, high ceilings, fine food and little modern luxuries. The pricier 'antique' rooms are especially special. Mobile phones aren't allowed in the hotel's public areas, a perfect place for celluphobes.

Eating

Decks (672 1538; Lido Kinneret Beach; mains 80-170NIS; lunch Sun-Fri, dinner Sat-Thu) Vegans and stoics beware, this local legend is the place to find char-grilled everything that once mooed, baaed, clucked or honked. The steaks are massive and juicy; the accompanying veggies locally grown and tender. Leave a bit of room, if you can, for dessert, a little bit of sin in an otherwise saintly region.

Yemenite Restaurant (Midrahov; mains from 25NIS; lunch Mon-Fri, dinner Sat-Thu) Perch on your plastic chair for a portion or two of deliciously oily Yemenite food. Many dishes are a variation on a pastry theme, served with strained tomatoes, boiled egg and spicy *zhug* (chilli relish). Try the *malawach*, a flat, round pastry pancake, with cheese and olives.

Pagoda (672 5513; Gdud Barak St; mains from 70NIS; lunch & dinner Sun-Thu) You know it's probably not all that 'authentic' when sashimi and sweet and sour appear on the same menu, but Pagoda remains a perennial favourite for its broad (though sometimes bland) interpretation of all things Asian. Don't worry about trying to find it, there aren't all that many faux-Chinese temples in town.

For good value, quick sit-down dining options, try the cafés at the top end of the *midrahov* (pedestrian mall). A long line of **felafel stalls** (HaYarden St; portions around 5NIS; 9am-7pm Sun-Thu, 9am-2pm Fri) runs along HaYarden St toward the bus station.

Entertainment

The cafés and bars around the *midrahov* attract crowds on weekend evenings, especially in summer.

Big Ben (Midrahov; 🕑 noon-late) Long popular with tourists, this easygoing bar is a good place to glug on a pint while taking in the match on the outdoor screen.

Papaya (Promenade; 🕑 5pm-late) Killer cocktails at this popular little waterfront bar, a decent destination for a sundowner or, should you be so inclined, a spot of karaoke on one of its weekly theme nights.

Getting There & Away

Egged (☎ 672 9222) buses 830, 835 and 841 depart for Tel Aviv (42NIS, 2½ hours, hourly) and bus 962 for Jerusalem (42NIS, three hours, every two hours) from the central bus station (just off HaShiloah St). There are also several daily (except Saturday) services to Haifa (Bus No 40, 35NIS, 1½ hours), Nazareth (21.50NIS, 45 minutes) and Tsfat (20NIS, one hour).

Outside the bus station, sheruts leave throughout the day, mostly to Tel Aviv (35NIS, two hours) and occasionally Haifa (20NIS, one hour). Sheruts also line up outside the Mizrahi Bank on HaBanim St.

SEA OF GALILEE ים כנרת البحر الجليل

Around 21km long and 55km in circumference, the Sea of Galilee (Kinneret in Hebrew), fed by the Jordan River, is a broad expanse of blue, cooled by balmy breezes. Though parts, especially around Tiberias and the southern coast, have been marred by modern development, the northern shores still hold the allure they must have done when the preaching Jesus gathered followers here to work a few nifty miracles. Base yourself in Tiberias and explore by bike, or camp at a laid-back site on the calm northeastern shores. The tourist office in Tiberias (p297) can provide maps and advice.

Western Shore

Migdal, 6km north of Tiberias, is said to have been the birthplace of Mary Magdalene. The connection is commemorated with a tiny white-domed shrine, overgrown with vegetation, near Restal Beach.

On Kibbutz Ginosar is the **Yigal Allon Centre** (Map p295; ☎ 672 1495; adult/child 20/15NIS; 🕑 8.30am-5pm Sat-Thu, 8.30am-1pm Fri), a museum whose most celebrated exhibit is the skeletal remains of an 8.2m fishing vessel that shrewd tour operators have dubbed 'the Jesus boat', dating back to the time of Christ's ministry.

Tabgha & Capernaum

כפר נחום & טבחה تبخا & كبرنحيم

Generally considered the most beautiful and serene of Christian holy places, **Tabgha** (Arabic, from the Greek *hepta pega*, meaning 'seven springs') is associated with three separate episodes from the New Testament. Modest dress (no shorts or tank tops) is required, and an attractive lakeside walkway links the Church of the Beatitudes to Capernaum.

The **Church of the Beatitudes** (Map p295; 🕑 8-11.40am & 2.30-4.40pm), which commemorates the Sermon on the Mount ('judge not, lest ye be judged' and other famous lines), sits in a lovely garden about 100m above the lake. The eight Beatitudes of Jesus are pictured in stained glass around the dome. Further on, the altar of the **Church of the Multiplication of Loaves & Fishes** (Map p295; 🕑 8am-5pm Mon-Sat, 10am-5pm Sun), also called the Heptapagon, is thought to include the rock where Jesus laid the five loaves and two fishes that multiplied to feed 5000 faithful listeners. In 1932, excavations uncovered some beautiful mosaic floors, including the topical 'loaves-and-fishes' motif. The wonderfully serene **Church of the Primacy of St Peter** (Map p295; 🕑 8am-4.50pm), with its lovely stained glass, was built by Franciscans in 1933 at Mensa Christi (Christ's Table), where Jesus and his followers ate fish from a table-like flat rock. In the 4th century, a now-ruined church was constructed here to commemorate the spot where the resurrected Jesus conferred the church leadership on St Peter.

Capernaum (Kfar Nahum; Map p295; admission 3NIS; 🕑 8am-4.40pm) was the home base of Jesus during the most influential period of his Galilean ministry and when he recruited some of his best-known apostles. An octagonal church stands over the ruins of a 3rd- or 4th-century synagogue that was built over his lodgings. The site now hosts a well-labelled museum, operated by the Franciscans.

Buses from Tiberias pass by Capernaum Junction (12NIS, 30 minutes, twice hourly), which is a 5km hike or hitch to any of the major sites.

Eastern Shore

There are plenty of scenic, uncrowded swimming spots along the eastern shore,

ZIMMER FREI

You can't come to the north of Israel and not know about 'zimmers', those ubiquitous glorified wooden cabins equipped with kitchen corners, hammocks, views and frequently a Jacuzzi, with which Israel is so bountifully blessed (though no one's exactly sure when the mantle 'zimmer' itself was taken up).

Up above the north and northeastern shores of the Sea of Galilee are two popular villages, filled with zimmers, to which weekending Israelis flock in their droves: zen-yoga-yin-and-yang leaning **Had Nes** to the north, and woodsy, relaxed **Ramot**, to the northeast. Prices per zimmer vary enormously, but most come in at around the US$100 mark per night, rising sharply at weekends and holidays. Far better value than most of Tiberias's hotels – especially outside high summer – and with lots more atmosphere, wander the villages until you find an option that suits, or check www.zimmer.co.il or www.weekend.co.il for the manifold options. Do like an Israeli, though, and insist on that most '70s of icons, the Jacuzzi, in yours.

many backed by campsites (see Sleeping, below). Just park your car or bike, and dip in. If you're in need of a rush of both water and adrenalin, spend your day slip-sliding away at the **Luna Gal Waterpark** (Map p295; ☎ 04-667 8000; adult/child 100/80NIS; 🕑 10am-5pm Apr-Oct).

Further south on the lake's shore, **Kursi National Park** (Map p295; ☎ 673 1983; adult/child 12/6NIS; 🕑 8am-5pm), designated by the Jewish Talmud as a site for idol worship, is said to be the place where Jesus cast a contingent of demon spirits into a herd of swine. The beautiful, recently excavated ruins feature an impressive 5th-century Byzantine-era monastery.

Sleeping

CAMPING

There's camping aplenty on the lake's eastern shores, and the two sites listed only charge for car parking, meaning that if you're hitching, busing or biking, your stay is free.

Ze'elon Beach (Map p295; per car for 24hr 50NIS; 🕑 year-round) Alternative, festivalish atmosphere beneath the trees and good facilities at this great choice, where swimming is officially prohibited – though everyone does it anyway.

Gofra Beach (Map p295; per car for 24hr 85NIS; 🕑 year-round) A well-developed site with nargilehs and even some fridges for hire, a palm-fringed beach bar, and a small supermarket.

HOSTELS & GUESTHOUSES

Karei Deshe HI Hostel (Map p295; ☎ 672 0601; s/d/tr US$75/100/129; ❄) A sparkling white building set in attractive grounds with date palms, eucalyptus trees, a rocky beach and a few peacocks, this place gets constant good feedback from travellers. Prices include breakfast, and you can even shoot a few hoops if you're in the mood. To get here, take bus 459 or 851 from Tiberias bus station, after which it's a 1.5km walk.

Ramot Resort Hotel (Map p295; ☎ 673 2636; www.ramot-nofesh.co.il; Ramot; r/cabin/chalet deluxe 680/880/1080NIS; ❄ 💻 🏊) Set in the village of Ramot, high above the northeastern banks of the Sea of Galilee, this large, pampering place has a pool, a spa and some lovely 'chalets deluxe' with views down over the lake. A particularly nice place for kids, who can splash and dash the days away with their Israeli counterparts. Guests can enjoy free jeep tours of the area (excluding entry fees to sites).

Getting There & Around

This region isn't really a convenient one to explore by bus, and if you're able to, the best thing to do is hire a car or bike; ask at your hostel or hotel in Tiberias, Jerusalem or Tel Aviv for the best local outfit.

If you do decide to bus it, buses 459, 841 and 963 depart regularly from the Tiberias bus station, going north around the lake to the northwestern shore sites; ask your driver to drop you at the appropriate spot.

To get to Ramot, bus 15 from Tiberias to Katzrin stops at the junction below Ramot around twice per day (14.80NIS, 35 minutes) and bus 843 from Tel Aviv to Katzrin (49NIS, three hours, 20 minutes) stops once per day in each direction. Your only other option, except for cycling, is to hitchhike. While we wouldn't recommend it, hitchhiking is very common in this area of the country.

UPPER GALILEE & THE GOLAN HEIGHTS

الجليل & الجولان

הגולן & הגליל העליון

It's all about green in the lush and lovely Upper Galilee and Golan Heights, where national parks are a hiker's delight, with a profusion of pools, rivers and waterfalls. But this peaceful, pastoral region of walking trails, national parks, and real-life cowboys hasn't always been so. Some of the fiercest battles between Israel and its neighbours took place in its now silent, windswept fields, traces of which you'll see in abandoned bunkers and modern war memorials. In 1967, during the Six Day War, Israel captured the area from Syria and 90% of its inhabitants were expelled. In 1973 Syrian forces invaded, only to be repelled to the current borders. And even today, whenever peace talks with Syria look likely, the crucial deciding factor will be whether Israel can ever truly bear to relinquish the much treasured, much disputed Golan Heights.

Meanwhile, whenever there's tension between Lebanon's Hezbollah and Israel, it's this region that bears the Israeli brunt. You never know when enmities might surface,

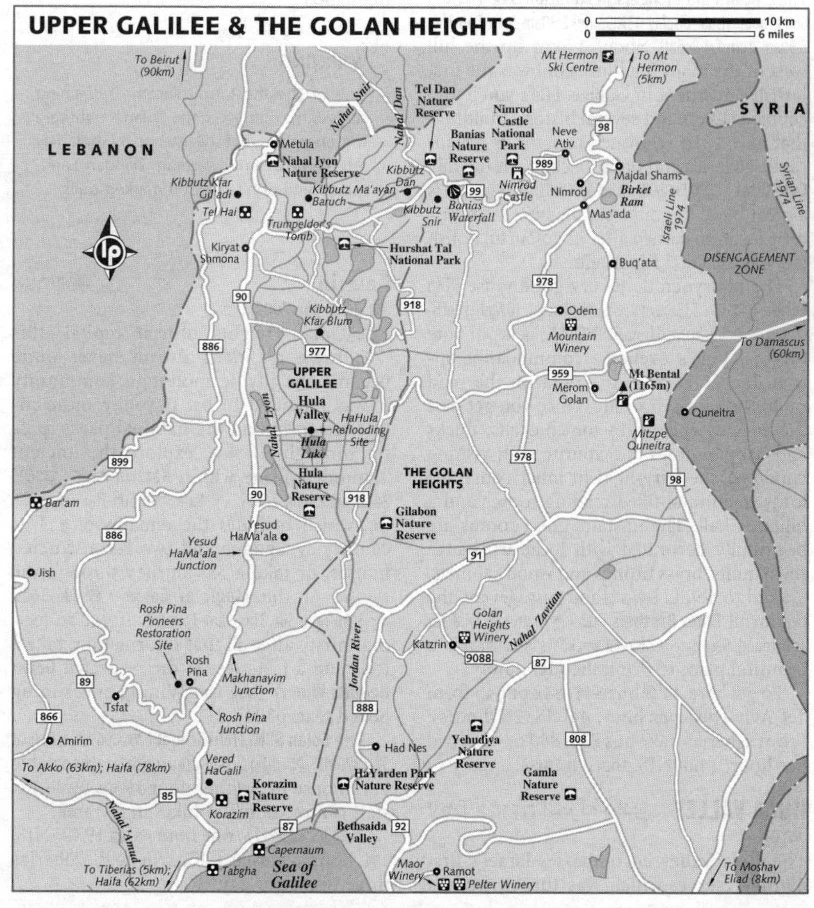

so keep abreast of the news while you're exploring the area.

The Upper Galilee and Golan is the most difficult part of the country to explore by public transport, since you're stuck with infrequent services and no Saturday buses at all. If possible, rent a car for a couple of days; this is especially economical if you can share with other travellers and combine your travel with camping on the eastern side of the Sea of Galilee.

ROSH PINA ראש פינה راس بنيا

☎ 04 / pop 2300

A popular and pricey rustic weekend getaway for Israelis, Rosh Pina has a bohemian reputation for its arts, both visual and culinary. The 1882 **Rosh Pina Pioneers Restoration Site** (☎ 693 6603; audiovisual display 15NIS; 8.30am-5pm Sun-Thu, 8.30am-1pm Fri & Sat), about 1.5km up the hill west of the main road junction, was the first Jewish settlement in Galilee. Here you'll find cobbled streets and several historic buildings that have been renovated to serve as restaurants, galleries and pubs. Back down the hill, **Café Gitel** (☎ 693 0808; mains 40-60NIS; 8am-late) is a great place to grab a simple bite, in an historic location named after its colourful Polish late owner, Gitel Kleinstein.

The idiosyncratic luxury guesthouse **Villa Tehila** (☎ 693 5336; www.villa-tehila.co.il; 10 Mabat Lachermon Hacholotzim St; d from 650NIS;) gets our vote for Rosh Pina's loveliest accommodation option. It's situated on the right on the road up to the restoration site. Once you get past the various enclosures for chickens, ducks and baby bunnies (a favourite with visiting children), the fairy-light-lit inner courtyard leads to antique-filled reading rooms and a billiards hall. The upstairs guest rooms are beautifully decorated with local art, handsewn quilts, brass fittings and wood cabinets. Linked to Tehila by a stone passageway, the colourful **Blues Brothers Pub** (9am-late Fri & Sat year-round, 9am-late occasional weekdays in summer) is a beautiful place to drink the night away.

To get here, take bus 841, 842 or 845 from Tel Aviv (two per hour, 44NIS, 2¾ hours). From Tiberias, take bus 835, 840 or 836 (two per hour, 14.80NIS, three hours).

HULA VALLEY עמק החולה الحولة وادي

☎ 04

The Hula Valley encompasses Israel's first nature reserve, which was turned from a malarial swampland into a prime migratory bird-watching destination in 1964.

Here, at the **Hula Nature Reserve** (☎ 693 7069; entry 18NIS, visitors centre extra 15NIS; 8am-5pm Sat-Thu, 8am-4pm Fri), over 200 bird species call in to make themselves at home, alongside less migratory water buffalo.

Bus 841 or 842 (twice per hour) between Rosh Pina and Kiryat Shmona will drop you off at the turning to the reserve, after which it's a 2.5km walk. Ask the driver to let you off at the right place.

GOLAN HEIGHTS הגולן الجولان

The beautiful, windswept Golan Heights bears plenty of echoes of the bloody, desperate battles played out on its pastures and highlands.

WARNING

One of the most troublesome remaining scars of the fighting in the Golan Heights are the landmines that still litter many spots. Pay attention to signs warning 'Danger: Landmines' and don't stray off marked trails.

Katzrin קצרין كترين

☎ 04 / pop 7000

The Golan Heights' official 'capital', this '70s town planner's dream never quite became the idyllic mountain community it was intended to be. If you're more interested in hiking the national parks, pass on through. If not, explore the ancient Talmudic village within **Katzrin Park** (☎ 696 2412; admission 24NIS; 8am-4pm Sun-Thu, 9am-2pm Fri), which includes the remains of a 3rd-century synagogue and two reconstructed houses, or take a 3D journey through the region at the **Magic of Golan** (☎ 696 3625; 9am-6pm Sun-Thu, 9am-3pm Fri). If you're feeling thirsty after all that information, take a tour and a taste-test at the respected **Golan Heights Winery** (see the Wining and Vining boxed text, p304).

The **Golan SPNI Field School** (☎ 696 1234; Daliyat St; d 320NIS;) has a clean and comfortable guesthouse in a rather dour 1960s building; staff can recommend hikes in the area.

Bus 15 (25NIS, one hour) and 19 (25NIS, 1¾ hours) connect Katzrin with Tiberias three times per day.

A-HIKING WE WILL GO

All of the region's national parks are overseen by the **Israel Parks & Nature Authority** (IPNA; ☎ 06-680 0086; www.parks.org.il). If you're planning on tackling a couple of parks, consider a one-week card (80NIS per person) or a two-week card (120NIS per person). Almost all reserves below have standard opening hours (8am to 5pm April to September, 8am to 4pm October to March) and admission fees (18NIS to 23NIS per adult). Here are five of the area's best hikes, all in IPNA-run parks.

- **Gamla Nature Reserve** (below) Hike down into the valley floor, and back up the other side to the once bustling – now desolate – fortress of Gamla and watch vultures wheel high overhead.
- **Banias Nature Reserve** (p304) Trek down to the impressive 33m-high Banias waterfall, especially beautiful in spring after the snow-melt runs off from the mountains.
- **Yehudiya Nature Reserve** (below) Take the challenging Upper Yehudiya Canyon Trail, crossing rivers and ice-cold pools along the way. Only for those with a taste for heights and a good strong freestyle.
- **Nimrod Castle National Park** (p304) Explore the romantic remains of a Crusader castle on this hilltop national park, with commanding, panoramic views of northern Israel from its ruined ramparts.
- **Tel Dan Nature Reserve** (p304) Not so much a hike as a gentle wander through a small and picturesque forest glade; pause at a natural wading pool to cool off hot feet.

Gamla & Yehudiya Nature Reserves

גמלא & שמורת הטבע של נחל יהודיה

South of Katzrin, the wilderness presents some terrific hiking along deep canyons and past gushing waterfalls and freshwater pools. **Gamla Nature Reserve** preserves both a large natural area and the ruins of Lord of the Rings–like ancient Jewish stronghold, **Gamla**, overlooking the Sea of Galilee, from which some 5000 Jewish inhabitants leapt to their deaths rather than be conquered by the Romans. Gamla Nature Reserve is especially notable for its colonies of griffon vultures, which can be observed from a purpose built observation post riding the thermals. There are several easy hikes here, as well as a wheelchair-friendly walkway to the vultures.

Between Gamla and Katzrin lies the star of Israel's northern national parks, the 66-sq-km **Yehudiya Nature Reserve**, where there's a pleasant **camping ground** (per person 14NIS) and some challenging hiking to be done. Trails include the four-hour Upper Zavitan Canyon Trail, which takes you to waterfalls and interesting hexagonal basalt formations, and the more challenging Upper Yehudiya Canyon Trail (see A Hiking We Will Go, above). Pick up a map at the entrance, or consult the park staff for hiking suggestions.

Both parks are difficult to reach without a car, though some people hitch from Katzrin. Egged bus 15 passes the Yehudiya stop twice per day in each direction between Tiberias and Katzrin; bus 843 from Tel Aviv to Katzrin passes once per day (49NIS, three hours, 20 minutes).

Majdal Shams & Mas'ada

מסעדה & מג'דל שאמס مجدل شمس و مسعده

The friendly Druze villages of Majdal Shams and Mas'ada, on the slopes of Mt Hermon, identify more strongly with Syria than with Israel, and continue to protest the Israeli occupation of the Golan Heights. They make interesting places to wander, and you'll find a plethora of good food places selling local Druze takes on Arabic mezze. In Majdal Shams, look out for the Shouting Hill, where Druze Israelis go on Friday mornings to shout news to their relatives on the Syrian side of the border. Later, when you get home, grab a copy of the 2004 movie *The Syrian Bride*, which deals with the separation of relatives between Israel and Syria.

Around 15km south of Mas'ada, at the **Mitzpe Quneitra** viewpoint, take a look across the border to the eerie Syrian ghost town of **Quneitra**, destroyed by Israel during the 1967 Six Day War. Along the road here, sample delicious floppy bread with *labneh* (soft, sourish white cheese), olive oil and *zaatar* (hyssop) sold by villagers at roadside stalls.

WINING & VINING

Israeli wines are quickly coming into their own on the international scene, and a trip to the north (if you're travelling by car) offers a great opportunity to visit the vineyards, and taste their vintages. Here's our pick of the crop; call or email in advance to make a tour appointment.

- **Golan Heights Winery** (☎ 04-696 8409/8435; www.golanwines.co.il; Katzrin Industrial Park; ⏲ 8.30am-5pm Sun-Thu, 8.30am-1.30pm Fri) Sip on the winery's famous Yarden wines, and visit the cellars and bottling plant.
- **Pelter Winery** (☎ 052 866 6385/4; www.pelterwinery.co.il; Ramot) Brothers Nir and Tal Pelter produce wine that's a firm favourite with Israeli restaurants.
- **Maor Winery** (☎ 052 851 5079; www.maorwinery.com; Ramot) The second of Ramot's wineries is run by friendly winemaker, Danny Maor.
- **Chateau Golan** (☎ 04-660 0026; www.chateaugolan.com; Moshav Eliad) In a moshav about 10km south-east of Ramot, this locally famous place creates an extensive list of tasty merlots, Syrahs (a local version of shiraz) and blended wines.

ISRAEL & THE PALESTINIAN TERRITORIES

Mt Hermon הר הרמון هرمن جبل

The uninitiated might never believe there's a ski resort in sunny Israel, but tucked away in the northeastern corner of the Israeli-controlled portion of the Golan Heights rises 2224m Mt Hermon, the highest peak in Israel, where skiing's the thing between around late December and the end of March. The **Mt Hermon Ski Centre** (☎ bookings 03-606 0640; www.skihermon.co.il; admission 38NIS, chair-lift 35NIS, day ski-pass 200NIS, equipment hire 135NIS; ⏲ 8am-4pm) makes a pricey way to traverse the white stuff, but it's the only opportunity you'll have in the Holy Land to do so.

Banias Nature Reserve & Nimrod Castle בניאס & קלעת נמרוד

One of the most spectacular spots in the region, the **Banias Nature Reserve** (Nahal Hermon Reserve; ☎ 04-695 0272; admission combined with entry to Nimrod 31NIS; ⏲ 8am-4pm Sun-Thu, 8am-2pm Fri), takes in the remains of a temple complex built by Agrippa II, as well as the gushing **Banias waterfall** about 1km away (and accessed by a separate gate – one ticket is good for both sites). Less than 2km east of Banias, you can explore the best-preserved Crusader fortress in Israel, which rises in fairytale style above its hilltop surroundings in **Nimrod Castle National Park** (☎ 04-694 9277; admission 18NIS). Bus 55 from Kiryat Shmona passes the Banias reserve twice daily and buses 25, 26 and 36 pass Kibbutz Dan, 6km to the west, from which you can walk, although some choose to hitchhike.

Tel Dan תל דן تيل دان هظبه

East of Kiryat Shmona is a cute little, Hundred Acre Wood–like area of natural springs and ancient Canaanite ruins (2700–2400 BC), preserved in the pretty **Tel Dan Nature Reserve**. The site was first settled in the 19th century BC as the city of Leshem, but was conquered in the 12th century BC by the tribe of Dan and became the northernmost Israelite outpost. Nowadays, it's home to four easy, wheelchair-accessible marked trails, and a cool natural wading pool.

Close to the park entrance, you'll find the **Beit Ussishkin Museum** (☎ 04-694 1704; admission 18NIS; ⏲ 9am-4.30pm Sun-Thu, 8am-3pm Fri, 9.30am-4.30pm Sat) which features interesting displays on the Hula Valley.

Another less challenging nature reserve is the nearby **Hurshat Tal ('Forest of Dew') National Park** (☎ 04-694 2440/2360; admission 33NIS, free if staying at the campsite). Here, a whole host of open-air pools fill with chilly water from the Dan River, enticing swimmers into their shoals. The reserve also boasts a terrific, grassy **campsite** (☎ 04-694 2360; per tent 50NIS, bungalow 300NIS) with simple bungalow units, each sleeping four.

Both reserves are very tricky to reach by public transport; if you're determined, consult Egged for precise times and bus lines.

TSFAT צפת تصفد

☎ **04 / pop 28,000**

The enticing hilltop town of Tsfat (also spelt Zefat, Tzfat or Safed) enjoys a temperate, high-altitude setting and a rich heritage of

Jewish mysticism. It makes a pleasant visit on weekdays, but don't turn up during Shabbat, when even the birds are grounded.

Orientation & Information

Central Tsfat is spread over a single hilltop, with the bus station on the east side and the old town centre directly opposite on the west side. The hill is scored by the restaurant-studded Yerushalayim (Jerusalem) St, which makes a complete loop between the two.

Sights

Just to the south of the city, the pleasant breeze-cooled park and viewpoint **Gan HaMetsuda** (Citadel Park) was once the site of a Crusader citadel. Central Tsfat's atmospheric old quarters slither down from Yerushalayim St, divided by the broad, stiff stairway that makes up **Ma'alot Olei HaGardom St**, which was built by the British after the 1929 riots, to divide the warring Arab and Jewish factions. The Arabs were then largely confined to what's now the Artists' Quarter, and the Jews to the easterly Synagogue Quarter.

The **Synagogue Quarter** is today a traditional Jewish neighbourhood, which centres on **Kikar HaMaganim** (Defenders' Sq). Two of its 19th-century synagogues are particularly worth a visit: the **Ha'Ari Ashkenazi Synagogue** and the **Cairo Synagogue**. Dress modestly; women should avoid bare ankles or shoulders and cardboard yarmulkes are available to male visitors. Photography is permitted except during Shabbat.

To the west, the **Artists' Quarter**, with its maze of traditional higgledy-piggledy Arab homes, is worth a wander even if you're not planning on investing in its output.

Courses

Courses in Torah teachings, the Kabbalah and general Jewish mysticism are available at the well-known **Ascent of Safed** (☎ 692 1364; www.ascentofsafed.com). Classes are open to anyone; for an introduction to the concept, check out the websites www.kabalaonline.org and www.thirtysevenbooks.com.

Sleeping

Ascent of Safed Hostel (☎ 692 1364; www.ascentofsafed.com; suggested donation dm/d 60/180NIS) This lovely hostel is particularly aimed at Jews who are studying at Ascent of Safed, and can offer an interesting way to meet local people. It's a five-minute walk from the centre of Yerushalayim St; beware that the enthusiastic staff will compel you to attend the institute's seminars.

Safed Guest House (☎ 692 1086; 1 Lohamei HaGeta'ot St; dm/s/d 89/153/224NIS;) Sitting at the edge of town, this hostel is about 2km (and a stiff slog) from the town centre. All rates include breakfast. It's more than a touch institutional, but remains one of the town's cheapest options. Take bus 6 or 7 from the central bus station.

Bar-El Bed & Breakfast (☎ 692 3661; www.bar-el.com; 23 Yod Zayin St; r for up to 2 people US$160, per extra guest US$30) A stay at this lovely suite in the backstreets of the Artists' Quarter will be a memorable one, with beautiful views from well-decorated quarters sleeping up to five. The highlight, though, is the dee-licious kosher feasts provided by Ronen Bar-El, who'll whip up one mean vegetarian buffet.

Eating

Tsfat's main attraction is a range of eating establishments on pedestrianised Yerushalayim St, which are accompanied by some of Israel's most inspiring views. If you're in town on Shabbat, pick up supplies well in advance, or you'll likely go ascetically hungry.

California Felafel (☎ 692 0678; Yerushalayim St; felafel 15NIS; 8am-11pm Sun-Thu, 8am-3pm Fri) An excellent felafel and shwarma option, just next to the bridge.

Canaan Gallery Café (☎ 697 4449; 47 Beit Yosef St; mains from 30NIS; 10am-6.30pm Sun-Fri) A soothing sanctuary in the midst of the Artists' Quarter; stop off here for a sandwich or a salad with a nice cup of coffee, gazing out at the gorgeous views.

Kappucino (☎ 052 595 5909; 35 Yerushalayim St; mains from 20NIS; breakfast & lunch Sun-Thu) Great coffee, big breakfasts, and free wi-fi at this cheery place on Yerushalayim St.

Getting There & Away

Bus 361 runs to Haifa (34NIS, two hours) every hour until 9pm (till 5.45pm on Friday), to Tel Aviv bus 846 runs twice each morning (51NIS, three hours). There is also a regular service to Tiberias (20NIS, one hour).

DEAD SEA

ים המלח البحر الميت

Who among us hasn't seen, at some point in their childhood, that classic image of the Dead Sea bather, toes to the sky, leisurely reading the *Sunday Times*? There's more to do here, though, than wallow below sea-level. After that obligatory float, don't miss the ruins at Masada, while the hiking tracks and springs of Ein Gedi Nature Reserve also merit exploration.

QUMRAN קומרן قمران

☎ 02

Described as 'the most important discovery in the history of the Jewish people', the **Dead Sea Scrolls**, now on display at the Israel Museum in Jerusalem, were discovered at the excavated ancient settlement of Qumran in 1947 by a Bedouin boy searching for a stray goat. Today the beautiful, barren site comprises **Qumran National Park** (☎ 994 2235; adult/child 18/8NIS; 8am-5pm) and includes the scant remains of the settlement (thought to date from the 2nd century BC to the 1st century AD) as well as caves believed to be those of the Essenes, the Jewish sect that authored the scrolls from 150 BC until AD 68, when the Essenes were disbanded by the Roman invaders.

Visitors can see a seven-minute multimedia program, and visit a small museum and shops selling books, souvenirs and Dead Sea mineral creams and beauty products.

Near Qumran, slather yourself in mud or float it out at one of the Dead Sea's **Kalia beaches**, which are far quieter than the beach at Ein Gedi. They comprise a string of private, paying places, the highlight being the **Biankini & Siesta Beach** (☎ 940 0033; admission 30NIS; 8am-8pm), a Moroccan-style place with basic shacks for rent for an overnight stay (80NIS); camping will cost you 40NIS per tent.

EIN GEDI עין גדי عين جدي

☎ 08 / pop 650

Ein Gedi Nature Reserve (☎ 658 4285; adult/child 23/12NIS; 8am-5pm summer, 8am-4pm winter) is a paradise of dramatic canyons, freshwater springs, waterfalls, and lush tropical vegetation (come wearing your swimming costume). Despite the busloads of rampaging school groups that descend on it daily, it continues to provide a haven for desert wildlife, and is especially lovely early in the morning. Note that food's not allowed in the reserve, so eat a hearty breakfast first.

The neighbouring **Ein Gedi National Antiquities Park** (adult/child 12/6NIS; 8am-4pm) includes the ruins of an ancient trapezoid synagogue with an especially inspiring mosaic floor, which was used from the 3rd to 6th centuries AD.

South of the reserve, you'll find the packed and stony **Ein Gedi spa bathing beach** (admission free, showers 8NIS): it's OK for a float, but keep an eye on your belongings as theft is rife. Better options for that Dead Sea experience are the Kalia Beaches (near Qumran).

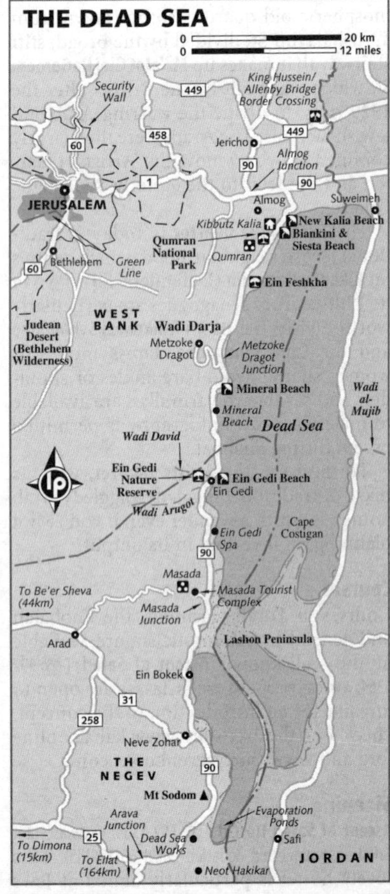

Sleeping & Eating

SPNI Field School (☎ 658 4288; www.teva.org.il; dm/s 75/130NIS, d 190-305NIS; ❄) Perched high on the hillside above Beit Sarah, this place enjoys great views and is an excellent launch point for early hikes, though it's a bit more basic than the youth hostel. Stay a few days and watch the magical light and changing scene over the lake. Rates include breakfast, and dinner is an extra 38NIS to 45NIS.

Ein Gedi Youth Hostel (Beit Sarah; ☎ 658 4165; eingedi@iyha.org.il; dm/s/d 97/250/280NIS; ❄) This highly popular place is uphill and 250m from the bus stop, and occupies one of the finest settings of any Israeli hostel. Rates include breakfast; ask at reception for the 15% discount on admission to the Nature Reserve.

Kibbutz Ein Gedi (☎ 659 4222; www.ein-gedi.co.il; s US$144-194, d US$180-230; ❄ 💻) Surrounded by nice gardens, this efficient kibbutz has plenty of organised activities (walks, yoga classes and the like) to keep you busy, as well as a terrific spa, where you can soak your aches and pains away. The rooms won't blow you away, but the frankincense and myrrh scents of a free night tour of the kibbutz botanical gardens might just do.

There aren't all that many eating options in Ein Gedi. Aside from the good, hearty buffets at **Kibbutz Ein Gedi** (buffets from 45NIS; 🕑 7-9.30am, noon-2pm, 6-9pm), try the self-service **Pundak Ein Gedi** (☎ 659 4761; mains from 39NIS, 🕑 10am-6pm) next to the petrol station, which has a decent salad bar.

MASADA מצדה مسعدا

☎ 08

Don't miss haunting Masada, a desert mesa rising high above the Dead Sea, which figures prominently in the Israeli psyche. During the Jewish First Revolt against the Romans in AD 66, after the sacking and burning of Jerusalem, the Zealots fled here to its high fortress, which became the last outpost of Jewish Resistance. Faced with imminent attack, 10 Jewish men were elected to slay the rest of their group. When the Romans stormed the fortress, they discovered 960 bodies; only seven people, who'd hidden in a water cistern, survived to relay the tale to the world. 'Masada shall not fall again', is the oath sometimes repeated at IDF swearing-in ceremonies, held here.

These days, Masada is guarded by a massive **tourist complex** (☎ 658 4207; 🕑 8am-4pm Apr-Sep, 8am-5pm Oct-Mar), including a restaurant and theatre that shows a short introductory video on the history of Masada. The summit ruins are accessible by foot via the steep and sinuous **Snake Path** (adult/child 23/12NIS) or on the considerably more popular **cable car** (adult one way/return 45/61NIS, child one-way/return 22/34NIS; 🕑 8am-4pm). Hand-held audio guides cost an extra 15NIS.

Sleeping & Eating

Isaac H Taylor HI Hostel (☎ 658 4349; fax 658 4650; dm/s/d from US$25/48/75; ❄ 💻 🏊) This hostel, near the Masada bus stop, provides excellent accommodation, with spacious dorms, attractive private rooms and even a swimming pool. Dinner costs an extra US$12, and guests get 15% off cable car fees. The hostel may let you pitch a tent in the garden; ask at reception.

Getting There & Away

There are around five daily buses (bus 444 or 486) from Jerusalem (39NIS, 2½ hours), which stop off at the Dead Sea en route from Jerusalem to Masada, and four buses from Eilat (55NIS, four hours).

THE NEGEV

הנגב العقبة سحرا

Many Israelis feel that the Negev, the sparsely inhabited southern wedge of Israel, is the country's biggest – but most overlooked – attraction. Taking in nearly half the area of the nation, the only towns of any size are Be'er Sheva, Arad, Mitzpe Ramon and Israel's subtropical toehold of Eilat, and none of them (except, perhaps, Mitzpe Ramon) are particularly enticing. A wonderful recent film, *The Band's Visit*, offers a fictional account of life in its sprinkling of one-camel outposts. Military bases, experimental agricultural projects, and the tent-dwellings of 75,000 seminomadic Bedouin aside, the region's biggest attraction lies undeniably in its hiking.

Whether you're walking the trails of Sde Boker, the Wilderness of Zin, En Avedat National Park, Maktesh Ramon, Timna National Park or the Eilat Mountains, you're bound be seduced by the magic of the barreness of the desert. Note, though,

NIGHT HIKES IN THE NEGEV

An amazing way to experience the wonders of the desert is on one of the Society for the Protection of Nature (SPNI)'s 'yarok tours' (green tours), which emphasise minimising our impact on Israel's wildernesses. One of the highlights is the 'Cold Nights on the Desert Heights' tour, which encompasses a full-moon desert hike, camping, and tai-chi in the Ramon Crater. The price (477NIS for non-SPNI members) includes all meals and one night's camping. Check out www.aspni.org for the full list of highly recommended tours.

that much of the Negev is a firing zone for the area's numerous military bases; take notice of military signs on the roads and don't wander into any fenced, signposted army areas.

BE'ER SHEVA באר שבע بير السبع

☎ 08 / pop 185,300

Travellers pressed for time are well advised to forego the hot, ugly and generally uninspiring 'capital' of the Negev and base themselves in more attractive, well-equipped Mitzpe Ramon. That is, of course, unless you're a tech wizard working at one of its plentiful state-of-the-art technology or research companies, or a student at the pioneering Ben-Gurion University, together the life and soul of this dusty, desert town.

Sights & Activities

Neither of Be'er Sheva's two most worthwhile attractions is actually in the town itself. The **Israeli Air Force Museum** (☎ 690 6855; www.iaf-museum.org.il; admission 26NIS; 8am-5pm Sun-Thu, 8am-1pm Fri), at the Khatserim IAF base 6km west of the centre, offers a gripping account of Israel's aeronautical history (even for nonenthusiasts) and about 100 planes to illustrate it. From the central bus station take bus 31 (9.80NIS, 10 minutes, once or twice per hour).

For something completely different, the worthy **Museum of Bedouin Culture** (☎ 991 3322; admission 20NIS; 9am-5pm Sun-Thu, 8am-2pm Fri) aims to preserve the Bedouin population's threatened culture, and employs local Bedouin guides to help do so. The museum is situated at Kibbutz Lahav; bus 42 runs directly to the kibbutz twice daily, but immediately heads back to Be'er Sheva without allowing time for a visit. Alternatively, take bus 369 towards Tel Aviv, which will drop you at the junction 8km from the kibbutz, after which you could walk or decide to thumb a ride.

Sleeping & Eating

Beit Yatziv Hostel (☎ 627 7444/5735; beit_yatziv@silverbyte.com; 79 Ha'Atzmaut St; dm/s/d 110/195/280NIS;) Popular with visiting university academics, this place is clean and welcoming, with a swimming pool that makes for welcome respite on summer days. To find it, look for the three large radio antennae.

Beit Ha-Ful (☎ 623 4253; 15 HaHistradut St; mains 15NIS; 8am-midnight Sun-Thu, 8am-3pm Fri, dinner Sat) For a hearty dollop of fuul look no further than this local favourite. It's a great town centre stop-off for refuelling on a long voyage through the desert.

Getting There & Away

On business days, bus 370 runs every 20 minutes to Tel Aviv (14NIS, 1½ hours) and buses 446 or 470 depart at least half-hourly to Jerusalem (32NIS, 1½ hours). For Eilat (55NIS, three hours), bus 397 departs more or less every hour via Mitzpe Ramon (23NIS, 1¼ hours). Bus services for Arad (14.80NIS, 45 minutes) run at least every half-hour.

From Be'er Sheva's central train station, which is adjacent to the central bus station, you can travel comfortably to Tel Aviv (25.50NIS, 1½ hours) roughly hourly from Sunday to Thursday.

SDE BOKER & AVDAT
שדה בוקר سدبوكار

☎ 08

Sde Boker Kibbutz, a popular stopping point for Jewish history buffs, contains the modest **home of David Ben-Gurion** (☎ 656 0320; adult/child 10/7NIS; 8.30am-4pm Sun-Thu, 8.30am-2pm Fri, 9am-3pm Sat), Israel's first Prime Minister. The home is preserved as it was at the time of his death in 1973. At the entrance to Sde Boker, a **visitor centre** shows a 20-minute film (7NIS) about the kibbutz. Around 3km south of the kibbutz, at a spectacular clifftop setting, are the graves of Ben-Gurion and his wife, Paula.

The gravesite is close to the northern entrance of beautiful, canyon-filled **En Avedat National Park** (☎ 655 5684; adult/child 23/12NIS;

THREE HIDDEN TREASURES

Israeli tour guide, Galit Zangwill, gives an inside peek into her three favourite undiscovered southern treasures (without the precise directions). 'The south is Israel's jewel,' she says, 'With the best night skies anywhere on the planet. Just lie back in your desert bed, and watch the stars.' Ask a local to show you the way to the following: though Galit was willing to disclose the destinations, she couldn't be cajoled into telling us exactly where they are located.

- **Hike Mount Saharonim** This hike on the slopes of the Maktesh Ramon Crater is one of its very best.
- **Ammonite wall** Fifteen minutes from a southern road, you'll find wall covered with ammonites, an extinct group of marine animals.
- **Climb Mount Tsfahot** (near Eilat) Set off early in the morning before sunrise for an extraordinary view, as the sun comes up, of the Red Sea, Eilat Mountains, Jordan, Saudi Arabia and Egypt.

Galit Zangwill works as a tour guide in Israel.

8am-5pm Sun-Thu, 8am-4pm Fri) where day-hikers can amble through the **Wilderness of Zin**, spotting ibex along the way, to the bizarrely chilly desert pools, **En Avedat**. A good place to start the hike is at the park's northern entrance. Take the steep trail after the pools, to the southern entrance (this takes about 2½ hours), from which you can hitch or take a bus (one every 1½ hours) back to your starting point, or loop back along the riverbed path to the northern entrance (this longer route takes four hours).

A great place to stay is the British-run **Krivine's Guest House** (052 712 304; krivjohn@netvision.net.il; s/d US$39/51) on the Ben-Gurion university campus. The guesthouse provides excellent tourist information, meals, mountain-bike rental and transport from the Sde Boker bus stop. Advance booking is essential.

Nearby **Avdat National Park** (655 1511; adult/child 23/12NIS; 8am-5pm Sun-Thu, 8am-4pm Fri), a ruins complex with Nabataean, Roman and Byzantine elements, is best known for the camel-caravan sculpture on the crest of the hill. Constructed by Nabataeans in the 2nd century BC, it served as a caravanserai along the trade route between Petra and the Mediterranean coast. More excitingly for some, parts of *Jesus Christ, Superstar* were shot here.

MITZPE RAMON

מצפה רמון متسزبئ رآمون

08 / pop 6000

Mitzpe is Hebrew for 'watchtower', and accordingly, this small but surprisingly engaging desert town, home to quite an eco-artsy-alternative young population, enjoys an impressive vista across the dramatic Maktesh Ramon crater, measuring 300m deep, 8km wide and 40km long. All along this dramatic 'watchtower' you'll find far-ranging views and an extensive network of hiking routes. This wild wonderland is good for days of wandering – but be sure to carry lots of water.

Information

The ammonite-shaped **visitors centre** (658 8754; adult/child 28/14NIS; 8am-5pm Sun-Thu, 8am-4pm Fri), perched on the crater rim, has a tourist office and presents an overview of Maktesh Ramon's intriguing natural history, along with a film about the park. Pick up a Makhtesh Ramon Nature Reserve map (2NIS) here.

Lots of companies run rugged jeep tours, but they come and go with the desert wind and you may need to muster a group; see the visitors centre for the latest offerings.

Sights

Downhill from the visitors centre, the **Bio-Ramon** (658 8755; adult/child 12/6NIS; 9am-6pm Sun-Thu, 9am-4pm Fri, 9am-5pm Sat) complex displays a collection of desert flora and fauna. Entrance is free if you've already bought a ticket to the visitors centre. East of town, the fun **Alpaca Farm** (658 8047; www.alpaca.co.il; adult/child 25/23NIS; 8.30am-4.30pm Sat-Thu) is home to a variety of cuddly, comical South American camelids.

Sleeping

Be'erot Camping (658 6713; www.beerot.com; campsites/Bedouin tent per person 25/40NIS) Camp in a dramatic setting, with local tents, Bedouin cuisine (meals are available for 30NIS), clean bathrooms and a modern shower block. It's 12km south of Mitzpe Ramon on the highway to Eilat, and then 5km down a bumpy access road. It's best to call ahead.

Silent Arrow (Hetzba Sheket; ☎ 052 661 1561; www.hetzbasheket.com; Bedouin/dome tents 80/120NIS) Environmentally sensitive Silent Arrow is an amazing place to relax and recuperate from the stresses of Eilat, Tel Aviv, or just life on the road. Choose from a mattress in a communal Bedouin tent or a private dome 'suite' tent, enjoy the twinkle of hanging lanterns (there's no electricity) and, most of all, revel in the silence. Volunteers are welcome, and archery workshops (hence the name) are frequent.

Succah in the Desert (Succah HaMidbar; ☎ 658 6280; www.succah.co.il; PO Box 272, Mitzpe Ramon; s/d Sat-Thu 250/400NIS, Fri 600/600NIS) Set 7km from town down a dusty track, this is an ecoretreat to get away from it all. Although short on creature comforts, the aims of the simple cabins are laudable: solar electricity, natural building materials and yummy vegetarian food. Advance bookings are essential and will avail you of free transport from Mitzpe Ramon.

Eating

Hannah's Restaurant (☎ 658 8158; mains from 25NIS; 🕑 9am-6pm Sun-Thu, 9am-3pm Fri) It is one of the wonders of Israel that petrol station restaurants are consistently some of the very best places to get simple, hearty food. Hannah's Restaurant, at the Paz petrol station, is no exception, turning out satisfyingly large portions of tasty Moroccan-influenced cuisine.

HaHavit (☎ 658 8226; mains 30-45NIS; 🕑 9am-2am) Located beside the visitors centre, HaHavit (Barrel) serves hearty pasta, sandwich and salad lunches, while on Tuesday nights you can party till late with locally based young soldiers.

Getting There & Away

From Sunday to Thursday, bus 392 travels to Eilat (44NIS, 2½ hours) at 8.55am, 10.25am, 12.55pm and 4.40pm. From 6am to 9.30pm, bus 60 shuttles hourly to and from Be'er Sheva (23NIS, 1¼ hours), via Sde Boker and Ein Avdat.

EILAT אילת أيلات

☎ 08 / pop 46,300

From Mitzpe Ramon to Eilat is the physical manifestation of the phrase 'from the sublime to the ridiculous'. Wedged between Jordan and Egypt, and separated from the Israel of international headlines by 200km of desert, Eilat is a resort town, incredibly popular with Israelis, where glitzy, much-of-a-muchness hotels line an artificial lagoon and glass-bottomed boats ply deteriorating coral reefs. Its founding fathers – convicts sent here in the 1950s to build the city – have been superseded by holidaying Spring Break–style student groups, and droves of French and Russian tourists intent on living it up. Chances are that if you've a vision of the Red Sea in your mind's eye, you'll be disappointed when you set foot, or touch down, in town.

Nevertheless, the city still serves as a good base for watersports, dive courses or exploring the dramatic surrounding mountainscape, or as a hop-off point to the decidedly more relaxed Red Sea beaches of Egypt's Sinai (see p189) and the nearby archaeological treasures of Jordan's rose-red Petra (p375).

Orientation

Eilat consists of a town centre, the hotel-fringed lagoon and beaches (the two exhilaratingly separated by the tiny airport and runway), and the 5km coastal strip between the town centre and the Egyptian border. The massive Jordanian flag down the coast to the east marks the Jordanian resort town of Aqaba (p383) next door.

Information

To change money, head for the many no-commission change bureaus in the town centre. ATMs are widespread.

Capish (☎ 632 5977; New Tourist Centre; 🕑 24hr) Internet is available at this coffeehouse.

E-Surf (☎ 634 4331; Bus station; 🕑 9am-11pm Sun-Thu, 9am-4pm Fri, 4-11pm Sat) Internet access at 15NIS per hour.

Police station (☎ 100) Located at the eastern end of Hativat HaNegev Ave.

Post office (🕑 8am-4pm Sun-Thu) Located in Red Kanyon Mall.

Tourist Information Office (☎ 630 9111; Bridge House, Yacht Marina; 🕑 8am-4pm Sun-Thu) Well stocked with maps and brochures.

Tourist police (🕒 10am-3am Sun-Wed, 10am-6am Thu-Sat) This station is near the Tourist Information Office at North Beach.

Sights & Activities

The first of Eilat's two biggest tourist treasures is the **Underwater Observatory Marine Park** (☎ 636 4200; www.coralworld.com/eilat; Taba Rd; adult/child 79/69NIS, oceanarium extra 10NIS; 🕒 9am-5pm), featuring the 'Oceanarium' mock submarine ride, tanks with sharks and rare green and hawksbill turtles (which live for 150 to 200 years). The highlight is the magical glassed-in underwater viewing centre – it's like snorkelling without getting wet. The adjacent aquarium displays many of

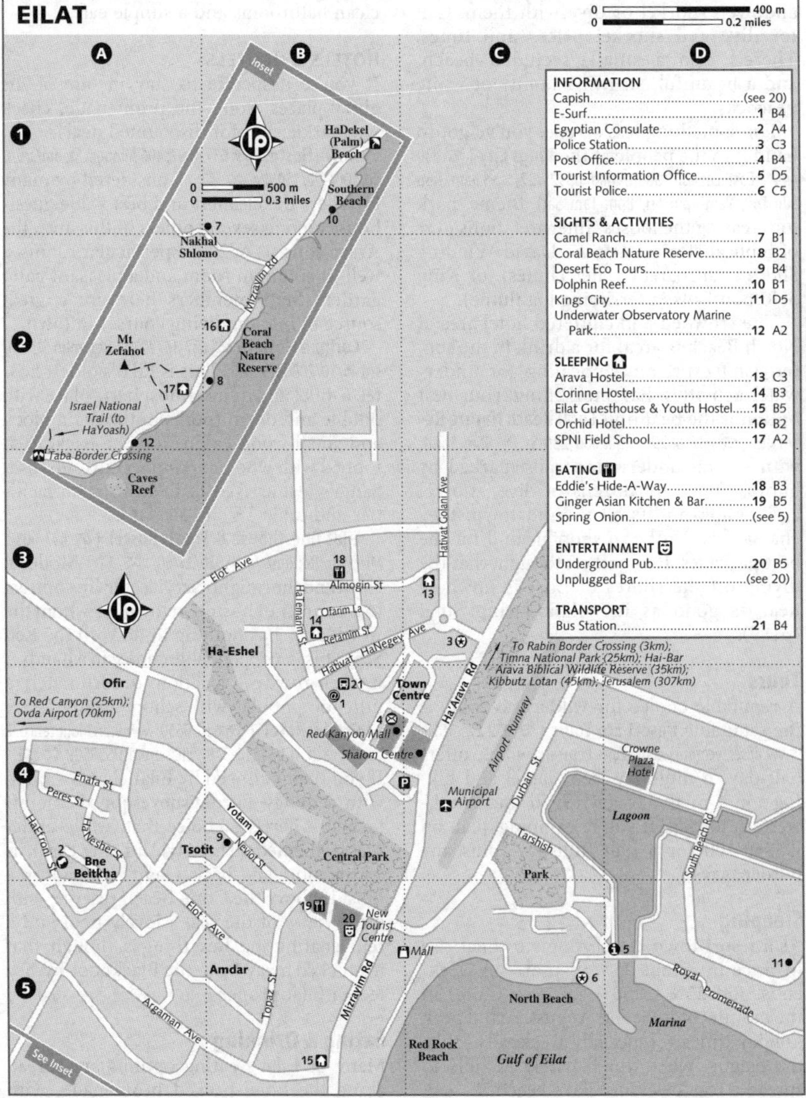

the tropical species you may have missed on the reef.

The second most popular attraction is the lovely **Dolphin Reef** (637 1846; www.dolphinreef.co.il; Southern Beach; adult/child 58/40NIS; 9am-5pm Sun-Thu, 9am-4.30pm Fri & Sat), on the road towards the Taba border, where visitors can observe dolphins from a floating boardwalk in a fenced-off stretch of sea, and even snorkel or dive with them. Call for dive and snorkel prices and times. There's also a small, secluded beach, and a beautiful, strutting family of white peacocks.

For something less serene, you've got to hand it to the people at the **Kings City** (630 4444; East Lagoon; adult/child US$25/22; 9am-1am Sun-Thu, 9am-4pm Fri, 8pm-1am Sat) theme park for creating the loosest interpretations ever of biblical stories. Try the David Winding Slides (transparent water chutes), or King Solomon Falls (a terrifying log flume).

The crowded and cluttered hotel area at North Beach is great for a drink in the sun, but isn't especially appealing for underwater activities. For snorkelling, your best option is the beautiful **Coral Beach Nature Reserve** (637 6829; admission 23NIS; 9am-5pm), with several underwater trails marked by buoys. There are dozens of dive, snorkel and sailing outfits all around town: they change frequently, so shop around for the best packages. Remember, though, that the diving off the shores of Eilat is nowhere near as good as in neighbouring Sinai (p189).

Tours

A reputable choice for wilderness tours is the reputable **Desert Eco Tours** (052 276 1598; www.desertecotours.com; Zofit Centre), which offers half-day to multiday jeep, camel and hiking tours in the Negev, Sinai and southwestern Jordan. If you're camping, plan on US$40/100 for a half-/full-day (plus any border taxes).

Sleeping

As a resort town, hotel rooms in Eilat rise in price by about 25% or more on weekends, and 25% to 50% (or even more) in the months of June and August. Avoid peak holiday times – especially weekends – like the plague, when you'll barely be able to spread a tea-towel on Eilat's beaches.

CAMPING

Camping is illegal on most beaches, and this is strictly enforced. If you really want to set up tent, people camp for free on the narrow stony shores on Taba Rd down to the border, but there are no facilities and it's not particularly pleasant. For better camping, pay 40NIS for a pitch at the **SPNI Field School** (637 1127), which is shady, with clean bathrooms and a simple café.

HOTELS & HOSTELS

If you're desperate to stay in one of the glitzy places along the promenade, check www.arkia.com for discounted deals.

Arava Hostel (637 4687; 106 Almogin St; dm/s/d/tr 40/100/120/150NIS;) Considered by many travellers the cleanest and best value guesthouse among several others in this area, the Arava consists of 27 unspectacular rooms, a well-lit common room and a pleasant patio garden. Staff members here are a great source of info on diving courses in town.

Corinne Hostel (637 1472; 127 Retamim St; dm/s/d 45/70/2000NIS;) This is Eilat's oldest hostel, a quiet and quite atmospheric place with double and dorm rooms in the main block and small wood cabins out the back, each topped with wooden reindeer cut-outs, as if Santa's just arrived in Eilat. Kitchen facilities and cable TV are available.

Eilat Guesthouse & Youth Hostel (637 0088; Mizrayim Rd; dm/s/d US$20/35/60;) Modern, clean and thoroughly serviceable (in contrast to a number of hostels in town for whom the word 'dive' has nothing to do with the Red Sea), this is a dependable choice in a handy – if often rowdy – location; unfortunately a little too popular with school groups.

Orchid Hotel (636 0630; www.orchidhotel.co.il; Coral Beach; d US$210-310, villas from US$850;) If you're not enticed by Eilat chains – often with a dodgy EuroDisneyesque theme attached – here's a choice that, while undeniably themed (Thai-style in this case), is a little more laid-back. Comfy huts adorn a hillside above the Coral Beach reserve, with great views of the sea, a lovely pool and a rejuvenating spa. Best thing is, though, that it's tucked away from the Blackpool-by-Sea feel of Eilat proper.

Eating & Drinking

Many of Eilat's eating options are spread along the hotel-packed promenade, with good-value Israeli chains such as Aroma (for coffee and sandwiches) and Giraffe (for noodles) well represented. There are cheap eats to be had at the market that spreads out along the seafront on weekends: look out for the sweetcorn stall, which sells over 50 sauces to top your corn cob. A number of small restaurants, cafés and shwarma stands can also be found in the New Tourist Centre.

Spring Onion (☎ 637 7434; Bridge House; mains 45-65NIS; 🕑 9am-3am; Ⓥ) This is a popular, mostly vegie place beside the lagoon bridge, serving huge portions of pizza and salad, and a mammoth Israeli breakfast.

Ginger Asian Kitchen & Bar (☎ 637 2517; www.gingereilat.com; Park Ave; mains from 60NIS; 🕑 lunch-late) If you're in the mood for pad thai accompanied by a stunning Fig Mojito, look no further than cool, loungey Ginger. Munch on sushi by all means, but make sure to leave space to slurp up the whisky-laced chocolate soup.

Eddie's Hide-A-Way (☎ 637 1137; 68 Almogin St; mains from 70NIS; 🕑 dinner Mon-Fri, lunch & dinner Sat) Succulent steaks are served at this Eilat institution, as well as good fish dishes and a nice line in vegetarian mains.

Entertainment

Eilat's nightlife is firmly bar-based, and the action focuses on the Promenade and New Tourist Centre, with frequently changing options.

Underground Pub (☎ 637 0239; www.underground-pub.com; New Tourist Centre; 🕑 noon-4am) The perennial traveller's favourite, with full English breakfasts, good value beer, easy music to listen to and nightly live entertainment.

Unplugged (☎ 632 6299; New Tourist Centre; 🕑 7pm-3am) Next door to the Underground Pub, this place, complete with outdoor tented area, attracts a teens-type crowd with a noisy, dance-bar atmosphere.

Getting There & Away

AIR

Eilat's **municipal airport** (☎ 637 3553) is amusingly situated slap bang in the middle of the city. Both **Arkia** (www.arkia.com) and **Israir** (www.israirairlines.com) fly several times daily to and from Tel Aviv (from US$70), and to Haifa three times per week (from US$80). Book online for the best rates.

BUS

From the **bus station** (☎ 636 5120; HaTemarim St) services depart to Tel Aviv (65NIS, five hours) with buses departing every hour from 5am to 10pm, with an additional overnight service at 1am. The last Friday bus is at 3pm and the first Saturday bus at 11.30am; this bus also stops in Be'er Sheva (55NIS, three hours). To Mitzpe Ramon (45NIS, 2½ hours), buses run more or less hourly on weekdays and at least twice on Saturday. To Jerusalem (65NIS, 4½ hours), Bus 444 runs six services daily. On Saturdays, the first Jerusalem bus departs at 4.30pm. Four buses per day depart to Masada (55NIS, four hours).

Getting Around

The town centre is walkable, but you'll need a bus or taxi for locations along Taba Rd (Dolphin Reef, the underwater observatory and Coral Beach). The hourly bus 15 connects the bus station with the Egyptian border at Taba (6.40NIS) from 8am to 6pm Sunday to Thursday, 8am to 3pm Friday and 9am to 7pm Saturday. A taxi to the Taba crossing should cost around 40NIS. To reach the Rabin border crossing into Jordan, you'll need to take a taxi (around 25NIS for the 15-minute journey). For destinations outside Eilat, it might make sense to rent a car: you'll see plenty of car rental outfits in town, but ask at your hotel or hostel for recommendations.

AROUND EILAT

Hikers will want to head for the Eilat Mountains, but be sure to pick up a copy of the 1:50,000 SPNI *Eilat Mountains* hiking map (82NIS), which is sold at the SPNI Field School in Eilat.

An excellent full-day hike will take you through the spectacular **Nakhal Gishron** (part of the Israel National Trail) from HaYoash to the Egyptian border. In the early 1990s the Dalai Lama walked part of this route, lecturing to a small collection of adherents atop one of its upper crests. Get an early start and carry at least three litres of water per person. You'll need the SPNI map to navigate this route.

Further north, the 600m-long **Red Canyon**, 1m to 3m wide and 10m to 20m deep, is readily accessed on foot via a 1.5km walking track from the car park. It makes a great short hike.

TOP THINGS TO DO ON A KIBBUTZ *gueritasmith*

- **Drink vodka** Let's face it, it's cheap to buy a litre bottle. It tastes as cheap as the asking price and could also double as bathroom cleaner. No volunteer should be without it.
- **Read and write ramblings** Graffiti is everywhere on the kibbutz. Write your own philosophical thoughts on the walls or read past volunteers' ramblings.
- **Be somebody else for a while** Nobody knows you so you can quite easily pretend to be somebody/something you're really actually erm, not. It works for volunteers only spending a short time on kibbutz. Longer-stayers will get found out eventually.
- **Get up at 6am** May not be everybody's cup of tea but believe me, it's not that bad, especially when you only got in at 4am.
- **Do menial tasks and get paid menial wages** If you like chickens, you could be in luck. Have competitions with fellow volunteers to see how many egg trays you can fill in one hour! It doesn't get any better than this.
- **Make fast, firm friends** Last, but definitely not least, if you're lucky enough to be based with a cool bunch of people, you'll have them as best friends for the rest of your life. Go. It's worth it.

What's your recommendation?
www.lonelyplanet.com/middle-east

If you'd prefer to take to the mountains on an alternative form of transport, **Camel Ranch** (Map p311; ☎ 08-637 0022; www.camel-ranch.co.il; Nakhal Shlomo; ⏲ 9am-1pm & 4-8pm) organises a whole host of camel trekking options (from 100NIS per person) from its base, less than 1km inland from the Eilat–Taba road. Try the sunset tour with Bedouin supper (no camel on the menu).

Timna National Park

תמנע פארק تمنه حديقه

About 25km north of Eilat, the **Timna National Park** (☎ 631 6756; www.timna-park.co.il; adult/child 38/33NIS; ⏲ 8am-4pm Sun-Thu & 8am-1pm Fri Sep-Jun, 6-8.30pm Sat-Thu & 8am-1pm Sun & Thu Jul & Aug) is the site of some stunning desert landscapes, enlivened with multicoloured rock formations. It was best known as a source of copper for 5th-century-BC Egyptian miners – the park is dotted with ancient mine shafts – but it also includes a wonderland of geological phenomena. The most intriguing are the **Natural Arch**, the eroded monolith known as the **Mushroom** and the photogenic **Solomon's Pillars**. There is also a range of excellent day hikes through one of Israel's wildest desert landscapes.

Buses between Eilat and Jerusalem pass the park turn-off, 2.5km from the park entrance. From there, it's a long walk to anything of interest; if you can, rent a car in Eilat (see p313).

Hai-Bar Arava Biblical Wildlife Reserve

שמורת חי–בר

Located 35km north of Eilat on Rte 90, the **Hai-Bar Arava Biblical Wildlife Reserve** (☎ 08-637 3057; admission 23NIS; ⏲ 8.30am-5pm Sun-Thu, 8.30am-4pm Fri & Sat) was created to establish breeding groups of threatened Negev wildlife. A private car is needed to navigate the wildlife reserve's gravelled roads, from where you can observe the animals in their 'natural state'. Just behind the ticket office is the **Predator Centre** (☎ 637 3057; admission 23NIS), housing animals endemic to the Negev. A combined ticket for both the Wildlife Reserve and the Predator Centre costs 39NIS.

Kibbutz Lotan

לוטן لوطان

If you are into anything organic, sustainable, environmental or ecological, **Kibbutz Lotan** (☎ 08-635 6935; www.kibbutzlotan.com; Rte 90), around 45km north of Eilat, might very well be the place for you. At the kibbutz's well-known Centre for Creative Ecology, you can take a 10-week 'Green Apprenticeship', or participate in a number of half- and day-long courses. There are also alternative therapies available, alongside plenty more earth and body-friendly stuff. Check the website for details of courses, activities the kibbutz runs and information about the pleasant guesthouse.

THE WEST BANK & GAZA STRIP

أضفة & غزة

הגדה המערבית & רצועת עזה

The West Bank and the Gaza Strip, predominantly Palestinian territories captured by Israel in 1967 during the Six Day War, have neither been annexed by Israel (as were East Jerusalem and the Golan Heights), nor granted outright autonomy. Instead, they lie in a grey area somewhere in between, their Palestinian citizens' movement impaired – or sometimes halted – by Israel's hundreds of checkpoints, road blocks, and its looming concrete 'security wall'.

The IDF's control over Palestinian cities, and their surrounding roads, has waxed and waned with the political tide. The 1993 Oslo Agreement brought Palestinians limited self-rule in the Gaza Strip and West Bank, but the IDF retook most urban areas during the second intifada. Today, the region is divided by Israel into several 'areas' – 'A,' 'B,' 'C,' etc – with a differing level of Israeli military intervention (and thus, Palestinian autonomy) in each.

Though talk of total Israeli disengagement from the area is frequently tossed around (with land swaps proposed in exchange for the largest West Bank Jewish settlements), the biggest disengagement plan yet occurred in August 2005 when some 9000 Israeli settlers were pulled out of their homes in Gaza's Gush Katif and forced to relocate in Israel proper. They left behind a US$200 million a year hothouse industry and 1500 homes, which were mostly demolished by Israel on the way out.

In recent years, the West Bank has remained a safe and fascinating place for international travellers to visit, to see how life really operates for Palestinian people. Avoid displaying outward signs of Judaism; read the news while you're in the region to keep abreast of events, but don't let propaganda

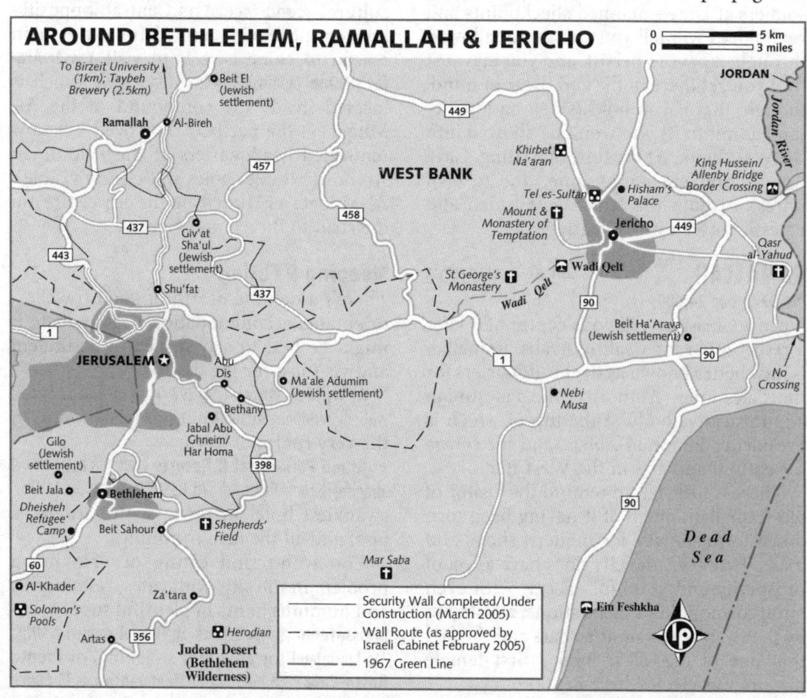

INSIDE THE WEST BANK

The West Bank, for all its recent troubles, is a fascinating place to learn about the real lives of Palestinians behind the often sensational news headlines. To make it all the more accessible, contact one of the following organisations.

- **Alternative Tourism Group** (☎ 02-277 2151; www.patg.org) Offers plenty of information, and recommended day tours of Hebron and Bethlehem (every Tuesday, 225NIS, 8am to 6pm).
- **Holy Land Trust** (☎ 02-276 5930; www.holylandtrust.org) Based in Bethlehem, the trust can arrange tours of the Territories, study programs, homestays and it helps organise the two-month annual Palestine Summer Encounter.
- **Palestinian Association for Cultural Exchange** (☎ 02-240 7611; www.pace.ps) Offers one-day and longer tours of Nablus, Hebron, Qalqilya (a West Bank town containing the West Bank's only zoo) and around, supports local cooperatives, and can arrange lecture programs.
- **Open Bethlehem** (☎ 02-277 2151; www.openbethlehem.org) Based on Manger Sq, a great first stop for an introduction to your travels in the West Bank.
- **Sabeel** (☎ 02-523 7136; www.sabeel.org) A highly respected ecumenical Christian organisation, offering regular conferences and programs.
- **Siraj Centre for Holy Land Studies** (☎ 02-274 8590; www.sirajcenter.org) Organises and coordinates plenty of activities and 'encounters' throughout the West Bank.

(on either side) put you off. You may find that occasionally (except Bethlehem, Taybeh and Jericho, which are usually accessible) soldiers at Israeli-manned checkpoints and roadblocks will tell you you're not allowed through; it pays to persist, and you may just find you get there in the end. Bear in mind, though, that if you hold Israeli nationality (and admit to it) you won't be allowed into the West Bank. At the time of writing, Gaza was a complete no-go zone, due to civil unrest, of both the Israeli/Palestinian and Palestinian/Palestinian variety.

RAMALLAH רמאללה رام الله

☎ 02 / pop 24,600

Once a Christian religious centre and later a resort town for wealthy Arabs, Ramallah is now better known as the headquarters for the Palestinian Authority, the Palestinian administrative body at the top of which is president Mahmoud Abbas, and the centre for culture and arts in the West Bank.

There is little left to remind the visitor of old Ramallah, much of it having been torn down to make way for modern shops and malls. However, the city does have a feel of prosperity and youthful energy, with even quite cosmopolitan inclinations, attested to by the swanky restaurants, bars and the fact that one of the West Bank's first female mayors was elected here in 2006.

Sights

Ramallah makes a good base if you're planning on extensively exploring the local cultural scene (see Arts Central, opposite) but for those with limited time, the main reason to come here is to visit **Yasser Arafat's tomb** (admission free; 8am-9pm), which is located inside the compound of the Al-Muqata'a, the partially destroyed but now renovated headquarters of the Palestinian Authority (bullet holes still clearly visible). Al-Muqata'a is 1km from the city centre, on the road to Birzeit and Nablus.

Sleeping & Eating

There's a definite dearth of good traveller-orientated accommodation in Ramallah; it might be best to stay in nearby Jerusalem and visit just for the day.

Al-Wihdeh Hotel (☎ 298 0412; Al-Nahda St; s/d without bathroom 80/100NIS) It has basic rooms in the very centre of town.

Grand Park Hotel & Resorts (☎ 298 6194; www.grandpark.com; Rafat Rd; s/d US$75/95;) The swankiest hotel in town, with gardens, a pool and all the luxe trimmings.

You won't find eating or drinking a problem in the city, with cafés, restaurants, and hummus joints in plentiful supply. Try **Maissareem** (Al-Se'a/Clock Sq; felafel sandwich 4NIS; lunch-late) for all-night snacking, or **Pronto Resto-Café** (☎ 298 7313; Al-Muntazah; mains 35-60NIS;

ARTS CENTRAL

One of the main reasons to come to Ramallah is if you're hoping to get an insight into the Palestinian arts scene. And it's a terrific place to do so, since Ramallah has arts centres in abundance. Here are a few of the best.

- **Al-Kasaba Theater & Cinematheque** (☎ 296 5292; www.alkasaba.org; Al-Manara) A well-known centre for arts, music, film and theatre, right in the city centre. Ask a local for directions.
- **AM Qattan Foundation** (☎ 296 0544; www.qatanfoundation.org; Al-Jihad St) Offers courses, readings and competitions in journalism, arts, script writing and poetry.
- **Khalil Sakakini Centre** (☎ 298 7374; www.sakakini.org; Al-Muntazah) Hosts exhibitions of local and international artists.
- **Popular Art Center** (☎ 240 3891; www.popularartcenter.org; Nablus Rd) Offers film screenings, events, and serves as the home of the Palestinian Dance School.
- **Ramallah Cultural Palace** (☎ 298 4704; www.ramallahculturalpalace.org; Industrial Zone) A large performance venue with regular events in all artistic genres.

lunch-late) for a nice glass of wine and a big bowl of pasta with the in-crowd.

Getting There & Away

To get to Ramallah, take a bus or sherut (4NIS) from outside the Damascus Gate in Jerusalem's Old City, which will drop you at Qalandia checkpoint. Cross on foot, and from there take a shared taxi (3NIS) to Al-Manara (Lighthouse Sq) in the city centre.

AROUND RAMALLAH

Taybeh Brewery (☎ 02-289 8868; www.taybehbeer.net), 15km from Ramallah in the small Christian village of Taybeh, is the Middle East's only microbrewery, brewing up several varieties of thirst-quenching Palestinian beer. Visit in September (rather than October) for the Oktoberfest, or call in advance to organise a tour and tasting. To get here, take a taxi or service taxi (50/10NIS) from anywhere in Ramallah.

With more than 6000 students (more than half of whom are women), the thriving **Birzeit University** (☎ 02-298 2153; www.birzeit.edu) is a Palestinian educational hub and hosts frequent public events and classes in Arabic. A service taxi from Al-Manara in Ramallah costs 5NIS.

JERICHO יריחו أريحا

☎ 02 / pop 19,800

Said to be one of the oldest continuously inhabited cities on earth, at 260m below sea level it's also the lowest town in the world. Its biblical history is rich, as the first place the Israelites conquered after 40 years of desert wandering, and later taken by Babylonians, Romans, Byzantines, Crusaders and Christians. While Jericho's archaeological sites remain impressive, they are readily surpassed by the surrounding desert landscapes and the views across the Dead Sea to the mysterious Mountains of Moab.

Ancient Jericho

Ancient Jericho's main sites are best accessed on the 6km anticlockwise loop formed by Ein as-Sultan St and Qasr Hisham St. Heading north out of the centre, the first site of interest is the **Mount & Monastery of Temptation**, a 12th-century Greek Orthodox monastery, rebuilt in the 19th century, which clings to the rocks at the traditional site where Jesus was tempted by Satan. You could walk here in 30 minutes or take the 1.3km-long **cable car** (☎ 232 1590; www.jericho-cablecar.com; adult/child US$9/6, under 3s free; 9am-6pm Mon-Sat), proclaiming itself triumphantly as the 'world's longest cable car below sea level' (we're sure the competition is stiff).

Across the street from the cable car is the archaeological site of **Tel es-Sultan** (adult/child 10/7NIS; 8am-5pm), whose remains date back 7000 years, though there's not much to observe except trenches, mounds and some ancient staircases.

Around 3km past the tourist complex, the road winds to the ruins of a 5th- or 6th-century synagogue and **Hisham's Palace** (adult/child 10/7NIS; 8am-5pm) – the impressive ruins of a 7th-century hunting lodge, replete with a beautiful, and oft photographed, Byzantine mosaic floor.

Back in town, look out for the **Zacchaeus Tree**, said to be the very same sycamore that Zacchaeus climbed 2000 years ago for a better view of the preaching Jesus (Luke 19:1-10).

Sleeping & Eating

Jericho Resort Village (☎ 232 1255; fax 232 2189; s/d 250/300NIS;) Near Hisham's Palace, this easy, breezy series of bungalows has a nice pool, bar and even a tennis court for that sub-sea level knockabout.

Intercontinental Hotel (☎ 231 1200; www.interconti.com; Jericho-Jerusalem Rd; d from US$90;) Near the checkpoint entrance to Jericho on the road from Jerusalem, this luxurious place has all the necessary perks of a big chain hotel, including pools, spa, casino and a nice restaurant. Nonguests can use the pools for the rather steep price of US$20/10 for an adult/child.

Abu Raed's Temptation Restaurant & Souvenir Centre (☎ 232 2614; Tel as-Sultan; mains from US$8; lunch-late) Worth dining here for the name alone, there's a delicious and extensive Middle Eastern lunch buffet (US$10) to fill up on so you won't be led astray on the Mount of Temptation. Just across the road from the cable car station.

Green Valley Park (☎ 232 2349; Ein es-Sultan St; mains 40-80NIS; lunch-late) Good grilled meats and scrummy mezze at this outdoor dining location on the road north to the Mount of Temptation.

Getting There & Away

Easy to access by car on Rte 1 from Jerusalem (follow signs for Jericho and the Dead Sea), it's possible to get here by shared taxi from Abu Dis, a southern suburb of Jerusalem. Get to Abu Dis by service taxi (7NIS) from the Damascus Gate in Jerusalem's Old City, then take a shared taxi from Abu Dis (10NIS) to the checkpoint. Alternatively, take a private taxi from Jerusalem (price according to the meter), or from Ramallah or Nablus (around 70NIS to 100NIS).

AROUND JERICHO

About 8km west of Jericho a road leads right to **Nebi Musa**, a small monastic complex built in 1269 and revered by Muslims as the tomb of Moses, with the Judean Desert as a dramatic backdrop.

Nearby, **Wadi Qelt** is a nature reserve in a steep canyon, with a natural spring where you can swim in a pool under a waterfall and hike along an aqueduct to the stunning 5th-century **St George's Monastery**, built into the cliff face of a canyon on the Mount of Temptation. The starting point for the four-hour hike is the Wadi Qelt turn-off on the Jerusalem–Jericho road (get the bus driver to drop you off here) and the finishing point is Jericho: follow signs for the settlement of Mitzpe Yericho to get you going. The route's easiest tackled, though, with a local Bedouin guide; ask around in Jericho beforehand.

BETHLEHEM בית לחם بيت لحم

☎ 02 / pop 29,000

Though the largely Christian town of Bethlehem has suffered in recent years from ongoing isolation caused by Israel's 'security wall', no trip to the region is complete without a visit to this serene, pretty destination, where golden afternoon light dapples centuries-old stones, and where those in search of kitsch can have their fill of Jesus hologram postcards, all-year Christmas shops, and life-size carved wooden nativities. Don't be put off by the ominous and intimidating Israeli checkpoint at the entrance to Bethlehem. Once through it, you'll emerge to a old-fashioned, quiet town that's struggled hard to survive as tourism here has plummeted.

Bethlehem is often visited as a daytrip from Jerusalem, but doing so would mean you miss out on its true charm. Stay a day or two at one of its pilgrims' hotels (only full these days during Christmas and Easter), eat on the street at cheap and delicious felafel and shwarma stands, browse its atmospheric souq and peruse its manifold sights, including the Grotto of the Nativity where Jesus is said to have been born. In Bethlehem, you'll find friendly locals eager to help you get your bearings or direct you to your destination, an unusually laid-back and parochial vibe, and an atmosphere that's remained spiritual despite the once-bustling and now fairly forlorn tourist trappings.

Orientation & Information

Bethlehem is a relatively small town, sandwiched between the two smaller Christian villages of Beit Sahour and Beit Jala. The old

ANOTHER BRICK IN THE WALL *Amelia Thomas*

Each time I return to Bethlehem, which, despite its troubles, remains one of my favourite towns in the world, more and more artwork has appeared on Israel's contentious 'security wall'. It's a stark contrast: on the Israeli side, there's nothing but the odd scrawled slogan, but on the Palestinian side, a riot of colours, blazing murals, and towering objections, in pictorial and word form, have appeared as a testament to the town's gradual imprisonment.

Like the Berlin Wall but more so (after all, it's more than twice as high), Bethlehem's stretch of sheer grey concrete has been turned into a rich canvas for social commentary. Look out for UK graffiti artist Banksy's irony-laden images, and Pink Floyd frontman Roger Waters' 'No Thought Control' slogan, sprayed on during a trip to the region in 2006. Though it's not officially allowed, Israeli soldiers seem fairly tolerant of the mural-makers, both local and international, and though you should heed any instructions (who wouldn't, if face to face with reflective sunglasses and a machine gun?), taking photos of the artwork shouldn't present any problems.

Though it's fast becoming a tourist attraction in its own right, let's hope that one day, just like the Berlin Wall, the wall's most famous images will be available, in chunk-form only, on eBay.

city spreads out on either side of a steep hill, which makes for some leg-acheing climbs up and down cobbled streets and seemingly hundreds of steps.

The centre of town is the pretty Manger Sq, on which stands the Church of the Nativity, the police station, post office, municipality buildings, a scattering of souvenir shops, and the **Peace Centre** (☎ 276 6677; www.peacenter.org; 🕑 9am-6pm Mon-Sat, 9am-4pm Sun, 9am-2am Christmas Eve), which offers tourist information and free maps, organises cultural events, and hosts a bookshop and public toilets. **Open Bethlehem**, also on Manger Sq, is the place to head for an inside picture into the West Bank. See Inside the West Bank (p316) for more details.

Sights

The venerable **Church of the Nativity** (🕑 5.30am-5pm), commissioned by the Emperor Constantine in AD 326, is one of the world's oldest functioning churches, and has had its fair share of sackings, lootings and invasions over the ages. The church also encompasses the underground **Grotto of the Nativity**, where Jesus is said to have been born and the **Chapel of the Manger** with its year-round nativity scene. Adjoining the church is the pinkish **St Catherine's Church**, from which Bethlehem's famous Midnight Mass in broadcast on Christmas Eve. The tour guides (around 50NIS for an hour) hanging around outside the church are usually highly knowledgeable and well worth taking along for the tour.

On Milk Grotto St is **Milk Grotto Chapel** (🕑 8-11am & 2-6pm), a shrine that commemorates the lactation of the Virgin Mary and to which women wanting children frequently make a quick pilgrimage. Across town, the **Old Bethlehem Museum** (☎ 274 2589; www.arabwomenunion.org; Star St; 🕑 8am-noon & 2-5pm Mon-Sat, closed Thu afternoon) offers a glimpse into a 19th-century Palestinian home, and there's also a gift shop vending crafts produced by the Arab Women's Union NGO.

Head to the **International Centre of Bethlehem (Dar Annadwa)** (☎ 277 0047; www.annadwa.org; Pope Paul VI St), for regular exhibitions of Palestinian artists, events, classes, and a quiet café.

BETHLEHEM'S FOOTBALL STARS

If, while in Bethlehem, you happen to see a group of young women – some in shorts and trainers, others in headscarves and long sleeves – kicking a football around a car park, don't be surprised: these are members of the Palestinian Women's National Soccer Team, whose Bethlehem members practice their dribbles and passes every Wednesday evening.

Though they have little in the way of resources – without even a grass pitch to train on – and though some of the team are from all the way to the west in inaccessible Gaza, the team won't be daunted. Despite checkpoints and permits, they have competed in Abu Dhabi and Amman, among other Middle Eastern locations. They may have yet to score a victory on the field, but the team members see their very existence as a victory against circumstances.

Sleeping

The only time you'll have to worry about room at the inn is at Christmas, when pilgrims still flock to Bethlehem for carols at the churches and prices may rise by up to 50%.

Arab Women's Union (☎ 277 5507; arwomenunion@yahoo.com; Beit Sahour; r US$20) In the nearby Christian village of Beit Sahour, this simple but comfy guesthouse is run by local women, who also undertake recycling, craft and community programs.

Bethlehem Star Hotel (☎ 274 3249; htstar@hall.net; s/d US$35/55) A plain, clean and simple choice, attracting aid workers and journalists who sip coffee while observing the wonderful city views from its breakfast room.

Casa Nova Oriental Palace (☎ 274 2798; www.casanovapalace.com; s/d US$45/60;) This solid value Franciscan-run guesthouse has 25 decent, recently renovated rooms in a stellar location right beside the Church of the Nativity.

our pick **Abu Gubran Guest House** (☎ 277 0047; www.annadwa.org; 109 Pope Paul VI St; d US$65;) Part of the Lutheran-run International Centre of Bethlehem (Dar Annadwa; see p319), Abu Gubran offers 13 lovely rooms, each decorated by a local art student and named after a Palestinian village. Double room prices include breakfast and dinner at the centre's airy rooftop restaurant.

Jacir Palace Inter-Continental (☎ 276 6777; www.ichotelsgroup.com; Jerusalem–Hebron Rd; s/d/ste US$80/90/120;) If you're looking for swish, this is the place to go. Opulent decorations, serene gardens and comfortable rooms grace this well restored palace; breakfast is included. Be aware, though, that since the hotel is rarely full these days, some facilities such as the gym or pool might not be open.

Eating

Eating out in Bethlehem is all about following your nose: the souq area and around has some mighty tasty street eats on offer, but anywhere you wander is likely to bring you within biting distance of a tasty, hole-in-the-wall restaurant treat. Manger Sq has a number of felafel and shwarma merchants. Look out, too, for the roving drinks vendors, in fez, embroidered outfit and cart topped with fake flowers. They serve sweet soft drinks for around 3NIS per plastic cup, and strong coffee for 4NIS.

Abu Shanab (☎ 275 0043; Manger St; mains 30-60NIS; closed Mon) Travellers are guaranteed a friendly welcome by the brothers who run this popular place, which serves up great lamb chops and *kofta* (spiced mincemeat grilled on a skewer) as well as a slew of vegetarian mezze.

Efteem (☎ 277 0157; Manger Sq; felafel sandwich 5NIS) Just down the ramp from Manger Sq, this is a particular favourite for yummy, filling felafel, shwarma, hummus and the like.

St George Restaurant (☎ 274 3780; Manger Sq; mains 45-60NIS; 8am-11pm) Especially popular with whistle-stop tour groups, this venerable place on the corner of Manger Sq serves up tasty grilled chicken, fish and meat dishes.

Getting There & Away

Most travellers enter Bethlehem from the ominous, prison-like checkpoint on the Jerusalem–Bethlehem road. Don't be discouraged by the checkpoint: despite intimidating appearances, it's easy for travellers to cross. Private/shared taxis (50/5NIS) make the journey from outside Jerusalem's Old City Damascus Gate, and terminate at the checkpoint. From there, you'll have to proceed through on foot: be sure to bring your passport, without which you'll be refused passage (note that if you're an Israeli passport holder, it's illegal to enter). Once on the Bethlehem side of the checkpoint, private taxis (50NIS; bargain hard) run the 3km to the town centre, though it's an interesting walk if you have the time.

You can also cross the checkpoint by car; bring your passport and rental papers. There's no shortage of on-street parking in Bethlehem and it's not considered dangerous to drive with Israeli registration plates. Though many car rental companies won't insure their fleet for trips into the West Bank, **Green Peace** (☎ 02-528 2179; www.greenpeace.co.il), based in Jerusalem, will.

AROUND BETHLEHEM

There are several sights around Bethlehem well worth striking out for, but most are inaccessible by public transport. Pick those you'd most like to see and negotiate a private taxi for the day to make the most of the area.

Around 1km east of Bethlehem, at Beit Sahour are the **Shepherds' Fields**, where the shepherds who visited Jesus in his manger are said to have tended their flocks. It's a pleasant stroll up here to a little old church, a favourite photo-op destination for local brides.

About 9km south of Beit Sahour stands **Herodion** (☎ 02-776 2251; adult/child 23/12NIS; 8am-5pm Sun-Thu, 8am-4pm Fri), the amazing volcano-shaped remains of the palace complex built by Herod between 24 and 15 BC.

Splendid architecture and a superb location combine to make the Greek Orthodox Monastery of **Mar Saba** (admission 20NIS; 8am-4pm Sun-Thu), clinging to the steep Kidron banks, one of the Holy Land's most impressive structures. The interior is open only to men, but there's a Women's Tower near the entrance where the fairer sex can survey the scenery. In nearby Beit Jala, don't miss the **Cremesian Salesian Monastery & Winery** (☎ 02-274 4826; Beit Jala), a wine-producing hilltop retreat for Salesian monks. Call in advance to arrange a tasting.

Not far from Bethlehem, on the road towards Hebron, ask your taxi driver to take you to **Daher's Vineyard**, an old Palestinian family farm still struggling against potential confiscation by Israel. Part of the youth organisation **Tent of Nations** (☎ 02-274 3071; www.tentofnations.org), visit the beautiful smallholding, and help the cause by buying your own US$25 patch (the price of a square metre) if you feel so inclined.

HEBRON חברון هبرن

☎ 02 / pop 160,500

It's a shame that Hebron has become known as a flashpoint for the Israeli-Palestinian conflict, since despite ongoing troubles, this ancient and vibrant town comprises the West Bank's major commercial centre, famous for its pottery, grapes and dairy products. As a place of pilgrimage, too, it's quite a hotspot; here you'll find the alleged graves of such notables as Adam and Eve, along with Abraham, Isaac, Jacob and their wives too. It's generally safe to visit, but to ensure your trip is trouble-free, avoid wearing a yarmulke, Star of David or any other suggestion of Judaism.

Hebron's main bone of contention is the disputed **Cave of Machpelah**, the traditional burial site of Abraham, and the **Ibrahimi Mosque** (8am-4pm Sun-Thu), which lies above it. For Jews and Christians, it's a highly revered site; for Muslims, its importance in the region is second only to Jerusalem's Dome of the Rock. Dress modestly, and bring a head covering if you're female.

There are around 17 Jewish settlements in the Hebron area, housing in total around 12,000 Jews, with a community of hard-core settlers inhabiting Hebron's souq itself. This has had a troubled effect on the town, with violence occasionally flaring. Most tragically, in February 1994, a Jewish settler stepped into the Ibrahimi Mosque and opened fire on Muslims at prayer. The building is thus now segregated into Muslim and Jewish sections, and security is tight.

Hebron's now sorrowful **souq** is a beautiful blend of Crusader and Mamluk facades, vaulted ceilings and narrow alleyways; repeated violence in the area has cleared out its shops and residents, making the place a sad and plaintive ghost town. Most commerce has moved to the adjoining new town, centred on a vibrant outdoor market. Don't miss the Ein Sara St factories here that produce Hebron's fabulous blue glass.

Sleeping & Eating

The **Hebron Tourist Hotel** (☎ 222 6760; Ein Sarah; s/d US$35/45), about 3km from the market, is one of the only – and fairly scruffy – budget places to stay in town.

A culinary highlight, far more popular than its presidential namesake, is **Abu Mazen** (☎ 222 6168; Nimra St; mains 25-35NIS; midday-late), where, for around 30NIS you'll get a whopping unlimited selection of salads, bread hot from the oven, a hot main, a bottle of water, a strong Arabic coffee, and a dessert. Otherwise, head to **King of Felafel** (☎ 222 8726; Al Haras; mid-morning–late) where you can stuff yourself silly for just 2NIS per felafel sandwich.

FOREIGN OBSERVERS IN HEBRON

As well as the 17 Jewish settlements in the Hebron area, around 600 settlers remain in Hebron city itself, heavily guarded by Israeli troops. International observers are consequently stationed here to monitor ongoing violence and settler activities. If you're interested in learning about the work of foreign observers in Hebron – or getting involved – contact **Christian Peacemakers Teams** (www.cpt.org) or **Temporary International Presence in Hebron** (☎ 222 4445; www.tiph.org).

Getting There & Away

Bear in mind that road blocks are frequent in this area, and entry to the town may be denied at any time. If roads are open, take a service taxi (20NIS) from Al-Musrara in Jerusalem, which takes about an hour to travel the 36km. You can also take a private taxi from Bethlehem (around 100NIS), which is a journey of 24km.

NABLUS שכם نابلس

☎ 09 / pop 130,300

Scenically situated between the Gerizim and Ebal peaks, this quite attractive, bustling town is the largest West Bank population centre and is well known for its production of soap, olive wood and olive oil – though also for its simmering angst against Israeli occupation. In the central Palestine/Al-Hussein Sq, you'll find the bus stops, the service taxi ranks and a small market. Immediately to the south, the Old Town stretches eastward along Nasir St. It's generally safe to visit but, as with everywhere in the West Bank, keep your ears open for current updates.

Sights

From Al-Hussein Sq head south towards the landmark minaret of **An-Nasir Mosque** (Nasir St) – one of 30 minarets punctuating the Nablus skyline. Nearby, at the heart of the atmospheric Ottoman-era Old City, is a privately owned old Turkish mansion known as **Touqan Castle**, where visitors can knock on the door to admire the architecture and garden. To get here from Nasir St, simply walk south through Al-Beik Gate and the entrance is up the slope on your left.

East of the An-Nasir Mosque, on An-Nasir St, is **Al-Shifa** (☎ 238 1176; men 8am-midnight Mon, Wed-Sat & 3pm-midnight Tue-Sun, women 8am-5pm Tue & Sun), the country's oldest functioning Turkish bath. Built around 1624 at the start of the Ottoman period, Al-Shifa offers massage, along with a stiff brush-down with a camel hair brush for around 20NIS. At the entrance to Balata refugee camp (the West Bank's largest UNRWA camp), you'll find **Jacob's Well** (☎ 8am-noon & 2-5pm) where the remains of a Crusader church marks the spot that Jesus is said to have been offered water by a Samaritan woman.

Sleeping & Eating

Al-Yasmeen Hotel (☎ 233 3555; yasmeen@palnet.com; s/d US$40/50) In the centre of town, this place is a favourite of aid workers and other foreigners.

The Nablus speciality is sweets, including Arabic pastries, halva, Turkish delight, and especially *kunafa* (vermicelli-like pastry over a vanilla base soaked in syrup). The best bakery at which to try this delicious delicacy is **Al-Aqsa** (Nasir St), in the Old City beside the An-Nasir Mosque.

Getting There & Away

Sherut taxis run to Nablus from Al-Nahda St in central Ramallah (13NIS). There are at least seven checkpoints en route, so how long it will take you is anybody's guess. The main Nablus checkpoint is Huwwara: this can be closed at any time, so find out if its open in advance if you can.

GAZA CITY עזה غزة

☎ 08 / pop 479,400

You might think that Israel's small compared to the size of its international coverage. But the Gaza Strip beats even Israel's square miles–to–newspaper column inches ratio. Would you believe that the tragically violence-plagued, explosive and intriguing piece of real estate is less than 10km wide, and just under 45km long?

Translations of the area's name offer a hint of its former glories: 'the treasure', 'the chosen place', and 'the ruler's prize' are just some of the interpretations. Throughout history, Gaza City – capital of the Gaza Strip – was a thriving deep-water port, coveted by such greats as the ancient Egyptians, Alexander the Great, the Emperor Hadrian, Saladin, Richard the Lionheart and even Napoleon.

Its more recent history, however, is more tragedy than treasure. Palestinian refugees flooded the area after the foundation of Israel in 1948, and poverty soon overshadowed affluence. Throughout the ensuing decades, Palestinian refugees came to loggerheads with Israeli settlers, and the outcome was frequently bloody. In 2005 Israel pulled out all settlers from Gaza, and there were hopes that life might stabilise. Recent events have proved the opposite. Nicknamed 'Hamas-stan', it's now Palestinian factions that are fighting each other, while despite intermittent attempts at a

NO-GO GAZA

Getting to Gaza, unless you're an aid worker, foreign diplomat or journalist was, at the time of writing, impossible. Check whether things have changed if you're intending on visiting (beware that the security situation is volatile and kidnappings alarmingly frequent) – but, sadly, it looks unlikely.

ceasefire, militants continue to lob missiles over the border to the troubled Israeli town of Sderot. Border gates bringing in valuable supplies are often blocked by Israel, while tunnels smuggle weapons and ammo from Egypt into Gaza. It's a bleak picture with few signs of hope, though stories from the inside show that, though unhappy, life does go on for Gaza City's troubled citizens.

Sights & Activities

Though it's not exactly tourist central, Gaza City does have a surprising amount to see. The area around central Palestine Sq holds most of the city's sites of historical interest. The most distinguished structure is the converted Crusader-era church, **Jama'a al-Akbar (Great Mosque)**. Along its southern wall runs the short, vaulted **Gold Market**, which has served prospective bridegrooms since the Mamluk era.

In 1799, during his Egyptian campaign, Napoleon Bonaparte camped in Gaza and established his base on Al-Wahida St in the attractive Mamluk-era building now called **Napoleon's Citadel**, currently awaiting inauguration as a UN-funded museum. From the citadel, head west and take the second right to reach the **Mosque of Said Hashim** (closed to non-Muslims Fri), built on the grave of the Prophet Mohammed's great-grandfather.

The city's beautiful, adobe **Arts & Craft Village** (☎ 284 6405; www.gazavillage.org; Gamal Abdul Nasser St) produces and then sells a range of local arts and crafts, including embroidery, copperware and glasswork, and has an attractive attached restaurant. You'll find the village about 800m south of the Islamic University on El-Khartoum St.

Sleeping & Eating

Al Deira (☎ 283 8100; Er-Rashid St; s/d from US$90/100;) An island of luxury in Gaza, the Al Deira has swish rooms, all with excellent sea views plus minibar and cable TV, and the best seafood in town at its downstairs restaurant, open for lunch and dinner daily.

Getting There & Away

When times are less troubled, the Erez border between Israel and Gaza is the main point of entry and exit. The best way to get here is by private car; public transport has currently given up the journey due to a dearth of passengers and you may not easily find an Israeli taxi willing to take you as far as the border.

ISRAEL & THE PALESTINIAN TERRITORIES DIRECTORY

ACCOMMODATION

Though Israel ranks as one of the most expensive destinations in the Middle East, its accommodation manages to cater to all budgets, with a good selection of hostels, midrange guesthouses and top-end luxury hotels. On summer weekends (June to September) and around Israeli holidays, though, prices can rise by as much as 50% to 70%.

The Palestinian Territories offers more limited, but cheaper, accommodation. A good base is Bethlehem, with its extensive range of pilgrims' hostels and budget to midrange hotels. There are also plenty of interesting options for homestays; see Inside the West Bank (p316) or sign up for a homestay exchange organisation such as **Hospitality Club** (www.hospitalityclub.org), which has a number of Palestinian members offering travellers a bed for the night.

Throughout the chapter, we have defined price ranges as: budget (double room up to US$75, or 255NIS), midrange (US$75 to US$100, or 255NIS to 510NIS), and top end (over US$150, or 510NIS), for a room during high season.

B&Bs

All over Israel you'll find accommodation in private homes, ranging from around US$25 to US$100 for a single or double. Facilities vary from simple rooms with shared facilities to self-contained studio apartments with kitchenettes and cable TV. Check the

PRACTICALITIES

- English-language daily (except Saturday) newspapers include, *Ha'aretz* (www.haaretzdaily.com) and the *Jerusalem Post* (www.jpost.com). In East Jerusalem you can pick up the weekly, Palestinian-produced *Jerusalem Times*.
- Tel Aviv's best station for English- and Hebrew-language rock music is 102FM. In Jerusalem, English news can be heard at 10pm on 88.2FM. English news and music is played sporadically on 100.7FM (Tel Aviv), 98.4FM (Jerusalem), 97.2FM (Haifa) and 94.4FM (Tiberias). The short-wave BBC World Service (1323 kHz) broadcasts news in English, as does the Voice of America broadcast (1260 kHz).
- Israel's two state TV channels feature plenty of English-language programming with Hebrew subtitles. These are supplemented by the Arabic-language Jordan TV. Nearly all hotels and guesthouses also have cable TV, which carries CNN, Sky and BBC World.
- The predominant video format in Israel is PAL.
- Electric power is 230 volts AC, 50Hz. The sockets are designed to accommodate two- and three-pin, round plugs. (European standard).
- Israel and the Palestinian Territories follow the international metric system.

Home Accommodation Association (www.bnb.co.il) for extensive listings.

Camping

Israel's campsites are usually beautifully positioned and very reasonably priced. A particular highlight are the sites around the northeastern shore of the Sea of Galilee, where many places don't charge a fee to pitch a tent, though you'll pay for parking if you bring a car. Several northern nature reserves have good value campsites attached, while there are numerous opportunities for wilderness camping in the Negev region (p307). It pays to employ a guide here and to ensure you bring sufficient water supplies.

It's not advisable to camp in the Palestinian Territories, due to general security concerns.

Hostels

Israel has an extensive network of roughly 30 official HI hostels, all of which are clean and well appointed. In most cities and towns, though, there are also private hostels which usually charge a little less than the HI outfits. For more on HI hostels, contact the **Israel Youth Hostels Association** (☎ 02-655 8405; www.iyha.org.il).

Hotels & Guesthouses

The standard of hotels and guesthouses in Israel runs from grim to gorgeous, with shades of everything in between. In most parts of the country, you'll find a few budget and top-end options (Israel is becoming especially strong in its unique boutique offerings), as well as good value midrange options. Israeli hotels are generally very good come breakfast time, with none of that European bread-cheese-and-jam-if-you're-lucky nonsense, even at the cheapest of places.

Note that some hotels may have a kosher policy, meaning the restaurant may not be in operation on holidays such as Yom Kippur; and if you see an ultraslow moving lift, that'll be the Shabbat elevator, which works automatically so that the devout need neither press the button nor strain their calf muscles on the stairs.

Kibbutz Guesthouses

In a bid to diversify their income, quite a few kibbutzim have turned to the guesthouse concept, with good (though often quite pricey for the standard of the rooms themselves) facilities. The **Kibbutz Hotels Reservations Office** (Map p278; ☎ 03-560 8118; www.kibbutz.co.il; 41 Montefiore St, Tel Aviv) offers full details of all kibbutz accommodation.

ACTIVITIES

Hiking

Don't miss the hiking opportunities in the region, even if it's only for a couple of days, which range from a wealth of waterfalls in the north, to desert desolation down south.

Most Israeli reserves are overseen by the **Israeli Nature & Parks Authority** (INPA; ☎ 02-500 6261; www.parks.org.il).

For hiking in the Palestinian Territories, consult local organisations (p316) for up-to-date information on areas considered safe; the area around Jericho (p317) is usually a great bet.

Watersports

Eilat's beaches are superbly overrated, despite its beautiful Red Sea position, but it's a good option for parasailing, waterskiing, and good value scuba courses (though the diving's better across the border in Sinai; see p189). Tel Aviv's beaches (p279), along with those heading north towards Haifa, are generally excellent. These, along with the Sea of Galilee (p299), all offer ample opportunities to swim, windsurf and sail, while the Dead Sea (p306) still provides that quintessential 'floating' experience.

BOOKS

Of course, if you want the ultimate companion to make sense of those most evocative of names – Sodom, Galilee, Bethlehem, or the Mount of Olives – simply lug along a copy of the Bible (Jewish or Christian) on your travels, and match the passages to the places on long-distance bus journeys. The Qu'ran, too, illuminates Jerusalem and the Holy Land environs.

For something more contemporary, a recommended duo, to get a lyrical perspective on life in both regions, are two autobiographies: *A Tale of Love and Darkness* (2005) by Amos Oz, and *Out of Place: A Memoir* (2000) by acclaimed Palestinian author, theorist and scholar, Edward Said.

A broader perspective on the region can be had if you're willing to wade through the *War and Peace*–like (without, sadly, much peace) tome, *The Great War for Civilisation: The Conquest of the Middle East* (2007) by stalwart journalist Robert Fisk. A more humorous, though historically questionable, account of the Holy Land can be had by dipping into Mark Twain's 1871 *The Innocents Abroad,* describing the bumpy, grumpy journey to Jerusalem and beyond.

And if you're interested in the everyday lives of West Bank Palestinians (and their zoo animals), this author's recent nonfiction novel *The Zoo on the Road to Nablus* (2008) makes (so I'm told) a very entertaining read.

BUSINESS HOURS

Israeli shopping hours are around 9am to 6pm (or later, especially in Tel Aviv) Sunday to Thursday, and 9am to 3pm Friday, with some places opening up after sundown on Saturday.

Banks are largely open from 8.30am to 12.30pm and 3pm to 5.30pm on Sunday, Tuesday and Wednesday; from 8.30am to 12.30pm on Monday and Thursday, and from 8.30am to noon on Friday. Some large city branches stay open all day, without the break for lunch, from Sunday to Thursday.

Post offices open from 8am to 6pm Sunday to Thursday, and 8am to noon on Friday; smaller branches may close for a couple of hours at lunchtime.

Bear in mind that in most parts of Israel (Tel Aviv not included), things grind to a halt during Shabbat, the Jewish Sabbath, which starts at sundown on Friday and ends one hour after sundown on Saturday. In Jerusalem and most other parts of the country, businesses close down around 3pm on Friday, and you might even have trouble locating dinner or a working ATM in observant areas. Public transport, too, ceases or is severely limited.

In largely secular Tel Aviv, Friday night is the biggest night out of the week, and Saturdays see scores of café-goers and diners hitting the pavement and beach cafés (most shops, though, do remain closed until Saturday sundown).

In predominantly Muslim areas – East Jerusalem, Akko, Jaffa, the West Bank and Gaza – businesses are closed all day Friday but remain open on Saturday. Christian-owned businesses (concentrated in Nazareth, Bethlehem and the Armenian and Christian Quarters of Jerusalem's Old City) are closed on Sunday.

CHILDREN

Travel in Israel and the Palestinian Territories is a breeze for children: the food's good, the distances are short and the natives are incredibly friendly. Baby food, powdered milk and nappies are readily available in shopping centres, and you'll find numerous helpful pharmacists able to tackle any minor health issues that might occur from life on the road.

One of the biggest drawcards for those with kids is inevitably Israel's beaches, which are usually clean, well-equipped with cafés and even playgrounds, and great for a paddle, a sandcastle or a swim. You'll notice that, unlike in much of Western Europe, local parents feel free to let their kids roam without fear of accident or abduction; it's such a child-friendly society that there's usually someone watching out for them, even when they're out of sight.

Most of Israel's parks and nature reserves are fantastic for kids, and older children will enjoy the hikes – some gentle, some more challenging – on offer throughout the country. The cities, too, have lots of diversions for children young and old, and there's always a toy shop, ice-cream parlour or other diverting activity for when a bribe's the only thing that will work.

Though the Palestinian Territories hold fewer obvious attractions for kids, children will nevertheless receive an extra-warm welcome, and will often be whisked away to meet local children or be treated to cakes and cookies. Kids will also enjoy Bethlehem's all-year Christmas shops and decorations, though younger kids (the author's included) may confuse the birthplace of Jesus for the hometown of Father Christmas.

COURSES

Some Israeli universities operate overseas programs for students of Hebrew, Arabic and Middle Eastern studies. Participants don't necessarily need to speak Hebrew, but may be required to study it as part of their curriculum. **Birzeit University** (www.birzeit.edu), 7km north of Ramallah, runs both beginners and advanced courses in Arabic language and literature for US$650 per course.

Travellers wishing to learn Hebrew will probably want to look for an *ulpan* – a language school catering mainly to new Jewish immigrants. Most programs cost under 500NIS per month; tourist information offices can give you details of *ulpanim* open for nonimmigrants.

For those who prefer not to study too hard, there are also kibbutz *ulpanim*, where you can take-on study in a rural atmosphere and work at the same time. The website www.kibbutzprogramcenter.org is an excellent source of information.

CUSTOMS REGULATIONS

Israel allows travellers to import duty free up to 1L of spirits and 2L of wine for each person over 17 years of age, as well as 250g of tobacco or 250 cigarettes. In theory, computer or diving equipment may need to be declared on arrival, and a deposit paid to prevent its sale in Israel, but in practice this regulation is rarely applied.

DANGERS & ANNOYANCES

Theft

Theft is as much a problem in Israel and the Palestinian Territories as it is in any other country, so take the usual precautions: for example, don't leave valuables in your room or vehicle. In hostels, it's wise to check your most valuable belongings into the desk safe. On intercity buses, it's fine to stow large bags in the luggage hold, but keep valuables with you inside. Crowded tourist spots and markets are obvious haunts for pickpockets, so stay aware of what's happening around you.

Security Situation

Security remains tight in Israel. When entering bus or rail terminals, shopping malls, government buildings and any place else that might conceivably be a terrorist target, your bags will be searched – and in some cases X-rayed. You will also be checked with a metal detector or by body search and probably asked the question: 'do you have a gun?' You'll get used to this – along with seeing armed soldiers strolling along the street – surprisingly quickly.

Roads into most West Bank towns have army roadblocks where you'll need to show a passport and answer questions about your reason for travel. Similarly, those leaving the country from Ben-Gurion airport are likely to be grilled about their stay and have their luggage thoroughly scrutinised.

Since the situation, particularly in the West Bank and Gaza (which is effectively off-limits), remains unpredictable, it's important to monitor the news closely before travelling in the area. Be aware that you may be warned off visiting these areas by concerned Israelis; while it's courteous to heed their warnings, it's also crucial to realise that they aren't necessarily accurate. So long as the Israeli army allows you through the checkpoints, you can assume that the area is relatively safe. Don't, though, exhibit any signs of Judaism or allegiance to Israel: no star-of-David yarmulkes or fake IDF T-shirts here.

DISCOUNT CARDS

A Hostelling International (HI) card is useful for obtaining discounts at HI hostels and an ISIC card entitles bearers to a 10% student discount on Egged buses, a 20% discount on Israel State Railways, as well as reductions on admissions to most museums and archaeological sites. Having said that, many places offer student discounts only to those studying in Israel, and cards issued by individual universities may not be recognised.

EMBASSIES & CONSULATES

Jerusalem may be Israel's capital, but most diplomatic missions are located in Tel Aviv; some also maintain consulates in Jerusalem, Haifa and/or Eilat.

Most diplomatic missions are open in the morning from Monday to Friday; some also open in the afternoon after closing for lunch. Unsurprisingly, there's no Lebanese, Iranian, Iraqi or Syrian embassy in Israel.

Australia (Map p276; ☎ 03-693 5000; www.australianembassy.org.il; 37 Sha'ul HaMelech Ave, Tel Aviv 64928)

Canada (Map p276; ☎ 03-636 3300; fax 03-636 3380; 3 Nirim St, Tel Aviv 67060)

Egypt Eilat (Map p311; ☎ 08-637 6882; 68 HaAfroni St 88119); Tel Aviv (Map p276; ☎ 03-546 4151; fax 03-544 1615; 54 Basel St, Tel Aviv 64239)

France (Map p278; ☎ 03-524 5371; 112 Herbert Samuel Esplanade, Tel Aviv 63572)

Germany (Map p278; ☎ 03-693 1313; www.tel-aviv.diplo.de; 19th fl, 3 Daniel Frisch St, Tel Aviv 64731)

Ireland (Map p278; ☎ 03-696 4166; fax 03-696 4160; 17th fl, 3 Daniel Frisch St, Tel Aviv 64731)

Jordan (off Map p276; ☎ 03-751 7722; fax 03-751 7722; www.jordanembassytelaviv.gov.jo; 14 Abbe Hillel St, Ramat Gan, Tel Aviv 52506)

Netherlands (off Map p276; ☎ 03-754 0777; www.netherlands-embassy.co.il; 14 Abbe Hillel St, Ramat Gan, Tel Aviv 52506)

Turkey (Map p276; ☎ 03-524 1101; fax 03-524 0499; 202 HaYarkon St, Tel Aviv 63405)

UK Embassy (Map p276; ☎ 03-725 1222, fax 03-527 1572, 192 HaYarkon St, Tel Aviv 64505); Consulate (Map p278; ☎ 03-510 0166, 1 Ben Yehuda St, Tel Aviv 63801) The consulate deals with for passport/visa issues.

USA Jerusalem (Map pp262-3; ☎ 02-625 3288; 27 Nablus Rd, Jerusalem 94190); Tel Aviv (Map p278; ☎ 03-519 7575; www.usembassy-israel.org.il; 71 HaYarkon St, Tel Aviv 63903)

FESTIVALS & EVENTS

The specific dates of Jewish festivals may vary from year to year. For the latest dates, ask at tourist offices.

January & February

International Tiberias Marathon (www.tiberias-marathon.co.il; Tiberias) Held in January.

Dead Sea Half-Marathon (www.marathon.deadsea.co.il) A race from Ein Gedi Spa to Masada and back; run in February.

Tel Aviv Jazz Festival (www.jazzfest.co.il) Held in February. Cool jazz from across the globe attracts jazz buffs and novices alike.

March & April

Boombamela Festival (www.boombamela.co.il; Netzanim Beach, Ashkelon) Naked bodies painted in rainbow colours, beach bonfires, bongo drums, art and hedonism. It's one of the wildest parties in the Middle East; held in March.

Jerusalem Half-Marathon (www.hmarathon.jerusalem.muni.il; Jerusalem) Run in March.

Arthur Rubinstein Piano Master Competition (www.arims.org.il) Usually held in Tel Aviv during March.

Ein Gev Music Festival (Ein Gev, Galilee) Ballet and orchestral music festival; held in April.

Haifa International Youth Theatre (Haifa) Street and theatre performances in April by Jewish and Arab companies.

May

Abu Ghosh Vocal Music Festival (Abu Ghosh, near Jerusalem) Haunting classical and choral performances in atmospheric, ancient venues.

Israel Festival (www.israel-festival.org.il; Jerusalem) A host of music, theatre and dance performances grace Jerusalem's stages for this huge annual event.

Jacob's Ladder Festival (www.jlfestifval.com; Sea of Galilee) Draws folk musicians and artists from around the world.

Jerusalem International Book Fair (www.jerusalembookfair.com; Jerusalem) Biennial event that attracts more than 1200 publishers from over 40 countries.

Shantipi New Age Festival (Kibbutz Lehavot Haviva, Pardesh Hanna) A free love–style New Age gathering in the spirit of Glastonbury.

June & July

Jerusalem Jazz Festival (www.jjf.org.il; Jerusalem) Jazz performances by Israeli and international performers across the city in June.

Jerusalem Film Festival (www.jff.org.il; Jerusalem) Prestigious international festival; held in July.

Karmi'el Dance Festival (www.dancefest.karmiel.israel.net; Karmi'el) Huge dance festival in July attracting more than 100 troupes from across the world.
White Night (Tel Aviv) All-night program of art, music, theatre and dance, with an outdoor fair held on Rothschild Blvd; July.

August & September

Klezmer Dance Festival (Tsfat) Held in August. Spirited festival of klezmer music, drawing happy international crowds.
Red Sea Jazz Festival (www.redseajazzeilat.com; Eilat) Four-day festival held during August with performers from across the world.
Nights of Love (Arad) Israeli pop festival in August.
Beresheet Festival(www.beresheet.co.il; Sea of Galilee) A Bohemian gathering, usually held in the Megiddo Forest, with lots of live music.
Ocktoberfest (www.taybehbeer.com; Taybeh) Beer festival at the Middle East's only microbrewery, in the Palestinian Christian village of Taybeh.

October

Fringe Theatre Festival (Akko) A lively program of street and theatre performances in Akko's picturesque Old City.
Haifa International Film Festival (www.haifaff.co.il; Haifa) Local and international films screen at this well-respected festival.
Love Parade (www.loveparade.co.il in Hebrew; Tel Aviv) Beachside festival and parade.

November & December

Olive Harvest Festival (Bethlehem) Olive farmers gather in Manger Sq during November for dancing, singing and displays of olive products.
Christmukkah (Haifa) A mixed citywide celebration, for Hannukah, Christmas and Ramadan.
Liturgical Festival of Choral Music (www.jso.co.il; Jerusalem) Sponsored by the Jerusalem Symphony Orchestra; held in December.

GAY & LESBIAN TRAVELLERS

Tel Aviv is the gay capital of Israel, if not the Middle East, and nearly all bars and nightspots that don't specifically cater to gays are gay-friendly. Other cities – even Jerusalem – have smaller, but active gay scenes; see individual destination listings.

Gay culture is nonexistent in the Palestinian Territories and many gay Palestinians have historically taken refuge in Israel. To better understand the difficult plight of gay and lesbian Palestinians, click on www.globalgayz.com/g-palestine.html or www.aswatgroup.org.

HOLIDAYS

Dates of Jewish holidays may vary from year to year, as they're based on the Jewish lunar calendar. The Orthodox Union website at www.ou.org/chagim has links to a calendar of Jewish holidays. For a list of Islamic holidays, see p628.

January & February

Eastern Orthodox Christmas 5 and 6 January
Armenian Christmas 19 January
Tu Bishvat (Arbour Day) The new year for trees; held in January. On this day different types of fruit and nuts are eaten and trees planted.
Black Hebrew Day of Appreciation & Love February festivities include art, music, food and dancing.

March & April

Purim The Feast of Lots commemorates the Persian Queen Esther's deliverance of her Jewish subjects from the despicable secular politician, Haman. Kids and adults alike dress up in costume and enjoy an evening of revelry. This is the time for the typically nondrinking Israelis to atone; according to tradition they get so plastered that they can't distinguish between 'bless Mordechai' and 'curse Haman'.
Good Friday Christian holiday commemorating the crucifixion of Jesus.
International Women's Day Palestinians celebrate this day on 8 March.
Easter Sunday Celebrated first by the Roman Catholics and Protestants and about two weeks later by the Armenian and Eastern Orthodox churches, Easter commemorates the resurrection of Jesus on the third day after the crucifixion. When times are calm, Catholic pilgrims throng the Via Dolorosa and Church of the Holy Sepulchre in Jerusalem's Old City, while many Protestants gather at the Garden Tomb for religious services.
Land Day (30 March) A Palestinian day of protest against the Israeli government's takeover of Palestinian lands.
Pesah (The Feast of Passover) Celebrates the exodus of the Children of Israel from Egypt, led by Moses. On the first and last days of this week-long festival, most businesses (including shops and markets) are closed and public transport shuts down; on other days of the festival, businesses may open for limited hours. Passover dinner, or Seder, consists of several prescribed dishes, each commemorating a different event, and during the entire period, bread is replaced with matzo, an unleavened wafer up to 1m in diameter.
Omer (Pesah to Shevuot) This is a Lent-like period solemnly commemorating the various trials of the Jewish people.
Soldiers Memorial Day This day commemorates fallen soldiers in various Israeli conflicts.
Armenian Holocaust Memorial Day 24 April
Mimouna North African Jewish festival.

Eastern Orthodox & Armenian Good Friday Takes place two weeks after the Protestant and Catholic Good Friday.

Eastern Orthodox & Armenian Easter This falls two weeks after the Protestant and Catholic Easter.

May

Yom HaSho'ah On Holocaust Day (22nd day of Omer) Sirens sound periodically throughout the day signalling two minutes of silence in memory of the six million Jewish victims of the Nazi Holocaust.

Labor Day (1 May) Day for Palestinian workers to celebrate their achievements.

Lag B'Omer Picnics Sports matches and bonfires and a permissible feast on the 33rd day of Omer commemorate the 2nd-century break in the plague that killed Rabbi Akiva's students (in some years, it may fall in late April).

Yom HaAtzma'ut This day commemorates 14 May 1948, when Israel became an independent state. The day before, Yom Hazikaron, is a memorial day dedicated to soldiers lost in Israel's various conflicts. For Palestinians, this day is called Al-Naqba, the Great Catastrophe.

June & August

Liberation of Jerusalem Day (4 June) This is a commemoration of the reunification of Jerusalem in June 1967.

Shevuot (Pentecost) Seven weeks after Pesah, this day celebrates the delivery of the Torah to Moses on Mt Sinai.

Tish'a BeAv This is a commemoration of the Destruction of the Temples.

September & October

Rosh HaShanah This is the 'head of the Year' (Jewish New Year) and prayer services begin on the eve of the holiday.

Independence Day (15 November) Marks the signing of the Palestine Declaration of Independence (signed in 1988).

Yom Kippur The Day of Atonement ends the 10 days of penitence that begin on Rosh HaShanah. The observant spend 25 hours in prayer and contemplation, confessing sins and abstaining from food, drink, sex, cosmetics (including soap and toothpaste) and animal products.

Sukkot On Sukkot (Tabernacles Festival) people erect homemade *sukkotim* (shelters) in commemoration of the 40 years which the ancient Israelites spent in the wilderness after the Exodus. The *sukkotim* walls are constructed of plywood with a roof of loose branches (so the sky is visible from inside); these sit on apartment balconies, gardens and even in hotels and restaurants.

Simhat Torah This falls seven days after Sukkot.

Yitzhak Rabin Memorial Day This day honours the assassinated prime minister, Yitzak Rabin (sometimes held in November).

December

Hanukkah Also called the Festival of Lights, Hanukkah celebrates the re-dedication of the Temple after the triumphant Maccabean revolt against the Seleucids. Each night for a week, families light a candle on a menorah (an eight-branched candelabrum) and exchange gifts.

Christmas Commemorating the humble birth of Jesus in Bethlehem, Christmas is celebrated by Catholics and Protestants on 25 December, while the Eastern Orthodox churches celebrate it on 7 January and the Armenians on 19 January. When things are calm on the West Bank, the event to attend is the Christmas Eve (24 December) midnight mass on Bethlehem's Manger Sq outside the Church of the Nativity. Note that space inside the church is reserved for observant Catholics who hold tickets (distributed free at the Christian Information Centre in Jerusalem's Old City).

INTERNET ACCESS

Most cities and towns have internet cafés, which are frequently open 24 hours and charge anywhere from 12NIS to 30NIS per hour. Free wi-fi access is widespread; almost every coffee chain and plenty of individual establishments have it on offer. Both internet cafés and wi-fi are less common in the Palestinian Territories, though not impossible to find.

LANGUAGE

Israel's national language is Hebrew, and the first language of most of the Arab population is the Syrian dialect of Arabic. Most Israelis and Palestinians speak some English, and most speak it well. You'll also hear a lot of Russian and French on the streets, courtesy of the large immigrant populations of both.

Because Israelis are largely of immigrant stock, other less common languages are also represented. Some older Ashkenazim, for example, still speak Yiddish (medieval German using the Hebrew alphabet) in everyday conversation. A very small number of Sephardic people still speak their traditional – but dying – Ladino, a blend of Hebrew and Spanish written in the Hebrew alphabet.

Most road signs appear in English, Hebrew and Arabic, but often with baffling transliterations – Caesarea, for example, may be rendered Qesariyya, Kesarya, Qasarya, and so on; and Tsfat may appear as Zefat, Zfat, or Safed. This doesn't stop at road signs, though: count the various spellings of 'foccaccia' and 'shakshuka' you'll see along the way.

MONEY

The official currency in both Israel and the Palestinian Territories is the new Israeli shekel (NIS), which is divided into 100 agorot. Coins come in denominations of 10 and 50 agorot (actually marked ½ shekel) and one, two and five shekels, and notes in 10, 20, 50, 100 and 200 shekels. Prices are also widely quoted in US dollars, though this is mostly if you're paying by credit card; few places will accept cash dollars as payment.

ATMs are widespread throughout Israel; less so in the Palestinian Territories, so take cash along with you. Travellers cheques may be changed at most banks, but commissions can be as high as 20NIS, regardless of the cheque amount. It's better to change them at a no-commission exchange bureau or the post office. Instant Western Union international money transfer services can be done at post offices.

Below are the rates for a range of currencies when this book went to print.

Country	Unit	New Israeli shekel (NIS)
Australia	A$1	2.58
Canada	C$1	3.16
Egypt	E£1	0.70
Euro zone	€1	5.07
Japan	¥100	4.14
Jordan	JD1	5.45
Lebanon	LL100	0.26
New Zealand	NZ$1	2.23
Syria	S£100	8.18
UK	UK£1	5.79
USA	US$1	3.92

POST

Letters and postcards to North America and Australasia take seven to 10 days to arrive, and to Europe, a bit less. Incoming mail takes three or four days from Europe and around a week from other places. An airmail postcard to Europe or Australia costs 5.40NIS and to the USA is 3.80NIS. A letter weighing 100g to 250g costs 10.20NIS to Europe or Australia, and 6.40NIS to the USA.

TELEPHONE

Mobile Phones

Most foreign providers operate in Israel and the Palestinian Territories (but it may be worth checking with your provider before you leave home). There are plenty of pay-as-you-go services; try Cellcom, which usually has the best deals on sim card purchase and subsequent calls, or the more pricey Orange. You'll find sim card and phone shops throughout the major Israeli cities.

Phone Codes

The country code for Israel and the Palestinian Territories is ☎ 972, followed by the local area code (minus the initial zero), then the subscriber number. Local area codes are given at the start of each city or town section in this guide. The international access code (to call abroad from Israel and the Palestinian Territories) is ☎ 001 with national provider Bezeq.

Phonecards

Phonecards can be bought at post offices, newsstands and phone shops and lottery kiosks. Most cost around 20NIS, and allow you to talk for 60 minutes for calls to standard destinations such as the UK, USA and Australia.

TRAVELLERS WITH DISABILITIES

For information on accessible facilities, contact **Access Israel** (☎ 057 723 9239; www.aisrael.com). The **Yad Sarah Organisation** (☎ 02-644 4444; www.yadsarah.org) loans wheelchairs, crutches and other mobility aids free of charge (a deposit is required). You may also want to look for the guidebook *Access in Israel & the Palestinian Authority* by Gordon Couch (www.accessinisrael.org), which provides the lowdown for travellers with mobility restrictions.

VISAS

With a few exceptions, visitors to Israel and the Palestinian Territories need only a passport valid for at least six months from the date of entry. Nationals of most Central American and African countries (but not South Africa), India, Singapore and some ex-Soviet republics also require a pre-issued visa.

Visas given at the border are valid for 90 days. Note that you'll only be allowed entry if you have a return ticket, otherwise, you'll most likely be detained and deported. Kibbutz and moshav volunteers must secure a volunteer's visa, which can be arranged with the assistance of the kibbutz or moshav.

Anyone who appears 'undesirable' or is suspected of looking for illegal employment may be questioned at length by immigration officials about the purpose of their visit and asked to provide evidence of sufficient funds for their intended length of stay. You'll also probably be detained for questioning if you have a Lebanese, Syrian, Pakistani or Sudanese stamp in your passport, though after a long wait, you'll probably be allowed in. Don't, if asked, mention that you'll be visiting the Palestinian Territories: travellers have been turned away at the border after answering in the affirmative.

Visa Extensions

To stay more than three months, visitors must apply for a visa through the **Ministry of the Interior** (☎ 02-670 1411; www.moin.gov.il, in Hebrew), with offices in most cities and towns. Join the queue by 8am or you could be waiting all day. You'll need 145NIS for the visa extension (plus 75NIS if you take the multientry visa option) and one passport-sized photo. You must also present evidence of sufficient funds for the extended stay. The Tel Aviv office is so backed up with applications that your first day of waiting in line is only to make an appointment to come back another day (usually one month later). For faster service try a smaller branch office.

Note that overstaying your allotted time elicits a fine of 135NIS per month – this can be sorted out at Ministry of the Interior offices or Ben-Gurion airport, but not at land borders. Travellers who overstay by just a few days report no hassles or fines.

WOMEN TRAVELLERS

Female travellers can expect the same sort of treatment they'd receive in most European countries, though it's important to dress modestly in religious areas such as the Old City and M'ea She'arim in Jerusalem, and in the West Bank and Gaza (where you'll be more of a novelty, but treated generally as a 'sister'). Note that the more religious male Jews and Muslims may not wish to shake a woman's hand.

WORK

While it isn't difficult to find casual work in Israel, to work legally you'll need a work permit from the Ministry of the Interior and they aren't easy to get.

In good times, eager international volunteers descend on Israel for a stint on a kibbutz or moshav. By definition, a kibbutz (plural kibbutzim) is a communal farm or other rural project staffed by volunteers, who trade their labour for food, lodging and a small stipend. After a short stint, though, quite a few volunteers are disappointed with what they encounter, and Tel Aviv hostels are crowded with dropouts who found things less utopian than anticipated. If another type of volunteering is more to your taste, contact **Ruach Tova** (www.ruachtova.org) for lots of opportunities in Israel, or one of the organisations listed on p316, for the Palestinian Territories.

Some volunteers organise a kibbutz stay through a kibbutz representative office in their own country. After collecting a basic registration fee (around US$50), the kibbutz representative will arrange flights and visas (individuals may make their own travel arrangements, which is generally cheaper). Alternatively, would-be volunteers can apply in person at **Kibbutz Program Centre** (Map p278; ☎ 03-527 8874; www.kibbutz.org.il; 18 Frishman St, cnr Ben Yehuda St, Tel Aviv; 🕒 8am-2pm Sun-Thu)

TRANSPORT IN ISRAEL & THE PALESTINIAN TERRITORIES

GETTING THERE & AWAY

Entering Israel & the Palestinian Territories

A frequent topic of conversation among travellers (a great source of annoyance for some and a breeze for others) is the entrance procedures for Israel and the Palestinian Territories. It's rigorous even at the best of times, and you can expect a barrage of questions about your recent travels, occupation, any acquaintances in Israel and possibly your religious or family background. If you are meeting friends in Israel, have their phone number handy. Anyone planning to work in Israel can expect delays.

Air

Israel's main air gateway, **Ben-Gurion airport** (TLV; ☎ 03-975 5555; www.ben-gurion-airport.co.il), is 20km southeast of Tel Aviv and 50km west

A STAMPED PASSPORT: A PROBLEM?

If you have an Israeli stamp in your passport (or an Egyptian or Jordanian border crossing stamp, which shows you've entered Israel), you'll be denied entry to Lebanon, Syria, Iran and Iraq. Egypt and Jordan, of course, are no problem.

Coming in the other direction, passport stamps from neighbouring Arab countries (Egypt and Jordan excepted) and Islamic destinations such as Pakistan and Sudan will slow your entry into Israel, and put you in line for questioning. Though you'll likely be granted entry in the end, there's nevertheless a chance that you might be turned away without a given reason.

The best solution to this problem is to get all visas and entry stamps stamped on pieces of paper, rather than on the passport itself, or, just to be sure, visit Israel last on your itinerary.

of Jerusalem. An ultramodern US$1 billion international terminal, unveiled in 2004, and handling 16 million passengers a year, it's easy to navigate and a well-organised port of entry and departure with El Al national carrier as its flagship line.

Only a handful of international charter flights touch down at the officially military Ovda airport outside Eilat; if you do end up here, the airport runs connecting buses to Eilat, or on to Tel Aviv or Jerusalem. To check on international flights, phone Ben-Gurion airport.

Note that airport security is tight, especially on El Al services, and international travellers should check in at least three hours prior to their flight. Fares into Israel aren't especially cheap and it's rarely an allowable stop on round-the-world itineraries. The best deals are normally available on the internet, frequently direct from the airlines' websites themselves. Tel Aviv is well served by European, US and Asian airlines.

Land

There are no open land borders between Israel and Syria or Lebanon. Egypt and Jordan both have open land borders with Israel and the Palestinian Territories, and you may cross on foot or by private vehicle, but not in a taxi or rental car. Drivers and motorcyclists will need the vehicle's registration papers and proof of liability insurance, plus a driving licence from home (but not necessarily an international driving licence).

EGYPT

The **Taba crossing** (☎ 08-637 2104, 08-636 0999; 🕑 24hr) is the only open border between Israel and Egypt. Here, travellers pay 69NIS departure tax to leave Israel, and around E£20 to enter Egypt. Driving your own vehicle across, you'll pay 32NIS departure tax on the car in Israel (as well as your individual fee) and a whopping E£180 on the Egyptian side.

Nearly all visitors require visas to enter Egypt, which cost 65NIS for US and German citizens and 100NIS for everyone else. They're available at the **Egyptian embassy** (Map p276; ☎ 03-546 4151; 54 Basel St, Tel Aviv; 🕑 for applications 9-11am Sun-Thu) and the **Egyptian consulate** (Map p311; ☎ 08-637 6882; 68 HaAfroni St, Eilat; 🕑 for applications 9-11am Sun-Thu). Deliver your passport, application and one passport-sized photo during opening hours in the morning and pick up the visa around 2pm the same day.

Alternatively, at the Taba border you can pick up a free Sinai-only entry permit, which is valid for 14 days and allows travel between Taba and Sharm el-Sheikh, and to Mt Sinai and St Katherine's Monastery; however, it is not valid for diving at Ras Mohammed National Park near Sharm el-Sheikh.

Access to the Taba border from Eilat is on city bus 15. From the Egyptian side, buses and shared taxis leave for Sinai; for details, see p208.

If you are trying to get to Cairo in a hurry, the best way is to hop on the **Mazada Tours** (Jerusalem Map p269; ☎ 02-623 5777; Pearl Hotel, 15 Jaffa Rd; Tel Aviv Map p276; ☎ 03-544 4454; www.mazada.co.il; 141 Ibn Gvirol St) direct bus service between Tel Aviv or Jerusalem and Cairo via Rafah (US$84, 12 hours). Buses leave Jerusalem/Tel Aviv at 9am/11am Sunday, Monday and Thursday. After picking up passengers in Cairo, they head back. Mazada is represented in Cairo by **Misr Travel** (☎/fax 02-335 5470).

JORDAN

There are three border crossing points with Jordan.

The least used of the three (since it's not especially convenient for anywhere unless you're travelling in your own car) is the **Jordan River/Sheikh Hussein Bridge crossing** (☎ 04-648 0018;

JUST ACROSS THE BORDER: PETRA, JORDAN

You simply can't get as far as Israel and not venture just across the southern border to visit the magical, fabled 'Rose red city, half as old as time'. Stunning at any time of year, Petra (p373) is especially beautiful after a light winter snow fall. From Eilat (p310), it's a short hop by taxi to the Yitzhak Rabin border crossing, a usually sleepy, easy crossing point; you can obtain your visa (JD10) at the border (open 6.30am to 10pm Sunday to Thursday, 8am to 8pm Friday and Saturday), so no need to plan in advance.

From here, take a taxi (JD5, 15 minutes) to the Aqaba minibus station and then a bus to Wadi Mousa (leaves when full between 7am and 2pm, JD4) or take a taxi (JD40), for the two hour ride through spectacular mountain scenery all the way up to Wadi Mousa, the closest town to Petra. Settle into your hotel room (we suggest the Cleopetra Hotel, see p378) or strike out for a quick drink in the Cave Bar (p380), where you can sip your beer in a 2000-year-old rock-cut tomb. But don't make too much of a night of it: you'll want to rise with the dawn, to see Petra's famous Treasury building in its best light the next morning, when the site (p375) opens at 6am .

8am-10pm), which is 6km east of Beit She'an in Galilee. Departure tax here is 70NIS, and there's an irritating 2km bus ride between the Israeli and Jordanian borders, which seems to take forever. To get here, take a bus to Beit She'an, and a taxi on to the border.

More popular is the **King Hussein/Allenby Bridge crossing** (☎ 02-548 2600; 8am-6pm Sun-Thu, 8am-2pm Fri & Sat), which is only 30km from Jerusalem and 40km from Amman. Note that the crossing is called Allenby Bridge when you are in Israel, but refer to it as King Hussein Bridge in Jordan. Traffic can be heavy here, especially between 11am and 3pm, and it's often chaotic due to Palestinian traffic. Departure tax here is 127NIS. A shared taxi from Jerusalem's Damascus Gate to the border crossing should cost you around 200NIS for the car; alternatively, take a bus from the **ABDO travel agency office** (☎ 628 3281) opposite the Damascus Gate; costs and frequencies vary, so call in to check.

In the south the **Yitzhak Rabin/Wadi Araba crossing** (☎ 08-630 0530; 6.30am-10pm Sun-Thu, 8am-8pm Fri & Sat) lies just 2km northeast of central Eilat, making it handy for day trips from Eilat to Aqaba, Petra and Wadi Rum. Exit tax here is 68NIS; take a taxi from central Eilat for the 10-minute journey.

Nearly all travellers require visas to enter Jordan; for details see p393. Visas can be purchased at both the Rabin (formerly called Arava) and Jordan River border crossings, but not at Allenby Bridge; single entry visas cost JD10 (around US$14). If you're travelling via Allenby, get a visa at the **Jordanian embassy** (off Map p276; ☎ 03-751 7722; fax 03-751 7712; 14 Abbe Hillel St, Ramat Gan, Tel Aviv), in the Tel Aviv suburb of Ramat Gan (take bus 66 from Ben Yehuda St). You can apply in the morning and pick the visa up around 2pm the same day; bring one passport-sized photo.

GETTING AROUND

Air

Israir (www.israir.co.il) flies at least once daily (including Saturday) between Ben-Gurion, Tel Aviv Sde Dov, Eilat and Haifa. **Arkia** (www.arkia.co.il), which also runs international charters, also operates flights between the same cities.

Bicycle

Cycle tourists should bear in mind the hot climate, winter rainfall, steep hills, and Israeli drivers with a death-wish. The best place for a leisurely cycle trip is around the Sea of Galilee; for such purposes, several of Tiberias' hostels hire out bicycles for quite reasonable rates.

Bus

Israel's small size and excellent road system combine to make bus travel the public transport of choice in the centre, though routes are very patchy in the north and far south of the country. The network is dominated by **Egged** (☎ 03-694 8888; www.egged.co.il), which runs fast and modern air-con buses on both long-distance and city bus routes; check online for information on schedules and prices, including city buses.

In Nazareth, East Jerusalem and the West Bank, a number of small Arab-run bus companies provide public transport on typically slow and antiquated vehicles. Note that Egged bus schedules are affected by public holidays and usually don't run during Shabbat, while Arab buses operate daily.

Car & Motorcycle

Drivers won't need an international licence, but must have their home drivers licence in order to rent a car or drive a private vehicle.

Because buses are less frequent in the Golan Heights and the Negev areas, these places are best seen with a rental car, and those on a budget will find that sharing a vehicle can be quite economical (US$250 per week, or less). Ask at your hotel or hostel to get an idea of the best rates and companies of the moment, which aren't always the international chains. Make sure your designated driver is good on both the offence and defence, and has a long fuse, since Israeli drivers aren't known for their caution or courtesy.

One highly recommended rental company for travel throughout Israel and on into the West Bank is **Green Peace** (☎ 02-528 2179; www.greenpeace.co.il), which offers cars daily from US$70, with discounts for longer rentals.

Hitching

Hitching is very popular countrywide – especially in the north and south – and the local method of soliciting a lift is to simply point an index finger at the road. For general safety reasons, though, we don't recommend you do it.

Local Transport

SHERUT

As in neighbouring Middle Eastern countries, the shared taxi (sherut) rules the roads of both Israel and the Palestinian Territories. In Israel, the sherut is usually a comfortable minibus; in the Palestinian Territories, it's known more commonly as simply a shared taxi or service taxi, and is often a smoking old Mercedes car with multiple passengers crammed in. During Shabbat, sheruts provide the only transport on certain major intercity routes, and on the West Bank, where Egged is limited to Jewish towns, the sheruts save hours of travelling time over the typically spluttering, smoke-belching Arab buses.

TAXI

Insist that Israeli taxi drivers use the meter (Palestinian yellow taxis rarely have a meter installed), and watch your progress on a map to ensure that the shortest route is followed. Taxi tariffs rise between 9pm and 5.30am.

Train

Israel State Railways (ISR; ☎ 03-577 4000; www.israrail.org.il) runs a limited but convenient, efficient and inexpensive network of passenger rail services between Be'er Sheva and Nahariya, as well as a route to Jerusalem. It is especially recommended for travel between Tel Aviv and Haifa or Akko. ISIC holders get a 20% discount. For the latest details, see its website.

Jordan

Ahlan wa sahlan! – 'Welcome to Jordan!' From the Bedouin of Wadi Rum to the taxi drivers of Amman, you'll be on the receiving end of this open-armed welcome every day. It's this, and a sense of peace and stability amidst a very tough neighbourhood, that makes travel in Jordan such a delight.

With heavyweight neighbours pulling big historical punches, Jordan easily holds its own, claiming some of the most significant sites in the region. Amman, Jerash and Umm Qais were cities of the ancient Roman Decapolis, while biblical sites range from Bethany-Beyond-the-Jordan, where Jesus was baptised, to Mt Nebo, where Moses is said to have looked out over the Promised Land. Grandest of all is the awe-inspiring Nabataean capital at Petra, crafted from sandstone cliffs.

But Jordan is not just about antiquities. It also offers the great outdoors, whether diving off the coast of Aqaba, trekking in the camelprints of Lawrence of Arabia, or hiking through stunning river gorges. Jordan's excellent nature reserves offer some of the most exciting adventure options in the Middle East – and some of the most heart-warming examples of environmental conservation in a region not known for its green credentials.

Like much of the Arab world, Jordan is trying to balance the time-honoured rhythms of a traditional society with a 'global lifestyle' that involves high-speed development. For travellers, this results in, for example, well-managed sites and reserves, but a lack of public transport between them. On the positive side, it means you can sleep under the stars on a goat-hair blanket one night and slip between starched linen at a spa resort the next.

Jordan is comparatively expensive for travellers and the cost of living is rising fast. That said, the country is compact and has enough compelling attractions (including spectacular landscapes) to absorb you for a good couple of weeks. Reserve some cash and don't miss it!

FAST FACTS

- **Area** 89,206 sq km
- **Capital** Amman
- **Country code** ☎ 962
- **Language** Arabic
- **Money** Jordanian dinar (JD); US$1 = JD0.707; €1 = JD1.109
- **Official name** Hashemite Kingdom of Jordan
- **Population** 6.2 million

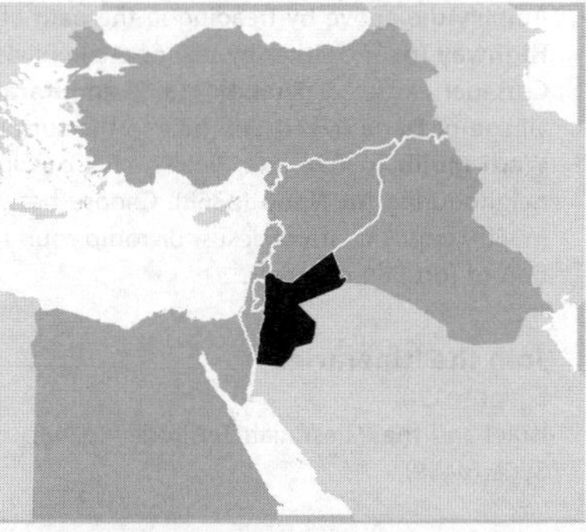

CLIMATE & WHEN TO GO

Average daily maximum temperatures in Amman range from 12°C in January to 32°C in August. Weatherwise, April/May and September/October are probably the best times to visit Jordan and these months are considered peak season.

Summer is an uncomfortable time to visit the Jordan Valley, Desert Castles, Aqaba and Wadi Rum: daily temperatures are well in excess of 36°C and can peak at 49°C. At the other extreme, snow in Amman and Petra is not unheard of in winter, and desert days and nights can be bitterly cold. Winter weather is pleasant and warm in Aqaba but with a high chance of rain.

See the Climate Charts (p625) for more information.

Note that most nature reserve facilities are closed from November until 1 April. One date for the calendar is the excellent Jerash Festival (p390), staged at the end of July.

HISTORY

Jordan has always been a crossroads for the Middle East's great civilisations, although most invaders have simply passed through en route to more prized possessions.

In 333 BC, Alexander the Great stormed through Jordan on his way to Egypt. After Alexander's death in 323 BC, Ptolemy I gained Egypt, Jordan and some parts of Syria. In southern Jordan, the Nabataeans, who were a semi-nomadic Arabian tribe that controlled lucrative trade routes, built a splendid capital at Petra, while the Roman Empire controlled much of the rest of the country.

After periods of occupation by the Seleucids, Sassanians and Byzantines, Jordan was the site of several initial key battles between the Byzantines and Arabs, before it was overrun by the armies of Islam in the 7th century AD. In the late 7th century, Jordan came under the control of the Umayyad Empire centred in Damascus.

JORDAN IN...

One Week

Arrive in Aqaba from Egypt, and party in Jordan's holiday town. Take the early-morning bus to spectacular **Wadi Rum** (p381) on day two. Hike from the visitor centre or share the cost of a 4x4 tour of the desert, made famous by Lawrence of Arabia. Hitch and bus back to Aqaba. On day three, take the early-morning bus to Wadi Musa and explore the rock-hewn wonders of neighbouring **Petra** (p373), a world-class site. On day four, catch the evening bus to **Amman** (p343) and spend day five exploring the frenetic capital. On day six, catch a chariot race in the Roman ruins of **Jerash** (p355) and leave the next day on a direct bus from Amman, either north to Damascus or west to Jerusalem via the King Hussein/Allenby Bridge crossing, taking note of visa restrictions (see p393).

For an easier border crossing into Israel and the Palestinian Territories, spend longer at Wadi Rum and Petra and use the Wadi Araba crossing from Aqaba into Eilat (p310).

Two Weeks

Amplify the above by treading in the path of the ancients from Petra to Amman via the **King's Highway** (p365), either by taxi or a combination of minibus and some hitching. Stop off at the Crusader castles of **Shobak** (p372) and **Karak** (p370); overnight at the remarkable escarpment village of **Dana** (p371) and hike in the surrounding reserve; pause for photo stops in dramatic **Wadi Mujib** (p369); and, finally, chill out in the travel-friendly town of **Madaba** (p366) and neighbouring **Mt Nebo** (p368). Choose between a tour of the **Dead Sea** (p360) and **Bethany** (p360), baptism site of Jesus, or romp round the **Eastern Desert** (p363) with its bizarre collection of fortified outposts.

Join the Itineraries

Egypt (p120)
Israel and the Palestinian Territories (p248)
Syria (p459)

In AD 747 an earthquake devastated much of Jordan, ushering in the rule of the Abbasids, who were in turn followed by the Cairo-based Fatimids in AD 969, and then, from 1037, by the Seljuk Turks.

In the 11th century, Pope Urban II launched the Crusades, capturing Jerusalem in 1099, slaughtering countless inhabitants and devastating the area. The Crusaders took control of most of Jordan by about 1115, and built fortresses at Karak, Shobak and Petra.

In the 12th century, the armies of Nur ad-Din, and later Salah ad-Din (Saladin), reunited the Arab and Islamic world and occupied most of the Crusader strongholds in Jordan. The Mamluks, former soldier-slaves, finally expelled the Crusaders in 1250. The Ottoman Turks defeated the Mamluks in 1516 and ruled until WWI.

In June 1916 the Arabs, with the assistance of TE Lawrence ('Lawrence of Arabia'), launched the Arab Revolt and helped the British drive the Turks from the region. In return, the Arabs were given British assurances that they would be allowed to establish an independent Arab state.

The newly formed League of Nations instead gave Britain a mandate over Palestine, and shortly afterwards the state of Transjordan, lying between Iraq and the East Bank of the Jordan River, was made a separate entity under King Abdullah. What remained of Palestine corresponded more or less to present-day Israel and the Palestinian Territories.

Directly after WWII, the British threw in the towel and handed over control of the region to the UN, which voted in favour of the partition of Palestine into separate Arab and Jewish states. Agreement could not be reached, however, and the Arab-Israeli War broke out in 1948, prompting many Palestinians to flee to Transjordan and ending with a comprehensive victory for Israel; it ensured Jewish occupation of the zones allocated to them under the UN partition plan as well as almost all those assigned to the Palestinian Arabs. Transjordan exploited the situation and occupied the West Bank and part of Jerusalem, whereupon King Abdullah shortened his fledgling country's name to Jordan.

King Abdullah was assassinated in 1951. He was succeeded the following year by his grandson Hussein, who took the throne at the age of just 17 and managed to hold it for 48 years through insurrection attempts, two wars with the Israelis and a virtual civil war with the Palestinians. He reigned until his death in 1999.

In the 1960s, aid poured in from the USA and Jordan enjoyed a boom in tourism, mainly in Jerusalem's old city. The situation was radically altered by the Six Day War of 1967, in which Jordan lost the West Bank and its half of Jerusalem to occupying Israeli forces. In return it gained a huge influx of Palestinian refugees.

These Palestinians, particularly the Palestine Liberation Organisation (PLO), became more militant against the Israeli occupation in the early 1970s and were angered in part by Hussein's claim to be the leader of the Palestinian people. After some bloody fighting in 1971, the bulk of the radicals were forced to cross the border to Lebanon, where they would later become one part among many of that country's woes.

King Hussein's diplomatic skills were stretched to the fullest when, during the 1991 Gulf War, he refused to side against Iraq, fearing unrest among Jordan's Palestinian populace. For the third time in 45 years, Jordan experienced a massive refugee inflow, with as many as 500,000 Palestinians previously working in the Gulf States fleeing to Jordan.

Jordan recovered remarkably well from that conflict and, despite fears of the threat of Islamic extremism, King Hussein went ahead and signed a full peace treaty with Israel in 1994.

When King Hussein finally succumbed in February 1999 to the cancer that had been ailing him for so long, his son and nominated heir, Abdullah II, became king of a comparatively stable and prosperous country.

Jordan Today

Inheriting much of the diplomatic flair of his father, King Abdullah belongs firmly to the new generation of Arab leaders in favour of social and economic reform. He has backed the promotion of women's rights (in 2007, 20% of seats in municipal councils were reserved for women) and supports freedom of the press, albeit tempered by local sensibilities. Jordan Media City, the country's state-of-the-art media hub, transmits 120 program channels.

JORDAN

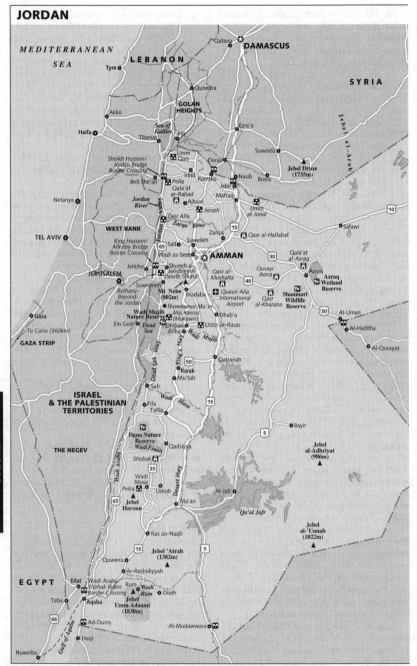

MEDITERRANEAN SEA
LEBANON
Qatana
DAMASCUS
Tyre
SYRIA
Quneitra
GOLAN HEIGHTS
Akko
Haifa
Sea of Galilee
Tiberias
Fiq
Ezra'a
Jebel al-Arab
Suweida
Umm Qais
Sheikh Hussein/ Jordan Bridge Border Crossing
Deraa
Jebel Druze (1735m)
Irbid
Ramtha
Nasib
Bosra
Beit She'an
Pella
Jabir
Qala'at ar-Rabad
Mafraq
Jordan River
Ajloun
Netanya
Jerash
Umm al-Jimal
10
Jordan Valley
Deir Alla
Zarqa River
Safawi
WEST BANK
15
Zarqa
Qasr al-Hallabat
TEL AVIV
King Hussein/ Allenby Bridge Border Crossing
Suweileh
65
Salt
Wadi as-Seer
AMMAN
30
Qala'at al-Azraq
Jericho
Shuneh al-Janubiyyeh (South Shuna)
JERUSALEM
Qasr al-Mushatta
Qusayr Amra
Azraq
Azraq Wetland Reserve
Suweimeh
40
Bethany-Beyond-the-Jordan
Mt Nebo (802m)
Madaba
Queen Alia International Airport
Qasr al-Kharana
Shaumari Wildlife Reserve
Hammamat Ma'in
Wadi Mujib Nature Reserve
Machaerus (Mukawir)
Dhab'a
30
Al-Umari
Gaza
Ein Gedi
Dead Sea
Dhiban
Umm ar-Rasas
Al-Haditha
To Cairo (360km)
Ariha
Wadi Mujib
GAZA STRIP
Al-Qurayat
Dead Sea Hwy
King's Hwy
Qatranah
50
Karak
Mu'tah
Safi
ISRAEL & THE PALESTINIAN TERRITORIES
Wadi Hasa
15
Fifa
Tafila
Bayir
5
Dana Nature Reserve
Wadi Finan
Qadsiyya
Jebel al-Adhriyat (986m)
THE NEGEV
Shobak
35
Desert Hwy
Wadi Araba
Wadi Musa
Petra
Udruh
Al-Jafr
Jebel Haroun
65
Ma'an
Qa'al Jafr
Jebel al-'Unnab (1022m)
Ras an-Naqb
15
Jebel 'Atrah (1382m)
5
Quweira
Ar-Rashidiyyah
EGYPT
Eilat
Wadi Araba/ Yitzhak Rabin Border Crossing
Rum
Wadi Rum
Diseh
Jebel Umm Adaami (1830m)
Taba
Aqaba
66
Ad-Durra
Al-Mudawwara
Gulf of Aqaba
Haql
Nuweiba

JORDAN

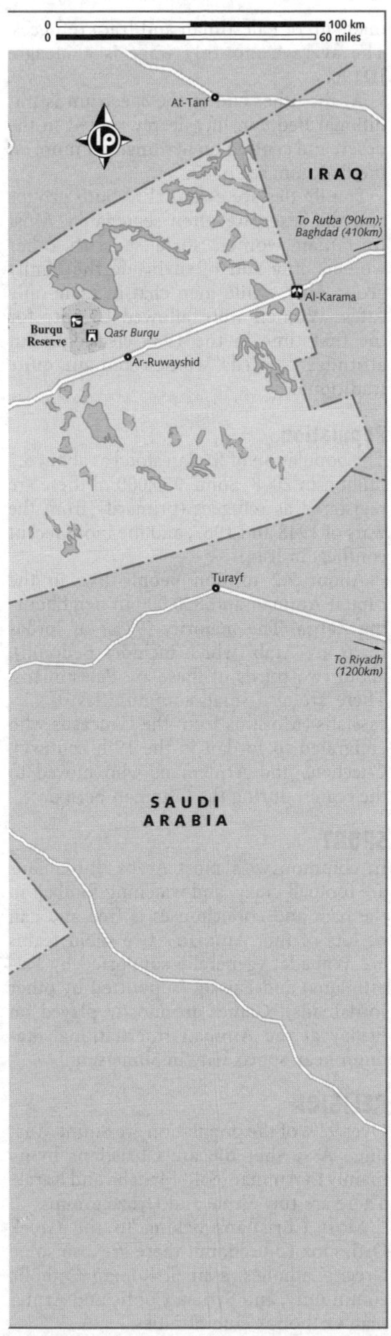

In common with other leaders in the region, the King has had to tread a fine line between cooperation with regional neighbours (especially Syria) while finding new ways of integrating with the rest of the world. His efforts in this regard have already won him international acclaim, especially in promoting a peaceful resolution to the Palestinian intifada (uprising).

Managing relations with Iraq (and the influx of 700,000 Iraqi refugees) has proved more problematic. This is especially the case as many of the refugees have greater spending power than average Jordanians and are being blamed for rising prices. Inflation topped 5.4% in 2007 and was expected to exceed that figure in 2008. Coupled with the rising price of fuel, inflation is now a major issue for the government.

Parliamentary elections last took place in November 2007, with independent, pro-government candidates winning the majority of seats. The new prime minister, Nader al-Dahabi, has a strong backing in parliament but has yet to convince the electorate of his abilities, especially in the light of continuing unemployment problems (the unemployment rate for 2007 was 13.5%), which has forced many Jordanian workers to move abroad – a trend the government is trying to reverse.

To help improve productivity and make Jordan a more attractive country for foreign investment, the government has reduced its debt-to-GDP ratio. A major challenge now facing Jordan is reducing dependence on foreign grants. The current resurgence of tourism is helping in this regard. Two incidents in recent times (the 2005 Al-Qaeda suicide bombing of three hotels in Amman, and the 2007 shooting by a lone gunman of tourists Downtown) momentarily cast doubt over Jordan's peaceful reputation. With so much at stake in terms of revenue, however, every effort is being made by Jordanian authorities to ensure the safety of travellers within the country.

THE CULTURE
The National Psyche

Jordanian people are extremely hospitable, with initial conversation inevitably leading to a heartfelt 'welcome'. This traditional sense of hospitality is mixed with an easy-going modernity and wonderful sense of

HOW MUCH?

- **Souvenir keffiyeh** from JD3
- **Cup of tea** from 300 fils
- **Midrange dinner** JD10
- **Museum admission** JD1
- **Mid-range hotel room** JD30 to JD80

LONELY PLANET INDEX

- **Litre of petrol** 600 fils and climbing
- **1.5L bottle of water** JD1
- **Bottle of Amstel beer** JD3.500
- **Souvenir T-shirt** JD8
- **Street stall felafel** 500 fils

humour that make Jordanians fun to get along with.

The modern Western outlook of Amman's young middle and upper classes contrasts with the conservative Bedouin morality of the countryside. This tension, along with the rapid social change linked to the rise of tourism, has led to a clash of values in places such as Wadi Musa.

Shared values include a deep respect for the Jordanian royal family, which is part of the ingrained tribal respect for elders. Islam dominates Jordanian views of the world, of course, as does the Palestinian experience, which is hardly surprising when you consider that 65% of Jordanians are Palestinian.

Being physically and ethnically close to Iraq, most Jordanians are often frustrated and at times angered by American policies towards Iraq but they are always able to differentiate a government from its people. You'll never be greeted with animosity, regardless of your nationality, only a courtesy and hospitality that are humbling.

Daily Life

More than 40% of Jordan's population lives in Amman, reflecting a big split between rural and urban lifestyles. The middle and upper classes of Amman shop in malls, drink lattes in mixed-sex Starbucks and obsess over the latest fashions. Mobile phones dominate life in Jordan as they do abroad. Yet urban unemployment is high, and entire neighbourhoods of Amman are made up of Palestinian and Iraqi refugees. The average monthly wage is a meagre JD190.

At the other end of the spectrum is traditional Bedouin life, deeply rooted in the desert and centred on herding. For more on the Bedouin, see p382.

Family ties are essential to both groups and the sexes are often segregated. Most Jordanian women socialise with other women only and often inside the family group only, while men chat in male-only cafés. Women were allowed to vote for the first time in the 1989 elections, but attitudes towards women remain quite traditional.

Population

The population of Jordan stood at about 6.2 million in 2008. Some 953,000 of these are registered as refugees (primarily from the wars of 1948 and 1967, and the more recent conflicts in Iraq).

About 2.2 million people live in the capital Amman and 850,000 in neighbouring Zarqa. The majority (98%) of Jordanians are Arab (which includes Bedouin); about two-thirds of these are Palestinians. There are also small communities of Circassians (Muslims from the Caucasus who emigrated to Jordan in the 19th century), Chechens and Armenians who moved to the region during the Ottoman period.

SPORT

In common with most Arabs, Jordanians are football crazy, and watching football in the bars and coffeehouses is free and can be lots of fun. Amman's two main teams are Wahadat (generally supported by Palestinians) and Faisaly (supported by other Jordanians). Games are mostly played on Friday at the Amman International Stadium near Sports City in Shmeisani.

RELIGION

Over 92% of the population are Sunni Muslims. A further 6% are Christians living mainly in Amman, Salt, Madaba and Karak. There are tiny Shiite and Druze groups.

Most Christians belong to the Greek Orthodox Church, but there are also some Greek Catholics, a small Roman Catholic community, and Syrian, Coptic and Armenian Orthodox communities.

ARTS

As Jordan has been at the crossroads of so many international 'caravans' of art and culture over the centuries, it's quite hard to define an essentially Jordanian aesthetic. The modern arts, especially popular literature, fine arts and music, are dominated by the Egyptian and Lebanese, and show strong Western influence. That said, there are a few local names to look out for and Jordanians will be well chuffed if you are able to identify them.

Literature

Mounis al-Razzaz, who died in 2002, was regarded by many as the driving force behind modern Jordanian literature. His works spoke of wider turmoil in the Arab world, notably in his satirical final work *Sweetest Night,* and of Amman's transition from a small village to a modern metropolis.

Diana Abu-Jaber, a celebrated Jordanian-American author, draws on her family's memories of Jordanian cultural identity, a love of Jordanian food and her life as an immigrant in the USA. Her works include *Arabian Jazz, Crescent* and *The Language of Baklava*.

Other modern novels include the Palestinian Yasmin Zahran's *A Beggar at Damascus Gate* and *Pillars of Salt* by Fadia Faqir, the tale of two women in a Jordanian asylum.

Jordan has produced several famous journalists in recent years. Rana Husseini is a human-rights activist dedicated to exposing the problem of crimes of honour through her writing. In 2003 she won the Ida B Wells award for Bravery in Journalism. Fouad Hussein is another high-profile journalist, investigating the so-called 'Grand Strategy' of Al-Qaeda: it makes for an uncomfortable read.

Cinema & TV

David Lean's epic masterpiece *Lawrence of Arabia* was partially filmed in Wadi Rum. Everyone headed to Petra will get to see *Indiana Jones and the Last Crusade* with its famous parting shots of Petra's Siq and Treasury.

Most Jordanians have access to satellite TV, which shows programs from across the Arab world. Jordanians are still wistful that it was a Jordanian singer who won the first ever *Superstar* competition, an Arab version of *Pop Idol.*

Music

Sakher Hattar (born 1963 in Amman) is renowned as the finest *oud* player in the region, winning many awards such as first place in the International Competition for Oud in Cairo in 1993. He has performed in Germany, USA, France and Tunisia.

Hani Naser is known as the 'Hand Drum Wizard' of Jordan, specialising in hand percussion instruments like the goblet drum and *djembe.* He has made recordings with the Rolling Stones, Ry Cooder, Santana, Lou Reed and many other famous international artists.

Jordan's traditional Bedouin music remains distinctive and vibrant. The most popular instrument is the *rubaba,* a melancholy one-stringed violin. If you take the Petra by Night Tour (see p380), you may well be treated to a performance in front of Petra's famous Treasury.

Painting

The 7th-century Umayyad frescoes at the desert castle, Qusayr Amra, in Jordan's eastern *badia* (basalt desert), and the Byzantine mosaics of the Madaba region, are high points of Jordan's historical visual arts.

To explore Jordan's contemporary art scene, visit Darat al-Funun (p347) and the Jordan National Gallery of Fine Arts (p349) in Amman. While you are there, you may come across Mohammed al-Saifi, a young Jordanian painter from Amman, renowned for employing industrial tools like aerosol sprays in work more usually expressed through a paintbrush. Another contemporary artist gaining local recognition is Hani Alqam, who has enjoyed success at a number of recent exhibitions in Amman.

Traditional Crafts

In Jordan, jewellery is an important indicator of wealth and status, especially among the Bedouin, who also produce wonderful weavings. Today more than 2000 Palestinian and Bedouin women produce kilims and camel bags under the guidance of several Jordanian organisations such as Beni Hamida. Palestinian embroidery is another important craft, and most visible on the Palestinian dresses known as *roza*.

If craft is your thing, then head for the **Wild Jordan Centre** in Amman (p347) for an overview of the country's diverse cottage industries and their locations.

ENVIRONMENT

The Land

Jordan can be divided into three major geographic regions: the Jordan Valley, the East Bank plateau and the desert. The fertile valley of the Jordan River is the dominant physical feature of the country's western region, running from the Syrian border in the north, along the border with Israel and the Palestinian Territories and into the Dead Sea. The valley (part of the larger African Rift Valley) continues under the name Wadi Araba and extends to the Gulf of Aqaba where Jordan claims a sneeze-sized stretch of the Red Sea. The majority of the population lives in a hilly 70km-wide strip running the length of the country known as the East Bank plateau. The remaining 80% of the country is desert, stretching into Syria, Iraq and Saudi Arabia.

Wildlife

Spring is the best time to see some of Jordan's two thousand flowers and plants, including the black iris, Jordan's redolent national flower.

Two of Jordan's most impressive animals are the Arabian oryx and Nubian ibex, which are resident at the Shaumari (p364) and Wadi Mujib (p362) nature reserves respectively. Jordan is an important corridor for migratory birds en route to Africa and southern Arabia.

Nature Reserves

The **Royal Society for the Conservation of Nature** (RSCN; www.rscn.org.jo) operates six reserves in Jordan, of which Wadi Mujib (p362) and Dana (p371) are the undoubted highlights. The Azraq Wetland Reserve (p364), located in eastern Jordan, is a good place for birdwatching.

Environmental Issues

According to the Environmental Sustainability Index (last updated in 2005), Jordan ranked higher than any other Arab country. The RSCN, under inspired leadership, has pioneered models for sustainable development and tourism by working closely with local communities and making them stakeholders in conserving local reserves. The society has also been responsible for reintroducing several endemic animals in Jordan, including the endangered oryx.

Despite these welcome environmental initiatives, there are still major problems including a chronic lack of water, pressure of tourism on fragile sites such as at Petra and in Wadi Rum, and increasing desertification through over-grazing.

Solutions to these problems are constantly under review and there are ambitious plans to build a pipeline, known as the 'Peace Conduit', connecting the Red and Dead Seas to provide desalinated water and also raising the dropping levels of the Dead Sea (see boxed text, p117).

FOOD & DRINK

While not as famous as the cuisine in Egypt or Turkey, Jordan nonetheless has a distinctive culinary tradition, largely thanks to the Bedouin influence.

The Bedouin speciality is *mensaf*, delicious spit-roasted lamb that is basted with spices until it takes on a yellow appearance. It is served on a platter of rice and pine nuts, flavoured with the cooking fat, and often centrally garnished with the head of the lamb. Honoured guests are served the eyes (which have a slightly almond flavour); less honoured guests are offered the tongue (a rich-flavoured, succulent meat). The dish is served with a sauce of yogurt, combined with the cooking fat. In Wadi Rum you might be lucky enough to be offered a Bedouin barbecue from the *zarb*, a pit oven buried in the desert sand.

Another Jordanian favourite is *maqlubbeh* (sometimes called 'upside down') – steamed rice pressed into a pudding basin, topped with meat, eggplant, tomato and pine nuts.

Dessert here, as in many parts of the Middle East, may be *kunafa* or *muhalabiyya* (a milk custard containing pistachio nuts).

The universal drink of choice is sweet black tea (coffee comes a close second); most social exchanges, including haggling over a kilim, are punctuated with copious glasses of it that are usually too hot to handle. Other options include *yansoon* (aniseed herbal tea) and *zaatar* (thyme-flavoured tea).

Bottled mineral water (1.5L bottle JD1) is widely available, as are the usual soft drinks, Amstel beer and locally produced wines.

Street eats – felafel, shwarma, fuul, roast chicken and hummus – are widely available. In mid-range restaurants, the most common way for a group to eat is to order mezze – a variety of small starters followed by several mains to be shared by all present.

AMMAN عمان

☎ 06 / pop 2.2 million

Amman is not one of the great cities of antiquity. Indeed, for those arriving from Damascus or Cairo, it can feel disappointingly grey and modern – though, alas, not in the visionary, expensive Dubai sense of the word. There are historic sites, as you would expect of a city once called Philadelphia: the 6000-seat Theatre, Odeon and Citadel are all fine, if relatively small, examples of Roman architecture.

The lack of historic sites shouldn't put you off, however. Amman has lots to offer the visitor, not least the balance it strikes between the demands of the past and the vision of its next generation. Residents talk openly of two Ammans, although in truth there are many. Eastern Amman (which includes Downtown and large Palestinian refugee camps on the fringes) is home to the urbanised poor and is generally more conservative. Western Amman is a world apart, the preserve of leafy residential districts, trendy cafés and bars, impressive contemporary art galleries and young men and women openly walking arm in arm.

So don't come to Amman looking for medieval bazaars or grand mosques. But do come to catch a glimpse of a tolerant and practical Arab city, embracing an international and culturally diverse vision of the future. It's also a great base from which to visit Jerash, the Dead Sea and the Eastern Desert Castles. Whatever your reason for visiting, the welcome is sure to be warm.

HISTORY

The site of Amman has been continuously occupied since 3500 BC. Biblical references to the city are numerous and indicate that by 1200 BC 'Rabbath Ammon' was the capital of the powerful Ammonites. When King David was insulted by the Ammonite king, Nahash, he sent Joab, commanding the Israelite armies, to besiege Rabbath. After taking the town, David burnt alive many inhabitants in a brick kiln.

Amman was taken by Herod around 30 BC, and fell under the sway of Rome.

Philadelphia (as it was then known) was the seat of Christian bishops in the early Byzantine period, but the city declined and fell to the Sassanians (from Persia) in about AD 614. At the time of the Muslim invasion of AD 636, the town was again thriving as a staging post of the caravan trade.

Amman was nothing more than a little village when a colony of Circassians resettled there in 1878. In 1900 it was estimated to have just 2000 residents. In 1921 it became the centre of Transjordan when King Abdullah made it his headquarters. Following the formation of the state of Israel in 1948, Amman absorbed a flood of

GIVING AMMAN A FACELIFT

Amman is on the rise, with several high-profile construction projects set to change the face of the city. Here are two initiatives that will be capturing headlines in the coming months:

- **National Museum** Amman's congested Downtown will eventually be home to public gardens, panoramic vantage points and pedestrian trails linking the Citadel and the Roman Theatre. The highlight of this project is the much-vaunted National Museum, located next to the City Hall. Despite construction delays, it is expected to welcome its first visitors in 2009 (*insha'allah!*).
- **Jordan Gate Towers** This high-profile US$1 billion business and retail complex at 6th Circle features twin 35-storey high-rise towers, and will include a five-star Hilton Hotel and a boutique shopping mall.

Palestinian refugees, and doubled its population in a mere two weeks. It continues to grow, currently swelled by many Iraqi refugees escaping the chaos across the border.

ORIENTATION

Built originally on seven hills (like Rome), Amman now spreads across 19 hills and is therefore not a city to explore on foot. That said, the Downtown area – known locally as *il-balad* – with its budget hotels and restaurants, banks, post offices and Amman's ancient sites are compacted into a relatively small area in the heart of the great metropolis.

The main hill is Jebel Amman, home to embassies and midrange and top-end hotels and restaurants. The traffic roundabouts (some now replaced with tunnels and major intersections) on Jebel Amman are numbered west of Downtown from 1st Circle to 8th Circle. The Jebel Weibdeh and Abdali areas have more hotels, the distinctive blue dome of the King Abdullah Mosque and the JETT and Abdali bus stations. West and south of these areas are glamorous Shmeisani and Abdoun, the most upmarket areas of Amman and the places to go for nightlife.

Maps

If you plan to stay for some time or intend to visit places out of the centre, *Maps of Jordan, Amman and Aqaba,* published by

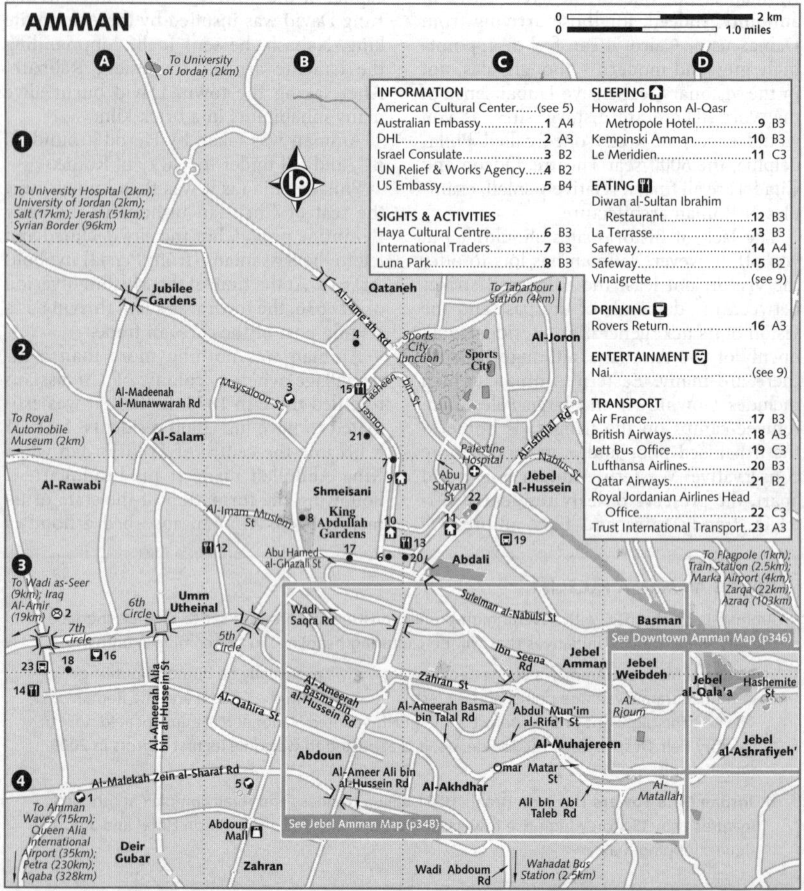

Luma Khalaf, is reliable and worth picking up from bookshops in Amman.

INFORMATION

Bookshops

Al-Aulama Bookshop (Map p346; ☎ 4636192; 44 Al-Amir Mohammed St; 8am-8pm Sat-Thu)
Amman Bookshop (Map p348; ☎ 4644013; Al-Amir Mohammed St; 9am-2pm & 3.30-6.30pm Sat-Thu)
Books@café (Map p346; ☎ 4650457; contact@books-café.com; Omar bin al-Khattab St; 10am-11.30pm) Grab a bite to eat (p351) while browsing.
Bustami's Library (Map p346; ☎ 4622649; Al-Amir Mohammed St; 5am-6pm Sat-Thu) Good for international newspapers.

Cultural Centres

The following cultural centres have a library and regular film nights, exhibitions and concerts. The two main local English-language newspapers, the *Jordan Times* and the *Star*, list current events.
American Cultural Center (Map p344; ☎ 5859102; US Embassy, Al-Umawiyeen St, Abdoun; 1-4.30pm Sat-Wed, 9am-4pm Thu) Has a library with American newspapers and magazines.
British Council (Map p348; ☎ 4636147; www.britishcouncil.org.jo; Abu Bakr as-Siddiq St, Jebel Amman; 9am-6.30pm Sun-Wed, to 3.30pm Thu) Southeast of 1st Circle. Has a library with current English newspapers and a pleasant café. Library hours are noon to 6.30pm Sunday to Wednesday, 11am to 3.30pm Thursday.
Centre Culturel Français (Map p346; ☎ 4612658; www.cccljor-jo.org; Kulliyat al-Sharee'ah St, Jebel Weibdeh; 8.30am-2pm & 4-6pm Sat-Thu)
Goethe Institut (Map p348; ☎ 4641993; www.goethe.de/na/amm/; 5 Abdul Mun'im al-Rifa'I St, Al-Radhwan; 9am-1pm Sun-Thu & 4.30-6.30pm Sun-Wed) Northwest of 3rd Circle.

Emergency

There is a small tourist police booth on Hashemi St near the Roman Theatre.
Ambulance (☎ 193)
Fire department (☎ 4617101, 199)
Police (☎ 192, 191)
Tourism police (toll-free ☎ 0800-22228)
Traffic police/accidents (☎ 4896390, 190)

Internet Access

Amman has plenty of internet cafés, particularly in the Downtown area.
Books@café (Map p346; ☎ 4650457; Omar bin al-Khattab St, Downtown; per hr JD2; 10am-11.30pm) A professional set-up (see p351) with fast connections.
Internet Yard (Map p346; ☎ 079 5509569; Al-Amir Mohammed St, Shmeisani; per hr JD1; 9.30am-midnight)
Welcome Internet (Map p346; ☎ 4620206; Al-Amir Mohammed St, Downtown; per hr JD1; 10.30am-1am)

Media

The *Jordan Times* and the *Star* are the two English-language newspapers and both are worth a read.

Jordan Today (www.jordantoday.com.jo) is a free monthly booklet that includes a yellow pages listing of embassies, airlines and the like. **Where to Go** (www.w2go.com) is similar and includes a useful collection of Amman restaurant menus. Pick them up in the better hotels and restaurants.

Medical Services

The two English-language daily newspapers list the current telephone numbers of doctors and pharmacies on night duty throughout the capital.
Al-Khalidi Medical Centre (Map p348; ☎ 4644281; www.kmc.jo; Bin Khaldoun St, southwest of 3rd Circle)
Italian Hospital (Map p346; ☎ 4777101; Italian St, Downtown)
Jacob's Pharmacy (Map p348; ☎ 4644945; 3rd Circle; 9am-3am)
Palestine Hospital (Map p344; ☎ 5607071; Queen Alia St)
University Hospital (Map p344; ☎ 5353444) Situated in the University of Jordan complex, northwestern Amman.

Money

Changing money is easy and the Downtown area especially has many banks, ATMs and moneychangers. See p391 for information and the Downtown map for locations.

Post

Central post office (Map p346; ☎ 4624120; Al-Amir Mohammed St, Downtown; 7.30am-5pm Sat-Thu, 8am-1.30pm Fri)
Customs office (Map p346; Omar al-Khayyam St, Downtown; 8am-2pm Sat-Thu) Diagonally opposite the parcel post office. Come here to send a parcel overseas.
Parcel post office (Map p346; Omar al-Khayyam St, Downtown; 8am-3pm Mon-Fri, to 2pm Sat, to 3pm Sun)

Telephone

The private telephone agencies around the Downtown area are the cheapest places for international and domestic calls.
Communication International (Map p346; Nimer bin Adwan St, Downtown)

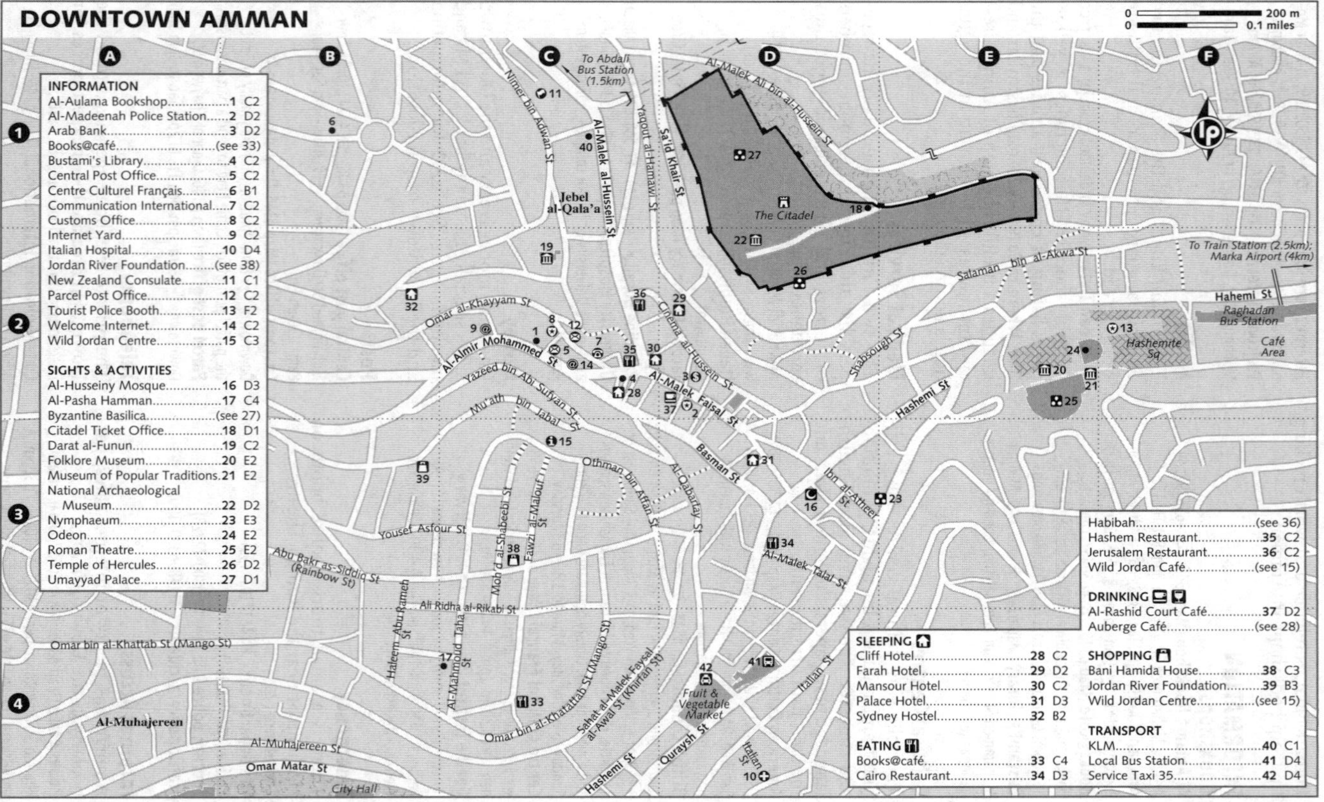
DOWNTOWN AMMAN
0 200 m
0 0.1 miles
INFORMATION
Al-Aulama Bookshop.....1 C2
Al-Madeenah Police Station.....2 D2
Arab Bank.....3 D2
Books@café.....(see 33)
Bustami's Library.....4 C2
Central Post Office.....5 C2
Centre Culturel Français.....6 B1
Communication International.....7 C2
Customs Office.....8 C2
Internet Yard.....9 C2
Italian Hospital.....10 D4
Jordan River Foundation.....(see 38)
New Zealand Consulate.....11 C1
Parcel Post Office.....12 C2
Tourist Police Booth.....13 F2
Welcome Internet.....14 C2
Wild Jordan Centre.....15 C3
SIGHTS & ACTIVITIES
Al-Husseiny Mosque.....16 D3
Al-Pasha Hamman.....17 C4
Byzantine Basilica.....(see 27)
Citadel Ticket Office.....18 D1
Darat al-Funun.....19 C2
Folklore Museum.....20 E2
Museum of Popular Traditions.....21 E2
National Archaeological Museum.....22 D2
Nymphaeum.....23 E3
Odeon.....24 E2
Roman Theatre.....25 E2
Temple of Hercules.....26 D2
Umayyad Palace.....27 D1
SLEEPING
Cliff Hotel.....28 C2
Farah Hotel.....29 D2
Mansour Hotel.....30 C2
Palace Hotel.....31 D3
Sydney Hostel.....32 B2
EATING
Books@café.....33 C4
Cairo Restaurant.....34 D3
Habibah.....(see 36)
Hashem Restaurant.....35 C2
Jerusalem Restaurant.....36 C2
Wild Jordan Café.....(see 15)
DRINKING
Al-Rashid Court Café.....37 D2
Auberge Café.....(see 28)
SHOPPING
Bani Hamida House.....38 C3
Jordan River Foundation.....39 B3
Wild Jordan Centre.....(see 15)
TRANSPORT
KLM.....40 C1
Local Bus Station.....41 D4
Service Taxi 35.....42 D4
To Abdali Bus Station (1.5km)
To Train Station (2.5km); Marka Airport (4km)
Jebel al-Qala'a
The Citadel
Al-Muhajereen
Hashemite Sq
Raghadan Bus Station
Café Area
Fruit & Vegetable Market
City Hall
Nimer bin Adwan St
Al-Malek al-Hussein St
Yaqout al-Hamawi St
Sa'id Khair St
Al-Malek Ali bin al-Hussein St
Salaman bin al-Akwa'St
Hahemi St
Hashemi St
Shabsough St
Cinema al-Hussein St
Al-Malek Faisal St
Omar al-Khayyam St
Al-Amir Mohammed St
Yazeed bin Abi Sufyan St
Mu'ath bin Jabal St
Othman bin Affan St
Al-Qabartay St
Basman St
Ibn al-Atheer St
Al-Malek Talal St
Yousef Asfour St
Moh'd al-Shabeebi St
Fawzi al-Malouf St
Abu Bakr as-Siddiq St (Rainbow St)
Ali Ridha al-Rikabi St
Haleem Abu Rameh St
Al-Mahmoud Taha St
Omar bin al-Khattab St (Mango St)
Omar bin al-Khatattab St (Mango St)
Sahat al-Malek Faysal al-Awal St (Khirfan St)
Quraysh St
Italian St
Al-Muhajereen St
Omar Matar St

Tourist Information

Jordan is one country where tourism complaints are taken seriously. If you have a question or problem, call the toll-free **Halla Line** (☎ 800-22228).

Ministry of Tourism & Antiquities (Map p348; ☎ 4642311; Al-Mutanabbi St, Jebel Amman; 8am-9pm) The information office on the ground floor can answer most queries, or call the Halla Line.

Wild Jordan Centre (Map p346; ☎ 4616523; www.rscn.org.jo; Othman bin Affan St) The place for information and bookings for Jordan's nature reserves, including Dana and Wadi Mujib. There's also an excellent craft shop (p353) and a superb café (p351) that sells organic food, making the centre worth a visit in its own right.

Visa Extensions

If you are staying in Jordan for longer than 30 days, you must obtain a (free) visa extension. Request your hotel to write a short letter confirming where you are staying. Your hotel will also need to fill out two copies of a small card, which states all their details (you fill in the details on the back). Take the form, the letter, a photocopy of the page in your passport with your personal details, your Jordanian visa page and your passport to the relevant police station (depending on which area of Amman you're staying in; ask at your hotel). If you're staying Downtown, go to the 1st floor of the **Al-Madeenah Police Station** (Map p346; ☎ 4657788; upstairs, Al-Malek Faisal St), opposite the Arab Bank.

After getting a stamp, take your passport to the **Al-Muhajireen Police Station** (Markez al-Muhajireen; Map p348; Al-Ameera Basma bin Talal Rd), west of Downtown, where you'll be granted a stay of up to three months. From Downtown take a taxi (600 fils) or service taxi No 35 from along Quraysh St. Police stations are usually open for visa extensions from 10am to 3pm Saturday to Thursday, although it's better if you go in the morning. Extensions are generally granted on the spot.

SIGHTS & ACTIVITIES

The restored **Roman Theatre** (Map p346; admission JD1; 8am-4pm Sat-Thu, 10am-4pm Fri Oct-Mar, 8.30am-7pm Apr-Sep) is the most obvious and impressive remnant of ancient Philadelphia. The theatre is cut into the northern side of a hill that once served as a necropolis, and can hold 6000 people. The theatre was built in the 2nd century AD during the reign of Antoninus Pius, who ruled the Roman Empire from AD 138 to 161. Performances are sometimes staged here in summer. The wings of the theatre are home to two quaint museums, the **Folklore Museum** (Map p346) and the **Museum of Popular Traditions** (Map p346); you can enter both as part of Roman Theatre admission. The museums have well-presented displays of traditional costumes and jewellery, as well as a mosaic collection.

The row of columns immediately in front of the theatre is all that's left of the **Forum**, once one of the largest public squares (about 100m by 50m) in imperial Rome. On the eastern side of what was the Forum stands the 500-seat **Odeon**. Built about the same time as the Roman Theatre, it served mainly as a venue for musical performances.

Hashemite Square, between the Roman Theatre and Raghadan station, is an ideal place to stroll, sip tea, smoke the nargileh (water pipe) and simply watch the world go by.

Philadelphia's chief fountain or **nymphaeum** (Map p346; admission free; daylight Sat-Thu) dates from AD 191 and stands with its back to Quraysh St, west of the theatre and not far from King Hussein Mosque. Excavations started in earnest in 1993, and restoration will continue for many years. Except for a few columns, an elegant archway and a few alcoves, there is still little to see.

The **Citadel** (Map p346; ☎ 4638795; admission JD2; 8am-4pm Sat-Thu Oct-Mar, to 7pm Sat-Thu Apr-Sep, 10am-4pm Fri year-round) sits on Jebel al-Qala'a – at 850m, Amman's highest hill. The complex includes some excavated ruins of an **Umayyad palace**, dating from about AD 720, of which the domed audience hall is the most impressive. There is an Umayyad cistern in the Citadel; a **Byzantine basilica** from the 6th or 7th century AD; and the **pillars of the Temple of Hercules**, which was constructed during the reign of Marcus Aurelius (AD 161 to AD 80).

Included in the Citadel's admission fee is the **National Archaeological Museum**, one of the best museums in Jordan. Exhibits include three 8500-year-old statues from Ain Ghazal, thought to be the world's oldest examples of sculpture.

Darat al-Funun (House of Arts; Map p346; ☎ 4643251; www.daratalfunun.org; Nimer bin Adwan St; admission free; 10am-7pm Sat-Wed, to 8pm Thu) is a tranquil complex dedicated to contemporary art. It

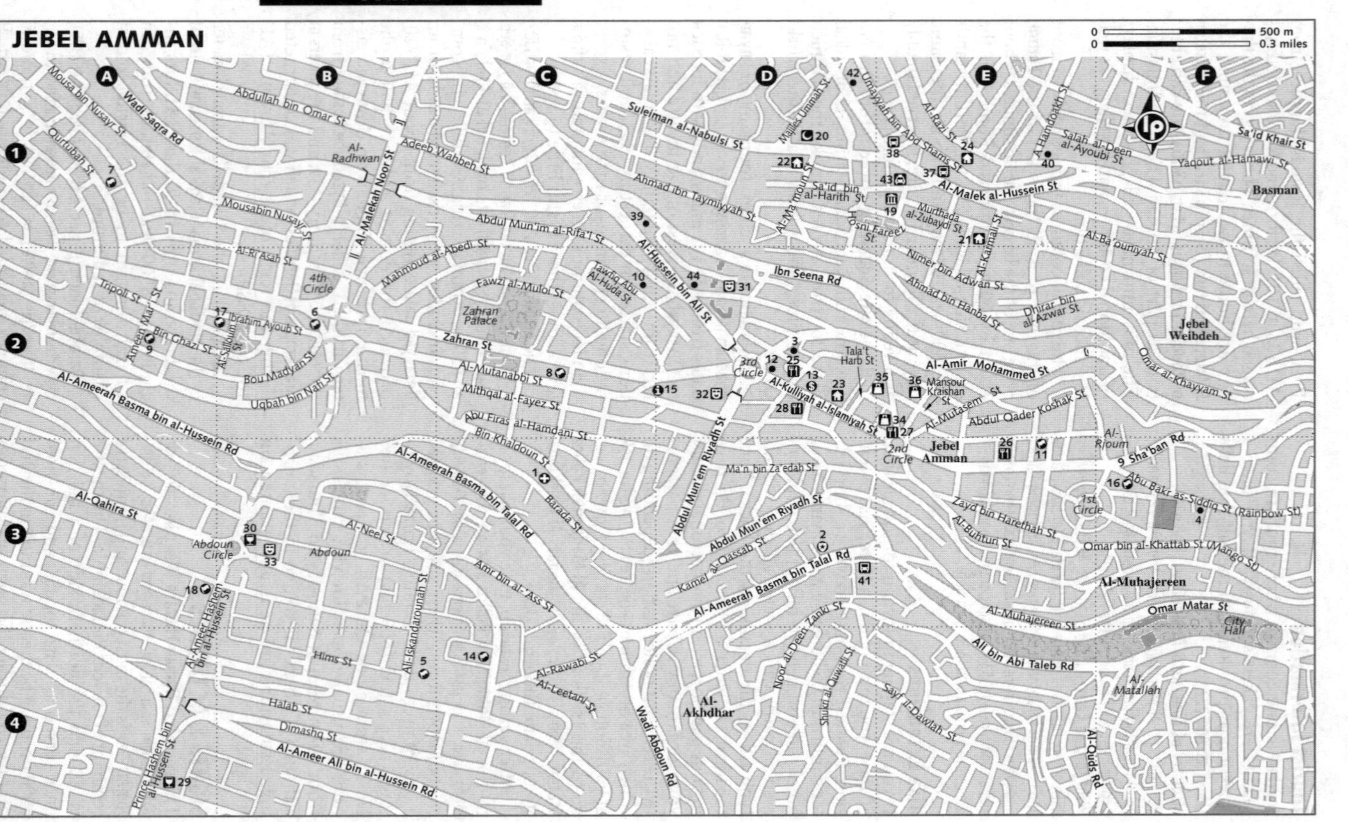
JORDAN
JEBEL AMMAN
0 500 m
0 0.3 miles
Mousa bin Nusayr St
Wadi Saqra Rd
Qurtubah St
Abdullah bin Omar St
Al-Radhwan
Al-Malekah Noor St
Adeeb Wahbeh St
Mousabin Nusayr St
Al-Ri'Asah St
4th Circle
Tripoli St
Ameen Mar'i St
Bin Ghazi St
Ibrahim Ayoub St
Al-Salloum St
Bou Madyan St
Uqbah bin Nafi St
Al-Ameerah Basma bin al-Hussein Rd
Al-Qahira St
Abdoun Circle
Abdoun
Al-Neel St
Al-Ameer Hashem bin al-Hussein St
Prince Hashem bin al-Hussein St
Halab St
Dimashq St
Al-Ameer Ali bin al-Hussein Rd
Hims St
Al-Iskandarounah St
Amr bin al-'Ass St
Al-Rawabi St
Al-Leetani St
Wadi Abdoun Rd
Suleiman al-Nabulsi St
Ahmad ibn Taymiyyah St
Abdul Mun'im al-Rifa'i St
Mahmoud al-Abedi St
Fawzi al-Mulqi St
Tawfiq Abu Al-Huda St
Zahran Palace
Zahran St
Al-Mutanabbi St
Mithqal al-Fayez St
Abu Firas al-Hamdani St
Bin Khaldoun St
Al-Ameerah Basma bin Talal Rd
Barada St
Al-Hussein bin Ali St
Ibn Seena Rd
3rd Circle
Abdul Mun'em Riyadh St
Ma'n bin Za'edah St
Kamel al-Qassab St
Noor al-Deen Zanki St
Shukri al-Quwatli St
Al-Akhdhar
Sayf il-Dawlah St
Majlies Ummah St
Al-Ma'moun St
Sa'id bin al-Harith St
Hosni Fareez St
Umayyah bin Abd Shams St
Al-Razi St
Murthada al-Zubaydi St
Al-Karmali St
Nimer bin Adwan St
Ahmad bin Hanbal St
Dhirar bin al-Azwar St
Tala't Harb St
Al-Kulliyah al-Islamiyah St
Mansour Kraishan St
Al-Mutasem St
Abdul Qader Koshak St
Al-Amir Mohammed St
2nd Circle
Jebel Amman
Zayd bin Harethah St
Al-Buhturi St
Al-Muhajereen
Al-Muhajereen St
Ali bin Abi Taleb Rd
Omar Matar St
City Hall
Al-Matallah
Al-Quds Rd
Al-Malek al-Hussein St
Al-Ba'ouniyah St
Jebel Weibdeh
Omar al-Khayyam St
Al-Rjoum
9 Sha'ban Rd
1st Circle
Abu Bakr as-Siddiq St (Rainbow St)
Omar bin al-Khattab St (Mango St)
A Hamdoakh St
Salah al-Deen al-Ayoubi St
Yaqout al-Hamawi St
Sa'id Khair St
Basman

features a small art gallery, an art library, artists' workshops and a program of exhibitions, lectures, films and public discussion forums.

The attraction at the **King Hussein Mosque** (Map p346; Hashemi St, Downtown) is the surrounding backstreet souqs rather than the building. This is definitely the best place in Amman to explore on foot. The first mosque was built on this site in AD 640 by Omar, the second caliph of Islam. The current mosque was built by King Abdullah I in 1924.

King Abdullah Mosque (Map p348; ☎ 5672155; Suleiman al-Nabulsi St, Jebel Wibdeh; admission JD2; 8-11am & 12.30-2pm Sat-Thu, 8-10am Fri) can house up to 7000 worshippers, with room for 3000 more in its courtyard. It welcomes non-Muslim visitors (women must cover their hair). Admission includes entry to a small Islamic museum.

The small but excellent **Jordan National Gallery of Fine Arts** (Map p348; ☎ 4630128; www.nationalgallery.org; Hosni Fareez St, Jebel Weibdeh; admission JD1; 9am-5pm Sun-Thu) exhibits contemporary Jordanian works including painting, sculpture and pottery.

Car enthusiasts might like the **Royal Automobile Museum** (Map p344; ☎ 5411392; www.royalautomuseum.jo; King Hussein Park; admission JD3; 10am-7pm Wed-Mon), which has a display of 70 classic cars and motorbikes from King Hussein's personal collection. It's in the northwestern suburbs, north of 8th Circle.

Al-Pasha Hammam (Map p346; ☎/fax 4633002; www.pashaturkishbath.com; Al-Mahmoud Taha St, Jebel Amman; 9am-2am, last booking midnight) is the perfect antidote to Amman's hills and bustle. The full service (JD22.500) includes a steam bath, sauna, Jacuzzi, body scrub, 40-minute massage and two soft drinks, all in a superb building architecturally faithful to Turkish hamam tradition. Bring a swimming costume. Women are welcome during the day but the evenings are men only.

WORLD'S TALLEST FLAGPOLE

From most places in the city, you can spot the huge Jordanian flag of the Raghadan palace compound, which at 127m high is said to be the world's largest free-standing flagpole. (A smaller but similarly impressive flag flies in Aqaba.) The award for the tallest flagpole in the world actually goes to those crazy North Koreans on the border with South Korea but that one is supported by cables, which, as everyone knows, is cheating.

AMMAN FOR CHILDREN

Amman Waves (Map p344; ☎ 64121704; www.ammanwaves.com; admission adult/child JD14/8; Airport Rd; 10am-7pm daily) Western-style water park, about 15km south of town on the highway to the airport.

Haya Cultural Centre (Map p344; ☎ 5665195; Ilya Abu Madhi St, Shmeisani; admission free; 9am-6pm Sat-Thu) Designed especially for children with a library, playground, an interactive ecomuseum and an inflatable castle.

Luna Park (Map p344; King Abdullah Gardens; admission JD1; 10am-10pm) Has rides and amusements.

INFORMATION
- Al-Khalidi Medical Centre 1 C3
- Al-Muhajireen Police Station 2 D3
- Amman Bookshop 3 D2
- British Council 4 F3
- British Embassy 5 B4
- Dutch Embassy 6 B2
- Egyptian Embassy 7 A1
- French Embassy 8 C2
- German Embassy 9 A2
- Goethe Institut 10 C2
- Iraqi Embassy 11 E3
- Jacob's Pharmacy 12 D2
- Jordan National Bank 13 D2
- Lebanese Embassy 14 C4
- Ministry of Tourism & Antiquities 15 D2
- Post Office (see 23)
- Saudi Arabian Consulate 16 F3
- Syrian Embassy 17 B2
- Tourist Police Centre (see 15)
- Yemeni Embassy 18 A3

SIGHTS & ACTIVITIES
- Jordan National Gallery of Fine Arts 19 E1
- King Abdullah Mosque 20 D1

SLEEPING
- Canary Hotel 21 E1
- Caravan Hotel 22 D1
- Jordan InterContinental Hotel 23 D2
- Toledo Hotel 24 E1

EATING
- Abu Ahmad Orient Restaurant 25 D2
- Haboob Grand Stores 26 E3
- Reem Cafeteria 27 E2
- Romero Restaurant 28 D2

DRINKING
- Blue Fig Café 29 A4
- Living Room (see 28)
- Tche Tche Café 30 B3

ENTERTAINMENT
- Century Cinemas 31 D2
- Cine Le Royal 32 D2
- Galleria Cinema 33 B3

SHOPPING
- Al-Alaydi Jordan Craft Centre 34 E2
- Al-Burgan 35 E2
- Artisana 36 E2

TRANSPORT
- Abdali Bus Station 37 E1
- Airport Express Bus 38 E1
- Emirates 39 C1
- Gulf Air 40 E1
- Hijazi (see 37)
- Muhajireen Bus Station (Minibuses to Dead Sea & Wadi as-Seer) 41 D3
- Royal Jordanian Airlines 42 D1
- Royal Jordanian Airlines (see 23)
- Service Taxis to Damascus, Beirut & Baghdad 43 E1
- Trust International Transport (booking office) (see 37)
- Turkish Airlines 44 D2

Wild Jordan Café (opposite) Offers a kid-friendly Friday brunch (9am to 11am) with entertainment and environmental education aimed at ages 8 to 11.

TOURS

For information on organised day trips from Amman, see p399.

SLEEPING

Budget

Downtown Amman has many cheap hotels. Budget places listed below have shared bathroom facilities unless stated otherwise; all promise hot water and some even deliver.

Cliff Hotel (Map p346; ☎ 4624273; Al-Amir Mohammed St; mattress on roof JD2, 3-bed dm JD23, s/d JD5/6) A long-standing shoestring favourite with friendly and accommodating staff. Cramped rooms are of questionable cleanliness, and it's cheeky to charge a dinar for the communal showers, but if you're sticking to a tight budget, this is the place to be.

Mansour Hotel (Map p346; ☎ 4621575; Al-Malek Faisal St; 4-bed dm JD5, s/d JD9/14, without bathroom JD7/10;) The Mansour is an old Arabic school converted into basic but attractive budget accommodation. The new management receives glowing reports from travellers, and it's quieter than most downtown hotels.

Farah Hotel (Map p346; ☎ 4651443; farahhotel@hotmail.com; Cinema al-Hussein St; 4- to 6-bed dm JD5, s/d JD15/22, without bathroom JD9/15;) The Farah is a backpacker-savvy place that gets consistently good reports from travellers. Private and shared rooms are tired, but the warm communal feel, knowledgable staff and popular movie nights compensate.

Sydney Hostel (Map p346; ☎ 4641122; sydney_hostel@yahoo.com; 9 Sha'ban St; dm/s/d/tr JD7/17/24/30;) A relative newcomer, the Sydney Hostel offers free internet and has a small onsite restaurant where guests gather to swap stories. The basic rooms are not as clean as they should be, however, and staffing is hit or miss.

our pick **Palace Hotel** (Map p346; ☎ 4624326; www.palacehotel.com.jo; Al-Malek Faisal St; s/d/tr JD17/24/30, without bathroom JD10/15/18;) The Palace is definitely the best budget option in the city, particularly because it understands the needs of backpackers, including providing reliable hot water, onsite internet café and top-value tours around Jordan. The fluorescent-lit rooms aren't much but they have air-con and satellite TV. The price includes a simple but filling breakfast, served in an attractive lounge where travellers congregate in front of the tube.

Midrange

Unless otherwise stated, all of the following hotels are located in the Jebel Amman area.

Caravan Hotel (Map p348; ☎ 5661195; caravan@go.com.jo; Al-Ma'moun St; s/d JD24/30;) Between hectic downtown and quieter Western districts, the Caravan is a good place to crash if you arrive at the station late. It's good value and reliable with a family feel and pleasant rooms.

Canary Hotel (Map p348; ☎ 4638353; canary_h@hotmail.com; 17 Al-Karmali St; s/d/ste JD24/31/40;) In the leafy Jebel Weibdeh area, the cosy B&B-style Canary is within easy walking distance of Abdali bus station. The rooms are comfortable and bathrooms sparkling.

Toledo Hotel (Map p348; ☎ 4657777; www.toledohotel.jo; Umayyah bin Abd Shams St; s/d from JD55/65;) The Moorish-style Toledo offers upmarket accommodation at a midrange price. Modern rooms with subdued lighting boast business-friendly amenities such as satellite TV and wireless internet, and the bathrooms are spacious. The hotel is conveniently located by Abdali bus station.

Ocean Hotel (Map p344; ☎ 5517280; www.oceanhotel.com.jo; Shatt al-Arab St, Umm Utheima; s/d from JD65/77;) A good choice if you want peace and quiet, the rooms here are warm and inviting and equipped with lots of amenities. The Ocean Hotel is also home to the renowned Lebanese Diwan al-Sultan Ibrahim Restaurant (p352). This hotel is not in Jebel Amman, but still centrally located.

Howard Johnson Al-Qasr Metropole Hotel (Map p344; ☎ 5689671; www.alqasr-hojo.com; 3 Arroub St; s/d JD90/100;) Located in fashionable Shmeisani, the HoJo has only 70 rooms, each incorporating pleasing design elements such as wood floors, crown moulding and soft lighting. The hotel has excellent restaurants and bars including Vinaigrette (opposite) and Nai (p352).

Top End

The following hotels are located in the Jebel Amman and Shmeisani areas. Note that cheaper prices are sometimes available if you book in advance online.

Le Meridien (Map p344; ☎ 5696511; www.lemeridien.com; Al-Malekah Noor St; r from JD120;)

While primarily targeting business travellers, the hotel wins guests over with its flawless rooms and world-class service.

Jordan InterContinental Hotel (Map p348; ☎ 464 1361, 0800 22666; www.intercontinental.com; Al-Kulliyah al-Islamiyah St; r from JD140;) The granddaddy of luxury hotels in Amman, the much-revered InterCon has been hosting foreign dignitaries for decades. Today, it still attracts an interesting mix of distinguished guests ranging from top American brass on R&R from Iraq to visiting royalty from the Gulf.

Kempinski Amman (Map p344; ☎ 5200200; www.kempinski.com; Abdul Hamid Shouman St; r from JD210;) Earning the title of Amman's most chic and sophisticated accommodation, this European-styled hotel offers designer rooms and regal bathrooms. Impressive entertainment facilities include a bowling alley, cinema and games centre for children.

EATING

Amman's budget restaurants are concentrated in Downtown and, to a lesser extent, Jebel Amman. More upmarket restaurants are found in Shmeisani and Abdoun.

Habibah (Map p346; Al-Malek al-Hussein St, downtown; pastries from 300 fils) This legendary shop is heaven for Middle Eastern sweets and pastries.

Reem Cafeteria (Map p348; ☎ 4645725; 2nd Circle, Jebel Amman; shwarma JD1) This shwarma stand has the punters queuing down the street at 3am. Even the royal family are rumoured to have dropped in here for a late-night kebab. And if it's good enough for them…

Hashem Restaurant (Map p346; Al-Amir Mohammed St; plates JD1-3; 24hr; V) A legendary place that overflows into the alley, Hashem is *the* place for felafel, hummus and fuul (fava-bean paste). A filling meal with bread and mint tea costs around JD1.

Jerusalem Restaurant (Al-Quds; Map p346; ☎ 463 0168; Al-Malek al-Hussein St; pastries from 500 fils, mains JD2-4; 7am-10pm) The Jerusalem Restaurant specialises in sweets and pastries but has a large restaurant at the back. Waiters get irritable translating the Arabic menu so if in doubt, opt for the *mensaf*, a Bedouin dish of lamb with yogurt.

Cairo Restaurant (Map p346; ☎ 4624527; Al-Malek Talal St; mains JD2-5; 6am-10pm) This has the best budget food downtown. Most of the locals opt for the mutton stews and boiled goats' heads, but if that doesn't appeal, the excellent *shish tawooq* (grilled chicken) is big enough for two.

Abu Ahmad Orient Restaurant (Map p348; ☎ 464 1879; 3rd Circle, Jebel Amman; meal JD4-6; noon-midnight) This excellent midrange Lebanese place has an outdoor terrace that bustles with life during the summer. The highlights are the hot and cold mezze – try a *buraik* (meat or cheese pie) or the *yalenjeh* (stuffed vine leaves).

Books@café (Map p346; ☎ 4650457; Omar bin al-Khattab, downtown; meals JD4-6; 10am-midnight) For coffeehouse chic and Western food, this mellow restaurant, bar and café is hard to beat. Genuine Italian pizzas and pasta are enjoyed by plenty of hip young Jordanians lounging on sofas in cosy corners.

Blue Fig Café (Map p348; ☎ 5928800; Prince Hashem bin al-Hussein St; mains JD4-8; 8.30am-1am) Travellers love the global coffeehouse vibe in this super-cool place near Abdoun Circle, which offers an extensive and imaginative mix of world fusion dishes. Throw in some seductive world music and the occasional poetry reading, and you've got a winner. And, really, where else could you get a 'Kyoto green tea and mint flavoured crème brûlée'?

our pick **Wild Jordan Café** (Map p346; ☎ 4633542; Othman Bin Affan St, downtown; 11am-midnight; mains JD5-10; V) After checking out the Wild Nature shop (featuring high-quality handmade crafts from Jordan's various regions), have lunch at this stylish café, where the emphasis is on light and healthy, with smoothies, wraps and vegetarian options like spinach and mushroom salad. The glass walls and open-air terrace offer terrific views over Amman, particularly at night. This spot is part of the Wild Jordan Centre; see p347.

Vinaigrette (Map p344; ☎ 5695481; Howard Johnson Al-Qasr Metropole Hotel, 3 Arroub St, Shmeisani; mains JD6-12; V) This stylish restaurant is located on the top floor of the Howard Johnson and, in keeping with the hotel's boutique theme, offers gourmet sushi and salads accompanied by mellow jazz.

La Terrasse (Map p344; ☎ 5662831; 11 August St, Shmeisani; meals JD20-25; 1pm-1am) This Shmeisani favourite offers high-end European cuisine in low-key luxury. The wine list is extensive, with labels representing Jordan and the Mediterranean rim (JD20 to JD25 a bottle). Most nights, after 10pm, the tiny stage hosts Arab singers and musicians.

Diwan al-Sultan Ibrahim Restaurant (Map p344; ☎ 5517383; Ocean Hotel, Shatt al-Arab St, Umm Utheina; meals JD10-15; ⏲ noon-midnight) The Diwan is highly recommended for high-quality Lebanese food. The fresh fish selection includes delicious *batrkh* (roe).

Romero Restaurant (Map p348; ☎ 4644227; www.romero-jordan.com; Mohammed Hussein Haikal St, Jebel Amman; pastas JD4, mains JD6-10) The best Italian restaurant in town: upmarket, formal and imaginative (try the chicken salad with rocca, mushroom, orange and pine nuts in a honey balsamic dressing). Desserts are divine – the crêpes with crème de banana, Grand Marnier and Cointreau are a must. Reservations recommended.

Of the larger supermarkets, around 500m southwest of the Sports City junction you will find a **Safeway** (Map p344; ☎ 5685311; Nasser bin Jameel St, Shmeisani; ⏲ 24hr). A second **Safeway** (Map p344; ☎ 5815558; ⏲ 24hr) is just southwest of 7th Circle in Sweifieh.

More central but smaller, **Haboob Grand Stores** (Map p348; ☎ 4622221; Al-Kulliyah al-Islamiyah St; ⏲ 7am-midnight) is located between 1st and 2nd Circles.

DRINKING

Cafés

Some of the cafés in Downtown are great places to watch the world go by, smoke a nargileh, meet locals and play cards or backgammon. In addition to the **Blue Fig Café** (see p351), there are plenty of other hip meeting places across town.

Auberge Café (Map p346; Al-Amir Mohammed St, downtown; ⏲ 10am-midnight) One floor below the Cliff Hotel, this is an authentic Jordanian coffeehouse. Grope your way through the tobacco haze to reach the balcony overlooking the main street.

Al-Rashid Court Café (Map p346; ☎ 4652994; Al-Malek Faisal St; tea or coffee 400 fils, nargileh JD1.250; ⏲ 10am-midnight Sat-Thu, 1-11pm Fri) Also known as the Eco-Tourism Café. The 1st-floor balcony here is *the* place to pass an afternoon and survey the chaos of Downtown. The entrance is hidden down a side alley.

Tche Tche Café (Map p348; ☎ 5932020; www.tchetchecafe.com; Abdoun Circle; ⏲ 10am-11pm) Far from traditional, this bright, buzzing teahouse is full of Jordanian women smoking the nargileh, sipping fruit smoothies and nodding to Arabic pop. Come early to get a seat.

A dozen or more cafés can be found around Hashemite Sq – a great place for people-watching in summer.

The place to be seen in Amman at night is Abdoun Circle (Map p348), where there are plenty of popular cafés overflowing with young, wealthy Ammanis.

Bars

Living Room (Map p348; ☎ 4655988; www.romero-jordan.com; Mohammed Hussein Haikal St; ⏲ 1pm-1am) Part lounge, part sushi bar, the Living Room is so coolly understated that it's easy to miss.

Rovers Return (Map p344; ☎ 5814844; Ali Nasouh al-Taher St, Sweifieh; drinks JD2-4, meals JD3-6; ⏲ 1pm-late) A popular and cosy English pub with wood panelling and a lively atmosphere. The comfort food includes authentic fish and chips and roast beef with gravy.

Blue Fig Café (Map p348; ☎ 5928800; www.bluefig.com; Prince Hashem bin al-Hussein St; starters from JD1.650, mains JD4-8; ⏲ 8.30am-1am) This is a great place to spend an afternoon or evening, with a trendy crowd, draught beer, good cocktails and a pleasant atmosphere. There's live music most Wednesday and Saturday nights.

ENTERTAINMENT

Nightclubs

Nai (Map p344; ☎ 5689671; Howard Johnson Al-Qasr Metropole Hotel, 3 Arroub St; ⏲ 6pm-2am) Currently one of the hottest places in town, Nai is a super-cool Ottoman-style lounge-club-cum-mezze bar. Mondays and Thursdays bring international DJs and a cover charge (JD10; bookings advised) and there's an Arabic band the first Thursday of the month.

Cinemas

Programs for these modern cinemas are advertised in the two English-language newspapers, the *Jordan Times* and the *Star*. Tickets cost JD5.

Century Cinemas (Map p348; ☎ 4613200; www.century-cinemas.com; 3rd Circle) In the Zara Centre behind the Grand Hyatt.

Cine Le Royal (Map p348; ☎ 4603022; Le Royal Hotel, 3rd Circle)

Galleria Cinema (Map p348; ☎ 5934793; Abdoun Circle)

SHOPPING

Amman is a good place to shop for souvenirs in Jordan, with everything from tourist kitsch to high-quality handicraft boutiques, many of which are run to benefit local communities.

The following are among the better places in Amman, and are generally open 9am to 6pm Saturday to Thursday. Prices are fixed.

Al-Alaydi Jordan Craft Centre (Map p348; ☎/fax 4644555; www.alaydijordan.1colony.com; off Al-Kulliyah al-Islamiyah St)

Al-Burgan (Map p348; ☎ 4652585; www.alburgan.com) Behind Jordan InterContinental Hotel.

Artisana (Map p348; ☎/fax 4647858; Mansour Kraishan St; 9.30am-6pm Sat-Thu)

Jordan River Foundation (Map p346; ☎ 4613081; www.jordanriver.jo; Bani Hamida House, Fawzi al-Malouf St; 8.30am-7pm Sat-Thu, 10am-6pm Fri) An emphasis on home design. Off Abu Bakr as-Siddiq St.

Wild Jordan Centre (Map p346; ☎ 4633587; Othman bin Affan St; 9am-7pm) Nature-inspired arts, crafts and products (silver, painted ostrich eggs, organic jam) made by communities living near Jordan's nature reserves. All profits go to the craftspeople and the nature reserve projects.

GETTING THERE & AWAY

Air

The only domestic air route is between Amman and Aqaba. For details, see p397. For a list of airlines serving Amman, see p394.

Bus

The three main bus stations in Amman are Abdali bus station (Map p348), for transport to the north and west; Wahadat bus station (Map p344) for the south; and Raghadan station (Map p346) for Amman and nearby towns.

Tickets for the following private buses should be booked at least one day in advance. The domestic **JETT bus office** (Map p344; ☎ 5664146; Al-Malek al-Hussein St, Shmeisani), about 500m northwest of the Abdali bus station, is the best option for buses to Aqaba (JD4.300, four hours, five buses daily). There is also a service to Petra (JD6, three hours) leaving at 6.30am.

Trust International Transport (Map p344; ☎ 5813427; Mataar al-Malekah Alya Rd) also has buses to Aqaba (JD7, five hours, seven daily) between 7.30am and 7pm. The location is inconvenient, near 7th Circle.

AMMAN TRANSPORT DISRUPTION

At the time of writing, the entire transportation grid in Amman was in the midst of a massive overhaul due to the renovation of Raghadan Station as well as the gradual closing of Abdali Station. Tabarbour Station in the northern suburbs is handling the overflow during the transition. Additionally, at the time of writing, fuel prices in Jordan were soaring due to factors such as the Iraq War, greater Middle Eastern instability and rampant inflation. As a result, it is almost certain that published prices for bus routes will increase significantly during the shelf life of this book.

FROM ABDALI BUS STATION

From Abdali station, minibuses leave regularly for the following destinations with all routes costing less than JD1: Ajloun (2 hours), Deir Alla (for Pella, 1 hour), Fuheis (45 minutes), Irbid (2 hours), Jerash (1¼ hours), Madaba (¾ hours), Ramtha (2 hours), Salt (¾ hours) and Zarqa (30 minutes).

FROM WAHADAT BUS STATION

From Wahadat station, minibuses depart regularly. For Petra (actually Wadi Musa), minibuses and service taxis (JD4, four hours) depart when full from the far corner of the lot between around 7am and 4pm. Buses to Aqaba (JD5, five hours) leave every hour or so until midnight. There are regular buses to Karak (JD1, two hours), Shobak (JD2, 2½ hours) and Ma'an (JD3, three hours). Most services dry up around 4pm.

For Dana, there is one bus a day at around 11am for Qadsiyya (JD3, three hours); otherwise take a bus to Tafila (JD2, 2½ hours) and change.

There are semiregular service taxis to Karak (JD2, two hours), Ma'an (JD3, three hours) and also infrequently to Aqaba (JD5, five hours).

To reach Wahadat station, take a service taxi or bus 23 from Abdali station, or service taxi 27 from Italian St (Map p346). A private taxi here will cost around JD1 to JD2 from downtown.

FROM OTHER BUS STATIONS

For the Dead Sea, minibuses leave from the small station opposite the Al-Muhajireen Police Station. You may find a local bus direct to Suweimeh (JD1, 1 hour) or even

Amman Beach – if not, you'll have to go to Shuneh al-Janubiyyeh (South Shuna; 1JD, 45 minutes) and change for Suweimeh, from where you'll have to hire a taxi or hitch for the last stretch. Minibuses also leave frequently for Wadi as-Seer (less than 1JD, 30 minutes).

The newly renovated Raghadan station in Downtown hadn't fully reopened at the time of research, but you can expect it to hold service taxis (for nearby suburbs), local city buses and, probably, minibuses to Madaba, Salt and Wadi as-Seer.

Car

All the major hotels have car rental offices. The largest selection of rental companies is at King Abdullah Gardens (Map p344). See p398 for details.

Service Taxi

Service taxis cover much the same territory as the minibus for slightly higher fares but faster services. They depart from the same stations as the minibuses. You'll find that departures are more frequent in the morning than in the afternoon.

Train

See p396 for information on the train between Amman and Damascus.

GETTING AROUND

To/From the Airport

Queen Alia International Airport is 35km south of the city centre.

The **Airport Express bus** (Map p348; ☎ 0880-022006, 4451531) runs between the airport and the upper end of Abdali bus station, passing through 4th, 5th, 6th and 7th Circles en route. The service (JD2, 45 minutes) runs every half hour or so between 7am and midnight. The last buses to the airport leave at 10pm and midnight; the first bus leaves at 6am.

A taxi costs JD15 to JD20 from the airport to Amman, slightly less in the opposite direction.

Private Taxi

The flag fall in a standard taxi is 150 fils, and cross-town journeys rarely cost more than JD2. Make sure your driver uses the meter, although most will do so automatically.

Service Taxi

Most fares on service taxis cost a few hundred fils per seat and you pay the full amount regardless of where you get off. After 8pm, the price for all service taxis goes up by 25%. Some of the more useful routes include the following (see map p346):

No 2 From Basman St, for 1st and 2nd Circles
No 3 From Basman St, for 3rd and 4th Circles
No 6 From Cinema al-Hussein St, for Abdali station and JETT offices
No 7 From Cinema al-Hussein St, past Abdali station and King Abdullah Mosque to Shmeisani
No 27 From Italian St for Wahadat station
No 35 From Quraysh St for Al-Muhajireen Police Station

AROUND AMMAN

WADI AS-SEER & IRAQ AL-AMIR عراق الأمير وادي السير

The narrow, pretty and fertile valley of Wadi as-Seer is a contrast to the bare and treeless plateau to the east of Amman. The caves of **Iraq al-Amir** (Caves of the Prince) and the ruins of **Qasr al-Abad** (Palace of the Slave) are a further 10km down the valley from the largely Circassian town of Wadi as-Seer.

The caves are arranged in two tiers – the upper forms a long gallery along the cliff face. The small but impressive ruins of Qasr al-Abad, thought to have been a 2nd-century-BC villa or minor palace, can be found about 700m further down the valley. The palace was built out of some of the biggest blocks of any ancient structure in the Middle East – the largest measures 7m by 3m.

Opposite the caves is the village of Iraq al-Amir, which is home to the aptly named **Iraq al-Amir Handicraft Village** (🕑 8am-4pm, closed Fri). Here you can buy handmade pottery, fabrics, foodstuffs, carpets and paper products. The project was founded by the Noor al-Hussein Foundation, which supports the initiatives of local women.

Minibuses leave Amman regularly for Wadi as-Seer (30 minutes) from the station opposite the Al-Muhajireen Police Station. From the town of Wadi as-Seer, take another minibus (100 fils) or walk about 10km, mostly downhill, to the caves. There is a signpost to the Iraq al-Amir Handicraft Village opposite the stairs to the caves.

JERASH & THE NORTH

Northern Jordan is the most densely populated area in the country, and is home to the major urban centre of Irbid as well as dozens of small towns and villages. It has been settled for centuries, as proved by the ancient tells and archaeological remains scattered around the pretty olive-clad hills.

Three cities of the ancient Decapolis (ten Roman city states bordering the Roman Empire) can be found in the region at Jerash (Gerasa), Umm Qais (Gadara) and Pella. Jerash in particular, which is often referred to as the 'Pompeii of Asia', is one of the most important and best-preserved Roman cities in the Near East. Much of the north remains off the beaten path, and you may well have the strawberry tree and pine forests of Ajloun and Dibeen to yourself.

The two main sites of Jerash and Ajloun are generally visited as day trips from Amman, whereas Umm Qais is accessible from Irbid. You can visit the area as part of an overland trip north to Syria.

JERASH جرش

☎ 02 / pop 160,000

These beautifully preserved Roman **ruins** (☎ 6351272; admission JD8; 8am-4pm Oct-Apr, to 7pm May-Sep), located 51km north of Amman, are deservedly one of Jordan's major attractions. Excavations have been going for 85 years but it is estimated that 90% of the city is still unexcavated. In its heyday the ancient city, known in Roman times as Gerasa, had a population of around 15,000.

Allow at least three hours to do Jerash justice. The best times to visit are before 10am or after 4pm, but this is tricky if you are relying on public transport. It's possible to leave luggage at the Jerash Rest House (p357) while you visit the site, for no charge.

In July and August, Jerash hosts the **Jerash Festival** (www.jerashfestival.com.jo), featuring local and overseas artists, music and drama performances inside the ancient city and displays of traditional handicrafts.

History

Although there have been finds to indicate that the site was inhabited in Neolithic times, the city only rose to prominence from the time of Alexander the Great (333 BC).

In the wake of the Roman general Pompey's conquest of the region in 64 BC, Gerasa became part of the Roman province of Syria and, soon after, a city of the Decapolis. Gerasa reached its peak at the beginning of the 3rd century AD, when it was bestowed with the rank of Colony, after which time it went into a slow decline as trade routes shifted.

By the middle of the 5th century AD, Christianity was the region's major religion and the construction of churches proceeded at a startling rate. With the Sassanian invasion from Persia in 614, the Muslim conquest in 636 and a devastating earthquake in 747, Jerash's heyday passed and its population shrank to about a quarter of its former size.

Sights & Activities

At the extreme south of the site is the striking **Hadrian's Arch**, also known as the Triumphal Arch, which was built in AD 129 to honour the visit of Emperor Hadrian. Behind the arch is the **hippodrome**, which hosted chariot races watched by up to 15,000 spectators.

In the summer of 2005, chariot races returned to Jerash for the first time in around 1500 years, thanks to a joint Swedish-Jordanian venture. Dubbed the **Roman Army and Chariot Experience** (tickets JD15; Sat to Thu, except Tue 11am & 2pm, Fri 10am; www.jerashchariots.com), the project runs chariot races in Jerash's hippodrome, recreated as authentically as possible, down to the use of Latin commands. Suspend comments about kitsch entertainment until you've watched the men in togas: not only is it enormous fun but also the commentary is suitably self-ironic to make sure you laugh with and not at the worthy men in feathers. The project also gives employment to local military veterans.

The **visitor centre** (☎ 6351272; admission JD8; 8am-4pm Oct-Apr, to 7pm May-Sep) is worth checking out for its reconstructions of many buildings in Jerash (and for its toilets). The **South Gate**, originally one of four along the city wall and built in AD 130, leads into the city proper.

The **Oval Plaza** (Forum) is one of the most distinctive images of Jerash, unusual because of its oval shape and huge size (90m long and 80m at its widest point). Some historians attribute this to the desire to gracefully link the main north–south axis (the *cardo maximus*)

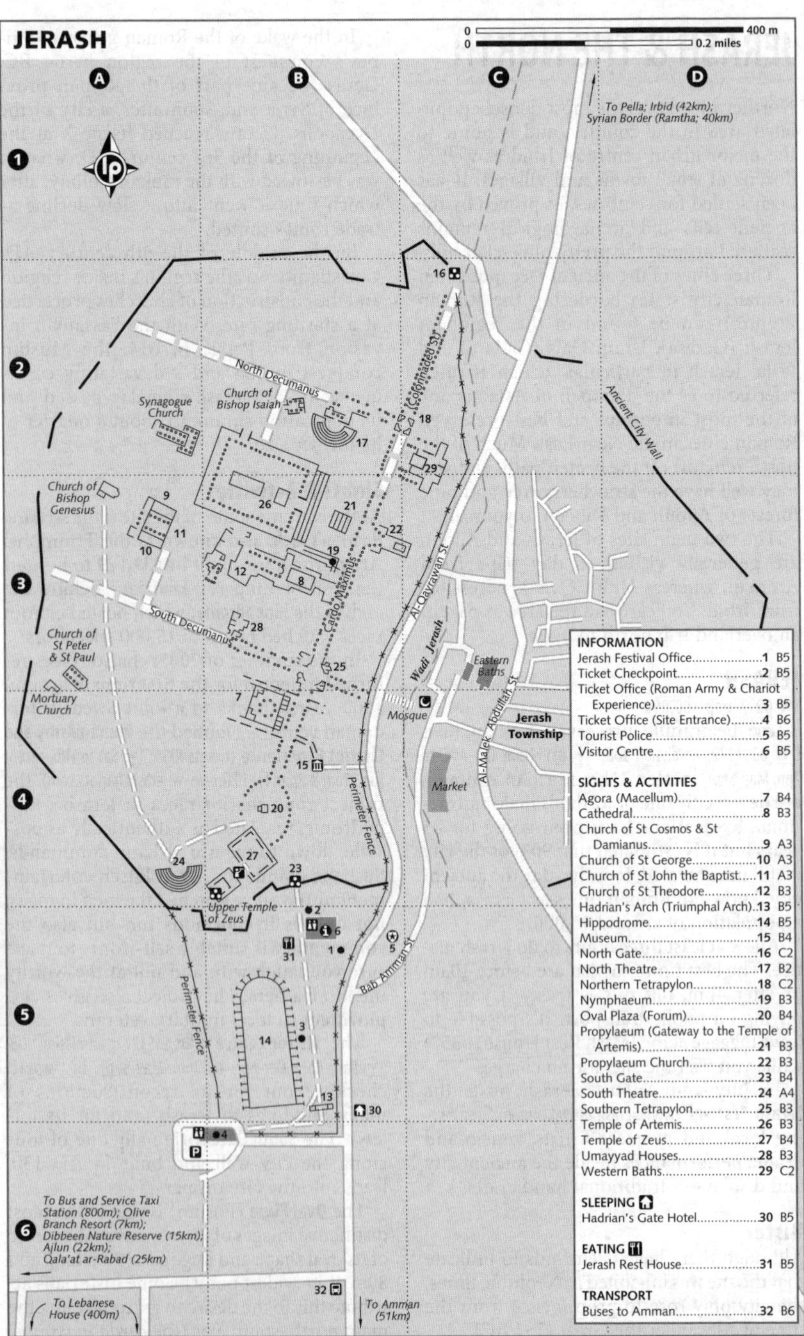

INFORMATION

Jerash Festival Office	1	B5
Ticket Checkpoint	2	B5
Ticket Office (Roman Army & Chariot Experience)	3	B5
Ticket Office (Site Entrance)	4	B6
Tourist Police	5	B5
Visitor Centre	6	B5

SIGHTS & ACTIVITIES

Agora (Macellum)	7	B4
Cathedral	8	B3
Church of St Cosmos & St Damianus	9	A3
Church of St George	10	A3
Church of St John the Baptist	11	A3
Church of St Theodore	12	B3
Hadrian's Arch (Triumphal Arch)	13	B5
Hippodrome	14	B5
Museum	15	B4
North Gate	16	C2
North Theatre	17	B2
Northern Tetrapylon	18	C2
Nymphaeum	19	B3
Oval Plaza (Forum)	20	B4
Propylaeum (Gateway to the Temple of Artemis)	21	B3
Propylaeum Church	22	B3
South Gate	23	B4
South Theatre	24	A4
Southern Tetrapylon	25	B3
Temple of Artemis	26	B3
Temple of Zeus	27	B4
Umayyad Houses	28	B3
Western Baths	29	C2

SLEEPING

Hadrian's Gate Hotel	30	B5

EATING

Jerash Rest House	31	B5

TRANSPORT

Buses to Amman	32	B6

with the Temple of Zeus. Fifty-six Ionic columns surround the paved limestone plaza.

On the south side of the Forum, the **Temple of Zeus** was built in about AD 162 over the remains of an earlier Roman temple; it's currently being restored. Next door, the **South Theatre** was built in the 1st century AD and could seat 5000 spectators. From the upper stalls, there are excellent views of ancient and modern Jerash, particularly the Forum, and the acoustics are still wonderful.

To the northeast of the Forum lies the **cardo maximus**, the city's main thoroughfare, also known as the colonnaded street, which stretches for 800m from the Forum to the **North Gate**. The street is still paved with the original stones, and the ruts worn by thousands of chariots can be clearly seen.

Halfway along the colonnaded street is the elegant **nymphaeum**, the main fountain of the city. The nymphaeum is followed by the imposing **Temple of Artemis**, reached via a fine propylaeum or monumental gateway, and a staircase. The Temple of Artemis was dedicated to the patron goddess of the city.

Further to the north is the **North Theatre**, built originally in AD 165 and now wonderfully restored.

The small **museum** (☎ 6312267; admission free; 🕑 8.30am-6pm Oct-Apr, to 5pm May-Sep) contains a good collection of artefacts from the site.

Sleeping & Eating

The modern town of Jerash comes to life after the sun sets and the air cools, making it well worth staying the night.

Hadrian Gate Hotel (☎ 77793907; walid friend.2007@yahoo.com; s/d/tr from JD18/35/45, with breakfast JD2.750) Run by the friendly Walid, the first and only hotel in Jerash proper boasts a spectacular location directly across from Hadrian's Gate. Private rooms with shared bathrooms are very modest but the owner more than compensates.

our pick Olive Branch Resort (☎ 6340555; www.olivebranch.com.jo; s/d JD20/40; ❄ 🏊) Around 7km from Jerash, off the Ajloun road, this hilltop hotel in attractive grounds has comfortable rooms with satellite TV, balconies with great views and a restaurant. You can camp for JD5 (JD4 with your own tent). A taxi from Jerash costs JD2 one way.

Jerash Rest House (☎ 6351437; lunch buffet JD5; 🕑 noon-5pm) Make no mistake – this restaurant near Hadrian's Gate is a tourist circus. That said, the buffet is great value and you can walk it off in the adjacent ruins.

our pick Lebanese House (☎ 6351301; mains JD3-5; 🕑 noon-11pm; V) Overlooking orchards, a 10-minute walk from central Jerash, this is a local favourite, with top-notch Lebanese dishes and attractive terrace seating. Culinary delicacies include buttery cow testicles… or you could just stick to the excellent vegetarian dishes.

You'll find more local fare opposite the visitor centre.

Getting There & Away

Buses and minibuses run frequently between Amman's Abdali bus station and Jerash (less than JD1, 1¼ hours), though they can take an hour to fill with enough passengers to warrant departure. From Jerash, minibuses travel regularly to Irbid (500 fils, 45 minutes) and Ajloun (300 fils, 30 minutes) until mid-afternoon. If you're still in Jerash after about 5pm, be prepared to hitch back to Amman (the tourist police are happy to cajole a passing motorist into taking you) because most buses stop running soon after that. A taxi to Amman costs around JD10 to JD15.

Jerash's bus station is a 15-minute walk west of the site, at the second set of traffic lights. If you don't fancy the walk, you can often jump on buses headed to Amman from the junction southeast of the main ticket office.

AJLOUN عجلون

☎ 02 / pop 125,000

Ajloun (or Ajlun) is another popular and easy day trip from Amman, and can be combined with a trip to Jerash if you leave early. The main attraction is **Qala'at ar-Rabad** (admission JD1; 🕑 8am-4pm Oct-Apr, to 7pm May-Sep), a fine example of Islamic military architecture, 3km west of town. Built in AD 1184–88 by the Arabs as protection against the Crusaders, it was enlarged in 1214 with the addition of a new gate in the southeastern corner, and once boasted seven towers as well as a surrounding dry moat that dropped to more than 15m deep.

The castle commands fine views of the Jordan Valley and was one in a chain of beacons and pigeon posts that allowed messages to be transmitted from Damascus to Cairo in a single day. Largely destroyed by Mongol invaders in 1260, it was almost immediately rebuilt by the Mamluks. In the

17th century, an Ottoman garrison was stationed here, after which it was used by local villagers. The castle was 'rediscovered' by the well-travelled JL Burckhardt, who also stumbled across Petra. Earthquakes in 1837 and 1927 badly damaged the castle, though slow and steady restoration is continuing.

The castle is an uphill walk (2.5km) from the town centre. Occasional minibuses (100 fils) go to the castle but a return trip by taxi from Ajloun (JD5), with 30 minutes to look around, is money well spent.

Sleeping & Eating

Ajloun Hotel (☎ 6420524; s/d from JD18/30) Located 500m down the road from the castle, this isn't a bad option assuming you don't mind claustrophobic rooms and unpredictable hot water. Choose one of the rooms on the top floor, all boasting spectacular views of the countryside.

Qalet al-Jabal Hotel (☎ 6420202; s/d/tr from JD35/45/50) About 1km before the castle, this is the better of the two hotels. The decor is outdated but the rooms are well equipped and have private balconies. The highlight is the outdoor terrace garden where slow-cooked meals are served – even if you're not staying here, stop by for supper.

Both **Abu-Alezz Restaurant** (meals JD2-3) and **Al-Raseed** (meals JD2-3) near the main roundabout in Ajloun offer cheap and tasty Jordanian fare including chicken, hummus and shwarma. There is also a small drink stand and snack shop next to the castle ticket office. Alternatively, head into the surrounding hills for a picnic.

Getting There & Away

From the centre of Ajloun, minibuses travel regularly to Jerash (less than 1JD, 30 minutes along a scenic road) and Irbid (less than 1JD, 45 minutes). From Amman (1JD, two hours), minibuses leave a few times a day from the Abdali bus station.

AJLOUN FOREST RESERVE محمية عجلون الطبيعية

Located in the Ajloun Highlands, this small (13 sq km) but attractive **nature reserve** (☎ 02-6475673; open year round) was established by the RSCN in 1988 to protect forests of oak, carob, pistachio and strawberry trees (look for the peeling, bright orange bark) and provide sanctuary for the endangered roe deer.

Several marked trails, some self-guided, weave through the hilly landscape of wooded valleys. Particularly worthwhile is the **Soap Maker's Trail**, a self-guided 7km trail (four hours, year round) that combines panoramic viewpoints with visits to a soap workshop. The products of this cooperative can be bought, along with other fair-trade products in the reserve's **craft shop**.

The reserve operates **tented bungalows** (Apr-Oct; s/d/tr/q from JD20/30/40/50). The ablution block contains composting toilets and solar-heated showers. There are also rustic **cabins** (s/d from JD55) equipped with private bathroom and terrace. Bring mosquito repellent in the summer.

In the tented **rooftop restaurant** (meals JD4-7; Ⓥ), there are lunchtime buffets with a good vegetarian selection. Outside, barbecue grills are available for public use.

To reach the reserve, charter a taxi for the 9km from Ajloun (around JD3 one way).

IRBID اربد

☎ 02 / pop 935,000

Irbid, Jordan's second largest city, is a university town and one of the more lively and progressive of Jordan's large towns. It's also a good base for exploring the historic site of Umm Qais, Pella and even Jerash. There's little to see in town apart from the excellent **Museum of Archaeology & Anthropology** (☎ 7271100, ext 4260; admission free; 🕒 10am-1.45pm & 3-4.30pm Sun-Thu) in the grounds of Yarmouk University. In the energetic area around the university, the streets are lined with restaurants and internet cafés. In the late afternoon, in particular, you'll find students out strolling.

Sleeping & Eating

The cheapest hotels are in the city centre in the blocks immediately north of King Hussein St. Most have shared bathrooms.

Al-Ameen al-Kabir Hotel (☎ 7242384; Al-Jaish St; dm/s/d from JD3/7/10) By far the best cheapie: friendly management, simple but well-tended rooms, and clean shared bathrooms (with hot showers). Women may feel more comfortable at either of the more upmarket hotels below.

Omayed Hotel (☎ 7245955; King Hussein St; s/d from JD20/25) Rooms are very basic and they've seen better days, but they come with satellite TV and large picture windows overlooking the city.

our pick **Al-Joude Hotel** (☎ 7275515; off University St; s/d/tr from JD30/40/50, ste JD75;) Located near the university, this hotel primarily caters for visiting families. It has a classy ambience, pleasing rooms and friendly staff, and deserves its four-star status.

Al-Saadi Restaurant (☎ 7242354; King Hussein St; meals JD3-5; 8.30am-9.30pm) If you're staying in downtown, this is one of the better places for Jordanian staples including roasted lamb and chicken, falafel, humus and fuul.

our pick **News Café** (Al-Joude Hotel; pizza JD2.500) Downstairs from the Al-Joude Hotel, this is a top spot for Irbid's smart set. It is a warm and inviting place for a milkshake and a snack.

There are dozens of restaurants to suit most budgets along University St.

Getting There & Away

Irbid, located approximately 85km north of Amman, is home to three main minibus and taxi stations.

From the North bus station, there are minibuses to Umm Qais (800 fils; 45 minutes).

From the large South bus station (New Amman bus station), air-conditioned Hejazi buses (2JD, 90 minutes) leave regularly for Amman's Abdali bus station until about 7pm. To Amman (Abdali bus station) there are also less comfortable buses and minibuses (less than 1JD, about two hours) and plenty of service taxis (1JD). Minibuses also leave the South station for Ajloun (45 minutes), Jerash (45 minutes) and the Syrian border, all for less than one dinar.

From the West bus station (locally known as Mujamma al-Gharb al-Jadid), about 1.5km west of the centre, minibuses go to Al-Mashari'a (5 minutes) for the ruins at Pella, Sheikh Hussein Bridge (for Israel and the Palestinian Territories; 45 minutes) and Shuneh ash-Shamaliyyeh (North Shuna, for the Dead Sea; one hour) for less than a dinar.

Irbid serves as a convenient jumping-off point for travellers heading to either Syria or Israel and the Palestinian Territories. The office of **Trust International Transport** (☎ 7251878; Al-Jaish St) near Al-Hasan Sports City is your best source of up-to-date information.

Getting Around

Service taxis (200 fils) and minibuses (100 fils) going to the south bus station can be picked up on Radna al-Hindawi St, three blocks east of the Al-Ameen al-Kabir Hotel. For the north station head to Prince Nayef St. For the west station take a bus from Palestine St, just west of the roundabout. A standard taxi fare from *il-bilad* (the town) to *al-jammiya* (the university) is 500 fils. A minibus from University St to the university gate costs 150 fils. Otherwise it's a 25-minute walk.

UMM QAIS أم قيس

☎ 02

Tucked in the far northwest corner of Jordan, and about 25km from Irbid, are the seldom-visited ruins of **Umm Qais** (Gadara; admission JD1; 8am-5pm), site of both the ancient Roman city of Gadara and an Ottoman-era village. The hilltop site offers spectacular views over the Golan Heights in Syria, the Sea of Galilee (Lake Tiberias) in Israel, the Palestinian Territories, which are north; and the Jordan Valley to the south.

Sights

The first thing you come to after the ticket office is the well-restored and brooding **west theatre**, which once seated about 3000 people. Like the north theatre, it was made from black basalt. Nearby is a colonnaded courtyard and the remains of a 6th-century **Byzantine church**. Beyond this is the **decumanus maximus**, Gadara's main road. A set of overgrown **baths** are to the west.

Leave some time for Beit Russan, a former residence of an Ottoman governor and now a **museum** (☎ 7500072; admission free; 8am-5pm Oct-Apr, to 6pm May-Sep). It is set around an elegant and tranquil courtyard. The main mosaic on display (dating from the 4th century and found in one of the tombs) contains the names of early Christian notables and is a highlight, as is the headless, white marble statue of the Hellenic goddess Tyche, which was found sitting in the front row of the west theatre.

Surrounding the museum are the ruins of the **Ottoman village** dating from the 18th and 19th centuries and also known as the acropolis.

Sleeping & Eating

Umm Qais Hotel (☎ 7500080; s/d from JD10/15) This modest, friendly option on the main street of the modern village has bright and airy rooms (some with en-suite bathrooms). There's a small ground-floor restaurant and rooftop café.

our pick **Umm Qais Resthouse** (☎ 7500555; meals JD5-10; ⏰ 10am-7pm, to 10pm Jun-Sep; Ⓥ) This much-loved restaurant, with lovely views of Galilee and the Golan Heights, is located inside a converted Ottoman house within the ruins of Gadara. The Resthouse offers an impressive seasonal menu highlighting fresh vegetarian produce and locally raised meats.

Getting There & Away

Minibuses leave Irbid's north bus station for Umm Qais (less than JD1, 45 minutes) on a regular basis. To continue to Pella on public transport, you'll have to backtrack to Irbid.

PELLA (TABAQAT FAHL) بيلا

☎ 02

Near the village of Al-Mashari'a are the ruins of the ancient city of Pella, 2km east (and uphill) of the road. The ruins require considerable imagination but the setting is superb.

Pella flourished during the Greek and Roman periods and, like Jerash and Amman, was one of the cities of the Decapolis. The city also came under the rule of the Ptolemaic dynasty, Seleucids and Jews, with the latter largely destroying Pella in 83 BC. Christians fled to Pella from Jerusalem to escape persecution from the Roman army in the 2nd century AD. The city reached its peak during the Byzantine era and there were subsequent Islamic settlements until the site was abandoned in the 14th century.

Of most interest are the ruins atop the hill on your right as you enter through the main gate. These include an **Umayyad settlement** with shops, residences and storehouses, the small, 14th-century **Mamluk mosque**, and the **Canaanite temple**, which was constructed around 1270 BC and was dedicated to the Canaanite god Baal.

Also of interest is the **Byzantine church**, which was built atop an earlier Roman civic complex, and the **east church**, up the hill to the southeast.

JORDAN

Sleeping & Eating

Pella Countryside Hotel (☎ 079 5574145; s/d half board JD25/30) The manager of the famous Pella Rest House also runs this charmer of a B&B, with a family feel and splendid views. The seven rooms are well kept, with private en-suite bathroom, hot shower and country-style flourishes. From February to May, black irises, the national flower of Jordan, bloom in the owner's garden.

our pick **Pella Rest House** (☎ 079 55574145; meals JD4-8; ⏰ noon-7pm) With exceptional views over Pella and the Jordan Valley, this famous restaurant offers an enticing menu highlighting regional cuisine – the fresh St Peter's fish is plucked straight from the Jordan River.

Getting There & Away

From Irbid's West bus station, minibuses go frequently to Al-Mashari'a (less than JD1, 45 minutes). Pella is a steep 2km walk up from the highway, which can be punishing in summer. Unlicensed minibuses (100 fils) run reasonably regularly up to the main entrance of Pella, but check the price first as overcharging is common. There is no direct transport from Amman.

THE DEAD SEA & AROUND

There are several excellent reasons to visit the Dead Sea region, not least for a float in the sea itself (opposite), especially if you're not visiting the Israeli side. Bethany-Beyond-the-Jordan is an important archaeological site that pinpoints a major event in the life of Jesus to a remarkably specific location on the banks of the Jordan River.

For something completely different, beautiful Wadi Mujib offers some of Jordan's wettest and wildest adventure opportunities.

Public transport is unreliable on the Dead Sea Hwy and this is one place to consider renting a car or taxi for the day. Most budget travellers visit the Dead Sea as part of a day trip from Amman or Madaba.

BETHANY-BEYOND-THE-JORDAN المغطس

Known in Arabic as Al-Maghtas (Baptism Site), this important site is claimed by Christians to be the place where Jesus was baptised by John the Baptist, where the first five apostles met and where the prophet Elijah ascended to heaven in a chariot. It wasn't until the 1994 peace treaty with Israel that the remains of churches, caves and baptism pools were unearthed. Pope John Paul II authenticated the site in March 2000.

Sights

Entry to the **site** (adult/child under 12 JD7/free; 8am-4pm winter & Ramadan, to 6pm summer) includes a mandatory guided tour. The shuttle bus makes a brief stop at Tell Elias, where the prophet Elias is said to have ascended to heaven after his death, and then normally continues to the **Spring of John the Baptist**, one of several places where John is believed to have baptised. The main archaeological site is the church complex next to the likely **site of Jesus's baptism**. The trail continues to the muddy **Jordan River**, where you too could be baptised if you had the foresight to bring your own priest.

Tours often return via the **House of Mary the Egyptian** and a two-room **hermit cave**. On the way back, you can ask to be dropped at the archaeological site of **Tell Elias** (Elijah's Hill), which includes a 3rd-century church, the cave of John the Baptist, baptism pools and the Byzantine **Rhotorius Monastery**.

Getting There & Away

Take any minibus to Suweimeh, en route to the Dead Sea. About 5km before the town, the road forks; the baptism site is well signposted to the right. From here, you'll need to walk or hitch the 5km to the visitor centre.

A taxi from Madaba to the site, taking in the Dead Sea and Mt Nebo en route, costs around JD25.

THE DEAD SEA البحر الميت

☎ 05

The Dead Sea is at the lowest point on earth and has such high salinity (due to evaporation) that nothing but the most microscopic of life forms can survive in it. Indeed, the only things you're likely to see in the Dead Sea are a few over-buoyant tourists. A dip in the sea is one of those must-do experiences but be warned: you'll discover cuts you didn't know you had, so don't shave before bathing! Sadly, the Dead Sea is under threat from shrinking water levels (see p117).

The most luxurious way to swim on the Jordanian side of the Dead Sea is at one of the upmarket resorts, which cost from JD20 (Dead Sea Spa Hotel) to JD35 (Mövenpick Resort & Spa) for day access to their sumptuous grounds, private beaches and swimming pools.

Most budget visitors head for **Amman Beach** (☎ 3560800; foreign adult/child JD10/6; 8.00am-midnight), about 2km south of the resorts. The landscaped grounds include a clean beach, sun umbrellas and freshwater showers. The vibrant local atmosphere makes it a great place to strike up conversation with a Jordanian family. Locals generally swim fully clothed, though foreigners shouldn't feel uncomfortable here in a modest swimming costume. Women on their own may prefer shorts and a T-shirt.

Opened in 2008, **Al-Wadi Resort** (adult/child JD25/18; 9am-6pm Sat-Thu, to 7pm Fri) has a variety of water games, including wave machine and slides. There are two restaurants (9am to midnight), one selling snacks and the other offering an Arabic menu. Children are measured on entry: those under 95cm are admitted for free! The resort is about 500m north of the Convention Centre at the head of the Resort strip.

A free alternative is **Herodus Spring**, where Herod himself is said to have sought the curative power of the hot springs for his itching body. The spring is about 10km south of the resort strip, but the area is neither clean nor inviting and there's little privacy. A better bet is to take a more private dip farther along the coast and wash off the salt (a necessity) with a bottle of water.

The resorts and public areas are very busy on Fridays – useful for finding a ride back to Amman if you missed the last bus. Take lots of water as the humidity and heat is intense (over 40°C in summer) and there's little shade.

If you've had enough of a splash for one day and feel like gaining the high ground, hop in a taxi (JD5) from Amman Beach to the **Dead Sea Panorama Complex** (admission JD2; 8am-midnight). This lookout, museum (8am-4.30pm) and restaurant complex is a great way to contextualise the Dead Sea and admire the panoramic view.

Sleeping & Eating

About 5km south of Suweimeh is a strip of opulent pleasure palaces that offer the latest in spa luxury.

Dead Sea Spa Hotel (☎ 3561000; www.jordandeadsea.com; s/d JD71/85, ste from JD156;) About 200m south of the Kempinski, this complex is not as refined as its luxury neighbours but is quality nonetheless. There's a medical/dermatological spa, private beach access, a big pool and separate kids' pool with slides.

JORDAN

Dead Sea Marriott (☎ 3560400; www.mariotthotels.com; s/d from JD175/190;) A grand resort with a poolside bar, good spa, lots of restaurants and facilities for children, cinemas, high-speed internet access and a jungle playground.

our pick Mövenpick Resort & Spa (☎ 3561111; www.moevenpick-deadsea.com; standard/superior/premium JD215/250/285;) The resort to beat, with Moroccan kasbah-style luxury accommodation, tennis courts, the gorgeous Zara spa (see boxed text, below), a fantastic assortment of bars and restaurants and a poolside bar.

Kempinski Hotel Ishtar (☎ 3568888; www.kempinski.com; from s/d JD200/220;) A Sumerian-style middle-level lobby overlooking the spectacular, circular infinity pool, together with a series of water features tumbling down to the Dead Sea, make this a palace among hotels.

Getting There & Away

The budget hotels in Amman sometimes organise day trips to Madaba, Mt Nebo and the Dead Sea if there are enough people. Buses from Amman direct to Amman Beach leave on a demand-only basis from Muhajireen bus station between 7am and 9am; the journey takes an hour and a half, and the last bus returns to Amman around 5pm (4pm in winter). JETT buses from Amman leave twice a week at 8am, returning at 6pm; in July, there is a daily service.

Minibuses usually run only as far as Suweimeh, but it may be possible to persuade them to take you the extra distance to the Dead Sea resorts for a few fils more. Some budget hotels in Amman organise day trips to the Dead Sea so ask around. For details of getting to/from the Dead Sea by public transport from the capital, see p353.

The Mariam Hotel (p367) in Madaba can often organise a day trip by taxi, taking in Bethany-Beyond-the-Jordan, Amman Beach and Hammamat Ma'in for around JD50, with an hour's stop at each site.

WADI MUJIB NATURE RESERVE

محمية الموجب

Wadi Mujib Nature Reserve (215 sq km) was established by the RSCN for the captive breeding of the Nubian ibex, but it also forms the heart of an ambitious ecotourism project.

First stop is the **visitor centre** (☎ 077 7422125), by the Dead Sea Hwy. The easiest hike on offer is the wet **Siq Trail** (JD12 per person); described by the guides as 'Petra with Water', this is an exciting 2km wade and scramble into the gorge, ending at a dramatic waterfall. Bring a swimming costume, towel and shoes that can get wet, and a watertight bag for valuables.

The most exciting option is the **Malaqi Trail** (per person JD53; 1 Apr-31 Oct), a guided half-day trip that involves a hike up into the wadi, a visit to some lovely swimming pools and then a descent (often swimming) through the siq, finally rappelling down the 18m waterfall (not appropriate for non-swimmers or those with a fear of heights). It's not exactly cheap, and you need a minimum of five people, but it's definitely one

IT'S A TOUGH JOB – BUT SOMEONE HAS TO DO IT *Jenny Walker*

As a die-hard traveller who felt that succumbing to a bed with a soft mattress was a sign of weakness, I was deeply suspicious of the whole spa circus. But if they were good enough for Herod the Great and Cleopatra, they ought to be good enough for a Lonely Planet author, so in the spirit of in-depth research, I forced myself out of the hiking boots and into the fluffy bath robes of the Zara Spa.

Stepping gingerly into the clinically white foyer, I expected to be routed by the security guard. Instead I was offered a mint tea, given a spa bag to stow boots and notebook, and shown to the pristine changing rooms. The spa experience starts in the cradling waters of the Dead Sea saltwater pool (27% salt), followed with a foot spa and a float in the Damascene-tiled Jacuzzi. Then I stepped outside for a bullying with jet sprays that exercised parts they probably shouldn't have. Best of all were the little pots that bubble when you sit in them and really ought to be X-rated.

Luxury of this kind is an extreme sport, and by the time I reached the spa's private infinity pool, I was so seduced by the ambience I hadn't the energy to try the saunas, steam rooms and tropical sprays. I laid under the oleander by the pool, sipping a chilled carrot juice, and wondering where the next tough assignment would take me.

of the most exhilarating things you can do in a day in Jordan.

Other options include the **Ibex Trail** (JD9.5), a half-day guided hike that leads up to the Nubian ibex enclosure.

Guides are compulsory for all but the Siq trail and should be booked in advance through the RSCN in Amman (see p347).

The reserve operates 15 **chalets** (☎ 079 7203888; s/d JD84/95; ❄) on the windy shores of the Dead Sea. They are very popular so book in advance. Each chalet has twin beds, and freshwater showers are available in the communal shower block. The small restaurant serves early breakfast (🕐 7am to 8.30am) for hikers. For JD25.500, chalet guests can also order a lunch or dinner of chicken, salad and mezze. A share of the profits is returned to the running of the reserve.

There's no public transport to the reserve so you need to rent a car or take a taxi from Amman, Madaba or Karak.

THE EASTERN DESERT

The landscape east of Amman quickly turns into a featureless stone desert, known as the *badia*, cut by twin highways running to Iraq and Saudi Arabia. It has its own haunting if barren beauty, partly because it seems so limitless: indeed this is what 80% of Jordan looks like, while supporting only 5% of its population. If you stray into this territory, you'll be surprised to find you're not the first to do so. A whole assortment of ruined hunting lodges, bathhouses and pleasure palaces, known collectively as 'desert castles', have lured people into the wilderness for centuries. Accommodation and public transport is almost nonexistent out here so most travellers visit the region on a tour from Amman. Alternatively, hire a car and make a thorough job of it by staying overnight in Azraq.

UMM AL-JIMAL أم الجمال

The strange, ruined basalt city of **Umm al-Jimal** (admission free; 🕐 daylight hr), only 10km from the Syrian border, is known by archaeologists as the 'Black Gem of the Desert'. It is thought to have been founded around the 2nd century AD and to have formed part of the defensive line of Rome's Arab possessions. It continued to flourish into Umayyad times as a city of 3000 inhabitants but was destroyed by an earthquake in AD 747. Much of what remains is urban (as opposed to monumental) architecture, including **houses**, **reservoirs**, various **churches**, a **Roman barracks** and the impressive **Western Church**. Umm al-Jimal is one of the region's most captivating sites, and the opportunity to scramble across huge basalt blocks warmed by the heat of the desert sun is simply too good to miss.

It's possible to see Umm al-Jimal on a day trip from Amman. Take a local minibus from Raghadan station to Zarqa (20 minutes), a minibus from there to Mafraq (45 minutes) and then another minibus 20km on to the ruins (20 minutes).

THE DESERT CASTLES قصور الصحراء

Most of the so-called 'desert castles' were built or adapted by the Damascus-based Umayyad rulers in the late 7th and early 8th centuries as desert retreats or hunting lodges, rather than actual castles. The most popular ruins can be visited in a loop from Amman via Azraq. It is just feasible to travel this loop in one long day using a combination of public transport and hitching, but most travellers join a tour from the Palace, Farah and Cliff Hotels in Amman (see p399).

Qasr al-Hallabat & Hammam as-Sarah قصر الحلابات & حمام الصرح

Crumbling Qasr al-Hallabat was originally a Roman fort built as a defence against raiding desert tribes. During the 7th century it was converted into a monastery and then the Umayyads fortified it into a country estate. The site consists of the square Umayyad fort and a partially restored mosque.

Some 2km down the road heading east is the **Hammam as-Sarah**, an Umayyad bathhouse and hunting lodge. It has been well restored and you can see the underground channels for the hot, cool and tepid bathrooms.

From Amman's Raghadan station, take a minibus to Zarqa (20 minutes), where you can get another to Hallabat (30 minutes) and ask to be dropped off outside either site.

Azraq الأزرق

☎ **05 / pop 8000**

The oasis town of Azraq ('blue' in Arabic) lies 80km east of Amman. For centuries an important meeting of trade routes, the town is still a junction of truck roads heading northeast to Iraq and southeast to Saudi

AN ECOLOGICAL DISASTER

A generation ago, Azraq was home to a vast oasis, but by 1991 the water table had dropped to over 10m below the ground and the wetlands had dried up completely. Salt was added to the wound, quite literally, when over-pumping destroyed the natural balance between the freshwater aquifer and the underground brine. As a direct result, salt water seeped into the wetlands, making the now brackish water unpalatable for wildlife and hopeless for drinking and irrigation.

Fortunately, there is hope that this once great oasis can be restored to its former glory. Since 1994, serious funding and a commitment from the UN Development Program (UNDP), the Jordanian government and the RSCN have successfully halted the pumping of water from the wetlands to urban centres. A brand new pipeline between Diseh (near Wadi Rum) and Amman has also helped ease pressure on the wetland springs.

Around 1.5 million cu metres of fresh water is now being pumped back into the wetlands every year by the Jordanian Ministry of Water, an ongoing process aimed at restoring about 10% of the wetlands to their former glory. However, a major hurdle still to overcome is the estimated 500 illegal deep wells that are still operating in the area.

Arabia. South Azraq was founded early last century by Chechens fleeing Russian persecution, while North Azraq is home to a minority of Druze, who fled French Syria in the 1920s.

SIGHTS

Azraq Wetland Reserve محمية الأزرق

Azraq is home to the **Azraq Wetland Reserve** (☎ 3835017; admission JD2; 🕒 9am-sunset), which is administered by the RSCN and is good for bird-watching. The Azraq Basin was originally 12,710 sq km (an area larger than Lebanon), but over-pumping of ground water sucked the wetlands dry in the 1970s and 1980s. The RSCN is trying to rehabilitate a small section (12 sq km) of the wetlands. An environmental recovery project of this magnitude is certainly worth your support, and the onsite visitor centre has well documented (if somewhat tragic) exhibits detailing the history of the basin's demise.

Qasr Al-Azraq قصر الأزرق

> 'It was to be Ali's first view of Azraq, and we hurried up the stony ridge in high excitement, talking of the wars and songs and passions of the early shepherd kings, with names like music, who had loved this place; and of the Roman legionaries who languished here as garrison in yet earlier times.'
>
> *TE Lawrence, Seven Pillars of Wisdom*

This brooding black basalt **castle** (admission JD1, ticket also valid for Qusayr Amra & Qasr Kharana; 🕒 daylight hr) dates back to the Roman emperor Diocletian (300 AD), but owes its current form to the beginning of the 13th century. It was originally three storeys high, but much of it crumbled in an earthquake in 1927. The Umayyads maintained it as a military base, as did the Ayyubids in the 12th and 13th centuries. In the 16th century the Ottoman Turks stationed a garrison here.

After the 16th century, the only other recorded use of the castle was during WWI when Sherif Hussein (father of King Hussein) and TE Lawrence made it their desert headquarters in the winter of 1917, during the Arab Revolt against the Ottomans. You can still visit Lawrence's room, which is directly above the southern entrance. Unfortunately, the ancient fort was almost destroyed in 1927 following a violent earthquake and it now requires some imagination.

Shaumari Wildlife Reserve محمية الشومري

This **reserve** (Mahmiyyat ash-Shaumari; www.rscn.org.jo; 🕒 8am-4pm), 10km south of Azraq, was established in 1975 to reintroduce endemic wildlife, particularly the endangered Arabian oryx (a white antelope with long, straight horns). Despite intense funding hurdles, the continuous threat of poaching and natural predators, oryx, Persian onagers (wild ass), goitered gazelle and ostrich have flourished here, a testament to RSCN efforts. At the time of research, the reserve was undergoing extensive redevelopment and was temporarily closed to visitors.

SLEEPING & EATING

Zoubi Hotel (☎ 3835012; r JD10) Located behind the Refa'i Restaurant in South Azraq, about 800m south of the T-junction, the rooms at this modest family-run hotel are comfortable, with clean bathrooms and charming old-fashioned furniture.

Azraq Resthouse (☎ 3834006; s/d/tr from JD30/35/50; ❄) Comprising spacious chalets equipped with satellite TV, the highlight of this comfortable resort is the swimming pool – just don't ask where the water comes from! The turn-off is about 2km north of the T-junction.

Azraq Palace Restaurant (☎ 079 5030356; buffet JD8, plates JD2-5; 🕑 noon-4pm & 6-11pm) This is probably the best place to eat in town and the place most groups stop for lunch. For a light lunch, choose the salad-only buffet.

our pick **Azraq Lodge** (☎ 3835017; s/d from JD 48/60, meals JD5-10; ❄ V) Sensitively renovated by the RSCN, this former 1940s British military hospital is run by a delightful family of Chechen descent, who serve their outstanding traditional cuisine in the on-site restaurant. There is a **handicraft workshop** (☎ 3835017; 🕑 9am-5pm) on site where local women craft (and sell) painted ostrich eggs and traditional textiles.

A string of truck-stop restaurants lines the 1km stretch of road south of the main T-junction.

GETTING THERE & AWAY

Minibuses run up and down the road along northern and southern Azraq in search of passengers before hitting the highway to Zarqa (less than 1JD, 1½ hours). If you're driving, Azraq is a long and straight drive along Route 30 from Zarqa.

Qusayr Amra قصر عمرا

One of the best-preserved desert buildings of the Umayyads, the Unesco World Heritage site of **Qusayr Amra** (admission JD1, ticket also valid for Qsar Azraq & Qasr Kharana; 🕑 8am-6pm May-Sep, to 4pm Oct-Apr) is the highlight of any trip into the Eastern Desert. Part of a much greater complex that served as a caravanserai, bath house and hunting lodge, the *qusayr* or 'little castle' is famous for its hedonistic (and somewhat risqué!) 8th-century frescoes of wine, women and wild good times. That said, the information boards in the visitor centre at Qusayr Amra delightfully assure the visitor that 'none of the paintings of Qusayr Amra portray scenes of unbridled loose-living or carryings-on'.

Qusayr Amra is on the main road, 26km from Azraq, southwest of the junctions of Hwys 30 and 40. From Azraq, take a minibus towards Zarqa as far as the junction, then you'll have to hitch as buses won't stop on the main road. Alternatively, charter a taxi from Azraq on a combined visit with Qasr al-Kharana, which is along the same road, nearer to Amman.

Qasr al-Kharana قصر الخرانه

Located in the middle of a vast treeless plain, this mighty **fortress** (admission JD1, ticket also valid for Qusayr Amra & Qasr Azraq; 🕑 8am-6pm May-Sep, to 4pm Oct-Apr) was most likely the inspiration for the somewhat incorrect 'desert castles' moniker. The intimidating two-storey structure is marked by round, defensive towers and narrow windows that appear to be arrow slits. If you take a closer look, however, you'll soon realize that the towers are completely solid, which means that they couldn't be manned by armed soldiers. Furthermore, it would be impossible to fire bows from the bizarrely shaped 'arrow slits', meaning that they most likely served as air and light ducts.

The origins of the building are something of a mystery: it was built either by the Romans or Byzantines, although what you see today is the result of renovations carried out by the Umayyads in AD 710. Around 60 labyrinthine rooms surround the central courtyard, suggesting that the building may have been used as a meeting place for the Damascus elite and local Bedouin.

Again, you'll need to hitch to reach this site. The complex is only signposted coming from Amman, so if you're coming from Azraq, keep an eye out for the nearby communication masts that disappointingly blight the site.

KING'S HIGHWAY

Of Jordan's three highways running from north to south, the King's Highway is by far the most interesting and picturesque, with a host of attractions lying on the road or nearby. The highway connects the mosaic town of Madaba to the pink city of Petra via Crusader castles, Roman forts, biblical sites, a windswept Nabataean temple and some epic landscapes – including the majestic Wadi Mujib and a gem of a nature reserve at Dana.

Unfortunately, public transport along the King's Hwy is patchy and stops altogether at Wadi Mujib, between Dhiban and Ariha; you can either take a private vehicle for part of the way or try to hitch. Alternatively, the Palace Hotel (p350) in Amman and the Mariam Hotel (opposite) in Madaba can organise transport along the highway.

MADABA مادبا

☎ 05 / pop 135,000

The relaxed market town of Madaba is best known for a collection of superb, Byzantine-era mosaics. The most famous of these is the mosaic map on the floor of St George's Church but there are many other mosaics carpeting different parts of the town, many of which are even more complete and vibrant in colour – look for the chicken. There's one in most mosaics and trying to spot it may save 'mosaic-fatigue' syndrome.

One third of Madaba's population is Christian (the other two-thirds are Muslim), making it one of the largest Christian communities in Jordan. The town's long tradition of religious tolerance is joyfully – and loudly – expressed on Fridays. This is one day when you shouldn't expect a lie-in. The imam summons the faithful before dawn. Then the carillon bells get the Orthodox Christians out of bed and finally Mammon gets a look-in with the honks and groans of traffic.

Madaba is worth considering as an alternative place to stay to Amman: Madaba is far more compact, has excellent hotels and restaurants, and is less than an hour by regular public transport from the capital. Madaba is also a good base for exploring the Dead Sea, Bethany and other sites such as Mt Nebo, Machaerus (Mukawir) and Hammamat Ma'in.

JORDAN

Information

Madaba's **visitor centre** (☎ 3253563; Abu Bakr as-Seddiq St; 8am-5pm) is a good place to begin a visit to Madaba. Benefiting from generous funding from US Aid, the well-run centre has a wide selection of free brochures, various displays, culturally revealing exhibits, very helpful staff and clean toilets.

Among Madaba's better internet cafés is **Tour.Dot internet** (Talal St; per hr 500 fils; 9am-2am).

All the town's half-dozen banks can change money and have ATMs.

Sights

Madaba's most famous site is the **Mosaic Map** in the 19th-century Greek Orthodox **St George's Church** (Talal St; admission JD1; 8am-5pm Sat-Thu Nov-Mar, 7.30am-6pm Apr-Oct; 9.30am-5pm Fri year-round). In 1884 Christian builders came across the remnants of an old Byzantine church on the site of their new construction. Among the rubble, having survived wilful destruction, fire and neglect, the mosaic they discovered had extraordinary significance: to this day, it represents the oldest map of Palestine in existence and provides many historical insights into the region.

The mosaic was crafted in AD 560 and has 157 captions (in Greek) depicting all the major biblical sites of the Middle East from Egypt to Palestine. It was originally around 15m to 25m long and 6m wide and once contained more than two million pieces. Although much of the mosaic has been lost, enough remains to sense the enormous scope of the original.

For the following places, admission is a combination ticket (JD2), which covers all three sites.

The **Archaeological Park** (☎ 3246681; Hussein bin Ali St; 8am-4pm Oct-Apr, to 5pm May-Sep) contains exceptional mosaics from all around the Madaba area. The large roofed structure in front as you enter contains the **Hippolytus Hall**, a former Byzantine villa with some superb classical mosaics (the upper image shows a topless Aphrodite sitting next to Adonis and spanking a naughty winged Eros). The other half of the structure is the 6th-century **Church of the Virgin Mary**. There are also remains of a Roman road.

The **Church of the Apostles** (Al-Nuzha St; 9am-4pm Oct-Apr, 8am-5pm May-Sep) contains a remarkable mosaic dedicated to the 12 apostles. The central portion shows a vivid representation of the sea, surrounded by fish and a comical little octopus.

Housed in several old Madaba residences, **Madaba Museum** (☎ 3244189; Al-Baiqa St; 9am-5pm) contains a number of ethnographic exhibits and some more good mosaics.

VOLUNTARY WORK

For those who like Madaba well enough to stay, there is an opportunity to teach English at the **New Orthodox School** (☎ 3250636; Talal St) that would make for a worthwhile gap year experience. Run by Father Innocent (Innokentios), who describes himself as 'Innocent by name, but guilty by any other means', the school is attached to St George's Church. It aims to promote 'mutual respect and peaceful coexistence' among youngsters of different religious communities and a nonprofit organisation, supporting needy students. Volunteers would receive free accommodation, pocket money and private Arabic lessons. Email Father Innocent for details (diodoros@wanadoo.jo).

Activities

If you've had just about enough mosaics for one day, you could always enjoy closely knit tiles of a different kind at **Madaba Turkish Bath** (☎ 3250999; Hashmi St). The baths are clean and intimate but opening hours appear to be ad hoc – it's best to call ahead. Women choose a female or male attendant and couples can share the facilities if they wish. Facilities include a steam room, Jacuzzi, scrub down, massage and a hot tiled floor. An hour's soak costs JD15 or JD20 with a massage.

Sleeping

Madaba Hotel (☎/fax 3240643; Al-Jame St; s/d JD10/18, s/d/tr without bathroom from JD8/16/21) The spartan rooms are clean with dorm-style beds and a heater and sporadic hot water. There's a ground-floor lounge and kitchen that guests can use. Breakfast (JD1) is better enjoyed elsewhere.

Lulu's Pension (☎ 3243678; fax 3247617; Hamraa al-Asd St; s/d/tr with bathroom & balcony JD15/25/35, without bathroom JD15/22/35) Comfortable rooms and a warm welcome characterise this family B&B.

Black Iris Hotel (☎ 3241959; www.blackirishotel.com; Al-Mouhafada Circle; s/d/tr JD18/25/35 For a feeling of 'home away from home', it's hard to beat this popular hotel run by one of Madaba's Christian families. The carpeted rooms are cosy and there's a spacious sitting area. It's a good bet for women travelling alone. The hotel is easy to spot from Al-Mouhafada Circle.

Moab Land Hotel (☎/fax 3251318; moabland hotel@wanadoo.jo; Talal St; s/d/t JD20/25/30) Directly opposite St George's Church and with wonderful views, this homely establishment is as central as it gets. The recently refurbished rooms have sprung mattresses and pine furniture, and there's a cosy communal area with TV. Breakfast is served on the glorious rooftop terrace in summer.

Salome Hotel (☎ 3248606; www.salomehotel.com; Aisha Umm al-Mumeneen St; s/d JD18/25; ❄ 💻) With the family-run appeal of a small residential hotel, the Salome is a good choice for a quiet stay. Rooms are small but they all have TV and are spotless. The hotel is next to the Mariam, a five-minute walk from the town centre.

our pick Mariam Hotel (☎ 3251529; www.mariam hotel.com; Aisha Umm al-Mumeneen St; s/d/tr JD25/30/36; ❄ 💻 🏊) The Mariam's friendly reputation is still intact despite ambitious recent expansions. Excellent facilities include a bar and a cheerful communal lobby. The modern, no-nonsense rooms have TV and sparkling bathrooms. The hotel can organise a taxi to/from the airport (around JD12) and transport along the King's Highway to Petra. Ask Charl, the owner, about a trip to see the local dolmens – neolithic structures with a stone slab supported by two stone uprights used most probably as burial chambers – a subject he is knowledgeable and passionate about.

Mosaic City Hotel (☎ 3251313; www.mosaiccity hotel.com; Yarmouk St; s/d JD25/35, extra bed JD10; ❄) This attractive 21-room hotel is a welcome new addition to Madaba's midrange accommodation. Some of the bright and spacious rooms have balconies overlooking lively Yarmouk St.

Madaba Inn Hotel (☎ 3259003; www.madabainn .com; Talal St; s/d/t JD45/60/75; ❄ 💻) This efficiently managed, 33-room hotel has comfortable rooms (all with TV and minibar), with great views across the Madaba plain and window seats. A generous breakfast of homemade local cheese, olives and yogurt is a bonus.

Eating

our pick Coffee Shop Ayola (☎ 3251843; ayolla@hot mail.com; Talal St; snacks around JD2; 🕑 8am-11pm; Ⓥ) If you want a toasted sandwich (JD2), Turkish coffee (JD1), glass of *arak* with locals or simply a cosy perch on which to while away some time with fellow travellers, then this is the place to come. With its friendly welcome, festoons of hand-loomed kilims, creeping vines and aroma of sheesha, it captures the essence of Jordan.

Petra Restaurant (Talal St; 8am-12 midnight; snacks JD1) Also known by its previous name of King Shwarma, this spot serves reliable fare including kebab sandwiches. Pick up dessert in one of the Arabic sweet shops round the corner.

Bowabit Restaurant (☎ 32403335; Talal St; mains JD7; 9am-midnight) With photographs of old Madaba and excellent Italian-style coffee (cappuccino JD2.500), this is a number-one place to relax after strolling round town. Alternatively, make a night of it over a dish of Madaba chicken and a beer (JD3).

Mystic Pizza (☎ 3243249; Prince Hassan St; small/medium/large pizza JD3/6/8; 9am-midnight; V) This tiny, trendy new venue with its heavy wood chairs and flat-screen TV prepares delicious pizzas including a fire-roasted vegetarian pizza. Follow it up with the best frappacino in town (JD2.500).

Haret Jdoudna (☎ 3248650; Talal St; starters from 800 fils, mains JD5-10 plus 26% tax; 9am-midnight; V) This attractive complex of craft shops (a share of the profit is returned to participating cooperatives) also runs a bar and a restaurant set in one of Madaba's restored old houses. Though popular with locals and discerning diners from Amman, the 'take it or leave it' attitude of restaurant staff can ruin the experience.

For freshly baked Arabic bread, head for the ovens opposite the Church of the Apostles. There are several grocery stores or 'supermarkets' in town. The most convenient for visitors is the so-called 'Tourist Supermarket' next to the Coffee Shop Ayola.

Getting There & Away

The bus station is 2km east of the King's Hwy.

Minibuses travel frequently between Madaba and Amman's Raghadan, Wahadat and (less often) Abdali bus stations (400 fils, one hour). The last bus back to Amman is around 9pm.

It is possible to travel to Karak on a twice-weekly university minibus (JD2, two hours) from the main bus/minibus station, although it travels via the less interesting Desert Hwy and doesn't always run in the university holidays.

The Mariam Hotel can arrange transport to Petra via the King's Hwy (JD15 per person, minimum three people) and to the Dead Sea (JD22). There is no public transport to Karak along the King's Hwy.

AROUND MADABA

Mt Nebo جبل نيبو

Mt Nebo, on the edge of the East Bank plateau and 9km from Madaba, is where Moses is said to have seen the Promised Land. He then died (aged 120!) and was buried in the area, although the exact location of the burial site is the subject of conjecture.

The entrance to the **complex** (admission JD1; 8am-4.30pm Oct-Apr, to 7pm May-Sep) is clearly visible on the Madaba–Dead Sea road. The first church was built on the site in the 4th century AD but most of the **Moses Memorial Church** you'll see today was built in the 6th century. The impressive main-floor mosaic measures about 9m by 3m, and is very well preserved. It depicts hunting and herding scenes interspersed with an assortment of African fauna, including a zebu (humped ox), lions, tigers, bears, boars, zebras, an ostrich on a leash and a camel-shaped giraffe. The inscription below names the artist. Even to the untrained eye, it's clear that this is a masterpiece.

From the **lookout**, the views across the valleys to the Dead Sea, Jericho, the Jordan Valley and the spires of Jerusalem are superb, especially on a cold day in winter when it is crystal clear. The new **museum** is worth a quick look before leaving.

From Madaba, shared taxis run to the village of Fasiliyeh, 3km before Mt Nebo (250 fils a seat). For an extra JD1 or so the driver will drop you at Mt Nebo. A return taxi, with about 30 minutes to look around, shouldn't cost more than JD5 per vehicle.

Hammamat Ma'in (Zarqa Ma'in) حمامات ماعين (زرقاء ماعين)

Drive anywhere in the hills above the Dead Sea and you'll notice occasional livid green belts of vegetation, a curtain of ferns across a disintegrating landscape of sulphurous rock, a puff of steam and the hiss of underground water. In fact, the hills are alive with the sound of thermal springs – there are about 60 of them suppurating below the surface and breaking ground with various degrees of violence.

The most famous of these is **Hammamat Ma'in** (admission per person JD10; 🕑 8am-11pm) in Wadi Zarqa Ma'in. Developed into a hot-springs resort, the water at the bottom of the wadi ranges from a pleasant 45°C to a blistering 60°C and contains potassium, magnesium and calcium, among other minerals. The water tumbles off the hillside in a series of waterfalls and less assuming trickles, and is collected in a variety of pools for public bathing.

The entrance fee permits use of the Roman baths, the family pool at the base of the waterfall closest to the entrance, and the swimming pool. It also includes a sandwich and a cold drink from the complex shop. The valley is overrun by people on Fridays during the spring and autumn seasons.

The **Janna Spa & Resort** (☎ 3245500; www.jannaspa.com; half board s/d JD119/129; ❄ 💻 🏊 Ⓥ) is currently closed for refurbishment. Minimal snacks and soft drinks are for sale in the shop near the entrance.

A taxi from Madaba costs about JD10/20 (one-way/return) including around an hour's waiting time at the springs.

MACHAERUS (MUKAWIR) مكاريوس (مكاور)

Just beyond the village of Mukawir is the spectacular 700m-high hilltop perch of **Machaerus** (admission free; 🕑 daylight hrs), the castle of Herod the Great. The ruins themselves are only of moderate interest but the setting is breathtaking and commands great views out over the surrounding hills and the Dead Sea.

Machaerus is known to the locals as Qala'at al-Meshneq (Gallows Castle). The ruins consist of the palace of Herod Antipas, a huge cistern, the low-lying remains of the baths and defensive walls. Machaerus is renowned as the place where John the Baptist was beheaded by Herod Antipas, the successor to Herod the Great, at the request of the seductive dancer Salome. The castle is about 2km past the village and easy to spot.

In Mukawir village, by the side of the road leading to the castle, is a weaving centre and gallery. This women's cooperative is run from the **Bani Hamida Centre** (☎ 3210155; www.jordanriver.jo; 🕑 8am-3pm Sun-Thu), where some of the gorgeous, colourful woven rugs and cushions are on sale. Profits are returned to the cooperative and make a substantial difference to local Bedouin lives.

From Madaba, minibuses (600fils, one hour) go to the village of Mukawir four or five times a day (the last around 5pm). Unless you have chartered a taxi from Madaba, you'll probably need to walk the remaining 2km (downhill most of the way). However, your minibus driver may, if you ask nicely and sweeten the request with a tip, take you the extra distance.

WADI MUJIB وادي الموجيب

Stretching across Jordan from the Desert Hwy to the Dead Sea is the vast and beautiful Wadi Mujib, sometimes known as the 'Grand Canyon of Jordan'. This spectacular valley is about 1km deep and over 4km from one edge to the other. The canyon forms the upper portion of the **Wadi Mujib Nature Reserve** (see p362), which is normally accessed from the Dead Sea Highway.

Even if you are not intending to make the crossing, it's worth travelling to the canyon rim. Just after Dhiban, the road descends after 3km to an awesome **lookout**. Some enterprising traders have set up a tea stall here, and fossils and minerals from the canyon walls are for sale. This is the easiest point on the road to stop to absorb the view, take a photograph and turn round if you're heading back to Madaba.

Dhiban is where almost all transport south of Madaba stops. The only way to cross the mighty Mujib from Dhiban to Ariha (about 30km) is to charter a taxi for JD8 each way. Hitching is possible, but expect a long wait.

Climbing out of the gorge on the southern side, you will come to the strategically placed **Trajan Rest House & Restaurant** (☎ 03-2310295/07, 95903302; trajan_resthouse@yahoo.com; bed in shared room JD5, with breakfast & dinner JD10). The rest house is mainly visited for its restaurant, a cavernous grotto of Bedouin artefacts, with handloomed rugs and benches at long trestle tables. The accommodation here is basic, with curtains for doors, but the nearby views from the canyon rim compensate. For those who have had to resort to hitching across this part of the highway, you may find a ride across the valley from here.

KARAK الكرك

☎ 03 / pop 210,000

The evocative ancient Crusader castle of Karak (or Kerak) became a place of legend during the 12th-century battles between the Crusaders and the Muslim armies of Salah ad-Din (Saladin). Although among the most famous, the castle at Karak was just one in a long line built by the Crusaders, stretching from Aqaba in the south to Turkey in the north. The fortifications still dominate the modern walled town of Karak.

At one point in its chequered history, the castle belonged to a particularly unsavoury knight of the cross, Renauld de Chatillon. Hated by Saladin for his treachery, de Chatillon arrived from France in 1148 to take part in the Crusades. He was renowned for his sadistic delight in torturing prisoners and throwing them off the walls into the valley 450m below; he even went to the trouble of having a wooden box fastened over their heads so they wouldn't lose consciousness before hitting the ground.

The **castle** (☎ 2351216; admission JD1; 🕑 8am-4pm Oct-Mar, to 7pm Apr-Sep) is entered through the **Ottoman Gate**, at the end of a short bridge over the dry moat. The path leading up to the left from inside the entrance leads to the **Crusader Gallery** (stables). At the end of the gallery, a long passageway leads southwest past the **soldiers' barracks** and **kitchen**. Emerging from the covered area, you will see the overgrown **upper court** on your right, and going straight ahead you will go past the castle's main **Crusader church**. At the far southern end of the castle is the impressive **Mamluk keep**, in front of which some stairs lead down to the **Mamluk palace**, built in 1311 using earlier Crusader materials. More stairs lead down to the delightful underground **marketplace**, which leads back to the entrance.

Sleeping & Eating

Towers Castle Hotel (☎ /fax 2354293; Al-Qala'a St; s/d/t JD12/20/27; ❄) Close to the castle, this friendly budget hotel is a good meeting place for younger travellers. Don't be put off by the rather dingy reception area: the rooms open onto balconies with wonderful views across Wadi Karak. You can find help with onward travel here.

our pick Karak Rest House (☎ 2351148; karakcastle@gmail.com; Al-Qala'a St; s/d JD28/47; ❄) If you want a bit more bang for your buck, then try this extravagantly decorated hotel, right next door to the castle, with sweeping views of Wadi Karak, elaborate Middle Eastern–style fixtures and fittings and an elegant lobby area. Sip mint tea under the pergola and enjoy the goings-on of Castle St.

King's Restaurant (☎ 2354293; Al-Mujamma St; mezze JD1, mains JD4; 🕑 8am-10pm) This boulevard restaurant attracts an assortment of travellers at all times of the day and night. It offers local, home-cooked Jordanian dishes like *maqlubbeh*. The neighbouring **Ram Peace Restaurant** (☎ 353789; Al-Mujamma St; mezze JD1, mains JD3; 🕑 8am-10pm) is similar. A few doors down, **Al-Fid'a Restaurant** (☎ 079 5037622; Al-Mujamma St; mains JD3; 🕑 8am-10pm) sells standard local fare of chicken, dips and salads.

our pick Kir Heres Restaurant (☎ 2355595; Al-Qala'a St; mains JD5-7; 🕑 9am-10pm; **V**) This wonderful, award-winning restaurant is a surprise find. The chef (and owner) is from Karak and has a passion for food. There are ostrich steaks prepared with local herbs (JD7), and vegetarians can choose from dishes like fried haloumi (JD2.250) and fresh mushrooms with garlic and thyme (JD2.250). Don't be alarmed by the smart striped tablecloths: the fare is extremely good value for money. Try the local wine (JD3 per glass) in the upper gallery at lunchtime and you can forget about visiting the castle afterwards!

King's Castle Restaurant (☎ 2396070; lunch buffet JD10; 🕑 noon-4pm) The daily buffet here is popular with day-tripping tour groups. With pleasant outdoor seating, castle views and over 20 salads to choose from, it's easy to understand why.

Al-Motaz Sweets (☎ 2353388; An-Nuzha St; 🕑 8am-10pm; **V**) This Arabic pastry shop is a must for those with a sweet tooth. The Al-Shubba supermarket on Al-Mujamma Street is ideal for stocking up on supplies for the next leg of the King's Highway.

Getting There & Away

From the bus/minibus station at the bottom of the hill just south of town, reasonably regular minibuses go to Amman's Wahadat station (JD1, two hours) via the Desert Hwy. Minibuses also run fairly frequently to Tafila (750 fils, one hour), the best place for connections to Qadsiyya (for Dana Nature Reserve) and Shobak. To Wadi Musa (for Petra), take a minibus to Ma'an (JD2, two hours) and change there. Minibuses to Aqaba (JD2.500, three hours) run about four times a day, mostly in the morning.

TAFILA الطفيله

☎ 03 / pop 80,000

Tafila is a busy transport junction and you may have to change transport here. Minibuses run frequently from Karak (750 fils, one hour) across the dramatic gorge of Wadi Hasa. There are also direct minibuses to/from the Wahadat station in Amman (JD2, 2½ hours) via the Desert Hwy, Aqaba (JD1.500, 2½ hours) via the Dead Sea Hwy, Ma'an (JD1.100, one hour) via the Desert Hwy, and down the King's Hwy to Shobak and Qadsiyya (for Dana Nature Reserve; JD1, 30 minutes).

DANA NATURE RESERVE محمية دانا الطبيعية

☎ 03

The RSCN-run **Dana Nature Reserve** (adult/student JD6/3; free admission for guests staying in RSCN accommodation) is one of Jordan's hidden gems and its most impressive ecotourism project. The gateway to the reserve is the charming 15th-century stone village of **Dana**, which clings to a precipice overlooking the valley and commands exceptional views. It's a great place to spend a few days hiking and relaxing. Most of the reserve is only accessible on foot.

The reserve is the largest in Jordan and includes a variety of terrain, from sandstone cliffs over 1500m high near Dana to a low point of 50m below sea level in Wadi Araba. Sheltered within the red-rock escarpments are protected valleys that are home to a surprisingly diverse ecosystem. About 600 species of plants (ranging from citrus trees and juniper, to desert acacias and date palms), 180 species of birds and over 45 species of mammals (of which 25 are endangered), including ibex, mountain gazelle, sand cat, red fox and wolf, thrive in the reserve. The reserve is also home to almost 100 archaeological sites including the 6000-year-old copper mines of Khirbet Feinan.

A WARDEN'S TALE

Malik Al-Nanah was born and brought up nearby in the village of Qadsiyya and has been working at Dana Nature Reserve for three years. He loves the reserve and told us more about it.

What was your first day here like?

The driver who brought me here congratulated me for getting the job, scolded me for throwing out an empty carton of juice and swerved to avoid a rock martin chick in the road. I knew then that I had a lot to learn.

Who visits the reserve?

All sorts, but there's been a change in the kind of tourists who come: more and more nature-lovers visit to take pictures or research special species.

Tell us about the cement factory.

It's owned by a French company and there are many rules in place to minimise its effect. Water springs include heavy elements released from the factory but good filters have helped reduce the dust clouds.

What role does the community cooperative play in the preservation of this reserve?

We hold workshops and plan how to include the local community by increasing employment – in transportation, for example, or by using local shops for supplies. The whole philosophy of the RSCN is to protect nature by supporting local people. We also have initiatives with local schools to get the children interested in nature.

What does the future hold for your reserve?

Dana is unique because it has four ecosystems – Arabian, Iranian/Asian, Semi-Desert and Desert, ranging from altitudes of 1700m to minus 50m – all of which occur within a very compact distance. As such, we hope Dana will soon achieve official 'biodiversity reserve' status, and within five years become the first National park in the Middle East.

What if travellers can't make it to Dana?

They should go and visit the RSCN's Wild Jordan Centre in Amman – we've taken nature to the city there and it's really inspiring!

Malik Al-Nanah is the Centre Manager at Dana Nature Reserve.

JORDAN

The **visitor centre** (☎ 2270497; dhana@rscn.org.jo; www.rscn.org.jo; 🕑 8am-3pm) in the Dana Guest House complex includes an RSCN craft shop, nature exhibits, craft workshops (closed by 3.30pm) and a food-drying centre for making organic food. This is also the place to obtain further information about the reserve and its hiking trails and to arrange a guide. Most trails require a guide, costing JD15 for up to two hours, JD25 for three to four hours and JD35 for five to six hours. Costs are for a group with a maximum of 18 people.

Hiking routes include the Steppe Trail (2½ hours, 8km) to Rummana camp ground, the Waterfalls Trail (2½ hours, 2.5km) and the short but steep Mysterious Nabataean Tomb Tour (two hours, 2.5km). The last two hikes require a shuttle to the trailhead (JD6). The main unguided option is the **Wadi Dana Trail** (14km) to Feinan Lodge, which switchbacks steeply down into the gorge (coming back is a real killer!).

Sleeping & Eating

Dana Hotel (☎ 2270537; www.danavillage.piczo.com; s/d JD12/20) This hotel, ethically run by the Sons of Dana Cooperative, is the oldest in the village, with simple but spotless rooms and helpful management. Meals (JD4) can be arranged.

Dana Tower Hotel (☎ 2270226, 079 5688853; dana_tower2@hotmail.com; s/d/t without bathroom JD5/10/12) This quirky assembly of rooms has a *majlis* (reception area) festooned with hanging memorabilia. With names like 'Flying Carpet' and 'Sunset Royal', the small, unheated rooms decorated with travellers' graffiti are grungy, but popular with younger backpackers. There is free tea and a washing machine.

our pick **Dana Guest House** (☎ 2270497; dhana@rscn.org.jo; d JD60, s/d/tr JD35/45/55 without bathroom; Ⓥ) With panoramic views across the reserve and a great roaring fire in winter, a welcome from enthusiastic park rangers and a collection of like-minded fellow travellers, this is one ecolodge that lives up to its hearty reputation. It is run by the RSCN and reservations are necessary in the high season. The balconies have breathtaking views. Book dinner (JD9) in advance.

our pick **Feinan Lodge** (s/d/tr JD40/50/65; Wadi Feinan; 🕑 1 Sep-30 Jun; Ⓥ) This unique ecolodge is only accessible on foot from Dana (six hours) or by 4WD via the Dead Sea Hwy (JD46, 2½ hours from Dana by taxi). At night, the monastic-style lodge is lit solely by hundreds of candles. Bring a torch and mosquito repellent. It's guaranteed to be a night to remember, not least for the exceptional, home-cooked vegetarian spread.

Rummana Campground (s/d/tr tent incl park entry fee JD20/35/50; 🕑 1 Mar-31 Oct; Ⓥ) The price may seem steep given the minimal facilities, but when you wake up to the sound of Dana's wildlife singing in your ear, it's easy to see why you have to book in advance. Fantastic hiking trails are just beyond the tent pegs. Tents, mattresses and blankets are provided. Book dinner (JD9 for a fabulous home-cooked feast) or bring your own food. Hike here in three hours from Dana village or arrange transport with the RSCN (JD10.500 for one to four people). The turn-off from the King's Hwy is around 5km north of Qadsiyya. Prices include park entry fee and there's a 45% discount for students.

If all the accommodation at Dana village is full, consider staying at **Al-Nawatef Camp** (☎ 2270413/77 7240378; nawatefcamp@hotmail.com; half board JD15). Perched on the edge of a neighbouring wadi to Dana, this small camp has a fabulous location and is run by an enterprising local man who knows the area because, he says, 'It runs in my blood.' The camp comprises goat-hair chalets with comfortable beds (and balconies) and a shared shower block. Many hiking options are possible.

Getting There & Away

Minibuses run every hour or so throughout the day between Tafila and Qadsiyya (JD1, 30 minutes). The turn-off to Dana village is 1km north of Qadsiyya – ask to be dropped off at the crossroads. From here it's a 2.8km steep downhill walk to Dana village. A single bus departs from Qadsiyya daily between 6am and 7am for Amman's Wahadat station (JD3, three hours), returning from Amman at around 11am.

A taxi from Tafila costs JD8 or the Dana Tower Hotel picks up travellers for free from Qadsiyya if you ring in advance and stay at the hotel. A taxi to Petra or Karak costs around JD30.

SHOBAK شوبك

Perched in a wild, remote landscape, **Shobak Castle** (admission free; 🕑 daylight hr) wins over even the most castle-weary, despite being less complete than its sister fortification at Karak. Formerly called Mons Realis (Mont Real, or

Montreal – the Royal Mountain), it was built by the Crusader king Baldwin I in AD 1115. It withstood numerous attacks from the armies of Saladin before succumbing in 1189, a year after Karak, after an 18-month siege. Rising above the surrounding plateau, it is an impressive sight from a distance.

Excavation on the castle's interior is ongoing and has revealed a market, two Crusader churches and, at the northern end of the castle, a semicircular keep whose exterior is adorned with Quranic inscriptions, possibly dating from the time of Saladin. The court of Baldwin I is also worth a look. The real highlight is the underground **escape tunnel** that winds down seemingly forever into the bowels of the earth, finally resurfacing way outside the castle at the base of the hill. Bring a torch and nerves of steel.

Most people visit Shobak en route to or from Petra but if you fancy staying over, try **Jaya Tourist Camp** (☎ 2164082/79, 5958958; jaya_camp@yahoo.com; JD15), which has 15 tents in a tranquil spot on high ground opposite Shobak Castle. To reach the camp, follow the signs for **Shobak Castle Campground** (☎ 2164265; currently closed), signposted from the King's Highway, and after 300m turn left and immediate right for 1km.

Occasional minibuses link Shobak village with Amman's Wahadat station (JD2, 2½ hours), and there are irregular minibuses to Karak from Aqaba via the Shobak turn off (ask the driver before setting out). Either way you'll still need a taxi for the last 3km or so to the fort.

PETRA & THE SOUTH

Travel along the King's Highway and you'll notice that somewhere after Dana the character of the countryside changes. As the fertile hilltop pastures of the north give way to the more arid landscapes of the south, you suddenly find you're in epic country – the country that formed the backdrop for *Lawrence of Arabia* and *Indiana Jones and the Last Crusade*. To make the most of this exciting part of Jordan, with its unmissable world wonders at Petra and Wadi Rum, you need to spend a day or two more than the map might suggest. Find some time to hike and stay with the Bedouin, and the experience is sure to become a highlight of your entire Middle Eastern trip. Before catching the ferry to Egypt or crossing into Israel and the Palestinian Territories, spare an evening for Aqaba, a popular night out with travellers.

PETRA & WADI MUSA

بترا & ادي موسى

☎ 03 / pop 15,600

If you can go to only one place in Jordan, make it Petra, the ancient rose-red city of the Nabataeans, Arabs who controlled the frankincense trade routes of the region in pre-Roman times. It was rediscovered by accident in 1812 by a Swiss explorer called Burckhardt (the same chap who stumbled on the temple at Abu Simbel in Egypt). Until his momentous journey, disguised as an Arab, the neglected city, hidden deep in the rocky valleys of Wadi Musa, had escaped the attention of the Western world for hundreds of years.

For the modern visitor, as for Burckhardt, the sublime experience of emerging from the Siq (canyon-like cleft in the rock, marking the entrance to Petra) is a hard act to follow, although there are other spectacles waiting in the wings, not least the Theatre and the imposing facades of the Royal Tombs. Magnificent as they are, these dramatic gestures of immortality may prove to be less memorable than the quiet amble through forgotten tombs, the illumination of a candy swirl of rock at sunset, the aroma from a chain of cloves, bought from a Bedouin stall holder, or the sense of sheer satisfaction, perched on top of a High Place, of energy well spent. Give it a couple of days to do this wonderful site justice!

Orientation

The village that has sprung up around Petra is Wadi Musa (Moses' Valley), a string of hotels, restaurants and shops stretching about 5km from Ain Musa, the head of the valley, down to the entrance to Petra. The village centre is at Shaheed roundabout, with shops, restaurants and budget hotels, while midrange hotels are strung out along the main road for the remaining 2km towards the entrance to Petra.

Information

Petra visitor centre (Map p374; ☎ 2156020; fax 2156060; 🕑 6am-9pm), just before the entrance to Petra, has a helpful information counter,

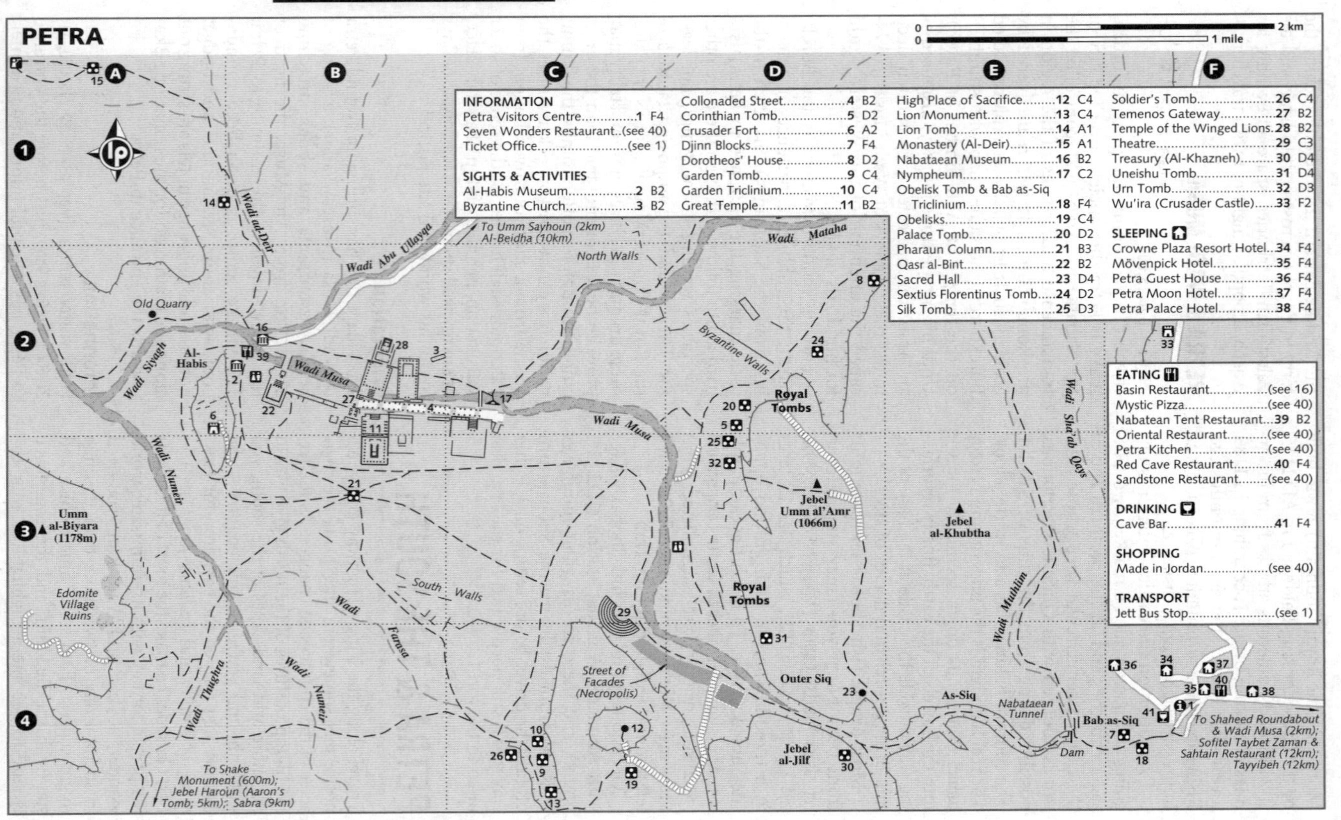
PETRA
0 2 km
0 1 mile
INFORMATION
Petra Visitors Centre....1 F4
Seven Wonders Restaurant..(see 40)
Ticket Office....(see 1)
SIGHTS & ACTIVITIES
Al-Habis Museum....2 B2
Byzantine Church....3 B2
Collonaded Street....4 B2
Corinthian Tomb....5 D2
Crusader Fort....6 A2
Djinn Blocks....7 F4
Dorotheos' House....8 D2
Garden Tomb....9 C4
Garden Triclinium....10 C4
Great Temple....11 B2
High Place of Sacrifice....12 C4
Lion Monument....13 C4
Lion Tomb....14 A1
Monastery (Al-Deir)....15 A1
Nabataean Museum....16 B2
Nympheum....17 C2
Obelisk Tomb & Bab as-Siq Triclinium....18 F4
Obelisks....19 C4
Palace Tomb....20 D2
Pharaun Column....21 B3
Qasr al-Bint....22 B2
Sacred Hall....23 D4
Sextius Florentinus Tomb....24 D2
Silk Tomb....25 D3
Soldier's Tomb....26 C4
Temenos Gateway....27 B2
Temple of the Winged Lions.28 B2
Theatre....29 C3
Treasury (Al-Khazneh)....30 D4
Uneishu Tomb....31 D4
Urn Tomb....32 D3
Wu'ira (Crusader Castle)....33 F2
SLEEPING
Crowne Plaza Resort Hotel..34 F4
Mövenpick Hotel....35 F4
Petra Guest House....36 F4
Petra Moon Hotel....37 F4
Petra Palace Hotel....38 F4
EATING
Basin Restaurant....(see 16)
Mystic Pizza....(see 40)
Nabatean Tent Restaurant....39 B2
Oriental Restaurant....(see 40)
Petra Kitchen....(see 40)
Red Cave Restaurant....40 F4
Sandstone Restaurant....(see 40)
DRINKING
Cave Bar....41 F4
SHOPPING
Made in Jordan....(see 40)
TRANSPORT
Jett Bus Stop....(see 1)
Wadi ad-Deir
Wadi Abu Ullayqa
To Umm Sayhoun (2km) Al-Beidha (10km)
North Walls
Wadi Mataha
Old Quarry
Al-Habis
Wadi Siyagh
Wadi Musa
Byzantine Walls
Royal Tombs
Wadi Sha'ab Qays
Wadi Numeir
Umm al-Biyara (1178m)
Jebel Umm al'Amr (1066m)
Jebel al-Khubtha
Edomite Village Ruins
South Walls
Wadi Farasa
Wadi Thughra
Street of Facades (Necropolis)
Outer Siq
As-Siq
Nabataean Tunnel
Wadi Mudhlim
Bab as-Siq
Dam
Jebel al-Jilf
To Shake Monument (600m); Jebel Haroun (Aaron's Tomb; 5km); Sabra (9km)
To Shaheed Roundabout & Wadi Musa (2km); Sofitel Taybet Zaman & Sahtain Restaurant (12km); Tayyibeh (12km)

ONE OF THE WORLD'S SEVEN WONDERS

So it's official: Petra is now one of the new Seven Wonders of the World. At least, that's according to a popularity poll organised by the privately run New 7 Wonders Foundation in Switzerland. The winners, which include Chichen Itza in Mexico, Christ the Redeemer in Brazil, the Colosseum in Italy, the Great Wall of China, Machu Picchu in Peru and the Taj Mahal in India, were selected in 2007 through a staggering 100 million votes cast by internet or telephone – the largest such poll on record.

To qualify for nomination, each wonder had to be manmade, completed before 2000 and in an 'acceptable state of preservation'. Jordan's nomination of Petra was a consistent favourite throughout the campaign, although it's a mystery how 14 million votes were cast from within a country of under 7 million people.

Already a list of seven *natural* wonders is being compiled, and authorities in Wadi Rum are eagerly eyeing the prize. The boost the 7 Wonders project has brought to local tourism is undeniable: 'I changed my name to Seven Wonders', said one café owner in Petra, 'in celebration of our success', and he's not the only one cashing in. Prices have risen and hotels are full, and that is at least partly thanks to Petra's newly endorsed status as one of the world's best-loved treasures.

several souvenir shops and toilets. The tourist police centre is opposite and there is a small post office behind the centre.

The Housing Bank (Visa; Map p378) and Jordan Islamic Bank (Visa and MasterCard; Map p378), up from the Shaheed roundabout, are good places to change money and both have ATMs. There are a couple of banks (but no ATMs) at the lower end of town near Petra. There are several internet cafés in Wadi Musa including **Rum Internet** (Map p378; per hr JD1; 10am-midnight), located downhill from Shaheed roundabout. **Seven Wonders Restaurant** (per hr JD3.50; 9am-11pm), near the entrance to Petra, a few doors up from the Mövenpick, serves a luxury hot chocolate (JD2.50). The **Wadi Musa Pharmacy** (Map p378) has a wide range of medications and toiletries and is located near the Shaheed roundabout.

Sights

PETRA

The spectacular sandstone city of Petra (Map p374) was built in the 3rd century BC by the Nabataeans, who carved palaces, temples, tombs, storerooms and stables from the sandstone cliffs. From here, they commanded the trade routes from Damascus to Arabia, and great spice, silk and slave caravans passed through, paying taxes and protection money. In a short time, the Nabataeans made great advances – they mastered hydraulic engineering, iron production, copper refining, sculpture and stone carving. Archaeologists believe that several earthquakes, including a massive one in AD 555, forced the inhabitants to abandon the city.

The ticket office is in Petra visitor centre. Admission fees are JD21/26/31 for a one-/two-/three-day pass (subsequent days are free with the three-day pass). Multiday tickets are nontransferable and signatures are checked. Children under 15 years are free.

The Site

You approach Petra through the legendary 1.2km-long, high-sided **Siq**. This is not a canyon but rather a rock landmass that has been rent apart by tectonic forces. Just as you start to think there's no end to the Siq, you catch breathtaking glimpses ahead of the most impressive of Petra's sights, the **Treasury**, known locally as Al-Khazneh. Carved out of iron-laden sandstone to serve as a tomb, the Treasury gets its name from the misguided local belief that an Egyptian pharaoh hid his treasure in the top urn. The Greek-style pillars, alcoves and plinths are truly masterpieces of masonry work.

From the Treasury, the way broadens into the **Outer Siq**, riddled by over 40 tombs known collectively as the **Street of Facades**. Just before you reach the weatherworn 7000-seat **Theatre**, notice a set of steps on the left. These ascend to the **High Place of Sacrifice**, a hill-top altar, an easy but steep 45-minute climb. Descend on the other side of the mountain via the **Garden Tomb**, **Soldier's**

SUGGESTED ITINERARIES IN PETRA

Instead of trying to see all the top spots, spare time to amble among unnamed tombs, have a picnic in the shade of a flowering oleander or sip tea and watch everyone else trying to 'see it all'. Begin early: the tour buses arrive between 8am and 9am and the Siq is best experienced before the crowds arrive. The Treasury is sunlit until 10am, while the Monastery and Royal Tombs are at their best after 3pm. The following suggestions combine obvious highlights with some off-the-beaten track exploration.

Half-Day (Five Hours)

Amble through the Siq, absorbing its special atmosphere and savouring the moment of revelation at the Treasury. Resist the temptation to head for the Theatre; instead, climb the steps to the High Place of Sacrifice. Pause for tea by the Obelisks and take the path into Wadi Farasa, enjoying wild flowers and the Garden Tomb en route. The path reaches the colonnaded street via a paintbox of rock formations. If there's time remaining, visit the Royal Tombs then return to the valley floor for a chat with Bedouin stallholders and a hunt for the perfect sand bottle.

One Day (Eight Hours)

Spend the morning completing the half-day itinerary but pack a picnic. After visiting the Royal Tombs, walk along to Qasr al-Bint and hike along the broad wadi that leads to Jebel Haroun as far as the Snake Monument – an ideal perch for a snack and a snooze. Return to Qasr al-Bint and slip into the nearby Nabataean Museum, saving some energy for the climb to the Monastery, a fitting finale for any visit to Petra.

Two Days

Spend a second day scrambling through exciting Wadi Muthlim and restore energies over a barbeque in the Basin Restaurant. Walk off lunch while exploring the hidden beauty of Wadi Siyagh with its pools of water, before strolling back along the Street of Facades. Sit in the Theatre to watch the sun go down on the Royal Tombs opposite – the best spectacle in Petra.

Tomb and **Garden Triclinium** and follow your nose back to the Street of Façades, not far after the Theatre.

Almost opposite the Theatre, you'll notice another set of steps that lead to a fine set of tomb facades cut into the cliffs above. These belong to the **Royal Tombs** and are worth a visit not just as they illustrate some of the best carving in Petra, but also because they give access to another of the city's mystic high places. To climb to the plateau above the Royal Tombs (one hour roundtrip), go past the **Urn Tomb** with its arched portico and look stairs just after the three-storey **Palace Tomb**. If the tea vendor at the top is available, ask him to show you an aerial view of the Treasury. Return the way you came or search out a set of worn steps leading down a gully to the Urn Tomb.

Returning to the Theatre, the main path turns west along the **colonnaded street**, which was once lined with shops, passing the rubble of the **nymphaeum** en route to the elevated **Great Temple** and the **Temple of the Winged Lions** on the opposite side of the wadi. At the end of the colonnaded street, on the left, is the imposing Nabataean temple known locally as **Qasr al-Bint** – one of the few free-standing structures in Petra.

From Qasr al-Bint, the path leads towards two restaurants, on either side of the wadi. The one on the left is the **Nabataean Tent Restaurant** (lunch buffet JD10, drinks JD2; 11.00am-4pm); the one on the right is the more up-market **Basin Restaurant** (lunch buffet JD12.800, fresh orange juice JD2.500; 11.00am-4pm), run by the Crown Plaza Resort. Both offer a good range of salads and hot dishes. If these don't appeal, there are plenty of stalls dotted around the site where you can buy water, herb tea and minimal snacks.

Behind the Nabataean Tent Restaurant is the small hill of Al-Habis (the prison). A set of steps winds up to **Al-Habis Museum** (8am-4pm), the smaller of Petra's two museums. From here you can take a path anticlockwise around the hill with fine views overlooking fertile **Wadi Siyagh**. Eventually you will come to another set of steps to the top of a hill, the site of a ruined **Crusader fort**, built in AD 1116. The views across Petra are spectacular. Allow an hour to circumnavigate the hill and reach the fort.

Beside the Basin Restaurant is the **Nabataean Museum** (9am-5pm Apr-Sep, to 4pm Oct-Mar), the opening to Wadi Siyagh and the start of the winding path that climbs to one of Petra's most beloved monuments, the **Monastery**. Known locally as Al-Deir, the Monastery is reached by a rock-cut staircase (a 45-minute walk to the top) and is best seen in late afternoon when the sun draws out the colour of the sandstone. Built as a tomb around 86 BC, with its enormous facade, it was most probably used as a church in Byzantine times (hence the name). Spare ten minutes to walk over to the two **viewpoints** on the nearby cliff tops. From here you can see the magnificent rock formations of Petra, Jebel Haroun and even Wadi Araba. On the way back down, look out for the **Lion Tomb** in a gully near the bottom of the path.

LONGER HIKES

There are numerous hikes into the hills and siqs around Petra. You need a guide for any hikes requiring overnight stops (it's not permitted to camp within Petra itself), but there are many other smaller trails that can be easily hiked alone.

This adventurous scramble through **Wadi Muthlim** to the Royal Tombs (1½ hours) is an exciting alternative route into Petra if you've already taken the main path through the Siq. The hike is not difficult or strenuous, but there are several places where you'll need to lower yourself down oversized boulders. Don't attempt the hike if it's been raining or is likely to rain. The trail starts by entering the **Nabataean Tunnel**, by the dam just before the entrance to the Siq. Turn left at the painted arrow at a junction at the narrowest part of the trail.

Longer hikes include the long haul up **Umm al-Biyara** (a steep hour each way) and the day return hike to **Jebel Haroun**, crowned

FIVE TIPS ON PETRA FROM TRAVELLERS

Imagine ancient caravans Hidden in the sandstone wilderness of Jordan is the ancient trading city of Petra, whose buildings and beautiful facades were carved out of the rock. Do yourself a favour and spend a few days exploring it while imagining the bustle of caravans full of exotic merchandise.

Wornoutboots79

Be there at the end of the day The Red Rose City turns into a palette of deep colours as the day ends. The sun's rays reach into areas of the carved facades unseen in the harsh desert light, and as the sun sets, a band of golden light gradually snakes to the top of the valley.

mscott

Pretend to be Indiana Jones Visiting the ancient ruins of Petra was a dream come true. No really, since watching *Indiana Jones* it was a lifetime goal! The immense structures carved straight out of the mountain side were stunning, and yup I saw where they filmed.

evilthecat

Give yourself time Give yourself at least three days, and explore the farther-off bits. Tip: hire a donkey if you're too tired to climb up all the steps to the Monastery. In decent shape? Then ask a local for the 'secret' path [above Royal Tombs] to overlook the Treasury.

santamonica811

Watch the sunset A beautiful and surprisingly peaceful view is from the main road south of Wadi Musa. The sun turned the rocks from red into a spectacular glowing red as it slowly sunk behind mountains into Wadi Araba.

louby_lou35

What's your recommendation?
www.lonelyplanet.com/middle-east

with the tomb of the biblical prophet Aaron (known to Muslims as Prophet Haroun). For each of these trails, walk to the Snake Monument and ask local Bedouin for the trailhead or follow a network of paths towards the obvious high points.

Sleeping

Prices for hotels in Wadi Musa fluctuate wildly, depending on the season and amount of business. Discounts are common.

BUDGET

Unless otherwise noted, all the following hotels are in Wadi Musa village, close to the central Shaheed Roundabout.

Valentine Inn (Map p378; ☎ 2156423; valentineinn@hotmail.com; s/d/tr JD10/15/18, dm without breakfast from JD3; V) Still struggling to slough off its past image as a hostel mainly for men, the Valentine is the quintessential backpackers' hotel with a raft of add-on services, including tours along the King's Highway. Rooftop sleeping costs JD2; the excellent vegetarian dinner is JD4.

Cleopetra Hotel (Map p378; ☎ 2157090; www.cleopetra.jeeran.com; s/d/tr JD12/16/21) One of the friendliest budget hotels in town, small rooms all have private bathroom (with hot water) or you can sleep on the roof (JD4, or JD5 with breakfast). There's a cosy communal sitting area that feels like your aunt's front room. Their recommended tours to Wadi Rum take the hassle out of finding transport.

Al-Anbat Hotel II (Map p378; ☎ 2157200; www.alanbat.com; s/d/tr JD15/20/30; breakfast JD1) The bright, white-marble lobby promises better accommodation than the rooms deliver – particularly as the plumbing needs attention and the staff are conspicuous by their absence. The double rooms at the front aren't bad and the excellent Salome Turkish Bath (JD20) is opposite.

Al-Anbat Hotel I (Map p378; ☎ 2156265; www.alanbat.com; s/d/tr JD18/30/36; buffet dinner JD6) Located out of town on the road between 'Ain Musa and Wadi Musa, this three-storey resort offers large rooms (mostly with views) with satellite TV and balconies. There's a Turkish bath (JD18 for guests) and small pool. Free transport to/from Petra is available. Campers (per person JD5) and camper vans are welcome, and there is access to toilets, showers and a kitchen.

MIDRANGE

El-Rashid Hotel (Map p378; ☎ 2156800; wailln@hotmail.com; Shaheed roundabout; s/d/tr from JD20/35/45) This is a well-run, friendly hotel with attractive, marble-floored lobby and elegant furniture. The rooms are not so appealing but the satellite TV will take your mind off the bright green walls.

Petra Moon Hotel (Map p374; ☎ 2156220; www.petramoonhotel.com; s/d/tr JD25/35/45) Behind the Mövenpick Hotel, this hotel is convenient for the entrance to Petra and is perennially popular with travellers (reservations advisable), who congregate in the foyer. The comfortable rooms have fridge, TV and two windows, good for enjoying the sunset.

our pick **Amra Palace Hotel** (Map p378; ☎ 2157070; www.amrapalace.com; s/d JD42/65; d with extra bed JD90;) This lovely hotel lives up to its name with magnificent lobby, marble pillars, giant brass coffeepots and Damascene-style furniture. Each room has spotless linen that's changed every day (there's a laundry on site), wooden headboards, upholstered furniture and satellite TV. Services include heated pool, Jacuzzi, summer terrace and an excellent Turkish bath (per person JD20). There is also a fun, cave-style internet café. With pretty gardens of roses and jasmine, this is undoubtedly one of the nicest hotels in Wadi Musa.

Petra Palace Hotel (Map p374; ☎ 2156723; www.petrapalace.com.jo; s/d/tr JD42/63/85;) Located 500m from the entrance to Petra, this attractive hotel, with its palm-tree entrance and helpful management, has a bar and restaurant. The corridors are a bit tired but the rooms are newly renovated. 'Garden rooms' open onto a terrace with two swimming pools.

TOP END

Petra Guest House (Map p374; ☎ 2156266; www.crowneplaza.com; s/d/t JD120/150/180;) You can't sleep closer to the entrance to Petra without bedding down in a cave. Although not of the same quality, the guesthouse does offer use of the Crown Plaza Resort Hotel's facilities. Choose from motel-like chalets or rooms in the recently renovated main building.

Mövenpick Hotel (Map p374; ☎ 2157111; www.moevenpick-petra.com; s/d JD155/170; V) This beautifully crafted, Arabian-style hotel, 100m from the entrance to Petra, is worth a visit simply to admire the inlaid furniture, marble fountains, wooden screens, antique dishes and brass salvers. There's a children's playground and small arcade of quality gift shops. The buffet breakfast and dinner are exceptional.

Sofitel Taybet Zaman (Map p374; ☎ 2150111; reservation@taybetzaman.com; s/d US$180/200; extra bed US$53; V) One of the most distinctive hotels in Jordan, the Taybet Zaman is a stylish reconstruction of a traditional Ottoman stone village, with luxurious and spacious rooms, handicraft shops and Turkish bath. The hotel is located in Tayyibeh village; a taxi from Petra (10km) costs about JD10 one way. Even if you don't stay, it's worth visiting the terrace restaurant called Sahtain, with its cavernous, vaulted interior. Simple fare for lunch includes the chef's salad (JD2.700), and there's a dinner buffet (JD19).

Eating

Central Wadi Musa is dotted with grocery stores where you can stock up for a picnic at Petra. There's a supermarket next to Al-Anbat Hotel I, slightly out of town on the road to 'Ain Musa.

Al-Afandi Quick Restaurant (Map p378; meals from JD2) A simple and friendly place located off the Shaheed roundabout, offering hummus, felafel and shwarma.

Al-Wadi Restaurant (Map p378; ☎ 2157151; salads JD1, mains JD4-5; 7am-late) Right on Shaheed roundabout, this lively spot offers pasta and pizza, as well as a range of vegetarian dishes and local Bedouin specialties such as *gallayah* (a traditional meal of chicken with tomatoes, other vegetables, garlic and Arabic spices) and *mensaf*, most of which come with salad and rice. The similar **Al-Arabi Restaurant** (Map p378; ☎ 2157661; mains from JD1; 6am-midnight) next door offers discounts to repeat customers.

Red Cave Restaurant (Map p374; ☎ 2157799; starters JD1, mains JD4-5; 9am-10pm) Cavernous, cool and friendly, this restaurant specialises in local Bedouin specialties including *mensaf* and *maqlubbeh*. Located very near the main entrance to Petra, it makes a good meeting point.

The **Oriental Restaurant** (Map p374; ☎ 2157087; mains JD4-5, pizzas from JD2.500; 11am-9.30pm), together with neighbouring **Sandstone Restaurant** (Map p374; ☎ 079 5542277; starters/mains JD1/6; 8.00am-midnight), offers simple fare of tasty mixed grills, salad and mezze with pleasant outdoor seating. These are good places for a beer (spare a good-natured chuckle at the English spelling of the menus).

Mystic Pizza (Map p374; ☎ 2155757; JD3-8; 8.30am-11pm; V) A welcoming new establishment serving fresh, tasty pizza including good vegetarian choices.

Consider cooking your own food (Jordanian mezze, soup and main course) at **Petra Kitchen** (Map p374; ☎ 2155700; www.petrakitchen.com; cookery course per person JD30; V). Located 100m from the Mövenpick Hotel, Petra Kitchen offers nightly cookery courses run by local chefs in a relaxed family-style atmosphere. Dishes change daily and the evening starts at 6.30pm (7.30pm in summer). The price

PETRA BY NIGHT

Like a grumbling camel caravan of snorting, coughing, laughing and farting miscreants, 200 people and one jubilantly crying baby make their way down the Siq 'in silence'. Asked to walk in single file behind the leader, breakaway contingents surge ahead to make sure they enjoy the experience 'on their own'. And eventually, sitting in 'reverential awe' outside the Treasury, the collected company shows their appreciation of Arabic classical music by lighting cigarettes from the paper-bag lanterns, chatting energetically, flashing cameras, and audibly farting some more. Welcome to public entertainment in the Middle East! If you really want the Siq to yourself, come in the winter, go at 2pm in the afternoon or take a virtual tour on the internet.

But silence and solitude is not what Petra by Night is all about. What this highly memorable tour does give you is the opportunity of experiencing one of the most sublime spectacles on earth in the fever of other people's excitement. As you pass huddles of whispering devotees staring up at the candlelit god blocks, help an elderly participant over a polished lozenge of paving stone, or hear the flute waft along the neck-hairs of fellow celebrants, this is surely much nearer to the original experience of the ancient city of Petra than walking through the icy stone corridor alone.

includes food and soft drinks, and best of all, you can skip the washing up.

Spare ten minutes between courses to nip upstairs to **Made in Jordan** (Map p374; ☎ 2155700; 10am-10pm) and select some olive oil from this excellent local craft shop.

Drinking

There's not a lot to do in the evening, other than recover from aching muscles and plan your next day in Petra. Most budget hotels screen *Indiana Jones and the Last Crusade* nightly until everyone is sick of it.

our pick **Cave Bar** (Map p374; ☎ 2156266; 8am-midnight; beer JD4.500, cocktail JD7, plus 26% tax & service) You can't come to Petra and miss the oldest bar in the world. Occupying a 2000-year-old Nabataean rock tomb, this blue-lit Petra hotspot has been known to stay open until 4am on busy summer nights. Sit among the spirits, alcoholic or otherwise, and you'll soon be getting a flavour of Petra you hadn't bargained on – the tasty Bedouin menu keeps them at bay. There's live Bedouin music from 9pm (except Saturday). The bar is next to the entrance to Petra Guest House, behind Petra visitor centre.

If you haven't seen enough of the old city for one day, consider taking the popular tour, **Petra by Night** (adult/child under 12 JD12/free), which starts from Petra visitor centre at 8.30pm on Monday, Wednesday and Thursday nights (cancelled when raining), and lasts two hours. It takes you along the Siq (lined with 1500 candles) as far as the Treasury in as much silence as is possible given the crowds.

Getting There & Away

A daily JETT bus connects Amman with Petra, largely designed for those wanting to visit on a day trip. The service leaves at 6.30am from Abdali Bus Station (single/return JD6/11) and drops passengers off at Petra visitor centre in Wadi Musa at 9.30am. The return bus leaves at 4.30pm.

Minibuses generally leave from the bus station in central Wadi Musa (Map p378). About eleven minibuses travel every day between Amman (Wahadat station) and Wadi Musa (JD5, three-four hours) via the Desert Highway. These buses leave Amman and Wadi Musa when full every hour or so between 6am and 1pm.

Minibuses leave Wadi Musa for Ma'an (JD1, 45 minutes) fairly frequently throughout the day (more often in the morning), stopping briefly at the university, about 10km from Ma'an. From Ma'an there are connections to Amman, Aqaba and (indirectly) Wadi Rum. Minibuses also leave Wadi Musa for Aqaba (JD4, two hours), via Tayyibeh, at about 6.30am, 8.30am and 3pm – ask around the day before to confirm or check through your hotel.

For Wadi Rum (JD4, 1½ hours), there is a daily minibus sometime around 6.30am. It's a good idea to reserve a seat the day before – your hotel should be able to contact the driver. Be wary of anyone charging you extra for 'luggage', offering to buy you overpriced water or hooking you onto a substandard tour – common complaints made by many readers. If you miss this bus, or the service isn't operating, take the minibus to Aqaba, get off at the Ar-Rashidiyyah junction and catch another minibus (or hitch) the remainder of the journey to Rum Village.

To Karak, a minibus sometimes leaves at around 8am (JD3), but demand is low so it doesn't leave every day. Alternatively, travel via Ma'an.

Getting Around

The standard, non-negotiable taxi fare from Petra to central Wadi Musa is JD1.

WADI RUM وادي رم

☎ 03

Western visitors have been fascinated by the magnificent desert and mountain landscape of Wadi Rum ever since TE Lawrence wrote so evocatively about its sculpted rocks, dunes and Bedouin encampments in *Seven Pillars of Wisdom* in the early 20th century. Lean's film, *Lawrence of Arabia*, which was party filmed here, not only contributed to the myth of the man who took part in the Arab Revolt but also gave epic status to Wadi Rum itself.

Wadi Rum is everything you'd expect of a quintessential desert: its extreme of summer heat and winter cold; violent and moody as the sun slices through chiselled siqs in the early morning or melts the division between rock and sand at sunset; exacting on the Bedouin who live in it, and vengeful on those who ignore its dangers. For most visitors, on half- or whole-day trips from Aqaba or Petra, Wadi Rum offers one of the easiest and safest glimpses of the desert afforded in the region. For those who can afford a day or two to sleep over at one of the desert camps, it can be an unforgettable way of stripping the soul back to basics.

Information

Admission to **Wadi Rum Protected Area** (per person JD2) is strictly controlled and all vehicles, camels and guides must be arranged either through or with the approval of the **visitor centre** (☎ 2090600; www.wadirum.jo; 🕑 7am-7pm), 7km before Rum Village.

Most people visit the desert as part of a 4WD trip arranged on arrival at the visitor centre; half-/full-day excursions cost around JD67/80. Prices are regulated, but do not include overnight stays in a Bedouin camp (around JD30 extra).

Baggy trousers or skirts and modest shirts or blouses, besides preventing serious sunburn, will earn you more respect from the conservative Bedouin, especially out in the desert.

Sights

Named in honour of Lawrence's book, the **Seven Pillars of Wisdom** is the large rock formation, with seven fluted turrets, easy to spot from the visitor centre. Farther along Wadi Rum, the enormous, dramatic **Jebel Rum** (1754m) towers above Rum Village. Of the sites closest to Rum Village (distances from the Rest House in brackets), there's a 1st-century BC **Nabataean temple** (400m) and good views from **Lawrence's Spring** (3km), named after Lawrence because he wrote so invitingly of it in *Seven Pillars of Wisdom*.

Further afield, the main highlights accessible by 4WD include:

Barrah Siq (14km) A long, picturesque canyon accessible on foot or by camel.

Burdah Rock Bridge (19km) This impressive 80m-high bridge can be viewed from the desert floor or, better still, you can scramble up to it with a guide (one hour).

Jebel Khazali (7km) Narrow siq with rock inscriptions.

Lawrence's House/Al-Qsair (9km) Legend has it that Lawrence stayed here during the Desert Revolt. The remote location and supreme views of the red sands are the main attraction.

Sand Dunes/Red Sands (6km) Superb red sand dunes on the slopes of Jebel Umm Ulaydiyya that seem to catch alight at sunset.

Sunset & Sunrise Points (11km) The places to be at dawn and dusk if you want to see the desert at its most colourful.

Umm Fruth Rock Bridge (13km) Smaller and more visited than Burdah, this bridge is tucked into an intimate corner of the desert.

Wadak Rock Bridge (9km) Easy to climb, this little rock bridge offers magnificent views across the valley.

Activities

If you don't fancy a 4x4 tour, there are several rewarding hikes in the area, though bear in mind that many of them require walking through soft sand – a tiring activity at the best of times and dangerously exhausting in the summer. Ask at the visitor centre for information on the great three-hour loop **hike** from the visitor centre to the **Seven Pillars of Wisdom** and up **Makharas Canyon** (take the left branch of the wadi), curving around the northern tip of Jebel Umm al-Ishrin back to the visitor centre.

MODERN CARETAKERS OF THE DESERT *Jenny Walker*

Pulling up outside an enclosure on the edge of Diseh, Mr Zawaedh proudly inspected the newest member of the community. The small bundle of pale fur and oversized legs belonged to a two-day-old camel, shivering in the winter winds. 'I call him Ibn Jinny, son of Jenny,' he said. I took this as a compliment and mused that this man belonged to roughly the same tribe of people whom Lawrence had called 'uncompromising, hard-headed' and 'unsentimental'. As I settled down to a glass of tea in time-honoured fashion, the more familiar Bedouin epithets of 'kind and hospitable' sprang to mind.

The Bedouin are universally proud of their claim to the area and welcoming to guests who visit it. Not surprising, then, that many of the 5000 Bedouin currently living in the area now make a living from tourism. 'This is the Bedouin life,' enthused one camp owner. 'This is our art, our craft, to reveal the wonders of Wadi Rum.' For centuries the Bedouin have been doing the same, offering bread and salt to those in need, knowing they can expect the same in return. The currency today is usually money, but the principle of easing the passage of strangers through traditional tribal territories remains unchanged.

Of course, the changes have required sacrifices. As we sat on the edge of the great arena of sand in the heart of Wadi Rum, our host cast a wistful eye over the landscape: 'Life before was simple and free,' he said, fidgeting with a mobile phone and a possible booking for the family camp. 'We managed goats and sheep and looked for water. Now there's education and working with tourists, even tribal conferences in New York – there's more money, but it's hard.' For most people, 'hard' means a goat-hair bed and scorpions, insufferable heat and freezing nights, not enough to eat and being forever thirsty. But for the few who are still brought up that way, this is the life where the 'herdsmen sing'.

We watched a camel drift across the horizon. 'Where is he going?' I asked. 'Probably south to Saudi Arabia.' 'How will you get him back?' 'He comes back when he's ready – in one month, or in six. We'll find him or he'll find us.' A wheatear hopped onto the rock and called out for prayers and our host dutifully disappeared to perform ablutions. Clearly and thankfully, it's going to take more than a computer and a tribal conference in New York to take the nomad out of the Bedouin: like the camel that returns when ready, the Bedouin know where home is.

With a guide you can make the excellent rock scramble through **Rakhabat Canyon**, crossing through Jebel Umm al-Ishrin.

A **camel ride** offers one of the best ways to understand the rhythms of the desert. A one-hour trip to the Alameleh rock inscriptions, for example, costs JD7. Full-day camel hire costs JD20 per day – see the rates posted at the visitor centre.

For ideas on more adventurous trips, see www.bedouinroads.com.

Sleeping

There are no hotels in Wadi Rum, but camping can range from a goat-hair blanket under the stars at an isolated Bedouin camp to a mattress under partitioned canvas in a 'party tent' in the neighbouring district of Diseh. Mattress, blankets and food are provided but bring your own linen.

Rest House (☎ 2018867; bedding in 2-person tent per person JD3) The frayed tents here offer the most accessible accommodation, recommended if you arrive in Wadi Rum too late to head into the desert. Pitch your own tent for JD1 (includes use of toilets and showers).

Mohammed Mutlak Camp (☎ 077 7424837; www.wadirum.org) This camp is in a beautiful spot overlooking Jebel Qattar. Half board costs JD30 per person, and dinner often includes delicious lamb cooked in a *zarb* (ground-oven). Transport by 4WD to the camp is free if you don't visit anywhere en route, or you could come by camel (JD20, two hours 15 minutes). There's no electricity but light is provided by gas lamp.

Sunset Camp (☎ 2032961, 079 5502421; www.mohammedwadirum.8m.com) This desert camp, around 12km from Rum village, has been recommended by many travellers. Prices, which include half-/full-day jeep excursions, accommodation and meals, are dependent on the size of your group. Call ahead for a quote.

our pick **Bait Ali** (☎ 2022626, 079 5548133; www.desertexplorer.net; half board in tent/chalet JD25/27;

☎ V) Tucked behind a hill, with a sublime view of the desert, this upmarket, eco-friendly camp is signposted 15km from the Desert Highway and 9km from the Wadi Rum visitor centre. The accommodation (either in army tents or twin-bed cabins) is basic but spotless as are the hot-water shower blocks. The facilities include an excellent restaurant with extensive nightly barbecue and a bar.

The following three desert camps are near the village of Diseh – clearly signposted off the Wadi Rum approach road, 16km from the Desert Highway. Hitch a ride near the police checkpoint to the village (8km – be prepared for a wait), or request someone from the camp to meet you.

Zawaideh Desert Camp (☎ 0795840664; zawaideh_camp@yahoo.com; half board per person JD14) This is a simple but atmospheric camp in the undercliff of the escarpment, on the edge of a wide plain.

Barrh Camp (☎ 079 5413563; hzawaydeh@yahoo.com; half board per person JD25) This small camp is run by Hilal Zawaedh, the president of the Diseh Village Touristic Cooperative (contact Mr Hilal with queries regarding any camps in Diseh). Tucked discreetly at the end of Siq Umm Tawaqi, beside a giant vertical slice of rock, the camp is within walking distance of some fine rock inscriptions.

Captain's Camp (☎ 2016905, 0795510432; captains@jo.com.jo; half board per person JD30) A well-run midrange camp with hot showers, a clean bathroom block and good buffets; popular with large tour groups. Contact Rafiq Suleiman.

Eating

Rest House (☎/fax 2018867; breakfast/lunch/dinner buffet JD3/8/10; 6am-midnight) Dining here is open air and buffet style. Sipping a large Amstel beer (JD2.500) while watching the sun's rays light up Jebel Umm al-Ishrin is the perfect way to finish off the day.

Rum Gate Restaurant (☎ 2015995; Wadi Rum visitor centre; buffet lunch JD10; 8am-5pm; V) Tasty dishes are offered in the buffet between noon and 4pm (popular with tour groups). Outside this time, the restaurant is buzzing with guides, weary hikers and independent travellers who congregate over a nonalcoholic beer (JD2) and a chicken sandwich (JD4.500). Profits contribute towards upkeep of the protected area.

Getting There & Away

At the time of research, there was at least one minibus a day to Aqaba (JD1.500, one hour) at around 7.30am; a second one may run at 8.30am. To Wadi Musa (JD5, 1½ hours), there is a fairly reliable daily minibus at 8.30am. Check current departure times at the visitor centre or Rest House when you arrive in Wadi Rum.

For Ma'an, Karak or Amman, the minibuses to either Aqaba or Wadi Musa can drop you off at the Ar-Rashidiyya crossroads with the Desert Highway (JD1.500, 20 minutes), where it is easy to hail onward transport.

Occasionally, taxis wait at the visitor centre (and sometimes the Rest House) for for a fare back to where they came from – normally Aqaba, Wadi Musa or Ma'an. It costs about JD25 to Aqaba and JD40 to Wadi Musa (Petra). A taxi from Rum village to the Ar-Rashidiyya crossroads with the Desert Highway costs around JD5.

AQABA العقبة

☎ 03 / pop 105,000

Aqaba is the most important city in southern Jordan and, with feverish development underway, is being groomed as the country's second city, if not in size at least in terms of status, revenue and tourism potential. Perched on the edge of the Gulf of Aqaba, ringed by high desert mountains and enjoying a pleasant climate for most of the year, Aqaba has what it takes to make a major resort. That's a fact not lost on hotel chains: a new InterContinental hotel is up and running and a neighbouring Kempinski hotel is nearly complete.

Surprisingly, given this radical makeover, Aqaba retains the relaxed small-town atmosphere of a popular, local holiday destination. For the visitor, although there's not much to see as such, it offers a sociable stopover en route to the diving and snorkelling clubs to the south or the big destinations of Wadi Rum and Petra to the northeast. It's also an obvious place to break a journey to/from Egypt, or Israel and the Palestinian Territories.

Information

BOOKSHOPS

Redwan Bookshop (☎ 2013704; redwanbook@hotmail.com; Zahran St; 7.30am-12.30pm & 4-9pm)

Extensive selection of newspapers, hard-to-find Jordanian titles and Lonely Planet guidebooks.

Yamani Library (☎/fax 2012221; Zahran St; 🕑 9am-2.30pm & 6-10pm)

INTERNET ACCESS

Aqaba has a good sprinkling of internet cafés, particularly along As-Sadah St, most of which charge around JD1 to JD2 per hour.

10zll internet Café (☎ 2022009; As-Sadah St; per hr JD1, 🕑 24hr) Next to Days Inn, this large establishment has coffee and soft drinks.

MONEY

There are plenty of banks (with ATMs) and moneychangers around town – see the map on p384 for locations.

POST

General post office (Al-Yarmuk St; 🕑 7.30am-7pm Sat-Thu, to 1.30pm Fri)

TOURIST INFORMATION

Tourist office (☎/fax 2013363; Baladiya Circle; 🕑 8am-2.30pm Sun-Thu) Located in a kiosk in the middle of a new park between carriageways, the brand-new tourist office has lots of leaflets and precious little else, despite friendly staff. There's another branch inside Aqaba Museum.

VISA EXTENSIONS

Aqaba is the only reliable place to get your visa extended outside Amman.

Aqaba Special Economic Zone Authority (ASEZA; ☎ 2091000; www.aqabazone.com) Behind Safeway, by the Central Bank of Jordan. You need to register here if you

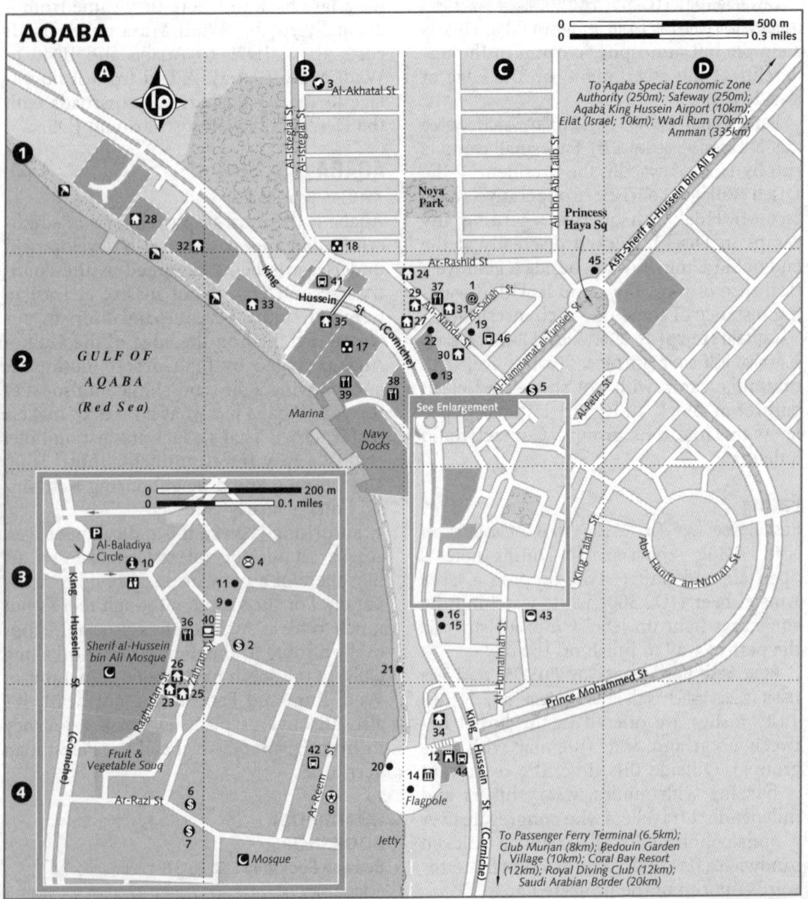

were given a free visa on arrival in Aqaba and are planning to stay in Jordan for more than 14 days (see p393).

Police station (☎ 2012411; Ar-Reem St; 🕑 7am-9pm Sat-Thu) Opposite the bus station. A three-month extension is usually available on the spot and is free. It's best to go earlier in the day (8am to 3pm).

Sights

Along King Hussein St (also known as the Corniche), and squeezed between the marina and the Mövenpick Resort, is the site of **Ayla** (Old Aqaba), which is the early medieval port city. The ruins are limited, but worth a quick look if you're passing.

Of more interest is **Aqaba Castle** (adult JD1 incl. Aqaba Museum; 🕑 8am-4pm Sat-Thu, 10am-4pm Fri), built originally by the Crusaders and expanded by the Mamluks in the early 16th century. The Ottomans occupied the castle until WWI, when it was substantially destroyed by shelling from the British Navy. The Hashemite coat of arms above the main entrance was raised soon afterwards as the Arab Revolt swept through Aqaba.

Nearby is the small but interesting **Aqaba Museum** (adult JD1 incl Aqaba Castle; 🕑 8am-4pm Sat-Thu, 10am-4pm Fri), which has a collection of artefacts including coins, late Byzantine reliefs, ceramics and stone tablets.

Activities

SWIMMING & HAMMAMS

The café-lined public beaches of Aqaba are aimed at sunset strollers rather than swimmers.

Aquamarina Beach Hotel (☎ 2016254; www.aquamarina-group.com; King Hussein St; 🕑 6am until sunset; day rate JD5) charges for use of their tiny scrap of sand, concrete pontoon, pool and restaurant.

Mövenpick Resort & Residence (☎ /fax 2034020; www.moevenpick-aqaba.com; King Hussein St; 🕑 7am until sunset; JD19) offers day use of a clean beach, three pools, health club, sauna and Jacuzzi, and includes vouchers worth JD5 for drinks.

Aqaba Turkish Baths (☎ 2031605; King Hussein St; 🕑 10am-10pm; JD12) has the full works – massage, steam bath and scrubbing – included in the rate. Readers have recommended this place highly: women and couples should call ahead for timings.

Keep your eyes skinned for the opening of the Tala Bay complex, south of Aqaba; it features a huge sandy bay in attractively landscaped gardens.

CRUISES

A company called **Sindbad** (☎ 2050077; www.sinbadjo.com; marina) operates popular cruises around the Gulf of Aqaba. Cruise prices range from JD15 per person for a two-hour sunset cruise to JD29 for a half-day trip with snorkelling (equipment is included in the cost) and barbeque. The cruises operate on a daily basis and depart from the end of the pier. Make sure that you buy your ticket half an hour before departure (1pm for the barbeque trip; 6pm for a sunset cruise).

INFORMATION

10zII Internet Café	1	C2
Arab Bank	2	B3
Arab Bank ATM	(see 28)	
Egyptian Consulate	3	B1
General Post Office	4	B3
Jordan Islamic Bank	5	C2
Jordan National Bank	6	A4
Moneychangers	7	A4
Police Station	8	B4
Redwan Bookshop	9	B3
Tourist Office	10	A3
Tourist Office	(see 14)	
Yamani Library	11	B3

SIGHTS & ACTIVITIES

Aqaba Castle	12	C4
Aqaba International Dive Centre	13	C2
Aqaba Museum	14	C4
Aqaba Turkish Baths	15	C3
Arab Divers	16	C3
Ayla (Old Aqaba) Ruins	17	B2
Ayla (Old Aqaba) Ruins (Old Church)	18	B1
Dive Aqaba	19	C2
Glass-bottom Boat Dock	20	B4
Glass-bottom Boats	21	B3
Red Sea Diving Centre	22	C2

SLEEPING

Al-Amer Hotel	23	A4
Al-Cazar Hotel	24	C2
Al-Kholil Hotel	25	A4
Al-Shula Hotel	26	A3
Aqaba Gulf Hotel	27	C2
Aquamarina Beach Hotel	28	A1
Aquamarina IV	29	C2
Captain's Hotel	30	C2
Golden Tulip	31	C2
Intercontinental Hotel	32	A1
Kempinski Hotel (under construction)	33	B2
Moon Beach Hotel	34	C4
Mövenpick Resort & Residence	35	B2

EATING

Al-Tarboosh Restaurant	36	A3
Floka Restaurant	37	C2
Formosa Restaurant	38	B2
Royal Yacht Club Restaurant	39	B2
Syrian Palace Restaurant	(see 26)	

DRINKING

Al-Fardos Coffee Shop	40	B3
Friends	(see 38)	

TRANSPORT

JETT	41	B2
Main Bus/Minibus Station	42	B4
Minibus/Service Taxi Station (to Karak & Safi)	43	C3
Minibuses (to Ferry Terminal, Southern Beaches & Royal Diving Club)	44	C4
Royal Jordanian	45	C2
Sindbad	(see 38)	
Trust International Transport	46	C2

JORDAN

GLASS-BOTTOM BOATS

If you can't spare time to go diving or snorkelling, the next best thing is a glass-bottom boat. Hire a boat for at least two to three hours to see the best fish.

Boats, which operate between 6.30am and 5pm, congregate along the central public beach or at a jetty in front of Aqaba Castle. The posted rate for a boat (holding about 10 people) is JD10/15/25 (half hour/45 minutes/hour). A three-hour trip costs JD75 and a half-day trip is JD100. Bring a swim suit and snorkelling equipment.

DIVING & SNORKELLING

According to the **Jordan Royal Ecological Society** (☎ 06-5679142; www.jreds.org), the Gulf of Aqaba has over 110 species of hard coral, 120 species of soft coral and about 1000 species of fish with some superb sites for diving and snorkelling. Access is south of the town centre and ferry-passenger terminal.

Aqaba's dive agencies are very professional. A one-/two-tank shore dive costs around JD20/35 and an additional JD10 for full equipment rental. Night dives and PADI courses (around JD200) are available.

Aqaba International Dive Centre (☎ 2031213; www.aqabadiving center.com; King Hussein St) Popular, well equipped and easily one of Aqaba's best.

Arab Divers (☎ 2031808; www.aqaba-arabdivers.com; King Hussein St) Highly recommended by readers year after year.

Dive Aqaba (☎ 079 6600701; www.diveaqaba.com; As-Sadah St) Known for its teaching staff.

Red Sea Diving Centre (☎ 2022323; off King Hussein St)

Royal Diving Club (☎ 2017035; www.rdc.jo) Twelve kilometres south of the city, this is virtually an institution.

For snorkelling, all the places listed above rent out flippers, mask and snorkel for JD3 to JD5 per day. Some offer snorkelling boat trips for around JD20 per person.

JORDAN

Sleeping

BUDGET

Unless otherwise stated, places listed here offer (nonsatellite) TV, air-conditioning and private bathroom with hot water (not always reliable); they don't include breakfast.

Al-Amer Hotel (☎ /fax 2014821; Raghadan St; s/d/tr JD12/15/20; ❄) Don't get too excited at the powder-blue reception with its chandelier: the French Rococo stops here! That said, the bright, clean rooms, especially at the front, make this a quality budget option. If you get peckish in the night, the Syrian Palace Restaurant (opposite) is right next door.

Al-Kholil Hotel (☎ /fax 2030152; Zahran St; s/d/tr JD14/16/22; ❄) This very basic hotel is central, at least. The low ceilings are a serious inconvenience to tall people. If you ignore the damp patches on the wall, this is a clean option if you get stuck for somewhere cheap.

Moon Beach Hotel (☎ 2013316; ashraf.saad77@yahoo.com; King Hussein St; s/d/tr JD17/25/30; ❄) Nearly next to the castle, this is undoubtedly the best of the budget options. The rooms mostly have sea views, satellite TV, a fridge and soap, though the dark-red furnishings won't be everyone's taste! The delightful management makes up for the dodgy decor.

Al-Shula Hotel (☎ 2015153; alshula@wanadoo.jo; Raghadan St; s/d/tr JD20/27/34; ❄) With its black-and-white marble reception desk, the hotel promises well but the rest is rather utilitarian. The rooms have TV and fridge, and most have good views.

Bedouin Garden Village (☎ 079 5602521; per person campsites/dm/r JD3/12/36; meals around JD5; 🅿 ❄) Sun worshippers and dive bums will love this funky spot on the coast between Aqaba port and Tala Bay. With cosy rooms and camping pitches, the appeal of the village is swapping stories with fellow travellers beneath the Bedouin tent.

MIDRANGE

The following places have a fridge, satellite TV, telephone and hot water, and prices include breakfast.

Al-Cazar Hotel (☎ 2014131; www.alcazarhotel.com; An-Nahda St; s/d/tr from JD25/35/45; ❄ 🅿) If you're looking for somewhere characterful to stay, this faded old grande dame of Aqaba, with two dozen overgrown palms in the front garden, is the place to come. Guests are entitled to free access to **Club Murjan** (JD7 for nonresidents), a beachfront sports centre south of Aqaba, reached by hotel transport twice a day at 9.30am and 1.30pm.

Golden Tulip (☎ 2051234; www.goldentulip.com; As-Sadah St; s/d JD65/80; ❄ 🅿) This thoroughly recommended hotel has a fashionable foyer and tasteful karaoke bar where the teetotal bartender mixes a superb cocktail. The rooms are cosy and bright, but beware knees and elbows in the surprisingly mean-sized bathrooms. The reception desk is manned by a uniformly charming staff.

Aquamarina IV (☎ 2051620; www.aqamarina-group.com; An-Nahda St; s/d JD40/60; ❄) This functional new hotel offers clean and comfortable rooms, somewhat marred by the smell of stale smoke. The lime green walls and yellow ceiling are designed to appeal to Ukrainian taste apparently!

Aquamarina Beach Hotel (☎ 2016254; www.aquamarina-group.com; King Hussein St; s/d JD37/64; ❄ 🏊) There's very little to commend this ugly, substandard Euro-resort except that it's the only midrange option to have sea access – albeit via a concrete pontoon. Solo women may feel uncomfortable here.

Coral Bay Resort (☎ 2017035; s/d from JD55/65; ❄ 💻 🏊) Part of the Royal Diving Club, this excellent camp, 12km south of Aqaba, is a quintessential divers' paradise. If you're planning on taking a dive course, or are interested in arranging a lengthy dive package, you couldn't ask for a better base.

our pick **Captain's Hotel** (☎ 2060710; www.captains-jo.com; An-Nahda St; s/d JD60/70; ❄ 💻 🏊) Aqaba's version of a boutique hotel, the Captain's began life as a fish restaurant (still functioning on the ground floor) and then evolved, one storey at a time, into this stylish new accommodation. The compact rooms (all with flat-screen TV), Arabian-style furniture and wonderful bathrooms with massage showers make this an upmarket choice for a midrange price.

Aqaba Gulf Hotel (☎ 2016636; www.aqabagulf.com; King Hussein St; r JD80; ❄ 💻 🏊) This was the first hotel to be built in Aqaba and it has quite an honour roll of guests. The stained-wood, split-level dining room looks thoroughly dated, as do the rest of the common-use areas, but this is not a criticism. The large, extremely comfortable rooms, copious breakfasts and excellent staff make this more of a lower top-end option.

TOP END

InterContinental Hotel (☎ 2092222; www.intercontinental.com; King Hussein St; standard/deluxe US$162/175; ❄ 💻 🏊 V) An imposing full stop at the end of the bay, the InterCon boasts less of an infinity pool than an 'infinity sea': on a calm day, the Gulf of Aqaba stretches in one seamless ripple all the way to Egypt. With exceptional landscape gardening, pools, a lazy river and a terracotta army of fully grown palm trees, the InterCon has stolen the top spot in Aqaba's luxury accommodation.

Mövenpick Resort Hotel (☎ 2034020; www.movenpick-aqaba.com; King Hussein St; standard/seaview/superior US$226/254/283; ❄ 💻 🏊 V) This stylish hotel, spreadeagled across the main road, has a palatial interior decorated with mosaics and Moroccan lamps. It's hard to beat.

Watch out for the **Kempinski Hotel**, expected to rival its neighbours on completion in 2009.

Eating

Aqaba's speciality is fish, particularly *sayadieh*: it's the catch of the day, delicately spiced, served with rice in an onion and tomato (or tahina) sauce.

Syrian Palace Restaurant (☎/fax 2014788; Raghadan St; mains JD2-6; 🕑 10am-midnight) Offers good local and Syrian food at moderate prices.

Al-Tarboosh Restaurant (☎ 2018518; Raghadan St; pastries around 200 fils; 🕑 7.30am-midnight) This hole-in-the-wall pastry shop does a great range of meat, cheese and vegie pastries that are heated up in a huge oven.

Floka Restaurant (☎ 2030860; An-Nahda St; starters JD4.500-6, mains JD5.500-11; 🕑 12.30-11.30pm; ❄) Choose sea bream, silver snapper, grouper or goatfish and select how you would like it cooked. Service can be slow but it's a friendly, unpretentious establishment.

our pick **Formosa Restaurant** (☎ 2060098; Aqaba Gateway complex; mains JD3-8; 🕑 8am-midnight; ❄ V) For a really excellent Chinese perspective on seafood (and with plenty of meat and vegetable options on the menu too), you couldn't better this cosy, intimate restaurant in the Aqaba Gateway.

Royal Yacht Club Restaurant (☎ 2022404; www.romero-restaurant.com; mains JD6-12; 🕑 noon-4.30pm & 6-11pm; ❄ V) Situated in the Royal Yacht Club, and with views of the marina, this classy Italian restaurant is a romantic place to enjoy a drink and watch the sunset.

Drinking

Al-Fardos Coffee Shop (just off Zahran St; coffee 500 fils) A traditional outdoor café where local men sip coffee, play backgammon and watch Arabic music videos. Foreign women are welcome.

Friends (☎ 2013466; upper storey, Aqaba Gateway; beer JD2.500-3; 🕑 3.30pm-3am) This is a relaxed and friendly place on a breezy terrace. Try the Dizzy Buddah cocktail (JD7); have two, and you may as well sleep over.

Getting There & Away

For information about crossing the border to/from Israel and the Palestinian Territories, see p396.

AIR

Royal Jordanian (☎ 2014477; www.rja.com.jo; Ash-Sherif al-Hussein bin Ali St; 9am-5pm Sun-Thu) Tickets to Amman cost JD55 one way.

BOAT

For details of boat services between Aqaba and Nuweiba in Egypt, see p397.

BUS & MINIBUS

JETT (☎ 2015223; King Hussein St) operates buses (JD7, five hours, five daily) to Amman between 7am and 5pm.

Trust International Transport (☎ 2032200; An-Nahda St) has buses to Amman (JD7.500, four hours, six daily) and Irbid (JD11, 5½ hours, 8.30am and 3.30pm).

Minibuses to Wadi Musa (for Petra), (JD4, two hours) leave when the bus is full between 7am and 2pm; you may have to wait up to an hour for a bus to leave. Otherwise, get a connection in Ma'an (JD2, 80 minutes).

Two minibuses go to Wadi Rum (JD1.500, one hour) at around 6.30am and 11am. Alternatively, catch a minibus towards Ma'an, get off at the turn-off to Wadi Rum at Ar-Rashidiyya and hitch a ride to Rum village.

Minibuses leave from the main bus/minibus station on Ar-Reem St. Minibuses to Karak (JD2, three hours), via Safi and the Dead Sea Hwy, are the exception, leaving from the small station next to the mosque on Al-Humaimah St.

For details about getting to Israel and the Palestinian Territories, see p396.

TAXIS

Chartering a taxi costs at least JD40 one way to Petra (1½ hours) and JD25 to Wadi Rum (one hour).

Getting Around

Handy minibuses (a trip costs around JD1) leave from near the entrance to Aqaba castle on King Hussein St for the Royal Diving Club via the southern beach camps, dive sites and the ferry terminal for boats to Egypt.

JORDAN DIRECTORY

ACCOMMODATION

Jordan offers a range of generally good-value accommodation. In this chapter, budget hotels are defined as those charging less than JD30, midrange hotels as those charging from JD30 to JD80, and top-end as hotels charging above JD80. These prices reflect a double room in peak season (September to October, and from March to early May), generally including breakfast and with a private bathroom, unless otherwise indicated. In Wadi Musa, you can sleep on a hotel roof in summer for around JD3.

The RSCN (p342) offers some of the country's most interesting accommodation options in nature reserves. These need to be booked in advance during peak seasons.

Note that holiday weekends are extremely busy in Aqaba and the Dead Sea. Outside these periods in nonpeak seasons, you can often negotiate discounts on published rates.

Some accommodation options offer 'half board', which includes bed, breakfast and one main meal.

ACTIVITIES

Diving and snorkelling are popular pastimes in the Gulf of Aqaba – see p386 for details.

Hiking is well organised in Dana Nature Reserve, Wadi Rum Protected Area and Wadi Mujib Nature Reserve. Wadi Mujib in particular offers some great canyoning and rappelling. Wadi Rum is the Middle East's premier climbing destination.

For details of outdoor activities in Jordan's nature reserves, contact the RSCN.

BOOKS

Lonely Planet offers a detailed *Jordan* guide.

Seven Pillars of Wisdom, by TE Lawrence, describes Lawrence's epic adventures in Jordan and the part he played in the Arab Revolt (he wrote a substantial portion of the book in Amman). It's dense going at times.

Annie Caulfield's *Kingdom of the Film Stars: Journey into Jordan* is an entertaining, personal account of the author's relationship with a Bedouin man in Jordan.

Petra: Lost City of the Ancient World, by Christian Augé and Jean-Marie Dentzer, is

PRACTICALITIES

- There are several English-language papers available, including the daily *Jordan Times* (200 fils; www.jordantimes.com) and weekly *Star* (500 fils; www.star.com.jo). Imported newspapers include *The Times* (JD4), *Guardian Weekly* (JD2), *Le Monde* and *Le Figaro* (JD2.250). The *International Herald Tribune* (JD1.250) has a regional section from Lebanon's *Daily Star*.
- Magazines include *Time* (JD2.700) and *Newsweek* (JD2.900).
- Check out Radio Jordan (96.3 FM) or the BBC World Service (1323AM). Try 99.6 FM for pop music.
- Channel 2 of Jordan TV broadcasts programs in French and English. Satellite stations such as the BBC CNN, MTV and Al-Jazeera can be found in most midrange hotels.
- Jordan's electricity supply is 220V, 50 AC. Sockets are mostly of a local two-pronged variety, although some places use European two-pronged and British three-pronged sockets.
- Jordan uses the metric system.

an excellent and very portable background introduction to Petra.

For an idea of life with the Bedouin at Petra, Marguerite van Geldermalsen's *Married to a Bedouin* is a modern classic.

Tony Howard and Di Taylor's books *Walking in Jordan* and *Walks & Scrambles in Rum* describe dozens of hikes in Jordan, from wadi walks to climbing routes up Jebel Rum.

BUSINESS HOURS

Government offices are open from 8am to 3pm Saturday to Thursday. Banks are open from 8.30am to 3pm Sunday to Thursday. Private businesses keep similar hours but are more flexible. Everything closes Friday lunchtime for weekly prayers. In Ramadan, business hours are reduced.

CHILDREN

Children are instant ice breakers in Jordan and you'll find people go out of their way to make families feel welcome.

Avoid a summer visit because the extreme heat is hard for children to tolerate. Stick to bottled mineral water, and if travelling with infants, bear in mind that disposable nappies are not readily available outside Amman and Aqaba.

For more comprehensive advice, see Lonely Planet's *Travel with Children* by Cathy Lanigan.

COURSES

If you fancy learning how to make your own mezze when you get home, try an evening course at **Petra Kitchen** (p379).

Jordan isn't a bad place to study Arabic, though living costs are a little higher than in Egypt or Syria.

British Council (☎ 06-4636147; www.britishcouncil.org/jordan.htm) Can put individuals in touch with a private tutor.

University of Jordan Language Center (☎ 06-5355000, ext 2370; www.ju.edu.jo; University of Jordan) Offers tailor-made courses with private instruction for individuals and small groups, geared to students' special interests. Rates are US$50 per hour per group, for groups of one to six students.

CUSTOMS REGULATIONS

Drugs and weapons are strictly prohibited. You can import 200 cigarettes and up to 1L of wine or spirits into Jordan duty free. There are no restrictions on the import and export of Jordanian or foreign currencies.

DANGERS & ANNOYANCES

Jordan is very safe to visit and travel around, remarkably so considering the political turmoil surrounding it. There is very little crime or anti-Western sentiment. The police keep a sharp eye on security, so carry your passport with you at all times and expect to show it at checkpoints near the border with Israel and the Palestinian Territories and roads that approach the Dead Sea.

During taxi rides, note that the fare quoted on the meter is in fils, not dinars. Perhaps understandably, it is rare for a taxi driver to point this out if you mistake the currency.

See p394 for advice for women travellers.

DISCOUNT CARDS

Student discounts are only occasionally available at tourist sites on production of an International Student Identity Card (ISIC). University ID cards are not accepted.

EMBASSIES & CONSULATES

The following embassies and consulates are in Amman (area code ☎ 06). Egypt also has a consulate in Aqaba. See p633 for an overview of visas for neighbouring countries. In general, the offices are open 9am to 11am Sunday to Thursday for visa applications and 1pm to 3pm for collecting visas.

Australia (Map p344; ☎ 06-5807000; www.jordan.embassy.gov.au; 3 Youssef Abu Shahhout, Deir Ghbar)

Egypt Embassy (Map p348; ☎ 06-5605175; fax 06-5604082; 22 Qortubah St; 9am-noon Sun-Thu) Located between 4th and 5th Circles. Consulate (Map p384; ☎ 03-2016171; cnr Al-Isteglal & Al-Akhatal Sts, Aqaba; 8am-3pm Sun-Thu)

France (Map p348; ☎ 06-4604630; www.ambafrance-jo.org; Al-Mutanabbi St, Jebel Amman)

Germany (Map p348; ☎ 06-5930367; www.amman.diplo.de; 31 Bin Ghazi St, Jebel Amman) Between 4th and 5th Circles.

Iraq (Map p348; ☎ 06-4623175; fax 06-4619172; Al-Kulliyah al-Islamiyah St, Jebel Amman) Located near the 1st Circle.

Israel Consulate (Map p344; ☎ 06-5503529; Maysaloon St, Shmeisani)

Lebanon (Map p348; ☎ 06-5929111; fax 06-5929113; Al-Neel St, Abdoun) Near the UK embassy.

Netherlands (Map p348; ☎ 06-5902200; www.netherlandsembassy.com.jo; 22 Ibrahim Ayoub St) Located near the 4th Circle.

New Zealand Consulate (Map p346; ☎ 06-4636720; fax 06-4634349; 99 Al-Malek al-Hussein St, downtown) Located on the 4th floor of the Khalaf Building.

Saudi Arabia Consulate (Map p348; ☎ 06-5924154; fax 06-5921154; 5th Circle, Jebel Amman)

Syria (Map p348; ☎ 06-5920684; Abdoun Prince Hashem bin Al-Hussein St, Jebel Amman) Located near the 4th Circle.

UK (Map p348; ☎ 06-5909200; www.britain.org.jo; Dimashq St, Wadi Abdoun, Abdoun)

USA (Map p344; ☎ 06-5906000; http://usembassy-amman.org.jo; 20 Al-Umawiyeen St, Abdoun)

Yemen (Map p348; ☎ 06-5923771; Al-Ameer Hashem bin al-Hussein St, Abdoun Circle)

FESTIVALS & EVENTS

Jordan's best-known cultural event is the **Jerash Festival** (www.jerashfestival.com.jo), a program of traditional music concerts and plays held in the spectacular Roman ruins of Jerash and Amman in July and August.

If an all-night party is more your style, then time your trip to Jordan with **Distant Heat** (www.distantheat.com), billed as one of the top-ten music festivals in the Middle East and organised to promote international youth peace. Featuring top international and local DJs, the festival is held at the end of July each year in Wadi Rum and often continues next day with beach pool parties in Aqaba.

GAY & LESBIAN TRAVELLERS

Most sources state that gay sex is not illegal in Jordan (though some dispute this) and that the age of consent for both heterosexuals and homosexuals is 16.

There is a subdued underground gay scene in Amman but public displays of affection are frowned upon. Two men or two women holding hands, however, is a normal sign of friendship.

There are a few places in Amman that are discreetly gay friendly, such as the multipurpose Books@café (p351) and Blue Fig Café (p351), which attract a young gay and straight crowd.

HOLIDAYS

In addition to the main Islamic holidays (p628), Jordan observes the following:

New Year's Day 1 January
Good Friday March/April
Labour Day 1 May
Independence Day 25 May
Army Day & Anniversary of the Great Arab Revolt 10 June
Christmas Day 25 December

INSURANCE

If you're planning to enjoy some of Jordan's many outdoor activities, you may want to check that your travel insurance policy covers them. See p628 for more on insurance.

INTERNET ACCESS

There are internet cafés in almost every town in Jordan, with costs averaging JD1.500 per hour. Connecting to the internet from your hotel room is possible, although only at limited midrange and top-end hotels. Jordan boasts numerous internet service providers (ISPs), including **Cyberia** (www.cyberia.jo).

INTERNET RESOURCES

Specific websites about Jordan include the following:

Jordan Jubilee (www.jordanjubilee.com) The best website about Jordan, it offers loads of extra detail on Petra and Wadi Rum among other practical tips.

Jordan Tourism Board (www.visitjordan.com) Good site with links to a range of Jordan-related websites.

Madaba (www.madaba.freeservers.com) Excellent description of Madaba's attractions and other nearby sites.

Ministry of Tourism and Antiquities (www.tourism.jo) Lots of tourist information.

Nabataea.Net (http://nabataea.net) 'Everything you wanted to know about the Nabataean empire.'

RSCN/Wild Jordan (www.rscn.org.jo) Ecotourism adventures in Jordan's nature reserves.

LANGUAGE

Arabic is the official language of Jordan. English is widely spoken, however, and in most cases is sufficient to get by. For a list of Arabic words and phrases, see p662.

LAUNDRY

There are laundries (mostly dry-cleaners) in Amman and Aqaba, although it's often easier to arrange through your hotel. It costs around JD4 for a 5kg load of washing, which comes back smelling divine and folded neatly.

MAPS

The Jordan Tourism Board's free *Map of Jordan* will suffice for most people.

The Royal Geographic Centre of Jordan's 2005 *Map of Petra* (JD3) is worth buying if you intend to do any hiking.

Jordan, by Kümmerly & Frey, is good, and probably the best if you're driving. GEO Project's *Jordan* (1:730,000) includes an excellent map of Amman.

MONEY

The currency in Jordan is the dinar (JD) – known as the *jay-dee* among hip young locals – and is made up of 1000 fils. A *piastre* refers to 10 fils. Often when a price is quoted, the ending will be omitted, so if you're told that something is 25, it's a matter of working out whether it's 25 fils, 25 piastre or 25 dinars! Although it sounds confusing, most Jordanians wouldn't dream of ripping off a foreigner, with the possible exception of taxi drivers (see p389).

It's not difficult to change money in Jordan; most hard currencies are accepted. Below are the rates for a range of currencies when this book went to print.

Country	Unit	Jordanian dinar (JD)
Australia	A$1	0.61
Canada	C$1	0.60
Egypt	E£1	0.13
Euro zone	€1	0.92
Israel and the Palestinian Territories	NIS1	0.19
Japan	¥100	0.78
New Zealand	NZ$1	0.42
Syria	S£10	0.15
UK	UK£1	1.31
USA	US$1	0.70

ATMs

ATMs abound in all but the smallest towns. Banks that accept both Visa and MasterCard include the Arab Bank and Jordan Gulf Bank, while the Housing Bank for Trade & Finance, Cairo-Amman Bank and Jordan Islamic Bank have numerous ATMs for Visa. The Jordan National Bank and HSBC ATMs allow you to extract dinars from your MasterCard and are Cirrus compatible. If an ATM swallows your card, call ☎ 06-5669123 (Amman).

Credit Cards

Credit cards are widely accepted in mid-range and top-end hotels and restaurants and a few top-end shops; a commission (up to 5%) is often added.

Moneychangers

There are plenty of moneychangers in Amman, Aqaba and Irbid, keeping longer hours than the banks. Many only deal in cash but some take travellers cheques, usually for a commission. Check the rates at banks or in the English-language newspapers.

Syrian, Lebanese, Egyptian, Israeli and Iraqi currency can all be changed in Amman, usually at reasonable rates, though you may have to shop around. Egyptian and Israeli currency is also easily changed in Aqaba.

Tipping

Tips of 10% are generally expected in the better restaurants, and loose change is appreciated by low-paid workers in cheaper places. A service charge of 10% is

A GOOD BUY

Several shops around Jordan sell high-quality handicrafts made by Jordanian women. Profits from the sale of all items go to local NGOs that aim to develop the status of women, provide income generation for marginalised families, nurture young artists or protect the local socio-cultural or natural environment. Products from these small-scale initiatives include silver jewellery from Wadi Musa; handmade paper products from Iraq al-Amir, Aqaba and Jerash; ceramics from Salt; painted ostrich eggs from Shaumari; weavings from Iraq al-Amir; and traditional clothing from across Jordan.

- **Bani Hamida Centre** (p369) Weaving cooperative with a store in Amman.
- **Jordan River Foundation** (www.jordanriver.jo) Profits go to support the foundation, which aims to preserve traditional communities of the Jordan River Valley. The main Jordan River shop (p352) is in Amman.
- **Noor Al-Hussein Foundation** (www.noor.gov.jo/nhf.htm) This organisation helps preserve traditional handicraft skills and supports vulnerable women's communities. Products are sold in shops throughout Jordan.
- **Wild Jordan** (p352) Proceeds from RSCN gift shops in Amman, Azraq, Dana and Wadi Rum contribute to environmental programs and to local communities.
- Other places that have an excellent range of ethically produced handicrafts include **Haret Jdoudna** (p368) in Madaba and **Made in Jordan** (p380) in Wadi Musa.

automatically added at most midrange and top-end restaurants.

Travellers Cheques

Travellers cheques are easily cashed by banks and some moneychangers, though commissions vary considerably so shop around. American Express travellers cheques seem to be the most widely accepted.

PHOTOGRAPHY

Digital accessories and memory cards are widely available for competitive prices (a 1GB memory card costs around JD20). Many camera shops can burn photos onto a CD and print digital pictures.

POST

Postcards cost 475 fils to send to the UK and Europe and 625 fils to the USA and Australia, and they can be posted in souvenir shops.

To send a 1kg parcel to the UK and Europe costs JD14.300 and JD4 for each subsequent 1kg; to the USA and Canada, it costs JD14.600, then JD8.100 per extra 1kg; to Australia, it costs JD13.600 and JD7.100 per extra 1kg. For detailed information, see **Jordan Post** (www.jordanpost.com.jo).

For typically reliable but expensive express mail services, try **DHL** (Amman Map p344; ☎ 06-5857136; info@amm-co.jo.dhl.com; behind C-Town Shopping Centre, 7th Circle, Amman; Aqaba Map p384; ☎ 03-2012039; Al-Petra St).

SHOPPING

Jordan is a great place to buy souvenirs. In Madaba, kilims make a great groundsheet for camping; in Wadi Musa, sand bottles have been elevated to an art form, and in Wadi Rum, you can find traditional Arab headcloths, or keffiyeh, and *agal* (the black cord used to keep it on your head) to keep the sand out of your hair.

For the ultimate portable souvenir, look for a piece of Bedouin silver jewellery in one of Aqaba's bead shops or design your own from lapis lazuli (blue), coral (red) and turquoise beads (from JD5). Alternatively, go local with a Bedouin necklace of cloves from Petra – their medicinal aroma is a better companion than a sweaty neighbour.

Bargaining is essential, but shopkeepers are less likely than their Syrian and Egyptian counterparts to budge much on price.

SOLO TRAVELLERS

Jordan is a great destination for solo travellers. The country is friendly, safe, compact and easy to travel around, with plenty of opportunities to mix both with fellow travellers (particularly in Amman, Madaba and Wadi Musa) and to meet the locals. During any bus ride, local people extend the hand of friendship and often the journey will end in an invitation to meet the family. One traveller in Jordan, Nathalie Ollier, found that her planned itinerary of a morning trip to Mukawir turned into an all-day tea-tasting event as she was taken from one shop owner, bus driver or village resident to another.

The tours run by the budget hotels in Amman and Madaba are a good way to share travel expenses and meet other travellers if you're short on time (see p399).

TELEPHONE

The local telephone system is reliable. For directory assistance, call ☎ 1212 (Amman) or ☎ 131 (elsewhere). Local calls cost around 150 fils. The easiest way to make a local call is from your hotel.

Overseas calls are cheapest at private telecommunication centres, which often consist of little more than a guy with a sign and a mobile phone! These international calls range from 350 fils to 700 fils per minute. Local phonecards are more expensive for international calls.

Mobile Phones

Mobile phones in Jordan use the GSM system. Two main service providers are **Fastlink** (☎ 06-5823111; www.fastlink.com.jo; code 079) and **Jordan Telecom Group** (☎ 06-4606666; http://jordantelecomgroup.com), both of which offer a full range of plans and prepaid SIM cards. Rates for signing up start at JD10 including 175 minutes of talk time.

Per minute mobile charges are around 350 fils to Europe and Australia and 700 fils to the USA.

Phone Codes

Jordan's country code is ☎ 962, followed by the local area code (minus the zero), then the six- or seven-digit number.

There are four area codes: ☎ 02 covers northern Jordan, ☎ 03 southern Jordan, ☎ 05 the Jordan Valley and central and eastern districts, and ☎ 06 the Amman area. Mobile phone numbers have eight digits and are preceded with ☎ 07. Toll-free numbers start with ☎ 0800.

TIME

Jordan is two hours ahead of GMT/UTC in winter and three hours ahead between 1 April and 1 October.

TOILETS

Many hotels and restaurants, except those in the budget category, have Western-style toilets. Squat toilets come with either a hose or water bucket provided for cleaning and flushing. Toilet paper should be thrown in the bin provided, as the sewerage system is not designed for paper. Public toilets are generally best avoided.

TOURIST INFORMATION

Jordan runs a good network of visitor centres inside the country, and the **Jordan Tourism Board** (www.visitjordan.com) has a good website. Contact the following offices for a package of brochures and maps:

France (☎ 01 55 60 94 46; gsv@articleonze.com; 122 rue Paris, 92100 Boulogne-Billancourt, Paris)

Germany (☎ 069-9231 8870; jordan@adam-partner.de; Weser Strasse 4 60329, Frankfurt)

UK (☎ 020-7371 6496; info@jordantourismboard.co.uk; 115 Hammersmith Rd, London, W14 0QH)

USA (☎ 1-877-733-5673, 703-243-7404; www.seejordan.org; Suite 102, 6867 Elm St, McLean, VA 22101)

TRAVELLERS WITH DISABILITIES

Jordanians are quick to help those with disabilities but cities are crowded and traffic is chaotic, and visiting most attractions, such as the vast archaeological sites of Petra and Jerash, involves long traverses over uneven ground. Horse and carriages are provided at Petra to help elderly travellers or those with disabilities.

The **Royal Diving Club** (p386), south of Aqaba, is a member of the **Access to Marine Conservation for All** (AMCA; www.amca-international.org), an initiative to enable people with disabilities to enjoy scuba diving and snorkelling.

VISAS

Visas are required by all foreigners entering Jordan. Single-entry visas are issued at both the border and airport on arrival (JD10).

If you plan to enter Jordan from Israel and the Palestinian Territories via King Hussein/Allenby Bridge (the only border crossing where visas are not issued), or you require a multiple-entry visa, then obtain them from

Jordanian embassies or consulates outside the country; they are generally issued within 24 hours. Single-/multiple-entry visas obtained this way cost JD10/20 and two photos are required.

If you arrive in Aqaba by sea from Nuweiba in Egypt (and, in theory, by land from Eilat in Israel), your visa should be free because Aqaba is designated as a Special Economic Zone set up for free trade. You must register at the ASEZA office in Aqaba (p384) if you plan to stay in Jordan for more than 14 days.

Tourist visas are valid for a stay of up to a month from the date of entry. If you want to stay more than a month, you must register with the police in Amman (p347) or Aqaba (p384); they will give you an extension for a stay of up to three months.

If you will be in Jordan for less than 24 hours en route to a third country, you can request a free-of-charge transit visa. This also exempts you from the JD5 departure tax, but you must leave Jordan within 24 hours of arrival.

For details of visas for other Middle Eastern countries, see the table, p633.

WOMEN TRAVELLERS

Most women who travel around Jordan experience no problems, and find they are welcomed with a mixture of warmth and friendly concern for their safety. That said, varying levels of sexual harassment do occur, especially in tourist areas where, rightly or wrongly, local men assume that 'anything goes'. Harassment can be somewhat mitigated by dressing modestly in baggy trousers or skirts with loose shirts or blouses that cover the cleavage, shoulders and upper arms. It's not necessary to cover your head.

Women will feel uncomfortable on public beaches in Aqaba and may prefer to wear shorts and a loose T-shirt over swimwear at the Dead Sea. Many restaurants in the country usher female customers into their family areas, where single men are not permitted.

Attitudes towards women vary greatly throughout the country. In the upmarket districts of Amman, women are treated the same as they would be in any Western country, whereas in rural areas more traditional attitudes prevail.

WORK

Work is not really an option for most foreigners passing through Jordan. Those hoping to work with Palestinian refugees might have luck with the public information office of the **UN Relief & Works Agency** (UNRWA; Map p344; ☎ 06-5609100, ext 165; jorpio@unrwa.org; Al-Zubeid Bldg, Mustapha bin Abdullah St, Shmeisani, Amman); contact them at least three months in advance.

Occasional vacancies for qualified English teachers occur at the **British Council** (Map p348; ☎ 06-4636147; www.britishcouncil.org.jo) or the **American Language Center** (☎ 06-5523901; www.alc.edu.jo), but you need to have solid teaching experience.

If you fancy staying in Jordan for a whole year, Father Innocent at the **Pilgrim's Guest House** (☎ 06-5523901; diodoros@wanadoo.jo) in Madaba is looking for volunteers to teach English in his school in return for board and keep, private Arabic lessons, participation in evening lessons run by the British Council and 'pocket money'.

TRANSPORT IN JORDAN

GETTING THERE & AWAY

Entering Jordan

For information on Jordanian visas and entry requirements, see Visas (p393).

Air

The main international airport is **Queen Alia International Airport** (☎ 06-4453187; www.qaia.gov.jo), 35km south of Amman.

Royal Jordanian (Map p344 ☎ 06-5678321; www.rja.com.jo; 9th fl, Housing Bank Centre, Shmeisani, Amman) is the excellent national carrier, but from the main European capitals you can generally get cheaper deals with other airlines. In Amman there are convenient offices in the Jordan InterContinental Hotel on **Al-Kulliyah al-Isalamiyah St** (Map p348; ☎ 06-4644267) and along **Al-Malek al-Hussein St** (Map p348; ☎ 06-5663525), uphill from the Abdali bus station.

DEPARTURE TAX

At the time of research, the departure tax from Jordan was JD5. If you are in the country for less than 72 hours, you are usually exempt from the tax.

The contact details in Amman of other airlines flying to/from Jordan are as follows:

Air France (AF; Map p344; ☎ 06-666055; www.airfrance.com; hub Charles de Gaulle, Paris)

British Airways (BA; Map p344; ☎ 06-5828801; www.ba.com; hub Heathrow, London)

Emirates (EK; Map p348; ☎ 06-643341; www.emirates.com; hub Dubai)

Gulf Air (GF; Map p348; ☎ 06-653613; www.gulfairco.com; hub Bahrain)

KLM (KL; Map p346; ☎ 06-655267; www.klm.com; hub Amsterdam)

Lufthansa Airlines (LH; Map p344; ☎ 06-601744; www.lufthansa.com; hub Frankfurt)

Qatar Airways (QR; Map p344; ☎ 06-684526; www.qatarairways.com; hub Doha)

Turkish Airlines (TK; Map p348; ☎ 06-659102; www.turkishairlines.com; hub İstanbul)

Land

In addition to the crossings below, Jordan has three borders with Saudi Arabia (at Al-Umari, Al-Mudawwara and Ad-Durra), but visas for Saudi are not given for casual travel, making it off-limits for most people.

IRAQ

Minibuses and service taxis leave from Amman's Abdali bus station for Baghdad, but the lack of security along the highway (via Fallujah) made this an extremely dangerous option at the time of research.

ISRAEL & THE PALESTINIAN TERRITORIES

Since the historic 1994 peace treaty between Jordan and Israel and the Palestinian Territories, three border crossings have opened to foreigners: Sheikh Hussein Bridge in the north, King Hussein Bridge near Amman and Wadi Araba in the south. These border crossings are known respectively as Jordan Bridge, Allenby Bridge and Yitzhak Rabin in Israel and the Palestinian Territories; you should refer to them as such only when travelling on the Israeli side of the border.

Trust International Transport (p398) has bus services from Amman to Nazareth (JD20), Haifa (JD20) and Tel Aviv (JD25) daily except Saturday. It also runs services from Irbid to Tel Aviv and Nazareth. Public transport doesn't run during the Jewish Shabbat (sunset Friday to sunset Saturday), so try to reach the border crossings early.

Note that one-month Israeli visas are issued at the Wadi Araba (Rabin) and Sheikh Hussein Bridge crossings, but those issued at the King Hussein Bridge are usually for three months. For more on Israeli visas, see p635.

Sheikh Hussein Bridge Crossing (Jordan Bridge)

Known in Arabic as 'Jisr Sheikh Hussein', this **border crossing** (🕒 6.30am-10pm Sun-Thu, 8am-8pm Fri & Sat) links northern Jordan with Beit She'an in Galilee.

Service taxis and minibuses leave Irbid's west bus station for the border (JD1, 45 minutes). From the bridge, it's a 2km bus ride to the Israeli side (usually excruciatingly slow, so if your bags aren't too heavy, it's best just to walk) from where you take a taxi 6km to Beit She'an for onward connections inside Israel and the Palestinian Territories.

King Hussein/Allenby Bridge Crossing

Known in Arabic as 'Jisr al-Malek Hussein', this **border crossing** (🕒 8am-2.30pm Sun-Thu, to 11.45pm Fri & Sat) offers travellers the most direct route between Amman and Jerusalem or Tel Aviv.

To reach this border from Amman, take a service taxi from Amman's Abdali (or Wahadat) bus station to King Hussein Bridge (JD4, 45 minutes), or there's a single daily JETT bus (JD8) at 6.30am.

Buses (JD2) shuttle between the two borders, and although the ride to the Israeli & Palestinian Territories side is short, it can last an eternity with repeated stops for passport and bag checks. At the time of research, it was not possible to walk, hitch or take a private car across this border.

To get to Jerusalem from the border, take a sherut (Israeli shared taxi; around 200NIS for the car) to Jerusalem's Damascus Gate.

If travelling in the other direction, you must pay an Israeli exit tax of 127NIS (around US$29, compared to around 69 NIS at other borders). Note that if you intend to return to Israel, you must keep the entrance form given to you by the Jordanians – you may have to prolong your stay in Jordan if you cannot find it.

If you intend to enter Jordan using this crossing from Israel and the Palestinian Territories, then you need to obtain a visa in advance (JD10) from one of Jordan's embassies or consulates abroad. This applies, however, only if you're entering Jordan through this crossing for the first time. If you are *re-entering* Jordan, you do not need to reapply for a Jordanian visa, providing you return through King Hussein Bridge within the validity of your Jordanian visa or extension. Keep the stamped exit slip and present it on returning. Note also that this option does not apply at any of Jordan's other border crossings.

At the Israeli border post, request officials to stamp the Jordanian exit slip rather than your passport if you intend to visit Syria and/or Lebanon. For entry to those countries, there must be no evidence in your passport of your trip to Israel, including use of any of Jordan's border crossings with Israel and the Palestinian Territories. For more information, see p332.

Wadi Araba Crossing (Yitzhak Rabin – formerly known as Arava)

This handy **border crossing** (6.30am-10pm Sun-Thu, 8am-8pm Fri & Sat) in the south of the country links Aqaba to Eilat. To get there from Aqaba, it's best to take a taxi (JD5, 15 minutes); you can walk across the border. On the other side, take a taxi to Eilat (25 NIS, 2km). All in all, Aqaba to Eilat takes about an hour.

> **JUST ACROSS THE BORDER: JERUSALEM, ISRAEL & THE PALESTINIAN TERRITORIES**
>
> Been peering across the Dead Sea at the Promised Land? Well, unlike Moses, you don't have to confine yourself to a long-distance view. Within half a day you can be slipping through Damascus Gate into the heart of old Jerusalem (p260). Take the 6.30am JETT bus (p395) to King Hussein Bridge border (45 minutes – closed Saturday and from noon on Friday) and put up with a long wait (three hours) at the crossing. Get a free visa at the border (but see p332 about Israeli stamp stigma). Take a bus to the Israeli side of the border and jump in a sherut (share taxi) to Jerusalem's Damascus Gate (30 minutes). Book in at the Lutheran Guest House (p271). Sit in the rose garden or antique sitting room to plan your visit to the Middle East's most historic, most holy and most disputed city.

SYRIA

The border crossings between Jordan and Syria are at Ramtha/Der'a and Jabir/Nasib. Note that most people need a visa from the Syrian Embassy in their home country: they are not available at the border nor from the Syrian Embassy in Amman.

Bus

Air-conditioned JETT buses make the journey between Amman (Abdali) and Damascus (JD7, seven hours) twice a day in either direction and there's a daily afternoon service to Aleppo (JD10, 11 hours). Book a day in advance for either.

To travel directly between Damascus and Amman, it's quicker and cheaper to take the direct bus or service taxi. If you want to explore Jerash and Umm Qais in Jordan or Ezra'a and Bosra ash-Sham in Syria, it's also possible to take a bus from Irbid's south bus station to Ramtha (JD1), another minibus or service taxi to the border and then transport to Der'a and Damascus beyond.

The Palace Hotel in Amman (p350) offers a useful minibus tour to Damascus, with stops in Jerash, Bosra and Shaba. A minimum of four passengers (hard to assemble, given the necessity of arranging visas in advance) is required; the price is around JD20 per person.

Service Taxi

The enormous yellow *servees* (shared taxis) leave regularly throughout the day from the lower (eastern) end of the Abdali bus station for Damascus (JD10). They generally cross at Jabir. From Irbid's south bus station, service taxis go to Damascus (JD5).

Train

A biweekly train service still leaves Amman for Damascus (JD3) along the Hejaz Railway on Monday and Thursday at 8am, but the dawdling service takes all day, with a change of trains at the border. The quaint old station is on King Abdullah I St, about 2.5km east of Raghadan bus station in Amman. The **ticket office** (06-4895413) is officially open from 7am on the morning of departure, although you may find someone around at other times. To get to the station, take a service taxi from Raghadan bus station, or a private taxi (around JD1).

Sea

There are two boat services from Aqaba to Nuweiba in Egypt. Departure times are subject to change, so call the **passenger terminal** (☎ 03-2013240; www.abmaritime.com.jo/english) before travelling and arrive at least 90 minutes before departure. Buy your tickets at the ferry port on the morning of departure (you'll need your passport).

The fast boat (one hour) leaves daily except Saturday and costs US$70. Children under 12 pay US$55.

The slow boat (a car ferry that takes three hours or more) officially leaves at noon but often doesn't get going until 5pm or later. Some days it doesn't leave at all. Tickets cost US$60 (children under 12 pay US$50).

Fares from Nuweiba must be paid for in US dollars.

There are money-exchange facilities at the terminals at Nuweiba and Aqaba. The Jordanian side offers a decent exchange rate but avoid travellers cheques, which attract a huge commission. You can get a free Sinai permit on arrival at Nuweiba. If you want a full Egyptian visa, enquire at the Egyptian consulate in Aqaba in advance (p390). Passports are collected on the boat in both directions and handed back on arrival at immigration.

JUST ACROSS THE BORDER: DAMASCUS & ALEPPO, SYRIA

Jordan has it all – biblical sites, Roman ruins, great castles and striking countryside – but even the most ardent Jordan traveller will agree that it lacks a good souq. This is easily remedied, however, by hopping on a JETT bus direct from Amman to Damascus, which will take seven hours (see opposite). Make sure you get your visa for Syria before you leave home (p633), as these are not generally available at the border nor from the Syrian Embassy in Amman. Note, too, you won't be allowed in with an Israeli stamp in your passport (see p332). Stay at the Sultan Hotel (p474) and the exceptional staff will point you in the right direction for the legendary Old City (p468). Or why not go the extra mile and take the JETT bus direct to Aleppo (opposite)? It takes eight hours for one of the best carpet-haggling, brass-polishing, labyrinthine markets in the world (p494).

JUST ACROSS THE BORDER: ST KATHERINE'S MONASTERY, EGYPT

If a couple of days of diving in Aqaba has whetted your appetite for the Dead Sea, then why not nip across the water and explore the spectacular coral gardens off Egypt's Mt Sinai coast? Simply hop on the fast boat from Aqaba at 3.30pm (left), obtain a free Sinai Peninsula permit on arrival (see Visas p633), and an hour later you can be sipping a beer by the waterfront in a camp in Nuweiba (p200). If you've had enough of the depths, then it's time to hit the heights by striking out early on the 2½-hour journey to St Katherine's Monastery (p201). A place of pilgrimage for Muslims, Jews and Christians, Mt Sinai is just a camel's ride away, and at sunrise or sunset it's a special place to be, whatever one's beliefs. Make the magic last by overnighting in the atmospheric Monastery Guesthouse (p199).

GETTING AROUND

Air

There is only one domestic air route, operated by Royal Jordanian twice daily between Amman and Aqaba (JD35 one way, one hour).

Royal Wings (www.royalwings.com.jo), a subsidiary of Royal Jordanian, flies daily between Aqaba and Amman's Marka airport (airport code ADJ), a smaller civil airport in the eastern suburbs of Amman. You can buy tickets for either of these airlines at any travel agency or Royal Jordanian office.

Bicycle

Cycling is not necessarily fun in Jordan. In summer, it's prohibitively hot, and cyclists on the King's Hwy have reported stone throwing by groups of young children. Cycling north or south can be hard work, as there is a strong prevailing western wind. Anywhere from the East Bank plateau down to the Dead Sea or Jordan Valley makes for exhilarating descents, but coming the other way will really test your calf muscles. Bring plenty of spare parts and contact **Cycling Association** (www.cycling-jordan.com) for tips before departure (see p646 for more information).

Bus

The national bus company **JETT** (Map p344; ☎ 06-5854679; www.jett.com.jo; Al-Malek al-Hussein St, Shmeisani, Amman) operates the most comfortable bus service from Amman to Aqaba and Petra. There are also services to King Hussein Bridge border crossing and Hammamat Ma'in.

Another reliable company with regular services from Amman is **Trust International Transport** (Map p344; ☎ 06-5813427; Mataar al-Malekah Alya Rd).

Just about all towns in Jordan are connected by 20-seat minibuses, although the King's Hwy, Dead Sea area and eastern Jordan are less well served. Minibuses leave when full and it can take an hour or more for the seats to fill up. Overcharging tourists is rare, except on routes to and from Wadi Musa (for Petra), where drivers often try to charge extra for 'luggage'.

Car & Motorcycle

Hiring a car is an ideal way to get the most out of Jordan. Distances are generally short and you'll have freedom to explore off the beaten track. Road conditions are generally good outside Amman.

DRIVING LICENCE

International Driving Permits (IDPs) are not needed. If you're driving, keep your driving licence, rental or ownership papers and car registration in an easily accessible place.

FUEL & SPARE PARTS

Petrol is available along the Desert and King's Hwys and in most sizeable towns. It costs about 540/620 fils for a litre of regular/super, though prices are rising weekly – one of the biggest bones of contention in Jordan at present. Diesel is about 320 fils a litre and unleaded is almost unheard of.

There are precious few mechanics in Jordan able to deal with the average modern motorcycle and its problems.

HIRE

Charges, conditions, drop-off fees, insurance costs and waiver fees in case of accident vary considerably, so it's worth shopping around. Daily rates are JD25 to JD30, weekly rates JD140 to JD200. You can normally drop off the rental car in another city (eg Aqaba) for around JD25 extra.

> **SCAMS**
>
> Be wary of taxi drivers who claim that your chosen hotel is closed, dirty or 'burnt down', only to recommend another hotel – where they get commission.

Many hire companies require a minimum three-days hire, and all require a deposit of up to JD400 payable upon pick up and refunded upon return of the car.

The following hire companies are reliable:

Avis (Map p344; ☎ 06-5699420, 777 397405; www.avis.com.jo; King Abdullah Gardens, Amman; 24hr) The biggest car hire company in Jordan, with offices at King Hussein Bridge and Aqaba and branches at the airport, Le Royal Hotel and Jordan InterContinental Hotel.

Budget (Map p344; ☎ 06-5698131; www.budget.com; 125 Abdul Hameed Sharaf St, Amman)

Europcar (Map p344; ☎ 06-5655581, 800-22270; www.europcar.middleeast.com; Isam Al-Ajlouni St, Amman) Branches at Radisson SAS, King Abdullah Gardens and in Aqaba (Map p384).

Hertz (Map p344; ☎ 24hr airport line 06-5624191, 06-4711771; www.hertz.com; King Abdullah Gardens, Amman) Offices at the airport, Grand Hyatt Amman, Sheraton and in Aqaba (Map p384).

Reliable Rent-a-Car (Map p344; ☎ 06-5929676, 079 5521358; www.rentareliablecar.com; 19 Fawzi al-Qawegli St, Amman) Cars JD20 to JD25. Offers free drop-off and pick-up in Madaba or the airport, and will deliver the car to you anywhere in Amman, and will even drive you to the edge of town if you are nervous about Amman traffic. Contact Mohammed Hallak.

INSURANCE

All car rentals come with some kind of insurance, but you should find out how much your excess is (ie the maximum you will have to pay in case of an accident), which may be as high as JD400. For JD5 to JD10 extra per day, you can buy Collision Damage Waiver (CDW), which takes your deductible down to JD100 or even to zero.

ROAD RULES

Vehicles drive on the right-hand side of the road in Jordan, at least in theory: more often, they loiter in the middle. The general speed limit inside built-up areas is 50km/h or 70km/h on multilane highways in Amman, and 90km/h to 110km/h on the highways. Note that indicators are seldom used, rules are only occasionally obeyed, the ubiquitous horn is a useful warning signal and pedestrians must take their chances. Wearing a seat belt is now compulsory.

Keep your passport, driver's licence, rental agreement and registration papers handy, especially along the Dead Sea Hwy where there are quite a few police check posts.

Hitching

In Wadi Rum and along the King's and Dead Sea highways, you may need to wave down a ride; it's customary to give a few dinars to the driver. For general information on hitching, see p650.

Local Transport

BUS

Local city buses are generally packed, routes are confusing and the chances of being pickpocketed are higher. Take a service taxi instead.

TAXI

Private taxis are quite cheap in the cities. Note that metered fares are displayed in fils not dinars, and if you proffer the fare in dinars by mistake, the driver is unlikely to correct you.

White *servees* are a little more expensive than minibuses and don't cover as many routes, but they are generally faster and take less time to fill up (there are generally only four seats). Inside cities like Amman, service taxis offer extensive coverage and are a good alternative to walking or taking private taxis. For more details on taxis in Jordan, see p354.

Tours

The Cliff (p350), Farah (p350) and Palace (p350) hotels in Amman offer useful day trips from the capital. The most popular ones run to the desert castles; to Jerash, Ajloun and Umm Qais; and along the King's Hwy to Petra, via Madaba, Mt Nebo, Mujib Gorge, Karak and Shobak (JD15 to JD25 per person). We've received varying reports about the quality of such tours, so it's worth asking other travellers before deciding. The tours are really just transport, so don't expect much from the guide.

One option that has been recommended by readers is the tour that leaves Amman at 8.30am and travels to Petra (9½ hours) via Madaba, Wadi Mujib, Karak, Shobak and Dana, with time spent at each of the various sites. The Mariam Hotel (p367) in Madaba can arrange a similar itinerary.

There are a few tour companies with a good reputation for comprehensive (but more expensive) tours around Jordan; try **International Traders** (Map p344; ☎ 06-5607075) in Shmeisani (Amman) and Aqaba, or call **Petra Moon** (☎ 03-2156665; www.petramoon.com) in Wadi Musa.

The Palace Hotel also runs a day trip from Amman to Damascus for around JD20 to JD25 per person. Note that for most nationalities, Syria does not issue visas at the border, so make arrangements from home if you're planning a trip to Damascus (see p633).

Lebanon

Beautiful, bountiful, beleaguered Lebanon is a tiny, chaotic and culturally colliding country like no other on earth. Blessed with serene mountain vistas and the majestic remains of ancient civilisations, it's also scarred both emotionally and physically by decades of civil war, invasions and terrorist attacks.

To the traveller, Lebanon comes across as a place of contradictions: home to a bubbling-hot nightlife in Beirut, a notorious Hezbollah (Party of God) headquarters in otherwise backwater Baalbek, a fistful of ski resorts in its loftier climes, and a dozen cramped and poverty-stricken Palestinian refugee camps. Combine all this with 18 'official' religions, three widely spoken languages, and an identity with one slipper in the East and one Jimmy Choo planted firmly in the West, and you can't help but believe that Lebanon's got it all – both good and bad.

Though welcoming, endearing and easy to get around, it's important to remember that Lebanon's also a troubled place that frequently sees violence and warfare. In recent times, there have been a slew of politically motivated assassinations and a 2006 war between the militant Hezbollah group and Israel, which saw countrywide destruction. Open fighting, moreover, broke out on Beirut's streets in May 2008, leading to civilian casualties and fears for the country's stability. Though things soon calmed down once more, it remains to be seen how long this peace and quiet will last.

Nevertheless, if you keep well abreast of the news, Lebanon remains a safe and undeniably fascinating destination for travellers. Hike the enchanting byways of the Qadisha Valley in the north of the country and you'll find it hard to imagine that a conflict has ever existed here; wander past the pockmarked shell of the Holiday Inn in Beirut and you'll wonder if there will ever be lasting peace. And this is Lebanon in a nutshell: a confusing, compelling conundrum in compact country form.

FAST FACTS

- **Area** 10,400 sq km
- **Capital** Beirut
- **Country code** ☎ 961
- **Language** Arabic
- **Money** Lebanese lira (also known as the Lebanese pound; LL); US$1 = LL1508; €1 = LL2232
- **Official name** Republic of Lebanon
- **Population** 4 million

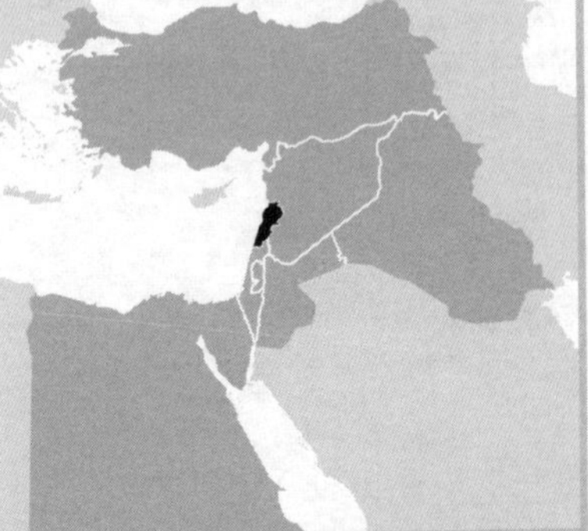

CLIMATE & WHEN TO GO

When's best to visit Lebanon depends on what you're planning on doing. Spring (March to May) is best for hiking, since the fields and slopes are green, lush and sprinkled with flowers. By May, the weather's often warm enough for a dip in the Mediterranean – and you could even try taking to the ski slopes in the morning and swimming on the coast in the afternoon, as the Lebanese are at great pains to point out.

Summer (June to September) is the time for sun seekers, when Beirut's beach clubs are hot, in more ways than one. It can, however, get very sticky on the coast, particularly in the polluted hearts of Beirut and Tripoli. Summer is also the season for festivals, many of which are held outdoors in spectacular locations, but be aware that during peaceful years, summer accommodation prices rise steeply as flocks of Lebanese expats descend.

Autumn (October to November) is another prime period for hiking, but be aware that outside Beirut things can be extremely quiet: summer tourist spots shut up shop while ski resorts are still oiling their ski lifts. Ramadan (usually September to October) shouldn't affect your travel plans too much in Lebanon, since most towns are a mixture of Christians and Muslims.

Winter is optimum if you're keen to hit the ski slopes, when resorts like the Cedars (p438) open for business; the ski season usually cranks up in early December and can last until early May. Make sure, countrywide, that your hotel room has some sort of heating and hot water, though, or you may have to wear your socks both in bed and in the shower. For more, see Climate Charts, p625.

HISTORY

Prior to its independence, Lebanon formed a part of Greater Syria. See p459 for information on the country pre-independence.

LEBANON IN...

One Week

Assuming all's quiet on Lebanon's eastern front and the Beirut–Damascus land border is open, take a bus from Damascus to **Beirut** (p415) for two days of indulging in the capital's cultural and hedonistic pursuits. From here, head north to pretty **Byblos** (p429), where ancient ruins are sprinkled beside an azure sea. If you've got your own transport, continue up to the **Qadisha Valley** (p437) on day four, for a long, soothing trek along the valley floor, past rock-cut monasteries and gushing waterfalls. If not, take the bus up to **Tripoli** (p432) to explore medieval souqs, munch on its famous sweets, and experience the ragged hustle and bustle of a working port city. From here, travel back down, via Beirut, to **Baalbek** (p447) to soak up the grandeur of the fabled 'Sun City' for days five and six, with a night in between at the historic **Palmyra Hotel** (p449). On day seven, stop in to admire **Aanjar** (p450), one of the world's few Umayyad city ruins, on your way back towards the Beirut–Damascus border.

Two Weeks

In addition to all the above, a fortnight will give you time to explore southern Lebanon and delve deeper into the country's great outdoors. If you're here in winter, don't miss two days skiing at **the Cedars** (p438), with an afternoon's wander around lovely, peaceful **Bcharré** (p437). If it's summer, take an extra day's walking in the **Qadisha Valley** (p438) and a second day to hike the stunningly barren mountains above the Cedars. Two more days can be happily spent exploring **Sidon** (p439) and **Tyre** (p442), two southern cities with tumultuous pasts and a wealth of ancient remains, then head over to **Deir al-Qamar** (p445) to soak up the small-town atmosphere and the wonders of **Beiteddine Palace** (p444) – not missing its incredible mosaic collection. Backtracking to Beirut, spend your final day or two relaxing beside the pool at one of its chi-chi beach clubs before boarding the bus back to Damascus.

Join the Itineraries

Syria (p459)

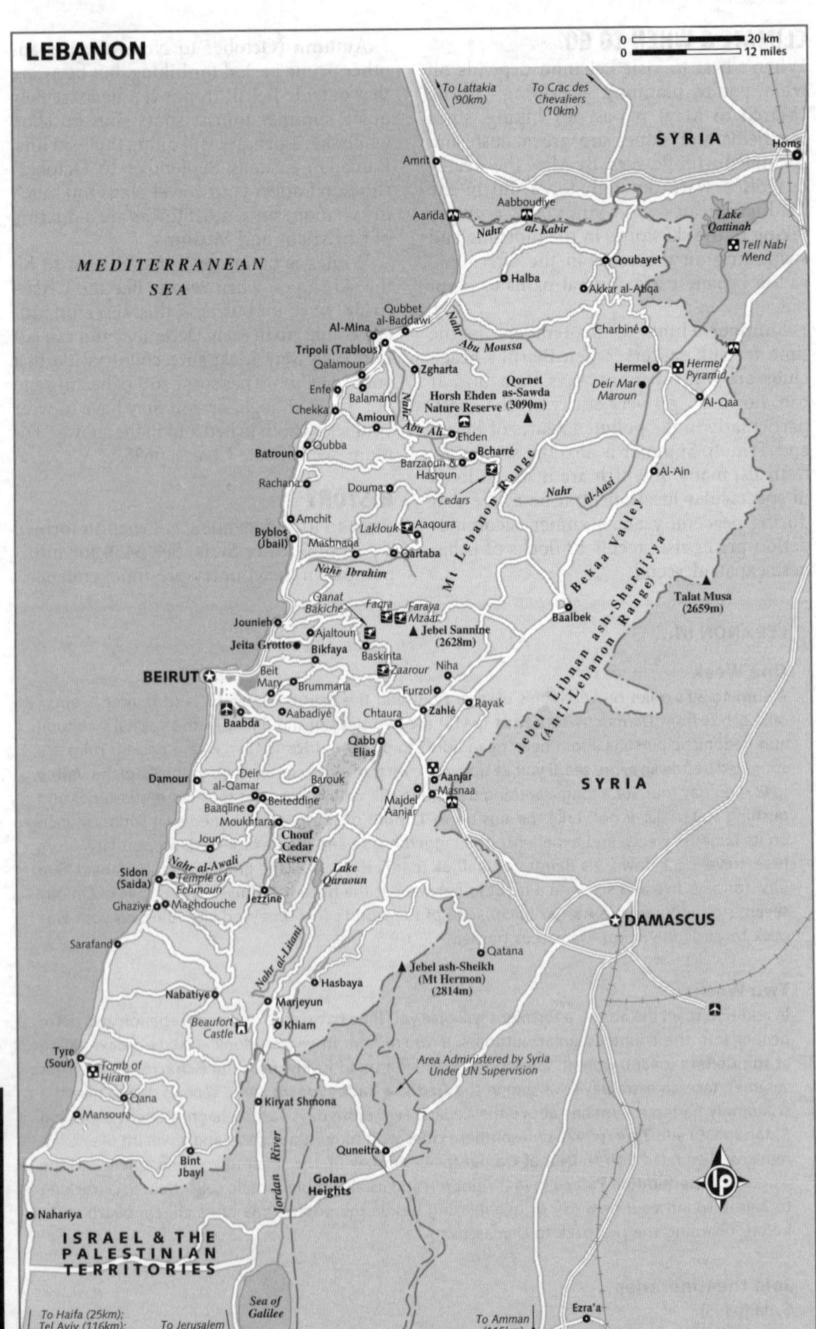
LEBANON
0 20 km
0 12 miles
To Lattakia (90km)
To Crac des Chevaliers (10km)
SYRIA
Homs
Amrit
Aarida
Aabboudiye
Nahr al-Kabir
Lake Qattinah
Tell Nabi Mend
MEDITERRANEAN SEA
Qoubayet
Halba
Akkar al-Atiqa
Qubbet al-Baddawi
Nahr Abu Moussa
Al-Mina
Tripoli (Trablous)
Charbiné
Qalamoun
Zgharta
Hermel
Hermel Pyramid
Enfe
Balamand
Qornet as-Sawda (3090m)
Deir Mar Maroun
Horsh Ehden Nature Reserve
Chekka
Nahr Abu Ali
Al-Qaa
Amioun
Ehden
Qubba
Batroun
Bcharré
Barzaoun & Hasroun
Al-Ain
Rachana
Douma
Cedars
Nahr al-Aasi
Amchit
Laklouk
Aaqoura
Mt Lebanon Range
Byblos (Jbail)
Mashnaqa
Qartaba
Bekaa Valley
Nahr Ibrahim
Talat Musa (2659m)
Qanat Bakiche
Faqra
Faraya Mzaar
Jounieh
Baalbek
Jebel Sannine (2628m)
Ajaltoun
Jeita Grotto
Bikfaya
Baskinta
Jebel Libnan ash-Sharqiyya (Anti-Lebanon Range)
BEIRUT
Beit Mary
Zaarour
Niha
Brummana
Furzol
Rayak
Baabda
Aabadiyé
Chtaura
Zahlé
Qabb Elias
Aanjar
SYRIA
Damour
Deir al-Qamar
Barouk
Masnaa
Beiteddine
Majdel Aanjar
Baaqline
Moukhtara
Chouf Cedar Reserve
Joun
Nahr al-Awali
Lake Qaraoun
Sidon (Saida)
Temple of Echmoun
Jezzine
Ghaziye
Maghdouche
DAMASCUS
Sarafand
Qatana
Jebel ash-Sheikh (Mt Hermon) (2814m)
Nahr al-Litani
Hasbaya
Nabatiye
Marjeyun
Beaufort Castle
Khiam
Tyre (Sour)
Tomb of Hiram
Area Administered by Syria Under UN Supervision
Qana
Kiryat Shmona
Mansoura
Jordan River
Quneitra
Bint Jbayl
Golan Heights
Nahariya
ISRAEL & THE PALESTINIAN TERRITORIES
Sea of Galilee
To Haifa (25km); Tel Aviv (116km); Jerusalem (180km)
To Jerusalem (150km)
To Amman (115km)
Ezra'a
LEBANON

The Early Years of Independence

Lebanon was officially declared independent in 1943, when, on 22 November, France – which had held its mandate since the end of WWI – gave in to the country's demands for independent rule. In 1946, the last French troops withdrew, and a jubilant Lebanon was left to fend for itself.

Prior to full independence, the government (also known as the National Assembly) had already been uniquely divided along religious lines: Christians and Muslims held parliamentary seats at a ratio of 6:5, broadly representing the religious make-up of the country established by a 1932 census. The president, the constitution stated, must be a Maronite Christian and the prime minister a Sunni Muslim. The speaker was to be a Shiite Muslim and the chief of staff a Druze. Though likely with lofty aims, dividing the country along sectarian lines from the very start was to be a major source of strife for years to come.

The early years of independence for the fledgling government weren't easy. First came economic strife and next, on 14 May 1948, the declaration of Israeli independence in former Palestine. Immediately, Lebanese soldiers joined pan-Arab armies and Palestinian fighters in the struggle against Israel. During 1948 and 1949, while war raged, Palestinian refugees flooded north into Lebanon; Amnesty International claims that the tiny nation absorbed more Palestinians than any other country, over 100,000 by the end of 1949 alone. Though initially welcomed into Lebanon, the Maronite majority soon became uneasy about the refugees, mostly Sunni Muslims, who threatened to tilt their precarious balance of power. In 1949, Lebanon accepted an armistice with Israel, but though 1948's UN Resolution 194 stated that refugees should be allowed to return home if they wanted to, this was largely not to be. The Palestinian refugees, largely against their own and locals' will, were in Lebanon to stay.

By the 1950s, the National Assembly was once again struggling against economic crisis, along with growing support for pan-Arabism, which advocated the creation of a united Arab entity in the Middle East. In 1952, staunchly pro-Western president Camille Chamoun quickly garnered Muslim enemies by refusing all notions of pan-Arabism, and in 1958, when his term was about to end, the unpopular president tried to extend his presidency to a second term. Lebanon's first civil war soon erupted, with pro-Western Maronites pitted against largely Muslim, pro–pan-Arabism opponents. Chamoun panicked, turning to the US for help, and on 15 July 1958, 15,000 US troops landed in Beirut.

The presence of US troops quelled trouble and Chamoun was finally persuaded to resign, to be replaced by a more even-handed president, Fouad Chehab. With Chehab's talent for smoothing ruffled feathers, Lebanon soon prospered, Beirut rapidly developing as the banking capital of the Arab world. Civil war, believed the optimistic Lebanese, was a thing of the past.

The Swinging '60s?

By the mid-'60s, Beirut, the newly crowned 'Paris of the East', was booming, but Palestinian refugees and the Shiites of the south remained in poverty. As Beirut basked in newfound riches, the less fortunate grew bitter and restive, and the good times were already numbered.

The collapse of the country's largest bank in 1966 and soon the 1967 Arab-Israeli Six Day War brought yet more Palestinian refugees fleeing into Lebanon. Refugee camps soon became centres of guerrilla resistance, and the government watched impotently as Palestinian attacks on Israel rapidly increased from Lebanese soil.

In May 1968, Israeli forces retaliated across the border. Meanwhile, with sectarian tensions growing, the Lebanese army clashed violently with Palestinian guerrillas. Palestinian forces proved too strong an opponent for the army, and in November 1969, Lebanon signed the Cairo Agreement with the Palestinian Liberation Organisation (PLO), agreeing to large-scale autonomy of its refugee camps and refugees' freedom 'to participate in the Palestinian revolution'.

Maronite opposition to the agreement was immediate. Many Muslims, on the other hand, felt an innate sympathy for their fellow Palestinians. In response, a group of Christians known as Phalangists began to arm and train young men, and by March 1970, fighting between Phalangists and Palestinians had erupted on Beirut's streets, as southern Lebanon suffered under Israeli reprisals against relentless guerrilla attacks. Rapidly, the country factionalised and took up arms.

Civil War

It's widely agreed that Lebanon's civil war began on 13 April 1975 when Phalangist gunmen attacked a Beirut bus, killing 27 Palestinian passengers. Soon, it was outright chaos. In December, Phalangists stopped Beirut traffic and killed Muslim travellers. Muslims did the same, prompting 'Black Saturday' during which around 300 people died.

The slaughter rapidly reached horrific proportions. In January 1976, Phalangists led a massacre of some 1000 Palestinians in Karantina, a Beirut slum. Two days later, Palestinians attacked the southern coastal town of Damour, and killed over 500 Christians. In August, Phalangists set their sights on the Tel al-Zaatar refugee camp, killing between 2000 and 3000 Palestinian civilians.

Soon Beirut was divided along the infamous Green Line, which split the city in two, with Christian enclaves to the east and Muslims to the west. Though allegiances and alliances along its border would shift many times in the coming strife, the Green Line would remain in place for another 15 years.

Syria & Israel Intervene

In 1976, the civil war gave Syria a reason to send tens of thousands of troops into Lebanon, initially sympathetic to the Palestinians and the pan-Arab cause. It wasn't long, though, before Syria switched allegiance to the Maronite side, occupying all but the far south and angering other Arab countries.

In October 1976, the Arab League nevertheless brokered a deal with Syria, allowing it to keep 40,000 troops in Lebanon as part of a peace-keeping 'Arab Deterrent Force'. Syria was left in primary control of Lebanon, and the first of the civil war's 150 short-lived ceasefires was declared.

But Palestinian attacks on Israel continued, prompting Israel to launch 'Operation Litani' in 1978, swiftly occupying most of southern Lebanon. Immediately, the UN demanded Israel's withdrawal and formed the UN Interim Force in Lebanon (UNIFIL) to 'restore international peace'. Though Israel withdrew to a 12-mile-wide 'Security Zone', it simultaneously installed a puppet South Lebanon Army (SLA) and proclaimed a 700-square-mile region south of Nahr al-Litani (the Litani River) 'Free Lebanon'. For the coming years, this area too would be knee-deep in war.

In 1982, Israeli 'Operation Peace for Galilee' troops marched into Lebanon, heading to Beirut, supported tacitly by Maronite and Phalangist leaders. By 15 June, Israeli forces had surrounded and besieged West Beirut, bombarding 16,000 PLO fighters entrenched there. Heavy fighting, unsurprisingly, ensued, and in just two months, the city was in ruins and 20,000, from both sides of the Green Line, were dead. On 21 August, the PLO left Beirut, guaranteed safe passage by multinational forces. By now, however, battle was also raging in the Chouf Mountains, the historic preserve of Druze and Christians and an area until now free from the ravages of war. The Lebanese army joined the Phalangists and Israelis against the Druze, who themselves were aided by the Shiite militia Amal, until the US intervened and another ceasefire was called.

The US, however, was becoming increasingly entrenched in the war, appearing to favour Israel and Lebanon's beleaguered government. In 1983 came the reprisals. In April, an Islamic jihad suicide attack on the US embassy in Beirut left 63 dead. In October, suicide bombers hit the US and French military headquarters in Beirut, killing over 300. In 1984, abductions and the torture of foreigners – whose involvement in Lebanese affairs the abductors deeply resented – began. The following year, international forces hastily left Lebanon.

Battle of the Camps

In early 1985, the last Israeli troops finally withdrew to their self-proclaimed 'security zone', leaving their interests in the hands of the SLA and Christian militias, who immediately clashed with Druze and Shiite opponents around Sidon. In West Beirut fighting continued between Shiite, Sunni and Druze militias, all battling for the upper hand.

In the midst of the chaos, PLO forces began to return to Lebanon. Concerned, however, that this would lead to a renewed Israeli invasion of the south, the Shiite Amal fought to remove them. Heavy fighting battered the Palestinian refugee camps during 1986, causing many more thousands of casualties.

THE DISPLACED & THE DISPOSSESSED

Most Palestinians who ended up refugees in Lebanon were relegated to UN Relief and Works Agency (UNRWA)–administered refugee camps, 12 of whose original 16 still house most of Lebanon's Palestinian population today.

According to UNRWA, there are now about 410,000 registered Palestinian refugees in Lebanon, and Amnesty International estimates that there are another 3000 to 5000 second-generation unregistered refugees living illegally and without rights.

Palestinian refugees in Lebanon still suffer from a lack of opportunities, prohibited from joining professions such as engineering and medicine, largely barred from owning property and with only limited access to public health care, education and welfare programs. Most are still provided for by UNRWA, which runs the camps' schools, hospitals, women's centres and vocational training programs.

They are not, however, Lebanon's only disadvantaged group. The Geneva-based Internal Displacement Monitoring Centre (IDMC) estimates there are between 216,000 and 800,000 Internally Displaced Persons in Lebanon, defined as individuals forced out of their homes due to war, persecution or natural disaster. Many, it states, remain displaced as a result of the 2006 war between Hezbollah and Israel, while the remainder are still displaced following Lebanon's civil war and Israeli invasions and occupation of southern Lebanon.

For more information, visit the IDMC website at www.internal-displacement.org or UNRWA at www.un.org/unrwa/english.

To add to the confusion, in 1987 the National Assembly government finally fell apart and split in two, with a Muslim government to the west of Beirut and a Christian administration to the east. Fighting along the Green Line continued to rage as Christian leaders attempted to drive Syria from Lebanon, angering Syria still more by accepting arms from Iraq, Syria's gravest enemy. It wasn't until 1989 that a road to peace finally seemed viable, with the drafting of the Taif Accord.

The Road to Peace

The Taif Accord, the product of a committee consisting of the Saudi and Moroccan kings and the Algerian president, proposed a comprehensive ceasefire and a meeting of Lebanon's fractured parliament to discuss a new government charter, which would redress the Christian-Muslim balance of power. The accord was formally ratified on 5 November 1989, and constitutional amendments included the expansion of the National Assembly from 99 to 128 seats, equally divided between Christians and Muslims.

Despite some resultant in-fighting, in August 1990 the National Assembly voted to accept the terms of the Taif Accord. With the exception of the still-occupied south, the country saw peace for the first time in 15 years, and the civil war officially ended on 13 October 1990.

Syria's continued presence in Lebanon beyond the civil war was justified with reference to Lebanon's weak national army and the government's inability to carry out Taif Accord reforms, including dismantling militias, alone. In 1990, Syria formalised its dominance over Lebanon with the Treaty of Brotherhood, Co-operation and Coordination, followed in 1992 by a defence pact. In May 1991, most militias – except Hezbollah, whose existence was justified by continuing Israeli occupation – were officially dissolved. In line with Taif Accord conditions, Syria began its military pull-out in March 1992, taking another 13 years to complete the job. The last Westerners kidnapped by Hezbollah were released in 1992.

Post-War Reconstruction

From 1993 onward the Lebanese army and life was slowly rebuilt and Rafiq Hariri, a Lebanese-born multimillionaire and entrepreneur, became prime minister.

Meanwhile, however, the south remained impoverished and the ground for Israeli-Hezbollah offensives. In 1993 Israel launched 'Operation Accountability' and in 1996 'Operation Grapes of Wrath' in response to Hezbollah and Palestinian attacks, the latter a land-sea-air offensive that devastated newly

WHO IS HEZBOLLAH?

The vicious 1983 suicide attacks on international forces heralded the first public appearance of Islamic Jihad, the armed wing of the radical, Iran-backed Shiite Hezbollah. Though relatively new, the group would soon prove a key figure in the civil war.

Historically, the Shiites had always been Lebanon's poor, concentrated in the south and having borne the brunt of Israeli retaliation against Palestinian guerrillas. As a minority group, they had little say in the country's government and had been displaced in vast numbers without adequate central aid.

With Syrian approval, Iranian revolutionary guards began to preach to the disaffected, who proved fertile ground for its message of overthrowing Western imperialism and the anti-Muslim Phalange. Alongside suicide bombings, its ruthless armed wing also resorted to hostage-taking, including CIA bureau chief William Buckley, who was tortured and killed; Associated Press bureau chief Terry Anderson; and UK envoy Terry Waite, who were held for almost seven and five years respectively.

Today, Hezbollah's armed tactics revolve around rocket attacks on Israel and kidnap missions against its soldiers, the group also concentrating on welfare projects in the still-stricken south, along with holding 14 seats in the Lebanese parliament. For more on the party's origins and social policies, see p448.

rebuilt structures, destroyed Beirut's power station, and killed around 106 civilians in the beleaguered southern village of Qana.

In 1999, Israel launched further attacks, targeting Beirut's power stations, while Hezbollah continued its offensives. Sustained losses, however, led to calls within Israel for military withdrawal, and its army finally withdrew from southern Lebanon on 24 May 2000. Hezbollah stated, however, that Israel would remain its target until Israeli troops were also withdrawn from Shebaa Farms, a 12-square-mile area southeast of Lebanon, captured by Israel in the 1967 Six Day War. In the years since the civil war, this bone of contention has frequently been the alleged reason for Hezbollah violence and Israeli retaliation.

In Lebanon, after 2000, discontent rumbled on. Maronite groups opposed Syria's refusal to withdraw from Lebanon while Shiites and Hezbollah continued to support its presence. On 2 September 2004, the UN issued Security Council Resolution 1559, which called 'upon all remaining foreign forces to withdraw from Lebanon'. Syria still did not comply, and on 20 October 2004, Prime Minister Hariri tendered his resignation, announcing that he would not be a candidate to head the next government.

The Killing of Rafiq Hariri

On 14 February 2005, a massive Beirut car bomb killed the former prime minister, Rafiq Hariri. The event triggered a series of demonstrations, with protestors placing blame firmly on Syria. Tens of thousands of protestors called for Syrian withdrawal from Lebanon, for an independent commission to investigate the murder of Hariri, and for the organisation of free parliamentary elections. Together, these events became known as the Cedar Revolution. On 14 March, Lebanon's largest-ever public demonstration was held in Martyrs' Sq, Beirut, with between 800,000 and one million attendees spanning sectarian divisions. The result was the March 14 Alliance, an anti-Syrian governmental alliance led by Saad Hariri, son of the murdered ex-prime minister, Samir Geagea and Walid Jumblatt.

With the UN, the USA, Russia and Germany all backing Lebanese calls for withdrawal, Syria finally bowed to pressure, withdrawing its 14,000 remaining troops from Lebanon on 27 April 2005 after almost 30 years of occupation. For the first time in more than two decades, Lebanon was completely free from military forces other than its own. This, however, was destined not to last.

Lebanon Today

The months after Syria's withdrawal were characterised by a spate of car bombs and targeted assassinations of anti-Syrian politicians and journalists, with growing calls for the expedition of a UN probe into Hariri's murder.

The 2005 parliamentary elections, the first after Syria's withdrawal, saw a majority win for the March 14 Alliance led by Saad Hariri, with Fouad Siniora elected Lebanon's new prime minister. The elections also saw Hezbollah become a legitimate governmental force, winning 14 seats in parliament while in the south its fighters continued to launch attacks on Israeli troops and towns. Though Siniora publicly denounced the attacks, it seemed that once again Lebanese authorities were powerless to stop them.

Meanwhile, the investigation into Hariri's death remained ongoing. The UN Security Council, along with the Lebanese cabinet, approved a special tribunal to prosecute those responsible for the crime. Currently, despite Syrian and Hezbollah protests, this is scheduled for some time after 2008, probably in The Hague.

On 12 July 2006, days after a Hezbollah incursion resulted in the deaths and kidnappings of several Israeli soldiers, Israel once again invaded Lebanon with the aim of destroying Hezbollah. For the following 33 days, Israeli warplanes pounded the country, resulting in the deaths of over 1000 Lebanese civilians. On 14 August fighting finally came to an end, though Israel maintained an air and sea blockade until 8 September.

Following the war Lebanon once again struggled back to its feet. Its tourist industry was hard hit, and homes and infrastructure countrywide were damaged or destroyed. Major contributors toward Lebanese reconstruction included Saudi Arabia, the European Union and a number of Gulf countries.

Lebanon's problems, however, are far from over. In December 2006, Hezbollah, Amal and various smaller opposition parties overran Beirut's centre in an attempt to bring down the government. Summer 2007 saw fierce fighting near Tripoli, with the Lebanese army battling Palestinian militants, while car bombs during the early part of the year killed two anti-Syrian members of parliament. More street fighting erupted in Beirut and Tripoli in early 2008, and a bus bombing in Tripoli in August 2008 prompted fears that Palestinian militant activity had still not been vanquished.

Meanwhile, the world's media continues to speculate that renewed conflict between Israel and Hezbollah – allegedly rearming furiously – is an ever-increasing likelihood.

TRAVEL WARNING: STAYING SAFE

Though its recent history has included several lengthy periods of relative calm, Lebanon's chequered religious, political and social fabric has frequently caused tensions to flare suddenly and violently.

Many countries, including the UK, Australia and the USA, currently include Lebanon on their list of countries to which all but essential travel should be avoided. Most specifically, foreign offices advise against travel south of Nahr al-Litani (the Litani River) or into Palestinian refugee camps, and suggest avoiding all public demonstrations.

Despite the bleak warnings, you'll find warm, welcoming people in Lebanon, eager to help travellers, and will quickly feel safe and at home.

Nevertheless, it's important to remember that circumstances can change extremely rapidly: in summer 2006, for example, many travellers suddenly found themselves stranded after Israel's attacks on the country shut down the international airport and rendered the main highway to the Syrian border impassable. Most crucially when in Lebanon, keep your eye on the news. **Ya Libnan** (www.yalibnan.com) and the **Daily Star** (www.dailystar.com.lb) are both good sources of up-to-the-minute online news.

More general suggestions include trying to avoid driving at night (largely due to Lebanon's hair-raising, headlight-free driving) and taking local advice when travelling in the south. If you're planning on visiting any Palestinian refugee camps, make sure you take a reliable local companion. Recent threats against UN Interim Forces in Lebanon (UNIFIL) troops have led some to warn against visiting restaurants or other establishments frequented by UNIFIL staff in Tyre. It may pay to talk with your embassy in Lebanon if you're in any doubt as to your safety.

Finally, theft is a minor problem, but random crime is far lower than in most Western cities. There are occasional spates of motor-scooter bag snatchings, particularly in Beirut but, as in any large city, you only need exercise normal precautions.

Though the Lebanese continue to live in hope, it seems fair to assume that the dark days are not over yet.

THE CULTURE

The National Psyche

Though Lebanon's 16 or so religions have fought quite consistently since the country's creation in 1943, one of the central paradoxes of the Lebanese psyche is the country's collective and overriding national pride in its tolerance of others. You're sure to hear this repeated throughout your trip, even when there's sectarian fighting going on just up the road.

You'll likely also experience the strange collective amnesia that seems to descend on the population if the country's civil war is ever brought up in conversation. A painful memory for most, reticence to talk about it (despite the physical scars that still pepper the landscape) is common. You usually won't encounter the same problem, however, if you mention current politics: everyone has an opinion they are keen to share on the political issue of the day. Another common feature among the Lebanese is the overriding optimism that 'everything's going to be all right', in the end.

While each of these three things may seem strange to a first-time visitor, you'll soon realise that each is essential to keeping the troubled country soldiering on, no matter how bad life gets.

The element of national identity, however, that will most profoundly affect visitors to the country is the justifiably legendary hospitality of the Lebanese towards their guests who, as the Lebanese saying goes, are a 'gift from God'. You'll be assured a warm welcome every step of the way, and will barely have to pause on a street corner for someone to offer you assistance, refreshingly free of strings. This makes Lebanon, despite its frequently violent reputation, a reassuringly comfortable place to spend time, and it won't take long for you to start reciprocating the Lebanese affection for their visitors ten-fold.

Daily Life

Though it's hard to generalise about such a traditionally factionalised country, family life, as in most Middle Eastern destinations, is central to all in Lebanon. Extended families often live close together, and many children live at home until married, either to save money for their own home or simply because they prefer it that way. Social life, too, is both close-knit and gregarious: everyone within a small community tends to know everything there is to know about everyone else.

Marriage is a second crucial factor throughout Lebanon, and members of all religions tend to marry young. An unmarried woman in her thirties will raise eyebrows, though a man still single at 30, as in most parts of the Middle East, is usually thought to be simply waiting for the right girl. And though there has traditionally been an expectation that people will marry within their religion, this barrier is slowly being broken down: many mixed-religion couples opt for marriage in Cyprus or Greece, if one half of the couple (usually the woman) doesn't choose to convert.

Alongside the importance of family and marriage, a university education is highly valued in Lebanon. Financial constraints aren't too much of an issue: those whose parents can't afford to subsidise them usually take part-time jobs alongside their classes. This is true for both men and women, since women of all religions are now readily accepted into all areas of the workplace, including the government. Many young people study with a view to emigrating overseas, lured by higher salaries and the promise of a safer, calmer lifestyle away from the unrest: for more on this, see the boxed text opposite.

HOW MUCH?

- **Cup of coffee** LL1500
- **Newspaper** LL2000
- **One-minute phone call to the UK** LL3000
- **Internet connection per hour** LL3000
- **Museum admission** LL5000

LONELY PLANET INDEX

- **Litre of petrol** LL1300
- **Litre of bottled water** LL600
- **Bottle of Almaza beer** LL3000
- **Souvenir T-shirt** LL8000
- **Sandwich** LL3000

As you'll notice from the pace of Beirut nightlife, young Christians – both male and female – usually have far greater social freedom than Muslims or members of other religions. But while these freedoms may at first appear similar to their Western counterparts, there are definite limits to acceptable behaviour. Drinking heavily, sleeping around or taking drugs is frowned upon in Lebanese society – not that you'd necessarily know it on a night out on Beirut's Rue Monot. And while party-central Beirut seems, on the surface, no different from any European capital city, venture just a few dozen kilometres north or south and you'll find people in traditional villages living and farming almost exactly as they did a century or more ago. Add to this a substantial Palestinian population almost entirely cut off from the mainstream – and rarely referred to in conversation by the Lebanese themselves – and you'll find that daily life in this tiny country is incredibly complex, and often wildly contrasting.

Population

Lebanon's official population of just under four million people is boosted by its Palestinian refugees, whom the UN Relief and Works Agency (UNRWA) puts officially at around 400,000.

It's a largely urban population, with around 90% of people living in cities, of which Beirut is the most highly populated, followed by Tripoli, Sidon and Tyre. According to the CIA World Factbook, the population growth rate currently stands at around 1.198%, with an average of 1.88 children per household, both figures very low for the Middle East. Lebanon has a youthful population: more than a quarter is currently under 14 years of age.

RELIGION

Lebanon hosts 18 'official' religious sects, which are Muslim (Shiite, Alawite, Ismaili and Sunni), Christian (Maronite, Greek Orthodox and Catholic, Armenian Catholic, Gregorian, Syrian Orthodox, Jacobite, Nestorian, Chaldean, Copt, Evangelical and Roman Catholic), Druze and Jewish. There are also small populations of Baha'is, Mormons, Buddhists and Hindus.

Muslims are today estimated to comprise around 60% of the population, though before the civil war, unofficial statistics put the ratio closer to 50:50, Muslim to Christian.

THE BRAIN DRAIN

A favourite topic of Lebanese conversation is the country's 'brain drain'. Current unofficial estimates suggest that one in three educated Lebanese citizens would like to live abroad, while a recent study by the Beirut Research and Development Centre (BRDC) found that 22% of the Lebanese population is actively working on an exit strategy. Another survey of university students showed that as many as 60% are hoping to leave Lebanon following graduation, for lives abroad.

There are a number of reasons why so many of Lebanon's bright young things are disappearing elsewhere, not the least the climate of fear that has lingered after the Israel-Hezbollah war of summer 2006. Terrorist attacks on Lebanese politicians, in which civilians are sometimes caught up, have also sent young Lebanese in pursuit of jobs overseas. Most popular tend to be the burgeoning Gulf States, which have the advantage of high salaries and being fairly close to home, with the USA, Canada and Europe all close seconds.

The second principal reason for the mass exit is that salaries in Lebanon are often simply too low to make for a comfortable, viable living. 'I've got a great job, a car, a high salary,' explains Mirvat Melki, a software engineer originally from Beirut, on leave from a lucrative position in Ghana. 'All the things I could never dream of having here in Lebanon, even though I'm pretty highly qualified. I earn about 10 times as much, per month, there as I would do here – if I could get a job at all.' People, he says, who have managed to acquire good jobs – often through family connections – hold tight to them and are reluctant to relinquish the security and move on. Many younger, educated people, he continues, are afraid for the country's future. 'Politics aren't safe; taxes are high; economics are bad. It cost me US$100,000 to go to university. In Lebanon, I'd have to work for a million years to pay that back. I miss home, but under these conditions, what choice do I have?' Perhaps one day, he says, he'll come home – but until then, like so many young Lebanese professionals, he's enjoying the financial freedom of a life overseas too much to think about it just yet.

The shift is attributed to the mass emigration of Christians during and since the civil war, and to higher birth rates among Muslims.

Traditionally, Muslim Shiites have largely inhabited the south of the country, the Bekaa Valley and southern suburbs of Beirut. Sunnis, meanwhile, have been concentrated in Beirut, Tripoli and Sidon; the Druze in the Chouf Mountains and Maronite Christians (the largest Christian group) have populated the Mt Lebanon region. Though recent years have seen population shifts, particularly in Beirut, this still largely holds true today.

ARTS

In summer, many towns and villages hold fabulous dance and music festivals (see p452), which are well worth looking out for. Baalbek's international festival is a particular highlight on the calendar. The nation's capital hosts its own lively arts scene, and is well equipped with theatres, cinemas and venues for the visual and performing arts.

Literature

Though for much of the 20th century Beirut was the publishing powerhouse of the Middle East, it suffered during the civil war and much of its recent literary output has been shaped by this long drawn-out and horrific event. Even today, a great deal of Lebanon's literary output remains concerned with themes drawn from these 15 years of hardship.

Of the writers who remained in Lebanon during the civil war, Emily Nasrallah is a leading figure, and her novel *Flight Against Time* is highly regarded. Those who work overseas include London-based Tony Hanania, born in 1964 and author of the 1997 *Homesick* and 2000 *Eros Island,* and Amin Maalouf, whose most enchanting book, *The Rock of Tanios,* is set in a Lebanese village where the Sheikh's son disappears after rebelling against the system.

Of those authors most widely available in translation, Lebanon's two major figures are Elias Khoury and feminist author Hanan al-Shaykh. Al-Shayk's *Story of Zahra* is a harrowing account of the civil war, while her *Beirut Blues* is a series of long letters that contrast Beirut's cosmopolitan past with the book's war-torn present. Elias Khoury has published 10 novels, many available in translation: his 1998 novel *Gate of the Sun* has achieved particular international acclaim.

Poet Khalil Gibran (1883–1931; for more, see p437) remains the celestial light in Lebanon's poetry scene. Interestingly, today poetry is once again flourishing in the largely Shiite south, partly due to a movement known as *Shu'ara al-Janub* (Poets from the South), for whom poetry has become a means of expressing the frustrations and despair of life in that most war-ravaged of regions.

Cinema & TV

Lebanese cinema managed to survive the raw civil war years and is today reappearing with vigour and verve, despite frequently difficult circumstances. Docudays (www.docudays.com), Beirut's annual documentary festival, is highly regarded internationally and attracts a global crowd, while

TOP 10 GREAT READS

Here's some fact, some fiction to accompany any journey through Lebanon.

- *Sitt Marie Rose: A Novel* (1982), by Etel Adnan
- *The Stone of Laughter* (1998), by Hoda Barakat
- *The Rock of Tanios* (1994), by Amin Maalouf
- *Memory for Forgetfulness: August, Beirut 1982* (1982), by Mahmoud Darwish
- *Death in Beirut* (1976), by Tawfiq Yusuf Awwad
- *Pity the Nation: Lebanon at War* (2001), by Robert Fisk
- *Bliss Street* (2004), by Kristin Kenway
- *Beirut Blues* (1994), by Hanan al-Shayk
- *The Prophet* (1923), by Khalil Gibran
- *Lebanon: A House Divided* (2006), by Sandra Mackey

MUSTN'T-MISS MOVIES

If you get the chance, don't fail to look up some of these cinematic treasures.

- *Towards the Unknown* (1957), directed by Georges Nasser
- *West Beirut* (1998), directed by Ziad Duweyri
- *The Little Wars* (1982), directed by Maroun Baghdadi
- *The Broken Wings* (1962), directed by Yousef Malouf
- *In the Shadows of the City* (2000), directed by Jean Chamoun
- *Caramel* (2007), directed by Nadine Labaki
- *Bosta* (2005), directed by Philippe Aractingi
- *Giallo* (2005), directed by Antoine Waked
- *Bint el-Haress* (1967), directed by Henry Barakat
- *Harab Libnan* (2001), directed by Omar al-Issawi

several film academies in the city churn out young hopefuls. A particular recent cinematic highlight occurred in 2007, when two Lebanese directors, Nadine Labaki and Danielle Arbid, made it to the prestigious Cannes Film Festival for their respective films *Caramel* and *Un Homme Perdu, Caramel* dealing daringly with inter-religious marriage and lesbianism.

The greatest of the cinematic lates was undoubtedly Georges Nasser, whose tragic 1958 *Ila Ayn?* (Whither?) is a classic of Lebanese cinema, and became the first to represent Lebanon in the Cannes festival. Later, the civil war temporarily brought Lebanon's film industry to a virtual halt, and most filmmakers were forced to work outside the country, seldom having their films shown within its boundaries. Ironically, though, many critics believe Lebanese cinema actually produced some of its best work under the highly restricted circumstances of the tragic war.

Modern classics to look out for are *West Beirut* (1998), directed by LA-based Ziad Duweyri (a former Tarantino cameraman), which tells the semi-autobiographical story of a teenager living in West Beirut during the first year of the civil war, and the award-winning documentary, *Children of Shatila*, of the same year, which looks at the history of the notorious refugee camp through children's eyes. On the lighter side of things, look out for Michel Kammoun's recent *Falafel*, a romantic comedy involving a young man on his perilous way to a Beirut party.

Music

Lebanon's two most famous female vocalists are the living legend Fairouz and the younger Najwa Karam, known as the 'Sun of Lebanese song'. Fairouz has enjoyed star status since her first recordings in Damascus in the 1950s, and later became an icon for Lebanon during the civil war (which she sat out in Paris). Now in her seventies, she still performs several concerts annually, composing new songs with her son Ziad, a renowned experimental jazz performer.

Najwa Karam, meanwhile, has managed to create an international audience for traditional Lebanese music, rising to stardom during the 1990s. With more than 16 albums under her belt, including the 2001 *Nedmaneh* with over four million copies sold worldwide, she remains a driving force on the Lebanese music scene.

Current hot names in mainstream pop include Nancy Ajram, Haifa and the 4 Cats, all with catchy tunes and raunchy videos. More good, solid pop is presented, from a male perspective, by Fadl Shakir. Another popular male musician, who marries classical Arabic music with contemporary sounds, is Marcel Khalife, hailing from Amchit, near Byblos. An oud player with a cult following, many of his songs have a controversial political side, such as his composition for the dead of the Sabra and Shatila refugee camps.

In the bars and clubs of Beirut's Rue Monot and Rue Gouraud, contemporary fusions of oriental trip-hop, lounge, drum and bass and traditional Arabic music, for both the dance floors and chilling out,

LISTEN TO THE BAND

Some travellers have told us that it's hard to track down live music in Lebanon. But armed with a few suggestions, you shouldn't have too much trouble finding yourself a memorable evening in the presence of some terrific local tunes.

In Beirut, your best first point of reference are newspaper and magazine listings (p417), along with flyers and posters, which you'll find largely on the streets of **Hamra** (p419) and at the **Virgin Megastore** (p417) on the Place des Martyrs. Along with one-off concerts, several Beirut venues offer reliable live music options almost every night of the week. Try the **Blue Note** (p425) for live jazz, the **Gemmayzeh Café** (p425) for traditional Lebanese sounds and **Bar Louie** (p425) for funky small live outfits.

Outside the capital, it may be more difficult to track down live music, though during the summer months you're likely to stumble across small local festivals with great local music performances in a variety of shapes and sizes. Across the country, there are also a few notable places to head to for evening drinks and tunes. The **Cafés du Bardouni** (p447) in Zahlé usually have live performances going on in the summer months, while up the coast from Beirut, the **Citadelle Café** (p432) at Byblos has nice live performances on Friday nights. Down south the **Al-Midane Café** (p445) at Deir al-Qamar has great live music on the atmospheric town square at summer weekends. And finally, if you see a wedding in swing anywhere, see if you can wangle yourself an invitation to step inside (usually not difficult, due to the Lebanese love of guests): the music's almost always live and the dance floor heaving with generations of Lebanese at their partying best.

have for the last few years dominated sound systems. Groups like the Beirut-based REG Project – Ralph Khoury, Elie Barbar and Guy Manoukian – specialise in Arab deep house and lounge. You'll hear these sounds, along with traditional belly-dancing tunes remixed to electronic music, almost anywhere you stop off for a strong drink and a good dance or two.

Architecture

Ancient architecture in Lebanon can be found at Baalbek's (p447) spectacular remains, in the traces of the Romans in Beirut (p419) and at the Umayyad ruins at Aanjar (p450).

Much of Lebanon's more recent heritage architecture has been damaged over the last century by the combined effects of war and redevelopment, though there remain a substantial number of examples of the country's traditional architecture dotted about the country. To the north, Tripoli's old city souqs contain a wealth of medieval and Islamic architecture, while Deir al-Qamar (p445), in the southern Chouf Mountains, is a well-preserved village with some beautiful 18th- and 19th-century villas and palaces. Beiteddine Palace (Beit ad-Din; see p444), also in the Chouf Mountains, is a melange of Italian and traditional Arab architecture, more remarkable for its lavish interiors than any architectural innovation.

Interior designers are doing wonderful work in Lebanon these days, and the B 018 nightclub (p426), designed by Bernard Khoury, is a top-notch example. Situated on the former Green Line, the club pays homage to the past at a site that was formerly a quarantine zone, a refugee camp and the site of an appalling massacre during the war – and is worth a visit as much for its appearance as its sizzling-hot DJs and crowd.

Painting

Lebanon's first art school was established in 1937, and by the 1950s and '60s a number of galleries opened to showcase the country's art, while the private Sursock Museum (p421), in Achrafiye, began to show new artists.

Though, like most of Lebanon's cultural output, the visual arts suffered during the civil war, the scene re-established itself with vigour soon afterwards. Apart from the earlier William Blake–style paintings of poet Khalil Gibran, famous 20th-century artists include the painters Hassan Jouni, Moustafa Farroukh and Mohammed Rawas. Better-known contemporary painters include Marwan Rechmawi, Bassam Kahwaji,

Amin al-Basha, Helen Khal, Salwa Zeidan and Etel Adnan (who, like Gibran, is also a writer) and Salwa Raodash Shkheir, a current Lebanese star of the sculpture world.

The photography and visual arts scene is the most vibrant and cutting-edge of all the arts in the region. The best places to experience the current Lebanese visual arts scene are the numerous small galleries around Hamra and Gemmayzeh and in the studios of Saifi Village (p419).

Theatre & Dance

Most theatre in Lebanon is based in Beirut, where prominent and established Lebanese playwrights such as Roger Assaf, Jalal Khoury and Issam Mahfouz are trying to encourage younger artists – though lack of funding remains a perennial problem – and a revitalised Lebanese theatre scene is gradually emerging. Beirut's Théâtre de Beyrouth (p426) in particular puts on high-quality performances (often experimental works) by young and emerging actors and playwrights.

As in other parts of the Middle East, both *dabke*, the traditional Levantine folk dance, and *raks sharki* (belly dancing) are very popular. Caracalla (www.caracalla.org) is the closest thing Lebanon has to a national dance troupe. Founded by Ahmed Caracalla, the choreographer of the Baalbek Festival in the 1960s, the group's performances are inspired by oriental dance, but also combine opera, dance and theatre. With colourful costumes and musicals based on diverse sources, from Shakespeare to modern Lebanese literature, they can be seen at some of Lebanon's summer festivals, and at the Monnot Theatre (p426) in Achrafiye.

ENVIRONMENT

The Land

Though Lebanon is one of the smallest countries in the world, its terrain is surprisingly varied and diverse. Four main geographical areas run almost parallel to each other from north to south. They are (from west to east): the coastal plain, the Mt Lebanon Range, the Bekaa Valley and the Anti-Lebanon Range.

The Mt Lebanon Range includes Lebanon's highest summit, Qornet as-Sawda

TRAVELLING SUSTAINABLY IN LEBANON

There are many simple but effective ways to have a positive impact while visiting oft-troubled Lebanon.

- Engage the services of a park guide at nature reserves, whose fee goes toward preserving and enhancing the area.
- Share the wealth among the lesser-known businesses: limiting your use of international chains will ensure a better distribution of tourist income.
- Don't stick solely to our Eating recommendations: you'll be evenly distributing the tourist dollar, and embarking on your own adventure of the senses, if you go where you tastebuds take you.
- Consider hiking with one of Lebanon's many trekking groups (see p452) who have valuable insights into low-impact tourism.
- If you're renting a car, try to team up with other travellers to split the cost: you're reducing the environmental impact substantially if you can cram four travellers into a Fiat Punto.
- Look for recycling points for your plastic water bottles, which bob with the tide in alarming numbers along the Beirut seashore.
- Take a registered guide to show you around ancient historic sites. In recent years, work has been sporadic for these invaluable sources of local knowledge.

Take a look at the Lebanese Greenpeace site (www.greenpeace.org.lb), the Ministry of the Environment (www.moe.gov.lb), the Society for the Protection of Nature in Lebanon (www.spnlb.org), or the UN site (www.unep.org/Lebanon) for more information on Lebanon's environment.

MEMORABLE MEALS IN LEBANON *heatherpavitt*

Breakfast in Beiteddine Go for the Lebanese breakfast at the Mir Amin Palace (p445). Fuul (fava bean paste); beans in lemon and olive oil; juicy mountain tomatoes; the tiniest sweet cucumbers; labneh (a thick curd yogurt); olives; the most delicious apricot jam and freshly made Lebanese bread. Sensational.

Lunch in Deir al-Qamar Ask for *lahm bi'ajeen* (meat pastry) at the small bakery opposite the main square in this picturesque 17th-century village (p445). The baker makes them on the spot, and two of these delicious pizza-like delicacies will fill you up and taste a treat.

Dinner in Baalbek After exploring the ancient ruins, enjoy a meal at the Palmyra Hotel (p449). For about US$15 I enjoyed *shish tawooq* (skewered, grilled chicken); *fattoosh* (a lettuce-based salad with Arabic bread croutons); hummus and a half bottle of local red wine. Sumptuous.

What's your recommendation?
www.lonelyplanet.com/middle-east

(3090m) and an example of the famous Cedars of Lebanon at the Cedars (p438). The Anti-Lebanon Range marks the border between Lebanon and Syria. Its highest summit is Jebel ash-Sheikh (Mt Hermon), at 2814m.

Environmental Issues

Ravaged by more than two decades of war, anarchy, unfettered construction and weak state control, Lebanon's environment remains very fragile, and some of the only areas to have escaped destruction are – ironically – the heavily landmined or cluster-bombed areas, still filled with unexploded ordinance.

The complete lack of basic service industries or infrastructure during the civil war meant that solid waste was dumped throughout the country, and many water sources are still polluted. Air pollution is another serious, ongoing problem particularly in Beirut, with a couple of million cars (many of them ancient, spluttering wrecks or petrol-guzzling SUVs) plying its crowded roads. Add to this catastrophic oil spills caused by the 2006 Israel-Hezbollah war (see www.oilspilllebanon.org for details) and it's not a pretty picture that emerges.

All, however, is not lost for Lebanon. A host of local and international NGOs are working to secure a better future for Lebanon's environment, while the government itself seems, in theory at least, committed to change. Huge national parks like Chouf Cedar Reserve (which makes up an incredible 5% of Lebanon's landmass) are, though underfunded and overstretched, working hard on protecting its wildlife. With time, money and persistence, there's still hope for the country to prove that, as the saying goes, great things come in small packages.

For a long list of Lebanese environment-related links, go to Leb Web at www.lebweb.com/dir/lebanon-environment.

FOOD & DRINK

Lebanese cuisine has a reputation as being one of the very best in the Middle East. The proof of the pudding, as they say, is in the eating, so sample as much of it as you possibly can.

Fresh ingredients, including numerous types of fruit, vegetables and pulses, are plentiful in Lebanon. Mezze, small dishes often served as starters, are a godsend for vegetarians even in the most far-flung parts of the country, with hummus, tabouleh and salads galore, while seafood and grilled meats are staunch favourites of carnivores. In Beirut, the diversity and quality of food on offer matches any international city: want tapas at two in the morning, or sushi at six? You'll find it all here.

Arabic or 'Turkish' coffee is particularly popular in Lebanon – look out for the men dispensing tiny, strong cups of it from the back of battered old Volkwagen vans – while delicious freshly squeezed vegetable and fruit juices are on offer almost everywhere throughout the summer. Alcohol, too, is widely available in Lebanon; Beirut's awash with cocktails, but the most popular alcoholic old-timer is the potent aniseed-flavoured arak, mixed liberally with water and ice, and sipped alongside meals or a long game of backgammon. The best local beer is Almaza, which lives up to its name ('diamond' in Arabic) when served ice-cold.

See p97 for a more general description of the region's culinary delights.

BEIRUT بيروت

☎ 01 / pop 1.3 million

Beirut, the nation's capital, is a fabulous place of glitz, glamour, restaurants and beach clubs – if, that is, you're one of the lucky ones. While the city centre is filled with suave sophistication, the outskirts of town comprise some of the most deprived Palestinian refugee camps of all, and its crowded slums provide a breeding ground for Hezbollah fighters. If you're looking for the real East-meets-West so talked about in the Middle East, this is precisely where it's at. Crowded and ancient, beautiful and blighted, hot and heady, home to Prada and Palestinians, Beirut is many things at once, most of them contradictory but all, without doubt, compelling.

HISTORY

Though there's evidence of a city on the site of modern Beirut dating back at least to ancient Egyptian times, it wasn't until the Roman era that the city really came into its own, both as a commercial port and military base and, by the 3rd century AD, as the location of a world-renowned school of law, one of the first three in the world. The city's fame continued until 551 AD, when a devastating earthquake and resultant tsunami brought massive death, destruction and decline. The law school was moved to Sidon, and Beirut didn't regain its importance as a trading centre and gateway to the Middle East until the 16th century, under local emir Fakhreddine.

In the 19th century Beirut enjoyed a commercial boom, but also the first of much meddling by European powers as French troops arrived at the city's port. The early years of the 20th century saw citywide devastation, the combined result of a WWI Allied blockade, famine, revolt and plague, which killed in total a quarter of its population. Following WWII, however, the city slowly became a major business, banking and publishing centre and remained so until the bloody, brutal civil war that ravaged the city's streets and citizens put paid to its supremacy.

Following the end of the war in 1990, rehabilitation of the city's infrastructure became the major focus of both the local and national governments, to restore its Paris of the East reputation. Beirut's battle scars, however, remain visible throughout the city.

ORIENTATION

Though there are lots of useful landmarks by which to navigate around town (the towering, derelict former Holiday Inn being the most obvious; see Map p420), navigating Beirut can still be a little tricky. The blue signs on street corners don't usually give the name of the street itself; instead, only the sector (suburb) name and rue (street) number. On top of this, numbered buildings are rare, and many streets don't have names at all, or are locally known by a different name from the one given on a map. That said, armed with a good street map (see below), getting familiar with this compact city is actually rather easy.

The university districts of Hamra and Ras Beirut, with their plethora of hotels, bookshops, cafés and restaurants, is the preferred base for many travellers. Directly north of Hamra runs the seafront Corniche, or Ave de Paris, along which are stringed Beirut's beach clubs and most of its top hotels. To the south is affluent Verdun, home to designer clothes shops that line the Rue Verdun. East from Hamra, you'll reach the beautifully restored Beirut Central District (BCD) or Downtown, at the centre of which is the landmark Place d'Étoile, also known as Nejmeh Sq, lined with pavement cafés. Just east again is the Place des Martyrs, where the huge Mohammed Al-Amin Mosque (reminiscent of İstanbul's Blue Mosque) is another useful landmark.

Edging the Place des Martyrs is the Rue de Damas, which was once the Green Line separating warring East and West Beiruts, and further west you'll find the funky Gemmayzeh district, centred on Rue Gouraud. A little south from here, you'll reach Achrafiye, another super-cool district, famous for its clubbing street, Rue Monot.

Maps

An invaluable aid to wandering Beirut is the English-language *Zawarib Beirut* (LL15,000 or US$10), which is a complete, large-scale A-Z-style street map of the entire city. Remember, though, that the street names listed here are in their English, rather than French, form (eg Damascus Blvd rather than Rue de Damas).

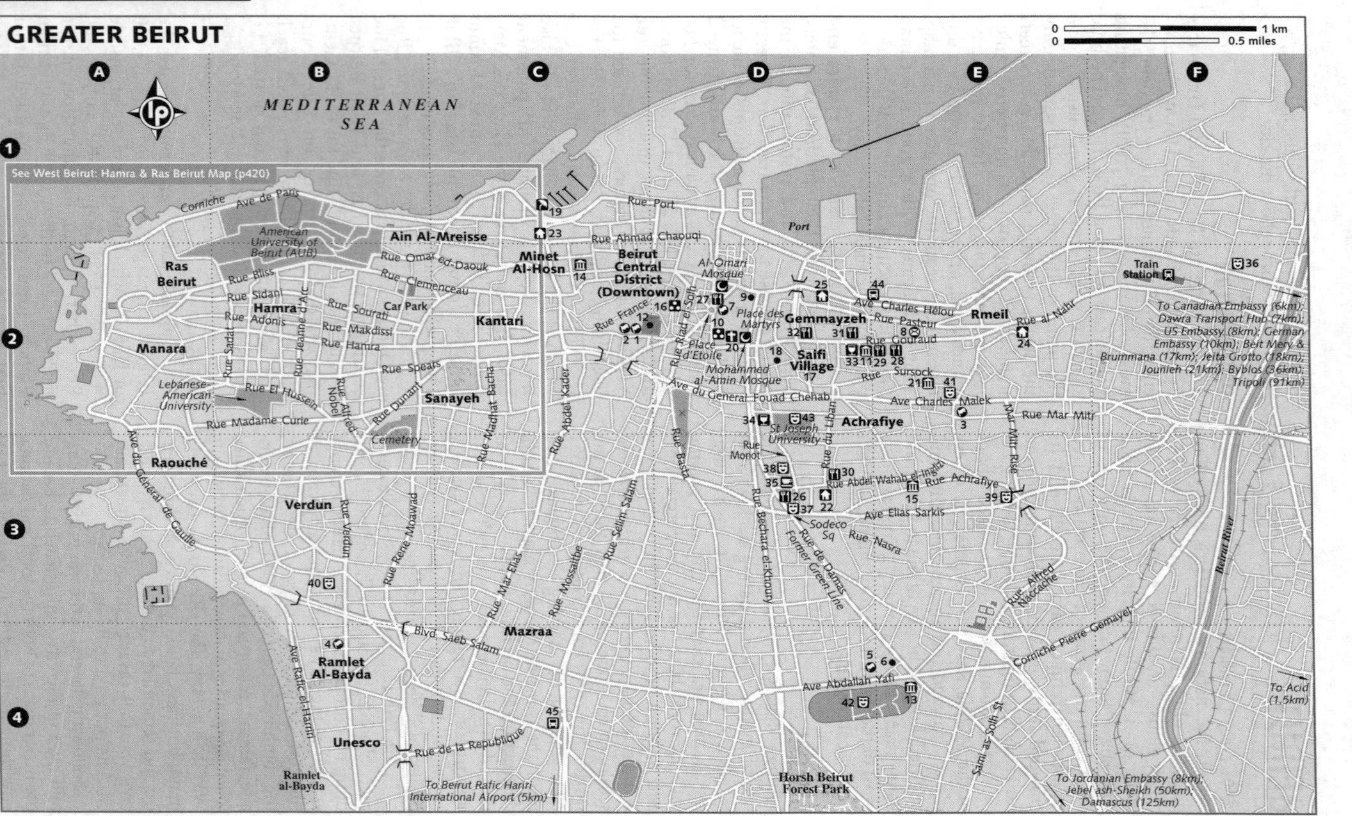
GREATER BEIRUT
0 1 km
0 0.5 miles
A B C D E F
1 2 3 4
MEDITERRANEAN SEA
See West Beirut: Hamra & Ras Beirut Map (p420)
Corniche
Ave de Paris
American University of Beirut (AUB)
Ain Al-Mreisse
Ras Beirut
Rue Bliss
Rue Sidani
Hamra
Rue Adonis
Rue Jeanne d'Arc
Rue Sourati
Car Park
Rue Makdissi
Rue Hamra
Rue Omar ed-Daouk
Rue Clemenceau
Kantari
Manara
Rue Sadat
Rue Spears
Lebanese-American University
Rue El Hussein
Rue Alfred Nobel
Rue Dunant
Sanayeh
Rue Madhat Bacha
Rue Madame Curie
Cemetery
Raouché
Ave du Général de Gaulle
Minet Al-Hosn
Rue Port
Rue Ahmad Chaouqi
Beirut Central District (Downtown)
Al-Omari Mosque
Port
Rue France
Rue Riad el-Solh
Place des Martyrs
Place d'Etoile
Mohammed al-Amin Mosque
Gemmayzeh
Saifi Village
Ave Charles Helou
Rue Pasteur
Rue Gouraud
Rue Sursock
Rmeil
Rue al Nahr
Train Station
To Canadian Embassy (6km); Dawra Transport Hub (7km); US Embassy (8km); German Embassy (10km); Beit Mery & Brummana (17km); Jeita Grotto (18km); Jounieh (21km); Byblos (36km); Tripoli (91km)
Ave du General Fouad Chehab
Ave Charles Malek
Rue Mar Mitr
Mar Mitr Rise
Achrafiye
St Joseph University
Rue du Liban
Rue Monot
Rue Abdel Wahab el-Inglizi
Rue Achrafiye
Ave Elias Sarkis
Sodeco Sq
Rue Nasra
Rue de Damas
Former Green Line
Rue Bechara el-Khoury
Rue Basta
Rue Abdel Kader
Rue Selim Salam
Rue Mossaitbe
Rue Mar Elias
Rue Rene Moawad
Rue Verdun
Verdun
Blvd Saeb Salam
Mazraa
Ramlet Al-Bayda
Ave Rafic el-Hariri
Unesco
Rue de la Republique
Ramlet al-Bayda
To Beirut Rafic Hariri International Airport (5km)
Horsh Beirut Forest Park
Ave Abdallah Yafi
Sami as-Solh St
Corniche Pierre Gemayel
Rue Alfred Naccache
Beirut River
To Acid (1.5km)
To Jordanian Embassy (8km); Jebel ash-Sheikh (50km); Damascus (125km)

Another useful street map is the city map provided on the back of the countrywide *Lebanon Tourist Map* (LL12,000), published by Paravision (www.paravision.org). Both are widely available in Beirut bookshops.

INFORMATION

Bookshops

Beirut has a good range of foreign-language bookshops (which keep standard opening hours unless indicated otherwise).

Books & Pens (Map p420; ☎ 741 975; Rue Jeanne d'Arc, Hamra; 8am-10pm Mon-Fri, 8am-8pm Sat) This stationers and bookshop stocks a decent selection of local and international newspapers and magazines.

Librairie Antoine (Map p420; ☎ 341 470; Rue Hamra, Hamra) If you're out of holiday reading, this place stocks literature (including Lebanese) in English, French and Spanish, and has a good children's section.

Naufal Booksellers (Map p420; ☎ 354 898; Rue Sourati, Hamra) Stockists of all things Lebanese, and a terrific place to browse for books and plan your onward travel.

Virgin Megastore (Map p416; ☎ 999 666; Opera Bldg, Place des Martyrs, Downtown; 9am-11pm Mon-Sat) A huge collection of books and maps on Lebanon, fiction and children's books, local and regional music, and the place to pick up tickets for Lebanon's summer festivals.

Emergency

Ambulance (☎ 140)
Fire brigade (☎ 175)
Police (☎ 160)
Tourist police (☎ 350 901)

Internet Access

There's no shortage of internet cafés all across Beirut; the highest concentration is in the vicinity of the AUB campus (p419). Opening hours are very flexible, though most open around 9am and stay open until well after midnight. Prices are generally around the LL3000 per hour mark.

PC Club (Map p420; ☎ 745 338; Rue Sidani, Hamra) A popular student hangout that rarely shuts up shop.

Virgin Café (Map p416; ☎ 999 777; 4th fl, Opera Bldg, Place des Martyrs, Downtown) Situated on the 4th floor of the Virgin Megastore, this is one of the only internet places currently operating in Downtown.

Web Café (Map p420; ☎ 03-283 456; Rue Makhoul, Hamra) Surf the internet while sipping an ice-cold beer.

Laundry

Most Beirut budget hotels can arrange laundry loads for around US$3 per four to five kilograms; the higher-end hotels will charge this just for one item.

Laundromatic (Map p420; ☎ 03-376 187; Rue Sidani, Hamra; load under/over 4.5kg LL4000/5500, dryer per 10 min LL2000; 9am-7pm Mon-Sat) Service wash and ironing services are also available for an extra charge.

Media

Beirut's two foreign-language newspaper dailies are the French language **L'Orient Le Jour** (www.lorientlejour.com; LL2000) and the English **Daily Star** (www.dailystar.com; LL2000). Online, the very best source of independent news is **Ya Libnan** (www.yalibnan.com).

The *Guide* (LL5000) is a useful glossy monthly that reviews the latest hotspots

INFORMATION		
Australian Embassy	1	C2
British Embassy	2	C2
Dutch Embassy	3	E2
Egyptian Embassy	4	B4
French Embassy	5	D4
General Security Office	6	E4
Italian Embassy	7	D2
Libanpost	8	E2
Virgin Café	(see 9)	
Virgin Megastore	9	D2
SIGHTS & ACTIVITIES		
Cardo Maximus	10	D2
Galerie Alice Mogabgab	11	D2
Grand Serail	12	C2
National Museum of Beirut	13	E4
Planet Discovery	14	C2
Robert Mouawad Private Museum	15	E3
Roman Baths	16	D2
Saifi Village	17	D2
Souq el-Tayeb	18	D2
St George Yacht Motor Club	19	C1
St George's Cathedral	20	D2
Sursock Museum	21	E2
SLEEPING		
Hotel Albergo	22	D3
InterContinental Phoenicia Hotel	23	C1
Pension al-Nazih	(see 25)	
Port View Hotel	24	E2
Talal's New Hotel	25	D2
EATING		
Abdel Wahab el-Inglezi	26	D3
Al Dente	(see 22)	
Al-Balad	27	D2
La Tabkha	28	E2
Le Chef	29	E2
Le Sushi Bar	30	D3
Olio	31	D2
Paul	32	D2
DRINKING		
Bar Louie	33	D2
Gemmayzeh Café	(see 31)	
Hole in the Wall	(see 34)	
Pacifico	34	D2
Torino Express	(see 33)	
Tribeca	35	D3
ENTERTAINMENT		
B 018	36	F2
Cassino	37	D3
Crystal	38	D3
Empire ABC	39	E3
Empire Dunes	40	B3
Empire Sofil Centre	41	E2
Hippodrome	42	D4
Monnot Theatre	43	D2
TRANSPORT		
Charles Helou Bus Station	44	E2
Cola Transport Hub	45	C4
Kurban Tours	(see 23)	

(including bars, cafés and restaurants) and details of forthcoming gigs, concerts, shows, exhibitions, festivals, and events for kids. Though its production is often beset by problems, *Time Out Beirut* (www.timeoutbeirut.com, LL5000), when it does appear, is an invaluable source of local information.

Medical Services

American University of Beirut Hospital (Map p420; ☎ 350 000, 354 911; Rue Sourati, Hamra) Considered one of the best hospitals in the Middle East, with English and French spoken.

Money

There are ATMs all over the city, most of which dispense both US dollars and Lebanese lira. Moneychangers are dotted plentifully along Rue Hamra.

Amir Exchange (Map p420; ☎ 341 265; Rue Hamra, Hamra; ⏲ 8am-8pm Mon-Sat). One of the very few moneychangers accepting travellers cheques, it charges US$2 to US$3 per US$100. Bring your passport and original purchaser's receipt.

Sogetour (Map p420; ☎ 747 111; www.sogetour.com.lb; 1st fl, Block A, Gefinor Center, Rue Maamari, Ras Beirut; ⏲ 8.30am-4pm Mon-Fri, 8.30am-1pm Sat) The best place to change Amex US-dollar travellers cheques (2% commission).

Post

Libanpost, the national post office, has plenty of branches scattered through town. Standard opening hours are 8am to 5pm Monday to Friday and 8am to 1.30pm Saturday. There are two convenient branches, **Hamra** (Map p420; ☎ 344 706; Matta Bldg, Rue Makdissi, Hamra) and **Gemmayzeh** (Map p416; ☎ 422 902; Zighbi Bldg, Rue Gouraud, Gemmayzeh).

Tourist Information

Tourist information office (Map p420; ☎ 343 073; www.destinationlebanon.gov.lb; Ground fl, Ministry of Tourism Bldg, 550 Rue Banque du Liban, Hamra; ⏲ 8am-1.30pm & 2-4.30pm Mon-Thu, 8am-3pm Fri, 8am-1pm Sat) Enter by the back door, through a covered car park, to find helpful staff, informative brochures, and LCC bus route maps.

Tourist police (Map p420; ☎ 752 428; fax 343 504; ⏲ 24hr) For complaints or problems (including robbery), contact this office opposite the Tourist information office.

Travel Agencies

The following are just two of the many Beiruti travel agencies:

Campus Travel (Map p420; ☎ 744 588; www.campus-travel.net; Maktabi Bldg, Rue Makhoul, Ras Beirut) Travel agency focused on student travel, which can arrange trips into Jordan and Syria, along with Lebanese ski jaunts.

Tania Travel (Map p420; ☎ 739 682; www.taniatravel.com; Rue Sidani, Hamra; ⏲ 8am-6pm Mon-Sat) On the 1st floor opposite the old Jeanne d'Arc theatre, this agency offers daytrips all over Lebanon, as well as to Damascus.

Visa Extensions

See Visas (p454) in the Lebanon Directory for details of how and where to extend your tourist visa.

DANGERS & ANNOYANCES

The biggest danger – and annoyance – in Beirut is the traffic. Rules both on and off the road are nonexistent, and pedestrians should take particular care when crossing the road. As with everywhere in Lebanon, it makes sense to keep abreast of the news and to avoid political demonstrations (at the time of research, the Hezbollah encampment on Place des Martyrs was also somewhere to avoid) and unaccompanied travel to Beirut's Palestinian refugee camps.

SIGHTS & ACTIVITIES

National Museum of Beirut

This must-see **museum** (Map p416; ☎ 612 295/7; www.beirutnationalmuseum.com; cnr Rue de Damas & Ave Abdallah Yafi; adult/student/child LL5000/1000/1000, guide US$15; ⏲ 9am-5pm Tue-Sun, except some public holidays) situated on the former Green Line has an impressive, but not overwhelming, collection of archaeological artefacts, and offers a great overview of Lebanon's history and the civilisations that made their home here.

Highlights include some beautifully observed Phoenician marble statues of baby boys (from Echmoun, 5th century BC), lovely 3rd- and 4th-century AD mosaics, Byzantine gold jewellery (found in a jar under the floor of a villa in Beirut) and the famous, much-photographed Phoenician gilded bronze figurines from Byblos (p429). A floor plan is distributed free with tickets, or you can opt for a more informative written guide (LL15,000) from the gift shop.

The museum screens a fascinating 12-minute documentary in its **theatrette** (ground fl; ⏲ every hr 9am-4pm) in English hourly or French on demand, detailing how curators saved the collection during the civil war and subsequently restored it to its former glory.

To get to the museum, walk 15 minutes south from Sodeco Sq along Rue de Damas, or hail a service taxi and ask for the Musée or the Hippodrome.

Hamra & Ras Beirut

Though not as impossibly hip as Achrafiye and Gemmayzeh, the university hubs of Hamra and Ras Beirut are home to hordes of students, giving the area a cheap and cheerful charm. You'll find good-value shopping opportunities strung along Rue Hamra, while Rue Bliss is home to lots of good bookshops and 24-hour cafés: perfect for a nargileh along with your Nietzsche.

AMERICAN UNIVERSITY OF BEIRUT (AUB)

One of the Middle East's most prestigious universities, the AUB is spread over 28 calm and tree-filled hectares, an oasis in the heart of a fume-filled city. Its **AUB museum** (Map p420; ☎ 340 549; http://ddc.aub.edu.lb/projects/museum; AUB campus, Ras Beirut; admission free; 🕑 10am-4pm Mon-Fri, except university & public holidays), just inside the university's main gate, is well worth a look. It was founded in 1868, making it one of the oldest museums in the Middle East. On display is a collection of Lebanese and Middle Eastern artefacts dating back to the early Stone Age, a fine collection of Phoenician glass and Arab coins from as early as the 5th century BC, and a large collection of pottery dating back to 3000 BC.

Downtown

In Beirut's swinging '60s heyday, a visit to Beirut's central Downtown district, filled with gorgeous Ottoman-era architectural gems, was akin to a leisurely stroll along Paris's Left Bank. By the 1980s, it had become the horrific, decimated centre of a protracted civil war; during the 1990s, it proved the focus of former prime minister Rafiq Hariri's colossally ambitious rebuilding program.

Today, Downtown's streets are surreally, spotlessly clean and traffic-free, and the whole area beautiful and impressive, though some locals suggest it lacks a little soul. Though in happier times Downtown could even have been described as touristy, much of the area is currently cordoned off to traffic (due to the ever-present threat of political assassinations and terrorism) by rolls of barbed wire and carefully stationed tanks; expect your bags to be searched as you enter.

While strolling Downtown's nevertheless quiet, soothing streets, don't miss the **Al-Omari Mosque** (Map p416), built in the 12th century as the Church of John the Baptist of the Knights Hospitaller and converted by the Mamluks into a mosque in 1291, and the new, Blue Mosque–like **Mohammed al-Amin Mosque** (Map p416), in which slain prime minister Rafiq Hariri is buried. Beside the Mohammed al-Amin Mosque, **St George's Cathedral** (Map p416; ☎ 561 980; services 7.15am & 6.30pm Mon-Thu & Sat, 9am & 11am Sun) is a Maronite church dating from the Crusades.

Worth exploring, too, are the magnificently restored **Roman baths** (Map p416), the **cardo maximus** (Map p416) and the **Grand Serail** (Map p416), a majestic Ottoman-era building now housing government offices.

For a spot of shopping, head to the nearby **Saifi Village** (Map p416; 🕑 10am-7pm Mon-Sat, late night shopping Thu), a cute, restored district filled with arts, crafts and clothing boutiques. On Saturdays **Souq el-Tayeb** (Map p416; ☎ 03-340 198; www.souqaltayeb.com; Saifi Village car park; 🕑 9am-2pm) sets up here, dispensing organic farmers' wares from around the country.

THE HOLIDAY INN

Though you might claim to have stayed in the world's worst Holiday Inn, this Beirut landmark takes things to another level entirely. Probably the most painful remaining monument to the civil war, it now rises above the Corniche like a huge concrete gravestone from behind the swanky Intercontinental Phoenicia.

Opened to great fanfare just weeks before the start of the civil war, the hotel quickly became a prime sniper position, which resulted in its forlorn and bullet-riddled appearance. Designed to withstand an earthquake, the building remains derelict, shreds of curtains still flapping at its windows, its only residents today a sizeable community of pigeons. Perhaps one day it will be a place of bustling porters and tinkling cocktail glasses once more; until then, it remains an enduring reminder of the dark days still uncomfortably close behind.

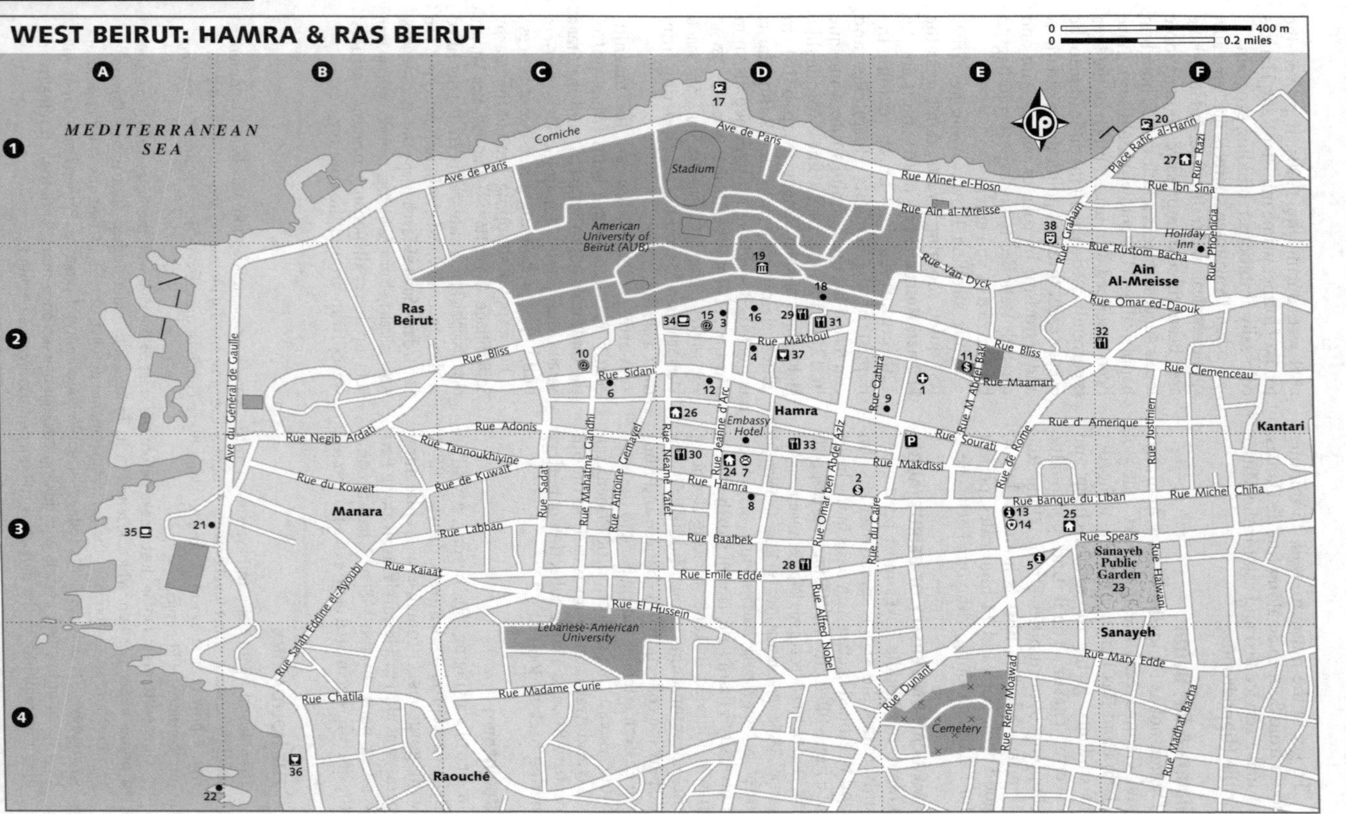
WEST BEIRUT: HAMRA & RAS BEIRUT
0 400 m
0 0.2 miles
MEDITERRANEAN SEA
Ain Al-Mreisse
Kantari
Hamra
Ras Beirut
Manara
Raouché
Sanayeh
Sanayeh Public Garden
American University of Beirut (AUB)
Lebanese-American University
Stadium
Cemetery
Corniche
Holiday Inn
Embassy Hotel
Ave de Paris
Ave du Général de Gaulle
Place Rafic al-Hariri
Rue Minet el-Hosn
Rue Ain al-Mreisse
Rue Van Dyck
Rue Bliss
Rue Graham
Rue Rustom Bacha
Rue Omar ed-Daouk
Rue Ibn Sina
Rue Razi
Rue Phoenicia
Rue Clemenceau
Rue Justinien
Rue d' Amerique
Rue Michel Chiha
Rue Banque du Liban
Rue de Rome
Rue Spears
Rue Halwani
Rue Madhat Bacha
Rue Mary Edde
Rue Rene Moawad
Rue Dunant
Rue Maamari
Rue M Abdel Baki
Rue Sourati
Rue Makdissi
Rue Qahira
Rue du Caire
Rue Omar ben Abdel Aziz
Rue Alfred Nobel
Rue Makhoul
Rue Jeanne d'Arc
Rue Hamra
Rue Baalbek
Rue Emile Eddé
Rue El Hussein
Rue Neamé Yafet
Rue Antoine Gemayel
Rue Sidani
Rue Mahatma Gandhi
Rue Sadat
Rue Adonis
Rue Tannoukhiyine
Rue de Kuwait
Rue Labban
Rue Kalaat
Rue Madame Curie
Rue Negib Ardati
Rue du Koweit
Rue Salah Eddine el-Ayoubi
Rue Chatila

Corniche

Stretching roughly from Pigeon Rocks in the south to the St George Yacht Club further north, the seafront Corniche is every Beiruti's favourite promenade spot, especially in the early evening around for sunset, and then on – aided by backgammon, nargilehs and barbeques – late into the night. Here, you'll find old-timers discussing the way things were, young hopefuls debating how they will be one day; pole fishermen, families, courting couples and cavorting children. Grab a piece of sea wall and a strong coffee, and delight in some people-watching par excellence. And if it's something more serene you're looking for, walk on down to **Pigeon Rocks** (Map p420), Beirut's famous natural offshore arches, where you can forget – for a few minutes at least – the trammels of the city.

If you fancy a dip, several of Beirut's chic, silicone-friendly **beach clubs** are situated along this stretch (note that the word 'beach' is used loosely, since there's barely a grain of sand to be found in any of them). Try out the **AUB beach** (Map p420; Ain al-Mreisse; admission AUB students LL3500, guests LL10,000), which is slightly scruffy but with a great student vibe, the swish **St George Yacht Motor Club** (Map p416; ☎ 356 350; Ain al-Mreisse; Mon-Fri LL15,000, Sat & Sun LL20,000), with its extensive facilities and upscale crowd, or the small but perfectly formed **La Plage** (Map p420; ☎ 366 222; Ain al-Mreisse; admission LL20,000; 🕑 9am-7pm May-Oct) filled with beautiful, bronzed bodies.

Achrafiye

Built on the site of a Roman City of the Dead, Achrafiye is an attractive and largely sedate area, historically one of the preserves of Beirut's Christian population and today dotted with galleries, antique shops and churches. Though eclipsed by neighbouring neighbourhood Gemmayzeh in terms of cool, Achrafiye's nightlife, centred on Rue Monot, remains legendary.

SURSOCK MUSEUM

With its stained glass dramatically illuminated at night, you won't miss this **museum** (Map p416; ☎ 334 133; Rue Sursock; admission free; 🕑 call for hrs), which opens only when there are exhibitions scheduled (check listings in the *Daily Star* or the *Guide*). Try, if you can, to get to see one, since the museum's spectacular marble and wood-panelled interior is every bit as dazzling as whatever is on display.

ROBERT MOUAWAD PRIVATE MUSEUM

Another worthwhile small **museum** (Map p416; ☎ 980 970; www.rmpm.info; cnr Rue Achrafiye & Rue Baroudi; 🕑 9am-5pm Tue-Sun), housed in a splendid old mansion, this place is filled with the findings of its one-time owner, the jeweller and collector Robery Mouawad. Like the Sursock Museum, it is a welcome, beautiful respite from a hot Beirut day.

Gemmayzeh

Gemmayzeh, centring on pretty Rue Gouraud, is for many locals Beirut at its best. Here's where hole-in-the-wall bars fill with revellers and the strains of live music as night sets in and where, during the day, you can peruse some cute and arty boutiques. There's also a scattering of art galleries for those interested in Beirut's contemporary arts scene: head to **Galerie Alice Mogabgab** (Map p416; ☎ 210 424, Rue Gouraud) to see it for yourself.

INFORMATION

Name	No	Grid
American University of Beirut Hospital	1	E2
Amir Exchange	2	D3
Books & Pens	3	D2
Campus Travel	4	D2
Helem	5	E3
Laundromatic	6	C2
Libanpost	7	D3
Librairie Antoine	8	D3
Naufal Booksellers	9	E2
PC Club	10	C2
Sogetour	11	E2
Tania Travel	12	D2
Tourist Information Office	13	E3
Tourist Police	14	E3
Web Café	15	D2

SIGHTS & ACTIVITIES

Name	No	Grid
American Language Center	16	D2
AUB Beach	17	D1
AUB Main Gate	18	D2
AUB Museum	19	D2
La Plage	20	F1
Luna Park	21	A3
Pigeon Rocks	22	A4
Sanayeh Public Garden	23	F3

SLEEPING

Name	No	Grid
Casa d'Or	24	D3
L'Hote Libanais	25	E3
Mayflower Hotel	26	D2
Regis Hotel	27	F1

EATING

Name	No	Grid
Barbar	28	D3
Bliss House	29	D2
Consumers Co-op	30	D3
Japanese, Please!	31	D2
Pasta di Casa	32	F2
Walimat Wardeh	33	D3

DRINKING

Name	No	Grid
Al-Kahwa	34	D2
Al-Raouda	35	A3
Bay Rock Café	36	B4
Blue Note	37	D2

ENTERTAINMENT

Name	No	Grid
Théâtre de Beyrouth	38	E1

VOLUNTEERING IN LEBANON

For those with time and energy to devote to a good cause, Lebanon has lots of volunteer opportunities. Visit these websites for more information.

- **Association for Volunteer Services Lebanon** (www.avs.org.lb) A great first point of contact for volunteering in Lebanon.
- **Daleel** (www.thedaleeel.com) An internet guide with many links to charities and other organisations.
- **Lebanon Association of SOS Children's Villages** (www.sos.org.lb) Part of the SOS global network.
- **Palestinian Human Rights Organisation** (PHRO; www.palhumanrights.org) Provides information on all aspects of Palestinian refugee life in Lebanon.

BEIRUT FOR CHILDREN

Beirutis go gaga for children, and you'll have no problem finding family-friendly activities, restaurants and hotels throughout town. Good brands of baby supplies – nappies, powdered milk and the like – are widely available at pharmacies.

At the southern end of the Corniche, kids will love all things flashy and screechy at **Luna Park** (Map p420; Manara; rides around LL5000; 10am-midnight), whose Ferris wheel offers great views from its pinnacle. Meanwhile, further up the Corniche, the **St George Yacht Motor Club** (see p421) has a nice children's pool, a playground, and grassy lawns to dash about on.

Though Beirut's hardly blessed with an abundance of open spaces, kids can let off steam somewhere green at the **Sanayeh Public Garden** (Map p420), with bike and skate hire available.

For something more cerebral, head to **Planet Discovery** (Map p416; ☎ 980 650; Espace Starco, Rue Omar ed-Daouk, Beirut Central District; admission LL5000; 9am-3pm Mon-Thu, 10am-7.30pm Fri & Sat), a fun and interactive science museum for ages three to 15. Puppet or magic shows are held most Fridays and Saturdays at 4pm and 5pm, for an additional fee of LL5000 per person.

FESTIVALS & EVENTS

Beirut International Film Festival (www.beirutfilmfoundation.org) Held in October, this festival showcases films from Lebanon and the wider Middle East.

Beirut International Marathon (www.beirutmarathon.org) Held each autumn, and popular with international athletes, the marathon includes various wheelchair and fun-run events.

Docudays (www.docudays.net) The wonderful Beirut International Documentary Festival, held every November or December, sees international audiences flock to the city.

SLEEPING

Budget

Decent budget accommodation is thin on the ground in Beirut, and Lonely Planet regularly receives traveller emails from those who booked a room – or an airport taxi – only to find none awaiting them. To try to guard against this, reconfirm your booking 24 hours before your arrival, and take along any email or fax correspondence as proof of dates, times or prices.

Talal's New Hotel (Map p416; ☎ 562 567; tnh@yahoo.com; Ave Charles Helou, Gemmayzeh; dm/s/d/tr US$7/16/20/24;) A friendly owner and a livelier vibe than nearby al-Nazih make this place probably the best budget bet in town. Rooms are small and simple but clean (some come with bathroom and TV), and the owner will strive to squeeze you in on the roof in summer if the place is full. There's a communal kitchen and internet access (first 15 minutes free, LL1000 per hour thereafter), and laundry costs US$3 per 5kg.

Pension al-Nazih (Map p416; ☎ 564 868; www.pension-alnazih.8m.com; Rue Chanty, Gemmayzeh; d LL37,500, dm/s/d LL15,000/22,500/45,000;) A decent, plain option just a few steps away from Talal's, the hotel's 10 rooms are ever popular with travellers and are clean, basic and quiet. The owner's particularly keen on filling the air with fresheners and fly sprays so, while hygienic, the atmosphere (definitely in terms of oxygen, rather than ambience) can be rather florid. Breakfast costs US$3 extra, and airport pick-up can be arranged for US$15. Note that only double rooms come with bathroom.

Regis Hotel (Map p420; ☎ 361 845; Rue Razi, Ain al-Mreisse; s/d/tr US$28/34/34;) It might look bleak and barren from the outside, but this basic place – while in no sense cozy – offers large rooms, helpful staff and a great proximity to Beirut's Corniche. Ask for a room with a sea view (rooms 101, 201, 301, 401 or 402); if you're a group of three travelling together, a big bonus is that a triple room costs the same as a double.

Midrange

Most of Beirut's midrange options are located in and around Hamra, though since most suffer from street noise, opt for a room at the back. It's well worth asking about discounts (sometimes as much as 40%) if you're visiting out of season.

our pick **L'Hote Libanais** (Map p420; ☎ 03-513 766; www.hotelibanais.com; Zico House, 174 Rue Spears, Sanayeh; s US$40-50, d US$60-70) If you really want to get under the skin of the country, stay with the people, an option made possible by L'Hote Libanais, which arranges B&B home stays in Beirut and beyond. Discounts for multiple-night stays and a range of accommodation are on offer. Email the helpful staff for the full list of excellent home-stay options.

Port View Hotel (Map p416; ☎ 567 500; www.portviewhotel.com; Rue Gouraud, Gemmayzeh; s/d/tr US$50/70/105;) A notch or two in terms of comfort above the budget options, the Port View is small, friendly and comfortable, and within easy walking distance of Rue Gouraud's bars and restaurants. Ask the knowledgable manager for his latest tips on exploring Beirut.

Casa d'Or (Map p420; ☎ 746 400; www.casadorhotel.com; Rue Jeanne d'Arc, Hamra; s/d/ste US$60/70/90;) One of Beirut's best midrange hotels, the Casa d'Or is a welcome addition to the often tired, beige-and-brown options of the Hamra sleeping scene. Its rooms are bright, cheery and well equipped, while equally appealing are its substantial off-season discounts.

Mayflower Hotel (Map p420; ☎ 340 680; www.mayflowerbeirut.com; Rue Neamè Yafet, Hamra; s/d/tr US$80/94/114;) An old-fashioned Beirut institution, the Mayflower claims to have been 'exceeding guests' expectations since 1957'. Don't necessarily expect quite so much from a stay here, but the rooms are certainly comfortable, the rooftop pool is a definite bonus, and a drink or two at the venerable Duke of Wellington bar a must.

Top End

Hotel Albergo (Map p416; ☎ 339 797; www.albergobeirut.com; 137 Rue Abdel Wahab el-Inglezi, Achrafiye; d from US$255, ste US$325-1400;) If it's unequivocal luxury you're after in that most perfect of boutique settings, look beyond the hefty price tag to the 33 glorious rooms of the Achrafiye-based Albergo. Attentive staff, divine Italian food at the hotel's Al Dente (p424) restaurant and a cute rooftop pool complete the plush picture in this delicious, antique-embellished old place.

InterContinental Phoenicia Hotel (Map p416; ☎ 369 100; www.ichotelsgroup.com; Rue Fakhr ed-Dine, Minet el-Hosn; s US$310-330, d US$275-540, ste from US$990;) Beirut's most prestigious pre–civil war address is now back on the luxury scene, with miles of marble and all the whistles and bells you could hope for. Heavy security is usually in place since this is the favourite haunt of Lebanese politicians and elite, meaning that you'll likely have your bag and body searched en route to your opulent, feather-pillowed suite.

EATING

Beirutis love to eat out, whether at chic top-end brasseries or at tiny hole-in-the-wall shwarma joints; and the city stays open late for its diners, with few arriving for dinner before 9pm or 10pm. The best thing about Beirut is the breadth of culinary choice, and things change fast on the culinary scene: by all means sample our own personal highlights, but don't miss the opportunity to branch out to seek your own.

Restaurants

HAMRA & RAS BEIRUT

Pasta di Casa (Map p420; ☎ 363 368; Rue Clemenceau, Ras Beirut; mains around LL9000; noon-midnight;) With its rafters, checked curtains and tablecloths, you'd be forgiven for thinking you'd stumbled into a tiny Italian backstreet eatery. The pasta portions are huge and delicious; the salads are fresh and tasty, and the prices are as tiny as its 10-tabled interior. Bring cash, since credit cards aren't accepted.

Walimat Wardeh (Map p420; ☎ 752 320; Rue Makdissi, Hamra; mains LL10,000; noon-3pm, 8pm-midnight;) Simple, stylish and well hidden, this place offers great music (with tango on Thursday nights) and a daily changing chalked-up menu, veering from Lebanese towards wider Mediterranean.

DOWNTOWN

Al-Balad (Map p416; ☎ 985 375, Rue Ahdab; mezze LL5000; ⏲ noon-midnight; ⊠) Sadly, Downtown's downturn in recent years has signalled the closure of many of its best lunch hangouts, but Al-Balad remains ever-popular and ever-present. With traditional Lebanese cooking prepared to its own special recipes, this is one of the best places for a tableful of mezze, including one mean red pepper hummus.

ACHRAFIYE

Abdel Wahab el-Inglezi (Map p416; ☎ 200 552; Rue Abdel Wahab el-Inglizi; mezze LL6500; ⏲ noon-4pm & 7pm-1am; ⊠) Set in a pretty old Ottoman house, this choice is renowned for its sumptuous buffets and high-quality hummus, of which it has more varieties than you can shake a chickpea at.

Le Sushi Bar (Map p416; ☎ 338 555; Rue Abdel Wahab el-Inglizi; sushi LL6000 per portion; ⏲ noon-midnight; ⊠) Credited with the launch of the sushi craze in Beirut, this place has also featured in *Vogue Paris*' feature '100 Best Restaurants in the World'. It's the place to splash out on all things that once splashed about; reservations for dinner are a must.

Al Dente (Map p416; ☎ 202 440; Hotel Albergo, 137 Rue Abdel Wahab el-Inglizi; mains LL14,500-38,000; ⏲ noon-3pm & 8.30-11pm Sun-Fri, 8.30-11pm Sat; ⊠) Suitably grand and resplendent as the Hotel Albergo's (p423) significant other, this restaurant's Italian dining is indulgent and divine. Bookings are essential, as are the melt-in-the-mouth risottos.

GEMMAYZEH

Olio (Map p416; ☎ 563 939; Rue Gouraud; pizza LL9000-15,000; ⏲ noon-midnight Mon-Sat; ⊠) Fill up on wood-fired pizza and delicious bruschettas washed down with stout red wines at this little Italian joint amid Rue Gouraud's manifold dining options. Get here early to secure a windowside table, perfect for watching the well-heeled crowds clattering by.

our pick **Le Chef** (Map p416; ☎ 445 373; Rue Gouraud; 2-course meals LL10,000; ⏲ 6am-6.30pm Mon-Sat) A beloved Beiruti institution; don't miss a lunch or two at this little Lebanese time warp, where waiters dish up vast platefuls of 'workers' food' to all and sundry. If it's on offer that day, try one of the regional specialities, including *molokhiyya*, a gloopy – and allegedly aphrodisiac – combination of rice, soup, mallow leaves, chicken and lamb.

La Tabkha (Map p416; ☎ 579 000; Rue Gouraud; mains LL8000; ⏲ noon-midnight Mon-Sat, 11am-5pm Sun; ⊠) A great bet for vegetarians, who'll love the lunchtime mezze buffet, this minimalist place offers good French and Lebanese dishes, with a menu that changes daily.

Cheap Eats

Every sector of Beirut is blessed with its own complement of felafel, kebab, fruit juice and shwarma stands, and a good rule of thumb, as ever, is to go where the locals seem to be going. A felafel sandwich should usually set you back around LL2500, a large fresh juice LL3000 and a hearty shwarma LL3000.

Barbar (Map p420; Rue Spears, Hamra; ⏲ 24hr) A phenomenally popular chain selling everything from mezze and shwarma to BBQ chicken wings and vegetarian pizza, as well as pastries, ice cream and fantastic fresh juice, to get stuck into on the pavement out front.

Bliss House (Map p420; Rue Bliss, Ras Beirut; ⏲ 7am-5am; ⊠) Always packed with AUB students grabbing a late-night snack or two, Bliss's three shop fronts offer decent-quality fast food at good prices including shwarma, kebabs, fruit cocktails and vitamin-boosting juices.

Japanese, Please! (Map p420; ☎ 361 047; Rue Bliss, Hamra; sushi from LL2000 per portion; ⏲ 11am-4pm & 7-11pm Mon-Sat) This tiny sushi bar offers welcome respite from yet another on-the-run shwarma, and does some tasty teriyaki and tempura too.

Paul (Map p416; Rue Gouraud, Gemmayzeh; ⏲ 8am-11pm; ⊠) A coffee chain but a good one, Paul makes a great place for a breakfast treat, with croissants and pastries coming in at around the LL3000 mark. The interior's cool, wooden and inviting, but there's also an outdoor terrace if you're in the mood for a spot of sun.

Self-Catering

Beirut is packed with small neighbourhood grocery shops, usually with a good greengrocers alongside. The **Consumers Co-op** (Map p420; Rue Makdissi, Hamra; ⏲ 7am-11pm) is the best supermarket that Hamra has to offer, with lots of local and imported goodies, and a great *charcuterie* a few doors down. For an organic, locally produced picnic, head to the **Souq el-Tayeb** (p419) on a Saturday, for tantalising farmers market treats.

GAY & LESBIAN BEIRUT

Though homosexuality is illegal in Lebanon, there's a thriving – if clandestine – gay scene in Beirut. Both **Acid** and **B 018** nightclubs (see nightclubs listings below) are very gay-friendly establishments, while Beirut's hammams and cafés provide plenty of opportunities to meet and greet.

Your first point of contact, though, should be **Helem** (Map p420; ☎ 745 092; www.helem.net; 1st fl, Yamout Bldg, 174 Rue Spears, Beirut) whose name derives from the Arabic acronym for the Lebanese Protection for Lebanese Gays, Bisexuals and Transgenders. The organisation's website and its offshoot, www.beirut.helem.net, offers plenty of information, listings and news.

Other useful gay and lesbian resources include:

- http://legal.20m.com
- www.bintelnas.org
- www.gaymiddleeast.com
- www.travelandtranscendence.com

DRINKING

Beirut has an embarrassment of riches when it comes to bars. For a drink in the afternoon, the coffee stops of the Corniche and Hamra are your best, and liveliest, bets; after dinner, the action moves to Gemmayzeh and Achrafiye, where you can bar-hop merrily into the wee hours.

Bars

Pacífico (Map p416; Rue Monot, Achrafiye; local beers LL6000; 7pm-late) Styling itself on 1920s Havana, this club prides itself on its food (Cuban-Mexican) and lengthy cocktail list (with more than 200 treats on offer). Happy hour, between 7pm and 8pm, is a good way to get an evening out started.

Hole in the Wall (Map p416; Rue Monot, Achrafiye; beer LL5000; 7pm-late) Particularly popular with expats, this is a great little pub where you can get a proper pint, and respite from the cooler-than-cool of many Rue Monot drinking destinations.

Bar Louie (Map p416; Rue Gouraud, Gemmayzeh; 11am-late) Laid-back and lively, this little bar hosts live music almost nightly. A couple of doors down, its 'shots bar' is the place to go if you're in need of a good strong pick-me-up, or advice on clubbing hotspots from its hip bartenders.

Torino Express (Map p416; ☎ 03-611 101; Rue Gouraud, Gemmayzeh; 8am-2am) One of Beirut's coolest small bars, this place is a café by day, transforming into a happy, friendly bar by night, aided by some delicious cocktails and a great DJ.

Blue Note (Map p420; ☎ 743 857; Rue Makhoul, Hamra; 11am-2am) This is one of the very best places to hear jazz and blues in Lebanon. Local – and sometimes international – bands perform at least every Thursday, Friday and Saturday, and admission (LL8800 for local bands, LL19,800 for international) is only charged on evenings when music is live.

Cafés

Bay Rock Café (Map p420; ☎ 796 700; Ave du Général de Gaulle, Raouché; 7am-2am) Spectacularly situated overlooking Pigeon Rocks, this café is an essential, if slightly pricey, port of call. Watch the sun go down over a cold beer, or wiggle with the belly dancers who usually perform at around midnight at weekends.

Al-Kahwa (Map p420; ☎ 362 232; Al-Kanater Bldg, Rue Bliss, Ras Beirut; 10am-1am) Permanently surrounded in a thick haze of nargileh smoke (a nargileh goes for LL10,000), this popular hangout for AUB students during the day also does some tasty snacks, including good quesadillas, and serves up a full English breakfast for LL6000.

Gemmayzeh Café (Map p416; ☎ 580 817; Rue Gouraud, Gemmayzeh; 8am-3am) This venerable Beiruti institution, dating back to Ottoman times, also has something of an aura of old Parisian bistro. Live Arabic music shows (10.30pm to midnight) take place every night except Tuesday; book in advance to make sure you don't miss this extra-special treat.

Tribeca (Map p416; ☎ 339 123; Rue Abdel Wahab el-Inglizi, Achrafiye; bagels LL5000-10,000; 8am-1am;) If you're craving a bagel or a piece of chocolate fudge cake, hurry to this mellow little place, which also serves huge lattes and cappuccinos, for your comfort food fix.

Al-Raouda (Map p420; ☎ 743 348; Corniche, Manara; grills LL8500; 7.30am-midnight summer, 8am-8pm winter;) A waterfront favourite with local families, stop in for a hit of strong coffee (LL1000) or a languid nargileh. It's a little tricky to find: walk down the lane right next to the Luna Park entrance, then look for the misspelt 'El Rawda' sign.

ENTERTAINMENT

Beirut's nightlife, along with Tel Aviv's in Israel, is justifiably considered among the best in the Middle East. Things don't usually get going until well after midnight (not surprising, considering the habitual dining hour is some time around 11pm) and continue on till dawn and long beyond.

Nightclubs

Acid (off Map p416; ☎ 03-714 678; Sin el-Fil; women free, men around US$20 incl open bar; 9pm-6am Fri & Sat) With pounding techno and a gay-friendly scene, Acid is massive, brash and loud, loud, loud. Frequent after-parties keep the energy going well into the weekend. It's a few kilometres out of town, south of the Sin el-Fil roundabout, beside the Futuroscope Exhibition Hall.

B 018 (Map p416; ☎ 03-800 018; Lot 317, La Quarantine; 9pm-7am) Easily the most famous club in town, this equally gay-friendly underground place, a couple of kilometres east of Downtown, is known for its mock-horror interior and sliding roof, which always opens at some point during the night. To get here, ask a cab driver to take you to the Forum de Beyrouth and follow the clubbers from there.

Crystal (Map p416; ☎ 332 523; Rue Monot, Achrafiye; admission free; 10pm-4am) Beirut's glitziest, glammest, camped-up club is where you go if you've got US$3000 to spend on a bottle of champagne, or a fistful of bling that just needs to be seen. Get here early or book a table in advance for ultimate dance-floor people-watching.

Cassino (Map p416; ☎ 656 777; cnr Sodeco Sq & Rue de Damas; admission free; 9pm-5am Sun-Thu) If you're tired of techno, head on over to chic Cassino for Arabic pop, champagne and cigars galore, but remember to dress the part if you want to make it past the choosy doormen.

Cinemas

There are several centrally located cinemas screening mainstream international movies. Try **Empire ABC** (Map p416; ☎ 209 298; ABC Mall, Achrafiye), **Empire Dunes** (Map p416; ☎ 792 123; Dunes Centre, Verdun) and **Empire Sofil Centre** (Map p416; ☎ 328 806; Sofil Centre, Ave Charles Malek, Achrafiye).

Theatre

Monnot Theatre (Map p416; ☎ 320 762/4; next to St Joseph's Church, Rue St Joseph University, Achrafiye) The Monnot Theatre hosts a regular program of French-language theatre, as well as live music performances.

Théâtre de Beyrouth (Map p420; ☎ 366 085; Rue Graham, Ain al-Mreisse) A small theatre offering cutting-edge performances from Lebanon and beyond, in Arabic, French and English.

Sport

Hippodrome (Map p416; ☎ 632 515; Ave Abdallah Yafi; admission LL5000-15,000; 11am-4pm Sun) This racing venue, just behind the National Museum of Beirut, is one of the few places in the Middle East where you can legally place a bet. Though its future is threatened due to land development, it remains, for now, wildly popular and lots of fun.

GETTING THERE & AWAY

For information on transport between Syria and Beirut, see p455.

Buses, minibuses and service taxis to destinations north of Beirut leave from Gemmayzeh's **Charles Helou bus station** (Map p416) and the **Dawra transport hub** (Dora; off Map p416), 7km northeast of town. To the south and southeast they leave from the **Cola transport hub** (Map p416) about 2km south of Beirut Central District. See p456 and the relevant town and city sections for further details.

For information on car hire, see opposite.

GETTING AROUND

To/From the Airport

Beirut Rafic Hariri International Airport (off Map p416; ☎ 628 000; www.beirutairport.gov.lb) is approximately 5km south of Beirut city centre. Though it's possible to take a bus from here to town, they're not exactly making it easy for you: the bus stop is a 1km walk from the terminal, at the airport roundabout, a hot walk in summer and a windy one on a winter's day.

The red-and-white LCC bus 1 will take you from the airport roundabout to Rue Sadat in Hamra (handy for all Hamra hotels); bus 5 will take you to Charles Helou bus station. Fares are LL700.

The blue-and-white OCFTC buses 7 and 10 also stop at the airport roundabout; bus 10 goes to Charles Helou bus station and bus 7 goes to Raouché, from where you can take bus 9 to Hamra. Fares are LL750. The buses operate between 5.30am and 9pm daily, and the maximum wait is generally about 10 to 15 minutes.

If you can stretch your budget, the most hassle-free way to get to town is to prearrange a taxi with your hotel. Even budget hostels offer this service, charging around US$15 for the ride; this is probably cheaper than you'll be offered at the airport itself without a fair amount of bargaining. If you do opt for a normal yellow cab, agree to the price before climbing inside.

Buses

Beirut is well serviced by its network of slow, crowded, but good-value buses. The red-and-white buses are owned by the private Lebanese Commuting Company (LCC; www.lccworld.com) and the blue-and-white buses (OCFTC) are government owned. All operate on a 'hail-and-ride' system: just wave at the driver and, in theory at least, the bus will stop. There are no timetables, but buses generally run from around 5.30am to 9pm daily at intervals of 15 minutes or so.

The bus routes most useful to travellers are listed below. A short trip will almost always cost LL750, a longer ride LL1000.

LCC BUSES

No 1 Hamra–Khaldé Rue Sadat (Hamra), Rue Emile Eddé, Hotel Bristol, Rue Verdun, Cola roundabout, Airport roundabout, Kafaat, Khaldé

No 2 Hamra–Antelias Rue Sadat (Hamra), Rue Emile Eddé, Radio Lebanon, Sassine Sq, Dawra transport hub, Antelias

No 5 Charles Helou–Hay as-Saloum Manara, Verdun, Yessoueiye, Airport roundabout, Hay as-Saloum

No 6 Cola–Byblos Antelias, Jounieh, Byblos (Jbail)

No 7 Museum–Bharssaf Museum, Beit Mery, Brummana, Baabdat, Bharssaf

OCFTC BUSES

No 1 Bain Militaire –Khaldé Bain Militaire, Unesco, Summerland, Khaldé

No 4 Dawra–Jounieh Dawra transport hub, Dbayé, Kaslik, Jounieh

No 5 Ministry of Information–Sérail Jdeideh Ministry of Information, Sodeco, Bourj Hammoud, Sérail Jdeideh

No 7 Bain Militaire–Airport Bain Militaire, Summerland, Bourj Brajné, Airport

No 8 Ain al-Mreisse–Sérail Jdeideh Ain al-Mreisse, Charles Helou bus station, Dawra transport hub, Sérail Jdeideh

No 9 Bain Militaire–Sérail Jdeideh Bain Militaire, Rue Bliss, Rue Adbel Aziz, Rue Clemenceau, Rue Weygand, Tabaris Sq, Sassine Sq, Hayek roundabout, Sérail Jdeideh

No 10 Charles Helou–Airport Charles Helou bus station, Shatila, Airport roundabout

No 15 Ain al-Mreisse–Nahr al-Mott Ain al-Mreisse, Raouché, Museum, Nahr al-Mott

No 16 Charles Helou–Cola Charles Helou bus station, Downtown, Cola transport hub

No 23 Bain Militaire–Dawra Bain Militaire, Ain al-Mreisse, Charles Helou bus station, Dawra transport hub

No 24 Museum–Hamra Museum, Barbir, Hamra

Car & Motorcycle

If you've nerves of steel and a penchant for *Grand Theft Auto*, you may well enjoy driving in Beirut and around. The best local car rental company is **Advanced Car Rental** (☎ 999 884/5; www.advancedcarrent.com), which offers great discounts on its published rates, and comes highly recommended over the international chains. And hey, they even throw in their very own CD, a sort of Arabic easy-listening compilation, for the ride.

Taxi & Service Taxi

Private taxi companies usually have meters; make sure your driver turns the meter on or agrees to a fare in advance. Within Beirut, taxis charge anywhere from LL2000 to LL10,000, depending on your destination.

Service (shared) taxis cover the major routes in Beirut. The fare is LL1000 or LL1500 (the difference seemingly depending on the driver) on established routes within the city and LL2000 to LL8000 to outlying suburbs.

AROUND BEIRUT

BEIT MERY & BRUMMANA بيت مرعي & برومانا

☎ 04

Set in pine forests some 800m above and 17km east of Beirut, Beit Mery – its name meaning 'House of the Master' in Aramaic –

is a lazy weekend getaway for Beirutis seeking respite from the city smog, and offers sweeping panoramic views over the capital. The town dates back to Phoenician times and is home to Roman and Byzantine ruins, including some fine **floor mosaics** in a nearby 5th-century Byzantine church (ask locally for directions). Also worth a visit is the 18th-century Maronite monastery of **Deir al-Qalaa**, built over the remains of a Roman temple; reconstruction work here continues, after having been occupied by Syrian troops until 2005.

Beit Mery's **Al Bustan Festival** (www.albustanfestival.com) is held in mid-February, with a varied program of chamber, choral and orchestral music. Many of the festival's performances take place at the Hotel Al Bustan (below).

About 4km northeast of Beit Mery is Brummana, a more bustling resort town connected to Beit Mery by a continuous strip full of hotels, eateries, cafés, shops and nightclubs. In summer it's equally popular with Beirutis escaping the city heat and has a carnival-like atmosphere, particularly on weekends. There's nothing particular to do here except to eat, drink and be merry (Beit Merry, perhaps); be aware that it's extremely quiet outside summer season and weekends.

Sleeping & Eating

There are dozens of places to stay and eat in both Beit Mery and Brummana, but unless you're in Lebanon for an extended stay, there's not much reason to favour them over Beirut itself.

Hotel Al-Bustan (☎ 972 980/82; www.albustanhotel.com; Beit Mery; s/d/ste from US$195/215/230; ❄ 💻 🏊) One of the smartest hotels in the two towns, this is a good choice during the popular Al Bustan Festival, since many concerts are performed in the hotel itself. Note that prices rise accordingly.

Restaurant Mounir (☎ 873 900; Main St, Brummana; mezze LL4000-7000; 🕑 noon-midnight) If you're especially hungry while flitting between the two towns, a culinary highlight is Mounir, which serves food on a pleasant terrace (equipped with a children's playground) with spectacular views over Beirut and the Mediterranean. Book in advance, request a table with a view, and settle in for a long lunch.

Getting There & Away

Service taxis from the National Museum or Dawra usually charge LL2500 to either Beit Mery or Brummana. The LCC bus 7 (LL750, 40 minutes) and OCFTC bus 7 both depart for here from Beirut from opposite the National Museum.

JEITA GROTTO مغارة جعيتا

☎ 09

For many visitors to Lebanon, the stunning **Jeita grotto** (☎ 220 840; www.jeitagrotto.com; adult/child under 12 LL18,150/10,075; 🕑 9am-6pm Tue-Fri, 9am-7pm Sat & Sun summer, 9am-5pm Tue-Sun winter, closed for 4 weeks late Jan-early Feb) is one of the highlights of their trip. One of the world's most impressive agglomerations of stalactites and stalagmites (remember the old rhyme, recalling that hanging 'stalactites hold on tight'?) it's also one of Lebanon's biggest tourist attractions. Extending around 6km back into the mountains, the caves were used as an ammunition store during the civil war, and their lower strata are flooded each winter due to the rising levels of the Nahr-el-Kalb (or Dog River) for which they form the source.

The incredible upper cavern, though, stays open all year, and can be explored on foot even when boat rides into the lower cavern are suspended due to flooding. And despite all kinds of tatty side attractions – including a toy train ride – the site remains a spectacular day trip from the city. Bear in mind that there's no photography allowed: you can stow your camera in lockers at the mouth of the caverns.

To get to the grotto, which lies about 18km northeast of Beirut, take a minibus (LL1500), or LCC bus 6 or OCFTC bus 4 (LL750) from Dawra and ask the driver to drop you at the Jeita turn-off on the Beirut–Jounieh Hwy. From here, negotiate a return price with a waiting taxi for the 5km journey (around US$12 to US$15), and make sure to figure in waiting time, since taxis one-way from the grotto back to the highway or Dawra charge a premium. Alternatively, a return taxi trip from Beirut should cost around US$25.

JOUNIEH جونيه

☎ 09 / pop 103,227

Once a sleepy fishing village, Jounieh, 21km north of Beirut, is now a high-rise strip mall hemmed in by the sea on one side and the mountains on the other. Famous as the home of noisy bars, camp restaurants catering to Saudi sheikhs and lurid 'super' nightclubs filled with bored exotic dancers, it's not somewhere you might want to spend too much time, but it does have two worthwhile distractions, both reachable on a day trip from Beirut: the soaring heights of the Teleferique, and the equally dizzying gaming tables of the venerable Casino du Liban.

Activities

Dubbed the Terrorifique by some, the **Jounieh Teleferique** (cable car; ☎ 936 075; adult/child return LL7500/3500; ⏲ 10am-11pm Jun-Oct, 10am-7pm Nov-May, closed Mon, Christmas Day & Good Fri) runs cable cars up from Jounieh to the mountaintop Basilica of Our Lady of Lebanon at Harissa. The views from the summit are spectacular, and for those with a peeping Tom penchant, so are the views from the cable cars themselves, which are whisked up close and personal past the living room windows of Jounieh's mountainside apartment blocks.

Your other must-do Jounieh diversion is the historic **Casino du Liban** (☎ 855 888; www.cdl.com.lb; Rue Maameltein; ⏲ slot-machines noon-5am, gaming rooms 8pm-4am), once host to celebrities like Liz Taylor and David Niven, though nowadays rather more Tony Clifton than Tony Bennett. Still, it has a kitsch charm for those longing for a taste of days gone by. Guests must be over 21 and wear smart casual gear (no jeans or sports shoes); a suit and tie are required (for men, of course) if you want to play the roulette wheels.

Eating

Jounieh has plenty of chain restaurants and glitzy, overpriced steak places, but a standout from the crowd is **Chez Sami** (☎ 910 520; Rue Maameltein; mains US$35; ⏲ noon-midnight), considered one of the best seafood restaurants in Lebanon. It's simple but stylish and offers great seaside views and a lovely summer terrace; there's no menu so take your pick from the catch of the day (500g of fish is around LL25,000) and come early – the crowds think it's the catfish's pyjamas.

Getting There & Away

You can get to Jounieh from Beirut by both LCC bus 6 and OCFTC bus 4, both departing from Dawra transport hub and charging LL1500 for the 40-minute ride. Service taxis also depart from the transport hub, and cost LL2000; ask the driver to drop you on the highway near the footbridge. A private taxi from Beirut to Jounieh costs around LL22,000.

NORTH OF BEIRUT

BYBLOS (JBAIL) بيبلوس

☎ 09 / pop 21,600

A pretty fishing port with a plethora of ancient remains and some interesting fishy fossils, Byblos is one of the highlights of the entire Middle Eastern Mediterranean coast. Although good accommodation options are regretfully thin on the ground, it nevertheless warrants a stop on the way north to Tripoli or the Qadisha Valley, or even a long day's trip from Beirut. Byblos also plays host to the annual summer Byblos Arts Festival.

History

Excavations have shown that Byblos (the biblical Gebal) was probably inhabited as early as 7000 years ago; by the middle of the 3rd millennium BC it had become the busiest trading port on the eastern Mediterranean and an important religious centre, all under the direction of the maritime Phoenicians. Close links to Egypt fostered its cultural and religious development, and as the city flourished it developed its own distinct art and architecture, part Egyptian, part Mesopotamian. It was in Byblos, too, that our modern alphabet is said to have had its roots, developed by the Phoenicians as a way of accurately recording its healthy trade transactions.

The city was renamed Byblos by the Greeks, who ruled here from 333 BC, named after the Greek word *bublos,* meaning papyrus, which was shipped from Egypt to Greece via Byblos' port. As the Greek empire fell into decline, the Romans, under Pompey, arrived in town, constructing temples, baths, colonnaded streets and public buildings galore. Later allied to Constantinople and conquered in the 7th century by the Islamic invasion, in 1104 AD the city fell to the Crusaders, who set about building a castle and moat with stone and columns taken from the earlier Roman temples.

Subsequent centuries under Ottoman and Mamluk rule saw Byblos' international reputation as a trading port decline, just as Beirut's star was in the ascendancy. It soon settled into a new incarnation as a small and sleepy fishing port, which it remains to this day. Excavations of its former glories began in 1860 and continue, at a snail's pace, today.

Orientation

The medieval town, with the most to attract visitors, stretches north from the perimeter of the seaside ruins, flanked to the north by Rue al-Mina and to the west by the harbour, home to a string of good restaurants. The modern town, hosting most useful services and cheap eateries, is centred on Rue Jbail, at the eastern end of Rue al-Mina.

Information

Banque Libanaise pour le Commerce (Rue Jbail) Can change US dollars or euros, and has an ATM.

Byblos Bank (Rue Jbail) Has an ATM.

Post office (☎ 540 003; Rahban St; 🕒 7.30am-5pm Mon-Fri, 8am-1pm Sat) Look for the Coral Petrol Station on Rue Jbail; 30m east of the station on a side street. It's around 20m up the hill on your right, on the 2nd floor.

Standard Chartered Bank (Rue Jbail) Has an ATM.

Tourist office (☎ 540 325; 🕒 8.30am-1pm Mar-Nov, closed Sun Dec-Feb) Located in the souq near the entrance to the archaeological site, it has maps of the site, but none of the town itself.

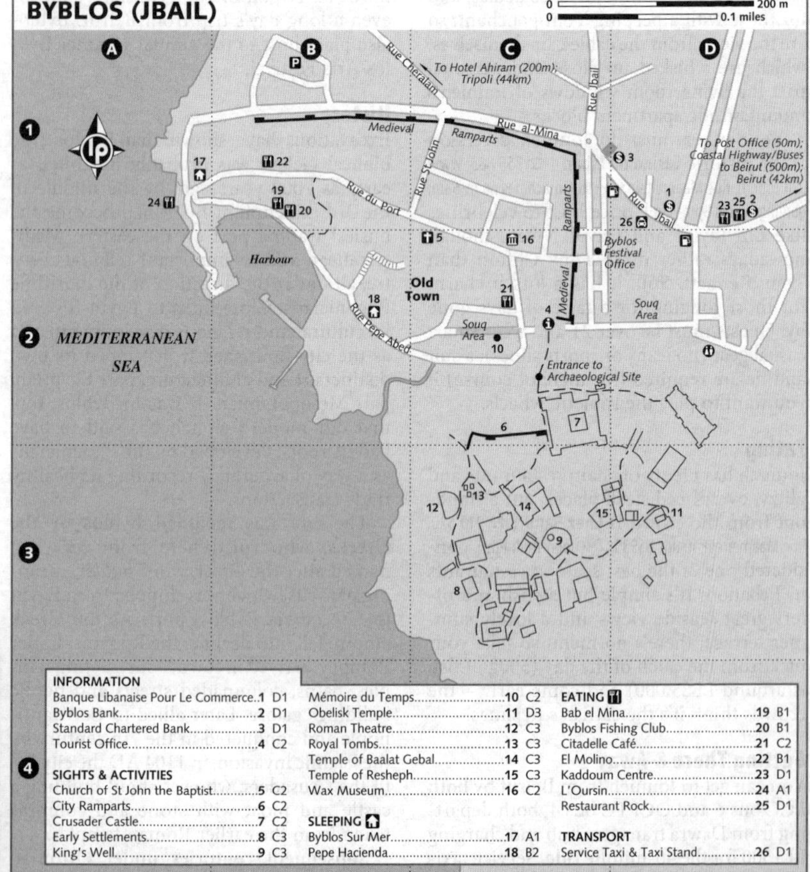

SOMETHING FISHY

Tucked away in an alleyway in the Byblos souq is the workshop of young local paleontologist Pierre Abi-Saad and his fascinating hundred-million-year-old haul of fishy history. Discovered in a quarry owned by his family for generations, almost 1km above sea level, his glimpses into a prehistoric, underwater world are today represented in almost every major international natural history museum, though he keeps his favourites for the long-awaited day when he, too, will open a museum of his own findings to the world.

More than 80% of the fossils Pierre has found represent species now extinct, and many haven't yet even been studied or named. Adorning the walls of his workshop and adjoining shop are eels, stingrays, octopi, jellyfish, eels, shrimp and coelacanths, one of the earliest fish ever to exist. His collection even includes such oddities as a fossil of a fish that had swallowed another fish before its ancient demise, and a 4m-long complete shark, the largest in the world.

While in Byblos, don't miss the chance to drop into Pierre's shop, **Mémoire du Temps** (☎ 547 083; www.memoryoftime.com; souq; 🕑 9am-7.30pm), where he's usually to be found chipping away enthusiastically at a hunk of limestone. His enthusiasm is infectious, his friendliness disarming, and you might even be invited up to the quarry yourself, to fish for your own ancient catch – without getting even your little toe wet.

Sights & Activities

The **Byblos Arts Festival** (www.byblosfestival.org) gets the town going each summer with a host of local and international performers. Check the website for up-to-date festival and ticket details, and events listings.

THE RUINS

This ancient **site** (☎ 540 001; adult/student/child LL6000/1500/1500; 🕑 8.30am-sunset) is entered through the restored 12th-century **Crusader castle** that dominates the sturdy 25m-thick **city ramparts** (which date from the 3rd and 2nd millennia BC). It's well worth taking a guide from here (LL10,000 to LL20,000 depending on the size of your group) to show you around the expansive site in detail. There are great views from the top of the ramparts, offering a good overview of the layout of the ancient city.

From the Crusader castle, turn left past the remains of the city gate and follow the path until you reach the L-shaped **Temple of Resheph** dating from the 3rd millennium BC. From here, move on to check out the intriguing **Obelisk Temple** from the early 2nd century BC, at which bronze votive offerings in the shape of human figures were discovered, and are now famously displayed at Beirut's National Museum (p418).

Following the path southwest, head past the **King's Well**, a spring that supplied the city with water until the end of the Hellenistic era (and where, according to legend, Isis sat weeping on her search for Osiris), to some of the earliest remains on the site, **early settlements** comprising the remnants of Neolithic (5th century BC) and Chalcolithic (4th century BC) enclosures, houses and huts. Throughout this area, large burial jars were found containing preserved bodies curled up in the foetal position.

Nearby, Byblos's old temple, the **Temple of Baalat Gebal** (the Mistress of Byblos) dates back to the 4th century BC. This was the largest and most important temple constructed at Byblos, dedicated to Aphrodite during the Roman period, and was rebuilt a number of times in the two millennia that it survived. Many temple findings, including alabaster vase fragments inscribed with the names of Old Kingdom pharaohs, are today also housed in the capital's National Museum (p418). The six standing columns approaching the temple are the vestiges of a Roman colonnaded street, built as the temple approach around 300 AD.

To the northwest of the temple, towards the sea, is the **Roman theatre**, a one-third size reconstruction of the original, situated near the cliff edge with great views across the sea. Behind this are nine **royal tombs**, cut in vertical shafts deep into the rock in the 2nd millennium BC; some of the sarcophagi found here are now housed in the National Museum, including that of King Hiram, whose sarcophagus has one of the earliest Phoenician alphabet inscriptions in the world. His grave shaft, too, is inscribed, this time with the eerie phrase, 'Warning here. Thy death is below.'

CHURCH OF ST JOHN THE BAPTIST (EGLISE ST JEAN MARC)

This Romanesque-style church, at the centre of the Crusader town, was begun in 1115 AD, and was slowly added to in subsequent centuries. It's thus an interesting mixture of Arab and Italian designs, with remains of Byzantine mosaics scattered about the area. It also features an unusual open-air baptistery, which sits against the north wall, its arches and four supporting pillars topped by a dome.

Almost opposite the church is the kitsch, for-waxwork-enthusiasts-only **Wax Museum** (☎ 540 463; admission LL6000; ⏰ 9am-5pm), a last-ditch diversion for that rare rainy day.

Sleeping

Currently, Byblos isn't blessed with a great many sleeping options.

Hotel Ahiram (☎ 540 440; www.ahiramhotel.com; s/d/tr US$50/65/75; ❄) Quite recently renovated, the Ahiram makes for a reasonable – if not memorable – sleep. All rooms have balconies with sea views, and the hotel has direct access to a small, pebbly beach. Ask about substantial off-season discounts.

Byblos Sur Mer (☎ 548 000; Rue du Port; s/d/ste US$65/75/105; ❄ 🏊) Alhough the rooms are small, tired and a mite overpriced, the central location of this Byblos old-timer can't be argued with, and neither can the harbour view from the room and seafront pool.

In summertime, it's worth enquiring at Byblos Fishing Club, which also operates the nearby informal **Pepe Hacienda** on Pepe Abed. Small bungalows can be rented here for US$20 per night.

Eating & Drinking

Citadelle Café (☎ 03-584 165; Souq; ⏰ 7am-midnight) On the corner of the square opposite the tourist office, this makes a fab place for a filling breakfast or an evening tipple. The hummus wraps (LL3000) are huge and yummy; top one off with a strong coffee and a chat with André, the knowledgeable owner, who'll give you tips on local attractions. There's usually live music on summer weekend evenings.

Bab El Mina (☎ 540 475; Old Port; mezze from LL3500, mains LL15,000; ⏰ 11am-midnight) Boasting a lovely location overlooking the port, the restaurant specialises in fish and traditional Lebanese mezze, at competitive prices. The fisherman's basket for two (LL45,000) is highly recommended by locals.

Byblos Fishing Club (Pepes; ☎ 540 213; Old Port; two-course meal per person US$25; ⏰ 11am-midnight) A Lebanese institution, the Fishing Club is still best known for its charismatic, now sadly deceased, Mexican owner Pepé, who, over the decades, dandled many a film star on his knee. The seafood's super fresh, courtesy of the restaurant's own private fishing fleet, and there's a little museum devoted to Pepe's memory, run, like the restaurant itself, by his spritely septuagenarian son, Roger.

El Molino (☎ 541 555; Rue du Port; 2-course meal & 2 margaritas LL35,000, beer LL4000; ⏰ noon-midnight Tue-Sun; ❄) This place offers tasty Mexican food and a fun atmosphere at night, fuelled by some strong tequilas and a spicy plate or two of nachos.

The Byblos Sur Mer hotel also operates the restaurant **L'Oursin** (⏰ lunch & dinner Apr-Sep; mains from LL7000), across the road, just beside the sea. For cheap eats, head to the many felafel and shwarma joints along Rue Jbail; local favourites include **Restaurant Rock** and the **Kaddoum Centre**, both open daily 8am to late, with prices starting at LL1500 for a felafel sandwich.

Getting There & Away

The **service taxi stand** (Rue Jbail) in Byblos is near the Banque Libanaise pour le Commerce. A service taxi to/from Beirut (the hub in Beirut is Dawra transport hub) costs LL3000 (about eight services depart between 7am and 6pm). The LCC bus 6 (LL750, around one hour) and minibuses (LL1000) also leave from Dawra transport hub and travel regularly along the coast road between Beirut and Byblos, stopping on Rue Jbail. It's a scenic and very pleasant trip.

TRIPOLI (TRABLOUS) طرابلس

☎ 06 / pop 237,909

Tripoli, 85km north of Beirut, is Lebanon's second largest city and the north's main port and trading centre. Famous for its medieval Mamluk architecture, including a large souq area considered the best in Lebanon, it might nevertheless seem more than a little run-down and provincial if you've come direct from Beirut. Recently troubled, with spates of street fighting and a bus bombing in August 2008, along with a protracted siege in a nearby Palestinian refugee camp the year before, Tripoli's not having an easy time of it. Do check the news before you go, but do visit: the city certainly warrants a day or so of souq-wandering and sweets-sampling, Tripoli's main speciality being *haliwat al-jibn,* a teeth-jarringly sweet confection made from curd cheese and served with syrup.

History

As early as the 8th century BC, Tripoli was already a thriving trading post, thanks to the constant comings and goings of traders from Tyre, Sidon and Arwad (the latter in present-day Syria). Each community settled in its own area, a fact reflected in the city's name, which derives from the Greek word *tripolis*, meaning 'three cities'.

Conquered in turn by the Seleucids, Romans, Umayyads, Byzantines and Fatimids, Tripoli was invaded by the Crusaders in 1102 AD, who held on to it for 180 years and built its imposing, and still-standing, hilltop fortress, the Citadel of Raymond de Saint-Gilles. In 1289 the Mamluk Sultan Qalaun took control of the city, and embarked upon an ambitious building program; many of the mosques, souqs, madrassas and khans that remain in the old city today date from sometime during either the Crusader or subsequent Sultan Qalaun era. The Turkish Ottomans took over the city in 1516 and ruled, in relative peace, until 1920, when it became part of the French mandate of Greater Lebanon.

With a large influx of Palestinian refugees from 1948 onward the city became the site of ferocious fighting during the civil war. Huge UN-administered refugee camps still hug Tripoli's outskirts, including the Nahr el-Bared camp, now infamous for its protracted Palestinian/Lebanese army deadlock in 2007.

Orientation

Tripoli comprises two main areas: the city proper, which includes modern Tripoli and the Old City, and Al-Mina, the rather down-and-out port area, 3km west along the sea front. The geographical centre of town is Saahat et-Tall (pronounced 'at-tahl'), a large square by the clock tower, where you'll find the service taxi and bus stands, and most of Tripoli's cheap hotels.

The old city sprawls east of Saahet et-Tall, while the modern centre is west of the square, along Rue Fouad Chehab. In Al-Mina you'll find the Corniche – shabby by day but alive with milling locals by night – as well as Tripoli's most fabulous hotel, Hotel Via Mina, and some nice, relaxed pavement cafés and bars.

Information

INTERNET ACCESS

Most of Tripoli's internet cafés are congregated on the main roads heading down to Al-Mina.

Dream Net 2 (☎ 03-858 821; Rue Riad al-Solh; per hr LL1000; 🕑 9am-midnight) On the opposite side of the road from the Hot Café.Com and less atmospheric, but cheaper and just as efficient.

Hot Café.Com (☎ 622 888; Rue Riad al-Solh; with own laptop per hr LL1500, with café laptop per hr LL2500; 🕑 9am-midnight) A large friendly place owned by an Australian expat.

MONEY

There are ATMs all over town, and lots on Rue Riad al-Solh.

Walid M el-Masri Co Exchange (☎ 430 115; Rue Tall; 🕑 8am-8pm Mon-Sat, 8am-1pm Sun) Exchanges US-dollar travellers cheques (US$2 per cheque).

POST

Al-Mina Post office (Rue ibn Sina; 🕑 8am-5pm Mon-Fri, 8am-noon Sat)

Main post office (Rue Fouad Chehab; 🕑 8am-5pm Mon-Fri, 8am-noon Sat) Around 400m south of Abdel Hamid Karami Sq.

TOURIST INFORMATION

Tourist office (☎ 433 590; www.lebanon-tourism.gov.lb; Abdel Hamid Karami Sq; 🕑 8am-5pm Mon-Sat) Staff members are friendly and helpful and speak English and French. Opening hours can be erratic, so try again if you find it closed.

Sights

OLD CITY

Dating from the Mamluk era (14th and 15th centuries), the compact Old City is a maze of narrow alleys, colourful souqs, hammams, khans, mosques and madrassas. It's a lively and fascinating place where craftspeople, including tailors, jewellers, soap makers and coppersmiths, continue to work as they have done for centuries. The **Souq al-Sayyaghin** (the gold souq), **Souq al-Attarin** (for perfumes and spices), the medieval **Souq al-Haraj** and **Souq an-Nahhassin**

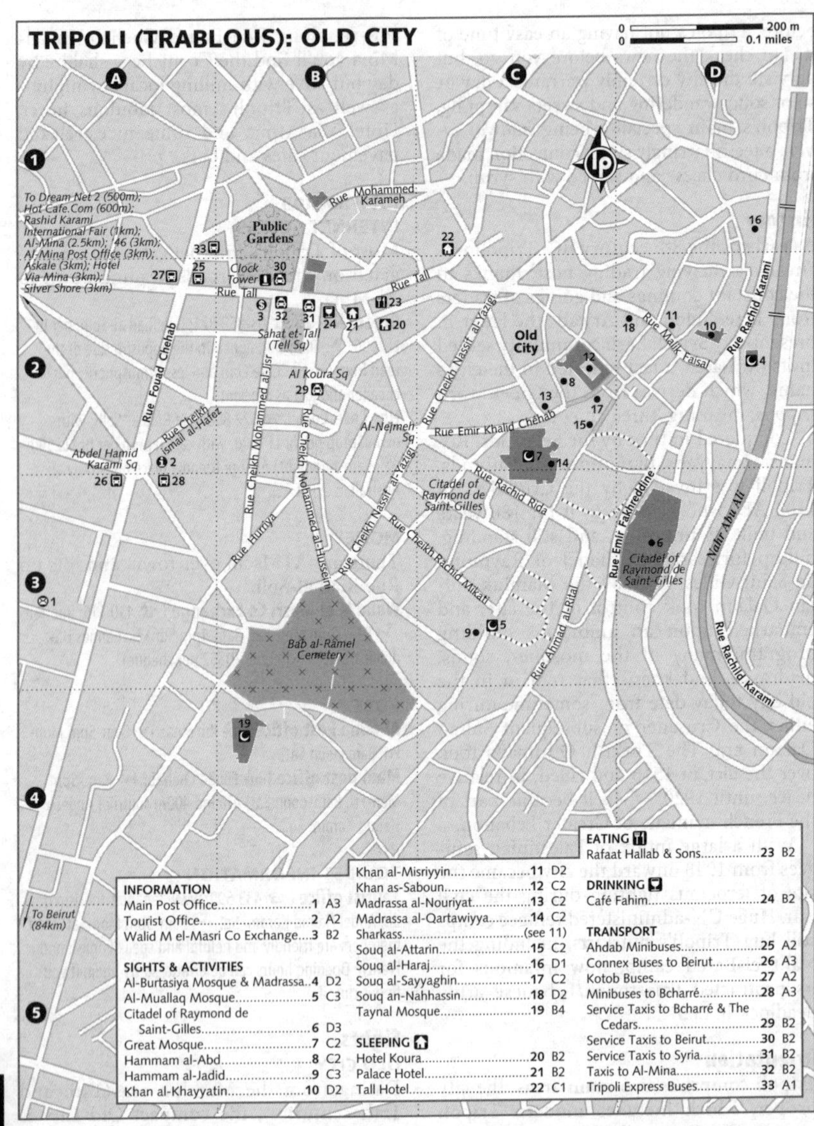

(the brass souq) are all well worth a wander.

The **Great Mosque**, built on the site of a 12th-century Crusader cathedral and incorporating some of its features, has a magnificent entrance and an unusual minaret that was probably once the cathedral bell tower. Opposite the mosque's northern entrance is the **Madrassa al-Nouriyat**, which has distinctive black-and-white stonework and a beautiful inlaid mihrab, and is still in use today. Attached to the east side of the Grand Mosque is the **Madrassa al-Qartawiyya**, converted between 1316 and 1326 from the former St Mary's church. Its elegant black-and-white facade and honeycomb-

ALL THE FUN OF THE FAIR *Amelia Thomas*

My favourite sight in Tripoli isn't actually much of a sight at all, a fact that somehow makes it even more evocative than the ancient souqs or the looming citadel. Today, it's little more than the vast, oval and barren central area of a traffic roundabout, on a road heading down from the centre of Tripoli towards Al-Mina.

Doesn't look like much? No, but this derelict space was once proudly known as the **Rashid Karami International Fair** (Map p434), commissioned in Lebanon's early '60s heyday, and filled with imposing concrete geometric forms, as a sort of modernist's answer to the great 19th-century World Fairs of Chicago, Paris and London.

Designed by the venerable architect Oscar Niemeyer, now over a century old and still going strong, the overgrown and underloved fairground stands as a testament to the changing fortunes of the country itself. Unlike its sister Niemeyer works – the most famous of which is undoubtedly the space-age concrete capital of Brasilia – the fairground has never received much international attention, though a band of Tripoli residents is working hard to prevent its demolition. Today, though sadly you can't wander through its half-finished pavilion, past its strange, desolate statues, a glance from the outskirts offers an artistic reflection of the plagued history of the city and the country as a whole.

patterned half-dome above the portal are well worth a look.

You have to glance up to see the **Al-Muallaq Mosque** (Hanging Mosque), a small and unusual 14th-century mosque, on the second floor of a building. Just opposite is the **Hammam al-Jadid**, the city's best-preserved bath house, in use from around 1740 well into the 1970s, which has some lovely coloured glass windows.

At the souq's centre, the **Khan as-Saboun** (Soap Khan; 10am-5pm Mon-Sat) was built in the 16th century and first used as an army barracks; since then, it has functioned as a point of sale for Tripoli's famous soaps for generations. Today, you can still stop in to pick up any of its 400 types of soap; check out the huge one carved into the shape of an open volume of the Quran.

To the west of the Khan as-Saboun is the 300-year-old **Hammam al-Abd** (basic bath LL12,000; 8am-10pm), the city's only functioning bathhouse. Unfortunately, it's only open to men, unless you are travelling with a group of women and can rent out the whole place.

One of the most beautiful buildings in the old city is the **Khan al-Khayyatin**, formerly a Crusader hospital and today a beautifully restored 14th-century tailors' souq lined with small workshops. To the northwest of the khan is **Khan al-Misriyyin**, which is believed to date from the 14th century when it was used by Egyptian merchants. On the first floor of the dilapidated khan, you can find **Sharkass** (bar of soap LL1000-3000, boxes of 3 LL4000, 1kg natural/perfumed soap LL6000/8000; 10am-5pm winter, to 7pm summer). Making soap since 1803, the family produces good-quality, authentic Tripoli soap; you're welcome to look around. Note that the shop is on the 1st floor (not the one with the same name on the ground). Close to the souq is the **Al-Burtasiya Mosque & Madrassa**, with its particularly fine mihrab inside.

Standing on its own to the south of the souqs on the outskirts of the Old City, but well worth the walk, is the restored **Taynal Mosque**. It dates from 1336 and represents probably the most outstanding example of Islamic religious architecture in Tripoli. As with all the Old City mosques, dress demurely (women should cover their legs, arms and head), take off your shoes outside, and check first that it's OK to enter. Some Old City mosques offer full cloaks for women to don, especially fun in the height of summer.

CITADEL OF RAYMOND DE SAINT-GILLES

Towering above Tripoli, this **Crusader fortress** (admission LL7500; 8am-6pm, closes earlier in winter) was originally built during the period from AD 1103 to AD 1104. It was burnt down in 1297 and partly rebuilt the following century by a Mamluk emir.

The most impressive part of the citadel is the imposing entrance, with its moat and three gateways (one Ottoman, one Mamluk, one Crusader). Guided tours are available and prices depend on group size: generally

LL5000/15,000/20,000 for one person/small group/large group. Since there's an architecturally muddled rabbit warren of parts inside, and very little labelling, it makes sense to employ their services if you want to learn more about the citadel's history.

Sleeping

Tourism has largely stayed away from Tripoli since the armed stand-offs of 2007, and several budget places have closed down as a result. Since, on top of this, there are really no decent midrange options, Tripoli's no longer a great base for exploring the north of the country – unless you stay either at the rock-bottom Hotel Koura or the top-end Hotel Via Mina, with a rental car to make travel in the far north far easier.

Tall Hotel (☎ 628 407; Rue Tall; s/d LL30,000/35,000; ❄) Unless you are pressed to find a bed for the night, the Tall Hotel shouldn't be your first choice: although the rooms themselves aren't too bad, the atmosphere is a little spooky since the corridors are very dim and eerily lit. Look for the red, misspelled 'Tell Hotel' sign, stencilled high on the building.

Hotel Koura (☎ 03-371 041; off Rue Tall; s/d/tr US$15/30/45, dm/d without bathroom US$10/15; ❄) Without doubt the best of Tripoli's budget bunch. This friendly, family-run place has bright, simple rooms with stone walls arranged around a central shared lounge. Breakfast is included in the price, and the extremely accomodating owners can arrange day trips.

Palace Hotel (☎ 429 993; Rue Tall; s/d/tr US$20/40/50; ❄) Don't be too encouraged by the freshly painted exterior of this atmospheric old building: as you climb the stairs, you'll realise that the interior is as creepy as the outside is cheerful. Still, if you can get the management to warm to you (and this might take some doing), it's a decent enough base, with plain rooms adequate for a sleep and a shower. The US$5 charge for turning on the air-con, though, might strike you as a little steep.

our pick **Hotel Via Mina** (☎ 222 227; www.via-mina.com; Al-Mina; d from US$100; ❄ 💻 🅿) A stay at the Via Mina is reason alone to head on up to Tripoli. This beautiful boutique place, tucked away in a quiet, cobbled backstreet, is a haven of wooden floors, iron spiral staircases, and a library filled with overstuffed armchairs and illustrated tomes. To get here, turn off the Corniche at the Tasty Café, then take a left on the street running parallel to the rear of the '46 restaurant.

Eating & Drinking

Tripoli's eating options aren't especially exciting, and if you're looking for cheap eats, it's best to either wander the area around the Old City (where you'll find street vendors selling sweetcorn cobs and felafel) or Rue Riad al-Solh, which has a plethora of budget fast-food joints. Al-Mina's Corniche is the place to go if you're in the mood for ice cream, while a string of floating coffeehouses on the water's edge dispense strong coffee and basic snacks.

Silver Shore (☎ 601 384; Corniche, Al-Mina; meals US$35; 🕑 11am-8pm; ❄) Considered the best seafood restaurant in northern Lebanon, this place is locally known for its hot sauce, made to a secret recipe. Be aware that it closes very early in the evening.

'46 (☎ 212 223; Corniche, Al-Mina; mains LL16,500; 🕑 7am-1am; ❄) Named after the year it first opened its doors, this place dispenses perfectly satisfactory pastas (try the spicy pasta arrabiata for LL9000), steaks and salads, making it a cut above Tripoli's other dining options. The entrance is around the back of the restaurant.

our pick **Rafaat Hallab & Sons** (Rue Tall; 🕑 5am-midnight; ❄) Founded in 1881, this is a popular central branch of what is probably the best Hallab patisserie in Lebanon and certainly the best place to sample Tripoli's famous sticky baklava-type sweets (from LL1500 per portion).

Café Fahim (☎ 444 516; Rue Tall; coffee/soft drink LL1500, nargileh LL1000-3000; 🕑 6am-10pm) A cavernous old café with an echoing, vaulted interior filled with local men, young and old, smoking nargileh and playing backgammon. Opposite the central clock tower, the terrace makes a good place for sipping tea and watching people.

The very best place for simple meals and a cold beer or two are the small streets just behind the Hotel Via Mina, which attract a young crowd for tasty salads, grills and mezze. They open up early evening, and are packed full into the night; **Askale** (pizzas & salads from LL5000; 🕑 6pm-late) is a particularly popular one.

Getting There & Away

For details of services from Tripoli to Syria, see p456.

TO/FROM BEIRUT

Three companies – Connex, Kotob and Tripoli Express – run bus services from Beirut to Tripoli. All leave from Zone C of Charles Helou bus station in Beirut; there's no need to book ahead.

Connex has 20 buses daily in either direction (LL2500, 90 minutes via Jounieh and Byblos, every 30 minutes from around 7am to 8.30pm). **Tripoli Express** runs smaller buses daily (LL2000, 90 minutes, every 10 to 15 minutes from 5am to 6pm). **Kotob**, which runs older buses daily, is the cheapest option and takes longer (LL1500, up to two hours, every 15 minutes from 6am to 6.30pm), stopping to let passengers off and on at Jounieh (LL1500, one hour), Byblos (LL1500, 30 minutes) and Batroun (LL1500, 1½ hours).

Ahdab also runs minibuses from Tripoli to Beirut (LL1500, around two hours, every 15 minutes from 6am to 8pm). All bus and minibus services depart from Rue Fouad Chehab and Rue Tall in Tripoli.

Service taxis leave about every half hour to Beirut (LL5000, 1½ hours) from near the service taxi booth, just in front of the clock tower.

TO BCHARRÉ, CEDARS & BAALBEK

Minibuses from Tripoli to Bcharré (cost LL2500, 80 minutes, three to four buses daily between 9am and 5pm) leave from outside the Marco Polo travel agency, which is about 25m from the tourist office on Abdel Hamid Karami Sq. For the Cedars, organise a taxi at Bcharré (cost around LL20,000).

A service taxi from Tripoli to Bcharré costs LL6000 (from 6am to 5pm daily) and to the Cedars costs LL10,000; both leave from Al-Koura Sq.

When there's no snow or ice to close the mountain road, it's possible to take a taxi from Bcharré or the Cedars to Baalbek (around US$60, 1½ hours).

Getting Around

Service taxis travel within the old and new parts of Tripoli (LL750) and to Al-Mina (LL1000).

BCHARRÉ & THE QADISHA VALLEY بشرى & وادي قاديشا

☎ 06

The trip up to the pretty town of Bcharré takes you through some of the most beautiful scenery in Lebanon. The road winds along mountainous slopes, continuously gaining in altitude and offering spectacular views of the Qadisha Valley, a Unesco World Heritage site and home to rock-cut monasteries and hermits' dwellings, and teeming with wildlife. Red-roofed villages perch atop hills or cling precariously to the mountainsides; the Qadisha River, with its source just below the Cedars ski resort, runs along the valley bottom, while Lebanon's highest peak, Qornet as-Sawda (3090m), soars overhead. With plentiful opportunities for hiking quiet valley trails or scaling bleak mountain wastes, this is the perfect antidote to all that's fiery, fraught or frivolous down the coast in Beirut.

Bcharré is the only town of any size in the area, and is particularly famous as the birthplace of Lebanese poet Khalil Gibran. If you're not here in skiing season (when the Cedars resort, further up the mountain road, should be your winter sports base: see p438) it's a nice place to relax for a few days, especially recommended as a launching point for hikes down into the stunning Qadisha Valley.

Orientation & Information

Bcharré's little town centre is dominated by the St Saba Church in the main square, Place Mar Sea. There's a string of shops heading both east and west along the main road, along with a pharmacy, several ATMS, a supermarket and the **L'Intime Internet Café** (per hr LL2000; 11am-11pm), which is about 20m from the church.

Sights & Activities

GIBRAN MUSEUM

According to his wishes, the famous poet and artist Khalil Gibran (1883–1931), author of the much-loved *The Prophet* (1923), was buried in a 19th-century monastery built into the rocky slopes of a hill overlooking Bcharré. The **museum** (☎ 671 137; adult/student LL3000/2000; 9am-5pm Mar-Nov, 10am-5pm Nov-Mar, closed Mon) that has been set up here houses a large collection of Gibran's paintings, drawings and gouaches and also some of his

HIKING IN THE QADISHA VALLEY

There are plentiful options for hiking in both the gorgeous Qadisha Valley and the surrounding mountains, and a number of groups offer guided walks in the area. Don't miss your chance to explore this little Garden of Eden in a turbulent Middle East.

The **Lebanon Mountain Trail** (www.lebanontrail.org) is a long-distance hiking path, running the whole length of Lebanon, which also passes through the area; its website offers useful information on walking in the valley. Below are three highly recommended organisations that offer regular treks here.

- **Esprit-Nomade** (☎ 70-813 001; www.esprit-nomade.com) Arranges weekly hikes, treks and snowshoeing, with an emphasis on responsible ecotourism. Highly recommended.
- **Lebanese Adventure** (☎ 03-360 027, 03-213 300; www.lebanese-adventure.com) Runs weekend outdoor evenings, including some great moonlight hikes with overnight camping.
- **Liban Trek** (☎ 01-329 975; www.libantrek.com) A trekking club running day and weekend hikes throughout Lebanon, as well as mountain sports.

To learn more about the Qadisha Valley itself, go to www.qadishavalley.com.

manuscripts. His coffin is in the monastery's former chapel, which is cut straight into the rock. Those unfamiliar with the poet's work will be able to stock up at the gift shop.

QADISHA GROTTO

This small **grotto** (admission LL4000; 🕑 8am-5pm summer, closed mid-Dec–mid-May) extends around 500m into the mountain and has some great limestone formations. Though not as extraordinary as Jeita Grotto (p428), its spectacular setting nevertheless makes it well worth a visit.

The grotto is a 7km walk from Bcharré; follow the signs to L'Aiglon Hotel and then take the footpath opposite. It's then a 1.5km walk to the grotto.

Sleeping & Eating

Hotel Tiger House (☎ 03-378 138; tigerhousepension@hotmail.com; Rue Cedre; dm US$10) On the high road out towards the Cedars ski resort, this is a comfy option with friendly owners. Outside the high summer or ski seasons, you'll likely have the bonus of a whole dorm room to yourself. Rates include breakfast.

Palace Hotel (☎ 671 460; s/d/tr US$30/40/48) Located just below the main road, about 100m west of St Saba Church, the hotel offers simple, clean rooms, with breakfast provided for an additional US$4.50. Rooms on the 2nd floor have balconies with views over the valley.

Hotel Chbat (☎ 671 270; Rue Gibran; s/d/tr US$45/70/85) More Swiss-looking than Lebanese, this friendly, chalet-style hotel has comfortable rooms with balconies, many of which have sitting rooms attached and lovely views across the valley. There are two restaurants, both serving hearty Lebanese food, and the lounge/bar usually has a roaring log fire in winter,

Makhlouf Elie Restaurant (☎ 672 585; Main St; 🕑 9am-midnight) This little place, with a rooftop terrace and beautiful views, serves standard Lebanese fast food – mezze, sandwiches and the like – and meals here come to about US$5 per person.

Getting There & Away

The bus and service taxi stop are outside the St Saba Church. See p437 for details of services between Tripoli, Bcharré and the Cedars.

There's also a minibus to Beirut's Dawra transport hub, which leaves every morning at 7am (LL5000), but double-check with a local that it's running outside ski season. When the road is open, you can take a taxi from Bcharré all the way to Baalbek (1½ hours) across the beautiful, bleak mountains for around US$60.

THE CEDARS الأرز

☎ 06

One of Lebanon's most attractive ski resorts, the Cedars is also Lebanon's oldest and most European in feel. The village takes its name from one of the country's few remaining groves of cedar trees, which stands on the right-hand side of the road as you head up towards the ski lifts. A few of these slow-growing trees are thought to be approaching 1500 years old, and fall under the protection of the Patriarch of Lebanon, who holds a festival here each August.

Since the trees are desperately trying to be protected, you can usually walk through the forest on marked trails (the area is reliably open 9am to 6pm between May and October; check at other times), except when the ground is soft and tree roots might be unwittingly damaged by visitors.

The ski season takes place here from around December to April, depending on snow conditions, and there are currently eight lifts in operation. Equipment can be rented from a number of small ski shops at the base of the lifts, coming in at around US$5 to US$12 per day. An adult day pass to the slopes costs US$20 Monday to Friday and US$27 at weekends; the price drops to US$10 and US$17 if it's just for the afternoon. A new, higher lift should be in operation by 2009, in time for the planned 2009 Asian Ski Championships to be held here. For more on skiing in Lebanon, visit the **Ski Lebanon** website (www.skileb.com), which offers information, packages, trips and accommodation bookings.

Sleeping & Eating

There's a good sweep of accommodation for all budgets at the Cedars, with great off-season discounts if you're here in summer for the hiking. Check, too, about mid-week rates during the winter, which are usually substantially cheaper than weekend prices. There aren't many dedicated restaurants in town, as most people eat at their hotels after a day on the slopes.

Hotel Mon Refuge (☎ 671 397; s/d/apt US$15/30/120; ❄) This simple place has pleasant rooms and apartments sleeping up to 12 people, all with open fires. There's a nice, cosy restaurant downstairs, serving a mixture of Western and Lebanese cuisine.

St Bernard Hotel (☎ 03-289 600; s/d/ste US$70/90/150; ❄) An old and ever-popular ski lodge near the cedar forest grove, this warm and welcoming place is great for its location just a couple of minutes from the ski slopes.

L'Auberge des Cedres (☎ 678 888; www.smresorts.net; s/d from US$110/145, luxury tents for 2 from US$205, chalets for 6 from US$435; ❄ 💻 🏊) Popular with well-heeled Beirutis, this place offers stylish, comfortable accommodation with the bonus of fabulous food, fresh croissants delivered to your doorstep every morning, and plentiful options for ballooning or quad biking during the snowless summer months.

Getting There & Away

See p437 for details of services from Tripoli and Bcharré to the Cedars. During the winter months, a daily minibus usually operates between Beirut's Dawra transport hub and the Cedars: check locally for timings and prices.

SOUTH OF BEIRUT

SIDON (SAIDA) صيدا

☎ 07 / pop 170,516

A small, workaday but attractive port town lying 40km south of Beirut amid thick citrus and banana groves, Sidon is most famous in modern times as the birthplace of assassinated former prime minister Rafiq Hariri. Delving back rather further into history, though, it was once a rich and flourishing Phoenician city, with tight trade links to ancient Egypt and a globally renowned glass-making industry.

Traces of Sidon's rich history can still be found all over town, with many ancient remnants tucked away in its intriguing medieval souqs. Unlike, for example, pretty Byblos to the north, Sidon makes few concessions to tourists: here, the history is very much part of everyday life, and while this means that options for accommodation and eating out are fairly limited, it also offers a stronger sense of exploration than some of Lebanon's more traveller-frequented destinations.

Orientation & Information

Almost everything of interest to visitors is along or just off the seafront, where you'll also find lots of eating options and Sidon's best hotel. Saahat an-Nejmeh, a huge roundabout, marks the centre of town, and is where you'll also find the bus and service taxi stands, along with the police station. On Rue Riad as-Solh, which runs south off Saahat an-Nejmeh, there are dozens of banks (most exchanging travellers cheques), ATMS, travel agencies and moneychangers. Currently, there are few long-lasting internet

TRAVEL WARNING: THE SOUTH

With a tragic history marred by frequent Israeli incursions, along with regular Palestinian and Hezbollah offensives, the south of Lebanon has suffered unlike any other region since the early days of the civil war right up to the present day. Most recently, the 2006 Hezbollah-Israeli war saw civilian casualties and widespread destruction in the countryside south of Sidon and Tyre, and thousands of UN Interim Forces troops (UNIFIL) remain stationed throughout the area.

While travelling here, don't venture too far off the main roads between Sidon and Tyre. Some foreign offices advise staying away from bars and restaurants popular with off-duty UN troops in Tyre. The land itself is still littered with unexploded mines and cluster bombs, so it's definitely not the place to set off on any kind of hike.

If you do wish to explore outside Sidon and Tyre, heed local advice: you can check with locals, embassy staff, UNIFIL or Lebanese soldiers and, as always, stay informed on the news front. For more information on UNIFIL itself, go to www.un.org/Depts/dpko/missions/unifil/.

cafés in town: ask at your hotel for the latest location with the swiftest connection.

Post office (☎ 722 813; Rue Rafiq al-Hariri; 🕑 8am-5pm Mon-Fri, 8am-noon Sat)

Tourist office (☎ 727 344; 🕑 8.30am-2pm Mon-Sat) A small office, with maps of Sidon's historic sites, operating inside the Khan al-Franj.

Sights & Activities

With the exception of the Sea Castle, all Sidon's sights are free to visit. Opening hours, though, can be a little erratic: if a place is closed, it pays to ask around since someone will probably be able to tell you where the keyholder is to be found.

THE OLD CITY

Old Sidon, a fascinating labyrinth of vaulted souqs, tiny alleyways and medieval remnants, stretches out behind the buildings fronting the harbour. Officially, there are 60 listed historic sights here, many in ruins, although renovation work is ongoing.

In the **souqs** you'll find craftspeople plying the same trades their ancestors did for centuries. There are plenty of opportunities to pick up the local fragrant orange-blossom water (good in both sweet and savoury cooking, or as a cordial for summer drinks) and *sanioura*, a light, crumbly, shortcake-like biscuit.

A highlight of the souq area is the **Khan al-Franj** (Inn of the Foreigners; admission free; 🕑 10am-6pm), the most beautiful and best preserved of all the limestone khans built by Fakhreddine (Fakhr ad-Din al-Maan II) in the 17th century. Wonderfully restored, it consists of vaulted arcades surrounding a large rectangular courtyard with a central fountain. Today, it houses the Hariri Foundation, founded by assassinated former PM Rafiq Hariri, which works on various restoration projects throughout the city and beyond.

Just behind the Khan al-Franj is the **Bab as-Saray Mosque**, the oldest in Sidon, dating from 1201 and filled with beautiful stonework. It may not always be open to non-Muslims, so check before entering. Another gem is the **Palace Debbané** (Al-Moutran St, Souq; admission free; 🕑 9am-6pm Sat-Thu) entered from the souq via a tall staircase marked with a sign. Built in 1721, this former Ottoman aristocrat's building has intricate Mamluk decoration, including tile work and cedar wood ceilings, and various historical exhibits.

Facing the northern tip of the harbour is the **Great (Omari) Mosque** (admission free), said to be one of the finest examples of Islamic religious architecture of the 13th century and originally converted from a fortified Knights Hospitaller structure. Severely damaged by the Israeli bombings of 1982, it underwent a long restoration, and now looks spectacular once again; it's open to non-Muslims outside prayer times and, as always, remember to dress appropriately.

SEA CASTLE

Erected in 1228 by the Crusaders, the **Sea Castle** (Qasr al-Bahr; admission LL4000; 🕑 9am-6pm summer, to 4pm winter) sits on a small island that was formerly the site of a temple dedicated to Melkart, the Phoenician version of Hercules, and is connected to the mainland by a fortified stone causeway. Like many other coastal castles, it was largely destroyed by the Mamluks to prevent the Crusaders returning to the region, but was renovated by Fakhreddine II in the 17th century. On calm days, you can see numerous broken rose granite columns lying on the sea floor beneath the castle; archaeologists think there's plenty more of this sort of history to be discovered further off Sidon's coast.

MUSEE DU SAVON (SOAP MUSEUM)

Located in an old soap factory dating from the 17th century, this surprisingly interesting **museum** (☎ 733 353; Rue al-Moutran; admission free; 9am-6pm Sat-Thu) is Lebanon's only museum of that most humble yet indispensable of products. Well laid-out, with trilingual explanations (Arabic, English, French) on the art of 'saponification' (which we non-saponifiers might simply call 'soapmaking'), the museum also hosts a stylish café and a boutique with some lovely illustrated history and cookery books, as well, of course, as the foaming white stuff itself.

Sleeping & Eating

Hotel d'Orient (☎ 720 364; Rue Shakrieh, Souq, Old City; dm/s with fan US$5/7, d with fan US$10-12) Grim and grimy, this is really only an option for those on their last Lebanese lira. It's on the right-hand side as you walk from the harbour to the soap museum: look for the faded 1st-floor sign.

Yacoub Hotel (☎ 737 733; Rue al-Moutrah; s/d US$40/60;) This clean, quiet choice is housed in a converted 200-year-old building and offers spotless, comfortable and attractive rooms. You'll see it signposted off to the left on your way up from the harbour to the soap museum.

our pick **Al-Qualaa Hotel** (☎ 734 777; www.alqualaa.com; Port Rd; s/d US$65/70;) Sidon's nicest accommodation lies on the main road in front of the town port, in a beautifully restored building. Ask for a room with a sea view to make the most of a stay in this light- and antique-filled place. There are also a couple of lovely rooftop cafés.

Rest House (☎ 722 469; mezze LL4000-6000, grills from LL10,000; 11am-11pm) On the seafront overlooking the Sea Castle and the lapping waves, this upscale government-owned restaurant in an old Ottoman khan has a pleasant, shaded garden terrace and a long menu of tasty mezze.

Al-Qualaa Hotel has a great rooftop café, with nice mezze lunches (mezze around LL3000 per portion) and soothing nargilehs for rent, open daily from 8am to late. For cheap eats, the strip beneath the hotel is filled with felafel, seafood and mezze joints, one of the most popular being **Abou Ramy** (felafel from LL2500; 8am-9pm). Otherwise, delve into the souq and follow your nose to find yourself dining on fresh food with ancient men in equally ancient surroundings.

Getting There & Away

TO/FROM BEIRUT

Buses and service taxis from Beirut to Sidon leave from the Cola transport hub. To Sidon, OCFTC buses (LL1000, one hour, every 10 minutes from 6am to 8pm) leave from the southwest side of the Cola roundabout. **Zantout** (☎ 03-223 414) also runs 14 express buses daily, roughly hourly from 6am to 9pm (LL1500, 30 minutes). Minibuses (without air-con) to/from Sidon leave every 10 to 15 minutes from 6.30am to 8.30pm and cost LL1000/1500 for day/evening trips, and service taxis cost LL2500. In Sidon, buses depart from the Lebanese Transport Office at Saahat an-Nejmeh, and service taxis from the service taxi stand just across from the roundabout.

TO TYRE

The Zantout bus from Sidon to Tyre (LL750, 45 minutes to one hour, roughly hourly from 6am to 7.30pm) leaves from the Lebanese Transport Office at the southern end of the town on Rue Fakhreddine, the continuation of Rue Riad as-Solh, near the Castle of St Louis. A service taxi from Sidon to Tyre costs LL3500 and a minibus costs LL1000 (both leaving from Saahat an-Nejmeh).

TEMPLE OF ECHMOUN معبد أشمون

About 2km northeast of Sidon, this **temple** (admission free; 8am-dusk) is Lebanon's only Phoenician site boasting more than mere foundations. Today it contains the remains of temples and shops as well as some interesting mosaics (although most are damaged).

Begun in the 7th century BC, the temple complex was devoted to Echmoun, god of the city of Sidon, and other buildings were later added by the Persians, Romans and Byzantines. Today, the highlight of the site is undoubtedly the throne of Astarte, flanked by two winged sphinxes.

From Sidon you can take a taxi (LL6000), service taxi (LL1000) or minibus (LL500) to the turn-off on the highway at the funfair, then walk a pleasant, orchard-lined 1.5km to the ruins.

TYRE (SOUR) صور

☎ 07 / pop 142,755

Famous most notoriously for its local hero Hassan Nasrallah and, most scenically, for its extraordinary Roman ruins, Tyre is an oft-troubled town filled with an abundance of both UN soldiers and Unesco World Heritage sites.

Tyre's origins date back to its foundation in approximately 2750 BC, after which it was ruled by the Egyptians and then the famous King Hiram (who sent cedar wood and skilled workers to Jerusalem so that the Hebrew King Solomon could build the Temple of Jerusalem) under whom it prospered. Later colonised variously by the Assyrians, Neo-Babylonians, Greeks, Seleucids, Romans, Byzantines, Arabs, Crusaders, Mamluks and Ottomans, Tyre began to languish from the 13th century onward and, despite many attempts, never quite recovered its former glory.

Every time the city attempts to get to its feet following disaster it seems to be struck down by a new catastrophe. Though it's generally proved safe to visit in recent times, be sure to heed local travel warnings, and it makes sense to avoid Palestinian refugee camps unless you're with a trusted local. Nevertheless, Tyre remains a picturesque and intriguing destination whenever

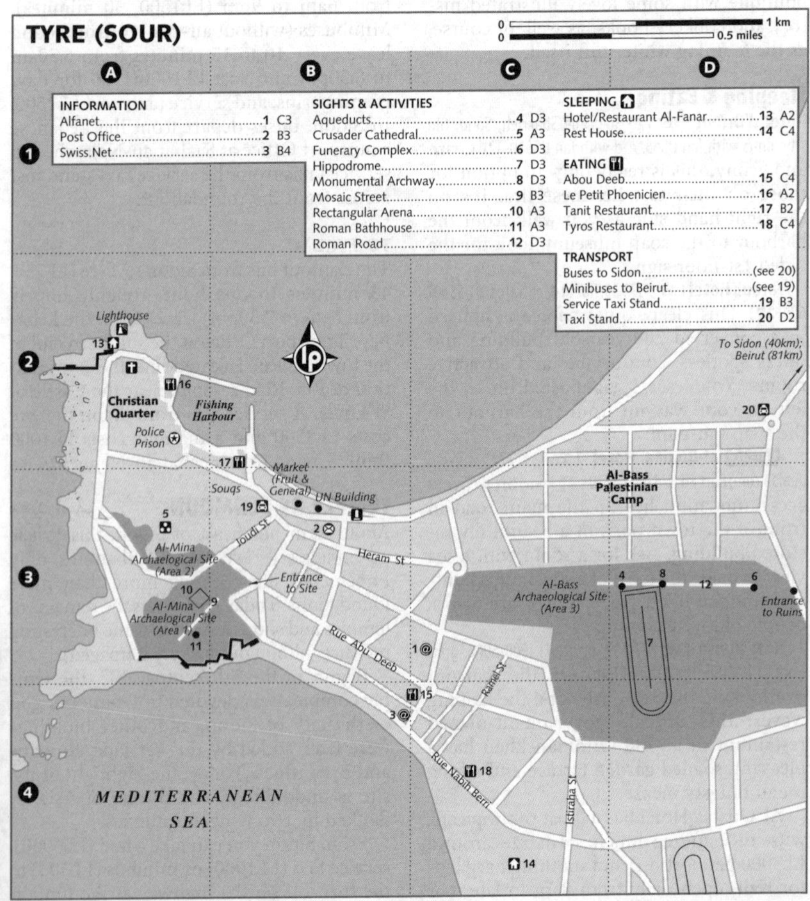

WHO IS HASSAN NASRALLAH?

Born in 1960 in a poor Beirut suburb, Hassan Nasrallah has gained international notoriety in recent years for being the public face and voice of Hezbollah, since becoming its Secretary-General in 1992.

His career began in 1975 when he joined the Amal movement, a Shiite militia, during the civil war. Following a period of religious study in Iraq, he joined Hezbollah in 1982 after Israel's invasion of Lebanon, and soon became known for his charismatic brand of fierce and fiery rhetoric. In 1992, he took on the role of Secretary-General after Hezbollah's former leader was killed in an Israeli helicopter attack. Nasrallah's own eldest son, Muhammed, was later killed in combat with Israel in 1997.

Often branded a terrorist by the West, Nasrallah has publicly criticised both the Taliban and Al-Qaeda, but remains set on the destruction of Israel. His leadership has seen Hezbollah responsible for kidnappings and bombings, as well as for far-reaching social, medical and educational programs throughout the impoverished south and beyond.

For a glimpse of 'Nasrallah, by Nasrallah', visit his website at http://english.wa3ad.org.

times are quieter down south, and if you can visit, you really should.

Orientation & Information

The old part of Tyre lies on the peninsula jutting out into the sea. The modern town is on the left-hand side as you arrive from Beirut. Behind the port is the Christian quarter, with its tiny alleys and old houses with shaded courtyards.

Banks with ATMs and the **post office** (☎ 740 565; 7.30am-5pm Mon-Fri, 8am-1pm Sat) are clustered near the service taxi stand in the town centre. Internet cafés include:

Alfanet (☎ 347 047; off Rue Abu Deeb; per hr LL1500; 10.30am-1am) Just north of the main roundabout.

Swiss.Net (☎ 03-446 154; Rue Nabih Berri; per hr LL1000; 9am-midnight)

Sights

In 1984, Tyre was declared a Unesco World Heritage site, and its archaeological remains are divided into three parts: Al-Mina (Areas 1 and 2) on the south side of the city, Al-Bass (Area 3) on the original mainland section, and a medieval site in the centre of town. Taking a guide is highly recommended here: a long tour should cost LL10,000 to LL15,000, or LL20,000 for a larger group.

The **Al-Mina Archaeological Site** (Areas 1 & 2; ☎ 740 115; adult/child LL6000/3500; 8.30am-30min before sunset) covers a large area leading down to the ancient Egyptian **submerged harbour,** created in the 3rd millennium BC. It features a **mosaic street** paved with impressive geometrical Roman and Byzantine mosaics, on each side of which are rows of large columns, made of green marble imported from Greece. Look out also for the unusually large public **Roman bathhouse** from the 2nd or 3rd century AD and a 4th-century **rectangular arena**, which would have held up to 2000 spectators, perhaps to watch some sort of ancient watersport.

A five-minute walk north of the main Al-Mina site brings you to the ruins of a 12th-century **Crusader cathedral**, along with a network of Roman and Byzantine roads.

The enormous **Al-Bass Archaeological Site** (Area 3; ☎ 740 530; adult/child LL6000/3500; 8.30am-30min before sunset) lies 2km from the Al-Mina site. Just past the entrance is a vast **funerary complex**, with hundreds of ornate stone and marble ancient sarcophagi lining the road, some intricately carved with the names of the occupants or reliefs drawn from the *Iliad.* A well-preserved **Roman road** stretches in a straight line for about 1.6km from an impressive 20m-high **monumental archway**, which probably dates from the time of Emperor Hadrian (2nd century AD). Beyond the archway is the largest and best preserved Roman **hippodrome** in the world (holding more than 20,000 spectators), built in the 2nd century AD for the ancient adrenalin sport of chariot racing. At the far end of the road are the remains of Roman **aqueducts**, parts of which are still held up by arcades.

Sleeping

Tyre's midrange sleeping options aren't really up to much at the moment; if you're staying in town, plump either for the budget or top-end choices listed, and forgo the mediocre middle.

our pick **Hotel/Restaurant al-Fanar** (☎ 741 111; www.alfanarresort.com; d US$40, with sea views US$50;) With its toes almost in the water, the location is the principal plus here. Run by a charming family, it's also homely, peaceful and welcoming, with rooms that are simple but clean; rates include breakfast. There are two little terraces, a pub in the cellar and, outside, a tiny beach. The restaurant (open from noon to 10pm or later) overlooks the lighthouse and serves homemade food and fish dishes (three-course meals including mezze and a fish dish for two/four people come to around US$30/50).

Rest House (☎ 742 000; www.resthouse-tyr.com.lb; Istiraha St; garden view d/ste US90/120, sea view r/junior ste US$115/145;) Large, bright, airy, tranquil, and with excellent facilities including a sandy beach, two pools, several restaurants and a pub, this makes a great place to rest (or dip) aching feet after a hot day exploring Tyre's ruins.

Eating

our pick **Le Petit Phoenicien** (☎ 740 564; Old Port; mezze LL3000-5500, fish LL40,000-70,000; noon-11pm winter, noon-2am summer) Also known locally as 'Hadeed', this place is widely considered the best in town for its fish, with a pleasant outdoor terrace overlooking the fishing harbour.

Tanit Restaurant (☎ 347 539; mezze LL4000, grills LL15,000; 10am-late) The atmospheric Tanit is popular with locals and UNIFIL troops for its bar as well as for its food, which ranges eclectically from mezze to stir-fries and steaks. The restaurant lies around the corner from the fishing harbour.

Tyros Restaurant (☎ 741 027; Rue Nabih Berri; mezze LL4500, grills LL6500-7500; 8am-late) This enormous, tent-like place is popular with the locals for its great atmosphere, a huge mezze menu and food at reasonable prices. There's live classical Arabic music most Saturday nights.

There are a few fast-food places at the roundabout on Rue Abou Deeb, including the large and very popular **Abou Deeb** (11am-late), which serves good felafels (LL1200) and shwarmas (LL2000).

Getting There & Away

For Beirut, microbuses (LL2000, after 8pm LL3000, one to 1½ hours, every 15 minutes from around 5am to 9pm) go direct from Tyre. Large minibuses also travel from Tyre to Beirut (LL2000 to LL3000, one to two hours, 6am to 8pm depending on passenger demand).

The first bus from Tyre to Sidon (LL1500, 30 to 45 minutes) leaves at 6am from the roundabout north of the entrance to the Al-Bass site. The last leaves at 8pm, and they come about twice per hour in between.

A service taxi from Beirut's Cola transport hub costs around LL7000; from Sidon to Tyre, a service taxi will cost LL4000.

CHOUF MOUNTAINS جبال الشوف

These spectacular mountains, southeast of Beirut, are the southernmost part of the Mt Lebanon Range. In places they're wild and beautiful; in others they're dotted with small villages and terraced for easy cultivation; throughout, they're a beautiful place for a day or two's exploration.

Beiteddine Palace (Beit ad-Din) بيت الدين

Located in otherwise unexceptional Beiteddine village, one of the highlights of the Chouf is undoubtedly the early 19th-century **Beiteddine Palace** (Beit ad-Din; ☎ 05-500 077; adult/student LL7500/5000; 9am-6pm Tue-Sun Apr-Oct, 9am-3.45pm Nov-May), around 50km southeast of Beirut.

Sitting majestically on a hill, surrounded by terraced gardens and orchards, the palace was built by Emir Bashir, Ottoman-appointed governor of the region, over a period of 30 years, starting in 1788. It's worth employing the services of a guide at the entrance (around LL10,000), since many of the palace's most sumptuous rooms are kept locked, and only guides hold the all-important key. Otherwise, you'll be reduced to tagging along behind another group, and hoping no one notices.

Meaning 'House of Faith', Beiteddine Palace was built over and around an older Druze hermitage. During the French mandate, the palace became used for local administration, after 1930 but, was declared a historic monument. In 1943, Lebanon's first president after independence declared it his summer residence. The palace was extensively damaged during the Israeli invasion; it's estimated that up to 90% of the original contents were lost during this time. When fighting ended in 1984, the palace was taken over by the Druze militia, and Walid Jumblatt, their leader, ordered its restoration and declared it a 'Palace of the People'. In 1999 the Druze returned it to the government.

Although conceived by Italian architects, the palace incorporates many traditional forms of Arab architecture. The main gate opens on to a 60m-wide **outer courtyard** (Dar al-Baraniyyeh) walled on three sides only; the fourth side has great views out over valleys and hills.

A double staircase on the outer courtyard's western side leads into a smaller **central courtyard** (Dar al-Wousta) with a central fountain. Beyond this courtyard is the third – and last – **inner courtyard** (Dar al-Harim). This was the centre of the family quarters, which also included a beautiful **hammam** and huge kitchens.

Underneath the Dar al-Wousta and Dar al-Harim are the former stables, now home to an outstanding collection of 5th- and 6th-century **Byzantine mosaics**. Found at Jiyyeh, 30km south of Beirut, they were brought by Walid Jumblatt to Beiteddine in 1982. Whatever you do, don't miss them: they're truly stunning.

The palace hosts a wonderful annual music festival during July and August. Check the festival website (www.beiteddine.org) for full details.

SLEEPING & EATING

Beiteddine Palace is really best experienced by a day trip from Beirut or from the lovely nearby Deir al-Qamar (right).

The only sleeping option nearby is the ultraluxurious **Mir Amin Palace** (☎ 05-501 315; www.miraminpalace.com; s/d US$123/155;), originally built by Emir Bashir for his eldest son. There are 24 beautifully decorated rooms here, and a lovely bar/restaurant worth a visit for the views alone. Expect to spend around US$30 to US$40 per person for a full meal of its delicious Lebanese cuisine.

Aside from a few snack bars, Beiteddine doesn't really have any other food options: pack yourself a picnic from Beirut or Deir al-Qamar, and eat it in the palace garden beside the beautiful open-air mosaics.

GETTING THERE & AWAY

Service taxis from Beirut's Cola transport hub run from Beirut to Beiteddine (LL5000, two hours, roughly hourly). The service taxi stand in Beiteddine is close to the palace on the main square; bear in mind that there are few service taxis after dark.

Deir al-Qamar دير القمر

☎ 05

Without question one of Lebanon's prettiest villages, this interesting small town, a few kilometres from Beiteddine, was the seat of Lebanon's emirates during the 17th and 18th centuries, and today is a sleepy, enchanting place for a lazy stroll and a sunset drink, while bats flit from ancient buildings all about you.

The main square has some fine examples of Arab architecture, including the **Mosque of Emir Fakhreddine Maan** built in 1493; a **silk khan** built in 1595 and now housing the French Cultural Centre; and the 18th-century **Serail of Youssef Chehab**, which saw a bloody factional massacre in its central courtyard in 1860.

On the main square, **Fakhreddine's Palace**, built in 1620, is now home to the dusty yet curiously endearing **Marie Baz Wax Museum** (☎ 511 666; adult/child LL10,000/5000; 8.30am-sunset), featuring a smattering of Lebanon's historic personalities, as well as George Bush senior and a weird, headless Jumblatt. If you listen politely to his lengthy commentaries, the elderly attendant might unlock the nearby Cheikh Jiriz Baz summer palace – now derelict – for you to see the fairytale views from the roof.

Just outside town, 2km down the road toward Beiteddine, don't miss Lebanon's most eccentric 'outsider art' masterpiece at **Castle Moussa** (☎ 041 144; admission LL7500; 8am-8pm summer, 8am-6pm winter), a modern castle built by a local businessman that houses an eclectic collection of moving dioramas, mechanical tableaux, and thousands upon thousands of guns. Prepare to be bemused and impressed in equal measure.

SLEEPING & EATING

La Bastide (☎ 505 320, 03-643 010; d/family r US$60/80) On the road towards Beiteddine, around 1km from Deir al-Qamar, this lovely, airy, flower-patterned place makes a great base for exploring the Chouf. Ask for a room with a view over the valley, or a family-sized room with three beds and a kitchenette.

Al-Midane Café (☎ 03-763 768; sandwiches & salads from LL6000; 10am-late) A lovely choice for light

LEBANON'S CEDARS

The most famous of the world's several species of cedar tree are the Cedars of Lebanon, mentioned in the Old Testament, and once covering great swathes of the Mt Lebanon Range.

Jerusalem's original Temple of Solomon was made from this sort of cedar wood, and the ancient Phoenicians, too, found it appealing for its fragrance and durability. Such a long history of deforestation, however, has meant that today, just a few pockets of cedars remain in Lebanon – despite the tree appearing proudly on the nation's flag.

Of these remnants of a once-abundant arboreal past, the best places to view the remaining cedars of Lebanon are either at the Chouf Cedar Reserve, or at the small grove at the Cedars ski resort (p438) in the north of the country. Still, with plenty of reforestation projects going on, there are hopes that Lebanon will one day be forested by its beautiful, long-living national emblem once more.

meals and lingering on Deir al-Qamar's central square, this place has live music at summer weekends until midnight and beyond.

GETTING THERE & AWAY

Service taxis from Beirut to Beiteddine (see Beitedinne Palace, p445) can drop you at Deir al-Qamar en route.

Chouf Cedar Reserve محمية ارز الشوف

The largest of Lebanon's three natural protectorates, the **Chouf Cedar Reserve** (☎ 05-502 230; www.shoufcedar.org; admission LL5000; 🕑 9am-7pm) comprises an incredible 5% of Lebanon's total land area. Within it are ancient rock-cut fortress remains as well as six of the country's last remaining cedar forests, some with trees thought to be around 2000 years old. More than 200 species of birds and animals (including wolves, gazelles and wild boar) inhabit or regularly pass through the area.

Tragically understaffed, not all parts of the park are open to visitors, so your best bet is to head to the ranger hut at the Barouk entrance, near the village of Barouk. Here, you can get advice on hiking trails (there are eight currently open to the public, ranging from 40 minutes to four hours), peruse the locally made produce at the shop, and employ the services of a guide for an enlightening tour of the Chouf Cedar Reserve.

If you're not coming here by your own car, negotiate a taxi fare from Beiteddine, some 10km away. If you want to stay overnight in the area, contact the **Association for Forests, Development & Conservation** (www.afdc.org.lb), which operates a forest ecolodge around 7km from the reserve.

BEKAA VALLEY
وادي البقاع

The fertile, pastoral Bekaa Valley is at once famous for its magnificent archaeological sites at Baalbek and Aanjar, and infamous for being the homeland of Hezbollah (Party of God), along with crops of 'Red Leb', high-quality cannabis. Heavily cultivated over millennia (it was one of Rome's 'breadbaskets'), it's actually a high plateau between the Mt Lebanon and Anti-Lebanon mountain ranges, less agriculturally burgeoning than in centuries past, due to a combination of deforestation and poor crop planning, but with plentiful vineyards slowly gaining an international reputation for their wines. Though you'll see Hezbollah's yellow flag fluttering around Baalbek, you'll find the locals (a mixture of Christians and Shiites) a welcoming lot and the attractions of the valley as intoxicating as its vintages.

ZAHLÉ زحله

☎ 08 / pop 79,803

A cheerful and bustling town with some nice riverside restaurants and a holiday feel in the summer months, Zahlé makes a great lunchtime or evening stop on the way between Beirut and Baalbek, or even an alternative base for exploring the Bekaa Valley if you find its happy atmosphere and cool climate (at 945m) particularly enticing. There are no particular sights as such: a visit to Zahlé is really all about hanging out at the Cafés du Bardouni, the open-air cafés that jostle along the water's edge, washed down with copious quantities of the local arak (aniseed liquor).

Orientation & Information

Most of the town's amenities are scattered along the main road, Rue Brazil, and Rue St Barbara, running parallel.

Dataland Internet (Rue Brazil; per hr LL5000; 8am-midnight)

Khoury General Hospital (Rue Brazil) Towards the head of the valley

Post office (Rue Brazil; 8am-5pm Mon-Fri, 8am-noon Sat)

Sleeping & Eating

In summer months, head down to the riverside, where the Cafés du Bardouni all offer mezze, grills and ice creams galore. Most open between 11am and noon, and stay open late into the night, for live music, a spot of gambling, and lots of whirring, flashing fairground attractions for the kids.

Hotel Akl (820 701; Rue Brazil; s/d/tr LL35,000/50,000/60,000, s/d without bathroom LL25,000/40,000) Though definitely dilapidated, this great budget choice has large rooms with lots of natural light, some overlooking the river, and a communal lounge with fireplace and a piano for a spot of Chopsticks. Check with the friendly management that the cheaper rooms have some sort of heating during the chilly winter months.

Hotel Monte Alberto (810 912; www.montealberto.com; d/tr US$60/70;) Located high above town, the hotel commands amazing views from its simple but spotless and comfortable rooms. If you're a fan of all things kitsch, you'll be able to choose between the vaguely cowboy funicular railway leading up the hill to the hotel and the revolving restaurant at the top.

Grand Hotel Kadri (813 920; www.grandhotelkadri.com; Rue Brazil; s/d/ste US$105/125/160;) Great facilities here include a health club, tennis court, nightclub and two restaurants, but the rooms at this grand and venerable place – once an Ottoman hospital – are a bit of a let-down. Note the name tags of the female receptionists: they all appear to have the same name (mystifyingly explained by one assistant on the grounds that it was 'so as not to confuse telephone callers').

Getting There & Away

Minibuses run from Beirut to Zahlé (LL3000, around one hour, approximately every 15 minutes from 4am to 1am) leaving from the southwest side of the roundabout at the Cola transport hub. Service taxis (LL6000) leave from the same spot. Both will drop you off at the highway roundabout turn-off, which is just over 1km from the centre of town. You can walk or negotiate a private taxi from there.

To get to Baalbek from Zahlé, take a service taxi (LL3000, 30 minutes) from the main taxi stand on a square off Rue Brazil, or walk to the highway roundabout at the southern end of town, where you can hail a passing microbus (LL1500, 45 minutes).

BAALBEK بعلبك

08 / pop 31,962

Known as the Heliopolis or 'Sun City' of the ancient world, Baalbek's ruins, without

FRUITS OF THE EARTH: THE BEKAA'S VINEYARDS

It'd be a shame to come to the Bekaa Valley and not have a quick tipple at one or two of its vineyards, which are fast becoming international names in wine. It's best to call in advance to make an appointment, and to ask for specific directions to the vineyards.

Lebanon's oldest and most famous winery, **Ksara Winery** (08-813 495; www.ksara.com.lb; Ksara; 9am-4pm), had its first vines planted here in the 18th century and has unique underground caves for maturing the wine. Take a 45-minute tour of the caves, and munch on cheese and cold cuts along with your wine tastings. To get here, take a southbound service taxi (LL1500) from Zahlé to Ksara Village, a five-minute walk from the winery.

Not far from Zahlé, **Chateau Kefraya** (08-645 333/444; www.chateaukefraya.com; Chateua Kefraya, Zahlé) is Lebanon's largest wine producer. If you're here between 25 August and 1 September, you'll witness the annual grape harvest. At other times, don't miss lunch at the stylist Dionysus restaurant, with French cuisine to complement the winery's best vintages.

Call in advance to experience a feast at the trendy **Massaya & Co** (03-735 795; www.massaya.com) vineyard's Le Relais restaurant, then stroll the vines overseen by Sami Ghosn, an LA architect-turned-winemaker.

doubt, comprise the most impressive ancient site in Lebanon and are arguably the best preserved in the Middle East. Their temples, built on an extravagant scale that outshone anything in Rome, have enjoyed a stellar reputation throughout the centuries, yet still manage to maintain the appealing air of an undiscovered wonder, due to their position in the middle of quiet, bucolic Baalbek. The town itself, 86km northeast of Beirut and administrative headquarters for both the Bekaa Valley and the Hezbollah party, is small, quiet and friendly, only really coming to life each July with the arrival of the famous annual Baalbek Festival (www.baalbek.org.lb), which runs whenever the political situation allows.

Orientation & Information

Baalbek is small and easily tackled on foot. The main road, Rue Abdel Halim Hajjar, is where you'll find the town's two banks, a number of ATMs, the ruins and the Palmyra Hotel. Note that neither of the banks cashes travellers cheques, and no hotels appear willing to accept credit cards.

Post office (8am-5pm Mon-Fri, 8am-2pm Sat) Heading along Ras al-Ain Blvd, it's up a side street before the Riviera Restaurant.

Network Center (370 192; off Rue Abdel Halim Hajjar; per hr LL3000; 9am-1am) Up a side street between the Palmyra and Jupiter Hotels.

Sights

BAALBEK RUINS

The very best time to visit the **site** (370 645; admission LL12,000, under 8yr free; 8.30am-30min before sunset) is during the early morning or – even better – late in the afternoon, when the light's great, the crowds thinnest and the temperatures cooler. It's highly recommended to take an accredited guide at the entrance to the site (around US$14 for an hour) who will really bring the stones to life.

The first of the two greatest temples at the main site is the **Temple of Jupiter**, completed around AD 60. Built on a massive substructure around 90m long, and incorporating some of the largest building blocks ever used, it was originally approached by a monumental staircase that rose high above the surrounding buildings. Today its remaining **six standing columns** (themselves also some of the very largest in the world) are a massive and spectacular reminder of the size and majesty of the original, ancient structure.

THE PARTY OF GOD

You'll probably hear far more in the world media about Baalbek's local Hezbollah party than you'll ever hear about its temples. From its roots as one of dozens of militia groups fighting during Lebanon's civil war, following a Shiite doctrine propagated by the Ayatollah Khomeini, Hezbollah has risen to become what many consider a legitimate resistance party, with its own radio station, TV network, countrywide network of social services, and 14 democratically elected seats in the Lebanese parliament.

Upon its foundation, the party initially aimed to bring to justice those accused of war crimes during the civil war (particularly Phalangist Christians), to create an Islamic government in Lebanon, and to eradicate 'Western colonialist' influences within the country. Since then, however, Hezbollah has given up on the second of these aims, replacing it with the desire to destroy the 'unlawful entity' that is present-day Israel. Regular vicious attacks on Israel's northern border attest to its attempts to carry this out.

Often represented to the outside world as a bloodthirsty and brutal organisation only interested in bombings, kidnappings and mayhem, Hezbollah nevertheless does far more than simply amassing arms and planning raids against Israel and potential aggressors. Its network of schools, hospitals, garbage disposal plants, training institutes for farmers, fresh water distribution points and childcare facilities are unsurpassed in Lebanon, bringing crucial aid to thousands of Lebanon's poor and needy. The money for all this, says the group, comes from 'donations', though many believe it's actually directly from deep Iranian high-profile pockets.

However the aid gets there, though, get there it does – to many impoverished communities in southern Lebanon and southern Beirut, who would, if Hezbollah did not exist, almost certainly go without.

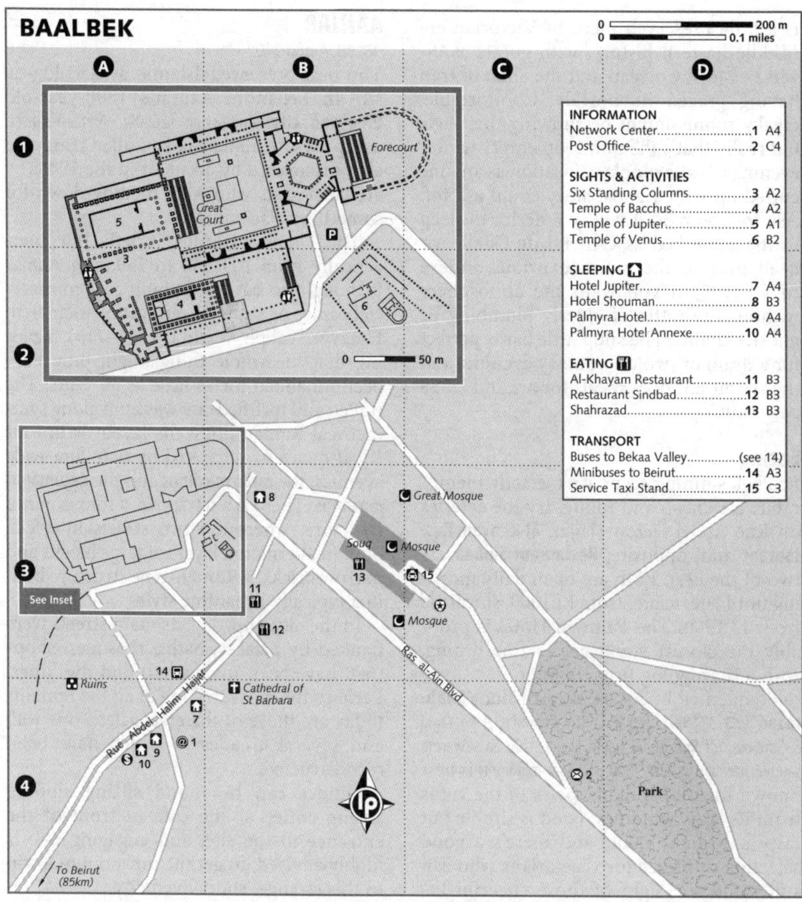

Adjacent to the Temple of Jupiter is the second of Baalbek's great temples, the **Temple of Bacchus**, known in Roman times as the 'small temple' and dedicated, in fact, to Venus/Astarte rather than to Bacchus. Completed around AD 150, it's amazingly well preserved and is still stunningly ornate, displaying tablatures decorated with images of the gods, from Mars and Victory to Diana, Vulcan and Ceres. Near the main ruins, look in on the exquisite **Temple of Venus**, a circular building with fluted columns. And if it looks vaguely familiar to any National Trust–going Brits, here's why: there's an exact 18th-century copy of the temple in the grounds of Stourhead, in Wiltshire.

Sleeping

Hotel Shouman (☎ 03-796 077; Ras al-Ain Blvd; dm/d/tr without bathroom LL10,000/25,000/25,000) Close to the ruins, three of the rooms here enjoy great views, including the triple Room 1. The beds are quite hard, but rooms are clean, as is the simple shared bathroom. Enter via a stone staircase; the pension is on the 1st floor.

Hotel Jupiter (☎ 376 715; Rue Abdel Halim Hajjar; s/d/tr US$10/20/25) Entered via an arcade northeast of the Palmyra Hotel, Jupiter has large, light, basic rooms equipped with fans off a central courtyard. The owners are friendly, and there's also a restaurant.

our pick **Palmyra Hotel** (☎ 376 011; fax 370 305; Rue Abdel Halim Hajjar; s/d/tr US$38/53/63) As unmissable as the ruins themselves, the Palmyra is a little preserved piece of Victorian-era Middle Eastern history, with guests as diverse as Jean Cocteau and the Shah of Iran having graced its portals. Comfortable, creaky rooms might be showing their age, but really that's the point: on empty winter evenings, it's as spooky a location as anyone curled up with a ghost story could ask for. Ask for room 30 if you've a desire to sleep in the same bed as General de Gaulle, or head over to the more luxurious annexe (d US$100) if you want the atmosphere without the rattle of elderly plumbing or ghostly chains. The snug little bar is perfect for a dram or two on a snowy evening, and the restaurant does meals for around US$8 per main.

Eating

Baalbek's dining scene isn't exactly memorable: for cheap and filling, try the eateries on Rue Abdel Halim Hajjar. **Al-Khayam Restaurant** and, opposite, **Restaurant Sinbad** are two of the best. Both are open daily morning until late; felafel from LL1000, shwarma from LL1500. The Palmyra Hotel is probably the closest you'll get to fine dining, with a roaring log fire in winter.

Frequented by locals, the 6th-floor **Shahrazad** (☎ 371 851; Top fl, Centre Commercial de Yaghi & Simbole, off Rue Abdel Halim Hajjar; chicken shwarma sandwich/kebab LL3500/7000; ⏰ 8am-midnight) is best known for the fabulous views of the ruins from its large windows. Food is simple but tasty and good value, and there's a good selection of mezze for vegetarians who can still stand the sight of those cheerful little plates. Access the restaurant via a signposted lift in the souq.

Getting There & Away

The only public transport options from Beirut to Baalbek are minibuses and service taxis. From the Cola transport hub, a minibus to Baalbek costs LL5000 (1½ hours); a service taxi costs LL7000. The bus stop in Baalbek is just up the road from the Palmyra Hotel, and the service taxi stand is in the souq area.

For information about how to get to Baalbek from Zahlé, see p447. In summer, you can negotiate a private taxi to take you across the barren, beautiful mountains to the Cedars or Bcharré (1½ hours) for around US$60.

AANJAR عنجر

☎ 08 / pop 2400

The best-preserved Islamic archaeological site in Lebanon, Aanjar's 1300-year-old **Umayyad city** (admission LL6000; ⏰ 8am-sunset) comprises the remains of a walled Umayyad city, discovered by accident in the 1940s by archaeologists who were digging down for something else entirely.

The Umayyads ruled briefly but energetically from AD 660 to 750, and Aanjar is thought to have been built as a commercial centre or strategic outpost by their sixth Umayyad caliph, Walid I (r 705–715), meaning that the whole thing might only have been inhabited for as little as 50 years. The walled and fortified city was built along symmetrical Roman lines; the layout is in four equal quarters, separated by two 20m-wide avenues, the **cardo maximus** and the **decumanus maximus**. There is a **tetrapylon**, a four-column structure, where the two streets intersect, built in alternating layers of large blocks and narrow bricks, a Roman-type structure built in a typically Byzantine style.

In the city's heyday, its main streets were flanked by palaces, baths, mosques, shops (600 have been uncovered) and dwellings. Perhaps the most striking of all the remains today are those of the **great palace**, one wall and several arcades of which have been reconstructed.

Guides can be found sitting sipping strong coffee at the café in front of the entrance to the site, and engaging one is highly advised, to get the most out of a trip to this strange, short-lived city.

Sleeping & Eating

Challalat Anjar Hotel (☎/fax 620 753; s/d/ste LL60,000/90,000/120,000; ❄) Aanjar's only hotel, situated amid the restaurants at the end of town, is bright and airy with, as the brochure points out, 'very considered prices'. All rooms have TVs and balcony, and its basic mezze-and-meats restaurant has live music on the terrace every night in summer.

Shams Restaurant (☎ 620 567; mezze from LL2500, grills from LL6000; ⏰ 10am-midnight) One of the most popular places to eat in town, this restaurant serves superb fresh fish and seafood, along with the usual array of tasty mezze. It's on the right hand side of the road into Aanjar, about 500m from the main Damascus highway.

For more dining choices (in summer only) follow signs for 'Restaurants Aanjar' down the town's main street. Here you'll find a range of nice Lebanese restaurants spread around blooming gardens, some with playgrounds and several with water wheels.

Getting There & Away

It's a bit tricky to get to Aanjar without your own car. If you're taking a service taxi heading south or to the Syrian border from Zahlé, ask to be dropped off at Aanjar town and walk from the highway (about 2km) to the site. Alternatively, negotiate a private taxi trip from Zahlé: a return, including a one-hour wait at the site, should cost around US$20.

LEBANON DIRECTORY

ACCOMMODATION

Where accommodation options have been divided into categories in the chapter, budget accommodation comes in at under US$40 per double room, midrange at between US$40 and US$90, and top-end at over US$90. Prices are quoted for a room in high season (June to September) except for the Cedars, which is for a room between December and March. Prices are either in US dollars or in Lebanese Lira (LL), depending on which is quoted by the establishment itself.

Note that in low season, large discounts are often available, sometimes as much as 50% or even more, so it's always worth checking. Some smaller places, however, may shut up shop if there seems to be no likelihood of travellers, so it might pay to call in advance if you've any doubts.

As an alternative to the places listed in this chapter, the **Lebanese Youth Hostel Federation** (www.lyhf.org) lists nine hostels serving the country, though no hostel in Beirut itself. Most are in small, rural villages, offering a taste of real local life, and have beds for around US$10 to US$15 per person per night. For upscale homestays across the country, look no further than **L'Hote Libanais** (p423), which can organise a single stay or an entire itinerary for very reasonable prices.

ACTIVITIES

The Lebanese passion for adventure translates into a wide variety of options for adventure activities.

Caving

Caving is possible in various places including the Jeita Grotto (p428). Contact the **Association Libanaise d'Etudes Speleologique** (ALES; ☎ 03-666 469; www.alesliban.org) for details of their trips, from beginners to advanced.

Cycling

Beirut by Bike (☎ 03-435 534) arranges bike tours in Beirut and beyond, and rents out bikes by the day, week or month. Give them a call to confirm their current location. The **Blue Carrot Adventure Club** (☎ 03-552 007; www.blue-carrot.com) organises mountain biking expeditions, along with a host of other adventure activities.

Diving

Watersports, including water-skiing, boating and jet-skiing (especially in Beirut and Jounieh) are available in Lebanon. Diving is a rapidly growing activity; there are some interesting wrecks to explore. A recommended website to check out for diving in Lebanon is that of the **Atlantis Diving College** (www.atlantisdivingcollege.com).

PRACTICALITIES

- The *Daily Star* provides good coverage of local news in English, the daily *L'Orient Le Jour* in French. The monthly magazine, the *Guide*, is useful for upcoming events, openings and exhibitions in Beirut. You can usually find it in Beirut's Virgin Megastore.
- The BBC World Service can be received on both 1323kHz and 72kHz; popular locally are Radio One, Light FM and Nostalgie. The major local TV channels are the government-run broadcaster Tele-Liban and five commercial channels: New TV, MTV, Future TV, NBN and LBC.
- European two-round-pin plugs are needed to connect to Lebanon's electricity supply (220VAC, 50Hz).
- Lebanon uses the metric system for weights and measures.

Skiing

Lebanon is also one of the few countries in the Middle East to offer extensive possibilities for skiing. Along with the Cedars (p438) there are almost half a dozen other resorts to ski or snowboard to your heart's content; your very best first stop is **Ski Lebanon** (www.skileb.com), which has information and booking options galore.

Trekking

For companies and resources on trekking, see the boxed text, p438.

BOOKS

As well as this book, Lonely Planet publishes a comprehensive guide, *Syria & Lebanon*. Jean Said Makdisi's *Beirut Fragments: A War Memoir* (1990) and *Teta, Mother and Me* (2004) illustrate the difficult and dangerous day-to-day life of one woman and her family during the civil war, chronicled by Palestinian writer Edward Said's sister. Thomas Friedman's *From Beirut to Jerusalem* (1998) also contains a grimly humorous account of life in Beirut during the difficult and dramatic war years.

There are few contemporary travel books dealing specifically with Lebanon; *The Hills of Adonis: A Journey in Lebanon* (1990) by Colin Thubron is one of the best. Also well worth reading are William Dalrymple's *From the Holy Mountain* (1998) and Robert D Kaplan's *Eastward to Tartary* (2001), both with chapters on travels in Lebanon.

For a lighter look at Lebanese life, grab a copy of *Life's Like That! Your Guide to the Lebanese* (2004) and its sequel *Life's Even More Like That* (2006) by Michael Karam, Peter Grimsditch and Maya Fldawi, with painfully accurate caricatures of Lebanese characters, from dog-walking Filipino maids to Hummer drivers, ladies who lunch, and frazzled foreign correspondents. It's a must-have companion to people-watching at Beirut's cafés, and is available in bookshops across the city.

BUSINESS HOURS

Shops and private businesses in Lebanon are generally open from 9am to 6pm Monday to Friday and from 9am to mid-afternoon on Saturday. Banks are open 8.30am to 2pm Monday to Friday and 8.30am to noon on Saturdays. Post offices and government offices are open 8am to 5pm Monday to Friday, and 8am to 1.30pm on Saturdays.

Restaurants have no standard opening hours, and in Beirut they may stay open all night. We've indicated opening hours, where possible, throughout the chapter.

COURSES

Many students come to Beirut to study Arabic. The following centres provide courses for foreigners:

American Language Center (Map p420; ☎ 01-366 002; www.alc.edu.lb; 1st fl, Choueiry Bldg, Rue Bliss, Beirut; 9am-6pm Mon-Sat)

American University of Beirut (Map p420; ☎ 01-374 444; www.aub.edu/lb/cames)

DANGERS & ANNOYANCES

See Travel Warning: Staying Safe (p407) for information on dangers and annoyances in Lebanon.

EMBASSIES & CONSULATES

Nationals of New Zealand should contact the UK embassy for assistance.

It's worth noting that at the time of research historic plans were afoot for the opening of a Syrian embassy in Beirut. Keep an eye out for developments on this front, but, as many Lebanese sceptics say, don't hold your breath.

Australia (Map p416; ☎ 01-974 030; Serail Hill, Downtown, Beirut)

Canada (off Map p416; ☎ 04-710 591; Coolrite Bldg, Autostrade, Jal ad-Dib, Beirut)

Egypt (Map p416; ☎ 01-867 917; Rue Thomas Edison, off Rue Verdun, Ramlet al-Bayda)

France (Map p416; ☎ 01-420 000; Rue de Damas) Near the National Museum.

Germany (☎ 04-914 444; near Jesus & Mary School, Mtaileb, Rabieh, Beirut)

Italy (Map p416; ☎ 01-985 200; Place d'Etoile, Downtown, Beirut)

Jordan (☎ 05-922 501; Rue Elias Helou, Baabda, Beirut)

Netherlands (Map p416; ☎ 01-204 663; Netherlands Tower, Achrafiye, Beirut)

UK (Map p416; ☎ 01-990 400; Serail Hill, Downtown, Beirut)

US (☎ 04-543 600; Awkar, PO Box 70-840 Antelias) Opposite the Municipality.

FESTIVALS & EVENTS

Many towns and villages host their own small festivals, which range from local fairs to full-on folkloric performances. The major arts festivals are listed here.

February

Al-Bustan Festival (www.albustanfestival.com) An annual festival held for five weeks in Beit Mery (north of Beirut). Daily events feature opera, chamber music and orchestral concerts.

July & August

Baalbek Festival (www.baalbeck.org.lb) Lebanon's most famous arts festival; held at the Roman ruins. Features opera, jazz, poetry and pop, and theatre productions.
Beiteddine Festival (www.beiteddine.org.lb) Music, dance and theatre held in the beautiful courtyard of the Beiteddine Palace.
Byblos International Festival (www.byblosfestival.org) Held in August among the ruins of Byblos's ancient harbour – includes pop, classic, opera and world music.

October

Beirut International Marathon (www.beirutmarathon.org) Also includes wheelchair events.
Beirut International Film Festival (www.beirutfilmfoundation.org) High-profile film festival with a growing reputation as one of the best in the Middle East.

November & December

Docudays (www.docudays.net) The wonderful Beirut International Documentary Festival, held every November or December, sees international audiences flock to the city.

GAY & LESBIAN TRAVELLERS

See the boxed text Gay and Lesbian Beirut (p425) for details, information and resources.

HOLIDAYS

New Year's Day 1 January
Feast of Saint Maroun 9 February – feast of the patron saint of the Maronites
Easter March/April – Good Friday to Easter Monday inclusive
Labour Day 1 May
Martyrs' Day 6 May
Assumption 15 August
All Saints Day 1 November
Independence Day 22 November
Christmas Day 25 December

Also observed are Muslim holidays; see p628 for dates.

MONEY

Lebanon's currency is the Lebanese lira (LL), also known locally as the Lebanese pound. Banknotes are of the following denominations: 1000, 5000, 10,000, 20,000, 50,000 and 100,000; there are also LL250 and LL500 coins.

US dollars are widely accepted countrywide, and higher-end establishments rarely quote prices in anything else.

Country	Unit	Lebanese lira (LL)
Australia	A$1	1002
Canada	C$1	1284
Euro zone	€1	2055
Israel and the Palestinian Territories	NIS1	407.18
Japan	¥100	1684
New Zealand	NZ$1	907.20
Syria	S£1	33.22
UK	UK£1	2248
USA	US$1	1519

ATMs are reliable and available countrywide, and dispense cash in both Lebanese lira and US dollars.

Budget hotels and restaurants generally do not accept credit cards. Tipping is widespread in Lebanon. For professional guides, hotel porters and parking valets tipping somewhere around LL2000 or more, depending on the level of service, will be appreciated. Waiters are usually tipped around 10%, but check your bill before doing so, since some places automatically add a 15% service charge.

PHOTOGRAPHY

There are plenty of shops selling memory cards and batteries for digital cameras all around Beirut, but especially along Rue Hamra. Outside Beirut, you may have problems finding memory cards, though batteries (rarely rechargeable) are widely on sale. A 1GB memory card goes for around US$25; a pack of four AA batteries costs around US$5.

TELEPHONE

Mobile Phones

Mobile-phone coverage extends throughout most of the country (bar a few remote, mountainous areas). Some car-hire agencies rent out mobile phones for around US$6 per day, plus a deposit and call charges. Otherwise, your mobile phone from home will probably work on a local network, though of course you'll pay heavily for the privilege of making calls or sending text messages.

Phone Codes

The country code for Lebanon is ☎ 961, followed by the local area code (minus the zero), then the subscriber number. Local area codes are given at the start of each city or town section in this chapter. The area code when dialling a mobile phone is ☎ 03 or ☎ 70. The international access code (to call abroad from Lebanon) is ☎ 00.

Phonecards

Prepaid calling cards come in two different types. The Telecard costs LL10,000 or LL30,000 and can be used in the many card-operated telephone booths on city streets. The alternative is the Kalam card, which costs LL15,000 or LL45,000 and allows you to make calls from any phone, public or private, with the use of a code. Cards can be bought at newsagents, post offices, kiosks, or anywhere an 'OGERO' sign is displayed. Calls cost LL100 per minute to a landline and LL300 to a mobile phone.

VISAS

All nationalities need a visa to enter Lebanon, though costs and visa requirements are constantly changing. For the most up-to-date information, visit the website of **Lebanon's General Security Office** (www.general-security.gov.lb). At the time of writing, tourist visas were free of charge.

Citizens of Jordan and Gulf Cooperation Countries (Kuwait, Saudi Arabia, United Arab Emirates, Qatar, Bahrain and Oman) are entitled to a free three-month visa at the airport.

Citizens of the countries below are entitled to a free one-month visa at the airport: Andorra, Antigua and Barbuda, Argentina, Armenia, Australia, Austria, Azerbaijan, the Bahamas, Barbados, Belarus, Belgium, Belize, Bhutan, Brazil, Bulgaria, Canada, Chile, China, Costa Rica, Croatia, Cyprus, Denmark, Estonia, Finland, France, Great Britain, Georgia, Germany, Greece, Hong Kong, Hungary, Iceland, Ireland, Italy, Japan, Kazakhstan, Kyrgyzstan, Latvia, Lithuania, Lichtenstein, Luxembourg, Macedonia, Macau, Malaysia, Malta, Mexico, Moldova, Monaco, the Netherlands, New Zealand, Norway, Palau, Panama, Peru, Poland, Portugal, Russia, Saint Kitts and Nevis, Samoa, San Marino, Singapore, Slovakia, Slovenia, South Korea, Spain, Sweden, Switzerland, Tajikistan, Trinidad and Tobago, Turkmenistan, Venezuela and Yugoslavia.

ISRAELI PASSPORT STAMPS

Lebanon denies entry to travellers with evidence of a visit to Israel in their passport (see p332 for more details). If asked at a border crossing or at the airport if you've ever been to Israel, bear in mind that saying 'yes' (if you have) will mean you won't be allowed into the country.

The same visa policy applies, in principle, at all Syrian–Lebanese border crossings, but be aware that visas may not always be issued free of charge (some travellers have reported being charged LL50,000 to obtain their one-month entry visa).

For other nationalities, visas must be obtained in advanced at any Lebanese embassy or consulate: you'll need two passport photos, and possibly a letter from your employers stating that you'll be returning to your job. Visas are usually issued the next day, but may take longer.

If you're planning onward travel into Syria, it's crucial to note that you can't get a Syrian visa in Lebanon (though some lucky travellers have nevertheless managed to do so at the border – not a method we'd recommend risking). Officially, only passport holders from countries that have no Syrian consulate (excluding, of course, Israel) can obtain visas at the Syrian border. If you want to travel overland, make sure you have a valid Syrian visa before you go to Lebanon. As this book went to press, however, there were plans to open a Syrian embassy in Beirut. If this indeed happens, it may finally be possible to obtain a Syrian visa in Lebanon. Monitor up-to-date news for details.

Visa Extensions

To extend your one-month visa to a three-month visa, go to the **General Security Office** (Map p416; ☎ 1717, 01-429 060/061; Rue de Damas, Beirut; ⏰ 8am-1pm Mon-Thu, 8-10am Fri, 8am-noon Sat) in Beirut, a few days before your first month ends. Take a passport photo, your passport, and photocopies of your passport ID page and the page where your entry visa was stamped.

WOMEN TRAVELLERS

Lebanon, in general, is an easy destination for solo female travellers, more akin in attitudes to neighbouring Israel than, for example, to next-door Syria. Revealing, Western-style clothes are common in Beirut and Jounieh, and in the beach clubs that line the sands from Sidon up to Byblos, but outside the main centres long-sleeved, loose clothing is still preferable. This is particularly the case in the south, the north around Tripoli and in the Bekaa Valley, all predominantly Muslim areas, and, of course, when entering holy places. For further advice for female travellers see p633.

TRANSPORT IN LEBANON

GETTING THERE & AWAY

You can travel to Lebanon by air, or by land from Syria. Note, though, that political tensions have often been known to close land borders between Lebanon and Syria, so check locally at your time of travel that the borders are open.

Air

Beirut Rafic Hariri International airport (BEY; ☎ 01-628 000; www.beirutairport.gov.lb) is Lebanon's only airport. The national carrier, **Middle East Airlines** (MEA; ☎ in Beirut 01-737 000; www.mea.com.lb), has an extensive network including flights to and from Europe and to the Arab world. It's reliable and has a decent safety record.

The following international airlines, among others, currently service Beirut:

Air France (AF; ☎ 01-977 977; www.airfrance.com; Beirut)
Cyprus Airways (CY; ☎ 01-362 237; www.cyprusairways.com; Beirut)
EgyptAir (MS; ☎ 01-973 330; www.egyptair.com.eg; Beirut)
Emirates (EK; ☎ 01-734 535; www.emirates.com; Beirut)
Gulf Air (GF; ☎ 01-323 332; www.gulfairco.com; Beirut)
Lufthansa (LH; ☎ 01-347 007; www.lufthansa.com; Beirut)
Malaysia Airlines (MH; ☎ 01-741 344; www.mas.com.my; Beirut)
Royal Jordanian Airline (RJ; ☎ 01-379 990; www.rja.com.jo; Beirut)
Turkish Airlines (TK; ☎ 01-999 849; www.turkishairlines.com; Beirut)

Land

BORDER CROSSINGS

The only land crossings from Lebanon are into Syria (the Israel–Lebanon land border has not been open for some years). Note, though, that these are often closed at short notice, so check in advance that they're open before travel. There are four in total, but the most reliably open crossing is at Masnaa, on the Beirut–Damascus highway. The other three are at Al-Qaa, at the northern end of the Bekaa Valley; Aarida, on the coastal road from Tripoli to Lattakia; and Aaboudiye on the Tripoli to Homs route.

So long as the borders are open, citizens of most countries can obtain a Lebanese visa at the border (see Visas, opposite for more details). Some travellers occasionally manage to obtain their Syrian visa at the Lebanese

JUST ACROSS THE BORDER: CRAC DES CHEVALIERS & DAMASCUS, SYRIA

Every traveller you've talked to in Lebanon who's already been to Syria has been raving about how unmissable its Crac des Chevaliers castle (Qala'at al-Hosn; p488) is, and how heady, historic Damascus (p464) is the highlight, so far, of their trip. How can you help, then, but yearn to see them for yourself?

Secure your Syrian visa (see Border Crossings above) before leaving home, to allow you to make the easy four-and-a-half-hour drive from Beirut to Damascus by bus or service taxi. Once in Damascus, meander the Ottoman lanes of the Old City (p468), haggle for spices in Souq al-Hamidiyya (p479) and marvel at its stately Umayyad Mosque (p469), before settling down for a single Thousand and One night at the delightful Dar al-Yasmin (p475).

The next morning, take a bus to Homs (p483) and another on to Crac des Chevaliers (p488), to transport yourself into a Crusader castle fantasy, with towers fit for a bevy of Rapunzels. Then it's back to Damascus, via Homs (staying the night, if you've time, to imbibe its laid-back, friendly air), to hop aboard a bus that will whisk you back from the thrum of life in ancient Damascene lanes to the pace of the Beirut fast lane, a few hours – and a century or two – away.

border, but this is a decidedly hit-and-miss affair, and could end up frustrating if you're denied entry. It's far better to arrange your Syrian visa in advance of travel to Lebanon.

BUS

Buses to Syria from Beirut leave from the **Charles Helou bus station** (Map p416). You must go there in person to book your ticket and, while buses are rarely full, it's still worth booking a seat the day before you travel and to check that services are actually running.

Buses for Damascus (LL7000, 4½ hours) depart half-hourly between 5.30am and 7am, after which they run every hour until around 7pm. Buses for Aleppo (ask for Halab; LL10,500, 6 hours) leave half-hourly from 7.30am to midday. There are also three buses per day to Lattakia (LL9000, 4 hours) at 10.30am, 2pm and 5.30pm; six to Homs (LL8500, 4 hours) at 7.30am, 9.30am, 1.30pm, 5pm, 7pm and 9.30pm; and four to Hama (LL9000, 6 hours) at 9.30am, 5pm, 7pm and 9.30pm.

From Tripoli – border openings and security situation allowing – there are also usually plenty of services running to Syria, with frequent departures throughout the morning to Homs (LL6000, 1½ hours), Hama (LL6500, two hours) and Aleppo (LL8000, four hours). Services to Lattakia (LL6000, two hours) and Damascus (LL10,000, four to 4 ½ hours) usually depart in the afternoon. Check with the companies on Tripoli's main square for details of times and prices.

At the time of writing, there were no services running from Tripoli to Amman in Jordan, Cairo in Egypt, or to İstanbul in Turkey, but it's worth checking to see if bus lines have been reinstated.

CAR & MOTORCYCLE

Since Lebanon levies a steep charge at the border for bringing in your car (calculated on a sliding scale, depending on the vehicle's value), it's not really advisable to try bringing your own vehicle into the country. If you're touring the Middle East in your own car, your best bet is to park it securely in Damascus, and take the bus into Lebanon from there.

GETTING AROUND

There are no air services or trains operating within Lebanon, but the country is so small (you can drive from one end to the other in half a day) that you don't really need them. In and around Beirut and the coastal strip, the bus, minibus and taxi network is extensive, cheap and fairly reliable. To fully explore the hinterland of the country, though (especially around the Qadisha Valley, Bekaa Valley and the south) it's well worth hiring a car or negotiating a private taxi, to avoid waiting for hours for a bus that eventually decides not to arrive at all.

Bicycle

Lebanon's steep terrain and the state of many urban roads demand a rugged, all-terrain bicycle. There are few designated bike lanes or routes, however, and drivers – whose driving style could politely be described as 'loose' or 'creative' – aren't exactly used to giving space to cyclists plying the country's roads. If you've thighs and nerves of steel, however, cycling the countryside is certainly stunningly scenic and the fresh mountain air a joy; see p451 for first contacts in the Lebanese cycling world.

Bus & Microbus

Buses travel between Beirut and all of Lebanon's major towns. There are three main bus pick-up and drop-off points in Beirut:

Charles Helou bus station (Map p416) Just east of downtown, for destinations north of Beirut (including Syria).
Cola transport hub (Map p416) This is in fact a confused bustling intersection (often known as Mazraa), generally serving the south, and the Bekaa Valley.
Dawra transport hub Northeast of Beirut, and covering the same destinations as Charles Helou bus station, it's usually a port of call on the way in and out of the city.

Charles Helou is the only formal station and is divided into three signposted zones:

Zone A For buses to Syria.
Zone B For buses servicing Beirut (where the route starts or finishes at Charles Helou bus station).
Zone C For express buses to Jounieh, Byblos and Tripoli.

Zones A and C have ticket offices where you can buy tickets for your journey. In the other stations (Cola and Dawra transport hubs) ask any driver for your bus (if someone doesn't find you first). Buses usually have the destination displayed in the front window, but largely in Arabic only.

There is a growing number of independently owned microbuses that cover the same routes. The advantages are that they're comfortable, frequent and often quicker than regular buses. The disadvantages are that they're more expensive and, since they're privately owned, you're taking a chance on the driver's motoring skills. You pay for your ticket on board, either at the start or end of the journey.

See individual town and city listings for detailed information on bus services.

Car

You need to be a competent driver with very steady nerves to contemplate driving in Lebanon, since there are few rules of the road, and a three-lane road, for example, can frequently become seven lanes. Hairpin bends and pot-holed roads are frequent in the mountains, and few roads are gritted after a snow fall. Beirut's traffic is often heavy, and road signs (where there are any at all) can be cryptic or misleading.

Having said all that, renting a car is a fantastic way to get to some of the most out-of-the-way parts of the country, especially if time is tight. With a car, you've got the freedom to explore the small villages peppering the Qadisha Valley, and make your own unexpected discoveries en route. Aside from being generally cautious, remember to stop at military checkpoints, and have your passport and car rental papers ready for inspection.

As well as the usual gamut of international operators (Avis, Budget, Thrifty and Sixt all have offices in Beirut), local outfit **Advanced Car Rental** comes highly recommended. See p427 for details.

Local Transport

BUS

Some towns, including Beirut, have both government and privately owned buses that operate a hail-and-ride system. Fares are generally LL750 for all except the most distant destinations; see individual town or city information for details.

TAXI & SERVICE TAXI

Most routes around Lebanese towns and cities are covered by service, or shared, taxis (see p651), which are usually elderly Mercedes with red licence plates and a taxi sign on the roof. You can hail them at any point on their route and also get out wherever you wish by saying *'anzil huun'* (drop me off here). Be sure to ask *'servees?'* before getting in (if it's an empty car), to ensure the driver doesn't try to charge you a private taxi fare. Going rates are generally LL1000 to LL1500 for trips within a town, and LL2000 to LL8000 for trips to outlying areas.

If you want to engage a private taxi, make sure the driver understands exactly where you want to go and negotiate the fare clearly before you get in (fares are suggested in relevant sections). Bear in mind that it might actually be cheaper, especially if you're planning on taking several day trips, to rent a car.

Tours

Several Lebanese operators organise reliable tours within Lebanon, and to Syria and Jordan from Lebanon. They cover most of Lebanon's highlights, are reasonably priced and usually include lunch, guide (in English or French), entrance fees and pick-up/drop-off at your hotel, and are comfortable (transport is in air-con coaches or minibuses). A day trip costs from US$22 per person for half-day trips and around US$50 to US$60 for full-day trips. For trekking tour operators, see boxed text p438.

Tour operators:

Adonis Travel (☎ 09-949 599; www.adonistravel.com/lebanon) Offers trips within Lebanon and multi-country itineraries.

Kurban Tours (Map p416; ☎ 01-371 013; www.kurbantravel.com; InterContinental Phoenicia Hotel, Minet al-Hosn, Beirut; 🕑 24hr)

Tania Travel (Map p416; ☎ 01-739 682; www.taniatravel.com; Rue Sidani, Hamra, Beirut; 🕑 8am-6pm Mon-Sat)

Syria

Syria could just be the friendliest, most hospitable rogue state on earth. There are many things you'll remember from your visit here, but the chances are it's the warmth and graciousness of the people that will live longest in the memory. In a wonderful antidote to what the US State Department would have you believe, it's the Syrians themselves who ensure most visitors develop a lifelong infatuation with the country's gentle charms.

So much of Syria bears the stamp of the grand epics of Middle Eastern history. The Old City of Damascus has watched it all, accumulating in the process an astonishing richness of architecture both sacred and profane, from the extraordinary Umayyad Mosque to jewel-like Damascene houses and souqs that you'll never want to leave. Aleppo, which vies with Damascus for the honour of the world's oldest city, is home to the finest medieval souq in the region. Then there's Palmyra, a glorious, alluring desert ruin that transports you back into the decadent Roman past. The World Heritage–listed castles of Crac des Chevaliers and Qala'at Saladin will also fulfil every childhood longing. And these are just the marquee attractions…

Best of all is the fact that these places are invariably woven into the fabric of daily life – the locals worship in the mosques, shop in the souqs, drink tea in the houses and picnic in the ruins. And they're happy for travellers to join them. And join them you must if Syrian food is on the menu, as the national cuisine is simply superb.

For all its wealth of historical associations, this is not a country stuck in the past. Since Bashar al-Assad took over the reins from his father in 2001, modernisation has been in the air. This is no Levantine backwater – Syria is a modern, efficient and very proud nation. It needs and deserves travellers to bear witness to this fact.

FAST FACTS

- **Area** 185,180 sq km
- **Capital** Damascus
- **Country code** ☎ 963
- **Language** Arabic
- **Money** Syrian pound (also known as the lira; S£); US$1 = S£51.85; €1 = S£80.15
- **Official name** Syrian Arab Republic
- **Population** 20.5 million

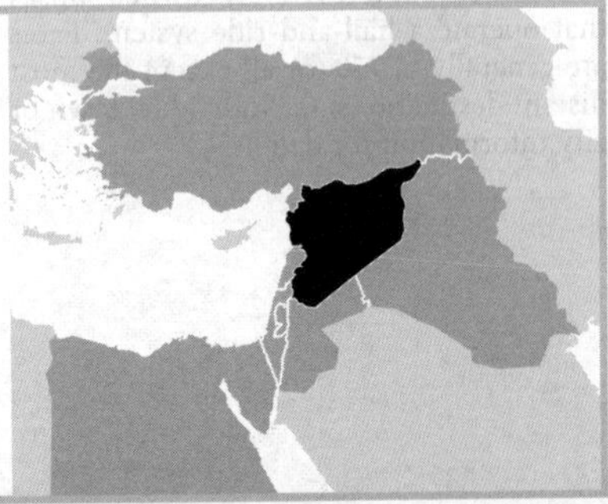

CLIMATE & WHEN TO GO

Syria has a Mediterranean climate with hot, dry summers (June to August) and mild, wet winters (December to February), especially close to the coast. Inland it gets progressively drier and more inhospitable. On the coast, average daily temperatures range from 29°C in summer to 10°C in winter and the annual rainfall is about 750mm. On the cultivated steppe area, temperatures average 35°C in summer and 12°C in winter. Rainfall varies from 250mm to 500mm. In the desert, the temperatures are high and rainfall is low. In summer, the days average 40°C and highs of 46°C are not uncommon. Winter can be extremely cold in mountainous areas, including Crac des Chevaliers.

Spring is the best time to visit as temperatures are mild and the winter rains have cleared the haze that obscures views for much of the year. Autumn is the next-best choice. The busiest tourism periods are Easter through to September and Islamic religious holidays; these months roughly coincide with what hotels call high season. During these times it's essential to book accommodation in advance.

For more information on Syria's climate, see p625.

HISTORY

Historically, Syria included the territories that now make up modern Jordan, Israel and the Palestinian Territories, Lebanon and Syria itself. Due to its strategic position, its coastal towns were important Phoenician trading posts. Later, the area became a pivotal part of the Egyptian, Persian and Roman empires, and many others in the empire-building business, for that matter.

Syria finally ended up as part of the Ottoman domains ruled from İstanbul, and was dished out to France (along with Lebanon) when the Ottoman Empire broke up after WWI. This caused considerable local resentment, as the region had been briefly independent from the end of WWI until the French took over in 1920.

SYRIA IN...

One Week

Arriving in Syria from Turkey, most roads lead to Aleppo (p491), where you should spend at least one day immersing yourself in the labyrinthine souqs, climbing up to the citadel and dining in Al-Jdeida. Next stop, Hama (p484), an engaging town in its own right, but also a base *par excellence* for the wonderful Crusader castle of Crac des Chevaliers (p488). A few buses run east into the desert and the iconic Roman ruins of Palmyra (p509), where you really should plan at least one sunset and one sunrise visit to the ruins. Then it's on to Damascus (p464), with its stunning Old City and wealth of architectural and other quintessentially Syrian charms. If you're coming from Lebanon, this is where you'll most easily begin your Syrian journey. Your week's almost up and you've just enough time to head to the Jordanian border (p525) from the Syrian town of Deraa.

Two Weeks

Two weeks in Syria is ideal, allowing an extra day each in Aleppo and Damascus. From Aleppo, a day trip taking in Qala'at Samaan (p502) and the Dead Cities (p503) is a must. You've the option of then taking the picturesque train ride to liberal Lattakia (p503), a base for a half-day trip to Qala'at Saladin (p508); from Lattakia, buses lead down the coast and around to Hama. The other alternative from Aleppo is a round trip to Rasafa (p518), although this can also be done from Hama (p486). Apamea (p490) is a jewel of a Roman city and can be visited as part of an excursion from Hama, or en route from Aleppo. Having visited Palmyra, day trips from Damascus include Maalula (p482) and Seidnayya (p482), while Bosra (p481) and its extraordinary theatre enables you to tick off the third of Syria's wonderful Roman cities.

Join the Itineraries

Jordan (p336)
Lebanon (p401)
Turkey (p530)

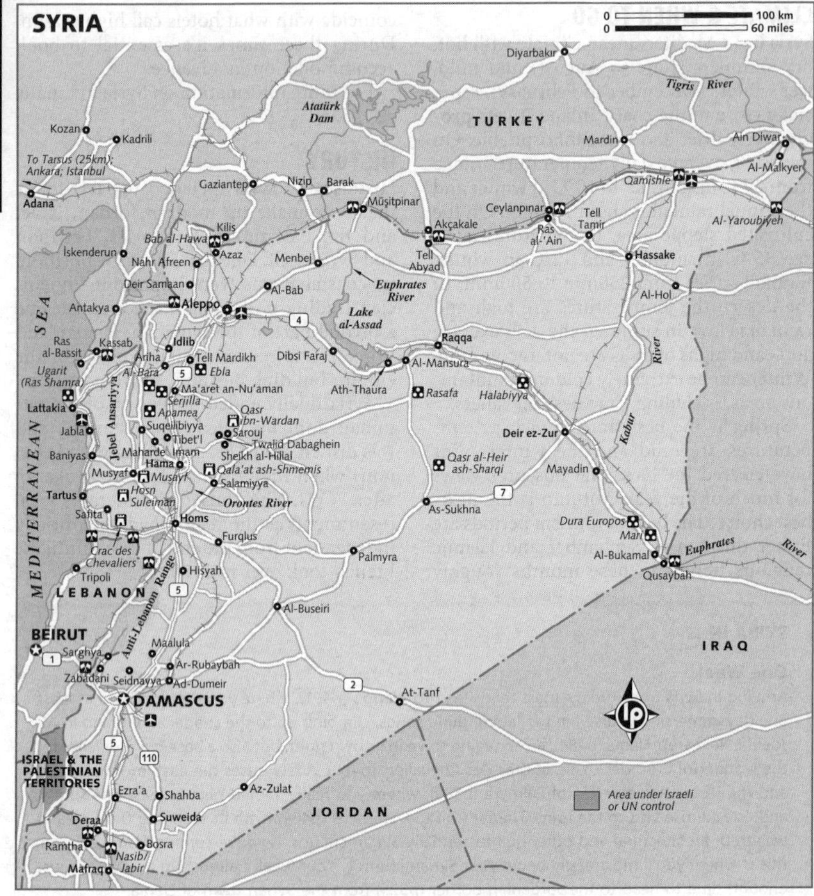

France never had much luck with its Syria–Lebanon mandate. Local opposition to its policy of carving up the country into mini-states (Grand Liban, Lebanon, Aleppo and Damascus) and minority enclaves (for the Druze and Alawites) led to revolts against French rule. Elections were held in 1928 and 1932, but moves to establish a constitution were stymied by the occupying power, which compounded its unpopularity in 1939 when it ceded the northern cities of Antioch (Antakya) and Alexandretta (Iskenderun) to encourage Turkey's neutrality in WWII.

A nationalist government was formed under Shoukri al-Quwatli in August 1943, but the French continued to be in denial about the waning of its influence in the region, bombing Damascus after locals had demonstrated in support of a final handover of administrative and military services to the new government. The situation was only resolved after the British intervened and oversaw the final departure of all French troops and administrators at the end of the war.

A period of political instability followed and by 1954, after several military coups, the nationalist Ba'ath Party ('Ba'ath' means 'renaissance') took power virtually unopposed. A brief flirtation with the Pan-Arabist idea of a United Arab Republic (with Egypt) in 1958 proved unpopular and coups in 1960, 1961 and 1963 saw the leadership change hands yet again. By 1966 the Ba'ath Party was back in power, but it was severely weakened by losses in two conflicts: the Six Day War with Israel in 1967 and the Black September hostilities in Jordan in 1970. At this point, Defence Minister Hafez al-Assad seized power.

Assad maintained control longer than any other post-independence Syrian government, with a mixture of ruthless suppression and guile. The most widely condemned example of the former came on 2 February 1982, when Assad ordered the shelling of the old city in Hama in response to a growing campaign by the Muslim Brotherhood. He followed this with a warning that anyone left in the city would be declared a rebel. In the fighting that followed, between 10,000 and 25,000 people were killed out of a total population of 350,000, and mosques, churches and archaeological sites were damaged and destroyed.

In 1998, he was elected to a fifth seven-year term with a predictable 99.9% of the vote. It took failing health to finally remove the man from power; his death was announced on 10 June 2000.

Syria Today

Following the death of Assad senior, his son Bashar acceded to power. A new government was formed in December 2001 with a mandate to push forward political, economic and administrative reforms. For a while, a wave of change swept Syria, the so-called 'Damascus Spring' buzzing with a proliferation of private newspapers, internet bloggers, and public debate not seen in the country in decades. Foreign goods flooded into Syria, private banks were allowed to open and mobile phones made a belated but wildly popular appearance. But 'not so fast' was the message that came from the old guard that had surrounded Bashar's father – anything perceived as opposing the government was quickly reined in. Reforming the country's unwieldy bureaucracy, whose membership depends more on political patronage and nepotism than on merit, also proved a road too far. As a result, while many of the economic reforms were left untouched and political reforms have stalled. Syrians generally agree that there is more freedom and less fear than there was during the rule of Assad senior, provided they don't become too involved in politics. But Syrians are chafing under low wages and rising prices and, more than political reform, it's the shackles of a still-stuttering economy that is, for the most part, their primary concern. Despite all the problems, it's a testament to the young president's political skill that he remains genuinely popular on the Syrian street. As many Syrians told us, 'it's the people around him who are the problem'.

Things are even more complicated in Syria's relations with the international community. Publicly branded a 'rogue state' by former US president, George W

ACCESS DENIED

You're casually surfing the internet and thought you'd update your Facebook profile. 'Access denied' flashes up on the screen. Must be the connection, you say to yourself. You try to watch a video on YouTube. Same problem. Before you start accosting the internet café owner about the quality of the connection, remember this: both Facebook and YouTube were banned in Syria in 2007 after the government claimed that Israel had infiltrated the sites. Some of the other banned websites are easy to understand, if not justify: Israeli newspapers, Kurdish and Islamist websites, and any sites which overtly criticise the Syrian government. Some of the other restricted sites are a little less obvious: Hotmail (but not Yahoo! … at least not yet) has been blocked at times, while Amazon.com suffers a similar fate, even as Amazon.co.uk slips through the net. The Arabic-language Wikipedia site is another casualty. Internet-connected phone calls made from internet cafés are technically illegal, although we've made Skype-connected calls from a private laptop on a Syrian server. Some internet cafés get around the restrictions using proxy addresses, but these can be extremely slow.

There is, of course, a serious side to internet censorship. Reporters without Borders (www.rsf.org), which places Syria 154th (out of 169) on its Worldwide Press Freedom Index, recently reported that seven so-called 'cyber dissidents' were, or have been, imprisoned. The most recent targets have been bloggers locked up for 'defaming and insulting the administrative bodies of the state'. That's not to say that Syria doesn't have a lively blogging community – check it out at Syria Planet (www.syplanet.com) – it's just that they have to be *very* careful what they write.

SYRIAN PRICES

Don't be surprised if the prices you find throughout this chapter are out of date by the time you arrive, especially in hotels. Prices have doubled over the past two years, and while we were there, the price of petrol increased by 350% at the stroke of a bureaucratic pen, increasing the cost for just about every aspect of Syrian life. Before you get shirty with your hotel receptionist about higher-than-expected prices, remember that he or she is probably suffering far more than you are. Days after the petrol increase, government (but not private) salaries were raised by 25% – small compensation for the skyrocketing prices which Syrian families have to pay. Please treat the prices throughout this chapter as a guide only and check with your hotel for the current prices when making a reservation.

And one other thing: Syrian hotels quote their prices in a mixture of US dollars, euros (increasingly the currency of choice) and, less often, Syrian pounds. Apart from top-end hotels, most places let you pay in any of the three currencies regardless of how they quote their prices, although make sure you're getting the best exchange rate.

Bush, Syria stands accused of fomenting political conflict in Lebanon, most notably through its support for Hezbollah. It has also been criticised by the US for allegedly turning a blind eye to the movements of Iraqi insurgents. In September 2007, Israeli planes bombed a site at Al-Kibar (on the Euphrates River, northwest of Deir ez-Zur), which the Israeli and US governments claimed was a partially completed, secret nuclear reactor and which Syria argued was a disused military facility. But the effect was to heighten tensions even further between Syria and the US.

On a more positive note, Syria confirmed in May 2008 that it was conducting indirect peace negotiations with Israel, with the Turkish government acting as intermediaries. Although still in their preliminary stages and with major outstanding issues not yet on the table – the status of Israeli-occupied Golan Heights and the fate of Palestinian refugees to name just two – the talks were the first, tentative signs that Syria's international isolation may one day be a thing of the past. More promisingly, in mid-2008 Syria and Lebanon entered a new period of détente, promising to open embassies in each other's capitals and improving co-operation.

For news of what's happening in Syria, albeit with restrictions, check out Syria News Wire (http://saroujah.blogspot.com).

THE CULTURE

Daily Life

In the public realm, Syrians face a number of challenges common to the region. On one level, Syrians are well educated with an overall literacy rate of around 80% (86% for men, 74% for women). School attendance is compulsory for children aged between six and 12, and there are four national public universities, which have combined enrolments of almost 200,000. At the same time, unemployment is far higher than the official rate of 10% suggests and inflation (officially around 10%) is threatening to run out of control. Compounding the problem, wages are low – average government salaries are just US$300 per month and university graduates such as doctors rarely earn more than US$700. The consequence is that the country faces a serious 'brain drain', with many graduates heading overseas to find better-paying work. The obligatory 30-months military service for all 18 year-old males may also be playing its part.

In the private sphere, family ties are extremely close, families are large, and extended families often live together. Rural–urban migration over recent years now means that about half of the country's population lives in the cities.

Population

Syria has a population of around 20.5 million, about 90% of which is Arab. Minorities such as the Bedouin Arabs (about 100,000) and smaller groupings of Armenians, Circassians and Turks are among the population. There are also around one million Kurds.

The country has an annual population growth of around 2.2%. Although this represents a decline from the 3.6% growth that was seen during the 1990s, it's still high by international standards. One-third of Syrians are under 15 years old, with the average age of the population just 21.4 years of age.

RELIGION

Islam is practised by about 84% of the population. Between 15% and 20% of this is made up of minorities such as Shiite, Druze and Alawite, while the remainder are Sunni Muslims. Christians account for the remaining 16% of the population and belong to various churches including Greek Orthodox, Greek Catholic, Syrian Orthodox, Armenian Orthodox, Maronite, Roman Catholic and Protestant.

ARTS

Syria has contributed some of the Arab world's best-loved cultural figures, but cultural life fell into decline during the reign of Hafez al-Assad, thanks largely to government repression and a critical lack of government funding. That said, the country's writers, musicians and cinematographers are starting to make waves again.

Literature

Most Syrian writers to have made their name beyond Syria's borders have done so from exile. The most famous contemporary example is Rafik Schami (b 1946), who left Syria in 1971. His *A Hand Full of Stars* is an outstanding work for teenagers, but *Damascus Nights* is his best-known (and most widely available) work.

Zakariya Tamir (b 1931), Syria's master of the children's story, deals with everyday city life marked by frustration and despair born of social oppression. Having been virtually forced to leave Syria in 1980, he was awarded the Syrian Order of Merit in 2002. His *Tigers on the Tenth Day and Other Stories* is wonderful.

But not everyone was forced to leave. The Damascene Nizar Qabbani (1923–98) became one of the Arab world's most beloved poets, credited with transforming formal Arabic poetry with the use of everyday language. He was adored in the 1950s for his love poems, and later for his expressions of the Arabs' collective feelings of humiliation and outrage after the wars with Israel.

Of the noted writers who remained in Syria, the most celebrated and outspoken was Ulfat Idilbi (1912–2007), who wrote about the late Ottoman Empire and French Mandate and the drive for liberation and independence. *Sabriya: Damascus Bitter Sweet* is critical of the mistreatment of women by their families, much of its anger stemming from Idilbi's own experience of being married off at 16 to a man twice her age. *Grandfather's Tale* is also worth tracking down.

In 2007, the release of *A Story Called Syria*, a collection of pieces by 40 writers, was celebrated and quickly followed by calls from Syria's writers and intellectuals to reinvigorate the literature scene.

Music

Syria's most famous musical star, Farid al-Atrache (1915–74), spent most of his career in Cairo and remains Syria's most beloved musical export across the region. Sometimes called the 'Arab Sinatra', he was a highly accomplished oud player and composer, who succeeded in updating Arabic music by blending it with Western scales and rhythms and the orchestration of the tango and waltz. His melodic improvisations on the oud (he's still known as 'King of the Oud') and his *mawal* (a vocal improvisation) were the highlights of his live performances, and recordings of these are treasured. By the time of his death, he was considered – and still is by many – to be the premier male Arabic music performer.

After a quiet period on the Syrian music scene, there are signs of a revival, thanks to the local success of albums by Kulna Sawa (*All Together*), Lena Chamamian, Itar Shameh, Anas and Friends, Gene and InsaniT, and a sold-out Woodstock-type concert that toured the country in 2007 featuring many of these bands.

Hailed as Syria's new diva, charismatic Lena Chamamian released her second CD, *Shamat* in 2007. Its heartfelt folk songs focused on social issues of concern to Syria's youth, such as Syrians having to leave their country to fulfil their dreams, and lovers weary of their families' interference in their romance.

ENVIRONMENT

Syria is one of the worst countries in the Middle East when it comes to both environmental awareness and government programs to protect the environment, despite facing the pressing issues of water scarcity, desertification and pollution. While Jordan, Lebanon and Israel are fast catching on to the benefits of ecotourism, Syria had, at the time of writing, just one lonely member of

HOW MUCH?

- **Cup of tea** S£50
- **Newspaper** S£5
- **One-minute phone call to the UK** S£100
- **Internet connection per hour** S£50 to S£100
- **Museum admission** S£15

LONELY PLANET INDEX

- **Litre of petrol** S£45
- **Litre of bottled water** S£25
- **Bottle of Barada beer** S£75 to S£100
- **Souvenir T-shirt (if you can find one)** S£500
- **Shwarma sandwich** S£30

their ranks: **Eco Tourism Syria** (www.ecotourismsyria.com). Although the company is something of a work-in-progress, its website is the best of its kind in Syria and tours can be organised to key biodiversity areas in the country. It's deserving of your support.

The only other environmental organisation of note in the country is the **Syria Environment Association** (Map pp470-1; ☎ 011-4467 7800; www.sea-sy.org, in Arabic; sea-sy@scs-net.org; Beit Jumaa, Sharia al-Hamrawi, Old City, Damascus), which has an office in Damascus. This NGO has initiated a number of tree-planting programs and is heavily involved in trying to save Damascus' Barada River. They also have an 'ecological garden' with a café (p478) just outside Bab al-Farag in Damascus.

DAMASCUS دمشق

☎ 011 / pop 4.6 million

Legend has it that on a journey from Mecca, the Prophet Mohammed cast his gaze upon Damascus but refused to enter the city because he wanted to enter paradise only once – when he died. In this city of legend, which vies for the title of the world's oldest continually inhabited city, this is but one of thousands of stories.

Damascus (Ash-Sham to locals) is a place of storytellers and of souqs, home to an Old City whose architecture traces millennia of history and where the assault on the senses sustains the romantic notion of the Orient unlike anywhere else in the Middle East. The weight of history has, above all else, bequeathed one special gift to those who visit: its polyglot inhabitants – whether Muslim or Christian – have, down through the centuries, perfected the art of hospitality and nowhere is the oft-heard refrain '*ahlan wa sahlan*, you are welcome', said with such warmth as it is in Damascus.

But this is not a city resting on its considerable laurels of historical significance – its conversion of countless elegant courtyard homes into restaurants and hotels and the vibrant life coursing through its streets has earned it a reputation as a dynamic cultural hub and even 'the new Marrakesh'. In short, the Prophet Mohammed may just have been right.

HISTORY

Excavations from the courtyard of the Umayyad Mosque have yielded finds dating back to the 3rd millennium BC. The name Dimashqa appears in the Ebla archives and also on tablets found at Mari (2500 BC), while hieroglyphic tablets found in Egypt make reference to 'Dimashqa' as one of the cities conquered by the Egyptians in the 15th century BC. The early conquerors include the

THINGS THEY SAID ABOUT…THE HISTORY OF DAMASCUS

'…no recorded event has occurred in the world but Damascus was in existence to receive news of it. Go back as far as you will into the vague past, there was always a Damascus…She has looked upon the dry bones of a thousand empires and will see the tombs of a thousand more before she dies…To Damascus, years are only moments, decades are only flitting trifles of time. She measures time, not by days and months and years, but by the empires she has seen rise, and prosper and crumble to ruin. She is a type of immortality.'

Mark Twain, The Innocents Abroad, 1869

'Some cities oust or smother their past. Damascus lives in hers.'

Colin Thubron, Mirror to Damascus, 1967

fabled King David of Israel, the Assyrians (732 BC), Nebuchadnezzar (around 600 BC), the Persians (530 BC), Alexander the Great (333 BC) and the Nabataeans (85 BC), before Syria became a Roman province in 64 BC.

With the coming of Islam, Damascus became an important centre as the seat of the Umayyad caliphate from 661 to 750. When the Abbasids moved the caliphate to Baghdad, Damascus was plundered once again. After the occupation of Damascus by the Seljuk Turks in 1076, the Crusaders tried to take the city. They made a second attempt in 1154 and a general of Kurdish origin, Nureddin (Nur ad-Din), came to the rescue, occupying Damascus himself and ushering in a brief golden era. A brief occupation by the Mongols was followed by the Mamluks of Egypt in 1260. During the Mamluk period, Damascene goods became famous worldwide and drew merchants from Europe. During the second Mongol invasion under Tamerlane, the city was flattened and the artisans and scholars were deported to the Mongol capital of Samarkand.

From the time of the Ottoman occupation in 1516, Damascus was reduced to the status of a small provincial capital in a large empire. The French occupied the city from 1920 to 1945. They met with massive resistance, bombarding the city to suppress rioting in 1925 and again in 1945; the latter episode led to full independence a year later when Damascus became the capital of an independent Syria.

ORIENTATION

There are two distinct parts to Damascus: the Old City and everything else. The Old City lies largely within imposing walls, with most visitors entering via Souq al-Hamidiyya (the eastern end of which begins immediately south of the citadel), which runs into the Umayyad Mosque. Another major thoroughfare through the Old City is Straight St (also known as Sharia Medhat Pasha and Sharia Bab Sharqi). The Christian Quarter, home to the Old City's boutique hotels, lies at the eastern end of the Old City, between Bab Sharqi and Bab Touma.

West and northwest of the Old City, the city centre is compact and finding your way around on foot is no problem. The main street, Sharia Said al-Jabri, begins at the Hejaz train station and runs northeast, changing its name to Sharia Bur Said. It finishes in Saahat Yousef al-Azmeh, the square that is at the heart of the modern city. The streets off this square are home to most of the airline offices, the main tourist office, the central branch of the Commercial Bank of Syria (CBS) and a host of hotels and restaurants. Souq al-Saroujah, the home of the city's backpacker hotels, is southeast of the square. South of Souq Saroujah is Martyrs' Sq (known to locals as Al-Merjeh), the city's 'downtown' district.

Maps

Librairie Avicenne (below) publishes a 2005 *Syria* map (S£100) with a detailed map of Damascus on the back. The tourist offices in town and at the airport stock a free *Damascus & Damascus Countryside* map.

INFORMATION

Bookshops

Bookshop (Map pp470-1; Sharia al-Qaimariyya; 🕒 11am-7pm) A small bookshop selling a handful of four-day-old international newspapers and an excellent selection of novels and some books about Syria. You can also leave your books here.

Librairie Avicenne (Map pp466-7; ☎ 221 2911; avicenne@net.sy; 4 Sharia Attuhami; 🕒 9am-8pm Sat-Thu) The best English-language bookshop in Syria.

Emergency

Ambulance (☎ 110)

Fire department (☎ 113)

Police (☎ 112)

Internet Access

Central post office (Map pp466-7; Sharia Said al-Jabri; per hr S£75; 🕒 8am-7pm Sat-Thu, 8am-1pm Fri & holidays) Reasonable connections upstairs in the main post office building.

Ci@o Net (Map pp466-7; per hr adult/student S£75/50; 🕒 7.30am-midnight) Off Sharia Yousef al-Azmeh, with fast connections and good for internet-connected phone calls.

E1 Café Net (Map pp470-1; Sharia Dehdaila; per hr S£60; 🕒 10am-midnight) Close to Bab Touma and one of the better options in the Old City.

Internet Café Smile (Map pp466-7; Sharia Souq Saroujah; per hr S£50 🕒 11am-midnight Sat-Thu, 2pm- midnight Fri) Convenient for Souq al-Saroujah's budget hotels.

Internet Corner (Map pp466-7; 1st fl, Abdin Bldg, Sharia Hammam al-Ward; per hr S£50; 🕒 10am-2am) Fast connections and good work stations in the backpacker quarter. It's still signposted as 'Fast Link'.

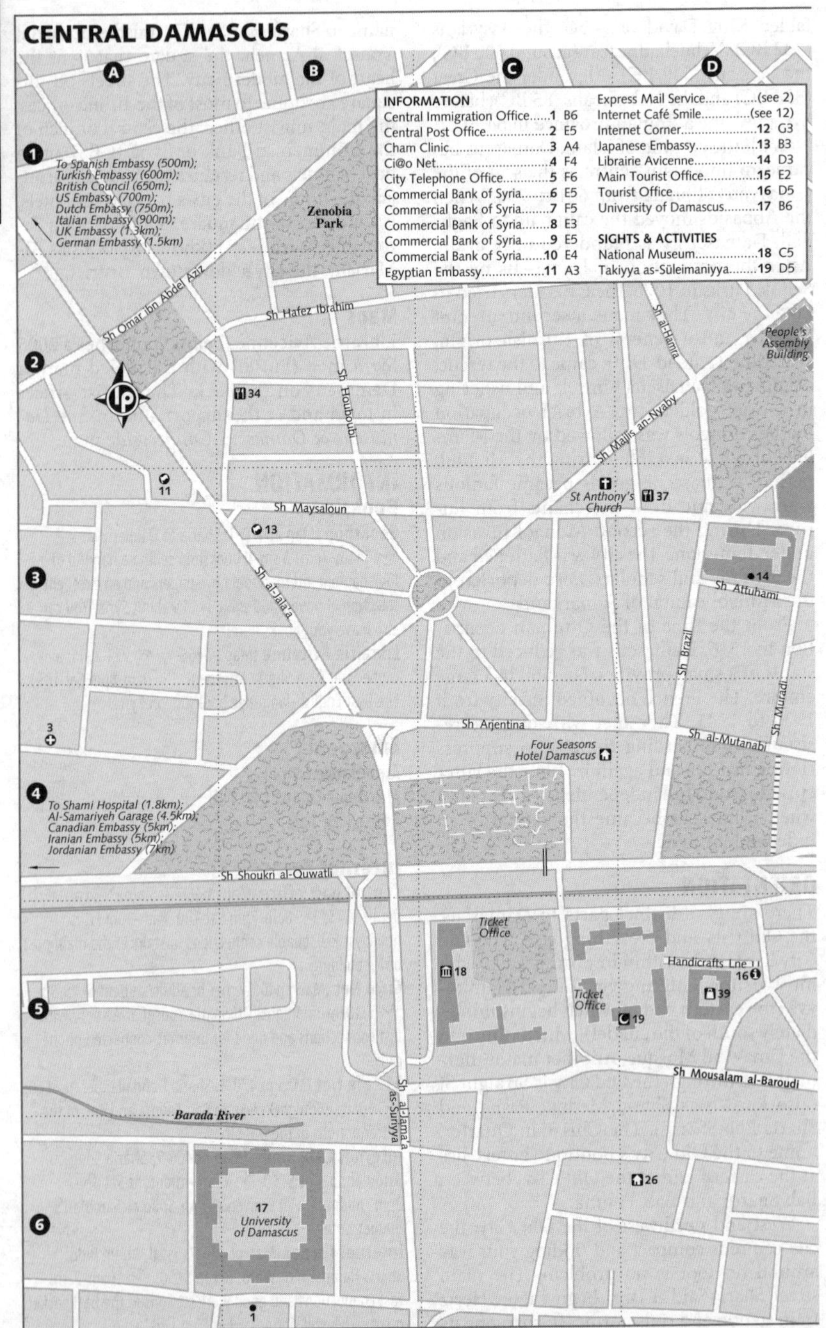
CENTRAL DAMASCUS
INFORMATION
Central Immigration Office......1 B6
Central Post Office..................2 E5
Cham Clinic...........................3 A4
Ci@o Net...............................4 F4
City Telephone Office.............5 F6
Commercial Bank of Syria........6 E5
Commercial Bank of Syria........7 F5
Commercial Bank of Syria........8 E3
Commercial Bank of Syria........9 E5
Commercial Bank of Syria.......10 E4
Egyptian Embassy..................11 A3
Express Mail Service.............(see 2)
Internet Café Smile..............(see 12)
Internet Corner......................12 G3
Japanese Embassy..................13 B3
Librairie Avicenne..................14 D3
Main Tourist Office................15 E2
Tourist Office.........................16 D5
University of Damascus..........17 B6
SIGHTS & ACTIVITIES
National Museum..................18 C5
Takiyya as-Süleimaniyya........19 D5
To Spanish Embassy (500m); Turkish Embassy (600m); British Council (650m); US Embassy (700m); Dutch Embassy (750m); Italian Embassy (900m); UK Embassy (1.3km); German Embassy (1.5km)
Zenobia Park
Sh Omar Ibn Abdel Aziz
Sh Hafez Ibrahim
Sh Houboubi
Sh al-Hamra
People's Assembly Building
Sh Majlis an-Nyaby
St Anthony's Church
Sh Maysaloun
Sh al-Jala'a
Sh Attuhami
Sh Brazil
Sh Muradi
Sh Arjentina
Sh al-Mutanabi
Four Seasons Hotel Damascus
To Shami Hospital (1.8km); Al-Samariyeh Garage (4.5km); Canadian Embassy (5km); Iranian Embassy (5km); Jordanian Embassy (7km)
Sh Shoukri al-Quwatli
Ticket Office
Handicrafts Lne
Sh Mousalam al-Baroudi
Sh al-Jama'a as-Sunyya
Barada River
University of Damascus

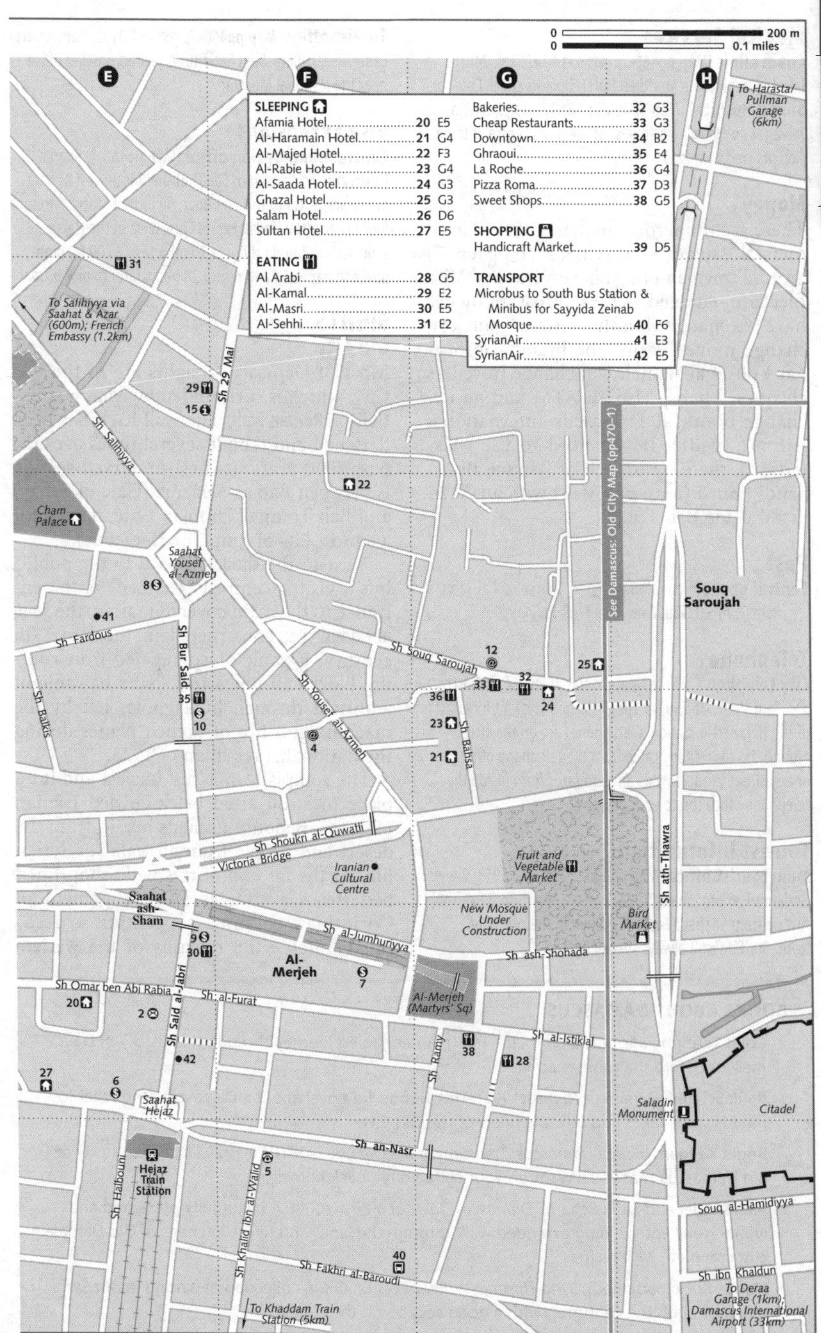
0 200 m
0 0.1 miles
E
F
G
H
SLEEPING
Afamia Hotel........................20 E5
Al-Haramain Hotel...................21 G4
Al-Majed Hotel......................22 F3
Al-Rabie Hotel......................23 G4
Al-Saada Hotel......................24 G3
Ghazal Hotel........................25 G3
Salam Hotel.........................26 D6
Sultan Hotel........................27 E5
EATING
Al Arabi............................28 G5
Al-Kamal............................29 E2
Al-Masri............................30 E5
Al-Sehhi............................31 E2
Bakeries............................32 G3
Cheap Restaurants...................33 G3
Downtown............................34 B2
Ghraoui.............................35 E4
La Roche............................36 G4
Pizza Roma..........................37 D3
Sweet Shops.........................38 G5
SHOPPING
Handicraft Market...................39 D5
TRANSPORT
Microbus to South Bus Station & Minibus for Sayyida Zeinab Mosque...40 F6
SyrianAir...........................41 E3
SyrianAir...........................42 E5
To Harasta/ Pullman Garage (6km)
To Salihiyya via Saahat & Azar (600m); French Embassy (1.2km)
Sh 29 Mai
Sh Salihiyya
Cham Palace
Saahat Yousef al-Azmeh
Sh Fardous
Sh Bur Said
Sh Balkis
Sh Souq Saroujah
Sh Yousef al-Azmeh
Sh Bahsa
See Damascus: Old City Map (pp470–1)
Souq Saroujah
Sh Shoukri al-Quwatli
Victoria Bridge
Iranian Cultural Centre
Fruit and Vegetable Market
Sh ath-Thawra
Saahat ash-Sham
New Mosque Under Construction
Bird Market
Sh al-Jumhuriyya
Sh ash-Shohada
Al-Merjeh
Al-Merjeh (Martyrs' Sq)
Sh Omar ben Abi Rabia
Sh al-Furat
Sh Said al-Jabri
Sh al-Istiklal
Sh Ramy
Saladin Monument
Citadel
Saahat Hejaz
Hejaz Train Station
Sh an-Nasr
Sh Halbouni
Sh Khalid ibn al-Walid
Souq al-Hamidiyya
Sh Fakhri al-Baroudi
Sh ibn Khaldun
To Khaddam Train Station (5km)
To Deraa Garage (1km); Damascus International Airport (33km)

Medical Services

Cham Clinic (Map pp466-7; ☎ 333 8742; 🕒 24hr) Located behind the Meridien Hotel. Doctors speak English.

Shami Hospital (Map pp466-7; ☎ 373 4925; Sharia Jawaher an-Nehru) Northwest of the main centre of town. Accepts credit cards.

Money

There are numerous branches of the Commercial Bank of Syria (CBS; Map pp466–7) around town and most have Visa- and Visa Electron–enabled ATMs. Most branches have exchange booths where you can change money easily; the branch on Saahat Yousef al-Azmeh will change travellers cheques. There's also an ATM and an exchange booth at Damascus International Airport (p481). If you need to use MasterCard, there's a branch of Banque Bemo Saudi Fransi (Map pp470–1) with an ATM just outside Bab Touma.

Post

Central post office (Map pp466-7; Sharia Said al-Jabri; 🕒 8am-7pm Sat-Thu, 8am-1pm Fri & holidays)

Telephone

City telephone office (Map pp466-7; Sharia an-Nasr; 🕒 8am-7pm Sat-Thu, to 1pm Fri & holidays) A block east of the Hejaz train station. Card phones are on the street around the corner (buy cards from the telephone office or any street vendor). You can send faxes from inside the telephone office (bring your passport).

Tourist Information

Main tourist office (Map pp466-7; ☎ 232 3953; www.syriatourism.org; Sharia 29 Mai; 🕒 9.30am-8pm Sat-Thu) Just up from Saahat Yousef al-Azmeh in the centre of town. Staff doesn't always speak English.

Tourist office (Map pp466-7; ☎ 221 0122; Handicrafts Lane; 🕒 9.30am-8pm Sat-Thu) A second, smaller office near the National Museum.

Visa Extensions

Central immigration office (Map pp466-7; Sharia Filasteen; 🕒 8am-2pm Sat-Thu) One block west of Baramke Garage. Go to the 2nd floor, fill in three forms, present four photos (the Kodak Express just west of the Hejaz train station can do them in 10 minutes; S£200 for eight photos), pay S£50 and return 24 hours later to pick it up.

SIGHTS

Old City

Most of Damascus's sights are in the Old City, which is surrounded by what was initially a **Roman wall**. The wall itself has been flattened and rebuilt several times over the past 2000 years. Its best-preserved section is between Bab as-Salaama (Gate of Safety) and Bab Touma (Thomas' Gate, named for a son-in-law of Emperor Heraclius).

Next to the **citadel** (closed to the public, but a visitor centre is planned) is the entrance to the main covered market, the **Souq al-Hamidiyya**, constructed in the late 19th century; a vault of corrugated-iron roofing blocks all but a few shafts of sunlight admitted through bullet holes left by the machine-gun fire of French planes during the nationalist rebellion of 1925.

The souq is Damascus' busiest and it's a place to stroll amid black-cowled Iranian pilgrims, Bedouin nomads just in from the desert and people from all walks of Syrian life. At the far end of this wide shop-lined pedestrian avenue is an arrangement of Corinthian columns supporting a decorated lintel – the remains of the **western**

BOOKS ABOUT DAMASCUS

- Colin Thubron, *Mirror to Damascus* (1967). An engaging journey through the history of Damascus before the tourists arrived.
- Rafik Schami, *Damascus Nights* (1997). This wonderful novel about a Damascus storyteller losing his voice takes you into the heart of the Old City.
- Brigid Keenan, *Hidden Damascus: Treasures of the Old City* (2001). Lavishly illustrated study of old Damascus that you'll want on your coffee table back home.
- Marie Fadel and Rafik Schami, *Damascus: Taste of a City* (2002). A beautifully presented and wonderfully entertaining extended walk through the lanes and home kitchens of Old Damascus, complete with recipes.
- Marius Kociejowski (ed), *Syria Through Writers' Eyes* (2006). A collection of writing about Syria down through the centuries, with a good section on the capital.

temple gate of the 3rd-century Roman Temple of Jupiter.

UMAYYAD MOSQUE

Welcome to the most beautiful **mosque** (Map pp470-1; admission S£50; dawn until after sundown prayers, closed 12.30-2pm Fri for noon prayers) in Syria and one of the holiest in the world for Muslims. Converted from a Byzantine cathedral (which in turn had occupied the site of the Temple of Jupiter), Damascus' crowning glory was built in AD 705. At the time, under Umayyad rule, Damascus had become the capital of the Islamic world and the caliph, Khaled ibn al-Walid, built what he called 'a mosque the equal of which was never designed by anyone before me or anyone after me'.

The mosque's outstanding feature is its golden **mosaics**, which adorn the facade of the prayer hall on the southern side of the courtyard, and a 37m stretch along the western arcade wall, which Damascenes believe represents the Barada Valley and the paradise that the Prophet Mohammed saw in Damascus. Traces remain elsewhere around the courtyard, leaving you to imagine the sublime aspect of the mosque in its heyday.

The expansive courtyard is flanked on three sides by a two-storey arched arcade and is occupied by an unusual **ablutions fountain** topped by a wooden canopy, and, on the western side, a small octagonal structure, the **Dome of the Treasury**, adorned with exquisite 14th-century mosaics and perched atop eight recycled Roman columns. The three minarets all date from different periods: the one on the northern side, the **Minaret of the Bride**, is the oldest; the one in the southwestern corner, the Mamluk-styled **Al-Gharbiyya minaret**, is the most beautiful; while the one on the southeastern corner, the **Minaret of Jesus**, is the tallest, and so named because local tradition has it that this is where Christ will appear on earth on Judgment Day.

The cavernous, rectangular **prayer hall** on the southern side of the courtyard is an Ottoman reconstruction that took place after a devastating fire in 1893. At the centre of the hall, resting on four great pillars above the transept, is the **Dome of the Eagle**, while looking somewhat out of place in the sanctuary is the green-domed, marble-clad **shrine of John the Baptist** (Prophet Yehia to Muslims) which supposedly holds the head of the man himself; other places around the Middle East make a similar claim. On the eastern side of the courtyard is the entrance to the **shrine of Hussein**, son of Ali and grandson of the Prophet. The shrine attracts large numbers of Shiite (mostly Iranian) pilgrims.

Such are the major landmarks of the Umayyad Mosque, but our favourite experience of a visit here is to find a quiet corner under the arches and watch as the devout explore one of Islam's foremost places of worship, mullahs rub shoulders with curious Western tourists and children gambol around the courtyard oblivious to the need for reverence. Mosques in the Islamic world are centres of community life and nowhere is this more true than here, especially close to sunset.

The tourist entrance to the mosque is on the north side, but first you'll need to buy a ticket outside the northwestern corner of the mosque; look for the 'Putting on Special Clothes Room' sign. Women are required to don the grey robes supplied.

Next to the ticket office in the small garden north of the mosque's walls is the modest, red-domed **Mausoleum of Saladin**, the resting place of one of the great heroes of Arab history. The mausoleum was originally built in 1193, and admission is included in the price of the Umayyad Mosque ticket.

NORTH OF THE MOSQUE

Northwest of Saladin's mausoleum is the 13th-century **Madrassa az-Zahiriyya** (Map pp470-1; 9am-5pm), within which is buried Sultan Beybars – another Islamic warrior hero, this time of the Mamluk dynasty. It was Beybars who won several decisive victories over the Crusaders, driving them from the region.

Also near the Umayyad Mosque is the modern, Iranian-built Shiite **Sayyida Ruqayya Mosque**, dedicated to the daughter of the martyr Hussein, son of Ali. Powerful in the passion it inspires in the (mostly Iranian) pilgrims, breathtaking in the extravagance of its decoration, this mosque is one of the most fascinating sights in Damascus and its presence ripples out through the surrounding streets.

This is one of the major pilgrimage sites for Shiite pilgrims to Damascus and although it has long been thus, the current mosque dates back only to the late 1980s. While the portico, courtyard and main

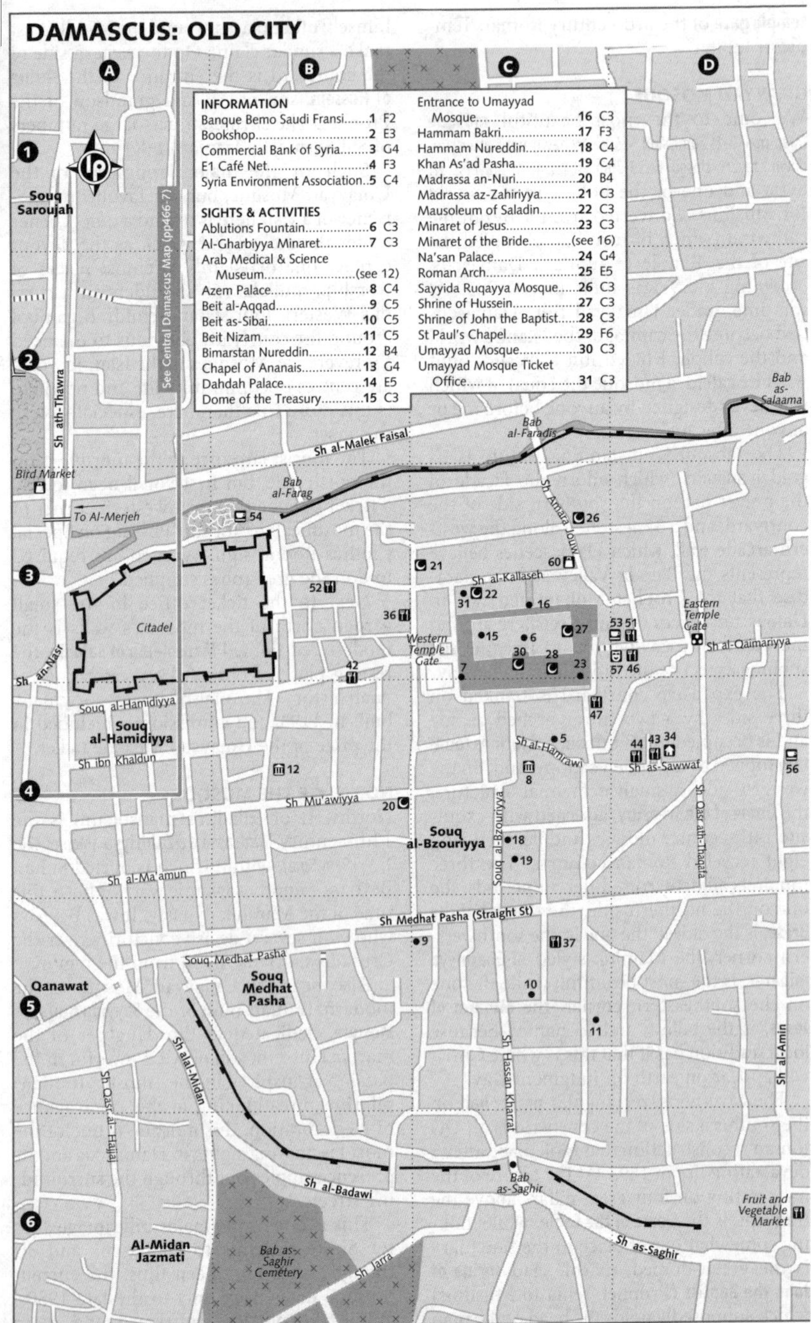
DAMASCUS: OLD CITY
INFORMATION
Banque Bemo Saudi Fransi........1 F2
Bookshop..............................2 E3
Commercial Bank of Syria........3 G4
E1 Café Net...........................4 F3
Syria Environment Association..5 C4
SIGHTS & ACTIVITIES
Ablutions Fountain.................6 C3
Al-Gharbiyya Minaret..............7 C3
Arab Medical & Science Museum..............(see 12)
Azem Palace..........................8 C4
Beit al-Aqqad.........................9 C5
Beit as-Sibai..........................10 C5
Beit Nizam.............................11 C5
Bimarstan Nureddin.................12 B4
Chapel of Ananais...................13 G4
Dahdah Palace.......................14 E5
Dome of the Treasury..............15 C3
Entrance to Umayyad Mosque..............16 C3
Hammam Bakri.......................17 F3
Hammam Nureddin..................18 C4
Khan As'ad Pasha...................19 C4
Madrassa an-Nuri...................20 B4
Madrassa az-Zahiriyya.............21 C3
Mausoleum of Saladin.............22 C3
Minaret of Jesus.....................23 C3
Minaret of the Bride...........(see 16)
Na'san Palace........................24 G4
Roman Arch...........................25 E5
Sayyida Ruqayya Mosque........26 C3
Shrine of Hussein...................27 C3
Shrine of John the Baptist.......28 C3
St Paul's Chapel.....................29 F6
Umayyad Mosque...................30 C3
Umayyad Mosque Ticket Office..............31 C3
See Central Damascus Map (pp466-7)
Souq Saroujah
Sh ath-Thawra
Bird Market
To Al-Merjeh
Sh an-Nasr
Citadel
Souq al-Hamidiyya
Sh ibn Khaldun
Sh al-Malek Faisal
Bab al-Farag
Bab al-Faradis
Bab as-Salaama
Sh Amara Jouw
Sh al-Kallaseh
Western Temple Gate
Eastern Temple Gate
Sh al-Qaimariyya
Sh al-Hamrawi
Sh as-Sawwaf
Sh Mu'awiyya
Souq al-Bzouriyya
Souq al-Bzouriyya
Sh Qasr ath-Thaqafa
Sh al-Ma'amun
Sh Medhat Pasha (Straight St)
Souq Medhat Pasha
Souq Medhat Pasha
Qanawat
Sh alal-Midan
Sh Qasr al-Hajjaj
Sh Hassan Kharrat
Sh al-Amin
Sh al-Badawi
Bab as-Saghir
Sh as-Saghir
Fruit and Vegetable Market
Al-Midan Jazmati
Bab as-Saghir Cemetery
Sh Jarra

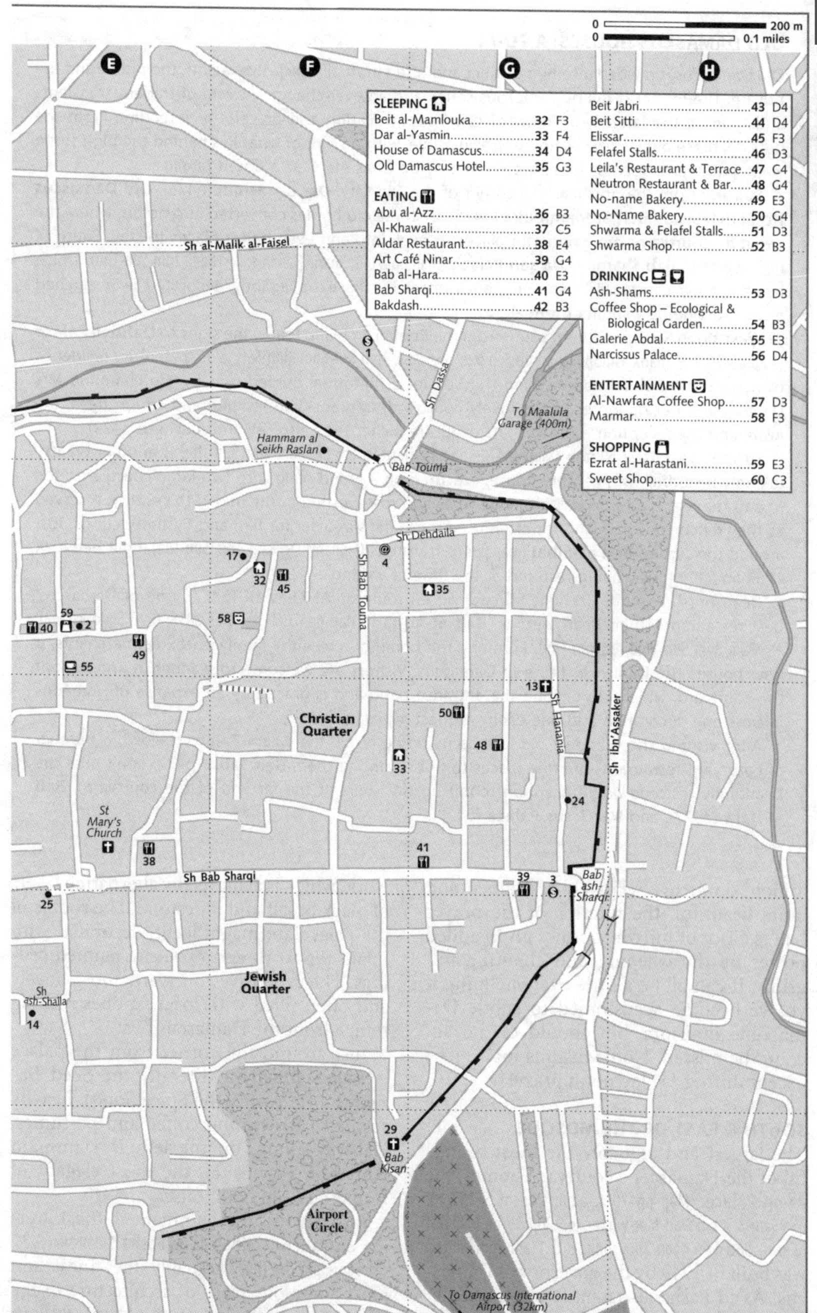
0 200 m
0 0.1 miles
E
F
G
H
SLEEPING
Beit al-Mamlouka.................32 F3
Dar al-Yasmin.....................33 F4
House of Damascus..............34 D4
Old Damascus Hotel.............35 G3
EATING
Abu al-Azz..........................36 B3
Al-Khawali..........................37 C5
Aldar Restaurant..................38 E4
Art Café Ninar......................39 G4
Bab al-Hara.........................40 E3
Bab Sharqi...........................41 G4
Bakdash..............................42 B3
Beit Jabri.............................43 D4
Beit Sitti..............................44 D4
Elissar.................................45 F3
Felafel Stalls.......................46 D3
Leila's Restaurant & Terrace...47 C4
Neutron Restaurant & Bar......48 G4
No-name Bakery...................49 E3
No-Name Bakery...................50 G4
Shwarma & Felafel Stalls........51 D3
Shwarma Shop.....................52 B3
DRINKING
Ash-Shams...........................53 D3
Coffee Shop – Ecological & Biological Garden..............54 B3
Galerie Abdal........................55 E3
Narcissus Palace...................56 D4
ENTERTAINMENT
Al-Nawfara Coffee Shop.......57 D3
Marmar...............................58 F3
SHOPPING
Ezrat al-Harastani.................59 E3
Sweet Shop..........................60 C3
Sh al-Malik al-Faisel
Sh Dassa
To Maalula Garage (400m)
Hammarn al Seikh Raslan
Bab Touma
Sh Dehdaila
Sh Bab Touma
Christian Quarter
Sh Hanania
Sh ibn'Assaker
St Mary's Church
Sh Bab Sharqi
Bab ash-Sharqi
Jewish Quarter
Sh ash-Shalla
Bab Kisan
Airport Circle
To Damascus International Airport (32km)
YRIA

OLD DAMASCUS HOUSES: A TOUR

Old Damascus is divided into two distinct and often mutually exclusive realms: the public and the private. The former is full of clamorous souqs and an ever-changing world of traders, transients and tourists; the latter is an oasis of calm, sophistication and graceful architecture. From the outside, these old Damascus homes are invisible, with no hint of what lies behind the high stone walls; courtyards such as these were often home to as many as a dozen families.

Starting from the northeastern corner of the Old City, **Dar al-Yasmin** (p475), **Old Damascus Hotel** (p475) and **Beit al-Mamlouka** (p475) are three old homes converted into hotels, where the beautiful courtyards are wonderful places to peek into and even better places to stay. South of here, close to Bab Sharqi, is **Na'san Palace** (Map pp470-1; Sharia Hanania; 8am-2pm Sun-Thu), which has a narrow courtyard in sombre tones offset by the extravagantly decorated *iwan* (arched alcove serving as a summer retreat).

West along Straight St, turn south from the Roman arch and follow the signs to **Dahdah Palace** (Map pp470-1; 9 Sharia ash-Shalla; admission free; 9am-1pm & 4-6pm Mon-Sat), a 17th-century residence owned by the Dahdah family. Ring the bell for an informal guided tour by the charming Mrs Dahdah and her daughter of the lovely courtyard, fragrant with jasmine and lemon trees, the *iwan,* and the reception room with its exquisite niche. They also sell antiques (see p479).

Further west, **Beit Nizam** (Map pp470-1; Sharia Nasif Pasha; 8am-2pm Sun-Thu) is another breathtakingly beautiful 18th-century house, executed on a grand scale with two large courtyards; the one to the rear is adorned with orange trees and rose bushes. In the mid-19th century, it served as the French consulate and it's often used these days as a set for film and TV productions. Just around the corner, **Beit as-Sibai** (Map pp470-1; Sharia al-Qabbani; 8am-2pm Sun-Thu), built between 1769 and 1774, was being restored at the time of writing.

Head north towards Straight St, pausing en route at **Al-Khawali** (p477), one of Damascus' best restaurants, then head west to **Beit al-Aqqad** (Map pp470-1; 223 8038; 8-10 Souq as-Souf; 9am-3pm Sun-Wed, to 1pm Thu). Formerly the home of a wealthy family of textile merchants, it now houses the Danish Institute in Damascus. Visitors are welcome to wander in and look at the courtyard, which lies beyond the entrance patio and is graced by an expanse of gorgeous inlaid-stone decoration and one of the highest *iwans* in the city.

After visiting the grandest old Damascus home of all, the **Azem Palace** (below), a number of courtyard restaurants are fine places to finish, among them **Beit Jabri** (p477; don't miss the beautifully restored *qa'a* (reception room) up the stairs at the far end of the courtyard), **Bab al-Hara** (p477), and **Narcissus Palace** (p478).

'onion' dome are relatively restrained and quite beautiful, the interior of the prayer hall is a riot of mirror mosaics given added power by the weeping and chanting pilgrims. It can all be a little overwhelming if you've become accustomed to subtle Damascene interiors, but should on no account be missed. Non-Muslims may enter, except during Friday noon prayers.

SOUTH & EAST OF THE MOSQUE

The largest and arguably the most beautiful of the Damascene courtyard homes, the **Azem Palace** (Map pp470-1; adult/student S£150/10; 9am-3.30pm Wed-Mon winter, to 5.30pm Wed-Mon rest of year, closed Fri noon-2pm summer & 11am-1pm winter) was built in 1749 by the governor of Damascus, As'ad Pasha al-Azem. It's fashioned in the typical Damascene style of striped stonework, which is achieved by alternating layers of black basalt and limestone. The rooms of the palace are magnificent, decorated with inlaid tile work and exquisite painted ceilings. The expansive courtyard, too, is lovely and often filled with local families seeking refuge from the Damascus heat.

Just around the corner from the palace is **Souq al-Bzouriyya** (literally the Seed Bazaar, but in reality the Spice Souq), heavily scented with cumin, coffee and perfumes. Halfway along, on the left, is Hammam Nureddin (opposite), the most elegant of Damascus' old bathhouses.

Just beyond the hammam is the towering entrance to **Khan As'ad Pasha** (admission S£75; 9am-3pm Sat-Thu), arguably the finest and most ambitious piece of architecture in the Old City – a cathedral among khans. Built in

1752 under the patronage of As'ad Pasha al-Azem, it's a supremely elegant arrangement of eight small domes around a larger circular aperture, allowing light to stream in above a circular pool. The domes are supported on four colossal grey-and-white piers that splay into graceful arches, with a backdrop of more horizontal grey-and-white magnificence. Don't fail to climb up to the first floor, where the cell-like rooms of the old khan surround the balconies that look down into the main courtyard with some marvellous interplays of light and shadow. It's a special place.

Swinging back to the west, the **Madrassa an-Nuri** is the mausoleum of Saladin's predecessor, Nureddin. Just south of the Souq al-Hamidiyya, the **Bimarstan Nureddin** was built in the 12th century as a mental hospital and was for centuries renowned in the Arab world as an enlightened medical-treatment centre. Inside, the hodgepodge exhibits of the **Arab Medical & Science Museum** (Map pp470-1; adult/student S£150/10; 9am-3pm Sat-Thu) are displayed around a cool, peaceful courtyard.

Heading east, about two-thirds of the way along Sharia Medhat Pasha – **Straight St** (Via Recta) – are the remains of a **Roman arch**. The arch roughly marks the starting point of what's referred to as the Christian quarter, although it's by no means exclusive.

St Paul's Chapel (Bab Kisan; admission free; 8am-6pm) marks the spot where, according to the biblical tale, the disciples lowered St Paul out of a window in a basket one night so that he could flee the Jews. The simple stone chapel occupies the gate itself; to get here, you have to leave the Old City via Bab Sharqi and follow the walls around to the southwest.

The old cellar of the **Chapel of Ananias** (Sharia Hanania; admission S£25; 9am-7pm) is reputedly the house of Ananias, an early Christian disciple who baptised St Paul. The crypt church has multilingual translations of the story of the two disciples, although scholars dispute whether this is Ananias' actual house.

National Museum & Around

Located off Sharia Shoukri al-Quwatli, the **National Museum** (Map pp466-7; ☎ 221 9938; adult/student S£150/10; 9am-4pm Wed-Mon Oct-Jan, to 6pm Wed-Mon Apr-Sep, closed for Fri prayers) is Syria's most important museum and well worth a visit. After passing the shady garden strewn with unlabelled antiquities, for which no room could be found within the museum's walls, you enter the museum proper through the imposing facade (the relocated entrance of Qasr al-Heir al-Gharbi, a desert fortress near Palmyra that dates to AD 688).

The exhibits are presented thematically and grouped into preclassical, classical and Islamic sections; labelling (in Arabic and English) is improving thanks to a joint Syrian-Italian overhaul. Highlights include the finely wrought stone friezes from the *qasr*, which you'll see immediately upon entering; tablets from the ruins of Ugarit (p508) showing one of the world's first alphabets; the downstairs Hypogeum of Yarhai, an extraordinary reconstruction of an underground burial chamber from Palmyra's Valley of the Tombs (p511); and the astonishing frescoed, 2nd-century synagogue from Dura Europos (p517), our favourite room in the whole museum.

Immediately east of the National Museum is the black-and-white-striped **Takiyya as-Süleimaniyya** (Map pp466–7), built in 1554 to the design of the Ottoman Empire's most brilliant architect, Mirmar Sinan. It's currently closed to the public, but the pencil-thin Ottoman-style minarets tower above the rooftops.

Hejaz Train Station

The grand Hejaz train station (Map pp466–7), completed in 1917, was the northern terminus of the Hejaz Railway, built to ferry pilgrims to Medina. Compared with the transport palaces of Europe, the station is a provincial affair, but the interior has a beautifully decorated ceiling. The actual platforms of the station are closed (although renovations have long been planned) and all trains now leave from Khaddam station. Outside there's a steam locomotive dating from 1908.

ACTIVITIES

There are a few hammams in the Old City, all of which offer a full service of massage, bath, exfoliation and sauna with towel, soap and tea.

Hammam Bakri (Map pp470-1; ☎ 542 6606; Sharia Qanayet al-Hattab; bath only S£150, full bath S£350; women 10am-5pm Sat-Thu, men 5pm-midnight Sat-Thu, 10am-midnight Fri) A local bath in the Christian quarter, near Bab Touma.

Hammam Nureddin (Map pp470-1; ☎ 222 9513; Souq al-Bzouriyya; bath only S£200, full bath S£450; 9am-midnight Sat-Thu) The oldest hammam in the city and strictly men only.

TOURS

Al-Rabie (☎ 231 8374) and Al-Haramain hotels (☎ 231 9489) organise popular day trips (minibus and private car). Prices depend on numbers, but are about US$35 to US$40 per person. Possibilities include day trips to: Bosra, Suweida and the Sayyida Zeinab Mosque; Crac des Chevaliers; Apamea; and Maalula, Seidnayya and Jebel Qassioun. Though considerably more expensive than by public transport, you'll save a lot of time.

FESTIVALS & EVENTS

Damascus Jazz Festival (July) In the citadel.
Silk Road Festival (late September) Celebrates Syria's long cultural history with events in Damascus, Aleppo, Palmyra and Bosra.
Damascus International Film Festival (November to December) Local and international films (you can see most of the films in Syria at other times too).

SLEEPING

The Damascus hotel scene is getting better all the time, although it remains the case that the best options are in the budget and top-end categories. It's not that there aren't good midrange choices; rather, there are very few that are especially exciting.

For student accommodation, try **House of Damascus** (Map pp470-1; ☎ 094 431 8068; www.houseofdamascus.com; per month S£10,000-15,000). Set in a lovely old Damascus house not far from the Umayyad Mosque, the rooms have shared bath and there's dial-up internet connections, a fridge, satellite TV and two shared kitchens.

Budget

Sharia Bahsa, in the Souq al-Saroujah district, is the budget travellers' ghetto. Here you'll find two perennial favourites, Al-Rabie and Al-Haramain, and the newcomer Ghazal House. These are usually full, making bookings essential.

Al-Saada Hotel (Map pp466-7; off Souq al-Saroujah; ☎ 231 1722; fax 231 1875; dm S£350, d S£800-1000, tr S£1500) From the same people who brought you the Hotel Al-Rabie, Al-Saada Hotel (also signed as Al-Saade), is a good option if the other three budget places are full. If that sounds like we're damning with faint praise, remember that those other three are top-notch. The rooms are simple and surround a small shady courtyard. Breakfast is S£100.

our pick Al-Rabie Hotel (Map pp466-7; ☎ 231 8374; alrabiehotel@hotmail.com; Sharia Bahsa; roof mattress/dm S£250/400, d/tr S£1500/1700, s/d without bathroom 600/1000) One of the best backpacker choices in all the Middle East, this enchanting 600-year-old house has a gorgeous courtyard featuring trailing vines, an orange tree and a fountain. Modern additions include a satellite TV and comfortable seating. Some rooms look onto the courtyard and some feature ornate high ceilings, large windows and exposed stonework; all are clean and have heating and fans. The staff is friendly and traveller-savvy. Breakfast is S£100.

Ghazal Hotel (Map pp466-7; ☎ 231 3736; www.ghazalhotel.com; Sharia Bahsa; roof mattress/dm/s/d S£250/400/800/1200) This friendly, clean hotel gets rave reviews from travellers. Its ample public areas don't quite have the character of the others further west, but the overall package is outstanding.

Al-Haramain Hotel (Map pp466-7; ☎ 231 9489; alharamain_hotel@yahoo.com; Sharia Bahsa; dm/d S£250/1800, s/d without bathroom S£720/1225) Another attractive old house, Al-Haramain has basic rooms and only two have private bathrooms, but the comfortable beds, clean linen and covered courtyard get the nod from us. Our only reservation is that management crams as many guests into dorm rooms as possible.

Midrange

Breakfast costs an additional €2 unless otherwise stated.

Salam Hotel (Map pp466-7; ☎ 221 6674; salamhotel@mail2world.com; Sharia ar-Rais; s/d/tr €20/25/30; ❄) In a quiet but central location just up the hill south of the National Museum, the Salam is clean and all rooms come with satellite TV. Some are looking a little worn, but it's a comfortable, tranquil choice that's more central than it appears on the map: a slow stroll to the Old City takes 15 minutes.

Sultan Hotel (Map pp466-7; ☎ 222 5768; sultan.hotel@mail.sy; Sharia Mousalam al-Baroudi; s/d €21/26, 5-bed room €90; ❄) Just west of the Hejaz station and a short walk to the Old City, this is the accommodation of choice for most archaeological missions to the country. Although the 31 rooms are basic but clean, what really makes this place is the level of service: the staff is exceptionally friendly and helpful.

There's a library of novels to borrow and a lounge/breakfast area with satellite TV.

Afamia Hotel (Map pp466-7; ☎ 222 8963; www.afamiahotel.com; classic s/d €25/30, executive s/d from €30/35;) The Afamia wins our vote for Damascus' best midrange hotel. Traveller-friendly, well-located close to the Hejaz train station and a 10-minute walk from the Old City, the hotel has a mix of rooms that were renovated recently (executive) and older rooms (classic). There are plans for all the rooms to be renovated which will make it a fine choice whichever room you get. The newer rooms aren't large but have plump doonas, comfortable beds, hairdryers, clean bathrooms and satellite TV; there are also plans for in-room ADSL internet access. Some rooms also have balconies.

Al-Majed Hotel (Map pp466-7; ☎ 232 3300; www.almajed-group.com; d low/high season €32/55;) This centrally located place has been built by a local who spent years working in the Gulf, and the decor and clientele reflect this fact. The clean rooms with pine furniture all come with satellite TV and some on the upper floors have views. The high-season price is more than it should be, low season is about right. For all its pluses, the quality of the rooms and service vary and get mixed reviews from travellers.

Top End

Prices in this category don't include 11% tax.

Old Damascus Hotel (Map pp470-1; ☎ 541 4042; www.old-damas.com; near Bab Touma; s/d US$75/95;) With an intimate courtyard, lovely spacious rooms and an attention to detail that has few rivals in the Old City, Old Damascus Hotel is outstanding. We also love the fact that it's run, at least in part, by women.

Beit al-Mamlouka (Map pp470-1; ☎ 543 0445/6; www.almamlouka.com; s/d US$120/135;) This courtyard house, which dates from 1650, has been converted into a sumptuous boutique hotel. Staying in the Süleyman the Magnificent room, with its painted ceiling and marble fountain, is a once-in-a-lifetime experience, made even better by the hotel's high level of service and great position within the walls of the Old City. There are only eight rooms, all of which are individually and beautifully decorated. The marmalade on your breakfast table comes from the trees in the courtyard and the rooftop terrace is a fine place to wile away an afternoon.

Dar al-Yasmin (Map pp470-1; ☎ 544 3380; www.daralyasmin.com; near Bab Touma; s/d/ste US$120/140/175;) Another lovely *hôtel de charme* (boutique hotel), arrayed around the courtyards of an old Damascene house, Dar al-Yasmin is one of the Old City's most agreeable places to stay. Rooms are decorated in an antique style with soaring ceilings and traditional furnishings. Some are on the small side with tiny bathrooms, others are spacious with modern amenities. There's wireless internet throughout and the service is gracious and discreet. If you're coming from Bab Touma along Sharia Bab Touma, take the second street on the left, then the first lane on the right.

EATING

The most atmospheric places to eat are the historic courtyard restaurants in the Old City, where prices are generally reasonable, at least by Western standards. If you want alcohol with your meal, you'll need to venture into the Christian quarter rather than the area around the Umayyad Mosque, although some places in the latter area will whisper in your ear that alcohol is available. In central Damascus, the best restaurants are found in the area around Saahat Yousef al-Azmeh.

Central Damascus

The side streets off Martyrs' Sq are crammed with cheap eateries, which mostly offer shwarma and felafel, but the southern perimeter of the square and the surrounding streets are more famous for their **sweet shops**, with windows dominated by great pyramids of baklava and other glorious Damascene sweets.

Another popular spot for cheap restaurants is just up the hill from Al-Rabie and Al-Haramain Hotels, in the Souq al-Saroujah district, where all the budget hotels are concentrated. There are places offering roast chicken, shwarma and some of the best *fatta* (an oven-baked dish of chickpeas, minced meat or chicken, and bread soaked in tahina) we tasted in Syria, as well as **bakeries** where the locals buy their bread. **La Roche** (Map pp466-7; ☎ 232 6579; Souq al-Saroujah; sandwiches S£75-125, meals S£250-300; 9am-midnight) is pleasant, serves pizza, pasta and a few other Syrian approximations of Western dishes; they also do local soups, *fatta* and fresh juices.

THE WORLD'S LARGEST RESTAURANT

Fancy an intimate dinner for…6014 people? It's official: Damascus now boasts the world's largest restaurant. Final recognition for Damascus Gate Restaurant (Bawabet Dimashq), in the suburbs of Damascus, came in May 2008, although the restaurant had been open since 2002. It's an astonishing project where the statistics speak for themselves: US$40 million to build, 1800 staff employed in summer, a dining area covering 54,000 sq metres with a 2500-sq-metre kitchen that the Guinness Book of Records describes as a 'mini factory'. With an aesthetic akin to a Las Vegas casino, Damascus Gate has decor that blends faux archaeological ruins, waterfalls and fountains with a menu of suitable breadth, ranging from local Syrian cuisine to Indian and Chinese 'zones'.

It's the brainchild of Muhammad Sannan, who told the BBC that size meant no diminishment in quality: 'In this part of the world, all people care about is their stomachs, so the food has to be the best'. We prefer a more cosy dining experience and we figure that you're not going to need our help in finding the world's largest restaurant. If you do go there, however, whatever you do, don't let them talk you into doing the washing up.

Pizza Roma (Map pp466-7; ☎ 331 6434; 3 Sharia Odai bin ar-Roqaa; pizza around S£100;) If you're keen on American-style (pan, rather than thinner Italian) pizzas, this is the most popular place in town. You'll find it west of the Cham Palace Hotel.

Al-Masri (Map pp466-7; ☎ 333 7095; Sharia Said al-Jabri; meals S£200; 7.30am-5pm) 'The Egyptian' is popular with local office workers, with a menu featuring the kind of home-cooked fare you'd find in Cairo's backstreets, along with local favourites such as *shakshuka* (fried egg and mince meat) and *shish tawooq* (grilled chicken kebab, often served with garlic and lemon sauce).

Al-Arabi (Map pp466-7; meals S£200) On a pedestrianised street off the southeastern corner of Al-Merjeh, Al-Arabi consists of two adjacent, cheap restaurants, one more casual, the other a little fancier with a separate family section. For the culinary adventurous, specialities include sheep testicles and sheep-brain salad with potatoes, but there are plenty of less challenging dishes including stuffed grape leaves, borek and *kibbeh* (cracked-wheat croquettes) with yogurt. We shudder to think what 'Jew's Mallow' is and we *think* we know what they mean by 'Unnatural Juice'…

Ghraoui (Map pp466-7; ☎ 231 1323; www.ghraouichocolate.com; Sharia Bur Said; confectionary per 100g S£200) We start salivating just thinking of the apricot half-coated with chocolate almost as much as the fresh cocoa truffle. There's a second branch in the departures lounge at Damascus International Airport.

Al-Sehhi (Map pp466-7; ☎ 221 1555; Sharia al-Abed; meals S£200; 11am-midnight) This modest family restaurant, off Sharia 29 Mai, confines itself to the basics – mezze, grilled meats, and very good *fatta* (S£100); they eat every part of the sheep here (brains, testicles, tongue…) and be aware that the '*fatta* with hummus and meat' is really hummus and tongue. There's a separate 'family area' for women diners.

Al-Kamal (Map pp466-7; ☎ 222 1494; Sharia 29 Mai; meals S£250; 11am-midnight) Located near the main tourist office, this place resembles a Parisian bistro. Regulars come for the good-value French *plats du jour* and home-style Syrian dishes including *kabsa* (spiced rice with chicken or lamb) and truly excellent *fatta*.

Downtown (Map pp466-7; ☎ 332 2321; Sharia al-Amar Izzedin al-Jazzari; meals S£500; 10am-1am) You're more likely to hear French being spoken than Arabic at this hip, contemporary café, off Sharia Maysaloun. It has Scandinavian-style decor (think chocolate-coloured wood and clean lines) and the most decadently delicious sandwiches, salads and fresh juices in Damascus. Try the caviar en croute sandwich with cucumber, dill, caviar, cream cheese and a boiled egg (S£500), and the strawberry and blackberry juice. Downtown is ideal if you've been on the road a while and crave tastes from home.

Old City

In the small alley east of the Umayyad Mosque, just past the Al-Nawfara Coffee Shop (p478), are a couple of very good shwarma places and a stall that does great felafel. There's another collection of felafel and shwarma hole-in-the-wall eateries in the covered market lane that runs north off Souq al-Hamidiyya.

Bakdash (Map pp470-1; Souq al-Hamidiyya; cone S£50; 9am-late) Find the queues close to the mosque-end of Souq al-Hamidiyya and you'll have found this wildly popular Damascene institution. A purveyor of scrumptious ice creams made with *sahlab* (a tapioca-root flavoured drink) and topped with crushed pistachio nuts, it's a souq-shopping must. Pay at the cash register before ordering.

Art Café Ninar (Map pp470-1; 542 2257; Sharia Bab Sharqi; pizza S£150; 10.30am-2am) Don't be surprised if you see local artists sitting at the wooden tables painting and sketching, or a poet jotting down lines of verse in a notebook. Damascus' intellectual set flocks to this casual eatery in a big stone building for the art exhibitions, excellent pizza and cheap beer. Be like the locals and drop by late.

Bab Sharqi (Map pp470-1; Sharia Bab Sharqi; meals S£175; 11am-midnight) It's hard to get a table out the front of this excellent pizzeria-cum-takeaway place, especially on a summer evening, when students linger over cold beers, bottles of Syrian wine, Italian-style pizzas and delicious *toshka* (Armenian toasted meat and cheese sandwiches).

Abu al-Azz (Map pp470-1; 221 8174; Souq al-Hamidiyya; lunch/dinner S£300/500; 9am-late) This place is popular with locals as much as tourists – Arab families pack the place over summer. Look for the sign 'Rest. Al Ezz Al Shamieh Hall', then pass through the bustling ground-floor bakery and up a narrow staircase to two floors of dining; the upper level is the most atmospheric. Expect mezze, salads and kebabs, live oriental music all day and whirling dervishes in the evening from around 10.30pm. No alcohol served.

Beit Jabri (Jabri House; Map pp470-1; 541 6254; 14 Sharia as-Sawwaf; meals around S£450; 9.30am-12.30am) This informal and phenomenally popular café is set in the partially restored courtyard of a stunning 18th-century Damascene house. The menu runs from breakfasts and omelettes to oriental mezze and mains. The quality of the food and service is OK, but doesn't always live up to the surrounds.

our pick **Bab al-Hara** (Map pp470-1; 541 8644; Sharia al-Qaimariyya; meals around S£450; 9.30am-midnight) West of the Umayyad Mosque, Bab al-Hara is one of our favourite Old City restaurants. The grills have that reassuring taste of charcoal, the *kibbeh* is some of the tastiest we've tried and the *fatta* is hearty and very good. Prices are a touch below the other courtyard eateries including the nargilehs (S£100), which draw a hip, young and local crowd. The service is casual and obliging. Highly recommended.

our pick **Leila's Restaurant & Terrace** (Map pp470-1; 544 5900; Souq al-Abbabiyya; meals S£500; 11am-2am) In the shadow of the Umayyad Mosque, opposite the Minaret of Jesus, this stylish place occupies, just for something different, a beautifully restored courtyard house with a glass ceiling. It's quieter than the more popular Beit Jabri, and we reckon the food is better as well. Vegetarians will love the lentil *kibbeh* and carnivores will be just as pleased with the delicious mixed grill. The fresh mint lemonade (S£75) hits the spot on a hot day, while the cheese *mamoul* (a shortbread-like pastry or cookie lightly filled with cheese) for desert is exquisite. The roof terrace is a great place to enjoy the Damascus night.

Neutron Restaurant & Bar (Map pp470-1; 544 5451; Ja'afar Ave; meals S£500;) One of a growing number of licensed restaurants in the Christian quarter of the Old City, Neutron is noteworthy for its French-influenced menu, full bar and nightly live music.

Al-Khawali (Map pp470-1; 222 5808; cnr Maazanet al-Shahim; meals from S£550; noon-2am) This is where Syria's president brings eminent international guests for a meal and it's not just because of the discreet, impeccable service or the beautifully renovated courtyard that was first built in 1368. A touch of class pervades this place, off Straight St, unlike the more casual atmosphere that you find elsewhere, and the food is first rate – devotees swear the Syrian cuisine is some of the best in the city. Try the aubergine and see what great mezze is all about, or the *jedy bzeit* (lamb with lemon sauce), but everything on the menu is subtly flavoured and delicious. Best of all, bread baked on the premises arrives on your table still warm from the oven. No alcohol or credit cards.

Elissar (Map pp470-1; 542 4300; Sharia ad-Dawamneh, Bab Touma; meals around S£600;) This elegant restaurant is named after a Phoenician princess, and its decor and menu are impressive enough to claim such a pedigree, although some locals reckon it's not what it was. Situated in an enormous old house with tables filling the courtyard and two upper levels of terraces, it serves up refined Syrian dishes and a few French-influenced mains, washed down by selections from a good wine and

SYRIA

BEST PLACES TO PEOPLE-WATCH IN SYRIA *Chocoloca*

Aleppo In the early evening, everyone promenades in Aleppo (p491).

Ice-cream shop in Damascus The famous ice-cream shop (p477) in Souq al-Hamidiyya is always a hub of activity. Watch ice cream being stretched and slapped, then rolled in pistachio nuts. Watch men smoke and chat downstairs, or join with the women and children upstairs.

Palmyra at sunset Just before sunset, tourists and locals alike journey to Zenobia's castle which overlooks the ancient city of Palmyra (p509). As the golden light paints the ruins, lovers and families appear, then disperse, each to a favourite place to dine alfresco.

By the sea in Lattakia Along Lattakia's (p503) seafront is a promenade where everyone goes to see and to be seen. Sit at a cliffside café to watch men watch ladies.

What's your recommendation? www.lonelyplanet.com/middle-east

arak list. They don't take credit cards and most menus don't list prices.

Aldar Restaurant (Map pp470-1; ☎ 544 5900; meals S£700; 🕑 11am-2am) In a chic conversion of an old Damascene building off Sharia Bab Sharqi, beside the Assieh School, and stylishly blending old and new, Aldar dishes up some of the tastiest Syrian cuisine in the city, with creative touches added to classics. For starters, don't miss the spicy *sojok* meatballs with a green pepper, onion and tomato sauce. Book a table for the live jazz on Tuesday night. Alcohol is served, and credit cards are accepted.

DRINKING

There are loads of places in the Souq al-Saroujah backpacker district, with the low outdoor stools a great place to discuss regional politics and local popular culture over a tea. Tea or coffee costs about S£50.

The finest places to relax in Damascus are the two historic coffeehouses, Al-Nawfara Coffee Shop (right) and **Ash-Shams** (Map pp470-1; Sharia al-Qaimariyya; 🕑 9am-midnight), nestled in the shadow of the Umayyad Mosque's eastern wall. Lingering over a tea here should be on every visitor's itinerary.

Coffee Shop – Ecological & Biological Garden (Map pp470-1; 🕑 9am-11pm) Just outside the north-eastern corner of the citadel, near Bab al-Farag and overlooking the trickle that is the Barada River, this agreeable modern coffee shop has outdoor and indoor tables alongside a garden set up by the Syria Environment Association. Although the plants need time to mature, it's an initiative worth supporting, quite apart from being a pleasant place to rest from the clamour of the Old City.

Galerie Albal (Map pp470-1; ☎ 544 5794; Sharia Shaweesh) For something a bit different, Galerie Albal, about a five-minute walk from the coffeehouses east along Sharia al-Qaimariyya, is a loud, Western-style café with an art gallery above. It's where the city's bohemian types congregate, and there are a handful of similar places alongside.

Narcissus Palace (Map pp470-1; ☎ 541 6785; 🕑 noon-1am) Packed to its very attractive rafters with young people catching up over a nargileh and tea, Narcissus Palace features music clips blaring from the satellite TV, backgammon pieces clinking, the fountain gently playing and extremely friendly staff to make sure everyone is happy. Great stuff.

A number of restaurants double as coffeehouses in Old City buildings. The better ones include Leila's Restaurant & Terrace (p477), Bab al-Hara (p477) and Beit Jabri (p477).

ENTERTAINMENT

our pick **Al-Nawfara Coffee Shop** (The Fountain Coffee Shop; Map pp470-1; Sharia al-Qaimariyya; 🕑 9am-midnight) Not only is this lovely old café an institution for imbibing tea and a nargileh, it's the home of Syria's last professional *hakawati* (storyteller). Every night after sunset prayers, Abu Shady takes to the stage to tell an epic tale of glorious days long past. Depending on the crowd, it can either be filled with banter or a little quiet as people come and go, often talking over the top of him. Either way, this is a Damascus must-see, not least because this is a dying art form (see boxed text opposite). A collection is taken near the end of the show.

The most popular nightclub in town is **Marmar** (Map pp470-1; ☎ 544 6425; Sharia ad-Dawanneh; admission incl 3 drinks S£750; 🔊), a bar-restaurant at Bab Touma that morphs into a club on Thursday and Friday nights and occasionally hosts live gigs on Sundays.

END OF STORY? *Terry Carter, Lara Dunston & Anthony Ham*

In one of the tales in *The Thousand and One Nights,* a king commissions a merchant to seek out the most marvellous story ever. The merchant sends out his slaves on the quest and at last success is achieved – a slave hears a wondrous story told in Damascus by an old man who tells stories every day, seated on his storyteller's throne. Jump forward several centuries, and in Damascus today there's still an old man who tells stories every day, seated on just such a throne. His name is Abu Shady and he's the last of the Syrian *hakawati* (professional storytellers).

Hakawati were a common feature of Middle Eastern city street life as far back as the 12th century. With the spread of coffee drinking during Ottoman times, the storytellers moved off the street and into the coffeehouses. As with many Arab traditions, the art of public storytelling has largely failed to survive the 20th century, supplanted in the coffeehouses first by radio, then by TV.

According to Abu Shady, the last professional storyteller before him in Syria went into retirement in the 1970s. As a boy, Abu Shady went with his father to watch the *hakawati* perform at the coffeehouses, and fell in love with stories. 'It was my habit to read too much,' he told us. 'When I was young I would run away from my job at the library to read books.' Abu Shady trained as a tailor but he would read every moment he could: Jean Paul Sartre, Victor Hugo, Ernest Hemingway, Khalil Gibran…

When the previous *hakawati* decided to retire and stop performing at Al-Nawfara Coffee Shop, its owner, Ahmed al-Rabat persuaded Abu Shady to take over, and in the early 1990s, he revived the profession. Since then, Abu Shady has been appearing nightly at Al-Nawfara in the shadows of the Umayyad Mosque. Costumed in baggy trousers and waistcoat with a tarboosh on his head, he recounts nightly from his volumes of handwritten tales. These include the legendary exploits of Sultan Beybars and Antar ibn Shadad, both Islamic heroes and – as Abu Shady tells it – regular doers of fantastic feats, sorcery and cunning roguery. He also invents his own stories, incorporating current events. The assembled listeners know the stories, but it's Abu Shady's delivery they come for: he interjects with jokes and comments, works the audience, punctuates the words with waves of his sword, and smashes it down on a copper-top table for startling emphasis. The audience responds with oohs and aahs, cheering and interjecting comments of their own.

Sadly, the audience is dwindling. Abu Shady says that nobody has the time to listen to stories anymore, although ever the optimist, he told us that the new generation 'are starting to get bored with satellite TV and internet and they are returning to stories'. We asked Abu Shady what the future is for the *hakawati*: 'It will die not because of a lack of interest, but because no one wants to take such a low-paying job.'

Even so, he hopes that his son, Shady, who already deputises when Abu Shady travels overseas for international festivals, will follow in his footsteps. Shady told us he stands ready to ensure that the era of the Arab storyteller doesn't end when his father hangs up his tarboosh.

SHOPPING

In the new part of town, the place to head for all manner of locally crafted souvenirs is **Handicrafts Lane**, a small shaded alleyway adjoining the Takiyya as-Süleimaniyya Mosque, just south of Sharia Shoukri al-Quwatli. Off the lane is a Turkish madrassa, now a **handicraft market** (Map pp466-7), where the former student cells are occupied by traders and craftspeople happy to demonstrate their skills at engraving and painting.

The Old City is awash with souqs. Apart from the bustling **Souq al-Hamidiyya** (Map pp470-1), the main souq in the city and with a wonderful atmosphere, the tributary souqs are roughly demarcated into specialties, one handling clothes, another sweets and spices, another jewellery, yet another stationery items and so on.

For handicrafts, some of the better shops are those along Sharia Hanania in the far east of the Old City, or along Sharia Medhat Pasha (Straight St), east of the Roman arch.

One excellent place for antiques is **Dahdah Palace** (p472), with a range of artefacts recovered from demolished Damascene houses.

For a range of beautiful and highly original handcrafted boxes, visit **Ezrat al-Harastani** (Map pp470-1; ☎ 541 2602; Sharia al-Qaimariyya), just east of the Eastern Temple Gate.

If you're looking for the famous Damascene sweets to take back home, you could try the stalls selling individually wrapped nougat-and-pistachio items in **Souq al-Bzouriyya** (Map pp470–1), the **sweet shop** (Map pp470–1) on the corner of Sharia al-Kallaseh and Sharia Amara Jouw, or the **sweet shops** (Map pp470–1) on Martyrs' Sq, with great pyramids of baklava to choose from.

GETTING THERE & AWAY

Air

Several SyrianAir offices are scattered about the city centre; one convenient **office** (Map pp466-7; ☎ 245 0097/8) is on Saahat Hejaz, just opposite the train station.

Most of the other airline offices are grouped across from the Cham Palace Hotel on Sharia Maysaloun, or one block south on Sharia Fardous.

Bus & Microbus

There are two main bus stations in Damascus: Harasta Garage (*Karajat Harasta,* also known as Pullman Garage), offering Pullman bus services to the north and international services to Turkey; and Al-Samariyeh Garage *(Karajat al-Samariyeh),* which has services to the south (eg Bosra) and departures for Jordan and Lebanon. In addition there are several other minibus and microbus stations serving regional destinations.

HARASTA/PULLMAN GARAGE

Harasta/Pullman Garage (off Map pp466–7) is about 6km northeast of the city centre. All the big private bus companies have their offices here.

Al-Kadmous runs a 24-hour service to Aleppo every hour on the hour (S£160, five hours); to Deir ez-Zur (S£200, six hours, hourly from 6am to 2.30am); 14 buses to Homs (S£70, two hours, from 6.15am to 8.15pm); to Hama (S£90, 2½ hours, four daily); to Tartus (S£110, 3½ hours, hourly from 5.30am to 11pm); and to Palmyra (S£150, four hours, hourly from 6am to 2.30am).

Al-Ahliah has services to Aleppo (S£150, hourly between 6am and 8pm), and to Lattakia (S£150, 4½ hours, five daily).

If you're travelling to Turkey, Hatay has Pullman services to Antakya (S£300, eight hours) and İstanbul (S£1300, 36 hours), leaving at 10pm daily. JETT buses also travel to Antakya (S£500) and İstanbul (S£1600) at 10pm daily.

To get to Harasta, you can take a microbus (S£10) from outside the fruit-and-veg market on Sharia al-Ittihad, just near Al-Haramain and Al-Rabie Hotels. A taxi will cost around S£150 – insist the meter be turned on.

AL-SAMARIYEH GARAGE

For services to the south (ie Bosra) and international destinations like Amman and Beirut (but not Turkey; see above), head to the new **Al-Samariyeh Garage** (Mezzeh West; (off Map pp466–7) on the western outskirts of the city.

For Bosra (S£90, two hours), we recommend Damas Tours, with new air-con buses heading south every two hours from 8am to 10pm. Al-Muhib also runs buses south at exactly the same times and prices as Damas Tours.

Private bus companies have frequent services from Al-Samariyeh Garage to Beirut (S£340, 4½ hours), departing every hour or so between 7.30am and 6.30pm, plus several buses daily to Amman (S£600, four to seven hours depending on border formalities). There's no bus service from Damascus to Baalbek.

OTHER BUS STATIONS

Microbuses to Deraa (for the Jordanian border) leave from the **Deraa Garage** (*Karajat Deraa;* Map pp466–7) in the south of the city. You're much better off getting a Pullman bus from Al-Samariyeh Garage.

For Maalula (S£50, one hour) and Seidnayya (S£40, 40 minutes), head to **Maalula Garage** (*Karajat Maalula;* Map pp470–1), just east of Saahat Abbasseen. A taxi to Maalula Garage from the centre costs around S£80.

Service Taxi

The main service-taxi station is at Al-Samariyeh Garage. Taxis leave throughout the day and night for Amman (S£600, four to seven hours, depending on border formalities) and Irbid (S£400, 3½ to five hours) in Jordan, and Baalbek (S£400, 2½ hours) and Beirut (S£450, from four hours, depending on border formalities) in Lebanon.

Train

All trains depart from the **Khaddam train station** (☎ 888 8678), about 5km southwest of the centre. A taxi there should cost around S£100. There are four daily express services to Aleppo (1st/2nd class S£240/200, 4½ hours) with a slower overnight service (S£110/75, six hours). Most of the trains on this line are new and comfortable.

The lines from the historic Hejaz station were, after lengthy delays, being renovated at the time of research but work proceeds at a snail's pace. This will be the terminus of a new Damascus–Beirut railway line, as well as for the resumption of Damascus–Amman services that ceased in 2006.

GETTING AROUND

To/From the Airport

Damascus International Airport is 32km southeast of Damascus. In the arrivals hall, there's an ATM next to the Commercial Bank of Syria exchange booth, enabled for Cirrus, Maestro, Visa and MasterCard. The booth exchanges cash, but not travellers cheques. There's a 24-hour tourist info office, supplying free city maps, but don't expect the staff to be either there or awake in the wee small hours.

The airport bus service (S£50, 30 minutes, half-hourly between 6am and midnight) runs between the airport forecourt and the southwest corner of the otherwise-empty Baramke Garage. Look for the orange-and-white bus to the right as you exit the arrivals hall.

A taxi into the city centre, organised at the desk just outside the arrivals hall, costs around S£1000 to most city-centre hotels, more for a minivan. If you're taking a taxi from the centre to the airport, you should pay around S£700, but you'll have to negotiate hard; hotel-arranged taxis generally cost S£1000 to make the trip.

Car-rental companies like Hertz and Europcar have booths in the arrivals hall, but it's rare that we've seen anyone behind the desk.

Bus & Taxi

Damascus is well served with a local bus and microbus network, but as the centre is so compact, you'll rarely have to use it. A microbus ride within the city costs S£10.

All taxis are yellow and there are thousands of them. A ride within the centre of town should never cost more than S£50; make sure they use their meters.

AROUND DAMASCUS

The major attractions within an easy day trip from the capital include the outstanding Roman ruins at Bosra and the important Christian sites of Seidnayya and Maalula.

BOSRA بصرى

☎ **015 / pop 28,800**

The black-basalt town of Bosra, 137km from Damascus, is an easy day trip from the capital. Once the capital of the Roman province of Arabia, it's now something of a backwater. But what a weird and wonderful backwater it is. Bosra's gigantic Roman theatre is alone worth the trip here and the surrounding ruins are brooding and atmospheric.

Information

Exchange booth (🕒 8am-2pm & 4-6pm Sat-Thu) You can change cash here (if they're open), just southeast of the citadel; the Cham Palace Hotel *may* change travellers cheques.

Tourist office (🕒 9am-7pm) Southeast of the citadel. Staff are willing but resources (and English) are limited.

Sights

The **citadel** (adult/student S£150/10; 🕒 9am-6pm Mar-Nov, to 4pm Dec-Feb) is a unique construction – it began life as a massive Roman theatre and later had its fortifications grafted on. The theatre was built early in the 2nd century AD, when Bosra was the capital of the Roman province of Arabia. The first walls were built during the Umayyad and Abbasid periods, with further additions being made in the 11th century by the Fatimids.

The magnificent 15,000-seat **theatre** is a rarity among Roman theatres in that it is completely freestanding rather than built into the side of a hill. It's a wonderful experience to be lost in the dark, oppressive fortress halls and dimly lit vaulted corridors and then to emerge through a sunlit opening to find yourself suddenly looking down on a vast, steeply terraced hillside of stone seating.

Other sites located in the Old Town north of the citadel include the old **Roman baths**, a 4th-century **monastery**, a **cathedral** (c 512) with an unfortunate concrete roof in one corner, various monumental gates, partially reconstructed **colonnades** of basalt corridors, the **Roman market** in lighter sandstone with mosaic-floor remnants off its northwestern side, vast cisterns and the **Mosque of Omar**, which dates to the 12th century.

Sleeping & Eating

All of the restaurants that occupy the open square outside the citadel entrance serve similar set menus of Syrian staples for around S£350.

Restaurant 1001 Nights (☎ 795 331) This is a long-standing traveller favourite, run by local entrepreneur Obeida Mekdad, but there's not much to distinguish it from half a dozen places alongside. The advantage here, apart from the 25% discount for students, is that budget travellers may be able to unfurl a sleeping bag to stay overnight; there's a shower and toilet but you'll need your own sleeping bag. Single women may not feel comfortable doing this. There are no fixed prices for overnight stays, ask when you arrive. Meals from S£350.

Bosra Cham Palace (☎ 790 881; www.chamhotels.com; s/d US$125/145;) The Cham Palace, a few hundred metres south from the citadel entrance, is the only hotel in town. On offer are well-presented rooms, nice gardens, a large swimming pool and a licensed coffeehouse (snacks around S£200). The restaurant (three-course meal S£660) is popular with tour groups.

Getting There & Away

Damas Tours runs new air-con buses between Bosra and Damascus (S£90, two hours, every two hours from 8am to 10pm). Al-Muhib runs similar services at the same times. Both leave from Damascus's Al-Samariyeh Garage.

Minibuses run between Bosra and Deraa (S£25) between 4.30am and 4pm. These leave when full from the front of the tourist information office.

SEIDNAYYA صيدنايا

Perched spectacularly on an enormous rocky outcrop, the Greek Orthodox Convent of Our Lady of Seidnayya is one of the most important places of Christian pilgrimage in the Middle East, due to the presence of a portrait of the Virgin Mary purportedly painted by St Luke. All manner of miracles have been attributed to this icon; at the time of the Crusades, the Christians considered Seidnayya second in importance only to Jerusalem. Veneration of the icon is fervent, and it's fascinating to witness Muslim pilgrims as well as Christians. Most of the structure dates from the 19th century.

Ascend the four flights of stairs (or take the lift), duck through the low wooden doorway, then pass to the courtyard on the right. Just off the courtyard is the pilgrimage shrine containing the famed relic, in a small dark room lit by candles amid the murmuring of the prayers of the devout and an aura of the sacred. Before entering, remove your shoes and ensure you're modestly dressed. The Feast of Our Lady of Seidnayya is held on 8 September each year, and the spectacle is worth attending if you're in the area. The main celebrations begin on the night of the 7th.

Travellers generally visit Seidnayya on a day trip from Damascus. There are regular microbuses to Seidnayya (S£40, 40 minutes) from Maalula Garage in northeastern Damascus. It's possible to combine Seidnayya with a visit to Maalula, although public transport between the two is infrequent.

MAALULA معلولا

☎ 011 / pop 5000

In a narrow valley in the foothills of Jebel Libnan ash-Sharqiyya, Maalula is a picturesque village huddled beneath a sheer cliff. If arriving by minibus, alight at the main village intersection, where there's a traffic island and the road splits. Head right up the hill, and at the top head right again; the road switches back, climbing steeply to the small **Convent of St Thecla** (Deir Mar Teqla), tucked snugly against the cliff. From here there are pretty views of the village.

Thecla was a pupil of St Paul and one of the earliest Christian martyrs. As one legend has it, after being cornered against the cliff at Maalula by soldiers sent to execute her, Thecla prayed to God, lightning stuck the cliff and a cleft appeared in the rock face, facilitating her flight. The shrine, beneath a rocky overhang at the top of the convent, is the highlight of any visit here. Otherwise, the convent, a sanctuary for nuns and orphans, is of minor interest, but ahead lies the legendary escape route, **St Thecla Gap**. Cut through the rock by run-off from the plateau above the village, this nar-

THE LANGUAGE OF CHRIST

The mainly Greek Catholic village of Maalula is one of just three villages where Aramaic, the language of Jesus Christ, is still spoken – the other two, Jabadeen and Sarkha, are nearby although they're now predominantly Muslim. Aramaic was once widely spoken in the Middle East and is one of the oldest continually spoken languages in the world, reaching its zenith around 500 BC. It bears similarities to both Arabic and Hebrew. The number of speakers has been steadily dwindling and remains under threat, but interest in keeping the language alive has increased dramatically.

Pilgrims from all over the world can study religion in Aramaic at St Ephrem's Clerical Seminary, in Seidnayya, while the Syrian Government recently established an Institute for Aramaic, and new texts and language-learning materials are being written in the ancient language which was, until recently, an oral language only; many of Maalula's Aramaic speakers cannot write it. In Maalula's Monastery and Church of St Sergius, Aramaic is proudly alive and well. Local worshippers all speak Aramaic (although the 7.30am liturgy is conducted in Arabic because the service has a written base), accounting for around half of the world's Aramaic speakers.

The language is being kept alive by Maalula's Aramaic speakers, who pass it along to their children; classes in local schools are taught in Arabic. So was the Aramaic spoken in Mel Gibson's epic, *The Passion of the Christ,* accurate? Maalula's locals say that although they could understand some of the words, it was actually a dialect known as Syriac, which is much more widespread than Maalula's brand of Aramaic. Locals claim that theirs is the true language of Christ.

row, steep-sided ravine resembles a modest version of the famed siq at Petra.

At the end of the canyon, head to the left and follow the road for picturesque views of the village and valley, and the Byzantine **Monastery and Church of St Sergius** (Deir Mar Sarkis or Convent of Sts Serge & Bacchus). Built in AD 325, it's one of the oldest churches in the world. According to legend, Sergius (Sarkis) was a Roman legionary who, after converting to Christianity and refusing to make sacrifices to the god Jupiter, was executed. The low wooden doorway leading into the monastery is over 2000 years old; however, the highlight is the small church itself, which still incorporates features of the pagan temple that previously stood here. The splendid collection of icons includes some 17th-century gems.

The hillside south of the church is riddled with small caverns that archaeologists believe were inhabited by prehistoric man some 50,000 to 60,000 years ago. This road loops back to the village, where it's possible to catch a minibus back to Damascus.

Sleeping & Eating

As Maalula is an easy half-day trip from Damascus, there's no need to stay overnight unless you want to attend the Festival of the Cross (13 September) or the St Thecla Festival (24 September). It's possible to stay overnight in simple rooms at the Convent of St Thecla, where there are no fixed rates; make a generous donation instead.

Maaloula Hotel (☎ 777 0250; maaloula@scs-net.org; s/d US$95/111; ✖ ❄) This comfortable four-star hotel offers clean, spacious rooms, and full amenities include a good restaurant serving Syrian and European food, and a coffeehouse and bar on its cliff-top perch.

La Grotta (☎ 777 0909; snacks from S£150) Adjacent to the Monastery and Church of St Sergius, this sparkling clean café in a light-filled stone building serves up excellent pizza, sandwiches, ice cream, cold beer and drinks.

Getting There & Away

From Damascus, minibuses (S£50, one hour) depart from Maalula Garage. In Maalula, buses stop at the main intersection in the village centre, just downhill from the Convent of St Thecla.

HOMS حمص

☎ 031 / pop 1.6 million

There's little of interest in Homs, although it does have an interesting old souq and an agreeable atmosphere. That said, for most travellers, it's one of those crossroads towns that you'll have to pass through at some stage, if only to change transport. Roads head north to Hama and Aleppo, east to

Palmyra and the Euphrates, south to Damascus and west to Tartus and the coast.

INFORMATION

There's no shortage of ATMs in Homs. For internet, **Messenger** (Sharia Tarablus; per hr S£50; ⌚ 24hr) is excellent. The **post office** (Sharia Abdel Moniem Riad) is about 200m north of the clock-tower roundabout, while the **telephone office** (Sharia Shoukri al-Quwatli; ⌚ 8am-8pm Sat-Thu, to 1pm Fri) is just east of the clock-tower roundabout.

SIGHTS

The only building of great note is the **Khaled ibn al-Walid Mosque**, on the Hama road, about 600m north of the town centre. Behind its black-stone facade and beneath its silver dome lies the tomb of the commander of the Muslim armies that brought Islam to Syria in AD 636.

Homs' restored old **souq**, with its grey stones, vaulted ceilings and elegant white lamp posts, is one of Syria's most attractive. Southeast of the souq, Homs' Christian Quarter is one of Syria's most welcoming and relaxed.

SLEEPING & EATING

An-Nasr al-Jedid Hotel (☎ 5227 423; Sharia Shoukri al-Quwatli; s/d S£250/450) Entered from a side street just off Sharia al-Quwatli, this is about the best of the budget places in town, but that's not saying much. It's grubby and has very uncomfortable beds, but the sheets are relatively clean and one of the showers along the corridor can sometimes be cranked up to give out some hot water (S£50 per shower). It is, however, set in a beautiful hundred-year-old building.

Lord Suites Hotel (☎ 5247 4008; www.lordsuiteshotel.com; Saahat Al Saa al-Jadida; s/d/tr US$50/70/100; ❄) This is a spotlessly clean, modern place and an excellent midrange choice. The rooms, which are actually one-, two- and three-bedroom suites, are enormous. Rooms come with fridge and satellite TV. Ask about discounts in winter.

Blue Stone (☎ 5245 9999; meals S£350; ⌚ 9am-late) In a big, greystone building looking out onto the street, this is the most happening bar-café-restaurant in the Christian Quarter. It positively hums in the evenings with the chatter of flirty young couples gazing into each other's eyes, same-sex groups of friends comparing rings (girls) and ring tones (boys), and families tucking into pizzas, pastas and big bowls of salad. It's on the corner of Sharias al-Jibawi and Qasr ash-Sheikh.

GETTING THERE & AWAY

There are two bus stations: the new 'hob-hob' minibus station, about 8km south of the city centre on the Damascus road; and the main 'luxury' bus station *(Karajat Pullman)*, about 2.5km northeast of the city on the Hama road. To get between town and the main bus station costs around S£40; between town and the microbus station costs up to S£60.

From the Pullman Garage, Al-Ahliah and Al-Kadmous have the most frequent departures, including at least hourly to Damascus (S£130, two hours) and Aleppo (S£140, 2½ hours). Other, less-regular departures include Tartus (S£70, one hour), Lattakia (S£180, 3½ hours) and Palmyra (S£135, two hours). Buses go to Hama (S£35, 30 minutes, half hourly).

Bright, new minibuses flit in and out of the 'hob-hob' bus station, most of them going to Hama (S£35, 45 minutes). They depart when full and you can generally turn up at any time, climb straight in, and expect to be away in less than 10 minutes.

See p490 for details of getting to Crac des Chevaliers.

HAMA حماه

☎ 033 / pop 1.6 million

The serenade of Hama's creaking ancient wooden *norias* (water wheels) is famous throughout the Middle East, and makes this attractive, though conservative, town one of the country's tourism hot spots. Hama also has terrific accommodation, which makes it the perfect base for visiting Crac des Chevaliers, Apamea and other sights in the area.

INFORMATION

Internet Access

Happy Net (☎ 216 057; per hr S£50; ⌚ 24hr) At the back of the Noria Hotel, off Sharia Shoukri al-Quwatli, this place has good connections.

Space Net (Sharia Abu al-Feda; per hr S£60; ⌚ 24hr) Free tea and fast connections.

Money

There are ATMs all over Hama, with at least three along Sharia Shoukri al-Quwatli. Two

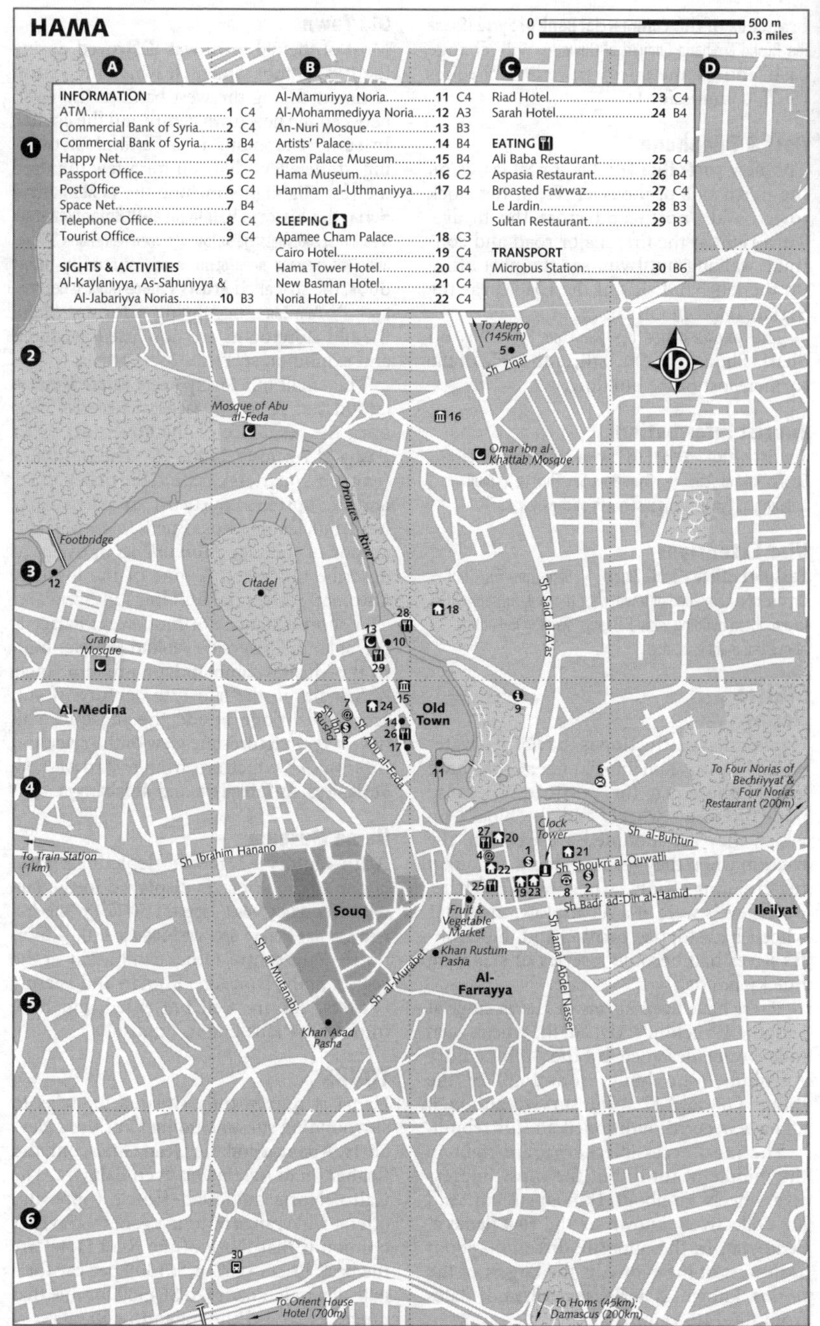
HAMA
0 500 m
0 0.3 miles
INFORMATION
ATM 1 C4
Commercial Bank of Syria 2 C4
Commercial Bank of Syria 3 B4
Happy Net 4 C4
Passport Office 5 C2
Post Office 6 C4
Space Net 7 B4
Telephone Office 8 C4
Tourist Office 9 C4
SIGHTS & ACTIVITIES
Al-Kaylaniyya, As-Sahuniyya & Al-Jabariyya Norias 10 B3
Al-Mamuriyya Noria 11 C4
Al-Mohammediyya Noria 12 A3
An-Nuri Mosque 13 B3
Artists' Palace 14 B4
Azem Palace Museum 15 B4
Hama Museum 16 C2
Hammam al-Uthmaniyya 17 B4
SLEEPING
Apamee Cham Palace 18 C3
Cairo Hotel 19 C4
Hama Tower Hotel 20 C4
New Basman Hotel 21 C4
Noria Hotel 22 C4
Riad Hotel 23 C4
Sarah Hotel 24 B4
EATING
Ali Baba Restaurant 25 C4
Aspasia Restaurant 26 B4
Broasted Fawwaz 27 C4
Le Jardin 28 B3
Sultan Restaurant 29 B3
TRANSPORT
Microbus Station 30 B6
To Aleppo (145km)
Sh Ziqar
Mosque of Abu al-Feda
Omar ibn al-Khattab Mosque
Orontes River
Footbridge
Citadel
Grand Mosque
Al-Medina
Sh Said al-A'as
Sh Ibn Rushd
Sh Abu al-Feda
Old Town
To Four Norias of Bechriyyat & Four Norias Restaurant (200m)
Clock Tower
Sh al-Buhturi
To Train Station (1km)
Sh Ibrahim Hanano
Sh Shoukri al-Quwatli
Sh Badr ad-Din al-Hamid
Ileilyat
Souq
Fruit & Vegetable Market
Khan Rustum Pasha
Sh al-Mutanabi
Sh al-Murabet
Al-Farrayya
Sh Jamal Abdel Nasser
Khan Asad Pasha
To Orient House Hotel (700m)
To Homs (45km); Damascus (200km)

branches of the **Commercial Bank of Syria** (Sharia ibn Rushd & Sharia Shoukri al-Quwatli) will change cash and (sometimes) travellers cheques (S£25 commission).

Post & Telephone

The new **post office** (8am-2pm Sat-Thu) is on the north side of the river. From the clock tower, walk north and cross the bridge. Turn right at the first major road and continue walking until you see the post office on the left-hand side of the road, near the Syrian Telecom Office.

The **phone office** (8am-7pm Sat-Thu) is off Sharia Shoukri al-Quwatli, at the side of the former post office building.

Tourist Information

Tourist office (☎ 511 033; www.syriatourism.org; Sharia Said al-A'as; 8am-8pm Sat-Thu) In a small building in the gardens just north of the river.

Visa Extensions

Passport office (Sharia Ziqar; 8am-2pm Sun-Thu) On the northern edge of town, near the new museum. It's in a modern building with 'Passport' written in English above the main entrance.

SIGHTS

Norias

Hama's main attraction is the *norias* (water wheels up to 20m in diameter) that have graced the town for centuries. Because both the water wheels and the blocks on which they are mounted are wooden, the friction when they turn produces a mournful groaning. Sadly, when we were here, water levels were at a record low, the water wheels had stopped turning and the Orontes River had become a series of stagnant, mucky ponds.

There have been *norias* in Hama since at least the 4th century AD, but the wheels seen today were designed by the 13th-century Ayyubids, who built around 30 of the things. Of these, 17 *norias* survive, although all have been reconditioned and/or rebuilt.

The most accessible *norias* are right in the middle of town, but the most impressive wheels lie about 1km upstream, and are collectively known as the **Four Norias of Bechriyyat**. In the opposite direction, about 1km west of the centre, is the largest of the *norias*, known as **Al-Mohammediyya**. It dates from the 14th century.

Old Town

Most of the old town was destroyed during the 1982 bombardment, leaving only a small remnant edging the west bank of the river, between the new town centre and the citadel. In sum, it amounts to a handful of twisting, stone alleys that run for a few hundred metres. Highlights include the **Al-Mamuriyya Noria**, the historic **Hammam al-Uthmaniyya** (bath & sauna S£200, massage S£150; men 8am-noon & 7pm-midnight, women noon-6pm) and, virtually next door, the so-called **Artists' Palace** (Ateliers des Peintures; 8am-3pm), occupying a former khan; the old storerooms are now used as studio and exhibition space for local artists.

The small but lovely **Azem Palace Museum** (adult/student S£75/5; 8am-3pm Wed-Mon) was once the residence of the governor, As'ad Pasha al-Azem (r 1700–42). The *haramlek* (women's quarters), behind the ticket office, and the upstairs courtyard are particularly beautiful, leading Ross Burns, historian and author of the sage *Monuments of Syria*, to describe this place as 'one of the loveliest Ottoman residential buildings in Syria'.

A short distance north of Azem Palace is the splendid riverside **An-Nuri Mosque**, built by the Muslim commander Nureddin, uncle of Saladin, in the late 12th century. If you cross the bridge beside the mosque, you have a very picturesque view of the river and three *norias*, which are, from east to west, **Al-Kaylaniyya**, **As-Sahuniyya** and **Al-Jabariyya**.

Hama Museum

A 4th-century-AD mosaic depicting a *noria* is one of the artefacts displayed in the **museum** (Sharia Ziqar; adult/student S£150/10; 9am-4pm Wed-Sun Nov-Mar, to 6pm Wed-Sun Apr-Oct), 1.5km north of the centre. Other exhibits cover the region in the Iron Age, Roman and Islamic periods. All are well presented and have informative labelling in English.

TOURS

Hama is conveniently situated for trips to surrounding sites including Crac des Chevaliers, Apamea and the Dead Cities, but also further on to Rasafa and even Palmyra. The Cairo, Noria and Riad Hotels (opposite) offer a wide range of tours; general traveller opinion is that those of the Riad Hotel are the best. Prices start at S£1300 per car for a half-day tour, and up to S£4500 for one that ranges as far as Palmyra and/or Rasafa.

EXCURSIONS FROM HAMA

You could easily spend a week exploring the attractions around Hama. Apart from the iconic sites of Crac des Chevaliers (p488), Apamea (p490), the Dead Cities (p503) and even Rasafa (p518), other popular excursions include: the beehive-house villages of **Sarouj**, **Twalid Dabaghein** and **Sheikh al-Hillal** (northeast of Hama); the lonely hilltop ruins of **Qala'at ash-Shmemis** (southeast); the temple ruins high in the Jebel Ansariyya at **Hosn Suleiman** (southwest); the solid castle of **Musayf** (west); the Byzantine ruins of **Qasr ibn Wardan** (northeast); and the extraordinary, recently unearthed mosaic fragment at **Tibetl'Imam** (north).

If you prefer to organise the trip yourself, one driver we recommend is **Abdurrahman Al-Asad** (☎ 0944 239 704), who charges S£1500 per car for a trip just to the Crac and up to US$60 for a full-day journey ranging further afield.

SLEEPING

Hama has some of the best accommodation in Syria.

Budget

our pick **Riad Hotel** (☎ 239 512; www.syriaphotoguide.com/riadhotel; Sharia Shoukri al-Quwatli; mattress on roof/dm S£150/200, s/d/tr from S£400/600/900, s/d without bathroom S£300/500; ❄ 💻) Wow! Freshly painted, large and extremely clean rooms have satellite TV and good beds; most have private bathrooms and those with shared bathrooms have one bathroom per two rooms. Some rooms have balconies onto the street and comfortable seating; others have queen-sized beds. Abdullah, your host, is friendly, knowledgeable and even has a decent Aussie accent. With a kitchen and ADSL internet (S£100 per hour) for guests at reception, it all adds up to one of Syria's best budget hotels. Breakfast costs S£100/150 (student/nonstudent).

Cairo Hotel (☎ 222 280; cairohot@aloola.sy; Sharia Shoukri al-Quwatli; mattress on the roof S£150, dm S£250, s/d S£550/700; ❄ 💻) The Cairo is also hugely popular with budget travellers and deservedly so. The rooms here are generally as good as those at the Riad and all come with private bathrooms, satellite TV and comfortable beds. Breakfast costs S£125 for travellers staying in dorm rooms or on the roof, free for others. There's internet (S£75 per hour) at reception and staff are friendly and knowledgeable.

Sarah Hotel (☎ 515 941; fax 217 240; s/d S£850/1100) Though it only opened in 2000, this place in the city's old quarter, off Sharia Abu al-Feda, isn't wearing too well: the rooms are a little tatty and the staff aren't very used to seeing Western travellers. Rooms are clean, quiet and light, with satellite TV. Breakfast costs S£150.

Midrange

New Basman Hotel (☎ 224 838; riadhotel@scs-net.org; Sharia Shoukri al-Quwatli; s/d US$20/30; ❄) After a recent overhaul by the owners of the Riad Hotel, this once down-at-heel place shines with enormous rooms, good bathrooms and a good central location.

Hama Tower Hotel (☎ 226 864; fax 521 523; s/d US$30/35; ❄) The rooms here are nothing special (they're fine, if a little tired), but the views from the north-facing 10th- and 11th-floor rooms are spectacular, looking out over the old town, the Al-Mamuriyya Noria and the citadel. If you get a south-facing room, it's probably not worth it, but staff assured us that foreign tourists are always given priority with these rooms. The hotel is off Sharia Shoukri al-Quwatli.

Noria Hotel (☎ 512 414; www.noria-hotel.com; older s/d US$30/40, new s/d/ste US$40/50/100; ❄) The older section of this two-star, 4th-floor hotel has spacious, clean and comfortable rooms, although beware the windowless ones, which are quieter but a tad claustrophobic. Rooms in the new section sparkle and are of a standard better than many four-star Syrian hotels – there are plans for the older rooms to undergo a similar overhaul. The stunning corner suite has a hydromassage bath, pleasing decor and views of the old town. Service is excellent and credit cards are accepted. Situated in the small streets between Sharia Shoukri al-Quwatli and the river.

Top End

Orient House Hotel (☎ 225 599; Sharia al-Jalaa; s/d/ste US$65/85/110; ❄) In a splendid, restored 18th-century building, with beautifully decorated ceilings, oriental lamps and a big, central, light-filled courtyard, this is Hama's most atmospheric accommodation. There's a new extension, so ask for one of the rooms in the Ottoman-era building. Rooms are well equipped with TV and fridge, and there's a good restaurant on site. The only downside is the location, at least a 20-minute walk from the centre; take a taxi.

Apamee Cham Palace (☎ 525 335; www.chamhotels.com; s/d US$110/130 plus tax 11%;) With a winning location just across the river from the old town, luxury rooms, tennis courts and a large swimming pool area, this five-star place is easy to recommend. Breakfast costs US$6 and credit cards are accepted.

EATING

Broasted Fawwaz (☎ 223 884; meals S£140; 8am-late) This long-standing favourite, off Sharia al-Buhturi, is known for its delicious hot chickens and freshly fried potato crisps with garlic sauce.

Le Jardin (☎ 525 335; Sharia abi Nawas; meals S£400; 4pm-late) Overlooking the splendid An-Nuri Mosque, river and water wheels, and serving alcohol, this leafy, terrace café-restaurant is a wonderful place to while away a few hours puffing on a nargileh (S£150). Local families love it here, and on weekends fill their tables with plates of mezze and kebabs.

Four Norias (Sharia al-Buhturi; meals S£400; 9am-late) On the banks of the river beside the *norias*, around 500m east of the centre, this large open-air terrace restaurant is popular with families and gets lively on summer evenings. There's a long list of mezze and kebabs, and costumed boys serving nargileh. No alcohol.

our pick **Aspasia Restaurant** (☎ 522 288; www.aspasia-hama.com; meals S£500; noon-midnight) Hama's best restaurant occupies a splendid, open-stone courtyard in the old town, but it's not just about atmosphere here. The food is delicious with an extensive menu that encompasses the usual range of mezze, as well as Western and local mains. The service is impeccable and there's an upstairs terrace that opens 6pm nightly for the tea-and-nargileh crowd, although the views are limited. No alcohol.

In the couple of blocks along Sharia Shoukri al-Quwatli and its side streets, there are a number of cheap felafel, shwarma, kebab and chicken restaurants. We highly recommend the excellent felafels at **Ali Baba Restaurant** (Sharia Shoukri al-Quwatli; felafel S£25; 10am-late).

Check to see if the Sultan Restaurant, in a lovely waterside stone building in the old town, has reopened after renovations. It used to be one of our favourite eating spots in Hama. To get here, pass through the low, vaulted tunnel beside the An-Nuri Mosque.

GETTING THERE & AWAY

The Pullman Garage is a 20-minute walk (or S£40 taxi ride) southwest of the town centre, just beyond the minibus station. The microbus station is on the same road, slightly closer to town. Minibuses from the town centre to the bus station (S£5) leave from the clock tower and run between 7.30am and 10pm.

Al-Ahliah and Al-Kadmous have the most frequent departures from Pullman Garage, with regular services to Damascus (S£150, 2½ hours) via Homs (S£35, 30 minutes) and Aleppo (S£105, 2½ hours). Al-Ahliah has four daily services to Lattakia (S£180, 3½ hours) via Homs and Tartus. Al-Kadmous also has four daily buses to Deir ez-Zur (S£315) via Homs and Palmyra (S£150).

Microbuses travel to Homs (S£30) every 10 minutes from 7am to 10pm, but you're much better off paying the little bit extra to travel with one of the luxury bus companies. Microbuses also travel to Suqeilibiyya (for Apamea) when full (S£30).

CRAC DES CHEVALIERS قلعة الحصن

☎ 031

Author Paul Theroux described Crac des Chevaliers as the epitome of the dream castle of childhood fantasies. TE Lawrence simply called it 'the finest castle in the world'. Impervious to the onslaught of time, Crac des Chevaliers (in Arabic Qala'at al-Hosn) is one of Syria's must-see sights. It was added to Unesco's World Heritage list in 2006.

HISTORY

The castle watches over the only significant break in the Jebel Ansariyya. Anyone who held this breach, known as the Homs Gap, between the southern end of the range and the northern outreaches of the Jebel Libnan ash-Sharqiyya (Anti-Lebanon Range), was virtually assured authority over inland Syria.

The first fortress known to have existed on this site was built by the emir of Homs in 1031, but it was the Crusader knights who, around the middle of the 12th century, largely built and expanded Crac into its existing form. Despite repeated attacks and sieges, including one led by Saladin, the castle held firm. In fact, it was never truly breached; the Crusaders just gave it up.

When the Mamluk sultan Beybars marched on the castle in 1271, the knights at Crac des Chevaliers were a last outpost. Jerusalem had been lost and the Christians were retreating. Numbers inside the castle, built to hold a garrison of 2000, were depleted to around 200. Even though they had supplies to last for five years, Crac des Chevaliers must have seemed more like a prison than a stronghold. Surrounded by the armies of Islam and with no hope of reprieve, the Crusaders departed after a month, having negotiated safe conduct to head to Tripoli.

SIGHTS

The remarkably well preserved **castle** (adult/student S£150/10; 9am-6pm Apr-Oct, to 4pm Nov-Mar) comprises two distinct parts: the outside wall with its 13 towers and main entrance; and the inside wall and central construction, built on a rocky platform. A **moat** dug out of the rock separates the two walls.

A suggested route for exploration is to walk from the main entrance up the sloping ramp and out to the moat. Visit the **baths**, which you can get down to by a couple of dogleg staircases over in the corner on your left, then move on to the **great hall**, which was also used as stables, from where you gain access to the three towers that punctuate the southern wall.

Continue around the wall and enter the **inner fortress** through the tower at the top of the access ramp into an open **courtyard**. The **loggia**, with its Gothic facade, on the western side of the yard, is the single most impressive structure in the castle, its delicate ceiling offering relief from the otherwise formidable aesthetic elsewhere.

Opposite the loggia is a **chapel** that was converted to a mosque after the Muslim conquest (the minbar, or pulpit, still remains). The staircase that obstructs the main door is a later addition and leads to the upper floors of the fortress. From here, you can climb to the round tower in the

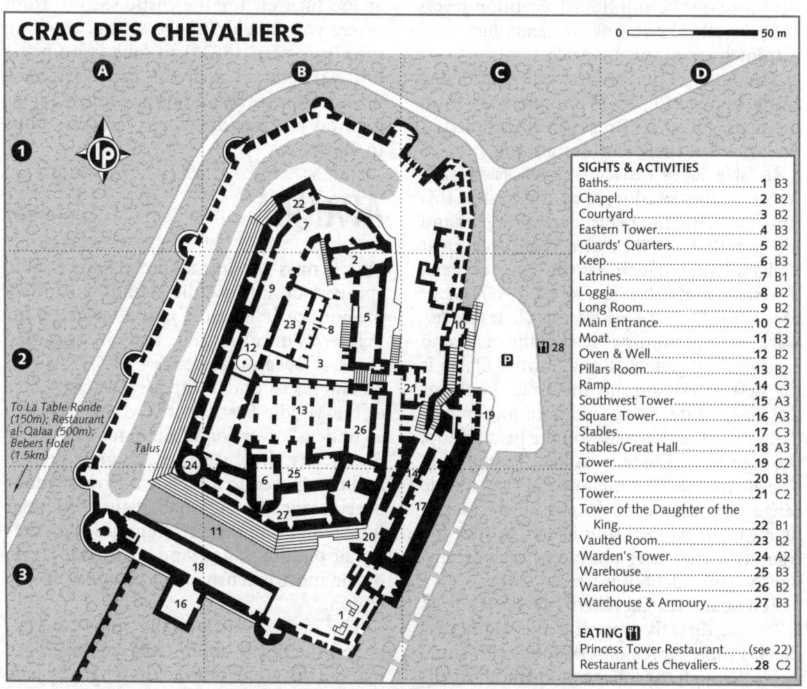

southwest corner, which is known as the **Warden's Tower** – on a clear day there are magnificent views from the roof.

After visiting the castle, drive or walk north from the entrance and follow the paved road that circles the castle perimeter and then climbs up to Restaurant al-Qalaa (below), from where you'll have the iconic, panoramic views of the castle that drew you here in the first place. It's about a 15-minute walk from the castle entrance.

SLEEPING & EATING

Crac des Chevaliers is just an hour or so from Tartus, Homs or even Hama, so most people visit on a day trip. Then again, a view of the Crac when you wake up is one the most romantic hotel views in Syria and possible if you stay at the Beibars Hotel.

Beibars Hotel (☎/fax 734 1201; akrambibars@mail.sy; Sharia Okbah Ben Nafee; s/d with view US$25/35, with view from balcony US$20/25; ❄) This comfortable hotel has stunning, sweeping views of the castle just across the valley. All rooms have views, although in the cheaper rooms you need to go onto the balcony to see the castle; those on the top floor (reception level) are the best. The rooms are clean, light and extremely good for the price.

The hotel is on the first hill west of the castle, about a 20- to 25-minute walk from the main entrance. Breakfast is included in the price but there's no restaurant.

La Table Ronde (☎ 740 280; meals around S£250) About 150m southwest of the castle, this run-down, mediocre place serves meals and it's here that you'll be directed if staying at Beibars Hotel, which has the same owners.

Restaurant al-Qalaa (☎ 734 1435, 0933 874 692; set menu S£300-350; 🕑 8.30am-10pm Apr-Oct, to 6pm Nov-Mar) Boasting stunning views of the castle and surrounding valleys, Restaurant al-Qalaa is the best eatery around the Crac. Look for the lone, white, two-storey building immediately west of the castle, on the next hilltop; the sign outside reads 'Alklaa Restaurant'. The all-you-can-eat menu comprises a wide range of mezze as well as grilled chicken or meat. In winter, ring ahead so that the friendly owner-chef can cater lunch or dinner for you. Alcohol is served.

Restaurant Les Chevaliers (☎ 740 411; meals S£300-350), directly opposite the main castle entrance, serves up OK food with some views through the foliage of the modern village of Hosn and surrounding valleys (but not the castle).

The **Princess Tower Restaurant** (meals S£300), in the castle's northwestern corner, serves mezze, grills and drinks. The setting is better than the food, although the latter is better than it used to be after a change of management.

GETTING THERE & AWAY

Crac des Chevaliers lies approximately 12km north of the Homs–Tartus highway. The castle is on the crest of the hill, perched above the village of Hosn.

Coming from Damascus or Hama, it's necessary to change buses in Homs. Buses from Homs to Crac des Chevaliers (S£40, 1½ hours) leave every hour on the hour; the last bus returning to Homs departs from the castle at 5.30pm in summer or 2.30pm in winter. Most hotels in Hama run organised tours to the castle (see p486); if you're just going to Crac des Chevaliers and back to Hama, expect to pay S£1300 to S£1500 per car.

From Tartus, catch a Homs microbus. You'll be dropped off on the main highway at the turn-off for the castle (S£35), from where you shouldn't have to wait too long for a microbus (S£35) to take you up the hill. To return, catch the microbus back down to the junction on the Homs–Tartus highway and flag down a passing microbus to Tartus.

APAMEA أفاميا

Don't miss Apamea (note that Arabic speakers do not use the sound 'p', so they pronounce it 'Afamia'). If it weren't for Palmyra's unsurpassable magnificence, the ruins of **Apamea** (adult/student S£150/10) would be famous as one of the great ancient sites of the Middle East. As it is, Apamea is like a condensed version of the pink-sandstone desert city, but executed in grey granite and transposed to a high, wild grassy moor overlooking the Al-Ghab Plain. Although little remains of the city's temples and other public buildings, its grand colonnade is one of the most extensive and beautiful in the region.

The main feature of the ruins of Apamea is the north–south **cardo** (main street), marked out along much of its length by parallel colonnades. At 2km, Apamea's cardo is longer than the one at Palmyra. Many of its columns, originally erected in the 2nd century AD, bear unusual carved designs and some have twisted fluting, a feature unique to Apamea. Visitors to this site as recently as 50 years ago would have seen nothing of this; in what's termed 'reconstructive archaeology', the columns have been recovered from where they once lay, scattered and overgrown with weeds, and have been re-erected by a Belgian team that's been working here since the 1930s.

North of the main junction, parts of the cardo still retain its original paving, visibly rutted by the wear of chariot wheels. The other monuments, such as the **nymphaeum** (monumental fountain) and **agora** (forum), require considerable imagination. There are ticket offices at both ends of the cardo.

Microbuses (S£40, 40 minutes) and minibuses (S£30, 40 minutes) regularly run the 45km from Hama to the village of Suqeilibiyya, where it's necessary to change to a microbus for Qala'at al-Mudiq (S£30, 10 minutes), the hilltop village adjacent to Apamea. The whole trip takes about an hour, except on Friday, when you can wait ages for a connection.

It's also possible to arrange a car and driver in either Aleppo (see p498; a day trip could be combined with a trip to the Dead Cities and even Qala'at Samaan) or Hama (p486).

ALEPPO

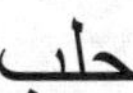

☎ 021 / pop 4.2 million

The Old City of Aleppo (Haleb in Arabic) can seem like an evocation of *The Thousand and One Nights*, and once lost in Aleppo's magical and labyrinthine souqs, you won't want to be found. But Aleppo has so much more, with the lovely and predominantly Christian district of Al-Jdeida, and it's here and in the Old City that you find some of Syria's best restaurants and boutique hotels. The city is outwardly more conservative than many of Syria's other cities (you'll see more women wearing the chador than elsewhere), but beneath the surface there are plenty of friendly fun-loving locals keen to introduce travellers to the city's many charms.

HISTORY

Written archives from the ancient kingdom of Mari indicate that Aleppo was already the centre of a powerful state as long ago as the 18th century BC, and the site may have been continuously inhabited for the past 8000 years. Its pre-eminent role in Syria came to an end with the Hittite invasions of the 17th and 16th centuries BC, and the city appears to have fallen into obscurity thereafter.

With the fall of Palmyra to the Romans, Aleppo became the major commercial link between the Mediterranean Sea and Asia. The town was destroyed by the Persians in AD 611 and fell easily to the Muslims later during their invasion in 637. The Byzantines overwhelmed the town in 961 and again in 968, but they could not take the citadel.

Three disastrous earthquakes also shook the town in the 10th century and Nureddin (Nur ad-Din) subsequently rebuilt the town and fortress. In 1124 the Crusaders under Baldwin laid siege to the town. After raids by the Mongols in 1260 and 1401, in which Aleppo was all but emptied of its population, the city finally came into the Ottoman Turkish orbit in 1516.

It prospered greatly until an earthquake in 1822 killed over 60% of the inhabitants and wrecked many buildings, including the citadel. The flood of cheap goods from Europe in the wake of the Industrial Revolution, and the increasing use of alternative trading routes, slowly killed off a lot of Aleppo's trade and manufacturing industry.

ORIENTATION

There are three main areas of Aleppo where you'll spend most of your time, and all are within a short walk of each other. Most of Aleppo's cheap hotels are clustered in the new city, a compact zone centred on Sharias al-Quwatli and al-Baron; restaurants, the National Museum and moneychangers are also here.

To the southeast are the citadel and the Old City with its souqs and two hotels, while northeast of the centre are the main Christian quarters including the charming cobbled Al-Jdeida district, where you'll find the best restaurants and numerous midrange hotels.

ALEPPO: NEW CITY

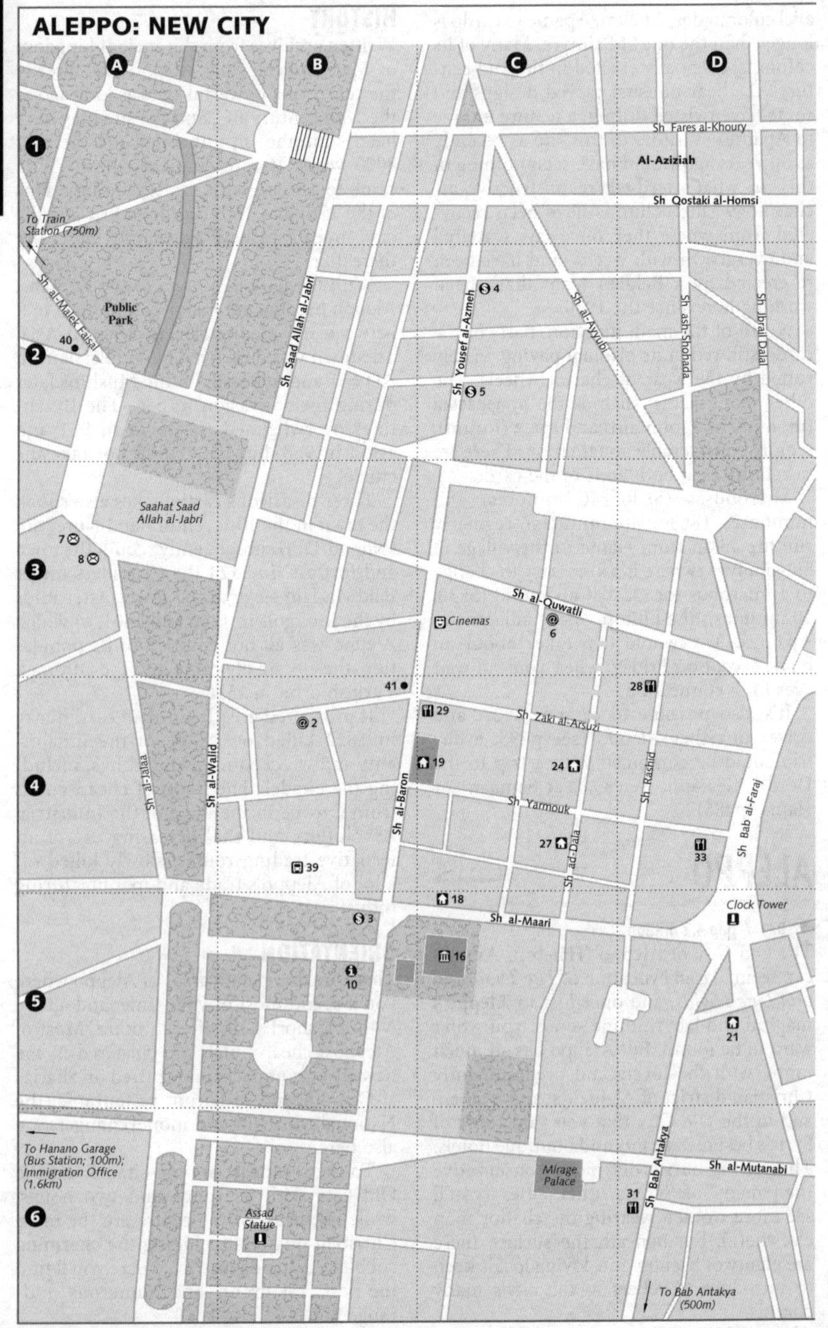

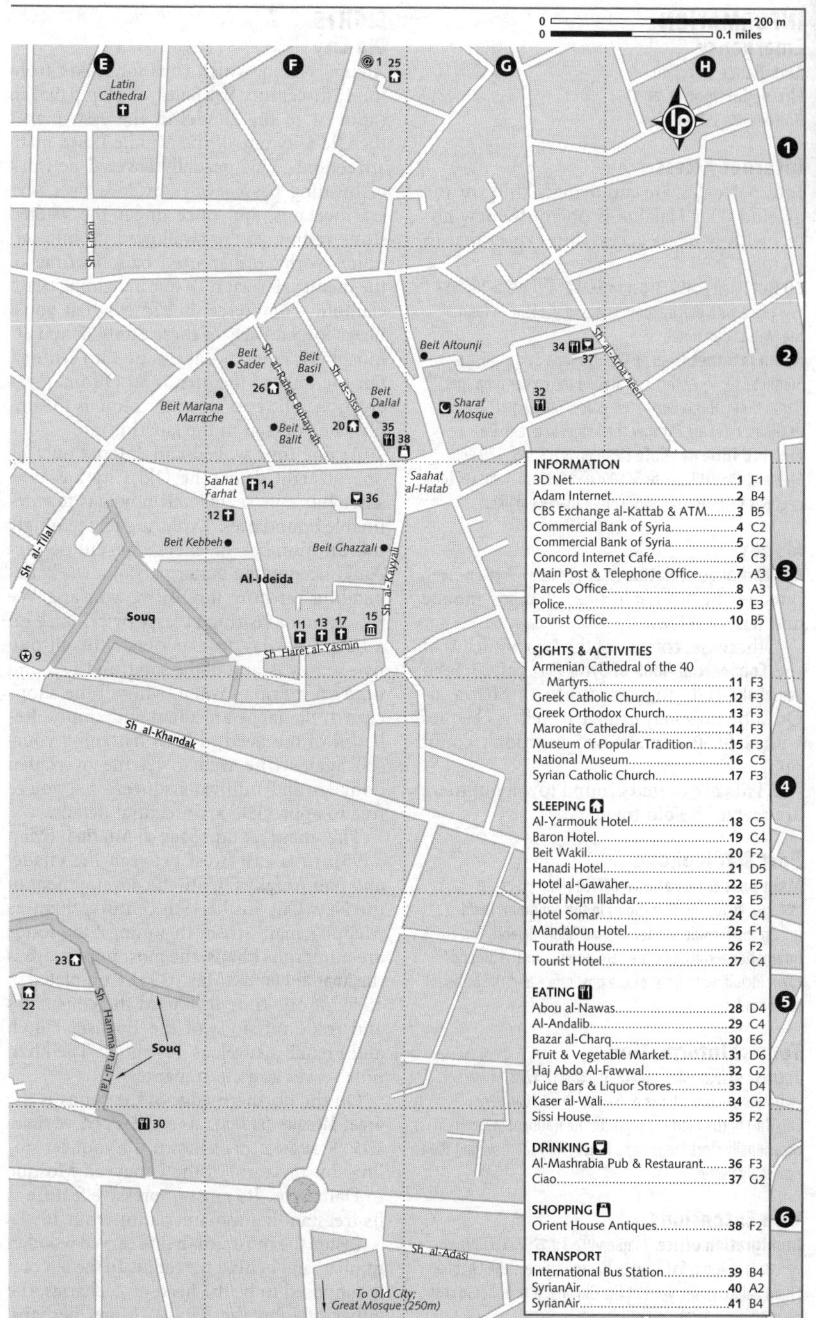
0 200 m
0 0.1 miles
Latin Cathedral
Sh Litani
Beit Sader
Beit Basil
Sh al-Raheb Buhayrah
Sh as-Sissi
Beit Dallal
Beit Altounji
Sharaf Mosque
Sh al-Arba'aeen
Beit Mariana Marrache
Beit Balit
Saahat Farhat
Saahat al-Hatab
Beit Kebbeh
Beit Ghazzali
Sh al-Kayyali
Al-Jdeida
Souq
Sh al-Tilal
Sh Haret al-Yasmin
Sh al-Khandak
Sh Hammam al-Tal
Souq
Sh al-Adasi
To Old City; Great Mosque (250m)
INFORMATION
3D Net 1 F1
Adam Internet 2 B4
CBS Exchange al-Kattab & ATM 3 B5
Commercial Bank of Syria 4 C2
Commercial Bank of Syria 5 C2
Concord Internet Café 6 C3
Main Post & Telephone Office 7 A3
Parcels Office 8 A3
Police 9 E3
Tourist Office 10 B5
SIGHTS & ACTIVITIES
Armenian Cathedral of the 40 Martyrs 11 F3
Greek Catholic Church 12 F3
Greek Orthodox Church 13 F3
Maronite Cathedral 14 F3
Museum of Popular Tradition 15 F3
National Museum 16 C5
Syrian Catholic Church 17 F3
SLEEPING
Al-Yarmouk Hotel 18 C5
Baron Hotel 19 C4
Beit Wakil 20 F2
Hanadi Hotel 21 D5
Hotel al-Gawaher 22 E5
Hotel Nejm Illahdar 23 E5
Hotel Somar 24 C4
Mandaloun Hotel 25 F1
Tourath House 26 F2
Tourist Hotel 27 C4
EATING
Abou al-Nawas 28 D4
Al-Andalib 29 C4
Bazar al-Charq 30 E6
Fruit & Vegetable Market 31 D6
Haj Abdo Al-Fawwal 32 G2
Juice Bars & Liquor Stores 33 D4
Kaser al-Wali 34 G2
Sissi House 35 F2
DRINKING
Al-Mashrabia Pub & Restaurant 36 F3
Ciao 37 G2
SHOPPING
Orient House Antiques 38 F2
TRANSPORT
International Bus Station 39 B4
SyrianAir 40 A2
SyrianAir 41 B4

INFORMATION

Emergency

Ambulance (☎ 110)
Fire department (☎ 113)
Police (☎ 362 4300)

Internet Access

Internet cafés are annoyingly thin on the ground. Dar Halabia is one of the few hotels with wireless access, but expect that to change.

3D Net (Map pp492-3; per hr S£100; 🕑 10am-10pm) A tiny place with patchy connections in the lane in front of the Mandaloun Hotel.

Adam Internet (Map pp492-3; Sharia Zaki al-Arsuzi; 50min S£50; 🕑 24hr) Just around the corner from the Baron Hotel, this is one of few places offering ADSL connections; rates are cheaper the longer you're there.

Concord Internet Cafe (Map pp492-3; ☎ 270 060; Sharia al-Quwatli; per hr S£100; 🕑 9.30am-3am) OK connections that drop out more often than we'd like.

Money

CBS Exchange al-Kattab (Map pp492-3; 🕑 8am-7pm), outside the tourist office, changes money and has an ATM.

Otherwise, try one of the two branches of the **Commercial Bank of Syria** (Map pp492-3; Sharia Yousef al-Azmeh), that are north of Sharia al-Quwatli; they may change travellers cheques with a S£50 commission but don't count on it.

ATMs are dotted around town, but there are few in the old town.

Post & Telephone

Main post & telephone office (Map pp492-3; ☎ 362 4010; 🕑 8am-5pm) In the enormous building on the far side of Saahat Saad Allah al-Jabri. For international calls, use the card phones dotted around town including in front of the post office and the National Museum.

Tourist Information

Tourist office (Map pp492-3; ☎ 212 1228; www.syriatourism.org; Sharia al-Baron; 🕑 8.30am-7pm Sat-Thu) In the gardens opposite the National Museum, it occasionally stocks maps and is generally more willing than especially useful.

Visa Extensions

Immigration office (Map pp492-3; ☎ 225 5330; 🕑 8am-1.30pm Sat-Thu) In the square near the Chabha Cham Palace Hotel, west of the Old City. A taxi should cost no more than S£50.

SIGHTS

Old City

Aleppo's souq, which runs for 1.5km from the 13th-century **Bab Antakya** (Map p495) in the west to the citadel in the east, makes the Old City one of the Middle East's main attractions. This partially covered network of bustling passageways extends over several hectares, and once under the vaulted stone ceiling you're swallowed up into another world, transported back in time to the medieval bazaars of our imaginings with clamour, commerce and smells that you'll never forget. Parts of these dimly lit and atmospheric markets date to the 13th century, but the bulk of the area is an Ottoman-era creation. The best way to explore is to simply lose yourself in the labyrinth.

At one time walled and entered only by one of eight gates, the Old City has long since burst its seams and now has few definable boundaries. Exploring its seemingly infinite number of alleys and cul-de-sacs could occupy the better part of a week, depending on how inquisitive you are. We recommend visiting at least twice: once on a busy weekday to experience the all-out, five-senses assault of the souq, and a second time on a Friday when, with all the shops closed, the lanes are silent and empty. Relieved of the need to keep flattening yourself against the wall to let the overladen donkeys and minivans squeeze by, you're free to appreciate architectural details.

The main souq, **Souq al-Attarine** (Map p495), runs east–west between the citadel and Bab Antakya. Until the development of the New City in the 19th century, this was Aleppo's main street. In amongst the souqs are numerous khans; the most impressive is the **Khan al-Jumruk** (Map p495). Completed in 1574, at one time it housed the consulates and trade missions of the English, Dutch and French, as well as 344 shops. The khan now serves as a cloth market.

On the northern edge of the souqs is the **Great Mosque** (Al-Jamaa al-Kebir; Map p495; admission S£25; 🕑 sunrise to just after sunset), the younger sibling (by 10 years) of the Umayyad Mosque in Damascus. Its most impressive feature is its freestanding minaret dating from 1090.

Inside the mosque is a fine carved wooden minbar, and behind the railing to the left of it is supposed to be the head of Zacharias, the father of John the Baptist. More, perhaps,

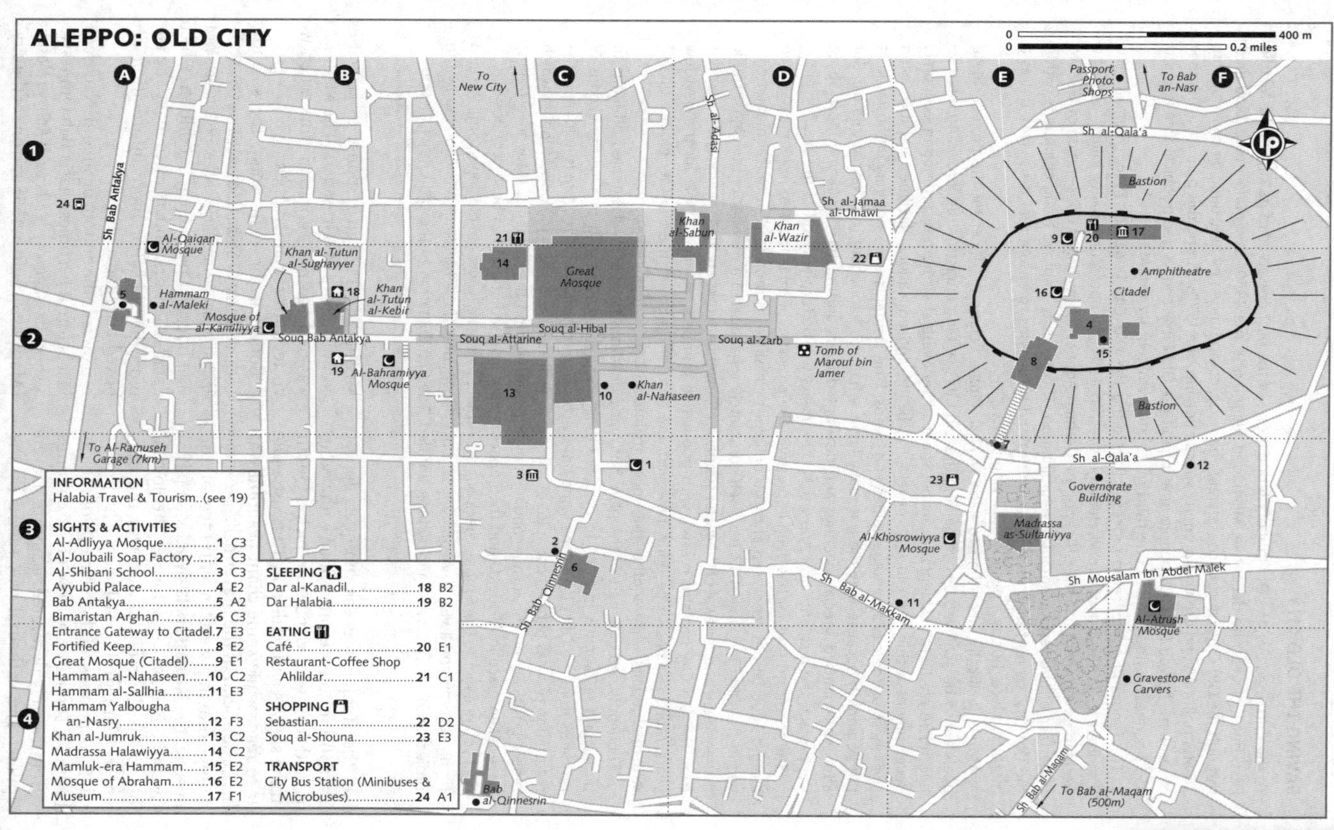
ALEPPO: OLD CITY
0 400 m
0 0.2 miles
To New City
Passport Photo Shops
To Bab an-Nasr
Sh al-Qala'a
Sh Bab Antakya
Sh al-Adasi
Bastion
Al-Qaiqan Mosque
Khan al-Tutun al-Sughayyer
Khan al-Sabun
Sh al-Jamaa al-Umawi
Khan al-Wazir
Great Mosque
Amphitheatre
Citadel
Hammam al-Maleki
Khan al-Tutun al-Kebir
Mosque of al-Kamiliyya
Souq Bab Antakya
Souq al-Hibal
Souq al-Attarine
Souq al-Zarb
Tomb of Marouf bin Jamer
Al-Bahramiyya Mosque
Khan al-Nahaseen
Bastion
To Al-Ramuseh Garage (7km)
Sh al-Qala'a
Governorate Building
Madrassa as-Sultaniyya
Al-Khosrowiyya Mosque
Sh Bab Qinnesrin
Sh Mousalam ibn Abdel Malek
Sh Bab al-Makkam
Al-Atrush Mosque
Gravestone Carvers
Sh Bab al-Maqam
To Bab al-Maqam (500m)
Bab al-Qinnesrin
INFORMATION
Halabia Travel & Tourism..(see 19)
SIGHTS & ACTIVITIES
Al-Adliyya Mosque....1 C3
Al-Joubaili Soap Factory....2 C3
Al-Shibani School....3 C3
Ayyubid Palace....4 E2
Bab Antakya....5 A2
Bimaristan Arghan....6 C3
Entrance Gateway to Citadel.7 E3
Fortified Keep....8 E2
Great Mosque (Citadel)....9 E1
Hammam al-Nahaseen....10 C2
Hammam al-Sallhia....11 E3
Hammam Yalbougha an-Nasry....12 F3
Khan al-Jumruk....13 C2
Madrassa Halawiyya....14 C2
Mamluk-era Hammam....15 E2
Mosque of Abraham....16 E2
Museum....17 F1
SLEEPING
Dar al-Kanadil....18 B2
Dar Halabia....19 B2
EATING
Café....20 E1
Restaurant-Coffee Shop Ahlildar....21 C1
SHOPPING
Sebastian....22 D2
Souq al-Shouna....23 E3
TRANSPORT
City Bus Station (Minibuses & Microbuses)....24 A1

SAVING THE OLD CITY

To the untrained eye, the Old City of Aleppo is one of the best preserved of its kind in the Middle East, but looks can be deceptive. Misguided planning in the 1950s saw major roads ploughed through the Old City, causing considerable damage, compounded by new building construction, greater pollution and growing property speculation into the 1970s. During this period the number of residents halved (120,000 people now inhabit the Old City), and its geographical area (around 355 hectares) is now around one-third of its late-19th-century extent.

The long and complicated process of restoring the Old City began in 1986, when Unesco inscribed it on the list of World Heritage sites. In 1994, Aleppo municipality joined with the German government (via the offices of the German Agency for Technical Cooperation or GTZ) to undertake a long-term program of rehabilitation. The aim is to improve living conditions within the Old City, by nurturing local communities and businesses to ensure that it survives, not as a museum piece, but as a historic but living entity.

More specifically, according to Rana Nakhal, Public Relations Officer for the project, these goals are to be achieved by overhauling the Old City's ageing infrastructure, providing interest-free micro-credit to residents to enable them to renovate their homes, promoting economic development within the Old City, developing health and educational facilities and increasing awareness of the city's heritage values and needs. 'The residents were not very enthusiastic at the beginning because they did not really know what was happening,' Ms Nakhal told us. 'But after we organised special meetings and distributed flyers and posters explaining more about the project, the residents now know that the project will be for the good of the area.'

The scorecard thus far has been impressive. The provision of small loans to residents has seen around 1000 homes renovated and 240 buildings classified as protected historical monuments within the Old City, while GTZ has itself completely rehabilitated a number of buildings. Traffic management and renewal of the water supply and sewer networks are also underway. The exodus from the Old City has also ceased, with population numbers relatively stable for the past few years. Much remains to be done, however: one third of houses in the Old City require urgent structural repairs while another third need maintenance or rehabilitation.

Tourism is certainly part of the plan, but many buildings have been designated off-limits to hotels and restaurants in a bid to preserve their original functions and to slow the exodus of residents from the Old City. At the same time, according to Ms Nakhal, 'tourism is helping in the restoration process (which costs a lot of money) as well as creating new job opportunities, which reflect positively on the local economic development and on the residents. Many investments have taken place in Al-Jdeida and the impact on the neighbourhood has been very positive.'

If you're eager to learn more, check out the project's website (www.gtz-oldaleppo.org). We also highly recommend a visit to Al-Shibani School (below), one of the buildings reinvigorated by the project, and which hosts an exhibition entitled 'The Rehabilitation of the Old City of Aleppo'.

than the architecture, the mosque's appeal lies in its life and it is often filled with young and old men who wander in, pick a Quran off the shelves and settle down against a pillar to read, while some chant beautifully at the western end of the prayer hall.

Opposite the western entrance of the mosque, the **Madrassa Halawiyya** (Map p495) was built in 1245 as a former theological college on the site of what was the 6th-century Cathedral of St Helen. The prayer hall incorporates all that remains of the cathedral, a semicircular row of six columns with intricately decorated, acanthus-leaved capitals. The cathedral was seized by the Muslims in 1124 in response to atrocities committed by the Crusaders. The Madrassa was undergoing restoration work when we visited, but remained open.

South of the main souq, the splendid 16th-century **Al-Shibani School** (Map p495; ☎ 331 9270; Al Jaloum quarter; admission free; 🕒 9am-4pm Wed-Mon) houses a permanent exhibition, which details the work underway to make the city more liveable. For more information see boxed text, above.

Towards the bottom of Souq al-Nahaseen, just before it becomes Sharia Bab Qinnesrin, a short passageway leads to **Al-Adliyya Mosque** (Map p495), built in 1555 and one of the city's major Ottoman-era mosques. It's worth a quick look inside for the fine tiling.

Heading south, follow your nose to **Al-Joubaili Soap Factory** (Map p495), ages old and still producing soaps the traditional way using olive oil and bay laurel. At the time of research it was closed to the public.

Directly across the street, behind railings, is the splendid **Bimaristan Arghan** (Map p495), one of the most enchanting buildings in Aleppo. Dating from the 14th century, it was converted from a house into an asylum. The main entrance gives access to a beautifully kept courtyard with a central pool overhung by greenery.

CITADEL

Sitting atop a huge, manmade, earthen mound east of the Old City, the **citadel** (Map p495; adult/student S£150/10; 9am-6pm Wed-Mon Apr-Sep, to 4pm Wed-Mon Oct-Mar) dominates the city skyline. The first fortifications were built by the Seleucids (364–333 BC), but everything seen today dates from much later. The citadel served as a power base for the Muslims during the 12th-century Crusades, when the moat, 20m deep and 30m wide, was dug. Much rebuilding and strengthening occurred during Mamluk rule from 1250 to 1517 and it's largely their work that survives.

On the southern side, its moat is spanned by a step-bridge that then climbs at a 45-degree angle to the imposing 12th-century **fortified gate**. As you climb up, it's easy to imagine just how the citadel's defenders were able to hold out against invaders; attacking armies would have been dangerously exposed on the bridge, as they confronted the massive fortifications of the gate, and the twisting entrance of five right-angled turns inside the gate made storming the structure a complicated task.

Once inside, the castle is largely in ruins, although the **throne room**, above the entrance, has been lavishly restored. On your right as you climb up through the ruins, note the **Ayyubid Palace** dating from the 13th century – it has a soaring entrance portal with stalactite stone decoration. To the rear of the palace is a recently renovated **Mamluk-era hammam**.

Back on the main path, off to the left is the small 12th-century **Mosque of Abraham**, attributed to Nureddin and one of several legendary burial places for the head of John the Baptist. Atop the hill, at the citadel's northern end, there's a sparsely endowed **museum** (S£75) in an Ottoman-era barracks, which is next to the **café** and **Great Mosque**.

Although the ruins themselves are interesting to pick your way through, the main attraction is the views from the battlements over the patchwork of roofs, domes and minarets.

Christian Quarter

The Christian quarter of **Al-Jdeida** is a charming, beautifully maintained warren of long, narrow stone-flagged alleyways. The quarter is undergoing something of a rebirth, with age-old townhouses being converted into hotels, restaurants and bars.

One of the main attractions here is the **Museum of Popular Tradition** (Le Musee des Traditions; Map pp492-3; ☎ 333 6111; Sharia Haret al-Yasmin; adult/student S£75/5; 8am-2pm Wed-Mon), housed in the lovely Beit Ajiqbash (1757). The artefacts showcasing everyday life in centuries past are interesting enough, but it's the splendid architecture and intricate interior decoration that will live in the memory, especially the guest room, with its amazing silver ceiling and snake-entwined light fitting, and the courtyard decoration. This is how many homes in Al-Jdeida once looked.

Close to the museum you'll find five major churches, each aligned to a different denomination.

Immediately west of the museum is the **Syrian Catholic Church** (Mar Assia al-Hakim; Map pp492–3), built in 1625 and happy to admit visitors who come knocking.

Next stop is the 19th-century **Greek Orthodox Church** (Map pp492–3) and further beyond that, still on Haret al-Yasmin, is the entrance to the 17th-century **Armenian Cathedral of the 40 Martyrs** (Map pp492–3); if possible, it's worth visiting on a Sunday to observe the Armenian mass performed here, which is still pervaded with a sensuous aura of ritual. It starts at 10am and lasts two hours.

North of these three, on Saahat Farhat, are the **Maronite Cathedral** (Map pp492–3) and a smaller **Greek Catholic Church** (Map pp492–3), which date to the 19th century.

National Museum

Aleppo's main **museum** (Map pp492-3; ☎ 221 2400; Sharia al-Baron; adult/student S£150/10; 9am-5.30pm Wed-Mon Apr-Sep, to 3.30pm Wed-Mon Oct-Mar) could be mistaken for a sports hall if it weren't for the extraordinary colonnade of giant granite figures that fronts the entrance. The wide-eyed characters are replicas of pillars that once supported the ceiling of an 8th- or 9th-century-BC temple-palace complex unearthed in Tell Halaf in northeastern Syria.

Inside, the collection is made up of other finds from northern Syria – there are some beautiful pieces including from Mari (p517), Ugarit (p508) and around Hama, with some fascinating cuneiform tablets from Ebla. But the labelling is abysmal and the presentation is otherwise poor, so only budding archaeologists with strong imaginations will find it worth the entry fee.

ACTIVITIES

At the foot of the citadel, on the southeast side, the **Hammam Yalbougha an-Nasry** (Map p495; Sharia al-Qala'a) was one of Syria's finest working bathhouses and something of a city showpiece, although it remained closed at the time of writing, after renovations, as the government looks for someone willing to pay the extortionate running costs.

Originally constructed in 1491, it has a splendid sun clock inside the dome above reception; if it's operational again, don't leave Aleppo without having a massage and scrub here.

If Hammam Yalbougha an-Nasry is still closed, women should try **Hammam al-Sallhia** (☎ 333 3572; Sharia Bab al-Makkam; complete massage & scrub S£600), around 300m south of the citadel entrance. It's open for women from 11am to 5pm but not necessarily every day.

The renovated, men-only **Hammam al-Nahaseen** (Map p495; hammam only S£300, complete massage & scrub S£500; 7am-8pm), in the heart of the souq just south of the Great Mosque, is open long hours and is still a local favourite, despite increasingly attracting tourists.

TOURS

For organising trips around the sights close to Aleppo and further afield, **Halabia Travel & Tourism** (☎ 224 8497, 0944 245 543; www.halabia-travel.com) is recommended. For a car and driver, you'll pay €30 to €50 for day trips and it also has plans for train tours and can arrange visas.

Most of the budget hotels offer a range of day trips to attractions in the area; you'll be looking at a base rate of S£1050 per person for shorter trips to Qala'at Samaan and surrounds, and up to S£1750 for a full-day trip to Qala'at Samaan, the Dead Cities, and Apamea.

SLEEPING

Aleppo has terrific accommodation across a range of budgets. All are well located, with the bulk of the budget hotels in the new part of town. The midrange and top-end places are clustered around the lovely Al-Jdeida district, with two midrange choices in the Old City near Bab Antakya. Reservations are recommended for much of the year.

Budget

Hotel Nejm Illahdar (Hotel Green Star; Map pp492-3; ☎ 223 9157; s/d from S£500/800;) On the 2nd floor of a building just off Bab al-Faraj, this place has been renovated in the not-too-distant past. Cheaper rooms come with fan, balcony and shower cubicle; the more expensive have air-con, comfortable beds and full (if tiny) bathrooms. When we visited, the cheaper rooms were a bit grubby. There's a lounge with satellite TV, as well as a fabulous rooftop terrace where breakfast (S£100) is served in summer.

Hotel al-Gawaher (Map pp492-3; ☎/fax 223 9554; gawaherh@aloola.sy; Bab al-Faraj; s/d/tr S£500/1000/1500) With Syrian hotel prices going through the roof in recent years, it's nice to see this backpacker mainstay hold firm. The simple rooms come complete with clean linen, private bathroom, toilet paper and soap, fans and electric heaters. Some have balconies onto the street, others have windows onto the interior salons, and some even have satellite TV. The 2nd-floor lounge is a pleasant place to hang out. Rooms on the top floor require a stiff climb.

Tourist Hotel (Map pp492-3; ☎ 211 6583; Sharia ad-Dala; d S£1000, s/d without bathroom S£500/1000;) Run by the formidable Madam Olga and her family, this small hotel is one of our budget favourites in Aleppo. It's famous throughout the country for its standards of cleanliness (it's immaculate), and rooms are well sized, light and comfortable. Some even have balconies and there's 24-hour hot water, fresh linen daily and an optional breakfast (S£150).

Hanadi Hotel (Map pp492-3; ☎ 223 8113; Sharia ad-Dala; s/d S£575/1150, without bathroom S£400/700;) This could just be the best place for budget travellers in town, with friendly, multilingual staff, an enormous sun terrace high above the Aleppo clamour and spotless freshly painted rooms (what's with so much pink?). Some travellers may not like the squat toilets and the entrance staircase could be Aleppo's steepest, but these are small drawbacks in a place with so much going for it. It also organises tours to surrounding sights (per person €15 to €25).

Hotel Somar (Map pp492-3; ☎ 211 3198; fax 211 4669; Sharia Yarmouk; s US$14-18, d US$16-25;) If you have no luck scoring a room at the Tourist Hotel, the old-fashioned Somar is a decent alternative. Rooms are comfortable and have satellite TV, and all come with tiny but very clean private bathrooms. Rooms at the front are the best, as those at the rear are dark, and there's a small but pleasant covered courtyard. The clientele is predominantly Arab.

Al-Yarmouk Hotel (Map pp492-3; ☎ 211 6154; fax 211 6156; Sharia al-Maari; s/d/tr S£700/1100/1500;) The Yarmouk may not see too many Western tourists – it mainly hosts Arab and Russian traders – but the chain-smoking English- and Russian-speaking staff are welcoming and it's a decent fallback if the other budget places are full. Having benefited from a makeover, each of the hotel's three floors has been painted a different colour, so take your pick from glossy lavender, pink and lemon. Rooms with bathrooms come with fridges, TVs, clean sheets and towels.

Midrange & Top End

Aleppo's midrange and top-end accommodation is outstanding and largely occupies restored courtyard houses in Al-Jdeida and just off the lanes of the souq in the old city. Unless indicated otherwise, all of these hotels provide comfortable rooms with heating and satellite TV. All except the Baron accept credit-card payment.

our pick **Dar Halabia** (Map p495; ☎ 332 3344; www.halabia-travel.com; s/d €29/39;) The Halabia bills itself as a 'Hotel de Charme' and it's entitled to do so. Located near Bab Antakya, it's one of only two hotels in the souq, and although its courtyard is not as polished as the boutique hotels in Al-Jdeida, it's an outstanding place to stay.

It occupies three old houses and has 19 rooms, the most attractive of which are on the ground floor around the courtyard of the main building, although all rooms are comfortable. The area's quite lonely at night when the whole quarter is deathly silent, but the hotel is lovely, spotlessly clean and great value. There are no TVs, but there's free wireless.

Dar al-Kanadil (Map p495; ☎ 332 4908; fax 363 3715; www.halabia-travel.com; s/d/tr €39/49/69;) Opened in mid-2008 and run by the same owners as Dar Halabia, this fine old house has tastefully decorated, large rooms arrayed around two open courtyards. The bathrooms here are lovely, and one of the upstairs terraces has partial views over the old city rooftops to the citadel.

Baron Hotel (Map pp492-3; ☎ 211 0880/1; www.the-baron-hotel.com; Sharia al-Baron; s/d/ste US$56/68/101;) Welcome to one of the most famous hotels in the Middle East, and while it may have lost most of its polish, it still retains plenty of ramshackle charm. Public areas (including the famous bar and the sitting room with a signed bill from TE Lawrence) are looking worse for wear, and rooms (even those that have been recently renovated) have peeling paintwork. Although it's overpriced, it's all about atmosphere and history here.

Tourath House (Map pp492-3; ☎ 211 8838; www.tourathhouse.com; Sharia al-Raheb Buhayrah; s/d US$65/85;) One of the newer courtyard hotels in Al-Jdeida, Tourath House follows the usual winning formula of lovely interior courtyard with simpler rooms, although all rooms have lovely restored ceilings. The service is friendly and helpful.

Mandaloun Hotel (Map pp492-3; ☎ 228 3008; www.mandalounhotel.com; s/d US$67/78;) Off Sharia Al-Telal, in the modern streets just north of Al-Jdeida, it's difficult to imagine what lies behind the facade of this boutique hotel. Gorgeous is the first word that comes to mind when describing the courtyard, complete with fountain and antique furniture, as well as a cosy restaurant and bar.

The downstairs rooms are knockouts, with four-star amenities and extremely attractive decor, although the exposed stone walls lend an almost monastic simplicity. Rooms on the top floor are cramped and nowhere near as nice as their downstairs counterparts, although some have exterior windows. There's also an annexe with old-style rooms.

Beit Wakil (Map pp492-3; ☎ 221 7169; www.beitwakil.com; Sharia as-Sissi; s/d/ste US$77/110/145;) In the Al-Jdeida quarter, this may well be Syria's most romantic hotel. Nineteen small rooms have an always understated, sometimes quite simple aesthetic compared to the enormous charm of the public areas, while one of the suites is stunning, located in the house's former reception room. Add 11% tax to your bill and don't expect internet access here. For details on the hotel's popular restaurant, see right.

EATING

Known for its richness and use of spices, Aleppine cuisine is distinctive within Syria and, in turn, the Middle East. Dining here is a real pleasure. Although street-food joints are ubiquitous, the good restaurants are mostly concentrated in Al-Jdeida.

The block bounded by Sharias al-Maari, Bab al-Faraj, al-Quwatli and al-Baron is full of cheap eateries offering the usual array of roast chicken, shwarma and felafel. A row of excellent juice stands lines up at the Bab al-Faraj end of Sharia Yarmouk. There are tiny stalls along the length of Souq Bab Antakya/az-Zarb/al-Attarine selling cheap felafel, kebabs, hummus, pastries and fuul.

Haj Abdo al-Fawwal (Map pp492-3; 7am-4pm) Opening early every morning, this is the best place to get Aleppine-style fuul, delicately seasoned with cumin, paprika, garlic, lemon juice and fresh parsley. Crowds start gathering around the tiny shop from 7am, bearing empty containers of every size and description, pushing and shoving their way to the front for their share of this aromatic dish. Don't leave Aleppo without trying some for yourself. It's off Saahat al-Hatab.

Al-Andalib (Map pp492-3; ☎ 222 4030; Sharia al-Baron; set menu S£200; noon-1am) The atmosphere at this rooftop restaurant one block north of the Baron Hotel is boisterous, and the place is packed most evenings. It serves a huge set meal of kebabs, salads, dips and fries. There's a S£50 service charge and a limited alcohol list. Come prepared to have a good time.

Abou al-Nawas (Map pp492-3; ☎ 211 5100; Sharia Rashid; meals from S£225) This long-standing favourite has a menu that stretches way beyond the basics to include the kind of dishes that are usually only ever served up at home (patrons are often invited into the kitchen to choose from the daily pots). There's an excellent-value set meal for S£225, which gives you a daily dish of your choice with rice or fries, pickles, tea or coffee, and a sweet. Be clear that this is what you're ordering, because the waiters inevitably encourage you to order a more expensive main dish instead. No alcohol.

Restaurant-Coffee Shop Ahlildar (Map p495; ☎ 333 0841; Souq ibn al-Khashab; meals from S£250; 8.30am-10pm) Overlooking the entrance to the Great Mosque, this fine restaurant means you can eat and then return to the souqs without having to traipse all the way back to Al-Jdeida for lunch. The food is fresh and tasty (we especially enjoyed the grilled cheese and well-priced *shish tawooq* for S£125), and there's a huge range of mezze, salads, soups, grills and a few Western dishes such as pizza. The inside tables are pleasant, but the upstairs terrace is the best.

Bazaar al-Charq (Map pp492-3; ☎ 224 9120; meals S£300) A pleasant alternative to the ubiquitous courtyard restaurants of Aleppo and Damascus, Bazar al-Charq is set in a reconstructed underground bazaar with vaulted ceilings, between Sharia al-Mutanabi and Sharia Hammam al-Tal. It has an extensive menu of mezze, grills, salads, soups and a few *plats de jour*; our lentil soup and mixed grill went down a treat. The live traditional music at 10.30pm Wednesday to Sunday rounds out a nice package. Our only complaint? When it came time to pay, 'service is not included' was whispered in our ears and they were disinclined to return our change.

Beit Wakil (Map pp492-3; ☎ 221 7169; Sharia as-Sissi; meals S£300;) Once Aleppo's best eatery, this hotel-restaurant does have a lovely setting in one of Al-Jdeida's most beautiful buildings. Guests sit in an atmospheric courtyard and can choose from an array of mezze and local specialities. The food is good though not spectacular, and service can be stuffy. It's licensed and accepts credit cards.

Sissi House (Map pp492-3; ☎ 221 9411; www.sissihouse.com; meals S£350-500;) Just off Saahat al-Hattab in the Al-Jdeida quarter, this upmarket restaurant is where Aleppo's glam set hangs out. Like the restaurant at Beit Wakil, it specialises in decent local variations on Levantine cuisine and offers a choice of over 50 mezze dishes. The licensed menu is in Arabic and French only, and doesn't list prices. Credit cards are accepted and there's often live music (oud from the stairs, followed by a wandering violinist).

Kaser al-Wali (Map pp492-3; ☎ 446 1389; meals S£350-500; 9am-1.30am;) In the northwestern corner of Al-Jdeida, off Sharia al-

Arba'aeen, Kaser al-Wali has fast become the restaurant of choice of many locals and travellers in Damascus. The expansive covered courtyard is rather lovely, the food contains all the usual suspects but they're especially good here, and there's live traditional music from 10.30pm Wednesday to Monday.

DRINKING

If you're after a drink only, the upstairs bar at Sissi House (opposite) is open until late and hosts a jazz pianist every night of the week, with a singer on Saturdays. It's the most sophisticated bar in town.

Nostalgia buffs may want to pop into the pricey, small bar at the venerable Baron Hotel (p499), but most visitors prefer the laidback **Al-Mashrabia Pub & Restaurant** (Map pp492-3; ☎ 211 5249; 🕑 4pm-1.30am) in Al-Jdeida, where the drinks are cheaper (local beer S£100) and the decor is more atmospheric; there's also an extensive snack menu here. **Ciao** (Map pp492-3; Sharia al-Arba'aeen; 🕑 4pm-1.30am) is another cool place for a drink.

The outdoor cafés on Sharia al-Qala'a, located opposite the entrance to the citadel, are great places to enjoy a coffee, fresh juice or nargileh and watch the world go by.

SHOPPING

Aleppo Souq

The best place to shop in Aleppo is without a doubt the souqs (Map p495) of the old city and great buys include textiles, brocade, gold, silver, carpets and olive soap. Although the pressure to buy has grown in recent years, the souq remains overwhelmingly targeted at a local market – apart from the architecture, that's what gives it its charm.

Like any Middle Eastern souq, Aleppo's bazaar is broken down into the usual demarcations: gold in one alley, spices in another, carpets in one spot, scarves across the way. The exception to this is bustling Souq al-Attarine (Map p495), which sells everything: hardware, clothing, spices, perfumes and even meat. South of Souq al-Attarine, the laneways almost exclusively give way to fabrics, clothing and shoes. North of Al-Attarine, the souq is at its most dense.

Squeezed around the Great Mosque are veins of parallel narrow alleys that in places are barely wide enough for people to pass each other. Here, Souq al-Hibal (Map p495) is devoted to shops selling cord, braid and rope, while Souq al-Tabush is crammed with stalls selling buttons, ribbons and all manner of things necessary for a woman to run up her family's clothes.

Souq az-Zarb (Map p495) is a good place to head for *jalabiyyas* (robes) or a keffiyeh.

Shops in the souq open from early in the morning until around 6pm Saturday to Thursday, while on Friday virtually the whole souq closes and is eerily deserted.

Sebastian (Map p495; ☎ 332 3672; Sharia al-Qala'a; 🕑 8am-8pm Sat-Thu) On the fringes of the souq, this place stocks a small but superb range of high-quality textiles, tablecloths, inlaid backgammon boards and boxes. However, the speciality is rustic kilims, silk rugs and antique carpets costing anything from US$50 to US$15,000. The multilingual owner, Mohammed, is highly knowledgeable, accepts credit cards and provides certificates.

Orient House Antiques (Map pp492-3; 1st fl, Saahat al-Hatab; 🕑 8am-8pm) Over in Al-Jdeida, the Beit Sissi store is a wonderful place to browse for antiques and bric-a-brac.

Souq al-Shouna (Map p495) is a handicrafts market behind the sheesha cafés on the southwestern side of the Citadel. While there are price tags, bargaining is still possible, although not required, and it's a good place to get an idea of prices before plunging into the souqs.

GETTING THERE & AWAY

Air

Aleppo's airport offers semi-regular connections to Turkey, Europe and other cities in the Middle East. Domestic services also run to Damascus (S£1500, one hour). A taxi between the airport and the city centre will cost at least S£500.

Bus

As of summer 2008, the main bus station, as far as most travellers are concerned, is Al-Ramuseh Garage, some 7km south of the city centre. All luxury, long-distance buses to destinations within Syria leave from here. A taxi to the old city or Al-Jdeida will cost around S£100. Although no services operate from the old Hanano Garage, buses connect the old bus station with the new.

From Al-Ramuseh, **Al-Kadmous** (☎ 224 8837; www.alkadmous.com) runs 24-hour services to Damascus on the hour (S£270, four hours) as well as regular services to Hama (S£105,

2½ hours), Homs (S£140, three hours) and Deir ez-Zur (S£230, five hours). Dozens of other private companies run similar services for the same prices, while a handful of companies cover the Aleppo-Lattakia route (S£170, 3½ hours). There are no direct services to Tartus or Palmyra – change at Homs for these.

Seven or eight companies offer daily services from Al-Ramuseh to Beirut (S£700, six hours) via Tripoli (S£600, five hours).

You'll find the International Bus Station north of the tourist office. Little more than a parking lot, it's the place for buses to Antakya (S£350), İstanbul (S£2500) and Amman (S£700 to S£750), with a handful of early-morning and late-night departures to each; travel times vary widely, depending on how long the border crossing takes. If you can't wait around for a bus to Antakya, a seat in a service taxi costs S£600. These leave when full from the International Bus Station.

Microbuses covering local routes around Aleppo leave from the sprawling City Bus Station outside Bab Antakya.

Train

The **train station** (☎ 221 3900) is housed in an attractive old building located about a 25-minute walk from the central hotel area, north of the big public park. Please note that all departure times listed below are subject to change, so check at the station for the latest departure times.

At the time of writing, there were four daily express services to Damascus at 4am, 5.40am, 10.05am and 3.30pm (1st/2nd class S£240/200, 4½ hours) and one slow service at midnight (1st/2nd class S£110/75, six hours). The services go via Homs (1st/2nd class S£130/110). The middle-of-the-night express services are considerably cheaper on the Damascus line.

To Lattakia, there are two daily express trains (1st/2nd class S£160/135, 2½ hours) at 6am and 5.45pm, and two slow trains (1st/2nd class S£70/50, 3½ hours) at 6.45am and 3.45pm. Two daily trains travel to Deir ez-Zur (4½ hours) at 11.15pm (1st/2nd class S£115/75) and 4.10pm (1st/2nd class S£175/145).

For long-haul travellers, there are services to Tehran (S£4050 in sleeper class) on Mondays at 1.30pm, and to İstanbul (S£3570 in sleeper class) on Tuesdays at 11.00am.

A taxi from the station to the Al-Jdeida, Bab Antakya or Bab al-Faraj areas should cost between S£35 and S£50.

QALA'AT SAMAAN
قلعة سمعان

Also known as the Basilica of St Simeon, the ruins of **Qala'at Samaan** (adult/student S£150/10; ⏰ 9am-6pm Apr-Sep, to 4pm Oct-Mar) are among the most atmospheric of Syria's archaeological sites. The basilica commemorates St Simeon Stylites, one of Syria's most eccentric early Christians.

Simeon was the son of a shepherd who opted at a young age for life in a monastery. Finding monastic life insufficiently ascetic, he retreated to a cave in the barren hills, where he lived under a regimen of self-imposed severity. Word spread and people began to visit to seek his blessing. Simeon apparently resented this invasion of his solitude so intensely that he was driven, in AD 423, to erect a 3m-high pillar upon which he took up residence so that people couldn't touch him. Legend goes that as his tolerance of people decreased he erected ever higher pillars. In all he's said to have spent close to 40 years on top of his pillars, the last of which was 18m in height. There was a railing around the top, and an iron chain attached to the stone to stop him toppling off in the middle of the night. Simeon would preach daily from his perch and shout answers to his audiences' questions; however, he refused to talk to women and even his mother was not allowed near the column. After his death in 459, an enormous church was built around the most famous pillar, and pilgrims from all parts of Christendom came to pay their respects.

The site today is remarkably well preserved, with the quite lovely Romanesque facade still standing and the arches of the octagonal yard still reasonably complete. There's plenty of ornamental carved stonework to admire, although Simeon's pillar is in a sad state and is nothing more than a boulder, reduced centuries ago by pilgrims chipping away at it for holy souvenirs.

The church had a unique design with four basilicas arranged in the shape of a cross, each opening onto a central octagonal yard covered by a dome. Beneath the dome stood the pillar. Completed in around 491 after about 14 years of building, it was the largest church in the world at the time. With the arrival of Islam in Syria, the Byzantine Christians were put on the defensive and the church complex was fortified, hence the name Qala'at (fortress). It eventually fell to the Islamic Fatimid dynasty in 1017.

Views of the surrounding countryside are simply stunning, especially towards the west and to Turkey in the north.

Qala'at Samaan is a 40-minute drive from Aleppo. Microbuses to the village of Daret' Azze (S£35, one hour) leave Aleppo every hour or so from the microbus bays, and this is as close to the site as you can get by public transport. From here, there are no local buses or taxis to take you the remaining 6km, so the only options are to hitch or walk, or convince the minibus driver to take you the extra distance. Aleppine taxi drivers will charge S£1000 to take you there, wait one hour and bring you back to town.

DEAD CITIES

These eerie and ancient ghost towns are dotted along the limestone hills that lie between the Aleppo–Hama highway in the east and the Orontes River in the west. By some estimates, there are hundreds, if not thousands, of such cities in northern Syria, ranging from single monuments to whole villages complete with houses, churches, mills, hammams and even wine presses. They date from the time when this area was part of the hinterland of the great Byzantine city of Antioch; the great mystery is why these towns and villages were abandoned. The latest theory is that they were emptied by demographic shifts – trade routes changed and the people moved with them.

Most travellers make a day trip taking in Al-Bara, Serjilla and Qala'at Samaan.

Al-Bara is the most extensive of the Dead Cities, dotted over a wide area of olive groves and intensively farmed land where vegetables, olives, grapes and apricots are grown alongside. The highlights are the striking pyramid tombs, 200m apart, decorated with Corinthian pilasters and carved acanthus leaves, a very visible testament to the one-time wealth of the settlement. The larger of the two still holds five sealed, decorated sarcophagi, although the interior (viewed through a metal grill) is strewn with graffiti.

The most evocative of the Dead Cities is undoubtedly **Serjilla** (adult/student S£75/5), especially in winter when the ruins might be shrouded in mist. It has the most semi-complete buildings, all sitting in a natural basin in windswept and hilly moorland. Although Serjilla has been deserted for about 15 centuries, the buildings' stone facades are remarkably well preserved and it's easy to get a feel for what the town would have looked like in its heyday. At Serjilla's centre is a small plaza flanked by a two-storey tavern and a large hammam. Next door lies an *andron* (men's meeting place), and further east, a small church along with substantial remnants of private houses and villas. It's a spooky place and the red hue of the building materials provides some quite beautiful interplays of light.

You're best off visiting the Dead Cities on a combined Qala'at Samaan/Dead Cities tour from Aleppo (p498) or in your own car, as they're extremely difficult to reach on public transport and are scattered over a large area.

LATTAKIA اللاذقية

☎ 041 / pop 1.05 million

Laid-back Lattakia has little in common with the rest of Syria and it's easily the country's most Westernised city. A busy port since Roman times, it has a Mediterranean feel, an outward-looking inclination and true *joie de vivre*. Its pavement cafés are inevitably packed with locals sipping espresso, smoking nargilehs, listening to imported music and telling slightly risqué jokes.

In Lattakia, young women don skin-tight jeans and apply their lipstick lavishly, eschewing the headscarf; young men dress in homeboy uniform, albeit with a Syrian slant. The place offers a refreshing change, particularly if you've travelled from conservative Aleppo and you've been on the Middle Eastern road for a while.

Apart from its atmosphere, Lattakia's major attraction is as a base for Qala'at Saladin and there are also some fine beaches north of town.

INFORMATION

Internet Access

Center Net (Sharia al-Mutanabi; per hr S£60; 11am-11pm) Good connections.

Fire Net (Sharia al-Maghreb al-Arabi; per hr S£60; 24hr) Quite fast connections and a room for wireless if you've a laptop.

Virus Internet Café (465 540; Sharia Baghdad; per hr S£30-60; 24hr) Worrying name, but fast connections and cool clientele.

Money

There are Syriabank ATMs all over Lattakia. One of the more central ones is at the **Commercial Bank of Syria No.2 Branch** (Sharia Baghdad); it may also change travellers cheques for a flat fee of S£25.

Post

Main post office (8am-2pm Sun-Thu) Some distance out of the centre, just north of the train station, in a little alley off Sharia Suria.

Telephone

Telephone office (Sharia Seif al-Dawla; 8am-11pm) To make an international call, buy a phone card then wait your turn for a free phone. You can also make calls from some internet cafés.

Tourist Information

Mohammed Ziadeh (093 337 6900; safwanhotel@go.com) Even if you're not staying at Safwan Hotel & Hostel (right), Mohammad has his finger on Lattakia's pulse and his mission in life seems to be keep travellers to his city well informed.

Tourist office (416 926; www.syriatourism.org; Sharia 14 Ramadan; 8am-8pm Sat-Thu) Opposite the Riviera Hotel. English-speaking staff supply maps and not much more.

Visa Extensions

Immigration office (8am-2pm Sun-Thu) Beyond the tourist office, near Saahat Jumhuriyya, and on the far side of a large traffic roundabout.

SIGHTS & ACTIVITIES

The small **National Museum of Lattakia** (Sharia Jamal Abdel Nasser; adult/student S£150/10; 9am-6pm Wed-Mon Apr-Sep, 8am-4pm Wed-Mon Oct-Mar) is housed in a charming old khan near the waterfront. Though its archaeological garden is attractive, the museum's displays are rather unimpressive, but do include some inscribed tablets from Ugarit, beautiful jewellery, coins and figurines, ceramics and pottery and a Crusader-era chainmail suit and swords.

Blue Beach is a good public beach at Shaati al-Azraq, 6km north of town. Minibuses (S£10) leave from a back alley down the side of the big, white school on Saahat al-Sheikh Daher. A taxi will cost S£150 one way.

The best beaches in Lattakia are monopolised by the large tourist resorts, which charge an extortionate S£700 for nonguests to use them.

Women will feel comfortable swimming at **Wadi Qandil**, 25km north of town, where the beach has black sand and clean water. To get here, catch a microbus (S£15) from the station near the stadium. Microbuses (S£20) also leave from here going to **Burj Islam**, where there's clean water and a stone beach. Ask to get off at Sakhra (the Rock). Women won't feel quite as comfortable here.

SLEEPING

As a seaside town that's popular with Syrians in summer, prices at some midrange hotels drop by as much as 15% in winter and rise by up to 20% in summer.

Budget

Hotel Lattakia (479 527; Sharia Yousef al-Azmeh; s/d S£500/700, without bathroom S£250/350;) Some of the cheapest beds in Lattakia are to be found here. The building's seen better days and the rooms (some with fan, some with air-con) are basic, but they're clean and the owner is friendly. Compared to other options in this price range around Syria, the bathrooms aren't at all bad. There's also a kitchen for use by guests. The hotel is tucked away in a central location, down a narrow alley north of the Al-Ajan mosque.

Safwan Hotel & Hostel (453 801, 093 337 6900; safwanhotel@go.com; Sharia Mousa bin Nosier; mattress on roof S£200, dm/s/d S£300/450/700, s/d without bathroom S£400/600) This could be our favourite backpackers' hotel in Lattakia. It's not that the rooms are anything special – they're basic and sometimes rundown, but clean (it pays to ask to see a few before choosing). Rather, the place is run by *Tintin* fan Mohammad Ziadeh and his family, and Mohammad is switched on to travellers' needs (see left). He's an engaging host.

Hotel al-Atlal (476 121; Sharia Yousef al-Azmeh; s/d from S£350/700) This simple, quiet establishment has immaculate rooms with snug beds and freshly laundered sheets; the bathrooms have squat toilets. There's a pleasant common area with free tea and satellite TV. The family who run the place add much warmth to your stay.

Hotel Riyad (☎ 479 778; fax 476 315; Sharia 14 Ramadan; s/d US$22/26; ❄) Overlooking a busy road but close to the centre, the Riyad has simple but tidy, well-sized rooms, most with balcony. Most rooms have fans but those with air-con cost no more.

Midrange & Top End

Hotel al-Nour (☎ 243 980; fax 245 340; Sharia 14 Ramadan; s/d US$30/35; ❄) A two-star place overlooking the motorway, Hotel al-Nour has

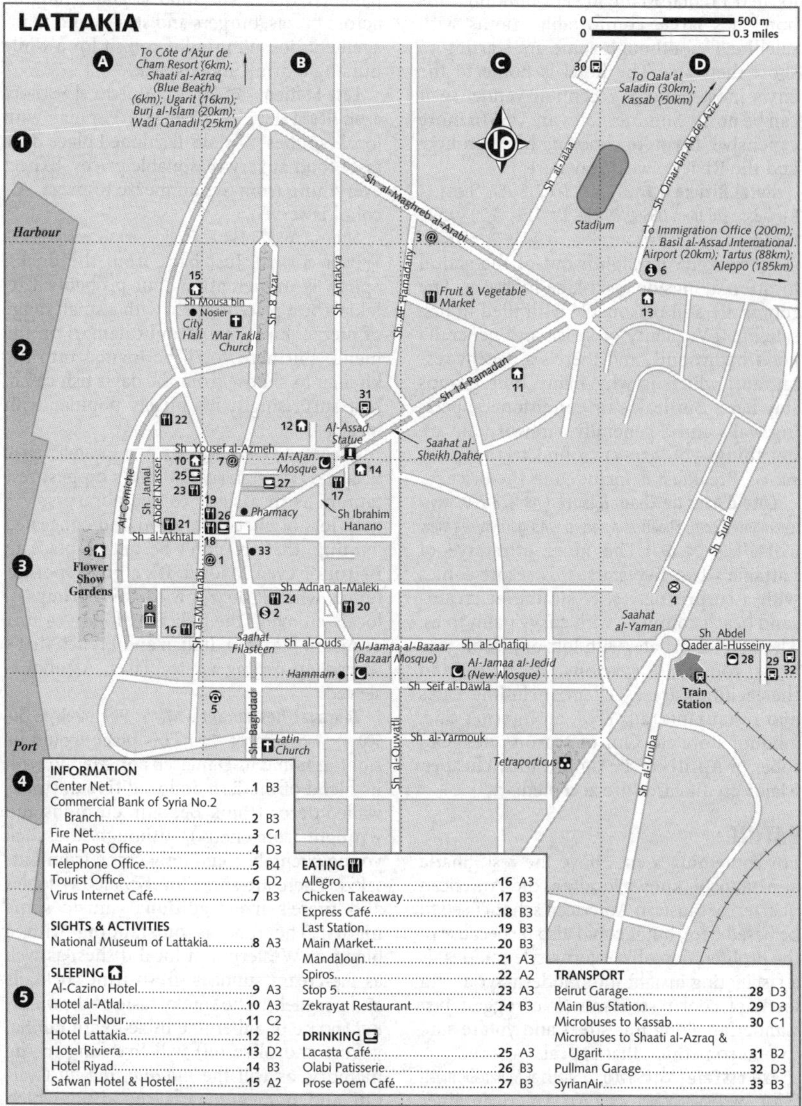

beds resembling concrete slabs; the rooms themselves are pretty good and come with satellite TV and some have balconies – those with carpet on the upper floors have a worn look to them. Ask for a room at the rear. It's all a touch overpriced, but only a touch.

Al-Cazino Hotel (☎/fax 461 140/142; Al-Corniche; s/d from US$40/50;) In an imposing and well-located French Mandate–era building, this hotel has large, comfortable rooms with satellite TV, although some are starting to show their age. The hotel is home to the city's most popular reception venue, so it can be noisy. Summer rates are US$10 more expensive. If you're choosing between here and the Riviera, we'd stay here.

Hotel Riviera (☎ 211 806; fax 218 287; Sharia 14 Ramadan; s/d from US$60/69 plus tax 11%;) Once the best hotel in Lattakia, it was for years easy to forgive its slightly out-of-the-action location alongside a six-lane highway. The rooms are still reasonable with tiled floors, satellite TV, plenty of space and generally good bathrooms, and there's a decent restaurant, which is why many tour groups stay here. But leaky air-conditioners, peeling walls and a generally careworn air are not things you expect to find in this price range. Breakfast is included in the price.

Côte d'Azur de Cham Resort (☎ 428 700; www.chamhotels.com; Shaati al-Azraq; d with garden/sea view US$140/180;) The more attractive of Lattakia's two five-stars, this resort comes with a surprisingly sexy swathe of cream-sand beach complete with curvy palm trees. The hotel is ornate, with lots of marble and brass, rooms are spacious and plush, and the facilities are excellent including cafés and restaurants, an ATM, an internet café, a liquor store etc. Out-of-season rates (October to April) can be significantly cheaper. Major credit cards are accepted.

EATING

For something a cut above the rest, Sharia al-Mutanabi (known locally as the 'American quarter' because an American school used to be based here, but it could also be because of the proliferation of Western-style eateries) is a fascinating insight into modern Syria with loads of cool restaurants. We suggest just wandering along this street and you're sure to find something that appeals.

Express Cafe (☎ 456 200; 22 Sharia al-Mutanabi; meals S£200; 9am-midnight;) An American diner in the Hard Rock Café style, this bright and noisy place offers burgers, steaks, pizza and hot and cold sandwiches. It also does great milkshakes, and there's a bar downstairs.

Stop 5 (☎ 477 919; 27 Sharia al-Mutanabi; meals around S£300; 11am-midnight;) Resembles a New York bar, with shelves of spirits, posters advertising happy hours and wood-panelled walls. The food is good, ranging across pizzas, burgers and steaks, and management doesn't mind if you sit for a while nursing a drink and a snack.

Last Station (☎ 468 871; 20 Sharia al-Mutanabi; meals around S£300; 11am-11pm) Popular with local families, this old-fashioned place does tasty food at very reasonable prices. Expect everything from Syrian mezze to pizza. Alcohol is served.

Spiros (☎ 478 238; Al-Corniche; meals around S£350; noon-midnight) Just back from the docks, Spiros is unpretentious but probably Lattakia's best place for fish, with a small range of mezze, meat mains and calamari on the menu. But here you'll be invited into the kitchen to choose from the day's fish catch. Not surprisingly, it's hugely popular with locals.

Allegro (☎ 458 000; Sharia al-Mutanabi; meals S£350; 11am-midnight) Lattakia's hippest restaurant is in a sleek contemporary space, with lots of chocolate wood and concealed lighting, that wouldn't be out of place in Beirut or even Madrid. It's a great spot for lunch, when it buzzes with noisy groups of locals enjoying the delicious food – a mix of Asian, Mexican, Italian and French that's served up on big white plates. Alcohol is served.

Zekrayat Restaurant (☎ 459 979; meals S£350-500; 9am-midnight;) This place would be right at home in Damascus or Aleppo with its blend of modern and traditional, stone-walled decor (think Bedouin cushions and wrought-iron chairs), although the slick young clientele could only come from Lattakia. There are some lovely balcony tables and there's live traditional music some nights. The food is outstanding with a blend of Western and local dishes, as well as ice-cream sundaes, fresh-fruit cocktails and nargilehs. The smoky taste of the *mutabal* (purée of aubergine mixed with tahina, yogurt and olive oil) will live long in the memory, as will the *mouhammarah* (walnut and pomegranate-syrup dip), which no longer appears on the menu but they'll prepare if asked. Our only complaint? No prices on the menu. It's off Sharia Adnan al-Maleki.

Mandaloun (☎ 454 400; Sharia al-Merkan; meals S£500-600; 🕑 1-11.30pm) Dress up for this elegant restaurant with stone walls and vaulted ceilings, where you'll be dining with Lattakia's affluent cigar-smoking set. The French and oriental cuisine is superb – try the tasty pink lentil soup or hearty traditional French onion soup for starters, and the melt-in-your-mouth filet mignon. There are excellent Lebanese wines on the menu and the service is faultless.

Snack stalls are located around the Saahat al-Sheikh Daher area, where you'll find fast-food places specialising in felafel, kebabs and shwarma. There's a good spit-rotisserie **chicken take-away** (S£150 for a whole chicken plus salad, hummus and bread) next door to the Hotel Riyad.

DRINKING

There's a real coffee culture in Lattakia, and many places serve up espresso that could stand up and be counted in Italy.

There are loads of good places around Sharia al-Mutanabi. Some of our favourites include the sleek **Lacasta Café** (Sharia al-Mutanabi; meal per person S£250; 🕑 noon-3am), where Lattakia's multitasking locals sip excellent espressos and puff on nargileh on white-leather sofas, and **Olabi Patisserie** (Sharia Yousef Shahour; 🕑 7am-midnight; 💻), off Sharia Baghdad, where they've free wireless and do great pastries, espresso and hot caramel.

For something a little different, try **Prose Poem Café** (Qasideh; 🕑 10am-11pm), a quiet little café off Sharia Baghdad, loved by a young, professional set and local intellectuals. There's Arabic poetry on the walls, a well-stocked bookshelf and the murmur of intelligent conversation.

GETTING THERE & AWAY

Air

Basil al-Assad International Airport lies about 25km southeast of Lattakia. A taxi to the centre of town costs around S£500. There are three weekly flights to Damascus (S£1200), but services increase considerably in summer. There's also one weekly flight to Cairo.

There's a local office of **Syrianair** (☎ 476 863/4; 8 Sharia Baghdad; 🕑 8am-8pm).

Bus

The Pullman Garage is on Sharia Abdel Qader al-Husseiny about 200m east of the train station. Numerous private companies have their offices here.

Al-Kadmous has a 24-hour service to Damascus (S£250, four hours) leaving on the hour; its regular minibus service to Tartus (S£65, one hour) runs between 6am and 9pm, stopping at Baniyas (S£35) en route. There are also four services daily to Homs (S£135, two hours), while Al-Ahliah has four daily buses to Hama (S£180). One or two companies also run services to Aleppo (S£170, 3½ hours), although we recommend you take the train (see below).

Microbus

At the time of writing, the main congregation of microbuses was 1.5km north of the town centre, near the sports stadium. From a huge lot, buses depart frequently for destinations such as Al-Haffa (S£20) for Qala'at Saladin (p508), and Kassab (S£45, 1½ hours) for the Turkish border. Changes are afoot, with plans to move most microbus destinations to east of the **Beirut Garage** (☎ 353 077). Check with the tourist office or Mohammed Ziadeh (see p504) for the latest locations.

Microbuses for Ugarit (Ras Shamra; S£10) go from a back alley down the side of the big white school on Saahat al-Sheikh Daher.

Microbuses to Baniyas (S£65, 45 minutes), Tartus (S£65, one hour), Homs (S£90, two hours) and Hama (S£100, three hours) leave from Beirut Garage, near the train station. From the same station, Izreq runs a daily minibus service (S£500) to Antakya in Turkey. If you call ☎ 352 021 it will collect you at your hotel.

Taxi

Taxis charge S£35 for trips within town.

Part of the service taxi station next to the train station is known locally as **Beirut Garage** (☎ 353 077), and it's from here that services run down the coast and across the border into Lebanon. They leave when full for Tripoli (S£450) and Beirut (S£700). If you call ☎ 353 077, they may collect you from your hotel.

Train

If you're travelling to Aleppo, we recommend you take a train rather than the bus, as they're extremely comfortable and the scenery is stunning, especially for the first 1½ hours from Lattakia. The train station is about 1.5km east of the city centre on Saahat al-Yaman. There are four daily departures for Aleppo: two express services (1st/2nd class S£160/135, 2½ hours) at 6.30am and 5.15pm, and two slow services (S£70/50 in 1st/2nd class, 3½ hours) at 7.20am and 3.40pm.

AROUND LATTAKIA

UGARIT رأس شمرا

The low-lying ruins at **Ugarit** (Ras Shamra; adult/student S£150/10; 9am-4pm Nov-May, to 6pm Jun-Oct) are all that remains of a city that was once the most important on the Mediterranean coast. From about the 16th to the 13th century BC, it was a centre for trade with Egypt, Cyprus, Mesopotamia and the rest of Syria. The writing on tablets found here is widely accepted as the earliest-known alphabet, and the tablets are on display in the museums in Lattakia, Aleppo and Damascus, as well as the Louvre in Paris. Today, the masonry left behind shows you the layout of the streets and gives you some vague idea of where the most important buildings were. Come here for the sense of history, not for the visual effect.

Regular microbuses (S£10) make the trip from Lattakia to Ugarit. They leave from a back alley down the side of the big white school on Saahat al-Sheikh Daher.

QALA'AT SALADIN قلعة صلاح الدين

Although Qala'at Saladin is less celebrated than Crac des Chevaliers, TE Lawrence was moved to write: 'It was I think the most sensational thing in castle building I have seen.' The sensational aspect is largely due to the site – the castle is perched on top of a heavily wooded ridge with precipitous sides dropping away to surrounding ravines. It's pretty amazing, a fact recognised by Unesco, who inscribed it on their World Heritage list in 2006.

The **castle** (adult/student S£150/10; 9am-4pm Wed-Mon Nov-Mar, to 6pm Wed-Mon Apr-Oct) is located 24km east of Lattakia and is a very easy half-day trip. Begun by the Byzantines in the 10th century, it was taken over by the Crusaders in the early 12th century and the construction of the castle as you see it today was carried out some time before 1188, the year in which the Crusaders' building efforts were shown to be in vain. After a siege of only two days, the armies of Saladin breached the walls and the Western knights were squeezed out of yet another of their strongholds.

After climbing up through the gate tower, the inner courtyard is watched over by two relatively intact **towers**; it is possible to climb the internal staircase in each tower up to the 1st floor and roof for fine views of the surrounding countryside. Other highlights include the **stables**, the **Ayyubid Palace** (1169–1260) and the **sunken cistern**.

To get here, take a microbus from Lattakia to the small town of Al-Haffa (S£20, 30 minutes). These leave from the minibus station near the stadium. Taxis and local cars wait at the bus stop at Al-Haffa and will take you the further 6km to the castle. They charge anywhere between S£150 to S£200 to take you there, although the minibus may take you up to the castle for the same fee. A taxi from Lattakia will charge S£1000 including waiting time.

THE GOLDEN AGE OF UGARIT

Until a worker ploughing a farm near the coast adjacent to Lattakia struck an ancient tomb, the site of Ugarit was unknown. This exciting and important discovery in 1928 led to the excavation of the site the next year by a French team led by Claude FA Schaeffer. What he found was astonishing.

The oldest finds at Ugarit date back to 6000 BC. Findings that date from around 1450 BC to 1200 BC reveal a sophisticated and cosmopolitan metropolis with palaces, temples and libraries with clay tablets bearing inscriptions. These clay tablets, representing a Semitic language – it is still thought by many to be the earliest-known alphabet in the world – became a celebrated finding. The site also revealed vast Mycenaean, Cypriot, Egyptian and Mesopotamian influences in the artefacts, a result of trade both by sea and by land.

PALMYRA تدمر

☎ 031

The rose-gold ancient ruins of Palmyra (known in Arabic as Tadmor) are one of the premier ancient sites in the Middle East, and for many travellers, the standout highlight of any visit to Syria. Rising out of the desert of central Syria, flanked by an expansive oasis, and just three hours from Damascus, Palmyra must rank high on your list of must-sees. Some travellers come on a day trip from Damascus, but sunrise and sunset are the most beautiful times here and we recommend an overnight stay as a minimum, preferably two.

Modern Palmyra is a typical tourist town along well-worn Middle Eastern trails. Expect camera shops selling memory cards, carpet shops, souvenir shops selling Crusader helmets and restaurants with faux-Bedouin decor. It's not without its problems (see boxed text, p511), but nor is it as challenging as some travellers will have you believe.

HISTORY

Tadmor is mentioned in texts discovered at Mari dating back to the 2nd millennium BC. Early rulers included the Assyrians, Persians and Seleucids, for whom it served as an indispensable staging post for caravans travelling between the Mediterranean, Mesopotamia and Arabia. It was also an important link on the old Silk Route from China and India to Europe, with the city prospering greatly by levying heavy tolls on the caravans.

But it was the Romans who made Tadmor their own. As they expanded their frontiers during the 1st and early 2nd centuries AD to occupy the eastern Mediterranean shores, Tadmor became stranded between the Latin realms to the west and those of the Parthians to the east. The oasis used this situation to its advantage, taking on the role of middleman between the two clashing superpowers. The influence of Rome grew, and the city they dubbed Palmyra (City of Palms) became a tributary of the empire and a buffer against rivals to the east.

The emperor Hadrian visited in AD 129 and declared Palmyra a 'free city', allowing it to set and collect its own taxes. In 212, under the emperor Caracalla (himself born of a Syrian mother), Palmyra became a Roman colony. Further wealth followed and Palmyra spent lavishly, enlarging its great colonnaded avenue and building more and larger temples.

After the interlude of Zenobia (see boxed text, below), a further rebellion in 273, in which the Palmyrenes massacred a garrison of 600 Roman archers, elicited a brutal response and Aurelian's legionaries slaughtered large numbers and put the city to the torch. Palmyra never recovered.

QUEEN OF THE DESERT

The most picaresque character in Palmyra's history was responsible for the city's most glorious historical moment, and also its subsequent rapid downfall. Palmyra's ruler, Odainat (also called Odenathus), was assassinated in 267. His second wife, Zenobia, took over in the name of their young son, Vabalathus. Rome refused to recognise this arrangement, not least because Zenobia was suspected of involvement in her husband's death. The emperor dispatched an army to deal with the rebel queen. Zenobia met the Roman force in battle and defeated it. She then led her army against the garrison at Bosra, then the capital of the Province of Arabia, and successfully invaded Egypt. With all of Syria and Palestine and part of Egypt under her control, Zenobia, who claimed to be descended from Cleopatra, declared her independence from Rome and had coins minted in Alexandria bearing her image and that of her son, who assumed the title of Augustus, or emperor.

The Roman emperor Aurelian, who had been prepared to negotiate, was not amused. After defeating Zenobia's forces at Antioch and Emesa (Homs) in 271, he besieged Palmyra itself. Zenobia was defiant to the last and instead of accepting the generous surrender terms offered by Aurelian, made a dash on a camel through the encircling Roman forces. She headed for Persia to appeal for military aid, only to be captured by Roman cavalry at the Euphrates. Zenobia was carted off to Rome in 272 as Aurelian's trophy and reputedly paraded in the streets, bound in gold chains. Later freed, she married a Roman senator and lived out her days in Tibur (now Tivoli), close to Rome.

The emperor Diocletian (r 254–305) later fortified the broken city as one in a line of fortresses marking the eastern boundary of the Roman Empire, and Justinian further rebuilt the city's defences in the 6th century. The city survived primarily as a military outpost and the caravan traffic all but dropped away.

In 634 the city fell to a Muslim army led by Khaled ibn al-Walid, and from this time Palmyra all but fades from history. It was finally and completely destroyed by an earthquake in 1089.

INFORMATION

Palmyra's helpful **tourist information office** (☎ 591 0574; www.syriatourism.org; Saahat ar-Rais; 🕑 8am-6pm Sat-Thu) is situated across from the museum. There is a **Commercial Bank of Syria exchange booth** (🕑 8am-8pm Sun-Thu, 10am-8pm Fri & Sat) in front of the museum; it doesn't change travellers cheques. The **post office** (🕑 8am-2pm Sat-Thu) is in front of the Al-Assad Gardens, just west of the tourist office.

Hani Internet (☎ 591 0878; per hr S£100; 🕑 8am-midnight), at the Traditional Palmyra Restaurant, has OK connections and also wi-fi for those toting laptops for the same price; you can also burn CDs here. For visa extensions, visit the office signed as **Passports** (Sharia al-Quwatli; 🕑 8am-1.30pm Sat-Thu) with three photos and pick up your passport the next day.

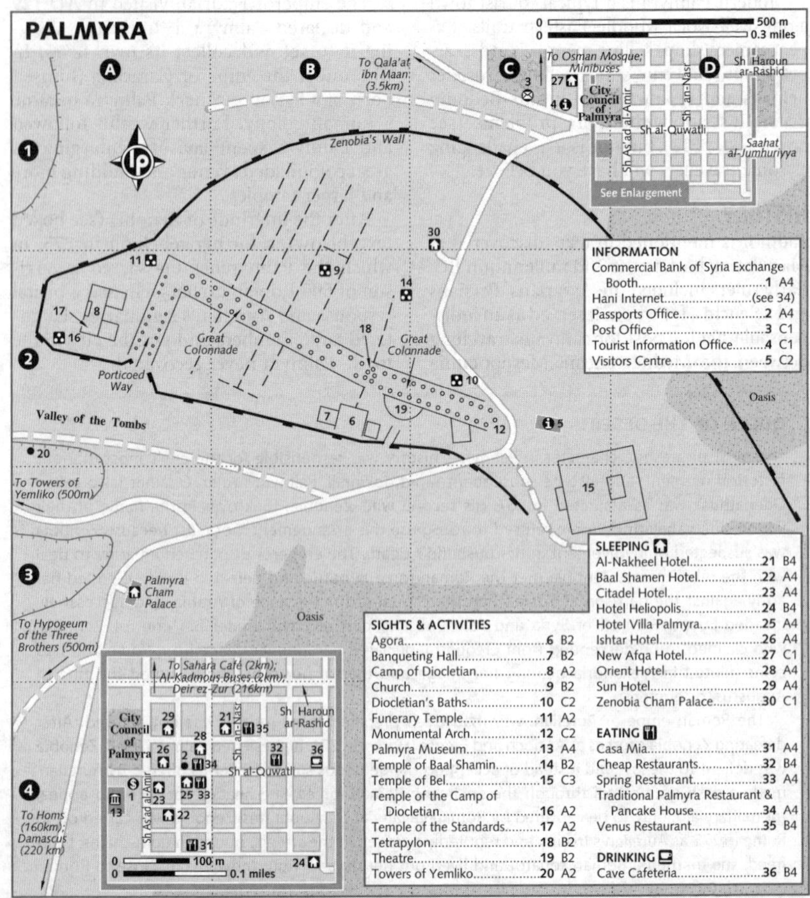

THE PROBLEM WITH PALMYRA

Palmyra is a once-small town and conservative Bedouin society that has, in recent decades, been inundated with tourists and its economy is almost entirely dependent on tourism. When tourist numbers plummeted after September 2001, these businesses hit hard times and competition between them became fierce – and sometimes nasty – as a result. The same happens whenever regional politics cause a downturn in tourist numbers. For example, the town's long-standing restaurants have a simmering feud and are known to regale travellers with rants about the competition. If they start sounding off to you, tell them you're not interested.

Competition is no less heated in the hotel scene, with some hotels meeting arriving buses, much to the annoyance of the others. Once in town, travellers may encounter another competition-fuelled annoyance: hotel touts. These guys (often kids) will try to take you to one of the hotels in town for a paying commission. Be aware that if you turn up with one of them, an extra 10% to 20% will be added to the quoted cost of a bed or room to cover his commission. And ignore the old 'That hotel is full/dirty/closed/a brothel' spiel about somewhere that you've already booked. If you're female and staff at any restaurant offer a massage, turn them down flat.

All of that said, be aware of the situation but don't be paranoid. Palmyra is not Egypt or Morocco. Most of what happens is pretty low level and the hassles are, in most cases, only bad by Syrian standards.

SIGHTS

The Ruins

There's no entry fee and no opening hours for the ruins, although three sites (the Temple of Bel, the Theatre and Elahbel, one of the funerary towers) do have set hours and require you to pay. Allow at least a day to explore the ruins, possibly with a break in the heat of the day and with a sunset trip up to Qala'at ibn Maan. Although Palmyra is Syria's singlemost popular attraction and tour groups spill from buses and into the ruins at regular intervals, the site is large enough to find a quiet corner and imagine you have the place to yourself. If you can do this at sunrise or sunset, when the columns and temple walls turn golden or rose pink, this is when you'll really understand the magic of Palmyra.

Bel was the most important of the gods in the Palmyrene pantheon, and the **Temple of Bel** (adult/student S£150/10; ⌚ 9am-6pm Apr-Sep, 8am-4pm Oct-Mar) is the most complete structure left in Palmyra. Once inside, you'll see that the complex consists of two parts: a huge walled *temenos* (courtyard), and at its centre, the *cella* (the temple proper), which dates from AD 32.

Just to the left of the entrance into the *temenos* is a sunken passage that enters the temple from the outside wall and gradually slopes up to the level of the courtyard. This was probably used to bring sacrificial animals to the precincts. The podium of the sacrificial altar is on the left, and beside it are the foundations of a banqueting hall. Inside the *cella* is a single chamber with *adytons* (large niches) at either end. To see how the temple once stood, visit room two of the Palmyra Museum (p512).

The earth-coloured building by the Temple of Bel was originally the residence of the Ottoman governor of Palmyra. It later became a prison, and at the time of research was about to open as the new **visitors centre** (⌚ 8am-6pm).

Formerly connected to the temple by a colonnade, the **monumental arch** across the road now serves as the entrance to the site proper, and it's one of the most evocative sites in Palmyra. The arch is interesting as it's actually two arches joined like a hinge to pivot the main street through a 30-degree turn. This slight direction switch, and a second one just a little further west, are evidence of the city's unique development – a crooked street like this would be quite unimaginable in any standard Roman city.

The section west of the arch is magnificent. This section lies at the heart of the ancient civic centre; it has been heavily restored and gives a very clear idea of how the city must have appeared in all its original splendour. The street itself was never paved, probably to save damage from camel caravans, but flanking porticoes on either side were. Each of the massive columns has a small, jutting platform about two-thirds of the way up, designed to hold the statue of some rich Palmyrene who had helped pay for the construction of the street.

South of the main colonnaded street is the city's **theatre** (admission S£75; 9am-6pm Apr-Sep, 8am-4pm Oct-Mar), which was buried by sand until the 1950s. Since its discovery it has been extensively restored.

About one-third of the way along the colonnaded street is the beautiful, reconstructed **tetrapylon**, a monumental structure that marked a junction of thoroughfares and marks the second pivot in the route of the colonnaded street. Its square platform bears at each corner a tight grouping of four columns. Each of the four groups of pillars supports 150,000kg of solid cornice. A pedestal at the centre of each quartet originally carried a statue. Only one of the 16 pillars is of the original pink granite (probably brought from Aswan in Egypt).

The **agora** was the hub of Palmyrene life, the city's most important meeting space, used for public discussion and as a market where caravans unloaded their wares and engaged in the trade that brought the desert oasis its wealth. What remains today is a clearly defined courtyard measuring 84m by 71m. The central area was once enclosed by porticoes on all four sides and the pillars carried statues. Adjoining the agora in the northwest corner are the remains of a small banqueting hall used by Palmyra's rulers.

After the detour to the agora, the main street continues northwest, and another smaller pillared street leads northeast to the **Temple of Baal Shamin**, a small shrine dedicated to the god of storms and fertilising rains.

Beyond the tetrapylon, the main street continues for another 500m. This stretch is littered with tumbled columns and assorted blocks of masonry and the views up towards Qala'at ibn Maan are quite lovely as the sun nears the horizon. The road ends in the impressive portico of a 3rd-century **funerary temple**.

South of the funerary temple, along the porticoed way, is the **Camp of Diocletian**, erected after the destruction of the city by Aurelian. It was possibly on the site of what had been the palace of Zenobia, although excavations so far have been unable to prove this. The camp lay near the Damascus Gate, which led on to a 2nd-century colonnaded street that supposedly linked Emesa (Homs) and the Euphrates.

To the south, at the foot of some low hills, is a series of tall, freestanding square-based towers known as the **Towers of Yemliko**. These were constructed as multistorey burial chambers, stacked with coffins posted in pigeonhole-like niches. The niches were sealed with stone panels carved with a head-and-shoulder portrait of the deceased; you can see many of these in the special displays at the National Museum in Damascus (p473).

It's possible to visit one of these towers, **Elahbel**, on a tour organised by the Palmyra Museum (adult/student S£75/5). Tours leave from the museum at 8.30am, 10am, 11.30am and 4.30pm (no 11.30am tour on Fridays, no 4.30pm tour October to March) and include a visit to the impressive **Hypogeum of the Three Brothers**, an underground burial chamber with beautiful frescoes.

Perched high on a hilltop to the west of the ruins is **Qala'at ibn Maan** (adult/student S£75/5; noon-sunset Wed-Mon), also known as the Arab Castle or citadel. From here, there are spectacular sunset views over the ruins. Though it's possible to walk here, many travellers choose to take one of the many tours sold by hotels in town (approximately S£150 per person).

Palmyra Museum

With improving but still patchy labelling in English and Arabic, **Palmyra Museum** (adult/student S£150/10; 8am-1pm & 4-6pm Wed-Mon Apr-Sep, 8am-4pm Wed-Mon Oct-Mar) is worth a quick visit to add some context to the ruins. There's a good, large-scale model of the Temple of Bel in its original state and some fine mosaics found in what are presumed to be nobles' houses, just east of the temple.

Other highlights include a collection of coins depicting Zenobia and her son, countless busts and reliefs that formed part of the panels used to seal the loculi in Palmyra's many funerary towers and *hypogea* (underground burial chambers), and an outstanding, 3m-high statue of the goddess Allat, associated with the Greek Athena.

Upstairs are newer exhibits that add a little depth to this otherwise modest collection: four mummies discovered in 2004 (note the shoes and children's bones arrayed in front of the four adult bodies) and a room exhibiting local Bedouin clothes and jewellery.

TOURS

Most hotels organise trips to surrounding sights, and those that don't can suggest a taxi driver who can.

Al-Nakheel Hotel (☎ 591 0744; www.heartofdesert.com) is our favourite. Its day trips include a one-day circuit taking in Qasr al-Heir ash-Sharqi (a desert Umayyad castle 120km northeast of Palmyra), Rasafa, Lake Asad and the Euphrates River (€25 per person), but its real specialty is camel safaris (€50 per person per night) into the surrounding desert, ranging from overnight to two-week expeditions.

SLEEPING

There are good options in the budget and midrange categories, with one of Syria's grandest old hotels a fine option at the top end. Prices vary seasonally and according to demand. This is one place where it pays to haggle.

Budget

Baal Shamen Hotel (☎ 591 0453; mattress on roof S£150, s/d S£200/400) The cheapest of Palmyra's budget options, Baal Shamen has spartan rooms that are generally pretty clean; all come with fan and heater. Better than the rooms is Mohammed Ahmed, the owner, who is a welcoming host.

Sun Hotel (☎ 591 1133; sunhotel-sy@hotmail.com; dm/s/d S£150/350/500;) This recommended small hotel is a mixed bag, although all rooms have fans and clean bathrooms; ask for one with an exterior window as the interior ones can be a bit gloomy. The three-bed room on the roof was nearing completion when we were there and it promises to be the best room in the house. Tidy but dark dorms (also with bathrooms) sleep three or four. Breakfast costs S£100 and the owner's mum is happy to cook dinner for S£150.

New Afqa Hotel (☎ 591 0386; mahran_afqa@hotmail.com; roof mattress S£150, s/d S£500/640;) This excellent budget choice is run by the genial Mahran and offers basic but clean boxlike rooms, most of which have bathrooms. The welcoming reception area has satellite TV and beer. You're slightly removed from the traveller scene elsewhere in Palmyra but closer to the ruins. Breakfast is S£100.

Citadel Hotel (☎ 591 0537; citadelhotel@hotmail.com; Sharia As'ad al-Amir; dm/s/d S£200/500/750;) Facing the side of the museum, this popular place has a comfortable foyer with satellite TV and 17 clean, basic rooms. All but the dorm rooms on the roof have small bathrooms. The pick of the rooms are those on the upper floors, although ask to see a few as some can be a bit on the nose. It's slightly overpriced, but is better value in low season when prices drop considerably.

our pick **Al-Nakheel Hotel** (☎ 591 0744; www.alnakheelhotel.net; s/d US$15/20;) Arguably the best-value accommodation in any price range in Palmyra, Al-Nakheel has traditional Bedouin styling in the public areas with some of it overflowing into the rooms; one has a balcony with views over the distant ruins. A Bedouin tent was under construction on the roof and meals are available, while the breakfasts are better than most. Best of all, it's all presided over by Mohamed, a local Bedouin who's an engaging host. It also organises tours (see left).

Midrange & Top End

Palmyra's midrange hotels are generally of a high standard, and there's one standout top-end choice. Quoted prices include breakfast and all offer satellite TV and heating. Credit cards are accepted in some places.

Ishtar Hotel (☎ 591 3073/4; www.ishtarhotel.net; Sharia al-Quwatli; s/d US$20/30;) It's not that the rooms here are anything special – as the management freely admits, they're 'simple and clean'. But this is one of the friendliest places in town, the rooms are comfortable, there's free internet for half an hour for guests, a reasonable restaurant and cave-themed basement bar (beers S£100 to S£150). A good package all round.

Orient Hotel (☎ 591 0131; orienthotel@hotmail.com; s/d/tw US$25/30/35;) A long-standing hotel in Palmyra, the Orient is popular with tour groups. The rooms are quite simple for the price, with worn carpets, but they're well sized and the service is friendly.

Hotel Villa Palmyra (☎ 591 0156; villapalmyra@mail.sy; Sharia al-Quwatli; s/d US$50/60;) This new hotel offers smallish rooms with attractive decor; probably the most comfortable midrange rooms in Palmyra and it's also the best-run hotel in the category. Ask for a room that faces the street unless you want to look out onto a wall… There's a rooftop restaurant, as well as a downstairs bar and pub.

Hotel Heliopolis (☎ 591 3921/2; heliopolis@mail.sy; s/d US$60/70;) In a quiet location behind

SYRIA

Saahat al-Jumhuriyya, this somewhat bland but well-maintained place offers comfortable, if overpriced, rooms. There are better hotels elsewhere for this price, but the Heliopolis has south-facing rooms that overlook the palm trees of the oasis with the Temple of Bel rising above them – these are the best hotel views in town if you can snaffle one. Breakfast costs an extra S£200.

Zenobia Cham Palace (☎ 591 8123; www.chamhotels.com; s US$62-96, d US$73-112; ❄ 💻) Long in a state of sad decline, the Zenobia, built in 1900 and one of the most famous grand old hotels of the Middle East, has finally received the overhaul it deserves. The rooms have understated traditional charm and are extremely comfortable, but best of all is the proximity to the ruins (they're on the doorstep) and the outdoor café and restaurant with fine views. Some rooms (101 to 106) have partial views, but the best views are from the terrace. It's easily the best place to stay in town.

EATING

Most places to eat are on or around the main drag, Sharia al-Quwatli. Most places serve alcohol.

You'll find cheap restaurants selling roast chicken, felafel and shwarma on Sharia al-Quwatli, between the Traditional Palmyra Restaurant and Saahat al-Jumhuriyya. Grocery and fruit-and-veg shops are also found in this area.

Venus Restaurant (☎ 591 3864; Sharia an-Nasr; meals S£250) Near the Traditional Palmyra and anything but its friend, this place has a similar menu. We're not in a position to judge whether this type of imitation constitutes a sincere form of flattery or an infringement of commercial rights, but its prices are a few notches cheaper, even if the atmosphere's not quite the same.

Spring Restaurant (☎ 591 0307; Sharia al-Quwatli; meals from S£250) The friendly Spring has a ground-floor dining area and a Bedouin tent on the roof where you can enjoy a meal and nargileh (S£100) in summer. The set *mensaf* (lamb on a bed of rice) meal is S£250, mezze cost around S£50 and grills start at S£150. Students get a 20% discount.

Traditional Palmyra Restaurant & Pancake House (☎ 591 0878; Sharia al-Quwatli; meals around S£300) The most popular restaurant in town, this long-standing place serves decent *mensaf*, lamb or chicken casseroles and a few other local specialties; all meals come with soup and complimentary tea. There are also delicious sweet and savoury pancakes (around S£200) if you don't want the full set meal.

Casa Mia (☎ 591 6222; meals around S£300) One of the newer restaurants in town, Casa Mia is fast drawing a tourist crowd, partly for its classy, if understated, traditional decor and partly for its local specialties such as *quaj* (oven-baked vegetables), *mjadarah* (burghul and lentils) and *kusa mahshi* (rice, meat and zucchini). The *mensaf* we had here was especially tasty. As a newcomer with no axe to grind, it's something of a haven from Palmyra's restaurant wars. The menu doesn't list prices. It's off Sharia al-Omar.

Of the hotel restaurants, the Ishtar Hotel serves a good set menu of mezze, soup, *mensaf* and dessert for around S£350, while the upstairs roof restaurant at the Hotel Villa Palmyra serves reasonable buffet-style meals (lunch/dinner S£330/495). The Zenobia Hotel (meals around S£500) gets mixed reviews, although the setting is lovely.

DRINKING

Locals can be found gossiping over cheap tea or playing cards at Cave Cafeteria near Saahat al-Jumhuriyya. Women won't feel comfortable here.

The outdoor terrace of the Zenobia Hotel is a more sophisticated world away where you can nurse a beer (around S£150) looking out over the ruins. Other good hotel bars include the cave-basement at Ishtar Hotel and the downstairs bar of the Hotel Villa Palmyra. Most restaurants also serve alcohol.

GETTING THERE & AWAY

Palmyra doesn't have a bus station. The most popular (and regular) buses are those of Al-Kadmous. They stop at the Sahara Café on the edge of town (2km from the museum; a taxi should cost S£50). The ticket office is in front of the café. Buses to Damascus (S£190) leave hourly from 6am to 7pm, at 9.30pm and hourly from 12.30am to 6am. Buses to Deir ez-Zur (S£150, two hours) leave hourly from 8am to 8pm. Services run less often to Homs (S£135) and Hama (S£150). Other private companies offer a similar service and leave from a spot 200m north of the Sahara Café.

Microbuses (S£65) and minibus service taxis (S£75) travel to Homs between 6am and sunset. They leave from outside the Osman Mosque.

THE EUPHRATES

One of the most historically significant rivers on earth, the Euphrates cuts a swathe through northeastern Syria, and arrayed along its banks, and in its hinterland, are a number of little-visited but rewarding sites.

DEIR EZ-ZUR دير الزور

☎ 051 / pop 285,000

Deir ez-Zur ('Deir' to the locals) is a busy market town by the Euphrates that, for travellers, serves as a gateway to the ancient riverbank sites of Dura Europos and Mari. On weekdays, the sometimes shady streets of Deir are filled with colourfully dressed farmers from the surrounding countryside, in town to buy and sell produce at the small but thriving souq off the main square.

The character of the town is heavily influenced by its proximity, both geographical and cultural, to Iraq. Although there really isn't that much to see in town, it has a pleasant riverside setting and an occasional fragrance of jasmine. They're not as accustomed to seeing tourists here as elsewhere in Syria, and solo women travellers may not always feel comfortable.

Orientation

The centre of town is the main square, Saahat 8 Azar, a scruffy, dusty place with the busy souq on its east side. The main north–south road, which runs from the canal through to the square, is bisected by the main east–west axis, which also runs through the square and is called Sharia Khaled ibn al-Walid to the east and Sharia Ali ibn Abi Taleb to the west. The body of water flowing just north of the square is not the Euphrates but a canal. The river is a further 500m north.

Information

Commercial Bank of Syria (Sharia Ali ibn Abi Taleb; ⌚ 8am-12.30pm Sat-Thu) About a 10-minute walk west of the main square; it has an ATM.

Immigration Office (Sharia ar-Rashid; ⌚ 8am-1.30pm Sat-Thu) A good place to extend your visa; the process takes only about half an hour. You need two photos and it costs S£25. To find the office, walk south from the telephone office, then diagonally across the square, turning right onto Sharia ar-Rashid; it's the low concrete building on your right.

Post Office (Sharia 8 Azar; ⌚ 8am-8pm Sat-Thu, to 1pm Fri) Halfway between the main square and the minibus station.

RIVER OF PARADISE: THE EUPHRATES

The significance of the Euphrates (a combination of Greek words that translates to 'gentle current') predates biblical times, but it's the mention of the river, known as 'Perath' in Hebrew and 'Al-Furat' in Arabic, in both the Book of Revelation and by the Prophet Mohammed that makes it most intriguing.

The river starts in northeast Turkey only 80km from its partner, the Tigris, and makes its way through Turkey, then Syria, meeting up with the Tigris in southern Iraq before heading into the Persian Gulf. The total length is about 2800 kilometres, and it's one of the four rivers that flow from the Garden of Eden, according to the Bible. Along with the Tigris, its water supply was important in the development of Mesopotamia. (The name Mesopotamia is Greek for 'between rivers', referring to the Euphrates and the Tigris.)

While the Euphrates languidly flows through Syria, political tension flows through the countries that it services. Turkey, Syria and Iraq all have a vested interest in the Euphrates for irrigation and the creation of hydroelectric power. The Southeast Anatolia Project in Turkey is the biggest development project ever in the country and involves the construction of 22 dams and 19 power plants, most of which are now completed, and which has prompted concern downriver. Syria has created the Tabaqah Dam on Lake Assad, which has doubled the amount of irrigated land in Syria. The consequences of a severe drought would severely affect the livelihood of millions of people across Turkey, Syria and Iraq. However, would it be a catastrophe of biblical proportions? The Book of Revelation in the New Testament of the Bible warns that when the river Euphrates runs dry, Armageddon follows. The Prophet Mohammed warned that the river will one day dry up, revealing unknown treasures that will cause widespread war. See it while you can.

Sights

MUSEUM

Museums elsewhere in Syria could take a lesson from Deir ez-Zur's small **museum** (Saahat ar-Rais, Sharia Ali ibn Abi Taleb; adult/student S£150/10; 8am-6pm Apr-Sep, to 4pm Oct-Mar, closed Tue). The pieces in the collection may not be as valuable or as striking as those in Damascus and Aleppo, but the presentation of the exhibits and labelling (in English and Arabic) is outstanding. The focus of the collection is on prehistoric and ancient Syria and it's well worth visiting if you're on your way to Dura Europos and Mari.

RIVER

The Euphrates River runs north of the city centre and is spanned by a 400m-long suspension bridge that provides fine views of the sluggish, eddying waters as they flow past islands and reeds along the riverbank. The bridge is an impressive structure and a favourite place with the locals for an evening promenade. On the other side of the bridge is a small recreation ground where the local boys swim.

To reach the main body of the river from the main square, Saahat 8 Azar, cross the canal and head north up Sharia 7 Nissan (the continuation of Sharia 8 Azar) for 500m; it runs into the southern end of the suspension bridge, which is open for pedestrians and bicycle users only.

Sleeping & Eating

Al-Jamia al-Arabiyya (☎ 351 371; Sharia Khaled ibn al-Walid & Sharia Maysaloun; s/d S£250/450) Though it has shabby, spartan rooms and the building is peeling away by the day, the hotel is kept reasonably clean and the owner, Nureddin, is a friendly host and speaks some English. Rooms are equipped with fans and basin and some have a balcony. Toilets (squat) and showers are shared.

Ziad Hotel (☎ 227 338; www.ziadhotel.com; Sharia Abu Bakr as-Siddiq; s/d US$35/45;) Easily the best hotel in Deir, Ziad Hotel is not far west of the main square and overlooks the canal. Its 33 rooms are large and spotlessly clean, with thick mattresses, fridge and satellite TV. There are plans to upgrade some of the rooms to four-star status and the breakfast is simple but fresh.

Lailati (☎ 229 648; Sharia Ali ibn Abi Taleb; meal per person S£250; noon-midnight) In a renovated art deco building with vivid orientalist paintings on the walls, this casual eatery 400m west of the main square is easily Deir's best and busiest. Attracting a chatty crowd of families, young couples and groups of women (a rarity in this part of the country), the menu is a mix of Syrian standards plus international dishes – everything from pizza to hamburgers – and it's all good.

There may not be many restaurants around in Deir but there are myriad eateries selling hot chicken, shwarma, kebabs, and burgers along Sharia Khaled ibn al-Walid. There's a handful of restaurants on the banks of the Euphrates, adjacent to the suspension bridge. The pleasant riverside setting doesn't quite compensate for the mediocre food; have a drink only and eat elsewhere.

Getting There & Away

AIR

The airport is about 7km east of town. The 'regular' flights (S£1500, one hour) between Deir ez-Zur and Damascus have been known to get cancelled – regularly. A shuttle bus runs to the airport from the office of **SyrianAir** (☎ 221 801; Sharia al-Ma'amoun; 8.30am-12.30pm Sat-Thu).

BUS

Several bus companies depart regularly from Deir ez-Zur's 'Pullman' station for Damascus (S£340, seven hours) via Palmyra (S£150, two hours) and to Aleppo (S£230, five hours) via Raqqa (S£100, two hours). Al Kadmous is the most popular choice. The luxury bus station is 2km south of town, at the far end of Sharia 8 Azar; a taxi costs S£50 from the town centre.

There's a local microbus service (S£15) to the airport from a stop about a five-minute walk south of the main square, on the right-hand side; otherwise a taxi will cost S£100.

MINIBUS & MICROBUS

The minibus station is on Sharia 8 Azar about 1km south of the main square. From here, there are regular departures for Raqqa (S£90, two hours), for Hassake in the north-east (S£125, 2½ hours) and south to Al-Bukamal (S£90, two hours) for Mari and Dura Europos.

SOUTHEAST OF DEIR EZ-ZUR

The Euphrates River empties down into Iraq southeast of Deir ez-Zur and two of Syria's most important ancient sites – Dura Europos and Mari – lie close to its banks, around 100km and 130km respectively from Deir ez-Zur.

To reach these sites, the road shadows the fertile Euphrates River flood, passing busy, if none too beautiful, market towns en route. With a car (a return taxi from Deir ez-Zur costs around S£2000, including waiting time), you could visit the lot and be back in Deir ez-Zur by midafternoon. With a very early start, it's also possible to do the same with a combination of microbuses and catching rides with locals. Whichever way you travel, the key is setting out as early as possible (both to avoid the worst of the heat and for better light for photography). Take lots of water and a hat.

Dura Europos تل الصلاحية

If you've only time to visit one ancient site in eastern Syria, make it **Dura Europos** (☎ caretaker 096 654 6597; adult/student S£75/5). With extraordinary views over the Euphrates and its flood plain, this extensive, Hellenistic/Roman fortress city amply rewards those who make it out here. Phone the caretaker, if he's not around, to let you in.

HISTORY

Founded by the Seleucids in around 280 BC, Europos retained the ancient Assyrian name of Dura (wall or fort), and is now known to locals as Tell Salhiye. It was the ideal place for a fortress – the desert plateau abruptly ends in a wall of cliffs dropping 90m into the Euphrates. In 128 BC the city fell to the Parthians and remained in their hands (although under the growing influence of Palmyra) until the Romans succeeded in integrating it into their defensive system in AD 165. Dura Europos was famous for its religious tolerance, seemingly confirmed by the presence of a church, synagogue and other Greek, Roman and Mesopotamian temples side by side. The Sassanian Persians seized control of the site in 256, and from then on its fortunes declined.

SIGHTS

The western wall stands out in the stony desert 1km east of the main road, and its most imposing element is the formidable **Palmyra Gate** – look for Greek inscriptions on the walls just inside the gate. The massive site sprawls away to the north, east and south, but just inside the gate there's a site map that's useful for getting your bearings.

Take the main path running northeast towards the river and you'll pass the low-lying remnants of **Roman baths** on the right, a **khan** on the left and then the site of the Greek **agora**. Opposite the agora are the sites (although little remains) of three **temples** dedicated to Artemis, Atargatis and the Two Gads. The original Greek temple to Artemis was replaced by the Parthians who added a tiny theatre for religious gatherings.

Around 300m northeast of the gate, the path drops down towards the riverbank. The Romans installed themselves at this end of the city, and it's from here that you'll get your first view of the river; here, the site begins to work its magic. Overlooking the river on the right, the partially rebuilt **Redoubt Palace** drops down to the delightful mud ruins of the **baths**, while the high wall of the **new citadel** dominates, away to the northeast.

Remarkably, all other visitors to the site on the day we were here ventured no further. Don't make the same mistake or you'll wonder what all the fuss is about. Instead, continue down the slope to the hill behind the citadel – from the summit there are stunning views out over the Euphrates and its fertile littoral, although tread carefully as the cliffs drop away steeply here. West of the new citadel, the Romans placed their **Palace of Dux Ripae**, built around a colonnaded courtyard of which nothing much is left, although from here there are some more fine river views.

GETTING THERE & AWAY

Any microbus between Al-Bukamal and Deir ez-Zur (S£50, two hours) will drop you near the ruins, which are clearly visible from the highway around 1km away.

Mari تل الحريري

The ruins of **Mari** (Tell Hariri; adult/student S£75/5), an important Mesopotamian city dating back some 5000 years, are about 10km north of Al-Bukamal. The mud-brick ruins are the single greatest key serving to unlock the door on the ancient past of Mesopotamia, but to everyone but archaeology buffs, they're not all that inspiring, with the most interesting finds in the museums of Damascus, Aleppo, Deir ez-Zur and in the Louvre in Paris.

The Babylonians under Hammurabi destroyed the city in 1759 BC. Before this, Mari had not only been a major commercial centre but also an artistic hothouse. Excavations were begun in 1933 and unearthed two palaces, five temples and a great many priceless archives in Akkadian – some 25,000 clay tablets were also discovered.

The **Royal Palace of Zimri-Lim**, named after an 18th-century-BC ruler who controlled the most important of the trade routes across Syria into Mesopotamia, was enormous, measuring 200m by 120m. Comprising a maze of almost 300 rooms disposed around two great courtyards, it was protected by earthen ramparts. Today, sheltered from the elements by a modern protective roof – which provides much-needed shade and protection for the site from the baking Mesopotamian heat – the palace remains Mari's main point of interest.

Adjacent to the palace, the crumbling mud mound is all that remains of an ancient **ziggurat**; the large concrete block on the summit will not be a highlight of your visit.

Microbuses travelling from Deir ez-Zur to Al-Bukamal (S£90, two hours) go right by Mari; buses will drop you at the turn-off from the highway (ask for Tell Hariri). From this same spot, it's normally possible to pick up a passing microbus for the return trip to Deir ez-Zur.

NORTHWEST OF DEIR EZ-ZUR

The road from Deir ez-Zur to Aleppo follows the Euphrates River for much of the way, with a number of worthwhile sights not far off the road. Rasafa is the stand-out highlight.

Rasafa الرصافة

Striking Rasafa, an ancient, long-abandoned walled city, lies 25km south of the Euphrates highway, rising up out of the featureless desert like a mirage. It's a fascinating place to explore, made all the more intriguing by its remote location. Bring a hat for protection against the sun as there's no shelter.

HISTORY

Diocletian established a fort here as part of a defensive line against the Sassanian Persians late in the 3rd century AD. About this time a cult to the local martyr St Sergius began to take hold. Sergius, a Roman soldier who converted to Christianity, was executed for refusing to perform sacrifices to Jupiter. By the 5th century Rasafa had become an important centre of Christian worship and an impressive basilica had been built.

A century later the city was at the height of its prosperity. The Byzantine emperor Justinian (r AD 527–65) further fortified the growing settlement against the threat of Persian assault. Ultimately, this was to no avail as Rasafa capitulated to the eastern empire in 616. Following the Muslim Arab invasion of Syria, the city was occupied by Hisham abd al-Malek, who pursued an energetic building policy, adorning the existing city with a palatial summer residence.

Just seven years after Hisham's death, the palace and city were razed by the Baghdad-based Abbasids, fierce rivals of the Umayyads. The city was finally abandoned when

VISITING RASAFA

With your own car, reaching Rasafa is relatively easy – the site lies 25km south of the main Aleppo-Deir ez-Zur highway; take the turn-off at Al-Mansoura. Some hotels in Palmyra (see p513) or Hama (p486) organise long day trips that take in some of the sights.

Otherwise, take a bus to Raqqa from Aleppo (S£135, 2½ hours) or Deir ez-Zur (S£135, 2½ hours). From Raqqa, catch a microbus to Al-Mansoura (S£30, 20 minutes) then negotiate a driver (at least S£500 return) or wait for a lift to take you the 25km to the ruins. It's just possible to visit Rasafa on a day trip by public transport from Aleppo or Deir ez-Zur (or even as a detour en route), but you have to be lucky with connections.

If you must stay overnight in dusty and largely unappealing Raqqa, the options are not impressive. The best of a bad lot is the overpriced **Lazaward Hotel** (☎ 216 120-22; Sharia Saqr Quraysh; s/d US$30/40; ❄), a three-star place with dirty carpets, sticky furniture and grotty bathrooms. There's a decent rooftop restaurant.

NORTHEASTERN SYRIA: CROSSING INTO TURKEY

If you're travelling into northeastern Syria from Turkey, or vice versa, there are no major monuments or must-see sites in this Kurdish region in northeastern Syria. The Syrian border is at Qamishle, a characterless Kurdish stronghold. The border is mainly used by Iraqi refugees crossing to renew their visas. As a result there are long lines and infuriatingly long waits; some travellers have reported waiting all day. The Turkish border is about 1km from the town centre; you have to walk across the border. Once on the Turkish side, it's a further five minutes' walk into Nusaybin, where it's possible to pick up a dolmuş (minibus) for onward travel. The crossing is officially open from 9am to 3pm.

The only accommodation we can recommend is the **Hotel Semiramis** (☎ 421 185; s/d US$20/25), 100m south of the bus station with basic, fairly clean rooms. Across from the Chahba Hotel, there's a nondescript restaurant (meals around S£200), where you can get fuul (fava bean soup), mezze and kebabs. Buses operate from Qamishle to major destinations including Damascus (S£400, 10 hours) and Aleppo (S£225, six to eight hours), departing from a station on Sharia Zaki al-Arsuzi.

invading Mongols swept across northern Syria in the 13th century.

SIGHTS

The walls, enclosing a quadrangle measuring 550m by 400m, are virtually intact; the main entrance is by the **North Gate**. Once inside, you're confronted by the immensity of the place, mostly bare now save for the churches inside. Little excavation has yet been done and you should stroll around the defensive **perimeter walls** before exploring the site.

Of the three churches that remain standing, the grandest is the partially restored **Basilica of St Sergius**. The wide central nave is flanked by two aisles, separated by a series of sweeping arches resting on pillars and a pair of less ambitious arch and column combinations. This and the two other churches date from the 6th century. In the southwestern corner of the complex lie huge underground **cisterns** that could keep a large garrison supplied with water through long sieges. There's a small café outside the east wall of the site selling snacks and drinks.

Lake al-Assad بحيرة الاسد

One of the Assad regime's most ambitious plans, to dam the Euphrates, went into effect in the 1960s with the creation of this glorious azure-coloured inland sea.

Appearing to rise out of the lake, **Qala'at Ja'abar** (student/student S£10/150; ⏲ 8am-6pm Apr-Sep, to 4pm Oct-Mar) is as impressive from a distance as the water vistas are from atop the citadel. Situated on the bank of Lake al-Assad, about 15km north of Ath-Thaura, the castle was built entirely of bricks in classic Mesopotamian style. Before the lake was dammed, the castle had rested on a rocky perch since before the arrival of Islam and had been rebuilt by Nureddin (Nur ad-Din) and altered by the Mamluks.

Without your own car, Qala'at Ja'abar can be difficult to get to. It's necessary to go via Ath-Thaura, either coming from Raqqa (S£40 by microbus) or Aleppo (S£115 by bus). You can then negotiate with a local driver in Ath-Thaura; expect to pay about S£500 return.

SYRIA DIRECTORY

ACCOMMODATION

Syria has some outstanding budget accommodation, with the best choices in Damascus, Hama and Aleppo, with other decent choices in Palmyra and Lattakia. In some cases, the rooms are terrific – simple, yet clean and sometimes with bathrooms and satellite TV. But best of all, these are places switched on to the travellers' network, great for meeting fellow travellers and arranging tours to nearby sites.

There's at least one good midrange hotel in most major tourist hotspots – expect comfortable rooms with good bathrooms, satellite TV and good service. But the real highlight is the new wave of boutique hotels that usually straddle the upper midrange and top-end categories. These are to be found in the old cities of Damascus and Aleppo, with a further option in Hama. These places invariably occupy traditional

PRACTICALITIES

- As well as the three state-run Arabic daily newspapers, there's one English-language daily, the *Syria Times* (S£5). This is published under direct government control and is big on propaganda and short on news.
- You can pick up the BBC World Service on a range of radio frequencies, including AM 1323 in Damascus and the Europe short-wave schedule in Aleppo. See www.bbc.co.uk/worldservice for details.
- CNN, BBC World and a handful of European satellite channels can be accessed in many hotel rooms.
- The country's electrical current is 220V AC, 50Hz. Wall sockets are the round, two-pin European type.
- Syria uses the metric system.

Syrian homes arrayed around an interior courtyard, making an art form of traditional decoration detail in the public areas and usually in the rooms themselves. While in Syria, you should stay in at least one, whatever your budget.

Prices cited are for rooms in the high season and include taxes and breakfast unless stated otherwise. We have defined budget hotels as any that charge up to US$25 for a double room; midrange as any that charge from US$20 to US$90; and top end as those that charge US$90 plus. In the low season (December to March) you should be able to get significant discounts at most hotels. Conversely, during July and August it can be extremely difficult to get a room in Damascus, Hama or Lattakia.

Although some will accept Syrian pounds, midrange and top-end hotels invariably require payment in US dollars or, increasingly, euros. Some also accept credit-card payments (often with a surcharge), but don't take this for granted.

BEST...

Budget Hotels

- **Al-Rabie Hotel** (Damascus; p474)
- **Ghazal Hotel** (Damascus; p474)
- **Al-Haramain Hotel** (Damascus; p474)
- **Riad Hotel** (Hama; p487)
- **Cairo Hotel** (Hama; p487)
- **Hanadi Hotel** (Aleppo; p498)
- **Tourist Hotel** (Aleppo; p498)
- **Safwan Hotel & Hostel** (Lattakia; p504)
- **Al-Nakheel Hotel** (Palmyra; p513)

Boutique Hotels

- **Dar al-Yasmin Hotel** (Damascus; p475)
- **Beit al-Mamlouka** (Damascus; p475)
- **Old Damascus Hotel** (Damascus; p475)
- **Orient House Hotel** (Hama; p487)
- **Dar Halabia** (Aleppo; p499)
- **Tourath House** (Aleppo; p499)
- **Beit Wakil** (Aleppo; p499)
- **Mandaloun Hotel** (Aleppo; p499)

Student Accommodation

Although you'll find flyers advertising shared student accommodation all over the Old City in Damascus, one place we recommend is House of Damascus (p474).

BUSINESS HOURS

The official weekend is Friday and Saturday. Most museums and sites are closed on Tuesday.

Banks Generally follow the government office hours but there are exceptions. Some branches keep their doors open for only three hours from 9am, while some exchange booths are open as late as 7pm.

Government offices 8am to 2pm daily except Friday and holidays. Post offices are open later in the large cities.

Restaurants Between noon and midnight daily. Cafés tend to open earlier and close later.

Shops 9am to 1.30pm and 4pm to 9pm summer, 9am to 1.30pm and 4pm to 8pm winter. Usually closed on Fridays and holidays. In Damascus souq, shops usually don't close at lunchtime and some stay open on Fridays. Aleppo souq shuts down on Friday, but doesn't close for lunch on other days.

CHILDREN

On the one hand, travelling in Syria with children can be a delight, as Syrians are extraordinarily welcoming to children; having children with you will quickly break down the barriers with locals and add a whole new dimension to your trip. Formula is readily available in pharmacies, and disposable nappies are stocked in supermarkets. Restaurants usually have highchairs and restaurants are extremely welcoming to families.

At the same time, very few Syrian hotels have child-friendly facilities and child-friendly sights are next to nonexistent (castles like Crac des Chevaliers and Qala'at Saladin may be exceptions for kids of a certain age). Few towns have easily accessible public gardens with playground equipment or shopping malls with amusement centres. As a result, you'd do well to come prepared with your own entertainment for the little ones.

COURSES

If you're a would-be student of the Arabic language, there are a number of options in Damascus.

British Council (Map pp466-7; ☎ 331 0631; www.britishcouncil.org/syria; Sharia Karim al-Khalil) Offers intensive courses in Modern Standard or Syrian Colloquial Arabic at three levels. You'll find it off Sharia Maysaloun.

Damascus University (Map pp466-7; ☎ 212 9494; www.arabicindamascus.edu.sy; Language Institute, Faculty of Human Arts, University of Damascus, Sharia Filasteen) Offers courses in Syrian Arabic.

DISCOUNT CARDS

Students get massive discounts on site admissions on presentation of an internationally recognised card such as the ISIC.

EMBASSIES & CONSULATES

Most embassies and consulates are open from around 8am to 2pm and are closed on Friday, Saturday and public holidays. The following are in Damascus. Note: the Canadian embassy currently provides emergency consular services to Australians; Irish and New Zealand interests are looked after by the UK embassy. One important development to watch out for is the possible opening of a Lebanese embassy in Damascus – see boxed text, p524, for more information.

Canada (Map pp466-7; ☎ 011-611 6692; www.damascus.gc.ca; Block 12 Autostrad al-Mezze)

Egypt (Map pp466-7; ☎ 011-333 3561; fax 011-333 7961; Sharia al-Jala'a, Abu Roumana)

France (Map pp466-7; ☎ 011-332 7992; www.amb-damas.fr; Sharia Ata Ayyubi, Salihiyya)

Germany (Map pp466-7; ☎ 011-332 3800/1; www.damaskus.diplo.de; 53 Sharia Ibrahim Hanano)

Iran (Map pp466-7; ☎ 011-222 6459; fax 011-222 0997; Autostrad al-Mezzeh)

Italy (Map pp466-7; ☎ 011-333 8338; www.ambdamasco.esteri.it; Sharia al-Ayyubi)

Japan (Map pp466-7; ☎ 011-333 8273; Sharia Shark Asiya al-Jala, Abu Roumana)

Jordan (Map pp466-7; ☎ 011-613 6261; damascus@fm.gov.jo; Miza Eastern Villas, Western Tarablus Street Bldg 27) Close to Al-Akram Mosque.

DAMASCUS WITH MY DAUGHTER *Anthony Ham*

Some Lonely Planet authors have families, too. And those of us with children don't like spending months away from them at a stretch. Thus it was that shortly after my daughter's nine-month 'birthday', she found herself on a plane to Damascus, accompanied by her mother and two of her grandparents. Seeing them emerge from the scrum at Damascus Airport was one of the highlights of my trip.

Before setting out, I had solicited the advice of a friend who had travelled extensively with her young son around the Middle East, including twice to Syria. Apart from telling us to just do it, she described Syria as 'one of the most child-friendly places I can think of'. How right she was. People went out of their way to be helpful (including one waiter who insisted on carrying the pram up three flights of stairs on his own), and our daughter soon got used to being picked up and cuddled by all manner of strangers. In the Umayyad Mosque, a lovely Syrian family invited us home so that they could spend more time with her. Outside the Sayyida Ruqayya Mosque, Iranian pilgrims insisted on having their photo taken with her. In restaurants and in our hotel, male waiters and hotel staff found any excuse to pick her up in the hope of receiving one of her newly minted smiles. And at Al-Nawfara Coffee Shop, she became best friends with Abu Shady, the *hakawati*, Syria's last storyteller.

Yes, it's true that my daughter probably won't remember her first visit to Damascus. But it was a wonderful experience that her parents will never forget.

Netherlands (Map pp466-7; ☎ 011-333 6871; fax 011-333 9369; Sharia al-Jala'a, Abu Roumana)
Spain (Map pp466-7; ☎ 011-613 2900/1; emb.damasco@mae.es; Sharia Shafi, east Mezze) Behind Hotel Al-Hayat.
Turkey (Map pp466-7; ☎ 011-333 1411; dakkabe@citechco.net; 58 Sharia Ziad bin Abi Soufian, Al Rawda)
UK (Map pp466-7; ☎ 0932 004 424; www.britishembassy.gov.uk/syria; Kotob Bldg, 11 Sharia Mohammed Kurd Ali, Malki)
USA (Map pp466-7; ☎ 011-3391 4444; http://damascus.usembassy.gov; 2 Sharia al-Mansour, Abu Roumana)

FESTIVALS & EVENTS

Visit the Syrian Ministry of Tourism website (www.syriatourism.org) for festival details.

Silk Road Festival Held annually in late September in the cities where the ancient caravans once met: Palmyra, Aleppo, Bosra and Damascus. A varied program features overseas acts, concerts, sporting events and dance performances.
Bosra Festival This festival of music and theatre is held every September or October in odd years. It offers the chance to be part of an audience in the town's spectacular Roman amphitheatre. Tickets cost from S£50.
Damascus International Film Festival This annual film festival in November is a 15-year veteran and sees 200 international and local films screened across Damascus.

GAY & LESBIAN TRAVELLERS

Homosexuality is prohibited in Syria and conviction can result in imprisonment.

Cleopatra's Wedding Present, by Robert Tewdwr Moss, is an entertaining account of a gay American's travels through Syria.

HOLIDAYS

In addition to the main Islamic holidays (p628), Syria celebrates the following public holidays:

New Year's Day 1 January
Revolution Day 8 March
Al-Adha Day 15 March
Mother's Day 21 March
Easter March/April
Hijra New Year's Day 6 April
National Day 17 April
May Day 1 May
Martyrs' Day 6 May
Liberation War of October Day 6 October
Christmas Day 25 December

MONEY

The official currency is the Syrian pound (S£), also called the lira. There are 100 piastres (also known as *qirsh*) to a pound but this is redundant as the smallest coin is one pound. Other coins come in denominations of two, five, 10 and 25. Notes come in denominations of 50, 100, 200, 500 and 1000.

There's at least one branch of the Commercial Bank of Syria in every major town and most will change US dollars or euros. There's also a small number of officially sanctioned private exchange offices, which change cash at official bank rates. The advantage is that whereas banks usually close for the day at 12.30pm or 2pm, the exchange offices are often open until 7pm.

Country	Unit	Syrian pound (S£)
Australia	A$1	31.77
Canada	C$1	40.33
Egypt	E£1	8.83
Euro zone	€1	62.46
Japan	¥100	52.90
Jordan	JD1	69.60
Lebanon	LL10	0.33
New Zealand	NZ$1	28.50
Turkey	TL1	31.63
UK	UK£1	93.51
USA	US$1	48.20

ATMs

There are now ATMs everywhere in Syria in most tourist centres and medium-sized towns, although Palmyra was a notable exception at the time of writing – expect that to change. Most ATMs accept Visa and are Cirrus or Maestro enabled, but only a handful (including at Damascus Airport and any branch of Banque Bemo Saudi Fransi) take MasterCard. Displays on each ATM announce which cards are accepted. One drawback for those hoping to survive from ATM cash withdrawals while in Syria is that most ATMs set a daily withdrawal limit, usually around S£3000.

Credit Cards

Major credit cards are increasingly being accepted by travel agencies, hotels and shops, but they're not yet accepted in most restaurants. This situation will change as soon as Visa and MasterCard are given permission to set up shop in Syria; at present all transactions must be processed through Lebanon, and a surcharge of around 10% is levied on the customer to cover this.

The contact number for Amex in Syria is ☎ 011-221 7813; for Visa, MasterCard and Diner's Club it's ☎ 011-222 1326.

Tipping & Bargaining

Tipping is expected in the better restaurants and by all tour guides. Whatever you buy, remember that bargaining is an integral part of the process and listed prices are always inflated to allow for it. If you're shopping in the souqs, bargain hard – even a minimum amount of effort will almost always result in outrageous asking prices being halved.

Travellers Cheques

It's becoming increasingly difficult to cash travellers cheques in Syria. If you do find a bank that will change your cheques, you must have the bank receipt with the cheque numbers detailed on it. Exchange offices never change them.

POST

The Syrian postal service is slow but trustworthy. Letters mailed from the main cities take about a week to get to Europe and up to a month to get to Australia or the USA.

TELEPHONE

Mobile Phones

You can purchase a Syriatel SIM card to use in your mobile phone while you're in the country. These cost S£400 and include a decent number of calls. MTN offers similar cards. Cards are available at mobile-phone shops throughout the country (these are ubiquitous) and at the arrivals hall at Damascus International Airport. Otherwise non-Syrian mobile phones work fine in Syria (usually through Syriatel), but roaming charges can be prohibitive.

Phone Codes

The country code for Syria is ☎ 963, followed by the local area code (minus the zero), then the subscriber number. The international access code (to call abroad from Syria) is ☎ 00. The numbers for directory assistance are ☎ 141 142 (national calls) and ☎ 143 144 (international calls).

Phonecards

Syrian Telecom cards are available from mobile-phone shops and kiosks and you'll find phones on the streets in most cities, especially outside the government telephone office. You'll need a S£200 card to make calls within Syria (S£20 per minute), a S£350 card to phone Europe and other Western destinations (around S£50 per minute).

VISAS

Everyone, except citizens of Arab countries, requires a visa to enter Syria. The basic rule is that you should obtain a visa at the Syrian embassy or consulate in your home country. Avoid applying in a country that's not your own or that you don't hold residency for, as the Syrian authorities don't like this: at best, they'll ask you for a letter of recommendation from your own embassy (often an expensive and time-consuming proposition); at worst, they'll turn you down flat. US citizens should be aware that many US embassies abroad have a policy of not issuing letters of recommendation – leading to the ridiculous situation where they issue letters stating that they don't issue letters of recommendation. If your home country doesn't have a Syrian embassy or consulate, there's no problem with you applying in another country; alternatively, you can obtain a visa on arrival.

Officially, the Syrian embassy in Amman issues visas only to nationals and residents of Jordan and to nationals of countries that have no Syrian representation. That said, we receive occasional reports that citizens without Jordanian residence were obtaining single-entry Syrian visas in Amman for JD90.

In Turkey, you can get Syrian visas in both Ankara and İstanbul, but you'll need a letter of recommendation from your embassy. There's no Syrian embassy in Lebanon, although that may have changed by the time you read this – see boxed text, p524.

There are three types of visa: transit, single entry and multiple entry. Transit visas are only good for airport stays. Both single- or multiple-entry visas are valid for 30 days inside Syria, although the embassy's visa stamp may say 15 days (see p524), and must be used within three months of the date of issue. Don't be misled by the line on the visa stating a validity of three months – this simply means the visa is valid *for presentation* for three months. You'll usually require two photographs and have to fill out two forms.

The cost of visas varies according to the reciprocal agreement Syria has made with your home country. For example, UK citizens pay

UK£35 for a single-entry visa, US citizens US$100 and Australian citizens A$45. If you book travel arrangements through a foreign tour operator that has a working relationship with a Syrian operator, you are entitled to a free visa, collectable at the point of entry.

Remember also that *any* evidence of a visit to Israel – most visa application forms ask if you've been to 'Occupied Palestine' – will see your application turned down flat. Later, if Syrian border officials see that you have an Israeli visa or stamp in your passport, or if a scan of recent stamps suggests that you have recently travelled through Israel and the Palestinian Territories, you will be refused entry to Syria (see boxed text, p332). However, slight changes may be afoot. There are tentative plans for this rule to be ever-so-slightly relaxed in the case of an organised tour group in which some members have an Israeli stamp. But it would take a peace treaty between Israel and Syria for us to recommend that you count on it.

Visas at the Border

If there's no Syrian representation in your country, you can obtain a visa on arrival at borders, airports or ports. Otherwise you MUST secure a visa in advance. Such is the official (and usually adhered to) position of the Syrian authorities. Even so, we continue to hear reports of travellers from countries with a Syrian embassy back home convincing immigration officials at land borders to waive the official rules and grant a visa. We don't recommend that you count on this, but if circumstances prevented you from getting a Syrian visa back home, you may want to try your luck, on the understanding, of course, that the chances of success are small and depend on the uncharacteristic goodwill of the Syrian authorities.

Visa Extensions

In one of the most welcome changes for travellers in Syria in recent years, you're no longer required to seek a visa extension if you wish to stay in the country longer than 15 days; at the time of writing, this requirement was still being stamped on visas by Syrian embassies around the world even though the requirement no longer applies. The rule change means that you must instead seek a visa extension after 30 days, which takes the need for extensions beyond the concern of most travellers.

If you're staying in Syria for more than 30 days you'll have to visit an immigration office, which you'll find in all main cities. Unless you ask for a longer extension, the usual length of the extension is a further 15 days, although up to one-and-a-half months is routinely granted upon request. They are usually only granted on the 29th or 30th day of your stay, so if you apply earlier expect to be knocked back. The specifics vary from place to place but there are always a couple of forms to complete and you need two to six passport photos. The cost is never more than S£50. For further details see the individual city sections.

WOMEN TRAVELLERS

Syria is an extraordinarily safe country in which to travel, and foreign women are generally treated with courtesy and respect; this is far from the most conservative country in the region. Even so, there will still always be a certain amount of unwanted predatory male attention, particularly in Palmyra and in the

TRAVEL BETWEEN SYRIA & LEBANON

In mid-2008 Syria and Lebanon began a period of unprecedented rapprochement, and it's one that could have important implications for those travelling between the two countries. Among the changes announced in mid-2008 were promises to open a Syrian embassy in Beirut and a Lebanese embassy in Damascus. Prior to the announcement, such embassies had not existed since independence, partly because relations have long been strained and in part because Syria considered Lebanon to be an extension of Syrian territory. Travellers report that it is becoming easier to obtain a Syrian visa at the Lebanese border, but this is a hit-and-miss affair, and could end up frustrating if you're denied entry. It's better to arrange your Syrian or Lebanese visa in advance. However, keep your ear to the ground by speaking to travellers and monitoring the Thorn Tree section of Lonely Planet's website (www.lonelyplanet.com) to find out if visas can be obtained at the border, and ask the staff at your friendly local Syrian or Lebanese embassy for the latest official position.

area around Sharia Baron in Aleppo. To minimise the chance of any unpleasant encounters, follow the advice given on clothing and behaviour on p633 and try to sit next to women on public transport. Clothing guidelines are particularly important in rural areas, which tend to be more conservative. But it's far from a universal picture: in Lattakia and much of Damascus, many local women dress much as they do in the West, while Hama and Aleppo are much more conservative.

While hitching a ride with locals is not unusual in Syria, we (and many locals) don't recommend that single women travellers hitch in Syria, especially since a young Canadian backpacker went missing in the area around Hama in 2007. It's worth noting that the young woman was the first foreigner ever to disappear in Syria and the case remains unsolved.

TRANSPORT IN SYRIA

GETTING THERE & AWAY

Entering Syria

For information on Syrian visas and entry requirements, see p523.

Air

Syria's main **international airport** (☎ 544 5983-9) is 32km southeast of Damascus and has regular connections to other cities in the Middle East, Europe, Africa and Asia on a variety of European- and Middle East-based airlines. There are also reasonable regional and occasionally European connections from **Aleppo** (☎ 421 1200). Lattakia has just one weekly Syrianair flight to Cairo.

Syrian Arab Airlines (Syrianair; www.syriaair.com) is the national airline. It has a small fleet, which includes some recently purchased Airbuses. From Damascus, Syrianair flies to destinations across Europe and the Middle East.

> **DEPARTURE TAX**
>
> There's an airport departure tax of S£200 payable in local currency at booths next to airport check-in counters. If you're leaving via one of Syria's land borders, the departure tax is S£500.

Land

Syria has borders with Lebanon, Turkey, Jordan and Iraq. It also shares a border with Israel, the hotly disputed Golan Heights, but it's a definite no-go zone that's mined and is patrolled by UN peacekeepers.

IRAQ

The only open border crossing with Iraq is just south of Al-Bukamal in the extreme east of the country, although whether it's open to foreign travellers depends on the prevailing political and security winds.

JORDAN

There are two border crossings between Syria and Jordan: at Nasib/Jabir and Deraa/Ramtha. These crossings are 3km apart. If crossing by car, service taxi or bus you'll cross through the main Nasib/Jabir post, on

> **JUST ACROSS THE BORDER: JERASH, JORDAN**
>
> If Syria's stirring Roman ruins of Palmyra, Apamea and Bosra have captured your imagination and you're eager for more, you'd be surprised how easy it is to visit Jerash (p355), Jordan's premier Roman site. Make sure you've a multiple-entry Syrian visa (p523) before setting out. With that sorted, catch either a private bus (p480) or service taxi (p480) from Damascus's Al-Samariyeh Garage, pick up your Jordanian visa at the border (p393) and continue on the same bus to Irbid (p358) in northern Jordan; setting out early will allow you to make the 3½- to five-hour journey and arrive in Irbid early enough to reach the ruins by sunset or for an early start the next morning. From Irbid, regular minibuses make the 45-minute trip to Jerash, where there is a handful of sleeping options (p357) that allow you to make an early start. Another alternative, if you're coming from Bosra (p482), is catch a minibus to Deraa, cross the border, then catch a Jordanian minibus down the highway to Irbid; you could, in theory, travel from Damascus to Bosra and on to Irbid in a single day, but you'd be hoping your minibuses fill up fast en route. Why bother? Well, for a start Jerash is stunning when bathed in the early morning and early evening light, especially its unique Oval Plaza (p355) and beautiful South Theatre (p357) with fine views over this lovely site.

the Amman-Damascus highway. If you're travelling by train or local transport, you'll use Deraa/Ramtha. Microbuses from the bus station at Deraa charge S£250 per person to take you across the border to Ramtha. The best way to get to Deraa from Damascus is to catch a bus from Baramke Garage.

From Damascus, there are daily buses to Amman (p480), for which you need to book in advance as demand for seats is high, or you can catch a service taxi. The famous Hejaz railway trip (p481) is also a possibility.

Jordanian visas are issued at the border (p393), or can be obtained in advance from the embassy in Damascus. It's cheaper to get it at the border.

LEBANON

There are plenty of buses from Damascus to Beirut (p480), although to travel direct to Baalbek the only option is a service taxi (see p480 for details). You can also travel by bus or service taxi to Beirut via Tripoli from Aleppo (p501) and Lattakia (p507).

See p454 for information on obtaining Lebanese visas.

TURKEY

There are several border crossings between Syria and Turkey. The busiest and most convenient links Antakya in Turkey with Aleppo, via the Bab al-Hawa border station. This is the route taken by all cross-border buses including those from Damascus and Aleppo (p501) bound for Antakya and onward Turkish destinations.

An interesting alternative to the bus might be the weekly train from Aleppo to İstanbul (p502).

You can also make your way by microbus from Lattakia, on the Syrian coast, to the border post on the outskirts of the village of Kassab and on to Antakya via Yayladağı. Over in the far northeast of Syria there's another crossing at Qamishle (see boxed text, p519) for the southeastern Turkish town of Nusaybin.

While Turkish visas are issued at the border (p614), you must already be in possession of a valid visa to enter Syria – see p523.

GETTING AROUND

Air

Syrianair has a monopoly on domestic flights in the country, and operates flights from Damascus to Aleppo, Deir ez-Zur, Lattakia and Qamishle. Students and under 26s can usually get discounted tickets.

Bus

Syria has a well-developed road network, and bus transport is frequent and cheap. Distances are short, so journeys rarely take more than a few hours. Carry your passport at all times as you'll need it to buy tickets.

Several kinds of buses ply the same routes, but the most safe and comfortable way to travel is by 'luxury' Pullman bus.

MINIBUS & MICROBUS

Minibuses operate on many of the shorter routes, eg Hama–Homs, Tartus–Lattakia and Homs–Lattakia. They take about 20 people, are often luridly decorated and have no schedule, departing when full. This means that on less-popular routes, you may have to wait quite some time until one fills up. Journey times are generally longer than with the other buses, as they set people down and pick them up at any and all points along the route – hence their common name of 'hob-

JUST ACROSS THE BORDER: BAALBEK, LEBANON

You're in Damascus and travellers coming from Lebanon are raving about the Roman ruins of Baalbek. Some even claim that it surpasses even Palmyra. So grab a visa to enter Lebanon, see p454, also see p524 for information about trying your luck at getting a visa at the border. Although there are no direct bus services between Damascus and Baalbek, service taxis (p480) regularly ply the route from Damascus's Al-Samariyeh Garage, covering the route in just 2½ hours. While you could conceivably return to Damascus the same day, what's your hurry? Baalbek rewards those who linger, especially early morning or late afternoon, and, besides, you also have to factor in time for a meal at Shahrazad (p450) with its astonishing views over the ruins. The ruins (p448) themselves are awash with temples to just about every known Roman deity and this is one ancient site where you can really imagine what it was like in its heyday.

JUST ACROSS THE BORDER: ŞANLIURFA (URFA), TURKEY

There are more famous cities in Turkey than Şanlıurfa (p604), but few offer such an exotic Middle Eastern feel, not to mention easy proximity to northern Syria. You might find a service taxi to the border crossing at Akçakale, which lies south of Şanlıurfa, from Aleppo's small International Bus Station (p501), but they can take an age to fill and you may be better off catching a much more frequent, early-morning cross-border bus to Antakya (p583) and change to a bus heading for Şanlıurfa. Alternatively you can aim for Gaziantep (p607), via İslahiye or Kilis; from Gaziantep there are departures on to Şanlıurfa. Before doing so, remember one very important point: you can pick up your Turkish visa (p614) at the border, but if you're planning to return to Syria, don't even think of setting out without a multiple-entry Syrian visa (p523) in your passport. Şanlıurfa has many calling cards, from the cave where Abraham is said to have been born to its evocative bazaar and *kale* (fortress). To return to Syria, catch a minibus to Harran (p605), one of the oldest continuously inhabited places in the world, then on to the Syrian border post at Akçakale. On the Syrian side of the border, service taxis run when full to Aleppo.

hob' (stop-stop) – and often detour from the main road.

The term 'microbus' is blurred, but in general refers to the little white vans (mostly Japanese) with a sliding door. These are used principally to connect the major cities and towns with surrounding small towns and villages. They are replacing the lumbering old minibuses with which they compete, and are faster and slightly more expensive. They follow set routes but along that route passengers can be picked up or set down anywhere. The fare is the same whatever distance you travel.

PULLMAN BUS

Dozens of private bus companies operate excellent services between the major cities. Routes are few and operators are in fierce competition for passengers. Every city bus station (known locally as *karajats*, or garages) has a row of prefab huts serving as booking offices for the various companies. There's no central information source for departure times or prices, so it's a case of walking around and finding out which company has the next bus to your destination, although chances are that the touts will find you before you get too far.

Fares vary little and buses are pretty much the same (large, newish, air-con). Seats are assigned at booking. A rigid no-smoking rule is imposed on most buses (although some drivers seem to be exempt), and during the journey a steward will distribute cups of water. A few companies do have the edge when it comes to the cleanliness and roadworthiness of their vehicles; particularly recommended are Al-Kadmous (sometimes signed 'KT') and Al-Ahliah.

Car & Motorcycle

You'll need an International Driving Permit (IDP) if you decide to drive in Syria. Traffic runs on the right-hand side of the road. The speed limit is 60km/h in built-up areas, 70km/h on the open road and 110km/h on major highways. The roads are generally quite reasonable, but when heading off into the backblocks you'll find that most signposting is in Arabic only.

Europcar (☎ 011-212 0624/5; www.europcar.com) has been joined by **Hertz** (☎ 011-221 6615; www.hertz.com) and a number of other international firms, including a gaggle of sometimes dodgy local companies. With the latter, keep your eye on insurance arrangements, which can be quite lackadaisical. Expect to pay at least US$50/325 per day/week for a small car including all insurance and unlimited mileage. The local companies can be cheaper. Most of the firms have desks at the airport, and offices on or around the Cham Palace Hotel on Sharia Maysaloun in central Damascus. You'll need an IDP and a sizeable cash or credit-card deposit; the minimum hire is usually three days.

Local Transport

Service taxis (shared taxis; ser-*vees*) only operate on the major routes and can cost twice the microbus fare – sometimes more.

Tours

Tours of some of the country's highlights can be organised in Damascus (p474),

Hama (p486) and Aleppo (p498), among other places.

Train

The once-neglected Syrian railway system is improving all the time due to recent government investment, including the purchase of new French-made locomotives. The main line connects Damascus, Aleppo, Deir ez-Zur, Hassake and Qamishle. A secondary line runs from Aleppo to Lattakia, along the coast to Tartus and again inland to Homs and Damascus.

Departures are often in the middle of the night, meaning that the only route where we recommend the train over the bus is between Lattakia and Aleppo; this goes through spectacular countryside, starts and terminates in centrally located stations, has at least one reasonable departure time and is very comfortable. At least one midmorning departure time and swish new trains also make the service a viable alternative to the bus between Damascus and Aleppo, although the scenery is uninspiring.

First class is air-con with aircraft-type seats; second class is the same without air-con – it's probably not worth it except in summer. Student discounts are only given on 2nd-class tickets.

Turkey

Hoş geldiniz (welcome) to the perfect introduction to the Middle East. Although most Turks see their country as European, the nation packs in as many wailing minarets and spice-trading bazaars as its southeastern neighbours, Iran, Iraq and Syria. This bridge between continents has absorbed Europe's modernism and sophistication, and Asia's culture and tradition. Travellers can enjoy historical hotspots, mountain outposts, expansive steppe and all the exoticism of the Middle East, without having to forego comfy beds and punctual buses.

Turkey's charms range from sun-splashed Mediterranean and Aegean beaches to Sultanahmet's mosques, and while these gems fit its reputation as a continental meeting point, the country can't be pigeonholed that easily. Many of its attractions are completely unlike anywhere else on the planet, such as Cappadocia's fairy chimneys and Pamukkale's white travertine (calcium carbonate) shelves and pools. The ethereal beauty of Mt Nemrut, littered with giant stone heads, and Olympos, where Lycian ruins peek from the undergrowth, is quintessentially Turkish.

Such potent mixtures of natural splendour and ancient remains result from millennia of eventful history, during which Middle Eastern empires such as the Hittites and the Seljuks establish capitals in Anatolia (Asian Turkey). So many names here are familiar from history lessons and Hollywood blockbusters, from Troy and Ephesus to Gallipoli, where Atatürk repelled Anzac and British forces. Travelling Turkey's beaches and plains is like turning the pages of a historical thriller, with mosques and medreses, hamams and *hans* (caravanserais) never far from view.

When it's time to close the book and seek worldly pleasures, Turkey shines as brightly as its red-and-white flag. This is, after all, the land that introduced the world to the kebap (and, less famously, the cherry). Vegetarians, meanwhile, can tuck into meze, ideally consumed on a panoramic terrace with rakı (aniseed spirit) or a tulip-shaped glass of *çay* (tea). And that's before you lace up your hiking boots or pull on a dive mask…

FAST FACTS

- **Area** 779,452 sq km
- **Capital** Ankara
- **Country code** ☎ 90
- **Language** Turkish
- **Money** Turkish lira (TL); US$1 = TL1.19; €1 = TL1.75
- **Official name** Türkiye Cumhuriyeti (Turkish Republic)
- **Population** 72 million

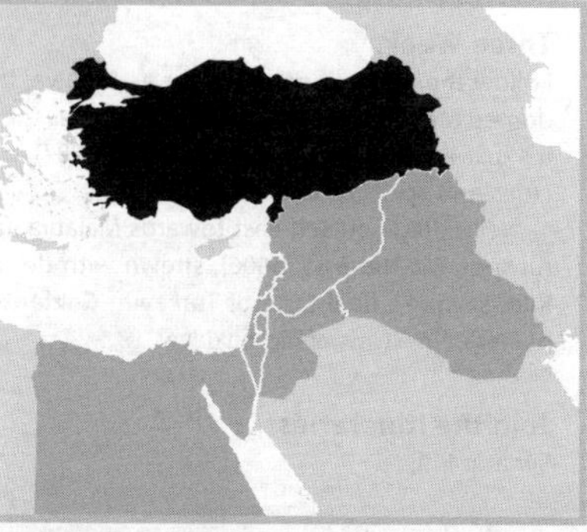

CLIMATE & WHEN TO GO

The Aegean and Mediterranean coasts have mild, rainy winters and hot, dry summers. The Anatolian plateau can be boiling hot (although less humid than the coast) in summer and freezing in winter. The Black Sea coast is mild with sporadic rain in summer, and chilly and wet in winter. Mountainous eastern Turkey is icy cold and snowy in winter, while temperatures shoot to the other end of the thermometer in high summer.

From late April to May (during spring) and from late September to October (during autumn) are the best times to visit; the weather is warm and dry, and there are fewer tourists. In the high season (July to mid-September) it can be suffocatingly hot and clammy, and major tourist destinations are crowded and overpriced.

Also see Climate Charts, p625.

HISTORY

Early Anatolian Civilisations

The Hittites, the greatest early civilisation in Anatolia, were a force to be reckoned with from 2000 to 1200 BC. Their capital, Hattuşa, is now an atmospheric site east of Ankara.

After the collapse of the Hittite empire, Anatolia splintered into small states and it wasn't until the Graeco-Roman period that parts of the country were reunited. Christianity later spread through the region, preached by the apostle Paul, crossing Anatolia on the new Roman roads.

Rome, then Byzantium

In AD 330 the Roman emperor, Constantine, founded a new imperial city at Byzantium (İstanbul). Renamed Constantinople, the strategic city became the capital of the Eastern Roman Empire and was the centre of the Byzantine Empire for 1000

TURKEY IN...

Two Weeks

Start the tour with pizazz in İstanbul, where the must-see sights include the famous **Aya Sofya** (p540), **Blue Mosque** (p540) and **Topkapı Palace** (p540).

After a few days of frenetic İstanbul, you'll be ready to blow town. Head southwest to the **Gallipoli battlefields** (p555), the site of horrendous Allied casualties in WWI. From there hop across the Dardanelles to the Aegean coast and **Troy** (p556), worth a visit even without Brad Pitt. You could pass a pleasant night in beachy **Assos** or **Behramkale** (p556), with its hilltop village and temple, en route to **Ephesus** (p563), the eastern Mediterranean's best-preserved classical city.

Nip inland to **Pamukkale's** (p566) gleaming white pools and ledges, then hit the coast again at **Olympos** (p577), with ruins in the undergrowth and hippies in tree houses. Spend the rest of your time ambling along the Mediterranean coast, stopping in spots such as **Antalya** (p578), with its Roman harbour and walled old city.

Prepare yourself for Syria in **Antakya** (p583), which was part of the French protectorate of Syria until 1938. Also known as Hatay and, in the Bible, Antioch, the former Roman settlement has some magnificent mosaics to look at before crossing the border at Reyhanlı/Bab al-Hawa (for Aleppo).

Three Weeks

Follow the above itinerary as far as Antalya, then veer northeast to Konya, where the turquoise-domed **Mevlâna Museum** (p586) occupies the former lodge of the whirling dervishes. From there, it's just a few hours to **Cappadocia** (p587), otherworldly home of fairy chimneys, underground cities and rock-cut churches.

Next, drag yourself east towards Malatya, from where you can visit another ethereally beautiful spot: **Mt Nemrut** (p606), strewn with decapitated stone heads. Before crossing to Aleppo at Kilis, savour a final taste of Turkey in **Gaziantep** (p607), home to 180-plus pastry shops and the planet's finest pistachio baklavas.

Join the Itineraries

Syria (p459)

years. During the European Dark Ages, the Byzantine Empire kept alive the flame of Roman culture, although it was intermittently threatened from the east (Persians, Arabs, Turks) and west (European powers such as the Goths and Lombards).

The Coming of the Turks: Seljuks & Ottomans

The Byzantine Empire began to decline from 1071, when the Seljuk Turks defeated its forces at Manzikert, north of Lake Van. The Seljuks overran most of Anatolia, establishing a provincial capital at Konya. Their domains stretched across the Middle East and their distinctive, conical-roofed tombs still dot Turkey.

The Byzantines endeavoured to protect Constantinople and reclaim Anatolia, but during the Fourth Crusade (1202–04), which was supposedly instigated to save Eastern Christendom from the Muslims, an unruly Crusader force sacked Constantinople.

The Seljuks, meanwhile, were defeated by the Mongols at Köse Dağ in 1243. The region fractured into a mosaic of Turkish *beyliks* (principalities) and Mongol fiefdoms, but by 1300, a single Turkish bey, Osman, established the Ottoman dynasty.

Having captured Constantinople in 1453, the Ottoman Empire reached its zenith a century later under Süleyman the Magnificent. It expanded deep into Europe, Asia and North Africa, but when its march westward stalled at Vienna in 1683, the rot set in. By the 19th century, European powers had begun to covet the Ottomans' domains.

Nationalism swept Europe after the French Revolution, and Greece, Romania, Montenegro, Serbia and Bosnia all won independence from the Ottomans. The First Balkan War removed Bulgaria and Macedonia from the Ottoman map, while Bulgarian, Greek and Serbian troops advanced on İstanbul. The empire was now known as the 'sick man of Europe'.

The Republic

WWI stripped the Turks of Syria, Palestine, Mesopotamia (Iraq) and Arabia, and the victorious Europeans intended to share most of Anatolia among themselves, leaving the Turks virtually nothing.

Enter Mustafa Kemal Atatürk, the father of modern Turkey. Atatürk made his name by repelling the British and Anzac forces in their attempt to capture Gallipoli. Rallying the tattered Turkish army, he outmanoeuvred the Allied forces in the War of Independence and, in 1923, pushed the invading Greeks into the sea at Smyrna (İzmir).

After renegotiation of the WWI treaties, a new Turkish Republic, reduced to Anatolia and part of Thrace, was born. Atatürk embarked on a modernisation program, introducing a secular democracy, the Latin script, European dress and equal rights for women (at least in theory). The capital shifted from İstanbul to Ankara. Many of the sweeping changes did not come easily and their reverberations can still be felt today. In population exchanges with Greece, more than a million Greeks left Turkey and nearly half a million Turks moved in; deserted 'ghost villages' can still be seen.

Since Atatürk's death in 1938, Turkey has experienced three military coups and, during the 1980s and '90s, had conflict with the Kurdistan Workers Party (PKK), which aimed to create a Kurdish state in Turkey's southeast corner.

Turkey Today

In the dramatic 2002 elections, the year-old Justice & Development Party (AKP) triumphed and its charismatic leader, Recep Tayyip Erdoğan, became prime minister. Intent on gaining EU entry for Turkey, the AKP has scrapped the death penalty, granted greater rights to the Kurds and cracked down on human rights violations.

By 2005 the economy was considered robust enough to introduce the new Turkish lira (YTL; Yeni Türk Lirası). The EU started accession talks with Turkey that October, but they have come to naught and the initial ardour for membership has cooled. In 2009 the new Turkish lira was renamed Turkish lira (TL; Türk Lirası).

Following the AKP's reelection in mid-2007, the tussle between 'secularists' and 'Islamists' intensified. A legal case to close the AKP for pursuing an antisecular agenda brought tensions to boiling point. In mid-2008, police arrested scores of people associated with the Ergenekon movement, alleging they were fomenting a coup against the government, and terrorist bombs exploded in İstanbul. Political meltdown was

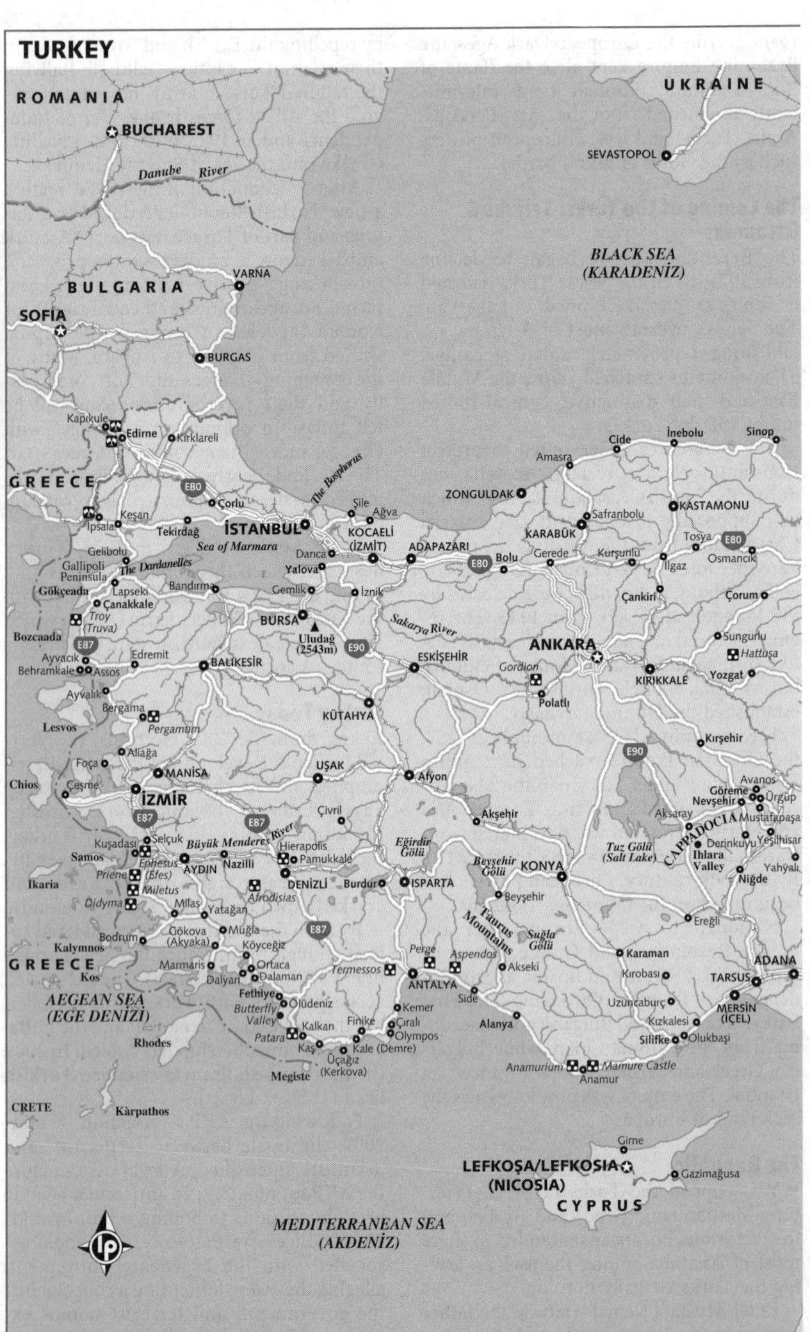
TURKEY
ROMANIA
BUCHAREST
Danube River
UKRAINE
SEVASTOPOL
BLACK SEA
(KARADENİZ)
BULGARIA
VARNA
SOFIA
BURGAS
Kapıkule
Edirne
Kirklareli
GREECE
E80
Çorlu
The Bosphorus
Şile
Ağva
İpsala
Keşan
Tekirdağ
İSTANBUL
KOCAELİ
(İZMİT)
ADAPAZARI
Sea of Marmara
Gelibolu
Gallipoli Peninsula
The Dardanelles
Darıca
Yalova
Gökçeada
Lapseki
Çanakkale
Bandırma
Gemlik
İznik
Troy
(Truva)
Bozcaada
E87
BURSA
Uludağ
(2543m)
E90
Sakarya River
Ayvacık
Behramkale
Assos
Edremit
BALIKESİR
ESKİŞEHİR
Ayvalık
KÜTAHYA
Bergama
Pergamum
Lesvos
Aliağa
Foça
MANİSA
UŞAK
Afyon
Chios
Çeşme
İZMİR
Çivril
Kuşadası
Selçuk
Büyük Menderes River
Hierapolis
Pamukkale
Samos
Ephesus
(Efes)
AYDIN
Nazilli
DENİZLİ
Priene
Miletus
Ikaria
Didyma
Milas
Yatağan
Afrodisias
Burdur
ISPARTA
Eğirdir Gölü
Bodrum
Gökova
(Akyaka)
Muğla
Köyceğiz
Kalymnos
GREECE
Marmaris
Ortaca
Dalyan
Dalaman
Kos
AEGEAN SEA
(EGE DENİZİ)
Fethiye
Ölüdeniz
Butterfly Valley
Patara
Kalkan
Kaş
Finike
Kemer
Çıralı
Olympos
Kale (Demre)
Üçağız
(Kerkova)
Megiste
Rhodes
CRETE
Kàrpathos
Termessos
Perge
Aspendos
ANTALYA
Side
Alanya
Zonguldak
Amasra
Cide
İnebolu
Sinop
Safranbolu
KASTAMONU
KARABÜK
Tosya
E80
Gerede
Kurşunlu
Osmancık
Bolu
Ilgaz
Çankırı
Çorum
ANKARA
Sungurlu
Hattuşa
Gordion
Polatlı
KIRIKKALE
Yozgat
Kırşehir
E90
Avanos
Göreme
Nevşehir
Ürgüp
Aksaray
Mustafapaşa
CAPPADOCIA
Derinkuyu
Yeşilhisar
Akşehir
Tuz Gölü
(Salt Lake)
Ihlara Valley
Yahyalı
Beyşehir Gölü
KONYA
Niğde
Beyşehir
Taurus Mountains
Suğla Gölü
Ereğli
Akseki
Karaman
ADANA
Kırobası
TARSUS
Uzuncaburç
MERSİN
(İÇEL)
Kızkalesi
Silifke
Olukbaşı
Anamurium
Mamure Castle
Anamur
Girne
LEFKOŞA/LEFKOSIA
(NICOSIA)
Gazimağusa
CYPRUS
MEDITERRANEAN SEA
(AKDENİZ)

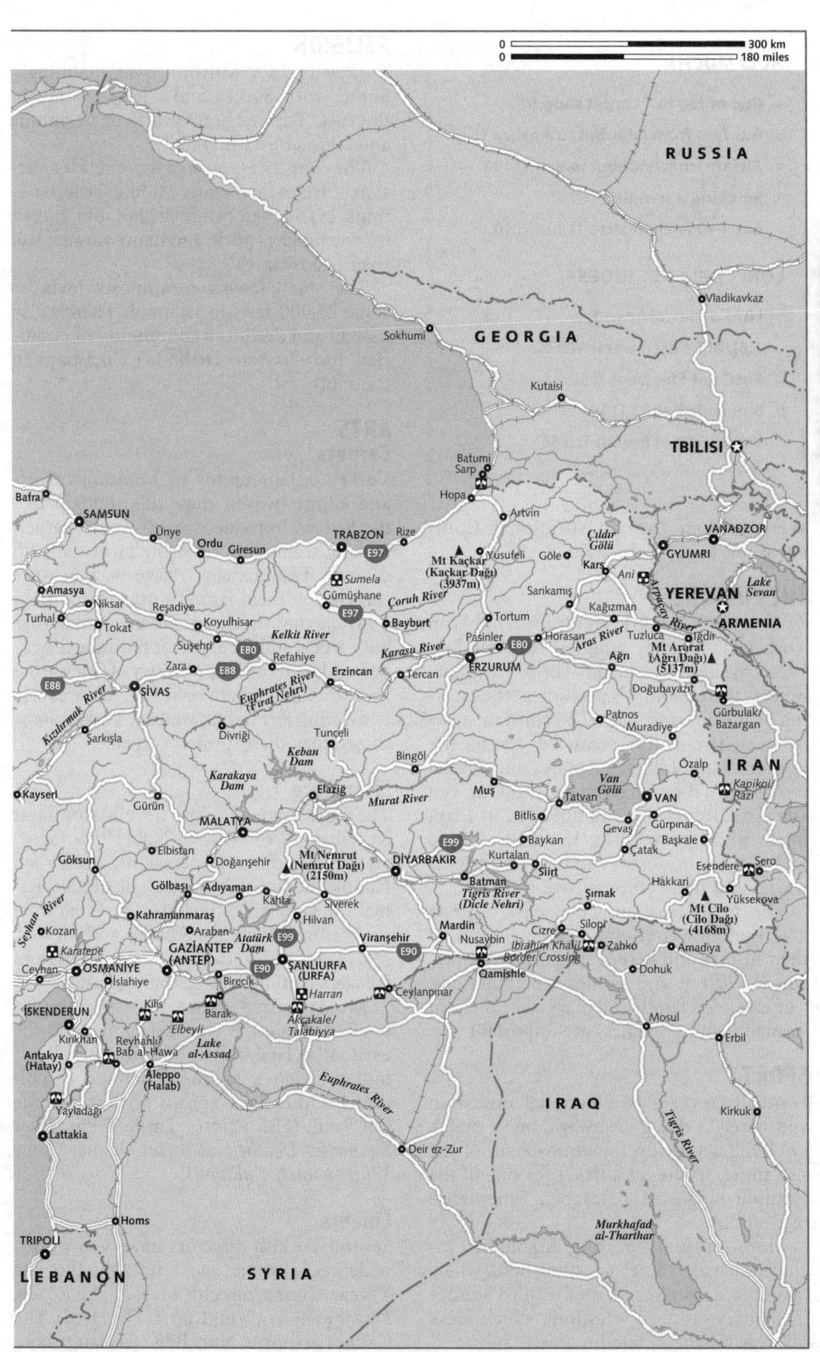

0 300 km
0 180 miles
RUSSIA
Vladikavkaz
GEORGIA
Sokhumi
Kutaisi
TBILISI
Batumi
Sarp
Hopa
Artvin
Bafra
SAMSUN
Ünye
Ordu
Giresun
TRABZON
Rize
E97
Mt Kaçkar (Kaçkar Dağı) (3937m)
Yusufeli
Göle
Çıldır Gölü
Kars
Ani
Arpaçay River
GYUMRI
VANADZOR
YEREVAN
Lake Sevan
ARMENIA
Amasya
Niksar
Turhal
Tokat
Reşadiye
Koyulhisar
Suşehri
Sumela
Gümüşhane
Çoruh River
Bayburt
Tortum
Sarıkamış
Kağızman
Kelkit River
E80
Refahiye
Karasu River
Pasinler
Horasan
Aras River
Tuzluca
Iğdir
Mt Ararat (Ağrı Dağı) (5137m)
Zara
E88
Erzincan
Tercan
ERZURUM
Ağrı
Doğubayazıt
SİVAS
Euphrates River (Fırat Nehri)
Kızılırmak River
Şarkışla
Divriği
Tunceli
Patnos
Muradiye
Gürbulak/ Bazargan
Keban Dam
Bingöl
Özalp
IRAN
Karakaya Dam
Kayseri
Elazığ
Murat River
Muş
Tatvan
Van Gölü
VAN
Kapıkoi/ Razi
Gürün
MALATYA
Bitlis
Gevaş
Gürpınar
Başkale
E99
Baykan
Çatak
Elbistan
Mt Nemrut (Nemrut Dağı) (2150m)
DİYARBAKIR
Kurtalan
Siirt
Göksun
Doğanşehir
Batman
Esendere
Sero
Hakkari
Gölbaşı
Adıyaman
Kahta
Siverek
Tigris River (Dicle Nehri)
Şırnak
Mt Cilo (Cilo Dağı) (4168m)
Yüksekova
Seyhan River
Kahramanmaraş
Hilvan
Mardin
Kozan
Araban
Atatürk Dam
Viranşehir
Nusaybin
Cizre
Silopi
Zahko
Amadiya
Karatepe
GAZİANTEP (ANTEP)
E90
Ibrahim Khalil Border Crossing
Ceyhan
OSMANİYE
İslahiye
ŞANLIURFA (URFA)
Qamishle
Dohuk
Birecik
Harran
Ceylanpınar
Kilis
Barak
İSKENDERUN
Elbeyli
Akçakale/ Talabiyya
Mosul
Erbil
Kırıkhan
Reyhanlı/ Bab al-Hawa
Lake al-Assad
Antakya (Hatay)
Aleppo (Halab)
Euphrates River
IRAQ
Yayladağı
Kirkuk
Lattakia
Tigris River
Deir ez-Zur
Homs
Murkhafad al-Tharthar
TRIPOLI
LEBANON
SYRIA

HOW MUCH?

- **Cup of tea in a carpet shop** free
- **Bus fare from İstanbul to Ankara** TL35
- **Airfare from İstanbul to Van** TL100
- **Smoking a nargileh** TL5
- **Entry to ancient sites** TL3 to TL10

LONELY PLANET INDEX

- **Litre of petrol** TL3.50
- **1.5L of bottled water** TL2.50
- **Bottle of Efes beer** TL5
- **Souvenir T-shirt** TL10
- **Simit (ring of bread)** TL0.50

averted when the Constitutional Court voted not to close the AKP.

THE CULTURE

As a result of Atatürk's reforms, republican Turkey has largely adapted to a modern Western lifestyle, but the Turks' mentality reflects their country's position at the meeting of Europe and Asia. The constant sway between two cultures can be disconcerting. In İstanbul, İzmir, Antalya and coastal resorts, you'd be forgiven for thinking you were in Europe; you will not need to adapt much in order to fit in. In smaller towns and villages, however, you may find people warier and more conservative.

The Turks have an acute sense of pride and honour. They are fiercely proud of their history and heroes, especially Atatürk, whose portrait and statues are ubiquitous. The extended family still plays a key role and formality and politeness are important.

SPORT

Football (soccer) is a national obsession and barely a day goes by without a match on TV. To soak up the atmosphere of the real thing, try to get a ticket for one of the İstanbul biggies: Galatasaray, Fenerbahçe or Beşiktaş.

More-unusual sporting highlights include the main camel-wrestling bout, which takes place near Selçuk on the third Sunday in January, and oil wrestling, which kicks off near Edirne in late June/early July.

RELIGION

Turkey is 98% Muslim, overwhelmingly Sunni, with Shiites and Alevis mainly in the east. The religious practices of Sunnis and Alevis differ markedly.

The country espouses a more relaxed version of Islam than many Middle Eastern nations. Many men drink alcohol, but almost no one touches pork, and many women still wear headscarves.

The small Jewish community includes some 25,000 Jews in İstanbul. There's also a small and declining community of Nestorian and Assyrian Orthodox Christians in the southeast.

ARTS

Carpets

Turkey is famous for its beautiful carpets and kilims (woven rugs). It's thought that the Seljuks introduced hand-woven carpet-making techniques to Anatolia in the 12th century. Traditionally, village women wove carpets for their family's use, or for their dowry; today, the dictates of the market rule, but carpets still incorporate traditional symbols and patterns. The Ministry of Culture has sponsored projects to revive age-old weaving and dyeing methods in western Turkey; some shops stock these 'project carpets'.

Literature

The most famous Turkish novelists are Yaşar Kemal, nominated for the Nobel Prize for literature on numerous occasions, and Orhan Pamuk, the Nobel Prize Laureate in 2006. Kemal's novels, which include *The Wind from the Plains, Salman the Solitary* and *Memed, My Hawk,* chronicle the desperate lives of villagers battling land-grabbing lords.

An inventive prose stylist, Pamuk's books include the Kars-set *Snow,* and the existential İstanbul whodunit *Black Book,* told through a series of newspaper columns. Other well-known writers include Elif Şafak *(Flea Palace),* Latife Tekin *(Dear Shameless Death)* and Buket Uzuner *(Long White Cloud, Gallipoli).*

Cinema

Several Turkish directors have won worldwide recognition, most notably the late Yılmaz Güney, director of *Yol* (The Road), *Duvar* (The Wall) and *Sürü* (The Herd). The Cannes favourite Nuri Bilge Ceylan probes the lives of village migrants in the big city in *Uzak* (Distant), and looks at male-female relationships in *İklimler* (Climates).

Ferzan Özpetek's *Hamam* (Turkish Bath) addresses the previously hidden issue of homosexuality in Turkish society. The new name to watch is Fatih Akin, who ponders the Turkish experience in Germany in *Duvara Karsi* (Head On) and *Edge of Heaven*.

Music

Turkey's successful home-grown pop industry managed to gain European approval faster than the country's politicians, when Sertab Erener won the Eurovision Song Contest with 'Every Way that I Can' in 2003.

The big pop stars include pretty-boy Tarkan, who Holly Valance covered, and chanteuse Sezen Aksu. Burhan Öçal is one of Turkey's finest percussionists; his seminal *New Dream* is a funky take on classical Turkish music. Ceza is the king of İstanbul's thriving hip hop scene.

With an Arabic spin, Arabesk is also popular. The genre's stars are Orhan Gencebay and the Kurdish former construction worker, Ibrahim Tatlıses.

Two Kurdish folk singers to listen out for are Aynur Doğan and Ferhat Tunç.

Architecture

Turkey's architectural history encompasses everything from Hittite stonework and Graeco-Roman temples to modern towerblocks in İstanbul, but perhaps the most distinctively Turkish styles are Seljuk and Ottoman. The Seljuks left magnificent mosques and medreses, distinguished by their elaborate entrances; the Ottomans also built grand religious structures, and fine wood-and-stone houses in towns such as Safranbolu and Amasya.

ENVIRONMENT

The Land

The Dardanelles, the Sea of Marmara and the Bosphorus divide Turkey into Asian and European parts. Eastern Thrace (European Turkey) comprises only 3% of the 779,452-sq-km land area; the remaining 97% is Anatolia, a vast plateau rising eastward towards the Caucasus mountains. With more than 7000km of coastline, snowcapped mountains, rolling steppes, vast lakes and broad rivers, Turkey is geographically diverse.

Environmental Issues

Turkey's embryonic environmental movement is making slow progress; discarded litter and ugly concrete buildings (some half-finished) disfigure the west in particular. Desertification is a long-term threat for the country.

Big dam projects have caused environmental problems. The 22-dam Güneydoğu Anadolu Projesi (GAP) project is changing southeastern Anatolia's landscape as it generates hydroelectricity for industry. Parched valleys have become fish-filled lakes, causing an explosion of diseases. GAP has also generated problems with Syria and Iraq, the countries downriver.

In 2008, dam-builders' plans to drown Hasankeyf saw the historic southeastern town named on the World Monuments Watch list (alongside four other Turkish sites).

On the plus side, Turkey is slowly reclaiming its architectural heritage; Central Anatolia's Ottoman towns Safranbolu and Amasya are masterpieces of restoration.

İstanbul has a branch of **Greenpeace Mediterranean** (☎/fax 0212-292 7619/7622; Kallavi Sokak 1/2, Beyoğlu).

FOOD

Turkish food is regarded as one of the world's greatest cuisines. Kebaps are, of course, the mainstay of restaurant meals; ubiquitous lokantas (restaurants) sell a wide range of them. Try the *durum* döner kebap – compressed meat (usually lamb) cooked on a revolving upright skewer over coals, then thinly sliced. Laid on pide bread, topped with tomato sauce and browned butter and with yogurt on the side, döner kebap becomes *İskender kebap,* primarily a lunchtime delicacy. Equally common are *köfte* (meatballs).

A quick, cheap fill, Turkish pizza is a freshly cooked pide topped with cheese, egg or meat. Alternatively, *lahmacun* is a paper-thin Arabic pizza with chopped onion, lamb and tomato sauce. Other favourites are *gözleme* (thin, savoury crêpes) and *simit* (ring of bread decorated with sesame seeds).

Fish dishes, although excellent, are often expensive; check the price before ordering.

For vegetarians, meze can be an excellent way to ensure a varied diet. Most restaurants should be able to rustle up *beyaz peynir* (ewe's- or goat's-milk cheese), *sebze çorbası* (vegetable soup), börek (flaky pastry stuffed

CLASSIC TURKISH EXPERIENCES *bingxian26*

Tavla and çay Turks are very fond of their *tavla* (backgammon) and *çay* (tea); spend an afternoon café-hopping and playing backgammon, and you'll feel Turkish in no time! You'll meet plenty of players who'll happily challenge you.

Bazaars Turkey's bazaars are wonderful – you can find anything from fish to headscarves and knockoff designer clothes. If you go to a local bazaar, you can practice your bargaining as the locals watch the funny foreigner.

Rakı Rakı, the aniseed-flavoured, clear spirit that turns white when mixed, is not for the faint of heart: it's strong stuff! But knock back a glass and you'll be an honorary Turk in no time.

Atatürk He's everywhere – wherever you are in Turkey, there's bound to be a building that Atatürk visited. Like any good Turk, you should check out the museum or monument commemorating the occasion.

What's your recommendation? www.lonelyplanet.com/middle-east

with white cheese and parsley), *kuru fasulye* (beans) and *patlıcan tava* (fried aubergine).

For dessert, try *fırın sütlaç* (rice pudding), *aşure* ('Noah's Ark' pudding, featuring up to 40 different ingredients), baklava (honey-soaked flaky pastry stuffed with walnuts or pistachios), *kadayıf* (syrup-soaked dough, often topped with cream) and *dondurma* (ice cream).

The famously chewy *lokum* (Turkish delight), widely available throughout Turkey, has been made here since the 18th century. For more information on Turkish cuisine, look out for Lonely Planet's *World Food Turkey* guide. Also see the Food & Drink chapter, p97.

DRINK

The national hot drink, *çay*, is served in tulip-shaped glasses with copious amounts of sugar. Tiny cups of traditional Turkish *kahve* (coffee) are served *şekersiz* (with no sugar), *az şekerli* (medium sweet) or *çok şekerli* (very sweet). Unfortunately, Nescafé is fast replacing *kahve* and, in tourist areas, it usually comes *sütlü* (with milk).

The Turkish liquor of choice is rakı, a fiery aniseed drink like the Greek ouzo or Arab arak; do as the Turks do and cut it by half with water. Turkish *şarap* (wine), both red *(kırmızı)* and white *(beyaz)*, is improving in quality and is worth a splurge. You can buy Tuborg or Efes Pilsen beers everywhere, although outside the resorts you may need to find a Tekel store (the state-owned alcoholic-beverage and tobacco company) to buy wine.

Ayran is a yogurt drink, made by whipping up yogurt with water and salt. Bottled water, packaged fruit juices and canned soft drinks are sold everywhere.

İSTANBUL

☎ Asian side 0216 / ☎ European side 0212 / pop 16 million

İstanbul's populous neighbourhoods, dating from the Byzantine era, from the golden age of the Ottoman sultans and from recent, less-affluent times, form a dilapidated but ultimately cohesive mosaic. Here, you can retrace the steps of the Byzantine emperors when visiting Sultanahmet's monuments and museums; marvel at the magnificent Ottoman mosques on the city's seven hills; and wander the cobbled streets of the ancient Jewish, Greek and Armenian neighbourhoods in the city's western districts. Centuries of urban sprawl unfurl before your eyes on ferry trips up the Bosphorus or Golden Horn.

The city's feeling of *hüzün* (melancholy) is being relegated to the past, replaced with a sense of energy, innovation and optimism not seen since the days of Süleyman the Magnificent. Stunning contemporary art galleries are opening around the city, and the possibility of a European-flavoured future is being embraced in the rooftop bars of Beyoğlu and the boardrooms of Levent. There has never been a better time to visit.

HISTORY

Late in the 2nd century, the Roman Empire conquered the small city-state of Byzantium – renamed Constantinople after Emperor Constantine moved his capital there in AD 330.

The city walls kept out barbarians for centuries while the western part of the Roman Empire collapsed. When Constantinople fell for the first time, it was to the misguided Fourth Crusade (1202–04).

In 1453, after a long, bitter siege, Mehmet the Conqueror marched to Aya Sofya (also known as Haghia Sofia or Sancta Sophia) and converted the church into a mosque.

As capital of the Ottoman Empire, the city experienced a new golden age. During the reign of Süleyman the Magnificent (1520–66), it was graced with many beautiful new buildings. Occupied by Allied forces after WWI, İstanbul came to be thought of as the decadent capital of the sultans, just as Atatürk's armies were shaping a new republican state.

When the Turkish Republic was proclaimed in 1923, Ankara became the new capital. Nevertheless, İstanbul remains the centre for business, finance, journalism and the arts.

ORIENTATION

The Bosphorus strait, between the Black Sea and the Sea of Marmara, divides Europe from Asia. On its western shore, European İstanbul is further divided by the Golden Horn (Haliç) into Old İstanbul in the south and Beyoğlu in the north.

Sultanahmet is the heart of Old İstanbul and boasts many of the city's famous sites. The adjoining area, with hotels to suit all budgets, is called Cankurtaran (*jan*-kur-tar-an), although if you say 'Sultanahmet' most people will understand where you mean.

Beyoğlu, on the northern side of the Golden Horn, was once the 'new', or 'European', city. The Tünel funicular railway runs uphill from Karaköy to the southern end of Beyoğlu's pedestrianised main street, İstiklal Caddesi. A tram runs from there to Taksim Sq, at the north end of the street, and the heart of 'modern' İstanbul; it's home to many luxury hotels and airline offices.

The International İstanbul Bus Station is in Esenler, about 10km northwest of Sultanahmet. North of Sultanahmet, on the Golden Horn, is Sirkeci Railway Station, terminus for European train services. Across the Bosphorus, Haydarpaşa station is the terminus for trains to Anatolia, Syria and Iran. For more information on getting around and into İstanbul, see p549.

INFORMATION

Emergency

Police ☎ 155

Tourist police (Map pp542-3; ☎ 0212-527 4503; Yerebatan Caddesi 6, Sultanahmet) Located across the street from the Basilica Cistern.

Internet Access

Most hotels and hostels have wi-fi access and a computer terminal with free internet access. There are also internet cafés throughout İstanbul, including:

Café Turka Internet Café (Map pp542-3; 2nd fl, Divan Yolu Caddesi 22, Sultanahmet; per hr TL2.50; 9am-midnight)

Robin Hood Internet Café (Map pp546-7; 4th fl, Yeni Çarşı Caddesi 8, Galatasaray; per hr TL2; 9am-11.30pm)

Medical Services

Alman Hastanesi (German Hospital; Map pp546-7; ☎ 0212-293 2150; Sıraselviler Caddesi 119, Taksim; 8.30am-6pm Mon-Fri, 8.30am-5pm Sat)

Amerikan Hastanesi (American Hospital; Map pp538-9; ☎ 0212-444 3777; Güzelbahçe Sokak 20, Nişantaşı; 24hr emergency department)

Money

Banks with ATMs are widespread, including in Sultanahmet's Aya Sofya Meydanı (Map pp542–3) and all along İstiklal Caddesi in Beyoğlu. The exchange rates offered at the airport are usually as good as those offered in town.

Post

İstanbul's central post office (Map pp542–3) is a few blocks southwest of Sirkeci Railway Station. In Sultanahmet there's a PTT booth on Aya Sofya Meydanı (Map pp542–3) and a PTT branch in the basement of the law courts (Map pp542–3); in Beyoğlu there are branches on İstiklal Caddesi (Map pp546–7) and near the Galata Bridge (Map pp546–7). There's also a PTT in the southwestern corner of the Grand Bazaar (Map pp538–9).

Tourist Information

Atatürk International Airport (IST; Atatürk Hava Limanı; off Map pp538-9; ☎ 0212-465 5555; www.ataturkairport.com; 24hr) Booth in international arrivals area.

Elmadağ (Map pp538-9; ☎ 0212-233 0592; 9am-5pm Mon-Sat) In the arcade in front of the İstanbul Hilton Hotel, just off Cumhuriyet Caddesi; about a 10-minute walk north of Taksim Sq.

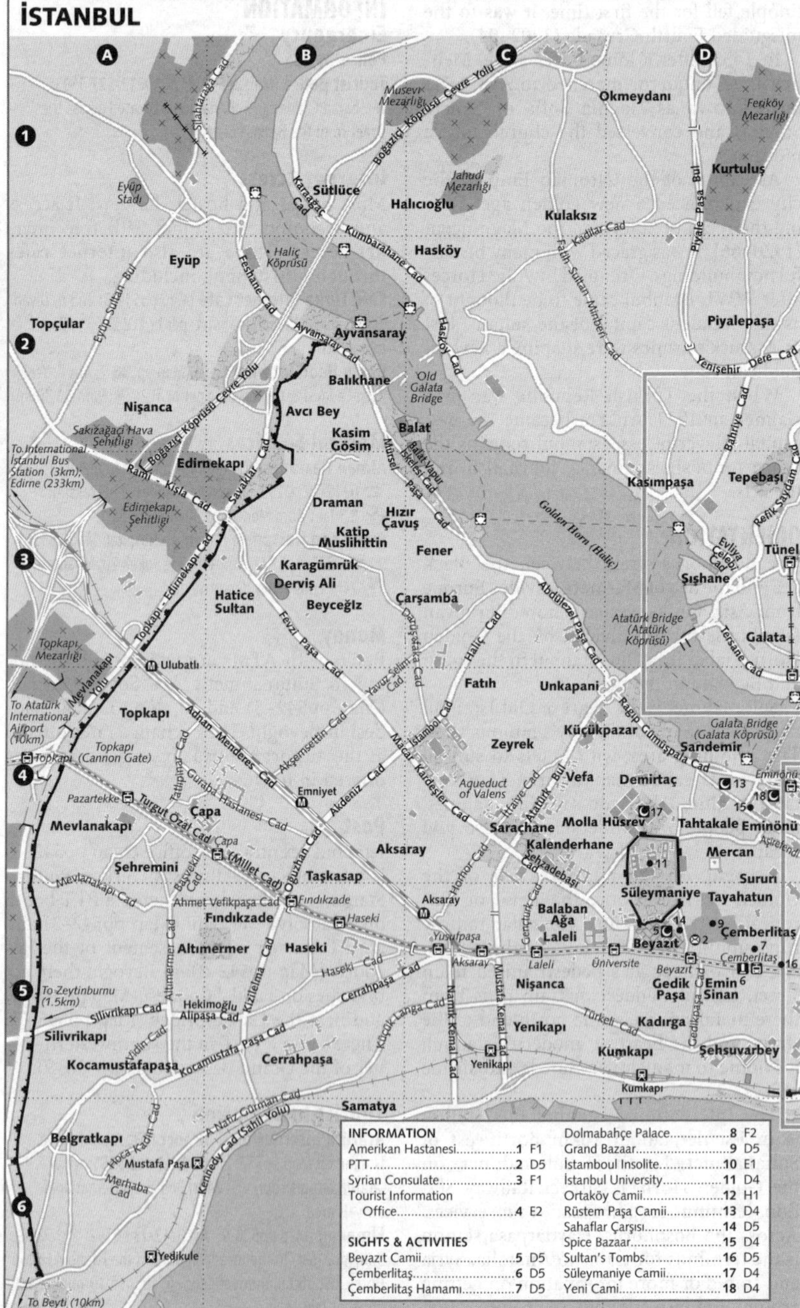

İSTANBUL
A
B
C
D
1
2
3
4
5
6
Okmeydanı
Feriköy Mezarlığı
Kurtuluş
Musevi Mezarlığı
Boğaziçi Köprüsü Çevre Yolu
Jahudi Mezarlığı
Sütlüce
Halıcıoğlu
Kulaksız
Kadilar Cad
Piyale Paşa Bul
Eyüp Stadı
Karaağaç Cad
Kumbarahane Cad
Hasköy
Haliç Köprüsü
Eyüp
Feshane Cad
Fatih Sultan Minberi Cad
Eyüp Sultan Bul
Topçular
Ayvansaray
Ayvansaray Cad
Hasköy Cad
Piyalepaşa
Yenişehir Dere Cad
Balıkhane
Old Galata Bridge
Nişanca
Avcı Bey
Bahriye Cad
Sakızağacı Hava Şehitliği
Kasim Gösim
Balat
Edirnekapı
To International İstanbul Bus Station (3km); Edirne (233km)
Rami Kışla Cad
Savaklar Cad
Mürsel Paşa Cad
Balat Vapur İskelesi Cad
Kasımpaşa
Tepebaşı
Refik Saydam Cad
Edirnekapı Şehitliği
Draman
Hızır Çavuş
Golden Horn (Haliç)
Katip Muslihittin
Fener
Evliya Çelebi Cad
Tünel
Edirnekapı Cad
Karagümrük
Derviş Ali
Şişhane
Hatice Sultan
Beyceğlz
Çarşamba
Abdülezel Paşa Cad
Atatürk Bridge (Atatürk Köprüsü)
Galata
Topkapı - Edirnekapı Cad
Fevzi Paşa Cad
Darüşşafaka Cad
Haliç Cad
Tersane Cad
Topkapı Mezarlığı
Ulubatlı
Yavuz Selim Cad
Fatih
Unkapani
Mevlanakapı Yolu
To Atatürk International Airport (10km)
Topkapı
Adnan Menderes Cad
Akşemsettin Cad
İstambol Cad
Zeyrek
Küçükpazar
Ragıp Gümüşpala Cad
Galata Bridge (Galata Köprüsü)
Sarıdemir
Topkapı (Cannon Gate)
Topkapı
Macar Kardeşler Cad
Tatlıpınar Cad
Guraba Hastanesi Cad
Akdeniz Cad
Vefa
Demirtaç
Eminönü
Pazartekke
Turgut Özal Cad (Millet Cad)
Emniyet
Aqueduct of Valens
İtfaiye Cad
Atatürk Bul
Molla Hüsrev
Tahtakale
Eminönü
Çapa
Mevlanakapı
Çapa
Saraçhane
Kalenderhane
Aşirefendi
Aksaray
Oğuzhan Cad
Şehzadebaşı Cad
Mercan
Şehremini
Taşkasap
Horhor Cad
Süleymaniye
Sururi
Mevlanakapı Cad
Başvekil Cad
Ahmet Vefikpaşa Cad
Fındıkzade
Aksaray
Tayahatun
Gençtürk Cad
Balaban Ağa
Fındıkzade
Haseki
Altımermer Cad
Laleli
Çemberlitaş
Altımermer
Haseki
Yusufpaşa
Beyazıt
Kızılelma Cad
Aksaray
Laleli
Üniversite
Çemberlitaş
Haseki Cad
Beyazıt
To Zeytinburnu (1.5km)
Cerrahpaşa Cad
Nişanca
Gedik Paşa
Emin Sinan
Hekimoğlu Alipaşa Cad
Namık Kemal Cad
Mustafa Kemal Cad
Silivrikapı Cad
Küçük Langa Cad
Türkeli Cad
Kadırga
Silivrikapı
Vidin Cad
Yenikapı
Gedikpaşa Cad
Kocamustafa Paşa Cad
Cerrahpaşa
Kumkapı
Şehsuvarbey
Kocamustafapaşa
Yenikapı
Kumkapı
Samatya
A Nafiz Gürman Cad
Kennedy Cad (Sahil Yolu)
Belgratkapı
Hoca Kadın Cad
Mustafa Paşa
Merhaba Cad
Yedikule
To Beyti (10km)
INFORMATION
Amerikan Hastanesi 1 F1
PTT 2 D5
Syrian Consulate 3 F1
Tourist Information Office 4 E2
SIGHTS & ACTIVITIES
Beyazıt Camii 5 D5
Çemberlitaş 6 D5
Çemberlitaş Hamamı 7 D5
Dolmabahçe Palace 8 F2
Grand Bazaar 9 D5
İstamboul Insolite 10 E1
İstanbul University 11 D4
Ortaköy Camii 12 H1
Rüstem Paşa Camii 13 D4
Sahaflar Çarşısı 14 D5
Spice Bazaar 15 D4
Sultan's Tombs 16 D5
Süleymaniye Camii 17 D4
Yeni Cami 18 D4

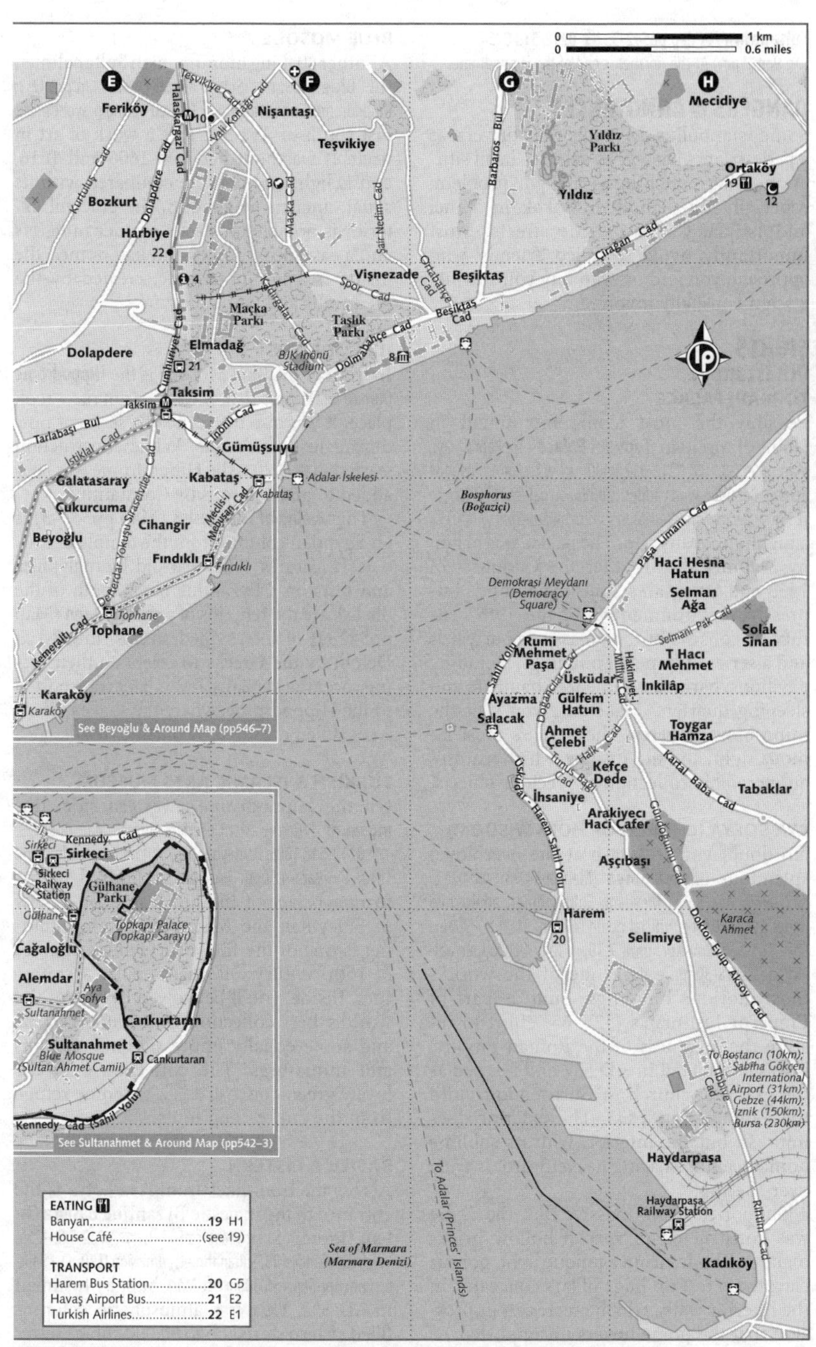

0 1 km
0 0.6 miles
E
F
G
H
Feriköy
Nişantaşı
Teşvikiye
Mecidiye
Yıldız Parkı
Ortaköy
Yıldız
Bozkurt
Harbiye
Vişnezade
Beşiktaş
Maçka Parkı
Taşlık Parkı
Elmadağ
Dolapdere
BJK İnönü Stadium
Taksim
Gümüşsuyu
Kabataş
Adalar İskelesi
Galatasaray
Çukurcuma
Cihangir
Beyoğlu
Fındıklı
Bosphorus (Boğaziçi)
Tophane
Karaköy
See Beyoğlu & Around Map (pp546–7)
Demokrasi Meydanı (Democracy Square)
Haci Hesna Hatun
Selman Ağa
Solak Sinan
Rumi Mehmet Paşa
T Hacı Mehmet
Üsküdar
İnkilâp
Ayazma
Gülfem Hatun
Salacak
Ahmet Çelebi
Toygar Hamza
Kefçe Dede
Tabaklar
İhsaniye
Arakiyeci Haci Cafer
Aşçıbaşı
Harem
Selimiye
Karaca Ahmet
Sirkeci
Sirkeci Railway Station
Gülhane Parkı
Topkapı Palace (Topkapı Sarayı)
Cağaloğlu
Alemdar
Aya Sofya
Cankurtaran
Sultanahmet
Blue Mosque (Sultan Ahmet Camii)
See Sultanahmet & Around Map (pp542–3)
To Bostancı (10km); Sabiha Gökçen International Airport (31km); Gebze (44km); İznik (150km); Bursa (230km)
Haydarpaşa
Haydarpaşa Railway Station
Kadıköy
To Adalar (Princes' Islands)
Sea of Marmara (Marmara Denizi)
EATING
Banyan 19 H1
House Café (see 19)
TRANSPORT
Harem Bus Station 20 G5
Havaş Airport Bus 21 E2
Turkish Airlines 22 E1
TURKEY

Sultanahmet (Map pp542-3; ☎ 0212-518 8754; 9am-5pm) At the northeast end of the Hippodrome.

DANGERS & ANNOYANCES

Some İstanbullus drive like rally drivers; as a pedestrian, give way to vehicles in all situations. Bag-snatching is a slight problem, especially on Galipdede Sokak in Tünel and İstiklal Caddesi's side streets. Most importantly, avoid so-called 'friends' who approach you and offer to buy you a drink; a scam is usually involved.

SIGHTS

Old İstanbul

TOPKAPI PALACE

Possibly the most iconic monument in İstanbul, opulent **Topkapı Palace** (Topkapı Sarayı; Map pp542-3; ☎ 0212-512 0480; www.topkapisarayi.gov.tr/eng; Babıhümayun Caddesi; admission palace TL20, harem TL15; 9am-7pm Wed-Mon summer, 9am-5pm winter) is a highlight of any trip. The palace was begun by Mehmet shortly after the Conquest of 1453 and Ottoman sultans lived in this impressive environment until the 19th century. It consists of four massive courtyards and a series of imperial buildings, including pavilions, barracks, audience chambers and sleeping quarters. Make sure you visit the mind-blowing **harem**, the palace's most famous sight, and the **Treasury**, which features an incredible collection of precious objects.

AYA SOFYA (CHURCH OF HOLY WISDOM)

No doubt you will gasp at the overblown splendour of **Aya Sofya** (Map pp542-3; ☎ 0212-522 0989; Aya Sofya Meydanı, Sultanahmet; adult/child under 6yr TL20/free, official guide (45min) TL50; 9am-5pm Tue-Sun Nov-Apr, until 7.30pm May-Oct, upper gallery closes 15-30min earlier), one of the world's most glorious buildings. Built as part of Emperor Justinian's (527–65) effort to restore the greatness of the Roman Empire, it was completed in AD 537 and reigned as the grandest church in Christendom until the Conquest in 1453. The exterior does impress, but the interior, with its sublime domed ceiling soaring heavenward, is truly over-the-top.

Supported by 40 massive ribs, the dome was constructed of special hollow bricks made in Rhodes from a unique light, porous clay; these rest on huge pillars concealed in the interior walls, which creates an impression that the dome hovers unsupported.

BLUE MOSQUE

Another striking monument in Sultanahmet, the **Blue Mosque** (Sultan Ahmet Camii; Map pp542-3; Hippodrome, Sultanahmet; closed during prayer times), just south of Aya Sofya, is a work of art in itself. It was built between 1606 and 1616, and is light and delicate compared with its squat, ancient neighbour. The graceful exterior is notable for its six slender minarets and a cascade of domes and half domes; the inside is a luminous blue, created by the tiled walls and painted dome.

HIPPODROME

In front of the Blue Mosque is the **Hippodrome** (Atmeydanı; Map pp542-3), where chariot races took place. It was also the scene of a series of riots during Justinian's rule. While construction started in AD 203, the Hippodrome was later added to and enlarged by Constantine.

The **Obelisk of Theodosius** (Map pp542–3) is an Egyptian column from the temple of Karnak. It features 3500-year-old hieroglyphics and rests on a Byzantine base. South of the obelisk are the remains of a **spiral column** (Map pp542–3) of intertwined snakes. Erected at Delphi by the Greeks to celebrate their victory over the Persians, it was later transported to the Hippodrome, where the snakes' heads were stolen during the Fourth Crusade.

TURKISH & ISLAMIC ARTS MUSEUM

On the Hippodrome's western side, this **museum** (Türk ve İslam Eserleri Müzesi; Map pp542-3; ☎ 0212-518 1805; Atmeydanı 46, Sultanahmet; admission TL10; 9am-4.30pm Tue-Sun) is housed in the former palace of İbrahim Paşa, son-in-law of Süleyman the Magnificent. The building is one of the finest surviving examples of 16th-century Ottoman secular architecture. Inside, you'll be wowed by one of the world's best collection of antique carpets and some equally impressive manuscripts and miniatures. The coffeehouse in the lovely green courtyard is a welcome refuge from the crowds and touts.

BASILICA CISTERN

Across the tram lines from Aya Sofya is the entrance to the majestic Byzantine **Basilica Cistern** (Yerebatan Sarnıçı; Map pp542-3; ☎ 0212-522 1259; Yerebatan Caddesi 13, Sultanahmet; admission TL10; 9am-6.30pm Apr-Sep, to 5.30pm Oct-Mar), built by Justinian in AD 532. This vast, atmospheric, column-filled cistern stored up to 80,000 cubic metres of water for regular summer use in the Great Palace, as well as for times of siege.

İSTANBUL ARCHAEOLOGY MUSEUM

Downhill from the Topkapı Palace, this superb **museum complex** (Arkeoloji Müzeleri; Map pp542-3; ☎ 0212-520 7740; Osman Hamdi Bey Yokuşu, Gülhane; admission TL10; ⌚ 9am-5pm Tue-Sun) is a must-see for anyone interested in the Middle East's ancient past. The main building houses an outstanding collection of Greek and Roman statuary, including the magnificent sarcophagi from the royal necropolis at Sidon in Lebanon. A separate building on the same site, the **Museum of the Ancient Orient** (Map pp542–3), houses Hittite relics and other older archaeological finds.

DIVAN YOLU CADDESI

Walk or take a tram westward along Divan Yolu from Sultanahmet, looking out on your right for a complex of **sultan's tombs** (Map pp538–9) that was constructed for 19th-century sultans, including Mahmut II (1808–39), Abdülaziz (1861–76) and Abdülhamid II (1876–1909).

A bit further along, on the right, you can't miss the **Çemberlitaş** (Map pp538–9), also known as the Banded Stone or Burnt Column. Constantine the Great erected the monumental column in AD 330 to celebrate the dedication of Constantinople as capital of the Roman Empire, and it has been covered with hoardings and awaiting renovation for years.

GRAND BAZAAR

Hone your haggling skills before dipping into the mind-boggling **Grand Bazaar** (Kapalı Çarşı; Map pp538-9; ⌚ 9am-7pm Mon-Sat). Just north of Divan Yolu, this labyrinthine medieval shopping mall consists of some 4000 shops selling everything from carpets to clothing, including silverware, jewellery, antiques and belly-dancing costumes. It's probably the most confusing and manic shopping precinct you could hope to experience. Sure, the touts are ubiquitous, but come in the right frame of mind and you'll realise it's part of the fun. With several kilometres of lanes, it's also a great place to ramble and get lost – which you will certainly do at least once.

Starting from a small masonry *bedesten* (market enclosure) built during the time of Mehmet the Conqueror, the bazaar grew to cover a vast area as shopkeepers put up roofs and porches so that commerce could be conducted comfortably in all weather.

BEYAZIT & SÜLEYMANIYE

Right beside the Grand Bazaar, the Beyazıt area takes its name from the graceful **Beyazıt Camii** (Map pp538–9), built between 1501 and 1506 on the orders of Sultan Beyazıt II. The **Sahaflar Çarşısı** (Old Book Bazaar; Map pp538–9) is nearby and the great gateway on the north side of the square belongs to **İstanbul University** (Map pp538–9).

Behind the university to the northwest is one of the city's most prominent landmarks and İstanbul's grandest mosque complex, the **Süleymaniye Camii** (Mosque of Sultan Süleyman the Magnificent; Map pp538-9; Prof Sıddık Sami Onar Caddesi; donation requested). It was commissioned in the 16th century by the most powerful of Ottoman sultans, Süleyman the Magnificent, and was designed by Mimar Sinan, the most famous of all imperial architects.

Eminönü

At the southern end of Galata Bridge looms large **Yeni Cami** (New Mosque; Map pp538-9; Yenicami Meydanı Sokak, Eminönü; donation requested), started in 1597 and completed, six sultans later, in 1663. Beside it is the atmospheric **Spice Bazaar** (Mısır Çarşısı; Map pp538-9; ⌚ 8.30am-6.30pm Mon-Sat), awash with spice and food vendors; it's a great place for last-minute gift shopping. To the west, on a platform above the fragrant market streets, is the 16th-century **Rüstem Paşa Camii** (Mosque of Rüstem Paşa; Map pp538-9; Hasırcılar Caddesi; donation requested), a small, richly tiled mosque designed by the great Ottoman architect Sinan.

Dolmabahçe Palace

Cross the Galata Bridge and follow the shore road along the Bosphorus from Karaköy towards Ortaköy and you'll come to the grandiose **Dolmabahçe Palace** (Dolmabahçe Sarayı; Map pp538-9; ☎ 0212-236 9000; Dolmabahçe Caddesi, Beşiktaş; admission selamlık TL15, harem-cariyeler TL10, selamlık & harem-cariyeler TL20, crystal palace & clock museum TL4; ⌚ 9am-4pm Tue-Wed & Fri-Sun summer, 9am-3pm winter), right on the waterfront. The palace was built between 1843 and 1856 as a home for some of the last Ottoman sultans. It was guaranteed a place in the history books when Atatürk died here on 10 November 1938 and all the palace clocks were stopped.

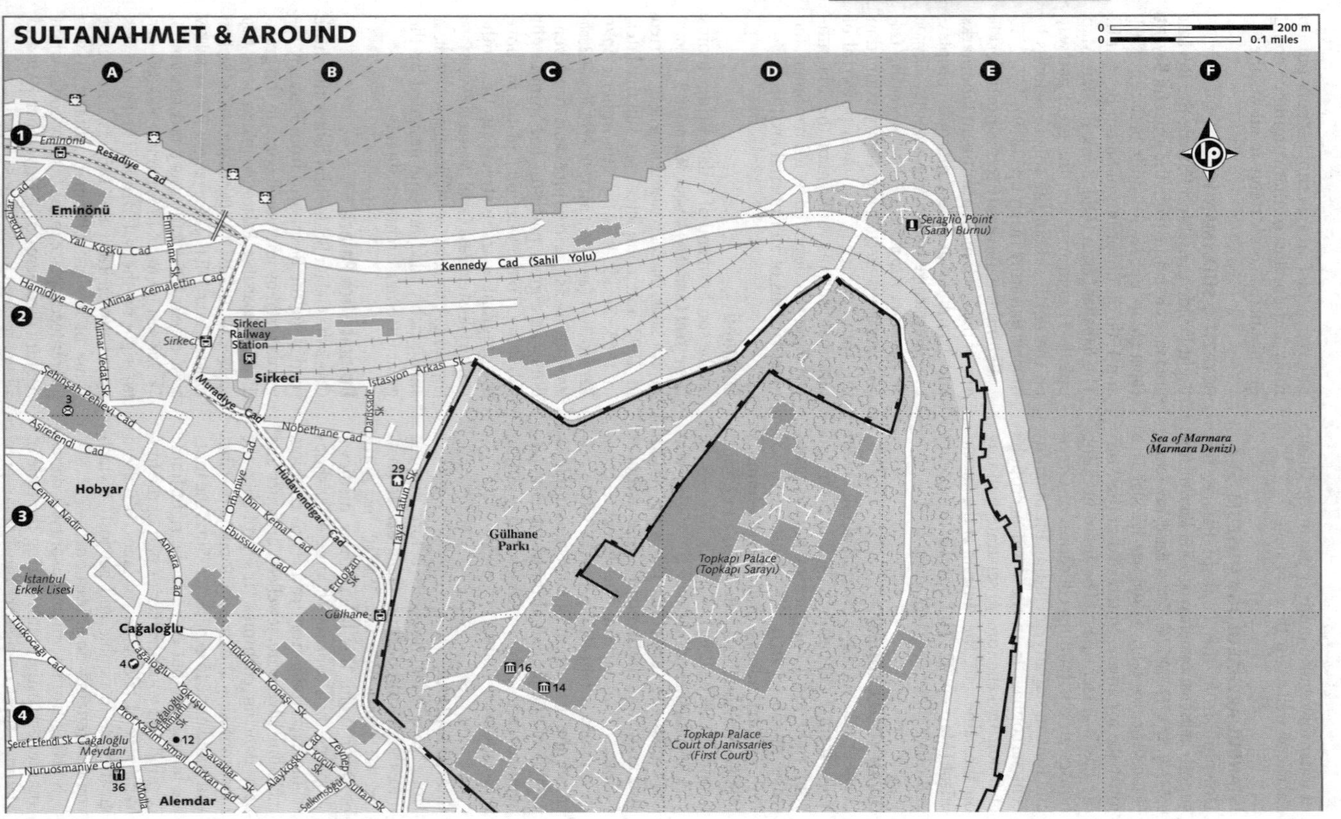
SULTANAHMET & AROUND
A
B
C
D
E
F
1
2
3
4
0 200 m
0 0.1 miles
Sea of Marmara
(Marmara Denizi)
Seraglio Point
(Saray Burnu)
Topkapı Palace
(Topkapı Sarayı)
Topkapı Palace
Court of Janissaries
(First Court)
Gülhane
Parkı
Kennedy Cad (Sahil Yolu)
Sirkeci
Railway
Station
Sirkeci
İstasyon Arkası Sk
Taya Hatun Sk
Nöbethane Cad
Hüdavendigar Cad
Muradiye Cad
Orhaniye Cad
İbni Kemal Cad
Ebussuut Cad
Gülhane
Hükümet Konağı Sk
Alayköşkü Cad
Zeynep Sultan Sk
Cağaloğlu
Ankara Cad
Cağaloğlu Yokuşu
Savaklar Sk
Prof Kazım İsmail Gürkan Cad
Alemdar
Molla
Emirname Sk
Mimar Kemalettin Cad
Mimar Vedat Sk
Yalı Köşkü Cad
Reşadiye Cad
Eminönü
Hamidiye Cad
Aşirefendi Cad
Şehinşah Pehlevi Cad
Hobyar
Cemal Nadir Sk
İstanbul
Erkek Lisesi
Türkocağı Cad
Şeref Efendi Sk
Cağaloğlu
Meydanı
Nuruosmaniye Cad
3
4
12
14
16
29
36

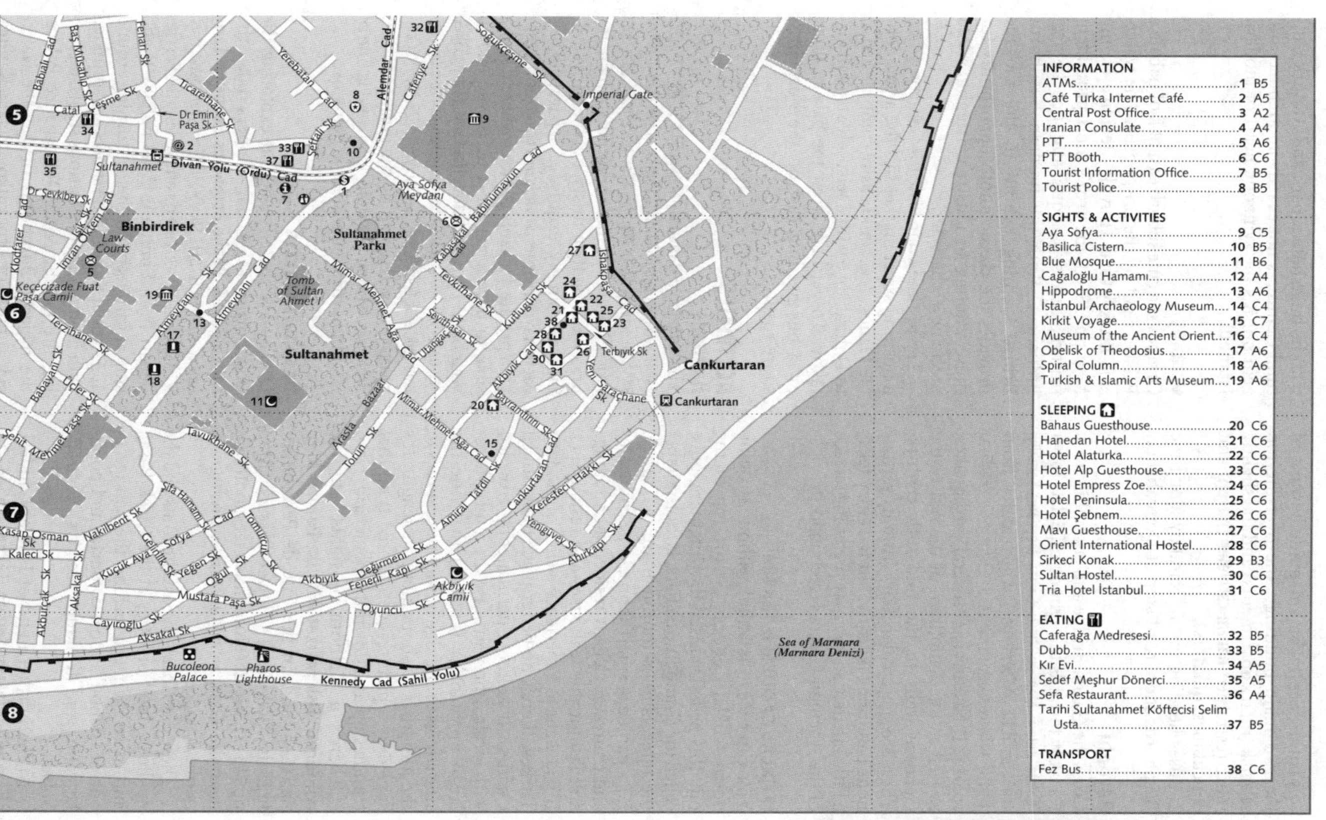
INFORMATION
ATMs 1 B5
Café Turka Internet Café 2 A5
Central Post Office 3 A2
Iranian Consulate 4 A4
PTT 5 A6
PTT Booth 6 C6
Tourist Information Office 7 B5
Tourist Police 8 B5
SIGHTS & ACTIVITIES
Aya Sofya 9 C5
Basilica Cistern 10 B5
Blue Mosque 11 B6
Cağaloğlu Hamamı 12 A4
Hippodrome 13 A6
İstanbul Archaeology Museum 14 C4
Kirkit Voyage 15 C7
Museum of the Ancient Orient 16 C4
Obelisk of Theodosius 17 A6
Spiral Column 18 A6
Turkish & Islamic Arts Museum 19 A6
SLEEPING
Bahaus Guesthouse 20 C6
Hanedan Hotel 21 C6
Hotel Alaturka 22 C6
Hotel Alp Guesthouse 23 C6
Hotel Empress Zoe 24 C6
Hotel Peninsula 25 C6
Hotel Şebnem 26 C6
Mavı Guesthouse 27 C6
Orient International Hostel 28 C6
Sirkeci Konak 29 B3
Sultan Hostel 30 C6
Tria Hotel İstanbul 31 C6
EATING
Caferağa Medresesi 32 B5
Dubb 33 B5
Kır Evi 34 A5
Sedef Meşhur Dönerci 35 A5
Sefa Restaurant 36 A4
Tarihi Sultanahmet Köftecisi Selim Usta 37 B5
TRANSPORT
Fez Bus 38 C6
Binbirdirek
Sultanahmet Parkı
Sultanahmet
Cankurtaran
Imperial Gate
Aya Sofya Meydanı
Tomb of Sultan Ahmet I
Law Courts
Keçecizade Fuat Paşa Camii
Akbıyık Camii
Bucoleon Palace
Pharos Lighthouse
Kennedy Cad (Sahil Yolu)
Divan Yolu (Ordu) Cad
Sea of Marmara (Marmara Denizi)
Arasta Bazaar

TURKEY

Visitors are taken on guided tours of the two main buildings: the over-the-top **selamlık** (men's apartments) and the slightly more restrained **harem-cariyeler** (harem and concubines' quarters).

Buses heading out of Karaköy along the Bosphorus shore road stop at Dolmabahçe.

Beyoğlu

Cross the Galata Bridge and cut uphill from Karaköy towards the cylindrical **Galata Tower** (Galata Kulesi; Map pp546-7; Galata Meydanı, Karaköy; admission TL10; 9am-8pm), which dates from 1348, when Galata was a Genoese trading colony. It has survived several earthquakes, as well as the demolition of the rest of the Genoese walls in the mid-19th century. There are spectacular views from its vertiginous panorama balcony, but the entry fee is a little inflated, so you may prefer the terrace of the Anemon Galata Hotel opposite.

İSTIKLAL CADDESI & TAKSIM

You can't leave İstanbul without strolling down İstiklal Caddesi. At the top of the hill, this pedestrianised thoroughfare, once called the Grand Rue de Péra, is indisputably the most famous thoroughfare in Turkey. It's a parade of smart shops, large embassies and churches, elegant residential buildings and fashionable teahouses and restaurants. If you want to experience a slice of modern Turkey, there's no better place than İstiklal Caddesi. It's almost permanently crowded with locals, who patronise the atmosphere-laden meyhaneler (taverns) that line the side streets or indulge in shopping sprees in the hundreds of shops along its length. It's served by a picturesque restored tram that trundles up and down the boulevard.

There's a plethora of sights, but the colourful **Fish Market** (Balık Pazar; Map pp546–7) and, in the Cité de Pera building, the **Çiçek Pasajı** (Flower Passage; Map pp546–7), are absolute must-sees; both are near the Galatasaray Lisesi (a prestigious public school).

These days locals bypass the touts and the mediocre food on offer at the Çiçek Pasajı and make their way behind the passage to one of İstanbul's most colourful and popular eating and drinking precincts, Nevizade Sokak.

At the northern end of İstiklal Caddesi, shambolic **Taksim Square** (Map pp546–7), with its huge hotels, park and Atatürk Cultural Centre, is not exactly an architectural gem but it's the symbolic heart of modern İstanbul.

Ortaköy

Ortaköy is a cute suburb east of Dolmabahçe Palace, right by the Bosphorus. The waterside **Ortaköy Camii** (Büyük Mecidiye Camii; Map pp538–9), the area's most prominent feature, mixes baroque and neoclassical influences. With the modern Bosphorus Bridge looming behind it, the mosque provides the classic photo opportunity for those wanting to illustrate İstanbul's 'old meets new' character.

Try to time your visit for Sunday, when a bustling street market fills the area's cobbled lanes. You could easily combine a visit to Dolmabahçe with a leisurely stroll in Ortaköy. To get here from the palace, jump on a bus heading east on the Bosphorus shore road.

ACTIVITIES

Hamams

The **Cağaloğlu Hamamı** (Map pp542-3; ☎ 0212-522 2424; www.cagalogluhamami.com.tr; Yerebatan Caddesi 34; bath services TL30-100; 8am-10pm men, 8am-8pm women) is the city's most beautiful hamam. It's pricey and pretty touristy, but the surroundings are simply exquisite. Separate baths each have a large *camekan* (reception area) with private, lockable cubicles where it's possible to have a nap or a tea at the end of your bath. The **Çemberlitaş Hamamı** (Map pp538-9; ☎ 0212-522 7974; www.cemberlitashamami.com.tr; Vezir Hanı Caddesi 8, Çemberlitaş; bath services TL29-79; 6am-midnight) was designed by the great Ottoman architect Mimar Sinan in 1584, and is one of İstanbul's most atmospheric hamams.

Bosphorus Cruise

Don't leave the city without exploring the Bosphorus. Most day-trippers take the much-loved **Public Bosphorus Excursion Ferry** (one way/return TL10/17.50; 10.35am year-round, noon & 1.35pm mid-Apr–Oct) up its entire length. Ferries depart from Eminönü (Map pp538–9) and stop at various points before turning around at Anadolu Kavağı. The shores are sprinkled with monuments and various sights, including the monumental Dolmabahçe Palace, the majestic Bosphorus Bridge, the waterside suburbs of Arnavutköy, Bebek, Kanlıca,

THE PLEASURES OF THE BATH

After a long day's sightseeing, few things could be better than relaxing in a hamam. The ritual is invariably the same. First, you'll be shown to a cubicle where you can undress, store your clothes and wrap the provided *peştamal* (cloth) around you. Then an attendant will lead you through to the hot room where you sit and sweat for a while.

Next you'll have to make a choice. It's cheapest to wash yourself with the soap, shampoo and towel you brought with you. The hot room will be ringed with individual basins that you fill from the taps above. Then you sluice the water over yourself with a plastic scoop. But it's far more enjoyable to let an attendant do it for you, dousing you with warm water and then scrubbing you with a coarse cloth mitten. Afterwards you'll be lathered with a sudsy swab, rinsed off and shampooed.

When all this is complete you're likely to be offered a massage – an experience worth having at least once during your trip.

Bath etiquette dictates that men should keep the *peştamal* on at all times.

Traditional hamams have separate sections for men and women, or admit men and women at separate times. In tourist areas most hamams are happy for foreign men and women to bathe together.

Emirgan and Sarıyer, as well as lavish *yalıs* (waterfront wooden summer residences) and numerous mosques.

Princes' Islands (Adalar)

With good beaches, open woodland, a couple of monasteries, Victorian villas and transport by horse-drawn carriages, this string of nine spotless islands, especially **Büyükada** (the biggest), make an ideal escape from the noise and hustle of İstanbul. Ferries (TL2.80) to the islands leave from the Adalar İskelesi dock at Kabataş (Map pp538–9), opposite the tram stop. Try to go midweek to avoid the crowds.

TOURS

İstamboul Insolite (Map pp538-9; ☎ 0212-241 2846; www.istanbulguide.net/insolite; Bahtiyar Sokak 6, Nışantaşı; full-day tours €50-150) This small agency runs a variety of offbeat tours.

Kirkit Voyage (Map pp542-3; ☎ 0212-518 2282; www.kirkit.com; Amiral Tafdil Sokak 12, Sultanahmet; half- & full-day tours €23-50) Kirkit specialises in small-group walking tours of the must-see sights.

FESTIVALS & EVENTS

The **İstanbul International Music Festival** (www.iksv.org/muzik), from early June to early July, attracts big-name artists from around the world who perform in venues that are not always open to the public (such as Aya İrini Kilisesi).

SLEEPING

İstanbul's accommodation is becoming quite pricey. For the time being, the best area to stay remains Cankurtaran, where the quiet streets have moderate hotels with stunning views from their roof terraces, and there are also more-luxurious options. Unless otherwise stated, rates include breakfast and private bathrooms; the exception is hostel dorms, which have shared bathrooms.

Budget

Private rooms are overpriced at some of these options.

Mavı Guest house (Map pp542-3; ☎ 0212-517 7287; www.maviguesthouse.com; Kutlugün Sokak 3, Sultanahmet; rooftop mattress/dm/d €8/12/36; 💻) Tiny Mavı's management is very friendly, which is just as well since some of its rooms are cramped and windowless, with uncomfortable beds. Diehard backpackers might want to claim one of the 24 mattresses on the decrepit rooftop.

Bahaus Guest house (Map pp542-3; ☎ 0212-638 6534; www.travelinistanbul.com; Akbıyık Caddesi, Cankurtaran; dm €15, d with/without bathroom €50/40; ☒ 💻) Generating great word of mouth, Bahaus' friendly and knowledgeable staff run a professional operation that avoids the institutional feel of some of its nearby competitors. Top marks go to the rooftop terrace bar.

Sultan Hostel (Map pp542-3; ☎ 0212-516 9260; www.sultanhostel.com; Akbıyık Caddesi 21, Cankurtaran; dm €14, d with/without bathroom €44/38; ☒ 💻) The Sultan offers freshly painted dorms with new bunk beds and good mattresses, and a 10% discount for HI cardholders.

Orient International Hostel (Map pp542-3; ☎ 0212-518 0789; www.orienthostel.com; Akbıyık Caddesi 13, Cankurtaran; dm/d €14/70, s without bathroom €70;

BEYOĞLU & AROUND

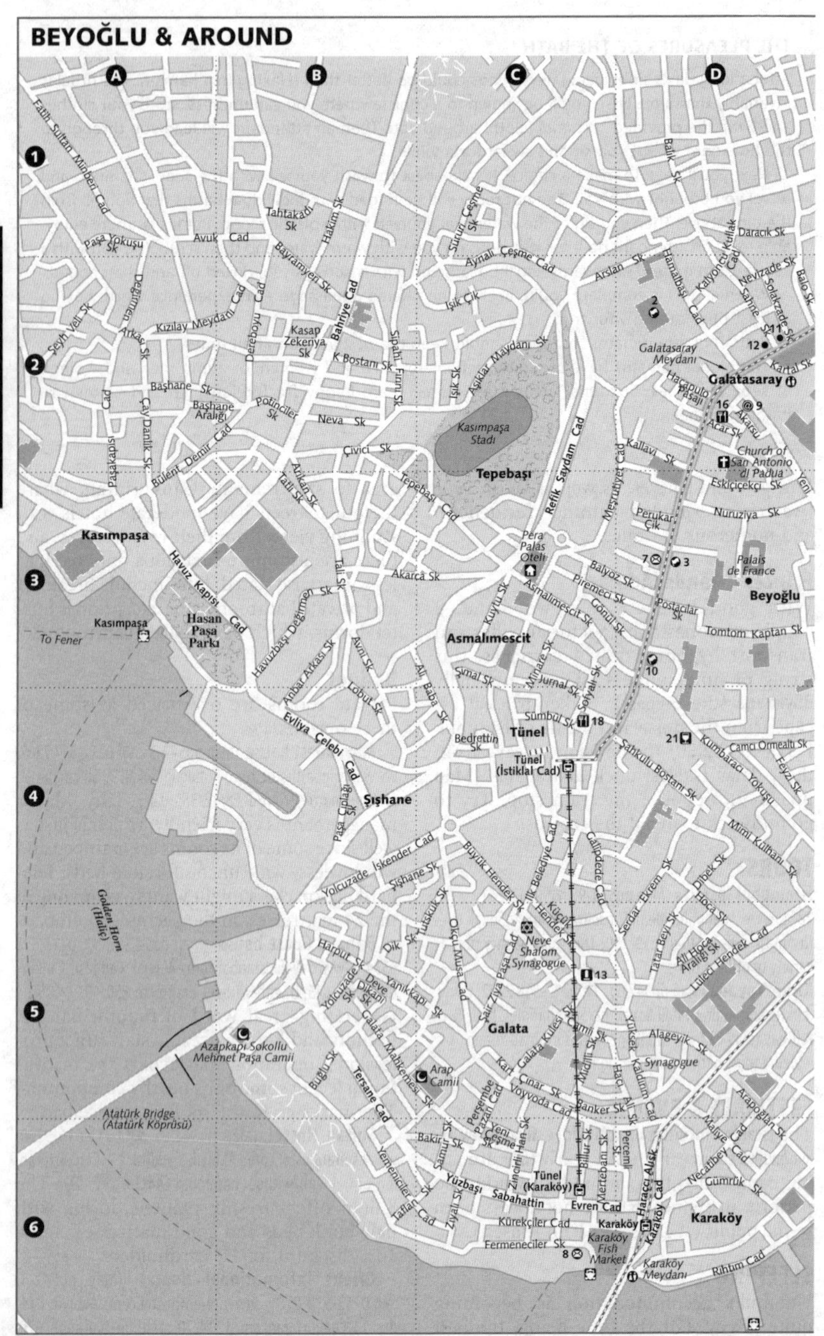

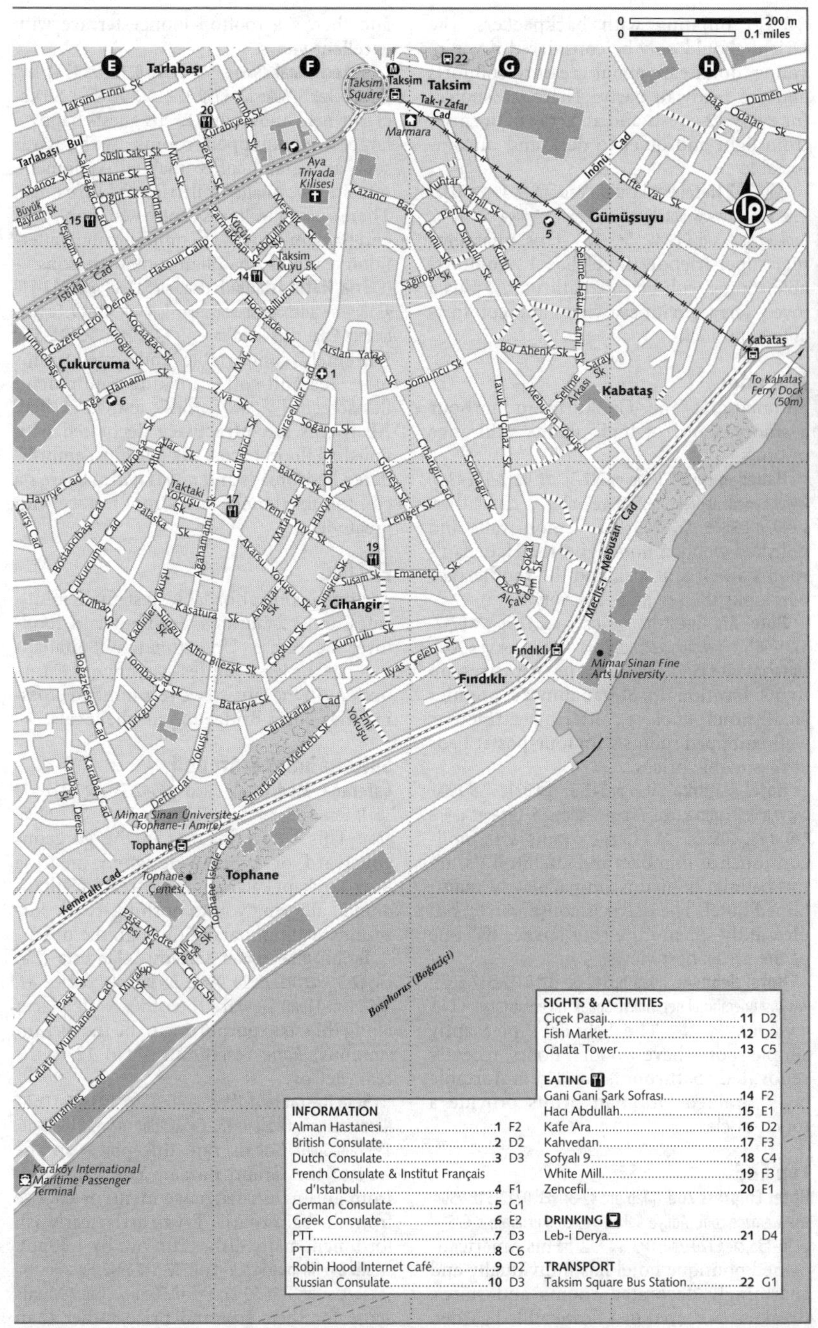
0 200 m
0 0.1 miles
E
F
G
H
Tarlabaşı
Taksim Square
Taksim
Tak-ı Zafar Cad
Marmara
22
Taksim Fırını Sk
Zambak Sk
Kurabiye Sk
Bekar Sk
Tarlabaşı Bul
Süslü Saksı Sk
Nane Sk
Abanoz Sk
İmam Adnan Sk
Mis Sk
Aya Triyada Kilisesi
Kazancı Başı
Meşelik Sk
Büyük Bayram Sk
Yeşilçam Sk
Sakızağacı Cad
Parmakkapı Sk
Küçük Abdullah Sk
Taksim Kuyu Sk
Muhtar Kamil Sk
Pembe Sk
Camii Sk
Osmanlı Sk
Kutlu Sk
Sağıroğlu Sk
Gümüşsuyu
İnönü Cad
Bağ Odaları Sk
Dümen Sk
Çifte Vav Sk
Selime Hatun Camii Sk
Hasnun Galip Sk
İstiklal Cad
Billurcu Sk
Hocazade Sk
Gazeteci Erol Dernek Sk
Koçaağaç Sk
Kuloğlu Sk
Turnacıbaşı Sk
Çukurcuma
Ağa Hamamı Sk
Mac Sk
Liva Sk
Arslan Yatağı Sk
Somuncu Sk
Bol Ahenk Sk
Saray Arkası Sk
Selime Sk
Kabataş
To Kabataş Ferry Dock (50m)
Mebusan Yokuşu
Tavuk Uçmaz Sk
Sıraselviler Cad
Soğancı Sk
Güllabici Sk
Oba Sk
Cihangir Cad
Sormağır Sk
Güneşli Sk
Bakraç Sk
Faikpaşa Sk
Altıpatlar Sk
Havyar Sk
Hayriye Cad
Taktaki Yokuşu Sk
Palaska Sk
Ağahamamı Sk
Yeni Yuva Sk
Matara Sk
Lenger Sk
Çarşı Cad
Bostancıbaşı Cad
Çukurcuma Cad
Akarsu Yokuşu Sk
Simsirci Sk
Susam Sk
Emanetçi Sk
Özoğul Sokak Sk
Alçakdam Sk
Meclis-i Mebusan Cad
Kulhan Sk
Kadirler Yokuşu
Süngü Sk
Kasatura Sk
Anahtar Sk
Cihangir
Kumrulu Sk
Coşkun Sk
Altın Bilezşk Sk
Tombaz Sk
İlyas Çelebi Sk
Fındıklı
Mimar Sinan Fine Arts University
Boğazkesen Cad
Türkgücü Cad
Batarya Sk
Sanatkarlar Cad
Enli Yokuşu
Sanatkarlar Mektebi Sk
Yokuşu
Karabaş Sk
Karabaş Cad
Deresi
Defterdar Yokuşu
Mimar Sinan Üniversitesi (Tophane-i Amire)
Tophane
Tophane İskele Cad
Kemeraltı Cad
Tophane Çeşmesi
Paşa Medrese Sesi Sk
Ali Sk
Kılıç Paşa Sk
Ciracı Sk
Murakıp Sk
Ali Paşa Sk
Galata Mumhanesi Cad
Kemankeş Cad
Bosphorus (Boğaziçi)
Karaköy International Maritime Passenger Terminal
TURKEY
SIGHTS & ACTIVITIES
Çiçek Pasajı....11 D2
Fish Market....12 D2
Galata Tower....13 C5
EATING
Gani Gani Şark Sofrası....14 F2
Hacı Abdullah....15 E1
Kafe Ara....16 D2
Kahvedan....17 F3
Sofyalı 9....18 C4
White Mill....19 F3
Zencefil....20 E1
DRINKING
Leb-i Derya....21 D4
TRANSPORT
Taksim Square Bus Station....22 G1
INFORMATION
Alman Hastanesi....1 F2
British Consulate....2 D2
Dutch Consulate....3 D3
French Consulate & Institut Français d'Istanbul....4 F1
German Consulate....5 G1
Greek Consulate....6 E2
PTT....7 D3
PTT....8 C6
Robin Hood Internet Café....9 D2
Russian Consulate....10 D3

) Bursting with backpackers, the Orient should only be considered if you're young, don't care about creature comforts and are ready to party. There's a shower for every 12 guests and an array of dorms – from light and quiet to dark and uncomfortable.

our pick **Hotel Peninsula** (Map pp542-3; ☎ 0212-458 6850; www.hotelpeninsula.com; Adliye Sokak 6, Cankurtaran; s/d €35/45;) This unassuming, super-friendly hotel has 12 comfortable rooms with private bathrooms, plus a lovely terrace with sea views and comfortable hammocks.

Midrange

Sultanahmet and Cankurtaran harbour a smorgasbord of high-quality midrange options.

Hanedan Hotel (Map pp542-3; ☎ 0212-516 4869; www.hanedanhotel.com; Adliye Sokak 3, Cankurtaran; s €40, d €60-65;) Pale lemon walls and polished wooden floors give the Hanedan's rooms an elegant feel, and the roof terrace overlooks the sea and Aya Sofya.

Hotel Alp Guest house (Map pp542-3; ☎ 0212-517 7067; www.alpguesthouse.com; Adliye Sokak 4, Cankurtaran; s/d €45/65;) The Alp lives up to its location in Sultanahmet's premier small-hotel enclave, offering attractive, well-equipped rooms with four-poster beds at reasonable prices.

Hotel Alaturka (Map pp542-3; ☎ 0212-458 7900; www.hotelalaturka.com; Akbıyık Caddesi 5, Cankurtaran; s €70, d €85-105;) Large rooms with mod-cons, such as minibars and satellite TVs, are the hallmarks of this immaculately maintained hotel. The decor is conservative, but pleasantly so, and the roof terrace has one of the area's best views.

Hotel Şebnem (Map pp542-3; ☎ 0212-517 6623; www.sebnemhotel.net; Adliye Sokak 1, Cankurtaran; s €70, d €90-100;) The Şebnem's pleasantly simple rooms have wooden floors, recently renovated bathrooms and comfortable beds. Framed Ottoman prints provide a touch of class.

Top End

Hotel Empress Zoe (Map pp542-3; ☎ 0212-518 2504; www.emzoe.com; Adliye Sokak 10, Cankurtaran; s €75, d €110-135, ste €120-240;) This American-owned boutique hotel has individually and charmingly decorated rooms and suites. Breakfast is served in a flower-filled garden and there's a rooftop lounge-terrace with excellent views.

Sirkeci Konak (Map pp542-3; ☎ 0212-528 43 44; Taya Hatun Sokak 5, Sirkeci; r €190-320;) Sirkeci's owners know what keeps guests happy – large, well-equipped rooms, with extras such as tea-and-coffee making equipment, satellite TV, quality toiletries and luxe linen. There's also a wellness centre with pool, gym and hamam, as well as complimentary afternoon teas and Anatolian cooking lessons.

Tria Hotel İstanbul (Map pp542-3; ☎ 0212-518 4518; www.triahotelistanbul.com; Turbıyık Sokak 7, Cankurtaran; s €180, d standard/superior €218/280;) Extremely comfortable and quiet rooms offer tea-and-coffee-making equipment, flat-screen TV, work desk and large bed. All rooms are attractively decorated with polished floorboards, silk curtains, embroidered bedspreads and *objets d'art*. There's a comfortable lounge and a roof terrace with great views.

EATING

Teeming with affordable fast-food joints, cafés and restaurants, İstanbul is a food-lover's paradise. Unfortunately, Sultanahmet has the least-impressive range of eating options in the city, so we recommend crossing the Galata Bridge to join the locals.

Sultanahmet & Around

Caferağa Medresesi (Map pp542-3; ☎ 0212-513 3601; Caferiye Sokak; soup TL3, köfte TL10; 8.30am-6pm) This teensy lokanta in the gorgeous courtyard of a Sinan-designed medrese near Topkapı Palace is a rare treat in Sultanahmet, allowing you to nosh in stylish surrounds without paying through the nose.

Tarihi Sultanahmet Köftecisi Selim Usta (Map pp542-3; ☎ 0212-520 0566; Divan Yolu Caddesi 12; 11am-11pm) Beware the other *köfte* places along this strip purporting to be the *meşhur* (famous) *köfte* restaurant – No 12 is the real McCoy.

Sefa Restaurant (Map pp542-3; ☎ 0212-520 0670; Nuruosmaniye Caddesi 17, Cağaloğlu; mains TL6.50-16; 7am-5pm) Locals rate this place on the way to the Grand Bazaar. You can order from an English-language menu or choose from the bain-marie. Try to arrive early-ish for lunch; many dishes run out by 1.30pm.

Kir Evi (Map pp542-3; ☎ 0212-512 6942; Hoca Rüstem Sokak 9; mains TL16.50-21; 10.30am-2.30am) Meals score for their size and price rather than their quality, but the biggest draw is the entertainment. Waiters serenade guests with everything from disco anthems to Arabesk numbers, and everyone joins in.

Dubb (Map pp542-3; ☎ 0212-513 7308; İncili Çavuş Sokak, Alemdar; TL12-24; 🕑 noon-3pm & 6-10.30pm) One of İstanbul's few Indian restaurants, Dubb specialises in mild tandoori dishes, but serves a range of fragrant curries, including vegetarian options. Its 4th-floor terrace offers views of Aya Sofya.

Nominating Sultanahmet's best takeaway döner kebap is a hard ask, but many locals are keen on the döner (TL4 to TL9) at **Sedef Meşhur Dönerci** (Map pp542-3; Divan Yolu), which is only open during the day.

Beyoğlu & Around

Gani Gani Şark Sofrası (Map pp546-7; ☎ 0212-244 8401; www.naumpasakonagi.com; Taksim Kuyu Sokak 11; pides TL7-9.50, kebaps TL7.50-10; 🕑 10am-11pm) Young Turkish couples love lolling on the traditional Anatolian seating at this cheap and friendly eatery. Tables and chairs are also available to the enjoy kebaps, *mantı* (Turkish ravioli) and pide.

Zencefil (Map pp546-7; ☎ 0212-243 8234; Kurabiye Sokak 8; mains TL10-12; 🕑 11am-11pm Tue-Sun) Comfortable and quietly stylish, this popular vegetarian café offers crunchy-fresh organic produce, homemade bread and guilt-free desserts.

Hacı Abdullah (Map pp546-7; ☎ 0212-293 8561; Sakızağacı Caddesi 9a; www.haciadbullah.com.tr; mains TL9-18; 🕑 11am-11pm; ☒) Just thinking about this İstanbul institution's *imam bayıldı* (eggplant stuffed with tomatoes, onions and garlic and cooked in olive oil) makes our taste buds go into overdrive.

Kafe Ara (Map pp546-7; ☎ 0212-245 4104; Tosbağ Sokak 8a; mains TL13-18; 🕑 8am-midnight) A converted garage with tables and chairs spilling into a wide laneway, Ara's a funky setting to enjoy panninis, salads and pastas.

Kahvedan (Map pp546-7; ☎ 0212-292 4030; Akarsu Caddesi 50, Cihangir; www.kahvedancafe.com/en; breakfast plates TL7-12, soups TL5-6, wraps TL9-14, mains TL13-21; 🕑 9am-2am Mon-Fri, 9am-4am Sat & Sun) This expat haven serves dishes such as bacon and eggs, French toast and falafel wraps.

White Mill (Map pp546-7; ☎ 0212-292 2895; www.whitemillcafe.com; Susam Sokak 13, Cihangir; breakfast plate TL17-19, mains TL15-23; 🕑 9.30am-1.30am) This industrial-chic bar-restaurant serves tasty, organic food and, in fine weather, its rear garden is a wonderful spot to enjoy a leisurely breakfast.

our pick **Sofyalı 9** (Map pp546-7; ☎ 0212-245 0362; Sofyalı Sokak 9, Tünel; meze TL4-8, mains TL10-16; 🕑 11am-1am Mon-Sat) Tables at this gem are hot property at weekends. It serves some of the city's best meyhane (tavern) food – notably the *Arnavut ciğeri* (Albanian fried liver), fried fish and meze – in surroundings as welcoming as they are attractive.

Ortaköy

The House Café (Map pp538-9; ☎ 0212-261 5818; İskele Sq 42, Ortaköy; breakfast platter TL24, sandwiches TL17.50-23.50, pizzas TL16.50-28.50) This casually chic café, a huge space on the waterfront, is one of the best spots for Sunday brunch (10am to 2pm), offering a good-quality buffet. Food at other times can be disappointing.

Banyan (Map pp538-9; ☎ 0212-259 9060; www.banyanrestaurant.com; 3rd fl, Salhane Sokak 3, Ortaköy; mains TL24-39; 🕑 11am-midnight) The excellent Asian food served at this stylish eatery is nearly as impressive as its view of the Bosphorus Bridge and Ortaköy Mosque. Get stuck into the three-course fixed menu lunch (TL40).

DRINKING

There's a thriving bar scene in Beyoğlu, and there's nothing better than swigging a few glasses of rakı around Balo Sokak and Sofyalı Sokak, or in the sleek rooftop bars on both sides of İstiklal. Sultanahmet is not as happening, but there are a few decent watering holes, particularly on Akbıyık Caddesi in summer.

On the top floor of a dishevelled building off İstiklal, **Leb-i Derya** (Map pp546-7; ☎ 0212-244 1886; www.lebiderya.com; 7th fl, Kumbaracı Yokuşu 115, Tünel; 🕑 11am-2am Mon-Fri, 8.30am-3am Sat & Sun) is unpretentious and a local favourite for its Bosphorus and Old İstanbul views.

GETTING THERE & AWAY

Air

İstanbul's **Atatürk International Airport** (IST; Atatürk Hava Limanı; off Map pp538-9; ☎ 0212-465 5555; www.ataturkairport.com) is 23km west of Sultanahmet. **Sabiha Gökçen International Airport** (off Map pp538-9; ☎ 0216-585 5000; www.sgairport.com), some 50km east of Sultanahmet, on the Asian side of the city, is increasingly popular for cheap flights from Europe.

Many foreign airlines have their offices north of Taksim, along Cumhuriyet Caddesi in Elmadağ. Travel agencies can also sell tickets and make reservations. **Turkish Airlines** (Map pp538-9; ☎ 0212-252 1106; www.thy.com; Cumhuriyet Caddesi 7) is the main domestic carrier, and Onur Air, Atlasjet and Fly Air also operate domestic flights from İstanbul.

For more details regarding flying to and from Turkey see p614; for details on flying around the country see p616.

Boat

Yenikapı (Map pp538–9), south of Aksaray Sq, is the dock for fast ferries across the Sea of Marmara to Yalova, Bursa and Bandırma (from where you can catch a train to İzmir). These carry both passengers and cars.

Bus

The huge **International İstanbul Bus Station** (Uluslararası İstanbul Otogarı; off Map pp538-9; ☎ 0212-658 0505) is the city's main otogar (bus station) for intercity and international routes. It's in Esenler, about 10km northwest of Sultanahmet. The Light Rail Transit (LRT) service stops here en route to/from the airport. If you're coming from Taksim Sq, bus No 83O (TL1.30, one hour) leaves about every 20 minutes from around 6.30am to 8.40pm. A taxi from Sultanahmet to the otogar costs around TL22 (20 minutes); from Taksim Sq around TL30 (30 minutes). Many bus companies offer a free *servis* (shuttle bus) to or from the otogar.

Buses leave from here for virtually anywhere in Turkey and for international destinations including Azerbaijan, Armenia, Bulgaria, Georgia, Greece, Iran, Romania and Syria.

If you're heading east to Anatolia, you might want to board at the smaller **Harem Bus Station** (Map pp538-9; ☎ 216-333 3763), north of Haydarpaşa Railway Station on the Asian shore, but the choice of service there is more limited. When arriving in İstanbul by bus from anywhere in Anatolia, it's considerably quicker to get out at Harem and take the car ferry to Sirkeci/Eminönü (TL1.40), which runs between 7am and 9.30pm daily, than stay on the bus until the international station.

Car & Motorcyle

It makes no sense to drive around İstanbul itself and have to deal with the traffic and parking problems. However, if you're heading out of the city, all the main car-hire agencies have desks at Atatürk International Airport, and some at Sabiha Gökçen International Airport.

Train

For services to Edirne and Europe go to **Sirkeci Railway Station** (Map pp542-3; ☎ 0212-527 0051). Daily international services from Sirkeci include the *Bosfor/Balakan Ekspresi*, stopping in Sofia (Bulgaria), Bucharest (Romania) and Belgrade (Serbia; TL92.40 to TL252.60), and the *Dostlu/Filia Ekspresi* to Thessaloniki (Greece; TL101.30 to TL178.20). European trains will terminate at Yenikapı after the completion of Marmaray, an ambitious public transport project aimed at relieving İstanbul's woeful traffic congestion, but this will not come about until 2012 at the earliest.

Trains from Anatolia and from countries to the east and south terminate at **Haydarpaşa Railway Station** (Map pp538-9; ☎ 0216-336 4470), on the Asian shore of the Bosphorus. International services from Haydarpaşa include the *Trans-Asya Ekspresi* to Tabriz (Iran) and the *Toros Ekspresi* to Aleppo (Syria).

GETTING AROUND

To/From the Airport

There's a quick, cheap and efficient LRT service from Atatürk International Airport to Zeytinburnu (TL1.40), from where you connect with the tram (TL1.40) that takes you directly to Sultanahmet – the whole trip takes about 50 minutes.

If you are staying near Taksim Sq, the **Havaş airport bus** (Map pp538-9; ☎ 0212-244 0487) is your best bet. Buses leave Atatürk airport (TL9) every 15 to 30 minutes from 4am to 1am, and Sabiha Gökçen airport (TL10) 25 minutes after planes land. From the Havaş office at Taksim, buses depart for the airports every 15 to 30 minutes from 4am to 1am (less frequently to Sabiha Gökçen).

Hostels and some of the smaller hotels in Sultanahmet can book minibus transport from the hostel to the airport for around TL10 per person. Unfortunately, this option only works going *from* town to the airport and not vice versa, and there are only six or so services per day.

A taxi to Atatürk airport from Sultanahmet costs from TL35; to Sabiha Gökçen, at least TL80.

Boat

The cheapest and most scenic way to travel any distance in İstanbul is by ferry. The main ferry docks are at the mouth of the Golden Horn (Eminönü, Sirkeci and Karaköy) and at Beşiktaş, a few kilometres northeast of the Galata Bridge, near Dolmabahçe Palace. *Jetons* (transport tokens) cost TL1.40.

Ferries for Üsküdar and the Bosphorus leave from Eminönü; ferries depart from Kabataş (Adalar İskelesi dock) for the Princes' Islands. From Karaköy, cruise ships dock and ferries depart for Kadıköy and Haydarpaşa on the Asian shore.

Public Transport

A *tramvay* (tramway) service runs from Zeytinburnu (where it connects with the airport LRT) to Kabataş (connecting with the funicular to Taksim Sq) via Sultanahmet, Eminönü and Karaköy (connecting with the funicular to Tünel). Trams run every five minutes or so from 6am to midnight.

A quaint antique tram rattles up and down İstiklal Caddesi in Beyoğlu, from the Tünel station to Taksim Sq via the Galatasaray Lisesi.

An LRT service connects Aksaray with the airport, stopping at 15 stations, including the main otogar, along the way. It operates from 5.40am until 1.40am.

İstanbul's efficient bus system has major bus stations at Taksim Sq, Beşiktaş, Aksaray, Rüstempaşa-Eminönü, Kadıköy and Üsküdar. Most services run between 6.30am and 11.30pm.

There is a one-stop Tünel funicular system between Karaköy and İstiklal Caddesi (TL1.40, every 10 or 15 minutes from 7.30am to 9pm). A newer funicular railway runs through a tunnel from Kabataş (where it connects with the tram) up to the metro station at Taksim Sq.

Every 30 minutes, suburban trains from Sirkeci Railway Station (TL1.40) run along the southern walls of Old İstanbul and west along the Marmara shore. There's a handy station in Cankurtaran for Sultanahmet. Services also connect Haydarpaşa Train Station with Gebze via Bostancı.

Taxi

İstanbul is full of yellow taxis, all of them with meters, although not all drivers want to use them. From Sultanahmet to Taksim costs around TL10; to the main otogar around TL22.

AROUND İSTANBUL

Since İstanbul is such a vast city, few places are within easy reach on a day trip. However, if you make an early start it's just possible to see the sights of Edirne in Thrace (Trakya), the only bit of Turkey that is geographically within Europe. The fast ferry link means that you can also just make it to Bursa and back in a day, although it's much better to plan to overnight there. Another must-see is İznik, a historic walled town on the shores of a peaceful lake, easily accessible from İstanbul.

EDİRNE

☎ 0284 / pop 136,000

European Turkey's largest settlement outside İstanbul, Edirne is disregarded by all but a handful of travellers who come to enjoy the stunning architecture. It was briefly the capital of the Ottoman Empire and many of its key buildings are in excellent shape. You'll find none of the razzmatazz or crowds of the Aegean or Mediterranean coasts here, but Edirne is hardly a backwater. With the Greek and Bulgarian frontiers a half-hour's drive away, the streets are crowded with foreigners, locals and off-duty soldiers. At the end of June is the oily **Kırpınar Wrestling Festival**.

Sights

Dominating Edirne's skyline like a massive battleship is the **Selimiye Mosque** (1569–75), the finest work of the great Ottoman architect Mimar Sinan. Its lofty dome and four tall (71m), slender minarets create a dramatic perspective. In the southeast corner of the complex is the 15-room **Turkish & Islamic Arts Museum** (Türk İslam Eserleri Müzesi; ☎ 225 1120; admission TL2; 🕒 8am-5pm Tue-Sun), which features displays on oil wrestling and dervishes. Smack-bang in the centre of town, you can't miss the 1414 **Eski Cami** (Old Mosque), which has rows of arches and pillars supporting a series of small domes. Another example of architectural magnificence is the **Üçşerefeli Cami** (Three-Balcony Mosque), which has four strikingly different minarets, all built at different times. The great imperial mosque built by the Ottoman architect Hayreddin, **Beyazıt II complex**

(1484–1512), stands in splendid isolation to the north of the town.

Sleeping & Eating

Hotel Aksaray (☎ 212 6035; fax 225 6806; Alipaşa Ortakapı Caddesi; s/d/tr/q TL35/65/80/100, s/d/tr without bathroom TL30/55/70;) This cheapie has basic rooms in a charmingly decrepit old building and bathrooms rammed into small spaces.

Tuna Hotel (☎ /fax 214 3340/3323; Maarif Caddesi 17; s/d/tr/q TL50/70/90/100;) An excellent choice for the price, the Tuna is at the quieter southern end of Maarif Caddesi.

Efe Hotel (☎ 213 6166; www.efehotel.com; Maarif Caddesi 13; s/d TL85/125;) The Efe is a stylish place, especially the lobby, which is filled with antiques and curios. The rooms, especially the 2nd-floor doubles, are big and bright, with fridges and electric kettles.

There's an assortment of eateries along Saraçlar Caddesi. The riverside restaurants south of the centre are more atmospheric, but most open only in summer and are booked solid at weekends.

Getting There & Away

The otogar is 9km east of the city centre. There are regular bus services for İstanbul (TL20, 2½ hours, 235km) and Çanakkale (TL25, four hours, 230km). If you're heading for the Bulgarian border crossing at Kapıkule, catch a dolmuş (TL5, 25 minutes) from opposite the tourist office on Talat Paşa Caddesi.

İZNİK

☎ 0224 / pop 20,000

A walled town laden with history and situated by a lake, İznik is popular with weekending İstanbullus but largely ignored by tourists, which has helped preserve its Turkish character. Stroll along the lakefront or mosey around the city centre, admiring the ruins of **Aya Sofya** (Church of Holy Wisdom; admission TL5; 9am-noon & 1-6pm Tue-Sun) and the Seljuk-style **Yeşil Cami** (Green Mosque), built between 1378 and 1387. The minaret, decorated with green-and-blue glazed zigzag tiles, is a wonder. It's also worth sparing an hour to visit the **İznik Museum** (İznik Müzesi; ☎ 757 1027; Müze Sokak; admission TL2; 8am-noon & 1-5pm Tue-Sun), which contains examples of İznik tiles. More-active types can follow a 5km circuit around most of İznik's **walls**, which were first erected in Roman times. Four main **gates** pierce the walls; the Lefke and İstanbul gates are most impressive.

Sleeping & Eating

Kaynarca Pansiyon (☎ 757 1753; www.kaynarca.s5.com; Kılıçaslan Caddesi, Gündem Sokak 1; dm/s/d/tr TL20/30/50/75;) This cheerful and central pension is a budget traveller's dream. It's pathologically clean and there's a spacious rooftop terrace for leisurely breakfasts (TL5).

Hotel Aydın (☎ 757 7650; www.iznikhotelaydin.com; Kılıçaslan Caddesi 64; s/d/tr TL50/80/100) Known locally for its onsite *pastanesi* (patisserie/bakery), the Aydın's smallish rooms come with TV, phone, balcony and chintzy bedspreads.

Çamlık Motel (☎ 757 1631; www.iznik-camlikmotel.com; Göl Sahil Yolu; s/d TL60/100;) At the southern end of the lakefront, this modern motel has spacious rooms and a restaurant with water views. It's a favourite with tour groups, so book ahead on summer weekends. The restaurant is recommended by locals as İznik's best spot to enjoy fish.

Köfteci Yusuf (☎ 757 3597; Atatürk Caddesi 75; mains from TL5) A favourite lunchtime spot for juicy *köfte* and other grills with chunky bread and hot green peppers. Leave room for the gorgeous desserts.

On the lakefront the Köşk Café, Sedef Aile Café Salonu and Lambada Café are all good for (nonalcoholic) drinks and snacks.

Getting There & Away

There are hourly buses from the İstanbul's main otogar to Bursa (TL7.50, 1½ hours) and frequent buses to Yalova (TL7.50, one hour), where you can catch a fast ferry to İstanbul.

BURSA

☎ 0224 / pop 1 million

Sprawling at the base of Uludağ, Bursa was the first capital of the Ottoman Empire. Today, Turkey's biggest winter-sports centre is a modern, prosperous city with lots of vitality and personality. Allow at least a day to take in the ancient mosques, medreses, hamams and their enthralling designs. If you feel in need of some pampering, the thermal springs in the village-like suburb of Çekirge are the perfect salve after exploring the city or Uludağ's tree-clad slopes.

The city centre, with its banks and shops, is along Atatürk Caddesi, between the Ulu

Cami (Grand Mosque) to the west and the main square, Cumhuriyet Alanı, commonly called Heykel (Statue), to the east.

Çekirge is a 10-minute bus or dolmuş ride from Heykel via Atatürk Caddesi. Bursa's otogar is an inconvenient 10km north of the centre; take bus No 38 or a taxi (around TL20).

Sights & Activities

About 1km east of Heykel is the supremely beautiful **Yeşil Cami** (Green Mosque; 1424) and its stunningly tiled **Yeşil Türbe** (Green Tomb; admission free; 8am-noon & 1-5pm). Right in the city centre, the largest of Bursa's mosques is the Seljuk **Ulu Cami** (Grand Mosque; Atatürk Caddesi), built in 1396. Behind the Ulu Cami, Bursa's sprawling **Covered Market** (Kapalı Çarşı) is proudly local, especially if you find İstanbul's Grand Bazaar too touristy.

Uphill and west of the Ulu Cami, on the way to Çekirge, don't miss the 14th-century **tombs of Osman and Orhan**, the first Ottoman sultans. A kilometre beyond lies the delightful **Muradiye Complex**, with a mosque and 12 decorated tombs dating from the 15th and 16th centuries. With a shady park in front, it's a peaceful oasis in a busy city.

Whether it's winter or summer, it's worth taking a cable-car ride up the 2543m-high **Uludağ** (Great Mountain) to take advantage of the view and the cool, clear air of Uludağ National Park. To get to the **teleferik** (cable car; return trip TL8) from Bursa, take a city bus from stop 1 or a dolmuş from behind the City Museum (Kent Müzesi). Bear in mind that the skiing facilities, while some of Turkey's best, are not European-resort standard.

Sleeping

There are a couple of decent options in Bursa, but also consider Çekirge, which has better, quieter options. The suburb's hotels are generally more expensive, but prices include the use of their mineral baths. To get here, take a 'Çekirge' bus, or a dolmuş from Heykel or along Atatürk Caddesi.

Hotel Güneş (☎ 222 1404; İnebey Caddesi 75, Bursa; s/d/tr/q without bathroom TL26/46/54/68) The family-run Güneş is Bursa's best budget pension, with small, neat rooms in a restored Ottoman house.

Mutlu Hotel (☎ 233 2829; mutluhotel@mynet.com; Murat Caddesi 19, Çekirge; s/d/tr TL50/78/90;) A reliable choice, the Mutlu combines a rustic wooden exterior with spacious marble thermal baths. The decor sometimes struggles to get past 1973, but the café outside is more modern.

Termal Hotel Gold 2 (☎ 235 6030; www.hotelgold.com.tr; I Murat Cami Aralığı, Çekirge; s/d TL60/90;) This restored 1878 house next to the I Murat Camii has wooden interiors and deep red drapery. Baths and parking are included, and the roof terrace is a bonus.

Hotel Artıç (☎ 224 5505; www.artichotel.com; Ulu Camii Karşısı 95, Bursa; s/d/tr TL60/90/100;) A decent option towards the western end of Atatürk Caddesi, with light, spacious rooms and good views of Ulu Cami from the breakfast salon. Ask for a discount on the posted rates.

TURKEY

Eating & Drinking

Sakli Bahçe (Çekirge Caddesi 2, Çekirge; mains TL4-8; 11am-11pm) The perfect place to watch the sunset, this chilled-out hilltop garden is the preferred meeting point for Bursa's bright young things, lured by excellent pizza and kebaps.

Yusuf (Culture Park; meze TL4-10; 11am-11pm) 'Joe's Place' features a meze- and grill-laden terrace set among shady trees. The service is so good that we saw waiters break out into a brisk trot to help customers.

Çiçek Izgara (☎ 221 6526; Belediye Caddesi 15; mains TL9-12; 11am-9.30pm) One block from Koza Parkı, behind the half-timbered *belediye* (town hall), this modern grillhouse is good for lone women and has a 1st-floor salon to watch the flower market below.

Make sure you spend an evening at one of the fish restaurants on Sakarya Caddesi, Bursa's most atmospheric eating precinct. After eating there, you'll find a few bars nearby, including Barantico and Gedikli Meyhane on Sakarya Caddesi and Müsadenızle on Altıparmak Caddesi.

If you're after a café, Mehfel Mado on Namazgah Caddesi is the city's oldest, with live music on its riverside terrace and a basement art gallery. Across the stream, the multiterraced Set Café, on Köprü Üstü, also offers live music.

Getting There & Away

The fastest way to get to İstanbul (TL20, 2½ to three hours) is to take a bus to Yalova, then a catamaran to İstanbul's Yenikapı docks. Get a bus that departs Bursa's bus terminal at least 90 minutes before the scheduled boat departure.

Karayolu ile (by road) buses to İstanbul take four to five hours and drag you around the Bay of İzmit. Those designated *feribot ile* (by ferry) go to Topçular, east of Yalova, and take the ferry to Eskihisar, a much quicker and more pleasant way to go.

AEGEAN COAST

While the Aegean coast may not be as scenic as the Mediterranean, its beaches define the western edge of the Anatolian landmass formerly known as Asia Minor, and the area is studded with fantastic historic sites. Come here to see Troy, Ephesus and Pergamum, and more-recent history at the battlefield sites on the Gallipoli Peninsula.

ÇANAKKALE

☎ 0286 / pop 86,600

The liveliest settlement on the Dardanelles, this sprawling harbour town would be worth a visit for its sights, nightlife and overall vibe even if it didn't lie opposite the Gallipoli Peninsula. Its sweeping waterfront promenade heaves during the summer months.

A good base for visiting Troy, Çanakkale has become a popular destination for weekending Turks; if possible, plan your visit for midweek.

Sleeping

Rooms are expensive around Anzac Day (25 April) and usually booked solid months before that date.

Anzac House Hostel (☎ 213 5969; www.anzachouse.com; 59-61 Cumhuriyet Meydanı; dm/s/d/tr without bathroom TL16/28/40/54;) Not to be confused with the three-star Anzac Hotel, central, cheap Anzac House is the main backpackers haunt.

Efes Hotel (☎ 217 3256; www.efeshotelcanakkale.com; Aralık Sokak 5; s/d TL30/50;) An excellent budget choice, with cheery decor and a welcoming owner. The best rooms have open showers and orthopaedic mattresses. The breakfasts are great, and there's a little garden with a fountain.

Yellow Rose Pension (☎ 217 3343; www.yellowrose.4mg.com; Aslan Abla Sokak 5; dm/s/d/tr TL17/30/55/60;) This bright, attractive guesthouse has a central but quiet location plus extras including a laundry service (TL15) and fully equipped kitchen.

our pick **Kervansaray Hotel** (☎ 217 8192; www.otelkervansaray.com; Fetvane Sokak 13; s/d/tr €35/50/60; P) Çanakkale's only boutique hotel is as lovely as you could hope for, laying on Ottoman touches in keeping with the restored house it occupies. The 19 rooms (including eight in a sympathetic new annexe) have a dash of character, without being overdone.

Çanak Hotel (☎ 214 1582; www.canakhotel.com; Dibek Sokak 1; s/d €35/60;) This excellent midrange option is just off Cumhuriyet Meydanı, with a stunning rooftop bar and games room, and a skylit atrium.

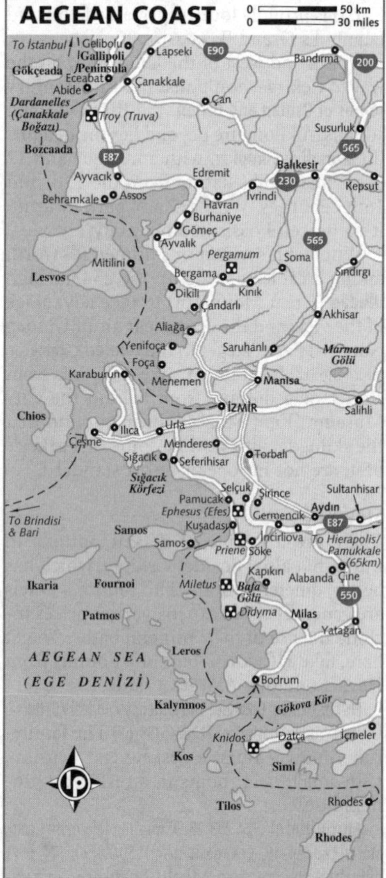

Eating & Drinking

To eat on the hoof, browse the stalls along the *kordon* (waterfront promenade) offering corn on the cob, mussels and other simple items. A local specialty is *peynir helvası*, made with soft white village cheese, flour, butter and sugar.

Köy Evi (☎ 213 4687; Yalı Caddesi 13; menu TL5; 🕑 8am-midnight) Proper home cooking rules in this tiny eatery, where local women make *mantı*, börek and *gözleme* (TL1.50).

Doyum (☎ 217 1866; Cumhuriyet Meydanı 13; main TL4.50-10) Generally acknowledged to be the best kebap and pide joint in town, a visit to Doyum is worth it for the good cheer alone.

Benzin (☎ 212 2237; Eski Balıkhane Sokak 11; pizzas TL8-12.50; 🕑 8.30am-1am) This 1960s-style waterfront café-bar is a relaxing spot for a drink and a bite, but gets packed at weekends.

Hayal Kahvesi (☎ 217 0470; Saat Kulesi Meydanı 6; admission free-TL5; 🕑 noon-1am, happy hour 4-9pm) Facing the clock tower, this café-bar (also called TNT Bar) with courtyard seating is Çanakkale's most popular live music venue.

Getting There & Away

There are regular buses to Ayvalık (TL20, 3½ hours), İstanbul (TL30, six hours) and İzmir (TL30, 5½ hours), and frequent ferry services to Eceabat (from TL2, 25 minutes).

ECEABAT (MAYDOS)

☎ 0286 / pop 5500

Just over the Dardanelles from Çanakkale, Eceabat (Maydos) is a small, easy-going waterfront town with the best access to the main Gallipoli battlefields.

Ferries dock by the main square, Cumhuriyet Meydanı, which has hotels, restaurants, ATMs, a post office, bus company offices and dolmuş and taxi stands. Like most of the peninsula, Eceabat is swamped with students and tour groups at weekends from April to mid-June and in late September.

Sleeping & Eating

Hotel Boss I (☎ 814 1464; www.heyboss.com; Cumhuriyet Meydanı 14; s/d/tr TL20/40/60; ❄) Behind its clapboard facade, this small, narrow place is as cheap and basic as you'll find here. Opt for a corner room or one facing the water (eg No 1) to get more space. It's no surprise that the same management run Hotel Boss II (Mehmet Akif Sokak), which charges the same rates, and the pricier Aqua Boss Hotel (İstiklal Caddesi).

TJs Hotel (☎ 814 2458; www.anzacgallipolitours.com; Cumhuriyet Meydanı 2/A; dm/s/d TL15/50/70; P ❄ 💻) With a commanding central position, the former Eceabat Hotel has rooms to suit every budget, from basic hostel bunk rooms upwards. The Ottoman-style rooftop bar has regular live events.

our pick **Hotel Crowded House** (☎ 814 1565; www.crowdedhousegallipoli.com; Huseyin Avni Sokak 4; dm/s/d/tr TL20/35/50/69; P ⊠ ❄ 💻) Eceabat's newest backpacker caravanserai, named after the antipodean band rather than the state of the accommodation, is housed in a four-storey building near the dock.

Liman Restaurant (☎ 814 2755; İstiklal Caddesi 67; mains TL6-15; 🕑 10am-12.30am) At the southern end of the waterfront, this is considered to be Eceabat's best fish restaurant; its covered terrace is a delight in all weather.

Getting There & Away

Long-distance buses pass through Eceabat on the way from Çanakkale to İstanbul (TL30, five hours). There are frequent ferry services to Çanakkale (from TL2, 25 minutes).

GALLIPOLI (GELİBOLU) PENINSULA

☎ 0286

Antipodeans and many Britons won't need an introduction to Gallipoli; it is the backbone of the 'Anzac legend' in which an Allied campaign in 1915 to knock Turkey out of WWI and open a relief route to Russia turned into one of the war's greatest fiascos. Some 130,000 men died, a third from Allied forces and the rest Turkish.

Today the Gallipoli battlefields are peaceful places, covered in brush and pine forests. But the battles fought here nearly a century ago are still alive in many memories, both Turkish and foreign, especially Australians and New Zealanders, who view the peninsula as a place of pilgrimage. The Turkish officer responsible for the defence of Gallipoli was Mustafa Kemal (the future Atatürk); his victory is commemorated in Turkey on 18 March. On Anzac Day (25 April), a dawn service marks the anniversary of the Allied landings.

The easiest way to see the battlefields is with your own transport or on a minibus tour from Çanakkale or Eceabat with **Hassle Free Tours** (☎ 213 5969; www.hasslefreetour.com;

Anzac House Hostel, Çanakkale; TL45-55), **Trooper Tours** (☎ 217 3343; www.troopertours.com; Yellow Rose Pension, Çanakkale; TL55) or **TJs Tours** (☎ 814 3121; www.anzacgallipollitours.com; TJs Hotel, Eceabat; TL45). With a tour you get the benefit of a guide who can explain the battles as you go along.

Most people use Çanakkale or Eceabat as a base for exploring Gallipoli. Car ferries frequently cross the straits from Çanakkale to Eceabat (from TL2). From Eceabat, take a dolmuş or a taxi to the Kabatepe Information Centre & Museum on the western shore of the peninsula.

Some travellers prefer to join an organised tour from İstanbul.

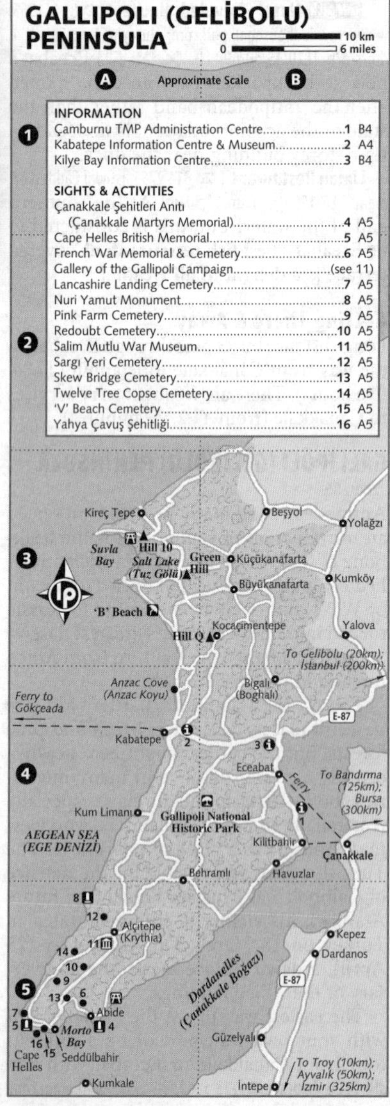

TROY (TRUVA)

☎ 0286

Of all the ancient sites in Turkey, the remains of the great city of Troy are among the least impressive; you'll have to use your imagination. However, it's an important stop for history buffs, and if you have read Homer's *Iliad*, the ruins have a romance few places on earth can match.

The ticket booth for the ruins of **Troy** (☎ 283 0536; admission per person/car TL10/3; 8.30am-7pm May–mid-Sep, to 5pm mid-Sep–Apr) is 500m before the site. The site is rather confusing for nonexpert eyes (guides are available), but the most conspicuous features, apart from the reconstruction of the Trojan Horse, include the **walls** from various periods; the Graeco-Roman **Temple of Athena**, of which traces of the altar remain; the Roman **Odeon**, where concerts were held; the **Bouleuterion** (Council Chamber), built around Homer's time (c 800 BC).

From Çanakkale, dolmuşes to Troy (TL2, 35 minutes, 30km) leave every hour on the half hour from 9.30am to 5.30pm from a station under the bridge over the Sarı, and drop you by the ticket booth. Dolmuşes run back to Çanakkale on the hour, until 5pm in high season and 3pm in low season.

The travel agencies offering tours to the Gallipoli battlefields (p555) also offer tours to Troy (around €25 per person).

BEHRAMKALE & ASSOS

☎ 0286

Behramkale, southwest of Ayvalık, is an old hilltop Greek village spread out around the ruins of a 6th-century temple. The Ionic **Temple of Athena** (admission TL5; 8am-dusk) has spectacular views of Lesvos and the dazzling Aegean – well worth the admission fee. Beside the entrance to the ruins, the 14th-century **Hüdavendigar Camii** is a simple early Ottoman mosque.

Just before the entrance to the village, a road winds 2km down to Assos harbour. It's a cluster of half-a-dozen old stone houses-turned-hotels overlooking a picture-perfect harbour, and is the ideal place to unwind over a cup of tea.

Behramkale and Assos make a fine combination, but are no longer sleeping beauties and get overcrowded. Over summer weekends and public holidays, İstanbullus and İzmirlis pour in by the bus load.

Sleeping

You can either stay in Behramkale village itself or in the hotels around Assos harbour.

BEHRAMKALE

Dolunay Pansiyon (☎ 721 7172; s/d TL25/50) In the centre of the village by the dolmuş stop, the homely Dolunay has six spotless, simple rooms set around a courtyard.

Timur Pansiyon (☎/fax 721 7449; timurpansiyon@yahoo.com; s/d TL35/60; Apr–mid-Sep) Remote, rustic and not unlike a shepherd's croft, the 200-year-old Timur's characterful rooms may prove too basic for some, but the setting above the village and beside the temple is fabulous.

Old Bridge House (☎ 721 7426; www.assos.de/obh; campsites TL10, dm TL20, d low/high season TL60/100; Mar-Nov) Near the Ottoman bridge at the entrance to town, this long-time travellers' favourite offers large double rooms, a six-bed dorm and garden cabins.

Eris Pansiyon (☎ 721 7080; erispansiyon.com; Behramkale Köyü 6; s/d TL90/130; Apr-Nov) Set in a stone house with gardens at the far end of the village, this has ordinary (for the price) but peaceful rooms. Afternoon tea is served on a terrace with views over the hills.

ASSOS

If you prefer to stay in the pricey hotels by Assos harbour, note that in high season virtually all of them insist on *yarım pansiyon* (half board).

Çakır Pansiyon (☎ 721 7048; www.assoscakirpansiyon.com; campsite per person TL8, s/d TL40/60, half board TL60/80) Around 100m east of the town entrance, this seafront pansiyon has simple but clean bungalows and a small camping site. Breakfast is served on a floating platform, dinner in a lantern-lit restaurant.

Yıldız Saray Hotel (☎ 721 7025; www.yildizsaray-hotels.com; r TL180) Though rooms are small, they're traditionally furnished, attractive and good value, with views across the harbour and three with access to a small terrace. The brassiere-style restaurant has a good reputation.

Hotel Behram (☎ 721 7044; www.behram-hotel.com; s/d half board TL120/180) On the front, by the town entrance, Behram has smallish rooms, although they are well-equipped and enlivened by bright decor.

our pick **Biber Evi** (☎ 721 7410; www.biberevi.com; s/d TL150/200, half board TL170/240) A real delight, this old stone house boasts a peaceful garden, a small terrace with lovely views and a gourmet restaurant. Rooms are Ottoman-rustic in style, complete with *gusulhane* – washing facilities hidden in a cupboard!

Eating

In contravention of the way these things usually work, the settlement at the bottom of the hill is actually the 'posh' part of town where prices, if not standards, are higher than at the top. Be sure to check the cost of fish and bottles of wine before ordering. You can eat for less than TL10 in Behramkale.

Getting There & Away

To get to Behramkale during the summer, catch the regular shuttle (TL1) from Assos. In winter, workers shuttle back and forth and you can normally jump on one of their buses.

Regular buses run from Çanakkale (TL7.50, 1½ hours) to Ayvalık, where you can pick up a dolmuş (which leaves when full) to Behramkale (TL3, 20 minutes). Some dolmuşes make a second stop down in Assos.

AYVALIK

☎ 0266 / pop 34,650

Back from the palm trees and touristy restaurants on Ayvalık's waterfront, the tumbledown old Greek village provides, in the words of hotelier Annette, a 'wonderful outdoor museum'. Horses and carts clatter down the village's narrow streets, past headscarf-wearing women holding court outside picturesque shuttered houses.

Olive-oil production is the traditional business here, although the town is now better known as a gateway to local islands and the Greek isle of Lesvos.

The otogar is 1.5km north of the town centre and the tourist office is 1.5km south; in summer there's an information kiosk on the waterfront south of the main square, Cumhuriyet Alanı. Offshore, you can visit Alibey

Island (Cunda), which is lined with open-air fish restaurants and linked by ferries and a causeway to the mainland. In summer, it is included in **cruises** (incl meal per person around TL10-12) around the bay's islands; cruises leave Ayvalık at about 11am and stopping here and there for sunbathing and swimming.

Sleeping & Eating

Taksiyarhis Pension (☎ 312 1494; www.taksiyarhispension.com; r without bathroom per person TL28, breakfast TL7) These 120-year-old Greek houses beside the eponymous church have exposed wooden beams and a jumble of cushions, rugs and handicrafts. Facilities include a communal kitchen, book exchange and bicycles for hire.

our pick **Annette's House** (☎ 312 5971; www.annetteshouse.com; Neşe Sokak 12; s/d €21/42) On a square that hosts a Thursday market, Annette's is an oasis of calm and comfort. Nothing is too much trouble for the eponymous German owner, who presides over a charming collection or large, clean, well-decorated rooms.

Şehir Kulübü (☎ 312 1088; Yat Limanı; fish per 500g TL15; 10am-2am) Jutting over the water, the 'city club' is the top choice for reasonably priced fish. You choose your fish from the giant freezer and mezes (TL4 to TL7) from the counter.

Martı Restaurant (☎ 312 6899; Gazinolar Caddesi 9; mains TL14-22; 7.30am-midnight) Another excellent choice, Martı specialises in Ayvalık and regional specialties as well as fish.

Getting There & Away

There are frequent direct buses from İzmir (TL7.50, three hours) and Bergama (TL7.50, 1¾ hours) to Ayvalık. Coming from Çanakkale (TL12, 3¼ hours), some buses drop you on the main highway to hitch to the centre.

For Alibey Island, take a dolmuş taxi (white with red stripes) from the main square (TL1.50) or a boat (TL2; June to August) from behind the tourist kiosk nearby.

Daily boats operate to Lesvos (Greece) between June and September (€40/50 one way/return). There are two boats a week from October to May. For information and tickets, contact **Jale Tours** (☎ 312 2740; Gümrük Caddesi 24).

BERGAMA & PERGAMUM

☎ 0232 / pop 58,210

As Selçuk is to Ephesus, so Bergama is to Pergamum: a workaday market town that's become a major stop on the tourist trail because of its proximity to the remarkable ruins of Pergamum, site of the preeminent medical centre of ancient Rome. During Pergamum's heyday (between Alexander the Great and the Roman domination of Asia Minor) it was one of the Middle East's richest and most powerful small kingdoms.

İzmir Caddesi (the main street) is where you'll find banks with ATMs and the PTT. There is a basic **Tourist Office** (☎ 631 2851; İzmir Caddesi 54; 8.30am-noon & 1-5.30pm), just north of the museum, and most pensions and hotels offer free internet access.

Sights

One of the highlights of the Aegean coast, the well-proportioned **Asclepion** (Temple of Asclepios; admission/parking TL10/3; 8.30am-5.30pm), about 3km from the city centre, was a famous medical school with a library that rivalled that of Alexandria in Egypt. The ruins of the **Acropolis** (admission TL10; 8.30am-5.30pm), 6km from the city, are equally striking. The hilltop setting is absolutely magical, and the well-preserved ruins are magnificent, especially the vertigo-inducing 10,000-seat **theatre** and the marble-columned **Temple of Trajan**, built during the reigns of emperors Trajan and Hadrian and used to worship them as well as Zeus.

The excellent **Archaeology Museum** (Arkeoloji Müzesi; ☎ 632 9860; İzmir Caddesi; admission TL2; 8.30am-5.30pm Tue-Sun) has a small but important collection of artefacts from both of these sites, including a collection of 4th-century statues from the so-called 'Pergamum School'.

Sleeping & Eating

Odyssey Guest house (☎ 653 9189; www.odysseyguesthouse.com; Abacihan Sokak 13; dm TL10, s/d without bathroom low season TL15/30, high season TL20/35) This 180-year-old house has clean (but sparse) rooms, furnished with copies of Homer's *Odyssey*. There's a trading library and breakfast is served on the rooftop terrace.

Gobi Pension (☎ 633 2518; www.gobipension.com; Atatürk Bulvarı 18; s/d €20/32, without bathroom €14/22;) On the main road behind a greenery-draped terrace, this is a great family-run place with bright, cheery rooms, most with new private bathrooms.

our pick **Akropolis Guest House** (☎ 631 2621; www.akropolisguesthouse.com; Kayalik Caddesi 5; s/d

TURKEY

€20/49; ⊠ ❋) This 150-year-old stone house is the closest Bergama gets to boutique, with eight attractively decorated rooms surrounding a pool and garden, a restaurant set in a barn and a terrace with Acropolis views.

Pala Kebap Salonu (☎ 633 1559; Kasapoğlu Caddesi 4; kebap €2.20; ⏰ 8am-11pm Mon-Sat) Though small and simple, this place is terrifically popular and the food's delicious. Try the spicy Bergama *köfte* (TL6).

Bergama Ticaret Odası Sosyal Tesisleri (☎ 632 9641; Ulucamii Mahallesi; meze TL5, mains TL6-8; ⏰ 10.30am-11pm) Run by Bergama municipality, this restaurant occupies a beautifully restored 200-year-old Greek house.

Sağlam Restaurant (☎ 632 8897; Cumhuriyet Meydanı 47; mains TL6-11; ⏰ 8am-11pm) This large, simple place is well known in town for its high-quality home cooking. It does a good selection of meze, which change daily, and delicious kebaps.

Getting There & Around

There are frequent buses to/from İzmir (TL10, two hours, 110km) and Ayvalık (TL7.50, 1¾ hours, 60km). Bergama's new otogar lies 7km from the centre at the junction of the highway and the main road into town. From here a dolmuş service shuttles into town (TL2); a taxi should cost around TL15 during the day.

There's no public transport to the archaeological sites. A taxi tour of sites including the Acropolis, the Asclepion and the museum costs from TL40 to TL60, depending on the time of year.

İZMİR

☎ 0232 / pop 2.6 million

Though you may eventually fall for its hectic nightlife, great shopping and top-notch museums, İzmir can take some getting used to. Certainly nowhere else in the region can prepare you for the sheer size, sprawl and intensity of the place.

At the water's edge, İzmir's traffic has been beaten back and the city really comes into its own. The seafront is one of its main attractions, the wide, pleasant esplanade of Birinci Kordon providing eating, drinking and sunset-watching opportunities. Inland, things are more hectic, but you'll find a buzzing bazaar, plenty of interesting ruins and a newly restored Jewish quarter.

Orientation & Information

İzmir's two main avenues run parallel to the waterfront. Atatürk Caddesi (Birinci Kordon or First Cordon), known locally as the Kordon, is on the waterfront; a block inland is Cumhuriyet Bulvarı, the İkinci Kordon (Second Cordon). Main squares Konak Meydanı (Government House Sq) and Cumhuriyet Meydanı are on these avenues.

Konak opens onto the bazaar and Anafartalar Caddesi, the bazaar's main street, leads to the train station, Basmane Garı. The Basmane-Çankaya area, near the station, has medium-priced hotels, restaurants and bus ticket offices.

İzmir's shopping, restaurant and nightclub district of Alsancak is to the north, while the otogar is 6.5km northeast of the centre.

The **tourist office** (☎/fax 483 5117/4270; Akdeniz Mahallesi 1344 Sokak 2) is on the seafront.

Sights

Since most of old İzmir was destroyed after WWI by a Greek invasion and a fire, there's little to see here compared with other Turkish cities. However, it does boast the remains of an extensive 2nd-century Roman **agora** (marketplace; admission TL2; ⏰ 8am-5pm), just southeast of the sprawling, atmospheric modern **bazaar**. It's also worth taking Bus 33 to the hilltop **Kadifekale** (*kale* means fortress),

DON'T FORGET YOUR NAZAR BONCUK

Nazar Boncuk is a ubiquitous Turkish 'evil-eye' charm. As in many cultures, Turks believe the 'evil eye' can bring you bad luck, and use Nazar Boncuks (literally 'evil-eye beads') to ward off malicious forces associated with envious eyes. Nazar Boncuks of various shapes and sizes are pinned to the clothes of babies, guard the doorways of restaurants and hang on walls and doors.

The bead reflects evil intent back to the onlooker. With its concentric dots of colours, it resembles an eye; its blue colour is said to help protect the user.

This tradition goes back to the Arabian craftsmen who settled in İzmir during the Ottoman Empire's decline. Today, the genuine eye beads are produced by a handful of glass masters in nearby Görece and Kurudere. Their methods and techniques have changed very little over the centuries.

where women still weave kilims on horizontal looms and the views are breathtaking.

Sleeping

İzmir's waterfront is dominated by high-end business hotels, which fill up quickly during the summer; inland are cheap and midpriced places, particularly around the train station. On 1296 Sokak, just southwest of the station, a number of hotels occupy restored Ottoman houses, but their interiors can be grungy and uninviting.

Otel Hikmet (☎ 484 2672; 945 Sokak 26; s/d TL20/45, without shower TL15/35) The sign outside says 'Hotel very good' and it's not wrong. Tucked away on cobbled streets off a café-lined square, this family-run house is full of character.

Imperial Hotel (☎ 425 6883; fax 489 4688; 1294 Sokak 54; s/d TL20/45; ❄) Past the grandiose entrance columns, marble floors and carpets, the rooms are more modest, but they're still of a decent size and terrific value.

Hotel Alican 2 (☎ 425 2912; alicanotel@hotmail.com; 1367 Sokak; s/d €19/35; ❄) One of the safer choices in the station area (there's a 24-hour reception), this has well-maintained rooms with modern bathrooms.

our pick Konak Saray Hotel (☎ 483 7755; www.konaksarayhotel.com; Anafartalar Caddesi 635; s/d €35/50; ⊠ ❄) This beautiful Ottoman house has been transformed into a superior boutique hotel. Rooms are a touch small, but stylish and modern, and soundproofed to keep bazaar noise out.

Eating

For fresh fruit, veg or freshly baked bread and delicious savoury pastries, head for the canopied market, just off Anafartalar Caddesi. *The* place to be seen on a romantic summer's evening is the sea-facing Kordon, though you pay for the location. In Alsancak, you lose the sunset views but gain on atmosphere; try 1453 Sokak (Gazi Kadinlar Sokağı).

Sakız (☎ 484 1103; Şehıt Nevresbey Bulvarı 9/A; mains TL8-12; ⏰ 11am-midnight; Ⓥ) It must have been a bold move opening a vegetarian café in carnivorous İzmir, but it has paid off. The food is traditional Turkish, just removed of its meat and fish elements, made with fresh local ingredients. Good wine list.

Kefi (☎ 422 6045; 1453 Sokak 17; meze TL5, mains TL14; ⏰ 11am-midnight) Kefi has stood the test of time with its superb cooking and elegant dining room in a restored Ottoman house. Fish and seafood dominate the menu, but it also does some mean meats; try the lamb with fennel.

Getting There & Away

AIR

Turkish Airlines offers nonstop flights to İstanbul (from TL109) and Ankara (from TL59) from İzmir, with connections to other destinations. Onur Air, Atlasjet, Fly Air, Sun Express Airlines and Izair also fly to İzmir. Flights to the city from European destinations have greatly increased in recent years.

BUS

İzmir is a major transport hub. From the otogar, frequent buses leave for Bergama (TL10, two hours), Kuşadası (TL10.50, 1¼ hours), Selçuk (TL6, one hour) and other destinations nationwide. Buses to Çeşme (TL10, two hours) leave from a local bus terminal in Üçkuyular, 6.5km southwest of Konak.

TRAIN

The daily *Alti Eylül Ekspresi* and, between April and October, the *Onyedi Eylül Ekspresi* go to Bandırma (TL16, 6½ hours), where you can catch a ferry across to İstanbul. Express trains also run to Ankara (sleeper TL26.50, 13 to 15 hours), Selçuk/Ephesus (TL3.50, 1½ hours) and Denizli (for Pamukkale; TL11, five hours).

ÇEŞME

☎ 0232 / pop 21,300

The Çeşme Peninsula is İzmir's summer playground, which means it can get busy with Turkish tourists at weekends and during the school holidays. Çeşme itself is a family-orientated resort and transit point for the Greek island of Chios, 8km west. It has a tangle of narrow backstreets and a dramatic Genoese fortress, and makes a good base for visiting the town of Alaçatı's old Greek stone houses and windsurfing beach.

The **tourist office** (☎ /fax 712 6653; İskele Meydanı 6; ⏰ 8.30am-noon & 1pm-5.30pm, Mon-Fri), ferry and bus ticket offices, banks with ATMs, restaurants and hotels are all within two blocks of the main square.

Sleeping & Eating

There's a wealth of good-value, homey pensions in Çeşme. Local pensions are usually open from May to October and bookings are essential in summer and at weekends. On the front are touristy restaurants specialising in seafood – and multilingual menus. For cheaper, more locally orientated places, head to İnkilap Caddesi.

Uz Pansiyon (☎ 712 6579; uzpansiyon@gmail.com; 3010 Sokak 7; s/d TL35/55; ❄) Near the bus station and 450m from the centre, this is one of Çeşme's cheapest pensions, but it's spotless and terrific value with a communal kitchen.

Otel Sesli (☎ 712 8845; www.otelsesli.com; 3025 Sokak 35; s/d €20/40; ❄) On a hill above the front, a 10-minute walk from the centre, this recently renovated place has bare rooms around a pool and potted plants.

Sahil Pansiyon (☎ 712 6934; www.cesmesahilpansiyon.com; 3265 Sokak 3; d from €40; ❄) This peaceful place is up some stairs in a rambling house and garden. The immaculate rooms have small balconies, some with sea views (ask for room No 9).

Ertan Oteli (☎ 712 6795; www.ertanotel.com.tr.tc; Hurriyet Caddesi 12; d low/high season €35/55; ❄) In the same block as the Rıdvan (also recommended), the Ertan has a better location on the seafront. Though by no means a good-looking hotel, the restaurant is reasonable, the staff helpful and the rooms have balconies.

Tokmak Hasan'in Yeri (☎ 712 0519; Çarsı Caddesi 11; mains TL4-8; 7am-8pm Mon-Sat) Rather hidden away, this simple place serves terrific home cooking at low prices.

Patika Restaurant Café & Bar (☎ 712 6357; Cumhuriyet Meydanı; mains TL10-16; 3pm-midnight) This is the place for fish at affordable prices. Between 9pm and 1am there's live Turkish music and sometimes belly dancing.

Pasifik Otel Restaurant (☎ 712 7465; 3264 Sokak; mains TL10-16; noon-9pm) If you fancy a walk and some fish, head to the Pasifik, at the northern end of the seafront, where you can enjoy a great fish casserole.

Getting There & Away

Buses from Çeşme's otogar run every 45 minutes to İzmir's otogar (TL10, two hours) and also go to Üçkuyular terminal (TL7.50, 1¼ hours).

In summer, there are five weekly ferries to the Greek island of Chios, and two ferries in winter. Buy your ticket (passenger return €65, car return €140 to €180) at the harbour; buy in advance if you have a car. See p644 for more information.

There are also twice weekly ferry services to Brindisi (Italy) and ferries to Ancona (Italy) from April and November. See p644 for more information.

SELÇUK

☎ 0232 / pop 27,280

Selçuk boasts one of the Seven Wonders of the Ancient World, an excellent museum, a fine basilica and mosque, a stork nest-studded aqueduct and, right on the town's doorstep, Ephesus. However, compared to the vast tourism factory of nearby Kuşadası, Selçuk's tourism industry is a small scale, workshop-sized affair.

Orientation & Information

Selçuk otogar lies just east of the İzmir–Aydın road (Atatürk Caddesi), with the town centre and some pensions immediately north of it. Pedestrianised shopping streets Namık Kemal, Cengiz Topel and Siegburg Caddesis run east from the main road to the train station.

On the western side of the main road a park spreads out in front of one wing of the Ephesus Museum. Many pensions can be found in the quiet, hilly streets between the museum and Ayasuluk Hill, northwest of the centre.

The **tourist office** (☎ 892 6945; www.selcuk.gov.tr; Agora Caddesi 35; 8am-noon & 1-5pm Mon-Fri winter, daily in summer) is opposite the museum.

It's a 30- to 45-minute walk from the tourist office in Selçuk to the main Ephesus admission gate. Many pensions in Selçuk offer free lifts there.

Sights

Selçuk is not only close to Ephesus, it's also blessed with superb monuments scattered around the centre. Don't miss the conspicuous **Basilica of St John** (St Jean Caddesi; admission TL2; 8am-5pm, to 7pm May-Sep), atop Ayasuluk Hill. It was built in the 6th century on the site where it was believed St John the Evangelist had been buried. The less-impressive **Temple of Artemis** (admission free; 8am-5pm, to 7pm May-Sep), between Ephesus and Selçuk, was once one of the Seven Wonders of the Ancient World. In its prime, it was larger than the Parthenon at Athens. Unfortunately, little more than one pillar now remains.

The **Ephesus Museum** (☎ 892 6010; Uğur Mumcu Sevgi Yolu Caddesi; admission €2.50; 8am-5pm, to 7pm

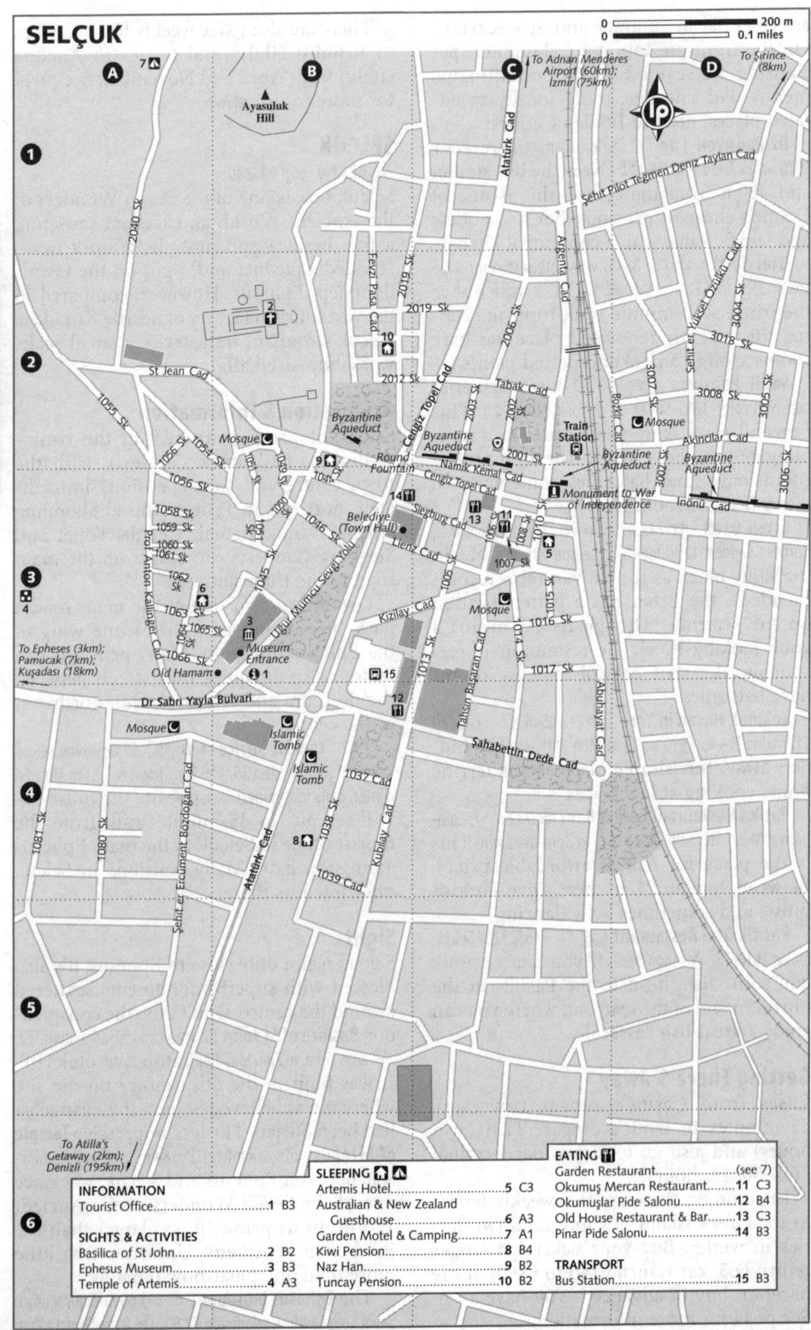
SELÇUK
0 200 m
0 0.1 miles
To Adnan Menderes Airport (60km); İzmir (75km)
To Şirince (8km)
Ayasuluk Hill
Atatürk Cad
Şehit Pilot Teğmen Deniz Taylan Cad
2040 Sk
Fevzi Paşa Cad
2019 Sk
Argenta Cad
Şehit er Yüksel Özülkü Cad
3004 Sk
3018 Sk
2006 Sk
St Jean Cad
2012 Sk
Cengiz Topel Cad
Tabak Cad
2003 Sk
2002 Sk
3007 Sk
3008 Sk
3005 Sk
Bozkir Cad
1055 Sk
Byzantine Aqueduct
Mosque
Train Station
Akincilar Cad
1054 Sk
1056 Sk
1051 Sk
1049 Sk
Round Fountain
Namik Kemal Cad
2001 Sk
3002 Sk
3006 Sk
1056 Sk
1047 Sk
Cengiz Topel Cad
Monument to War of Independence
İnönü Cad
1058 Sk
1059 Sk
1060 Sk
1061 Sk
1050 Sk
1046 Sk
Siegburg Cad
Belediye (Town Hall)
1010 Sk
1008 Sk
1006 Sk
1007 Sk
Prof Anton Kallinger Cad
1062 Sk
1045 Sk
Lienz Cad
1005 Sk
1063 Sk
1065 Sk
1064 Sk
1066 Sk
Uğur Mumcu Sevgi Yolu
Kizilay Cad
1015 Sk
1016 Sk
Museum Entrance
Old Hamam
To Epheses (3km); Pamucak (7km); Kuşadası (18km)
1013 Sk
Tahsin Başaran Cad
1014 Sk
1017 Sk
Dr Sabri Yayla Bulvari
Islamic Tomb
Şahabettin Dede Cad
Abuhayat Cad
1037 Cad
1081 Sk
1080 Sk
Şehit er Ercument Bozdoğan Cad
Atatürk Cad
1038 Sk
Kubilay Cad
1039 Cad
To Atilla's Getaway (2km); Denizli (195km)
INFORMATION
Tourist Office.......................1 B3
SIGHTS & ACTIVITIES
Basilica of St John...................2 B2
Ephesus Museum......................3 B3
Temple of Artemis....................4 A3
SLEEPING
Artemis Hotel.........................5 C3
Australian & New Zealand Guesthouse...6 A3
Garden Motel & Camping................7 A1
Kiwi Pension..........................8 B4
Naz Han...............................9 B2
Tuncay Pension.......................10 B2
EATING
Garden Restaurant..................(see 7)
Okumuş Mercan Restaurant.............11 C3
Okumuşlar Pide Salonu................12 B4
Old House Restaurant & Bar...........13 C3
Pinar Pide Salonu....................14 B3
TRANSPORT
Bus Station..........................15 B3

May-Sep) houses a striking collection of artefacts, including the effigy of Priapus, the Phallic God, as seen on every postcard from İstanbul to Antakya.

Sleeping

Garden Motel & Camping (☎ 892 6165; info@galleriaselciukidi.com; Kale Altı 5; per person/tent/car/campervan TL10/5/5/10, tent hire TL12; 🖳 🏊) Located 200m north of the mosque, this grassy camping ground is large and well designed, with facilities including a good restaurant and children's amusements.

Atilla's Getaway (☎ 892 3847; www.atillasgetaway.com; dm/r €8/16, bungalow without bathroom €8; 🖳 🏊) An attractive camping and bungalow complex 2.5km south of Selçuk. Run by a welcoming Turkish-Australian, it's packed with facilities and has a fun atmosphere.

Australia & New Zealand Guest house (☎ 892 6050; www.anzguesthouse.com; 1064 Sokak 12; dm/d TL12.5/45, d without bathroom TL30; ⊠ ❄) Despite the rules posted in the rooms, this is a welcoming place with sofas and comfortable clutter in its courtyard, and a great covered roof terrace. Bikes are free or you can hire a motor scooter.

Kiwi Pension (Alison's Place; ☎ 892 4892; www.kiwipension.com; 1038 Sokak 26; dm/s/d TL12/25/40, s/d without bathroom TL20/32; 🖳 🏊) Presided over by the energetic Alison, the Kiwi receives glowing reports. Rooms are simple but spotless and bright, and there's a private pool set 1km away in a mandarin orchard.

Artemis Hotel (☎ 892 6191; www.artemisguesthouse.net; 1012 Sokak 2; s/d €25/40; ❄) Spruced up by a renovation, the Artemis, near the train station, has large, new beds, fresh linen and decent bathrooms.

Tuncay Pension (☎ 892 6260; www.tuncaypension.com.tr; 2019 Sokak 1; d with/without air-con €50/35; ❄) It's a touch expensive for a pension, but a good, friendly choice nonetheless. There's a cool courtyard with a fountain where generous breakfasts are served.

Naz Han (☎ 892 8731; nazhanhotel@gmail.com; 1044 Sokak 2; r €50-70; ⊠ ❄) Living up to its name, which means 'coy', the Naz Han hides behind high walls. This 100-year-old Greek house has five simple but comfortable rooms arranged around a courtyard.

Eating

Okumuşlar Pide Salonu (☎ 892 6906; Şahabettin Dede Caddesi 2; pide TL4; 🕒 10am-11pm) Next to the bus station, this busy branch of the pide chain does fabulous pides (including vegie options).

Pinar Pide Salonu (☎ 892 9913; Siegburg Caddesi 3; pide TL4; 🕒 9am-midnight) Some travellers claim that this little place serves the best pide anywhere. It also does some good kebaps and salads.

Old House Restaurant & Bar (Eski Ev; ☎ 892 9357; 1005 Sokak 1/A; mains TL6-9; 🕒 8am-midnight) Set in a courtyard among fruit trees, this cool, intimate place serves tasty Turkish dishes. Try the Old House kebap.

Okumuş Mercan Restaurant (☎ 892 6196; 1006 Sokak 44; meze TL4-5, mains TL7-9; 🕒 7am-11pm) This place is loved locally for its traditional home fare, served in a courtyard beside a fountain in the shade of a mulberry tree.

Garden Restaurant (☎ 892 6165; Garden Motel, Kale Altı 5; meze TL5.50, mains TL7-11; 🕒 8am-11pm) About as organic as it gets in Selçuk, the restaurant enjoys a bucolic setting amid plots and the majority of the produce on your plate is grown. The selection of mezes is particularly good.

Getting There & Away

Selçuk's otogar is across from the tourist office. While it's easy enough to get to Selçuk direct from İzmir (TL6, 1½ hours), coming from the south or east you generally have to change at Aydın.

Frequent minibuses head for Kuşadası (TL4, 30 minutes) and over to the beach at Pamucak.

EPHESUS (EFES)

Even if you're not an architecture buff, you can't help but be dazzled by the sheer beauty of the ruins of **Ephesus** (☎ 892 6010; admission TL15, parking TL3; 🕒 8am-5pm Oct-Apr, 8am-7pm May-Sep), the best-preserved classical city in the eastern Mediterranean. If you want to get a feel for what life was like in Roman times, Ephesus is an absolute must-see.

There's a wealth of sights to explore, including the **Great Theatre**, reconstructed between AD 41 and 117, and capable of holding 25,000 people; the marble-paved **Sacred Way**; the 110-sq-metre **agora** (marketplace), heart of Ephesus' business life; and the **Library of Celsus**, adorned with niches holding statues of the classical Virtues. On Curetes Way, you can't miss the impressive Corinthian-style **Temple of Hadrian**, on the left, with lovely

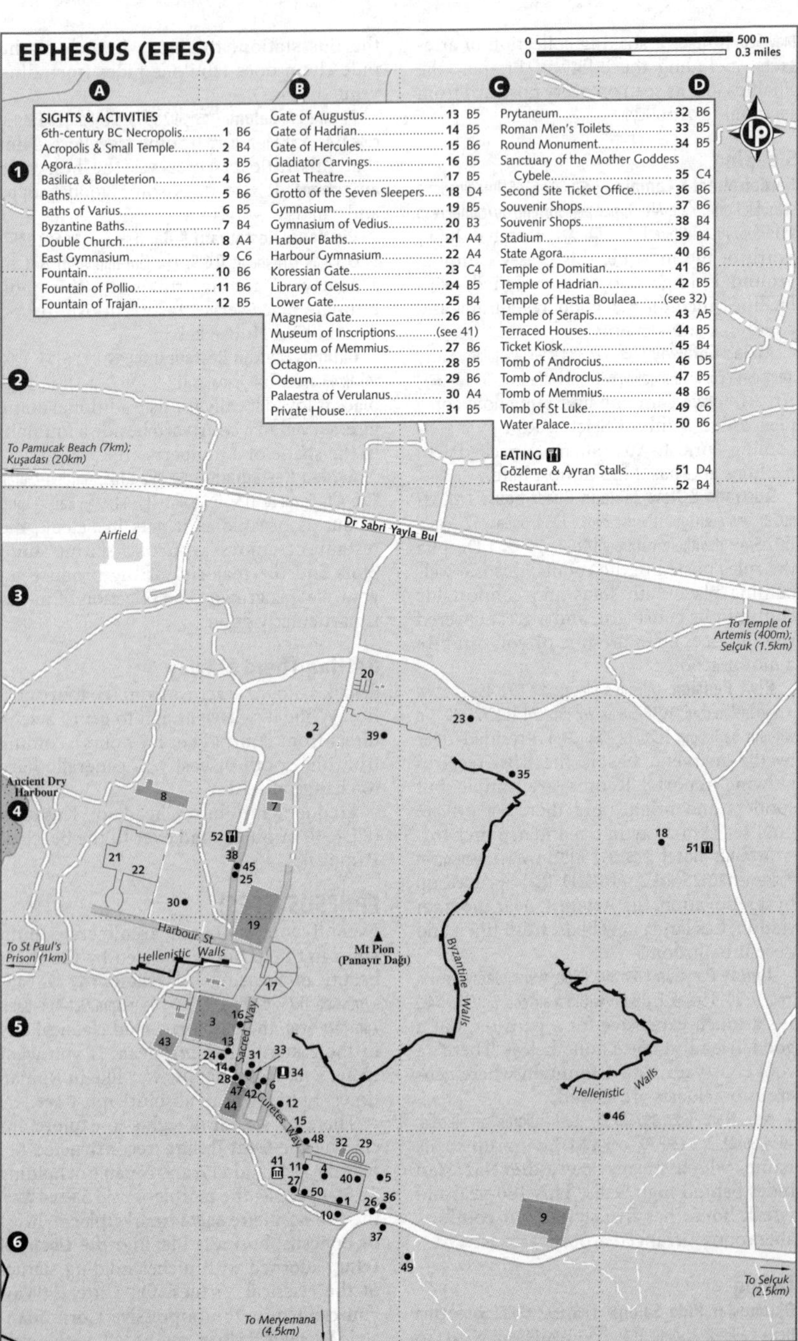

EPHESUS (EFES)
0 500 m
0 0.3 miles
SIGHTS & ACTIVITIES
6th-century BC Necropolis 1 B6
Acropolis & Small Temple 2 B4
Agora 3 B5
Basilica & Bouleterion 4 B6
Baths 5 B6
Baths of Varius 6 B5
Byzantine Baths 7 B4
Double Church 8 A4
East Gymnasium 9 C6
Fountain 10 B6
Fountain of Pollio 11 B6
Fountain of Trajan 12 B5
Gate of Augustus 13 B5
Gate of Hadrian 14 B5
Gate of Hercules 15 B6
Gladiator Carvings 16 B5
Great Theatre 17 B5
Grotto of the Seven Sleepers 18 D4
Gymnasium 19 B5
Gymnasium of Vedius 20 B3
Harbour Baths 21 A4
Harbour Gymnasium 22 A4
Koressian Gate 23 C4
Library of Celsus 24 B5
Lower Gate 25 B4
Magnesia Gate 26 B6
Museum of Inscriptions (see 41)
Museum of Memmius 27 B6
Octagon 28 B5
Odeum 29 B6
Palaestra of Verulanus 30 A4
Private House 31 B5
Prytaneum 32 B6
Roman Men's Toilets 33 B5
Round Monument 34 B5
Sanctuary of the Mother Goddess Cybele 35 C4
Second Site Ticket Office 36 B6
Souvenir Shops 37 B6
Souvenir Shops 38 B4
Stadium 39 B4
State Agora 40 B6
Temple of Domitian 41 B6
Temple of Hadrian 42 B5
Temple of Hestia Boulaea (see 32)
Temple of Serapis 43 A5
Terraced Houses 44 B5
Ticket Kiosk 45 B4
Tomb of Androcius 46 D5
Tomb of Androclus 47 B5
Tomb of Memmius 48 B6
Tomb of St Luke 49 C6
Water Palace 50 B6
EATING
Gözleme & Ayran Stalls 51 D4
Restaurant 52 B4
To Pamucak Beach (7km); Kuşadası (20km)
Dr Sabri Yayla Bul
Airfield
To Temple of Artemis (400m); Selçuk (1.5km)
Ancient Dry Harbour
Harbour St
To St Paul's Prison (1km)
Hellenistic Walls
Mt Pion (Panayır Dağı)
Byzantine Walls
Sacred Way
Curetes Way
Hellenistic Walls
To Selçuk (2.5km)
To Meryemana (4.5km)
TURKEY

friezes in the porch; the magnificent **Terraced Houses** (admission TL15; 9am-4.30pm); and the **Fountain of Trajan**. Curetes Way ends at the two-storey **Gate of Hercules**, constructed in the 4th century AD, which has reliefs of Hercules on both main pillars. Up the hill on the left are the ruined remains of the **Prytaneum** (municipal hall) and the **Temple of Hestia Boulaea**, in which a perpetually burning flame was guarded. Finally, you reach the **Odeum**, a small theatre dating from AD 150 and used for musical performances and meetings of town council.

Audio guides are available, as are water and snacks, but bring your own as prices are high. Heat and crowds can be problematic so come early or late and avoid weekends and public holidays.

Many pensions in Selçuk offer free lifts to Ephesus. Note that there are two entry points roughly 3km apart. A taxi from Selçuk to the main entrance should cost about TL12.

KUŞADASI

0256 / pop 50,000

It's easy to sneer at Kuşadası's package hotels, fast-food restaurants, in-your-face bazaar, karaoke bars, tattoo parlours and holiday crowds. But many locals are very proud of the place, seeing it as exemplifying a can-do, make-the-best-of-yourself spirit, and those who revile it as snobs.

There are internet cafés and banks with ATMs in the centre. The most useful dolmuş stand is 1.5km inland on Adnan Menderes Bulvarı. The otogar is right out on the bypass road.

Sights

Kuşadası is short on specific sights, although there's a minor stone **fortress** once used by pirates on an island in the harbour, and an old **caravanserai** near the harbour. Just beyond the PTT, a passage leads to the old **Kaleiçi** neighbourhood, which has narrow streets packed with restaurants and bars.

Kuşadası also makes a good base for visits to the superb ancient cities of **Priene**, **Miletus** and **Didyma** (all 3 sites admission TL2; 8.30am-6.30pm May-Sep, 9am-5.30pm Oct-Apr) to the south; if you're pushed for time, a 'PMD' tour from Kuşadası tour operators costs around €30. Perched high on the craggy slopes of Mt Mykale, Priene has a beautiful, windswept setting; Miletus boasts a spectacular theatre; and in Didyma is the stupendous Temple of Apollo.

Kuşadası's most famous beach is **Kadınlar Denizi** (Ladies Beach), 2.5km south of town and served by dolmuşes running along the coastal road.

Sleeping

Beware the touts at the otogar and harbour; it's best to decide where you're heading before arrival and stick with the choice.

Panorama (614 6619; www.otelpanorama.com; Kıbrıs Caddesi 14; s/d low season €15/20, high season €20/28;) A few steps from the bazaar, this used to be Sammy's Palace, a long-standing backpacker favourite. The rooms are spartan and dog-eared, but there's a rooftop terrace for the breakfasts and optional dinners.

our pick **Sezgin's Guest house** (614 4225; www.sezginhotel.com; Aslanlar Caddesi 68; s/d €20/24;) Perhaps the top budget choice, with large, almost Swiss-style wood-panelled rooms, comfortable beds, armchairs, TVs, fridges and balconies overlooking a garden.

Villa Konak (612 2170; www.villakonakhotel.com; Yıldırım Caddesi 55; s/d €40/50;) Hidden in the old quarter of town is this restored 140-year-old stone house. The rooms, attractively updated with the odd orientalist flourish, are arranged around a rambling courtyard-garden. It's peaceful and cool and there's a bar, restaurant and library.

Eating & Drinking

There's an abundance of eateries to suit every wallet. As ever, check the cost before ordering fish. If looking for a drink, Barlar Sokak (Bar St) is chock-a-block with Irish-theme pubs. It's a scruffy-around-the-edges kind of street, but after a few drinks it can be lots of fun.

Köfteci Ali (Aslanlar Caddesi 14; 9am-midnight winter, 24hr summer) Situated near Bar St, ready to hoover up the post-club traffic, this street booth does some terrific spicy wrapped pide kebaps (TL5).

Avlu (614 7995; Cephane Sokak 15; mains TL5-8; 8am-midnight) In the old town, Avlu offers first-class home cooking in a clean and cheerful environment. A long-standing local fave, it has a great pick-and-point counter, some tasty vegie options and delectable Turkish puds.

Saray (612 0528; Bozkurt Sokak 25; mains TL10-18; 9am-2am) Enjoying a following among both locals and expats, the Saray has a refined courtyard and, inside, an unpretentious dining room that often rocks with happy-hour sing-a-longs. The menu, a typical Kuşadası calling-all-ports affair, includes some decent Turkish and vegetarian choices.

Getting There & Away

BOAT

All Kuşadası travel agencies sell tickets to the Greek island of Samos. There's at least one daily boat to/from Samos (€30 one way, €35 same-day return) between April and October, but ferries do not operate in the winter.

BUS

From the otogar, direct buses depart for several far-flung parts of the country, or you can change at İzmir. In summer, three buses run daily to Bodrum (TL20, 2½ hours); in winter, take a dolmuş to Söke (TL4, every 30 minutes). For Selçuk (TL4, 30 minutes), pick up a minibus on Adnan Menderes Bulvarı.

PAMUKKALE

☎ 0258

Way inland, east of Selçuk, Pamukkale is renowned for gleaming white ledges (travertines) with pools that flow down over the plateau edge. It used to be one of the most familiar images of Turkey, but these days it has lost a bit of its gloss. Sadly in recent years the water supply has dried up and it is no longer possible to bathe in the travertine pools. Behind this fragile natural wonder lie the magnificent ruins of the Roman city of Hierapolis, an ancient spa resort.

Pamukkale is also a good base from which to explore the ruined city of Afrodisias (Geyre), near Karacasu southeast of Nazilli.

Sights

TRAVERTINES & HIERAPOLIS RUINS

As you climb the hill above Pamukkale village, you pay to enter the **travertines and Hierapolis** (admission TL10; daylight). The ruins of Hierapolis, including a huge theatre, a colonnaded street, a latrine building and a vast necropolis, are spread over a wide area; allow at least half a day to do them justice.

Afterwards you can swim amid sunken Roman columns at Hierapolis' **Antique Pool** (adult/child TL18/9; 9am-7pm) and visit the excellent **Hierapolis Archaeology Museum** (admission TL2; 9am-12.30pm & 1.30-7.15pm Tue-Sun), which contains some spectacular sarcophagi and friezes from Hierapolis and nearby Afrodisias. As you return to the village, keep looking back for great views of the glittering travertines.

AFRODISIAS

Ephesus may be the *crème de la crème* of western Anatolia's archaeological sites, but the ruined city of **Afrodisias** (admission TL5; 9am-7pm May-Sep, 9am-5pm Oct-Apr) is thought by many to rival it. Because of its isolation, it is less overrun with coach parties. Most of what you see dates back to at least the 2nd century AD. If it's not too busy, the site exudes an eerie ambience that is unique and unforgettable. The 270m-long **stadium**, one of the biggest in the classical world, is a startling vision, as are the **Temple of Aphrodite** and the white-marble **theatre**.

The only downside is that access by public transport is not easy. It's more sensible to arrange a tour (TL30) from Pamukkale. Tours leave with a minimum of four people, a figure that's usually achievable.

Sleeping & Eating

Competition between Pamukkale's many pensions is intense, and the services on offer are much better than in most other towns. Most places provide good, cheap home-cooked meals and serve wine and beer. Several welcoming, family-run pensions are clustered at the junction of İnönü and Menderes Caddesis.

Hotel Dört Mevsim (☎ 272 2009; www.hoteldortmevsim.com; Hasan Tahsin Caddesi 19; dm TL10, s/d TL20/35;) The 'Four Seasons' is quite different to its top-end namesakes, but has simple and clean family-run rooms in a quiet lane. Expect lots of bright decor, and an even brighter welcome. Camping is TL10 for two people.

Aspawa Pension (☎ 272 2094; www.aspawapension.com; Turgut Özal Caddesi 28; s/d €13/22;) Another centrally located pension, the Aspawa ticks all the value boxes. Pool, air-con, wi-fi and good food in a family atmosphere.

Beyaz Kale Pension (☎ 272 2064; www.beyazkalepension.com; Menderes Caddesi; s/d €15/25;) The 'White Castle' is handy for the centre of the village and has spotless rooms arranged around a pool. Welcoming family hostess Haçer is a whiz in the kitchen, especially when it comes to vegetarian food. Larger rooms are also available.

Artemis Yoruk Hotel (☎ 272 2073; www.artemisyorukhotel.com; Atatürk Caddesi; dm/s/d/tr/q €7/15/19/25/32;) With a super-central location, this sprawling edifice has a wide range of rooms from four-bed dorms to private and family rooms. The bar offering 'bloody cold beer' can get pleasingly raucous.

Melrose Hotel (☎ 272 2767; www.allgauhotel.com; Hasan Tahsin Caddesi; r TL35-50;) Renovations have installed an outdoor dining area at this friendly, family-run spot with clean-as-a-whistle rooms and two swimming pools. The flasher rooms (TL70 to TL80) have bijou balconies and kitschly romantic circular beds.

Getting There & Away

In summer, Pamukkale has several direct buses to Selçuk, but it's best to assume for most destinations you'll have to change in Denizli (TL2, 30 minutes). Pamukkale has no proper otogar; buses drop you at the Denizli dolmuş stop.

BODRUM

☎ 0252 / pop 28,580

Some people will tell you Bodrum is an unsophisticated low-end resort town; they obviously haven't been to Kuşadası. In fact, Bodrum manages to welcome the summer hordes without diluting its character and charm. With laws in place restricting the height of buildings, the town has neat architectural uniformity. Out of season, the whitewashed houses and subtropical gardens can appear almost idyllic.

Orientation & Information

The **otogar** (Cevat Şakir Caddesi) is 500m inland from the Adliye (Yeni) Camii, a small mosque at the centre of the town. The PTT and several banks with ATMs are on Cevat Şakir. There are internet cafés on Üçkuyular Caddesi, all charging about TL2 per hour. The **tourist office** (☎ 316 1091; Kale Meydanı; 9am-6pm Mon-Fri, daily in summer) is beside the Castle of St Peter, and there is an information booth at the otogar entrance.

Sights & Activities

Bodrum's star attraction is the conspicuous **Castle of St Peter**. Built in 1437 by the Crusaders, the castle houses the **Museum of Underwater Archaeology** (☎ 316 2516; admission TL10; 8am-noon & 1-5pm winter, 9am-noon & 1-7pm Tue-Sun summer), containing finds from shipwrecks dating back to 1025; and a model of a Carian princess' tomb, inside the **French Tower** (admission €2.75; 10am-noon & 2-4pm Tue-Fri). Sadly there's little left of the **Mausoleum of Halicarnassus** (admission TL5; 8.30am-5.30pm Tue-Sun), the monumental tomb of King Mausolus, which was once among the Seven Wonders of the Ancient World.

Bodrum is famous for its scuba diving. Look for the dive centres on the boats moored near the tourist office, including **Snorkel & Dive Center** (☎ 313 6017; Cevat Şakir Caddesi 5). Numerous yachts moored along Neyzen Tevfik Caddesi on the western bay run day trips (about €12) around the bay.

TURKEY

Sleeping

There are plenty of budget hotels and pensions in the centre and along the Eastern Bay, although be aware that the closer you are to the front the less chance you'll have of getting a good nights sleep. A number of upmarket boutique hotels line the coast just east of the Eastern Bay.

Sevin Pension (☎ 316 7682; www.sevinpension.com; Türkkuyusu Caddesi 5; dm €9-11, s/d €14/24 in winter; dm €13, s €18-22, d €25-36, tr €39-45 in summer;) It may be basic, but for the price it offers a lot: a prime (albeit noisy) location, TV, free wi-fi, good breakfasts and helpful staff.

Sedan Pansiyon (☎ 316 0355; off Türkkuyusu Caddesi 121; s/d €12/24, without bathroom €10/16) It's at the basic end of the spectrum, with rooms of varying sizes and states of repair arranged around a ramshackle, peaceful courtyard.

Bahçeli Ağar Aile Pansiyonu (☎ 316 1648; 1402 Sokak 4; s/d €20/36) This endearing little pension is located in a passageway off Neyzen Tevik Caddesi, opposite the marina. With a little courtyard overhung by vines, it has an intimate feel, and guests have use of the kitchen.

Mylasa Pansiyon (☎ 316 1846; Cumhuriyet Caddesi 34; s/d €25/35;) The archetypal Bodrum pension, back from the beach but very much at the heart of the party scene. Rooms are small with TVs, but none too modern looking. The café-restaurant is lively and there are great panoramic views from the terrace.

Kilavuz Otel (☎ 316 3892; www.kilavuzotel.com; cnr Atatürk Caddesi & Adliye Sokak 17; s/d €35/40;) Striking a good balance between proximity to the front and the need for peace and quiet, this family-run place offers 15 simply furnished, clean rooms.

Baç Pansiyon (☎ 316 2497; bacpansiyon@turk.net; Cumhuriyet Caddesi 14; s €28-33, d €45-65; ❄) Small but stylish and all in marble, wood and wrought iron, this central hotel also boasts about the best views in Bodrum. It sits right above the water and four of its 10 comfortable room have delightful balconies over the waves.

El Vino Hotel (313 8770; www.elvinobodrum.com; Pamili Sokak; s/d €80/120; ❄ 🅿) The dark backstreet location doesn't look that promising, but behind the stone wall is one of the town's loveliest hotels. The El Vino's rooms are large and well appointed with wooden floors, large beds, TVs and writing desks.

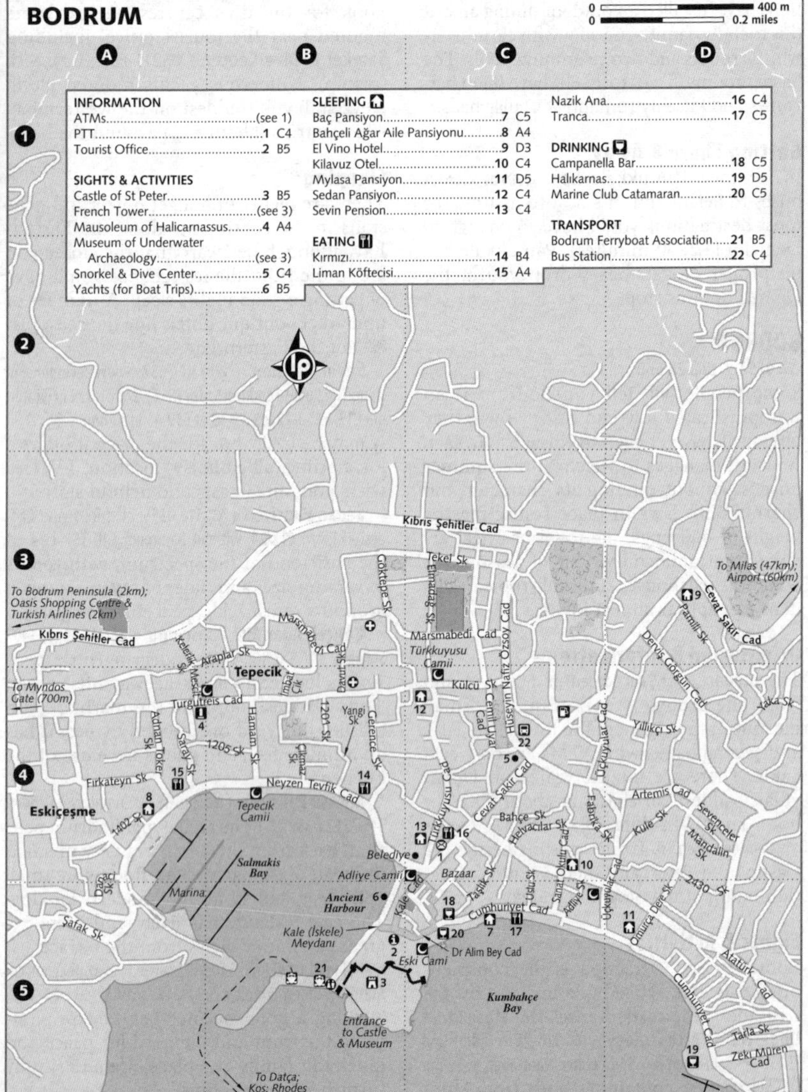

Eating & Drinking

Bodrum's finest, and most-expensive restaurants are all located along the Western Bay; its worst on the Eastern Bay. In between, on Cevat Şakir Caddesi and in the bazaar are the best value options. Here you'll find a collection of Turkish restaurants and *büfes* (snack bars), where you can pick up a döner wrapped in pide for TL4. As elsewhere, check prices before ordering fish.

Nazik Ana (☎ 313 1891; Eski Hukumet Sokak 7; meat mains TL4-5, vegetarian mains TL2-3; 🕒 9am-10pm, closed Sun in winter) Hidden away down a narrow alley and definitely worth hunting out, this simple but atmospheric place is a huge hit locally. With its point-and-pick counter, it's a great place to sample different Turkish dishes.

Liman Köftecisi (☎ 316 5060; Neyzen Tevfik Caddesi 172; mains TL7-12.50; 🕒 8am-midnight) The famous Liman serves delicious food at decent prices. *Köfte* is the specialty. Of the six types, the TL10 *Liman köfte* (with yogurt, tomato sauce and butter) is the top dish.

Kırmızı (☎ 316 4918; Neyzen Tevik Caddesi 44; meze TL5-8, mains TL10-14; 🕒 11.30am-midnight) Serving Mediterranean food made from fresh local ingredients, the Kırmızı is a characterful place with three floors and a garden terrace. The walls are used to exhibit the works of local artists.

Tranca (☎ 316 6610; Cumhuriyet Caddesi 36; meze TL8-10, mains TL12-24; 🕒 11am-midnight) Jutting out into the bay, the family-run Tranca boasts about the best views of anywhere in Bodrum. Its specialties are *tuzda balık* (fish baked in salt) and *testi kebabı* (casserole served in a clay pot); both cost TL40 to TL50 with a minimum of two people.

For drinking and entertainment follow the normal rule of thumb: for cheap and cheerful head to the Eastern Bay, for expensive and classy, think Western Bay. Nightclubs such as Halıkarnas and the floating Marine Club Catamaran are famous party hotspots, but there are quieter hangouts, too. Try the small orientalist-style **Campanella Bar** (☎ 316 5302; Cumhuriyet Caddesi; 🕒 noon-4am), adorned with flower boxes set above a shop on a small alley. This spot is full of atmosphere and usually has live music playing.

Getting There & Away

Airlines including Turkish Airlines fly from İstanbul and elsewhere to Bodrum International Airport, 60km away and connected to Bodrum by Havaş shuttle bus.

By bus, there are services to more or less anywhere you could wish to go. Useful services include those to İstanbul (TL70), Kuşadası (TL20) and Marmaris (TL20).

Daily ferries (€25 same-day return) link Bodrum with Kos (Greece); hydrofoils (€35 same-day return) operate from Monday to Saturday between May and October. In summer there are also two weekly hydrofoils to Rhodes (Rhodos; €50 one way, €60 same-day return); check with the **Bodrum Ferryboat Association** (☎ 316 0882; www.bodrumferryboat.com; Kale Caddesi Cümrük Alanı 22), on the dock past the western entrance to the castle.

MEDITERRANEAN COAST

The western Mediterranean, known as the 'Turquoise Coast', is a glistening stretch of clear blue sea where Gods once played in sublime pebble coves and spectacular ruins abound. In villages too pretty to postcard, sun-kissed locals yawn and smile at travellers' never-ending quest for the 'Med Life'.

The region's seamless mix of history and holiday inspires and enchants. At places such as Patara and Olympos, your hand-packed sandcastles are humbled by vine-covered ruins and Lycian tombs. If you prefer to interact with your surroundings, plunge into activities such as scuba diving at Kaş and kayaking atop the underwater city in Kekova.

The eastern Mediterranean, meanwhile, has long lived in its more fashionable western neighbour's shadow. But the Arab-spiced area has at least as many pristine beaches as the Turquoise Coast.

MARMARİS

☎ 0252 / pop 35,160

An unashamedly brash harbour town that swells to over 200,000 people during summer, Marmaris is heaven or hell depending which way your boat floats. It sports one of Turkey's swankiest marinas, and a stunning natural harbour where Lord Nelson organised his fleet for the attack on the French at Abukir in 1798. Not far away, the deeply indented Reşadiye and Hisarönü Peninsulas hide bays of azure backed by pine-covered mountains and gorgeous fishing villages.

Orientation & Information

İskele Meydanı (the main square) and the **tourist office** (☎ 412 1035; İskele Meydanı 2; 🕑 8am-noon & 1-5pm Mon-Fri mid-Sep–May, daily Jun–mid-Sep) are by the harbour, north of the castle. The post office is on 51 Sokak. Hacı Mustafa Sokak, also called 39 Sokak or Bar St, runs inland from the bazaar; action here keeps going until the early hours.

The otogar is 3km north of town, near the turnoff to Fethiye.

Sights & Activities

The small **castle** (admission TL2; 🕑 8am-noon & 1-5pm Tue-Sun) houses a modest museum and offers lovely views of Marmaris.

Numerous yachts along the waterfront offer day tours of Marmaris Bay, and its beaches and islands. A day's outing usually costs between TL50 and TL80 per person, but you'll have to negotiate.

On a day tour you'll usually visit Paradise Island, Aquarium, Phosphoros Cave, Kumlubuku, Amos, Turunç, Green Sea and İçmeler. Two- and three-day trips often go to Dalyan and Kaunos.

Marmaris is also a popular place to scuba dive, and there are several dive centres on the waterfront.

Sleeping

Marmaris has hundreds of good-value sleeping options, especially for self-caterers. The following listings include high-season prices; off-season, expect serious discounts.

Interyouth Hostel (☎ 412 3687; interyouth@turk.net; 42 Sokak 45; dm or s without bathroom with/without ISIC card TL10/15, d without bathroom TL30; 💻) Located inside the covered bazaar, this hostel is efficiently run and a great source of travel information. Rooms, though smallish and rather spartan, are spotless and well maintained. There are bags of extras, even free pasta nights on the rooftop from June to September.

Maltepe Pansiyon (☎ 412 1629; 66 Sokak 9; s/d TL30/50; ☒ ❄ 💻) The shady garden is the main attraction of this longstanding budget choice. Rooms are small but spotless, and internet access is free.

Otel 47 (☎ 412 4747; www.hotel47.com; Atatürk Caddesi 10; s/d TL60/90; ☒ ❄) Amid the bright lights and swaying palm trees of Atatürk Caddesi, there's a certain Miami Beach vibe going on at 47. Regulars return for the prime location and white terrace overlooking the traffic.

Royal Maris Otel (☎ 412 8383; www.royalmarisotel.com; Atatürk Caddesi 34; s/d TL100/150; ❄ 🏊) It offers two pools, a private beach, a hamam, fitness centre and spacious balconies with stunning views – remarkably affordable.

Eating & Drinking

For something cheap and cheerful, try the bazaar area between the post office and the mosque, or the old town area around the castle, where there's a host of small Turkish restaurants. On 39 Sokak (Bar St), stalls cater to ravenous late-night revellers.

Meryem Ana (☎ 412 7855; 35 Sokak 62; mains TL5-6) Simple and understated, this place serves terrific traditional home cooking. A firm family affair, you can see the mother and aunt hard at work in the kitchen. A large mixed vegie plate costs TL10.

Fellini (☎ 413 0826; Barboras Caddesi 61; meals TL20; 🕑 9am-midnight) Perennially popular with both locals and visitors in the know, this attractive waterfront restaurant does great thin-crust pizzas and pasta.

Aquarium Restaurant (☎ 413 1522; Barboras Caddesi; meals TL20; 🕑 9am-midnight) Run by a Turkish-Kiwi couple, this loud and proud port-side restaurant serves grills and steaks to a jovial crowd. Slightly overpriced, but it's got the location covered.

For quick eats head to the **Doyum** (☎ 413 4977; Ulusal Egemenlik Bulvarı 17; 🕑 24hr), a good place for an early breakfast (TL5) and vegie dishes (TL4 to TL5); chicken joint **Alin's Cafe and Grill** (☎ 413 0826; Barboras Caddesi 61; meals TL12), full of young Turkish families feasting on healthy grills and kebaps; and **İdil Mantı Evi** (☎ 413 9771; 39 Sokak 140; meze TL5-6, mains TL8-20; 🕑 4pm-4am), a great spot on Bar St for the night-nibbles.

Marmaris is a party town, so drinkers and hedonists should stagger straight to the aptly named Bar St.

Getting There & Away

The nearest airports to Marmaris are at Dalaman and Bodrum.

The otogar in Marmaris has frequent buses and minibuses to Bodrum (TL20, four hours), İzmir (TL30, 4½ hours) and Fethiye (TL14, three hours).

Catamarans to Rhodes sail daily in summer (one way/same-day return/open return €50/50/75 including port tax, 50 minutes). They do not operate from November to mid-April. Buy your ticket in any Marmaris travel agency.

KÖYCEĞİZ

☎ 0252 / pop 7520

The star attraction here is the beautiful and serene Lake Köyceğiz Gölü. As it's so tough to rival the Med, this farming town attracts only modest tourism, and still depends mostly on citrus fruits, olives, honey and cotton for its livelihood. This region is also famous for its liquidambar trees, source of precious amber gum. Despite its sleepiness, the surrounding Köyceğiz-Dalyan Nature Reserve has a growing reputation among outdoor types for its excellent hiking and cycling. Köyceğiz town can also be reached by an easy boat trip across the lake from Dalyan.

Sleeping

Most of the accommodation lies west of the mosque, and managers can organise tours on and around the lake. There are lots of cheap and cheerful restaurants off the main square.

Fulya Pension (☎ 262 2301; fulyapension@mynet.com; Ali İhsan Kalamaz Caddesi 100; s/d TL20/40; ⊠ ❄) The bubbly young owner maintains Fulya as a brilliant budget option. Rooms are clean and cheap, all have balconies and there's a large roof terrace. Bikes are available for free, and the TL15 boat trips are a bargain.

Flora Hotel (☎ 262 4976; www.florahotel.info; Kordon Boyu 96; s/d/apt TL20/40/60; ⊠ ❄) The foyer is filled with flags in tribute to the foreign guests who often come for arranged walks in the nearby Gölgeli Mountains. The rooms here have only side views of the lake, however, while apartments sleep two adults and two children.

Alila Hotel (☎ 262 1150; Emeksiz Caddesi 13; s/d TL40/70; ❄ 🅿) By far the most character-filled hotel in town, 12 of the Alila's rooms also boast direct views of the water. Friendly owner Ömar attends to every detail (right down to the swan-folded towels).

Tango Pansiyon (☎ 262 2501; www.tangopension.com; Ali İhsan Kalmaz Caddesi 112; dm/s/d per person TL15/30/50; ⊠ ❄) Managed by the local school sports teacher, this place is big on activities. Rooms are bright, cheerful and well maintained, and there's a pleasant garden.

Mutlu Kardeşler (☎ 262 2480; Tören Alanı 52; soup TL3, köfte TL5, kebap TL6, pide TL2-3; 🕑 7am-1am) Funky in a rural kind of way, this simple place is much-loved locally and has tables on a little terrace out the back.

Colıba (☎ 262 2987; Cengiz Topel Caddesi 64; köfte TL6; 🕑 10am-1am) Cool-headed staff serve meze, grills and house specialty *alabalık* (trout) to young couples and businessmen. Whitewashed and wooden, Colıba has a shaded terrace with views of the lake front.

Next to Colıba, the pink-and-purple **Pembe Restaurant** (☎ 262 2983; Cengiz Topel Caddesi 70; meals around TL8-10) does cheap seafood and meat dishes.

Getting There & Away

There are frequent buses and dolmuşes to Fethiye (TL8, 1¾ hours), Marmaris (TL5, one hour) and Dalyan (TL4, 30 minutes).

DALYAN

☎ 0252

Dalyan is a laid-back river-mouth community with a strong farming pedigree and a growing penchant for tourism. It makes an entertaining base for exploring the surrounding fertile waterways, in particular the popular turtle nesting grounds of İztuzu Beach and Lake Köyceğiz.

In summer, excursion boats go out to explore the river and the lake. You can save yourself a lot of money, and ensure your lira is spread evenly around town, by taking boats run by the local **Dalyan Kooperatifi** (☎ 284 7843), located near the turtle statue. The cooperative's cruises cost about TL20 and take in the **Sultaniye hot springs** and **mud baths** on the shores of Lake Köyceğiz, the ruined city of **Kaunos** (admission TL5; 🕑 8.30am-5.30pm) and the unspoilt **İztuzu beach** on the Mediterranean coast.

Sleeping

Dalyan Camping (☎/fax 284 4157; Maraş Caddesi 144; per tent/caravan TL15/25, 2-/3-/4-person bungalows TL20/40/60; 🕑 Apr-Oct) This compact, well-shaded site is centrally located by the river. The eight pinewood bungalows are simple, clean and quite attractive.

Midas Pension (☎ 284 Kaunos Sokak 30; www.midasdalyan.com; Kaunos Sokak 32; s/d TL50/60; ❄) Selçuk and Saadet Nur are the wonderful hosts of this riverside pension raised on stilts. The 10 rooms are smartly decked out, with private bathrooms attached.

Kilim Hotel (☎ 284 2253; www.kilimhotel.com; Kaunos Sokak 7; s/d TL35/70; 🕑 Apr-Nov; ❄ 🅿) The

TURKEY

active English owner Becky presides over this buzzing midrange hotel with a pool and palm-shaded seating area, and spacious rooms containing king-size beds. There's a ramp for wheelchair access, complimentary use of bicycles, and daily yoga and aerobic workouts.

Eating & Drinking

Dalyan's restaurant scene swings between high quality and lousy value, so be selective. For a drink, keep your ears pricked along Maraş Caddesi.

A good spot for a beer and a meal is **Caretta Caretta** (☎ 284 3039; Maraş Caddesi 124; meze TL5, mains incl fish TL10-20; 8am-1am Mar-Nov). This signature riverbank restaurant is scattered with wagons and wooden platforms; the *bonfile ve tavuk ciğerli börek* (beef fillet with chicken livers baked in puff pastry) leads the impressive menu.

Getting There & Away

There are some direct dolmuşes to Dalyan from Köyceğiz (TL4, 30 minutes), but getting here normally involves changing at Ortaca (TL1.50). To get to Dalaman from Dalyan you must change in Ortaca and Köyceğiz. Dalyan's minibuses leave from the stop behind the mosque.

FETHİYE

☎ 0252 / pop 50,700

In 1958 an earthquake levelled the old harbour city of Fethiye, sparing only the ancient remains of Telmessos (400 BC) from its wrath. Fifty years on and Fethiye is once again a prosperous and proud hub of the western Mediterranean. Its natural harbour, tucked away in the southern reaches of a broad bay scattered with pretty islands, is perhaps the region's finest.

Orientation & Information

Fethiye's otogar is 2.5km east of the centre. Atatürk Caddesi, the main street, has banks with ATMs. Most pensions are either up the hill or west of the marina; the **tourist office** (☎ 614 1527; İskele Meydanı; 10am-noon & 1-5.30pm daily May-Sep, Mon-Sat Oct-Apr) is opposite the marina, just past the Roman theatre.

Tours

Be sure to sign up for the **12-Island Tour** (per person TL25), which mixes swimming, cruising and sightseeing around Fethiye Bay. Hotels and agencies sell tickets or you can negotiate a price with the boat companies at the marina. The boats usually stop at six islands and cruise by the rest.

Sleeping

Fethiye has some good-value midrange digs, but not much at the deluxe end.

Ideal Pension (☎ 614 1981; www.idealpension.net; 26 Sokak 1; dm/s/d from TL20/35/40) For the past two decades Ideal Pension has provided high-quality, cheap beds to weary travellers. Aside from the clean (albeit small) rooms, there's a large terrace with bay views and generous breakfasts.

Tan Pansiyon (☎ /fax 614 1584/1676; 30 Sokak 43; s/d TL30/50) When the backpacker grind wears thin, try this traditional Turkish pension run by a charming elderly couple. Rooms are small (the bathrooms smaller), but it's sparkling clean and quiet.

Villa Daffodil (☎ 614 9595; www.villadaffodil.com; Fevzi Çakmak Caddesi 115; s/d TL50/90) This large Ottoman-designed guesthouse is one of the few older buildings to survive. The rooms have slanted ceilings and a homely feel; the best have sea views and ante-rooms. Hussein, a retired colonel, is a genial manager.

Eating & Drinking

One way to taste Fethiye's fabulous fish without losing too many Turkish lira is to bring your own! Follow fishy smells to find the market, browse what's on offer and check the day's prices chalked up on the boards. Next, ferry the fish to one of the restaurants surrounding the market (pick the most popular) and ask them to cook it. For just €2.75, they will cook your flipper and throw in a sauce, green salad, garlic bread, fruit and coffee.

Paşa Kebab (☎ 614 9807; Çarşı Caddesi 42; meze TL3-4, pide TL2-6, pizza TL8-10; 9am-midnight) Considered locally to offer the best kebaps in town, this honest and unpretentious place has a well-priced menu. Try the Paşa special, an oven-baked beef, tomato and cheese concoction.

Café Oley (☎ 612 9532; 38 Sokak 4; breakfast €3.35-6, meals TL8-10; 8am-midnight) The superstar Atilla is famed for her smoothies, Vegemite and pancakes. She also does good salads and sandwiches.

Meğri Lokantasi (☎ 614 4047; Çarşı Caddesi 26; mains TL14-25; 8am-2am low season, to 4am high season) Packed with locals who spill onto the

BLUE VOYAGES

For many travellers a four-day, three-night cruise on a gület (traditional wooden yacht) between Fethiye and Kale (Demre) is the highlight of their trip to Turkey. Usually advertised as a Fethiye–Olympos voyage, the boats actually start or stop at Kale and the trip to/from Olympos (1¼ hours) is by bus. From Fethiye, boats call in at Ölüdeniz and Butterfly Valley and stop at Kaş, Kalkan and Üçağız (Kekova), with the final night at Gökkaya Bay. A less-common route is between Marmaris and Fethiye, also taking four days and three nights.

Food and water is usually included in the price, but you have to buy your booze on the boat. All boats are equipped with showers, toilets and smallish but comfortable double cabins (usually six to eight of them). In practice, most people sleep on mattresses on deck.

Depending on the season the price is €100 to €180 per person, which is not at all cheap, so it makes sense to shop around. Here are some of our suggestions to get the best price possible:

- Do ask for recommendations from other travellers
- Do bargain, but don't necessarily go for the cheapest option because the crew might skimp on food and alcohol
- Do check out your boat (if you are in Fethiye) and ask to see the guest list
- Do ask whether your captain and crew speak English
- Don't go for gimmicks such as free watersports, which often prove to be empty promises
- Don't buy your ticket in İstanbul, as pensions and commission agents take a healthy cut selling tickets
- Don't take a boat just because it is leaving that day

We recommend owner-operated outfits, as they run a much tighter ship. During summer some larger companies may farm out unknowing tourists to lazy captains with suspect boats. Boats come and go just about every day of the week between late-April and October. Competition is stiff between the following companies:

Almila Boat Cruise (☎ 0535-636 0076; www.beforelunch.com)
Big Backpackers (☎ 0252-614 9312; www.bluecruisefethiye.com)
Interyouth Hostel (☎ 0252-412 3687; interyouth@turk.net)
Olympos Yachting (☎ 0242-892 1145; www.olymposyachting.com)

streets, the Meğri does excellent and hearty home-style cooking. The *güveç* (casseroles) are a specialty.

Hilmi et Balık Restaurant (☎ 612 6242; Hal ve Pazar Yeri 53; meze TL5, 400g fish TL15-20; ⌚ 10am-midnight) Set inside the fish market building, this place does meat dishes as well as fish (its specialty) and is a firm favourite locally. You can also bring-your-own fish.

Fethiye's bars and nightclubs are mostly cheek-by-jowl on one little street, Hamam Sokak, just off İskele Meydanı. **Val's Bar** (☎ 612 2363; Müge Sokak; beer TL4; ⌚ 9am-1am) is a cute little bar run by Englishwoman Val and located near the new Cultural Centre – it stocks a mean selection of poison and suitably strong coffee. Alternatively, try **Club Bananas** (☎ 612 8441; beer TL5; ⌚ 10pm-5am) because any venue where staff set fire to the bar then dance on it is hard to overlook on a big night out.

Getting There & Away

For northbound buses, you must change at Antalya or Muğla. Buses from the otogar to Antalya (TL20, 7½ hours) head east along the coast via Kalkan (TL7, 1½ hours), Kaş (TL8, three hours) and Olympos (TL15, five hours). The inland road to Antalya (TL16, four hours, 222km) is quicker. Minibuses to more-local destinations, including Ölüdeniz, leave from behind the big white mosque (Yeni Cami) in the town centre.

ÖLÜDENİZ

☎ 0252

Over the mountains to the south of Fethiye, lovely Ölüdeniz's sheltered blue-ish lagoon beside lush national park and a long spit of sandy beach have been a curse as much as a blessing. Ölüdeniz (Dead Sea) is now one of the most famous beach spots on the Mediterranean, with far too many package-holiday hotels backed up behind the sands. Still, the **lagoon** (admission TL2; 8am-8pm) itself remains tranquillity incarnate and is a gorgeous place to sun yourself. Ölüdeniz is also a mecca for **tandem paragliding** (and parasailing). Companies here offer tandem paragliding flights off 1960m-high Baba Dağ (Mt Baba) for TL150 to TL200.

Sleeping & Eating

Sugar Beach Club (☎ 617 0048; www.thesugarbeachclub.com; Ölüdeniz Caddesi 20; campsite per person TL10, car & caravan TL10, bungalow per person TL70, without bathroom TL35-45; Apr-Oct;) About 600m to the right of the main drag, this is a well-run theme park for beach-party backpackers. It has a private strip of beach shaded by palms, shaded lounging areas, a beach café-bar and spotless bungalows. Bikes can be hired and small shops are onsite.

Oba Restaurant (☎ 617 0158; Mimar Sınan Caddesi; mains TL15-25; 8am-midnight) Built like a log cabin, the Oba Hostel's restaurant has a great reputation for home-style food at a palatable price. It also does great Turkish/European breakfasts, including homemade muesli with mountain yogurt and local pine honey.

Getting There & Away

Frequent minibuses run between Ölüdeniz and Fethiye (TL3, 25 minutes).

PATARA

☎ 0242

Scruffy little Patara, outside of Gelemiş, is the perfect spot to mix your ruin-rambling with some dedicated sand-shuffling on 20-odd kilometres of wide, golden **beach** (admission to beach & ruins TL2). With its rural setting and unhurried pace of life, it's a great place to chill out for a few days. The extensive **ruins** include a triple-arched triumphal gate at the entrance to the site, with a necropolis containing several Lycian tombs nearby. All in all, it's a good combination of nature and culture.

Sleeping & Eating

All the places to stay and most of the places to eat are in Gelemiş village, 1.5km inland from the ruins and 2.5km from the beach.

Rose Pension (☎ 843 5165; www.rosepensionpatara.com; s/d TL20/35;) This large, sand-coloured pension is favoured by shrewd travellers who can spot genuine hospitality from the arse-end of a dolmuş. Extra efforts such as garden-fresh produce and a stylish lounge make this an affectionate place to stay.

Sema Hotel (☎ 843 5114; www.semahotel.com; s/d TL25/40;) The Sema is not a luxurious hotel, but is ideal for those who prefer to share their travel experience with warm locals. Perched 60 steep steps above town, the rooms are basic, but spotless, cool and (pretty much) mosquito-free.

Golden Pension (☎ 843 5162; www.goldenpension.com; s/d TL30/40;) Offering homely rooms with balconies, a pretty shaded terrace and a friendly family that's not over-eager to please, this spot is peaceful and private. There are plans for a pool and the restaurant (mains TL10 to TL20) enjoys good foot traffic thanks to a comprehensive menu of meat, fish and vegetarian dishes.

Akay Pension (☎ 843 5055; www.pataraakaypension.com; s/d/t TL25/35/45;) Run by super-keen-to-please Kazım and family, the pension has well-maintained little rooms and comfortable beds with balconies overlooking orange trees.

Getting There & Away

Buses on the Fethiye–Kaş route drop you on the highway 4km from Gelemiş village. From here, dolmuşes run to the village every 45 minutes.

Minibuses run from the beach through the village to Fethiye (TL6, six daily), and also as regularly to Kalkan (TL5, 25 minutes) and Kaş (TL8, 45 minutes).

KALKAN

☎ 0242

Kalkan is a stylish hillside harbour town that slides steep into a sparkling blue bay. It's as rightly famous for its restaurants as its sublimely pretty beach and makes a smart alternative to the better-known, neighbouring Kaş.

Although Kalkan was once an Ottoman-Greek fishing village called Kalamaki, the town is now devoted to upscale tourism. Development continues unchecked on the outskirts of town, but thankfully Kalkan's charms are found right in the middle. Spend a night or two in one of many great-value pensions and you'll quickly see why foreign investors have driven up property prices.

Sleeping

Çelik Pansiyon (☎ 844 2126; Süleyman Yılmaz Caddesi 9; s/d TL30/40; ❄) One of the few cheap guesthouses open year-round, the Cçlik has rather spartan rooms, though they're quite spacious and spotless, and a roof terrace.

Holiday Pension (☎ 844 3777; Süleyman Yılmaz Caddesi; d TL50, without breakfast TL35) The rooms are simple but charming, some with old wooden beams, antique lace curtains and delightful balconies with good views.

Türk Evi (☎ 844 3129; www.kalkanturkevi.com; Hasan Altan Caddesi; d TL60-80; ❄) Multilingual and multitalented Önder and Selma Elitez run one of the more endearing places to stay on the western Mediterranean coast. The beautifully restored stone house has eight rooms filled with rare antique furniture, some with original bathtubs.

OUR PICK **The Elixir** (☎ 843 5032; Kalamar Yolu 8; d €100-120; ❄ 💻 🏊) It's always exciting to see a hotel attempt something new, especially when they pull it off. Part body-focused retreat, part designer hotel, The Elixir features two swimmingly handsome pools (one on the roof), and a smooth-edged Turkish bath.

Eating & Drinking

İstanbul Restaurant (☎ 844 2282; Süleyman Yılmaz Caddesi; mains TL10-20) This understated eatery's few white-clothed tables are usually filled with knowing diners, enjoying dishes such as a*li nazik* (aubergine, pepper and beef puree) and *ahtapot güveç* (octopus casserole).

Belgin's (☎ 844 3614; Hasan Altan Caddesi; mains TL12-20; 🕑 10am-midnight Apr-Oct) In a 150-year-old former olive-oil press, Belgin's serves traditional Turkish food at tempting prices. The specialty is *mantı*. There's usually live Turkish music from 8pm.

Korsan Kebap (☎ 844 2116; Atatürk Caddesi; meals TL20) With tables on a terrace by the harbour, it does delicious, upmarket kebaps and pide. Try the specialty, the *dürüm kebap* with spicy tender steak.

Aubergine (☎ 844 3332; İskele Sokak; meals €13; 🕑 9am-midnight) With tables right on the yacht marina, as well as cosy seats inside, the restaurant is famous for its slow-roasted wild boar, as well as its swordfish fillet served in a creamy vegetable sauce.

Daphne Restaurant (☎ 844 3547; Kocakaya Caddesi; mains TL15-30; 🕑 May-Oct) Owned by the same crowd as the heralded Aubergine, big things were expected of the former Daphne Hotel. It certainly delivers, with an emphasis on wok-style dishes and seafood. Live music is played on most nights.

Moonlight Bar (☎ 844 3043; Süleyman Yılmaz Caddesi 17; beer €2; 🕑 10am-4am or later mid-Apr–Oct) Kalkan's oldest bar is still its most 'happening', though 95% of people at the tables outside, or on the small dance floor, are tourists.

Getting There & Away

In high season, minibuses connect Kalkan with Fethiye (TL7, 1½ hours, 81km) and Kaş (TL2.50, 30 minutes, 29km). Around eight minibuses also run daily to Patara (TL5, 25 minutes, 15km).

KAŞ

☎ 0242 / pop 7700

The 500m-high mountain known as 'Sleeping Man' (Yatan Adam) has watched Kaş evolve from a beautiful place of exile for political dissidents, to a funky boutique shopping and café strip, to a seaside adventure playground. While Kaş proper may not sport the finest beach culture in the region, it's a yachties' haven and the atmosphere of the town is wonderfully mellow. The surrounding areas are ideal for day trips by sea or scooter and a plethora of adventure sports are on offer, in particular, some world-class diving.

Sights & Activities

Apart from enjoying the town's mellow atmos' and small pebble beaches, you can walk west a few hundred metres to see the well-preserved **theatre**. You can also step to the Lycian **rock tombs** in the cliffs above the town – the walk is strenuous so go at a cool time of day. It's also well worth going up the hill on the street to the east of the tourist office to reach the **Monument Tomb**, a Lycian sarcophagus mounted on a high base.

The most popular **boat trip** (TL25 to TL30) is to Kekova Island and Üçağız, a three-hour excursion that includes time to see several interesting ruins as well as stops for swimming. Other standard excursions go to the Mavi Mağara (Blue Cave), Patara and Kalkan, or to Liman Ağzı, Longos and several nearby islands. There are overland excursions to the wonderful 18km-long Saklıkent Gorge.

If you want to do anything active while you are in Kaş, contact **Bougainville Travel** (☎ 836 3737; www.bougainville-turkey.com; İbrahim Selin Caddesi 10). This long-established English-Turkish tour operator offers scuba diving, trekking, mountain biking and canyoning trips in the area. The sea-kayaking day trips over the Kekova sunken city (TL50), suitable for all fitness levels, will be the highlight of your stay in Kaş.

Sleeping

Cheap pensions are mostly west of Atatürk Bulvarı, and more-expensive hotels and restaurants to the east.

Kaş Camping (☎ 836 1050; Yaşar Yazici Caddesi; 2-person campsites TL20) Situated on an attractive rocky site 800m west of town, this has long been the most popular place for camping, with a lovely swimming area and bar.

Santosa Pension (☎ 836 1714; Recep Bilgin Caddesi 4; s/d TL20/40; ⊠ ❄) Clean, quiet and cheap is how best to describe this backpacker hangout. The rooms are bare and simple, but excellent for the price.

Ateş Pension (☎ 836 1393; www.atespension.com; Amfi Tiyatro Sokak 3; s/d TL30/50; ⊠ ❄ 💻) Well run by Ahmed and family, this is a friendly place with a pleasant roof terrace where barbecues are held. Guests also have free use of the kitchen and internet.

Hilal Pansiyon (☎ 836 1207; www.korsan-kas.com; Süleyman Çavuş Caddesi; dm/s/d TL15/30/50; ⊠ ❄) The friendly Hilal has a plant-potted terrace where barbecues take place. The travel agency below it offers guests 10% discounts on activities including kayaking, diving and trips to Saklıkent.

Hideaway (☎ 836 1887; www.kasturkey.com; Amfi Tiyatro Sokak; s TL50, d TL70-80; ❄ 🅿) Aptly named, the quiet Hideaway is located at the far end of town. Rooms are simple but in good order and all have a balcony. There's a roof terrace with sea views over the water and amphitheatre.

Eating

Oba Restaurant (☎ 836 1687; İbrahim Serin Caddesi 26; meze TL4, moussaka TL6) With a pleasant walled terrace under orange trees, the Oba offers Turkish dishes cooked by Nuran, the owner's mother. Hearty, tasty and great value, it's simple Turkish home cooking at its best.

Bi Lokma (☎ 836 3942; Hukumet Caddesi 2; mains TL8-12; ⏰ 9am-midnight) The Bi Lokma has tables meandering around a terraced garden overlooking the harbour. Sabo (Mama) turns out great traditional dishes, including famous *mantı* and Mama's pastries. The wine list is also reasonably priced.

Çinarlar (☎ 836 2860; Mütfü Efendi Sokak 4; pide TL5-8, pizza TL8-15; ⏰ 8am-1am) Perennially popular among Kaş' young, who come for the affordable pide and pop music, it also has a pleasant courtyard tucked away off the street.

Natur-el (☎ 836 2834; Gürsöy Sokak 6; meals TL15-20) With its dishes cooked to old Ottoman recipes passed down from generation to generation, Natur-el provides a chance to sample Turkish cuisine at its brilliant best. If you haven't yet tried *mantı*, then chose from three varieties here.

Sultan Garden Restaurant (☎ 836 3762; Hükümet Caddesi; mains TL15-25; ⏰ 10am-midnight) This is a very pretty place complete with original Lycian tombs and a functional cistern. The vegie burger is awesome and the *hünkar beğendı* (spiced lamb pieces on aubergine puree) is soft and flavoursome.

Mercan (☎ 836 1209; Balıkçı Barınağı 2; mains TL15-30; ⏰ 9am-midnight) Since 1956, when the owner's father was working his magic, the Mercan has been satisfying customers with fish and meat creations and confident, disarming service. The swordfish kebap should win awards.

Bahçe Restaurant (☎ 836 2370; Likya Caddesi 31; meals TL25; ⏰ dinner) Up behind the Lycian sarcophagus, it has a pretty garden and serves excellent dishes at decent prices, including a terrific range of meze. The fish in paper receives rave reviews.

Drinking

Rejoice! There are a couple of buzzing bars in Kaş. Not the kind of boisterous places you would find in Marmaris or Kuşadası, but more civilised venues heavy on atmosphere. Check out **Echo Bar** (Gürsöy Sokak), **Mavi Bar** (Mütfü Efendi Sokak) or, run by a retired New York taxi driver with a few stories to tell, **Hi-Jazz Bar** (Zümrüt Sokak 3). For caffeinated concoctions, make for **Café Merhaba** (İbrahim Serin Caddesi 19) or **Hideaway Café & Bar** (Cumhuriyet Caddesi 16a).

Getting There & Away

There are half-hourly dolmuşes to Kalkan (TL2.50, 30 minutes), Olympos (TL8, 2½ hours) and Patara (TL8, 45 minutes), and daily buses to İstanbul (TL65, 15 hours), Ankara (TL50, 11 hours) and İzmir (TL25, 8½ hours). For other destinations, connect at Fethiye (TL8, three hours) or Antalya (TL9, 3½ hours).

OLYMPOS & ÇIRALI

☎ 0242

Olympos has long had an ethereal hold over its visitors. It was an important Lycian city in the 2nd century BC, when the Olympians devoutly worshipped Hephaestus (Vulcan), the god of fire. No doubt this veneration sprang from reverence for the mysterious Chimaera, an eternal flame that still springs from the earth not far from the city. Along with the other Lycian coastal cities, Olympos went into a decline in the 1st century BC, before its fortunes twisted and turned through Roman rule, 3rd-century-AD pirate attacks and fortress building during the Middle Ages by the Venetians, Genoese and Rhodians (you can still see remains hanging from the clifftops). By the 15th century the site had been abandoned.

Neighbouring, 1km to the east, is another gem of a place. While Olympos has a well-established party reputation (though it has gentrified considerably during the last decade), Çıralı is the perfect place to experience the fine art of *keyif* (quiet relaxation).

The drive here is also a treat, strewn with mountain views all the way from Kaş.

Sights

Don't miss the fascinating ruins of **ancient Olympos** (admission per day TL2). A skip away from the beach, it's a wild, abandoned place where ruins peek out from forested coppices, rock outcrops and riverbanks.

If you just want to spend a lazy day, nothing beats the **beach** in Olympos. Çıralı also boasts a fine stretch of clear sand.

Most pensions in Olympos and Çıralı run tours (TL10) to **Chimaera**, a cluster of flames that blaze from crevices on the rocky slopes of Mt Olympos. It's located about 7km from Olympos.

Sleeping & Eating

OLYMPOS

Staying in an Olympos tree house has long been the stuff of travel legend – it offers fabulous-value, community-minded accommodation in a stunning natural setting. The tree-house dream is fading in the face of modern conveniences, but all camps include breakfast and dinner in the price, although drinks are extra. Bathrooms are generally shared, but many bungalows (offered as an alternative to tree houses) have private bathrooms and some have air-con.

Not all tree houses have reliable locks, so store valuables at reception. It's also worth being extra attentive with personal hygiene while staying here – every year some travellers get ill. The huge influx of visitors, over the summer in particular, can overwhelm the camps' capacity for waste disposal. Be vigilant when it comes to eating and don't swim around the point area.

Kadir's Yörük Top Treehouse (☎ 892 1250; www.kadirstreehouses.com; dm/bungalow TL20/40; ☒ ❄) Kadir's started the tree-living trend. For the first time in many years, the quirky place has grown smaller due to a fire damaging a large section of the property. But the fun has not gone away: there are three bars (including the time-honoured Bull Bar) and a rock-climbing wall. A range of other activities are also on offer.

Şaban (☎ 892 1265; www.sabanpansion.com; dm/tree house TL20/30, bungalow TL35-40; ☒ ❄) The sight of travellers laid out in hammocks snoozing in the shade soon confirms the local lore: that you come here to chill. Şaban is not a party place, and instead sells itself on tranquillity, space, a family feel and great home cooking. It's a good choice for single women.

Orange Pension (☎ 892 1317; www.olymposorangepension.com; bungalow with/without bathroom TL40/35; ❄) A long-standing favourite that's especially big with Turkish university students and Japanese guests, the Orange has grown in size in recent years, but Yusuf and friends still run a good show. The wooden en suite rooms upstairs have a futuristic Swiss Family Robinson feel, while the concrete rooms downstairs are perhaps the future of Olympos. It's got a great communal dining area and the same guys run a nightclub hidden in the valley.

Bayram's (☎ 892 1243; www.bayrams.com; tree house TL30, bungalow with/without air-con TL50/40; ☒ ❄) Here chilled-out 20-somethings sit on cushioned benches in post-party states. Backgammon, books and the odd swim in the sea are Bayram's activities of choice.

Varuna (☎ 892 1347; mains TL10-15; 🕑 8am-2.30am) Next to Bayram's, this popular spot serves snacks and mains including fresh trout, *gözleme* and *şiş kebaps* (roast skewered meat) in attractive open cabins, or you can just grab a beer (TL3).

ÇIRALI

Çıralı, to put it crudely, is just two dirt roads lined with pensions. To put it another way, it's a delightful beach community for nature lovers and post-backpackers. There are about 60 pensions here, some near the path up to the Chimaera and others close to the beach and the Olympos ruins.

Olympia Treehouse & Camping (☎ 8257 311; campsite/tree house per person incl breakfast TL10/20) Offering a tree-house experience without being in Olympos (and sans party atmosphere), this is a pleasant, peaceful place set by the beach amid fruit trees. Boat and snorkelling excursions can be organised.

Orange Motel (☎ 825 7327; www.orangemotel.net; s/d TL50/90; ⊠ ❄) Another smart and affordable choice right on the beach. The garden is hung with hammocks and the stairs leading to the agreeable rooms are wrought in iron design. The evening meal is about as wild as it gets in Çıralı; non-guests often drop by for a taste of what's cooking.

Hotel Canada (☎ 825 7233; www.hotelcanada.com; s/d TL80/100; ❄ 💻 ♿) This is a beautiful place to stay, offering pretty much the quintessential Çıralı experience – warmth, friendliness and steady relaxation among hammocks and citrus trees. It's ideal for families and children. Carrie and Saban are impeccable hosts.

Arcadia Hotel (☎ 825 7340; www.arcadiaholiday.com; d with half board TL200; ❄) The Canadian-Turkish owners of these four luxury bungalows have established a lovely escape amid verdant gardens at the northern end of the beach, across the road from Myland Nature (also recommended). The place is well laid out and well managed, and the restaurant is of a high standard.

Getting There & Away

Buses and minibuses plying the Fethiye–Antalya road will drop you at a roadside restaurant from where hourly minibuses go on to Çıralı and Olympos (TL2.75, 20 minutes). From October to April they wait until enough passengers arrive, which can sometimes take a while.

ANTALYA

☎ 0242 / pop 603,200

Once seen by travellers as the gateway to the 'Turkish Riviera', Antalya is generating a buzz among culture-vultures. Situated directly on the Gulf of Antalya (Antalya Körfezi), the largest Turkish city on the Mediterranean is both stylishly modern and classically beautiful. It boasts the creatively preserved Roman-Ottoman quarter of Kaleiçi, a pristine Roman harbour, plus stirring ruins in the surrounding Bey Mountains (Beydağları). The city's restaurants and boutique hotels rival those throughout the country, the archaeological museum is world class, there are a number of chic Med-carpet clubs, and the opera and ballet season at the Aspendos amphitheatre continues to draw attention.

Orientation & Information

The otogar is 4km north of the centre on the D650 highway to Burdur. The city centre is at Kale Kapısı, a major intersection marked by a clock tower. To get into Kaleiçi, head south down the hill from the clock tower or cut in from Hadrian's Gate (Hadriyanüs Kapısı), just off Atatürk Caddesi.

There are several post offices within walking distance of Kaleiçi and a small **tourist office** (☎/fax 241 1747; Yavuz Ozcan Parkı; 🕒 8am-7pm). **Natural Internet Café** (🕒 8am-11pm; Kaleiçi), next to Cumhuriyet Meydanı, is the city's most atmospheric café.

Sights & Activities

Around the harbour is the lovely historic district called **Kaleiçi**, whose walls once repelled raiders. It's a charming hill full of twisting alleys, atmosphere-laden courtyards, souvenir shops and lavishly restored mansions, while cliffside vantage points on either side of the harbour provide stunning views over a beautiful marina and the soaring Bey Mountains.

Heading down from the **clock tower** you will pass the **Yivli Minare** (Grooved Minaret), which rises above an old church that was converted into a mosque. In the southern reaches of Kaleiçi, the quirky **Kesik Minare** (Cut Minaret) is built on the site of a ruined Roman temple.

Just off Atatürk Caddesi, the monumental **Hadrian's Gate** was erected during the Roman emperor Hadrian's reign (AD 117–38).

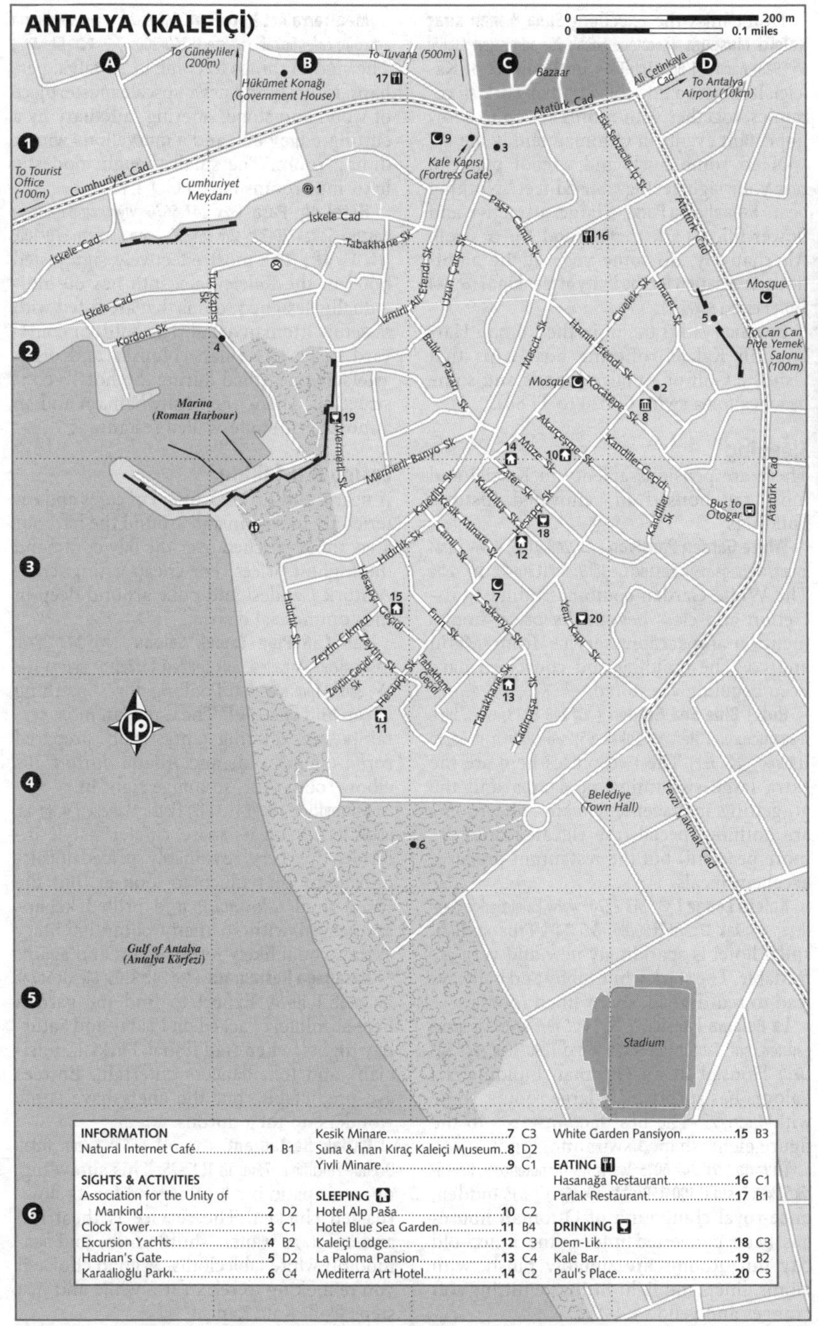
ANTALYA (KALEİÇİ)
0 200 m
0 0.1 miles
A
B
C
D
1
2
3
4
5
6
To Güneyliler (200m)
Hükümet Konağı (Government House)
To Tuvana (500m)
17
Bazaar
Ali Çetinkaya Cad
To Antalya Airport (10km)
Atatürk Cad
9
3
Kale Kapısı (Fortress Gate)
Eski Sebzeciler İç Sk
To Tourist Office (100m)
Cumhuriyet Cad
Cumhuriyet Meydanı
1
İskele Cad
Tabakhane Sk
Paşa Camii Sk
16
Uzun Çarşı Sk
İzmirli Ali Efendi Sk
Tuz Kapısı Sk
Kordon Sk
4
Mosque
Civelek Sk
İmaret Sk
5
Hamit Efendi Sk
To Can Can Pide Yemek Salonu (100m)
Mescit Sk
Balık Pazarı Sk
Marina (Roman Harbour)
Mosque
Kocatepe Sk
2
8
19
Mermerli Sk
Mermerli Banyo Sk
Akarçeşme Sk
14
Müze Sk
10
Kandiller Geçidi
Zafer Sk
Kaledibi Sk
Kurtuluş Sk
Hesapçı Sk
18
Kesik Minare Sk
Bus to Otogar
Kandiller Sk
Atatürk Cad
Hıdırlık Sk
12
Camii Sk
7
Hesapçı Geçidi
15
2 Sakarya Sk
20
Yeni Kapı Sk
Hıdırlık Sk
Fırın Sk
Zeytin Çıkmazı
Zeytin Sk
Zeytin Geçidi Sk
Tabakhane Geçidi
Hesapçı Sk
Tabakhane Sk
13
Kadırpaşa Sk
11
Belediye (Town Hall)
Fevzi Çakmak Cad
6
Gulf of Antalya (Antalya Körfezi)
Stadium
INFORMATION
Natural Internet Café 1 B1
SIGHTS & ACTIVITIES
Association for the Unity of Mankind 2 D2
Clock Tower 3 C1
Excursion Yachts 4 B2
Hadrian's Gate 5 D2
Karaalioğlu Parkı 6 C4
Kesik Minare 7 C3
Suna & İnan Kıraç Kaleiçi Museum 8 D2
Yivli Minare 9 C1
SLEEPING
Hotel Alp Paša 10 C2
Hotel Blue Sea Garden 11 B4
Kaleiçi Lodge 12 C3
La Paloma Pansion 13 C4
Mediterra Art Hotel 14 C2
White Garden Pansiyon 15 B3
EATING
Hasanağa Restaurant 16 C1
Parlak Restaurant 17 B1
DRINKING
Dem-Lik 18 C3
Kale Bar 19 B2
Paul's Place 20 C3

TURKEY

Don't miss the excellent **Suna & İnan Kıraç Kaleiçi Museum** (Kocatepe Sokak 25; admission €0.85; 9am-noon & 1-6pm Thu-Tue), in the heart of Kaleiçi. It houses a fine collection of Turkish ceramics, together with rooms set up to show important events in Ottoman family life.

Need some hush and a cool place to rest your sightseeing-abused feet? Nothing beats **Karaalioğlu Parkı**, a large, attractive and flower-filled park that's good for a stroll. Alternatively, do some yoga at the ambitious **Association for the Unity of Mankind** (244 5807; Hesapçı Sokak 7).

Excursion yachts tie up in the Roman Harbour in Kaleiçi, offering boat trips that visit the Gulf of Antalya islands and some beaches for a swim (TL20 to TL80).

Sleeping

There are pensions aplenty in Kaleiçi and most are housed in renovated historic buildings.

White Garden Pansiyon (248 9115; www.xhost.co.uk/whitegarden; Hesapçı Geçidi 9; s/d TL30/40) The White Garden combines tidiness, discretion and class beyond its price, not to mention impeccable service from Metin and co. The building and courtyard have been begulingly restored.

Hotel Blue Sea Garden (248 8213; www.blueseagarden.com; Hesapçı Sokak 65; s/d with half board TL40/60) The two pluses here are the extra large swimming pool area and the go-getting management team. The rooms are nothing special (the elevated ones are more peaceful) but the restaurant prepares excellent meals.

Kaleiçi Lodge (243 2270; www.kaleicilodge.com; Hesapçı Sokak 37; s/d TL50/80) This stylish, small hotel is sparklingly new and very affordable. The stark white lobby and hallways lead to red-draped, sharp-lined rooms.

La Paloma Pansion (244 8497; www.lapalomapansion.com; Tabakhane Sokak 3; s/d TL80/100) Housed in an Ottoman building, La Paloma has surprisingly large rooms, some with Jacuzzi. The best face inwards to the figure eight–shaped swimming pool.

Tuvana (247 6015; www.tuvanahotel.com; Karanlýk Sokak 7; s/d TL100/150) This hidden, once-royal compound of Ottoman houses has been converted into a fine inner–old city inn. Rooms are suitably plush, with kilims, linen and light fittings emitting soft oranges and yellows.

Mediterra Art Hotel (244 8624; www.mediterraart.com; Zafer Sokak 5; d/ste TL160/200) The sign of things to come in Antalya, perhaps, is this brand new, upscale masterpiece of wood and stone, offering sanctuary by a cutting-edge pool, and a marvellous winter dining room. The small though modestly luxurious rooms have LCD TVs.

Hotel Alp Paşa (247 5676; www.alppaşa.com; Hesapçı Sokak 30-32; s/d €65/90, with Jacuzzi €70/100) The most effectively signposted hotel in the Kaleiçi labyrinth has 60 individually designed rooms that are fitted with tasteful Ottoman detail. The outdoor courtyard displays Roman columns and other artefacts unearthed during the hotel's construction. There's an onsite hamam and an atmospheric stone-walled restaurant.

Eating & Drinking

A nearly endless assortment of cafés and eateries are tucked in and around the harbour area; those perched over the bay command the highest prices. For cheap eating, cross Atatürk Caddesi and poke around deep in the commercial district.

Can Can Pide Yemek Salonu (243 2548; Hasim Iscan Mahallesi, Arik Caddesi 4a; Adana durum TL6; 9am-11pm Mon-Sat) Looking for something cheap and cheerful? The Can Can most certainly can, offering fantastically prepared *çorba* (soup), pide and Adana *durum*. It's elbow room only, so nudge right in.

Güneyliler (241 1117; Elmali Mahallesi 4 No 12; meals TL12) With its spare, cafeteria-style interior, this *very* reasonably priced locals-only joint isn't much to look at. But the wood-fired *lahmacun* and grilled kebaps are served with so many complimentary extras, you'll likely return again and again.

Hasanağa Restaurant (242 8105; Mescit Sokak 15; meals TL10-20) Expect to find the garden here absolutely packed on Friday and Saturday nights, when traditional Turkish musicians and folk dancers entertain. Entrées are predictable, but the chefs have some wonders up their aprons.

Parlak Restaurant (241 6553; Kazım Özlap Qvenue Zincirlihan 7; meals TL12-25) This sprawling, open-air patio is a local legend for its slow-roasted chicken. The service is theatrical and exact, as waiters shuffle meze and seafood off white tablecloths. A good choice if you're looking to relax for a while and just steps from Kale Kapısı.

There are many bars in Kaleiçi and around the yacht harbour. It's worth seeking out the atmospheric **Kale Bar** (☎ 248 6591; Mermerli Sokak 2), attached to the Tütav Turk Evi Hotel and artfully constructed around the old city wall; the lively **Dem-Lik** (☎ 247 1930; Zafer Sokak 16), filled with Turkish students; and the religiously inclined **Paul's Place** (☎ 244 6894; Yeni Kapı Sokak 24). The good word comes in coffee cups at this informal expat 'club' on the 2nd-floor of St Paul Cultural Center.

Getting There & Away

Antalya's airport is 10km east of the city centre on the Alanya highway. Turkish Airlines offers frequent flights to/from İstanbul and Ankara. Atlasjet also has flights to/from İstanbul.

From the otogar, buses head for Göreme (TL38, 10 hours), Konya (TL18, six hours), Olympos (TL8, 1½ hours) and Manavgat/Side (TL8, 1½ hours).

AROUND ANTALYA

Between Antalya and Alanya there are several magnificent Graeco-Roman ruins to explore. You can't help but be dazzled by the sheer beauty of the ruins at **Perge** (admission TL10; 9am-7.30pm), 15km east of Antalya and 2km north of Aksu. The site has a 12,000-seat stadium and a 15,000-seat theatre. Another stunning place is **Aspendos** (admission TL10, parking TL4; 8am-7pm), 47km east of Antalya. Here you'll see the world's best-preserved Roman theatre, dating from the 2nd century AD and still used for performances during the Aspendos Opera & Ballet Festival every June or July. The former capital of the fierce Termessians, who fought off Alexander the Great, **Termessos** (admission TL10; 8am-5.30pm) is high in the mountains, 34km inland from Antalya. The ruins have a spectacular setting but demand some vigorous walking and climbing. Unless a coach party turns up, these places are all eerily deserted.

The only gripe is that it's not convenient to get to these sights by public transport. The easiest way to see them is with your own transport or on a tour from Antalya. A full-day tour to Perge and Aspendos, with side trips to spots such as Side, costs TL80 per carload; a half-day tour taking in Termessos costs TL60. Ask at your pension or hotel in Antalya. There are also plenty of agencies in Antalya hiring out cars for TL50 to TL70 per day.

SİDE

☎ 0242 / pop 18,000

The seasonal village of Side (*see*-duh) is the Turkish version of a carnival by the sea. With its souvenir-peddlers, quaint beaches, family-friendliness and peculiar slapstick charm, this once-docile fishing town is now a firmly established playground. It's almost like a film set; glorious Roman and Hellenistic ruins mark out the road and the evening performance at the ancient amphitheatre is spectacularly showbiz. The touts are a tedious downside, but visitors to Side often return, happy to get fleeced now and then by the same 2000-year-old tricks, happy to swim in the sea, happy to bask on the rocks, happy to unwind in Side.

You'll find ATMs on the main drag.

Sights

Side's impressive ancient structures include a huge **theatre** (admission TL10; 8am-7pm) with 15,000 seats, one of the largest in Anatolia; a Roman bath, now a **museum** (admission TL5; 9am-7pm) with an excellent small collection of statues and sarcophagi; and seaside **temples** to Apollo and Athena, dating from the 2nd century AD. It's also blessed with sandy **beaches**.

Sleeping & Eating

Beach House Hotel (☎ 753 1607; www.beachhouse-hotel.com; Barbaros Caddesi; s/d TL35/70; P) Run a long-term Australian expat, this justifiably popular spot has a prime beachside locale, yet still promotes restfulness. Most rooms face the sea and all have spacious balconies. The neighbouring Soundwaves Restaurant, run by the same crew, is also recommended.

Chillout Side (☎ 753 2041; www.chilloutside.com; Zambak Sokak 32; dm/s/d TL25/40/60) The backpacker scene is set to return to Side with the opening of this keenly run new premises. Set around a pretty garden of mulberry trees, palms and roses, the hostel features a smart little bar and a genuine travel vibe.

While the number of restaurants increases every season, the menus tend to repeat. Fresh fish (TL15 to TL25) is usually the way forward here – check what's included in the price. The classiest joint in town is probably **Moonlight Restaurant** (☎ 753

TURKEY

1400; Barbaros Caddesi 49; meals around TL25), with an extensive Turkish wine list and unfussy service. The mostly seafood offerings are well presented and very fresh. The biggest drawcard, however, is the romantic back patio.

Getting There & Away

In summer, Side has direct bus services to Ankara, İzmir and İstanbul. Otherwise, frequent minibuses connect Side with Manavgat otogar, 4km away, from where buses go to Antalya (TL8, 1¼ hours), Alanya (TL8, 1¼ hours) and Konya (TL25, 5½ hours).

ALANYA

☎ 0242 / pop 110,100

Alanya has mushroomed from a sparsely populated highway town on a silky sand beach to a densely populated tourist haven. Aside from the odd boat cruise or beach stroll, many visitors to Alanya shuffle between the airport shuttle and the hotel pool, perhaps venturing to a restaurant and banging nightclub after dark. But Alanya has something special up its dusty sleeve. Looming high above the modern centre is a brilliant fortress district, with trappings of a fine Seljuk castle, a wonderful mess of ruins, active remnants of village life and a touch of revamped 'Ottomania'.

The otogar is on the coastal highway (Atatürk Caddesi), 3km west of the centre. You'll find numerous banks with ATMs in the centre.

Sights & Activities

Alanya's crowning glory is the Seljuk **fortress** on top of the promontory, overlooking the city as well as the Pamphylian plain and the Cilician mountains. The octagonal **Kızıl Kule** (Red Tower; admission TL2; 9am-7.30pm Tue-Sun), down by the harbour, was built in 1226.

Every day at around 10.30am **boats** (per person TL35, incl lunch) leave from near Gazipaşa Caddesi for a six-hour voyage around the promontory, visiting several caves and **Cleopatra's Beach**.

Many local operators also organise tours for landlubbers. A typical tour to sights including Aspendos and Side costs around TL55 per person, while a village-visiting **4WD safari** into the Taurus Mountains costs about TL40.

Sleeping

Sadly, Alanya is low on cheap accommodation, as pensions have been superseded by faceless concrete lumps. There are, however, two cheap options close to the main drag:

Baba Hotel (☎ 513 1032; İskele Caddesi 6; s/d TL35/45) Baba is about the cheapest pad in town, but you pay for what you get (which is not much). The front entrance is located on the left side of a cement stairway just off the street.

Otel Temiz (☎ 513 1016; fax 519 1560; İskele Caddesi 12; s/d TL50/100;) Hotel 'Clean' is just that. Plus the rooms are spacious and the balconies offer a bird's-eye view of the thumping club and bar action below.

Eating & Drinking

The cheap restaurant scene is being swallowed by rising rents, so if you're tired of tourist traps, look for a *köfte* joint or any lokanta popular with workers.

Köfte D' Köfte (☎ 512 1270; Kale Caddesi; meals around TL12) A flashy yellow-and-red sign greets diners at this new 'boutique' fast-food joint. Attentive service and generous meat, rice and salad combinations are all part of the deal.

Gaziantep Sofrası Restaurant (☎ 513 4570; İzzet Azakoğlu Caddesi; meals TL15) For something more adventurous than standard grills and seafood, this is one of central Alanya's best options. Traditional food from Gaziantep is on offer.

Mahperi Restaurant (☎ 512 5491; www.mahperi.com; Rıhtım Caddesi; meals €15-25) A much-loved fish-and-steak restaurant that's been in operation since 1947 (an astonishing feat in Alanya), this place is quite the class act, offering an escape from the tourism glitz.

Red Tower Brewery Restaurant (☎ 513 6664; İskele Caddesi 80) If EU membership were dependent on a good brewpub, then the Red Tower would be Turkey's sole delegate. Not only is this place rare, it also makes staggeringly good Pilsen.

Cuba (☎ 511 8745; İskele Caddesi) The newest addition to the Alanya party junket, this stylish and relatively small club is a (slightly) less manic alternative. Ladies dressed in white get a free mojito.

Getting There & Away

There are frequent buses to Antalya (TL10, two hours) and to Adana (TL25, 10 hours), stopping in a number of towns (including Anamur) en route.

Fergün Denizcilik (☎ 511 5565; www.fergun.net) runs ferries to Girne (Cyprus) three twice a week (TL148 return, including taxes).

THE EASTERN COAST

East of Alanya, the coast sheds some of its touristic freight. The ghostly ruins of Byzantine **Anamurium** (admission TL2; 8am-8pm), 8.5km west of **Anamur**, are definitely worth a stop. About 7km east of the town, it would really be a shame to miss the wonderful **Mamure Castle** (Mamure Kalesi; admission TL2; 8am-6pm), built right on the beach by the Christian leaders of the Armenian kingdom of Cilicia in the 12th century.

Anamur is a good base to break your journey. In the harbour district, **Hotel Bella** (☎ 816 4751; www.mybellahotel.com; Kursat Caddesi 5; s/d/tr TL35/60/75;) offers clean rooms and excellent facilities. It's particularly popular with young Turks, while the fine restaurant is the best meeting place in town. Operated by the same energetic owner, **Eser Pansiyon** (☎ 814 2322, 814 9130; www.eserpansiyon.com; İnönü Caddesi 6; s/d/tr TL25/40/50, 5-person flat TL70;) offers by far the best value in town. If you want to be next to the otogar, **Hotel Dedehan** (☎ 814 7522; D400 Hwy; d TL30;) also makes a good base for excursions, as the owner lends guests cycles and rents out motorbikes. If hunger beckons, try the busy central **Asmaaltı Lokantası** (☎ 814 8040; Solyu Caddesi; meals TL10), a hit with the locals for its cheap stews. **Kap Restaurant** (☎ 814 2374; İskele Meydanı; meals around TL15) is the fish restaurant of choice. The mezes are also delicious, but service can be sloppy.

ANTAKYA (HATAY)

☎ 0326 / pop 140,700

The biblical Antioch, Antakya (confusingly, also called Hatay) was a major Roman settlement and, until 1938, part of the French protectorate of Syria. Both St Paul and St Peter dropped by to preach here, and you can visit the ancient **Church of St Peter** (St Pierre Kilisesi; admission TL5; 8.30am-noon & 1.30-4.30pm Tue-Sun), 3km northeast of town. The magnificent Roman mosaics in the **Antakya Archaeology Museum** (☎ 214 6168; Gündüz Caddesi; admission TL5; 8.30am-noon & 1.30-5pm Tue-Sun) more than justify an overnight stop on the way to Syria.

Divan Oteli (☎ 215 1518; İstiklal Caddesi 62; s/d TL20/40;) is the best budget option in town. **Hotel Orontes** (☎ 214 5931; www.oronteshotel.com; İstiklal Caddesi 58; s/d TL50/80;) is conveniently located near the otogar. If you want to kick back in style, the **Antik Beyazıt Otel** (☎ 216 2900; beyazit@antikbeyazitoteli.com; Hükümet Caddesi 4; s/d TL85/110;) occupies a French colonial building.

The otogar has direct buses to most western and northern points. There are also frequent services to Gaziantep (TL12, four hours) and Şanlıurfa (TL24, seven hours).

The Jet bus company has direct daily buses across the Syrian border to Aleppo, leaving at 9am and noon, and to Damascus at noon. Alternatively, for Aleppo catch a local bus to Reyhanlı (TL2, 45 minutes) and a dolmuş to the Turkish border, where you have to walk a few kilometres to the Syrian post. See also p616.

CENTRAL ANATOLIA

On central Turkey's hazy plains, the sense of history is so pervasive that the average kebap chef can remind you that the Romans preceded the Seljuks. This is, after all, the region where the whirling dervishes first swirled, Atatürk began his revolution, Alexander the Great cut the Gordian knot and King Midas turned everything to gold. Julius Caesar came here to utter his famous line, *'Veni, vidi, vici'* ('I came, I saw, I conquered').

In Safranbolu and Amasya, drinking in the history involves sipping *çay* and gazing at the half-timbered Ottoman houses. While these are two of Turkey's most beautiful towns, offering Ottoman digs with cupboard-bathrooms, other spots are so little-visited that foreigners may find themselves entered as just *turist* (tourist) in hotel guest books. This offers the opportunity to get to grips with everyday Anatolian life in a coach party–free environment – where historical heavyweights from the Hittites to Atatürk established major capitals.

ANKARA

☎ 0312 / pop 4.5 million

İstanbullus may quip that the best view in Ankara is the train home, but the Turkish capital has more substance than its reputation as a staid administrative centre suggests. The capital established by Atatürk offers a mellower, more manageable vignette of urban Turkey than İstanbul, and two of the country's most important sights: the Anıt

Kabir, Atatürk's hilltop mausoleum; and the Museum of Anatolian Civilisations, which will help you solve clues at sites left on the Anatolian plains by Hittites, Phrygians and other ancient folk. It can be a disjointed place, but two or three neighbourhoods have some charm: the historic streets in the hilltop citadel, the chic Kavaklıdere district and Kızılay, one of Turkey's hippest urban quarters.

Orientation & Information

Ankara's citadel crowns a hill 1km east of Ulus Meydanı (Ulus Sq), the heart of Old Ankara and near most of the inexpensive hotels. The newer Ankara lies further south, with better hotels, restaurants and nightlife in Kızılay and Kavaklıdere.

Atatürk Bulvarı is the main north–south axis. Ankara's mammoth otogar is 5.5km southwest of Ulus and 4.5km west of Kızılay. The train station is just over 1km southwest of Ulus Meydanı along Cumhuriyet Bulvarı.

The **tourist office** (☎ 310 8789, 231 5572; Anafartalar Caddesi 67, Ulus; 9am-5pm Mon-Fri, 10am-5pm Sat), southeast of Ulus Meydanı, plans to move to a new office at the train station. The main **PTT** (Atatürk Bulvarı) is just south of Ulus Meydanı. There are internet cafés and banks with ATMs around Ulus Meydanı, and Karanfil Sokak in Kızılay.

Sights

With the world's richest collection of Hittite artefacts, the state-of-the-art **Museum of Anatolian Civilisations** (Anadolu Medeniyetleri Müzesi; ☎ 324 3160; admission TL15; 8.30am-5pm), housed in a beautifully restored 15th-century *bedesten*, is Turkey's best museum outside İstanbul. Just up the hill, it's also well worth exploring the side streets of the **citadel**, the most scenic part of Ankara. Inside it, local people still live as if in a traditional Turkish village.

About 400m north of Ulus Meydanı, take a look at the surprisingly well preserved remains of the **Roman baths** (Roma Hamaları; admission TL3; 8.30am-12.30pm & 1.30-5.30pm), dating back to the 3rd century. Southeast of the baths, you'll find more Roman ruins, including the **Column of Julian** (AD 363) in a square ringed by government buildings, and the **Temple of Augustus & Rome**.

If you're an Atatürk devotee, you can't leave the city without having paid your respects to the founder of modern Turkey at the **Anıt Kabir** (Mausoleum of Atatürk; admission free; 9am-5pm mid-May–Oct, to 4pm Nov-Jan, to 4.30pm Feb–mid-May), 2km northwest of Kızılay Meydanı.

Sleeping

The first three listings are in the citadel or on the hill leading to it from Ulus Meydanı. However, locals advise against wandering Ulus' streets after about 9pm, so you may prefer to stay in Kızılay, which is pricier but has better restaurants and bars. Book ahead to beat the businessmen and bureaucrats to a room.

Kale Otel (☎ 311 3393; Şan Sokak 13, Ulus; s/d TL30/50) One of the closest hotels to the museum, the Kale's yellow-and-red facade is rather off-putting but its pink-and-red interior is more palatable. Wi-fi is available. This is one of Ulus' more-pleasant budget options.

Hitit Oteli (☎ 310 8617; www.otelhitit.com; Hisarparkı Caddesi 12, Ulus; s/d TL75/100) A noticeable step up in quality compared to the nearby budget places. The rooms are not as smart as the reception, with its fish tank and budgie, but it is a reasonable option near the museum.

our pick **Angora House Hotel** (☎ 309 8380; angorahouse@gmail.com; Kalekapısı Sokak 16-18, Ulus; s/d/tr €45/60/75; Mar-Oct;) Ankara's original boutique hotel is in a great location inside the citadel and offers beautiful, individually decorated rooms in a restored house, benefiting from some fine half-timbering and a walled courtyard.

Hotel Metropol (☎ 417 3060; www.hotelmetropol.com.tr; Olgunlar Sokak 5, Kızılay; s/d TL70/100;) Quite a snip at these prices, the three-star Metropol provides quality and character across the board. The breakfast is excellent, but laundry rates are high.

Eating

Head to Ulus Meydanı for cheap eats.

our pick **Le Man Kültür** (☎ 310 8617; Konur Sokak 8a-b, Kızılay; mains TL6-11; 10am-11pm) One of Kızılay's coolest hangouts, this restaurant packs in the ripped denim and beehives (of the Amy Winehouse variety) between walls decorated with subversive cartoons. The menu ranges from kebaps to Mexican and even Argentinean dishes.

Zenger Paşa Konağı (☎ 311 7070; www.zengerpasa.com; Doyran Sokak 13, Ulus; mains TL12-17; noon-12.30am;) Built in 1721 for governor Mehmet Fuat Paşa, the Zenger Paşa is crammed with Ottoman ephemera. It

SAFRANBOLU & AMASYA: RELAX IN (OTTOMAN) STYLE

Bored with the ubiquitous concrete eyesores that disfigure almost every city in Turkey? Make a beeline for Safranbolu and Amasya, respectively 145km north and 270km northeast of Ankara. These picture-postcard towns are slightly off the beaten track, but beckon savvy travellers with their ethereal settings and historical atmosphere. Both retain many of their original Ottoman buildings.

Safranbolu is such an enchanting city that it was declared a Unesco World Heritage site, on a par with Florence, Italy. It boasts a wonderful old Ottoman quarter bristling with 19th-century half-timbered houses. Most of them have been restored, and as time goes on, more and more are being saved from deterioration and turned into hotels or museums.

Blissfully located on riverbanks beneath cliffs, Amasya is one of Turkey's best-kept secrets. One of the country's prettiest towns, it harbours numerous historic sites, including the rock-hewn tombs of the kings of Pontus, a lofty citadel, Seljuk buildings and enough picturesque Ottoman piles to satisfy the fussiest sultan.

Good news: both Safranbolu and Amasya boast excellent accommodation, with a profusion of lovely B&Bs set in restored Ottoman mansions. There are a few direct buses from Ankara to both Safranbolu (TL20, three hours) and Amasya (TL30, five hours); the latter is closer to Sivas.

looks at first like a deserted ethnographic museum, but the pide, meze and grills, still cooked in the original oven, plus the perfect citadel views, attract wealthy Ankaralıs.

Köşk (☎ 432 1300; İnkılap Sokak 2, Kızılay; mains TL15-30; 🕑 9am-midnight) Ankara's best fish restaurant has a glass-fronted dining room with views of the pedestrianised boulevards and a chanteuse warbling away. Meze such as fresh calamari with peppers, and simple but effective grills and fish mains, are just as alluring.

Getting There & Away

AIR

Ankara's Esenboğa airport, 33km north of the city centre, is the hub for Turkish Airlines' domestic-flight network; there are daily nonstop flights to most Turkish cities with Turkish Airlines or Atlasjet. International flights are generally cheaper using one of İstanbul's airports.

BUS

Ankara's huge otogar (Ankara Şehirlerarası Terminali İşletmesi; AŞTİ) is the vehicular heart of the nation, with coaches going everywhere all day and night. They depart for İstanbul (TL25 to TL33, six hours) at least every 30 minutes.

TRAIN

There are useful services to Adana, İstanbul, Kayseri, Sivas and a few other cities, but some of the long-haul services can be excruciatingly slow.

SİVAS

☎ 0346 / pop 294,000

Sivas lies at the heart of Turkey geographically as well as politically, thanks to its role in the run-up to the War of Independence. The Congress building resounded with plans, strategies and principles as Atatürk and his adherents discussed their great goal of liberation. With a colourful, sometimes tragic history and some of the finest Seljuk buildings ever erected, Sivas is a good stopover en route to the wild east.

The **tourist office** (☎ 222 2252; 🕑 9am-5pm Mon-Fri) is in the *valılık* (provincial government headquarters) building on the main square. Don't miss the buildings in the adjoining park: the **Çifte Minare Medrese** (Seminary of the Twin Minarets) with a grand Seljuk-style gateway; the fabulous **Şifaiye Medresesi**, a former medical school that's one of the city's oldest buildings; and the 13th-century **Bürüciye Medresesi**. Southeast of the park are the 1197 **Ulu Cami** (Great Mosque) and the glorious **Gök Medrese** (Blue Seminary); west of it is the **Atatürk Congress & Ethnography Museum** (Atatürk Kongre ve Etnografya Müzesi; Inonü Bulvarı; admission TL2; 🕑 8.30am-noon & 1.30-5pm Tue-Sun), in the imposing Ottoman school building that hosted the Sivas Congress in September 1919.

Hotels line Eski Belediye Sokak, just east of the main square. Among them are **Sultan Otel** (☎ 221 2986; www.sultanotel.com.tr; Eski Belediye Sokak 18; s/d/tr TL90/140/170) and **Otel Madımak** (☎ 221 8027; Eski Belediye Sokak 2; s/d/tr TL60/90/115), although be aware that the site has sad resonances as a hate crime took place here in

MADIMAK MEMORIAL

The original Otel Madımak was the site of one of modern Turkey's worst hate crimes, on 2 July 1993, when 37 Alevi intellectuals and artists were burned alive in a mob arson attack. The victims, who had come for a cultural festival, included Aziz Nesin, the Turkish publisher of Salman Rushdie's *Satanic Verses*. A crowd of more than 1000 extreme Islamist demonstrators gathered outside the hotel after Friday prayers to protest about the book's publication, and in the ensuing chaos the hotel was set alight and burned to the ground.

The Madımak has since reopened (with a kebap shop in the foyer!), although many human rights groups are calling for the site to be turned into a memorial and museum. The government has already rejected this plan once, sparking accusations that some ministers were directly involved or at least sympathetic to the arsonists.

As well as a memorial, many protesters want to see the trial of the Madımak suspects reopened, believing they were let off too lightly. Thirty-one death sentences, upheld in a 2001 appeal, were commuted to life in prison when Turkey abolished the death sentence the following year.

The scars from the tragedy show no signs of fading, and Sivas' name has become synonymous with the incident. Demonstrations and vigils take place in Sivas on the anniversary of the attack; in 2008, tens of thousands of people attended a service to mark the 15th anniversary.

1993 (see the boxed text, above for more information).

At the rustic, wood-panelled **Sema Hanımın Yeri** (☎ 223 9496; İstasyon Caddesi Öncü Market; mains TL2.50-5; ⌚ 8am-midnight), the welcoming Madame Sema serves home-cooked food such as *içli köfte* (meatballs stuffed with spices and nuts). Friendly café-restaurant **Yeşil Café** (☎ 222 2638; Selçuklu Sokak; mains TL4-8; ⌚ 7.30am-11pm) has a tiny balcony upstairs with the best-ever views of spotlit twin minarets.

Buses go to destinations including Amasya (TL20, 3½ hours), Ankara (TL30, six hours) and Erzurum (TL30, seven hours). Services are not that frequent, so you may want to book ahead at one of the ticket offices just east of Hükümet Meydanı, along Atatürk Caddesi.

Sivas is a main rail junction. The *Doğu Ekspresi* and *Erzurum Ekspresi* go through Sivas to Erzurum and Kars daily; the *Güney Ekspresi* (from İstanbul to Kurtalan) runs four times a week in either direction.

KONYA

☎ 0332 / pop 762,000

Turkey's equivalent of the 'Bible Belt', conservative Konya treads a delicate path between its historical significance as the home town of the whirling dervish orders and a bastion of Seljuk culture on the one hand, and its modern importance as an economic boom town on the other. Luckily the city derives considerable charm from this juxtaposition of old and new, and boasts one of Turkey's finest and most characteristic sights, the Mevlâna shrine.

Orientation & Information

The town centre stretches from Alaaddin Tepesi, the hill topped by the Alaaddin Camii mosque (1221), along Mevlâna Caddesi to the tomb of Mevlâna, now called Mevlâna Müzesi. The otogar is 14km north of the centre; free *servis* take half an hour for the trip into town.

The **tourist office** (☎ 353 4020; Mevlâna Caddesi 21; ⌚ 8.30am-5.30pm Mon-Sat) is across the square from the Mevlâna Müzesi. You'll find numerous banks with ATMs and internet cafés around Alaaddin Tepesi, and the PTT just south of Mevlâna Caddesi near Hükümet Meydanı.

Sights

Join the pilgrims and head straight to the wonderful **Mevlâna Museum** (☎ 351 1215; admission TL2; ⌚ 9am-6.30pm Tue-Sun, 10am-6pm Mon), at the eastern end of Mevlâna Caddesi. The former lodge of the whirling dervishes, it is topped by a brilliant turquoise-tiled dome – one of the most inspiring images of Turkey. Although it's virtually under siege from devout crowds, there's a palpable mystique here.

It's also well worth visiting two outstanding Seljuk buildings near Alaaddin Tepesi. **Karatay Müzesi** (☎ 351 1914; Alaaddin Meydanı; admission TL3; ⌚ 9am-noon & 1.30-5.30pm), once a Muslim theological seminary, is now a museum housing a superb collection of ceramics (although it was closed for renovations when we visited). **İnceminare Medresesi** (Seminary of the Slender Minaret; ☎ 351 3204; Adliye Bulvarı; admission TL3; 🕑 9am-noon & 1.30-5.30pm), now the Museum of Wooden Artefacts & Stone Carving, has an extraordinarily elaborate doorway.

Sleeping

Otel Mevlâna (☎ 352 0029; Cengaver Sokak 2; s/d/tr from TL40/60/85) Across Mevlâna Caddesi from Otel Bera Mevlâna, this friendly central option is a good choice for backpackers of both sexes. The rooms have firm beds and fridges.

Otel Derya (☎ 352 0154; Ayanbey Sokak 18; s/d/tr TL50/80/100; P ❄) Quiet and spotless, the three-year-old Derya is a good choice for families and female travellers. The rooms, although slightly bland, have TVs and minibars, and the management is friendly and efficient.

Hotel Rumi (☎ 353 1121; www.rumihotel.com; Durakfakih Sokak 5; s/d/tr/ste €50/75/100/125; P ❄ 💻) Boasting a killer position near the Mevlâna Museum, the stylish Rumi has 33 rooms and suites with curvy chairs, slender lamps and mirrors. There's a hamam in the basement.

Hotel Balıkçılar (☎ 350 9470; www.balikcilar.com; Mevlâna Karşısı 2; s/d/tr/ste €89/120/140/157, breakfast €12; ❄) Easily the best reception area in town, styled as a cobbled Ottoman street. Facilities include a large lobby bar, restaurant, sauna, hamam and occasional *sema* (dervish ceremony) performances.

Eating & Drinking

Gülbahçesı Konya Mutfağı (☎ 351 0768; Gülbahçe Sokak 3; mains TL4-8; 🕑 8am-10pm) One of Konya's best restaurants, mostly because of its upstairs terrace with views of the Mevlâna Museum's gardens. Dishes include *yaprak sarma* (stuffed grape leaves), spicy Adana kebap and *etli ekmek* (bread with meat); no beer is served.

Osmanlı Çarşısı (☎ 353 3257; İnce Minare Sokak) Looking like an apple smoke–spewing pirate ship, this early-20th-century house near Alaaddin Tepesi has terraces and seats on the street. Nargilehs are being lit or bubbling away everywhere you look.

Getting There & Away

There are three daily flights to and from İstanbul with Turkish Airlines.

From the otogar, 7km north of Alaaddin Tepesi and accessible from there by tram, there are frequent buses to all major destinations, including Ankara (TL20, four hours), İstanbul (TL45, 11½ hours), Kayseri (TL25, four hours) and Sivas (TL30, seven hours). There are lots of ticket offices in the centre.

Two express trains link Konya and İstanbul.

CAPPADOCIA (KAPADOKYA)

Between Kayseri and Nevşehir, Central Anatolia's mountain-fringed plains give way to a land of fairy chimneys and underground cities. The fairy chimneys – rock columns, pyramids, mushrooms and a few camels – were formed, alongside the valleys of cascading white cliffs, when Erciyes Dağı (Mt Erciyes) erupted. The intervening millennia added to the remarkable Cappadocian canvas, with Byzantines carving cave churches and subterranean complexes to house thousands of people.

You could spend days touring rock-cut churches and admiring frescoes (technically seccos; one of many factoids visitors learn on a hike through the canyons). Alternatively, view the troglodyte architecture from far above on a dawn hot-air balloon ride or from a panoramic hotel terrace. Whether it's a pension or a boutique hideaway with as few rooms as it has fairy chimneys, Cappadocia's accommodation rates as some of Turkey's best and allows guests to experience cave dwelling first hand.

Tours

The following Göreme-based agencies offer good daily tours (costing around TL60) of local highlights, including Ihlara Valley.

Heritage Travel (☎ 271 2687; www.turkishheritagetravel.com; Yavuz Sokak 31)

Neşe Tour (☎ 271 2525; www.nesetour.com; Avanos Yolu 54)

Nomad Travel (☎ 271 2767; www.nomadtravel.com.tr; Müze Caddesi 35)

Kirkit Voyage (☎ 511 3148; www.kirkit.com; Avanos) and **Argeus Tours** (☎ 341 4688; www.argeus.com.tr, www.cappadociaexclusive.com; Ürgüp) are experienced travel agencies with varied programs

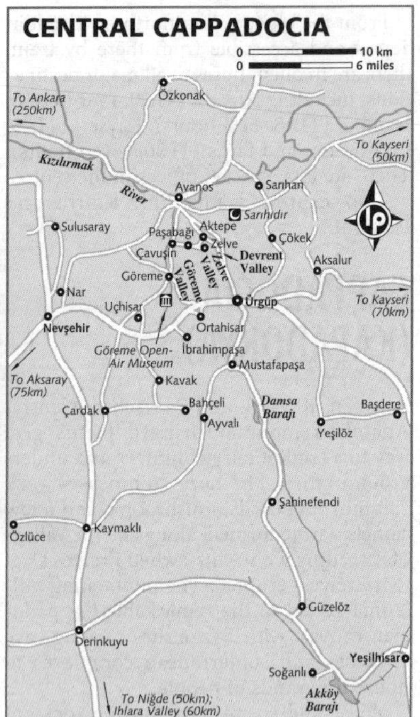

including horse-riding and cycling tours. **Middle Earth Travel** (☎ 271 2559; www.middleearthtravel.com; Göreme) offers walking tours and activities such as abseiling.

GÖREME

☎ 0384 / pop 2250

Göreme is the archetypal travellers' utopia: a beatific village where the surreal surroundings spread a fat smile on everyone's face. Beneath the honeycomb cliffs, the locals live in fairy chimneys – or increasingly, run hotels in them. The wavy white valleys in the distance, with their hiking trails, panoramic viewpoints and rock-cut churches, look like giant tubs of vanilla ice cream. Rose Valley, meanwhile, lives up to its name; watching its pink rock slowly change colour at sunset is best accompanied by meze in one of the excellent eateries.

Tourism is having an impact on this destination and these days a visitor can start the day in a hot-air balloon, before touring a valley of rock-cut Byzantine churches at Göreme Open-Air Museum. Nonetheless, rural life is still apparent around Göreme, where once upon a time, if a man couldn't lay claim to one of the rock-hewn pigeon houses, he would struggle to woo a wife.

All the services useful to travellers are in the centre, including the otogar (where there are four ATMs), the PTT and internet cafés.

Sights & Activities

Cappadocia's top attraction is **Göreme Open-Air Museum** (Göreme Açık Hava Müzesi; admission TL10; ⏰ 8am-5pm). It's pricey but it's worth every lira. Medieval frescoes can be seen in the rocky monastic settlement, where some 20 monks lived. The best-preserved churches are from the 10th to 13th centuries, although some are even older than that. The stunning **Karanlık Kilise** (Dark Church; admission TL8) is one of the most famous and fresco-filled of the churches, and is worth paying the extra admission fee. Across the road from the main entrance, the **Tokalı Kilise** (Buckle Church) is also impressive, with an underground chapel and fabulous frescoes.

There are a number of **hiking** options around Göreme village. It's surrounded by a handful of gorgeous valleys that are easily explored on foot, allowing about one to three hours for each of them. The valleys are

CAPPADOCIA FROM ABOVE

If you've never taken a flight in a hot-air balloon, Cappadocia is one of the best places in the world to do it. Flight conditions are especially favourable here, with balloons operating most mornings from the beginning of April to the end of November. The views across the valleys and fairy chimneys are simply unforgettable – it's a magical experience (see p37 for a full account of the experience). It's pricey but definitely worth blowing your budget on, costing about €155 to €250 per person for a one- to two-hour flight in an eight- to 20-passenger balloon. 'VIP flights' for two people cost a mere €600.

Operators offer different packages (and safety standards), so shop around. The following have good credentials:

Kapadokya Balloons (☎ 271 2442; www.kapadokyaballoons.com; Adnan Menderes Caddesi, Göreme)

Sultan Balloons (☎ 353 5249; www.sultanballoons.com; Sarıgüvercinlik Mevkii, Mustafapaşa Kasabası, Ürgüp)

remote in places and there have been attacks in them, so walk with a companion if possible. Most pension owners will be happy to guide you on the trails for a minimal fee.

Sleeping

With about 100 hostels, pensions and hotels in Göreme, competition keeps prices low. If you're visiting between October and May, pack warm clothes as it gets very cold at night.

Kaya Camping Caravaning (☎ 343 3100; kayacamping@www.com; campsites per adult/child TL13/8.50; 💻 🏊) This impressive camping ground is 2.5km from the centre of town, uphill from the Göreme Open-Air Museum. Set among fields of vines and a good sprinkling of trees, it has magnificent views and top-notch facilities.

Köse Pension (☎ 271 2294; www.kosepension.com; Ragıp Üner Caddesi; dm TL12, s without bathroom TL20, tw hut TL40, d/tw with bathroom TL60/60, tr with/without bathroom TL75/60; 🏊) Köse Pension has some rough edges, but unlike most hostels, it has a swimming pool in the garden and a terrace where communal meals are served. Run by Edinburgh-born Dawn Köse and family, the backpacker institution is cheerily painted with grinning spiders and winding creepers. On the roof are wooden huts and a 20-bed dorm.

Flintstones Cave (☎ 271 2555; www.theflintstonescavehotel.com; dm with/without breakfast TL15/10, s/d TL20/40, with Jacuzzi TL40/60; 💻 🏊) Among fields on the edge of the village, this lively hostel has hosted a pool-side barbecue for every fairy chimney in Cappadocia. Manager Fatih, who claims to be Fred Flintstone's nephew, advertises heaps of activities in the bar-restaurant, a cavernous hangout with a pool table. Ask to see a few rooms because there is a range of choices.

Kookaburra Pension (☎ 271 2549; kookagoreme@hotmail.com; Konak Sokak 10; dm without breakfast TL10, s/d TL20/40; 💻) This small pension, with agricultural tools and pot plants decorating its stone passages, has tidy, spacious rooms with private bathrooms. The roof terrace is a knockout and there's internet access in the bar-restaurant up top.

Kemal's Guest House (☎ 271 2234; www.kemalsguesthouse.com; Karşıbucak Sokak; dm with/without breakfast €9/6, s/d/tr/q €24/30/42/52) Entered via a flowery garden and reception with big bookshelves and battered sofas, popular Kemal's is run by a genial Turkish-Dutch couple. Barbara offers guided hikes and her eponymous beau, a cookery teacher, rustles up Turkish feasts. There are cave, Ottoman and modern rooms, and single-sex cave dorms with private bathrooms.

our pick **Kelebek Hotel & Cave Pension** (☎ 271 2531; www.kelebekhotel.com; Yavuz Sokak 31; s/d standard €28/35, s/d deluxe €36/45, ste €65-220; 💻 🏊) Pioneering Ali Yavuz converted his family home into Göreme's first boutique hotel, which boasts the village's best terrace for surveying the Cappadocian dreamscape. Divided into the modestly named Kelebek Pension and the newer Kelebek Suites, the 32-room complex ranges across stone houses and two fairy chimneys. More than the hamam, garden and small swimming pool, it's the helpful staff and Yavuz' passion for village life that make this a magical spot.

Fairy Chimney Inn (☎ 271 2655; www.fairychimney.com; Güvercinlik Sokak 5/7; s/d/tr from €44/55/66, students €22; ⊠ 💻) This fairy chimney high on Aydınlı Hill has been wonderfully converted by its owner, a German anthropologist. Rooms are beautifully decorated, with simple furniture, cushions and carpets, and a refreshing lack of TVs and Jacuzzis. Other treats include the cave hamam, communal lounge, home-cooked meals and glorious garden terrace.

Kismet Cave House (☎ 271 2416; www.kismetcavehouse.com; Kağnı Yolu 9; d standard/deluxe €60/80) Opened in 2007, this eight-room guesthouse has quickly built a strong reputation. The arched rooms up top have the edge on the chimney chambers, but both options offer Afghani bedspreads, Jacuzzis and views of Rose Valley. Owner Faruk encourages communal Anatolian living at long dining tables.

Eating

Most of Göreme's pensions provide good, cheap meals but you could also take advantage of some fine eateries in town.

Cappadocia Kebap Center (☎ 271 2682; Müze Caddesi; mains TL3.50) This tiny, friendly joint is a great place for a fast feed. You can enjoy a chicken döner kebap sandwich or a spicy *acılı kebap* sandwich, accompanied by freshly squeezed orange juice (TL3).

Nazar Börek (☎ 271 2441; Müze Caddesi; mains TL5) If you're after a cheap and filling meal, sample the börek, *gözleme* and *sosyete böregi* (stuffed spiral pastries with yogurt and tomato sauce) served at this simple place. Friendly staff and a pleasant outdoor eating area on the canal make it a perennially popular option.

Fırın Express (☎ 271 2266; Eski Belediye Yanı Sokak; pide & pizza TL4-8, mains TL8-13; ⏰ 11am-11pm) Set slightly back from the main strip, this wood cabin–like eatery is praised by carnivores and vegetarians for its pide and pizza. More substantial claypot dishes are also available.

Cappadocia Pide Salonu (☎ 271 2858; Hakki Paşa Meydanı; pide TL5-9) Göreme's pide hotspot has a more local feel than most of the village's eateries. Sitting under the canalside umbrellas, you can tuck into 12 types of pide, as well as spaghetti, grills, pottery kebaps, beer and rakı.

Point Café (Müze Caddesi; mains TL10) Missing your favourite comfort foods? A Turkish–South African couple dishes up curries, burgers, fruit smoothies, filter coffee and homebaked cakes.

our pick Dibek (☎ 271 2209; Hakkı Paşa Meydanı 1; mains TL10-15; ⏰ 9am-11pm) Dibek is one of Göreme's most original restaurants, and the best place to try a *testi kebap* (kebap cooked in a terracotta pot, broken at the table to serve). You must give three hours' notice before eating, so the dish can be slow-cooked in an oven in the stone floor.

Local Restaurant (☎ 271 2629; Müze Caddesi 38; mains TL11) At the start of the road to the Göreme Open-Air Museum, the Local is one of Göreme's best eateries, with an outdoor terrace and an elegant, stone-walled dining room. The service is attentive, ingredients are fresh, and prices are reasonable for the scrumptious dishes.

Manzara Restaurant (☎ 271 2712; Harim Sokak 14; mains TL12) With its bird's-eye view of Göreme's flat roofs and less-flat rock formations, Manzara is a prime spot to spend a meze-and-rakı evening. Choose between two terraces and an indoor dining room with a fireplace.

Getting There & Away

There are daily long-distance buses to all sorts of places from Göreme otogar; you may have to transfer in Nevşehir.

Minibuses travel from Ürgüp to Avanos (TL2) via Ortahisar, Göreme Open-Air Museum, Göreme village, Çavuşin and (on request) Paşabağı and Zelve every two hours. There's also an hourly municipal bus running from Avanos to Nevşehir (TL3) via Çavuşin, Göreme and Uçhisar.

UÇHİSAR

☎ 0384 / pop 6350

Between Göreme and Nevşehir is picturesque, laid-back yet stylish Uçhisar, built around a **rock citadel** (admission TL3; ⏰ 8am-8.15pm) that offers panoramic views from its summit. There are some excellent places to stay; the following, all located on the same street, are brilliant value and have formidable views of Pigeon Valley, Rose Valley and the rest of the rocky gang.

Uçhisar Pension (☎ 219 2662; www.uchisarpension.com; Kale Yani 5; s/d TL30/60)

La Maison du Réve (☎ 219 2199; www.lamaisondureve.com; Tekelli Mahallesi 32; s/d/tr €20/30/40; 💻)

Les Terrasses d'Uçhisar (☎ 219 2792; www.terrassespension.com; Eski Göreme Yolu; s/d/tr/ste €38/38/46/80; 💻)

A half-hourly municipal bus runs from Avanos to Nevşehir via Göreme and Uçhisar (TL1.50 to TL2.50). Services also link the village with Ortahisar and Ürgüp.

ZELVE VALLEY

Make sure to visit the excellent **Zelve Open-Air Museum** (admission TL5, parking TL2; ⏰ 8am-5pm, last admission 4.15pm), off the road from Göreme to Avanos. It is less visited than the Göreme Valley (though the monastic seclusion once offered here is long gone) and has rock-cut churches, a rock-cut mosque and some opportunities for serious scrambling. In the same area, some of the finest fairy chimneys can be seen at **Devrent Valley**, also known as Imagination Valley for its chimneys' anthropomorphic forms; and **Paşabağı**, where you can climb inside one formation to a monk's quarters, decorated with Hellenic crosses.

AVANOS

☎ 0384 / pop 11,800

Avanos is famous for pottery, made with red clay from the Kızılırmak (Red River), which runs through its centre, and white clay from the mountains. Its old town is rundown and its riverside setting does not match the other Cappadocian centres. However, it boasts some superb views of Zelve and, when the pottery-purchasing tour groups have moved on, it's an appealingly mellow country town.

Sleeping & Eating

Ada Camping (☎ 511 2429; www.adacampingavanos.com; Jan Zakari Caddesi 20; campsites per person TL10 incl electricity;) Take the Nevşehir road and bear right to reach this large, family-run camping ground that's in a superb setting near the river.

Kirkit Pension (☎ 511 3148; www.kirkit.com; Atatürk Caddesi; s/d/tr €30/40/55;) Set in converted old stone houses, this long-running pension is known throughout Cappadocia for its congenial, laid-back atmosphere. The simple rooms are decorated with kilims, historical photographs of the region and Uzbek bedspreads.

Sofa Hotel (☎ 511 5186; www.sofa-hotel.com; Orta Mahallesi Baklacı Sokak 13; s/d TL60/100;) Lots of Cappadocian cave establishments have their idiosyncrasies, but this hotel is downright bonkers. Staircases, bridges and terraces lead you up the hill, past eyes suddenly staring out from a mosaic fragment or a pottery face, to 33 rooms crammed with knick-knacks.

Sanço-Panço Restaurant (☎ 511 4184; Çarşi Sokak; mains TL6-7) This basic but welcoming eatery on the main square is a great people-watching spot. Given Avanos' pottery trade, it's hardly surprising that the specialty is *güveç* (beef stew baked in a clay pot).

Dayının Yeri (☎ 511 6840; Atatürk Caddesi 23; mains TL10) This shiny, modern *ocakbaşıs* (grill restaurant) is one of Cappadocia's best, and is an essential stop on any visit to Avanos. The kebaps and pide are equally sensational.

Getting There & Away

Half-hourly buses connect Avanos with Göreme, Uçhisar, Nevşehir and Ürgüp, costing TL1.50 to TL3.

ÜRGÜP

☎ 0384 / pop 15,500

If you have a soft spot for upmarket hotels and fine dining, you need look no further – Ürgüp is the place you're after. The ever-growing battalion of boutique hotels in the town's honey-coloured stone buildings (from pre-1923 when the town had a large Greek population) are proving very popular with travellers. With a spectacular natural setting and a wonderful location at the very heart of central Cappadocia, this is one of the most seductive holiday spots in the whole of Turkey.

There are internet cafés, banks with ATMs and restaurants around Cumhuriyet Meydanı, the main square. Many of the boutique hotels are on Esbelli Hill.

Sleeping

Hotel Elvan (☎ 341 4191; www.hotelelvan.com; Barbaros Hayrettin Sokak 11; s/d/tr TL35/60/80;) A friendly welcome and homely atmosphere await you at this unpretentious but immaculate guesthouse. There's a small roof terrace and comfortable dining room. It's excellent value.

Yıldız Hotel (☎ 341 4610; www.yildizhotel.com; Kayseri Caddesi; s TL30-60, d TL60-100) Nowhere near as impressive as the other budget options mentioned here, Yıldız offers old-fashioned rooms that are clean but in need of a paint job and new carpet.

Cappadocia Palace (☎ 341 2510; www.hotel-cappadocia.com; Duayeri Mahallesi Mektep Sokak 2; standard s/d/tr TL35/70/85, cave TL60/120/140;) This large, comfortable hotel is housed in a converted Greek mansion near Cumhuriyet Meydanı. There's a lovely arched restaurant-lounge and an attractive foyer area. Book ahead.

Razziya Evi (☎ 341 5089; www.razziyaevi.com; Cingilli Sokak 24; s/d/tr TL70/80/120) This lovingly restored *evi* (house) has seven cheerful rooms (some in slightly musty caves). There's a hamam, a salon with satellite TV, a pretty courtyard and a kitchen that guests can use.

Kemerli Evi (☎ 341 5445; www.kemerliev.com; Dutlu Camii Mahallesi Çıkmaz Sokak 12; s/d €60/80;) This converted 13th-century house is lost up backstreets inhabited by friendly locals. The eight rooms have antique chairs and carpets, nooks and crannies are everywhere, and an air of calm hangs between the thick stone walls. The elevated terrace has a beautiful swimming pool and panoramic views.

our pick **Esbelli Evi** (☎ 341 3395; www.esbelli.com; Esbelli Mahallesi Sokak 8; s/d/ste €80/90/200;) Consummate host Süha Ersöz opened Cappadocia's first boutique hotel. Having bought surrounding properties to preserve Esbelli's atmosphere of hilltop serenity, his complex now has 10 rooms and five suites in nine houses. However, it feels small and intimate, thanks to the welcoming atmosphere and the communal areas where guests are encouraged to congregate.

Melekler Evi (☎ 341 7131; www.meleklerevi.com.tr; Dereler Mahallesi Dere Sokak 59; d €90-145) This seven-room hotel's name, House of Angels, could refer to its lofty position at the top of the old town, eye-to-eye with pigeon houses. Restored by an architect and an interior designer, the cave and arch rooms are tastefully decorated in subtle shades.

Eating & Drinking

Micro Café & Restaurant (☎ 5341 5110; Cumhuriyet Meydanı; mains TL11) It's not the plaza's most popular restaurant, but Micro's diverse menu, ranging across Ottoman chicken, spinach crêpe and peppered T-bone steak, attracts some tourists and locals.

Şömine Cafe & Restaurant (☎ 341 8442; Cumhuriyet Meydanı; meze TL5, salads TL5-7, mains TL9-15) This popular restaurant on the plaza has a roof terrace and an attractive indoor dining room. Start with a salad or a meze choice such as *sosyete mantısı* (one large ravioli), then attack a *kiremit* (clay-baked meat or vegetable dish).

our pick **Ziggy's** (☎ 341 7107; Yunak Mahallesi, Teyfik Fikret Caddesi 24; mains TL13-16, set menu TL30) Cool Ziggy's, named after a David Bowie song, has a series of terraces. Whether you opt for a cocktail or the 12-course set menu, which features 10 meze plates, such as the distinctive smoked aubergine, hosts Selim and Nuray add some İstanbul sophistication to the Cappadocian views.

Dimrit (☎ 341 8585; Yunak Mahallesi, Teyfik Fikret Caddesi 40; mains TL10-21) With meze served in curvy dishes and three types of rakı, Dimrit's hillside terraces are top spots to spend a sunset. The extensive menu features salads, fish, classic grills and house specials.

Ehlikeyf (☎ 341 6110; Cumhuriyet Meydanı; mains TL12-25) Competing with nearby Şömine in the sophistication stakes, Ehlikeyf occupies a sleek dining room with a wavy ceiling. Dishes such as the fabulous Ehlikeyf kebap (steak served on slivered fried potatoes, garlic yogurt and a demiglace sauce) arrive on glass plates.

The main square is the best place to grab an alcoholic or caffeinated beverage at an outside table and watch Cappadocia cruise by. *Pastanes* and cafés such as Şükrüoğlu and Café Naturel vie for attention with their sweet eats and shiny window displays. Local institution **Han Çirağan Restaurant** (☎ 341 2566; Cumhuriyet Meydanı) has a good terrace for a beer, but we wouldn't recommend eating here as the service is lacklustre and the food is bog-standard Turkish fare.

Getting There & Away

There are daily long-distance buses to nationwide destinations from Ürgüp's otogar.

Minibuses travel to Avanos (TL2) via the Göreme Open-Air Museum, Göreme village and (on request) Zelve every two hours.

MUSTAFAPAŞA

☎ 0384 / pop 1600

Mustafapaşa is the sleeping beauty of Cappadocia, a peaceful village with pretty old stone-carved houses, some minor rock-cut churches and a few good places to stay. If you want to get away from it all, this is the place to base yourself. Until WWI, it was called Sinasos and was predominantly an Ottoman-Greek settlement.

If you want to bed-down for the evening, **Hotel Pacha** (☎ 353 5331; www.pachahotel.com; Sinasos Meydanı; s/d €20/30) is the real thing: a family-run business that offers a warm welcome and home-cooking by the lady of the house, Demra. The restored Ottoman-Greek pile has a great feel about it from the moment you enter its pretty, vine-trellised courtyard.

There is decayed elegance to **Hotel Natura** (☎ 353 5030; www.clubnatura.com; Sümer Sokak 16; r incl dinner TL70), which occupies a 19th-century Ottoman-Greek mansion. Carpets are everywhere in the expansive 'antique' rooms, alongside lamps, pictures, hat stands and the odd broken window.

Inhabited by the same family since 1938, the **Old Greek House** (☎ 353 5306; www.oldgreekhouse.com; Şahin Caddesi; s TL60, d TL80-120) is just about the best place to try Ottoman cuisine in Cappadocia (mains TL6 to TL20, menu TL22 to TL30). Prepared by half a dozen village women, the dishes include unusual choices and some of the best baklava we tasted. The hotel is an excellent place to stay thanks to its historic aura.

Seven buses per day (less on Sunday) travel between Mustafapaşa and Ürgüp (TL1).

IHLARA VALLEY

☎ 0382

A beautiful canyon full of rock-cut churches dating back to Byzantine times, **Ihlara Valley** (Ihlara Vadısı; admission TL5; 🕑 8am-6.30pm) is a must-see. Footpaths follow the course of the river, Melendiz Suyu, which flows for 13km between the narrow gorge at Ihlara village and the wide valley around **Selime Monastery** (🕑 dawn-dusk).

In the words of one Slovakian traveller, Radovan: 'The deep canyon with lots of churches and trees opens up as you approach Selime. After that you're in a sleepy valley with the river flowing, big mountains typical of Cappadocia in the distance, and a gorgeous monastery in Selime.'

The easiest way to see the valley is on a day tour from Göreme (p587), which allows a few hours to walk through the central part of the gorge. To get there by bus, you must change in Nevşehir and Aksaray, making it tricky to get there and back from Göreme and walk the valley in a day.

KAYSERİ

☎ 0352 / pop 1.2 million

Mixing Seljuk tombs, mosques and modern developments, Kayseri is both Turkey's most Islamic city after Konya and one of the country's economic powerhouses, nicknamed the 'Anatolian tigers'. Colourful silk headscarfs are piled in the bazaar (one of the country's biggest) and businesses shut down at noon on Friday when many Muslims go to the mosque for prayers, but Kayseri's religious leanings are less prominent than its manufacturing prowess. Its populates are often less approachable than folk in Göreme and around, and this can be frustrating and jarring if you arrive fresh from the fairy chimneys. However, if you are passing through this transport hub, it's worth taking a look at a Turkish boomtown with a strong sense of its own history.

Orientation & Information

The basalt-walled citadel at the centre of the old town, just south of Cumhuriyet Meydanı (the huge main square) is a good landmark. The train station is at the northern end of Atatürk Bulvarı, 500m north of the old town. The futuristic otogar is about 3km northwest of the centre.

You'll find banks with ATMs and a helpful **tourist office** (☎ 222 3903; Cumhuriyet Meydanı; 8am-5pm Mon-Fri) in the centre. To check your emails, head to **Soner Internet Café** (Düvenönü Meydanı; per hr TL1.50; 8am-midnight), west of the old town.

Sights

The fabulous **citadel** was constructed in the early 13th century, during the Seljuk sultan Alaattin Keykubat's reign, then restored over the years (twice in the 15th century). Just southeast of the citadel is the wonderful **Güpgüpoğlu Konağı** (admission TL2; 8am-5pm Tue-Sun), a fine stone mansion dating from the 18th century, which now houses an interesting ethnographic museum.

Among Kayseri's distinctive features are important building complexes founded by Seljuk queens and princesses, such as the impressive **Mahperi Hunat Hatun Complex**, east of the citadel. On the other side of the bazaar is the **Ulu Cami** (Great Mosque), a good example of early Seljuk style. Another striking monument is the **Çifte Medrese** (Twin Seminaries). The adjoining religious schools of Çifte Medrese, in Mimar Sinan Parkı north of Park Caddesi, date back to the 12th century.

Scattered about Kayseri are several conical **Seljuk tombs**.

Sleeping & Eating

Hotel Sur (☎ 222 4367; Talas Caddesi 12; s/d/tr TL40/60/75) Beyond the dark reception and institutional corridors, the Sur's rooms are bright, comfortable and some overlook the city walls.

Elif Hotel (☎ 336 1826; elifotelkayseri@elifotelkayseri.com; Osman Kavuncu Caddesi 2; s/d/tr TL40/70/90) Despite their slightly worn bathrooms, the rooms are a bargain, with satellite TV and minibar. Ask for a spot at the rear of the building, which is quieter.

Hotel Çapari (☎ 222 5278; www.hotelcapari.com; Gevher Nesibe Mahellesi Donanma Caddesi 12; s/d/tr/ste TL60/90/110/120;) With thick red carpets and friendly staff, this three-star hotel on a quiet street off Atatürk Bulvarı is one of the best deals in town.

Bent Hotel (☎ 221 2400; www.benthotel.com; Atatürk Bulvarı 40; s/d/tr TL75/100/120) Its name may not inspire confidence, but the Bent is a good midrange choice overlooking the pedal boats in Mimar Sinan Parkı.

The western end of Sivas Caddesi has a strip of fast-food joints that still seem to be pumping when everything else in town is quiet, including the fish-loving **İstanbul Balık Pazarı** (☎ 231 8973; Sivas Caddesi; mains TL3; 8am-11pm).

Kayseri's best restaurants are **Tuana** (☎ 222 0565; 2nd fl, Sivas Caddesi; mains TL7), with views of the citadel and Erciyes Dağı and a roll-call of classic dishes such as kebaps and Kayseri *mantı;* and **Elmacioğlu İskender et Lokantası** (☎ 222 6965; 1st & 2nd fl, Millet Caddesi 5; mains TL8-13; 9am-10.30pm), where *İskender kebaps* are the house specialty, available with *köfte* or in 'double' form. Mmmm…

Getting There & Away

Turkish Airlines and Onur Air have daily flights to/from İstanbul. Sun Express serves İzmir twice a week.

On an important north–south and east–west crossroads, Kayseri has lots of bus services. Destinations include Sivas (TL18, three hours) and Ürgüp (TL6, 1¼ hours) and Göreme (TL10, 1½ hours).

By train, there are useful services to Adana, Ankara, Diyarbakır, Kars and Sivas, mostly daily.

THE BLACK SEA & NORTHEASTERN ANATOLIA

Travel no further: you've found what you're looking for. A place where resorts are non-existent, where you can really feel a sense of wilderness and adventure, and where superb archaeological sites and hidden treasures are set among eerie landscapes – welcome to the Black Sea coast and eastern Turkey.

If you're overlanding to Iran, Iraq or Syria, you will certainly need to transit parts of these fascinating areas; bear in mind that the weather can be bitterly cold and snowy in winter, especially in eastern Turkey.

It's only travellers that have been slow to catch on to the appeal of the Black Sea. The craggy and spectacular coastline is scattered with the legacy of the civilisations and empires that have ebbed and flowed in this historic region. Often bereft of other travellers, the local castles, churches and monasteries, as important as the must-see sights in other parts of Turkey, remember the kings of Pontus, the Genoese and the Ottomans.

From the Black Sea coast, it's fairly straightforward to get to northeastern Anatolia. This far-flung outpost is almost a void on the tourist radar due to its remoteness, making it a red flag to those hungry for the unknown. Here the flavours of the neighbouring Caucasus, Central Asia and Iran are already palpable. The *saklı cennet* (secret paradise) is a perfect blend of nature and culture, with many palaces, castles, mosques and churches dotted around the steppe.

> **DRIVING THE BLACK SEA COAST**
>
> To see some of the Black Sea region's best views, looking north out to sea, travel the glorious, vertigo-inducing curves on the coastal road from **Amasra**, with its Roman and Byzantine ruins, to beachy **Sinop**.
>
> Continuing east, **Samsun** has little of interest for tourists, but there are excellent beaches around the cheerful resort town of **Ünye**, on a wide bay 95km east of Samsun. About 80km further to the east, **Ordu** is a bustling city with a palmlined seafront boulevard. **Giresun** is famous for its hazelnuts and cherries, having introduced the latter to Italy, and from there to the rest of the world.

TRABZON

☎ 0462 / pop 400,000

Trabzon is one of those 'love it or hate it' kind of places. Its slightly seedy port-town character puts some people off, while others appreciate the city's cosmopolitan buzz. Arguably the Black Sea coast's most sophisticated city – sorry, Samsun – Trabzon centres upon the whirl of activity on its main square. Beeping dolmuşes hurtle anticlockwise like a modern chariot race, while local students team headscarves with Converse All Stars, beneath a giant screen showcasing the city's beloved Trabzonspor football team.

Orientation & Information

Modern Trabzon is centred on Atatürk Alanı (also known as Meydan Parkı), uphill from the port. There are cafés and restaurants to the west, on Uzun Sokak (Long Lane) and Kahramanmaraş Caddesi (Maraş Caddesi for short), where you will also find banks with ATMs, exchange offices and the PTT. The otogar is about 3km from the centre.

The helpful **tourist office** (☎/fax 326 4760; Camii Sokak; 🕑 8am-5.30pm daily Jun-Sep, 8am-5pm Mon-Fri Oct-May) is south of Atatürk Alanı. There's a **Georgian consulate** (☎ 326 2226; trabzoncons@gul.net; Pertev Paşa Sokak 10) and, west of the centre, a **Russian consulate** (☎ 326 2728; rusconsultrb@ttnet.net.tr; Şh Refik Cesur 6, Ortahisar).

Sights

Without doubt, Trabzon's star attraction is the 13th-century **Aya Sofya** (☎ 223 3033; admission TL2; 9am-6pm Tue-Sun Apr-Oct, 9am-5pm Tue-Sun Nov-Mar), 4km west of town and reachable by dolmuş from Atatürk Alanı. Marvel at the vividly coloured frescoes and mosaic floors.

Another draw is the **Atatürk Köşkü** (Atatürk Villa; admission €1.25; 8am-7pm May-Sep, 8am-5pm Oct-Apr). This beautiful 19th-century mansion is set high above the town and is accessible by bus from the northern side of Atatürk Alanı.

The ancient **bazaar** is west of Atatürk Alanı, accessible by the pedestrianised Kunduracılar Caddesi, which cuts through the lively district's tightly packed streets. Further west, **Ortahisar** is a picturesque old neighbourhood straddling a ravine, not to be confused with the Cappadocian village.

SUMELA MONASTERY

Of all the dreamy spots in eastern Turkey that make you feel like you're floating through another time and space, **Sumela** (admission TL5; 9am-6pm), 46km south of Trabzon, wins the time-travel prize by a long shot. Carved out of a sheer cliff like a swallow's nest, this Byzantine monastery features superb frescoes (partially damaged by vandals). Some of them date from the 9th century.

The monastery is in the Altındere Vadısı Milli Parkı (Altındere Valley National Park), which you must pay TL3 to enter (plus TL8 for private vehicles). If you're visiting by public transport, try and catch a dolmuş from Trabzon at around 8am to avoid the midmorning flow of tour groups.

You can also visit on a tour (TL20) from Trabzon; contact **Eyce Tours** (☎ 326 7174; www.eycetours.com).

Sleeping

Many of the cheapies off the northeastern corner of Atatürk Alanı and along the coastal road double as brothels.

Hotel Nur (☎ 323 0445; Camii Sokak 15; s/d 40/60;) A long-standing, but often overly popular, travellers' favourite, the Nur has amiable, English-speaking staff and small, brightly painted rooms. The lounge is good for getting the travellers' lowdown on going to Georgia.

Hotel Anıl (☎ 326 7282; Güzelhisar Caddesi 12; s/d TL50/80;) A promisingly flash reception lures travellers in, and the rooms in pink and yellow are actually good value; even the downstairs rooms have views.

Hotel Nazar (☎ 323 0081; www.nazarhotel.net; Güzelhisar Caddesi 5; s/d TL70/100;) Look beyond the flagrant photoshopping in the brochure (flower gardens in central Trabzon? Yeah right), and the Nazar is a smart business-class option.

Otel Horon (☎ 326 6455; www.otelhoron.com; Sıramağazalar Caddesi 125; s/d TL90/125;) Inside the aubergine-coloured walls, any shortcomings in design are overcome by wi-fi, well-stocked minibars, city views from the rooftop bar-restaurant and some female reception staff (guaranteeing propriety).

Eating

Trabzon is not the Black Sea's gastronomic highpoint, but scores of good eateries line Atatürk Alanı and the two streets to the west.

İstanbul Kır Pidesi (☎ 321 2212; Uzun Sokak 48; mains TL3-5) Three-floors of wood-fired goodness for the pide and börek aficionado within.

Hürrem Sultan Sofrası (☎ 321 8651; Maraş Caddesi 30; mains TL4-10) This popular lunch den sometimes serves regional dishes such as *muhlama* and *kuymak* (melted cheese dishes). Businessmen, students and cops are all regulars at this friendly spot.

Üstad (☎ 326 5406; Atatürk Alanı 18b; meals TL5-8) Locals squeeze into this compact lokanta right on Trabzon's main square. We can thoroughly recommend the *biber dolması* (stuffed peppers) that come with a robust pinch of chilli.

Bordo Mavi (☎ 326 2077; Halkevi Caddesi 12; meals TL6-10; 11am-10pm) This cosmopolitan garden café adjoins the clubhouse of Trabzonspor, the local football team. It's not at all boozy or noisy though, and the excellent pizzas and pasta have an authentic tinge of Italy.

Reis'in Yeri (meals TL8-14; Liman Mukli İdare; 11am-11pm) It can be easy to forget Trabzon is a coastal city, until you head downhill, away from the traffic and over the pedestrian overbridge, to this sprawling fish/chicken/*köfte* grill place. It doubles as a beer garden and you can hire rowboats to steer around the tiny cove.

Drinking

Stress Café (☎ 321 3044; Uzun Sokak) Stress? You must be joking. One of Trabzon's best live

TURKEY

music and nargileh spots, the Stress Café is so laid-back it's almost horizontal.

Café Life (☎ 321 2955; Halkevi Caddesi 15) Two floors up, past wildlife pics from *National Geographic,* this is one of Trabzon's more vibrant venues, with live music, fast food and free-flowing booze.

Kalendar (Zeytinlik Caddesi 10) Low tables and mood lighting give this place near the Trabzon Museum a cosmopolitan vibe. It's perfect for a coffee and brunch.

Getting There & Away

Turkish Airlines, Pegasus Airlines, Onur Air and Sun Express fly to/from Turkish locations including İstanbul. At the time of writing, Azerbaijan Airways was trialling a weekly flight from Trabzon to Baku.

Two shipping offices down by the harbour sell tickets for ferries going to Sochi in Russia (about €55), but you need to have your Russian visa sorted. There are two to three weekly services.

From Trabzon's otogar, you can reach numerous destinations in Turkey as well as Tbilisi (Tiflis) in Georgia and Erivan in Armenia (via Georgia). There are regular services to Erzurum (TL25, six hours), Kars (TL35, 10 hours) and Kayseri (TL45, 12 hours).

ERZURUM

☎ 0442 / pop 402,000

Erzurum is a contradictory place: it's Islamic to its core, with deep roots in tradition, but has adapted to Western consumerism. Here you can shop till you drop and quaff rakı – all while the muezzins call the faithful to prayer. A gregarious student population adds a liberal buzz to the air. The city promotes itself as the architectural capital of eastern Anatolia and an impressive array of Seljuk monuments make this tag well deserved. If oohhing and aahhing over the wonderful medreses and mosques on the main drag isn't your thing, come in winter and enjoy the nearby Palandöken ski resort.

Orientation & Information

The otogar is 2km from the centre along the airport road. The centre is compact, with the main sights within walking distance of each other. You'll find lots of banks with ATMs, the PTT and internet cafés on or around Cumhuriyet Caddesi, the main drag.

The **Iranian consulate** (☎/fax 316 2285/1182; Atatürk Bulvarı; 🕑 8.30am-noon & 2.30-4.30pm Mon-Thu & Sat) is about 2km west of the centre, towards Palandöken.

Sights

The well-preserved walls of the 5th-century **citadel** (admission TL2; 🕑 8am-5pm) loom over a maze of narrow streets, offering good views of the town and the surrounding steppe.

Another must-see is the beautifully symmetrical **Çifte Minareli Medrese** (Twin Minaret Seminary; Cumhuriyet Caddesi), a famous example of Seljuk architecture dating from the 1200s. The eye-catching carved portal is flanked by twin brick minarets decorated with small blue tiles.

Next to the Çifte Minareli is the **Ulu Cami** (Great Mosque; Cumhuriyet Caddesi), built in 1179. Unlike the elaborately decorated Çifte Minareli, the Ulu Cami is restrained but elegant.

Further west along Cumhuriyet Caddesi is the **Yakutiye Medrese**, a seminary built by the local Mongol emir in 1310 and now a museum.

Sleeping

Otel Çınar (☎ 213 2055; Ayazpaşa Caddesi; s/d TL20/30, s without bathroom TL13) If the Yeni Çınar is full, the adjoining Çınar has diminutive singles, which will do the trick for unfussy backpackers. Rooms are daubed a gaudy shade of green and have well-scrubbed bathrooms.

Yeni Çınar Oteli (☎ 213 6690; Ayazpaşa Caddesi; s/d TL25/35) This place may not look like much, but has plenty of virtues for true budget-seekers. It's clean, safe, quiet and within walking distance of everything you might need. The only flaw is the deserted, dimly lit street at night.

Yeni Ornek (☎ 233 0053; Kazım Karakebir Caddesi; s/d TL30/40) Style? Erm, no. The Yeni Ornek is as no-frills as it gets but the rooms are well kept and the staff pleasant. After a long day's turf pounding, sink into the comfy leather armchairs in the lobby.

Grand Hotel Hitit (☎/fax 233 5001/2350; Kazım Karabekir Caddesi; s/d TL40/70) A good lair in this price bracket, with rooms that seemingly get plenty of TLC. Convenient location and good views from the rooftop breakfast room.

our pick **Esadaş Otel** (☎ 233 5425; www.erzurumesadas.com.tr, in Turkish; Cumhuriyet Caddesi; s/d TL45/80; P) Right on the main thoroughfare and close to everything, including our beloved

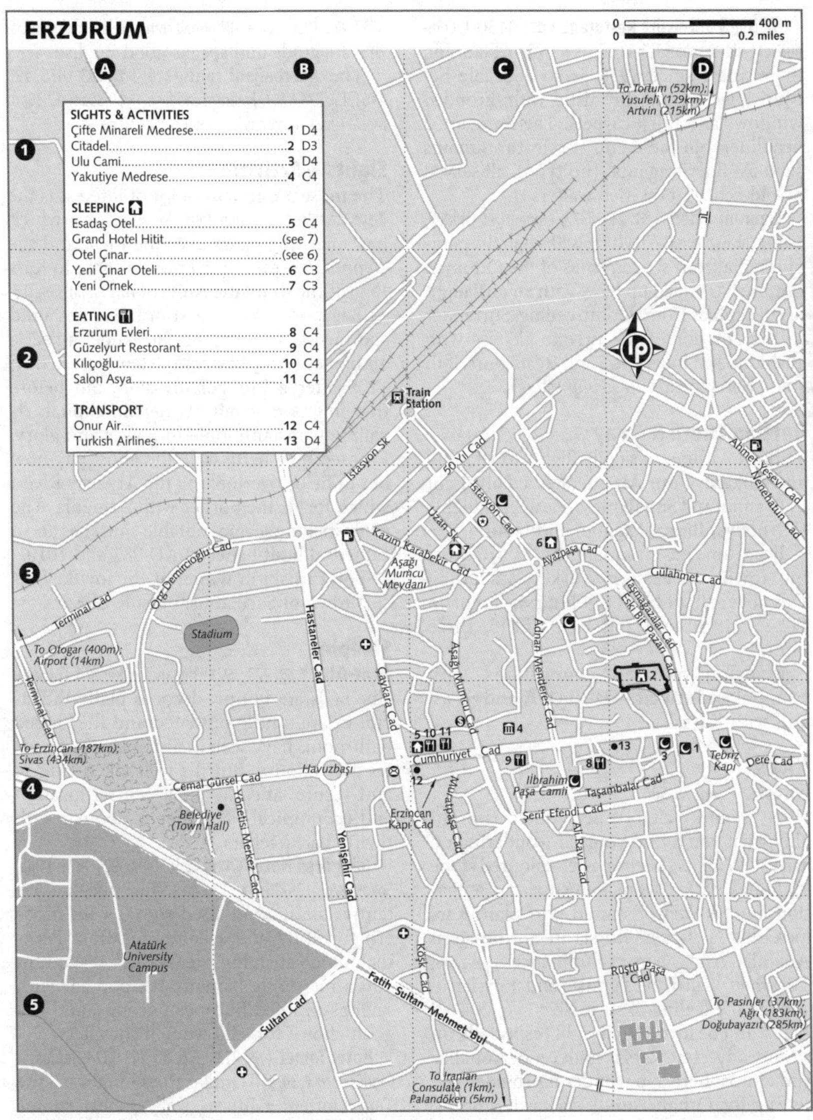

Kılıçoğlu pastry shop. Terrific breakfast, with five varieties of local cheese, sausages and yogurt. Bargain down the prices a bit if business is slack.

Eating

You'll find plenty of eateries sprinkled around Cumhuriyet Caddesi.

Kılıçoğlu (☎ 235 3233; Cumhuriyet Caddesi; snacks & pastries from TL2) A smart pastry shop that turns out snacks, 27 kinds of baklava and 23 ice-cream flavours.

Salon Asya (☎ 234 9222; Cumhuriyet Caddesi; mains TL4-8) Buzzing and packed, come here for satisfying kebaps and meals in rosy surrounds. The food is fresh and hygienically prepared.

our pick **Güzelyurt Restorant** (☎ 234 5001; Cumhuriyet Caddesi; mains TL5-13) This iconic restaurant, in business since 1928, is so adorable because it feels so anachronistic, with shrouded windows and thick carpets. The meze are a headliner, but the menu also features mains such as 'Bof Straganof' (no typo), all served by old-school, bow-tied waiters.

Erzurum Evleri (☎ 212 8372; Cumhuriyet Caddesi, Yüzbaşı Sokak; mains TL7-12) It feels like half the paraphernalia from six centuries of the Ottoman Empire has ended up here, with an onslaught of collectibles from floor to ceiling. Surrender to the languor of the private alcoves with cushions and low tables, and treat yourself to soup, börek or *tandır kebap* (stew).

Getting There & Away

Turkish Airlines has daily flights to İstanbul and Ankara. Onur Air operates a daily flight to İstanbul and Sun Express has weekly flights to Antalya, Bursa, İstanbul and İzmir.

Erzurum has frequent buses to most big towns in eastern Turkey, including Doğubayazıt (TL20, 4½ hours), Trabzon (TL25, six hours) and Kars (TL15, three hours).

Erzurum has rail connections with İstanbul and Ankara via Kayseri and Sivas, and with Kars.

KARS

☎ 0474 / pop 78,500

What a quirky city. 'Where am I?' is probably what you'll find yourself wondering on arrival. With its stately, pastel-coloured stone buildings dating from the Russian occupation and its well-organised grid plan, Kars looks like a slice of Russia in northeastern Anatolia. And the mix of influences – Azeri, Turkmen, Kurdish, Turkish and Russian – adds to the feeling of surprise.

It won't be love at first sight (especially on a rainy day), but Kars is high on personality and atmosphere. No wonder it provided the setting for Orhan Pamuk's award-winning novel *Kar (Snow)*.

Information

Most banks (and ATMs), internet cafés, hotels and restaurants are on or close to Atatürk Caddesi, the main street. The **tourist office** (☎ 212 6817; Lise Caddesi; 🕑 8am-noon & 1-5pm Mon-Fri) can help you organise a taxi to Ani, but your best bet is to contact **Celil Ersoğlu** (☎ 212 6543, 0532-226 3966; celilani@hotmail.com), who acts as a private guide and speaks good English.

The **Azerbaijani consulate** (☎ 223 6475, 223 1361; fax 223 8741; Erzurum Caddesi; 🕑 9.30am-12.30pm Mon-Fri) is northwest of the centre.

Sights & Activities

The most prominent point of interest is the **Kars Castle** (admission free; 🕑 8am-5pm), which has smashing views over the town and the steppe. However, most people come to Kars to visit the dramatic ruins of **Ani** (admission TL5; 🕑 8.30am-5pm), 45km east of town. Set amid spectacular scenery, the site exudes an eerie ambience. Ani was completely deserted in 1239 after a Mongol invasion, but before that it was a stately Armenian capital, rivalling Constantinople in power and glory. Fronted by a hefty wall, the ghost city now lies in fields overlooking the Arpaçay River, which forms the border with Armenia. The ruins include several notable churches and a cathedral built between AD 987 and 1010.

You can ski in winter at the low-key resort town of Sarıkamış, outside of Kars.

Sleeping

Kent Otel (☎ 223 1929; Hapan Mevkii; s/d TL15/30) The beds are lumpy, decor is plain, the facilities are a little outdated and the shared bathrooms have seen their fair share of bodies and odours. But it's well taken care of and secure, and the great central location and economical rates keep it popular with thrifty backpackers.

Güngören Hotel (☎ 212 5630; fax 223 4821; Millet Sokak; s/d TL30/50; P) This fine pile has attentive staff, good-sized rooms with modern furniture and a handy location. Perks include a satisfying breakfast, a restaurant and a men-only hamam. It's popular with savings-minded European groups, and is a good choice for solo women travellers.

Hotel Temel (☎ 223 1376; fax 223 1323; Yenipazar Caddesi; s/d TL30/45) Unlike the Güngören, the Temel offers a lift, as well as neat rooms with immaculate sheets and a soothing blue-and-yellow colour scheme. The management gets mixed reviews.

our pick **Kar's Otel** (☎ 212 1616; www.karsotel.com; Halit Paşa Caddesi; s/d TL190/260; ⊠ ❄) Seeking a luxurious cocoon with homely qualities, efficient hosts and a big dollop of atmosphere? Look no further than this savvy boutique hotel, housed in an old Russian mansion. It breathes an air of repose, though some might find the white colour scheme a bit too clinical, and its Ani Restaurant (mains TL6 to TL15) is also recommended. Well worth the splurge.

Eating

Kars is noted for its excellent honey. It's on sale in several shops, which also sell the local *kaşar peyniri* (mild yellow cheese) and *kuruyemiş* (dried fruits) – perfect ingredients for a picnic on the steppe.

Antep Lahmacun Salonu (☎ 223 0741; Atatürk Caddesi; mains TL2-4) Pide and *lahmacun* aficionados head straight to this humble joint to gobble a flavoursome local-style pizza at paupers' prices.

our pick **Ocakbaşı Restoran** (☎ 212 0056; Atatürk Caddesi; mains TL5-8) This well-established restaurant is the pinnacle of Kars' eating scene. Sample its signature dishes, *ali nazık* (eggplant puree with yogurt and meat) and Anteplim pide (sesame bread stuffed with meat, cheese, parsley, nuts and eggs), and you'll understand why. It has two rooms, including a mock troglodytic one (wow!), but it's not licensed (boo!).

Getting There & Away

There are frequent minibuses to Erzurum (TL15, three hours) and one morning bus to Van (TL30, six hours). If you're heading to Doğubayazıt, you'll have to change in Iğdır.

For Ani take the taxi dolmuşes organised by Kars tourist office, or private guide Celil Ersoğlu (see opposite). It costs about TL30 per person in a taxi, provided there's a minimum of six people. If not, the full fare is TL100 return plus waiting time. You can hire a taxi from TL70, but ensure the driver understands you want a few hours at the site.

DOĞUBAYAZIT

☎ 0472 / pop 36,000

What an awesome backdrop: on one side, Mt Ararat (Ağrı Dağı, 5137m), Turkey's highest mountain; on the other, İshak Paşa Palace, a breathtakingly beautiful palace-mosque-fortress complex. Not bad for a charmless frontier town high on testosterone (read: lots of soldiers, policemen, moustached men and the occasional tout, but, alas, very few women on the streets).

A lack in charm doesn't, however, mean a lack in character. This is a quintessentially Kurdish town that prides itself on its strong Kurdish heritage, which it celebrates during the **Kültür Sanat ve Turizm Festival** (Culture and Arts Festival) in late June. Doğubayazıt is also the main kicking-off point for the overland trail through Iran (the border is 35km away).

Information

Doğubayazıt is small and easily negotiated on foot. For tourist information, travel agencies including **Ararat Trek** (☎ 535-616 0267; www.ararattrek.com; Dr İsmail Beşikçi Caddesi; 8am-8pm) can help with your queries. Most banks have ATMs. Moneychangers including **Nişantaş Döviz** (Dr İsmail Beşikçi Caddesi; 7am-7pm Mon-Sat, 7am-noon Sun) sometimes have Iranian rials. There are several internet cafés on the main drag.

Sights & Activities

Your jaw will drop in amazement the minute you see **İshak Paşa Palace** (İshak Paşa Sarayı; admission TL2; 8.30am-5.30pm Tue-Sun Apr-Oct, 8.30am-5pm Nov-Mar). Perched romantically among rocky crags, 6km southeast of town, this fortress-palace-mosque is the epitome of *The Thousand and One Nights* castle. Built between 1685 and 1784, it blends elements of Seljuk, Ottoman, Georgian, Persian and Armenian architecture.

Minibuses (TL1) rattle between the otogar and the palace, but there's no fixed schedule; they leave when they are full. A taxi driver will want about TL20 for a return trip, waiting time included. Walking back down is pleasant, although women in particular might feel rather isolated.

Now that the troubles in the east have died down, it is once again possible to climb **Mt Ararat**, although you need a permit and a guide. At the time of research you needed to apply at least 45 days in advance. You can apply through any reputable travel agency in Turkey.

Sleeping & Eating

A word of warning: the two camping ground-cum-pensions near İshak Paşa Palace are not recommended for women travellers.

Lale Zar Camping (☎ 544-269 1960; lalezarcamping@hotmail.com; İshakpaşa Yolu Üzeri; campsite per person TL8 incl tent rental) Yes, it looks like a bit of a schlep from downtown Doğubayazıt (on the road to İshak Paşa Palace). But this Kurdish/Dutch campsite is in a well-tended property dotted

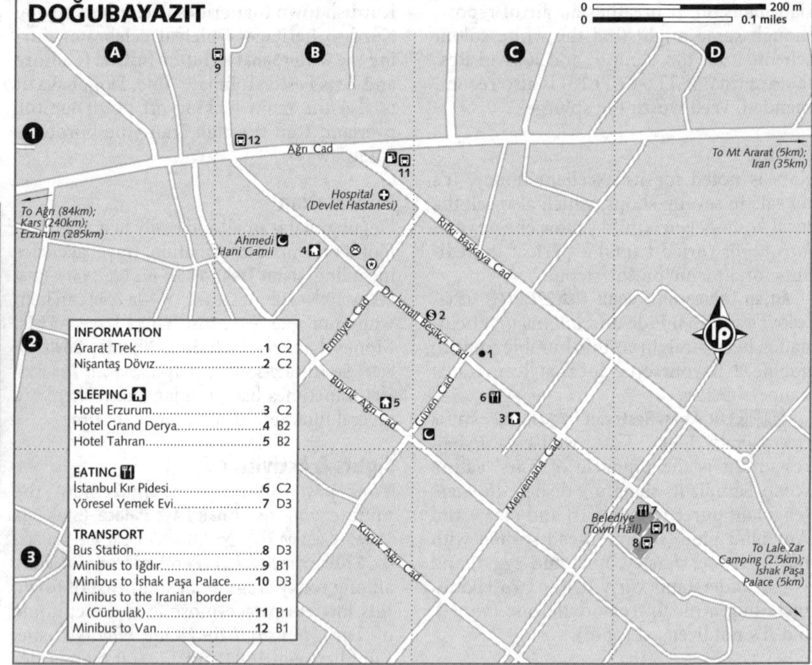

with a few grassy patches (but no shade to speak of), and its location means a multitude of stars in the night sky and quiet nights. There's a food store and restaurant.

Hotel Erzurum (☎ 312 5080; Dr İsmail Beşikçi Caddesi; s/d without bathroom TL10/20) The Erzurum is an old warhorse of the Doğubayazıt backpacker scene, and it shows. But at these prices you almost expect cell-like, threadbare rooms and saggy mattresses. It's conveniently located and the shared bathrooms won't have you squirming.

Hotel Tahran (☎ 312 0195; www.hoteltahran.com; Büyük Ağrı Caddesi 124; s/d TL20/36; 💻) The Tahran's recipe for success is to keep prices low, standards high and employ attentive (in a good way) staff. Although on the small side, the rooms come equipped with crisp sheets and views of Mt Ararat. Bilal, the affable manager, is well clued up on Iran. A safe bet for solo women travellers, too.

Hotel Grand Derya (☎ /fax 312 7531/7833; Dr İsmail Beşikçi Caddesi; s/d TL50/90; Ⓟ) An ideal retreat after a few days' clambering in knee breeches and hiking boots, this excellent venue offers comfortable rooms with all the mod cons. For Ararat views, request a room ending with 01 or 12 (avoid those ending in 02). Bring earplugs for the 5am call to prayer emanating from the nearby mosque.

İstanbul Kır Pidesi (☎ 312 8352; Dr İsmail Beşikçi Caddesi; pide TL1) This modest eatery serves up the best value pide this side of Mt Ararat. Choose between the cheese, potato and meat (and that's about it).

our pick **Yöresel Yemek Evi** (☎ 312 4026; Dr İsmail Beşikçi Caddesi; mains TL3-5) Yay! Some feminine touches in this male-dominated city! This place is run by an association of Kurdish women whose husbands are imprisoned. They prepare lip-smacking *yöresel* (traditional) meals at bargain-basement prices.

Getting There & Away

There are about four daily minibuses to Van (TL10, three hours). To get to Kars, change minibus at Iğdır (TL5, 45 minutes); the journey should cost about TL10 total.

Minibuses (TL4) to the Iranian border (Gürbulak) leave from near the junction of Ağrı and Rıfkı Başkaya Caddesis, just past the *petrol ofisi* (petrol station), approximately every hour. The last one departs around 5pm.

SOUTHEASTERN ANATOLIA

Turkey's wild child, southeastern Anatolia feels different from the rest of the country, and that's part of its appeal. Apart from a few Arabic and Christian pockets, this huge chunk of territory is predominantly Kurdish.

What does it have on its menu? For starters, you can choose from a wealth of historical cities, such as Mardin, the region's trophy piece, perched on a hill dominating Mesopotamia; Şanlıurfa, swathed in historical mystique, and the old city of Diyarbakır, ensnared in mighty basalt walls.

For the main course, how about natural wonders? Adjust your camera to 'panoramic' and shoot life-enhancing images of Mt Nemrut (Nemrut Dağı), topped with colossal ancient statues, or shimmering Van Gölü (Lake Van).

Best of all, you can savour these sights without any tourist hustle and bustle. Oh, and southeastern Anatolia has its fair share of gastronomic pleasures (hmmm, pistachio baklavas…).

VAN

☎ 0432 / pop 391,000

Young couples walking hand in hand on the main drag, students flirting in the pastry shops, live bands knocking out Kurdish tunes in pubs, unscarved girls sampling ice cream and daring eye contact with foreigners. Frontier towns never looked so liberal! Van is different in spirit from the rest of southeastern Anatolia – more urban, more casual – and boasts a brilliant location, near the eponymous lake.

Everything you'll need (hotels, restaurants, banks, the PTT and the bus-company offices) lie on or around Cumhuriyet Caddesi, the main commercial street.

SAFETY IN THE EAST

The security situation in southeastern Turkey has improved considerably since it was the epicentre of the Kurdish rebellion during the 1980s and '90s. Although it's always wise to keep your ear to the ground, there is currently little reason to think travellers would suffer anything worse than delays at checkpoints along their way. If there is any trouble, the military will simply not let you get anywhere near it. The only road that was closed at the time of research was the long stretch from Şırnak to Hakkari, on the Iraqi border.

Sights

Van's main claim to fame is its **castle** (admission TL2; 9am-dusk), about 3km west of the city centre, where you'll also find the foundations of **Eski Van** (the old city). The small **Van Museum** (Van Müzesi; Kışla Caddesi; admission TL2; 8am-noon & 1-5pm Tue-Sun) boasts an outstanding collection of Urartian exhibits, with gold jewellery, bronze belts, helmets, horse armour and terracotta figures.

Around the city, Van's 8th-century Armenian rulers took refuge on **Akdamar Island** in Van Gölü (Lake Van) when the Arab armies flooded through from the south. The recently restored Akdamar Kiliseli (Church of the Holy Cross) is one of the wonders of Armenian architecture. The island is a day trip from Van by minibus or the occasional boat.

A slightly longer excursion to the southeast takes you to the spectacular **Hoşap Castle** (admission TL2), a Kurdish castle perched on top of a rocky outcrop. To get to there, catch a Başkale- or Yüksekova-bound minibus on Cumhuriyet Caddesi, and say you want to get out at Hoşap (TL5). After seeing the castle, flag down a bus to Çavuştepe, where you can pick up a bus to Van. Frequent minibuses and buses ply the route.

Sleeping

Otel Aslan (☎ 216 2469; Özel İdare İş Merkezi Karşısı; s TL15-20, d TL20-35) The great central location and budget rates keep this hotel-cum-hostel popular with thrifty backpackers. Cheaper rooms share bathrooms; pray you're not the last in line to shower. No breakfast is served. Don't leave valuables in your room.

Büyük Asur Oteli (☎ 216 8792; asur_asur2008@hotmail.com; Cumhuriyet Caddesi, Turizm Sokak; s/d TL45/75; P) Even if you're on a tight budget, consider spending a little more to enjoy the comforts of this reliable midrange venture. The rooms come complete with fresh linen,

TURKEY

back-friendly beds, TV and well-scrubbed bathrooms. It has an ultra-central location, a vast lobby where you can unwind over a beer, and can organise tours to Akdamar Island and Hoşap Castle.

Otel Akdamar (☎ 214 9923; www.otelakdamar.com; Kazım Karabekir Caddesi; s/d TL60/90; P) The Akdamar has long been a key player on Van's accommodation scene. The location is excellent, the hotel is well organised and amenities are solid, but it needs to move with the times if it's not to be left resting on former glories.

Eating & Drinking

Safa 3, Çorba 1 Paça Salonu (☎ 215 8121; Kazım Karabekir Caddesi; soups TL2; 24hr) Gastronomic adventurers, head to this quirky little restaurant. Regulars swear by the *kelle* (mutton's head); we're happy for them to be the judge! The spicy lentil soup takes you into more traditional culinary territory.

Ayça Pastaneleri (☎ 216 0081; Kazım Karabekir Caddesi; snacks TL2-4) With its see-and-be-seen glass front and modern furnishings, this place lures in students in search of a pleasant spot to flirt and relax over toothsome baklavas and decent snacks.

Akdeniz Tantuni (☎ 216 9010; Cumhuriyet Caddesi; sandwiches TL3) Make a beeline for this delightful little den on the main drag, which prepares devilish chicken sandwiches at low prices.

Halil İbrahim Sofrası (☎ 210 0070; Cumhuriyet Caddesi; mains TL6-12) One word describes this downtown hotspot: yum. The eclectic food is well presented and of high quality, with service and sleek surrounds to match. Ahh, the *İskender kebap:* so rich, so tender.

Barabar Türk Evi (☎ 214 9866; Sanat Sokak) The closest thing Van has to a pub, the Barabar is a rare breed in eastern Turkey. There is a fever-pitch energy with its mainly student crowd of both sexes gulping down pints of frothy draught beer.

YUMMY BREAKFASTS

Van is famed for its tasty *kahvaltı* (breakfast), best tried on pedestrianised Eski Sümerbank Sokak, also called 'Kahvaltı Sokak' (Breakfast St). Here, a row of eateries offers complete Turkish breakfasts (around TL8), including the buzzing **Sütçü Fevzi** (☎ 216 6618; Eski Sümerbank Sokak; 7am-noon) and **Sütçü Kenan** (☎ 216 8499; Eski Sümerbank Sokak; 7am-noon). Sample *otlu peynir* (cheese mixed with a tangy herb, Van's specialty), *beyaz peynir* (a mild yellow cheese), honey from the highlands, olives, *kayma* (clotted cream), butter, tomatoes, cucumbers and *sucuklu yumurta* (omelette with sausage).

Getting There & Away

There are daily flights to/from Ankara and İstanbul with Turkish Airlines and Pegasus Airlines. Sun Express operates weekly flights to/from İzmir and Antalya.

There are also regular daily bus services to Diyarbakır (TL30, seven hours) and morning minibuses to Doğubayazıt (TL10, three hours) via Çaldıran. For services to Iran, see p615.

DİYARBAKIR

☎ 0412 / pop 665,400

Tension, violence? What tension, what violence? Since the 1980s, this animated city has been the centre of the Kurdish resistance movement and violent street demonstrations still occur from time to time. But oh, how things are changing. Filled with soul, heart and character, Diyar has recently begun to tap into its tourism potential. Behind its basalt walls, the old city is crammed full of historical buildings and Arab-style mosques. Stroll along the narrow, twisting alleyways and soak up the ancient ambience.

Banned until a few years ago, the **Nevruz Festival** (21 March) is a great occasion to immerse yourself in Kurdish culture.

Orientation & Information

Most services useful to travellers are in Old Diyarbakır, on or around Gazi Caddesi, including the PTT, internet cafés and banks with ATMs. The **tourist office** (☎ 228 1706; Kapısı; 8am-5pm Mon-Fri) is housed in a tower of the wall. The otogar is some 14km from the centre, on the Urfa road (about TL20 by taxi). The train station is 1.5km west of the centre.

Sights

Diyarbakır's single most conspicuous feature is the old city's 6km circuit of **walls**, probably dating from Roman times. They make a striking sight whether you're walking along the top or the bottom.

Of Diyarbakır's many mosques, the most impressive is the **Ulu Cami** (Gazi Caddesi), built in 1091 by an early Seljuk sultan. The **Nebi Camii** (Gazi Caddesi), at the main intersection of Gazi and İzzet Paşa/İnönü Caddesis, has a quirky detached minaret sporting a stunning combination of black-and-white stone.

Sleeping

Aslan Palas (☎ 228 9224; fax 223 9880; Kıbrıs Caddesi; s/d TL20/30; ❄) A worthwhile backup for cash-strapped (male) travellers. Prices don't include breakfast but you'll find several *kahvaltı salonu* (breakfast eateries) nearby.

Hotel Surkent (☎ 228 1014; İzzet Paşa Caddesi; s/d TL30/45; ❄) Tangerine frames and aluminium plates on the facade, flamingo-pink walls, technicolour bed linen and flashy orange curtains: the owners of the Surkent certainly like your life to be colourful. The top-floor rooms boast good views, it's in a peaceful street and close to everything. One downside: there's no lift.

Hotel Birkent (☎/fax 228 7131/7145; İnönü Caddesi; s/d TL40/60; P ❄ 💻) We saw some female travellers at this mostly hassle-free venture, which is a good sign. Expect neat bathrooms, spotless rooms, turquoise bedspreads, a convenient location and copious breakfast.

our pick **Otel Büyük Kervansaray** (☎/fax 228 7131/7145; Gazi Caddesi; s/d/ste TL80/120/250; P ❄ 🏊) This is your chance to sleep in the 16th-century Deliller Han; a converted caravanserai. It's not the height of luxury, but it scores high on amenities, with a restaurant, a bar, a hamam and a nifty pool.

Eating & Drinking

A stroll along Kıbrıs Caddesi reveals plenty of informal places to eat and tantalising pastry shops.

Şafak Kahvaltı & Yemek Salonu (Kıbrıs Caddesi; mains TL5-8) Nosh on freshly prepared meat dishes and expertly cooked pide in this brisk Diyarbakır institution. It's also a good place for a restorative morning *kahvaltı* (breakfast).

Otel Büyük Kervansaray (☎ 228 7131; Gazi Caddesi; mains TL5-10) Even if you're not staying in this historic hotel it's worth popping in for a meal in the restaurant, a converted camel stable. There's live music here most nights and it's licensed.

our pick **Selim Amca'nın Sofra Salonu** (☎ 224 4447; Ali Emiri Caddesi; mains TL6-12, set menu TL19) This bright eatery outside the city walls is famous for its *kaburga dolması* (lamb or chicken stuffed with rice and almonds). Round it off with a devilish *İrmik helvası* (a gooey dessert).

Şeyhmus Tatlıcısı (Kıbrıs Caddesi; 🕒 7am-8pm) Keep up your strength with a delectable baklava or a sticky *kadayıf*.

Getting There & Away

Diyarbakır is connected with İstanbul and Ankara by daily Turkish Airlines, Onur Air, Sun Express and Pegasus Airlines flights. Pegasus has weekly flights to/from İzmir and Sun Express has weekly flights to/from Antalya, Bursa and İzmir.

Several buses a day link Diyarbakır with Şanlıurfa (TL15, three hours) and Van (TL25, seven hours), among others. For Mardin (TL7, 1¼ hours), take a minibus from the minibus terminal (İlçe Garajı), 1.5km southwest of the city.

To get to Iraq, take a bus to Cizre (TL17, four hours) or Silopi (TL20, five hours) from the main otogar. There are about four services per day. See p615 for more details.

MARDİN

☎ 0482 / pop 55,000

What a beauty! Pretty as a picture, Mardin is a highly addictive, unmissable spot with a fabulous setting, a breathtaking layout and a wealth of architectural treasures. With its minarets poking out of a labyrinth of brown lanes, its castle dominating the old city and the honey-coloured stone houses that trip down the hillside, it emerges like a phoenix from the roasted Mesopotamian plains.

Another draw is the mosaic of people. With Kurdish, Yazidi, Christian and Syrian cultures, among others, it has a fascinating social mix.

Mardin has started to become popular with Turkish travellers. We recommend getting here before it becomes too touristy.

Sights

Strolling through the rambling **bazaar**, keep your eyes open for the ornate **Ulu Cami**, a 12th-century Iraqi Seljuk structure.

Mardin Museum (Mardin Müzesi; admission TL2; 🕒 8am-5pm), prominently positioned on Cumhuriyet Meydanı, is housed in a superbly restored mansion dating from the late 19th century. Back on Cumhuriyet

Caddesi, head east and keep your eyes peeled for the three-arched facade of an ornately carved **house**.

Continue east, looking for steps on the left (north) that lead to the **Sultan İsa Medresesi** (daylight), which dates from 1385 and is the town's prime architectural attraction.

Opposite the post office, housed in a 17th-century caravanserai, you can't miss the minaret of the 14th-century **Şehidiye Camii**. It's superbly carved, with colonnades all around and three small domes superimposed on the summit.

Also worth visiting is the 15th-century **Forty Martyrs Church** (Kırklar Kilisesi; Sağlık Sokak), with the martyrs depicted above the doorway of the church as you enter. If it's closed, bang on the door to alert the caretaker.

The **Kasımiye Medresesi** (1469), 800m south of Yeni Yol, is another must-see. It sports a sublime courtyard walled in by arched colonnades, as well as a magnificent carved doorway.

Sleeping & Eating

Otel Bilem (☎ 213 0315; fax 212 2575; Yenişehir; s/d TL60/120; P) A safe albeit unsexy choice in the new part of Mardin (Yenişehir), 2km northwest of Cumhuriyet Meydanı. Although its facade and lobby have been renovated, the Bilem is no architectural beauty queen, but it's often full to the brim with tour groups.

Artuklu Kervansarayı (☎ 213 7353; www.artuklu.com; Cumhuriyet Caddesi; s/d TL90/140; P) Dark floorboards and furniture, stone walls, sturdy wooden doors: you'll feel like you're in a castle. We're not sure how to take this self-proclaimed 'boutique hotel', but they certainly broke the mould when they conceived the 'medieval' interior.

our pick **Erdoba Konakları** (☎ 212 7677; www.erdoba.com.tr; Cumhuriyet Caddesi; s/d TL100/160; P) Right in the heart of the old town, this serene boutique hotel comprises four finely restored mansions, with lots of period charm. Downside: only five rooms come with a view (but a few terraces look onto the Mesopotamia plain). There's a high-quality onsite restaurant.

our pick **Cercis Murat Konağı** (☎ 213 6841; Cumhuriyet Caddesi; mains TL10-18) The Cercis occupies a traditional Syrian Christian home with two finely decorated rooms and a terrace affording stunning views. Conjured up by local women (there's a TV screen where you can watch them at work in the kitchen), the dainty dishes include *mekbuss* (eggplant pickles with walnut), *kitel raha* (Syrian-style meatballs) and *dobo* (piece of lamb with garlic, spices and black pepper).

Getting There & Away

Turkish Airlines has a daily flight to/from İstanbul and Pegasus Airlines has weekly flights to/from İzmir. There are frequent minibus to Diyarbakır (TL7, 1¼ hours) and, if you are heading to Iraq, Silopli (TL15, three hours) via Cizre. See p615 for more information about the Iraqi border.

ŞANLIURFA (URFA)

☎ 0414 / pop 463,800

Mystical and pious, Şanlıurfa (the Prophets' City) is a spiritual centre *par excellence* and a great pilgrimage town. This is where the prophets Job and Abraham left their marks. As has been the case with centuries of pilgrims before you, the first sight of the Dergah complex of mosques and the holy Gölbaşı area (with the call to prayer as a soundtrack) will be a magical moment that you will remember for a long time to come.

It's also in Urfa that you begin to feel you've reached the Middle East, courtesy of its proximity to Syria. Women cloaked in black chadors elbow their way through the odorous crush of the bazaar streets; moustached gents in *şalvar* (traditional baggy Arabic pants) swill tea and click-clack backgammon pieces in shady courtyards. Welcome to one of Turkey's most exotic cities.

Orientation & Information

Along different stretches, the city's main thoroughfare is called Atatürk, Köprübaşı, Sarayönü and Divan Yolu Caddesis. The otogar is about 1km from the centre (but should be relocated out of town in the near future).

The PTT, most banks with ATMs and internet cafés are on or near the main drag. For tourist information, contact **Harran-Nemrut Tours** (☎ 215 1575, 0542-761 3065; Köprübaşı; ozcan_aslan_teacher@hotmail.com; 8.30am-6pm). The owner speaks very good English.

Sights

Gölbaşı park, surrounded by a complex of mosques, is a symbolic recreation of a legend in which the Islamic prophet Abraham (İbrahim) ended up, quite literally, in a bed of roses after a tussle with Nimrod, the Assyrian king. Pilgrims come to pay their respects, then feed fat, sacred carp in a pool nearby. After doing this, you can explore the wonderful **bazaar**. It's a jumble of streets, some covered, some open, selling everything from sheepskins and pigeons to jeans and handmade shoes.

The **kale** (fortress; admission TL2; 8am-8pm) on Damlacık hill, from which Abraham was supposedly tossed, is Urfa's most striking feature. It looks magnificent when floodlit and can be reached via a flight of stairs or a tunnel cut through the rock. Come up here for unobstructed views over Urfa.

It's also worth visiting the numerous **mosques** dotted in the centre.

About 50km to the southeast, **Harran** is one of the oldest continuously occupied settlements in the world. Its ruined walls, Ulu Cami, crumbling fortress and beehive houses are powerful, evocative sights.

Getting to Harran is straightforward – you don't need to take a tour. Minibuses (TL5, one hour) leave Urfa's otogar approximately every hour and drop you in the new part of Harran near the *belediye* and PTT, a 10-minute walk from the old part. Harran-Nemrut Tours is a good operator if you want to go on a tour.

Sleeping

Otel Doğu (215 1228; Sarayönü Caddesi; s/d TL15/25) The minimalist 'reception' is off-putting, but the rooms are fine for the price, with clean-smelling bathrooms, bare floors, a super-central location and double glazing. Some have shared bathrooms. The catch? No air-con and no fan.

Hotel Bakay (/fax 215 8975/4007; Asfalt Yol Caddesi; s/d TL30/50) A safe bet that won't hurt the pocket, the Bakay is remarkably clean, but be prepared to trip over your backpack in the tiny rooms. Some are brighter than others, so ask to ogle a few before settling in. It's popular with Turkish families: a good sign for female travellers.

Hotel İpek Palas (215 1546; Köprübaşı Dünya Hastanesi Arkası; s/d TL30/50, without bathroom TL20/30) Despite its peeling walls and tatty carpets, the İpek delivers the goods perfectly adequately, with friendly staff, functional bathrooms and an ace location. Breakfast is skimpy, but Zahter Kahvaltı, a good spot to eat on Köprübaşı Caddesi, is nearby.

Hotel Rabis (216 9595; www.hotelrabis.com, in Turkish; Sarayönü Caddesi; s/d TL60/80) Urfa's latest arrival is a model of shiny midrange quality, with thick carpets, flat-screen TVs and double glazing. There's good views from the rooftop terrace, too. One of the best deals in town.

Hotel Arte (314 7060; www.otel-arte.com.tr; Atatürk Bulvarı; s/d TL60/90) Style and sleekness in Urfa? Yes, it's possible. The design-led interior of the Arte features Barbie-esque plastic chairs, laminate floors, contemporary furniture and floor-to-ceiling windows.

Eating & Drinking

It pays to be a bit careful what you eat in Urfa, especially in summer, because the heat makes food poisoning more likely. The city is famed for its atmospheric *konuk evi*, charming 19th-century stone mansions that have been converted into restaurants and, to a lesser extent, hotels.

Hacıbaba Kadayıf (Sarayönü Caddesi; pastries TL2) Back home, don't tell your dietician about the *peynirli kadayıf* (cheese-filled shredded wheat doused in honey) at this little den near the Yusuf Paşa Camii.

our pick **Çift Mağara** (215 9757; Çift Kubbe Altı Balıklıgöl; mains TL4-9) The dining room is directly carved into the rocky bluff that overlooks the Gölbaşı, but the lovely terrace for dining alfresco beats the cavernous interior. It's famed for its delicious *içli köfte*.

Büyükfırat (215 8552; Sarayönü Caddesi; mains TL4-9) With its fountain and breezy outdoor seating, this restaurant-café-fast-food joint is the perfect salve after a day's sightseeing. Nosh on burgers, pizzas, stews and kebaps or slug down a freshly squeezed orange juice.

Cevahir Konuk Evi (215 4678; www.cevahirkonukevi.com; Yeni Mahalle Sokak; mains TL6-10) This *konuk evi* offers excellent tabouleh and faultlessly cooked *tavuk şiş* (chicken kebap). You can also stay the night (single/double TL70/130).

Pinarbaşı Konağı (215 3919; Eylül Caddesi 12; mains TL8-10) Another *konuk evi*, with an eclectic menu of kebaps, grills and stews.

Gülhan Restaurant (313 3318; Atatürk Bulvarı; mains TL6-11) Razor-sharp waiters; well-presented food; the right mood; slick and salubrious surrounds – all good ingredients. The dishes are all pretty good, but if you want a recommendation, go for the Bursa *İskender kebap*.

Head for the *çay bahçesis* in the Gölbaşı park to relax over a cup of tea in leafy surrounds.

Getting There & Away

Turkish Airlines has daily flights to/from Ankara and İstanbul.

Frequent buses connect Şanlıurfa with Gaziantep (TL15, 2½ hours) and Diyarbakır (TL15, three hours). To get to Syria, take a minibus to Akçakale (TL5), then catch a taxi over the border to Talabiyya. The border is open 11am to 3pm on the Syrian side (closed Friday).

MT NEMRUT

Mt Nemrut (Nemrut Dağı; 2150m) is one of the great must-see attractions of eastern Turkey. Two thousand years ago, right on top of the mountain and pretty much in the middle of nowhere, an obscure Commagene king chose to erect fabulous temples and a funerary mound. The fallen heads of the gigantic decorative statues of gods and kings that now lie on the mountain, toppled by earthquakes, form one of Turkey's most enduring images.

Access to Nemrut Dağı Milli Parkı (Mt Nemrut National Park) costs TL5. There are a few possible bases for visiting Mt Nemrut. To the north is Malatya, where the tourist office organises all-inclusive daily minibus tours (TL80, early May to late September/early October), with a sunset visit to the heads, a night at a hotel below the summit and a second, dawn visit.

Alternatively, visit the mountain from the south via Kahta, where sunrise and sunset tours are available. The Kahta trip is notorious for hassles and rip-offs, but this route is more scenic.

Two-day tours (TL120, minimum four people) or sunset/sunrise tours (TL80, minimum four people) are also available from **Harran-Nemrut Tours** (☎ 215 1575, 0542-761 3065; Köprübaşı; ozcan_aslan_teacher@hotmail.com; 8.30am-6pm) in Şanlıurfa.

Some people take a two-day tour (about TL250) from Cappadocia, but it's a tedious drive. If you have enough time, it's better to opt for a three-day tour, which should also include a few stops such as Harran, Şanlıurfa and Gaziantep.

Sleeping

MALATYA

Malatya Büyük Otel (☎ 325 2828; fax 323 2828; Halep Caddesi, Yeni Cami Karşısı; s/d TL35/60;) This sharp-edged monolith wins no awards for character but sports serviceable (if small) rooms with salubrious bathrooms and dashing views of a huge mosque. Location is handy – the bazaar is one block behind – and staff are obliging.

Yeni Hotel (☎ 323 1423; yenihotel@turk.net; Yeni Cami Karşısı Zafer İşhanı; s/d TL35/60;) Quite transparently intended to rival the neighbouring Malatya Büyük, this well-run establishment has rooms in pastel hues, with electric-blue bedspreads.

Grand Akkoza Hotel (☎ 326 2727; www.grandakkozahotel.com; Çevre Yolu Üzeri Adliye Kavşağı; s/d TL75/110;) This glass-fronted three-star venture provides a good level of comfort and service. There's also a hamam, sauna and gym. It's awkwardly placed (if you're not driving) on the busy ring road, but within easy access of the city centre.

KAHTA

In high summer the nicest places to stay, especially if you have your own transport, are not in Kahta itself but on the slopes of the mountain. The final three spots listed here are in Kahta itself, the rest of the options are out of town.

Damlacık Garden Camping (☎ 0416-741 2027; campsites per person TL5;) At Damlacık, about 2km from the junction for the entrance gate of Mt Nemrut National Park.

Arsemia Kafeterya & Kamping (☎ 0416-741 2118, 0505-320 0882; arsemia_52@hotmail.com; campsites per person TL5, d per person TL15) In Eski Kale, about 1km past the entrance gate of the national park.

Karadut Pension (☎ 0416-737 2169; www.karadutpansiyon.net; campsites per person TL5, d per person TL20;) This pension-cum-hostel at the northern end of Karadut has 11 neat rooms (some with air-con), cleanish bathrooms and a kitchen you can use.

Pension Kommagene (☎/fax 725 9726/5548; Mustafa Kemal Caddesi; campsites per person TL7, s/d without breakfast TL35/50;) The most obvious choice for tight-fisted travellers, primarily because of the lack of competitors in this price bracket. Rooms are not flashy but clean, secure and well organised. Add TL6 for breakfast.

Hotel Nemrut (☎ 725 6881; www.hotelnemrut.net; Mustafa Kemal Caddesi; s/d TL45/70; P) Your run-of-the-mill motel, with uninspiring yet well-maintained rooms. Tour groups stop here on their way to Nemrut. A few smiles in reception would sweeten the deal.

Zeus Hotel (☎ 725 5694; www.zeushotel.com.tr; Mustafa Kemal Caddesi; campsites per person TL20, s/d TL80/100; P) Another group-friendly stalwart, this solid three-star option gets an A+ for its swimming pool in the manicured garden. Angle for the renovated rooms, which feature top-notch bathrooms and flat-screen tellies.

GAZİANTEP (ANTEP)

☎ 0342 / pop 1.1 million

Antep is a greatly underrated city that proclaims a modern, laissez-faire attitude while thumbing its nose at Urfa's piety. It's one of the most desirable places to live in eastern Anatolia, with the biggest city park this side of the Euphrates and a buzzing café culture. It also boasts one attraction that makes the trip across Turkey well worth the fare: the Mosaic Museum.

Orientation & Information

The throbbing heart of Gaziantep is the intersection of Atatürk Bulvarı/Suburcu Caddesi and Hürriyet/İstasyon Caddesis, marked by a large statue of Atatürk. Most hotels, banks with ATMs and sights are within walking distance of this intersection. The otogar is about 6km from the town centre. The train station is 800m north.

The **tourist office** (☎ 230 5969; 100 Yıl Atatürk Kültür Parkı İçi; 8am-noon & 1-5pm Mon-Fri) is in the city park.

Sights

The unmissable **kale** (citadel; admission free; 8.30am-4.30pm Tue-Sun) offers superb vistas over the city. Not far south of the citadel is a buzzing bazaar area, which has recently been restored and includes Zincirli Bedesten. Scattered in the centre are numerous old **stone houses** and **caravanserai**, also being restored as part of Gaziantep's ongoing regeneration.

Don't skip the **Gaziantep Museum** (Mosaic Museum; ☎ 324 8809; İstasyon Caddesi; admission TL2; 8.30am-noon & 1-5pm Tue-Sun), with its display of fabulous mosaics unearthed at the rich Roman site of Belkıs-Zeugma.

Sleeping

Gaziantep is rolling in accommodation, much of it on or near Suburcu, Hürriyet and Atatürk Caddesis.

Yunus Hotel (☎ 221 1722; hotelyunus@hotel.com; Kayacık Sokak; s/d TL30/50; P) As far as physical beauty goes, this a real plain Jane, but it's a secure spot to hang your rucksack, the rates are good and it's handily set in the centre of town.

Hotel Veliç (☎ 221 2212; www.velicotel.com; Atatürk Bulvarı; s/d TL35/55; P) A recent lick of paint (yellow and lilac) has elevated this concrete lump on the main drag a couple of notches up the comfort ladder. The rooms are on the small side, but top marks go to the bright top-floor breakfast area.

Yesemek Otel (☎ 220 8888; www.yesemekotel.com; İsmail Sokak; s/d TL50/70; P) Bang in the thick of things, this well-regarded pile offers great service and facilities, including a restaurant and a private *otopark*, although its executive look doesn't really scream 'holidays'.

our pick **Anadolu Evleri** (☎ 220 9525, 0533-558 7996; www.anadoluevleri.com; Köroğlu Sokak; s/d TL105/135, 1-/2-person ste TL135/170;) A tastefully restored old stone house in a lovely position, this oasis celebrates local tradition: a beguiling courtyard, beamed or painted ceilings, mosaic floors, secret passageways, and antique furniture and artefacts. It's spitting distance from the bustling bazaar, yet it feels quiet and restful.

Eating & Drinking

This fast-paced and epicurean city is reckoned to harbour more than 180 pastry shops and to produce the best *fıstık* (pistachio) baklavas you can gobble down in Turkey, if not in the world.

Çavuşoğlu (☎ 231 3069; Eski Saray Caddesi; mains TL4-8) This sprightly outfit rustles up dishes that will fill your tummy without emptying your wallet. Portions are copious, the meat is perfectly slivered and the salads are fresh.

our pick **İmam Çağdaş** (☎ 231 2678; Kale Civarı Uzun Çarşı; mains TL4-10) This talismanic pastry shop and restaurant is run by Imam Çağdaş, our culinary guru, who concocts wicked pistachio baklavas that are delivered daily to customers throughout Turkey. And if there was a kebap Oscar awarded, this place would also be a serious contender.

Çulcuoğlu Et Lokantasi (☎ 231 0241; Kalender Sokak; mains TL5-10; 11.30am-10pm Mon-Sat) Just

TURKEY

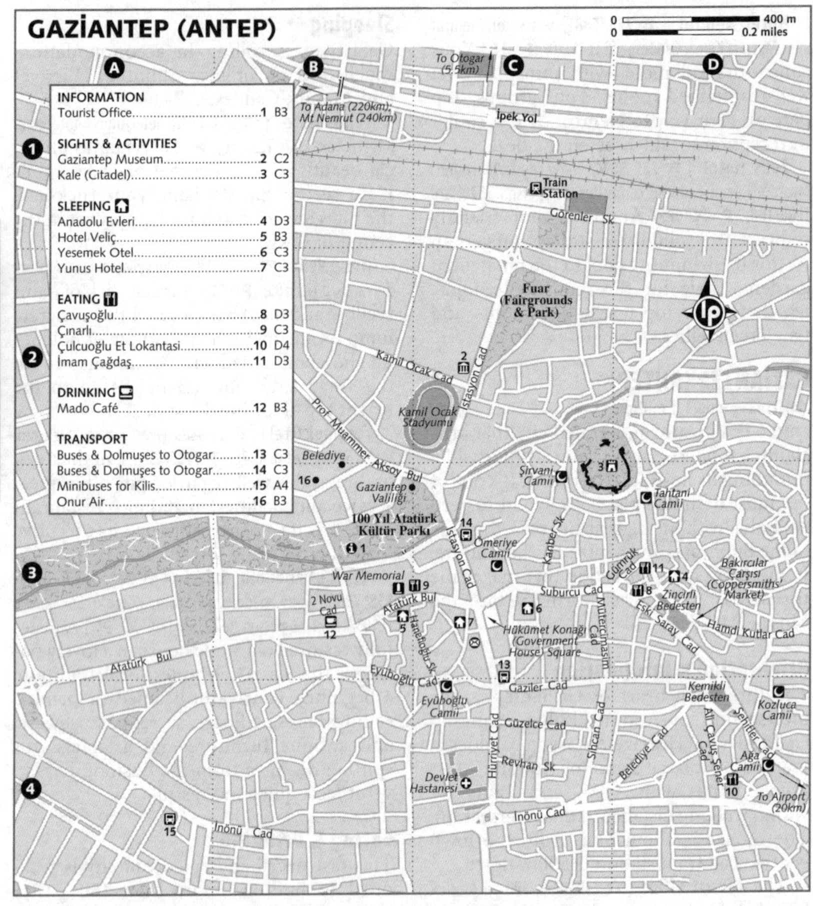

surrender helplessly to your inner carnivore at this Gaziantep institution. The yummy kebaps are the way to go, but grilled chicken also puts in menu appearances. Don't be discouraged by the unremarkable entrance.

Çınarlı (☎ 221 2155; Çınarlı Sokak; mains TL4-11) The Çınarlı has long enjoyed a great reputation for its *yöresel yemeks* (traditional dishes). Choose between three small rooms, decorated with rugs, weapons and other collectibles, and a bigger dining room, where you can enjoy live music in the afternoon.

Mado Café (☎ 221 1500; Atatürk Bulvarı) The super-slick Mado is *the* place to meet Gaziantep's movers and shakers in a smart setting. You can nosh on snacks (mains TL7 to TL9) and sip fruity cocktails, but the pastries and ice creams make the place tick.

Getting There & Away

Turkish Airlines has daily flights to/from Ankara and İstanbul. Onur Air and Pegasus also serve İstanbul, Sun Express serves İzmir and Cyprus Turkish Airlines has a weekly flight to London Stansted.

From the otogar you can reach many destinations, including Şanlıurfa (TL15, 2½ hours) and Antakya (TL18, four hours).

There's no direct bus to Syria; you'll have to go to Kilis first, then taxi to the border or to Aleppo. Minibuses to Kilis (TL6, 65km) leave every 20 minutes or so from a separate *garaj* (minibus terminal) on İnönü Caddesi.

To get to Aleppo and Damascus by train, you'll need to go to İslahiye to catch the twice-weekly train to Syria.

TURKEY DIRECTORY

ACCOMMODATION

Camping

Camping facilities are dotted about Turkey, although sometimes not as frequently as you might hope. Some hotels and pensions will also let you camp in their grounds for a small fee, and they sometimes have facilities especially for campers.

Hostels

Given that pensions are so cheap, Turkey has no real hostel network. The best place to find hostels are backpacker hangouts such as Göreme, where many pensions offer dormitories and hostel-style facilities.

Pensions & Hotels

Most tourist resorts offer simple, family-run pensions where you can get a good, clean single room from around TL20 a night (and a dorm bed from around TL10). Pensions are often cosy and represent better value than full-blown hotels. These places usually offer a choice of simple meals (including breakfast), laundry services, international TV services and so on, and it's these facilities that really distinguish them from traditional small, cheap hotels. Many pensions also have staff who speak English.

In most cities there is a variety of old and new hotels, which range from the depressingly basic to full-on luxury. The cheapest nonresort hotels (around TL30 a night per person) are mostly used by working Turkish men travelling on business and are not always suitable for lone women, as they may face stares whenever they enter the lobby. Moving up a price bracket, one- and two-star hotels vary from TL70 to TL120 for a double room with shower – these hotels are less oppressively masculine in atmosphere, even when the clientele remains mainly male.

If you fancy top-notch accommodation at reasonable prices, Turkey is the place to do it. Boutique hotels are all the rage in the country. Increasingly, old Ottoman mansions and other historic buildings are being refurbished or completely rebuilt as hotels equipped with all the mod cons and bags of character. The best boutique hotels are located in İstanbul, Cappadocia, Safranbolu and Amasya, but almost every city boasts some character-filled establishments.

In tourist-dependent areas such as the coast and Cappadocia, many hotels close from November to April. Some stay open, but your choices will still be diminished. One consolation is that rates fall in winter.

Unless otherwise stated, breakfast and private bathrooms are included in the room rates quoted in this book. Dorms in İstanbul often have shared bathrooms. Some spots offer half-board accommodation, which includes bed, breakfast and one main meal, and this is stated in the review.

Tree Houses

Olympos, on the coast southwest of Antalya, is famous for its 'tree houses', wooden shacks of minimal comfort in forested settings near the beach. Increasingly, these basic shelters are being converted into chalets with more comfort.

PRACTICALITIES

- For the news in English, pick up the *Turkish Daily News*. The APA Group's guides to İstanbul, Ankara, Bodrum and Antalya, which retail at tourist gathering points, feature listings and articles.
- TRT3 (Türkiye Radyo ve Televizyon) provides short news broadcasts in English, French and German, and can be found on 88.2MHz, 91.6MHz, 92.8MHz, 94MHz or 99MHz depending on where you are in the country. BBC World Service broadcasts on 12095kHz in İstanbul.
- Digiturk offers hundreds of Turkish and international TV channels, including CNN International and BBC World.
- The electrical current is 220V AC, 50Hz. Wall sockets are the round, two-pin European type.
- Turkey uses the metric system for weights and measures.

RESIST THE TOUTS!

In smaller tourist towns such as Fethiye, Pamukkale and Selçuk, touts for the pensions may accost you as you step from your bus and string you whatever line they think will win you over. Of course they are after a commission from the owner. Taxi drivers often like to play this game too. Avoid letting these faux friends make your choices for you by deciding where you want to stay and sticking to your guns.

ACTIVITIES

Popular activities include hiking and trekking in the Kaçkar Mountains and southern Cappadocia's Ala Dağlar National Park. Another popular stroll is the Lycian Way, a 30-day, 509km walk around the coast and mountains of Lycia, starting at Fethiye and finishing near Antalya. The spectacular valleys of central Cappadocia are also excellent for hiking. If you're a serious hiker you could consider conquering Turkey's highest mountain, the 5137m-high Mt Ararat (p599) near Doğubayazıt, but you need a permit.

All sorts of watersports, including diving, waterskiing, rafting and kayaking, are available on the Aegean and Mediterranean coasts. The best diving is offered off Kaş (p576), Bodrum (p567) and Marmaris (p570). You can also try tandem paragliding at Ölüdeniz (p574).

Skiing is becoming more popular, with the best facilities at Palandöken, near Erzurum (p596), and the most scenic runs at conifer-studded Sarıkamış (p598), near Kars. However, their facilities do not meet the standards of the better European resorts.

Those of a lazier disposition may want to take a gület (traditional wooden yacht) trip along the Mediterranean coast, stopping off to swim in bays along the way (p573).

The laziest 'activity' of all consists of paying a visit to a hamam (p545), where you can get yourself scrubbed and massaged for a fraction of what it would cost in most Western countries.

BUSINESS HOURS

Government and business offices, and banks usually open from 8.30am to noon and 1.30pm to 5pm Monday to Friday. Main post offices in large cities are open every day. Smaller post offices may be closed on Saturday afternoon and all day Sunday. During the hot summer months the working day in some cities begins at 7am or 8am and finishes at 2pm.

The working day gets shortened during the holy month of Ramazan (Ramadan), and more-Islamic cities such as Konya and Kayseri virtually shut down during noon prayers on Friday. Apart from that, Friday is a normal working day in Turkey. The day of rest, a secular one, is Sunday.

In tourist areas food, souvenir and carpet shops are often open virtually around the clock. Elsewhere, shops are open 9am to 6pm Monday to Saturday, and markets often get going earlier than that. Shopkeepers generally don't close for lunch, even if it means munching on a kebap behind their counter.

CUSTOMS REGULATIONS

Two hundred cigarettes and 50 cigars or 200g of tobacco, and five 1L or seven 700mL bottles of alcohol can be imported duty free.

It's strictly illegal to export antiquities. Customs officers spot-check luggage and will want proof that you have permission from a museum before letting you leave with an antique carpet.

DANGERS & ANNOYANCES

Although Turkey is one of the safest countries in the region, you must take precautions. Conceal your money in a safe place (such as a discreet money belt, or loose in a zippable shirt pocket) and be wary of pickpockets on buses, in markets and in other crowded places. Keep an eye out for anyone suspicious lurking near ATMs.

In İstanbul, single men are sometimes approached in areas such as Sultanahmet and Taksim and lured to a bar by new 'friends'. The scammers may be accompanied by a fig leaf of a woman. The victim is then made to pay an outrageous bill, regardless of what he drank. Drugging is also a problem, especially for lone men. Again, it most commonly happens in İstanbul, and involves so-called friends, a bar and perhaps a willowy temptress. Sometimes on the bus, the person in the seat next to you buys you a drink, slips a drug into it and then makes off with your luggage. So be a tad wary of who you befriend, especially when you're new to the country.

More commonly, the hard-sell tactics of carpet sellers can drive you to distraction. Despite their idyllic appearances, tourist hotspots are driven by foreign spenders and there is often no such thing as a free kebap. 'Free' lifts and other cheap services often lead to near-compulsory visits to carpet showrooms or hotel commission for touts.

Travelling in the southeast is now safe, although roads do close due to military activity against the PKK (PKK/Kongra-Gel) rebels in the mountains on the Iraqi border. When we visited, the only road that was closed to foreigners was between Hakkari and Şırnak. For more information, see p601.

EMBASSIES & CONSULATES

Foreign embassies are in Ankara but many countries also have consulates in İstanbul. In general they are open from 9am to noon Monday to Friday, and some open in the afternoon. For more information, visit http://tinyurl.com/6ywt8a.

Australia Ankara (☎ 0312-459 9521; www.embaustralia.org.tr; 7th fl, Uğur Mumcu Caddesi 88, Gaziosmanpaşa); İstanbul (☎ 0212-243 1333; 2nd fl, Suzer Plaza, Asker Ocağı Caddesi 15, Elmadağ)

Bulgaria (☎ 0312-467 2071; Atatürk Bulvarı 124, Kavaklıdere, Ankara)

Canada (☎ 0312-409 2700; Cinnah Caddesi 58, Çankaya, Ankara)

Egypt Ankara (☎ 0312-426 1026; fax 427 0099; Atatürk Bulvarı 126, Kavaklıdere); İstanbul (☎ 212-324 2180; Akasyalı Sokak 26, 4 Levent)

France Ankara (☎ 0312-455 4545; Paris Caddesi 70, Kavaklıdere); İstanbul (Map pp546-7; ☎ 0212-334 8730; İstiklal Caddesi 8, Taksim)

Germany Ankara (☎ 0312-455 5100; Atatürk Bulvarı 114, Kavaklıdere); İstanbul (Map pp546-7; ☎ 0212-334 6100; İnönü Caddesi 16-18, Taksim)

Greece Ankara (☎ 0312-448 0873; greekemb@superonline.com; Zia Ur Rahman Caddesi 9-11, Gaziosmanpaşa); Edirne (☎ 0284-235 5804; Nolu Caddesi 2); İstanbul (Map pp546-7; ☎ 0212-245 0596; Turnacıbaşı Sokak 32, Galatasaray)

Iran Ankara (☎ 0312-427 4320; Tahran Caddesi 10, Kavaklıdere); Erzurum (☎ 0442-315 9983; fax 316 1182; Alparslan Bulvarı, 201 Sokak); İstanbul (Map pp542-3; ☎ 0212-513 8230; 2nd fl, Ankara Caddesi 1, Cağaloğlu)

Iraq (☎ 0312-468 7421; fax 468 4832; Turan Emeksiz Sokak 11, Gaziosmanpaşa, Ankara)

Ireland Ankara (☎ 0312-446 6172; fax 446 8061; Uğur Mumcu Caddesi, MNG Binasi B-Bl 88/3, Gaziosmanpaşa); İstanbul (☎ 0212-482 2434; fax 482 0943; Ali Riza Gurcan Caddesi 2/13, Merter)

Israel Ankara (☎ 0312-459 7500; fax 459 7555; Mahatma Gandhi Caddesi 85, 06700 Gaziosmanpaşa); İstanbul (☎ 212-317 6500; Yapı Kredi Plaza, Blok C, Kat 7, Levent)

Jordan (☎ 0312-440 2054; fax 440 4327; Mesnevi Dede Korkut Sokak 18, Çankaya, Ankara)

Lebanon Ankara (☎ 0312-446 7485; fax 446 1023; Kıkulesi Sokak 44, Gaziosmanpaşa); İstanbul (☎ 0212-236 1365; fax 227 3373; Teşvikiye Caddesi 134/1, Teşvikiye)

Netherlands Ankara (☎ 0312-409 1800; fax 409 1898; Hollanda Caddesi No 3, Yıldız); İstanbul (Map pp546-7; ☎ 0212-393 2121; fax 292 5031; İstiklal Caddesi 393, Tünel)

New Zealand Ankara (☎ 0312-467 9054; www.nzembassy.com/turkey; 4th fl, İran Caddesi 13, Kavaklıdere); İstanbul (☎ 0212-244 0272; nzhonconist@hatem-law.com.tr; 3rd fl, İnönü Caddesi 48, Taksim)

Russia Ankara (☎ 0312-439 2122; www.turkey.mid.ru; Karyağdi Sokak 5, Çankaya); İstanbul (Map pp546-7; ☎ 0212-292 5101; visavi@turk.net; İstiklal Caddesi 443, Beyoğlu)

Syria Ankara (☎ 0312-440 9657; fax 438 5609; Abdullah Cevdet Sokak 7, Çankaya); İstanbul (Map pp538-9; ☎ 0212-232 6721; Maçka Caddesi 59, Ralli Apt 3, Nişantaşı)

UK Ankara (☎ 0312-455 3344; fax 455 3320; Şehit Ersan Caddesi 46a, Çankaya); İstanbul (Map pp546-7; ☎ 0212-334 6400; fax 334 6401; Meşrutiyet Caddesi 34, Tepebaşı, Beyoğlu)

USA Ankara (☎ 0312-455 5555; fax 467 0019; Atatürk Bulvarı 110, Kavaklıdere); İstanbul (☎ 0212-335 9000; fax 335 9102; Kaplıcalar Mevkii 2, İstinye)

FESTIVALS & EVENTS

Following are some of the major annual festivals and events in Turkey:

Anzac Day The WWI battles at Gallipoli are commemorated with dawn services on 25 April.

International İstanbul Music Festival Held from early June to early July in İstanbul.

Kırkpınar Oil Wrestling Championship Huge crowds watch oil-covered men wrestling in a field near Edirne in late June or early July.

Mevlâna Festival The dervishes whirl in Konya from 10 to 17 December.

Nevruz Festival Kurds and Alevis celebrate the ancient Middle Eastern spring festival on 21 March. Banned until recent years, Nevruz is now an official holiday.

Note that for the week-long festival of Kurban Bayramı (Eid al-Adha) at the end of November, hotels are jam-packed, banks close and transport is booked up weeks ahead. See also Holidays, p612.

GAY & LESBIAN TRAVELLERS

Although not uncommon in a culture that traditionally separates men and women, overt homosexuality is not socially acceptable except in a few small pockets in İstanbul, Bodrum and other resorts. In İstanbul there is an increasing number of openly gay bars and nightclubs, mainly around the Taksim Sq end of İstiklal Caddesi. Some hamams are known to be gay meeting places.

For more information, contact Turkey's own gay and lesbian support group, **Lambda İstanbul** (www.lambdaistanbul.org).

HOLIDAYS

As well as the major Islamic holidays (see p628), Turkey observes the following national holidays:

New Year's Day 1 January
Children's Day 23 April
Youth & Sports Day 19 May
Victory Day 30 August
Republic Day 29 October
Anniversary of Atatürk's Death 10 November

INTERNET ACCESS

Wherever you go, you'll never be far from an internet café. Fees are generally TL1 to TL2 for an hour. Throughout the country, hotels of all standards typically offer free wi-fi access, as do many restaurants and cafés. In accommodation listings, we have used the internet icon where the hotel provides a computer with internet access for guest use.

LANGUAGE

Turkish is the official language and almost everyone understands it. It's been written in the Latin script since Atatürk rejected Arabic in 1928. In southeastern Anatolia, most Kurds speak Turkish, but in remote places you'll hear Kurmancı and Zazakı, the two Kurdish dialects spoken in Turkey. South of Gaziantep you'll also hear Arabic being spoken alongside Turkish.

For words and phrases in Turkish, see p666.

MAPS

Turkish tourist offices supply an excellent free *Tourist Map* (1:850,000), plus local maps.

MONEY

Turkish lira (TL) comes in notes of five, 10, 20, 50 and 100, and one lira coins. One Turkish lira is worth 100 kuruş, which is available in one, five, 10, 25 and 50 kuruş coins. The Turkish lira superseded the new Turkish lira (YTL) in January 2009. After 31 December 2009, new Turkish lira notes and the associated kuruş coins will no longer be accepted for payment, but can be exchanged for the new currency at branches of the bank Türkiye Ziraat Bankasi.

Inflation is an ongoing problem in Turkey and many businesses quote prices in the more-stable euro. We have used both lira and euros in listings, according to the currency quoted by the business in question.

Below are the exchange rates for a range of currencies when this book went to print.

Country	Unit	Turkish lira (TL)
Australia	A$1	1.03
Canada	C$1	1.30
Euro zone	€1	2.02
Japan	¥100	1.68
New Zealand	NZ$1	0.90
Syria	S£10	0.33
UK	UK£1	2.31
USA	US$1	1.56

ATMs

ATMs readily dispense Turkish lira to Visa, MasterCard, Cirrus, Maestro and Eurocard holders; there's hardly a town without a machine. Some tellers also dispense euros and US dollars. Provided that your home bank card only requires a four-digit personal identification number (PIN), it's possible to get around Turkey with nothing else. But remember to draw out money in the towns to tide you through the villages, and keep some cash in reserve for the inevitable day when the ATM decides to throw a wobbly.

Note that some overseas banks charge an arm and a leg for the conversion – check before you leave home.

Cash

US dollars and euros are the easiest currencies to change, although many banks and exchange offices will change other major currencies such as UK pounds and Japanese yen. You may find it difficult to exchange Australian or Canadian currency, except at banks and offices in major cities.

Credit Cards

Visa and MasterCard are widely accepted by hotels, restaurants, carpet shops etc, although many pensions and local restaurants do not accept them outside the main tourist areas. You can also get cash advances on these cards. Amex cards are not accepted as often.

Moneychangers

It's easy to change major currencies in most exchange offices, some PTTs, shops and hotels, although banks may make heavy weather of it. Places that don't charge a commission usually offer a worse exchange rate instead.

Foreign currencies are readily accepted in shops, hotels and restaurants in main tourist areas. Taxi drivers accept foreign currencies for big journeys, which may drive down the price if the exchange rate is working in your favour.

Tipping

Turkey is fairly European in its approach to tipping and you won't be pestered by demands for baksheesh, as elsewhere in the Middle East. Leave waiters and bath attendants around 10% of the bill; in restaurants, check a tip hasn't been automatically added to the bill. It's normal to round off metered taxi fares.

Travellers Cheques

Banks, shops and hotels often see it as a burden to change travellers cheques and will probably try to get you to go elsewhere or charge a premium. In case you do have to change them, try Akbank.

POST

The base rate for sending postcards and letters to Europe is TL0.85; TL0.90 to Australia, New Zealand and the USA. Parcels sent by surface mail to Europe cost around TL40 for the first 1kg, then TL12 per extra kg; to North America, Australia and New Zealand, TL58 for the first 1kg, then TL17 per extra kg.

Turkish *postanes* (post offices) are indicated by black-on-yellow 'PTT' signs.

Most central post offices in tourist areas offer a poste restante service.

TELEPHONE & FAX

Türk Telekom payphones can be found in many major public buildings and facilities, public squares and transportation termini. International calls can be made from payphones.

Türk Telekom centres have faxes, but using them requires lots of paperwork and they may insist on retaining your original! It's easier to use your hotel fax, although you should always check the cost first.

Mobile Phones

The Turks just love *cep* (mobile) phones. But calling a mobile costs roughly three times the cost of calling a landline, no matter where you are. Mobile phone numbers start with a four-figure code beginning with ☎ 05. If you set up a roaming facility with your home phone provider, you should be able to connect your own mobile to the Turkcell or Telsim network.

If you buy a Turkcell (the most comprehensive network) SIM card and use it in your home mobile, the network detects and bars foreign phones within a fortnight. Removing your phone from the blacklist requires a convoluted bureaucratic process. You can pick up a basic mobile phone for about TL50, or get one thrown in with the SIM card for a little extra. New Turkcell credit is readily available at shops displaying the company's blue-and-yellow logo, found on every street corner.

Phone Codes

The country code for Turkey is ☎ 90, followed by the local area code (minus the zero), then the seven-digit subscriber number. Local area codes are given at the start of each city or town section in this book. Note that İstanbul has two codes: ☎ 0212 for the European side and ☎ 0216 for the Asian side. The international access code (to call abroad from Turkey) is ☎ 00.

Phonecards

All Türk Telekom's public telephones require phonecards, which can be bought at telephone centres or, for a small mark-up, at some shops. If you're only going to make one quick call, it's easier to look for a booth with a sign saying '*köntörlü telefon*', where the cost of your call will be metered.

TOILETS

Most hotels and public facilities have toilets that are Western-style, but you'll sometimes see squat toilets. Carry toilet paper and place it in the bin, if one is provided, to avoid inadvertently flooding the premises.

Almost all public toilets require a payment of about 50 kuruş.

VISAS

Nationals of the following countries don't need to obtain a visa when visiting Turkey for up to three months: Denmark, Finland, France, Germany, Ireland, Israel, Italy, Japan, New Zealand, Sweden and Switzerland. Although nationals of Australia, Austria, Belgium, Canada, the Netherlands, Norway (one month only), Portugal, Spain, the UK and the USA need a visa, this is just a stamp in the passport that you buy on arrival at the airport or at an overland border, rather than at an embassy in advance.

Make sure you join the queue to buy your visa before joining the one for immigration. How much you pay depends on your nationality; at the time of writing, Australians and Americans paid US$20 (or €15), Canadians US$60 (or €45), and British citizens UK£10 (or €15 or US$20). You *must* pay in hard currency cash. The customs officers expect to be paid in one of these curriencies and may not accept Turkish lira. They also don't give any change.

The standard visa is valid for three months and, depending on your nationality, usually allows for multiple entries. Your passport must be valid for at least six months from the date you enter the country.

For details of visas for other Middle Eastern countries, see p633 and the Visas sections in the Directory of the other country chapters.

In theory, a Turkish visa can be renewed once after three months, but the bureaucracy and costs involved mean that it's much easier to leave the country (usually to a Greek island) and then come back in again on a fresh visa.

WOMEN TRAVELLERS

Some women travel around virtually unmolested while others report constant harassment. Whatever your own experience and feeling, your best bet is to dress modestly and be sensitive to the society's customs. Cover the upper legs and arms and avoid shorts or skimpy T-shirts, except in the resorts. Provided you stick to these recommendations, most men will treat you with kindness and generosity. Wearing a wedding ring and carrying a photo of your 'husband' and 'child' will help immeasurably, as can wearing dark glasses to avoid eye contact.

Men and unrelated women are not expected to sit beside each other in long-distance buses, and lone women are often assigned seats at the front, near the driver.

Women can sit where they like in eateries in tourist areas. Elsewhere, restaurants that aim to attract women often set aside a section for families. Look for the term *aile salonu* (family dining room). The same applies to *çay bahçesi* (tea gardens).

TRANSPORT IN TURKEY

GETTING THERE & AWAY

Entering Turkey

For information on Turkish visas and entry requirements, see left.

Air

Turkey's most important airport is İstanbul's **Atatürk International Airport** (IST; Atatürk Hava Limanı; off Map pp538-9; ☎ 0212-465 5555; www.ataturkairport.com), 25km west of the city centre. The cheapest fares are almost always to İstanbul, and to reach other Turkish airports, even Ankara, you often have to transit in İstanbul. Other international airports are at Adana, Ankara, Antalya, Bodrum, Dalaman and İzmir.

Turkey's national carrier is **Turkish Airlines** (THY; Türk Hava Yolları; Map pp538-9; ☎ 0212-252 1106; www.thy.com), which has direct flights from İstanbul to most capital cities around the world, including Beirut, Cairo, Damascus, Dubai, Jeddah, Kuwait, Riyadh, Tehran and

SMUGGLING TROUBLE *Jean-Bernard Carillet*

One of the Turkish taxi drivers waiting on the Iraqi side of the border with Turkey (at the Ibrahim Khalil border post) offered to drive us to Silopi, and while we were at the immigration counter, he returned to his car and stuffed our backpack with smuggled cigarettes. Smuggling is taken very seriously by Turkish customs, and officers searched all cars and scanned luggage. Luckily, we discovered the contraband and avoided a *Midnight Express* scenario. The moral of the story: never leave your luggage unattended.

Tripoli in the Middle East. Turkish Airlines also recently began flying to Iraqi Kurdistan five times a week. It has a good safety record.

Other airlines flying to and from Turkey:

Air France (AF; ☎ 0212-310 1919; www.airfrance.com; İstanbul) Hub: Paris Charles de Gaulle Airport.

American Airlines (AA; ☎ 0212-237 2003; www.aa.com; İstanbul) Hub: Dallas/Fort Worth Airport.

Azerbaijan Airlines (AHY; ☎ 0212-296 3733; www.azal.az; İstanbul) Hub: Baku Airport.

British Airways (BA; ☎ 0212-317 6600; www.britishairways.com; İstanbul) Hub: Heathrow Airport, London.

Emirates Airlines (EK; ☎ 0212-315 4545; www.emirates.com; İstanbul) Hub: Dubai Airport.

Iran Air (IR; ☎ 0212-225 0255; www.iranair.com; İstanbul) Hub: Tehran Mehrabad Airport.

KLM (KL; ☎ 0212-230 0311; www.klm.com; İstanbul) Hub: Amsterdam Schipol Airport.

Lufthansa (LH; ☎ 0212-315 3400; www.lufthansa.com; İstanbul) Hub: Frankfurt Airport.

Olympic Airways (OA; ☎ 0212-296 7575; www.olympicairlines.com; İstanbul) Hub: Athens Airport.

Qantas Airways (QF; ☎ 0212-325 5536; www.qantas.com; İstanbul) Hub: Sydney Airport.

Singapore Airlines (SIA; ☎ 0212-463 1800; www.singaporeair.com; İstanbul) Hub: Singapore Changi Airport.

Land

Turkey shares borders with Armenia, Azerbaijan, Bulgaria, Georgia, Greece, Iran, Iraq and Syria. There are plenty of ways to get into and out of the country by rail or bus. For details on getting to Turkey from countries outside the Middle East, see p641.

IRAN

There are regular buses from İstanbul and Ankara to Tabriz and Tehran. You may also want to consider taking a dolmuş from Doğubayazıt, 35km east of the border at Gürbulak, for about TL5, and then walking across the border. The crossing might take up to an hour. From Bazargan there are onward buses to Tabriz; from Sero there are buses to Orumiyeh. You can catch buses to Iran from Van.

By train, the *Trans-Asya Ekspresi* leaves İstanbul every Wednesday and arrives two nights later in Tehran (TL111.20), travelling via Ankara, Kayseri and Van before crossing the border at Kapikoi/Razi and stopping in Salmas, Tabriz and Zanjan. The journey involves a five-hour ferry crossing of Lake Van. See the Iranian Railways site, **RAJA Passenger Train Co** (www.rajatrains.com), for more information about this service and the train from Tehran to Damascus (Syria), which passes through Van and across the lake.

For more information about travel to Iran, see p642.

IRAQ

Crossing the Turkish–Iraqi border at Habur, 15km southeast of Silopi (reached by bus from Mardin or Diyarbakır via Cizre), is surprisingly straightforward and safe. At Silopi's otogar, you'll soon realise that the crossing is a well-organised business that's in the hands of the local taxi mafia. For TL60 (or the equivalent in euros or US dollars), a taxi driver will handle all formalities

TURKEY

JUST ACROSS THE BORDER: AMADIYA, IRAQ

Across the border from southeastern Anatolia is an Iraqi reflection of this Kurdish corner of Turkey. Iraqi Kurdistan (p226) shows a positive side of the troubled country. Beneath snow-capped peaks, construction engineers are giving substance to the region's slogan, 'The Other Iraq'. In the village of Amadiya (p230), several fine churches, a 400-year-old mosque and a huge marble gate sit on a mountain plateau.

Iraq is still a dangerous country and you should read our warning, p213 before considering visiting. The good news, if you decide to go for it, is that crossing the Turkey–Iraq border at Habur (Ibrahim Khalil border post) is surprisingly painless (see above). It can take less than an hour.

To get to nearby Silopi, catch one of the frequent buses from Mardin (p604) or Diyarbakır (p603) via Cizre. On the other side of the border, taxis wait to run you to the provincial capital, Dohuk (p227), 90km southwest of Amadiya.

The Kurdish Regional Government issues its own tourist visa, which is good for travelling within Iraqi Kurdistan only. Citizens of most countries, including the USA, Australia and New Zealand as well the EU, are automatically issued a free, 10-day tourist visa at the point of entry. Extensions are available; see p245 for more information.

JUST ACROSS THE BORDER: ALEPPO (HALAB), SYRIA

Why cross the border to Syria when there's so much to see in southeast Turkey? The answer is simple: the world's longest roofed market. Beneath their vaulted stone ceilings, Aleppo's labyrinthine souqs (p494) are a window-shopping opportunity for every sense. Several hectares of traders push everything from plastic trinkets to the same goods that camels once transported along the Silk Road.

Getting to Aleppo is considerably faster than it was in those caravanserai days, with two direct daily buses from Antakya (see p583 for travel information).

Traffic builds up at the Reyhanlı/Bab al-Hawa border crossing to Syria, so try to pass through before 8am or take a taxi (Antakya to Aleppo TL60), which can weave between stationary vehicles.

From southeastern Anatolia, it's not quite as easy to cross into Syria. If you're starting the trip in Gaziantep, you'll need to go to İslahiye to catch the train or to Kilis to pick up a taxi; see p608. From Şanlıurfa, take a minibus to Akçakale and catch a taxi over the border; see p606 for more information.

All foreigners need a visa to enter Syria (p523). Getting a single-entry visitor visa (€20) is a straightforward, same-day process at the embassy in Ankara or İstanbul (p611); you need two passport photos. Do not leave the application until the border.

up to the Iraqi border post. After the Turkish customs post, the taxi drives you to the Ibrahim Khalil border post (the Iraqi side; p246), over the bridge on the Tigris. Here you might be asked where you are staying in Iraq – be honest and clear. It can help if you have an Iraqi contact. Then you can take one of the Iraqi (well, Kurdish) taxis that wait in a car park just outside customs, and head to nearby Zakho or the provincial capital, Dohuk.

SYRIA

There are eight border posts between Syria and Turkey, but the border at Reyhanlı/Bab al-Hawa is by far the most convenient, and therefore the busiest. Daily buses link Antakya in Turkey with the Syrian cities of Aleppo (Halab; TL6, four hours) and Damascus (TL11, eight hours). Also close to Antakya is the border post at Yayladağı, convenient for Lattakia (Syria). Other popular crossings to Syria include via Kilis, 65km south of Gaziantep; the Akçakale border, 54km south of Şanlıurfa; and the Nusaybin–Qamishle border 75km east of Mardin.

It's possible to buy bus tickets direct from İstanbul to Aleppo or Damascus, with buses leaving daily. A better option is the very comfortable *Toros Ekspresi* train, which departs İstanbul on Sunday morning for Aleppo (TL101.20, 30 hours) via Adana, Konya and Eskişehir. Several comfortable trains link Aleppo and Damascus daily.

Sea

Turkey has passenger-ship connections with Greece, Italy and northern Cyprus. For details see p644.

GETTING AROUND

Air

The state-owned **Turkish Airlines** (THY; Türk Hava Yolları; Map pp538-9; ☎ 0212-252 1106; www.thy.com) connects all the major cities and resorts, via its two main hubs, İstanbul and Ankara.

The most useful destinations for travellers include Ağrı (for Doğubayazıt), Ankara, Antalya, Bodrum, Dalaman (for Marmaris), Diyarbakır, Erzurum, Gaziantep, İstanbul, İzmir, Kars, Kayseri, Konya, Mardin, Şanlıurfa, Trabzon and Van. You can buy tickets through travel agencies or directly from the airlines (often using their websites).

Cheaper domestic flights are also available with the following airlines:

Atlasjet (☎ 0216-444 3387; www.atlasjet.com) A growing network, with flights from İstanbul, Çanakkale, İzmir and Antalya to cities throughout the country.

Onur Air (☎ 0212-444 6687; www.onurair.com.tr) Flights from Antalya, Bodrum, Dalaman, Diyarbakır, Erzurum, Gaziantep, İstanbul, İzmir, Kayseri and Trabzon, among others.

Pegasus Airlines (www.pegasusairlines.com) Flights between İstanbul and locations from Antalya to Van.

Sun Express Airlines (www.sunexpress.com.tr) A Turkish Airlines subsidiary.

Bus

Turkish buses go just about everywhere you could possibly want to go, and what's more

FEZ BUS

A hop-on, hop-off bus service, the **Fez Bus** (Map pp538-9; ☎ 0212-516 9024; www.feztravel.com; Akbıyık Caddesi 15, Sultanahmet, İstanbul) links the main tourist resorts of the Aegean and the Mediterranean with İstanbul and Cappadocia. The bonuses of using the Fez Bus are convenience (you don't carry your bags), flexibility (passes are valid from June to October and you can start anywhere on the circuit) and atmosphere (it's fun and energetic, with a strong party vibe). The downsides? You spend most of your time with travellers rather than locals, and it can rapidly become boring once you've had your fill of the backpacker fraternity. Also, it doesn't work out to be cheaper than doing it yourself with point-to-point buses.

A Turkish Delight bus pass (adult/student €176/164) allows you to travel from İstanbul to Çanakkale, Ephesus, Köyceğiz, Fethiye, Olympos, Cappadocia and then back to İstanbul via Ankara.

they do so comfortably and cheaply (it costs around TL80 to cross the whole country).

A town's otogar is often on the outskirts, but the bigger bus companies usually have free *servis* to ferry you into the centre and back again. Most otogars have an *emanet* (left-luggage room) that will charge a small fee, or you can sometimes leave luggage at the bus company's ticket office. Besides intercity buses, the otogar often handles dolmuşes that operate local routes, although some locations have a separate station for such services.

All Turkish bus services are officially smoke-free.

Car & Motorcycle

In the major cities, plan to leave your car in a parking lot and walk – traffic is terrible.

DRIVING LICENCE

An international driving permit (IDP) may be handy if your driving licence is from a country likely to seem obscure to a Turkish police officer.

FUEL

There are plenty of modern petrol stations in the west, many open 24 hours. In the east, they are a bit less abundant but you won't have trouble finding one. Be warned: petrol prices are high and are not showing any signs of going down.

HIRE

Hiring a car is quite expensive (often around TL70 to TL120 per day with unlimited mileage, less for long-term hire). All the main car-hire companies are represented in the main towns and resorts. It's better to stick to the well-established companies (such as Avis, Budget, Europcar, Hertz and Thrifty) as they have bigger fleets and better emergency backup. You can get great discounts through **Economy Car Rentals** (www.economycarrentals.com), which covers most of the country, but you need to book at least 24 hours in advance.

INSURANCE

You must have third-party insurance, valid for the entire country. If you don't have it, you can buy it at the border.

ROAD RULES

Drink-driving is a complete no-no. Maximum speed limits, unless otherwise posted, are 50km/h in towns, 90km/h on highways and 120km/h on an *otoyol* (motorway). Driving is hair-raising during the day because of fast, inappropriate driving and overladen trucks, and dangerous at night, when you won't be able to see potholes, animals, or even vehicles driving with their lights off!

Local Transport

With a few exceptions, you probably won't use public buses in large cities. In İstanbul, the underground metro and the tram are quick and efficient ways of getting around.

Taxis are plentiful. They have meters – just make sure they're switched on.

Train

Turkish State Railways (TCDD; www.tcdd.gov.tr/tcdding) runs services across the country, but it has a hard time competing with long-distance buses for speed and comfort. Don't plan a trans-Turkey train trip in one go as the country is large and trains can be slow. For example, the *Vangölü Ekspresi* from İstanbul to Lake Van (1900km), takes almost two days. Buses take less than 24 hours, planes less than two hours. Only between Ankara and İstanbul is travel fast and pleasant.

Middle East Directory

CONTENTS

This chapter provides a general overview of essential things you need to know about the Middle East, covering, in alphabetical order, everything from Accommodation and Activities to Women Travellers and Work. Each individual country chapter also has a Directory section that includes more specific information about these headings as they relate to each country. Please consult both when searching for information.

ACCOMMODATION

In most countries of the Middle East, you'll find accommodation that ranges from cheap and nasty to plush and palatial; most places sit comfortably somewhere in between. Throughout this book, accommodation is divided into price categories (budget, midrange and top end); within each category prices run from cheapest to most expensive. For the way these price categories are defined and the amenities you can expect from country to country, read the Accommodation section in the Directory section of each individual country chapter.

> **BOOK YOUR STAY ONLINE**
>
> For more accommodation reviews and recommendations by Lonely Planet authors, check out lonelyplanet.com/hotels. You'll find the true, insider lowdown on the best places to stay. Reviews are thorough and independent. Best of all, you can book online.

Generally Syria and Egypt have the cheapest accommodation, while Turkey, Jordan, Israel and the Palestinian Territories and Lebanon will cost a little more. However, travel through the Middle East is now such a well-worn path that in most major destinations covered by this book you'll find at least one high-quality place to suit your budget, whether you're travelling on a shoestring or an expense account.

Camping

Camping in the Middle East is possible. Stick to officially sanctioned campsites because many areas that are military or restricted zones aren't always marked as such and erecting a tent on an army firing range won't be a highlight of your trip. There are official camping grounds in Egypt, Lebanon, Turkey and Israel and the Palestinian Territories.

Hostels

There are youth hostels in Egypt, Israel and the Palestinian Territories. It's not usually necessary to hold a Hostelling International card to stay at these places, but it will get you a small discount.

Hotels

Standards vary between countries but price usually (not always) reflect quality.

In hotels at the bottom end of the price scale, rooms are not always clean. In fact, let's be honest: they can be downright filthy, and shared showers and toilets often bear traces of the previous users. Very cheap hotels are just dormitories where you're crammed into a room with whoever else fronts up. Some of the cheapest places are probably too basic for many tastes; they're rarely suitable for women travelling alone.

That said, there are some places that stand out and while they may have no frills, nor do their bathrooms give any indication of the good health or otherwise of previous occupants. Some places even treat you like a king even as you pay the price of a pauper. The happy (and most common) medium is usually a room devoid of character, but containing basic, well-maintained facilities.

In the midrange, rooms have private bathrooms, usually with hot water, fans to stir the air, a bit more space to swing a backpack and (sometimes) TVs promising international satellite channels.

Hotels at the top end of the range have clean, self-contained rooms with hot showers and toilets that work all the time, not to mention satellite TV, shampoo and regularly washed towels in the bathrooms, air-con to provide refuge from the Middle Eastern sun and a few luxuries to lift the spirits.

An increasing (and entirely welcome) trend is the proliferation of tastefully designed boutique hotels that make a feature of traditional design. Syria is leading the way with wonderful old courtyard homes and palaces converted into atmospheric hotels in Aleppo (p498), Damascus (p475) and even Hama (p487). Although most such places straddle the midrange/top-end price categories, even budget travellers should consider indulging in this fabulous sensory experience at least once on their travels.

For further details and other types of accommodation, see the Accommodation sections in the Directory of each individual country chapter.

GRAND OLD HOTELS OF THE MIDDLE EAST

If you're hankering after the Middle East of TE Lawrence and other stiff-upper-lipped colonial types, a few grand old hotels from the era still exist. Some have been tarted up with only hints remaining of their former glories, but a few are fraying around the edges a little, adding to the appeal for nostalgia buffs.

- Windsor Hotel, Cairo (p139)
- Old Winter Palace Hotel, Luxor (p161)
- Palmyra Hotel, Baalbek (p449)
- Zenobia Cham Palace (p514)
- Baron Hotel, Aleppo (p499)

ACTIVITIES

From deep-desert safaris in the Sahara to snow-skiing in Lebanon, from hiking the high valleys of central Jordan to diving and snorkelling beneath the surface of the Red Sea, there aren't too many activities that you *can't* do in the Middle East.

In addition to the following activities, you can also go caving in Lebanon (see p451), tandem paragliding or parasailing in Turkey (see p573) or, also in Turkey, sea-kayaking (see p575).

Cycling

The Middle East offers some fantastic, if largely undeveloped, opportunities for cyclists. Unlike in Europe, you're likely to have many of the trails to yourself. However, the heat can be a killer (avoid June to September) and you'll need to be pretty self-sufficient as spare parts can be extremely scarce. That said, many people particularly enjoy cycling the flatter roads of Syria. One of the highlights of travelling in this way is that locals in more out-of-the-way places will wonder what on earth you're doing – an ideal way to break the ice and meet new friends. For cycling in Lebanon, see p451.

For advice about cycling around the Middle East, see p646.

Desert Safaris

If you are the kind of traveller who loves deserts – the solitude, the gravitas of an empty landscape, the interplay of light and shadow on the sands – as an antidote to the clamour of cities, then the Middle East has some stirring examples of the kind. The most accessible deserts are those around Wadi Rum (Jordan), but Egypt's Sinai interior, and the vast tracts of Saharan sands, and Israel's Negev Desert also have considerable appeal.

Wadi Rum (p381) has many calling cards that are guaranteed to inspire even the most city-bound traveller: the orange sand, the improbable rocky mountains, the soulful Bedouin inhabitants who are the ideal companions around a desert campfire and the haunting echoes of TE Lawrence. When you add to this the ease of getting here and exploring – it's accessible from major travel routes and is compact enough to explore within short time frames – and the professional operators that run expeditions here, it's hardly surprising that Wadi Rum is the desert experience that travellers to the Middle East love most. The official **Wadi Rum Protected Area visitor centre** (www.wadirum.jo) should be your first port of call – the staff can arrange anything from afternoon camel treks to 4WD safaris and hikes lasting several days.

In the tourist towns of Egypt's Sinai Peninsula, you'll find plenty of small Bedouin operators who lead groups into the interior (p195) on overnight, two- or three-day camel treks. Even more conducive to leaving the modern world behind is an expedition from one of Egypt's Western Oases on a 4WD safari into the Sahara; such expeditions can be arranged in any of the oases, but Bahariya Oasis (p178) and Siwa Oasis (p180) are the most popular departure points.

Israel's Negev Desert is less attractive than deserts elsewhere, but dusty jeep tours are possible (see the boxed text, p308), while Desert Eco Tours (see p312) in Eilat runs some of the best Negev expeditions.

Diving

Put simply, the Red Sea is one of the world's premier diving sites. For beginners, you'll be blown away by this dazzling underwater world of colourful coral and fish life, extensive reef systems and the occasional shipwreck. Even snorkelling in these areas is a glorious introduction. For experienced divers, there are plenty of sites to escape the wide-eyed newbies and see underwater landscapes that are both challenging and exceptionally beautiful.

The best place to experience the Red Sea is from one of the resorts on Egypt's Sinai Peninsula, with outstanding diving off Sharm el-Sheikh (p191), Dahab (p194) and, to a lesser extent, Nuweiba (p200). Over on the Red Sea coast of the Egyptian mainland, Marsa Alam (p188) is easily their match.

There are also Red Sea dive centres in Eilat (p310) in Israel and Aqaba (p383) in Jordan with good offshore sites, but if you're travelling on to Egypt, it's worth the wait – for our pick of the best dive sites in the Red Sea, see the boxed text, p191.

Most dive centres offer every possible kind of dive course. The average open-water certification course for beginners, either with CMAS, PADI or NAUI, takes about five days and usually includes several dives. The total

UNDERWATER CRIMES

Most divers are natural environmentalists, which is hardly surprising given that the more pristine the environment, the better the experience for everyone. Indeed, responsible divers know well the unwritten rule of underwater exploration: look but don't touch. But you'd be surprised what a small number of rogue divers get up to.

For a start, buying coral or shells, or removing objects from marine archaeological sites (mainly shipwrecks), otherwise known as looting, still happens. Then there are those divers who'd never dream of throwing their rubbish on the street, but don't bother to carry their debris out with them – out of sight from land, perhaps, but not for the marine life that's under threat from discarded plastics. Absurd as it seems, some people even think that the fish that comes for a closer look is hungry and can't resist, despite everyone telling them that feeding the fish is a big no-no. Worst of all, a small minority of divers think it's fun to ride on the backs of turtles.

Then there are those underwater 'crimes' that are more due to carelessness than greed. Whatever the motivation, the potential to damage the underwater environment forever is equally strong. Practices to be avoided include: using anchors on reefs; grounding boats on coral; touching or standing on living marine organisms (polyps can be damaged by even the gentlest contact, and if you must hold on to the reef, touch only exposed rock or dead coral); dragging equipment across the reef; ignoring the power of fin strokes (surges of water and clouds of sand can damage or smother delicate organisms); not maintaining proper buoyancy control (divers descending too fast and colliding with the reef cause serious damage); and spending too long in underwater caves (the longer you stay, the more likely it is that your air bubbles may be caught within the roof, thereby leaving organisms high and dry).

LEAVING THE WORLD AS YOU FOUND IT

Nothing spoils a good walk through the wilderness quite like discovering that the hikers who preceded you have left their mark upon the environment. A cigarette butt, a rusting tuna can, a mound of human waste that the former owner didn't cover up – multiplied by even a small proportion of the tens of thousands of hikers who trek through the Middle East, these signifiers of the human presence add up to a whole lot of rubbish. Today wilderness, tomorrow a landscape spoiled for everyone.

Most of the rules for responsible hiking are common sense: don't remove plant life or cut down trees for open fires; don't forge new trails or take shortcuts as many areas are prone to erosion; do make sure any fire is fully extinguished before you move on; do bury all your bowel movements in a deep hole and at least 100m from the nearest watercourse; don't bury your rubbish (animals *will* dig it up) and do carry it all out with you; avoid the use of detergents or toothpaste near waterways; never buy souvenirs made from endangered species; and don't leave food scraps behind or otherwise feed the wildlife.

In some ways, it's all about preparation. Carrying a lightweight kerosene, alcohol or Shellite (white gas) stove means you won't go hungry and your environmental impact is minimal. Also carry reusable containers or stuff sacks. And if you must light a fire, spend your day with one eye out for dead, fallen wood and always remember the adage 'the bigger the fool, the bigger the fire'.

cost starts from around US$285; prices depend on the operator and location. A day's diving (two dives), including equipment and air fills, costs US$65 to US$115. An introductory dive is around US$70. Full equipment can be hired for about US$20 per day. Essential reading for anyone planning on taking a course is the boxed text on p194.

For more details, see the Activities sections in each country's Directory.

Hammams

One of the great sensual indulgences of the Middle East, the hammam (hamam in Turkey) is better known in the West as a 'Turkish bath'. There's nothing quite like a robust massage on tiled slabs, a sweltering steam-room session, and a hot tea taken afterwards while swathed in towels, all under vaulted domes that have changed little in centuries (the architecture is invariably exceptional). Even if you've showered beforehand, you'll never consider yourself clean again until you've had a hammam. For years afterwards, you'll remember your masseur as you would a scary teacher who taught you some of the more invigorating lessons in life. For a rundown on the complete experience, see the boxed text, p545.

The following is a list of the best hammams in the Middle East.

Çemberlitaş Hamamı (p544) İstanbul, Turkey.
Cağaloğlu Hamamı (p544) İstanbul, Turkey.
Hammam Yalbougha an-Nasry (p498) Aleppo, Syria.
Hammam Nureddin (p473) Damascus, Syria.
Al-Pasha Hammam (p349) Amman, Jordan.
Al-Shifa (p322) Nablus, Israel and the Palestinian Territories.

Hiking & Climbing

Jordan is a trekkers' paradise, most notably in the spectacular landscapes around Wadi Rum (p381), Petra (p375) and the steep valleys of Dana Nature Reserve (p371) and Wadi Mujib (p369). For climbing possibilities in Jordan, see p388.

Maktesh Ramon (the Middle East's largest crater; p309) and the canyons and pools of En Avdat in Israel and the Palestinian Territories' Negev Desert are great trekking areas, but those who don sturdy boots and head to the higher, cooler Upper Galilee and Golan regions will also be amply rewarded; for more information on the best hiking spots in Israel, see the boxed text, p303.

In Lebanon, the Qadisha Valley is hiking central (see the boxed text, p438), while in Turkey some fine trails pass through the Kaçkar Mountains, the Ala Dağlar (near Niğde), the mountains of Lycia, Cappadocia and Mt Ararat (5137m) near Doğubayazıt. For more information, see p610.

See the Activities section in the relevant country chapters for further details.

Sailing

With its whitewashed villages, idyllic ports and mountainous backdrop, Turkey's Mediterranean and Aegean coasts are ideal for yacht cruising, especially given its proximity to the Greek Islands. Possibilities

DESERT HIKING: WATER & WARM CLOTHES

While the Middle East offers a host of hiking opportunities, the conditions are quite different from those most visitors are accustomed to. For this reason, you have to be careful in picking the right time of year for your visit so that you don't expire by lunchtime on the first day.

In the summer, hiking can be extremely dangerous, and in 40°C heat most hikers will go through one litre of water every hour. Even in the cooler months, your main issue will be water, and hikers should have available at least four litres per person per day.

The most effective way to conserve water isn't necessarily to drink sparingly, as this tends to psychologically focus attention on water availability, and may lead to an unhealthy hysteria. Before setting off in the morning, flood your body's cells with water. That is, drink more water than you feel you can possibly hold! After a few hours, when you grow thirsty, do the same again from the supply you're carrying. Believe it or not, with this method you'll actually use less water and feel less thirsty than if you drink sparingly all day long.

Another major concern is the desert sun, which can be brutal. Wear light-coloured and lightweight clothing; use a good sunscreen; and never set off without a hat or Arab-style head covering to shelter your neck and face from the direct sun. You'll also value a light, semitransparent veil to protect your eyes, nose, mouth and ears from blowing sand and dust.

If the heat's a major problem, it's best to rise before the sun and hike until the heat becomes oppressive. You may then want to rest (in the shade) through the heat of midday and begin again after about 3pm. During warmer months, it may also be worthwhile timing your hike with the full moon, which will allow you to hike at night.

Because many trails follow canyons and wadis, it's also important to keep a watch on the weather. Rainy periods can render normally dry wadis impassable, and those with large catchment areas can quickly become raging – and uncrossable – torrents of muddy water, boulders and downed trees. Never camp in canyons or wadis and always keep to higher ground whenever there's a risk of flash flooding.

And just because you're in the desert, don't for a second imagine that you're in for a balmy night – with no cloud cover to trap the earth's heat, night-time temperatures in the desert can plummet, even below freezing in winter. As a result, make sure you've warm clothing in your backpack unless you want to pass the most uncomfortable of nights.

include everything from day trips to two-week luxury charters. Kuşadası (p565), Bodrum (p567), Fethiye (p572) and Marmaris (p569) are the main centres, with more resorts developing yachting businesses all the time. You can hire crewless bareboats or flotilla boats, or take a cabin on a boat hired by an agency. Ask anywhere near the docks for details. For more information, see the boxed text, p573.

For one of the Middle East's most leisurely and enjoyable experiences, try a slow cruise up the Nile aboard a felucca (p170).

Snow Skiing

'Snow sports in the Middle East' probably sounds like it belongs in the tall-tales-told-to-gullible-travellers category, but not if you're Lebanese. In the 1970s, Beirut was famous for the fact that you could swim in the Mediterranean waters of the Lebanese capital in the morning, then ski on the slopes of Mt Makmel, northeast of Beirut, in the afternoon. No sooner had the guns of civil war fallen silent than the Lebanese once again reclaimed the slopes from the militias, and their infectious optimism has seen the ski resorts going from strength to strength. For information on skiing in Lebanon, turn to p439 and p452.

Watersports

Any Red Sea resort worth its salt – from the expensive package tour resorts of Sharm el-Sheikh (Egypt) to the chilled, backpacker-friendly Dahab (Egypt) – will let you indulge your passion for watersports from windsurfing to water-skiing.

Eilat (p311) in Israel is arguably the Middle East's watersports capital with waterskiing, parasailing and a host of other water-borne thrills on offer. In Egypt, Sharm el-Sheikh (p191) has a full range of options, while Hurghada (p184) has a happening kite-surfing scene. For the region's best windsurfing spot, though, head to Moon Beach in Sinai (p191). Aqaba (p383) in Jordan, Beirut and Jounieh (p451) in Lebanon, and many of Turkey's Mediterranean beach resorts all offer ample opportunities for year-round snorkelling, water-skiing and windsurfing.

For more details, see the Activities sections in each country's Directory.

BUSINESS HOURS

With just a few exceptions, the end-of-week holiday throughout the Middle East is Friday. In Israel and the Palestinian Territories it's Saturday (Shabbat), while in Lebanon and Turkey it's Sunday. In countries where Friday is the holiday, many embassies and offices are also closed on Thursday, although in areas where there are lots of tourists, many private businesses and shops are open on Thursday and many stores will reopen in the evening on Friday.

It's worth remembering that shops and businesses may have different opening hours for different times of the year – they tend to work shorter hours in winter and open earlier in summer to allow for a longer lunchtime siesta. During Ramadan (the month-long fast for Muslims), almost everything shuts down in the afternoon.

Where possible, throughout this book we give the opening times of places of interest. The information is usually taken from notices posted at the sites. However, often the reality on the ground is that sites open pretty much as and when the gate guard feels like it. On a good day he'll be there an hour early, on a bad day he won't turn up at all. Who can blame him when in out-of-the-way places he may never see a visitor for days anyway? With the exception, perhaps, of those countries with a more Western concept of timekeeping (Israel and the Palestinian Territories and Turkey, for example), all opening hours must be prefaced, therefore, with a hopeful *insha'allah* (God willing).

CHILDREN

People who've never visited the region may tell you you're crazy, but we have a simple message for those of you considering travelling with your children to the Middle East: go for it. Our confidence is well placed: at least two of the authors writing this book have travelled in the

TOP MIDDLE EAST SIGHTS FOR KIDS

- **Dahab** (p194) Diving in the Red Sea at Dahab will open up a whole new world that they never imagined (except when watching *Nemo*).
- **The Nile** (p173) A felucca trip up the Nile, from Aswan to Luxor (p153), offers a break from sardine-can shared taxis.
- **Temple of Karnak** (p155) The sound-and-light show here is a great alternative to history books for learning about ancient Egypt.
- **Jerusalem** (p260) A host of child-friendly activities and the perfect place to bring Sunday school lessons to life.
- **Dead Sea** (p361) Leave your kids giggling at the buoyancy of it all – yes, even Dad floats!
- **Petra** (p375) If they've seen *Indiana Jones*, watch them go wide-eyed with recognition.
- **Aleppo** (p491) Labyrinthine souqs made for legends like Ali Baba and Aladdin.
- **Damascus** (p464) Some of the world's friendliest people will make your kids feel part of the fun in the world's oldest city.
- **Crac des Chevaliers** (Syria; p488) and **Karak** (Jordan; p370) Castles replete with legends of kings and knights and damsels in distress.
- **İstanbul** (p536) A great place to make geography interesting by visiting two continents in one day.
- **Cappadocia** (p587) A fairytale landscape made for a child's fertile imagination.

region with their kids (see, for example, the boxed text, p521) and not only lived to tell the tale but also plan to do so again at the earliest available opportunity. If you don't believe us, look around – you won't see many families of travellers, but the ones you do see will probably be having a pretty good time. On the all-important question of security, any place that's safe for you to visit will generally be similarly safe for your children.

The advantages of travelling with your kids are many. For a start, most people you'll meet in the region come from large extended families, love kids and will make sure that your children are made to feel welcome. More than that, your chances of meeting locals (especially local families) is greatly enhanced – most kids are much better at connecting with locals and overcoming language difficulties than adults will ever be.

In the process of visiting the Middle East, you'll also be giving your children a priceless gift. Unlike any vaguely news-savvy adult, most children have yet to have their perceptions of the Middle East distorted by stereotypes. Seeing for themselves just how friendly (and just like us) the people of the Middle East can be is a lesson that will last a lifetime.

Practicalities

If we've convinced you to bring your children with you, there are a few provisos that you should bear in mind. First, it's a good idea to avoid travel in the summer as the extreme heat can be quite uncomfortable and energy sapping. If you'll be travelling by taxi or minibus, you may consider bringing a child's seat-belt adjuster as few such vehicles have child seats. As for hotels, you'll almost certainly want something with a private bathroom and hot water, thereby precluding most budget accommodation.

Otherwise, disposable nappies, powdered milk, formula and bottled water are widely available throughout the region.

For more comprehensive advice on the dos and don'ts of taking the kids in your luggage, see Lonely Planet's *Travel with Children* by Cathy Lanigan. For more details, turn to the Directory in each individual country chapter.

CHILDREN'S BOOKS ABOUT THE MIDDLE EAST

- *The Thousand and One Nights (The Arabian Nights)* – if you buy one book for your kids about the Middle East, make it this one, with a variety of editions to suit most ages.
- *The Librarian of Basra: A True Story from Iraq,* by Jeanette Winter, recounts the true tale of Basra's librarian who saved the library's books in the aftermath of the American invasion (ages 4-8).
- *The Magic Apple: A Folktale from the Middle East,* by Rob Cleveland, follows three boys' journeys (complete with flying carpets) to fulfil their father's last wish (ages 4-8).
- *Sitti's Secrets,* by Naomi Shihab Nye, is a heart-warming book that follows Mona as she returns to the Palestinian Territories (ages 4-8).
- *The Day of Ahmed's Secret,* by Florence H Parry, is a beautifully illustrated story of a young Cairo boy on the streets of this beguiling city (ages 6-9).
- *The Enchanted Storks: A Tale of Bagdad,* by Aaron Shepard, has it all: a caliph who turns into a stork, a wicked magician and an enchanted princess (ages 6-10).
- *Sami and the Time of the Troubles,* by Florence Parry Heide and Judith Heide Gilliland, brings a child's hopes and an adult's war together in Beirut (ages 9-12).
- *Samir and Yonatan,* by Daniella Carmi, tells of an improbable friendship between two boys – one Israeli, the other Palestinian (ages 9-12).
- *A Handful of Stars,* by Rafik Schami, is a coming-of-age novel about life for teenagers in modern Syria (ages 12+).
- *Children in the Muslim Middle East,* by Elizabeth Warnock Fernea, is more for adults than kids, but what you'll learn about the children of the region will be invaluable in introducing your children to the region.

CLIMATE CHARTS

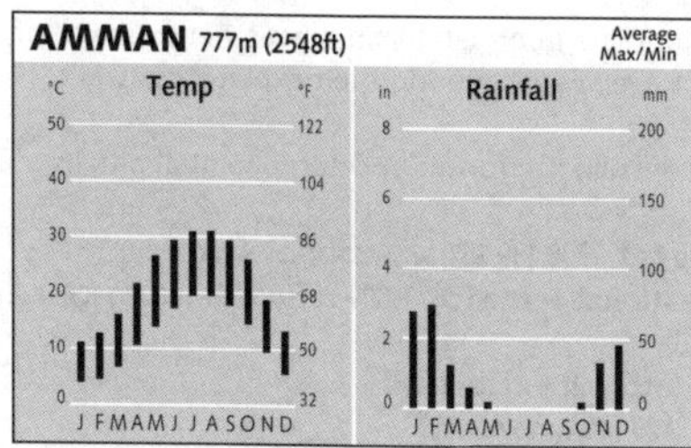

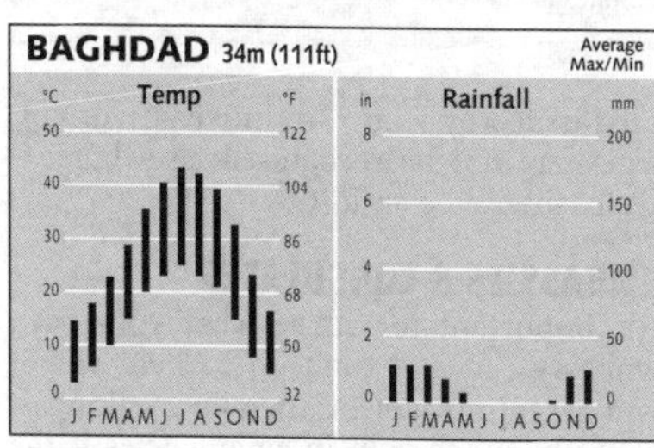

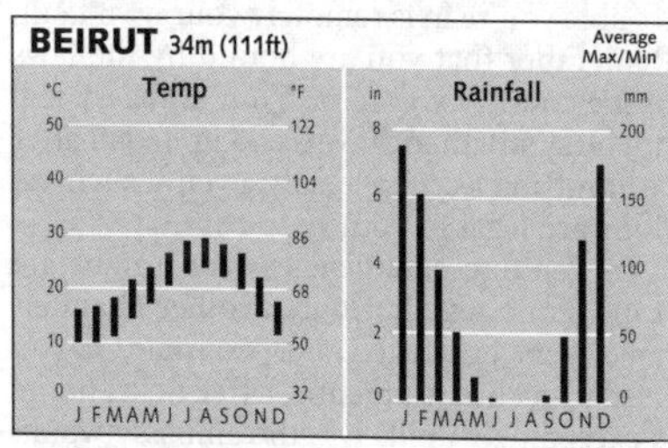

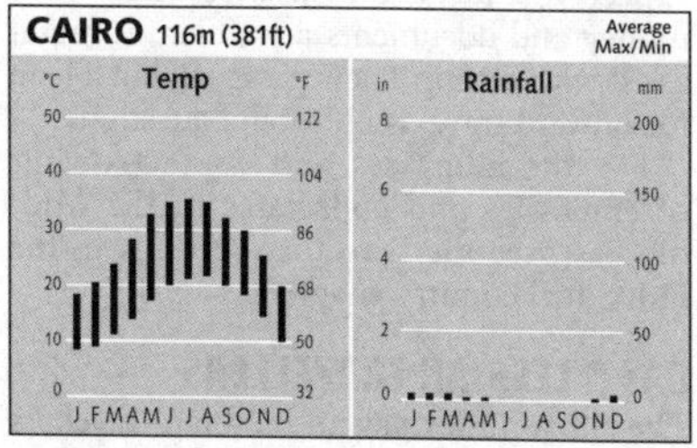

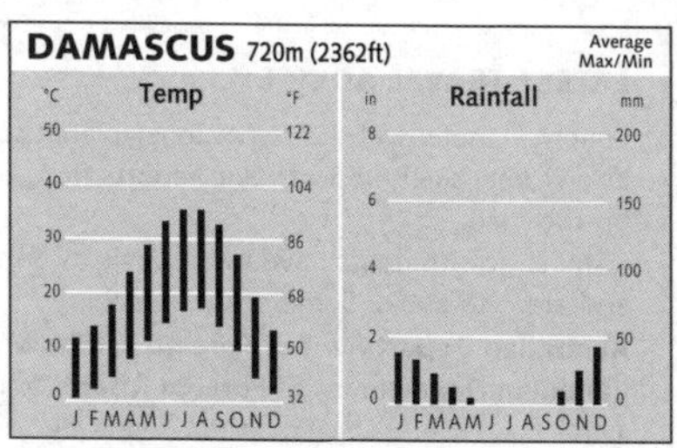

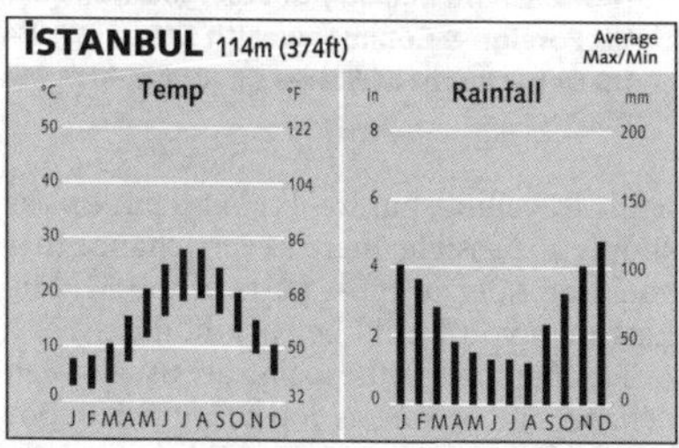

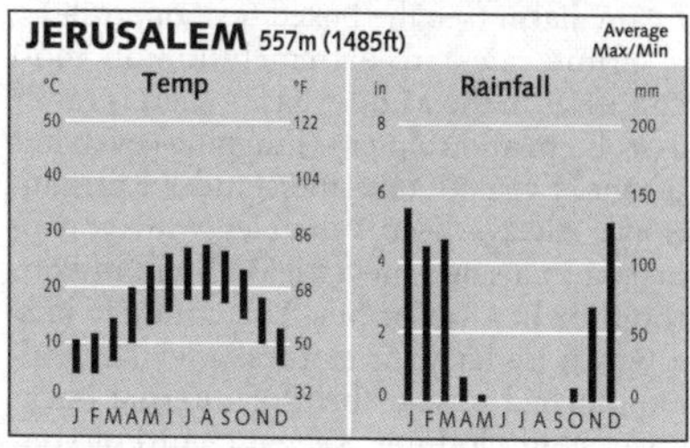

CUSTOMS REGULATIONS

Customs regulations vary from country to country, but in most cases they aren't that different from what you'd expect in the West – a couple of hundred cigarettes and a couple of bottles of booze.

There was a time when electronics used to arouse interest when entering or leaving Egypt and Syria, but it's becoming increasingly rare. If they do pull you up, items such as laptop computers and especially video cameras may be written into your passport to ensure that they leave the country with you and are not sold. If you're carrying this sort of thing, it's better not to be too obvious about it. This same principle of discretion applies to printed material that could be interpreted as being critical of the government, although customs officials at major entry/departure points rarely search the bags of tourists.

DANGERS & ANNOYANCES

Don't believe everything you read about the Middle East. Yes, there are regions that travellers would be ill advised to visit. But alongside the sometimes disturbing hard facts is more often a vast corpus of exaggeration, stereotyping and downright misrepresentation. You should always be careful

LATEST TRAVEL ADVICE

Lonely Planet's website (www.lonelyplanet.com) contains information on what's new, as well as any new safety reports, and reports from other travellers recounting their experiences while on the road.

Most governments have travel-advisory services detailing terrorism updates, potential pitfalls and areas to avoid. Some of these include:

Australian Department of Foreign Affairs & Trade (☎ 1300 139 281; www.smartraveller.gov.au)
Canadian Department of Foreign Affairs & International Trade (☎ 1-800-267-6788; www.voyage.gc.ca)
New Zealand Ministry of Foreign Affairs & Trade (www.mft.govt.nz/travel)
UK Foreign & Commonwealth Office (☎ 0845 850 2829; www.fco.gov.uk)
US Department of State (☎ 202-647-4000; www.travel.state.gov)

while travelling, but we'll try and put this as simply as possible: there's every chance that you'll be safer in most parts of the Middle East than you would be back home.

Trouble spots in the region are usually well defined, and as long as you keep track of political developments, you're unlikely to come to any harm (see the boxed text, opposite).

Crime rates are extremely low in most countries in the Middle East – theft is rarely a problem and robbery (mugging) even less of one. Even so, take the standard precautions. Always keep valuables with you or locked in a safe – never leave them in your room or in a car or bus. Use a money belt, a pouch under your clothes, a leather wallet attached to your belt, or internal pockets in your clothing. Keep a record of your passport, credit card and travellers cheque numbers separately; it won't cure problems, but it will make them easier to bear. We're sorry to say this, but beware of your fellow travellers; there are more than a few backpackers who make their money go further by helping themselves to other people's.

DISCOUNT CARDS

An International Student Identity Card (ISIC) can be useful in the Middle East. Egypt, Israel and the Palestinian Territories, Syria and Turkey have various (and often considerable) student discounts for admission to museums, archaeological sites and monuments. In Syria, it slashes admissions to almost all historical sites to about a 10th of the normal foreigners' price, while elsewhere discounts usually range from 25% to 50%. In Israel, cardholders also qualify for 10% reductions on some bus fares and 20% on rail tickets. Bear in mind that a student card issued by your own university or college may not be recognised elsewhere; it really should be an ISIC.

EMBASSIES & CONSULATES

It's important to realise what your own embassy can and can't do to help you if you get into trouble. Generally speaking, it won't be much help in emergencies if the trouble you're in is remotely your own fault. Remember that you are bound by the laws of the country you're in. Your embassy will not be sympathetic if you end up in jail after committing a crime locally, even if such actions are legal in your own country.

In genuine emergencies, you might get some assistance, but only if other channels have been exhausted. For example, if you need to get home urgently, a free ticket home is exceedingly unlikely – the embassy would expect you to have insurance. If all your money and documents are stolen, it might assist with getting a new passport, but a loan for onward travel is out of the question.

For the addresses and contact details of embassies and consulates in the Middle East, see the Directory sections in the individual country chapters.

GAY & LESBIAN TRAVELLERS

The situation for gay and lesbian travellers in the Middle East is more diverse than you might imagine. Israel is the best place in the region to be gay – homosexuality is legal, and Tel Aviv and Eilat in particular have thriving gay and lesbian scenes. The same doesn't apply to the Palestinian Territories, and hundreds of Palestinian gays have been forced to seek refuge in Israel. Homosexuality is also legal in Turkey, with

IS IT SAFE?

Imagine somebody whose image of the USA was built solely on the 9/11 attacks, or who refused to visit Spain or the UK as a result of terrorist attacks in Madrid and London in recent years. Just as the USA, the UK and Spain are rarely considered to be dangerous destinations so, too, day-to-day life in the Middle East very rarely involves shootings, explosions and other elements of terror; major international news sources rarely, if ever, report the good news. Picture the scene on CNN: 'Today all was quiet on the streets of Damascus, Amman and Cairo. Now, back to the studio…' There are trouble spots where violence persists, such as Iraq – visiting the country is a serious undertaking and not for your average traveller. And there are places where violence flares from time to time (such as in the Palestinian Territories or Lebanon). But such outbreaks of violence usually receive widespread media coverage, making it relatively easy to avoid these places until things settle down.

Terrorist incidents also do occur, and there have been attacks in Israel and the Palestinian Territories and the Red Sea resorts of Egypt's Sinai Peninsula in recent years. While such incidents are clearly major causes for concern, these are definitely the exception rather than the norm. The sad fact about modern terrorism is that you may face similar dangers anywhere in the world and that you're probably no more at risk in the Middle East than you may be in your home country. As one holidaymaker was reported saying in the wake of the 2005 Sharm el-Sheikh bombings: 'Actually, I live in central London. I don't really want to go home!'

In our experience, most people in the Middle East are perfectly able to distinguish between the policies of Western governments and individual travellers. You may receive the occasional question ('Why does the West support Israel?'), but you'll almost never be held personally accountable, except perhaps in deeply troubled Iraq. Once in Tehran we stood, obviously Westerners, with cameras and pasty complexions, and watched a crowd march by chanting 'Death to America! Death to Britain!' Several marchers grinned, waved and broke off to come over and ask how we liked Iran.

So, while right now we'd advise against visits to Gaza, Hebron or Baghdad, rarely should events in the news make you reconsider your travel plans. Keep abreast of current affairs, and if you need to phone your embassy for travel advice, then do. Otherwise, just go.

İstanbul and Ankara both home to a small but thriving gay culture. Whether that's about to change remains unclear, however, after the gay rights group Lambda (www.lambdaistanbul.org) was closed down by the authorities in May 2008 for violating Turkish morality laws.

It is slightly more complicated in Egypt and Jordan, where, although the criminal code doesn't expressly forbid homosexual acts, laws regarding public decency have been used to prosecute gays, especially in Egypt; the Jordanian capital Amman nonetheless has a few gay-friendly spots. Homosexuality is illegal in Lebanon, Syria and Iraq, although Beirut takes a fairly liberal approach with a small but vibrant gay scene (see the boxed text, p425). In those countries where homosexuality is illegal or ambiguous in a legal sense, penalties include fines and/or imprisonment. That does not mean that gays aren't active, but it does mean that gay identity is generally expressed only in certain trusted, private spheres.

Even in those countries in which homosexuality is not prohibited by law, it remains fairly low key, with the exceptions of Tel Aviv (see the boxed text, p283) and İstanbul. In general, however, as a Westerner, you're unlikely to encounter prejudice or harassment as long as you remain discreet; that may not be the case if you become involved with a local. As a general rule, the same rules of discretion apply for everyone in this conservative region, whether homosexual or heterosexual.

For a good rundown on the prevailing situation in most countries of the Middle East – including news updates, the legal situation and postings by locals and gay visitors – visit www.gaymiddleeast.com, which has sections on all countries covered in this book. Another worthwhile site is www.globalgayz.com.

For more information on gay-friendly bars and hotels, see the *Spartacus International Gay Guide* (www.spartacusworld.com/gayguide) and the Gay & Lesbian Travellers sections in the individual country chapters of this book.

HOLIDAYS

All Middle Eastern countries, save Israel, observe the main Islamic holidays listed below. Countries with a major Shiite population also observe Ashura, the anniversary of the martyrdom of Hussein, the third imam of the Shiites. Most of the countries in this book also observe both the Gregorian and the Islamic New Year holidays. Every country also has its own national days and other public holidays – for details refer to the individual country chapters.

Eid al-Adha (Kurban Bayramı in Turkey) This feast marks the time that Muslims make the pilgrimage to Mecca.

Eid al-Fitr (Şeker Bayramı in Turkey) Another feast, this time to herald the end of Ramadan fasting; the celebrations last for three days.

Islamic New Year Also known as Ras as-Sana, it literally means 'the head of the year'.

Lailat al-Mi'raj This is the celebration of the Ascension of the Prophet Mohammed.

Prophet's Birthday This is also known as Moulid an-Nabi, 'the feast of the Prophet'.

Ramadan (Ramazan in Turkey) This is the ninth month of the Muslim calendar, when Muslims fast during daylight hours. Foreigners are not expected to follow suit, but it's considered impolite to smoke, drink or eat in public during Ramadan. As the sun sets each day, the fast is broken with *iftar* (the evening meal prepared to break the fast). See also p74 for further details.

Islamic Calendar

All Islamic holidays fall according to the Muslim calendar, while secular activities are planned according to the Christian system.

The Muslim year is based on the lunar cycle and is divided into 12 lunar months, each with 29 or 30 days. Consequently, the Muslim year is 10 or 11 days shorter than the Christian solar year, and the Muslim festivals gradually move around our year, completing the cycle in roughly 33 years.

Year zero in the Muslim calendar was when Mohammed and his followers fled from Mecca to Medina (AD 622 in the Christian calendar). This Hejira (migration) is taken to mark the start of the new Muslim era, much as Christ's birth marks year zero in the Christian calendar.

INSURANCE

Travel insurance covering theft, loss and medical problems is highly recommended. Some policies offer travellers lower and higher medical-expense options; the higher ones are chiefly for countries such as the USA, which have extremely high medical costs. There's a wide variety of policies available, so shop around. Watch particularly for the small print as some policies specifically exclude 'dangerous activities', which can include scuba diving, motorcycling and even trekking.

For further details on health insurance, see p654, and for car insurance, see p650.

INTERNET ACCESS

You're never too far from an internet café in all major cities and larger towns across the Middle East. If you need to track one down and you're not close to one of those listed in this book, your best bet is to ask your hotel reception or to head to the university district (if there is one) and ask around.

If you're travelling with a laptop, wireless internet access is increasingly the norm in most top-end hotels as well as many in the midrange categories. It's also getting easier to connect in upmarket cafés and restaurants. Expect the number of hotspots to

ISLAMIC HOLIDAYS

Hejira year	New Year	Prophet's Birthday	Lailat al-Mi'raj	Ramadan begins	Eid al-Fitr	Eid al-Adha	Ashura
1430	31 Dec 2008	9 Mar 2009	19 Jun 2009	23 Aug 2009	21 Sep 2009	29 Nov 2009	8 Jan 2009
1431	20 Dec 2009	27 Feb 2010	8 Jun 2010	12 Aug 2010	10 Sep 2010	18 Nov 2010	28 Dec 2009
1432	9 Dec 2010	16 Feb 2011	29 May 2011	1 Aug 2011	31 Aug 2011	7 Nov 2011	17 Dec 2010
1433	29 Nov 2011	5 Feb 2012	18 May 2012	21 Jul 2012	20 Aug 2012	28 Oct 2012	6 Dec 2011
1434	18 Nov 2012	25 Jan 2013	7 May 2013	10 Jul 2013	9 Aug 2013	17 Oct 2013	26 Nov 2012

Actual dates may occur a day later, but probably not earlier, depending on western hemisphere moon sightings.

have grown considerably by the time you arrive in the region.

Given its reputation for political censorship, there are surprisingly few websites that are blocked by governments in the region. That's not to say it doesn't happen. In Syria, for example, sites criticising the government are often blocked, while access is occasionally denied to Hotmail, Wikipedia and Amazon.com (although, strangely, Amazon.co.uk slips through the net).

MONEY

Details on each country's currency, places to change money and advice on specific exchange rates are given in the Directory of the individual country chapters. Throughout this general section, we have quoted prices in US dollars (US$), as these rates are more likely to remain stable than local currencies (which may go up and down).

If we had to choose our preferred way of carrying our money to the Middle East, it would be a combination of withdrawing money from ATMs and carrying a supply of US dollar or euro cash.

See the Money section in the individual country chapters for more details.

ATMs

ATMs are now a way of life in most Middle Eastern countries and, with a few exceptions, it's possible to survive on cash advances. This is certainly the case in Turkey, Lebanon, Israel and the Palestinian Territories, Jordan and Egypt, where ATMs are everywhere and they're all linked to one of the international networks (eg MasterCard, Maestro, Cirrus, Visa, Visa Electron or GlobalAccess systems). Syria increasingly has similar ATMs, but they've yet to reach beyond the major towns (eg there was no ATM in Palmyra at the time of research) and most ATMs set a daily withdrawal limit of around US$50, making it more difficult to get by on this method alone. That will almost certainly change during the life of the book, but don't turn up counting on it.

Another thing to consider is whether the convenience of withdrawing money as you go is outweighed by the bank fees you'll be charged for doing so. It's a good idea to check the transaction fees both with your own bank back home and, if possible, with the banks whose machines you'll be using while you travel.

Cash

Although credit cards are increasingly accepted, cash remains king in the Middle East. And not just any cash. US dollars and, increasingly, euros are the currency of choice in most countries of the Middle East, and not just for changing money – many midrange and top-end hotels prefer their bills to be settled in either currency. If the prevalence of straight US$ transactions strikes you as odd in a region with such a strained relationship with the US, you're not the only one. The graffiti we saw in the backstreets of the Old City in Damascus speaks for itself: 'Every US dollar we deal with today is a bullet in the heart of an Arab citizen tomorrow.'

If your funds have run dry and you've no means of withdrawing money, Western Union (www.westernunion.com) has representatives in every country covered by this book.

The only danger in relying solely on travelling with cash is that if you lose it, it's lost forever – insurance companies simply won't believe that you had US$1000 in cash.

Credit Cards

Credit cards (especially Visa and MasterCard) are accepted by an ever-growing number of Middle Eastern hotels, top-end restaurants and handicraft shops, but the situation is still a long way from one where you could pay your way solely by flashing the card. Israel and the Palestinian Territories, Lebanon and Turkey are the most credit-card-friendly countries in the region, while Syria lags far behind – while some Syrian businesses accept credit cards, most still do so via Lebanese banks, which can add considerably to the cost of your purchase. You should always be wary of surcharges for paying by card, and not just in Syria – many Egyptian and Jordanian businesses also sting for commissions over and above the purchase price.

Tipping

Tipping is expected to varying degrees in all Middle Eastern countries. Called baksheesh, it's more than just a reward for having rendered a service. Salaries and wages are much lower than in Western countries, so baksheesh is regarded as an often essential means of supplementing income. To a cleaner in a one- or two-star hotel who may earn the equivalent of US$50 per month, the accumulated daily dollar tips given by guests can constitute the mainstay of his or her salary.

For Western travellers who aren't used to continual tipping, demands for baksheesh for doing anything from opening doors to pointing out the obvious in museums can be quite irritating. But it is the accepted way. Don't be intimidated into paying baksheesh when you don't think the service warrants it, but remember that more things warrant baksheesh here than anywhere in the West. One hint: carry lots of small change with you, but keep it separate from bigger bills, so that baksheesh demands don't increase when they see that you can afford more.

Tipping of around 10% to 15% is increasingly expected in midrange and top-end restaurants in Israel and the Palestinian Territories, Lebanon, Turkey and, to a lesser extent, Syria. Check your bill closely, however, as many such restaurants include an additional charge for service, in which case a further tip is not necessary. One country where baksheesh or tipping isn't as prevalent is Jordan, where many locals feel irritated when tourists throw their money around, not least because some employers are known to deduct anticipated tips from their employees, resulting in even lower wages!

Other circumstances in which a tip is expected is where you've taken a tour either with a guide or a taxi driver or both. How much to leave depends on the length of the expedition and the helpfulness of the guide.

Travellers Cheques

Does anyone out there still use travellers cheques? If you're among their dwindling ranks, perhaps you should reconsider. Yes, they're secure and replaceable, but so too are most credit and other bank cards. The main reason for not using travellers cheques is that only a limited number of banks will change them, they'll always charge a commission for doing so and it always means you'll spend longer in the bank.

If you do take travellers cheques, carry a mix of high- and low-denomination notes, as well as cheques, so that if you're about to leave a country, you can change just enough for a few days and not end up with too much local currency to get rid of.

PHOTOGRAPHY & VIDEO

Equipment

Memory cards are widely available in most countries of the Middle East, although you'll have a wider choice of brands in major cities. Expect prices to be broadly similar to what you'd pay back home. The situation for batteries is also similar, although for more professional cameras, you'd be better off bringing your own supply. When it comes to burning photos onto CDs, most internet cafés will do so without batting an eyelid.

Cameras and lenses collect dust quickly in desert areas. Lens paper and cleaners can be difficult to find in some countries, so bring your own. A dust brush is also useful.

Photographing People

As a matter of courtesy, don't photograph people without asking their permission first. While that's a general rule for photography anywhere, it's especially important in the Middle East. Children will almost always say yes, but adults may say no. In more conservative areas, including many rural areas, men should never photograph women and in most circumstances should never even ask. In countries where you can photograph women, show them the camera and make it clear that you want to take their picture. Digital cameras have the advantage of being able to show people their photo immediately after you've taken it, which is usually temptation enough for most people to say yes.

Restrictions

In most Middle Eastern countries, it is forbidden to photograph anything even vaguely military in nature (bridges, train stations, airports, border crossings and other public works). The definition of what is 'strategic' differs from one country to the next, and signs are not always posted, so err on the side of caution and, if in doubt, ask your friendly neighbouring police officer for permission.

Photography is usually allowed inside religious and archaeological sites, unless there are signs indicating otherwise. As a rule, do not photograph inside mosques during a service. Many Middle Easterners are sensitive about the negative aspects of their country, so exercise discretion when taking photos in poorer areas.

SHOPPING FOR THAT SPECIAL SOMETHING

For the connoisseur of kitsch, the Middle East is an absolute dream. How about one of the following?

Blinking Jesus Kitsch is king at many Christian sites in Israel, but it's perhaps best represented by the 3D postcards portraying a very Nordic-looking Jesus whose eyes open and close, depending on the angle of view.

Ephesus clock A plastic version of a Roman gate with arch stones for nine o'clock through to three o'clock. However, the time between three and nine o'clock (in the open portal) is anybody's guess.

Inflatable Arafat Just put your lips to the back of his head and blow for a life-size, pear-shaped, air-filled bust of everybody's favourite keffiyeh-wearing world leader. Gathering dust on shelves in Gaza City.

King Tut galabiyya Perfect for lounging around the house, a short-sleeved, brightly coloured robe that is usually too short and festooned with a giant iron-on reproduction of the famous funerary mask.

King Tut hologram lamp White-plaster bust of the famous boy-king that appears to float like a hologram when plugged in. Available in Cairo's Khan al-Khalili (p134) for a mere US$50.

Mother-of-pearl telephone A real telephone, but in a wooden casing with inlaid mother-of-pearl (actually plastic) patterning. Not only is it hideous but also it's about the shape and size of a typewriter. Available in the Souq al-Hamidiyya, Damascus (p468).

Priapus from Ephesus A small replica of the (in)famous, generously endowed statue on display at the museum here. Attach to the wall for a splendid coat hook.

Pyramid paperweight A clear-resin pyramid with a golden sphinx inside. When you shake it, golden 'snow' rains down. Or maybe it's acid rain. Available in Egypt anywhere tourists congregate.

SMOKING

Being a nonsmoker is a relative term in the Middle East because you'll inhale more than your fair share of passive smoke in most of the countries in the region. While much of that smoke will be of the less-offensive scented variety emanating from nargilehs, you'll encounter plenty of cigarette smoke in most restaurants, cafés and even public transport across the region.

There are two notable exceptions to the general rule. Smoking is banned in Israel in all enclosed public places and places serving food must have nonsmoking sections, while a law banning smoking in bars, cafés and restaurants came into effect in Turkey on 1 September 2008. Although the Turkish law was far from universally welcomed, the law applies only to cigarettes, hence exempting nargilehs or sheeshas.

Otherwise, it's a pretty smoky picture in all the other countries. The American University of Beirut has declared itself a smoke-free campus, but that's about the only sliver of good news we can report for anti-smoking campaigners.

SOLO TRAVELLERS

You're watching the sun rise from high on Mt Sinai, or setting over the ruins of Palmyra. Do you wish there was someone alongside to share it with, or do you try to find a quiet spot to enjoy the view in peace and solitude? How you answer that question should give you a pretty good idea whether travelling solo is for you.

Logistically, travelling on your own in the Middle East is as easy as travelling with others – you don't need two people to buy a bus ticket or arrange accommodation. More importantly, you wake up in the morning and the day is yours and yours alone, thereby allowing you to have the trip of your choosing, rather than one held back by the compromises inherent in taking other people into account. The opportunity to meet locals is greatly enhanced by travelling on your own rather than in a larger group. Few people like to travel alone 24/7, but solo travellers who want to come into the fold or simply a few hours' company can easily meet other travellers wherever there's a travellers' scene, such as in İstanbul, Damascus or Dahab.

The downside of travelling alone is that it can prove to be a little more expensive, not least because hotel rooms generally cost more for individual travellers (a single room is rarely half the price of a double room). Although many hotels organise tours to surrounding sights, organising your own taxi will invariably prove pricey unless you can find other travellers to share costs.

Women travellers often travel alone through the Middle East without any problem, although we'd probably only recommend it only for seasoned travellers or those who have visited the region before. A woman travelling solo is still rare enough to draw attention, and although most of that will be benign, you'll almost certainly attract a following of male admirers.

For more advice for women travellers, see opposite.

TELEPHONE

In most countries of the Middle East, the cheapest way to make international calls is at your friendly local internet café for a fraction of the cost of calling on a normal land line. Staff at these cafés (most of which are equipped with webcams, microphones and headsets) are generally pretty tech-savvy, and can sell you the relevant card (there are usually a number of brands to choose from) and show you how to use it. Most internet cafés will also let you use operators such as Skype (www.skype.com) – remember to take your sign-in details.

If you're a traditionalist, or if internet-connected phone calls aren't possible, head for the public telephone office, which usually sits adjacent to the post office. Here, you can generally make operator-connected calls or buy cards for use in phone booths around the city; kiosks dotted around most major cities generally sell the same cards. There are also privately run call centres (although many of these have three-minute call minimums), where you can make international calls and send faxes. Costs for international calls start at about US$3 per minute, and a few countries offer reduced rates at night.

If cash is tight, many travellers make an international call and then make their (long-suffering) parents call them back later at their hotel. If that's the case, the least you can do is buy them a calling card back home before you leave, so that they don't dread every time they hear from you.

Mobile Phones

Mobile networks in Middle Eastern countries all work on the GSM system, and it's extremely rare that your mobile brought from home won't automatically link up with a local operator. That's fine for receiving calls, but roaming charges can make for a nasty surprise back home if you've made a few calls while away. If you plan to be in a country for a while, making calls while there, your best option is to buy a local SIM card – an easy process in every country of the region.

See the Telephone section in the relevant country chapters for further details.

TIME

Egypt, Israel and the Palestinian Territories, Jordan, Lebanon, Libya, Syria and Turkey are two hours ahead of GMT/UTC, with Iraq three hours ahead. Of the countries covered by this book, only Jordan does not operate daylight-saving hours.

Time is something that Middle Eastern people always seem to have plenty of; something that should take five minutes will invariably take an hour. Trying to speed things up will only lead to frustration. It is better to take it philosophically than try to fight it.

TOILETS

Outside the midrange and top-end hotels and restaurants (where Western-style loos are the norm), visitors will encounter their fair share of Arab-style squat toilets (which, incidentally, according to physiologists, encourage a far more natural position than the Western-style invention!).

It's a good idea to carry an emergency stash of toilet paper with you for the times when you're caught short outside the hotel as most of these toilets have a water hose and bucket for the same purpose.

TOURIST INFORMATION

Most countries in the region have tourist offices with branches in big towns and at tourist sights. That said, don't expect much. Usually, the most the offices can produce is a free map; help with booking accommodation or any other service is typically beyond the resources of the often nonetheless amiable staff. The exceptions to this rule are some of the offices in Israel and the Palestinian Territories, which are in fact very useful. You'll usually get better results relying on the knowledge and resourcefulness of your hotel reception or a local guide. Tourist-office locations are given in the individual town and city sections throughout this book.

TRAVELLERS WITH DISABILITIES

Generally speaking, scant regard is paid to the needs of disabled travellers in the Middle East. Steps, high kerbs and other assorted obstacles are everywhere, streets are often badly rutted and uneven, roads are made virtually uncrossable by heavy traffic, and many doorways are low and narrow. Ramps and specially equipped lodgings and toilets are an extreme rarity. The happy exception is Israel and the Palestinian Territories; see p330 for details. Elsewhere, you'll have to plan your trip carefully and will probably be obliged to restrict yourself to luxury-level hotels and private, hired transport.

If it all sounds difficult, remember that where Middle Eastern governments have singularly failed to provide the necessary infrastructure, local officials, guides and hotel staff almost invariably do their best to help in any way they can.

Before setting out for the Middle East, disabled travellers should consider contacting any of the following organisations who can help with advice and assistance:

Access-able Travel Source (☎ 303-232-2979; www.access-able.com; PO Box 1796, Wheatridge, CO, 80034, USA)

Accessible Travel & Leisure (☎ 0145-272 9739; www.accessibletravel.co.uk) Claims to be the biggest UK travel agent dealing with travel for the disabled. The company encourages the disabled to travel independently.

Holiday Care (☎ 0845 124 9971; www.holidaycare.org.uk; The Hawkins Suite, Enham Place, Enham Alamein, Andover SP11 6JS, UK)

Mobility International USA (☎ 541-343-1284; www.miusa.org; 132 East Broadway, Suite 343, Eugene, OR 97401, USA)

Royal Association for Disability & Rehabilitation (RADAR; ☎ 020-7250 3222; www.radar.org.uk; 12 City Forum, 250 City Rd, London, EC1V 8AF, UK) Publishes a useful guide called *Holidays & Travel Abroad: A Guide for Disabled People*.

Society for Accessible Travel and Hospitality (☎ 212-447-7284; www.sath.org; 347 5th Ave, Suite 610, New York, NY 10016, USA)

VISAS

If you do one piece of research before setting out on your trip, it should be to familiarise yourself with the requirements for obtaining visas for the countries that you intend to visit. For the unwary, it can be a minefield. For the well informed, it shouldn't pose too many difficulties. For more information on the visa requirements for each country, see Visas in the Directory of the relevant country chapter. For a broad overview of visas and border crossings for Middle Eastern countries, see the table Visas & Borders at a Glance that follows this section.

If Israel and the Palestinian Territories loom on your horizon, the most obvious thing to consider is how to get around the problem of an Israeli stamp in your passport if you intend to later visit Syria, Lebanon or Iraq. For advice, see the boxed text, p332.

There are other things you need to consider. Although it's becoming less frequent, some embassies request a letter from an employer or, if you're applying abroad, a letter of introduction from your embassy. Then there are the Israeli officials who, if they don't like the look of you, may ask to see that you have a sufficient amount of money to cover your stay. Some embassies also ask to see a 'ticket out', which means that before you can obtain a visa to get into a country you must have a ticket to prove that you intend leaving again.

Depending on the country, you can get them either before you go, along the way or, increasingly frequently, at the airport or border. The advantage of predeparture collection is that it doesn't waste travelling time, and 'difficult' embassies are sometimes less difficult when you're in your own country – they can usually explain things in your own language and that seemingly meaningless, but utterly essential, document they require is much easier to find back home. It's also true that if you're turned down in your home country, there's usually nothing to stop you trying again while on the road.

WOMEN TRAVELLERS

Some women imagine that travel to the Middle East is both difficult and dangerous. In reality, there's no reason why women can't enjoy the region as much as their male counterparts. In fact, some seasoned women travellers consider their gender a help, not a hindrance, in the Middle East and you'll likely meet more women travellers having the time of their lives than come across those doing it tough.

For more information on the situation in specific countries, see the Women Travellers section in the Directory of each individual country chapter.

Attitudes Towards Women

Some of the biggest misunderstandings between Middle Easterners and Westerners

VISAS & BORDERS AT A GLANCE

To/From	From/To	Border Crossing Notes
Egypt	Israel & the Palestinian Territories	the Taba crossing is the only one open to foreign travellers (p202)
Egypt	Jordan	joined by ferry, the entry points are at Nuweiba (Egypt; p200) & Aqaba (Jordan; p383)
Jordan	Israel & the Palestinian Territories	the crossings are at King Hussein/Allenby Bridge (close to Jerusalem), Jordan River/Sheikh Hussein Bridge (close to Beit She'an/Irbid) & Yitzhak Rabin (close to Eilat/Aqaba)
Jordan	Iraq	the Karama/Tarbil crossing, 330km east of Amman, is not recommended
Jordan	Syria	the fastest of the 2 crossings is at Ramtha/Deraa
Syria	Lebanon	of the 4 main crossings, the 2 main ones are along the Beirut-Damascus Highway & on the Tripoli-Tartus coastal road
Syria	Iraq	the only open crossing is just south of Al-Bukamal in eastern Syria, but is not recommended for foreign travellers
Syria	Turkey	the most popular crossing is Bab al-Hawa between Antakya (p583) & Aleppo (p491)
Turkey	Iraq	the crossing is at Zakho (p226)

*The situation regarding visas for travel between Syria and Lebanon may have changed by the time you read this. See the boxed text, p524 for more information.

occur over the issue of women. Half-truths and stereotypes exist on both sides: many Westerners assume all Middle Eastern women are veiled, repressed victims, while a large number of locals see Western women as sex-obsessed and immoral.

For many Middle Easterners, both men and women, the role of a woman is specifically defined: she is mother and matron of the household. The man is the provider. However, as with any society, generalisations can be misleading and the reality is far more nuanced. There are thousands of middle- and upper-middle-class professional women in the Arab World who, like their counterparts in the West, juggle work and family responsibilities. Among the working classes or in conservative rural areas, where adherence to tradition is strongest, the ideal may be for women to concentrate on home and family, but economic reality means that millions of women are forced to work (but are still responsible for all domestic chores).

The issue of sex is where differences between Western and Middle Eastern women are most apparent. Premarital sex (or, indeed, any sex outside marriage) is taboo, although, as with anything forbidden, it still happens. Nevertheless, it's the exception rather than the rule – and that goes for men as well as women. However, for women the issue is potentially far more serious. With occasional exceptions among the upper classes, women are expected to be virgins when they marry and a family's reputation can rest upon this. In such a context, the restrictions placed on a young girl – no matter how onerous they may seem to a Westerner – are intended to protect her and her reputation from the potentially disastrous attentions of men.

The presence of foreign women presents, in the eyes of some Middle Eastern men, a chance to get around these norms with ease and without consequences. That this is even possible is heavily reinforced by distorted impressions gained from Western TV and by the comparatively liberal behaviour of foreign women in the country. As one hopeful young man in Egypt remarked, when asked why he persisted in harassing every Western woman he saw: 'For every 10 that say no, there's one that says yes.'

Visa Obtainable at Border?	Visa Information	Border Crossing Information
to Egypt: only with letter from Egyptian travel agency to Israel & the Palestinian Territories: yes	p207 & p330	p208 & p332
to Egypt: at Aqaba Port to Jordan: yes	p207 & p393	p209 & p397
to Jordan: yes (except at King Hussein/Allenby Bridge) to Israel & the Palestinian Territories: yes	p393 & p330	p395 & p332
to Jordan: yes to Iraq: no	p393 & p245	p395
to Jordan: yes to Syria: yes, if no Syrian embassy in your home country	p393 & p523	p396 & p525
not officially*	p523 & p454	p526 & p455
to Syria: no to Iraq: no	p523 & p245	p525
to Syria: yes, if no Syrian embassy in your home country to Turkey: yes	p523 & p614	p526 & p616
to Turkey: yes to Iraq: Iraqi Kurdish visas are issued at Zakho & at Erbil & Sulaymaniyah airports (travellers of Arab descent need not apply)	p614 & p245	p615 & p246

What to Expect

Women travellers are no different from their male counterparts in that meeting local people is a highlight of travelling in the Middle East. Where women have an advantage is that, unlike male travellers, they can meet Middle Eastern women without social restrictions. In this sense, women have access to a whole Middle Eastern world that men can never hope to see. Local women are as curious about life for women beyond the Middle East as you are about their lives, and they love to chat to women visitors. They are, of course, far more likely to approach you as a female if you're on your own or in a group of women. That said, local women are less likely than men to have had an education that included learning English – you'll find this to be the only major barrier to getting to meet and talk with them.

One other advantage, and it's one which you should exploit to the full, is that it's often perfectly acceptable for a woman to go straight to the front of a queue or to ask to be served first before any men who may be waiting!

That's not to say that everything is perfect. Far from it. Sexual harassment is a problem worldwide and the Middle East is no exception. Harassment can come in many forms: from stares, muttered comments and uncomfortably close contact on crowded public transport, to the difficulty of eating in public on your own, where you may receive endless unwanted guests – even the wandering hands of waiters can be a problem. Women also report being followed and hissed at by unwanted male admirers on a fairly regular basis.

That said, although 'mild' harassment can be common in some countries, physical harassment is rare and sexual harassment is considered to be a serious crime in many Middle Eastern countries. In fact, incidents of sexual assault or rape are far lower in the region than in the West. It's also true that, contrary to prevailing stereotypes, the treatment of foreign women can be at its best in more conservative societies, providing, of course, you adhere to the prevailing social mores.

The treatment of women can also be a factor of age: older women will find they are greatly respected. As one seasoned Middle Eastern expat and traveller told us, she was so traumatised after travelling in Israel as a 21-year-old that she took up karate. Now in her forties, she's been going back to the region ever since. 'I realise the older I get, the less harassment I receive,' said, and she's now 'wonderfully relieved I've reached that age where I can have a meaningful conversation with men without inviting other expectations. Having a husband is also immensely useful!'

What to Do When You're There

What sort of experience you have will depend partly on situations beyond your control, but also on your reaction to them. Expatriate women and those who've travelled extensively throughout the region maintain that the most important thing is to retain your self-confidence and sense of humour. Another recurring theme is that you should always be alert, but a certain detachment can be an equally powerful weapon: ignoring stares and refusing to dignify suggestive remarks with a response generally stops unwanted advances in their tracks.

It may be unfair, even discriminatory in the eyes of many travellers, but how women travellers dress will, considering the stereotypes at large in the region, go a long way towards determining how you're treated. To you, short pants and a tight top might be an expression of your right to do whatever the hell you want. To many local men, your dress choice will send an entirely different message, confirming the worst views held of Western women.

The best way to tackle the stereotypes is to visibly debunk them: in other words, do as the locals do, dress and behave more modestly than you might at home and always err on the side of caution. As with anywhere, take your cues from those around you: if you're in a rural area and all the women are in long, concealing dresses, you should be conservatively dressed.

Dressing 'modestly' really means covering your upper legs and arms, shoulders and cleavage. A scarf is also useful, both to cover your neckline and to slip over your head when you want to look even more inconspicuous or when the occasion requires it (such as when visiting a mosque). For all the inconvenience, dressing conservatively has the following advantages: you'll get a much warmer reception from the locals (who will really appreciate your willingness to respect their culture and customs), you'll attract less unwanted attention, and you may well feel more comfortable (long baggy clothes don't just keep you cooler, they also protect you from the fierce Middle Eastern sun).

There are other ways to avoid unwelcome attention. Eat in a restaurant's family section, where one exists, or at places more used to tourists. If you're not married, invent or borrow a husband, wear a wedding ring, even carry a photo of your 'kids'. While this may cause some consternation – what sort of mother/wife are you to have left your family to travel alone? – it will deter many suitors, especially if you assure them that you're on your way to meet them right now. Most women travellers also find that avoiding direct eye contact with local men – dark sunglasses help – works wonders, although a cold glare can also be an effective riposte if deployed at the right moment.

Maximising your interaction with local women can also help you avoid uncomfortable situations. In taxis, avoid sitting in the front seat unless the driver is female and, on all forms of public transport, sit next to another woman whenever possible. You're lost? Try asking a local woman for directions.

If none of this works and you can't shake off a hanger-on, going to the nearest public place, such as the lobby of a hotel, usually works well. If they still persist, asking the receptionist to call the police usually frightens them off.

WORK

It's possible to pick up work in the Middle East in order to extend your stay and eke out your savings – but you have to know where to look and what you're looking for. Forget Syria; realistically, your best options are in Egypt, Israel and the Palestinian Territories, and Turkey, in the places where other foreigners gather in numbers.

For information about working on a kibbutz or a moshav, see p331.

Teaching English

Teaching centres – both the respectable kind and the 'cowboy' outfits – can be found throughout the Middle East. The cowboys are often desperate for teachers, and they'll take on people whose only qualification is that their mother tongue is English. In general, the pay is minimal and you'll probably have to stay on a tourist visa, which it will be up to you to renew. However, numerous long-term travellers finance their stays this way, particularly in Cairo and İstanbul.

Your chances of getting a better job are greatly improved if you have a certificate in CELTA (Certificate in English Language Teaching to Adults). This is what used to be known as TEFL, and basically it's your passport to work abroad. To get the qualification, you'll need to attend a one-month intensive course, which you can do in your home country via an English-language training centre. In the UK, contact **International House** (IH; ☎ 020-7611 2400; www.ihlondon.com; 16 Stukeley Street, London WC2B 5LQ), which runs more than a dozen courses a year and has 110 affiliated schools in 30 countries worldwide, including Egypt (Cairo) and Turkey (İstanbul). Once you've completed the course, you can apply for any advertised positions.

Alternatively, you could fly out to Cairo and do the CELTA course at Cairo's **International Language Institute** (www.arabicegypt.com), which is affiliated to International House. Depending on the price of your flight, this may be a cheaper way to do it than at IH in London, as the cost of the course is generally around half the equivalent of doing it in the UK.

The other major employer of English-language teachers is the **British Council** (www.britishcouncil.org). Its overseas teaching centres very rarely take on people who just turn up at the door, as most recruiting is done in the UK. Well in advance of your departure date, check its website, which has a list of upcoming vacancies and British Council addresses in the Middle East.

Qualified teachers should also check out **Dave's ESL Café** (www.eslcafe.com) for regular job postings.

Working at a Hostel

In Israel (Jerusalem, Tel Aviv and Eilat) and various places in Turkey (particularly İstanbul, Selçuk, Bodrum, Fethiye and Cappadocia), it's usually possible to pick up work in a hostel, typically cleaning rooms or looking after reception. It doesn't pay much, but it does usually get you a free room, a meal or two a day plus some beer money. The only way to find this kind of work is to ask around.

Transport in the Middle East

CONTENTS

GETTING THERE & AWAY

This section tells you how to reach the Middle East by air, land and sea from other parts of the world, and outlines the routes for onward travel from the region. For details of travel between one country and its neighbours within the region, see the Getting There & Away section at the end of the relevant country chapter.

ENTERING THE MIDDLE EAST

For visa requirements, see the Visa section of each country's Directory; information on crossing borders is covered in each chapter's Transport section.

> **THINGS CHANGE...**
>
> The information in this chapter is particularly vulnerable to change. Check directly with the airline or a travel agent to make sure you understand how a fare (and ticket you may buy) works and be aware of the security requirements for international travel. Shop carefully. The details given in this chapter should be regarded as pointers and are not a substitute for your own careful, up-to-date research.

Please note that neither Israeli citizens nor anyone with an Israeli stamp in their passport will be allowed to enter Iran, Iraq, Lebanon or Syria. For advice on how to get around this decades-old Middle Eastern conundrum, see the boxed text, p332.

AIR

All the major European and Middle Eastern, and some Asian, airlines serve the principal cities of the region; the most frequent flights head for Cairo, İstanbul and Tel Aviv. Another route to consider is via the Gulf region, thanks to the burgeoning power (and growing routes) of Emirates, Qatar Airways and Gulf Air.

A proliferation of budget or low-cost carriers, especially in Turkey and the Gulf region, has revolutionised flying to and within the region. Many of these fly into Middle Eastern cities that are not connected to the outside world by national airlines; others offer domestic services, while others are charter airlines.

Airlines

The following all fly into the Middle East:

Afriqiyah Airways (www.afriqiyah.aero)
Air Arabia (www.airarabia.com) UAE low-cost airline.
Air Canada (www.aircanada.com)
Air France (www.airfrance.com)
Al-Buraq (www.buraqair.com; Libya) Private Libyan Airline.
Alitalia (www.alitalia.com)
American Airlines (www.aa.com)
Atlasjet (www.atlasjet.com) Turkish international charter airline.
Austrian Airlines (www.aua.com)
Bahrain Air (www.bahrainair.net)
British Airways (www.britishairways.com)
Corendon Airlines (www.corendon-airlines.com) Turkish airline with flights around Europe.
Delta Air Lines (www.delta.com)
EgyptAir (www.egyptair.com.eg)
El Al (www.elal.co.il)
Emirates (www.emirates.com)
Ethiopian Airlines (www.ethiopianairlines.com)
Free Bird Airlines (www.freebirdairlines.com) Turkish charter airline.
Golden International Airlines (www.goldenairlines.com) Turkish charter airline.
Gulf Air (www.gulfair.com)

CLIMATE CHANGE & TRAVEL

Climate change is a serious threat to the ecosystems that humans rely upon, and air travel is the fastest-growing contributor to the problem. Lonely Planet regards travel, overall, as a global benefit, but believes we all have a responsibility to limit our personal impact on global warming.

Flying & Climate Change

Pretty much every form of motor travel generates CO_2 (the main cause of human-induced climate change) but planes are far and away the worst offenders, not just because of the sheer distances they allow us to travel, but because they release greenhouse gases high into the atmosphere. The statistics are frightening: two people taking a return flight between Europe and the US will contribute as much to climate change as an average household's gas and electricity consumption over a whole year.

Carbon Offset Schemes

Climatecare.org and other websites use 'carbon calculators' that allow jetsetters to offset the greenhouse gases they are responsible for with contributions to energy-saving projects and other climate-friendly initiatives in the developing world – including projects in India, Honduras, Kazakhstan and Uganda.

Lonely Planet, together with Rough Guides and other concerned partners in the travel industry, supports the carbon offset scheme run by climatecare.org. Lonely Planet offsets all of its staff and author travel.

For more information check out our website: lonelyplanet.com.

Inter Airlines (www.interekspres.com) Turkish charter airline.
Iran Air (www.iranair.com)
Iran Aseman (www.iaa.ir)
Jazeera Airways (www.jazeeraairways.com) Kuwaiti low-cost airline that flies to all Middle Eastern countries except Israel and Iraq.
Kenya Airways (www.kenya-airways.com)
KLM Royal Dutch Airlines (www.klm.com)
Kuwait Airways (www.kuwait-airways.com)
Libyan Arab Airlines (www.ln.aero)
Lotus Air (www.lotus-air.com) Egyptian charter airline.
Lufthansa (www.lufthansa.com)
Mahan Air (www.mahan.aero)
Middle East Airlines (www.mea.com.lb)
Nasair (www.flynas.com) Saudi low-cost carrier.
Olympic Airlines (www.olympicairlines.com)
Onur Air (www.onurair.com.tr) Turkish airline.
Pegasus Airlines (www.flypgs.com) Turkish charter airline.
Qantas Airways (www.qantas.com)
Qatar Airways (www.qatarairways.com)
Royal Jordanian (www.rja.com)
Sama (www.flysama.com) Saudi budget airline.
Singapore Airlines (www.singaporeair.com)
Sudan Airways (www.sudanair.com)
Sun D'Or (www.sundor.co.il) Israeli budget carrier airline.
SunExpress (www.sunexpress.com) Turkish charter airline.
Swiss International Airlines (www.swiss.com)
SyrianAir (www.syriaair.com)
Tarhan Tower Airlines (www.ttairlines.com) Turkish charter airline.
Tunis Air (www.tunisair.com)
Turkish Airlines (www.thy.com)
Turkmenistan Airlines (www.turkmenistanairlines.com)
Uzbek Airways (www.uzairways.com)

Africa

Despite the proximity, there's nothing cheap about flying from the Middle East into Africa. In fact, for most African capitals a ticket bought in London will be cheaper than one bought in the Middle East. The best bet may be to buy your African ticket with a stopover in the Middle East.

As a general rule, the widest choice of direct African destinations is offered by EgyptAir. They're now being challenged by Afriqiyah Airways, which flies to 12 sub-Saharan African capitals, including Bamako (Mali), Accra (Ghana), Lagos (Nigeria) and Khartoum (Sudan) from Cairo, provided you don't mind going via Tripoli (Libya). South African Airways is another option, connecting the Middle East (Cairo, Amman and Beirut) with Johannesburg. Other airlines that connect the Middle East (usually Cairo) with African cities include Ethiopian Airlines (Addis Ababa), Kenya Airways (Nairobi), Sudan Airways (Khartoum) and Tunis Air (Tunis).

INTERNET AIR FARES

Most airlines, especially budget ones, encourage you to book on their websites. Other useful general sites to search for competitive fares include the following.

- www.atrapalo.com (in Spanish)
- www.cheaptickets.com
- www.ebookers.com
- www.expedia.com
- www.expedia.de (in German)
- www.fr.lastminute.com (in French)
- www.lastminute.com
- www.lastminute.de (in German)
- www.lowestfare.com
- www.opodo.com
- www.orbitz.com
- www.planesimple.co.uk
- www.rumbo.es (in Spanish)
- www.sta.com
- www.travel.com.au
- www.travelocity.com

Australia & New Zealand

Airlines that fly directly to the Middle East from Melbourne and Sydney include Emirates and Qatar Airways; Emirates also operates services to Brisbane and Perth. Although they require a stopover in Dubai and Doha respectively, they have connections throughout the Middle East, they're generally counted among the world's best airlines and their prices can be surprisingly reasonable.

If you're headed for Tel Aviv, Qantas Airways and El Al via Asia are the best. Other options include Alitalia via Milan, Lufthansa Airlines via Frankfurt or KLM Royal Dutch Airlines via Amsterdam.

Both **STA Travel** (☎ 134 782; www.statravel.com.au) and **Flight Centre** (☎ 133 133; www.flightcentre.com.au) have offices throughout Australia.

In New Zealand, both **Flight Centre** (☎ 0800 243 544; www.flightcentre.co.nz) and **STA Travel** (☎ 0800 474 400; www.statravel.co.nz) have branches throughout the country.

Central Asia & the Caucasus

Look no further than İstanbul as your gateway to the Middle East from Central Asian and Caucasus destinations. There are regular flights between İstanbul and Almaty (Kazakhstan), Bishkek (Kyrgyzstan), Baku (Azerbaijan), Tashkent (Uzbekistan) and Ashghabat (Turkmenistan) with Turkish Airlines and/or the national airlines of each country.

From Tel Aviv, Uzbekistan Airways flies to Tashkent.

Europe

With the rise of online booking services, there's not much variation in airfare prices for departures from the main European cities, but prices do vary considerably depending on your date of travel and when you booked. All the major airlines also usually offer some sort of deal and travel agencies generally have a number of special offers, so shop around.

Look out for cheap charter-flight packages from Western Europe to destinations in Turkey, Egypt and Israel. Some of the flight-plus-accommodation packages offered by travel agencies can work out to be cheaper than a standard flight, although often the dates can be very restrictive.

Most European carriers fly into the major cities of the Middle East (usually several times a week); the most frequent connections are with Paris, Frankfurt, Rome and Athens.

Recommended agencies on the mainland in Europe:

Airfair (☎ 0900-7717 717; www.airfair.nl; Netherlands)
Barcelo Viajes (☎ 902 116 226; www.barceloviajes.com; Spain)
CTS Viaggi (☎ 199 501 150; www.cts.it; Italy)
Nouvelles Frontières (☎ 08 25 00 07 47; www.nouvelles-frontieres.fr; France)
STA Travel (☎ 069-743 032 92; www.statravel.de; Germany)

UK

Although charter flights leave for Turkey and the Red Sea resorts of Egypt's Sinai Peninsula from many UK airports, most regular flights leave from London and a handful of other international airports. There are few dedicated specialists for Middle East flights and your best bet is to call **STA Travel** (☎ 0871 230 0040; www.statravel.co.uk) and **Trailfinders** (☎ 0845 058 5858; www.trailfinders.co.uk), both of which have branches throughout the UK.

If you're looking to fly into Egypt then it's also worth calling **Soliman Travel** (☎ 020-7244

6855; www.solimantravel.com), a reputable Egypt specialist that often manages to undercut the competition, usually with charter flights.

USA & Canada

There are more flights to the Middle East from the USA than from Canada, but still not that many: Royal Jordanian flies between Amman and New York/Chicago or Montreal, as well as a handful of other US cities; EgyptAir flies between New York and Cairo; El Al connects Tel Aviv to a number of US cities as well as Montreal; and Delta Air Lines flies from Tel Aviv, Cairo and İstanbul to New York with connections elsewhere in North American cities.

STA Travel (☎ 800-781-4040; www.statravel.com) has offices in many major US cities; call the toll-free 800 number for office locations or visit its website.

Travel CUTS (☎ 1866-246-9762; www.travelcuts.com) is Canada's national student travel agency and has offices in all major cities.

LAND

Border Crossings

Border crossings in the Middle East can be slow and it can take hours to pass through immigration and customs formalities, especially if you bring your own car. Showing patience, politeness and good humour is likely to speed up the process. For further details, see p633 for visa information and p649 for information on bringing your own vehicle, as well as the Transport sections in each individual country chapter.

If travelling overland independently to or from the Middle East – whether hitching, cycling, driving your own car or riding by train or by bus – you can approach the region from Africa, the Caucasus, Iran or Europe.

AFRICA

For details of ferry services between Aswan (Egypt) and Wadi Halfa (Sudan), see p645. Before setting out, check the security situation in Sudan; many East African overlanders skip Sudan by flying from Egypt to Addis Ababa in Ethiopia.

Egypt's only border crossing with Libya is at Amsaad, on the Mediterranean coast 12km west of Sallum. Service taxis run up the mountain between the town and the Egyptian side of the crossing for E£4. If that sounds suspiciously easy, you're right to be sceptical. Tourist visas for Libya require an invitation from an accredited Libyan tour company, and you'll be required to sign up for an escorted tour for the duration of your stay. Such an invitation should be arranged weeks in advance. *Never* just turn up at the border hoping that visa regulations have been relaxed.

THE CAUCASUS

Armenia

At the time of writing, the Turkish–Armenian border was closed to travellers. The situation could change, so it's worth checking (the Russian embassy handles Armenian diplomatic interests in Turkey). If you want to travel from Turkey to Armenia (or vice versa), you can fly or travel by bus via Georgia. At least three buses weekly depart from Trabzon's otogar heading for Yerevan.

Azerbaijan (Nakhichevan)

At least two daily buses depart from Trabzon's otogar heading for Tbilisi (Georgia), where you can change for Baku. You can cross from Turkey to the Azerbaijani enclave of Nakhichevan via the remote Borualan–Sadarak border post, 105km southeast of Iğdır. From there, you'll need to fly across Armenian-occupied Nagorno-Karabakh to reach the rest of Azerbaijan and Baku.

Georgia

The main border crossing is at Sarp on the Black Sea coast, between Hopa (Turkey) and Batum (Georgia). You can also cross inland at the Türkgözü border crossing near Posof, north of Kars (Turkey) and southwest of Akhaltsikhe (Georgia). The Sarp border crossing is open 24 hours a day; Türkgözü is open from 8am to 8pm, though in winter you might want to double check it's open at all. At least two daily buses depart from Trabzon's otogar heading for Tbilisi (19 hours).

If you're heading to the Türkgözü border from the Turkish side, a convenient starting point is Kars. You need to get to Posof first, then hire a taxi or minibus to take you to the border post 16km away. From the border, hire another taxi to take you to the Georgian town of Akhaltsikhe, from where regular buses head to Tbilisi (which can take up to seven hours). A more direct option consists of taking a minibus to

Ardahan, where you can hop on the daily İstanbul–Tbilisi bus, which leaves from Ardahan at around 10am.

EUROPE

It's fairly easy to get to İstanbul by direct train or bus from many points in Europe via Bulgaria. Despite the romantic appeal of train journeys, getting to Turkey overland is usually cheaper and faster by bus. Several Turkish bus lines offer reliable and quite comfortable services between İstanbul and Germany, Italy, Austria and Greece.

Bulgaria & Other Eastern European Countries

There are three border crossings between Bulgaria and Turkey. The main border crossing is the busy Kapitan–Andreevo/Kapıkule, 18km west of Edirne on the E5. The closest town on the Bulgarian side is Svilengrad, some 10km from the border. You have to hitch a lift or hire a taxi rather than walk between the Greek–Turkish border posts. This crossing is open 24 hours daily. There's a second crossing at Lesovo–Hamzabeyli, some 25km north of Edirne; it's a quieter option during the busy summer months than Kapitan–Andreevo/Kapıkule, but takes a little longer to get to and there's no public transport. The third crossing is at Malko Târnovo–Kırıkkale, some 70km northeast of Edirne and 92km south of Burgas.

There are several bus departures daily to Sofia, and the coastal cities of Varna and Burgas in Bulgaria from İstanbul's otogar. There are also daily departures to Skopje, Tetovo and Gostivar in Macedonia, and to Constanta and Bucharest (Romania).

The daily *Bosphorus Express* (*Bosfor Ekspresi*) train, for example, runs from İstanbul to Bucharest, from where you can travel onwards by train to Moldova and Hungary. You can also catch the *Bosphorus Express* as far as Dimitrovgrad (Bulgaria) from where you can travel onwards to Sofia (Bulgaria) and on to Belgrade (Serbia). You'll need to take your own food and drinks as there are no restaurant cars on these trains.

Greece

The crossing points between western Thrace in Greece and eastern Thrace in Turkey are at Kipi–İpsala, and Kastanies/Pazarkule, near Edirne.

One of the most popular ways of getting to Turkey from Europe is to make your way to Alexandroupolis in Greece and cross at Kipi–İpsala, 43km northeast of Alexandroupolis, or Kastanies–Pazarkule, 139km northeast, near the Turkish city of Edirne. Both borders are open 24 hours.

At least six weekly buses travel from Athens' Peloponnese train station to İstanbul. You can also pick up the bus in Thessaloniki and at Alexandroupolis. Alternatively, you can make your own way to Alexandroupolis and take a service from the intercity bus station to the border town of Kipi. You can't walk across the border, but it's easy enough to hitch (you may be able to get a lift all the way to İstanbul). Otherwise, take a bus to İpsala (5km east beyond the border) or Keşan (30km east beyond the border), from where there are many buses to the capital.

The best option for travelling by train between Greece and Turkey is the overnight train between Thessaloniki and İstanbul called the *Filia-Dostluk Express*. The 1400km journey takes 12 to 14 hours, including an hour or two's delay at the border, and accommodation is in comfy, air-conditioned sleeper cars. You can buy tickets at the train stations but not online. For more information see the websites of **Turkish State Railways** (TCDD; www.tcdd.gov.tr) or the **Hellenic Railways Organisation** (www.ose.gr).

IRAN

There are two border crossings between Iran and Turkey: the busier Gürbulak–Bazargan, near Doğubayazıt (Turkey) and Şahabat (Iran); and the Esendere–Sero border crossing, southeast of Van (Turkey). Gürbulak–Bazargan is open 24 hours. Esendere–Sero is open from 8am until midnight, but double-check in winter as the border might be closed. Travellers are increasingly using this second crossing into Iran, which has the added bonus of taking you through the breathtaking scenery of far southeastern Anatolia. And to make things easy, there is a direct bus running between Van (Turkey) and Orumiyeh (Iran).

There are regular buses from İstanbul and Ankara to Tabriz and Tehran. You may also want to consider taking a dolmuş from Doğubayazıt 35km east to the border at Gürbulak and then walking across the border. The crossing might take up to an hour. From

CARNETS

A carnet de passage is like a passport for your car, a booklet that is stamped on arrival at, and departure from, a country to ensure that you export the vehicle again after you've imported it. It's usually issued by an automobile association in the country where the vehicle is registered. Most countries of the Middle East require a carnet, although rules change frequently.

The sting in the tail is that you usually have to lodge a deposit to secure it. If you default on the carnet – that is, you don't have an export stamp to match the import one – then the country in question can claim your deposit, which can be up to 300% of the new value of the vehicle. You can get around this problem with bank guarantees or carnet insurance, but you still have to fork out in the end if you default.

Should the worst occur and your vehicle is irretrievably damaged in an accident or catastrophic breakdown, you'll have to argue it out with customs officials. Having a vehicle stolen can be even worse, as you may be suspected of having sold it.

The carnet may also need to specify any expensive spare parts that you're planning to carry with you, such as a gearbox, which is designed to prevent any spare-part importation rackets. Contact your local automobile association for details about all necessary documentation at least three months in advance.

Bazargan there are onward buses to Tabriz; from Sero there are buses to Orumiyeh.

The *Trans-Asya Ekspresi* train runs between Tehran and İstanbul, travelling via Tabriz, Van and Tatvan. Expect a comfortable journey on connecting Turkish and Iranian trains, a ferry ride across Lake Van, and no showers. See the Iranian Railways site, **RAJA Passenger Train Co** (www.rajatrains.com), for more information. There's also a weekly train service between Tehran (Iran) and Damascus (Syria) via Van, Malatya and Aleppo. See www.tcdd.gov.tr for more information.

Of the five major crossing points between Iraq and Iran, the only one that *may* be open to tourists is at the busy Iraqi border town of Haji Omaran, 180km northeast of Erbil. To cross here, you will need a prearranged Iranian visa. Check with the local authorities before travelling.

Car & Motorcycle

Anyone planning to take their own vehicle with them needs to check in advance what spare parts and petrol are likely to be available (see p648).

A number of documents are also required (if you're unsure what to take, check with the automobile association in your home country):

Carnet de passage See the boxed text, above.

Green card Issued by insurers. Insurance for some countries is only obtainable at the border.

International Driving Permit (IDP) Although most foreign licences are acceptable in Middle Eastern countries, an IDP issued by your local automobile association is highly recommended, and is required for entry with a vehicle at some border crossings.

Vehicle registration documents In addition to carrying all ownership papers, check with your insurer whether you're covered for the countries you intend to visit and whether third-party cover is included.

SEA

Ferries shuttle reasonably regularly between southern Europe and Israel, Turkey and Egypt. There are other less-frequented routes connecting Egypt with Sudan and the Arabian Peninsula. In summer, you might also come across services operating between Cyprus and Syria, but these are highly seasonal and change from year to year.

As well as the services listed below, some cruise liners call at Middle Eastern ports such as Suez or Alexandria, but these are beyond the scope of this book. A good travel agent should be able to tell you what's available in the season you are travelling.

Unless stated otherwise, all services run in both directions. When booking, remember that a slight discount may apply on return tickets; student, youth or child fares may be possible on some lines. Schedules tend to change at least annually according to demand; fares, too, often fluctuate according to season, especially on the Mediterranean routes.

Although vehicles can be shipped on most of the following routes, bookings may have to be made some time in advance. The charge usually depends on the length or volume of the vehicle and should be checked with the carrier. As a rule, motorcycles cost almost nothing to ship while bicycles are free.

You're unlikely to regret taking an adequate supply of food and drink with you on any of these ships; even if it's available on board, you're pretty stuck if it doesn't agree with you or your budget.

Cyprus

From Haifa (Israel and the Palestinian Territories), there are overnight passenger and cargo ferries to Limassol in Cyprus (10 hours). From Limassol, there are ferry connections to Greek ports, including Piraeus (the port for Athens). The ferry is operated by **Rosenfeld Shipping** (☎ 04-861 3671; www.rosenfeld.net). Note that when demand is low, the service may be suspended.

From Port Said (Egypt), boats to Limassol in Cyprus depart twice weekly from May to November. For information and tickets, visit one of the many shipping agencies in Port Said, such as **Canal Tours** (☎ 066-332 1874, 012-798 6338; canaltours@bec.com.eg).

The main crossing point between northern Cyprus and Turkey is between Taşucu (near Silifke, in Turkey) and Girne on the northern coast of northern Cyprus; **Akgünler Denizcilik** (www.akgunler.com.tr) makes this journey. You can also travel between Alanya (Turkey) and Girne with **Fergün Denizcilik** (www.fergun.net), or between Mersin (Turkey) and Gazimağusa (Famagusta), on the east coast of Northern Cyprus, with **Turkish Maritime Lines** (☎ 324-231 2688) in Mersin.

If you have a multiple-entry visa for Turkey, you should be able to cross over to Northern Cyprus and back again without buying a new one. However, if your visa has expired, you should anticipate long queues at immigration.

Greece

Private ferries link Turkey's Aegean coast and the Greek islands, which are in turn linked by air or boat to Athens. Services are usually daily in summer, several times a week in spring and autumn, and perhaps just once a week in winter. Please note that all the information that follows covers travelling to Greece from Turkish cities and towns.

Daily boats operate from Ayvalık to Lesvos (Greece) from June to September, with two weekly services from October to May. Çeşme is a transit point to the Greek island of Chios, 10km away across the water; in summer, there are five weekly ferries to Chios, and at least two weekly services in winter. Buy your ticket from any travel agency at the harbour.

All Kuşadası travel agencies sell tickets to the Greek island of Samos; a daily boat runs from April to October. There may be more-frequent departures in summer.

There are daily ferries between Bodrum and Kos (Greece), with daily hydrofoils (except Sunday) servicing the same route from May to October. Two weekly hydrofoils also link Bodrum with Rhodes (Rhodos) in summer. From Marmaris, catamarans to Rhodes sail daily in summer and do not operate from November to mid-April. Buy your ticket in any Marmaris travel agency.

There are also services between Datça and Rhodes, and between Kaş and Kastellorizo (Greece).

Car-ferry services operate between Greek ports and several Turkish ports, but not to İstanbul.

Italy

From Çeşme (Turkey), situated about 85km west of İzmir, **Marmara Lines** (www.marmaralines.com; 2½ days) ferries run twice weekly to Brindisi via Corfu and Patras in Greece (once weekly in winter). Marmara Lines also connects Ancona in Italy from Çeşme between April and November (2½ days). **Turkish Maritime Lines** (www.tdi.com.tr, in Turkish) also operates twice-weekly ferries between Brindisi and Çeşme.

Car-ferry services operate between Italian and several Turkish ports, but not to İstanbul.

Russia & Ukraine

There are also a handful of routes over the Black Sea to Turkey. **Ferrylines** (www.ferrylines.com) is a good starting point for information about ferry travel in the region.

Ferries travel between Trabzon (Turkey) and Sochi in Russia three times a week, while **UKR Ferry** (www.ukrferry.com) has a comfortable, 36-odd hour weekly service crossing the Black Sea between Odessa and İstanbul. Another weekly service runs between Sevastopol and İstanbul; for more information, check out www.aroundcrimea.com.

Sudan & Saudi Arabia

The **Nile River Valley Transport Corporation** (☎ in Aswan 097-303 348, in Cairo 02-575 9058) runs one passenger ferry per week between Aswan in Egypt and Wadi Halfa in Sudan (16 to 24 hours). Options include 1st class with bed in a cabin, an airline seat and deck class. To board the ferry, you must have a valid Sudanese visa in your passport.

Telestar Tours (☎ in Cairo 02-794 4600, in Suez 062-332 6251) runs an irregular service between Suez (Egypt) and Jeddah (about 36 hours). Once in Jeddah, you can arrange an onward ticket to Port Sudan. Note that getting a berth during the hajj is virtually impossible. There's a daily fast ferry that runs between Hurghada and Duba (three hours), though prices and schedules vary depending on the time of year.

For more information, try **International Fast Ferries Co** (☎ 065-344 7571; www.internationalfastferries.com) or inquire at the Hurghada port. You will not be allowed to board any of these services unless you have a valid Saudi visa in your passport.

TOURS

International tour companies offer a host of tour possibilities for visiting the Middle East – everything from a package tour by the beach to a more gruelling six-week overland expedition. These can usually be booked directly through the tour company, but you'll also have plenty of choice if you visit any travel agent in your home country.

For tour companies specialising in individual countries, see the Transport section of the relevant country chapter.

Australia

In Australia, most of the companies that offer tours to the Middle East do so as agents for the UK packages; check out the websites that are listed under the UK companies for the local affiliate closest to you.

There are also a few interesting home-grown outfits:

Adventure Associates (☎ 1800 222 141; www.adventureassociates.com)
Intrepid (☎ 1300 364 512; www.intrepidtravel.com)
Passport Travel (☎ 03-9500 0444; www.travelcentre.com.au)
Tempo Holidays (☎ 1300 362 844; www.tempoholidays.com)

France

Ailleurs.com (☎ 08 92 16 11 92; www.ailleurs.com)
Atalante (☎ 04 72 53 24 80; www.atalante.fr)
Hommes et Montagnes (☎ 04 38 86 69 19; www.hommes-et-montagnes.fr)
Voyageurs du Monde (☎ 01 40 15 11 15; www.vdm.com)
Voyailes (☎ 01 34 70 40 89; www.voyailes.fr)
Zig-Zag Randonnées (☎ 01 42 85 13 93; www.zigzag-randonnees.com)

Germany

Dabuka Expeditions (☎ 0605-987 9896; www.dabuka.de)
Djoser (☎ 0221-920 1580; www.djoser.de)

Italy

Antichi Splendori Viaggi (☎ 011 812 67 15; www.antichisplendori.it in Italian)
NBTS Viaggi (☎ 011 051 95 75; www.nbts.it)
Shiraz Travel Tours (☎ 065 115 708; www.shiraztravel.com)

Spain

Oriente Medio (www.orientemedio.eu)
Viajes Tuareg (☎ 932 652 391; www.viajestuareg.com)

UK

Adventure Company (☎ 0845 450 5316; www.adventurecompany.co.uk)
Ancient World Tours (☎ 020-7917 9494; www.ancient.co.uk)
Andante Travels (☎ 01722 713800; www.andantetravels.co.uk)
Cox & Kings (☎ 020-7873 5000; www.coxandkings.co.uk)
Crusader Travel (☎ 020-8744 0474; www.crusadertravel.com)
Dragoman (☎ 01728 861133; www.dragoman.com)
Exodus (☎ 020-8675 5550; www.exodus.co.uk)
Explore Worldwide (☎ 0845 013 1537; www.explore.co.uk)
Imaginative Traveller (☎ 0800 316 2717; www.imaginative-traveller.com)
Kumuka (☎ 0800 068 8855; www.kumuka.com)
Oasis Overland (☎ 01963 363400; www.oasisoverland.co.uk)
On the Go (☎ 020-7371 1113; www.onthegotours.com)
Peregrine (☎ 0844 736 0170; www.peregrineadventures.com)
Silk Road and Beyond (☎ 020-7371 3131; www.silkroadandbeyond.co.uk)

USA

Bestway Tours & Safaris (☎ 1-800-663-0844; www.bestway.com)
Yalla Tours (☎ 1-800-644-1595; www.yallatours.com)

GETTING AROUND

This chapter should be used for general planning only. If you want to travel, for instance, between Turkey and Israel and the Palestinian Territories, it will give you a broad overview of the options: air, land or sea, train versus bus, and so on. Then, if you decide to go by bus from İstanbul to Damascus, from Damascus to Amman, and Amman to Jerusalem, you should begin by going to the Getting There & Away section at the back of the Turkey chapter (p616) for further details on buses to Syria. The destination-specific sections will tell you where the border crossing points are. Once in Syria, consult p525 for the best way to continue to Amman in Jordan. Simple.

AIR

With no regional rail network to speak of, and distances that make the bus a discomforting test of endurance, flying is certainly the most user-friendly method of transport in the Middle East if your time is tight. Tickets are more flexible than buses or trains, schedules more rigidly adhered to, refunds easier to get and information more readily available.

Flying isn't a safe option for getting to or from Iraq, nor is flying possible between Israel and the Palestinian Territories and other Middle Eastern countries, except for Egypt, Jordan and Turkey. But, these exceptions aside, almost every Middle Eastern capital is linked to each of the others.

If you're in a capital city, it's usually worth buying your ticket through a reputable local travel agency or, increasingly, over the internet. It can give you all the available choices without having to visit several different airline offices, and the price will usually be the same, if not less.

Airlines in the Middle East

Until recently, most flights were operated by state airlines. Of these, when it comes to service, punctuality and safety, El Al (Israel), Royal Jordanian, Turkish Airlines and Middle East Airlines (Lebanon) are probably the pick of the bunch, while SyrianAir has a solid if unspectacular reputation. EgyptAir is probably best avoided.

The growth of private (usually low-cost) airlines, especially in Turkey and Israel, means that flying domestic routes within these countries has become a lot more feasible.

For a full list of airlines flying to and from the Middle East, see p638. Those that fly domestically within the Middle East:

Anadolujet (www.anadolujet.com) Low-cost Turkish domestic airline with an extensive network.
Arkia Israel Airlines (☎ 03-690 3712; www.arkia.co.il; Israel) Connects Tel Aviv, Eilat and Haifa.
Atlasjet (www.atlasjet.com) Domestic Turkish services.
Egypt Air Express (www.egyptair.com) Domestic Egyptian airline operated by Egypt Air.
Israir Airlines (☎ 516-593 1785; www.israirairlines.com; Israel) Connects Tel Aviv, Eilat and Haifa.
Onur Air (www.onurair.com.tr; Turkey) Extensive domestic flights within Turkey.
Pegasus Airlines (www.flypgs.com) Extensive domestic network within Turkey.
Sun Express (www.sunexpress.com) Turkish domestic routes.
Tarhan Tower Airlines (www.ttairlines.com) Turkish domestic flights.

Detailed information on many airlines' safety records (including reams of statistics) can be found at www.airsafe.com/index.html.

Air Passes

Emirates (www.emirates.com) offers the 'Arabian Airpass' that allows cut-price travel around the Middle East. To qualify, you need to buy a flight to Dubai. Onward flight 'coupons' (a minimum of two, maximum of six) are then available to cities such as Cairo, Alexandria, Amman, Beirut or Damascus. The coupons are valid for three months from when the first coupon is redeemed. Prices are based upon zones, with the above cities coming within Zone C (except, for some reason, Alexandria, which is in the cheaper Zone B).

BICYCLE

Although the numbers doing it are small, cycling round the Middle East is a viable proposition, provided that cyclists are self-sufficient and able to carry litres of extra water.

Most of the people we spoke to reckoned that the most enjoyable cycling was in Turkey and Syria (this is backed up by letters from readers). Although hilly, the scenery in Turkey is particularly fine and accommodation is fairly easy to come by, even in the smallest villages. This is definitely not the case elsewhere, and in Syria in particular you may have to spend the odd night in a tent. In Turkey, if you get tired of pedalling, it's also no problem to have your bike transported in the luggage hold of the big modern buses.

One big plus about cycling through the region is the fact that cyclists are usually given fantastic welcomes (a trademark of the Middle East in any case) and are showered with food and drink. Cyclists in Syria frequently receive invitations from people along the way to come home, meet the family, eat and stay over. Even the police are helpful and friendly. There are a couple of exceptions, with isolated reports of kids throwing stones at cyclists (maybe because of the cycling shorts, we don't know) along Jordan's King's Hwy and in Sinai. But these are minor blips of annoyance.

By far the major difficulty cited by all cyclists was the heat. This is at its worst from June to August, and cycling in these summer months is definitely not recommended. May to mid-June and September through October are the best times. Even then, you're advised to make an early morning start and call it a day by early afternoon.

There are bicycle-repair shops in most major towns and the locals are excellent 'bush mechanics', with all but the most modern or sophisticated equipment.

The following additional tips may help:

- Carry a couple of extra chain links, a chain breaker, spokes, a spoke key, two inner tubes, tyre levers and a repair kit, a flat-head and Phillips-head screwdriver, and Allen keys and spanners to fit all the bolts on your bike.
- Check the bolts daily and carry spares.
- Fit as many water bottles to your bike as you can – it gets hot.
- Make sure the bike's gearing will get you over the hills.
- Confine your panniers to a maximum weight of 15kg.
- Carrying the following equipment in your panniers is recommended: a two-person tent (weighing about 1.8kg) that can also accommodate the bike where security is a concern; a sleeping bag rated to 0°C and an inflatable mattress; a small camping stove; cooking pot; utensils; a water filter (two microns) and a compact torch.
- Wear cycling shorts with a chamois bum and cleated cycling shoes.
- Don't worry about filling the panniers with food, as there will be plentiful and fresh supplies along the route.

CYCLING CONTACTS

If you're considering cycling in the Middle East, but have a few pressing questions that first need answering, you can post your query on the Thorn Tree on Lonely Planet's website (www.lonelyplanet.com) under the Activities branch. There's a strong likelihood somebody will respond with the information you're looking for.

Alternatively, you could contact the **Cyclists' Touring Club** (CTC; ☎ 0844 736 8450; www.ctc.org.uk), a UK-based organisation that offers good tips and information sheets on cycling in different parts of the world; the website itself is quite useful.

BOAT

Boat services between Middle Eastern countries definitely play second fiddle to air and land transport, with a notable exception: getting between Jordan and Egypt.

The most popular services are the two ferry services between Nuweiba in Egypt and Aqaba in Jordan. The fast-ferry service takes one hour, while the slow (and cheaper) ferry makes the journey in 2½ to three hours. The only other option may be a catamaran trip between Aqaba and Sharm el-Sheikh, but this wasn't operating at the time of research. Vehicles can usually be shipped on these routes, but advance arrangements may have to be made. For more information on these ferry services, see p397 and p209.

Practicality is the essence of Middle East ferry services, not luxury. Even in 1st class, you're not in for a pleasure cruise, while deck class often means just that. While food and drink of some sort may be available on board, many passengers prefer to take their own.

BUS

Buses are the workhorses of the Middle East, and in most places they're probably you're only option for getting from A to

B. Thankfully, most buses are reliable and comfortable.

The cost and comfort of bus travel vary enormously throughout the region. One typical nuisance is bus drivers' fondness (presumably shared by local passengers) for loud videos; sleep is almost always impossible. Another potential source of discomfort is that in most Middle Eastern countries, the concept of a 'nonsmoking bus' is that this is something that other regions have, although that is changing.

Most Middle Eastern countries can be reached by taking a direct international bus from other parts of the region. For example, Damascus has several daily bus services to İstanbul (30 hours), Ankara (14 hours), Beirut (four hours) and Amman (seven hours), while Aleppo also has daily services to İstanbul (22 hours), Ankara (10 hours) and Beirut (six to seven hours). From Amman, it's also possible to travel to the King Hussein/Allenby Bridge (for Israel and the Palestinian Territories; 45 minutes), Cairo (a daily bus-ferry combination; 16 hours) or even Baghdad (14 hours), although the latter journey is chronically unreliable and probably unsafe. There are also services from Cairo to Jerusalem and from Cairo to Tel Aviv via Sinai (at least 10 hours).

For further details of these services, see the Getting There & Away sections of the relevant city sections and the Transport sections of the individual country chapters.

Even in those countries without any international bus services, it's usually possible to get to at least one neighbouring country by using domestic services, making your own way across the border and picking up another domestic service or taxi in the next country. This method is usually cheaper and it avoids one of the big problems of international services: waiting for the vehicle to clear customs at each border, which can mean delays of several hours. However, if you're planning on using domestic buses, make sure that there will be onward transport on the other side of the border.

Reservations

It's always advisable to book bus seats in advance at the bus station, which is usually the only ticket outlet and source of reliable information about current services. Reservations are a must over the Muslim weekend (Friday) as well as during public holidays (see p628).

CAR & MOTORCYCLE

Bringing your own car to the Middle East will give you a lot more freedom, but it's certainly not for everyone. For information on the paperwork required, see p643.

Throughout the Middle East, motorcycles are fairly popular as a means of racing around in urban areas, but are little used as long-distance transport. If you do decide to ride a motorcycle through the region, try to take one of the more popular Japanese models if you want to stand any chance of finding spare parts. Even then, make sure your bike is in very good shape before setting out. Motorcycles can be shipped or, often, loaded as luggage on to trains.

Driving Licence

If you plan to drive, get an IDP from your local automobile association. An IDP is compulsory for foreign drivers and motorcyclists in Egypt, Iran, Iraq and Syria. Most foreign (or national) licences are acceptable in Israel and the Palestinian Territories, Lebanon and Turkey, and for foreign-registered vehicles in Jordan. However, even in these places an IDP is recommended. IDPs are valid for one year only.

Fuel & Spare Parts

Mechanical failure can be a problem as spare parts – or at least official ones – are often unobtainable. Fear not, ingenuity often compensates for factory parts; your mechanic back home will either have a heart attack or learn new techniques when you show them what's gone on under your hood in the Middle East.

Generally, Land Rovers, Volkswagens, Range Rovers, Mercedes and Chevrolets are the cars for which spare parts are most likely to be available, although in recent years Japan has been a particularly vigorous exporter of vehicles to the region. In Syria, spare parts for US vehicles may be very hard to find. One tip is to ask your vehicle manufacturer for a list of any authorised service centres it has in the countries you plan to visit. The length of this list is likely to be a pretty good reflection of how easy it is to get parts on your travels.

Usually two grades of petrol are available; if in doubt get the more expensive one.

THE PROS & CONS OF BRINGING YOUR OWN VEHICLE

Pros

- You aren't tied to schedules.
- You can choose your own company, set your own pace, take the scenic route, declare your vehicle a smoking or nonsmoking zone, and you won't be at the mercy of taxi drivers or have to fight for a place on a bus.
- You can avoid all the hassles that go with carrying your world on your back.
- Fuel is generally much cheaper than at home, although times are changing in this regard.

Cons

For all the positives, it's difficult to imagine a route through the Middle East that would justify the expense and hassle of bringing a car and getting it out again. Indeed, for the vast majority of short-term visitors to the Middle East, the advantages of being attached to one vehicle are far outweighed by the disadvantages. Primary among these are:

- The mountains of paperwork and red tape before you leave home – documents usually take a month or more to obtain, and just finding out the current regulations can be difficult. It's best to get in touch with your automobile association (eg AA or RAC in the UK) at least three months in advance.
- The expense of getting hold of a carnet de passage (see p643).
- The often hair-raising driving in unfamiliar territory.
- The variability in the quality of the roads themselves.
- The sheer distance between places of interest.
- The millstone-around-the-neck worry of serious accident, breakdown or theft.
- If trouble flares in a particular region, the option of circumventing it by travelling by air won't be possible; air freighting even a motorcycle can be prohibitively expensive. Selling or dumping a temporarily imported vehicle in the Middle East is more or less ruled out by customs regulations. Car ferries can get around some of these problems, but shipping a car isn't cheap, often requires an advance booking and won't help you out in every eventuality.

Petrol stations are few and far between on many desert roads. Away from the main towns, it's advisable to fill up whenever you get the chance. Locally produced maps often indicate the locations of petrol stations. Diesel isn't readily available in every Middle Eastern country, nor is unleaded petrol.

Hire

Car hire is possible in all Middle Eastern countries, and international hire companies such as **Hertz** (www.hertz.com), **Avis** (www.avis.com) and **Europcar** (www.europcar.com) are represented in many large towns. Local companies are usually cheaper, but the cars of international companies are often better maintained and come with a better back-up service if problems arise. Local companies sometimes carry the advantage of including a driver for a similar cost to hiring the car alone. A good place to find competitive rates is **Imakoo Cars** (www.imakoocars.co.uk/directory-in.php/middle-east), a clearing house for cheap rates of international companies with services in all countries covered in this guide, except Egypt.

Reputable tour agencies can also be a good source of cars, offering competitive rates, decent cars and often a driver thrown in for little extra – usually the best option for short-term travellers. Some agencies can arrange vans, minibuses and buses for groups, but most deal only in cars; very few rent out motorcycles or bicycles.

To hire a car, you'll need any or all of the following: a photocopy of your passport and visa; deposit or credit-card imprint; and your driving licence or IDP. The minimum age varies between 21 and 25 – the latter is most common, particularly with international companies.

Always make sure that insurance is included in the hire price, familiarise yourself with the policy – don't hire a car unless it's insured for every eventuality.

Before hiring a self-drive vehicle, ask yourself seriously how well you think you can cope with the local driving conditions and whether you know your way around well enough to make good use of one. Also compare the cost with that of hiring a taxi for the same period.

Insurance

Insurance is compulsory in most Middle Eastern countries, apart from being highly advisable. Given the large number of minor accidents, not to mention major ones, fully comprehensive insurance (as opposed to third-party) is strongly advised, both for your own and any hire vehicle. Car-hire companies customarily supply insurance, but check the cover and conditions carefully.

Make certain you're covered for off-piste travel, as well as travel between Middle Eastern countries (if you're planning cross-border excursions). A locally acquired motorcycle licence is not valid under some policies.

In the event of an accident, make sure you submit the accident report as soon as possible to the insurance company or, if hiring, the car-hire company, and do so before getting the car repaired.

Road Conditions

The main roads are good, or at least reasonable, in most parts of the Middle East, but there are plenty of unsurfaced examples and the international roads are generally narrow and crowded. Conditions across the Middle East vary enormously, but in almost all cases, they'll be worse than you're used to back home. Turkey, Jordan and Israel and the Palestinian Territories probably have the best roads, but those in Lebanon and Syria adhere to the following rule: worse than they should be but probably better than you'd expect. Some of Egypt's roads are fine, others are bone-jarringly bad.

Road Hazards

One of your enduring (and, hopefully, not too painful) memories of the Middle East will undoubtedly be the driving standards: the driving can be appalling by Western norms. Fatalism and high speed rule supreme. Many regulations are, in practice, purely cautionary, although prison terms for speeding in Syria does seem to have noticeably improved the situation. Car horns, used at the slightest provocation, take the place of caution and courtesy. Except in well-lit urban areas, try to avoid driving at night, as you may find your vehicle is the only thing on the road with lights.

In desert regions, particularly in Egypt, beware of wind-blown sand and wandering, free-range camels – the latter can be deadly at night.

Remember that an accident in the more remote parts of the region isn't always handled by your friendly insurance company. 'An eye for an eye' is likely to be the guiding principle of the other party and their relatives, whether you're in the wrong or not. Don't hang around to ask questions or gawp. Of course we're not saying that you shouldn't report an accident, but it may be more prudent to head for the nearest police station than to wait at the scene.

Road Rules

You're unlikely even to know what the speed limit is on a particular road, let alone be forced to keep to it – the rules exist more in theory than they are enforced in reality. As a rule, only non-Middle Easterners wear motorcycle helmets or car safety belts in most countries of the region, but that doesn't mean you shouldn't if one is available.

A warning triangle is required for vehicles (except motorcycles) in most Middle Eastern countries; in Turkey two triangles and a first-aid kit are compulsory.

In all countries, driving is on the right-hand side of the road (although many motorcyclists seem to consider themselves exempt from this convention) and the rules of when to give way (at least officially) are those which apply in Continental Europe.

HITCHING

Although many travellers hitchhike, it is never an entirely safe way of getting around and those who do so should understand that they are taking a small but potentially serious risk. There is no part of the Middle East where hitching can be recommended for unaccompanied women travellers. Just because we explain how hitching works, doesn't mean we recommend you do it.

Hitching as commonly understood in the West hardly exists in the Middle East (except in Israel and the Palestinian Territories). Although in most countries you'll often see people standing by the road hoping for a lift, they will nearly always expect (and be expected) to offer to pay. Hitching in the Middle Eastern sense is not so much an alternative to the public transport system as an extension of it, particularly in areas where there's no regular public transport. The going rate is often roughly the equivalent of the bus or shared taxi fare, but may be more if a driver takes you to an address or place off their route. You may well be offered free lifts from time to time, but you won't get very far if you set out deliberately to avoid paying for transport.

Hitching is not illegal in any Middle Eastern country and in many places it's extremely common. However, while it's quite normal for Middle Easterners, Asians and Africans, it isn't something Westerners are expected to do. In many Middle Eastern countries, Westerners who try to set a precedent of any kind often attract considerable (and sometimes unwelcome) attention. While this can work to your advantage, it can also lead to suspicion from the local police.

Throughout the Middle East a raised thumb is a vaguely obscene gesture. A common way of signalling that you want a lift is to extend your right hand, palm down.

LOCAL TRANSPORT

Bus

In most cities and towns, a minibus or bus service operates. Fares are very cheap, services are fast, regular and run on fixed routes with, in some cases, fixed stops. However, unless you're very familiar with the town, they can be difficult to get to grips with (few display their destinations and fewer still do so in English and they are often very crowded). Unless you can find a local who speaks your language to help you out, your best bet is to stand along the footpath (preferably at a bus stop if one exists) of a major thoroughfare heading in the direction you want to go, and call out the local name (or the name of a landmark close to where you're heading) into the drivers' windows when they slow down.

Few countries have public minibuses to/from the airport, but top-end hotels and travel agencies (if you're taking a tour) can usually send a complimentary minibus if they're given sufficient advance notice.

Taxi

In the West, taxis are usually considered a luxury. In the Middle East they're often unavoidable. Some cities have no other form of urban public transport, while there are also many rural routes that are only feasible in a taxi or private vehicle.

Taxis are seemingly everywhere you look and, if you can't see one, try lingering on the footpath next to a major road and, within no time, plenty of taxis will appear as if from nowhere and will soon toot their horns at you just in case you missed them, even if you're just trying to cross the street.

The way taxis operate varies widely from country to country and city to city. So does the price. Different types of taxis are painted or marked in different ways, or known by different names, but, often, local people talking to foreigners in English will just use the blanket term 'taxi'. If you want to save money, it's important to be able to differentiate between the various kinds.

Details of local peculiarities are given in the Getting Around sections at the end of the country chapters.

REGULAR TAXI

Regular taxis (variously known as 'agency taxis', 'telephone taxis', 'private taxis' or 'special taxis') are found in almost every Middle Eastern town or city. Unlike shared taxis, you pay to have the taxi to yourself, either to take you to a preagreed destination or for a specified period of time. In some places, there's no other public transport, but in most, regular taxis exist alongside less expensive means of getting around (although these usually shut down overnight). They are primarily of use for transport within towns or on short rural trips, but in some countries hiring them for excursions of several hours is still cheap. They are also often the only way of reaching airports or seaports.

SHARED TAXI

A compromise between the convenience of a regular taxi and the economy of a bus, the shared taxi picks up and drops off passengers at points along its (generally fixed) route and runs to no particular schedule.

TIPS FOR CATCHING TAXIS

On the whole, taxi drivers in the Middle East are helpful, honest and often humorous. Others – as in countries all over the world – find new arrivals too tempting a target for minor scams or a spot of overcharging. Here are a few tips:

- Not all taxi drivers speak English. Generally, in cities used to international travellers, they will (or know enough to get by), but not otherwise. If you're having trouble, ask a local for help.
- Always negotiate a fare (or insist that the meter is used if it works) before jumping in. Town taxis occasionally have meters, which sometimes work and are even used from time to time. This book quotes local rates but, if in doubt, inquire at your point of departure.
- Don't rely on street names (there are often several versions and the driver may recognise your pronunciation of none of them). If you're going to a well-known destination (such as a big hotel), find out if it's close to a local landmark (check the Lonely Planet map if there is one) and give the driver the local name for the landmark. Even better, get someone to write down the name in Arabic or whatever the local language is.
- Make sure you're dropped off at the right place.
- Avoid using unlicensed cab drivers at airports or bus stations.

It's known by different names – collect, collective or service taxi in English, *servees* in Arabic, sherut in Hebrew and dolmuş in Turkish. Most shared taxis take up to four or five passengers, but some seat up to about 12 and are indistinguishable for most purposes from minibuses.

Shared taxis are much cheaper than private taxis and, once you get the hang of them, can be just as convenient. They are dearer than buses, but more frequent and usually faster, because they don't stop so often or for so long. They also tend to operate for longer hours than buses. They can be used for urban, intercity or rural transport, but not necessarily all three in a particular place.

Fixed-route taxis wait at the point of departure until full or nearly full. Usually they pick up or drop off passengers anywhere en route, but in some places they have fixed halts or stations. Sometimes each service is allocated a number, which may be indicated on the vehicle. Generally, a flat fare applies for each route, but sometimes it's possible to pay a partial fare.

Shared taxis without routes are supreme examples of market forces at work. If the price is right you'll quickly find a taxi willing to take you almost anywhere, but if you're prepared to wait a while, or to do your journey in stages, you can get around very cheaply. Fares depend largely on time and distance, but can also vary slightly according to demand.

Beware of boarding an empty one, as the driver may assume you want to hire the vehicle for your exclusive use and charge you accordingly. It's advisable to watch what other passengers pay and to hand over your fare in front of them. Passengers are expected to know where they are getting off. 'Thank you' in the local language is the usual cue for the driver to stop. Make it clear to the driver or other passengers if you want to be told when you reach your destination.

TRAIN

There are train networks in Egypt, Israel and the Palestinian Territories, Syria and Turkey and these can represent the best transport option on some routes, such as between Cairo and Luxor in Egypt, or between Aleppo and Lattakia in Syria, for example. Levels of comfort vary from country to country – many of Egypt's trains are badly in need of an overhaul, while Syria and Turkey use new trains on some routes and the entire system is improving all the time.

Most railway lines in the region were built primarily for strategic or economic reasons, and many are either no longer in use or only carry freight, meaning that networks are not as extensive as they first appear. In general, trains are less frequent and usually slower than buses, while many stations are some distance out of the town centres they serve.

In general, tickets are only sold at the station and reservations are either compulsory or highly recommended.

International train services are few and far between in the Middle East. There is a once-weekly train service that runs between Damascus and İstanbul (via Aleppo) – see p502 and p616 for details. Check to see whether service has resumed along the Amman–Damascus line and whether the planned Damascus–Beirut service has opened.

Health

CONTENTS

Prevention is the key to staying healthy while travelling in the Middle East. Infectious diseases can and do occur in the Middle East, but these are usually associated with poor living conditions and poverty and can be avoided with a few precautions. The most common reason for travellers needing medical help is as a result of accidents – cars are not always well maintained, seatbelts are rare and poorly lit roads are littered with potholes. Medical facilities can be excellent in large cities, but in remoter areas may be more basic.

BEFORE YOU GO

A little planning before departure, particularly for pre-existing illnesses, will save you a lot of trouble later. See your dentist before a long trip; carry a spare pair of contact lenses and glasses (and take your optical prescription); and carry a first-aid kit with you.

It's tempting to leave it all to the last minute – don't! Many vaccines don't ensure immunity until two weeks, so visit a doctor four to eight weeks before departure. Ask your doctor for an International Certificate of Vaccination (otherwise known as the yellow booklet), which will list all the vaccinations you've received. This is mandatory for countries that require proof of yellow fever vaccination upon entry, but it's a good idea to carry it wherever you travel.

> **TRAVEL HEALTH WEBSITES**
>
> It's usually a good idea to consult your government's travel health website before departure, if one is available.
>
> **Australia** (www.smartraveller.gov.au)
> **Canada** (www.hc-sc.gc.ca/index-eng.php)
> **UK** (www.nhs.uk/Healthcareabroad) Also check the private www.traveldoctor.co.uk.
> **USA** (wwwn.cdc.gov/travel)

Travellers can register with the **International Association for Medical Advice to Travellers** (IMAT; www.iamat.org). Its website can help travellers to find a doctor with recognised training. Those heading off to very remote areas may like to do a first-aid course (Red Cross and St John Ambulance can help), or attend a remote medicine first-aid course, such as those offered by the **Royal Geographical Society** (www.rgs.org).

Bring medications in their original, clearly labelled containers. A signed and dated letter from your physician describing your medical conditions and medications, including generic names, is also a good idea. If carrying syringes or needles, be sure to have a physician's letter documenting their medical necessity.

INSURANCE

Find out in advance if your insurance plan will make payments directly to providers or reimburse you later for overseas health expenditures (in many Middle Eastern countries doctors expect payment in cash). It's also worth making sure that your travel insurance will cover repatriation home or to better medical facilities elsewhere. Your insurance company may be able to locate the nearest source of medical help, or you can ask at your hotel. In an emergency, contact your embassy or consulate. Your travel insurance will not usually cover you for anything other than emergency dental treatment. Not all insurance covers emergency aeromedical evacuation home or to a hospital in a major city, which may be the only way to get medical attention for a serious emergency.

RECOMMENDED VACCINATIONS

The World Health Organization (WHO) recommends that all travellers, regardless of the region they are travelling in, should be covered for diphtheria, tetanus, measles, mumps, rubella and polio, as well as hepatitis B. While making preparations to travel, take the opportunity to ensure that all of your routine vaccination cover is complete. The consequences of these diseases can be severe and outbreaks do occur in the Middle East.

MEDICAL CHECKLIST

Following is a list of other items you should consider packing in your medical kit.

- acetaminophen/paracetamol (eg Tylenol) or aspirin
- adhesive or paper tape
- antibacterial ointment (eg Bactroban) for cuts and abrasions
- antibiotics (if travelling off the beaten track)
- antidiarrhoeal drugs (eg containing loperamide)
- antihistamines (for hay fever and allergic reactions)
- anti-inflammatory drugs (eg containing ibuprofen)
- bandages, gauze, gauze rolls
- insect repellent that contains DEET (for skin)
- insect spray that contains permethrin (for clothing, tents and bed nets)
- iodine tablets (for water purification)
- oral-rehydration salts
- pocket knife
- scissors, safety pins, tweezers
- steroid cream or cortisone (for allergic rashes)
- sunscreen
- syringes and sterile needles (if travelling to remote areas)
- thermometer

INTERNET RESOURCES

There is a wealth of travel health advice on the internet. For further information, lonelyplanet.com is a good place to start. The **WHO** (www.who.int/ith/en) publishes a good book, *International Travel and Health*, which is revised annually and available online at no cost. Another website of general interest is **MD Travel Health** (www.mdtravelhealth.com), which provides complete travel health recommendations for every country, updated daily, also at no cost. The website of the **Centers for Disease Control & Prevention** (www.cdc.gov) is a very useful source of traveller health information.

FURTHER READING

Recommended references include *Traveller's Health* by Dr Richard Dawood (Oxford University Press), *International Travel Health Guide* by Stuart R Rose, MD (Travel Medicine Inc), and *The Travellers' Good Health Guide* by Ted Lankester (Sheldon Press), an especially useful health guide for volunteers and long-term expatriates working in the Middle East.

IN TRANSIT

DEEP VEIN THROMBOSIS (DVT)

Deep vein thrombosis occurs when blood clots form in the legs during plane flights, chiefly due to prolonged immobility. The longer the flight, the greater the risk. Most blood clots are reabsorbed uneventfully, but some may break off and travel through the blood vessels to the lungs, where they may cause life-threatening complications.

The chief symptom of DVT is swelling or pain of the foot, ankle or calf, usually but not always on just one side. When a blood clot travels to the lungs, it may cause chest pain and difficulty breathing. Travellers with any of these symptoms should immediately seek medical attention.

To help prevent the development of DVT on long flights you should walk about the cabin, perform isometric compressions of the leg muscles (ie contract the leg muscles while sitting), drink plenty of fluids, and avoid alcohol and tobacco.

JET LAG & MOTION SICKNESS

Jet lag is common when crossing more than five time zones, and results in insomnia, fatigue, malaise or nausea. To avoid jet lag try drinking plenty of fluids (nonalcoholic) and eating light meals. Upon arrival, seek exposure to natural sunlight and readjust your schedule (for meals, sleep etc) as soon as possible.

Antihistamines such as dimenhydrinate (Dramamine) and meclizine (Antivert, Bonine) are usually the first choice for treating motion sickness. Their main side-effect is drowsiness. A herbal alternative is ginger, which works like a charm for some people.

IN THE MIDDLE EAST

AVAILABILITY & COST OF HEALTH CARE

The health care systems in the Middle East are varied. Medical care can be excellent in Israel, with well-trained doctors and nurses, but can be patchier elsewhere. Reciprocal health arrangements with countries rarely exist and you should be prepared to pay for all medical and dental treatment.

Medical care is not always readily available outside major cities. Medicine, and even sterile dressings or intravenous fluids, may need to be bought from a local pharmacy. Nursing care may be limited or rudimentary as this is something families and friends are expected to provide. The travel assistance provided by your insurance may be able to locate the nearest source of medical help, otherwise ask at your hotel. In an emergency, contact your embassy or consulate. Also see Medical Services in the Information section of the capital city in each country chapter.

Standards of dental care are variable and there is an increased risk of hepatitis B and HIV transmission via poorly sterilised equipment. Keep in mind that your travel insurance will not usually cover you for anything other than emergency dental treatment.

For minor illnesses such as diarrhoea, pharmacists can often provide valuable advice and sell over-the-counter medication. They can also advise when more specialised help is needed.

INFECTIOUS DISEASES

Diphtheria

Diphtheria is spread through close respiratory contact. It causes a high temperature and severe sore throat. Sometimes a membrane forms across the throat requiring a tracheostomy to prevent suffocation. Vaccination is recommended for those likely to be in close contact with the local population in infected areas. The vaccine is given as an injection alone, or with tetanus, and lasts 10 years.

Hepatitis A

Hepatitis A is spread through contaminated food (particularly shellfish) and water. It causes jaundice, and although it is rarely fatal, can cause prolonged lethargy and delayed recovery. Symptoms include dark urine, a yellow colour to the whites of the eyes, fever and abdominal pain. Hepatitis A vaccine (Avaxim, VAQTA, Havrix) is given as an injection: a single dose will give protection for up to a year, while a booster 12 months later will provide a subsequent 10 years of protection. Hepatitis A and typhoid vaccines can also be given as a single-dose vaccine (hepatyrix or viatim).

Hepatitis B

Infected blood, contaminated needles and sexual intercourse can all transmit hepatitis B. It can cause jaundice, and affects the liver, occasionally causing liver failure. All travellers should make this a routine vaccination. (Many countries now give hepatitis B vaccination as part of routine childhood vaccination.) The vaccine is given singly, or at the same time as the hepatitis A vaccine (hepatyrix). A course will give protection for at least five years, and can be given over four weeks or six months.

HIV

Countries in the Middle East covered by this book that require a negative HIV test as a visa requirement for some categories of visas (not tourist visas) include Egypt, Jordan and Lebanon.

Leishmaniasis

Spread through the bite of an infected sand fly, leishmaniasis can cause a slowly growing skin lump or ulcer. It may develop into a serious life-threatening fever usually accompanied by anaemia and weight loss. Sand fly bites should be avoided whenever possible. Infected dogs are also carriers. Leishmaniasis is present in Iraq, Israel and the Palestinian Territories, Jordan, Lebanon, Syria and Turkey.

Leptospirosis

Leptospirosis is spread through the excreta of infected rodents, especially rats. It can cause hepatitis and renal failure that may be fatal. It is unusual for travellers to be affected unless living in poor sanitary conditions; the greatest risk is in Turkey. The disease causes a fever and jaundice.

Malaria

The prevalence of malaria varies throughout the Middle East. Many areas are considered to be malaria free, while others have seasonal risks. The risk of malaria is minimal in most cities; however, check with your doctor if you are considering travelling to any rural areas. It is important to take antimalarial tablets if the risk is significant. For up-to-date information about the risk of contracting malaria in a specific country, contact your local travel health clinic.

Anyone who has travelled in a country where malaria is present should be aware of the symptoms of malaria. It is possible to contract malaria from a single bite from an infected mosquito. Malaria almost always starts with marked shivering, fever and sweating. Muscle pains, headache and vomiting are common. Symptoms may occur anywhere from a few days to three weeks after the infected mosquito bite. The illness can start while you are taking preventative tablets if they are not fully effective, and may also occur after you have finished taking your tablets.

Poliomyelitis

Generally spread through contaminated food and water, polio is present, though rare, throughout the Middle East. It is one of the vaccines given in childhood and should be boosted every 10 years, either orally (a drop on the tongue), or as an injection. Polio may be carried asymptomatically, although it can cause a transient fever and, in rare cases, potentially permanent muscle weakness or paralysis.

Rabies

Spread through bites or licks on broken skin from an infected animal, rabies (present in all countries of the Middle East) is fatal. Animal handlers should be vaccinated, as should those travelling to remote areas where a reliable source of postbite vaccine is not available within 24 hours. Three injections are needed over a month. If you have not been vaccinated you will need a course of five injections starting within 24 hours or as soon as possible after the injury. Vaccination does not provide you with immunity, it merely buys you more time to seek appropriate medical help.

Rift Valley Fever

This haemorrhagic fever, which is found in Egypt, is spread through blood or blood products, including those from infected animals. It causes a 'flu-like' illness with fever, joint pains and occasionally more serious complications. Complete recovery is possible.

Schistosomiasis

Otherwise known as bilharzia, this is spread through the freshwater snail. It causes infection of the bowel and bladder, often with bleeding. It is caused by a fluke and is contracted through the skin from water contaminated with human urine or faeces. Paddling or swimming in suspect freshwater lakes or slow-running rivers should be avoided. There may be no symptoms. Possible symptoms include a transient fever and rash, and advanced cases of bilharzia may cause blood in the stool or in the urine. A blood test can detect antibodies if you have been exposed and treatment is then possible in specialist travel or infectious-disease clinics. Be especially careful in Egypt, Iraq and Syria.

Tuberculosis (TB)

Tuberculosis is spread through close respiratory contact and occasionally through infected milk or milk products. BCG vaccine is recommended for those likely to be mixing closely with the local population. It is more important for those visiting family or planning on a long stay, and those employed as teachers and health-care workers. TB can be asymptomatic, although symptoms can include coughing, weight loss or fever months or even years after exposure. An X-ray is the best way to confirm if you have TB. BCG gives a moderate degree of protection against TB. It causes a small permanent scar at the site of injection, and is usually only given in specialised chest clinics. As it's a live vaccine it should not be given to pregnant women or immunocompromised individuals. The BCG vaccine is not available in all countries.

Typhoid

Typhoid is spread through food or water that has been contaminated by infected human faeces. The first symptom is usually fever or a pink rash on the abdomen. Septicaemia (blood poisoning) may also occur. Typhoid vaccine (typhim Vi, typherix) will give protection for three years. In some countries, the oral vaccine Vivotif is also available.

Yellow Fever

Yellow fever vaccination is not required for any areas of the Middle East. However, the mosquito that spreads yellow fever has been known to be present in some parts of the region. It is important to consult your local travel health clinic as part of your predeparture plans for the latest details. For this reason, any travellers from a yellow fever endemic area (eg parts of sub-Saharan Africa) will need to show proof of vaccination against yellow fever before entry. This normally means if arriving directly from an infected country or if the traveller has been in an infected country during the last 10 days. We would recommend, however, that travellers carry a certificate if they have been in an infected country during the previous month to avoid any possible difficulties with immigration. There is always the possibility that a traveller without an up-to-date certificate will be vaccinated and detained in isolation at the port of arrival for up to 10 days, or even repatriated. The yellow fever vaccination must be given at a designated clinic, and is valid for 10 years. It is a live vaccine and must not be given to immunocompromised or pregnant travellers.

TRAVELLER'S DIARRHOEA

To prevent diarrhoea, avoid tap water unless it has been boiled, filtered or chemically disinfected (with iodine tablets). Eat only fresh fruits or vegetables if cooked or if you have peeled them yourself, and avoid dairy products that may contain unpasteurised milk. Buffet meals are risky, as food should be piping hot; meals freshly cooked in front of you in a busy restaurant are more likely to be safe.

If you develop diarrhoea, be sure to drink plenty of fluids, preferably an oral rehydration solution containing salt and sugar. A few loose stools don't require treatment but, if you start having more than four or five stools a day, you should start taking an antibiotic (usually a quinolone drug) and an antidiarrhoeal agent (such as loperamide). If diarrhoea is bloody, persists for more than 72 hours, is accompanied by fever, shaking chills or severe abdominal pain you should seek medical attention.

ENVIRONMENTAL HAZARDS

Heat Illness

Heat exhaustion occurs after heavy sweating and excessive fluid loss with inadequate replacement of fluids and salt. It is particularly common in hot climates when taking unaccustomed exercise before full acclimatisation. Symptoms include headache, dizziness and tiredness. Dehydration is already happening by the time you feel thirsty – aim to drink sufficient water so that you produce pale, diluted urine. The treatment of heat exhaustion consists of fluid replacement with water or fruit juice or both, and cooling by cold water and fans. The treatment of the salt-loss component consists of taking in salty fluids (such as soup or broth), and adding a little more table salt to foods than usual.

Heat stroke is much more serious. This occurs when the heat-regulating mechanism in the body breaks down. An excessive rise in body temperature leads to sweating ceasing, irrational and hyperactive behaviour, and eventually loss of consciousness and death. Rapid cooling by spraying the body with water and fanning is an ideal treatment. Emergency fluid and electrolyte replacement by intravenous drip is usually also required.

Insect Bites & Stings

Mosquitoes may not carry malaria but can cause irritation and infected bites. Using DEET-based insect repellents will prevent bites. Mosquitoes also spread dengue fever.

Bees and wasps only cause real problems to those with a severe allergy (anaphylaxis). If you have a severe allergy to bee or wasp stings you should carry an adrenaline injection or similar.

Sand flies are located around the Mediterranean beaches. They usually only cause a nasty itchy bite but can carry a rare skin disorder called cutaneous leishmaniasis. Bites may be prevented by using DEET-based repellents.

Scorpions are frequently found in arid or dry climates. They can cause a painful bite, which is rarely life threatening.

Bed bugs are often found in hostels and cheap hotels. They lead to very itchy lumpy bites. Spraying the mattress with an appropriate insect killer will do a good job of getting rid of them.

Scabies are also frequently found in cheap accommodation. These tiny mites live in the skin, particularly between the fingers. They cause an intensely itchy rash. Scabies is easily treated with lotion available from pharmacies; people who you come into contact with also need treating to avoid spreading scabies between asymptomatic carriers.

Snake Bites

Do not walk barefoot or stick your hand into holes or cracks. Half of those bitten by venomous snakes are not actually injected with poison (envenomed). If bitten by a snake, do not panic. Immobilise the bitten limb with a splint (eg a stick) and apply a bandage over the site using firm pressure, similar to a bandage over a sprain. Do not apply a tourniquet, or cut or suck the bite. Get the victim to medical help as soon as possible so that antivenene can be given if necessary.

Water

Tap water is not safe to drink in the Middle East. Stick to bottled water, boil water for 10 minutes, or use water-purification tablets or a filter. Do not drink water from rivers or lakes; this may contain bacteria or viruses that can cause diarrhoea or vomiting.

TRAVELLING WITH CHILDREN

All travellers with children should know how to treat minor ailments and when to seek medical treatment. Make sure the children are up to date with routine vaccinations, and discuss possible travel vaccines well before departure as some vaccines are not suitable for children aged under one year.

In hot, moist climates any wound or break in the skin may lead to infection. The area should be cleaned and then kept dry and clean. Remember to avoid potentially contaminated food and water. If your child is vomiting or experiencing diarrhoea, lost fluid and salts must be replaced. It may be helpful to take rehydration powders for reconstituting with boiled water. Ask your doctor about this.

Children should be encouraged to avoid dogs or other mammals because of the risk of rabies and other diseases. Any bite, scratch or lick from a warm blooded, furry animal should immediately be thoroughly cleaned. If there is any possibility that the animal is infected with rabies, immediate medical assistance should be sought.

WOMEN'S HEALTH

Emotional stress, exhaustion and travelling through different time zones can all contribute to an upset in the menstrual pattern. If using oral contraceptives, remember some antibiotics, diarrhoea and vomiting can stop the pill from working and lead to the risk of pregnancy – remember to take condoms with you just in case. Condoms should be kept in a cool, dry place or they may crack and perish.

Emergency contraception is most effective if taken within 24 hours after unprotected sex. The **International Planned Parent Federation** (www.ippf.org) can advise about the availability of contraception in different countries. Tampons and sanitary towels are not always available outside of major cities in the Middle East.

Travelling during pregnancy is usually possible but there are important things to consider. Have a medical check-up before embarking on your trip. The most risky times for travel are during the first 12 weeks of pregnancy, when miscarriage is most likely, and after 30 weeks, when complications such as high blood pressure and premature delivery can occur. Most airlines will not accept a traveller after 28 to 32 weeks of pregnancy, and long-haul flights in the later stages can be very uncomfortable. Antenatal facilities vary greatly between countries in the Middle East and you should think carefully before travelling to a country with poor medical facilities or where there are major cultural and language differences compared with home. Taking written records of the pregnancy, including details of your blood group, are likely to be helpful if you need medical attention while away. Ensure your insurance policy covers pregnancy, delivery and postnatal care, but remember insurance policies are only as good as the facilities available.

Language

CONTENTS

ARABIC

Arabic is the official language of all Middle Eastern countries except Iran, Israel and Turkey. While English (and to a lesser extent, French – mainly in Lebanon and Syria) is widely spoken in the region, any effort to communicate with the locals in their own language will be well rewarded. No matter how far off the mark your pronunciation or grammar might be, you'll often get the response (usually with a big smile), 'Ah, you speak Arabic very well!' Unlike English, the language is written from right to left, and it's a very good idea to at least familiarise yourself with the alphabet (see opposite).

Learning the basics for day-to-day travelling doesn't take long at all, but to master the complexities of Arabic would take years of constant study. Lonely Planet's *Egyptian Arabic Phrasebook* will prove very useful in this region – thanks in no small way to the predominance of Egyptian TV programs being broadcast throughout the Middle East. Or, for a guide that includes four varieties of Arabic, try Lonely Planet's *Middle East Phrasebook*.

TRANSLITERATION

It's worth noting here that transliterating from Arabic script into English is at best an approximate science. The presence of a number of sounds unknown in European languages, and the fact that the script is 'incomplete' (most vowel sounds are not written), combine to make it nearly impossible to settle on one method of transliteration. A wide variety of spellings are therefore possible for words when they appear in Roman script.

The matter is further complicated by the wide variety of dialects and the imaginative ideas Arabs themselves often have on appropriate spelling in, say, English. Words spelt one way in Egypt may look very different in Syria, which is heavily influenced by French. Not even the most venerable of Western Arabists have been able to come up with an ideal solution.

PRONUNCIATION

Pronunciation of Arabic can be tongue-tying for someone unfamiliar with the intonation and combination of sounds. Much of the vocabulary in this language guide would be universally understood throughout the Arab world, although some of it, especially where more than one option is given, reflects regional dialects. For best

HOW DO YOU SPELL THAT?!

While we have tried to standardise all spellings in this book there are some instances in which flexibility seemed to be more appropriate than consistency. For example, if two alternative transliterations for the same thing exist in different countries, we may go with both if it's clear that these are the spellings any visitor to those countries will find on local maps and road signs.

Differences in spelling also arise through the same word having several variants in the different languages of the region – 'square' in Arabic is traditionally transliterated as *midan*, but in Turkish it's written *maydan* and in Persian *meidun* (or *meidun-é*; 'the square of'). Here lies great potential for confusion, as in the case with hamam, which is Turkish for the famed 'bathhouse', but Arabic for 'pigeon'; if you're looking for a good steam-cleaning, in Arabic you ask for a hammam, with the two syllables sounded distinctly.

We have also been forced to modify some spellings because of regional differences in Arabic pronunciation. The most obvious example of this occurs with the hard Egyptian sounding of the letter *jeem*, like the 'g' in 'gate', whereas elsewhere in the Arab world it's a softer 'j' as in 'jam' – hence we have used both *gadid* and *jadid* (new), and gebel and jebel (mountain).

THE STANDARD ARABIC ALPHABET

Final	Medial	Initial	Alone	Transliteration	Pronunciation
ـا			ا	**aa**	as in 'father'
ـب	ـبـ	بـ	ب	**b**	as in 'bet'
ـت	ـتـ	تـ	ت	**t**	as in 'ten'
ـث	ـثـ	ثـ	ث	**th**	as in 'thin'
ـج	ـجـ	جـ	ج	**j (g/zh)**	as in 'jet'; (**g** or as the 's' in 'measure' in Egypt)
ـح	ـحـ	حـ	ح	**H**	a strongly whispered 'h', like a sigh of relief
ـخ	ـخـ	خـ	خ	**kh**	as the 'ch' in Scottish *loch*
ـد			د	**d (z)**	as in 'dim' (as **z** in Egypt)
ـذ			ذ	**dh**	as the 'th' in 'this'; also as **d** or **z**
ـر			ر	**r**	a rolled 'r', as in the Spanish word *caro*
ـز			ز	**z**	as in 'zip'
ـس	ـسـ	سـ	س	**s**	as in 'so', never as in 'wisdom'
ـش	ـشـ	شـ	ش	**sh**	as in 'ship'
ـص	ـصـ	صـ	ص	**ṣ**	emphatic 's'
ـض	ـضـ	ضـ	ض	**ḍ**	emphatic 'd'
ـط	ـطـ	طـ	ط	**ṭ**	emphatic 't'
ـظ	ـظـ	ظـ	ظ	**ẓ**	emphatic 'z'
ـع	ـعـ	عـ	ع	**'**	the Arabic letter *'ayn*; pronounce as a glottal stop – like the closing of the throat before saying 'Oh-oh!' (see Other Sounds, p662)
ـغ	ـغـ	غـ	غ	**gh**	a guttural sound like Parisian 'r'
ـف	ـفـ	فـ	ف	**f**	as in 'far'
ـق	ـقـ	قـ	ق	**q**	a strongly guttural 'k' sound; also often pronounced as a glottal stop
ـك	ـكـ	كـ	ك	**k**	as in 'king'
ـل	ـلـ	لـ	ل	**l**	as in 'lamb'
ـم	ـمـ	مـ	م	**m**	as in 'me'
ـن	ـنـ	نـ	ن	**n**	as in 'name'
ـه	ـهـ	هـ	ه	**h**	as in 'ham'
ـو			و	**w**	as in 'wet'
				oo	long, as in 'food'
				ow	as in 'how'
ـي	ـيـ	يـ	ي	**y**	as in 'yes'
				ee	as in 'beer', only softer
				ai/ay	as in 'aisle'/as the 'ay' in 'day'

Vowels Not all Arabic vowel sounds are represented in the alphabet. For more information on the vowel sounds used in this language guide, see Vowels (p662).

Emphatic Consonants To simplify the transliteration system used in this book, the emphatic consonants have not been included.

results, pronounce the transliterated words slowly and clearly.

Vowels

Technically, there are three long and three short vowels in Arabic. The reality is a little different, with local dialect and varying consonant combinations affecting their pronunciation. This is the case throughout the Arabic-speaking world. At the very least, five short and three long vowels can be identified:

a	as in 'had'
e	as in 'bet'
i	as in 'hit'
o	as in 'hot'
u	as in 'push'
aa	as in 'father' or as a long pronunciation of the 'a' in 'had'
ee	as the 'ea' in 'eagle'
oo	as the 'oo' in 'food'

Consonants

Pronunciation for all Arabic consonants is covered in the Arabic alphabet table (p661). Note that when double consonants occur in transliterations, both are pronounced. For example, *el-hammaam* (toilet, bathhouse), is pronounced 'el-ham-mam'.

Other Sounds

Arabic has two sounds that are very tricky for non-Arabs to produce, the *'ayn* and the glottal stop. The letter *'ayn* represents a sound with no English equivalent that comes even close. It is articulated from deep in the throat, as is the glottal stop (which is not actually represented in the alphabet), but the muscles at the back of the throat are gagged more forcefully – it has even been described as the sound of someone being strangled!

In many transliteration systems *'ayn* is represented by an opening quotation mark, and the glottal stop by a closing quotation mark. To make the transliterations in this language guide (and throughout the rest of the book) easier to use, we have not distinguished between the glottal stop and the *'ayn*, using the closing quotation mark to represent both sounds. You should find that Arabic speakers will still understand you through the context of your topic of conversation.

LANGUAGE

CONVERSATION & ESSENTIALS

Arabs place great importance on civility, and it's rare to see any interaction between people that doesn't begin with profuse greetings, inquiries into the other's health and other niceties.

Arabic greetings are more formal than greetings in English, and there is a reciprocal response to each. These sometimes vary slightly, depending on whether you're addressing a man or a woman. A simple encounter can become a drawn-out affair, with neither side wanting to be the one to put a halt to the stream of greetings and well-wishing. As an *ajnabi* (foreigner), you're not expected to know all the ins and outs, but if you come up with the right expression at the appropriate moment, they'll love it.

The most common greeting is *salaam 'alaykum* (peace be upon you), to which the correct reply is *wa alaykum as-salaam* (and upon you be peace). If you get invited to a birthday celebration or are around for any of the big holidays, the common greeting is *kul sana wa intum bi-kher* (I wish you well for the coming year).

After having a bath or a haircut, you will often hear people say to you *na'iman*, which roughly means 'heavenly' and boils down to an observation along the lines of 'nice and clean now!'.

Arrival in one piece is always something to be grateful for. Passengers will often be greeted with *al-hamdu lillah 'al as-salaama*, meaning 'thank God for your safe arrival'.

Hi.	*marhaba*
Hello.	*ahlan wa sahlan/ahlan* (literally 'welcome')
(response)	*ahlan beek or ya hala*
Goodbye.	*ma'a salaama/ Allah ma'ak*
Good morning.	*sabah al-khayr*
(response)	*sabah an-noor*
Good evening.	*masaa al-khayr*
(response)	*masaa an-noor*
Good night.	*tisbah 'ala khayr*
(response)	*wa inta min ahlu*
Yes.	*aywa/na'am*
No.	*la*
Please. (request)	*min fadlak* (m)/ *min fadlik* (f)
Please. (polite, eg in restaurants)	*law samaht* (m)/ *law samahtee* (f)

Please. (come in/ go ahead)	*tafadal* (m)/*tafadalee* (f)/ *tafadalu* (pl)
Thank you.	*shukran*
Thanks a lot.	*shukran jazeelan*
You're welcome.	*'afwan or ahlan*
How are you?	*kayf haalak?* (m)/ *kayf haalik?* (f)
Fine. (literally 'thanks be to God')	*al-hamdu lillah*
Pleased to meet you. (departing)	*fursa sa'ida*
Pardon/Excuse me.	*'afwan*
Sorry!	*'assif!*
Congratulations!	*mabrook!*
What's your name?	*shu-ismak?* (m)/*shu-ismik?* (f)
My name is ...	*ismee ...*
Where are you from?	*min wayn inta?*

Do you speak ...?	*btah-ki ...?/hal tatakallam ...?*
I speak ...	*ana bah-ki .../ana atakallam ...*
English	*ingleezi*
French	*faransi*
German	*almaani*

I understand.	*ana af-ham*
I don't understand.	*ma bif-ham/la af-ham*
What does this mean?	*yaanee ay?*
I want an interpreter.	*ureed mutarjem*
I (don't) like ...	*ana (ma) bahib/ana (la) uhib ...*
No problem.	*mish mushkila*
Never mind.	*ma'alesh*

Questions like 'Is the bus coming?' or 'Will the bank be open later?' generally elicit the inevitable response *in sha' Allah* (God willing), an expression you'll hear over and over again. Another less common one is *ma sha' Allah* (God's will be done), sometimes a useful answer to probing questions about why you're not married yet!

HEALTH

I'm ...	*'andee ...*
asthmatic	*azmit raboo*
diabetic	*is sukkar*

I'm allergic ...	*'andee Hasasiyya ...*
to antibiotics	*min mudād Haiowi*
to aspirin	*min asbireen*
to nuts	*min mukassarāt*
to penicillin	*min binisileen*

antiseptic	*mutahhir*
diarrhoea	*is-haal*
doctor	*duktoor/tabeeb*

EMERGENCIES – ARABIC

Help me!	*saa'idoonee!*
I'm sick.	*ana mareed* (m)/ *ana mareeda* (f)
Call the police!	*ittusil bil bolees!*
Go away!	*rouh min hoon!*
Shame on you!	*istiHi a'la Haalak!* (said by a woman to a man bothering her)

headache	*sudaa'*
hospital	*mustashfa*
medicine	*dowa*
pharmacy	*agzakhana/saydaliyya*

ACCOMMODATION & SERVICES

Do you have ...?	*fee'andakum ...?*
a room	*ghurfa*
a single room	*ghurfa mufrada*
a double room	*ghurfa bee sareerayn*
a shower	*doosh*
hot water	*mayy harr*
a toilet	*twalet/mirhad/hammaam*
air-con	*kondishon/takyeef*
electricity	*kahraba*

Where is (the) ...?	*wayn ...?*
bank	*al-masraf/al-bank*
hotel	*al-funduq*
market	*as-sooq*
Mohammed St	*sharia Mohammed*
mosque	*al-jaami'/al-masjid*
museum	*al-mat'haf*
passport & immigration office	*maktab al-jawaazaat wa al-hijra*
police	*ash-shurtaal-bolees*
post office	*maktab al-bareed*
restaurant	*al-mat'am*
tourist office	*maktab as-siyaaHa*

How much?	*qaddaysh/bikam?*
How many?	*kam wahid?*
How much money?	*kam fuloos?*
money	*fuloos/masaari*
big	*kabeer*
small	*sagheer*
good	*kwayyis*
bad	*mish kwayyis/mu kwayyis*
cheap	*rakhees*
expensive	*ghaali*
cheaper	*arkhas*
open	*maftooh*
closed	*maghlooq/musakkar*

TIME & DAYS

What is the time?	*adaysh as-saa'a?*
It's 5 o'clock.	*as-sa'a khamsa*
When?	*mata/emta?*
yesterday	*imbaarih/'ams*
today	*al-yom*
tomorrow	*bukra/ghadan*
minute	*daqiqa*
hour	*sa'a*
day	*yom*
week	*usbu'*
month	*shaher*

Monday	*al-itneen yom*
Tuesday	*at-talaata yom*
Wednesday	*al-arba'a yom*
Thursday	*al-khamees yom*
Friday	*al-jum'a yom*
Saturday	*as-sabt yom*
Sunday	*al-ahad yom*

MONTHS

The Muslim Hejira calendar year has 12 lunar months and is 11 days shorter than the Western (Gregorian) calendar year, so important Muslim dates will fall 11 days earlier each (Western) year.

There are two Gregorian calendars used in the Arab world. In Egypt and the Gulf States, the months have virtually the same names as in English (eg January is *yanaayir*, October is *octobir*), but in Lebanon, Jordan and Syria, the names are quite different. Talking about, say, June as 'month six' is the easiest solution, but for the sake of completeness, the months from January are:

January	*kaanoon ath-thaani*
February	*shubaat*
March	*aazaar*
April	*nisaan*
May	*ayyaar*
June	*huzayran*
July	*tammooz*
August	*'aab*
September	*aylool*
October	*tishreen al-awal*
November	*tishreen ath-thani*
December	*kanoon al-awal*

The Hejira months also have their own names:

1st	*moharram*
2nd	*safar*
3rd	*rabee' al-awwal*
4th	*rabee' ath-thaani*
5th	*jumada al-awwall*
6th	*jumada al-akheera*
7th	*rajab*
8th	*sha'baan*
9th	*ramadaan*
10th	*shawwaal*
11th	*zool-qe'da*
12th	*zool-hijja*

SIGNS – ARABIC

Entrance	مدخل
Exit	خروج
Open	مفتوح
Closed	مغلق
Prohibited	ممنوع
Information	معلومات
Hospital	مستشفي
Police	شرطة
Men's Toilet	حمام للرجال
Women's Toilet	حمام للنساء

NUMBERS

0	*sifr*	٠
1	*waaHid*	١
2	*itneen*	٢
3	*talaata*	٣
4	*arba'a*	٤
5	*khamsa*	٥
6	*sitta*	٦
7	*saba'a*	٧
8	*tamaniya*	٨
9	*tis'a*	٩
10	*ashra*	١٠
11	*Hida'ash*	١١
12	*itna'ash*	١٢
13	*talata'ash*	١٣
14	*arbatash*	١٤
15	*khamistash*	١٥
16	*sittash*	١٦
17	*sabi'tash*	١٧
18	*tamanta'ash*	١٨
19	*tisita'ash*	١٩
20	*'ishreen*	٢٠
21	*waaHid wa 'ishreen*	٢١
22	*itneen wa 'ishreen*	٢٢
30	*talateen*	٣٠
40	*arbi'een*	٤٠
50	*khamseen*	٥٠
60	*sitteen*	٦٠
70	*saba'een*	٧٠
80	*timaneen*	٨٠

90	*tis'een*	٩٠
100	*imia*	١٠٠
200	*imiatayn*	٢٠٠
1000	*'alf*	١٠٠٠
2000	*'alfayn*	٢٠٠٠
3000	*thalath-alaf*	٣٠٠٠

TRANSPORT

How many kilometres?	*kam kilometre?*
airport	*al-mataar*
bus station	*mahattat al-baas*
train station	*mahattat al-qitaar*
car	*as-sayaara*
1st class	*daraja awla*
2nd class	*daraja thani*
here	*hena*
there	*henak*
left	*yasaar*
right	*shimal/yameen*
straight ahead	*'ala tool*

HEBREW

Written from right to left, Hebrew has a basic 22-character alphabet – but from there it starts to get very complicated. Like English, not all these characters have fixed phonetic values and their sound can vary from word to word. You just have to know that, for instance, Yair is pronounced 'Ya-ear' and doesn't rhyme with 'hare' or 'fire'.

As with Arabic, transliteration of Hebrew script into English is at best an approximate science. The presence of sounds not found in English, and the fact that the script is 'incomplete' (most vowels are not written) combine to make it nearly impossible to settle on one consistent method of transliteration. Numerous spellings are therefore possible for words when they appear in Roman script, and that goes for place and people's names as well.

If you'd like a more comprehensive guide to Hebrew, get a copy of Lonely Planet's *Hebrew Phrasebook.*

CONVERSATION & ESSENTIALS

Hello.	*shalom*
Goodbye.	*shalom*
See you later.	*lehitra'ot*
Good morning.	*boker tov*
Good evening.	*erev tov*
Goodnight.	*layla tov*
Thank you (very much).	*toda (raba)*
Please.	*bevakasha*
You're welcome.	*al lo davar*
Yes.	*ken*
No.	*lo*
Excuse me.	*slikha*
Wait.	*regga*
What?	*ma?*
When?	*matai?*
Where is ...?	*eifo ...?*
Do you speak English?	*ata medaber anglit?* (m)/ *ata medaberet anglit?* (f)

ACCOMMODATION & SERVICES

bill	*kheshbon*
hotel	*malon*
room	*kheder*
toilet	*sherutim*
How much is it?	*kama ze ole?*
money	*kesef*
bank	*bank*
post office	*do'ar*
letter	*mikhtav*
stamps	*bulim*
envelopes	*ma'atafar*
air mail	*do'ar avir*
pharmacy	*bet mirkakhat*
shop	*khanut*
cheap	*zol*
expensive	*yakar*
right (ie correct)	*nakhon*

TIME & NUMBERS

What is the time?	*ma hasha'a?*
seven o'clock	*hasha'a sheva*
minute	*daka*
hour	*sha*
day	*yom*
week	*shava'a*
month	*khodesh*
Monday	*yom sheni*
Tuesday	*yom shlishi*
Wednesday	*yom revi'i*
Thursday	*yom khamishi*
Friday	*yom shishi*
Saturday	*shabbat*
Sunday	*yom rishon*

Hebrew uses standard Western numerals for written numbers.

0	*efes*
1	*akhat*

2	*shta'im*
3	*shalosh*
4	*arba*
5	*khamesh*
6	*shesh*
7	*sheva*
8	*shmone*
9	*tesha*
10	*eser*
11	*eakhat-esre*
12	*shteim-esre*
20	*esrim*
21	*esrim ve'akhat*
30	*shloshim*
31	*shloshim ve'akhat*
50	*khamishim*
100	*me'a*
200	*matayim*
300	*shalosh mayat*
500	*khamaysh mayat*
1000	*elef*
3000	*shloshet elefim*
5000	*khamayshet elefim*

TRANSPORT

Which bus goes to ...?	*eize otobus nose'a le ...?*
Stop here.	*atsor kan*
airport	*sde te'ufa*
bus	*otobus*
near	*karov*
railway station	*rakevet takhana*

LANGUAGE

TURKISH

Ottoman Turkish was written in Arabic script, but this was phased out when Atatürk decreed the introduction of Latin script in 1928. In big cities and tourist areas, many locals know at least some English and/or German. In the southeastern towns, Arabic or Kurdish is the first language.

For a more in-depth look at the language, including a list of useful words and phrases, get a copy of Lonely Planet's *Turkish Phrasebook*.

PRONUNCIATION

The letters of the new Turkish alphabet have a consistent pronunciation; they're reasonably easy to master, once you've learned a few basic rules. All letters except **ğ** (which is silent) are pronounced, and there are no diphthongs.

Vowels

A a	as in 'shah'
E e	as in 'fell'
İ i	as 'ee'
I ı	as 'uh'
O o	as in 'hot'
U u	as the 'oo' in 'moo'
Ö ö	as the 'ur' in 'fur'
Ü ü	as the 'ew' in 'few'

Note that **ö** and **ü** are pronounced with pursed lips.

Consonants

Most consonants are pronounced as in English, but there are a few exceptions:

Ç ç	as the 'ch' in 'church'
C c	as English 'j'
Ğ ğ	not pronounced – it draws out the preceding vowel
G g	as in 'go'
H h	as in 'half'
J j	as the 's' in 'measure'
S s	as in 'stress'
Ş ş	as the 'sh' in 'shoe'
V v	as the 'w' in 'weather'

CONVERSATION & ESSENTIALS

Hello.	*Merhaba.*
Goodbye/Bon Voyage.	*Allaha ısmarladık/Güle güle.*
Please.	*Lütfen.*
Thank you.	*Teşekkür ederim.*
That's fine/You're welcome.	*Bir şey değil.*
Excuse me.	*Affedersiniz.*
Sorry. (Excuse me/Forgive me.)	*Pardon.*
Yes.	*Evet.*
No.	*Hayır.*
How much is it?	*Ne kadar?*
Do you speak English?	*Ingilizce biliyor musunuz?*
Does anyone here speak English?	*Kimse Ingilizce biliyor mu?*
I don't understand.	*Anlamiyorum.*
Just a minute.	*Bir dakika.*
Please write that down.	*Lütfen yazın.*

HEALTH

I'm ...	*... var.*
asthmatic	*astımım*
diabetic	*şeker hastalığı*

EMERGENCIES – TURKISH

Help!/Emergency! *İmdat!*
I'm ill. *Hastayım.*
Could you help us, please? *Bize yardım edebilirmisiniz lütfen?*
Call a doctor! *Doktor çağırın!*
Call the police! *Polis çağırın!*
Go away! *Gidin!/Git!/Defol!*
I'm lost. *Kayboldum.*

I'm allergic to ... *... alerjim var.*
to antibiotics *antibiyotiklere*
to nuts *çerezlere*
to peanuts *fıstığa*
to penicillin *penisiline*

antiseptic *antiseptik*
diarrhoea *ishali*
hospital *hastane*
medicine *ilaç*
nausea *mide bulantum*
pharmacy *eczane*

ACCOMMODATION & SERVICES

Where is a cheap hotel? *Ucuz bir otel nerede?*
What is the address? *Adres ne?*
Please write down the address. *Adresıyazar mısınız?*
Do you have any rooms available? *Boş oda var mı?*

I'd like ... *... istiyorum.*
a bed *bir yatak*
a single room *tek kişilik oda*
a double room *Ikıkişilik oda*
a room with a bathroom *banyolu oda*
to share a dorm *yatakhanede bir yatak*

How much is it per night? *Bir gecelik nekadar?*
May I see it? *Görebilir miyim?*
Where is the bathroom? *Banyo nerede?*

I'm looking for the/a ... *... arıyorum.*
bank *bir banka*
city centre *şehir merkezi*
... embassy *... büyükelçiliğini*
hotel *otelimi*
market *çarşıyı*
police *polis*
post office *postane*
public toilet *tuvalet*
telephone centre *telefon merkezi*
tourist office *turizm danışma bürosu*

TIME & NUMBERS

What time is it? *Saat kaç?*
today *bugün*
tomorrow *yarın*
in the morning *sabahleyin*
in the afternoon *öğleden sonra*
in the evening *akşamda*

Monday *Pazartesi*
Tuesday *Salı*
Wednesday *Çarşamba*
Thursday *Perşembe*
Friday *Cuma*
Saturday *Cumartesi*
Sunday *Pazar*

January *Ocak*
February *Şubat*
March *Mart*
April *Nisan*
May *Mayıs*
June *Haziran*
July *Temmuz*
August *Ağustos*
September *Eylül*
October *Ekim*
November *Kasım*
December *Aralık*

0 *sıfır*
1 *bir*
2 *iki*
3 *üç*
4 *dört*
5 *beş*
6 *altı*
7 *yedi*
8 *sekiz*
9 *dokuz*
10 *on*
11 *on bir*
12 *on iki*
13 *on üç*
14 *on dört*
15 *on beş*
16 *on altı*
17 *on yedi*
18 *on sekiz*
19 *on dokuz*

20	*yirmi*
21	*yirmıbir*
22	*yirmıiki*
30	*otuz*
40	*kırk*
50	*elli*
60	*altmış*
70	*yetmiş*
80	*seksen*
90	*doksan*
100	*yüz*
200	*ikıyüz*
1000	*bin*
2000	*ikıbin*
1,000,000	*bir milyon*

TRANSPORT

Where is the bus/ tram stop?	*Otobüs/tramvay durağınerede?*
I want to go to (İzmir).	*(İsmir)'e gitmek istiyorum.*
Can you show me on the map?	*Haritada gösterebilir misiniz?*
Go straight ahead.	*Doğru gidin.*
Turn left.	*Sola dönün.*
Turn right.	*Sağa dönün.*
near	*yakın*
far	*uzak*

SIGNS – TURKISH

Giriş/Çıkış	Entrance/Exit
Danışma	Information
Açık/Kapalı	Open/Closed
Polis/Emniyet	Police
Polis Karakolu/ Emniyet Müdürlüğü	Police station
Yasak(tır)	Prohibited
Tuvalet	Toilet

When does the ... leave/arrive?	*... ne zaman kalkar/gelir?*
ferry/boat	*feribot/vapur*
city bus	*şehir otobüsü*
intercity bus	*otobüs*
train	*tren*
tram	*tramvay*

next	*gelecek*
first	*birinci/ilk*
last	*son*
timetable	*tarife*
train station	*istasyon*

I'd like a ... ticket.	*... bileti istiyorum.*
one-way	*gidiş*
return	*gidiş-dönüş*

LANGUAGE

Also available from Lonely Planet: *Middle East Phrasebook*

Glossary

This glossary contains some English, Arabic (Ar), Egyptian (E), Farsi (Far), Hebrew (Heb), Jordanian (J), Kurdish (K), Lebanese (Leb) and Turkish (T) words and abbreviations you may encounter in this book. See p99 for useful words dealing with food. For other useful words and phrases, see Language (p660).

Abbasid dynasty – Baghdad-based successor dynasty to the *Umayyad dynasty;* ruled from AD 750 until the sacking of Baghdad by the Mongols in 1258
abu (Ar) – father or saint
acropolis – high city; hilltop citadel of a classic Hellenic city
agora – open space for commerce and politics in a classic Hellenic city, such as a marketplace or forum
ahwa – see *qahwa*
Ashkenazi – a Jew of German or Eastern European descent
Ayyubid dynasty – Egyptian-based dynasty (AD 1169–1250) founded by *Saladin*

Baath Party – secular, pan-Arab political party that ruled in Iraq until 2003 and still holds power in Syria
badia (J) – stone or basalt desert
bait – see *beit*
baksheesh – alms or tip
balad (Ar) – land or city
bawwab (Ar) – doorman
beit (Ar) – house; also *bait*
bey (T) – junior officer in Ottoman army; a term of respect that corresponds to Mr

calèche (E) – horse-drawn carriage
caliph – Islamic ruler
cami(i) (T) – mosque
caravanserai – see *khan*
cardo – road running north–south through a Roman city
carnet de passage – permit allowing entry of a vehicle to a country without incurring taxes
çarşı (T) – market or bazaar
çay (T) – see *shai*
centrale – telephone office
chador (Ar) – black, one-piece, head-to-toe covering garment; worn by many Muslim women

Decapolis – league of 10 cities, including Damascus, in the northeast of ancient Palestine
decumanus – road running east–west through a Roman city
deir (Ar) – monastery or convent
dervish – Muslim mystic; see also *Sufi*
Diaspora – community in dispersion or exile from their homeland
dolmuş (T) – minibus that sometimes runs to a timetable but more often sets off when it's full
döner kebap (T) – see *shwarma*

Eid al-Adha – Feast of Sacrifice marking the pilgrimage to Mecca
Eid al-Fitr – Festival of Breaking the Fast celebrated at the end of *Ramadan*
emir – literally 'prince'; Islamic ruler, military commander or governor
evi (T) – house

Fatimid dynasty – Shiite dynasty (AD 908–1171) from North Africa, later based in Cairo, claiming descent from Mohammed's daughter Fatima
felafel – deep-fried balls of chickpea paste with spices served in a piece of flat bread with tomatoes or pickled vegetables; *ta'amiyya* in Egypt
felucca – traditional wooden sailboat used on the Nile in Egypt
fuul – paste made from fava beans

gebel (E) – see *jebel*
gület (T) – traditional wooden yacht

hajj – annual Muslim pilgrimage to Mecca; one of the five pillars of Islam
hamam (T) – see *hammam*
Hamas – militant Islamic organisation that aims to create an Islamic state in the pre-1948 territory of Palestine; the word is an acronym (in Arabic) for Islamic Resistance Movement
hammam (Ar) – bathhouse; *hamam* in Turkish
han – see *khan*
haram – anything that is forbidden by Islamic law; also refers to the prayer hall of a mosque
hared – (plural *haredim*) member of an ultra-orthodox Jewish sect; also *hasid* (plural *hasidim*)
hasid – see *hared*
Hejira – Mohammed's flight from Mecca to Medina in AD 622; the starting point of the Muslim era and the start of the Islamic calendar
Hezbollah – 'Party of God'; Lebanon-based organ of militant *Shiite* Muslims
hypostyle hall – hall in which the roof is supported by columns

imam – prayer leader or Muslim cleric
intifada – Palestinian uprising against Israeli authorities in the West Bank, Gaza and East Jerusalem; literally 'shaking off'
iwan – vaulted hall, opening into a central court in a *madrassa* or a mosque

jamaa – see *masjid*
jebel (Ar) – hill, mountain; *gebel* in Egypt
jihad – literally 'striving in the way of the faith'; holy war

kale(si) (T) – fortress
keffiyeh (Ar) – chequered scarf worn by Arabs
khan – travellers' inn, usually constructed on main trade routes, with accommodation on the 1st floor and stables and storage on the ground floor; also *caravanserai, han, wikala* in Egypt
kibbutz – (plural kibbutzim) Jewish communal settlement run cooperatively by its members
kilim – woven rug
kippa – skullcap
Knesset – Israeli parliament
konak (T) – mansion
Koran – see *Quran*
kosher – food prepared according to Jewish dietary law
köy(ü) (T) – village

Likud – Israeli right-wing political party
liman(ı) (T) – harbour
lokanta (T) – restaurant

madrassa – Muslim theological seminary; modern Arabic word for school; *medrese(si)* in Turkey
mahalle(si) (T) – neighbourhood, district of a city
Mamluk – slave-soldier dynasty that ruled out of Egypt from AD 1250–1517
masjid (Ar) – mosque; also *jamaa*
mastaba – Arabic word for 'bench'; mud-brick structure above tombs from which the pyramids were developed
medina – city or town, especially the old quarter of a city
medrese(si) (T) – see *madrassa*
Mesopotamia – ancient name for Iraq from the Greek meaning 'between two rivers'
meydan(ı) – see *midan*
meyhane (T) – (plural meyhaneler) tavern
meze (T) – see *mezze*
mezze – a collection of appetisers or small plates of food; *meze* in Turkish
midan (Ar) – town or city square; *meydan(ı)* in Turkish (plural *meydanlar*)
midrahov (Heb) – pedestrian mall
mihrab – niche in a mosque indicating direction of Mecca
minbar – pulpit used for sermons in a mosque
mitzvah (Heb) – adherence to Jewish commandments

moshav (Heb) – cooperative settlement, with private and collective housing and industry
muezzin – cantor who sings the call to prayer
mullah – Muslim scholar, teacher or religious leader

nargileh (Ar) – water pipe used to smoke tobacco; *sheesha* in Egypt
norias – water wheels

obelisk – monolithic stone pillar with square sides tapering to a pyramidal top; used as a monument in ancient Egypt
otogar (T) – bus station
oud – pear-shaped, stringed instrument; the forerunner of the Western lute

pansiyon – pension, B&B or guesthouse
pasha – Ottoman governor appointed by the sultan in Constantinople
Peshmerga – Kurdish soldiers, literally 'those who face death'
PKK – Kurdistan Workers Party
PLO – Palestine Liberation Organisation
PTT (T) – Posta, Telefon, Telğraf; post, telephone and telegraph office
pylon – monumental gateway at the entrance to a temple

qahwa (Ar) – coffee, coffeehouse; *ahwa* in Egypt
qasr – castle or palace
Quran – the holy book of Islam; also *Koran*

Ramadan – ninth month of the lunar Islamic calendar during which Muslims fast from sunrise to sunset; Ramazan in Turkish
ras (Ar) – cape, headland or head

sahn (Ar) – courtyard of a mosque
Sala – the Muslim obligation of prayer, ideally to be performed five times a day; one of the five pillars of Islam
Saladin – (Salah ad-Din in Arabic) Kurdish warlord who retook Jerusalem from the Crusaders; founder of the *Ayyubid dynasty*
Sawm – the Muslim month of *Ramadan;* one of the five pillars of Islam
servees – shared taxi with a fixed route
settler – term used to describe Israelis who have created new communities on Arab territory, usually land captured from the Arabs during the 1967 War
Shabbat – Jewish Sabbath observed from sundown on Friday to one hour after sundown on Saturday
Shahada – Islam's basic tenet and profession of faith: 'There is no god but Allah, and Mohammed is the Prophet of Allah'; one of the five pillars of Islam

shai (Ar) – tea; *çay* in Turkish
sheesha (E) – see *nargileh*
sheikh – venerated religious scholar; also shaikh
sherut (Heb) – shared taxi with a fixed route
Shiite – one of the two main branches of Islam
shwarma – grilled meat sliced from a spit and served in pita-type bread with salad; also *döner kebap* in Turkish
siq (Ar) – narrow passageway or defile such as the one at Petra
souq – market or bazaar
stele – (plural stelae) stone or wooden commemorative slab or column decorated with inscriptions or figures
Sufi – follower of any of the Islamic mystical orders that emphasise dancing, chanting and trances in order to attain unity with God; see also *dervish*
sultan – absolute ruler of a Muslim state
Sunni – one of the two main branches of Islam
sura – chapter in the *Quran*

ta'amiyya (E) – see *felafel*
Talmud – a collection of 63 Jewish holy books that complement the *Torah*
tell – ancient mound created by centuries of urban rebuilding
Torah – five books of Moses, the first five Old Testament books; also called the Pentateuch

UAE – United Arab Emirates
Umayyad dynasty – first great dynasty of Arab Muslim rulers, based in Damascus (AD 661–750); also Omayyad dynasty

wikala (E) – see *khan*
willayat – village

Zakat – the Muslim obligation to give alms to the poor; one of the five pillars of Islam
ziggurat (Far) – rectangular temple tower or tiered mound built in *Mesopotamia* by the Akkadians, Babylonians and Sumerians

The Authors

ANTHONY HAM

Coordinating Author; Syria

Anthony first landed in Damascus in 1998 and couldn't bear to leave. He stayed three months and returns at every available opportunity, including with three generations of his family. His first job for Lonely Planet was the Iraq chapter of this guide back in 1999 and he has since written or contributed to guides for Jordan, Iran, Saudi Arabia and Libya, and four editions of this *Middle East* guide. He has also worked in Australia as a refugee lawyer with clients from the Middle East and has a Masters degree in Middle Eastern politics. A full-time freelance writer and photographer, Anthony is now based in Madrid and writes for magazines and newspapers around the world.

JAMES BAINBRIDGE

Turkey

James first visited Turkey as a student at the end of an inter-railing trip through Eastern Europe. He lived on bread and cheese triangles for a week in İstanbul and the Princes' Islands, before using the last of his meagre funds to get home to Britain. His latest Turkish trip was more successful: wandering Anatolia and making up for student starvation by spending his entire fee on kebaps. When he's not investigating various countries' national dishes, James lives in London on Green Lanes, the city's 'little Turkey'. He has contributed to half a dozen Lonely Planet guidebooks, and coauthored *A Year of Festivals*, which features Turkey's oil- and camel-wrestling festivals alongside hundreds of other events.

CÉSAR SORIANO

Iraq

As a career journalist and former *USA Today* staff writer, César has worked and travelled extensively throughout the Middle East, from Beirut to Bahrain. His love affair with Iraq began in April 2003 when he took a taxi from Kuwait City to Baghdad to witness the fall of Saddam Hussein's regime. He's since returned repeatedly to cover the war and soak up the country's legendary culture and hospitality over countless cups of sweet tea and plates of *masgoof* (grilled fish). His previous Lonely Planet titles include *Mexico*, *Flightless* and *Colombia*. When he's not collecting passport stamps (50 countries and counting), the Washington DC native lives in London with his lovely wife, Marsha.

LONELY PLANET AUTHORS

Why is our travel information the best in the world? It's simple: our authors are passionate, dedicated travellers. They don't take freebies in exchange for positive coverage so you can be sure the advice you're given is impartial. They travel widely to all the popular spots, and off the beaten track. They don't research using just the internet or phone. They discover new places not included in any other guidebook. They personally visit thousands of hotels, restaurants, palaces, trails, galleries, temples and more. They speak with dozens of locals every day to make sure you get the kind of insider knowledge only a local could tell you. They take pride in getting all the details right, and in telling it how it is. Think you can do it? Find out how at **lonelyplanet.com**.

AMELIA THOMAS
Israel & the Palestinian Territories, Lebanon

Amelia Thomas is a writer and journalist working in the Middle East, India and beyond. She has worked on numerous Lonely Planet titles, especially loves spending atmospheric nights in the Middle East's old Victorian hotel relics, and writes regularly about the region for *CNN Traveller*. She has four children – aged four, three, two and six months – who enjoy tagging along on far-flung jaunts. Her book *The Zoo on the Road to Nablus* tells the story of the last Palestinian zoo, and she is currently working on two new books, involving a Beiruti magician, an American medicine show and a Pakistani circus.

JENNY WALKER
Jordan

Jenny Walker's first involvement with the Middle East was as a student, collecting butterflies for her father's book on entomology in Saudi Arabia. Convinced her mother and she were the first Western women to brew tea in the desolate interior, she returned to university to see if that were true. Her studies resulted in a dissertation on Doughty and TE Lawrence (Stirling University) and a thesis entitled *Perception of the Arabic Orient* (Oxford University). She has written extensively on the Middle East for Lonely Planet and, with her husband, authored *Off-Road in the Sultanate of Oman*. Although deeply attached to the Middle East, Jenny has travelled in 94 countries from Panama to Mongolia.

RAFAEL WLODARKSI
Egypt

After completing degrees in Marketing and Psychology in Melbourne, Rafael vowed never to use either of them and set off on a six-month around-the-world trip. Eight years and five passports later and he is yet to come home. Rafael spent most of his twenties travelling overland through the Middle East, the Indian subcontinent, and North and South America. He has returned to Egypt several times and has managed to cover every inch of that dusty land – from Abu Simbel to the tip of the Sinai desert. He's currently based somewhere between San Francisco, London and Zanzibar.

CONTRIBUTING AUTHORS

Dr Alon Tal wrote the boxed text, The Dead Sea is Dying, p117. He founded the Israel Union for Environmental Defense and the Arava Institute for Environmental Studies, and has served as chair of Life and Environment, Israel's umbrella group for green organisations. Professor of the Desert Ecology Department at Ben-Gurion University, he heads the Jewish National Fund's sustainable development committee and still finds time to hike and bike around Israel with his wife and daughters.

Behind the Scenes

THIS BOOK

This 6th edition of *Middle East* was researched and written by Anthony Ham (coordinating author), James Bainbridge, Amelia Thomas, César Soriano, Jenny Walker and Rafael Wlodarski. For details of who wrote which chapters, see p672. Dr Caroline Evans wrote the text that formed the basis of the Health chapter. The previous edition of this book was researched and written by a team of authors also led by coordinating author Anthony Ham.

This book was commissioned in Lonely Planet's Melbourne office and produced by the following:

Commissioning Editors Kerryn Burgess, Emma Gilmour
Coordinating Editor Anna Metcalfe
Coordinating Cartographers Erin McManus, Andy Rojas
Coordinating Layout Designer Jacqui Saunders
Managing Editor Bruce Evans
Managing Cartographers Shahara Ahmed, Adrian Persoglia, Mandy Sierp
Managing Layout Designer Sally Darmody
Assisting Editors Nigel Chin, Andrea Dobbin, Cathryn Game, Carly Hall, Evan Jones, Simon Sellars
Assisting Cartographers Anita Banh, Marion Byass, Clare Capell, Di Duggan, Tadhgh Knaggs, Joanne Luke, Peter Shields
Cover Designer Pepi Bluck
Colour Designer Carlos Solarte
Project Manager Eoin Dunlevy
Language Content Coordinator Quentin Frayne
Thanks to Adam Bextream, Lucy Birchley, David Carroll, Laura Jane, Lisa Knights, Chris Love, Gina Tsarouhas

THANKS

ANTHONY HAM

Shukran to Abu Shady and Shady (Damascus), Ammar Saleh (Damascus), Simon and Amer (Damascus), Tariq (Damascus), Baha (Aleppo), Mohammed Ziadeh (Lattakia), Nisrine Haddad (Maalula), and to fellow travellers Beatriz Castaño, Juan Olazabal, Emilie Aris, Martin Wade, Suzanne West (and Carys), Robin and Saima Nichols, Cameron Powers and Kristina Sophia. Thanks also to my coauthors, editor extraordinaire Kerryn Burgess and Virginia Maxwell. It has been my immense good fortune to share Damascus with my father Ron, parents-in-law Alberto and Marina, and my wife and daughter who made one of my favourite cities so much more special. To Marina and Carlota – *sois mi vida* wherever we find ourselves in the world.

JAMES BAINBRIDGE

Teşekkür ederim (thank you) to Padi and Hulya for the bed in İstanbul, and to Jahid, Aziz and the Hemi posse for the paragliding demo in Sivas; to Pat, Süha, Ali Mustafa, Maggie, Kaili, Osman and

THE LONELY PLANET STORY

Fresh from an epic journey across Europe, Asia and Australia in 1972, Tony and Maureen Wheeler sat at their kitchen table stapling together notes. The first Lonely Planet guidebook, *Across Asia on the Cheap,* was born.

Travellers snapped up the guides. Inspired by their success, the Wheelers began publishing books to Southeast Asia, India and beyond. Demand was prodigious, and the Wheelers expanded the business rapidly to keep up. Over the years, Lonely Planet extended its coverage to every country and into the virtual world via lonelyplanet.com and the Thorn Tree message board.

As Lonely Planet became a globally loved brand, Tony and Maureen received several offers for the company. But it wasn't until 2007 that they found a partner whom they trusted to remain true to the company's principles of travelling widely, treading lightly and giving sustainably. In October of that year, BBC Worldwide acquired a 75% share in the company, pledging to uphold Lonely Planet's commitment to independent travel, trustworthy advice and editorial independence.

Today, Lonely Planet has offices in Melbourne, London and Oakland, with over 500 staff members and 300 authors. Tony and Maureen are still actively involved with Lonely Planet. They're travelling more often than ever, and they're devoting their spare time to charitable projects. And the company is still driven by the philosophy of *Across Asia on the Cheap*: 'All you've got to do is decide to go and the hardest part is over. So go!'

everyone who brought Cappadocia to life, and to Crazy Ali for giving a poem to the Queen of Spain; to Mustafa in Boğazkale and Nazlı in Konya (good luck in Ibiza); to Ollagh for the whisky and manly companionship in Kayseri, and to the Kurds in Çorum for the beers and more manly companionship. *Şerefe* (cheers)!

CÉSAR SORIANO

Special thanks to Lonely Planet's Kerryn Burgess for believing in the Iraq chapter and pioneer traveller Daniel Parsons, whose Backpack Iraq blog served as an inspiration. In Iraq, thanks to Zaid Sabah for translations and years of friendship over many games of PlayStation football *(Viva Mexico!)*; travel buddy Chase Winter; fellow CouchSurfers Josh Overcast and Rachel for their locals' insight; and all the people of Iraqi Kurdistan for their warmth and hospitality, especially my saviour Akre Peshmerga Commander Ayoub. I dedicate this chapter to my loving wife Marsha, whose love and support always guides me home.

AMELIA THOMAS

Thanks, as always, to Kerryn Burgess for her thorough, supportive and inspirational approach, to Anthony Ham for being a fabulous coordinating author, and to the whole terrific team at Lonely Planet. Special thanks, in Israel and the Palestinian Territories, to Yoran Bar, Galit Zangwill, Jet van Wijk, Maia Rushby, Abdelfattah, Sami and my good friends in Bethlehem. My gratitude once again, in Lebanon, to Pierre in Byblos, and to the many travellers who provided so many helpful hints and suggestions. And, of course, thanks to Cassidy, Tyger, Cairo, Zeyah and Gal for being such good travelling companions.

JENNY WALKER

It has been a great pleasure meeting the people of Jordan for this project and I was quickly reminded why Jordan's such a wonderful country. Special thanks to Chris Johnson (Director, Wild Jordan) and other RSCN officials; Ruth, Jordan Jubilee; Marguerite van Geldermalsen; Tyler Norris, Executive Director; Daniel Adamson and Mahmoud Twaisi, Abraham Path Initiative; Charl, Owner of Mariam Hotel. Thanks to Kerryn Burgess and Anthony Ham for their ever-professional input. As usual, I'm forever grateful to my beloved husband, Sam Owen, who was so entirely integral to the research of my chapter that it should bear both our names.

RAFAEL WLODARSKI

Thanks goes out to the all the people who helped smooth my journey through Egypt's dusty plains. A huge helping of thanks goes out to the people who went beyond the call of duty to make this book possible, including Michael Snarr and Khaled Ibrahim in Cairo, and Jedediah and Andrea in Dahab. A big thanks also goes to Kerryn Burgess for sending me back to Egypt, and for sharing those gruelling Dahab research days with me. Very special thanks are reserved, as always, for Suzanna.

OUR READERS

Many thanks to the travellers who used the last edition and wrote to us with helpful hints, useful advice and interesting anecdotes:

Jeanette Aakvik, Carles Acero, Keith Adams, Roberta Attenhofer, Craig Baguley, Katrina Baylis, Julia Benn, Mike Bloom, Chris Brailsford, Francis Breyer, Michael Brunner, Tim Bugansky, Celia Burgess, Grace Burson, Helen Bussell, Corr Chris, Andrew Curtis, Katarina Cvetkovic, Glenna Drisko, Gerald Drissner, Camille Dunn, Heinz Effertz, Gianni Filippi, John Fioretta, Ismail Gaffaz, Klaus Meyer Garcia, Thomas George, Ruth Gordon, Alan Gray, Kevin Gray, James Gronsand, Matthew Harnack, Rosie Hatton, Tii Heikkinen, Richard Heyer, Johnathon Hinks, Alison Hood, Jende Huang, Nam Seok Hwang, William Izard, Simon Jenkins, K, Demian Khan, Sara Kilani, Lea Kirkwood, Peter Koch, Katherine Krabel, Stacy Krachun, Susanne Lane, Greg Laufer, Lavik Lavik, Katie Lee, Kurt Leodolter, Paul Li, Henrik Pryser Libell, Chris Louie, Sonja Magnuson, Mark Makowiecki, Ras Malai, Jesse McClelland, Simon McPherson, Meg Menke, Ben Merven, Christopher Mesbah, Babak

SEND US YOUR FEEDBACK

We love to hear from travellers – your comments keep us on our toes and help make our books better. Our well-travelled team reads every word on what you loved or loathed about this book. Although we cannot reply individually to postal submissions, we always guarantee that your feedback goes straight to the appropriate authors, in time for the next edition. Each person who sends us information is thanked in the next edition – and the most useful submissions are rewarded with a free book.

To send us your updates – and find out about Lonely Planet events, newsletters and travel news – visit our award-winning website: **lonelyplanet.com/contact**.

Note: we may edit, reproduce and incorporate your comments in Lonely Planet products such as guidebooks, websites and digital products, so let us know if you don't want your comments reproduced or your name acknowledged. For a copy of our privacy policy visit lonelyplanet.com/privacy.

Mirzai, Dabet Morales, Anissa Morgenstern, Ruth Orli Mosser, Eshragh Motahar, Neil Multack, Jerry Neufeld-Kaiser, Johan Olsen, Esmé Palliser, Paulo Eduardo Palmerio, Judith Pasternak, Gordon Picken, David Pin, Chris Ploegaert, Simon Purdy, Carol Purfield, Walter Raubeson, Judy Roberts, Kyle Rogerson, Marcela Ruggeri, Fia Salesa, Rafael Sánchez, Rani Sanghera, Elie Sasson, Joe Sibbald, Scott Skinner, Julie Small, Barney Smith, Henrik Stabell, Jesse Sutton, Fateme Tajalli, Graeme Thorley, Victor Lopez Toonen, Matthew Tschoegl, Paula Van Hennik, Michael Voggenauer, Mari Von Hoffmann, James Walker, Nick Walter, Fionna Ward, Rebbekka Warner, Martin Westrick, Tim Wisleder, Armin Zomorodi.

ACKNOWLEDGMENTS

Many thanks to the following for the use of their content:

Globe on title page ©Mountain High Maps 1993 Digital Wisdom, Inc.

Index

ABBREVIATIONS

E	Egypt
Irq	Iraq
I & PT	Israel & the Palestinian Territories
J	Jordan
Leb	Lebanon
S	Syria
T	Turkey

000 Map pages
000 Photograph pages

INDEX

000 Map pages
000 Photograph pages

D

INDEX

N

INDEX

000 Map pages
000 Photograph pages